BENSON and HEDGES
CRICKET YEAR
SEVENTH EDITION

BENSON and HEDGES
CRICKET YEAR
SEVENTH EDITION

SEPTEMBER 1987 to SEPTEMBER 1988

EDITOR – DAVID LEMMON

PELHAM BOOKS/STEPHEN GREENE PRESS

Editor's note

The aim of *Benson and Hedges Cricket Year* is that the cricket enthusiast shall be able to read through the happenings in world cricket, from each October until the following September (the end of the English season). Form charts are printed and a player's every appearance will be given on these charts, and date and place allow these appearances to be readily found in the text.

The symbol * indicates 'not out' or 'wicket-keeper' according to the context and the symbol † indicates captain.

The editor wishes to express his deepest thanks to Brian Croudy, Les Hatton, Victor Isaacs, Anthony Lalley, Qamar Ahmed, Peter Sichel, Sudhir Vaidya, John Ward and Graeme Wright, whose advice and help over statistics have been invaluable.

PELHAM BOOKS/STEPHEN GREENE PRESS

Published by the Penguin Group
27 Wrights Lane, London W8 5TZ, England
Viking Penguin Inc., 40 West 23rd Street, New York, New York 10010, USA
Penguin Books Australia Ltd, Ringwood, Victoria, Australia
Penguin Books Canada Ltd, 2801 John Street, Markham, Ontario, Canada L3R 1B4
Penguin Books (NZ) Ltd, 182–190 Wairau Road, Auckland 10, New Zealand

Penguin Books Ltd, Registered Offices: Harmondsworth, Middlesex, England

First published 1988

Copyright © Pelham Books Ltd and David Lemmon, 1988

Typeset by Goodfellow and Egan, Cambridge
Printed and bound in Great Britain by
Richard Clay Ltd, Bungay, Suffolk

A CIP catalogue record for this book is available from the British Library
ISBN 0 7207 1829 5

PREVIOUS PAGES: *England* v. *Australia at Old Trafford. (David Munden)*

Sponsor's message

With the events of England's tour of Pakistan fresh in the mind, administrators and enthusiasts everywhere must have been hoping for a little more success and a little less controversy during the 1988 domestic season. Four England captains and a heavy defeat at the hands of a formative West Indian touring team later, it is difficult to argue that hopes have been realised. It has however given us plenty to review.

The *Benson and Hedges Cricket Year*, now in its Seventh Edition, reports not only on the English season but on all first-class cricket played throughout the world during the past twelve months. Superbly illustrated, I am sure the book will prove both informative and highly entertaining.

BARRY JENNER
Marketing Manager
Benson and Hedges

Comment

From the moment that Gatting attempted to reverse sweep Border's first delivery in the World Cup final and succeeded only in lobbing the ball into the wicket-keeper's gloves, English cricket appeared to pass into a state of decline and disquiet. The events in Pakistan, Australia and New Zealand are dealt with elsewhere in this volume, but none can take pride in much that has happened in the past twelve months. If Gatting and Broad were two of the sinners who were also sinned against, nevertheless, they found themselves financially rewarded in spite of their lapses, and only latterly were they disciplined, too late and for the wrong reasons.

Professional cricketers are fortunate men in that they earn their livings by playing a game that they profess to love and enjoy, few are so lucky; yet the position in which the professional sportsman finds himself places him in a position of great responsibility. He must, like Caesar's wife, seem above suspicion, for he is the idol and model for many, young and old, and his every word and movement is watched with adulation. When he errs he is being untrue to others as well as himself. If the cricketer needs reminding of this fact, then he should watch the Kwik Cricket which was presented as lunch-time entertainment at Test matches and on other occasions. The TCCB are to be congratulated on the way in which they have taken this game into schools and excited and interested children, but cricketers should heed the comment of one viewer at The Oval who remarked that while few of the children knew how to hold a bat properly, all of them were able to ape the postures and attitudes that they saw on the field and on television to perfection.

Several reasons have been forwarded for the recent poor standard of English cricket. Too much cricket, overseas players and the limited-over game are the favourite scapegoats, yet none of those excuses bears too close an examination. Players do not play as much today as they did fifty years ago. A statistical comparison will reveal that few, if any, cricketers play as many innings or bowl as many overs as they did in the nineteen-thirties, and a cricketer will only improve if he is tested against the best, although one could argue that too many places in club sides are being filled by cricketers from overseas and local talent is being suffocated. Chris Cowdrey makes a defence of one-day cricket later in this book.

The cause of our malaise that rarely seems to be offered is whether or not the application, mental attitude and fitness of some of our players is all that it should be. Before he left county cricket Clive Rice was in despair at the lack of application and hard work in many young cricketers that he knew, and one recalls being told of an incident by two Warwickshire committee members a few years ago. They called into the ground one day when there was no match, and at a time when the County was struggling, and noted that there were only three players practising in the nets – Amiss, Moles and Kallicharran – one desperate and eager to establish himself in the side, the other two with more than a hundred Test caps and more than one hundred and fifty centuries between them.

It is impossible to legislate for attitudes, as an attempt to insist on over-rates has proved, but perhaps there is a need for some self-questioning in certain areas. In 1987, there was a tendency to insist that although England had lost a Test series to Pakistan, they had actually won on points and were really the better side. Recent events have proved that to have been a fallacy, and a more realistic appraisal in 1987 might have brought better results in 1988.

At the beginning of last season, after a series of defeats, Kent asked themselves some questions about ability and attitude. The result was that they played the rest of the year with a joy and determination that brought them to within one point of winning the Britannic Assurance County Championship. It should be noted, too, that nine of their squad of thirteen were born in Kent and three of the others very close by in the home counties.

One gives Kent as an example because their staff and administration never forgot that their main concern was to entertain and cater for the paying spectator. It was not the same in all counties, and one dismays at those who hanker after large memberships and then wish to give those members little or nothing in return. There is a danger that players and administrators will become further removed from those who pay to come through the turnstiles. One accepts that gate receipts are now a small part of a club's income, but there is no atmosphere, no reason for advertisers and ultimately no professional cricket itself without the support of the paying customer, yet one has not heard of too many of them being co-opted onto panels of enquiry or having their advice sought on the suitability of four-day cricket.

Cricket faces problems, not all of its own making, but it would do well to consider the plight of soccer, brought to the brink of disintegration by short-sightedness, greed, lack of concern for the average spectator and the want of the smack of firm government.

DAVID LEMMON

Contents

World XI

For the first time, we are including a World XI in *Benson and Hedges Cricket Year*. The selection has not been an easy one, nor will it please everyone, but it is made on the basis of consistency of performance at all levels throughout the year. It would be best first to explain some notable exclusions.

The young Indian leg-spinner Hirwani is not chosen because, in spite of his outstanding achievement on his Test début and his fine form in Sharjah, the evidence for his inclusion above Abdul Qadir is insufficient. The same must apply to Vengsarkar. He played brilliantly against West Indies, but his first-class season was so limited by injury that it would be unfair to others to choose him on the basis of two Test matches and little else. Neither Martin Crowe nor Richard Hadlee makes the XI because both were troubled by injury and loss of form after some excellent performances for New Zealand in Australia. Hadlee returned for the tournament in Sharjah, but he was not impressive. The Indian batsman Lamba just loses out because, in spite of his prolific scoring in domestic cricket, he has yet to prove himself at the top level. Allan Lamb is unlucky that there is so much batting talent in the world, and Greenidge did not show the consistency in all conditions that Boon did, although there are many who would not leave him out of a World XI to play Mars or anyone else. It is likely that Crowe and Hadlee would force their way into that side, too.

The Benson and Hedges Cricket Year World XI for 1988

Graham Gooch (England)

Consistent at county and Test level, Gooch was also outstanding in the World Cup. Like all great batsmen, it is not just the number of runs that he scores but the way in which he scores them that is a delight, yet he showed in 1988 a quality of defence and concentration which we had not seen before.

David Boon (Australia)

Solid and determined, Boon was the outstanding batsman of the Australian season and was prominent in their World Cup triumph.

Graeme Hick (Worcestershire and Northern Districts)

The dominant batsman in world cricket in 1988, Hick excelled in New Zealand and England where records fell to him almost weekly.

Steven Waugh (Australia)

As a replacement for Martin Crowe, Waugh scored pro-

Graham Gooch. (Sporting Pictures UK Ltd)

David Boon. (Adrian Murrell/Allsport)

lifically in county cricket for Somerset. He was a vital member of Australia's Test side and was outstanding in the World Cup.

Graeme Hick. (Trevor Jones/Allsport)

Allan Border. (Adrian Murrell/Allsport)

Steven Waugh. (Allsport)

Allan Border (Australia)

Border established new records for Australia and led the side with dignity and discipline. He served Essex as a model professional and a prolific run-scorer, adapting to the most difficult conditions.

Javed Miandad. (Allsport)

Javed Miandad (Pakistan)

Javed proved himself against England and, at last, against West Indies, and he must now be considered as a batsman with no superior in the world.

Abdul Qadir (Pakistan)

Qadir's triumphs in the West Indies as well as in Pakistan and his success at the one-day game as well as in Test and domestic cricket make him supreme among spinners.

Abdul Qadir. (David Munden)

Kiran More. (Sporting Pictures UK Ltd)

Malcolm Marshall. (Adrian Murrell/Allsport)

Malcolm Marshall (West Indies)

The greatest fast bowler in the world, Marshall's absence from the West Indian side on occasions during the year showed them to be a very ordinary side without him.

Kiran More (India)

His record-breaking performances at Test level and in one-day international cricket mark him as a wicket-keeper of exceptional ability who has matured significantly in the past 18 months. Dujon batted brilliantly in England and kept acrobatically to the quick bowlers, but More's all-round wicket-keeping places him in the side.

Imran Khan (Pakistan)

Imran just edges out Curtley Ambrose on account of his outstanding bowling in West Indies and in the World Cup, but it was sad that his career with Sussex ended so lamely.

Viv Richards (West Indies)

Viv Richards was the 11th choice for the side, and a selection which cost much thought. He is not the batsman

Imran Khan. (Adrian Murrell/Allsport)

Clive Rice. (Mike King/Allsport)

Viv Richards. (Adrian Murrell/Allsport)

he once was, as was apparent from his performances in England, but he saved his side against India, and West Indies were lost without him against Pakistan. He may be near to the close of one of the greatest of careers, but he still sends a shudder of delight and expectation through the crowd when he comes down the pavilion steps.

Clive Rice (South Africa)

If Rice were able to play at international level, he would be first choice for a World XI. As it is, he was still the outstanding all-rounder in South Africa and, if one considers the Silk Cut Challenge, in the world. There is no better captain in the world. He makes a formidable 12th man.

Top of the World

The Reliance World Cup in
India and Pakistan.

Fireworks mark the end of a highly successful World Cup.
(Allsport)

The withdrawal from the competition of leading players like Botham, Gower, Hadlee, Greenidge and Marshall and the general scepticism expressed in the British press as to the advisability of holding the fourth World Cup tournament outside England created an impression that the whole exercise was doomed to fail. Never could an impression have been so wrong. All four World Cup competitions have proved to be both exciting and highly successful, and the first to be staged outside England proved to be the best of all in quality of cricket and entertainment while the organisation could not be faulted.

Pakistan, England, Sri Lanka and West Indies comprised the first group while India, Australia, New Zealand and Zimbabwe competed in Group Two. The tournament began at Hyderabad on 8 October.

Round One
PAKISTAN v. SRI LANKA

A capacity crowd of 15,000 welcomed the hosts, Pakistan, and were rewarded with a victory which was considerably narrower than had been expected. The Pakistan innings was founded on a third-wicket partnership of 113 between Rameez Raja and Javed Miandad. Rameez took 30 overs to reach fifty, but Pakistan were aided by some wayward opening bowling from the Sri Lankans. Javed's 103 came off 96 balls and included 6 fours. It was his fifth century in

one-day internationals, and he joined Viv Richards and Desmond Haynes as the scorers of four thousand runs in this type of cricket.

When Sri Lanka batted Kuruppu was soon caught at the wicket off an outswinger and Dias was deceived by Abdul Qadir's googly which hit his middle stump. It was Qadir who presented the Sri Lankans with major problems, frequently beating the bat and proving most economical. Mahanama played an intelligent and forceful innings and hit the first six of the tournament. He and Gurusinha added 79 for the fourth wicket, and there was some enterprising batting by de Silva, but the Sri Lankans could never match the required run rate.

Round One
ENGLAND v. WEST INDIES

An outstanding innings by Allan Lamb took England to an improbable victory in their opening match. England needed 91 from the last 10 overs, and 34 from the last 3, but snatched victory in remarkable circumstances.

Gatting won the toss and asked West Indies to bat. Foster and De Freitas, who was unwell, bowled with commendable accuracy. Best chopped the ball on to his wicket and Haynes foolishly ran himself out. Both Richardson and Richards were competent rather than commanding. Richardson was yorked by Foster, and when

England hero against West Indies – Allan Lamb. (Adrian Murrell/Allsport)

Javed Miandad – the first centurion in the fourth World Cup. (Adrian Murrell/Allsport)

ROUND ONE – PAKISTAN v. SRI LANKA
8 October 1987 at Niaz Stadium, Hyderabad

PAKISTAN				SRI LANKA			
Rameez Raja	c R.J. Ratnayake, b Anurasiri	76		D.S.B.P. Kuruppu*	c Saleem Yousuf, b Imran Khan	9
Ijaz Ahmed	c Kuruppu, b R.J. Ratnayeke	16		R.S. Mahanama	c Javed Miandad, b Mansoor Akhtar	89
Mansoor Akhtar	c R.J. Ratnayake, b J.R. Ratnayeke	12		R.L. Dias	b Abdul Qadir	5
Javed Miandad	b J.R. Ratnayeke	103		A. Ranatunga	b Tauseef Ahmed	24
Wasim Akram	run out	14		L.R.D. Mendis†	run out	1
Saleem Malik	not out	18		A.P. Gurusinha	b Abdul Qadir	37
Imran Khan†	b R.J. Ratnayake	2		P.A. de Silva	b Imran Khan	42
Saleem Yousuf*	not out	1		J.R. Ratnayeke	c Saleem Yousuf, b Wasim Akram	7
Mudassar Nazar				R.J. Ratnayake	c Mudassar Nazar, b Wasim Akram	8
Abdul Qadir				V.B. John	not out	1
Tauseef Ahmed				S.D. Anurasiri	run out	0
Extras	lb 15, w 9, nb 1	25		Extras	b 7, lb 14, w 7, nb 1	29
(50 overs)	(for 6 wkts)	267		(49.2 overs)		252

	O	M	R	W		O	M	R	W
John	10	2	37	–	Imran Khan	10	2	42	2
R.J. Ratnayake	10	–	64	2	Wasim Akram	9.2	1	41	2
J.R. Ratnayeke	9	–	47	2	Mudassar Nazar	9	–	63	–
de Silva	10	–	44	–	Abdul Qadir	10	1	30	2
Anurasiri	10	–	52	1	Tauseef Ahmed	10	–	48	1
Gurusinha	1	–	8	–	Mansoor Akhtar	1	–	7	1

FALL OF WICKETS
1–48, 2–67, 3–180, 4–226, 5–259, 6–266

FALL OF WICKETS
1–29, 2–57, 3–100, 4–103, 5–182, 6–190, 7–209, 8–223, 9–251

Umpires: S.J. Woodward & V.K. Ramaswamy

Pakistan won by 15 runs

ROUND ONE – ENGLAND v. WEST INDIES
9 October 1987 at Municipal Stadium, Gujranwala

WEST INDIES				ENGLAND			
D.L. Haynes	run out	19		G.A. Gooch	c Dujon, b Hooper	47
C.A. Best	b De Freitas	5		B.C. Broad	c Dujon, b Walsh	3
R.B. Richardson	b Foster	53		R.T. Robinson	run out	12
I.V.A. Richards†	b Foster	27		M.W. Gatting†	b Hooper	25
P.J.L. Dujon*	run out	46		A.J. Lamb	not out	67
A.L. Logie	b Foster	49		D.R. Pringle	c Best, b Hooper	12
R.A. Harper	b Small	24		P.R. Downton*	run out	3
C.L. Hooper	not out	1		J.E. Emburey	b Patterson	22
W.K.M. Benjamin	not out	7		P.A.J. De Freitas	b Patterson	23
C.A. Walsh				N.A. Foster	not out	9
B.P. Patterson				G.C. Small		
Extras	lb 9, nb 3	12		Extras	lb 14, w 6, nb 3	23
(50 overs)	(for 7 wkts)	243		(49.3 overs)	(for 8 wkts)	246

	O	M	R	W		O	M	R	W
De Freitas	10	2	31	1	Patterson	10	–	49	2
Foster	10	–	53	3	Walsh	9.3	–	65	1
Small	10	–	45	1	Harper	10	–	44	–
Emburey	10	1	22	–	Benjamin	10	2	32	–
Pringle	10	–	83	–	Hooper	10	–	42	3

FALL OF WICKETS
1–8, 2–53, 3–105, 4–122, 5–205, 6–235, 7–235

FALL OF WICKETS
1–14, 2–40, 3–98, 4–99, 5–123, 6–131, 7–162, 8–209

Umpires: A.R. Crafter & R.B. Gupta

England won by 2 wickets

Richards was out in the 31st over West Indies were 122 for 4. Emburey and De Freitas maintained a stranglehold on the batting, and Logie and Dujon could add only 32 in 12 overs. Pringle, however, proved to be the Achilles heel, bowling a line that suited all batsmen, particularly Harper, who took 22 off the penultimate over. Pringle's 83 runs from his 10 overs proved to be an unwanted record for an England bowler in limited-over internationals. West Indies had plundered 84 runs from the last eight overs of the innings.

Walsh and Patterson extracted lift and life from the wicket and Broad was soon caught behind. Robinson unwisely tried to steal a run to Harper with the inevitable result. Gooch and Gatting looked assertive until Gatting was caught in two minds by Hooper, who bowled a mixture of off-breaks and gentle seamers and was bowled. Two balls later, the young all-rounder had Gooch caught behind. Pringle and Downton went cheaply, and the innings appeared to be in a state of disintegration, but Emburey straight drove Patterson for six and hit 22 from 15 balls. De Freitas hit 23 off 21 balls and played a major part in an astounding win. Walsh bowled the 48th over and was hit for 16 runs, 15 of these were scored by Allan Lamb who out-thought Walsh as the bowler tried to bowl a full length on or outside the leg stump and moved away to crash the ball to the off-side boundary. Patterson conceded 6 runs so that 13 were needed from Walsh's last over.

Lamb turned the first ball to mid-wicket for two, manoeuvred the second to third man for four as Walsh bowled a full pitch outside leg stump and then stood amazed as the usually rhythmical Walsh bowled four wides down the leg side. A no-ball produced another single, and Foster hit the next ball to third man for four and an England victory. The batsmen ran from the field arms aloft. Walsh crumpled in despair, and an exhausted Lamb was hero of the hour.

Round One
INDIA v. AUSTRALIA

Holders of the World Cup and favoured to reach the final, India suffered a dreadful shock in their opening match. Put in to bat, Australia were given a splendid start by Boon and Marsh. They kept the score moving with sensible attacking shots and brisk, intelligent running between the wickets. The hundred came up in the 21st over, and Boon was out in the 25th. Jones played an innings of delight, and a total of 300 always looked probable, but the Australian middle order lost its way, and the final total of 270 owed much to Marsh's 110 from 140 deliveries.

Gavaskar began at a thrilling rate. McDermott was savaged for 31 in four overs, and when Gavaskar was out Srikkanth and Sidhu continued the violent assault on the bowling. Sidhu hit 5 sixes and India were well ahead of the 5.4 an over that they needed. In the 37th over, they had reached 207, and it was not until then that the third wicket fell. The loss of a few wickets seemed to matter little, for, with four overs remaining, only 15 runs were needed and four wickets were standing, but Kapil Dev played a casual shot and Binny was spectacularly run out by Jones. Nine

The last-over specialist, an all-rounder who played a most important part in Australia's triumph – Steve Waugh. (Adrian Murrell/Allsport)

runs were scored before Prabhakar tempted Border 15 yards away and paid the price. Maninder came to face the last over with six runs needed. Steve Waugh was the bowler. Twice Maninder tucked the ball away for two, but he swung exotically at the fifth ball of the over and was bowled to give Australia victory by one run. Had Hanif Mohammad, the match adjudicator, not credited Jones with six runs after umpire Archer had first signalled two, the result would have gone the other way, but nothing could disguise Australia's advance in maturity, discipline and confidence and India's old temperamental failing under pressure of their own making.

Round One
NEW ZEALAND v. ZIMBABWE

The final game in the first round of matches exposed the limitations of a New Zealand side bereft of Hadlee and weakened by recent retirements. Put in to bat, New Zealand were well served by makeshift opener Snedden and Martin Crowe, who added 84 for the second wicket. An accurate spell by Traicos blunted the middle order, and a target of 243 seemed within Zimbabwe's capabilities. At 104 for 7, they looked in ruins, however, but Iain Butchart joined Dave Houghton in a stand of 117 in 20 overs, an eighth wicket record for limited-over internationals. Houghton was quite magnificent. He hit 3 sixes and 13 fours in an innings which lasted only 136 balls and he was not dismissed until the 47th over when he was brilliantly caught on the boundary by Wright. Brandes was run out in the same over without addition, and the last over arrived with six needed. The valiant Butchart was run out when he slipped in going for a leg-bye.

John Traicos, captain of Zimbabwe and consistently accurate and economic with his off-breaks. (Adrian Murrell/Allsport)

Zimbabwe wicket-keeper Dave Houghton played one of the finest innings of the tournament, 141 v. New Zealand at Hyderabad. (Adrian Murrell/Allsport)

ROUND ONE – INDIA v. AUSTRALIA
9 October 1987 at Chidambaram Stadium, The Chepauk, Madras

AUSTRALIA					INDIA			
D.C. Boon	lbw, b Shastri		49		S.M. Gavaskar	c Reid, b Taylor		37
G.R. Marsh	c Azharuddin, b Prabhakar		110		K. Srikkanth	lbw, b Waugh		70
D.M. Jones	c Sidhu, b Maninder		39		N.S. Sidhu	b McDermott		73
A.R. Border†	b Binny		16		D.B. Vengsarkar	c Jones, b McDermott		29
T.M. Moody	c Kapil Dev, b Prabhakar		8		M. Azharuddin	b McDermott		10
S.R. Waugh	not out		19		R.N. Kapil Dev†	c Boon, b O'Donnell		6
S.P. O'Donnell	run out		7		R.J. Shastri	c and b McDermott		12
G.C. Dyer*					K.S. More*	not out		12
P.L. Taylor					R.M.H. Binny	run out		0
C.J. McDermott					M. Prabhakar	run out		5
B.A. Reid					Maninder Singh	b Waugh		4
Extras	lb 18, w 2, nb 2		22		Extras	b 2, lb 7, w 2		11
(50 overs)	(for 6 wkts)		270		(49.5 overs)			269

	O	M	R	W		O	M	R	W
Kapil Dev	10	–	41	–	McDermott	10	–	56	4
Prabhakar	10	–	47	2	Reid	10	2	35	–
Binny	7	–	46	1	O'Donnell	9	1	32	1
Maninder Singh	10	–	48	1	Taylor	5	–	46	1
Shastri	10	–	50	1	Waugh	9.5	–	52	2
Azharuddin	3	–	20	–	Border	6	–	39	–

FALL OF WICKETS
1–110, 2–174, 3–228, 4–237, 5–251, 6–270

FALL OF WICKETS
1–69, 2–131, 3–207, 4–229, 5–232, 6–246, 7–256, 8–256, 9–265

Umpires: D.M. Archer & H.D. Bird

Australia won by 1 run

ROUND ONE – NEW ZEALAND v. ZIMBABWE
10 October 1987 at Lal Bahadur Stadium, Hyderabad

NEW ZEALAND				ZIMBABWE			
M.C. Snedden	c Waller, b Rawson	64		R.D. Brown	c J.J. Crowe, b Chatfield	1
J.G. Wright	c Houghton, b Traicos	17		A.H. Omarshah	lbw, b Snedden	5
M.D. Crowe	c and b Rawson	72		D.L. Houghton*	c M.D. Crowe, b Snedden	141
A.H. Jones	c Brandes, b Omarshah	0		A.J. Pycroft	run out	12
J.J. Crowe†	c Brown, b Curran	31		K.M. Curran	c Boock, b Watson	4
D.N. Patel	lbw, b Omarshah	0		A.C. Waller	c Smith, b Watson	5
J.G. Bracewell	not out	13		G.A. Paterson	c Smith, b Boock	2
I.D.S. Smith*	c Brown, b Curran	29		P.W.E. Rawson	lbw, b Boock	1
S.L. Boock	not out	0		I.P. Butchart	run out	54
W. Watson				E.A. Brandes	run out	0
E.J. Chatfield				A.J. Traicos†	not out	4
Extras	b 4, lb 5, w 4, nb 3	16		Extras	lb 8, w 1, nb 1	10
(50 overs)	(for 7 wkts)	242		(49.4 overs)		239

	O	M	R	W		O	M	R	W
Curran	10	–	51	2	Chatfield	10	2	26	1
Rawson	10	–	62	2	Snedden	9	–	53	2
Brandes	7	2	23	–	Watson	10	2	36	2
Traicos	10	2	28	1	Bracewell	7	–	47	–
Butchart	4	–	27	–	Patel	5	–	27	–
Omarshah	9	–	42	2	Boock	8.4	–	42	2

FALL OF WICKETS
1–59, 2–143, 3–145, 4–166, 5–169, 6–205, 7–240

FALL OF WICKETS
1–8, 2–10, 3–61, 4–67, 5–86, 6–94, 7–104, 8–221, 9–221

Umpires: Mahboob Shah & P.W. Vidabagamage

New Zealand won by 3 runs

ROUND TWO – PAKISTAN v. ENGLAND
13 October 1987 at Pindi Club Ground, Rawalpindi

PAKISTAN				ENGLAND			
Mansoor Akhtar	c Downton, b Foster	6		G.A. Gooch	b Abdul Qadir	21
Rameez Raja	run out	15		B.C. Broad	b Tauseef Ahmed	36
Saleem Malik	c Downton, b De Freitas	65		R.T. Robinson	b Abdul Qadir	33
Javed Miandad	lbw, b De Freitas	23		M.W. Gatting†	b Saleem Jaffer	43
Ijaz Ahmed	c Robinson, b Small	59		A.J. Lamb	lbw, b Abdul Qadir	30
Imran Khan†	b Small	22		D.R. Pringle	run out	8
Wasim Akram	b De Freitas	5		J.E. Emburey	run out	1
Saleem Yousuf*	not out	16		P.R. Downton*	c Saleem Yousuf, b Abdul Qadir	0
Abdul Qadir	not out	12		P.A.J. De Freitas	not out	3
Tauseef Ahmed				N.A. Foster	run out	6
Saleem Jaffer				G.C. Small	lbw, b Saleem Jaffer	0
Extras	lb 10, w 3, nb 3	16		Extras	b 6, lb 26, w 8	40
(50 overs)	(for 7 wkts)	239		(48.4 overs)		221

	O	M	R	W		O	M	R	W
De Freitas	10	1	42	3	Wasim Akram	9	–	32	–
Foster	10	1	35	1	Saleem Jaffer	9.4	–	42	2
Small	10	1	47	2	Tauseef Ahmed	10	–	39	1
Pringle	10	–	54	–	Abdul Qadir	10	–	31	4
Emburey	10	–	51	–	Saleem Malik	7	–	29	–
					Mansoor Akhtar	3	–	16	–

FALL OF WICKETS
1–13, 2–51, 3–112, 4–123, 5–202, 6–210, 7–210

FALL OF WICKETS
1–52, 2–92, 3–141, 4–186, 5–206, 6–207, 7–207, 8–213, 9–221

Umpires: A.R. Crafter & R.B. Gupta

Pakistan won by 18 runs

Round Two
PAKISTAN v. ENGLAND

The euphoria that greeted England's success over West Indies was muted by a dismal performance against Pakistan, who were severely handicapped when food poisoning deprived them of the services of Imran Khan in the field. Gatting asked Pakistan to bat first and there was early reward when Mansoor was caught behind off Foster, who was troubled by a knee injury. Broad ran out Rameez Raja, but Javed and Saleem Malik put on 61 and took the score to 112 in the 20th over when Javed was adjudged lbw. Clearly, he did not like umpire Crafter's decision and exchanged angry words with Gatting. Javed later apologised, but this was an unhappy incident, the precursor of worse that was to follow some weeks after the World Cup had ended.

In the 38th over, Pakistan were 132 for 4, and it looked unlikely that they would reach 200, but Ijaz Ahmed hit 59 off 60 balls, including a six and a four off successive deliveries from Small. Pringle was again punished severely, three overs in late innings costing 31 runs, and the last over of the innings, bowled by Emburey, produced 15 runs.

Gooch and Broad gave England an encouraging start so that the target of 240 looked to be easily attainable, particularly as Saleem Malik and Mansoor Akhtar had to bowl ten overs between them. Gooch was bowled by Qadir's quicker ball, and Broad fell to Tauseef, who turned a ball sharply into the batsman. This was the last ball of the 25th over, and left England still comfortably placed at 92 for 2. Robinson fretted and dithered for 62 balls before he swung at Qadir, but Lamb and Gatting pushed the score along comfortably until, in the 43rd over, with only 54 needed and seven wickets in hand, Gatting gave himself room to try to hit Saleem Jaffer past cover and was bowled. It was a dreadful shot, and so unnecessary.

Pringle had a nightmare. He found it difficult to hit the ball anywhere but straight to mid-on or mid-off and ran out Emburey before running himself out in frustration. Running between the wickets is not the strongest part of his cricket.

Emburey was out in the 47th over, which was bowled by Qadir, who had Lamb lbw and Downton caught behind so that England began the over on 206 for 4 and ended it at 211 for 7. Only further misery remained, and England pondered on their disorder and tactics.

Round Two
WEST INDIES v. SRI LANKA

Having put West Indies in to bat, Sri Lanka had hopes of a miracle when Ravi Ratnayeke dismissed Best and Richardson with successive deliveries with the score on 45. It was to be 182 runs later before they achieved another success. Desmond Haynes hit 105 off 109 balls with a six and 9 fours, his ninth century in limited-over internationals, but he was overshadowed by Viv Richards, whose tenth one-day international hundred beat Kapil Dev's World Cup record set up at Tunbridge Wells in 1983. Richards' 181 was made off only 125 balls, and he hit 6

Navjot Singh Sidhu acknowledges the applause for his fifty. Sidhu emerged as one of the most exciting young batting discoveries of the World Cup. (Adrian Murrell/Allsport)

sixes and 16 fours. It was a devastating performance, and he and Logie added 116 in 58 minutes for the fourth wicket. The West Indies total was a record for one-day internationals.

Sri Lanka began bravely with 24 off the first two overs, but thereafter they settled for batting practice.

Round Two
AUSTRALIA v. ZIMBABWE

Zimbabwe again promised more than they achieved, and ultimately Australia were comfortable winners. Border chose to bat first on a low, slow wicket when he won the toss, but Curran bowled with fire and had Boon caught behind. At 20, Jones was run out and one run later, Border offered Jarvis a simple return catch. The left-arm

ROUND TWO – WEST INDIES v. SRI LANKA
13 October 1987 at National Stadium, Karachi

WEST INDIES			
D.L. Haynes	b Gurusinha	105
C.A. Best	b J.R. Ratnayeke	18
R.B. Richardson	c Kuruppu, b J. R. Ratnayeke	0
I.V.A. Richards†	c Mahanama, b de Mel	181
A.L. Logie	not out	31
R.A. Harper	not out	5
P.J.L. Dujon*		
C.L. Hooper		
W.K.M. Benjamin		
C.A. Walsh		
B.P. Patterson		
Extras	b 4, lb 8, w 4, nb 4	20
(50 overs)	(for 4 wkts)	360

SRI LANKA			
R.S. Mahanama	c Dujon b Walsh	12
D.S.B.P. Kuruppu*	lbw, b Patterson	14
A.P. Gurusinha	b Hooper	36
P.A. de Silva	c Dujon, b Hooper	9
A. Ranatunga	not out	52
L.R.D. Mendis†	not out	37
R.S. Madugalle		
J.R. Ratnayeke		
A.L.F. de Mel		
V.B. John		
S.D. Anurasiri		
Extras	b 1, lb 2, w 6	9
(50 overs)	(for 4 wkts)	169

	O	M	R	W
John	10	1	48	–
J.R. Ratnayeke	8	–	68	2
Anurasiri	10	–	39	–
de Mel	10	–	97	1
de Silva	6	–	35	–
Ranatunga	2	–	18	–
Gurusinha	4	–	43	1

	O	M	R	W
Patterson	7	–	32	1
Walsh	7	2	23	1
Harper	10	2	15	–
Benjamin	4	–	11	–
Hooper	10	–	39	2
Richards	8	–	22	–
Richardson	4	–	24	–

FALL OF WICKETS
1–45, 2–45, 3–227, 4–343

FALL OF WICKETS
1–24, 2–31, 3–57, 4–112

Umpires: S.J. Woodward & V.K. Ramaswamy

West Indies won by 191 runs

ROUND TWO – AUSTRALIA v. ZIMBABWE
13 October 1987 at Chidambaram Stadium, The Chepauk, Madras

AUSTRALIA			
G.R. Marsh	c Curran, b Omarshah	62
D.C. Boon	c Houghton, b Curran	2
D.M. Jones	run out	2
A.R. Border†	c Omarshah, b Butchart	67
S.R. Waugh	run out	45
S.P. O'Donnell	run out	3
G.C. Dyer*	c Paterson, b Butchart	27
P.L. Taylor	not out	17
C.J. McDermott	c Brown, b Curran	1
T.B.A. May	run out	1
B.A. Reid		
Extras	w 8	8
(50 overs)	(for 9 wkts)	235

ZIMBABWE			
R.D. Brown	b O'Donnell	3
G.A. Paterson	run out	16
D.L. Houghton*	c O'Donnell, b May	11
A.J. Pycroft	run out	9
K.M. Curran	b O'Donnell	30
A.C. Waller	c and b May	19
A.H. Omarshah	b McDermott	2
P.W.E. Rawson	b Reid	15
I.P. Butchart	c Jones, b O'Donnell	18
A.J. Traicos†	c and b O'Donnell	6
M.P. Jarvis	not out	1
Extras	b 2, lb 3, w 3, nb 1	9
(42.4 overs)		139

	O	M	R	W
Curran	8	–	29	2
Jarvis	10	–	40	–
Rawson	6	–	39	–
Butchart	10	1	59	2
Traicos	10	–	36	–
Omarshah	6	–	32	1

	O	M	R	W
McDermott	7	1	13	1
Reid	7	1	21	1
O'Donnell	9.4	1	39	4
Waugh	6	3	7	–
May	8	–	29	2
Taylor	5	–	25	–

FALL OF WICKETS
1–10, 2–20, 3–133, 4–143, 5–155, 6–202, 7–228, 8–230, 9–235

FALL OF WICKETS
1–13, 2–27, 3–41, 4–44, 5–79, 6–97, 7–97, 8–124, 9–137

Umpires: Khizar Hayat & D.R. Shepherd

Australia won by 96 runs

Still the master batsman. A World Cup record score of 181 by Viv Richards, West Indies v. Sri Lanka, Karachi. (Allsport)

seamer, playing his first game in the competition, put down the chance, and Border and Marsh went on to add 113 for the third wicket. Waugh hit 45 off 37 balls, and, in reply, Zimbabwe could find no one to master the Australian attack or to hint at scoring at the necessary rate.

Round Two
INDIA v. NEW ZEALAND

Put in to bat, India were 21 for 3 inside 10 overs, yet the wounds were self-inflicted. Srikkanth, at his most eccentric, ran out Gavaskar and himself, but Navjot Singh Sidhu played another spectacular innings, 4 sixes and 4 fours in his 75 off 71 balls. Azharuddin gave him excellent support, but the great spark of the innings came at the close when Kapil Dev and More added an unbeaten 82 in 51 balls of glorious improvisation and excellent running. Kapil Dev hit a six and 4 fours and faced 58 balls. More's 42 not out was his highest score in a one-day international.

Rutherford, standing in for Wright, who had influenza, and Snedden gave New Zealand a sensible start, but Martin Crowe was lured forward and beaten by Maninder's spin. It was the Indian spin bowling, Maninder in particular, which denied New Zealand. Jones batted well without ever suggesting dominance, and the New Zealanders floundered as they searched for quick runs.

Round Three
PAKISTAN v. WEST INDIES

The fourth World Cup continued its thrilling course when Pakistan gained a memorable last-ball victory over West Indies to place themselves firmly at the top of Group B, a position in the semi-finals seemingly assured. The excitement of another capacity crowd was intense.

Richards won the toss and West Indies batted first. They were given an excellent start by Haynes and new cap Phil Simmons, who hit 8 fours in his fifty off 51 balls. He was first out, in the 21st over, after which the innings lost its way, Saleem Jaffer taking three wickets in 16 balls. Richards steadied his side with a highly responsible innings, but Imran, who had suffered against Simmons early on, returned to cut down the tail and leave West Indies with a very disappointing 216.

Mansoor and Saleem Malik were early victims, and Walsh bowled Ijaz Ahmed with a fine delivery which cut back sharply and hit the off stump. When Javed was caught and bowled by Hooper in the 35th over, Pakistan, 110 for 5, looked doomed. Saleem Yousuf, missed twice, hit with gusto and enterprise, and he and Imran added 73 in 11 overs.

At the start of the 48th over, Pakistan were 196 for 6, needing 21 off 18 balls, but Saleem Yousuf was caught at square-leg, sweeping at Walsh, and when, in the next over, Wasim Akram drove Patterson into the hands of

The master. Abdul Qadir proved that a leg-spinner could dominate batsmen in one-day cricket as easily as he could bemuse them in a Test match. (Allsport)

Richardson and Tauseef ran himself out the first ball he faced, Pakistan were left comtemplating a final over from which 14 runs were needed with only one wicket remaining.

Again Walsh was the bowler. As against England, he was to suffer the cruellest of fates. Qadir took a single off the first ball, Jaffer a single off the second. A misfield allowed Qadir to snatch two from the third delivery, and the fourth Qadir, having given himself room, hit high over long-off for six. A drive into the covers brought two runs so that two were needed from the last ball. Walsh stopped in his run-up to warn Jaffer about backing up too soon, a sporting gesture, and when he bowled Qadir sliced the ball past slip for the winning runs as the ground erupted with Pakistan ecstasy.

For his sportsmanship in not running out Saleem Jaffer and for his general demeanour in face of the barrage twice inflicted upon him, Walsh was presented with a hand-woven carpet by a Karachi firm.

Round Three
ENGLAND v. SRI LANKA

England made two changes in their side, bringing in Athey for Robinson and replacing the injured Foster with a second spinner, Hemmings. The limited Sri Lankan attack posed few problems for an England batting side which approached the game positively. Gooch and Broad laid the foundation. Gooch and Gatting added 53 off 55 balls, Gatting and Lamb 76 off 71 balls. From the last five overs, Lamb and Emburey pillaged 69 runs.

The young and talented Sri Lankan batsmen were soon in a mist, the target too daunting to give hope of a serious challenge, and only rain and bad light threatened to stop an overwhelming English victory.

Round Three
INDIA v. ZIMBABWE

Zimbabwe hoped to change their luck by batting first when they won the toss, but Manoj Prabhakar took four wickets in 17 balls to reduce Zimbabwe to 13 for 4 and to give India a grip on the game which they never relaxed. Pycroft batted bravely, hitting 61 off 102 balls, but India's three spinners perplexed the other batsmen, and the holders romped to an emphatic and early victory. Gavaskar hit 9 fours in his 43.

Round Three
AUSTRALIA v. NEW ZEALAND

The first October rain in Indore for 35 years prevented any play on the first scheduled day and reduced the game to 30 overs. Put in to bat, Australia owed much to Boon and Jones, who added 117 off 98 balls. Boon scored at the rate of a run a ball. Jones was even quicker, and Border supplemented them with 34 off 26 balls. The New Zealand spinners, Patel and Bracewell, were particularly severely treated and were a visible weakness in the attack.

Wright and Rutherford were reunited as New Zealand's openers and gave their side a splendid start with 83 in 12 overs. O'Donnell accounted for them both, but Martin

Prabhakar – a devastating opening spell for India against Zimbabwe at Bombay. (Adrian Murrell/Allsport)

Crowe played with calm authority to take New Zealand to the brink of victory. When the last over began they needed seven to win with four wickets in hand.

Steve Waugh, a hero against India, was again entrusted with the final over. If Walsh was a last-over sufferer, Waugh was the end of the match World Cup superman. Waugh's first ball to Martin Crowe was just short of a length. The batsman played rather lazily at it and scooped a catch to cover. Smith was yorked next ball. From the next four accurate deliveries, New Zealand could manage only three singles and a run out. They had certainly plucked defeat from the jaws of victory, and a well-organised, well-disciplined Australian side seemed assured of a place in the semi-finals.

Round Four
PAKISTAN v. ENGLAND

Pakistan became the first side to reach the semi-finals when they beat England for a second time in the tournament. Their win was never in doubt once England had frittered away a strong position in mid-innings. Unwisely, England chose Robinson in place of Broad while Foster returned for Pringle. Robinson had a lucky escape when Saleem Yousuf put down a straightforward chance off Imran after England had been put in, and it was Gooch

ROUND TWO – INDIA v. NEW ZEALAND
14 October 1987 at KSCA Stadium, Bangalore

INDIA			
K. Srikkanth	run out		9
S.M. Gavaskar	run out		2
N.S. Sidhu	c Jones, b Patel		75
D.B. Vengsarkar	c and b Watson		0
M. Azharuddin	c Boock, b Patel		21
R.J. Shastri	c and b Patel		22
R.N. Kapil Dev†	not out		72
M. Prabhakar	c and b Chatfield		3
K.S. More*	not out		42
L. Sivaramakrishnan			
Maninder Singh			
Extras	lb 4, w 2		6
(50 overs)	(for 7 wkts)		252

	O	M	R	W
Chatfield	10	1	39	1
Snedden	10	1	56	–
Watson	9	–	59	1
Boock	4	–	26	–
Bracewell	7	–	32	–
Patel	10	–	36	3

FALL OF WICKETS
1–11, 2–16, 3–21, 4–86, 5–114, 6–165, 7–170

NEW ZEALAND			
M.C. Snedden	c Shastri, b Azharuddin		33
K.R. Rutherford	c Srikkanth, b Shastri		75
M.D. Crowe	st More, b Maninder Singh		9
A.H. Jones	run out		64
J.J. Crowe†	c Vengsarkar, b Maninder Singh		7
D.N. Patel	run out		1
J.G. Bracewell	c Maninder, b Shastri		8
I.D.S. Smith*	b Prabhakar		10
S.L. Boock	not out		7
W. Watson	not out		2
E.J. Chatfield			
Extras	b 5, lb 9, w 5, nb 1		20
(50 overs)	(for 8 wkts)		236

	O	M	R	W
Kapil Dev	10	1	54	–
Prabhakar	8	–	38	1
Azharuddin	4	–	11	1
Sivaramakrishnan	8	–	34	–
Maninder Singh	10	–	40	2
Shastri	10	–	45	2

FALL OF WICKETS
1–67, 2–86, 3–146, 4–168, 5–170, 6–189, 7–206, 8–225

Umpires: H.D. Bird & D.M. Archer

India won by 16 runs

ROUND THREE – PAKISTAN v. WEST INDIES
16 October 1987 at Qaddafi Stadium, Lahore

WEST INDIES			
D.L. Haynes	b Saleem Jaffer		37
P.V. Simmons	c and b Tauseef Ahmed		50
R.B. Richardson	c Ijaz Ahmed, b Saleem Jaffer		11
I.V.A. Richards†	c Saleem Malik, b Imran Khan		51
A.L. Logie	c Mansoor, b Saleem Jaffer		2
C.L. Hooper	lbw, b Wasim Akram		22
P.J.L. Dujon*	lbw, b Wasim Akram		5
R.A. Harper	c Mansoor, b Imran		0
E.A.E. Baptiste	b Imran Khan		14
C.A. Walsh	lbw, b Imran Khan		7
B.P. Patterson	not out		0
Extras	b 1, lb 14, w 2		17
(49.3 overs)			216

	O	M	R	W
Imran Khan	8.3	2	37	4
Wasim Akram	10	–	45	2
Abdul Qadir	8	–	42	–
Tauseef Ahmed	10	2	35	1
Saleem Jaffer	10	–	30	3
Saleem Malik	3	–	12	–

FALL OF WICKETS
1–91, 2–97, 3–118, 4–121, 5–169, 6–184, 7–184, 8–196, 9–207

PAKISTAN			
Rameez Raja	c Richards, b Harper		42
Mansoor Akhtar	b Patterson		10
Saleem Malik	c Baptiste, b Walsh		4
Javed Miandad	c and b Hooper		33
Ijaz Ahmed	b Walsh		6
Imran Khan†	c Logie, b Walsh		18
Saleem Yousuf*	c Hooper, b Walsh		56
Wasim Akram	c Richardson, b Patterson		7
Abdul Qadir	not out		16
Tauseef Ahmed	run out		0
Saleem Jaffer	not out		1
Extras	b 5, lb 12, w 7		24
(50 overs)	(for 9 wkts)		217

	O	M	R	W
Patterson	10	1	51	2
Walsh	10	1	40	4
Baptiste	8	1	33	–
Harper	10	–	28	1
Hooper	10	–	38	1
Richards	2	–	10	–

FALL OF WICKETS
1–23, 2–28, 3–92, 4–104, 5–110, 6–183, 7–200, 8–202, 9–203

Umpires: A.R. Crafter & S.J. Woodward

Pakistan won by 1 wicket

ROUND THREE – ENGLAND v. SRI LANKA
17 October 1987 at Shahi Bagh Stadium, Peshawar

ENGLAND			
G.A. Gooch	c and b Anurasiri		84
B.C. Broad	c de Silva,		
	b J.R. Ratnayeke		28
M.W. Gatting†	b R.J. Ratnayake		58
A.J. Lamb	c de Silva,		
	b J.R. Ratnayeke		76
J.E. Emburey	not out		30
C.W.J. Athey	not out		2
D.R. Pringle			
P.R. Downton*			
P.A.J. De Freitas			
E.E. Hemmings			
G.C. Small			
Extras	lb 13, w 5		18
(50 overs)	(for 4 wkts)		296

	O	M	R	W
J.R. Ratnayeke	9	–	62	2
John	10	–	44	–
de Silva	7	–	33	–
R.J. Ratnayake	10	–	60	1
Anurasiri	8	–	44	1
Ranatunga	6	–	40	–

FALL OF WICKETS
1–89, 2–142, 3–218, 4–287

SRI LANKA			
R.S. Mahanama	c Gooch, b Pringle		11
D.S.B.P. Kuruppu*	c Hemmings,		
	b Emburey		13
A.P. Gurusinha	run out		1
A. Ranatunga	lbw, b De Freitas		40
R.S. Madugalle	b Hemmings		30
L.R.D. Mendis†	run out		14
P.A. de Silva	c Emburey,		
	b Hemmings		6
J.R. Ratnayeke	c Broad, Emburey		1
R.J. Ratnayake	not out		14
V.B. John	not out		8
S.D. Anurasiri			
Extras	b 2, lb 9, w 6, nb 3		20
(45 overs)	(for 8 wkts)		158

	O	M	R	W
De Freitas	9	2	24	1
Small	7	–	27	–
Pringle	4	1	11	1
Emburey	10	1	26	2
Hemmings	10	1	31	2
Gooch	2	–	9	–
Athey	1	–	10	–
Broad	1	–	6	–
Lamb	1	–	3	–

FALL OF WICKETS
1–31, 2–32, 3–37, 4–99, 5–105, 6–113, 7–119, 8–137

Umpires: R.B. Gupta & V.K. Ramaswamy

England won on faster scoring rate

ROUND THREE – INDIA v. ZIMBABWE
17 October 1987 at Wankhede Stadium, Bombay

ZIMBABWE			
G.A. Paterson	b Prabhakar		6
K.J. Arnott	lbw, b Prabhakar		1
D.L. Houghton*	b Prabhakar		0
A.J. Pycroft	st More, b Shastri		61
K.M. Curran	c More, b Prabhakar		0
A.C. Waller	st More, b Maninder		16
I.P. Butchart	c Sivaramakrishnan,		
	b Maninder		10
A.H. Omarshah	c More, b Maninder		0
M.A. Meman	run out		19
A.J. Traicos†	c Gavaskar,		
	b Sivaramakrishnan		0
M.P. Jarvis	not out		8
Extras	b 2, lb 6, w 6		14
(44.2 overs)			135

	O	M	R	W
Kapil Dev	8	1	17	–
Prabhakar	8	1	19	4
Maninder Singh	10	–	21	3
Azharuddin	1	–	6	–
Sivaramakrishnan	9	–	36	1
Shastri	8.2	–	28	1

FALL OF WICKETS
1–3, 2–12, 3–13, 4–13, 5–47, 6–67, 7–67, 8–98, 9–99

INDIA			
K.Srikkanth	c Paterson, b Traicos		31
S.M. Gavaskar	st Houghton,		
	b Traicos		43
M. Prabhakar	not out		11
D.B. Vengsarkar	not out		46
N.S. Sidhu			
M. Azharuddin			
R.J. Shastri			
R.N. Kapil Dev†			
K.S. More*			
L. Sivaramakrishnan			
Maninder Singh			
Extras	lb 1, w 4		5
(27.5 overs)	(for 2 wkts)		136

	O	M	R	W
Curran	6	–	32	–
Jarvis	4	–	22	–
Butchart	3	–	20	–
Traicos	8	–	27	2
Meman	6.5	–	34	–

FALL OF WICKETS
1–76, 2–80

Umpires: Mahboob Shah & D.R. Shepherd

India won by 8 wickets

More and Maninder Singh proved a match-winning combination for India against Zimbabwe. Waller is stumped . . . (Adrian Murrell/Allsport)

. . . and Omarshah is caught first ball. (Adrian Murrell/ Allsport)

who was the first to go, mishooking Imran to long leg. Robinson had seemed to settle when he was bowled trying to cut Abdul Qadir's quicker ball.

Gatting again showed a reluctance to come in at number three, but he and Athey were soon together in a fruitful partnership which brought 135 runs in 24 overs. England had seemed to have gained total ascendancy when they began the 37th over at 179 for 2. Athey pulled two half-volleys from the bowler, Tauseef, for four and then, in a fit of insanity, played a wretched reverse sweep and was bowled. Two balls later, Gatting essayed a sweep at Abdul Qadir and spooned the ball to the wicket-keeper. Emburey, dizzily at number six, swept and was lbw and Imran, bowling at great pace, had Downton caught at the wicket and knocked back Lamb's leg stump in successive overs so that five England wickets had fallen for 19 runs.

ROUND THREE – AUSTRALIA v. NEW ZEALAND
19 October 1987 at Nehru Stadium, Indore

AUSTRALIA			
D.C. Boon	c Wright, b Snedden	87
G.R. Marsh	c J.J. Crowe, b Snedden	5
D.M. Jones	c Rutherford, b Patel	52
A.R. Border†	c M.D. Crowe, b Chatfield	34
S.R. Waugh	not out	13
T.M. Moody	not out	0
S.P. O'Donnell		
G.C. Dyer*		
T.B.A. May		
C.J. McDermott		
B.A. Reid		
Extras	b 1, lb 5, w 2	8
(30 overs)	(for 4 wkts)	199

	O	M	R	W
Snedden	6	–	35	2
Chatfield	6	–	28	1
Watson	6	–	34	–
Patel	6	–	45	1
Bracewell	6	–	51	–

FALL OF WICKETS
1–17, 2–134, 3–171, 4–196

NEW ZEALAND			
K.R. Rutherford	b O'Donnell	37
J.G. Wright	c Dyer, b O'Donnell	47
M.D. Crowe	c Marsh, b Waugh	58
A.H. Jones	c Marsh, b McDermott	15
J.J. Crowe†	c and b Reid	3
D.N. Patel	run out	13
J.G. Bracewell	c and b Reid	6
I.D.S. Smith*	b Waugh	1
M.C. Snedden	run out	1
E.J. Chatfield	not out	0
W. Watson	not out	2
Extras	b 4, lb 5, w 4	13
(30 overs)	(for 9 wkts)	196

	O	M	R	W
McDermott	6	–	30	1
Reid	6	–	38	2
May	6	–	39	–
O'Donnell	6	–	44	2
Waugh	6	–	36	2

FALL OF WICKETS
1–83, 2–94, 3–133, 4–140, 5–165, 6–183, 7–193, 8–193, 9–195

Umpires: D.M. Archer & Khizar Hayat

Australia won by 3 runs

One of the most valuable all-rounder cricketers in the competition, Simon O'Donnell, who, sadly, was unable to play in the Australian season due to illness. (Allsport)

Foster and De Freitas conjured some heroics, but England's total was some forty runs short of what might have been expected in mid-innings.

That they were short of an adequate total became quickly apparent when Pakistan batted. Mansoor was run out when Rameez sent him back and Emburey's throw to Hemmings was fast and true. Rameez and Saleem Malik made light of this mishap, however, and seemed to be running singles every ball as England's bowling erred consistently towards leg stump. Rameez, in fact, scored 62 singles and Saleem 43, yet Rameez's fine 113 occupied only 148 balls and Saleem Malik's 88 was from 94 deliveries. Their stand was worth 167 in 29 overs.

Well as he batted, Rameez had the fortune to be missed by Gatting at square-leg when 5, by Athey at mid-wicket when 52 and by Robinson, whose under-arm throw when Rameez was well out of his ground missed the wicket, when 77. All of them were simple chances.

Rameez eventually fell to De Freitas, who was much troubled by a stomach ailment, and Saleem went to Emburey, but by then England, and Gatting, had no control of affairs.

Round Four
WEST INDIES v. SRI LANKA

Sri Lanka gave their best exhibition of the competition when, having put West Indies in to bat, they came close to beating opponents who still appeared to be short of confidence. Haynes seemed not quite at his best, but Simmons gave further indication of his potential with a rich and free array of strokes which brought him 11 fours in his 89 and marked him, along with Sidhu, as the most exciting newcomer in the tournament. The rest of the West Indian innings was surprisingly patchy, and but for Logie's continued delight in the one-day game, Sri Lanka could well have been faced by a modest target.

They began badly, but found an exciting hero in Arjuna Ranatunga, the bulky 23-year-old. He hit Walsh for two successive sixes and battered him out of the attack. With eight overs left, Sri Lanka were 168 for 5, and four overs later, Ranatunga having launched his assault on Walsh, only 37 were needed for victory. It was Patterson who thwarted Sri Lanka's bid. Bowling off a short run, he

Brendon Kuruppu attempts unsuccessfully to run out Roger Harper, Sri Lanka v. West Indies. (Adrian Murrell/ Allsport)

ROUND FOUR – PAKISTAN v. ENGLAND
20 October 1987 at National Stadium, Karachi

ENGLAND

G.A. Gooch	c Wasim Akram, b Imran Khan	16
R.T. Robinson	b Abdul Qadir	16
C.W.J. Athey	b Tauseef Ahmed	86
M.W. Gatting†	c Saleem Yousuf, b Abdul Qadir	60
A.J. Lamb	b Imran Khan	9
J.E. Emburey	lbw, b Abdul Qadir	3
P.R. Downton*	c Saleem Yousuf, b Imran Khan	6
P.A.J. De Freitas	c Saleem Yousuf, b Imran Khan	13
N.A. Foster	not out	20
G.C. Small	run out	0
E.E. Hemmings	not out	4
Extras	lb 7, w 4	11
(50 overs)	(for 9 wkts)	244

	O	M	R	W
Imran Khan	9	–	37	4
Wasim Akram	8	–	44	–
Tauseef Ahmed	10	–	46	1
Abdul Qadir	10	–	31	3
Saleem Jaffer	8	–	44	–
Saleem Malik	5	–	35	–

FALL OF WICKETS
1–26, 2–52, 3–187, 4–187, 5–192, 6–203, 7–206, 8–230, 9–230

PAKISTAN

Rameez Raja	c Gooch, b De Freitas	113
Mansoor Akhtar	run out	29
Saleem Malik	c Athey, b Emburey	88
Javed Miandad	not out	6
Ijaz Ahmed	not out	4
Imran Khan†		
Saleem Yousuf*		
Wasim Akram		
Abdul Qadir		
Tauseef Ahmed		
Saleem Jaffer		
Extras	lb 6, w 1	7
(49 overs)	(for 3 wkts)	247

	O	M	R	W
De Freitas	8	2	41	1
Foster	10	–	51	–
Hemmings	10	1	40	–
Emburey	10	–	34	1
Small	9	–	63	–
Gooch	2	–	12	–

FALL OF WICKETS
1–61, 2–228, 3–243

Umpires: A.R. Crafter & V.K. Ramaswamy

Pakistan won by 7 wickets

ROUND FOUR – WEST INDIES v. SRI LANKA
21 October 1987 at Modi Stadium (Green Park), Kanpur

WEST INDIES

D.L. Haynes	b Anurasiri	24
P.V. Simmons	c Madugalle, b J.R. Ratnayeke	89
R.B. Richardson	c Mahanama, b Jeganathan	4
I.V.A. Richards†	c R.J. Ratnayake, b de Silva	14
A.L. Logie	not out	65
C.L. Hooper	st Kuruppu, b de Silva	6
P.J.L. Dujon*	c Kuruppu, b J.R. Ratnayeke	6
R.A. Harper	b J.R. Ratnayeke	3
W.K.M. Benjamin	b R.J. Ratnayake	0
C.A. Walsh	not out	9
B.P. Patterson		
Extras	b 2, lb 7, w 7	16
(50 overs)	(for 8 wkts)	236

	O	M	R	W
J.R. Ratnayeke	10	1	41	3
John	5	1	25	–
R.J. Ratnayake	5	–	39	1
Jeganathan	10	1	33	1
Anurasiri	10	1	46	1
de Silva	10	–	43	2

FALL OF WICKETS
1–62, 2–80, 3–115, 4–155, 5–168, 6–199, 7–213, 8–214

SRI LANKA

R.S. Mahanama	b Patterson	0
D.S.B.P. Kuruppu*	c and b Hooper	33
J.R. Ratnayeke	lbw, b Benjamin	15
R.S. Madugalle	c Haynes, b Harper	18
A. Ranatunga	not out	86
L.R.D. Mendis†	b Walsh	19
P.A. de Silva	b Patterson	8
R.J. Ratnayake	c Walsh, b Patterson	5
S. Jeganathan	run out	3
V.B. John	not out	1
S.D. Anurasiri		
Extras	b 2, lb 11, nb 10	23
(50 overs)	(for 8 wkts)	211

	O	M	R	W
Patterson	10	–	31	3
Walsh	9	2	43	1
Harper	10	1	29	1
Benjamin	10	–	43	1
Hooper	8	–	35	1
Richards	3	–	17	–

FALL OF WICKETS
1–2, 2–28, 3–66, 4–86, 5–156, 6–184, 7–200, 8–209

Umpires: Amanullah Khan & Mahboob Shah

West Indies won by 25 runs

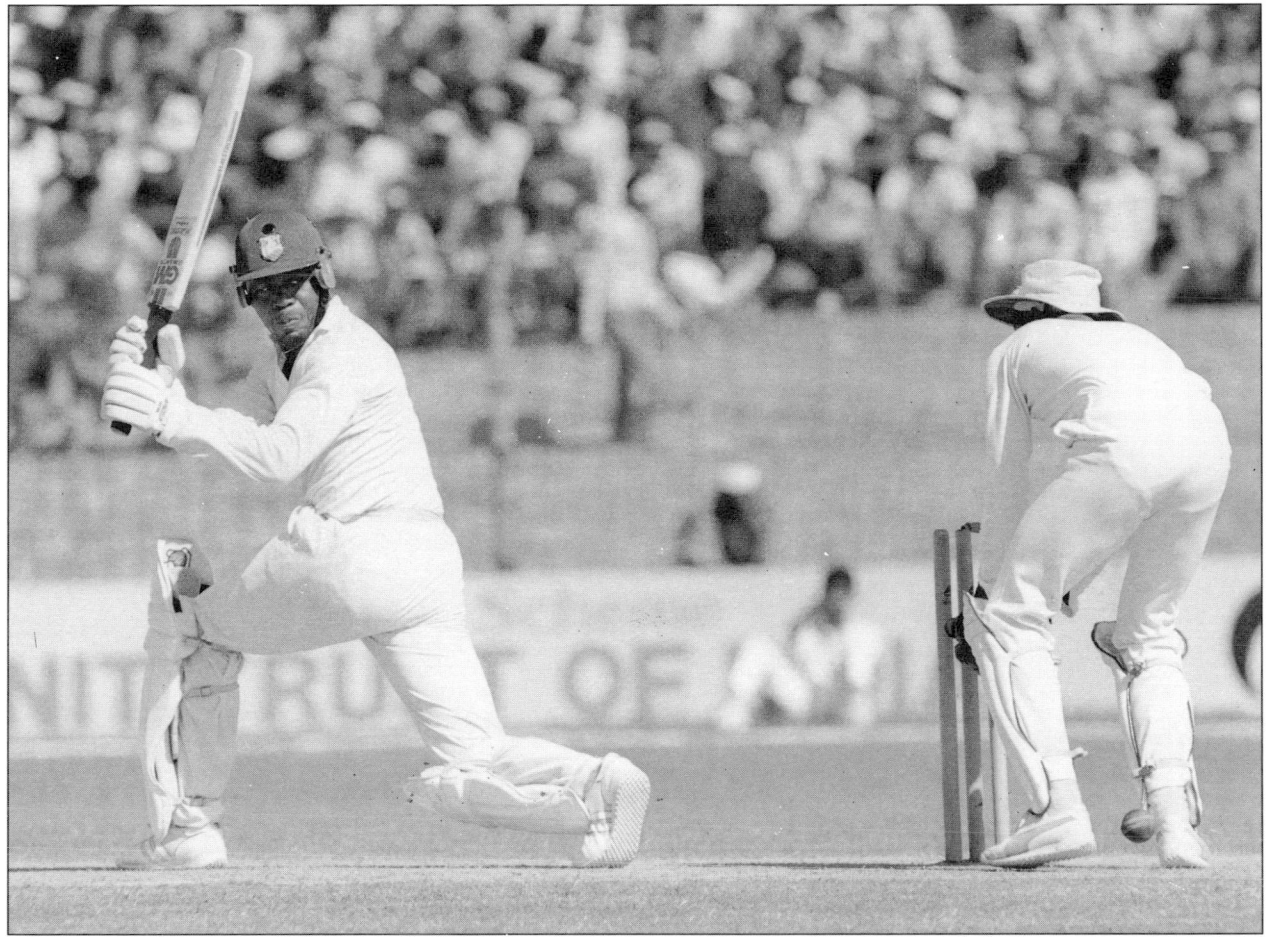

LEFT: *Boon – Man of the Match. (Allsport)*

ABOVE: *Desmond Haynes is bowled by Don Anurasiri, West Indies against Sri Lanka, Kanpur. (Adrian Murrell/ Allsport)*

dismissed de Silva and Ratnayake so that 28 were needed from the last over, bowled by Benjamin, which proved impossible.

Ranatunga's glorious innings, which raised Sri Lankan hopes, was made off 92 balls.

Round Four
INDIA v. AUSTRALIA

Border's decision to put India in to bat on a beautiful batting pitch had little to commend it. The Australian all-seam attack laboured against a constant battery of delightful shots. They bowled accurately and were well supported in the field, but little could be done to stem the flow of runs.

In reply, Australia were given a rollicking start by Boon and Marsh, who were both severe on the Indian pace bowlers. They put on 88 in 18 overs to give Australia every chance of success, but the advent of the Indian spinners changed the complexion of the game. Maninder and Shastri removed both openers and so restricted the middle-order batting that the run rate required soon reached proportions which made an Indian victory inevitable.

Round Four
NEW ZEALAND v. ZIMBABWE

The excitement and interest engendered by the World Cup was never better exemplified than by the fact that 50,000 people watched two of the less fancied sides in the competition meet at Eden Gardens. Again batting first, although this time not by choice, Zimbabwe began disastrously when Grant Patterson was run out in the second over. Thereafter they gave their most impressive batting display of the tournament with Omarshah and Arnott making their best scores and Houghton hitting 50 off 58 balls at a time when an increase in the run rate was very necessary. Pycroft, too, showed increasing aggression, but, even so, the final score of 227 hardly seemed likely to trouble the New Zealanders.

When Rutherford, Wright and Patel, who was finding international cricket difficult to adjust to, were out for 56 New Zealand were struggling, and their struggle became

ROUND FOUR – INDIA v. AUSTRALIA
22 October 1987 at Ferozeshah Kotla, New Delhi

INDIA					AUSTRALIA			
K. Srikkanth	c Dyer, b McDermott		26		G.R. Marsh	st More, b Maninder		33
S.M. Gavaskar	b O'Donnell		61		D.C. Boon	c More, b Shastri		62
N.S. Sidhu	c Moody, b McDermott		51		D.M. Jones	c Kapil Dev, b Maninder		36
D.B. Vengsarkar	c O'Donnell, b Reid		63		A.R. Border†	c Prabhakar, b Maninder		12
R.N. Kapil Dev†	c Dyer, b McDermott		3		S.R. Waugh	c Sidhu, b Kapil Dev		42
M. Azharuddin	not out		54		T.M. Moody	run out		2
R.J. Shastri	c and b Waugh		8		S.P. O'Donnell	b Azharuddin		5
K.S. More*	not out		5		G.C. Dyer*	c Kapil Dev, b Prabhakar		15
M. Prabhakar					C.J. McDermott	c and b Azharuddin		4
C.J. Sharma					A.K. Zesers	not out		2
Maninder Singh					B.A. Reid	c Sidhu, b Azharuddin		1
Extras	b 1, lb 6, w 11		18		Extras	lb 11, w 8		19
(50 overs)	(for 6 wkts)		289		(49 overs)			233

	O	M	R	W		O	M	R	W
O'Donnell	9	1	45	1	Kapil Dev	8	1	41	1
Reid	10	–	65	1	Prabhakar	10	–	56	1
Waugh	10	–	59	1	Maninder Singh	10	–	34	3
McDermott	10	–	61	3	Shastri	10	–	35	1
Moody	2	–	15	–	Sharma	7.1	–	37	–
Zesers	9	1	37	–	Azharuddin	3.5	–	19	3

FALL OF WICKETS
1–50, 2–125, 3–167, 4–178, 5–243, 6–274

FALL OF WICKETS
1–88, 2–104, 3–135, 4–164, 5–167, 6–182, 7–214, 8–227, 9–231

Umpires: D.R. Shepherd & Khalid Aziz

India won by 56 runs

ROUND FOUR – NEW ZEALAND v. ZIMBABWE
23 October 1987 at Eden Gardens, Calcutta

ZIMBABWE					NEW ZEALAND			
G.A. Paterson	run out		0		K.R. Rutherford	b Brandes		22
A.H. Omarshah	c M.D. Crowe, b Watson		41		J.G. Wright	b Omarshah		12
K.J. Arnott	run out		51		M.D. Crowe	c Butchart, b Omarshah		58
D.L. Houghton*	c M.D. Crowe, b Boock		50		D.N. Patel	c Arnott, b Brandes		1
A.J. Pycroft	not out		52		J.J. Crowe†	not out		88
K.M. Curran	b Boock		12		A.H. Jones	c Jarvis, b Traicos		15
A.C. Waller	not out		8		M.C. Snedden	b Jarvis		4
I.P. Butchart					I.D.S. Smith*	not out		17
E.A. Brandes					S.L. Boock			
A.J. Traicos†					W. Watson			
M.P. Jarvis					E.J. Chatfield			
Extras	lb 7, w 6		13		Extras	b 1, lb 5, w 4, nb 1		11
(50 overs)	(for 5 wkts)		227		(47.4 overs)	(for 6 wkts)		228

	O	M	R	W		O	M	R	W
Snedden	10	2	32	–	Curran	2	–	12	–
Chatfield	10	2	47	–	Jarvis	7.4	–	39	1
Patel	10	1	52	–	Brandes	10	1	44	2
Watson	10	1	45	1	Omarshah	10	–	34	2
Boock	10	1	44	2	Butchart	8	–	50	–
					Traicos	10	–	43	1

FALL OF WICKETS
1–1, 2–82, 3–121, 4–180, 5–216

FALL OF WICKETS
1–37, 2–53, 3–56, 4–125, 5–158, 6–182

Umpires: Khizar Hayat & P.W. Vidabagamage

New Zealand won by 4 wickets

greater when they slipped to 158 for 5 in the 38th over. It was skipper Jeff Crowe, playing with admirable composure, who led New Zealand through this difficult period. His 88 not out was his highest score in one-day internationals and came off 105 balls. He hit Jarvis for the winning run with 14 balls to spare.

Round Five
PAKISTAN v. SRI LANKA

Pakistan assured themselves of first place in Group B when they overwhelmed Sri Lanka, who had struggled throughout most of the competition. Imran won the toss and Rameez and Mansoor gave Pakistan a sound start. The real foundation of the Pakistan innings came from Saleem Malik, however, who hit his first century in limited-over internationals. His hundred came off 85 balls and included 10 fours. His innings was followed by some violent hitting from Wasim Akram, Ijaz and Imran.

Sri Lanka lost two wickets very quickly and settled for batting practice even though Imran retired from the fray with a bruised ankle.

Round Five
ENGLAND v. WEST INDIES

West Indies suffered a misfortune when Gray, who had been expected to play in this match, broke his left wrist at net practice. Fortune did favour West Indies when Richards won the toss and asked England to bat first on a grassy pitch on which the dew still lingered. Robinson was far from happy and, having been dropped at the wicket in the third over, he had his off stump broken in two by Patterson in the ninth. Richards crowded the uncertain Athey, but Gooch's solidity and some profligate bowling by West Indies, who conceded 38 extras, 22 of them unforgivable wides, helped England out of a difficult period.

Harper had replaced Walsh to bowl his 10 overs in a single spell, but Hooper, who replaced Patterson, bowled three leg-side wides in his first over and failed completely to settle. Gooch and Athey prospered until Athey swept Harper into the hands of Patterson on the long-leg boundary.

Gatting was quickly into his stride and after 30 overs, England were 150 for 2, but Richards showed his bowlers the virtues of line and length. Not only did he curb the scoring, but he had Gatting lbw playing across the line.

Gooch's mighty innings came to an end when he was caught at deep mid-wicket off the 137th ball that he faced. He had hit 7 fours and had given the England innings the substance that it so desperately needed. Lamb, De Freitas and Emburey pillaged 83 from the last 10 overs, and England had something to bowl at.

Haynes was caught off a long hop in the fifth over, but

ROUND FIVE – PAKISTAN v. SRI LANKA
25 October 1987 at Iqbal Stadium, Faisalabad

PAKISTAN				SRI LANKA			
Rameez Raja	c and b Anurasiri	32		R.S. Mahanama	run out		8
Mansoor Akhtar	b Jeganathan	33		D.S.B.P. Kuruppu*	c Saleem Yousuf,		
Saleem Malik	b J.R. Ratnayeke	100			b Imran Khan		0
Javed Miandad	run out	1		J.R. Ratnayeke	run out		22
Wasim Akram	c Ranatunga,			R.S. Madugalle	c Saleem Yousuf,		
	b de Silva	39			b Manzoor Elahi		15
Ijaz Ahmed	c and b John	30		A. Ranatunga	c and b Abdul Qadir		50
Imran Khan†	run out	39		L.R.D. Mendis†	b Abdul Qadir		58
Manzoor Elahi	not out	4		P.A. de Silva	not out		13
Saleem Yousuf*	not out	11		A.L.F. de Mel	b Abdul Qadir		0
Abdul Qadir				S. Jeganathan	c Saleem Yousuf,		
Tauseef Ahmed					b Javed Miandad		1
Extras	lb 6, w 2	8		V.B. John	not out		1
				S.D. Anurasiri			
(50 overs)	(for 7 wkts)	297		Extras	b 4, lb 4, w 6, nb 2		16
				(50 overs)	(for 8 wkts)		184

	O	M	R	W		O	M	R	W
J.R. Ratnayeke	10	–	58	1	Imran Khan	3.2	1	13	1
John	8	1	53	1	Wasim Akram	7	–	34	–
de Mel	10	–	53	–	Manzoor Elahi	9.4	–	32	1
Jeganathan	9	1	45	1	Tauseef Ahmed	10	1	23	–
Anurasiri	7	–	45	1	Abdul Qadir	10	–	40	3
de Silva	6	–	37	1	Saleem Malik	7	1	29	–
					Javed Miandad	3	–	5	1

FALL OF WICKETS
1–64, 2–72, 3–77, 4–137, 5–197, 6–264, 7–285

FALL OF WICKETS
1–4, 2–11, 3–41, 4–70, 5–150, 6–173, 7–173, 8–179

Umpires: R.B. Gupta & S.J. Woodward

Pakistan won by 113 runs

England v. *West Indies at Jaipur. (Allsport)*

RIGHT: *The moment of truth. Richards is bowled by Hemmings for 51. (Adrian Murrell/Allsport)*

Simmons and Richardson looked purposeful until Simmons was deceived by Emburey. Richards now took the stage and he and Richardson added 82 in under 18 overs. Richards erupted with 3 enormous sixes. Twice he hit Hemmings over square leg, and one massive hit off Emburey sent the ball soaring over mid-wicket. Then he stepped back towards leg to play Hemmings through the off-side field, but he was beaten in the flight and bowled.

Richard's 51 had come off as many balls, and his dismissal changed the course of the match. Hemmings caught Logie, who had batted briskly, and ran out Harper when he hit the stumps from 20 yards. Richardson's fine innings ended on the 130th ball he faced when he was splendidly caught by Downton, who had an outstanding match behind the stumps. The last six West Indian wickets went down in eight overs for 30 runs.

Round Five
INDIA v. ZIMBABWE

India comfortably brushed aside Zimbabwe, but they failed to lift their rate of scoring, which would have taken them ahead of Australia. Gavaskar occupied 114 balls for his fifty, and it was left to Kapil Dev with 41 off 25 balls including 3 sixes to give the innings any impetus.

Round Five
AUSTRALIA v. NEW ZEALAND

Electing to bat first, Australia were admirably served by Geoff Marsh, who batted throughout the 50 overs to record his second century of the competition. Boon ran himself out in the 10th over, and although Jones and Marsh added 126 in 26 overs, the innings never really came alight. The middle order disintegrated woefully, and it was not until May joined Marsh that good sense replaced the suicidal tendencies that had been the characteristic of the Australian innings. The bonus for Australia came with the last over of their quota, when Chatfield, usually so accurate and controlled, erred down the leg side and conceded 19 runs, a total which proved to be a great misfortune to New Zealand.

Snedden and Wright began purposefully, and their stand of 72 gave New Zealand every hope of victory, but the Kiwis suffered another piece of misfortune when Wright drove Waugh, and the bowler deflected the ball onto the stumps with Martin Crowe out of his ground. Wright continued to bat well, and there was a valuable contribution from Rutherford, but the rest of the New Zealand batting looked to be struggling and, in spite of a

ROUND FIVE – ENGLAND v. WEST INDIES
26 October 1987 at Sawai Mansingh Stadium, Jaipur

ENGLAND			
G.A. Gooch	c Harper, b Patterson	92
R.T. Robinson	b Patterson	13
C.W.J. Athey	c Patterson, b Harper	21
M.W. Gatting†	lbw, b Richards	25
A.J. Lamb	c Richardson,	
	b Patterson	40
J.E. Emburey	not out	24
P.A.J. De Freitas	not out	16
P.R. Downton*		
N.A. Foster		
E.E. Hemmings		
G.C. Small		
Extras	b 5, lb 10, w 22, nb 1	38
(50 overs)	(for 5 wkts)	269

	O	M	R	W
Patterson	9	–	56	3
Walsh	10	–	24	–
Benjamin	10	–	63	–
Harper	10	1	52	1
Hooper	3	–	27	–
Richards	8	–	32	1

FALL OF WICKETS
1–35, 2–90, 3–154, 4–209, 5–250

WEST INDIES			
D.L. Haynes	c Athey, b De Freitas	9
P.V. Simmons	b Emburey	25
R.B. Richardson	c Downton, b Small	93
I.V.A. Richards†	b Hemmings	51
A.L. Logie	c Hemmings,	
	b Emburey	22
C.L. Hooper	c Downton,	
	b De Freitas	8
P.J.L. Dujon*	c Downton, b Foster	1
R.A. Harper	run out	3
W.K.M. Benjamin	c Foster, b De Freitas	8
C.A. Walsh	b Hemmings	2
B.P. Patterson	not out	4
Extras	lb 7, w 1, nb 1	9
(48.1 overs)		235

	O	M	R	W
De Freitas	9.1	2	28	3
Foster	10	–	52	1
Emburey	9	–	41	2
Small	10	–	61	1
Hemmings	10	–	46	2

FALL OF WICKETS
1–18, 2–65, 3–147, 4–182, 5–208, 6–211, 7–219, 8–221, 9–224

Umpires: Mahboob Shah & P.W. Vidanagamage

England won by 34 runs

ROUND FIVE – INDIA v. ZIMBABWE
26 October 1987 at Gujarat Stadium, Ahmedabad

ZIMBABWE			
R.D. Brown	c More, b Sharma		13
A.H. Omarshah	run out		0
K.J. Arnott	b Kapil Dev		60
A.J. Pycroft	c More, b Sharma		2
D.L. Houghton*	c Kapil Dev, b Shastri		22
A.C. Waller	c Shastri, b Maninder		39
I.P. Butchart	b Kapil Dev		13
P.W.E. Rawson	not out		16
E.A. Brandes	not out		3
M.P. Jarvis			
A.J. Traicos†			
Extras	b 1, lb 12, w 9, nb 1		23
(50 overs)	(for 7 wkts)		191

INDIA			
K. Srikkanth	lbw, b Jarvis		6
S.M. Gavaskar	c Butchart, b Rawson		50
N.S. Sidhu	c Brandes, b Rawson		55
D.B. Vengsarkar	not out		33
R.N. Kapil Dev†	not out		41
M. Azharuddin			
R.J. Shastri			
K.S. More*			
M. Prabhakar			
C.J. Sharma			
Maninder Singh			
Extras	lb 6, w 3		9
(42 overs)	(for 3 wkts)		194

	O	M	R	W
Kapil Dev	10	2	44	2
Prabhakar	7	2	12	–
Sharma	10	–	41	2
Maninder Singh	10	1	32	1
Shastri	10	–	35	1
Azharuddin	3	–	14	–

	O	M	R	W
Brandes	6	–	28	–
Jarvis	8	1	21	1
Omarshah	8	–	40	–
Traicos	10	–	39	–
Rawson	8	–	46	2
Butchart	2	–	14	–

FALL OF WICKETS
1–4, 2–36, 3–40, 4–83, 5–150, 6–155, 7–184

FALL OF WICKETS
1–11, 2–105, 3–132

Umpires: D.M. Archer & H.D. Bird

India won by 7 wickets

ROUND FIVE – AUSTRALIA v. NEW ZEALAND
27 October 1987 at Sector 16 Stadium, Chandigarh

AUSTRALIA			
G.R. Marsh	not out		126
D.C. Boon	run out		14
D.M. Jones	c Smith, b Watson		56
A.R. Border†	b Snedden		1
M.R.J. Veletta	run out		0
S.R. Waugh	b Watson		1
G.C. Dyer*	b Chatfield		8
C.J. McDermott	lbw, b Chatfield		5
T.B.A. May	run out		15
A.K. Zesers	not out		8
B.A. Reid			
Extras	lb 10, w 7		17
(50 overs)	(for 8 wkts)		251

NEW ZEALAND			
M.C. Snedden	b Waugh		32
J.G. Wright	c and b Zesers		61
M.D. Crowe	run out		4
K.R. Rutherford	c Jones, b McDermott		44
J.J. Crowe†	c and b Border		27
D.N. Patel	st Dyer, b Border		3
J.G. Bracewell	run out		12
I.D.S. Smith*	c Boon, b Waugh		12
S.L. Boock	run out		12
W. Watson	run out		8
E.J. Chatfield	not out		5
Extras	b 1, lb 7, w 4, nb 2		14
(48.4 overs)			234

	O	M	R	W
Snedden	10	–	48	1
Chatfield	10	2	52	2
Boock	10	1	45	–
Bracewell	4	–	24	–
Patel	8	–	26	–
Watson	8	–	46	2

	O	M	R	W
McDermott	10	1	43	1
Reid	6	–	30	–
Waugh	9.4	–	37	2
Zesers	6	–	37	1
May	10	–	52	–
Border	7	–	27	2

FALL OF WICKETS
1–25, 2–151, 3–158, 4–158, 5–175, 6–193, 7–201, 8–228

FALL OF WICKETS
1–72, 2–82, 3–127, 4–173, 5–179, 6–186, 7–206, 8–208, 9–221

Umpires: Khizar Hayat & D.R. Shepherd

Australia won by 17 runs

Geoff Marsh, 126 not out for Australia against New Zealand. His opening partnerships with Boon were a source of inspiration to Australia. (Adrian Murrell/ Allsport)

few lusty blows from the tail, they were never truly in contention.

Paradoxically, Australia's run rate slipped in spite of this victory and India moved above them in Group A. Both sides were now certain to qualify for the semi-finals.

Round Six
ENGLAND v. SRI LANKA

The last round of matches began with the four semi-finalists virtually decided although England had to beat Sri Lanka to confirm their place. This they did with comparative ease, but four missed chances, none of them too hard, made the task a little more difficult than was necessary. The first catch went down in the opening over when Gooch dislocated a finger when he dropped Ratnayeke off De Freitas. Gooch left the field for repairs and was off for the entire innings. Substitute Jarvis also put down a catch. Emburey held one at slip and after 10 overs, Sri Lanka were 25 for 2. Roy Dias, dropped on one, then played an innings of great delight as he and the punishing left-hander Gurusinha added 88. Dias has been one of the most

accomplished and entertaining batsmen in world cricket. Sri Lanka's elevation to Test status came a little too late for him, but those of us lucky enough to have seen him bat will cherish a memory of power and elegance, of a classicism now all too rare. Having faced 105 balls, he was beaten by Hemmings as he advanced down the wicket. One suspects that this was his last innings in international cricket. Sri Lanka still managed 75 from their last 10 overs with the highly promising but inconsistent de Silva and Jeganathan in particularly thumping form.

Gooch and Robinson soon put England on the road to victory with 123 in 23.3 overs against a very limited attack, and after this victory was a formality. Sri Lanka were handicapped by the absence of Mendis, also playing his last international, who had a stomach upset, but the inescapable fact is that their cricket in the competition had been bitterly disappointing. Two years earlier, they had promised so much and one felt that an exciting and thoroughly entertaining Test side was taking shape, but the bowling has failed to develop, the spirit has often been weak and the batting inconsistent. Players like de Silva and Mahanama still have much to offer, but sounder application and maturity are now needed.

Round Six
PAKISTAN v. WEST INDIES

With Pakistan already assured of first place in Group B,

Roy Dias – an elegant farewell? (Adrian Murrell/Allsport)

ROUND SIX – ENGLAND v. SRI LANKA
30 October 1987 at Nehru Stadium, Pune

SRI LANKA			
R.S. Mahanama	c Emburey, b De Freitas	14	
J.R. Ratnayeke	lbw, b Small	7	
A.P. Gurusinha*	run out	34	
R.L. Dias	st Downton, b Hemmings	80	
L.R.D. Mendis†	b De Freitas	7	
R.S. Madugalle	c sub (Jarvis), b Hemmings	22	
P.A. de Silva	not out	23	
A.L.F. de Mel	c Lamb, b Hemmings	0	
S. Jeganathan	not out	20	
V.B. John			
S.D. Anurasiri			
Extras	lb 3, w 3, nb 5	11	
(50 overs)	(for 7 wkts)	218	

	O	M	R	W
De Freitas	10	2	46	2
Small	10	1	33	1
Foster	10	–	37	–
Emburey	10	1	42	–
Hemmings	10	–	57	3

FALL OF WICKETS
1–23, 2–25, 3–113, 4–125, 5–170, 6–177, 7–180

ENGLAND			
G.A. Gooch	c and b Jeganathan	61	
R.T. Robinson	b Jeganathan	55	
C.W.J. Athey	not out	40	
M.W. Gatting†	not out	46	
A.J. Lamb			
P.R. Downton*			
J.E. Emburey			
P.A.J. De Freitas			
N.A. Foster			
G.C. Small			
E.E. Hemmings			
Extras	b 1, lb 13, w 3	17	
(41.2 overs)	(for 2 wkts)	219	

	O	M	R	W
J.R. Ratnayeke	8	1	37	–
John	6	2	19	–
de Mel	4.2	–	34	–
Jeganathan	10	–	45	2
Anurasiri	10	–	45	–
de Silva	3	–	25	–

FALL OF WICKETS
1–123, 2–132

Umpires: D.M. Archer & Khizar Hayat

England won by 8 wickets

ROUND SIX – PAKISTAN v. WEST INDIES
30 October 1987 at National Stadium, Karachi

WEST INDIES			
D.L. Haynes	c Imran, b Mudassar	25	
P.V. Simmons	b Wasim Akram	6	
R.B. Richardson	c Abdul Qadir, b Imran Khan	110	
I.V.A. Richards†	b Wasim Akram	67	
A.L. Logie	c Mudassar, b Imran	12	
R.A. Harper	b Wasim Akram	2	
C.L. Hooper	not out	5	
W.K.M. Benjamin	c Mudassar, b Imran	0	
P.J.L. Dujon*	not out	1	
C.A. Walsh			
B.P. Patterson			
Extras	b 3, lb 10, w 16, nb 1	30	
(50 overs)	(for 7 wkts)	258	

	O	M	R	W
Imran Khan	9	–	57	3
Wasim Akram	10	–	45	3
Abdul Qadir	10	1	29	–
Mudassar Nazar	10	–	47	1
Saleem Jaffer	6	–	37	–
Saleem Malik	5	–	30	–

FALL OF WICKETS
1–19, 2–84, 3–221, 4–242, 5–248, 6–255, 7–255

PAKISTAN			
Mudassar Nazar	b Harper	40	
Rameez Raja	c Hooper, b Patterson	70	
Saleem Malik	c Richards, b Walsh	23	
Javed Miandad	b Benjamin	38	
Ijaz Ahmed	b Benjamin	6	
Imran Khan†	c Harper, b Walsh	8	
Saleem Yousuf*	b Patterson	7	
Wasim Akram	lbw, b Patterson	0	
Abdul Qadir	not out	8	
Shoaib Mohammad	b Benjamin	0	
Saleem Jaffer	not out	8	
Extras	b 4, lb 6, w 10, nb 2	22	
(50 overs)	(for 9 wkts)	230	

	O	M	R	W
Patterson	10	1	34	3
Walsh	10	1	34	2
Harper	10	–	38	1
Benjamin	10	–	69	3
Richards	10	–	45	–

FALL OF WICKETS
1–78, 2–128, 3–147, 4–167, 5–186, 6–202, 7–202, 8–208, 9–208

Umpires: R.B. Gupta & V.K. Ramaswamy

West Indies won by 28 runs

Srikkanth made a furious assault on the New Zealand bowling at Nagpur and shared an opening partnership of 136 with . . . (Adrian Murrell/Allsport)

Sunil Gavaskar, who hit a breathtaking 103 not out. (Adrian Murrell/Allsport)

this match only had meaning if England failed to beat Sri Lanka. As it was, West Indies showed something of their old form, batting with control and sense and bowling with a hostility and accuracy which they had hitherto lacked. Richardson batted with great confidence, facing 136 balls and hitting 2 sixes and 8 fours. He and Richards put on 137 in 23 overs and took their side to a strong position.

Pakistan began convincingly with Mudassar, recalled to the side, and Rameez putting on 78 in 19 overs, but thereafter the necessary acceleration eluded them and they drifted to defeat. They were, however, still in the semi-final and West Indies, for the first time in the history of the competition, were not.

Round Six
AUSTRALIA v. ZIMBABWE

A ruggedly efficient innings of 93 in 33 overs by David Boon was the backbone of the Australian innings. Dean Jones was strangely out of touch, labouring through 27 overs, but Veletta played with a flourish towards the end of the innings.

Waller was forced to retire when he was hit on the

forehead by a rising ball from Reid. He returned later, but by then the Zimbabwe cause was lost, and their total was boosted by some friendly overs from Boon and Jones.

Like Sri Lanka, Zimbabwe had had a disappointing tournament, and they face a desperate search for fresh, young talent. Australia's victory and run rate placed them at the top of the table in Group A, with a rate of 5.19 to India's 5.18.

Round Six
INDIA v. NEW ZEALAND

Once more New Zealand failed to play with conviction and ended a most disappointing tournament by being trounced by an Indian side who were breathtakingly brilliant. New Zealand were shattered by Chetan Sharma, who performed the first hat trick in the history of the World Cup when he bowled Rutherford, Smith and Chatfield with the last three balls of the 42nd over. Watson and Snedden recovered some pride with a stand of 39 in the last eight overs.

To overhaul Australia and finish top of Group A, India had to reach their target in 42.2 overs. From the outset

Chetan Sharma – the first hat trick in World Cup cricket, Nagpur, 31 October. (George Herringshaw)

ROUND SIX – AUSTRALIA v. ZIMBABWE
30 October 1987 at Barabati Stadium, Cuttack

AUSTRALIA				ZIMBABWE			
D.C. Boon	c Houghton, b Butchart	93		A.H. Omarshah	b Waugh	32
G.R. Marsh	run out	37		A.C. Waller	c Waugh, b McDermott	38
D.M. Jones	not out	58		K.M. Curran	c Waugh, b May	29
C.J. McDermott	c Rawson, b Traicos	9		A.J. Pycroft	c Dyer, b McDermott	38
A.R. Border†	st Houghton, b Traicos	4		D.L. Houghton*	lbw, b May	1
M.R.J. Veletta	run out	43		I.P. Butchart	st Dyer, b Border	3
S.R. Waugh	not out	10		P.W.E. Rawson	not out	24
S.P. O'Donnell				E.A. Brandes	not out	18
G.C. Dyer*				M.P. Jarvis		
T.B.A. May				K.J. Arnott		
B.A. Reid				A.J. Traicos†		
Extras	b 3, lb 3, w 6	12		Extras	lb 5, w 6, nb 2	13
(50 overs)	(for 5 wkts)	266		(50 overs)	(for 6 wkts)	196

	O	M	R	W		O	M	R	W
Rawson	9	–	41	–	McDermott	10	–	43	2
Jarvis	6	–	33	–	Reid	9	2	30	–
Omarshah	7	–	31	–	Waugh	4	·	9	1
Brandes	10	1	58	–	O'Donnell	7	1	21	–
Traicos	10	–	45	2	May	10	1	30	2
Butchart	8	–	52	1	Border	8	–	36	1
					Jones	1	–	5	–
					Boon	1	–	17	–

FALL OF WICKETS
1–90, 2–148, 3–159, 4–170, 5–248

FALL OF WICKETS
1–55, 2–89, 3–92, 4–97, 5–139, 6–156

Umpires: Mahboob Shah & P.W. Vidanagamage

Australia won by 70 runs

ROUND SIX – INDIA v. NEW ZEALAND
31 October 1987 at Vidarbha C.A. Ground, Nagpur

NEW ZEALAND				INDIA			
J.G. Wright	run out	35		K. Srikkanth	c Rutherford, b Watson	75
P.A. Horne	b Prabhakar	18		S.M. Gavaskar	not out	103
M.D. Crowe	c Pandit, b Azharuddin	21		M. Azharuddin	not out	41
J.J. Crowe†	b Maninder Singh	24		N.S. Sidhu		
D.N. Patel	c Kapil Dev, b Shastri	40		D.B. Vengsarkar		
K.R. Rutherford	b Sharma	26		R.N. Kapil Dev†		
M.C. Snedden	run out	23		R.J. Shastri		
I.D.S. Smith*	b Sharma	0		C.S. Pandit*		
E.J. Chatfield	b Sharma	0		M. Prabhakar		
W. Watson	not out	12		C.J. Sharma		
D.K. Morrison				Maninder Singh		
Extras	lb 14, w 7, nb 1	22		Extras	lb 1, w 2, nb 2	5
(50 overs)	(for 9 wkts)	221		(32.1 overs)	(for 1 wkt)	224

	O	M	R	W		O	M	R	W
Kapil Dev	6	–	24	–	Morrison	10	–	69	–
Prabhakar	7	–	23	1	Chatfield	4.1	1	39	–
Sharma	10	2	51	3	Snedden	4	–	29	–
Azharuddin	7	–	26	1	Watson	10	–	50	1
Maninder Singh	10	–	51	1	Patel	4	–	36	–
Shastri	10	1	32	1					

FALL OF WICKETS
1–46, 2–84, 3–90, 4–122, 5–181, 6–182, 7–182,
8–182, 9–221

FALL OF WICKETS
1–136

Umpires: H.D. Bird & D.R. Shepherd

India won by 9 wickets

Boon is stumped by acting wicket-keeper Javed Miandad, Australia v. Pakistan semi-final. (Allsport)

RIGHT: *A victim of frustration and Tauseef Ahmed, Dean Jones is bowled for 38 in the semi-final match at Lahore. (Allsport)*

Final Tables

Group A

	P	W	L	Pts	R/R
India	6	5	1	20	5.39
Australia	6	5	1	20	5.19
New Zealand	6	2	4	8	4.88
Zimbabwe	6	–	6	0	3.76

Group B

	P	W	L	Pts	R/R
Pakistan	6	5	1	20	5.01
England	6	4	2	16	5.12
West Indies	6	3	3	12	5.16
Sri Lanka	6	–	6	0	4.04

that never seemed in doubt. Srikkanth and Gavaskar took 18 from the first two overs, and the sixth of the innings, bowled by Chatfield, produced 21 runs. Gavaskar hit sixes straight and over mid-wicket and then drove majestic fours. The opening stand realised 136 in 17 overs. Srikkanth hit 3 sixes and 9 fours in his 58-ball innings, and Gavaskar's first hundred in limited-over internationals came off 85 balls. Azharuddin helped him to continue the rout so that India won with nearly 18 overs to spare, having scored at just under seven runs an over.

The competition now entered its final stages with the climax looming that most people had predicted, India v. Pakistan at Calcutta.

Semi-Final
PAKISTAN v. AUSTRALIA

For the third time in successive World Cups Pakistan were

SEMI-FINAL – PAKISTAN v. AUSTRALIA
4 November 1987 at Qaddafi Stadium, Lahore

AUSTRALIA				PAKISTAN			
G.R. Marsh	run out		31		Rameez Raja	run out	1
D.C. Boon	st Javed Miandad,				Mansoor Akhtar	b McDermott	9
	b Saleem Malik		65		Saleem Malik	c McDermott,	
D.M. Jones	b Tauseef Ahmed		38			b Waugh	25
A.R. Border†	run out		18		Javed Miandad	b Reid	70
M.R.J. Veletta	b Imran Khan		48		Imran Khan†	c Dyer, b Border	58
S.R. Waugh	not out		32		Wasim Akram	b McDermott	20
S.P. O'Donnell	run out		0		Ijaz Ahmed	c Jones, b Reid	8
G.C. Dyer*	b Imran Khan		0		Saleem Yousuf*	c Dyer,	
C.J. McDermott	b Imran Khan		1			b McDermott	21
T.B.A. May	not out		0		Abdul Qadir	not out	20
B.A. Reid					Saleem Jaffer	c Dyer, b McDermott	0
Extras	b 1, lb 19, w 13, nb 1		34		Tauseef Ahmed	c Dyer, b McDermott	1
					Extras	lb 6, w 10	16
(50 overs)	(for 8 wkts)		267				
					(49 overs)		249

	O	M	R	W		O	M	R	W
Imran Khan	10	1	36	3	McDermott	10	–	44	5
Saleem Jaffer	6	–	57	–	Reid	10	2	41	2
Wasim Akram	10	–	54	–	Waugh	9	1	51	1
Abdul Qadir	10	–	39	–	O'Donnell	10	1	45	–
Tauseef Ahmed	10	1	39	1	May	6	–	36	–
Saleem Malik	4	–	22	1	Border	4	–	26	1

FALL OF WICKETS
1–73, 2–155, 3–155, 4–215, 5–236, 6–236, 7–241, 8–249

FALL OF WICKETS
1–2, 2–37, 3–38, 4–150, 5–177, 6–192, 7–212, 8–236, 9–247

Umpires: H.D. Bird & D.R. Shepherd

Australia won by 18 runs

beaten in the semi-final, but defeat by Australia at Lahore was by far the most bitter disappointment that they have ever had to face.

Border was happy to win the toss and bat first, and once again Australia were well served by their openers Boon and Marsh. Imran's pace and accuracy was nullified by Saleem Jaffer's wayward bowling and by the inability of Wasim Akram to pitch in line with the stumps, and it was not until the 18th over that Saleem Malik hit the stumps from square-leg to run out Marsh and break the stand. Jones settled into fluency and, in spite of an accurate spell from Qadir, Pakistan had no further success until the 31st over when Boon overbalanced and was stumped down the leg side by Javed, who had taken over from Saleem Yousuf after the wicket-keeper had been hit in the mouth. At the end of the next, Jones, frustrated, was bowled by Tauseef, and Pakistan had edged back into the match.

Veletta now played extremely well as he and Border negotiated a difficult time to add 60 before the Australian captain was run out as he attempted a second run. Imran now returned and, bowling at a considerable pace, he inspired his side with a magnificent spell, taking 3 for 17 in five overs, wrecking the stumps three times.

Waugh had survived a controversial decision by umpire Shepherd, who ruled that O'Donnell was run out even though he was standing in his ground and Waugh was on his way back to the pavilion. The decision proved to be vital. At the end of the 49th over, Australia were 249 for 8, and Imran had given his side a hold on the game, but he was forced to entrust the last over to Saleem Jaffer, who bowled no better than he had done at the outset. Waugh

hit his first ball over long-on for six and took 18 runs off the over. It proved to be a significant figure.

Pakistan made a wretched start. Rameez was sent back and run out by Border on the third ball of the innings. Mansoor, looking nothing like the batsman who had played such an important part in Pakistan's success in England, drove down the wrong line and was bowled while Saleem Malik was caught at mid-off so that Pakistan were 38 for 3 in 10.1 overs.

Javed and Imran began a careful process of repair and gradually increased the run rate. By the 36th over they had taken the score to 150 and there was more than a glimmer of a Pakistan victory, but Imran suddenly swung wildly at Border and was caught behind. Wasim Akram hit 2 sixes and with Javed at the crease, Pakistan still breathed hope, but in the 44th over he took an extravagant swing at Reid and was bowled. This left the last three Pakistan wickets six overs in which to make 56 runs, which, against some tight out-cricket, proved a task beyond them. The margin between the two sides was 18 runs, the toll that Waugh had exacted from Saleem Jaffer's last over. A nation mourned.

Semi-Final
INDIA v. ENGLAND

It seemed that winning the toss would be all important, for there was every indication that the ball would swing, but when England were asked to bat first it was soon apparent that swing was not to be the problem. By the fifth over, there was only one slip in operation and Maninder was bowling in the 11th over. It was he who accounted for

---

SEMI-FINAL – INDIA v. ENGLAND
5 November 1987 at Wankhede Stadium, Bombay

ENGLAND					INDIA			
G.A. Gooch	c Srikkanth, b Maninder Singh		115		K. Srikkanth	b Foster		31
R.T. Robinson	st More, b Maninder Singh		13		S.M. Gavaskar	b De Freitas		4
C.W.J. Athey	c More, b Sharma		4		N.S. Sidhu	c Athey, b Foster		22
M.W. Gatting†	b Maninder Singh		56		M. Azharuddin	lbw, b Hemmings		64
A.J. Lamb	not out		32		C.S. Pandit	lbw, b Foster		24
J.E. Emburey	lbw, b Kapil Dev		6		R.N. Kapil Dev†	c Gatting, b Hemmings		30
P.A.J. De Freitas	b Kapil Dev		7		R.J. Shastri	c Downton, b Hemmings		21
P.R. Downton*	not out		1		K.S. More*	c and b Emburey		0
N.A. Foster					M. Prabhakar	c Downton, b Small		4
G.C. Small					C.J. Sharma	c Lamb, b Hemmings		0
E.E. Hemmings					Maninder Singh	not out		0
Extras	b 1, lb 18, w 1		20		Extras	b 1, lb 9, w 6, nb 3		19
(50 overs)	(for 6 wkts)		254		(45.3 overs)			219

	O	M	R	W		O	M	R	W
Kapil Dev	10	1	38	2	De Freitas	7	–	37	1
Prabhakar	9	1	40	–	Small	6	–	22	1
Maninder Singh	10	–	54	3	Emburey	10	1	35	1
Sharma	9	–	41	1	Foster	10	–	47	3
Shastri	10	–	49	–	Hemmings	9.3	1	52	4
Azharuddin	2	–	13	–	Gooch	3	–	16	–

FALL OF WICKETS
1–40, 2–79, 3–196, 4–203, 5–219, 6–231

FALL OF WICKETS
1–7, 2–58, 3–73, 4–121, 5–168, 6–204, 7–205, 8–218, 9–219

Umpires: A.R. Crafter & S.J. Woodward

England won by 35 runs

ABOVE: *A nervous Mansoor Akhtar makes his ground, but he was soon to fall to McDermott. (Allsport)*

BELOW: *Gooch sweeps his way to 115 for England against India in the semi-final. (Adrian Murrell/Allsport)*

Robinson, stranding him half-way down the wicket and beating him with flight and turn. Like Robinson, Athey struggled, but Gooch was in fine form, employing the sweep to great effect, nullifying the Indian spin attack and keeping the score moving.

When he was joined by Gatting runs flowed freely. Both batsmen swept time and again, and Kapil Dev seemed strangely reluctant to adjust his field accordingly. Gooch and Gatting added 117 in 19 overs. Gooch was missed by Srikkanth, a running chance, when he was 82, but otherwise dominated, and it was Gatting who was the first to go, sweeping a ball from outside his off stump onto his leg stump in the 41st over. Two overs later, Gooch was caught on the mid-wicket boundary. He had played with great composure, a Colossus of a batsman.

The last 7.5 overs, with Lamb again in rollicking form, produced 51 runs, and India were left with a stiff although not impossible task.

India were handicapped by the absence of Vengsarkar, who was unwell, but with the most exciting batting side in the competition they still posed a great threat to England. Gavaskar caused crowd hysteria when he opened his account with a boundary, but then there was total silence when De Freitas knocked back his off stump, and the little man left the international arena for the last time, head bowed. This was the saddest failure of the day, indeed of the tournament.

Although not finding the boundary, Srikkanth and Sidhu began to repair the damage with some crisp shots against bowling that was not as demanding as it should have been, but alas, Srikkanth, head up, swung wildly at Foster and was bowled. He was not the last Indian batsman to have a fatal rush of blood. Sidhu was looking impressive until he clipped Foster to extra cover. Pandit bustled chirpily until he was deceived by a slower ball.

Foster had taken three vital wickets and India, ever eager for runs, were 121 for 4. Azharuddin looked assured, and now he was joined by Kapil Dev, capable of blasting any attack, and there were soon indications that this was a day that he had chosen to blast. Hemmings' first three overs cost 27 runs and Gooch had to bowl three tidy overs to try to compensate. In 32 balls, Azharuddin and Kapil Dev added 47, the Indian captain scoring 30 of them. India were racing to the final in front of an adoring crowd. Hemmings had suffered badly on the leg side. Azharuddin was dropped by Small at square-leg, another running chance, and Kapil Dev smote lustily in the same direction. Gatting posted himself on the leg-side fence as reinforcement and, incredibly, Kapil Dev hit the ball into his hands at the first opportunity. He was destroyed by his own excesses, attempting a six on the longest boundary when a four would have been easy fodder. It was a crucial lapse of concentration or of common sense.

TOP LEFT: *The turning point of the semi-final match between England and India. Kapil Dev swings Hemmings high to the square-leg boundary . . . (Adrian Murrell/ Allsport)*
LEFT: *. . . where Gatting takes the catch. (Adrian Murrell/ Allsport)*

ABOVE: *World Cup semi-final. (Allsport)*
BELOW: *Hemmings has Azharuddin lbw and England smell victory. (Adrian Murrell/Allsport)*

The moment that rocked Bombay. De Freitas bowls Gavaskar in his second over, and the most prolific run-scorer in Test cricket leaves the international scene for the last time. (Adrian Murrell/Allsport)

RIGHT: *Cup Final Day, Calcutta. (Allsport)*

Still Shastri was able to help Azharuddin push the score along and and the two hundred was passed with just under 10 overs remaining so that India were strolling to victory. Azharuddin, who had batted so well, underestimated Hemmings, however, and was lbw as he played across the line to a ball which kept low. More was caught and bowled by Emburey one run later off a casual shot, and India's temperamental weaknesses of the past returned to haunt them as a corporate insanity gripped them and they lost nerve and the match in a frightful scurry of woeful shots.

Prabhakar swung at Small. Chetan Sharma clouted the first ball he received to mid-wicket where Lamb took a fine tumbling catch and Shastri skied to Downton. It was all over. India had had success in their sights and, suddenly, were beaten by 35 runs with 4.3 of their overs unused.

Final
ENGLAND v. AUSTRALIA

Fate had decreed that England and Australia would contest the final of the fourth World Cup when human beings had believed an India–Pakistan meeting the most likely, with West Indies the strongest challengers to that pairing. Australia's arrival in the final was remarkable. In the months before the competition they had been seen as one of the weaker sides, but astute management and a wise policy which opted for young, dedicated players with a sense of discipline had paid dividends. They had played consistently well throughout the tournament. They were also happy to win the toss once again and bat first, which was better suited to their plans and temperament.

They began with a flourish, aided by the inaccuracy of Small and the inconsistency of De Freitas, and Boon and Marsh, the most reliable opening pair in the competition, took 49 off the first nine overs. It was Foster who put on the brakes and then ripped out Marsh's off stump with a fine delivery. Foster conceded only 16 runs in eight overs, and he and the two spinners gave England new heart.

Jones swept the first ball of Hemmings' second spell for six, but then scooped to mid-wicket. As the scoring had become becalmed, McDermott was promoted and hit 14 off eight balls, was dropped by Gooch off his own bowling and then bowled by the Essex man, who bowled a most commendable spell until Veletta and Border attacked him.

Boon skied the ball to Downton as he attempted to sweep Hemmings, and in the 10 overs that followed his dismissal, Border and Veletta added 73. Foster had been taken off after 10 economical overs, but he returned for two overs, which cost 22 runs as Veletta moved down the

FINAL – ENGLAND v. AUSTRALIA
8 November 1987 at Eden Gardens, Calcutta

AUSTRALIA				ENGLAND			
D.C. Boon	c Downton, b Hemmings		75	G.A. Gooch	lbw, b O'Donnell		35
G.R. Marsh	b Foster		24	R.T. Robinson	lbw, b McDermott		0
D.M. Jones	c Athey, b Hemmings		33	C.W.J. Athey	run out		58
C.J. McDermott	b Gooch		14	M.W. Gatting†	c Dyer, b Border		41
A.R. Border†	run out		31	A.J. Lamb	b Waugh		45
M.R.J. Veletta	not out		45	P.R. Downton*	c O'Donnell, b Border		9
S.R. Waugh	not out		5	J.E. Emburey	run out		10
S.P. O'Donnell				P.A.J. De Freitas	c Reid, b Waugh		17
G.C. Dyer*				N.A. Foster	not out		7
T.B.A. May				G.C. Small	not out		3
B.A. Reid				E.E. Hemmings			
Extras	b 1, lb 13, w 5, nb 7		26	Extras	b 1, lb 14, w 2, nb 4		21
(50 overs)	(for 5 wkts)		253	(50 overs)	(for 8 wkts)		246

	O	M	R	W		O	M	R	W
De Freitas	6	1	34	–	McDermott	10	1	51	1
Small	6	–	33	–	Reid	10	–	43	–
Foster	10	–	38	1	Waugh	9	–	37	2
Hemmings	10	1	48	2	O'Donnell	10	1	35	1
Emburey	10	–	44	–	May	4	–	27	–
Gooch	8	1	42	1	Border	7	–	38	2

FALL OF WICKETS
1–75, 2–151, 3–166, 4–168, 5–241

FALL OF WICKETS
1–1, 2–66, 3–135, 4–170, 5–188, 6–218, 7–220, 8–235

Umpires: R.B. Gupta & Mahboob Shah

Australia won by 7 runs

wicket to him. The 44th, 46th and 48th over each cost 12 runs while the last over, bowled by De Freitas, went for 11 runs, which meant that 65 runs had been scored from the final six overs of the innings. England had erred badly.

The fourth ball of McDermott's opening over had Robinson lbw, beaten for pace. It was the first ball that Robinson faced and his selection ahead of Broad was a mystery. Gooch and Athey put on 65 in 17 overs before Gooch fell to O'Donnell, a most valuable cricketer.

As usual, Athey found it difficult to lift the scoring rate, but Gatting was hitting and running briskly. After 31 overs, England were 135 for 2. There were signs of disarray in the Australian side, and Border brought him-

self on to bowl in order to calm his team, one felt. To his first delivery, pitched on leg stump, Gatting played the most stupid shot one can remember seeing played by a first-class cricketer in any form of cricket. He attempted a reverse sweep, although the shot would have brought him no runs for the area was tenanted, and the ball hit him on the shoulder and looped into Dyer's gloves. Gatting, obstinately, would not admit that the shot was injudicious, yet others felt that the crassness of it should be seared in his memory as it is in the memory of those who saw it.

Athey and Lamb put on 35 in eight overs, and Athey's 104-ball innings was ended when he was run out by Waugh's throw as he went for a third run. As he was to do

LEFT: *Foster bowls Marsh. England's first success. (All-sport)*
RIGHT: *Arjuna Ranatunga gave Sri Lanka some compensation for their lack of success by being the leading batsman in the World Cup averages. (Adrian Murrell/Allsport)*

with some regularity in the coming weeks, Athey debated the umpire's decision, but the television replay showed quite clearly that the umpire was correct. Athey's innings had spanned 39 overs.

From the last 10 overs, England needed 75, but this slipped to a more difficult 46 from the last five. Waugh bowled Lamb in the 47th over, but De Freitas suddenly brought a glimpse of the unlikely when he hit McDermott for 14 in three balls, 15 coming from the 48th over. Waugh, however, was as steady and reliable as O'Donnell had been earlier and had him caught at long-off in the next over. McDermott began the last over with England 17 short of victory, but there were to be no heroics, and a thoroughly professional, enthusiastic and well organised side won a deserved victory and restored pride to Australian cricket.

BELOW: *Mike Veletta played an invaluable innings of 45 not out at a crucial time. (Adrian Murrell/Allsport)*

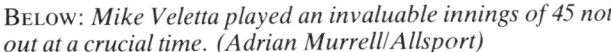

ABOVE: *McDermott has Robinson lbw first ball. (Adrian Murrell/Allsport)*

To the victor the spoils. Border chaired by his ecstatic team-mates. (Patrick Eagar)

Man-of-the-Match Awards

Round One
Javed Miandad, A.J. Lamb, G.R. Marsh, D.L. Houghton

Round Two
Abdul Qadir, I.V.A. Richards, S.R. Waugh, R.N. Kapil Dev

Round Three
Saleem Yousuf, A.J. Lamb, M. Prabhakar, D.C. Boon

Round Four
Imran Khan, P.V. Simmons, M. Azharuddin, J.J. Crowe

Round Five
Saleem Malik, G.A. Gooch, R.N. Kapil Dev, G.R. Marsh

Round Six
G.A. Gooch, R.B. Richardson, D.C. Boon, S.M. Gavaskar and C.J. Sharma

Semi-Finals
C.J. McDermott, G.A. Gooch

Final
D.C. Boon

RELIANCE WORLD CUP – AVERAGES

AUSTRALIA BATTING

	M	Inns	NOs	Runs	HS	Av	100s	50s
G.R. Marsh	8	8	1	428	126*	61.14	2	1
D.C. Boon	8	8		447	93	55.87		5
S.R. Waugh	8	8	5	167	45	55.66		
M.R.J. Veletta	4	4	1	136	48	45.33		
D.M. Jones	8	8	1	314	58*	44.85		3
A.R. Border	8	8		183	67	22.87		1
G.C. Dyer	8	4		50	27	12.50		
T.B.A. May	6	3	1	16	15	8.00		
C.J. McDermott	8	6		34	14	5.66		
T.M. Moody	3	3	1	10	8	5.00		
S.P. O'Donnell	7	4		15	7	3.75		

Also batted: B.A. Reid 1 (8 matches); P.L. Taylor 17* & 0 (2 matches); A.K. Zesers 2* & 8* (2 matches)

AUSTRALIA BOWLING

	Overs	Mds	Runs	Wkts	Av	Best	Runs/Ov
C.J. McDermott	73	3	341	18	18.94	5/44	4.67
S.R. Waugh	63.3	4	288	11	26.18	2/36	4.53
A.R. Border	32		166	6	27.66	2/27	5.18
S.P. O'Donnell	60.4	6	261	9	29.00	4/39	4.30
B.A. Reid	68	7	303	6	50.50	2/38	4.45
T.B.A. May	44	1	213	4	53.25	2/29	4.84
P.L. Taylor	10		71	1	71.00	1/46	7.10
A.K. Zesers	15	1	74	1	74.00	1/37	4.93

Also bowled: D.C. Boon 1-0-17-0; D.M. Jones 1-0-5-0; T.M. Moody 2-0-15-0

AUSTRALIA FIELDING FIGURES

11 - G.C. Dyer (ct 9/st 2); 4 - B.A. Reid, D.M. Jones and S.P. O'Donnell; 3 - S.R. Waugh; 2 - D.C. Boon, G.R. Marsh and C.J. McDermott; 1 - A.R. Border, T.B.A. May, T.M. Moody and A.K. Zesers

ENGLAND BATTING

	M	Inns	NOs	Runs	HS	Av	100s	50s
A.J. Lamb	8	7	2	299	76	59.80		2
G.A. Gooch	8	8		471	115	58.87	1	3
C.W.J. Athey	6	6	2	211	86	52.75		2
M.W. Gatting	8	8	1	354	60	50.57		3
N.A. Foster	7	4	3	42	20*	42.00		
B.C. Broad	3	3		67	36	22.33		
R.T. Robinson	7	7		142	55	20.28		1
P.A.J. De Freitas	8	6	2	79	23	19.75		
J.E. Emburey	8	7	2	96	30*	19.20		
D.R. Pringle	3	2		20	12	10.00		
P.R. Downton	8	5	1	19	9	4.75		
G.C. Small	8	3	1	3	3*	1.50		

Also batted: E.E. Hemmings 4* (6 matches); P.W. Jarvis was in the party but did not appear in a match

ENGLAND BOWLING

	Overs	Mds	Runs	Wkts	Av	Best	Runs/Ov
E.E. Hemmings	59.3	4	274	13	21.07	4/52	4.60
P.A.J. De Freitas	69.1	12	283	12	23.58	3/28	4.09
N.A. Foster	70	1	313	9	34.77	3/47	4.47
J.E. Emburey	79	4	295	6	49.16	2/26	3.73
G.C. Small	68	2	331	6	55.16	2/47	4.86
G.A. Gooch	15	1	79	1	79.00	1/42	5.26
D.R. Pringle	24	1	148	1	148.00	1/11	6.16

Also bowled: C.W.J. Athey 1-0-10-0; B.C. Broad 1-0-6-0; A.J. Lamb 1-0-3-0

ENGLAND FIELDING FIGURES

9 - P.R. Downton (ct 8/st 1); 4 - C.W.J. Athey; 3 - J.E. Emburey; 2 - G.A. Gooch, E.E. Hemmings and A.J. Lamb; 1 - B.C. Broad, N.A. Foster, M.W. Gatting, R.T. Robinson and sub (P.W. Jarvis)

INDIA BATTING

	M	Inns	NOs	Runs	HS	Av	100s	50s
M. Azharuddin	7	5	2	190	64	63.33		2
K.S. More	6	4	3	59	42*	59.00		
D.B. Vengsarkar	6	5	2	171	63	57.00		1
N.S. Sidhu	7	5		276	75	55.20		4
R.N. Kapil Dev	7	5		152	72*	50.66		1
S.M. Gavaskar	7	7	1	300	103*	50.00	1	2
K. Srikkanth	7	7		248	75	35.42		2
R.J. Shastri	7	4		63	22	15.75		
M. Prabhakar	7	4		23	11*	7.66		

Also batted: R.M.H. Binny 0 (1 match); Maninder Singh 4 & 0* (7 matches); C.S. Pandit 24 (2 matches); C.J. Sharma 0 (4 matches); L. Sivaramakrishnan played in two matches but did not bat

INDIA BOWLING

	Overs	Mds	Runs	Wkts	Av	Best	Runs/Ov
Maninder Singh	70	1	280	14	20.00	3/21	4.00
M. Azharuddin	23.5		109	5	21.80	3/19	4.57
M. Prabhakar	59	4	235	9	26.11	4/19	3.98
C.J. Sharma	36.1	2	170	6	28.33	3/51	4.70
R.J. Shastri	68.2	1	274	7	39.14	2/45	4.00
R.N. Kapil Dev	62	6	259	5	51.80	2/38	4.17
L. Sivaramakrishnan	17		70	1	70.00	1/36	4.11

Also bowled: R.M.H. Binny 7-0-46-1 (1 innings)

INDIA FIELDING FIGURES

11 - K.S. More (ct 6/st 5); 5 - R.N. Kapil Dev; 3 - N.S. Sidhu; 2 - M. Azharuddin, R.J. Shastri and K. Srikkanth; 1 - S.M. Gavaskar, Maninder Singh, C.S. Pandit, M. Prabhakar, L. Sivaramakrishnan and D.B. Vengsarkar

NEW ZEALAND BATTING

	M	Inns	NOs	Runs	HS	Av	100s	50s
K.R. Rutherford	5	5		204	75	40.80		1
M.D. Crowe	6	6		222	72	37.00		3
J.J. Crowe	6	6	1	180	88*	36.00		1
J.G. Wright	5	5		172	61	34.40		1
M.C. Snedden	6	6		157	64	26.16		1
W. Watson	6	4	3	24	12*	24.00		
A.H. Jones	4	4		94	64	23.50		1
S.L. Boock	4	3	2	19	12	19.00		
I.D.S. Smith	6	6	1	69	29	13.80		
J.G. Bracewell	4	4	1	39	13*	13.00		
D.N. Patel	6	6		58	40	9.66		
E.J. Chatfield	6	3	2	5	5*	5.00		

Also batted: P.A. Horne (1 match); D.K. Morrison played in one match but did not bat

NEW ZEALAND BOWLING

	Overs	Mds	Runs	Wkts	Av	Best	Runs/Ov
W. Watson	53	3	270	7	38.57	2/36	5.09
S.L. Boock	32.4	2	157	4	39.25	2/42	4.80
E.J. Chatfield	50.1	8	231	5	46.20	2/52	4.60
M.C. Snedden	49	3	253	5	50.60	2/35	5.16
D.N. Patel	43	1	222	4	55.50	3/36	5.16
J.G. Bracewell	24		154	0	–	0/24	6.41

Also bowled: D.K. Morrison 10-0-69-0 (1 innings)

NEW ZEALAND FIELDING FIGURES

4 - M.D. Crowe; 3 - I.D.S. Smith; 2 - S.L. Boock, J.J. Crowe and K.R. Rutherford; 1 - E.J. Chatfield, A.H. Jones, D.N. Patel, W. Watson and J.G. Wright

RELIANCE WORLD CUP – AVERAGES

PAKISTAN BATTING

	M	Inns	NOs	Runs	HS	Av	100s	50s
Saleem Malik	7	7	1	323	100	53.83	1	2
Rameez Raja	7	7		349	113	49.85	1	2
Javed Miandad	7	7	1	274	103	45.66	1	1
Saleem Yousuf	7	6	3	112	56	37.33		1
Imran Khan	7	6		147	58	24.50		1
Ijaz Ahmed	7	7	1	129	59	21.50		1
Mansoor Akhtar	6	6		99	33	16.50		
Wasim Akram	7	6		85	39	14.16		
Saleem Jaffer	5	3	2	9	8*	9.00		
Tauseef Ahmed	6	2		1	1	0.50		

Also batted: Abdul Qadir 12*, 16*, 8* and 20* (7 matches); Manzoor Elahi 4* (1 match); Mudassar Nazar 40 (2 matches); Shoaib Mohammad 0 (1 match)

PAKISTAN BOWLING

	Overs	Mds	Runs	Wkts	Av	Best	Runs/Ov
Imran Khan	49.5	6	222	17	13.05	4/37	4.45
Abdul Qadir	68	2	242	12	20.16	4/31	3.55
Mansoor Akhtar	4		23	1	23.00	1/7	5.75
Saleem Jaffer	39.4		210	5	42.00	3/30	5.29
Wasim Akram	63.2	1	295	7	42.14	3/45	4.65
Tauseef Ahmed	60	4	230	5	46.00	1/35	3.83
Mudassar Nazar	19		110	1	110.00	1/47	5.78
Saleem Malik	31	1	157	1	157.00	1/22	5.06

Also bowled: Javed Miandad 3-0-5-1 (1 innings); Manzoor Elahi 9.4-0-32-1 (1 innings)

PAKISTAN FIELDING FIGURES
9 - Saleem Yousuf; 3 - Mudassar Nazar; 2 - Abdul Qadir, Mansoor Akhtar and Javed Miandad (ct 1/st 1); 1 - Ijaz Ahmed, Imran Khan, Saleem Malik, Tauseef Ahmed and Wasim Akram

SRI LANKA BATTING

	M	Inns	NOs	Runs	HS	Av	100s	50s
A. Ranatunga	5	5	2	252	86*	84.00		3
R.L. Dias	2	2		85	80	42.50		1
L.R.D. Mendis	6	6	1	136	58	27.20		1
A.P. Gurusinha	4	4		108	37	27.00		
P.A. de Silva	6	6	2	101	42	25.25		
R.S. Mahanama	6	6		134	89	22.33		1
R.S. Madugalle	5	4		85	30	21.25		
D.S.B.P. Kuruppu	5	5		69	33	13.80		
R.J. Ratnayake	3	3	1	27	14*	13.50		
S. Jeganathan	3	3	1	24	20*	12.00		
J.R. Ratnayeke	6	5		52	22	10.40		
A.L.F. de Mel	3	2		0	0	0.00		

Also batted: V.B. John 8*, 1*, 1* and 1* (96 matches); S.D. Anurasiri 0 (6 matches)

SRI LANKA BOWLING

	Overs	Mds	Runs	Wkts	Av	Best	Runs/Ov
S. Jeganathan	29	2	123	4	30.75	2/45	4.24
J.R. Ratnayeke	54	2	313	10	31.30	3/41	5.79
R.J. Ratnayake	25		163	4	40.75	2/64	6.52
A.P. Gurusinha	5		51	1	51.00	1/43	10.20
S.D. Anurasiri	55	1	271	4	67.75	1/44	4.92
P.A. de Silva	42		217	3	72.33	2/43	5.16
A.L.F. de Mel	24.2		184	1	184.00	1/97	7.56
V.B. John	49	7	226	1	226.00	1/53	4.61
A. Ranatunga	8		58	0	–	0/18	7.25

SRI LANKA FIELDING FIGURES
4 - D.S.B.P. Kuruppu (ct 3/st 1); 3 - R.J. Ratnayake; 2 - S.D. Anurasiri, P.A. de Silva and R.S. Mahanama; 1 - S. Jeganathan, V.B. John, R.S. Madugalle and A. Ranatunga

WEST INDIES BATTING

	M	Inns	NOs	Runs	HS	Av	100s	50s
I.V.A. Richards	6	6		391	181	65.16	1	3
A.L. Logie	6	6	2	181	65*	45.25		1
R.B. Richardson	6	6		271	110	45.16	1	2
P.V. Simmons	4	4		170	89	42.50		2
D.L. Haynes	6	6		219	105	36.50	1	
P.J.L. Dujon	6	5	1	59	46	14.75		
C.L. Hooper	6	6	2	42	22	14.00		
C.A. Best	2	2		23	18	11.50		
C.A. Walsh	6	3	1	18	9*	9.00		
R.A. Harper	6	6	1	37	24	7.40		
W.K.M. Benjamin	5	4	1	15	8	5.00		

Also batted: B.P. Patterson 0* & 0* (6 matches); E.A.E. Baptiste 14 (1 match); A.H. Gray was in the party, but did not appear in a match

WEST INDIES BOWLING

	Overs	Mds	Runs	Wkts	Av	Best	Runs/Ov
B.P. Patterson	56	2	253	14	18.07	3/31	4.51
C.A. Walsh	55.3	6	229	9	25.44	4/40	4.12
C.L. Hooper	41		181	7	25.85	3/42	4.41
R.A. Harper	60	4	206	4	51.50	1/28	3.43
W.K.M. Benjamin	44	2	218	4	54.50	3/69	4.95
I.V.A. Richards	31		126	1	126.00	1/32	4.06

Also bowled: R.B. Richardson 4-0-24-0; E.A.E. Baptiste 8-1-33-0

WEST INDIES FIELDING FIGURES
4 - P.J.L. Dujon and C.L. Hooper; 2 - R.B. Richardson, I.V.A. Richards and R.A. Harper; 1 - D.L. Haynes, C.A. Best, A.L. Logie, C.A. Walsh, B.P. Patterson and E.A.E. Baptiste

ZIMBABWE BATTING

	M	Inns	NOs	Runs	HS	Av	100s	50s
D.L. Houghton	6	6		225	141	37.50	1	1
K.J. Arnott	4	3		112	60	37.33		2
A.J. Pycroft	6	6		174	61	34.80		2
P.W.E. Rawson	4	4	2	56	24*	28.00		
A.C. Waller	6	6	1	125	39	25.00		
E.A. Brandes	4	3	2	21	18*	21.00		
I.P. Butchart	6	5		98	54	19.60		1
K.M. Curran	5	5		75	30	15.00		
A.H. Omarshah	6	6		80	41	13.33		
G.A. Paterson	4	4		24	16	6.00		
R.D. Brown	3	3		17	13	5.66		
A.J. Traicos	6	3	1	10	6	5.00		

Also batted: M.P. Jarvis 8* and 1* (5 matches); M.A. Meman 19 (1 match)

ZIMBABWE BOWLING

	Overs	Mds	Runs	Wkts	Av	Best	Runs/Ov
K.M. Curran	26		124	4	31.00	2/29	4.76
A.H. Omarshah	40		179	5	35.80	2/34	4.47
A.J. Traicos	58	2	218	6	36.33	2/27	3.75
P.W.E. Rawson	33		188	4	47.00	2/46	5.69
I.P. Butchart	35	1	222	3	74.00	2/59	6.34
E.A. Brandes	33	4	153	2	76.50	2/44	4.63
M.P. Jarvis	35.4	1	155	2	77.50	1/21	4.34

Also bowled: M.A. Meman 6-5-0-34-0 (1 innings)

ZIMBABWE FIELDING FIGURES
5 - D.L. Houghton (ct 3/st 2); 3 - R.D. Brown; 2 - E.A. Brandes, I.P. Butchart, G.A. Paterson and P.W.E. Rawson; 1 - K.J. Arnott, K.M. Curran, M.P. Jarvis, A.H. Omarshah and A.C. Waller

Renaissance

The season in Australia.
Sheffield Shield. McDonald's Cup.
Test series Australia *v.* New Zealand,
Australia *v.* Sri Lanka. Bicentennial
Test and One-Day International.
Benson and Hedges World Series.
Form charts.
First-class averages.
Review of the season by Chris Harte.

Celebratory season. Sydney Harbour prepares for the Bicentennial Test Match, Australia v. England. (Allsport)

Australian cricket emerged from the doldrums of the past few years. Triumph in the World Cup had been hard earned and the planning had been intelligent. There was enthusiasm, youth and discipline, and an element of self-belief had returned. The arrival of Ian Botham at Queensland encouraged the belief that the state could at last win the Sheffield Shield, and there was a general reawakening of interest in this premier competition. The 'rebels' had returned from South Africa, and, although banned from Test cricket, were able to take their places in the Sheffield Shield sides, if selected. There was to be a three-match Test series against New Zealand, a visit from Sri Lanka, a Bicentennial Test against England and, inevitably, a long programme of one-day internationals for the Benson and Hedges World Series. Australian cricket faced the future more optimistically than it had done for some time. The sad note to intrude was the news that Simon O'Donnell was suffering from cancer and would miss the season as he underwent a course of treatment. The joyous news at the end of the season was that the treatment had proved successful, and the likeable O'Donnell was restored to fitness.

13, 14, 15 and 16 November 1987

at Sydney

South Australia 171 (A.M.J. Hilditch 57, M.R. Whitney 5 for 33) and 131 (G.F. Lawson 6 for 31)
New South Wales 206 (P.L. Taylor 78, P.W. Gladigau 5 for 48) and 98 for 4

New South Wales won by 6 wickets
New South Wales 6 pts, South Australia 0 pts

at Brisbane

Victoria 226 (D.F. Whatmore 51, C.J. McDermott 5 for 65) and 293 (D.M. Jones 75)
Queensland 405 for 9 dec (A.R. Border 168, G.S. Trimble 112, I.T. Botham 58, A.I.C. Dodemaide 4 for 89) and 115 for 5

Queensland won by 5 wickets
Queensland 6 pts, Victoria 0 pts

at Perth

Tasmania 135 and 189 (D.C. Boon 69, G.A. Hughes 55, S.J. Milosz 4 for 53)
Western Australia 461 for 6 dec (T.M. Moody 144, M.R.J. Veletta 106, G.M. Wood 83, W.S. Andrews 72)

Western Australia won by an innings and 137 runs
Western Australia 6 pts, Tasmania 0 pts

A crowd of over 4,000 arrived to see Ian Botham's début for Queensland. He did not disappoint, taking four fine slip catches, having Bright lbw and then on the second day, before a crowd of 10,000, hitting 58 off 34 balls, including 4 sixes and 7 fours. One over from left-arm spinner Emerson produced 21 runs, 20 of them to Botham. The highlight of the game at Brisbane, however, was a fifth wicket stand between Border and Glenn Trimble. They came together at 35 for 4 and took the score to 266 before Trimble fell to Dodemaide. Victoria were below strength, missing Hughes and Jackson as well as O'Donnell, but Queensland were superior throughout the match.

Geoff Lawson reasserted himself as a contender for a Test place as New South Wales brushed aside South Australia in three days. Led by Greg Dyer, who had succeeded Wellham as captain, New South Wales owed much to night-watchman Peter Taylor, who followed his maiden first-class century in Zimbabwe with his highest Shield score.

In Perth, nothing went right for Tasmania. Veletta and Moody put on 234 for Western Australia's second wicket at a run a minute. Wood hit 83 in three hours, and Andrews made 72 off 108 deliveries. Tasmania's opening bowler Cooley collided with the fence when he tried to stop a big hit by Ken MacLeay and could not bat in the second innings. Milosz had match figures of 7 for 66.

18 November 1987

at Perth

Western Australia 192
New Zealanders 193 for 8 (A.H. Jones 84 not out, K.R. Rutherford 54)

New Zealanders won by 2 wickets

Wood and Andrews hit 62 in 42 minutes, with Andrews hitting 48 off 55 balls. Snedden was the most successful of the tourists' bowlers in this day/night match, and Jones and Rutherford, who added 100 for the third wicket, were

A return to fitness and form. Geoff Lawson, 6 for 31 as New South Wales beat South Australia in the opening match of the season. (Mark Leech)

the most impressive batsmen as New Zealand won with eight balls to spare.

20, 21, 22 and 23 November 1987

at Melbourne

Victoria 501 for 5 dec (D.M. Jones 191, P.W. Young 164 not out)
Tasmania 324 (G.A. Hughes 147, A.I.C. Dodemaide 5 for 43) and 354 for 9 (G.A. Hughes 95, M.D. Taylor 59, A.J. de Winter 51)

Match drawn
Victoria 2 pts, Tasmania 0 pts

at Adelaide

South Australia 387 (D.W. Hookes 89, P.R. Sleep 70, M.D. Haysman 60, A.M.J. Hilditch 56, J.N. Maguire 5 for 60) and 209 for 3 dec (A.M.J. Hilditch 91 not out, D.W. Hookes 67)
Queensland 318 (R.B. Kerr 91, I.T. Botham 66, T.B.A. May 4 for 55) and 210 for 8 (R.B. Kerr 63, G.M. Ritchie 55)

Match drawn
South Australia 2 pts, Queensland 0 pts

at Perth

Western Australia 131 (R.J. Hadlee 5 for 37) and 117 (R.J. Hadlee 5 for 30, W. Watson 4 for 42)
New Zealanders 344 for 9 dec (M.D. Crowe 119, D.N. Patel 105, K.H. MacLeay 4 for 75)

New Zealanders won by an innings and 96 runs

With skipper Dean Jones hitting a glorious century on the

South Australia v Queensland at Adelaide. Anderson is lbw to Tim May for 16. (Chris Harte)

opening day and Peter Young reaching a career best, Victoria gave the Tasmanian bowlers another drubbing to supplement the one they had received in Perth. Glenn Hughes hit a maiden century, which nearly helped save the follow-on, and he followed his first innings with 95 in the second before being caught at cover. Victoria looked like completing an innings victory, but de Winter, a late inclusion in place of Peter Faulkner, who withdrew for personal reasons, batted doggedly to save the visitors.

In spite of Botham's three wickets and five from Maguire, South Australia took a first innings lead over Queensland. Border rested his main bowlers and offered some fodder on which the home side could feed in their second innings and so consider a declaration. Hookes finally asked Queensland to make 279 in as many minutes. The visitors were challenging for victory until a middle-order collapse against spinners May and Sleep. South Australia gave a first-class début to pace bowler Shane George, who, at 17 years, 31 days, was the youngest player to represent the state. He dismissed Courtice and Kerr in the first innings.

Richard Hadlee took five wickets in an innings for the 93rd time, and 10 wickets in a match for the 11th, as the New Zealanders romped to victory over Shield holders Western Australia in three days. Martin Crowe and Dipak Patel added 164 for the tourists' fifth wicket.

25 November 1987

at Renmark

New Zealanders 197 for 8
South Australia Country XI 112

New Zealanders won by 85 runs

27, 28, 29 and 30 November 1987

at Melbourne

Western Australia 291 (G.M. Wood 74) and 237 for 3 (G.R. Marsh 120 not out, M.R.J. Veletta 52)
Victoria 431 for 4 dec (D.F. Whatmore 127, P.W. Young 93 not out, M.B. Quinn 81, A.I.C. Dodemaide 71 not out)

Match drawn
Victoria 2 pts, Western Australia 0 pts

at Newcastle

Queensland 210 (G.M. Ritchie 64, G.F. Lawson 4 for 41) and 345 for 6 dec (R.B. Kerr 107, A.R. Border 101, G.S. Trimble 68 not out)
New South Wales 139 and 83 (C.J. McDermott 7 for 54)

Queensland won by 333 runs
Queensland 6 pts, New South Wales 0 pts

at Adelaide

New Zealanders 360 for 7 dec (M.D. Crowe 144, A.H. Jones 65, T.B.A. May 4 for 92) and 267 for 6 dec (M.D. Crowe 56 not out)
South Australia 242 (D.W. Hookes 128, J.G. Bracewell 7 for 98) and 386 for 7 (G.A. Bishop 123, W.B. Phillips 75)

South Australia won by 3 wickets

Queensland secured the second win in three matches and moved to the top of the Shield table with an emphatic win over New South Wales. The match was over in three days, and 17,795 people watched it. Queensland struggled in their first innings, but New South Wales fared even worse against McDermott, Tazelaar and Botham. A third wicket stand of 206 between Kerr and Border took Queensland to a commanding position. Border reached his 50th first-class hundred. Needing over 400 runs to win, New South Wales were shot out in 95 minutes for 83. McDermott and Tazelaar bowled unchanged. McDermott returned his best Shield figures, 7 for 54 in 11 overs, and Tazelaar had 3 for 22 in 10.

Western Australia's ambitions suffered something of a reverse at Melbourne, where a late start and some laborious Victorian batting determined the course of the match. Whatmore, who reached 5,000 runs in first-class cricket, and Quinn began with a stand of 197, a record for Victoria against Western Australia, and Young and Dodemaide added an unbeaten 170 at the close. Geoff Marsh hit a patient century to save the game on the last day.

Martin Crowe and Andrew Jones produced some sparkling batting in a stand of 138 for the New Zealanders, and, in spite of a 128 in 172 minutes from David Hookes, South Australia trailed. The rest of the state side fumbled before off-spinner John Bracewell. Jeff Crowe set South Australia a formidable target, 386, but Glenn Bishop hit bravely for 3½ hours, and Wayne Phillips showed some exciting stroke-play. There were valuable contributions from

Haysman, O'Connor and May, and South Australia won most commendably.

4, 5, 6 and 7 December 1987

at Devonport

Tasmania 134 and 295 (D.J. Buckingham 112, G.F. Lawson 5 for 72)
New South Wales 467 for 4 dec (M.D. O'Neill 130 not out, M.E. Waugh 101 not out, S.B. Smith 84, M.A. Taylor 72)

New South Wales won by an innings and 38 runs
New South Wales 6 pts, Tasmania 0 pts

Once more Tasmania were overwhelmed. They were bowled out in 61.1 overs by a varied attack, and then their bowlers were put to the sword yet again. Steve Smith returning to the New South Wales side for the first time since the South African venture, and Mark Taylor put on 113 for the first wicket. Mark Waugh hit a maiden first-class century as he and O'Neill shared an unbeaten stand of 187. In three matches, Tasmania had conceded 1,429 runs and taken only 15 wickets. Buckingham, batting with a runner, battled bravely for 330 minutes, but Lawson was again in fine form, and an innings victory for New South Wales always looked probable.

Craig McDermott returned his best figures in the Sheffield Shield, 7 for 54, as Queensland bowled out New South Wales for 83. McDermott was Australia's leading bowler in the Test series with New Zealand. (Adrian Murrell/ Allsport)

First Test Match
AUSTRALIA v. NEW ZEALAND

Winning the toss on a cloudy, breezy morning, Allan Border had no hesitation in asking New Zealand to bat first, and his decision was more than justified by the end of the first day. Veletta and Morrison made their débuts in Test cricket.

Although there were doubts as to his fitness, Bruce Reid was the pick of the Australian bowlers and he began the New Zealand slide when he had Rutherford taken at silly mid-on off the fourth ball of the match. Wright batted dourly, and Jones was at the wicket 90 minutes before being bowled by McDermott. Martin Crowe at last brought some suggestion of class and stroke-play to the batting and hit 67 in just over three hours, but six wickets went down for 48 runs in the last part of the first day, and New Zealand, 181 for 9 at the close, were already struggling to keep in the match.

That the Australians had not put the match totally out of reach of the New Zealanders by the end of the second day was due to lapses towards the close. McDermott brought the New Zealand innings to a prompt close when he had Bracewell caught, and Boon and Marsh set about giving Australia the solid start which had now become customary. Hadlee could not find his rhythm until the post-lunch session, when he had Marsh taken at slip and caused

Dean Jones to play a rising ball down into his stumps. Danny Morrison captured a notable first Test wicket when he had Allan Border lbw at 131, and shortly after tea John Bracewell had Veletta taken close in.

Throughout these mishaps David Boon batted with a decisive authority which now marks him as a batsman of the highest calibre. His footwork was positive, and he punched, drove and cut with confident power. His fifth Test hundred arrived when he cut Bracewell, and this was followed by two boundaries off Hadlee. He moved to the highest Test score of his career. It was a resounding innings, worthy of any Man-of-the-Match award, but its end was silly. Waugh pushed a ball from Bracewell to mid-wicket and called for a sharp single. Slow to react, Boon was beaten by Martin Crowe's accurate throw. Obviously shaken by this disaster, Steve Waugh clipped the second ball of the last over to square-leg, and Australia finished on 219 for 6.

The last four Australian wickets realised another 86 runs on the third day. Peter Sleep was the main contributor, being last out for 39. Poor Rutherford again made one feel that Test cricket was not for him, struggling for two before offering a straightforward catch to Dyer behind the stumps. Two runs earlier, New Zealand had lost Wright to Reid, and three more wickets were to fall before the arrears were cleared. Andrew Jones batted grittily, but he was out when he flashed wildly at Reid, and Martin Crowe

---

FIRST TEST MATCH – AUSTRALIA v. NEW ZEALAND
4, 5, 6 and 7 December 1987 at Wooloongabba, Brisbane

NEW ZEALAND

	FIRST INNINGS		SECOND INNINGS	
K.R. Rutherford	c Veletta, b Reid	0	(2) c Dyer, b McDermott	2
J.G. Wright	c Dyer, b Hughes	38	(1) lbw, b Reid	15
A.H. Jones	b McDermott	4	c Border, b Reid	45
M.D. Crowe	c Waugh, b Hughes	67	c Jones, b Hughes	23
J.J. Crowe†	lbw, b Waugh	16	lbw, b Reid	12
D.N. Patel	c Dyer, b McDermott	17	c Dyer, b Hughes	62
R.J. Hadlee	c Boon, b Hughes	8	c Marsh, b McDermott	24
J.G. Bracewell	c Veletta, b McDermott	11	c Dyer, b McDermott	0
I.D.S. Smith*	lbw, b Reid	2	c Veletta, b Reid	9
D.K. Morrison	c Waugh, b McDermott	0	c Dyer, b Waugh	2
E.J. Chatfield	not out	0	not out	1
Extras	b 1, lb 7, w 4, nb 11	23	b 6, lb 1, w 1, nb 9	17
		186		**212**

	O	M	R	W	O	M	R	W
Reid	25	10	40	2	25	6	53	4
McDermott	22.2	6	43	4	21	2	79	3
Hughes	18	5	40	3	17	7	57	2
Waugh	22	9	35	1	2	1	2	1
Sleep	6	1	20	–	14	5	14	–

FALL OF WICKETS
1–0, 2–28, 3–80, 4–133, 5–143, 6–153, 7–175, 8–180, 9–181
1–18, 2–20, 3–66, 4–103, 5–104, 6–142, 7–142, 8–152, 9–204

AUSTRALIA

	FIRST INNINGS		SECOND INNINGS	
G.R. Marsh	c Bracewell, b Hadlee	25	(2) not out	31
D.C. Boon	run out	143	(1) lbw, b Bracewell	24
D.M. Jones	b Hadlee	2	not out	38
A.R. Border†	lbw, b Morrison	9		
M.R.J. Veletta	c Rutherford, b Bracewell	4		
S.R. Waugh	c Jones, b Morrison	21		
P.R. Sleep	c and b Bracewell	39		
G.C. Dyer*	lbw, b Hadlee	8		
C.J. McDermott	c Wright, b Morrison	22		
M.G. Hughes	c Smith, b Morrison	5		
B.A. Reid	not out	8		
Extras	b 3, lb 5, w 2, nb 9	19	lb 1, w 1, nb 2	4
		305	(for 1 wkt)	**97**

	O	M	R	W	O	M	R	W
Hadlee	31	5	95	3	8	3	14	–
Morrison	28	7	86	4	8	–	32	–
Chatfield	34	11	58	–				
Bracewell	24.5	3	58	2	13	3	32	1
Patel					3.1	–	18	1

FALL OF WICKETS
1–65, 2–72, 3–110, 4–131, 5–219, 6–219, 7–250, 8–286, 9–291
1–37

Umpires: A.R. Crafter & M.W. Johnson

Australia won by 9 wickets

Danny Morrison made his Test début for New Zealand against Australia at Brisbane and took 4 for 86 in the first innings. (Patrick Eagar)

hooked Hughes into the hands of square-leg. Jeff Crowe, still struggling for form, was lbw, and New Zealand led by only 12 runs at the end of the day.

The game was over 17 minutes after tea on the fourth day. Dipak Patel offered resistance, but the eager Australian pace attack was not to be denied, and Boon, Marsh and Jones wasted little time in hitting off the runs.

The winning of the toss had played a decisive part in the winning of the match, but it was hard to escape from the fact that New Zealand, in a period of reconstruction, were carrying three or four players who were not of Test standard. Sadly, their captain appeared to be one of them.

11, 12, 13 and 14 December 1987

at Melbourne

South Australia 468 (W.B. Phillips 126, D.W. Hookes 93, G.A. Bishop 79, H.B. Jolly 65, S.P. Davis 4 for 70) and 158 for 2 dec (G.A. Bishop 82 not out)
Victoria 345 for 8 dec (W.G. Whiteside 84 not out, I.D. Frazer

76, D.F. Whatmore 69, J.D. Siddons 64, S.P.G. George 4 for 81) and 285 for 4 (J.D. Siddons 124 not out, P.W. Young 60)

Victoria won by 6 wickets
Victoria 6 pts, South Australia 0 pts

at Perth

New South Wales 115 (T.M. Alderman 5 for 35) and 131 (G.R.J. Matthews 53, C.D. Matthews 6 for 56)
Western Australia 256 (K.J. Hughes 76, G.R.J. Matthews 5 for 49)

Western Australia won by an innings and 10 runs
Western Australia 6 pts, New South Wales 0 pts

South Australia introduced two newcomers to the Sheffield Shield in Lehmann and Jolly. Darren Lehmann, at 17 years old, was further testimony to the southern state's desire to encourage youth. With Wayne Phillips reaching his 13th first-class hundred and David Hookes hitting fiercely, the visitors reached an impressive total, but determined batting enabled Victoria to avoid the follow-on at which point they declared. South Australia scored at more than five an over, and then declared, leaving Victoria 68 overs in which to make 282. Jamie Siddons played a sparkling innings, hit 15 fours, and saw Victoria to their target with 23 balls to spare.

Hughes, Shipperd and Alderman returned to the Western Australian side, and Hughes, used as an opener, and Alderman played a significant part in the reigning champions' victory, which came inside three days. Matthews, the left-arm medium-pacer had nine wickets in the match.

Second Test Match
AUSTRALIA *v.* NEW ZEALAND

New Zealand recovered from the trauma of losing skipper Jeff Crowe to the third ball of the match to reach 268 for 2 by the close of the first day. Crowe, who had promoted himself in an attempt to rediscover his form, looped a simple catch to short leg. Wright and Andrew Jones repaired the damage with a stand of 128, and Australia suffered a setback when Reid left the field with torn ligaments in his back. It transpired that his season was at an end.

Wright became the first victim of débutant off-spinner Tim May, but Martin Crowe hit a six and 3 fours in his first 22 runs and reached 88 by the end of the day, having been at the wicket for 2½ hours. Meanwhile, Andrew Jones had scored a lusty first Test hundred. He reached three figures with a boundary off the 247th ball he received. Not always orthodox, he presented a brave and aggressive front and played commendably.

On the second day, Martin Crowe soon completed his eighth Test hundred, a New Zealand record, and he and Jones took their stand to 213. Crowe was caught at long-off, a fine running catch, having hit a six and 17 fours and faced 184 balls. Jones was run out by McDermott, who bowled with great determination, and thereafter New Zealand lost their way, failing to press home the advantage that they had gained.

Australia began the third day on 17 for 0, but Hadlee dismissed Boon and Jones in four balls, and Marsh went at 85. New Zealand again had a chance to take charge of the match, but Allan Border played a defiant innings. He should have been stumped off Gray when he was 57, and Jeff Crowe sportingly indicated that he had not taken a catch cleanly when Border was 65, but by the end of the day the Australian captain had reached his 22nd Test century.

He turned this into his first double hundred in Test cricket on the fourth day when he overtook Bradman and Greg Chappell to become the leading run-scorer in Australian Test history. In all, he batted for 599 minutes and hit 20 fours.

Dyer played some fierce shots to reach a maiden Test fifty, and Hadlee finished the innings with the sixth ball of the final day. It gave him figures of 5 for 68, remarkable in the circumstances, and it was the 30th time that he had taken five wickets in a Test innings.

New Zealand had an uncomfortable last day against spin, but a draw had long been apparent.

Border was rightly named as Man of the Match, but Martin Crowe, Hadlee and Andrew Jones, who hit 11 fours and batted for 444 minutes, all deserved special mention.

Andrew Jones, unorthodox but effective. Jones hit 150 for New Zealand in the second Test, at Adelaide. (David Munden)

SECOND TEST MATCH – AUSTRALIA *v.* NEW ZEALAND
11, 12, 13, 14 and 15 December 1987 at Adelaide Oval

NEW ZEALAND

	FIRST INNINGS		SECOND INNINGS	
J.J. Crowe†	c Veletta, b Reid	0	c Boon, b May	19
J.G. Wright	c Waugh, b May	45	b McDermott	8
A.H. Jones	run out	150	c Border, b Sleep	64
M.D. Crowe	c sub (Hughes), b Sleep	137	c Border, b Sleep	8
D.N. Patel	c Marsh, b McDermott	35	c Boon, b May	40
E.J. Gray	c Boon, b McDermott	23	c Border, b May	14
R.J. Hadlee	c and b Jones	36	(9) not out	3
J.G. Bracewell	c Sleep, b McDermott	32		
I.D.S. Smith*	not out	8	(8) c Dyer, b Sleep	5
M.C. Snedden	c Veletta, b McDermott	0	(7) not out	8
D.K. Morrison				
Extras	b 3, lb 7, w 1, nb 8	19	b 2, lb 4, nb 7	13
	(for 9 wkts, dec)	485	(for 7 wkts)	182

AUSTRALIA

	FIRST INNINGS	
G.R. Marsh	c Gray, b Hadlee	30
D.C. Boon	b Hadlee	6
D.M. Jones	c Smith, b Hadlee	0
A.R. Border†	st Smith, b Bracewell	205
S.R. Waugh	lbw, b Snedden	61
P.R. Sleep	c Smith, b Morrison	62
M.R.J. Veletta	c sub (Rutherford), b Bracewell	10
G.C. Dyer*	run out	60
C.J. McDermott	lbw, b Hadlee	18
T.B.A. May	not out	14
B.A. Reid	c Smith, b Hadlee	5
Extras	b 2, lb 13, w 1, nb 9	25
		496

	O	M	R	W	O	M	R	W
Reid	7	–	21	1				
McDermott	45.5	10	135	4	10	3	29	1
Waugh	31	11	71	–	10	4	17	–
May	54	13	134	1	30	10	68	3
Sleep	34	5	109	1	32	14	61	3
Jones	3	1	5	1	3	2	1	–

	O	M	R	W
Hadlee	42	16	68	5
Morrison	22	–	89	1
Bracewell	48	8	122	2
Snedden	32	6	89	1
Gray	44	10	102	–
Patel	7	3	11	–

FALL OF WICKETS
1–0, 2–128, 3–341, 4–346, 5–398, 6–405, 7–473, 8–481, 9–485
1–16, 2–57, 3–77, 4–139, 5–153, 6–170, 7–179

FALL OF WICKETS
1–29, 2–29, 3–85, 4–201, 5–355, 6–380, 7–417, 8–451, 9–489

Umpires: R.C. Bailhache & S.G. Randell

Match drawn

18, 19, 20 and 21 December 1987

at Brisbane

Western Australia 217 (T.M. Moody 89, D.Tazelaar 6 for 52) and 192 (T.J. Zoehrer 51)
Queensland 318 (R.B. Kerr 102, I.T. Botham 53) and 92 for 0 (T.J. Barsby 50 not out)

Queensland won by 10 wickets
Queensland 6 pts, Western Australia 0 pts

at Sydney

New South Wales 438 for 9 dec (S.R. Waugh 170, M.E. Waugh 114 not out, A.I.C. Dodemaide 5 for 114)
Victoria 195 for 9 (M.R. Whitney 5 for 68)

Match drawn
No points

at Devonport

New Zealanders 410 for 7 dec (P.A. Horne 125, I.D.S. Smith 62) and 143 (P.I. Faulkner 4 for 37)
Tasmania 305 (M.D. Taylor 85) and 208 for 8 (D.C. Boon 101 not out)

Match drawn

Queensland finished 1987 on top of the Sheffield Shield table when career-best bowling by Dirk Tazelaar shot out the reigning champions Western Australia on the opening

day of the match at Brisbane. Rob Kerr hit his 14th first-class hundred, and Ian Botham, with 3 sixes in one over off leg-spinner Milosz, hit 53 off 38 balls. Western Australia were handicapped by the loss of skipper Graeme Wood with an injured hand and succumbed placidly in their second innings to leave Queensland a simple task.

In Sydney, where only five overs were possible on the last day, the Waugh twins scored centuries in the same first-class innings for the first time. It took Steve more than five hours to reach his hundred, but Mark reached his century in three hours and hit 15 fours as he dominated a ninth-wicket stand of 105 with Lawson. Victoria were saved by the rain.

A century by opener Phil Horne suggested that the New Zealanders may have solved one of their problems. His 125 occupied 294 minutes. The tourists held the upper hand in Devonport until Faulkner's medium pace disrupted them in the second innings. There was just time for David Boon to register another century.

23 December 1987

at Canberra

New Zealanders 201 (K.R. Rutherford 63, G. Irvine 5 for 42)
Prime Minister's XI 164 (J.G. Bracewell 4 for 40)

New Zealanders won by 37 runs

Ken Rutherford asserted a claim for a recall to the New Zealand side for the final Test in the 50-over match in Canberra. The tourists were out on the fifth ball of the last over. Mr Hawke's XI began well, with Mark Taylor and Greg Matthews putting on 59, but Man of the Match John Bracewell tore the heart out of the middle order.

26 December 1987

at Perth

Sri Lankans 291 for 5 (P.A. de Silva 112, R.S. Mahanama 64, A. Ranatunga 51)
Western Australia 230 for 9

Sri Lankans won by 61 runs

Sri Lankans made a heartening start to their tour. Mahanama, who hit 6 fours, and Aravinda de Silva, who hit 2 sixes and 6 fours, added 119 for the second wicket. The home side fell far short in their 49 overs.

Third Test Match
AUSTRALIA v. NEW ZEALAND

Australia gave a first Test cap to Tony Dodemaide, New Zealand brought back Horne in an attempt to solve their opening problem, Whitney replaced the injured Reid, and Border asked New Zealand to bat first before a crowd of 51,087 when he won the toss.

Horne took 45 minutes to get off the mark, but lost concentration when he flashed wildly at Dodemaide. Andrew Jones once more showed considerable resilience, playing within his limitations, but matching Wright in

An outstanding Test début for Dodemaide, fifty and 6 for 58 in a fine all-round performance in the third Test at Melbourne. (Adrian Murrell/Allsport)

run-scoring as the pair added 87. Jones' end was unfortunate. He glanced McDermott down the leg side where Dyer held the ball as he tumbled. The camera, however, revealed that he had dropped the ball as he rolled over, and post-match debate left Dyer wishing to apologise and more fuming over umpires.

Wright batted for 310 minutes and played an innings of great merit. He was out one short of his century when, pinned down by McDermott, he was tempted into a rash drive. Jeff Crowe became tangled and was lbw, and Patel was beaten by a ferocious yorker, but Bracewell stayed with Martin Crowe until the end, which came at 242 for 5.

Martin Crowe had batted with an accomplishment, authority and charm which mark him as one of the very greatest of players, and, 76 not out at the end of the first day, he appeared to be marching serenely towards a century, but, on the second morning, he added only six before edging to Veletta, who took a fine slip catch. The next ball Bracewell touched to the wicket-keeper to give Whitney his first Test wicket in Australia, his previous appearance having been six years earlier. Smith alone, with some brave blows, offered any late resistance, and New Zealand were out for a disappointing 317.

Whitney took four wickets and gave McDermott fine

support, for once again the young Queensland pace bowler showed the extent of his improvement in recent months and bowled splendidly. His achievements paled before those of Hadlee, however. The veteran all-rounder trapped Boon at 24, beat Marsh off the pitch and had him taken in the gully and had Border dropped in the slips by Bracewell first ball. Undismayed, Hadlee had Jones caught behind to bring him 3 for 6 in 19 balls.

Veletta countered with aggression, but Hadlee returned to dismiss him after tea, and Bracewell accounted for Border to leave Australia 121 for 5 and in trouble. Waugh replied with some bravely attacking shots, and Australia were 170 for 5 at the close of the second day.

Waugh fell in the first over of the third day, but Australia were reprieved by some rather unimaginative captaincy by Jeff Crowe, who failed to grasp the advantage his bowlers had given him. Sleep reached his highest Test score in 309 minutes' batting, Dyer gave ample support and Dodemaide celebrated his Test début with a fifty in four hours so that Australia took a surprising first-innings lead.

On the fourth day, the game swung in favour of Australia. Martin Crowe prevented Australia from taking complete command with another fine innings during the

---

THIRD TEST MATCH – AUSTRALIA v. NEW ZEALAND
26, 27, 28, 29 and 30 December 1987 at Melbourne Cricket Ground, Melbourne

NEW ZEALAND

	FIRST INNINGS		SECOND INNINGS	
P.A. Horne	c Dyer, b Dodemaide	7	c Boon, b Dodemaide	27
J.G. Wright	c Dyer, b McDermott	99	b Sleep	43
A.H. Jones	c Dyer, b McDermott	40	run out	20
M.D. Crowe	c Veletta, b McDermott	82	c Border, b Dodemaide	79
J.J. Crowe	lbw, b McDermott	6	c Boon, b Sleep	25
D.N. Patel	b McDermott	0	c Dyer, b Dodemaide	38
J.G. Bracewell	c Dyer, b Whitney	9	(8) c Veletta, b Dodemaide	1
R.J. Hadlee	c Dodemaide, b Whitney	11	(7) lbw, b Sleep	29
I.D.S. Smith	c Jones, b Whitney	44	c Dyer, b Dodemaide	12
D.K. Morrison	c Border, b Whitney	0	b Dodemaide	0
E.J. Chatfield	not out	6	not out	1
Extras	b 1, lb 4, nb 8	13	b 2, lb 8, nb 1	11
		317		**286**

AUSTRALIA

	FIRST INNINGS		SECOND INNINGS	
D.C. Boon	lbw, b Hadlee	10	(2) c M. Crowe, b Morrison	54
G.R. Marsh	c sub (Rutherford), b Hadlee	13	(1) c Bracewell, b Hadlee	23
D.M. Jones	c Smith, b Hadlee	4	c M. Crowe, b Chatfield	8
A.R. Border	c J. Crowe, b Bracewell	31	lbw, b Hadlee	43
M.R.J. Veletta	lbw, b Hadlee	31	c Patel, b Bracewell	39
S.R. Waugh	c Jones, b Bracewell	55	c Patel, b Bracewell	10
P.R. Sleep	lbw, b Hadlee	90	lbw, b Hadlee	20
G.C. Dyer	run out	21	c Smith, b Hadlee	4
A.I.C. Dodemaide	c Smith, b Morrison	50	lbw, b Hadlee	3
C.J. McDermott	b Morrison	33	not out	10
M.R. Whitney	not out	0	not out	2
Extras	lb 8, nb 11	19	b 1, lb 9, nb 4	14
		357	(for 9 wkts)	**230**

	O	M	R	W	O	M	R	W
McDermott	35	8	97	5	10	1	43	–
Whitney	33.3	6	92	4	20	5	45	–
Dodemaide	20	4	48	1	28.3	10	58	6
Waugh	10	1	44	–				
Sleep	12	1	31	–	26	5	107	3
Jones					8	3	23	–

	O	M	R	W	O	M	R	W
Hadlee	44	11	109	5	31	9	67	5
Morrison	27.4	5	93	2	16	2	54	1
Chatfield	30	10	55	–	21	6	41	2
Bracewell	32	8	69	2	24	5	58	1
Patel	12	6	23	–				

FALL OF WICKETS
1–32, 2–119, 3–187, 4–221, 5–223, 6–254, 7–254, 8–280, 9–294
1–73, 2–76, 3–158, 4–178, 5–220, 6–272, 7–272, 8–281, 9–285

FALL OF WICKETS
1–24, 2–30, 3–31, 4–78, 5–121, 6–170, 7–213, 8–293, 9–354
1–45, 2–59, 3–103, 4–147, 5–176, 6–209, 7–209, 8–216, 9–227

Umpires: A.R. Crafter & R.A. French

Match drawn

course of which he passed 4,000 runs in the calendar year. He is only the seventh player to have achieved this feat.

Openers Horne and Wright cleared off the arrears, but they left in quick succession. Jones and Martin Crowe then added 80, and the partnership was broken when Jones was run out attempting a fourth run. Crowe's 79 off 111 balls gave the New Zealand innings impetus, but he was out to an angled shot. Jeff Crowe and Patel batted doggedly, and Hadlee took the fight to the enemy. Hadlee fell to Sleep, and Dodemaide took two quick wickets to give him five in the innings to add to his fifty, a memorable Test début.

Dodemaide took a sixth wicket on the last morning when he had Smith caught behind with only one run added to the overnight score. This left Australia to make 247 to win, and there was an encouraging crowd of 23,859 to see them attempt to do it. Marsh and Boon gave them a solid enough start although both were dropped in the slips by the Crowe brothers. Jones fell to Chatfield's accurate medium pace, and Marsh became Hadlee's first victim of the innings, but when Border took his side to within a hundred of their target Australia looked comfortable winners. Border fell to a mighty delivery from Hadlee, and Waugh became the second victim of the nagging Chatfield.

Sleep and Veletta moved on to the attack, and the score moved past 200. Hadlee trapped Sleep lbw, and Veletta was seventh out, well caught by Patel. Dyer was caught behind, and Dodemaide was lbw. Dodemaide was Hadlee's 373rd victim in Test cricket, so bringing the great

New Zealander alongside Ian Botham as the leading wicket-taker in Test cricket. The capture of Dodemaide also meant that Australia were 20 short of victory with their last pair together and five overs remaining. Faced by Hadlee, Whitney, in his first Test in Australia, could have been forgiven for immediate surrender, but he coped spendidly. He faced 18 balls, scored two and, with McDermott, saved the game. Whitney defended against the last over of the match, bowled by Hadlee, and punched the air happily when he kept out the last ball. It was a fitting end to a fine match which had brought Allan Border his first series victory as Australia's captain. It was the eighth series in which he had led his country.

28 and 29 December 1987

at Perth

Western Australia 484 for 8 dec (M.W. McPhee 131, T.G. Breman 71 not out, W.S. Andrews 70, G. Shipperd 64, T.M. Moody 57, P.A. de Silva 4 for 109)
Sri Lankans 383 for 7 (A.P. Gurusinha 202, M.A.R. Samarasekera 55, P.A. de Silva 52)

Match drawn

A joyful time for batsmen in two days at Perth. McPhee hit 131 off 129 balls with 3 sixes and 17 fours, and Moody and skipper Andrews put on 109 in 73 minutes. On the second day, Gurusinha hit 202 off 275 deliveries with 27 fours.

AUSTRALIA v. NEW ZEALAND – TEST MATCH AVERAGES

AUSTRALIA BATTING

	M	Inns	NOs	Runs	HS	Av	100s	50s
A.R. Border	3	4		288	205	72.00	1	
P.R. Sleep	3	4		211	90	52.75		2
D.C. Boon	3	5		237	143	47.40	1	1
S.R. Waugh	3	4		147	61	36.75		2
G.R. Marsh	3	5	1	122	31*	30.50		
C.J. McDermott	3	4	1	83	33	27.66		
G.C. Dyer	3	4		93	60	23.25		1
M.R.J. Veletta	3	4		84	39	21.00		
D.M. Jones	3	5	1	52	38*	13.00		
B.A. Reid	2	2	1	13	8*	13.00		

Played in one Test: M.G. Hughes 5; T.B.A. May 14*; A.I.C. Dodemaide 50 & 3; M.R. Whitney 0* & 2*

NEW ZEALAND BATTING

	M	Inns	NOs	Runs	HS	Av	100s	50s
M.D. Crowe	3	6		396	137	66.00	1	3
A.H. Jones	3	6		323	150	53.83	1	1
J.G. Wright	3	6		248	99	41.33		1
D.N. Patel	3	6		192	62	32.00		1
R.J. Hadlee	3	6	1	111	36	22.20		
I.D.S. Smith	3	6	1	80	44	16.00		
J.J. Crowe	3	6		78	25	13.00		
J.G. Bracewell	3	5		53	32	10.60		
D.K. Morrison	3	4		2	2	0.50		

Played in two Tests: E.J. Chatfield 0*, 1*, 6* & 1*.
Played in one Test: P.A. Horne 7 & 27; K.R. Rutherford 0 & 2;
E.J. Gray 23 & 14; M.C. Snedden 0 & 8*

AUSTRALIA BOWLING

	Overs	Mds	Runs	Wkts	Av	Best	10/m	5/inns
A.I.C. Dodemaide	48.3	14	106	7	15.14	6/58		1
B.A. Reid	57	16	114	7	16.28	4/53		
M.G. Hughes	35	12	97	5	19.40	3/40		
C.J. McDermott	144.1	30	426	17	25.05	5/97		1
D.M. Jones	14	6	29	1	29.00	1/5		
M.R. Whitney	53.3	11	137	4	34.25	4/92		
P.R. Sleep	124	31	342	7	48.85	3/61		
T.B.A. May	84	23	202	4	50.50	3/68		
S.R. Waugh	75	26	169	2	84.50	1/2		

NEW ZEALAND BOWLING

	Overs	Mds	Runs	Wkts	Av	Best	10/m	5/inns
R.J. Hadlee	156	44	353	18	19.61	5/67		3
J.G. Bracewell	141.5	27	339	8	42.37	2/58		
D.K. Morrison	101.4	14	354	8	44.25	4/86		
E.J. Chatfield	85	27	154	2	77.00	2/41		
D.N. Patel	22.1	9	52	0	–	0/11		

Bowled in one innings: M.C. Snedden 32 - 6 - 89 - 1; E.J. Gray 44 - 10 - 102 - 0

AUSTRALIA FIELDING FIGURES

13 - G.C. Dyer; 7 - M.R.J. Veletta; 6 - A.R. Border and D.C. Boon; 3 - S.R. Waugh and D.M. Jones; 2 - G.R. Marsh; 1 - P.R. Sleep, A.I.C. Dodemaide and sub (M.G. Hughes)

NEW ZEALAND FIELDING FIGURES

8 - I.D.S. Smith (ct 7/st 1); 3 - J.G. Bracewell and K.R. Rutherford (two as sub); 2 - M.D. Crowe, A.H. Jones and D.N. Patel; 1 - J.G. Wright, E.J. Gray and J.J. Crowe

Richard Hadlee, 10 for 176 at Melbourne, and level with Botham as the taker of the record number of wickets in Test cricket. (Adrian Murrell/Allsport)

31 December 1987

at Mandurah

Sri Lankans 245 for 5 (A. Ranatunga 106 not out, D.S.B.P. Kuruppu 51)
Western Australian Country XI 102 (S.M.S. Kaluperuma 4 for 15)

Sri Lankans won by 143 runs

Arjuna Ranatunga hit 106 off 83 balls and off-spinner Kaluperuma took four wickets in 6.2 overs to give Sri Lankans a comfortable win and encouragement for the Benson and Hedges World Series.

1, 2, 3 and 4 January 1988

at Adelaide

South Australia 158 (C.D. Matthews 4 for 41) and 328 (A.M.J. Hilditch 166, T.M. Alderman 4 for 67)
Western Australia 237 (W.S. Andrews 55) and 250 for 7 (G.M. Wood 82, K.J. Hughes 62)

Western Australia won by 3 wickets
Western Australia 6 pts, South Australia 0 pts

at Brisbane

Queensland 278 (G.S. Trimble 67, D. Tazelaar 56, T.V. Hohns 55, D.R. Gilbert 4 for 61) and 203 (G.M. Ritchie 100 not out, P.W. Anderson 54)
New South Wales 129 and 300 (M.E. Waugh 88, M.A. Taylor 71, M.D. O'Neill 70, C.G. Rackemann 4 for 54)

Queensland won by 52 runs
Queensland 6 pts, New South Wales 0 pts

Western Australia and Queensland moved ahead of the pack with hard-earned victories over South Australia and New South Wales. Chris Matthews again impressed as South Australia were bowled out for 158 on the opening day in Adelaide. The Western Australian batting was dogged in reply, and it was by tenacity rather than brilliance that they took a first innings lead. The home side lost three wickets in clearing the arrears, but their innings was totally dominated by Andrew Hilditch who batted 6½ hours for his 10th first-class hundred. Needing 250 to win, Western Australia lost McPhee at 7, and Shipperd and Moody had both gone by the time the score reached 59. Wood and Hughes added 110 in two hours to rekindle hope, and the challenge was maintained by Andrews, Zoehrer and Matthews so that the winning runs came with 16 balls to spare.

Steve Rixon reached a record number of appearances behind the stumps for New South Wales before announcing his retirement from first-class cricket. (Allsport)

Queensland recovered from an uneven start to reach 278, with Tazelaar hitting a career best 56 at number nine. New South Wales crumpled before the four Queensland seamers, and Ritchie helped to consolidate the home side's strong position with his first century of the season after Queensland had slipped to 61 for 6 and shown signs of losing their nerve. Reaching 131 for 2, New South Wales looked as if they might surprise the home side, but they lost three wickets for two runs, and it was only late spirited resistance from Mark Waugh which delayed Queensland.

Benson and Hedges World Series

First One-Day International
AUSTRALIA v. SRI LANKA

Sri Lanka's poor form in the World Cup was continued in the opening match of the World Series, where an even batting display took Australia to a solid total which proved far too much for the visitors.

Aravinda de Silva took three wickets in a one-day international for the first time, but he was soon out, one of the first seven to fall for 82 runs when Sri Lanka batted. Guy de Alwis and Labrooy showed some spirit with a ninth wicket stand of 50, but by then the match had long been decided.

Following his successful Test début, Tony Dodemaide began his one-day international career in equally remark-able fashion, taking 5 for 21 in 7.2 overs, including three of the first four wickets.

Benson and Hedges World Series

Second One-Day International
AUSTRALIA v. NEW ZEALAND

Deciding to bat first, New Zealand were well served by makeshift opener Andrew Jones, who hit 87 off 107 balls. He and Martin Crowe put on 106 in 78 minutes for the second wicket, and the stand was ended in controversial manner. Crowe was given out caught behind when he swept at Taylor, but clearly the ball had hit Crowe on the arm. Thereafter the New Zealand batting was moderate, and their total of 232 for 9 looked unlikely to trouble Australia duly.

Marsh and Boon put on 70 in 20 overs to give an excellent foundation, but in the next 10 overs five wickets went down while 35 runs were scored. Inevitably, it was Hadlee who caused most of the damage with three wickets in four overs. Dean Jones, however, held firm, and he and Peter Taylor put on 51 for the seventh wicket.

Jones was run out by a fine throw from Jeff Crowe in the 49th over, and it was left to McDermott and Whitney to try to scramble the 12 runs needed to win. With two runs needed and three balls left, Whitney heaved at Martin Snedden and John Bracewell took a splendid running catch at mid-off.

FIRST ONE DAY INTERNATIONAL – AUSTRALIA v. SRI LANKA
2 January 1988 at Perth

AUSTRALIA				SRI LANKA			
D.C. Boon	c and b P.A. Silva	56		R.S. Mahanama	c Dodemaide, b Waugh	19
G.R. Marsh	c de Alwis, b Ramanayake	14		A.P. Gurusinha	c Dyer, b Dodemaide	0
D.M. Jones	c Gurusinha, b P.A. de Silva	55		P.A. de Silva	b Dodemaide	11
A.R. Border†	c Mahanama, b P.A. de Silva	31		A. Ranatunga	c Border, b Dodemaide	7
M.R.J. Veletta	run out	27		R.S. Madugalle†	c Border, b Waugh	7
S.R. Waugh	not out	35		H.P. Tillekeratne	c Dyer, b May	9
G.C. Dyer*	run out	9		J.R. Ratnayeke	b Whitney	19
A.I.C. Dodemaide	c Mahanama, b Ratnayeke	4		R.G. de Alwis*	c Marsh, b Dodemaide	44
C.J. McDermott	not out	0		C.P. Ramanayake	c Jones, b Waugh	6
T.B.A. May				G.F. Labrooy	lbw, b Dodemaide	33
M.R. Whitney				K.N. Amalean	not out	0
Extras	b 4, lb 7, w 4, nb 3	18		Extras	b 4, lb 3, w 2, nb 4	13
(50 overs)	(for 7 wkts)	249		(44.2 overs)		168

	O	M	R	W		O	M	R	W
J.R. Ratnayeke	9	–	35	1	Dodemaide	7.2	–	21	5
Labrooy	9	–	38	–	McDermott	5	1	15	–
Amalean	6	1	27	–	Whitney	10	–	26	1
Ramanayake	7	1	33	1	Waugh	10	2	34	3
P.A. de Silva	10	–	58	3	May	10	3	49	1
Ranatunga	9	–	47	–	Jones	2	–	16	–

FALL OF WICKETS
1–57, 2–84, 3–143, 4–189, 5–199, 6–224, 7–238

FALL OF WICKETS
1–2, 2–20, 3–33, 4–49, 5–50, 6–78, 7–82, 8–118, 9–168

Umpires: T.A. Prue & P.J. McConnell

Man of the Match: S.R. Waugh

Australia won by 81 runs

Benson and Hedges World Series

Third One-Day International
NEW ZEALAND v. SRI LANKA

Once again Sri Lanka were brushed aside with ease so that, after only three games in the World Series competition, the finalists already seemed determined.

Mahanama inadvertently diverted the ball onto his wicket on the fourth delivery of the match, and apart from Ranatunga, who hit 35 off 51 balls with 5 fours, none of the early batsmen showed confidence. A belated stand of 52 off 40 balls between de Alwis and Ravi Ratnayeke was the only sign of encouragement for Sri Lanka, who were frustrated by the accuracy of Chatfield and Hadlee.

An opening stand of 80 between Jones and Wright gave New Zealand a fine start. They fell in quick succession, but Martin Crowe hit 52 from 68 balls before being caught magnificently by Aravinda de Silva. Patel, who had helped him to add 85, fell at the same score, but New Zealand cruised to victory.

Benson and Hedges World Series

Fourth One-Day International
AUSTRALIA v. NEW ZEALAND

Having chosen to bat first, Australia were in deep trouble when, with Gillespie dismissing Marsh and Border with his

One of Sri Lanka's few successes in the Benson and Hedges World Series, opening batsman Mahanama. (Michael King/Allsport)

SECOND ONE-DAY INTERNATIONAL – AUSTRALIA v. NEW ZEALAND
3 January 1988 at Perth

NEW ZEALAND			
J.G. Wright	c and b McDermott	13
A.H. Jones	c Boon, b Waugh	87
M.D. Crowe	c Dyer, b Taylor	45
J.J. Crowe†	c Taylor, b Whitney	0
D.N. Patel	c Dyer, b Taylor	3
T.E. Blain*	c Border, b McDermott	16
R.J. Hadlee	c Taylor, b Dodemaide	23
J.G. Bracewell	run out	4
M.C. Snedden	not out	11
S.R. Gillespie	run out	6
E.J. Chatfield	not out	1
Extras	lb 16, w 5, nb 2	23
		232

AUSTRALIA			
G.R. Marsh	c sub (Horne), b Bracewell	24
D.C. Boon	c Patel, b Bracewell	44
D.M. Jones	run out	92
A.R. Border†	lbw, b Hadlee	3
M.R.J. Veletta	b Hadlee	7
S.R. Waugh	c Blain, b Hadlee	0
G.C. Dyer*	c sub (Horne), b Snedden	4
P.L. Taylor	c J.J. Crowe, b Chatfield	16
C.J. McDermott	c Patel, b Chatfield	7
A.I.C. Dodemaide	not out	9
M.R. Whitney	c Bracewell, b Snedden	3
Extras	lb 11, w 6, nb 5	22
(49.4 overs)		231

	O	M	R	W
Dodemaide	10	1	43	1
McDermott	10	–	37	2
Waugh	10	–	49	1
Whitney	10	–	46	1
Taylor	10	–	41	2

	O	M	R	W
Hadlee	10	–	35	3
Chatfield	10	1	39	2
Bracewell	10	1	27	2
Snedden	9.4	–	51	2
Gillespie	7	1	48	–
Patel	3	–	20	–

FALL OF WICKETS
1–27, 2–133, 3–134, 4–146, 5–177, 6–189, 7–203, 8–219, 9–228

FALL OF WICKETS
1–78, 2–82, 3–84, 4–102, 5–105, 6–132, 7–183, 8–198, 9–221

Umpires: R.C. Bailhache & P.J. McConnell

Man of the Match: A.H. Jones

New Zealand won by 1 run

THIRD ONE-DAY INTERNATIONAL – NEW ZEALAND v. SRI LANKA
5 January 1988 at Sydney

SRI LANKA			
R.S. Mahanama	b Morrison		0
A.P. Gurusinha	run out		23
P.A. de Silva	c Blain, b Chatfield		5
A. Ranatunga	c Blain, b Snedden		35
R.S. Madugalle†	c M.D. Crowe, b Morrison		13
H.P. Tillekeratne	lbw, b Snedden		0
R.G. de Alwis*	c Patel, b Bracewell		32
J.R. Ratnayeke	c Wright, b Chatfield		41
G.F. Labrooy	c Patel, b Chatfield		3
E.A.R. de Silva	b Chatfield		6
C.P. Ramanayake	not out		11
Extras	lb 3, w 2		5
(48.2 overs)			174

	O	M	R	W
Morrison	10	2	43	2
Hadlee	9	4	12	–
Chatfield	9.2	1	32	4
Bracewell	10	–	41	1
Snedden	10	1	43	2

FALL OF WICKETS
1–0, 2–14, 3–40, 4–76, 5–76, 6–82, 7–134, 8–147, 9–159

NEW ZEALAND			
J.G. Wright	c Mahanama, b Ramanayake		41
A.H. Jones	c and b Ramanayake		34
M.D. Crowe	c P.A. de Silva, b Labrooy		52
D.N. Patel	c de Alwis, b J.R. Ratnayeke		29
T.E. Blain	not out		5
J.J. Crowe	not out		6
J.G. Bracewell			
R.J. Hadlee			
M.C. Snedden			
D.K. Morrison			
E.J. Chatfield			
Extras	b 1, lb 6, w 4		11
(48.4 overs)	(for 4 wkts)		178

	O	M	R	W
J.R. Ratnayeke	9.4	–	40	1
Labrooy	10	1	37	1
Ramanayake	10	2	28	2
E.A.R. de Silva	10	1	17	–
Ranatunga	5	–	27	–
P.A. de Silva	4	–	22	–

FALL OF WICKETS
1–80, 2–82, 3–167, 4–167

Umpires: A.R. Crafter & R.A. French

Man of the Match: E.J. Chatfield

New Zealand won by 6 wickets

FOURTH ONE-DAY INTERNATIONAL – AUSTRALIA v. NEW ZEALAND
7 January 1988 at Melbourne

AUSTRALIA			
D.C. Boon	b Chatfield		9
G.R. Marsh	c Patel, b Gillespie		12
D.M. Jones	b Snedden		48
A.R. Border†	c Wright, b Gillespie		0
M.R.J. Veletta	c Blain, b Snedden		4
S.R. Waugh	b Snedden		68
G.C. Dyer*	c Jones, b Chatfield		38
P.L. Taylor	run out		2
A.I.C. Dodemaide	c Gillespie, b Hadlee		8
C.J. McDermott	c M.D. Crowe, b Chatfield		9
M.R. Whitney	not out		2
Extras	lb 12, nb 4		16
(49.4 overs)			216

	O	M	R	W
Chatfield	10	2	31	3
Hadlee	8.4	1	42	1
Snedden	10	1	36	3
Gillespie	9	–	41	2
Bracewell	8	–	32	–
Patel	4	–	22	–

FALL OF WICKETS
1–17, 2–31, 3–31, 4–39, 5–127, 6–192, 7–195, 8–197, 9–211

NEW ZEALAND			
J.G. Wright	run out		20
A.H. Jones	c Dodemaide, b McDermott		59
D.N. Patel	b Whitney		12
M.D. Crowe	c Dodemaide		37
J.J. Crowe†	c and b Taylor		9
T.E. Blain*	b Dodemaide		7
R.J. Hadlee	c Taylor, b Waugh		23
J.G. Bracewell	c Boon, b McDermott		9
M.C. Snedden	c Waugh, b McDermott		3
S.R. Gillespie	not out		8
E.J. Chatfield	not out		0
Extras	b 4, lb 10, w 6, nb 3		23
(50 overs)	(for 9 wkts)		210

	O	M	R	W
Dodemaide	10	1	25	2
McDermott	10	–	50	3
Whitney	10	–	46	1
Waugh	10	–	41	1
Taylor	10	–	34	1

FALL OF WICKETS
1–47, 2–79, 3–121, 4–138, 5–157, 6–168, 7–180, 8–188, 9–209

Umpires: R.C. Bailhache & P.J. McConnell

Man of the Match: S.R. Waugh

Australia won by 6 runs

first two deliveries, they slumped to 39 for 4. Dean Jones and Steve Waugh came to the rescue with a stand of 88 off 113 balls.

Jones was bowled by Snedden, but Waugh continued to strike the ball cleanly. His half century came off 74 balls, and he had added 65 with Dyer when he chopped a ball into his own stumps. Australia were all out in the last over of their quota, and their score of 216 hardly looked enough to win the match on a good batting wicket which was a little slow.

Andrew Jones and Wright again gave New Zealand a brisk and valuable start before Wright was run out by Dean Jones. Patel helped Andrew Jones to keep the score moving, and Martin Crowe and Jones took the total to 121 so that New Zealand were seemingly well on top. Martin Crowe was not in his usual fluent form, however, and Border frustrated him with some intelligent field settings. Dodemaide and McDermott then gained the upper hand. Jones and Martin Crowe were both dismissed, and New Zealand began to struggle.

Hadlee revived hopes with some lusty blows, and the

Determination from Tazelaar. He had an outstanding season for Queensland. (Adrian Murrell/Allsport)

last over began with New Zealand needing 13 to win. Waugh, the World Cup last-over specialist, had Hadlee caught at long-off, and eight off the last two balls proved too much for Gillespie and Chatfield.

8, 9, 10 and 11 January 1988

at Brisbane

Queensland 324 (A.B. Henschell 89, R.B. Kerr 64, P.W. Anderson 55)
Tasmania 173 (C.G. Rackemann 4 for 51) and 147 (D.Tazelaar 5 for 54)

Queensland won by an innings and 4 runs
Queensland 6 pts, Tasmania 0 pts

at Perth

Victoria 333 (D.F. Whatmore 170, C.D. Matthews 4 for 107) and 256 for 5 (P.W. Young 66 not out, J.D. Siddons 52, D.F. Whatmore 51)
Western Australia 427 for 8 dec (G.M. Wood 150 not out, T.J. Zoehrer 109, W.S. Andrews 50)

Match drawn
Western Australia 2 pts, Victoria 0 pts

With the Benson and Hedges World Series occupying most of the attention, Queensland and Western Australia took another step closer to ensuring that they would compete in the Sheffield Shield final. Queensland won with more than a day to spare against the hapless Tasmanian side. Queensland's win was based on an essentially sound team performance. Stuart Saunders reappeared for Tasmania after an absence of two years.

Dav Whatmore, missed four times, hit his highest score in first-class cricket in the match at Perth, as did Graeme Wood. Wood and Zoehrer added 165 in 210 minutes for the sixth wicket to clinch first innings points for Western Australia in a match in which the scoring was often slow.

Benson and Hedges World Series

Fifth One-Day International
NEW ZEALAND v. SRI LANKA

Sri Lanka gave an improved display in the fifth match of the series, but were checked by Hadlee just as they threatened a late surge for runs. In his eighth over, Hadlee had Ranatunga caught at deep mid-on and bowled Labrooy to leave Sri Lanka on 207 for 8. Ravi Ratnayeke hit 23 off 26 balls in a spirited climax to the innings.

Wright and Jones put on 102 for New Zealand's second wicket after the luckless Rutherford had again gone cheaply, but New Zealand never found the required run rate easy to maintain. Hadlee gave the innings a necessary boost with 25 off 33 balls. He was out on the third ball of the final over, but Blain killed Sri Lanka's lingering hopes by hitting the next two balls for two and a four through mid-wicket.

Benson and Hedges World Series

Sixth One-Day International
AUSTRALIA v. SRI LANKA

Boon and Marsh began the Australian innings with a partnership of 115 in 100 minutes off 147 balls. Marsh was

run out in the 24th over, and Boon and Jones then added 84 off 82 balls in 49 minutes. Boon was out at 199, and his fine innings was all the more commendable in that it had been played in a temperature close to 100 degrees and the batsman was near exhaustion.

Asked to score at a rate of 5.8 an over, Sri Lanka never looked like reaching their target.

Benson and Hedges World Series

Seventh One-Day International
NEW ZEALAND v. SRI LANKA

Sri Lanka won their first, and as it transpired their only, match in the competition when they beat New Zealand in Hobart with 3.3 overs and four wickets to spare. New Zealand were restricted by some tight bowling and were in considerable trouble at 70 for 5. Hadlee, playing his 100th one-day international, lifted them with 52 off 68 balls, but their final score never looked likely to be good enough.

Sri Lanka began uneasily, losing Kuruppu and Gurusinha for 33, but Mahanama and Aravinda de Silva hit 103 off 141 balls in 96 minutes to set up Sri Lanka's victory.

Carl Rackemann was recalled to the Queensland side and his pace bowling had much to do with the northern state reaching the Sheffield Shield final. (Adrian Murrell/ Allsport)

FIFTH ONE-DAY INTERNATIONAL — NEW ZEALAND v. SRI LANKA
9 January 1988 at Adelaide

SRI LANKA				NEW ZEALAND			
R.S. Mahanama	c Blain, b Snedden	51		K.R. Rutherford	c Kuruppu, b J.R. Ratnayeke	1
D.S.B.P. Kuruppu*	c Hadlee, b Morrison	23		J.G. Wright†	run out	61
A.P. Gurusinha	c and b Gillespie	7		A.H. Jones	b Ramanayake	63
P.A. de Silva	c Jones, b Chatfield	51		M.D. Crowe	c Gurusinha, b Ramanayake	39
A. Ranatunga	c Gillespie, b Hadlee	42		D.N. Patel	st Kuruppu, b P.A. de Silva	9
R.S. Madugalle†	c M.D. Crowe, b Gillespie	3		R.J. Hadlee	c Gurusinha, b J.R. Ratnayeke	25
M.A.R. Samarasekera	b Gillespie	3		T.E. Blain	not out	25
J.R. Ratnayeke	c Rutherford, b Hadlee	23		M.C. Snedden	not out	0
G.F. Labrooy	b Hadlee	0		S.R. Gillespie		
E.A.R. de Silva	c Chatfield, b Morrison	15		D.K. Morrison		
C.P. Ramanayake	not out	3		E.J. Chatfield		
Extras	lb 12, w 2, nb 6	20		Extras	b 2, lb 3, w 8, nb 6	19
(49.5 overs)		241		(49.5 overs)	(for 6 wkts)	242

	O	M	R	W		O	M	R	W
Morrison	5.5	1	39	2	Labrooy	10	2	39	–
Hadlee	10	1	35	3	J.R. Ratnayeke	9.5	–	44	2
Chatfield	10	1	43	1	Ramanayake	7	–	47	2
Gillespie	10	–	40	3	E.A.R. de Silva	10	2	40	–
Snedden	10	–	47	1	P.A. de Silva	9	–	41	1
Patel	4	–	25	–	Samarasekera	4	–	26	–

FALL OF WICKETS
1–35, 2–66, 3–121, 4–160, 5–187, 6–192, 7–206, 8–207, 9–234

FALL OF WICKETS
1–1, 2–103, 3–164, 4–186, 5–204, 6–236

Umpires: L.J. King & P.J. McConnell

Man of the Match: R.J. Hadlee

New Zealand won by 4 wickets

13 January 1988

at Manly Oval, Sydney

Prime Minister's XI 174 (Bagshaw 4 for 25)
Aboriginal XI 175 for 3 (G. James 51)

Aboriginal XI won by 7 wickets

The match attracted a crowd of about 6,000 and the start was delayed by a demonstration against the Bicentenary celebrations. Bob Hawke, the 58-year-old Prime Minister, batted 15 minutes, but failed to score. He played the ball on without removing the bails. Lillee, Walker, Ian Chappel, Marsh and Cosier were among those who played for the Prime Minister's XI.

Benson and Hedges World Series

Eighth One-Day International
AUSTRALIA v. SRI LANKA

With Allan Border hitting his only fifty of the series and Peter Taylor the hero, Australia beat Sri Lanka in this day/night match to make sure of a place in the final. For once Boon and Marsh failed, and Australia were never at ease until Border's innings and until Peter Taylor helped nurse 71 from the closing overs of the innings.

Sri Lanka began badly, but a stand of 97 between Ranatunga and Madugalle rallied them. Taylor again came to Australia's rescue, dismissing Madugalle and taking four of the last six wickets, which fell for 42 runs.

15, 16, 17 and 18 January 1988

at Devonport

Tasmania 111 (S.P.G. George 6 for 51) and 282 (M.D. Taylor 166, P.I. Faulkner 57, J.K. Pyke 5 for 47)
South Australia 463 for 9 dec (D.W. Hookes 132, W.B. Phillips 85, J.K. Pyke 64, E.J. Harris 4 for 57, D.K. Lillee 4 for 99)

South Australia won by an innings and 70 runs
South Australia 6 pts, Tasmania 0 pts

at Perth

Queensland 303 (G.M. Richie 76, I.T. Botham 70, R.B. Kerr 59, T.M. Alderman 4 for 87, P.A. Capes 4 for 87) and 238 (I.T. Botham 58, K.H. MacLeay 5 for 99)
Western Australia 348 (W.S. Andrews 66, G.M. Wood 61, C.G. Rackemann 4 for 56) and 194 for 7 (J. Brayshaw 60 not out, C.G. Rackemann 4 for 65)

Western Australia won by 3 wickets
Western Australia 6 pts, Queensland 0 pts

In the crucial top of the table match in Perth, Western Australia won a hard-fought contest with 9.4 overs remaining. The game attracted much interest and was well promoted by local businessmen and the Western Australian Cricket Association. The Queensland first innings was

---

SIXTH ONE-DAY INTERNATIONAL – AUSTRALIA v. SRI LANKA
10 January 1988 at Adelaide

AUSTRALIA				SRI LANKA			
G.R. Marsh	run out		37	R.S. Mahanama	c Veletta, b Whitney		50
D.C. Boon	c Madugalle, b P.A. de Silva		122	D.S.B.P. Kuruppu	b McDermott		5
D.M. Jones	c Gurusinha, b Labrooy		69	A.P. Gurusinha	run out		43
A.R. Border†	c E.A.R. de Silva, b Ratnayeke		13	P.A. de Silva	run out		43
M.R.J. Veletta	run out		5	A. Ranatunga	c Veletta, b Dodemaide		23
S.R. Waugh	not out		8	R.S. Madugalle†	lbw, b Dodemaide		7
C.J. McDermott	run out		8	J.R. Ratnayeke	b Dodemaide		1
G.C. Dyer*	not out		3	R.G. de Alwis*	not out		11
A.I.C. Dodemaide				E.A.R. de Silva	c Veletta, b McDermott		3
P.L. Taylor				G.F. Labrooy	not out		3
M.R. Whitney				C.P. Ramanayake			
Extras	b 4, lb 16, w 4		24	Extras	b 1, lb 11, w 6, nb 1		19
(50 overs)	(for 6 wkts)		289	(50 overs)	(for 8 wkts)		208

	O	M	R	W		O	M	R	W
J.R. Ratnayeke	10	–	49	1	Dodemaide	10	1	27	3
Labrooy	10	–	44	1	McDermott	10	–	31	2
Ramanayake	8	–	46	–	Whitney	10	–	53	1
E.A.R. de Silva	4	–	27	–	Waugh	10	–	37	–
Ranatunga	8	–	50	–	Taylor	10	1	48	–
P.A. de Silva	10	–	53	1					

FALL OF WICKETS
1–115, 2–199, 3–244, 4–268, 5–274, 6–282

FALL OF WICKETS
1–9, 2–106, 3–132, 4–172, 5–187, 6–189, 7–190, 8–197

Umpires: A.R. Crafter & M.W. Johnson

Man of the Match: D.C. Boon

Australia won by 81 runs

a thing of fits and starts. Barsby went early, but Kerr and Ritchie added 121. Then four wickets fell for 30 runs before Botham and Hohns added 85. The home side's batting was much more consistent, but they did not claim first innings points until eight wickets were down.

Against Western Australia's all pace attack, Queensland showed grit and determination in their second innings and left the home side with no easy task to make 191 on a difficult wicket. Western Australia found their hero in Jamie Brayshaw, son of Ian, a former stalwart of the state. Playing his first Shield game, Brayshaw played with courage and skill to steer his side to victory.

There was equal romance in Devonport. Having done very well in Perth grade cricket, the great Dennis Lillee made himself available for Western Australia's Sheffield Shield side, but he was not invited to play. With the approval of the ACB and the states concerned, Lillee suddenly found himself in the Tasmanian side, the three-month residential qualification being waived. On a green wicket, Tasmania were shot out for 111 in 203 minutes so that the first-day crowd had the chance to see Lillee bowl.

Romantic return. Dennis Lillee took a wicket with his first ball for Tasmania against South Australia at Devonport, 15 January, the occasion of his return to first-class cricket. (David Munden)

SEVENTH ONE-DAY INTERNATIONAL – NEW ZEALAND v. SRI LANKA
12 January 1988 at Bellerive Oval, Hobart

NEW ZEALAND			
K.R. Rutherford	b Ranatunga		24
J.G. Wright	c Madugalle,		
	b J.R. Ratnayeke		8
J.J. Crowe†	run out		0
M.D. Crowe	c de Alwis,		
	b Ramanayake		25
D.N. Patel	c P.A. de Silva,		
	b Ranatunga		0
T.E. Blain	not out		49
R.J. Hadlee	c sub (Tillekeratne),		
	b J.R. Ratnayeke		52
I.D.S. Smith*	c Mahanama,		
	b J.R. Ratnayeke		9
S.R. Gillespie	not out		9
D.K. Morrison			
E.J. Chatfield			
Extras	lb 9, w 11, nb 3		23
(50 overs)	(for 7 wkts)		199

	O	M	R	W
J.R. Ratnayeke	9	1	33	3
Labrooy	10	–	43	–
Ranatunga	10	1	34	2
Ramanayake	10	2	30	1
Gurusinha	2	–	15	–
E.A.R. de Silva	5	1	16	–
P.A. de Silva	4	–	19	–

FALL OF WICKETS
1–29, 2–32, 3–67, 4–67, 5–70, 6–165, 7–179

SRI LANKA			
R.S. Mahanama	run out		58
D.S.B.P. Kuruppu	c M.D. Crowe,		
	b Morrison		12
A.P. Gurusinha	c Smith, b Hadlee		5
P.A. de Silva	c Chatfield,		
	b Gillespie		55
A. Ranatunga	c Morrison, b Hadlee		11
R.S. Madugalle†	c Wright,		
	b Rutherford		10
J.R. Ratnayeke	not out		21
R.G. de Alwis*	not out		7
C.P. Ramanayake			
E.A.R. de Silva			
G.F. Labrooy			
Extras	b 1, lb 10, w 5, nb 5		21
(46.2 overs)	(for 6 wkts)		200

	O	M	R	W
Chatfield	10	1	30	–
Hadlee	10	1	22	2
Morrison	8.2	1	36	1
Gillespie	10	–	51	1
Patel	3	–	25	–
Rutherford	5	–	25	1

FALL OF WICKETS
1–24, 2–33, 3–136, 4–151, 5–167, 6–185

Umpires: M.W. Johnson & S.G. Randell

Man of the Match: R.S. Mahanama

Sri Lanka won by 4 wickets

He did not disappoint. His first ball caught the edge of Hilditch's bat and was caught by wicket-keeper Soule. Thereafter things became harder. Hookes and Phillips added 187 for the third wicket, and Pyke and Plummer 108 for the eighth. In spite of Mick Taylor's hundred and a stand of 188 with Faulkner, Tasmania were well beaten. Pyke, like George in the first innings, returned career-best bowling figures for South Australia.

Lillee bowled on each of the first three days and sent down 45 overs to take 4 for 99.

Benson and Hedges World Series

**Ninth One-Day International
NEW ZEALAND v. SRI LANKA**

What had been expected since the opening matches of the competition became an actuality as New Zealand beat Sri Lanka to qualify to meet Australia in the final. The Sri Lankan batting was kept well in check by Hadlee and Chatfield, and New Zealand, who were heavily fined for bowling four overs short, won when Hadlee on-drove Ratnayeke to the boundary with 11 balls remaining.

Benson and Hedges World Series

**Tenth One-Day International
AUSTRALIA v. NEW ZEALAND**

As both sides had qualified for the final, the match had little significance. New Zealand were handicapped when rain interrupted their innings in the 41st over. The game was reduced to 44 overs, and the visitors did well to score 39 runs from the last 21 balls.

Australia began badly, losing Marsh and McDermott in Chatfield's opening over, but Boon and Jones steadied them, and they won with great ease. Boon and Jones put on 77 in 74 minutes.

Benson and Hedges World Series

**Eleventh One-Day International
AUSTRALIA v. SRI LANKA**

Out of the competition, Sri Lanka had only honour and experience to play for. Their enthusiasm remained undiminished, but again they started uncertainly as Whitney took three quick wickets and it was left to Aravinda de Silva and Gurusinha to revive them with a fourth wicket stand of 79. De Silva, who had an excellent tournament, hit 7 fours in his innings of 79.

For a time, Australia looked in danger of defeat as, with Ramanayake claiming three wickets, they slipped to 91 for 5 and 100 for 6. It was not until the aggressive Veletta found a confident partner in Dodemaide that victory looked possible, and it was achieved with only three balls to spare.

EIGHTH ONE-DAY INTERNATIONAL – AUSTRALIA v. SRI LANKA
14 January 1988 at Melbourne

AUSTRALIA				SRI LANKA			
D.C. Boon	c Ranatunga, b J.R. Ratnayeke	1		R.S. Mahanama	b Dodemaide	7
G.R. Marsh	c de Alwis, b Labrooy	0		D.S.B.P. Kuruppu	lbw, b Waugh	22
D.M. Jones	c Mahanama, b Ranatunga	31		A.P. Gurusinha	c Border, b McDermott	7
M.R.J. Veletta	b Jeganathan	46		P.A. de Silva	c Boon, b McDermott	10
S.R. Waugh	c de Alwis, b Labrooy	27		A. Ranatunga	run out	67
A.R. Border†	c Labrooy, b P.A. de Silva	61		R.S. Madugalle†	c and b Taylor	44
G.C. Dyer*	c Madugalle, b Labrooy	4		R.G. de Alwis*	c Veletta, b Taylor	0
P.L. Taylor	not out	27		J.R. Ratnayeke	c Dyer, b Dodemaide	16
C.J. McDermott	c Gurusinha, b Labrooy	19		G.F. Labrooy	c McDermott, b Taylor	13
A.I.C. Dodemaide	not out	10		S. Jeganathan	c Border, b Taylor	1
T.B.A. May				C.P. Ramanayake	not out	6
Extras	lb 11, w 6	17		Extras	lb 8, w 3, nb 1	12
(50 overs)	(for 8 wkts)	243		(44.5 overs)		205

	O	M	R	W		O	M	R	W
J.R. Ratnayeke	8	–	24	1	Dodemaide	7.5	2	36	2
Labrooy	10	1	39	4	McDermott	10	2	42	2
Ramanayake	5	–	32	–	Waugh	7	–	33	1
Ranatunga	10	–	47	1	May	10	–	48	–
Jeganathan	7	–	36	1	Taylor	10	1	38	4
P.A. de Silva	10	–	54	1					

FALL OF WICKETS
1–2, 2–6, 3–66, 4–90, 5–158, 6–172, 7–190, 8–220

FALL OF WICKETS
1–14, 2–27, 3–38, 4–66, 5–163, 6–163, 7–164, 8–183, 9–189

Umpires: R.C. Bailhache & R.A. French

Man of the Match: P.L. Taylor

Australia won by 38 runs

NINTH ONE-DAY INTERNATIONAL – NEW ZEALAND v. SRI LANKA
16 January 1988 at Wooloongabba, Brisbane

SRI LANKA			
D.S.B.P. Kuruppu	c Patel, b Morrison	47
R.S. Mahanama	c Blain, b Chatfield	12
A.P. Gurusinha	run out	0
P.A. de Silva	run out	25
A. Ranatunga	run out	25
R.S. Madugalle†	c Blain, b Morrison	5
M.A.R. Samarasekera	c Snedden, b Chatfield	8
J.R. Ratnayeke	not out	15
R.G. de Alwis*	c Rutherford, b Chatfield	2
G.F. Labrooy	not out	2
C.P. Ramanayake		
Extras	lb 9, w 12, nb 2	23
(39 overs)	(for 8 wkts)	164

NEW ZEALAND			
K.R. Rutherford	b Labrooy	1
J.G. Wright†	c Ranatunga, b Ramanayake	22
A.H. Jones	c de Alwis, b Ranatunga	29
M.D. Crowe	run out	43
D.N. Patel	c Ranatunga, b Ramanayake	1
T.E. Blain*	b Ranatunga	17
R.J. Hadlee	not out	21
M.C. Snedden	not out	15
S.R. Gillespie		
D.K. Morrison		
E.J. Chatfield		
Extras	b 2, lb 5, w 10, nb 1	18
(37.1 overs)	(for 6 wkts)	167

	O	M	R	W
Hadlee	9	1	25	–
Morrison	6	–	39	2
Chatfield	9	2	27	3
Gillespie	8	–	39	–
Snedden	7	–	25	–

	O	M	R	W
J.R. Ratnayeke	7.1	–	40	–
Labrooy	8	1	32	1
Ramanayake	8	2	28	2
Samarasekera	3	–	18	–
Ranatunga	8	–	35	2
P.A. de Silva	3	1	7	–

FALL OF WICKETS
1–52, 2–54, 3–97, 4–103, 5–111, 6–139, 7–142, 8–148

FALL OF WICKETS
1–1, 2–43, 3–78, 4–90, 5–122, 6–139

Umpires: R.C. Bailhache & C.D. Timmins

Man of the Match: M.D. Crowe

New Zealand won by 4 wickets

TENTH ONE-DAY INTERNATIONAL – AUSTRALIA v. NEW ZEALAND
17 January 1988 at Wooloongabba, Brisbane

NEW ZEALAND			
J.G. Wright	c Dyer, b Waugh	19
A.H. Jones	b Waugh	65
J.J. Crowe†	c McDermott, b Taylor	41
M.D. Crowe	c Davis, b Taylor	1
R.J. Hadlee	not out	9
V.R. Brown	c Dyer, b McDermott	10
T.E. Blain*	not out	8
K.R. Rutherford		
M.C. Snedden		
S.R. Gillespie		
E.J. Chatfield		
Extras	lb 13, w 8, nb 2	23
(44 overs)	(for 5 wkts)	176

AUSTRALIA			
G.R. Marsh	c Blain, b Chatfield	1
D.C. Boon	lbw, b Snedden	48
C.J. McDermott	c Blain, b Chatfield	0
D.M. Jones	c Brown, b Snedden	31
M.R.J. Veletta	not out	32
S.R. Waugh	c Blain, b Snedden	45
A.R. Border†	not out	9
G.C. Dyer*		
A.I.C. Dodemaide		
P.L. Taylor		
S.P. Davis		
Extras	lb 8, w 2, nb 1	11
(33.2 overs)	(for 5 wkts)	177

	O	M	R	W
Dodemaide	9	1	26	–
McDermott	10	–	49	1
Davis	10	–	33	–
Waugh	8	1	23	2
Taylor	7	–	32	2

	O	M	R	W
Chatfield	5	2	19	2
Hadlee	7	–	28	–
Snedden	8	2	40	3
Gillespie	6.2	–	31	–
Brown	7	–	51	–

FALL OF WICKETS
1–42, 2–128, 3–131, 4–156, 5–168

FALL OF WICKETS
1–2, 2–2, 3–79, 4–90, 5–154

Umpires: A.R. Crafter & M.W. Johnson

Man of the Match: S.R. Waugh

Australia won by 5 wickets

Benson and Hedges World Series

Twelfth One-Day International
AUSTRALIA v. NEW ZEALAND

With both sides on the verge of meeting in the final, this match had an unreal quality. Marsh showed his worth with a fine century which was the substance of Australia's victory. New Zealand rested Hadlee and Wright. Hadlee was strong in his complaints about the treatment he had received from the Australian crowds.

Benson and Hedges World Series					
Qualifying Table					
	P	*W*	*L*	*Pts*	*R/R*
Australia	8	7	1	14	4.74
New Zealand	8	4	4	8	4.08
Sri Lanka	8	1	7	2	4.02

Dean Jones. His batting won him the individual award in the Benson and Hedges World Series finals. (Adrian Murrell/Allsport)

ELEVENTH ONE-DAY INTERNATIONAL – AUSTRALIA v. SRI LANKA
19 January 1988 at Sydney

SRI LANKA		
R.S. Mahanama	c Border, b Whitney	12
D.S.B.P. Kuruppu	b Whitney	2
A.P. Gurusinha	c Jones, b Whitney	37
S.A.M. Kaluperuma	b Waugh	4
P.A. de Silva	c Dyer, b Waugh	79
A. Ranatunga	c Marsh, b Waugh	16
R.S. Madugalle†	lbw, b Waugh	0
J.R. Ratnayeke	c Boon, b Whitney	1
R.G. de Alwis*	c Marsh, b Dodemaide	4
G.F. Labrooy	not out	6
C.P. Ramanayake	not out	5
Extras	b 2, lb 16, w 3, nb 1	22
(50 overs)	(for 9 wkts)	188

AUSTRALIA		
D.C. Boon	c Mahanama, b J.R. Ratnayeke	15
G.R. Marsh	c Gurusinha, b Ramanayake	8
D.M. Jones	c de Alwis, b Ramanayake	9
M.R.J. Veletta	not out	68
S.R. Waugh	c Mahanama, b Ramanayake	16
A.R. Border†	c and b P.A. de Silva	12
G.C. Dyer*	b Ranatunga	4
A.I.C. Dodemaide	c Kaluperuma, b Labrooy	30
P.L. Taylor	not out	10
T.B.A. May		
M.R. Whitney		
Extras	lb 10, w 3, nb 4	17
(49.3 overs)	(for 7 wkts)	189

	O	M	R	W
Whitney	10	2	34	4
Dodemaide	10	1	34	1
Waugh	10	–	33	4
May	10	–	22	–
Taylor	10	1	47	–

	O	M	R	W
J.R. Ratnayeke	10	1	32	1
Labrooy	9.3	1	43	1
Ramanayake	10	–	35	3
Ranatunga	9	–	35	1
P.A. de Silva	10	–	31	1
Kaluperuma	1	–	3	–

FALL OF WICKETS
1–16, 2–27, 3–39, 4–113, 5–140, 6–148, 7–162, 8–172, 9–179

FALL OF WICKETS
1–25, 2–30, 3–49, 4–72, 5–91, 6–100, 7–173

Umpires: T.A. Prue & S.G. Randell

Man of the Match: M.R.J. Veletta

Australia won by 3 wickets

TWELFTH ONE-DAY INTERNATIONAL – AUSTRALIA *v.* NEW ZEALAND
20 January 1988 at Sydney

AUSTRALIA				NEW ZEALAND			
G.R. Marsh	c Brown, b Chatfield	101		T.E. Blain*	c Jones, b McDermott	1	
D.C. Boon	c Blain, b Snedden	8		A.H. Jones	c Dyer, b Davis	19	
D.M. Jones	c Bracewell, b Gillespie	15		J.J. Crowe†	c Veletta, b Dodemaide	6	
M.R.J. Veletta	c Gillespie, b Bracewell	19		K.R. Rutherford	c McDermott, b Davis	10	
S.R. Waugh	c J. J. Crowe, b Watson	0		D.N. Patel	b Davis	13	
A.R. Border†	run out	22		V.R. Brown	st Dyer, b Taylor	32	
G.C. Dyer*	c J. J. Crowe, b Brown	11		J.G. Bracewell	b Waugh	38	
C.J. McDermott	c Jones, b Chatfield	18		M.C. Snedden	c Veletta, b Taylor	6	
A.I.C. Dodemaide	not out	11		S.R. Gillespie	lbw, b Taylor	2	
P.L. Taylor	not out	3		W. Watson	c Boon, b Waugh	1	
S.P. Davis				E.J. Chatfield	not out	1	
Extras	b 2, lb 6, w 4, nb 1	13		Extras	lb 7, w 5, nb 2	14	
(50 overs)	(for 8 wkts)	221		(44.5 overs)		143	

	O	M	R	W		O	M	R	W
Snedden	10	1	36	1	Dodemaide	9	1	21	1
Chatfield	10	3	26	2	McDermott	8	1	31	1
Watson	10	1	49	1	Davis	10	1	27	3
Gillespie	6	–	31	1	Waugh	7.5	–	33	2
Bracewell	10	1	47	1	Taylor	10	2	24	3
Brown	4	–	24	1					

FALL OF WICKETS
1–17, 2–50, 3–88, 4–88, 5–145, 6–162, 7–194, 8–217

FALL OF WICKETS
1–3, 2–30, 3–34, 4–48, 5–73, 6–119, 7–134, 8–138, 9–141

Umpires: A.R. Crafter & L.J. King

Man of the Match: G.R. Marsh

Australia won by 78 runs

BENSON AND HEDGES WORLD SERIES FIRST FINAL – AUSTRALIA *v.* NEW ZEALAND
22 January 1988 at Melbourne

NEW ZEALAND				AUSTRALIA			
J.G. Wright	c Dyer, b Davis	16		D.C. Boon	c Bracewell, b Watson	47	
A.H. Jones	c Dyer, b Dodemaide	4		G.R. Marsh	b Watson	9	
M.D. Crowe	c Dyer, b Dodemaide	48		D.M. Jones	not out	58	
J.J. Crowe†	run out	33		M.R.J. Veletta	not out	57	
R.J. Hadlee	c Boon, b McDermott	34		A.R. Border†			
T.E. Blain*	run out	1		S.R. Waugh			
V.R. Brown	c Waugh, b Davis	2		G.C. Dyer*			
J.G. Bracewell	c Border, b Waugh	17		C.J. McDermott			
M.C. Snedden	c Taylor, b McDermott	15		P.L. Taylor			
W. Watson	c Border, b Waugh	1		A.I.C. Dodemaide			
E.J. Chatfield	not out	3		S.P. Davis			
Extras	lb 2, w 1	3		Extras	b 2, lb 3, w 2, nb 2	9	
(49.5 overs)		177		(44.5 overs)	(for 2 wkts)	180	

	O	M	R	W		O	M	R	W
Dodemaide	10	2	29	2	Chatfield	7.5	2	19	–
McDermott	9.5	–	37	2	Hadlee	9	–	36	–
Davis	10	1	27	2	Snedden	10	3	39	–
Waugh	10	–	47	2	Watson	10	3	36	2
Taylor	10	–	35	–	Bracewell	8	–	45	–

FALL OF WICKETS
1–11, 2–47, 3–91, 4–126, 5–129, 6–132, 7–143, 8–161, 9–169

FALL OF WICKETS
1–33, 2–73

Umpires: R.C. Bailhache & P.J. McConnell

Australia won by 8 wickets

Benson and Hedges World Series

First Final
AUSTRALIA v. NEW ZEALAND

Australia, as expected on recent form, disposed of New Zealand with some ease in the first of the best-of-three final matches. Wicket-keeper Greg Dyer played a significant part in undermining the New Zealand innings. He helped dismiss both Jones and Martin Crowe and took a spectacular diving catch to his left to account for John Wright. Boon and Steve Waugh also took diving catches to send back Hadlee and Vaughan Brown, while Border completed an impressive Australian performance in the field with a remarkable stop and throw to run out Jeff Crowe. All of the Australian bowlers kept a tight line and length and offered the New Zealand batsmen little scope for quick runs.

Australia lost Marsh at 33, but David Boon, exuding confidence, hit a brisk 47. He become Watson's second victim, after which Mike Veletta and Dean Jones hit 107 off 131 balls to take their side to a most comfortable win with 5.1 overs to spare.

There was no individual award for the first final, an award being made over the two matches.

Greg Dyer, Australia's wicket-keeper throughout the season. (Adrian Murrell/Allsport)

BENSON AND HEDGES WORLD SERIES SECOND FINAL – AUSTRALIA v. NEW ZEALAND
24 January 1988 at Sydney

NEW ZEALAND						AUSTRALIA						
T.E. Blain*	c Veletta, b McDermott				9		G.R. Marsh	c Wright, b Hadlee				5
J.G. Wright	c Waugh, b Dodemaide				8		D.C. Boon	c Snedden, b Watson				43
M.D. Crowe	b Davis				8		C.J. McDermott	c M.D. Crowe, b Snedden				24
A.H. Jones	not out				56		D.M. Jones	not out				53
R.J. Hadlee	c Border, b Waugh				19		M.R.J. Veletta	c sub (Rutherford), b Snedden				30
J.J. Crowe†	c Jones, b McDermott				42		A.R. Border†	not out				11
D.N. Patel	not out				11		S.R. Waugh					
J.G. Bracewell							G.C. Dyer*					
M.C. Snedden							A.I.C. Dodemaide					
W. Watson							P.L. Taylor					
E.J. Chatfield							S.P. Davis					
Extras	lb 11, w 4				15		Extras	lb 3				3
(38 overs)	(for 5 wkts)				168		(34.1 overs)	(for 4 wkts)				169

	O	M	R	W			O	M	R	W
Dodemaide	8	–	27	1		Hadlee	8	2	22	1
McDermott	8	–	29	2		Chatfield	6	2	34	–
Davis	8	1	23	1		Snedden	8	–	45	2
Taylor	7	–	27	–		Bracewell	7	–	37	–
Waugh	7	–	51	1		Watson	5.1	–	28	1

FALL OF WICKETS
1–20, 2–21, 3–31, 4–79, 5–139

FALL OF WICKETS
1–12, 2–48, 3–91, 4–145

Umpires: A.R. Crafter & P.J. McConnell

Man of the Finals: D.M. Jones

Australia won by 6 wickets

Benson and Hedges World Series

Second Final
AUSTRALIA v. NEW ZEALAND

Rain cost two hours' play in the second final and reduced the contest to one of 38 overs. The rain arrived when the New Zealand innings was only five overs old, and the visitors were always struggling to build a respectable total from that point. Andrew Jones, as he had done throughout most of the tour, salvaged some pride with a resolute 56 not out after three quick wickets had fallen, and Jeff Crowe, for whom the tour had not been a happy one, hit 42 off 40 balls with a six and 4 fours.

Marsh again went early, but Craig McDermott, promoted to number three to give the innings an initial boost, hit 4 fours and made 24 off 16 balls. Veletta and Boon were no less positive, and Dean Jones, whose batting won him the individual award for the finals, hit 53 off 70 balls to steer Australia to victory and trophy with 23 balls to spare.

22, 23, 24 and 25 January 1988

at Adelaide

South Australia 319 (D.W. Hookes 82, G.A. Bishop 67, P.R. Sleep 58, D.R. Gilbert 5 for 94) and 113 for 3 dec

New South Wales 150 for 2 dec (J. Dyson 60 not out) and 219 (M.E. Waugh 72, S.B. Smith 51)

South Australia won by 63 runs
South Australia 6 pts, New South Wales 0 pts

23, 24 and 25 January 1988

at Bellerive Oval, Hobart

Tasmania 339 for 6 dec (D.J. Buckingham 71, P.I. Faulkner 61 not out, E.J. Harris 56)
Sri Lankans 303 (A.P. Gurusinha 118, R.S. Madugalle 56, T.J. Cooley 4 for 95)

Match drawn

Adverse weather had an effect on both matches. Bishop and Hookes brought South Australia from 26 for 2 to 142 before Bishop fell to Jones. Earlier, Hilditch had been caught at the wicket by Emery off Gilbert, who returned his best figures of an unhappy season. Emery was making his first-class début, Rixon having retired after making a record 94 appearances for New South Wales. With so much play lost, Murray Bennett declared on the third day although the visitors were still 169 runs behind. Hookes responded as his side scored quick runs and left New South Wales a day in which to make 283.

Steve Smith batted purposefully early on the last day,

BENSON AND HEDGES WORLD SERIES – AVERAGES

AUSTRALIA BATTING

	M	Inns	NOs	Runs	HS	Av	100s	50s
D.M. Jones	10	10	2	461	92	57.62		5
M.R.J. Veletta	10	10	3	295	68*	42.14		2
D.C. Boon	10	10		393	122	39.30	1	1
S.R. Waugh	10	8	2	199	68	33.16		1
P.L. Taylor	9	5	3	58	27*	29.00		
A.I.C. Dodemaide	10	6	3	72	30	24.00		
A.R. Border	10	9	2	162	61	23.14		1
G.R. Marsh	10	10		211	101	21.10	1	
G.C. Dyer	10	7	1	73	38	12.16		
C.J. McDermott	9	8	1	85	24	12.14		
M.R. Whitney	5	2	1	5	3	5.00		

Played in four matches: S.P. Davis did not bat
Played in three matches: T.B.A. May did not bat

NEW ZEALAND BATTING

	M	Inns	NOs	Runs	HS	Av	100s	50s
A.H. Jones	9	9	1	416	87	52.00		5
R.J. Hadlee	9	8	2	206	52	34.33		1
M.D. Crowe	9	8		298	52	33.11		1
J.G. Wright	9	9		208	61	23.11		1
T.E. Blain	10	10	4	138	49*	23.00		
J.J. Crowe	8	8	1	137	42	19.57		
J.G. Bracewell	6	4		68	38	17.00		
M.C. Snedden	8	6	3	50	15*	16.66		
V.R. Brown	3	3		44	32	14.66		
S.R. Gillespie	7	4	2	25	9*	12.50		
D.N. Patel	8	8	1	78	29	11.14		
K.R. Rutherford	5	4		36	24	9.00		
W. Watson	3	2		2	1	1.00		

Played in ten matches: E.J. Chatfield 1*, 0*, 1* and 3*
Played in four matches: D.K. Morrison did not bat
Played in one match: I.D.S. Smith 9

AUSTRALIA BOWLING

	Overs	Mds	Runs	Wkts	Av	Best	4/inns
A.I.C. Dodemaide	91.1	10	189	18	16.05	5/21	1
S.P. Davis	38	3	110	6	18.33	3/27	
C.J. McDermott	80.5	4	321	15	21.40	3/50	
S.R. Waugh	89.5	3	381	17	22.41	4/33	1
M.R. Whitney	50	2	205	8	25.62	4/34	1
P.L. Taylor	84	5	326	12	27.16	4/38	1
T.B.A. May	30	3	119	1	119.00	1/49	
D.M. Jones	2	–	16	0	–		

NEW ZEALAND BOWLING

	Overs	Mds	Runs	Wkts	Av	Best	4/inns
E.J. Chatfield	87.1	17	300	17	17.64	4/32	1
D.K. Morrison	30.1	4	157	7	22.42	2/39	
K.R. Rutherford	5	–	25	1	25.00	1/25	
R.J. Hadlee	80.4	10	257	10	25.70	3/35	
M.C. Snedden	82.4	8	362	14	25.85	3/36	
W. Watson	25.1	4	113	4	28.25	2/36	
S.R. Gillespie	56.2	1	281	7	40.14	3/40	
J.G. Bracewell	53	2	229	4	57.25	2/27	
V.R. Brown	11	–	75	1	75.00	1/24	
D.N. Patel	14	–	92	–	–		

AUSTRALIA FIELDING FIGURES

13 - G.C. Dyer (ct 12/st 1); 9 - A.R. Border; 7 - M.R.J. Veletta; 6 - D.C. Boon and P.L. Taylor; 4 - D.M. Jones and C.J. McDermott; 3 - G.R. Marsh, S.R. Waugh and A.I.C. Dodemaide; 1 - S.P. Davis

NEW ZEALAND FIELDING FIGURES

11 - T.E. Blain; 6 - D.N. Patel; 5 - M.D. Crowe; 4 - J.G. Wright and S.R. Gillespie; 3 - A.H. Jones, J.J. Crowe, J.G. Bracewell and K.R. Rutherford (inc one as sub); 2 - M.C. Snedden, E.J. Chatfield, V.R. Brown and P.A. Horne (both as sub); 1 - R.J.Hadlee, D.K. Morrison and I.D.S. Smith

and Mark Waugh hit 72 off 86 balls with 4 sixes and 7 fours, but Andrew Zesers bowled Waugh shortly before tea, and New South Wales subsided to Sleep and Zesers in the closing session.

The first first-class fixture played at the Bellerive Oval was badly affected by rain, and the match was, in effect, reduced to one innings. Consistent batting enabled Tasmania to declare late on the second day. The Sri Lankans spent the rest of the game in consolidating their batting form before the Test match. Gurusinha hit a patient century. Courtney and Young made their first-class débuts for Tasmania, and Claye Young, who, like Troy Cooley bowled impressively, began his career by dismissing Kaluperuma and Aravinda de Silva in his first two overs without conceding a run.

27 January 1988

at Manuka Oval, Canberra

Sri Lankans 238 for 6 (A.P. Gurusinha 95, A. Ranatunga 78, G. Irvine 4 for 49)
Australian County XI 224 for 9

Sri Lankans won by 14 runs

Ranatunga and Gurusinha put on 219 for the third wicket after the Sri Lankans had been put in to bat.

BENSON AND HEDGES WORLD SERIES – AVERAGES

SRI LANKA BATTING

	M	Inns	NOs	Runs	HS	Av	100s	50s
P.A. de Silva	8	8		279	79	34.87		3
C.P. Ramanayake	8	6	5	31	11*	31.00		
A. Ranatunga	8	8		226	67	28.25		1
R.S. Mahanama	8	8		209	58	26.12		3
J.R. Ratnayeke	8	8	2	137	41	22.83		
R.G. de Alwis	7	7	2	100	44	20.00		
D.S.B.P. Kuruppu	6	6		111	47	18.50		
A.P. Gurusinha	8	8		122	43	15.25		
G.F. Labrooy	8	7	3	60	33	15.00		
R.S. Madugalle	8	8		89	44	11.12		
E.A.R. de Silva	4	3		24	15	8.00		
M.A.R. Samarasekera	2	2		11	8	5.50		
H.P. Tillekeratne	2	2		9	9	4.50		

Played in one match: K.N. Amalean 0*; S. Jeganathan 1; S.A.M. Kaluperuma 4

SRI LANKA BOWLING

	Overs	Mds	Runs	Wkts	Av	Best	4/inns
C.P. Ramanayake	65	7	279	11	25.36	3/35	
J.R. Ratnayeke	72.4	2	297	10	29.70	3/33	
S. Jeganathan	7	–	36	1	36.00	1/36	
G.F. Labrooy	76.3	6	315	8	39.37	4/39	1
P.A. de Silva	60	1	285	7	40.71	3/58	
A. Ranatunga	59	1	275	6	45.83	2/34	
S.A.M. Kaluperuma	1	–	3	0	–		
A.P. Gurusinha	2	–	15	0	–		
K.N. Amalean	6	1	27	0	–		
M.A.R. Samarasekera	7	–	44	0	–		
E.A.R. de Silva	29	4	100	0	–		

SRI LANKA FIELDING FIGURES

7 - R.S. Mahanama and R.G. de Alwis; 6 - A.P. Gurusinha; 4 - P.A. de Silva; 3 - A. Ranatunga and R.S. Madugalle; 2 - D.S.B.P. Kuruppu (ct 1/st 1); 1 - C.P. Ramanayake, G.F. Labrooy, E.A.R. de Silva, S.A.M. Kaluperuma and sub (H.P. Tillekeratne)

29, 30, 31 January and 1 February 1988

at Launceston

Victoria 409 for 8 dec (G.M. Watts 176, D.F. Whatmore 52) and 135 for 1 dec (D.F. Whatmore 71 not out)
Tasmania 287 for 5 dec (D.J. Buckingham 103 not out) and 144 for 9

Match drawn
Victoria 2 pts, Tasmania 0 pts

Gary Watts returned to first-class cricket after an absence of four years and hit his maiden first-class century. He and Dav Whatmore began the match with a stand of 102. Victoria also recalled Ray Bright and gave first-class débuts to pace bowler Paul Reiffel and batsman Warren Ayres, who played two seasons for Woodford Wells in the Essex league. Tasmania's innings was blighted by rain, and Davison declared 122 in arrears after Danny Buckingham had reached his second hundred of the season. Set to make 258 in 2¾ hours, Tasmania struggled on a difficult pitch and were saved by their last pair, Cooley and Young, who survived 32 deliveries.

30 January 1988

at Traegar Park, Alice Springs

Sri Lankans 252 for 5 (A. Ranatunga 85, P.A.R. de Silva 70)
Northern Territories Invitation XI 236 (C.P. Ramanayake 4 for 12)

Sri Lankans won by 115 runs

31 January 1988

at Traegar Park, Alice Springs

Sri Lankans 131
South Australia 132 for 4 (A.M.J. Hilditch 53 not out)

South Australia won by 6 wickets

Bicentennial Test Match
AUSTRALIA v. ENGLAND

England broke from their tour of New Zealand to participate in Australia's Bicentennial celebrations. In every sense, this was a joyous occasion, but the cricket was serious, keenly contested, although below what one accepts as Test standard.

This lack of class was never more apparent than on the opening day when Gatting won the toss, England batted and closed at 221 for 2. Chris Broad survived the day with admirable resolution, benefiting from being missed by McDermott off his own bowling when 36, to reach his fourth hundred in six Tests against Australia. Broad was not the only one to prosper as the result of some lapses in the field by the Australians. Moxon, never at ease, was dropped at short-leg by Boon when five and by Border at slip when 15. Both were simple chances. He eventually played over a ball of full length from Sleep after the opening stand had realised 93.

The second wicket put on 99 before Robinson steered Dodemaide to second slip. Gatting, received with some hostility, made three in 67 minutes before the close of a

BICENTENNIAL TEST MATCH – AUSTRALIA *v.* ENGLAND
29, 30 and 31 January 1988 at Sydney Cricket Ground

ENGLAND

	FIRST INNINGS	
B.C. Broad	b Waugh	139
M.D. Moxon	b Sleep	40
R.T. Robinson	c Veletta, b Dodemaide	43
M.W. Gatting†	c Dyer, b Waugh	13
C.W.J. Athey	c and b Taylor	37
D.J. Capel	c Sleep, b Taylor	21
J.E. Emburey	st Dyer, b Sleep	23
B.N. French*	st Dyer, b Taylor	47
N.A. Foster	c Border, b Taylor	19
E.E. Hemmings	not out	8
G.R. Dilley	b Waugh	13
Extras	b 4, lb 9, w 1, nb 8	22
		425

AUSTRALIA

	FIRST INNINGS		SECOND INNINGS	
D.C. Boon	c French, b Foster	12	(2) not out	184
G.R. Marsh	c French, b Capel	5	(1) c Athey, b Emburey	56
D.M. Jones	c Emburey, b Hemmings	56	c Moxon, b Capel	24
A.R. Border†	c Broad, b Capel	2	not out	48
M.R.J. Veletta	c Emburey, b Hemmings	22		
S.R. Waugh	c French, b Dilley	27		
P.R. Sleep	c Athey, b Foster	41		
G.C. Dyer*	lbw, b Dilley	0		
P.L. Taylor	c French, b Hemmings	20		
A.I.C. Dodemaide	not out	12		
C.J. McDermott	c Foster, b Dilley	1		
Extras	lb 10, w 1, nb 5	16	b 3, lb 7, nb 6	16
		214	(for 2 wkts)	328

	O	M	R	W
McDermott	35	8	65	–
Dodemaide	36	10	98	1
Taylor	34	10	84	4
Waugh	22.5	5	51	3
Sleep	45	8	114	2

	O	M	R	W	O	M	R	W
Dilley	19.1	4	54	3	13	1	48	–
Foster	19	6	27	2	15	6	27	–
Capel	6	3	13	2	17	4	38	1
Emburey	30	10	57	–	38	5	98	1
Hemmings	22	3	53	3	52	15	107	–

FALL OF WICKETS
1–93, 2–192, 3–245, 4–262, 5–313, 6–314, 7–346, 8–387, 9–410

FALL OF WICKETS
1–18, 2–25, 3–34, 4–82, 5–116, 6–147, 7–153, 8–183, 9–209
1–162, 2–218

Umpires: A.R. Crafter & P.J. McConnell

Match drawn

LEFT: *The setting for the Bicentennial Test – Sydney Cricket Ground, The Pavilion. (Adrian Murrell/Allsport)*

day which is best remembered for the parade of great players of the past.

By lunch-time on the second day, England, 295 for 4, were immune from defeat, but not from criticism as to their attitude to the game. Gatting's innings of 13 occupied 109 minutes, and Broad, having batted 7¼ hours, attempted to leave a ball from Waugh but deflected it onto his stumps off his arm. It was bad luck. Broad's reaction was to knock his leg stump out of the ground in fury at himself. That was petulant bad manners in keeping with much that had been seen in Pakistan. The reaction by the English management was to fine Broad £500 instantly. Had such swift action been taken when Broad refused to leave the wicket after being given out in Pakistan a few months earlier, a much more serious crime, the agonies of the winter tour may have been avoided, or at least lessened. Is one to think that shameful behaviour in Pakistan is more acceptable than in Australia?

England failed to build significantly on the advantage that Broad's long innings had given them. Australia

ABOVE: *Sir Donald Bradman receives the plaudits of the crowd. (Adrian Murrell/Allsport)*

BELOW: *Knock back in anger! Chris Broad plays on to end his mighty innings in the Bicentennial Test and turns to knock down a stump in self-disgust. (Patrick Eagar)*

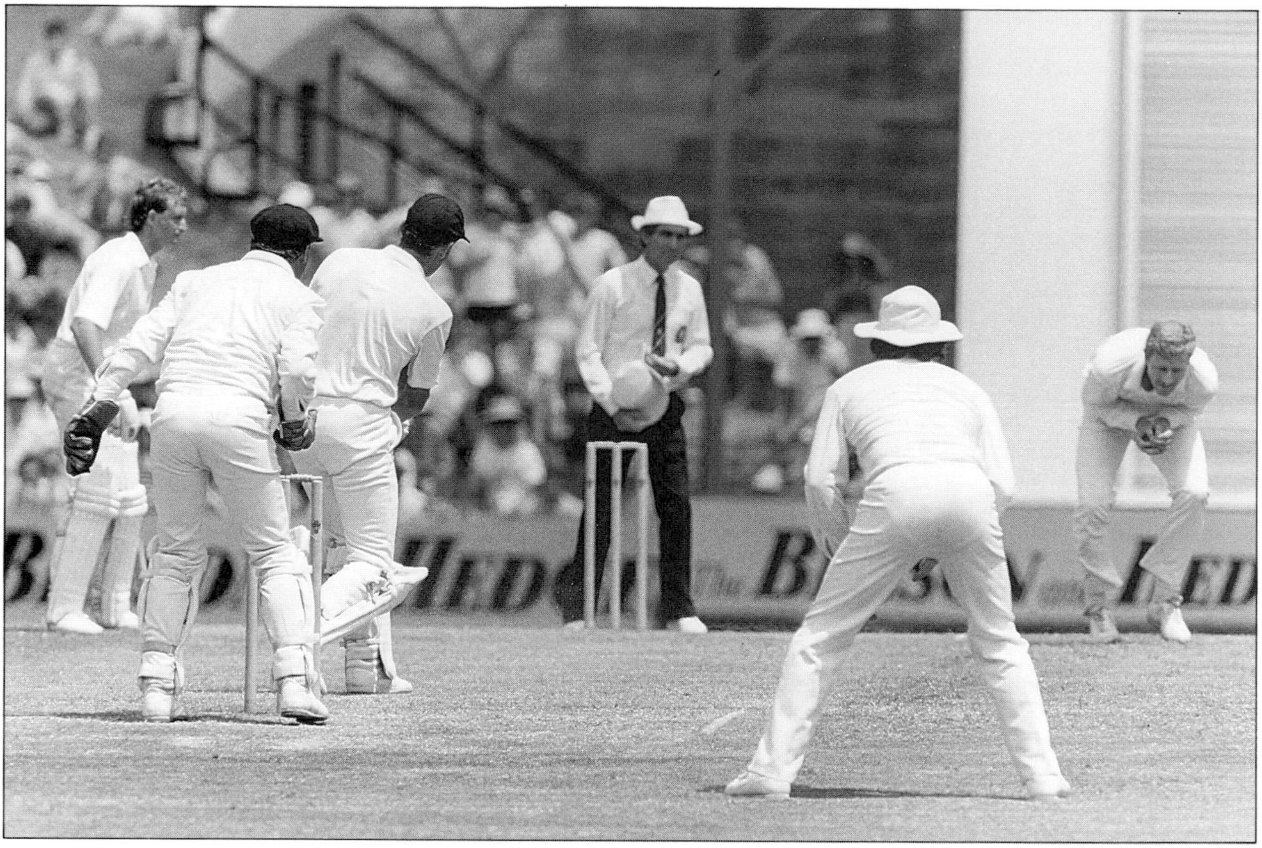

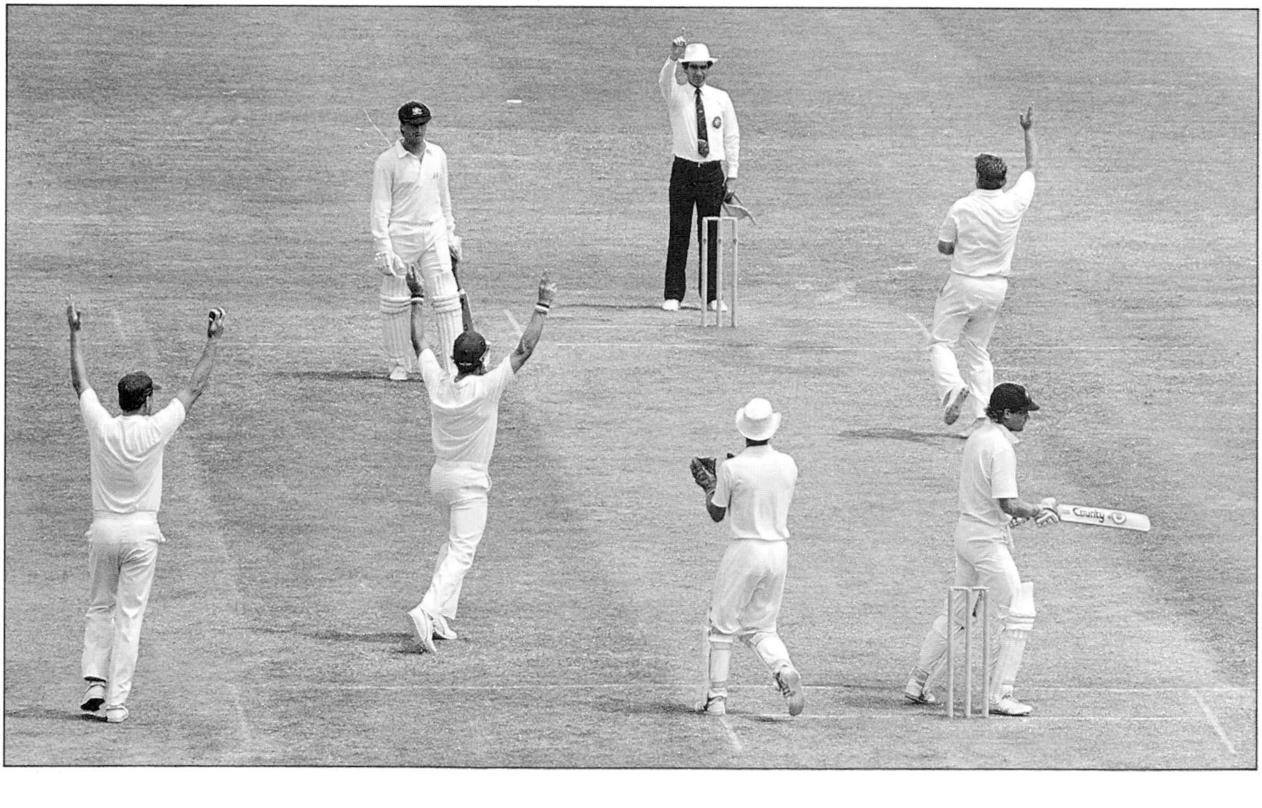
County

LEFT: *Athey – caught and bowled by Peter Taylor. (Patrick Eager)*
BELOW LEFT: *Dean Jones is caught by Emburey off Hemmings. (Patrick Eagar)*

missed more chances, but Peter Taylor bowled well, Foster and French blasted well, and Boon and Marsh hit 14 in 10 overs before the close.

The third day saw the game swing dramatically in favour of England. Three wickets fell in the first session and four in the second. England emulated Australia in putting down several chances, but they also held some. Boon gloved the ball to French, and Marsh glanced to the wicket-keeper too. Border rather irresponsibly pulled Capel to long-leg. Jones was far from happy against the spinners, and Veletta, having been badly missed, was taken at short-leg.

Jones reached a frenetic fifty and fell almost immediately. He had enjoyed much luck, being dropped by Emburey and missed off an easy stumping chance. French atoned in some way by taking Waugh one-handed, and Dyer, who had had to leave the field and have stitches in an injured nose after being hit while keeping wicket, was lbw to Dilley, who was in lively mood in the afternoon. Sleep and Taylor offered defiance until bad light ended play early with Australia 164 for 7.

Australia failed to avoid the follow-on on the fourth day. They had seemed to be heading for safety, but Taylor

cut at Hemmings and was caught off the underedge. Then the new ball accounted for Sleep, spectacularly caught at second slip, and McDermott, even more spectacularly caught by the acrobatic Foster at mid-on.

Poor light again ended play early, but this was due in part to silliness in bowling Dilley, and Dilley's silliness in bowling a bouncer. By the time that play ended, Boon and Marsh had batted through 43.3 overs and scored 101.

They extended their stand to 162 the next, and last, day, the highest opening partnership for Australia against England at Sydney. Boon reached his hundred before lunch and altogether batted for 492 minutes, faced 431 balls and hit 14 fours. He was named Man of the Match. A draw pleased most people, even if the overall standard of play did not.

3 February 1988

at Queen Elizabeth Oval, Bendigo

Sri Lankans 262 for 5 (A.P. Gurusinha 116 not out, R.S. Mahanama 61)
Victorian Country XI 152 (G.F. Labrooy 4 for 26)

Sri Lankans won by 110 runs

Bicentennial One-Day International
AUSTRALIA v. ENGLAND

The Australian celebrations continued with, inevitably, a one-day international against England, and were completed as they gained their ninth consecutive victory in

---

BICENTENNIAL ONE-DAY INTERNATIONAL – AUSTRALIA v. ENGLAND
4 February 1988 at Melbourne Cricket Ground

AUSTRALIA				ENGLAND			
D.C. Boon	c and b Capel	33		B.C. Broad	c Dyer, b Waugh	25
G.R. Marsh	run out	87		R.T. Robinson	c Dodemaide, b Whitney	35
D.M. Jones	c sub (Moxon), b Emburey	30		P.A.J. De Freitas	run out	21
M.R.J. Veletta	c Capel, b Emburey	13		C.W.J. Athey	c Border, b Davis	4
S.R. Waugh	run out	27		N.H. Fairbrother	st Dyer, b Taylor	22
A.R. Border†	c Gatting, b De Freitas	19		M.W. Gatting†	c Border, b Whitney	37
A.I.C. Dodemaide	not out	7		D.J. Capel	c Taylor, b Davis	18
P.L. Taylor	not out	1		J.E. Emburey	b Dodemaide	26
G.C. Dyer*				C.J. Richards*	not out	14
S.P. Davis				N.V. Radford	not out	0
M.R. Whitney				P.W. Jarvis		
Extras	lb 6, w 5, nb 7	18		Extras	lb 9, w 1, nb 1	11
(48 overs)	(for 6 wkts)	235		(48 overs)	(for 8 wkts)	213

	O	M	R	W		O	M	R	W
De Freitas	10	1	43	1	Whitney	10	1	37	2
Radford	10	–	61	–	Dodemaide	10	1	35	1
Capel	8	1	30	1	Davis	10	–	55	2
Jarvis	10	–	42	–	Waugh	10	–	42	1
Emburey	10	–	53	2	Taylor	8	–	35	1

FALL OF WICKETS
1–70, 2–133, 3–169, 4–184, 5–222, 6–233

FALL OF WICKETS
1–58, 2–65, 3–82, 4–96, 5–123, 6–172, 7–175, 8–213

Umpires: A.R. Crafter & R.C. Bailhache

Man of the Match: G.R. Marsh

Australia won by 22 runs

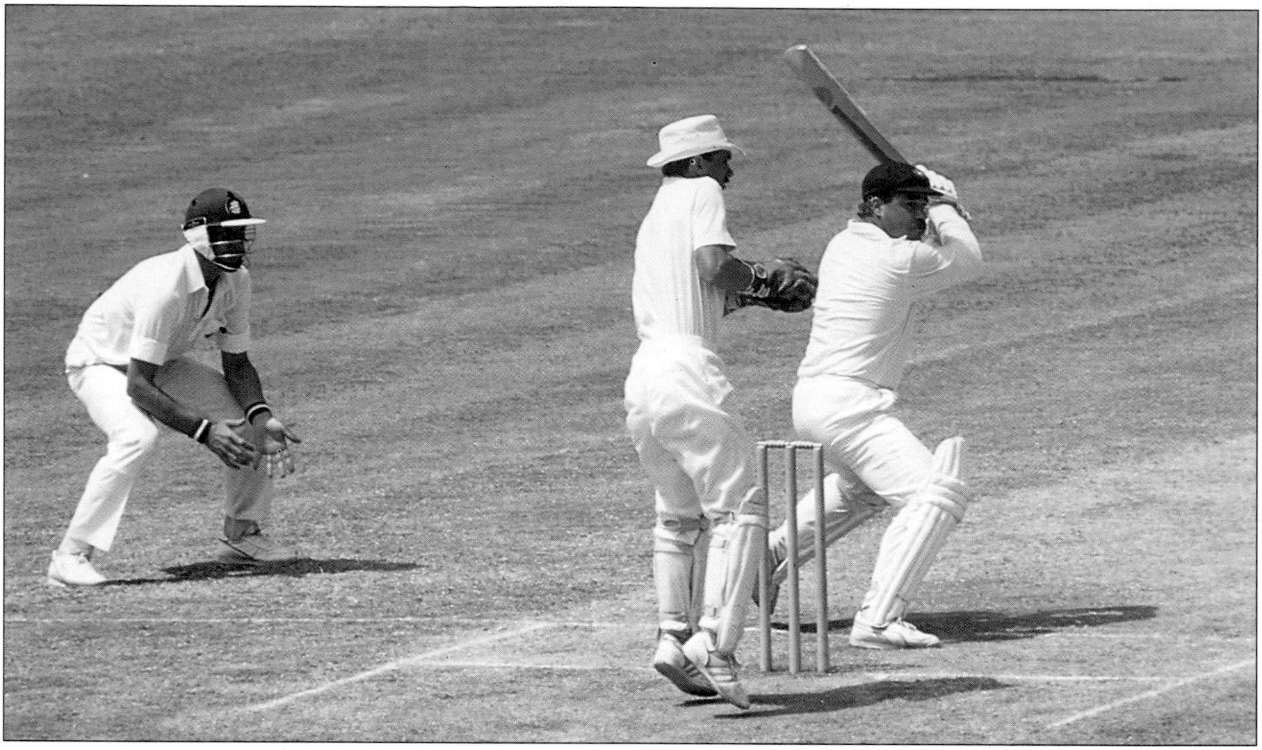

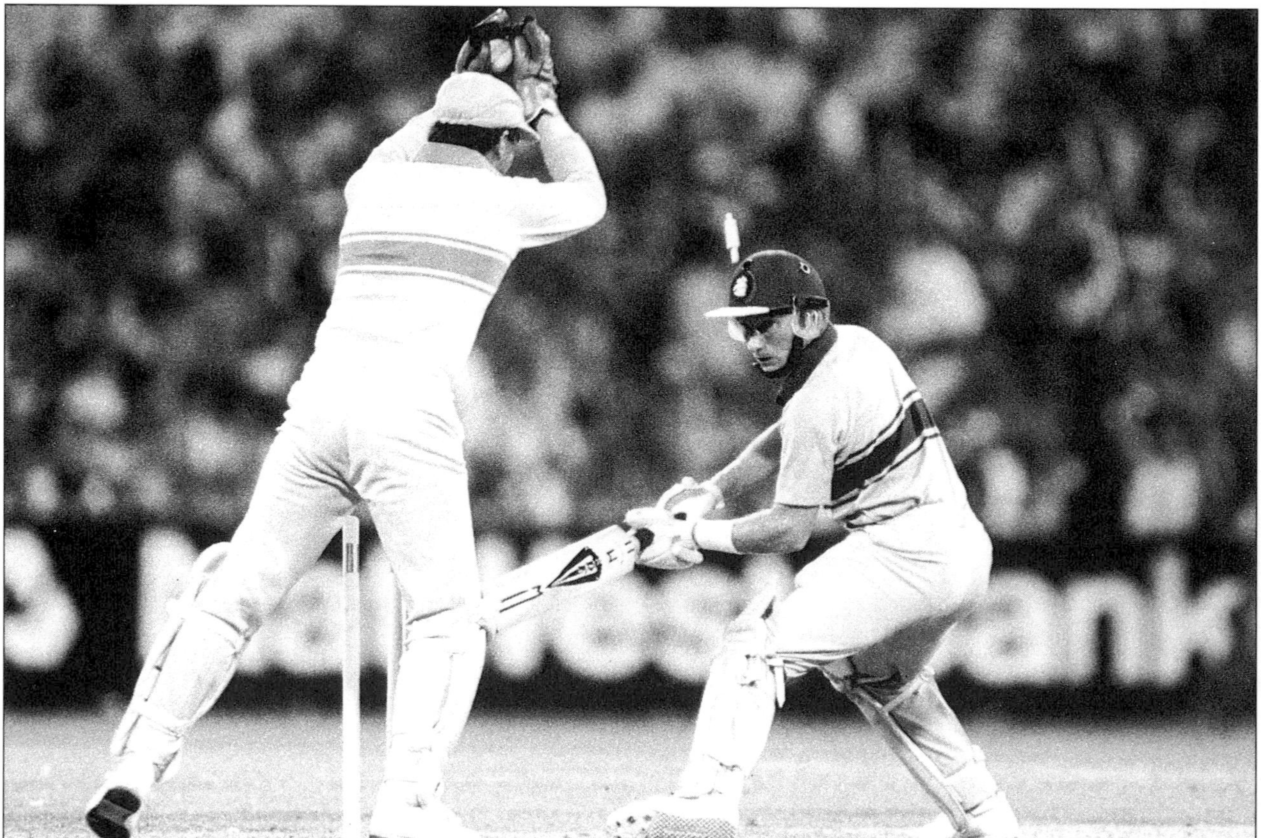

LEFT: *David Boon drives through the off side during his match-saving innings which won him the individual award. (Adrian Murrell/Allsport)*
BELOW LEFT: *Fairbrother, stumped Dyer, bowled Taylor for 22 in the Bicentennial One-Day International. (Adrian Murrell/Allsport)*

limited-over cricket. Boon and Marsh gave Australia the sound and solid start that had played so important a part in the country's success in 1987–8. They put on 70 in 19 overs although they should have been caught by both Capel and Gatting, first at point then at mid-wicket. Jones was dropped by Robinson, who hurt his hand in missing the catch, and the brightest spot for England was in the brisk bowling of Jarvis, who conceded only nine runs in his first five overs.

Jarvis was not rewarded with a wicket, however, but Emburey, whose bowling was less impressive, accounted for both Jones and Veletta and ran out Marsh with a fine throw. Waugh, too, was adjudged run out, and Border was very well caught by Gatting running back from mid-on. England bowled two overs fewer than they should have done and were duly fined approximately £700.

Robinson showed a great sense of freedom at the start of the England innings, but he mis-timed a drive and was caught. De Freitas played purposefully until he was run out by Border's direct throw from extra cover. Gatting raised hopes with 37 off 47 balls, but after he was caught by the tumbling Border there was little doubt as to which way the match would go.

Marsh was named Man of the Match to the delight of the crowd of 54,159.

6, 7, 8 and 9 February 1988

at Brisbane

Queensland 385 (T.J. Barsby 102, I.T. Botham 60, G.S. Trimble 57, P.R. Sleep 4 for 91) and 271 (A.R. Border 118 not out)
South Australia 364 (D.W. Hookes 112, G.A. Bishop 100, T.V. Hohns 5 for 100) and 247 for 8 (W.B. Phillips 53, P.R. Sleep 52, A.B. Henschell 4 for 101)

Match drawn
Queensland 2 pts, South Australia 0 pts

at Bellerive Oval, Hobart

Western Australia 334 (G.R. Marsh 86, W.S. Andrews 57, K.H. MacLeay 57) and 263 for 7 dec (M.R.J. Veletta 95, G.M. Wood 79)
Tasmania 273 (B.F. Davison 59, D.C. Boon 53, C.D. Matthews 6 for 77) and 209 (D.C. Boon 89, P.I. Faulkner 59, T.G. Hogan 6 for 57)

Western Australia won by 115 runs
Western Australia 6 pts, Tasmania 0 pts

at Melbourne

Sri Lankans 157 (S.P. Davis 5 for 80) and 362 for 6 dec (A. Ranatunga 68, P.A. de Silva 68)
Victoria 146 (G.F. Labrooy 7 for 71) and 297 for 5 (G.M. Watts 122, J.D. Siddons 103)

Match drawn

Trevor Barsby, 102 for Queensland v. South Australia, Brisbane, 6 February. (Adrian Murrell/Allsport)

With the only interest in the Sheffield Shield as to who would finish top of the table and claim ground advantage in the final, Queensland failed to produce their pre-Christmas form in their match against South Australia at Brisbane. Trevor Barsby hit his first hundred of the season and shared a second wicket stand of 163 with Trimble, while Ian Botham gave the innings later impetus to take Queensland to 385. South Australia responded with an opening stand of 157 between Bishop and Hilditch, who made 49. This was followed by a swashbuckling hundred from Hookes, but South Australia lost their last five wickets for 10 runs inside an hour to concede first innings points. Allan Border hit a five-hour century when Queensland batted again and set South Australia to make 293 in approximately 53 overs. In fact, Queensland bowled 60 overs in the remaining time, but after a promising start South Australia lost their way and settled for a draw.

Tasmania welcomed back Boon and looked an altogether stronger side but still bowed to Western Aus-

LEFT: *Botham and Healy leap in appeal as Zesers is caught behind off Henschell, Queensland* v. *South Australia, 6–9 February (Adrian Murrell/Allsport)*

RIGHT: *Allan Border steers the ball through the off-side field during his innings of 118 not out for Queensland against South Australia. Border enjoyed a memorable season, leading Australia to success over New Zealand and Sri Lanka, hitting his first double century in Test cricket, and becoming Australia's leading run-maker in Test history. (Adrian Murrell/Allsport)*

A result never looked likely in a game that was dominated by batsmen. Siddons played two fine innings as did Mark Waugh. Waugh's third hundred of the season strengthened his claim to join his brother in the national side for he had a most consistent season with the bat. Greg Matthews had a good all-round match, and Gavin Robertson, making his first-class début, claimed the wicket of Dimattina in the second innings as well as scoring 38.

Test Match
AUSTRALIA v. SRI LANKA

An inexperienced and ill-prepared Sri Lankan side was no match for Australia, who completed their most successful

tralia, who recovered from the shock of losing Veletta and Moody for 16 at the beginning of the match. Matthews was again in fine form with his medium-pace bowling, and after Veletta and Wood had added 115 for the third wicket, Wood declared, setting Tasmania to make 325 in a minimum of 87 overs. At 127 for 2, they were well placed, but Tom Hogan, playing his first match since his return from South Africa, brought about a collapse with his slow left-arm spin so that seven wickets fell for 30 runs. Some honour was saved when Peter Faulkner hit 59 off 86 balls and added 52 in half an hour for the last wicket with Lillee, who scored five.

The Sri Lankans batted disappointingly in their last game before the Test match. Graeme Labrooy returned the best bowling figures of his career and gave his side a slender lead after which they batted with more resolution. Set to make 374 on a slightly shortened last day, Victoria were well served by left-hander Gary Watts and by Jamie Siddons, who put on 198 for the third wicket, but the task of scoring 374 proved to be too great.

12, 13, 14 and 15 February 1988

at Melbourne

Victoria 403 (W.G. Whiteside 80, J.D. Siddons 71, G.M. Watts 66, M.G. Dimattina 60, D.F. Whatmore 55, G.R.J. Matthews 6 for 97) and 212 for 5 dec (J.D. Siddons 130)
New South Wales 279 (M.E. Waugh 69, G.R.J. Matthews 62, D.J. Hickey 4 for 90) and 206 for 5 (M.E. Waugh 100 not out)

Match drawn
Victoria 2 pts, New South Wales 0 pts

Ranjan Madugalle. A difficult time as Sri Lanka's new captain. (Adrian Murrell/Allsport)

international season in recent years with an emphatic innings victory inside four days.

Sri Lanka were handicapped from the start when injury ruled out Gurusinha, their most prolific run-scorer. They gave a first Test cap to medium-pace bowler Ramanayake while Australia brought back Mervyn Hughes in place of Peter Sleep.

Border won the toss, and Boon and Marsh began, almost inevitably, with a stand of 120. Boon, having been missed at square-leg off a difficult chance, was bowled by the persevering Ratnayeke some 20 minutes after Marsh had fallen to Labrooy. Dean Jones and Allan Border added 156 in 151 minutes, and although Border was surprisingly bowled when in sight of a century, Jones reached three figures with a cross-batted swat to mid-wicket where he was dropped by substitute Tillekeratne. Jones was on 98 at the time and ran two for the dropped catch. Australia closed on 333 for 3.

Sri Lanka's out-cricket was better on the second day. Jones fell to Labrooy after hitting 13 fours and batting for 251 minutes, and the rest of the batting never quite came

to fruition. Sri Lanka ended the day on 85 for 3, defeat already looming.

Mahanama was out early on the third morning, and Ranatunga was the only other batsman to show anything approaching international quality. Ravi Ratnayeke began with five boundaries and hit 24 in an hour while Ranatunga's innings occupied 225 minutes and included 5 fours. He was twice dropped, and Dyer put down Ramanayake first ball. Even so, Border enjoyed the rare luxury of being able to ask Sri Lanka to follow-on.

Mahanama again looked impressive, but he was run out by Boon at 36. Kuruppu and Kaluperuma followed on 42, and the disappointing Avarinda de Silva was out at 66. Sri Lanka closed at 78 for 4, Ranatunga and Madugalle hanging on gamely.

Madugalle was out quickly on the fourth morning. He had had a most unhappy time since becoming Sri Lanka's captain. Ranatunga, who hit 6 fours and batted 92 minutes, was the next to go, and Ratnayeke, with Mahanama and Ranatunga the only Sri Lankan to show any kind of form in the match, was last out after hitting 5

TEST MATCH – AUSTRALIA v. SRI LANKA
12, 13, 14 and 15 February 1988 at the WACA Ground, Perth

AUSTRALIA

FIRST INNINGS		
G. R. Marsh	b Labrooy	53
D.C. Boon	b J. R. Ratnayeke	64
D.M. Jones	lbw, b Labrooy	102
A.R. Border†	b J.R. Ratnayeke	88
M.R.J. Veletta	c de Alwis, b J.R. Ratnayeke	21
S.R. Waugh	c Labrooy, b Amalean	20
G.C. Dyer*	c Ramanayake, b Amalean	38
P.L. Taylor	c Amalean, b J.R. Ratnayeke	18
A.I.C. Dodemaide	not out	16
C.J. McDermott	c de Alwis, b Amalean	4
M.G. Hughes	b Amalean	8
Extras	lb 12, w 5, nb 6	23
		455

	O	M	R	W
J.R. Ratnayeke	40	6	98	4
Labrooy	36	5	108	2
Ramanayake	17	2	58	–
Amalean	22.2	1	97	4
Kaluperuma	13	–	62	–
Ranatunga	8	2	18	–
de Silva	1	–	2	–

FALL OF WICKETS
1–120, 2–133, 3–289, 4–346, 5–346, 6–380, 7–418, 8–434, 9–443

SRI LANKA

	FIRST INNINGS		SECOND INNINGS	
R.S. Mahanama	c Dyer, b Dodemaide	41	run out	28
D.S.B.P. Kuruppu	c Marsh, b McDermott	19	c Dyer, b Dodemaide	3
S.M.S. Kaluperuma	lbw, b McDermott	0	c and b Hughes	6
P.A. de Silva	lbw, b Waugh	6	lbw, b Dodemaide	7
A. Ranatunga	c and b Waugh	55	lbw, b Dodemaide	45
R.S. Madugalle†	c Border, b Dodemaide	6	c Waugh, b Hughes	7
J.R. Ratnayeke	c Marsh, b McDermott	24	c Dyer, b Dodemaide	38
R.G. de Alwis*	c Dyer, b Waugh	0	c Waugh, b Hughes	8
C.P. Ramanayake	c Dyer, b Waugh	9	c Veletta, b Hughes	0
G.F. Labrooy	c Dyer, b Dodemaide	4	b Hughes	4
K.N. Amalean	not out	7	not out	0
Extras	b 1, lb 6, w 2, nb 14	23	lb 6, nb 1	7
		194		**153**

	O	M	R	W	O	M	R	W
McDermott	20	3	50	3	4	2	8	–
Hughes	18	2	61	–	21	7	67	5
Dodemaide	22.3	6	40	3	19.1	7	58	4
Waugh	20	7	33	4	8	4	14	–
Taylor	2	1	3	–				

FALL OF WICKETS
1–51, 2–51, 3–60, 4–93, 5–107, 6–147, 7–148, 8–181, 9–182
1–36, 2–42, 3–42, 4–66, 5–83, 6–111, 7–130, 8–131, 9–153

Umpires: R.C. Bailhache & P.J. McConnell

Australia won by an innings and 108 runs

---

fours and batting for an hour. The game was over at 12.15 p.m., and only 10,382 had watched the three days, 1¼ hours' play.

Mervyn Hughes took five wickets in a Test innings for the first time, and Dodemaide again showed his appetite for international cricket although some might say that to put this match in that class was being presumptuous.

18, 19, 20 and 21 February 1988

at Adelaide

Tasmania 592 (M.D. Taylor 216, D.J. Buckingham 126, B.F. Davison 55)
South Australia 673 (A.M.J. Hilditch 185, D.W. Hookes 112, G.A. Bishop 101, D.F.G. O'Connor 75, W.B. Phillips 67, P.R. Sleep 57 not out, D.K. Lillee 4 for 165)

Match drawn
South Australia 2 pts, Tasmania −0.2 pts

This was the ultimate irony of Tasmania's season. Mick Taylor hit his highest score in first-class cricket, and he and Danny Buckingham shared a Tasmanian record fourth wicket stand of 258. Tasmania reached 592, the highest score that they have made in first-class cricket. Bishop and Hilditch replied with an opening stand of 199. Hookes hit his fourth hundred of the season, and Tasmania's score was passed with seven wickets down. The game ended

when South Australia were all out, having batted for 815 minutes, 214.4 overs. Tasmania were penalised 0.2 points for a slow over rate, and Lillee bowled 55 overs to take 4 for 165.

McDonald's Cup

19 February 1988

at Perth

Western Australia 170
Victoria 168 (D.M. Jones 54)

Western Australia (2 pts) won by 2 runs

21 February 1988

at Brisbane

New South Wales 287 for 7 (J. Dyson 79, S. Hookey 77, S.R. Waugh 56)
Queensland 134

New South Wales (2 pts) won by 153 runs

Davis was run out on the penultimate ball of the last over to give Western Australia victory at Perth. Zoehrer, with three catches and a stumping, took the individual award. Dyson and Hookey began the game against Queensland

Mervyn Hughes, 5 for 67 for Australia against Sri Lanka, his best bowling performance in Test cricket. (Adrian Murrell/Allsport)

with a stand of 128, and Hookey was named Man of the Match as New South Wales won with ease.

24, 25, 26 and 27 February 1988

at Sydney

New South Wales 295 (M.E. Waugh 95, M.D. O'Neill 68) and 213 for 8 dec (T.H. Bayliss 68)
Western Australia 176 (G.R.J. Matthews 4 for 58) and 201 (G.R. Marsh 82, S.R. Waugh 4 for 30)

New South Wales won by 131 runs
New South Wales 6 pts, Western Australia 0 pts

at Adelaide

Victoria 178 (J.D. Siddons 58, P.W. Gladigau 7 for 85) and 455 for 5 dec (J.D. Siddons 241 not out, D.M. Jones 101)
South Australia 161 (D.W. Hookes 60, A.I.C. Dodemaide 4 for 37) and 385 for 6 (P.R. Sleep 104 not out, A.M.J. Hilditch 67, D.W. Hookes 65)

Match drawn
Victoria 2 pts, South Australia 0 pts

at Launceston

Tasmania 481 (D.C. Boon 108, M.D. Taylor 89, P.I. Faulkner 78 not out, B.F. Davison 73, G.A. Hughes 71, T.V. Hohns 5 for 115) and 290 for 8 dec (D.C. Boon 143, G.A. Hughes 56)
Queensland 363 for 5 dec (G.S. Trimble 138 not out, R.B. Kerr 62, I.A. Healy 58 not out) and 314 (R.B. Kerr 96, G.M. Ritchie 85, C. Young 6 for 120)

Tasmania won by 94 runs
Tasmania 6 pts, Queensland 0 pts

Shock defeats for the two leading states left the venue of the Sheffield Shield final undecided until the last round of matches. Mark Waugh and Mark O'Neill added 155 for the fourth wicket to rouse New South Wales in their first innings, and the visitors then slumped before the off-spin

Healy won a place in the Queensland side when wicket-keeper Anderson was injured, but at the end of the season he was named in the Australian side to tour Pakistan, the only wicket-keeper in the party. (Adrian Murrell/Allsport)

of Greg Matthews and Peter Taylor. Leading by 119 on the first innings, New South Wales were 38 for 5 in their second before Greg Matthews and Bayliss put on 79. Set to make 333 to win in a little over a day, Western Australia offered little resistance.

Tasmania gained their first first-class win since February 1984, when they overcame pre-season favourites Queensland, who had lost their way since Christmas. Missed off the first ball of the match, David Boon hit a century in each innings, and Queensland were asked to make 409 from a minimum of 89 overs. Against a depleted attack Kerr and Ritchie gave their side hope as the score reached 221 before the second wicket fell, but Claye Young returned his best figures to give Tasmania their first points of the season.

Peter Gladigau returned his best bowling figures as Victoria were shot out for 178, but South Australia could still not manage first innings points. Jamie Siddons then hit the highest score of his career, his 241 coming off 239 balls. He hit a six, a five and 30 fours. Peter Sleep hit a comfortable hundred as the game petered to a draw.

McDonald's Cup

28 February 1988

at Launceston

Queensland 150 for 8 (R.J. Tucker 4 for 31)
Tasmania 151 for 5 (D.C. Boon 73)

Tasmania (2 pts) won by 5 wickets

at Adelaide

Victoria 232 (G.M. Watts 81, C. Killen 4 for 33, P.W. Gladigau 4 for 46)
South Australia 226 for 6 (J.K. Pyke 76 not out, P.W. Jackson 4 for 26)

Victoria (2 pts) won by 6 runs

Tasmania romped to victory with 9.2 overs to spare to put Queensland out of the Mcdonald's Cup. David Boon took the individual award. A valiant, unbroken stand of 106 was not enough to give South Australia victory over Victoria who had the Man of the Match winner in Gary Watts.

2, 3, 4 and 5 March 1988

at Melbourne

Victoria 256 (D.F. Whatmore 85, D. Tazelaar 5, for 55) and 328 (G.M. Watts 116, J.D. Siddons 76, J.N. Maguire 5 for 89)
Queensland 209 (M.G. Hughes 4 for 43, P. Reiffel 4 for 80) and 168

Victoria won by 207 runs
Victoria 6 pts, Queensland 0 pts

at Perth

South Australia 138 (B.A. Reid 5 for 34) and 331 (D.W. Hookes 65, A.M.J. Hilditch 59, W.B. Phillips 59, G.A. Bishop 55, C.D. Matthews 4 for 79)
Western Australia 434 (G.M. Wood 186, K.H. MacLeay 67, C.D. Matthews 64, A.K. Zesers 4 for 86) and 36 for 3

Western Australia won by 7 wickets
Western Australia 6 pts, South Australia 0 pts

at Sydney

Tasmania 327 (D.C. Boon 93, M.D. Taylor 81, S.R. Waugh 5 for 50, M.R. Whitney 5 for 54) and 204 (M.D. Taylor 86, G.F. Lawson 6 for 40, G.R.J. Matthews 4 for 54)
New South Wales 460 (M.A. Taylor 144, M.E. Waugh 116, S.R. Waugh 55) and 72 for 2

New South Wales won by 8 wickets
New South Wales 6 pts, Tasmania 0 pts

Having led the Sheffield Shield table from the start of the season, Queensland found themselves pushed into second place at the last, so conceding home advantage to Western Australia in the Shield final. Jamie Siddons reached a thousand runs for the season in a generally solid Victorian first innings, but it was Watts and Siddons in the second innings who virtually put the game out of Queensland's reach. Watts batted 5½ hours and hit 11 fours. Needing 376 in just under four hours, Queensland never looked like avoiding defeat.

Bruce Reid returned to the Western Australian attack and helped shoot out South Australia as 16 wickets fell on the opening day. That the home side recovered from 88 for 6 was almost entirely due to skipper Graeme Wood, who hit his highest score in first-class cricket and led his side to an impregnable position. South Australia batted with consistent application in their second innings, but there was to be no denying Western Australia. Wood and MacLeay added 160 for the home side's eighth wicket, a Western Australian record.

Tasmania were swept aside by New South Wales, but Mick Taylor passed a thousand runs for the state. Mark Waugh reached his fourth hundred of the season and he and Mark Taylor, who hit his only century of the summer, added 142 for the fourth wicket.

Sheffield Shield – Final Table					
	P	W	L	D	Pts
Western Australia	10	6	2	2	38
Queensland	10	5	3	2	32
New South Wales	10	4	4	2	24
Victoria	10	2	1	7	22
South Australia	10	2	4	4	16
Tasmania	10	1	6	2	5.8
(Tasmania penalised 0.2 points for slow over rate)					

McDonald's Cup

6 March 1988

at Perth

Western Australia 225 for 7 (G.R. Marsh 105)
South Australia 229 for 6 (G.A. Bishop 119 not out)

South Australia (2 pts) won by 4 wickets

at Sydney

Tasmania 154
New South Wales 123 for 6

New South Wales (2 pts) won on faster scoring rate

New South Wales became the only state to come through the qualifying rounds of the McDonald's Cup unbeaten when they beat Tasmania in a rain-interrupted match. They owed their victory to all-rounder Graham Smith, who took the individual award for his 2 for 19 in 6 overs and 22 not out, and off-spinner Peter Taylor. There were two centuries at Perth, but Glenn Bishop's 119 not out proved to be the match-winning innings.

McDonald's Cup Semi-Finals

12 March 1988

at Adelaide

Tasmania 220 for 8 (D.C. Boon 62)
South Australia 194 for 3 (D.W. Hookes 57 not out)

South Australia won on faster scoring rate

13 March 1988

at Sydney

Victoria 180 for 7
New South Wales 184 for 5 (G.L. Smith 58 not out)

New South Wales won by 5 wickets

Graham Smith again took the honours as New South Wales swamped Victoria with seven overs to spare. The semi-final in Adelaide was marred by rain, but South Australia reached their reduced target with ease, Darryl Scott taking the individual award.

McDonald's Cup – Final Tables

Group A

	P	W	L	Pts	R/R
South Australia	2	1	1	2	4.58
Victoria	2	1	1	2	4.00
Western Australia	2	1	1	2	3.95

Group B

	P	W	L	Pts	R/R
New South Wales	2	2	–	4	4.61
Tasmania	2	1	1	2	3.36
Queensland	2	–	2	0	2.84

Sheffield Shield Final
WESTERN AUSTRALIA v. QUEENSLAND

The Shield final, held in Perth in mid-March, had drama and controversy two days before a ball was bowled. On the flight from Brisbane to Perth, a number of incidents took place, resulting in Ian Botham's appearance in the East Perth court. It took Botham's old friend and rival Dennis Lillee, who put up $5,000 (£1,950) bail surety, to keep the English champion out of gaol. With such a cloud hanging over them, Queensland seemed to lose the invincibility

SHEFFIELD SHIELD FINAL – WESTERN AUSTRALIA v. QUEENSLAND
18, 19, 20, 21 and 22 March 1988 at WACA Ground, Perth

QUEENSLAND

	FIRST INNINGS		SECOND INNINGS	
R.B. Kerr	c Marsh, b Matthews	46	c Andrews, b Alderman	2
T.J. Barsby	c Zoehrer, b Matthews	48	b MacLeay	21
G.M. Ritchie	c MacLeay, b Matthews	33	lbw, b Alderman	34
A.R. Border†	c Andrews, b MacLeay	66	c Veletta, b Matthews	6
G.S. Trimble	c Zoehrer, b Mullally	15	lbw, b Alderman	3
I.T. Botham	c MacLeay, b Matthews	9	c MacLeay, b Alderman	54
D. Tazelaar	c Zoehrer, b Matthews	6	(10) c Wood, b Alderman	5
T.V. Hohns	lbw, b Matthews	14	(7) not out	59
I.A. Healy*	lbw, b Matthews	14	(8) c Zoehrer, b Alderman	0
C.J. McDermott	not out	8	(9) c Andrews, b Mullally	1
C.G. Rackemann	b Matthews	0	b MacLeay	8
Extras	b 9, lb 9, w 8, nb 4	30	b 9, lb 7, nb 7	23
		289		216

	O	M	R	W	O	M	R	W
Mullally	17	2	55	1	12	6	17	1
MacLeay	27	10	53	1	17.2	6	40	2
Alderman	26	10	62	–	28	4	91	6
Matthews	32.5	7	101	8	27	9	52	1

FALL OF WICKETS
1–63, 2–115, 3–161, 4–200, 5–234, 6–253, 7–253, 8–266, 9–289
1–9, 2–38, 3–46, 4–49, 5–88, 6–162, 7–164, 8–169, 9–194

Umpires: P.J. McConnell & A.R. Vrafter

Western Australia won by 5 wickets

WESTERN AUSTRALIA

	FIRST INNINGS		SECOND INNINGS	
G.R. Marsh	c Healy, b Rackemann	41	b Tazelaar	39
M.R.J. Veletta	c Barsby, b Rackemann	23	lbw, b Tazelaar	59
J. Brayshaw	c Border, b Rackemann	24	c Botham, b Tazelaar	4
G.M. Wood†	run out	141	c Healy, b Tazelaar	0
K.J. Hughes	run out	11	c sub (Maguire), b Botham	21
K.H. MacLeay	lbw, b McDermott	2	(6) not out	20
W.S. Andrews	lbw, b Rackemann	71	(7) not out	10
T.J. Zoehrer*	c Healy, b Rackemann	0		
C.D. Matthews	c Barsby, b Hohns	2		
T.M. Alderman	lbw, b Hohns	0		
A. Mullally	not out	2		
Extras	lb 15, nb 12	27	lb 8, nb 1	9
		344	(for 5 wkts)	162

	O	M	R	W	O	M	R	W
McDermott	24	4	80	1	7	1	21	–
Tazelaar	32	10	79	–	22.4	6	65	4
Rackemann	30	7	69	5	14	4	29	–
Botham	24	7	66	–	16	3	33	1
Hohns	19.5	7	35	2	4	1	6	–

FALL OF WICKETS
1–61, 2–75, 3–140, 4–153, 5–186, 6–322, 7–326, 8–335, 9–335
1–78, 2–82, 3–82, 4–125, 5–133

LEFT: *Career-best figures of 8 for 101 in the Sheffield Shield final confirmed Chris Matthews as the leading bowler of the Australian season. His 57 wickets was 11 more than his nearest rival. (Adrian Murrell/Allsport)*
BELOW: *Triumph again for Western Australia's skipper Graeme Wood and a recall to the Australian side for the tour of Pakistan. (Adrian Murrell/Allsport)*

they had created earlier in the season. This incident, linked with other Botham incidents during the season, was to lead to the abrupt end of the English all-rounder's stay with Queensland.

In front of a large crowd at the WACA ground – 31,905 over five days – Graeme Wood won the toss and put Queensland in to bat on a strip which had behaved erratically when used earlier in the season. As Australian paceman Bruce Reid had cried off with injury, the home selectors gambled by bringing in 18-year-old Alan Mullally for his début, but it was second change bowler Chris Matthews who did the damage with his left-arm deliveries which cut across the batsmen.

His 4 for 75 on the first day, as Queensland crawled to 245 for 6, became a career best 8 for 101 as he crashed through the visitors' tail. Their 289 would have been far worse had Allan Border not been dropped before he had scored.

Western Australia were always going to claim a first

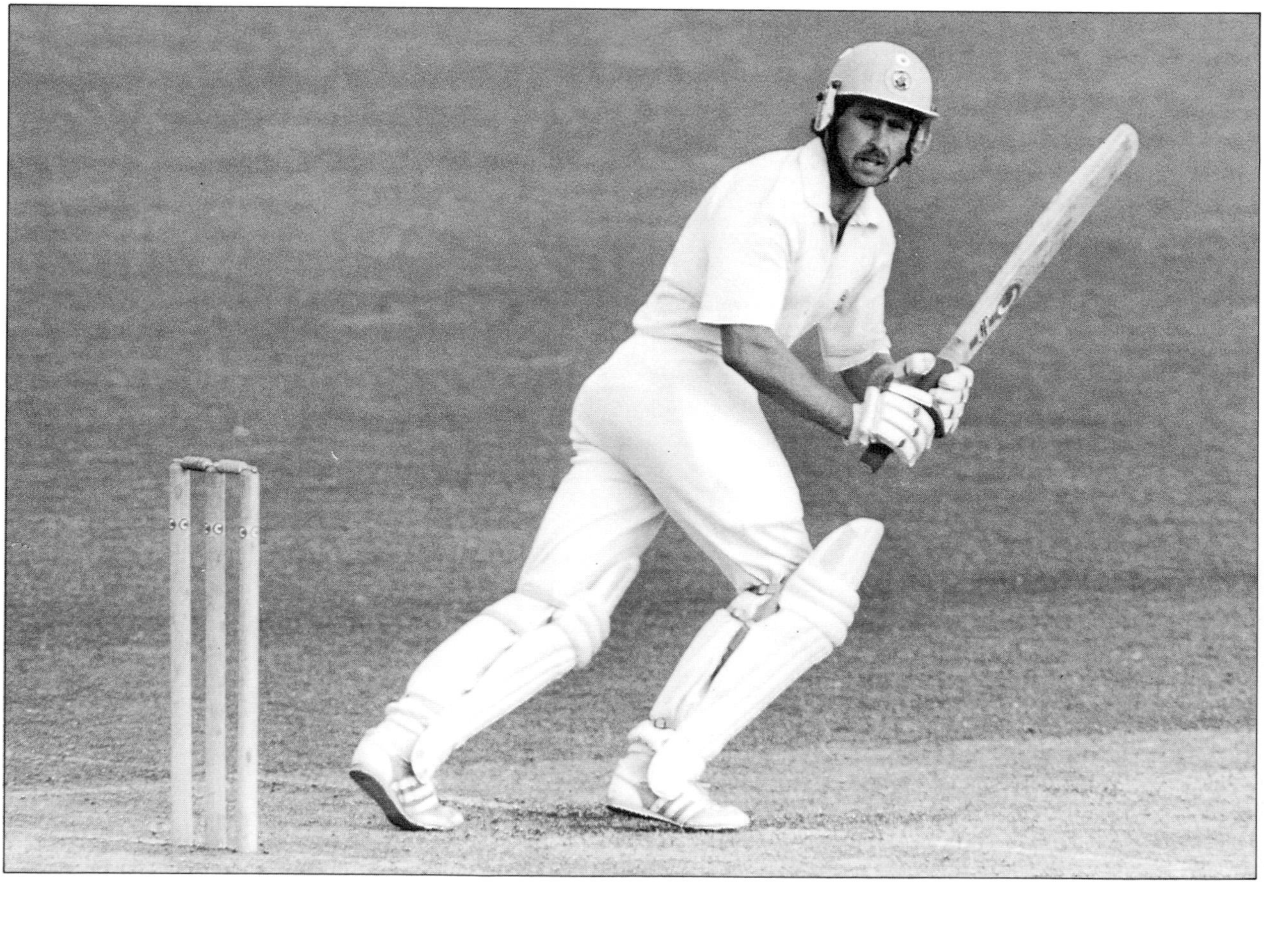

McDONALD'S CUP FINAL – NEW SOUTH WALES v. SOUTH AUSTRALIA
27 March 1988 at Sydney Cricket Ground

NEW SOUTH WALES

S. Hookey	c Hookes, b Zesers	8
M.A. Taylor	c Phillips, b Johnston	30
S.R. Waugh	c Hookes, b Scott	23
M.E. Waugh	c Bishop, b Scott	38
T.H. Bayliss	b Gladigau	44
G.R.J. Matthews	c Johnston, b Scott	11
G.L. Smith	c Zesers, b May	42
P.L. Taylor	not out	9
G.C. Dyer*†	not out	2
G.F. Lawson		
M.R. Whitney		
Extras	b 2, lb 7, w 2, nb 1	12
(50 overs)	(for 7 wkts)	219

	O	M	R	W
Gladigau	10	–	41	1
Johnston	10	–	27	1
Zesers	10	1	32	1
Scott	10	–	41	3
Pyke	2	–	28	–
May	8	–	41	1

FALL OF WICKETS
1–40, 2–40, 3–98, 4–107, 5–155, 6–174, 7–217

SOUTH AUSTRALIA

G.A. Bishop	c P.L. Taylor, b S.R. Waugh	26
A.M.J. Hilditch	b P.L. Taylor	28
D.B. Scott	c Hookey, b Matthews	15
D.W. Hookes†	run out	31
W.B. Phillips*	run out	0
P.R. Sleep	not out	48
J.K. Pyke	b S.R. Waugh	38
D.A. Johnston	not out	2
T.B.A. May		
A.K. Zesers		
P.W. Gladigau		
Extras	lb 4, w 1, nb 3	8
(50 overs)	(for 6 wkts)	196

	O	M	R	W
Whitney	10	–	42	–
Lawson	10	1	55	–
S.R. Waugh	10	2	37	2
P.L. Taylor	10	–	29	1
Matthews	10	1	29	1

FALL OF WICKETS
1–55, 2–57, 3–99, 4–100, 5–105, 6–193

Man of the Match: G.L. Smith

New South Wales won by 23 runs

---

innings lead, the only question being, by how much? The fact that it was only 55 was due to former rebel Carl Rackemann, who bowled splendidly in the sapping heatwave Perth experienced during the match. His 5 for 69 from 30 overs claimed five top batsmen – Marsh, Veletta, Brayshaw, Andrews and Zoehrer – but it was Wood who took the praise. A captain's innings of 141 in 399 minutes from 278 deliveries with 15 fours and a six, under a blazing sun and a temperature in excess of 41 degrees, was heroic by any standards. Wood caressed the ball affectionately through the covers and hooked and pulled with a subtle grace. It was a delightful innings to watch.

Queensland made a disastrous reply. At stumps they were 58 for 4, a lead of only three runs, due to some swing bowling of the highest calibre from another ex-rebel, Terry Alderman. On the fourth morning, he sunk Queensland with 6 for 91, breaking their hearts yet again. This left Western Australia to score 162 in just under nine hours for victory and their 11th Shield win.

Test colleagues Geoff Marsh and Mike Veletta put on 78 for the first wicket before a mini-collapse saw the score move to 133 for 5, Dirk Tazelaar claiming four wickets. However, the experience of vice-captain Wayne Andrews and former Test wicket-keeper Tim Zoehrer saw Western Australia home.

Andrews, very appropriately, scored the winning runs with a six high over square-leg. The Queensland hoodoo had struck again.

Chris Harte

McDonald's Cup Final
NEW SOUTH WALES v. SOUTH AUSTRALIA

New South Wales gained consolation from the season when they took Australia's limited-over one-day competition with a competent rather than dramatic performance. A solid start was nullified when Hookey and Taylor fell at the same score, but the home side kept their heads and were again well served by Graham Smith, who took the individual award for the third time in four matches in the tournament. He hit 42 out of 62 and gave the later part of the innings the impetus that it needed.

The South Australian innings followed a similar pattern, but when Wayne Phillips was run out without scoring there was no one who could lift the run rate to the standard required, and the visitors never came to terms with the demands of the game.

First-Class Averages

BATTING

	M	Inns	NOs	Runs	HS	Av	100s	50s
G.M. Wood	12	18	3	1050	186*	70.00	3	5
D.C. Boon	12	21	2	1287	184*	67.73	5	6
J.D. Siddons	11	18	2	1077	241*	67.31	4	5
M.E. Waugh	10	16	3	833	116	64.07	4	4
A.R. Border	13	22	3	1164	205	61.26	4	2
D.W. Hookes	11	20	1	1149	132	60.47	4	7
P.W. Young	9	14	5	543	164*	60.33	1	3
G.M. Watts	5	10		563	176	56.30	3	1
D.F. Whatmore	11	19	1	912	170	50.66	2	7
A.M.J. Hilditch	11	20	1	922	185	48.52	2	5

First-Class Averages continued

	M	Inns	NOs	Runs	HS	Av	100s	50s
M.D. Taylor	12	22		1003	216	45.59	2	5
P.L. Taylor	8	9	3	269	78	44.83		1
G.A. Bishop	11	20	1	833	123	43.84	3	4
D.M. Jones	12	19	1	751	191	41.72	3	2
P.R. Sleep	14	22	3	775	104*	40.78	1	6
R.B. Kerr	11	21	1	793	107	39.65	2	6
G.M. Ritchie	10	18	1	638	100*	37.52	1	4
W.B. Phillips	11	19	1	669	126	37.16	1	5
S.R. Waugh	10	15	1	517	170	36.92	1	3
G.S. Trimble	11	20	2	660	138*	36.66	2	3
G.A. Hughes	12	22	1	754	147	35.90	1	4
G.R. Marsh	13	21	2	671	120*	35.31	1	4
D.J. Buckingham	11	20	1	668	126	35.15	3	3
W.A. Andrews	11	19	2	594	72	34.94		6
P.I. Faulkner	10	18	3	512	78*	34.13		4
I.T. Botham	11	19		646	70	34.00		7
M.D. O'Neill	9	16	3	436	130*	33.53	1	2
W.G. Whiteside	7	11	1	333	84*	33.30		2
W.G. Ayres	3	6	1	161	46	32.20		
M.G. Dimattina	11	14	3	354	60	32.18		1
A.I.C. Dodemaide	11	17	6	353	71*	32.09		2
M.W. McPhee	3	5	1	121	44	30.25		
T.M. Moody	11	19		568	144	29.89	1	1
T.H. Bayliss	4	6		179	68	29.83		1
J.K. Pyke	4	6	1	149	64	29.80		1
I.D. Frazer	3	5		148	76	29.60		1
T.J. Barsby	8	15	1	412	102	29.42	1	1
I.A. Healy	4	8	2	580	176	29.33		1
J.A. Brayshaw	3	6	1	144	60*	28.80		1
K.H. MacLeay	9	13	4	254	67	28.22		2
H.B. Jolly	8	12	2	280	65	28.00		2
M.R.J. Veletta	13	21	1	552	106	27.60	1	3
M.B. Quinn	5	7		188	81	26.85		1
B.F. Davison	11	21	1	530	73	26.50		3
M.D. Haysman	7	12	1	287	60	26.09		1
G.R.J. Matthews	10	16	2	358	62	25.57		2
M.A. Taylor	10	18		459	144	25.50	1	2
T.V. Hohns	7	12	2	252	59*	25.20		2
S.B. Smith	6	10		252	84	25.20		2
D.F.G. O'Connor	7	12	1	261	75	23.72		1
T.J. Zoehrer	12	19	3	376	109	23.50	1	1
C.L. Broadby	5	10	5	114	42*	22.80		
D.Tazelaar	11	17	5	273	56	22.75		1
C.D. Matthews	12	18		409	64	22.72		1
P.W. Anderson	7	12	1	250	55	22.72		2
K.J. Hughes	6	10		223	76	22.30		1
J. Dyson	5	10	2	157	60*	19.62		1
N. Courtney	5	8		146	39	18.25		
A.B. Henschell	8	14	1	225	89	17.30		1
A.J. de Winter	5	10		164	51	16.40		1
G.C. Dyer	10	13		193	60	14.84		1
C.J. McDermott	10	13	3	138	33	13.80		
R.E. Soule	12	21	3	228	45	12.66		

	M	Inns	NOs	Runs	HS	Av	100s	50s
P.A. Capes	10	14	4	116	23	11.60		
G.F. Lawson	10	13	2	119	28	10.81		
P.W. Gladigau	10	15	1	145	25	10.35		

(Qualification – 100 runs, average 10.00)

BOWLING

	Overs	Mds	Runs	Wkts	Av	Best	10/m	5/inns
G.F. Lawson	336.3	102	792	42	18.85	6/31		3
S.R. Waugh	218.3	59	499	23	21.69	5/50		1
C.D. Matthews	443.3	83	1277	57	22.40	8/101		3
D. Tazelaar	375	92	1036	46	22.52	6/52		3
G.R.J. Matthews	335.4	103	746	32	23.31	6/97		2
C.G. Rackemann	280.1	68	733	31	23.64	5/69		1
M.R. Whitney	290.2	63	762	32	23.81	5/33		3
T.M. Alderman	394	114	944	39	24.20	6/91		2
P. Reiffel	146.2	36	416	17	24.47	4/80		
K.H. MacLeay	271.3	78	690	28	24.64	5/99		1
A.I.C. Dodemaide	420.4	103	1125	45	25.00	6/58		3
C.J. McDermott	376.1	75	1087	41	26.51	7/54	1	3
P.A. Capes	325.1	69	887	32	27.71	4/87		
I.T. Botham	311.5	82	805	29	27.75	3/12		
P.W. Gladigau	349.3	76	1104	38	29.05	7/85		2
M.G. Hughes	319.5	74	930	32	29.06	5/67		1
B.A. Reid	178	51	429	14	30.64	5/34		1
J.N. Maguire	293	64	810	25	32.40	5/60		2
A.B. Henschell	200.2	59	560	17	32.94	4/101		
C. Young	69.3	6	363	11	33.00	6/120		1
P.L. Taylor	199.2	57	505	15	33.66	4/84		
T.V. Hohns	270.4	64	743	22	33.77	5/100		2
S.P.G. George	206.1	21	778	23	33.82	6/51		1
A.K. Zesers	423.2	141	983	29	33.89	4/86		
J.K. Pyke	128	25	408	12	34.00	5/47		1
D.R. Gilbert	170.4	31	541	15	36.06	5/94		1
P.W. Jackson	371.1	116	947	26	36.42	3/55		
T.B.A. May	309	73	812	22	36.90	4/55		
D.K. Lillee	223.2	45	600	16	37.50	4/99		
S.P. Davis	312	64	814	21	38.76	5/50		1
P.I. Faulkner	348.4	102	896	21	42.66	4/37		
S.J. Milosz	193.3	54	486	11	44.18	4/53		
P.R. Sleep	512	123	1479	32	46.21	4/91		
D.J. Hickey	239	27	942	20	47.10	4/90		
G.A. Hughes	188.5	34	621	10	62.10	2/20		
T.J. Cooley	308	28	1275	20	63.75	4/95		

(Qualification – 10 wickets)

LEADING FIELDERS

47 - T.J. Zoehrer (ct 44/st 3); 38 - G.C. Dyer (ct 34/st 4); 33 - M.G. Dimattina (ct 30/st 3); 28 - R.E. Soule (ct 25/st 3); 27 - P.W. Anderson (ct 26/st 1); 24 - M.R.J. Veletta; 22 - W.B. Phillips (ct 18/st 4); 18 - I.T. Botham, D.W. Hookes and M.E. Waugh; 17 - I.A. Healy (ct 15/st 2) and P.W. Young; 16 - M.A. Taylor; 15 - G.S. Trimble, D.M. Jones and D.F. Whatmore; 13 - D.C. Boon and R.B. Kerr; 12 - W.S. Andrews, A.R. Border, G.R. Marsh, G.R.J. Matthews and S.R. Waugh; 10 - J.D. Siddons

---

AUSTRALIAN SHEFFIELD SHIELD SEASON
1987–8
by Chris Harte

There can have been few more moving moments in the history of Australian cricket than at a few minutes before 5 p.m. on Friday 15 January 1988.

At the Devonport Oval, Tasmania had been bundled out for 111 in 57.1 overs by South Australia. Now, with a slight Bass Strait breeze at his back, 38-year-old Dennis Lillee set off to bowl the first ball of his come-back trail.

Andrew Hilditch patted his bat into his crease as Lillee pounded in: the hair on his head rather sparse, the hair on his chest now grey.

The run-up, the action, the rhythm were the same as of old. Lillee was nervous, he had said so during Tasmania's woeful innings.

In he came and bowled what was probably a leg-cutter. It pitched in line with off stump and moved away ever so slightly. Hilditch, a former Australian vice-captain, pushed forward.

The ball took the edge of the bat and flew to wicket-keeper Richard Soule, who threw the ball high into the air. Lillee was surrounded by his team mates – captain Brian

Davison from Rhodesia via Leicesteshire, Mick Taylor from Melbourne, Glenn Hughes from Perth, Errol Harris from Cairns and those other Tasmanians. Now they were one.

The crowd went wild. Boosted by the news of Lillee's return, they had flocked to the ground. Those in the Eric Webster Stand stood and cheered wildly, stamping their feet in a presumably local custom. Those on the outer mounds thumped the tin fence while those in their cars parked around the ground tooted their horns.

Richard Soule was ecstatic. Later on, in the dressing room, he provided surely the quote of the season when he said: 'Since I was a little kid in short pants, I always had a dream. Today it came true: caught Soule, bowled Lillee.'

And from that point on in the season, the dismal Tasmanian team just kept on improving. Bolstered by a new General Manager – former South Australian Cricket Association Secretary, Richard Watson – an extra $50,000 sponsorship from an insurance company and the promise of a Test match in late 1989 at the new Bellerive Oval ground in Hobart, the tide could well have turned for Tasmanian cricket.

The 1987–8 Sheffield Shield season had its latest start since 1948, as, owing to the World Cup, the initial matches were originally scheduled to start on 13 November. However, after Australia's success in the tournament, the matches were put back an extra 24 hours in order 'to let the returning players recover'. A move, one could suggest, not previously tried in the Country Championship.

Prior to the season, the Australian media concerned themselves with two domestic cricket matters. Would the returning South African rebels be chosen for their States again? And would teenage cricket prodigy Thanh Chi Nguyen become the first Vietnamese refugee to play for Australia?

Just before the season's first match got under way in Sydney, the Cricket Ground Trust announced the opening of the Members' area to the public. This did not please one elderly woman who had officially complained within an hour about a shapely blonde wearing a bikini.

South Australian captain David Hookes had already complained, as, on losing the toss, his side were sent in to bat on an underprepared Sydney pitch. With over 140 mm of rain the previous three days, curator Peter Leroy and his staff had had their preparation severely hampered.

Only a fine 57 by Andrew Hilditch gave the visitors any sense of respectability as they clawed their way to 171. Geoff Lawson (3 for 18) and Mike Whitney (5 for 33) were the main destroyers, with Whitney's wickets all coming in his final burst when switched to the Randwick end.

At the close New South Wales were 2 for 17 with two night-watchmen holding the fort. The following day one of them, Peter Taylor, assisted by schoolboy field placings, virtually won the match for the home side. Taylor scored a Shield best 78 in a remarkably easy way. Facing South Australia's spin pair of Tim May and Peter Sleep, Taylor took one pace down the pitch and hit the ball over the massed infield. His 16 boundaries were testimony to his success.

After gaining a first innings lead of 35, New South Wales had Lawson (6 for 31) and Whitney (2 for 29) to bowl South Australia out for 131. Needing 97 for victory, New South Wales won by six wickets late on the third day, beating an approaching thunderstorm by minutes.

The 7,353 crowd in Sydney was beaten on one day alone in Brisbane when a total of 18,008 turned up to watch Ian Botham and Queensland defeat Victoria by five wickets.

Craig McDermott opened the home attack with Botham, his second wicket – that of Victorian captain Dean Jones – being his 200th in first-class matches. McDermott took 5 for 65 as Victoria declared at 9 for 226 half an hour before stumps on the first day. At 3 for 10 then 4 for 35, Queensland looked broken, but captain Allan Border and Glenn 'Son of Sam' Trimble then proceeded to equal Queensland's record fifth-wicket partnership against Victoria.

Their 231 in 224 minutes equalled Ken Mackay and Ron Archer's stand made in 1953-4, and delighted the second-day attendance of 10,812. Trimble's departure after scoring 112 off 185 balls with 2 sixes and 12 fours gave Ian Botham his chance to delight the adoring crowd.

Botham hit – and hit is the correct word – 58 runs in 42 minutes with 4 sixes into the stand, and 7 fours from just 34 deliveries, which had his partner Allan Border saying that he felt sorry for the Victorian bowlers.

Border finally reached 168 before being bowled by Tony Dodemaide, and to think that only seven days earlier he was in Calcutta holding the World Cup.

Queensland easily took maximum points on the fourth day with Victoria's only high note being Davenell Whatmore's passing of Warwick Armstrong's Victorian fielding record of 102 catches.

In Perth, where Western Australia thrashed Tasmania by an innings and 137 runs, the action seemed to be everywhere but out in the centre. Before the match began the WACA announced a 15-year inflation-proofed sponsorship deal with a local bank, worth some $2.1 million (£850,000). Then on the second day, batsman Wayne Andrews was fined $200 (£78) for a breach of the Australian Cricket Board's dress code.

Andrews' heinous crime? He was not wearing batting gloves manufactured by the ACB's approved sponsor. Andrews' argument that he was not comfortable in the approval apparel was not considered to be a suitable excuse.

And to top it all off, at 12.18 p.m. on the third day a swallow intercepted a delivery from Peter Faulkner to WA captain Graeme Wood, and immediately departed from this mortal coil. The remains were to be stuffed (if they weren't already) and put on display in the WACA museum.

On the field Tasmania, captained by Brian Davison on his return to first-class cricket after a two-year absence, fell for 135 after having been put into bat.

Western Australia replied with 6 declared for 461, Tom Moody a career-best 144, Mike Veletta 106, and Wood 83. Wood's 12th run was his 10,000th in first-class cricket. Only a second wicket stand of 64, between David Boon (69) and Glenn Hughes (55), helped Tasmania reach 189 – and a sound defeat.

The Tasmanian team then flew to Melbourne for the fourth match of the season, and quickly found themselves in more trouble. Batting for five sessions, Victoria declared at 5 for 501 with Dean Jones making 191 in 288 minutes from 251 balls with 25 fours. Peter Young made a career-best unbeaten 164; his 224-run fourth wicket partnership with Jones being an all-wicket record for matches between the two sides which stretch back to the 1850–1 season.

Tasmania were 1 for 8 when Glenn Hughes went to the crease, and 9 for 310 when he left. Living in the shadow of elder brother Kim had not been easy, and only a move to Tasmania could guarantee top-level cricket. Hughes certainly came of age with a maiden century, 147 in six hours.

The previous season he had scored eight half-centuries in 688 runs, but this three figures was well deserved. As Tony Dodemaide was claiming 5 for 43, mainly with his newly discovered outswinger, so Hughes piled on his runs. Hit on the helmet twice by paceman Merv Hughes (definitely no relation although they shared a birthday on the third day), Hughes showed many of his brother's mannerisms although none of his elegance.

Forced to follow on, Tasmania's openers gave Hughes a 58-minute rest before he was back in action. Only a stupid shot mid-way through the last day stopped Hughes claiming a century in each innings. He fell when 95, caught in the covers from spinner David Emerson.

And wasn't Emerson pleased! It had been four years and 543 runs since his last first-class wicket. When bad light finished the match, the visitors had reached 9 for 354 and a draw.

In Adelaide, South Australia threw a surprise for their match against Queensland. Into the team came Shane Peter George George, at 17 years and 31 days, the third-youngest player to represent the state. Ahead of him were Clem Hill (16 years 9 days) and Affie Jarvis (17 years 23 days). George also knocked Victor Trumper out of 12th spot in the youngest Australian cricketer list.

David Hookes won the toss and batted, making 89 out of South Australia's first-day 5 for 272. The home side strung out their innings until just before tea on the second day reaching 387, with Michael Haysman (60) and Peter Sleep (70) playing vital roles.

Queensland's first wicket fell at 21 when Andrew Courtice was adjudged leg before wicket giving George his first victim. On the third day in front of 6,312 spectators (17,863 for the match, the highest since December 1972), Ian Botham delighted the crowd with 66 cracking runs. Only Robbie Kerr (91) made any other impression as the visitors made 318.

A fourth day declaration by South Australia at 3 for 209 left Queensland too little time to win and a draw resulted.

Queensland's third match in 11 days saw them at the Newcastle Sports Ground to take on New South Wales in a match which had yet another first for Australian cricket: a female streaker on the second day.

The match, which lasted only three days, pulled in 17,795 spectators and, for the eighth year running, a handsome profit for the Newcastle Cricket Association: $55,378 (£22,705). The Botham factor had struck again.

Twelve wickets fell on the first day as Queensland were bundled out for 210 in 65 overs as New South Wales dropped five regulation catches. The home side 2 for 43

overnight fell for 139 in three hours' play with Queensland's four paceman sharing the spoils.

The visitors' response, after being 2 for 26, was swift. A 206-run stand between Allan Border (101) and Robbie Kerr (107) saw Queensland out of trouble. After Border had been dismissed on completing his 50th first-class hundred, Glenn Trimble (68 not out) saw the total to 6 for 345 before the declaration.

Ian Botham (20) hit a delivery from Peter Taylor high over the H.L. Wheeler Stand and out of the ground. The ball was never seen again.

Needing 417 to win in a day and a half, New South Wales crumpled in 21 overs and 95 minutes. Craig McDermott with 7 for 54 and Dirk Tazelaar 3 for 22 bowled unchanged as a sorrowful New South Wales batting display saw them reach just 83.

Meanwhile, in Melbourne, rain had delayed the start of Victoria's match against Western Australia. When play finally got under way, the visitors took their time scoring 291 at fractionally above two runs an over. Captain Graeme Wood's 74 in 4½ hours sent the crowd to sleep.

When Victoria batted mid-way during the second day, it was a totally different story. At a run a minute Michael Quinn and Davenell Whatmore saw the score to 0 for 180 at stumps, a new record first wicket partnership between the teams, passing the 175 set by Bill Lawry and Ian Redpath at Melbourne in 1968–9.

Wood had gambled by opening his attack with the medium pace of Peter Capes and Ken MacLeay instead of fast men Chris Matthews and Bruce Reid. The ploy failed and it was Matthews on the third morning who made the breakthrough, claiming Whatmore (127) caught at mid-on.

Dean Jones (29) and Quinn (81) made 61 together and after three wickets fell for three runs, Peter Young (93 not out) and Tony Dodemaide (71 not out) saw the score to 4 for 431 before Jones declared. The Victorian team were starting to hit their straps and it was apparent that coach Ian Redpath was blending together a good quality team.

Realising they had no chance of gaining maximum points, Western Australia used the rest of the match for batting practice. Geoff Marsh batted through for an unbeaten 120, aided by 52 from Mike Veletta and Tom Moody (46) in 3 for 237.

For the statistically minded, the Sheffield Shield match between Tasmania and New South Wales at the Devonport Oval starting on 4 December 1987 was the 1,196th of the competition. Moreso it was the 2,300th Australian first-class match.

Brian Davison won the toss, elected to bat on a good pitch albeit with some bounce, and top-scored with 41 as his colleagues crashed around him and the score reached 134. Although Lawson (3 for 22) and Peter Taylor (3 for 19) took most wickets, it was the home side's lack of confidence which saw them fall.

The first New South Wales wicket fell at 113, when Steve Smith (84), playing his first game since returning from the wilds of Africa, put together an innings described as 'dynamic'. He hooked and cut the short ball with blistering power, pinching a dozen boundaries in his run-a-minute knock. Smith was finally caught behind, attempting to glide a ball to third man. Trevor Bayliss (38) took over the attacking role and after his dismissal Mark Taylor (72) hit out.

Mark O'Neill and Mark Waugh came together late on the second day and added an unbeaten 187 in exactly 2½ hours of brilliant cricket.

Norman O'Neill would have been proud of his son, who scored 130 not out in a way reminiscent of his father's style. Although the third morning's play was delayed half an hour by a clearing coastal shower from Mount Rowland, it was Mark Waugh who caught the eye.

With the nickname of 'Afghanistan' (the forgotten Waugh: get it?), he scored his maiden first-class century from 125 balls in 145 minutes and 11 delightfully struck fours.

At 4 for 467 New South Wales acting captain Murray Bennett declared, to end the locals' misery. Lawson and Whitney then combined to take two wickets each and Tasmania hobbled to 6 for 168 at the close.

The final day saw an innings of courage from the injured Danny Buckingham. Batting with a runner he scored 112 as his team slid to defeat by an innings and 38 runs.

Lawson with 5 for 72 – his 20th five in a innings haul – celebrated his 30th birthday with a win.

Four days later the erratic captaincy of South Australia's David Hookes gave Victoria a victory they did not deserve. Batting first on a tranquil Melbourne Cricket Ground pitch, South Australia made 5 for 352 on the first day, Hookes contributing 91, which took him past the 6,000 run mark in Sheffield Shield matches.

Wayne Phillips (126) posted his 13th century on the second morning, and Harvey Jolly 65 on his début, as the visitors reached 468.

Victoria had Whatmore (60), Frazer (76), Siddons (64) and Whiteside (84 not out) as the main contributors as acting captain Simon Davis declared half an hour before stumps on the third day at 8 for 345. For the visitors, Michael Haysman took his initial wicket in first-class cricket to at last give him an average – which read as 429.00!

South Australia were ambling along at 2 for 158 the next morning, Glenn Bishop on 82, when a surprise declaration came.

Victoria could not believe their luck and won by six wickets with 35 minutes to spare. Needing 282, Whatmore (46) and Young (60) set the pace for young Jamie Siddons to record his then highest score, a delightful unbeaten 124. The mood in the South Australian dressing room after the game was, regretfully, only a taste of things to come.

New South Wales went to Perth for a thrashing in two days and 27 minutes. Western Australia had recalled three of their South African rebel players, and their presence made all the difference. Terry Alderman took 5 for 35 on the first afternoon as New South Wales collapsed for 115. Kim Hughes scored 76 as the home team answered with 256 despite Greg Matthews taking 5 for 49.

New South Wales fell in a heap on the second day in reply with only the unrelated Matthews – Chris and Greg – dominating. Left-armed paceman Chris took 4 for 39, finally 6 for 56 next morning, and Greg top-scored with 53 out of 131. Western Australia winning by an innings and 10 runs.

Recalled New South Wales wicket-keeper Steve Rixon played in his 92nd Shield match for his state, passing the record he had jointly held with Doug Walters.

The 11th Shield match of the season, at Sydney between New South Wales and Victoria, was so badly affected by rain that a draw was inevitable.

On the first day in fine conditions, New South Wales made 3 for 226 from 97 overs after slowing to a crawl after lunch. When Steve Waugh went to the wicket in the first over, he started as if he was after the fastest century of the season. When 42 he became stuck for 50 minutes, going scoreless. From then on, he took 320 minutes for his next 86 runs, being unbeaten on 128 at the close.

Saturday 19 December at the Sydney Cricket Ground saw Victoria facing a Waugh on both fronts as Steve and twin brother Mark both scored centuries – for the first time together in any grade of cricket.

Steve went on to a career-best 170, with Mark unbeaten on 114 when Greg Dyer declared at tea on 9 for 438. Only Tony Dodemaide with 5 for 114 from 45 tight overs, and Paul Jackson 3 for 128 from 53, had stemmed the onslaught.

New South Wales paceman Mike Whitney took three quick wickets as the visitors stayed overnight on 4 for 88. Rain interrupted all but the middle session on the third day as Whitney's figures became 5 for 68 and Victoria went to 9 for 191. Only 17 minutes' play was possible on the final day in which just four runs came from five overs.

In Brisbane a Botham-inspired crowd of 15,674 saw the Queensland machine grind on relentlessly, defeating Western Australia in three days by 10 wickets.

Allan Border put the visitors in to bat with only a defiant 89 by Tom Moody stopping a complete rot. Dismissed for 217, Dirk Tazelaar 6 for 52, Western Australia had some modicum of revenge having Queensland 1 for 9 at stumps.

The second day saw Robbie Kerr record his 15th three-figure score, 102 in 325 minutes. His dismissal, caught by Alderman at second slip from spinner Steve Milosz, was the signal for a Botham hitting spree.

In just 37 minutes, 7 boundaries flowed from his bat, 3 consecutively from Todd Breman's medium-pacers. Then 3 sixes off Milosz, each one further into the cavernous Clem Jones Stand, the last one bouncing off the front of the roof. This was power hitting at its best. Botham's 53 came from 38 balls and on his departure the crowd went home.

Last man Tazelaar remained on 43 – and a batting average of 83 – as Queensland's last wicket fell, from the final ball of the day, with the total on 318, a lead of 101.

Western Australia were soon in trouble on the final morning at 4 for 38, in reality 5 for 38 as Graeme Wood had a cracked knuckle and could not bat.

A tail-end resistance led by former Australian wicket-keeper Tim Zoehrer (51) saw the score to 192, not enough to deny Queensland a 10-wicket win.

As the old year faded out with 40 per cent of the matches completed, Queensland had such a huge lead in the competition, it was just a matter of finding out who would play them in the Shield final in Brisbane.

Officials of the Brisbane Cricket Ground Trust were already making preparations for the five-day final to be

New South Wales 1987–8
First-Class Matches

BATTING

Match column key:
- SA Syd = v. South Australia (Sydney) 13–15 November 1987
- Qld New = v. Queensland (Newcastle) 27–9 November 1987
- Tas Dev = v. Tasmania (Devonport) 4–7 December 1987
- WA Per = v. Western Australia (Perth) 11–13 December 1987
- Vic Syd = v. Victoria (Sydney) 18–21 December 1987
- Qld Bri = v. Queensland (Brisbane) 1–4 January 1988
- SA Ade = v. South Australia (Adelaide) 22–5 January 1988
- Vic Mel = v. Victoria (Melbourne) 12–15 February 1988
- WA Syd = v. Western Australia (Sydney) 24–7 February 1988
- Tas Syd = v. Tasmania (Sydney) 2–5 March 1988

	SA Syd 1	SA Syd 2	Qld New 1	Qld New 2	Tas Dev 1	Tas Dev 2	WA Per 1	WA Per 2	Vic Syd 1	Vic Syd 2	Qld Bri 1	Qld Bri 2	SA Ade 1	SA Ade 2	Vic Mel 1	Vic Mel 2	WA Syd 1	WA Syd 2	Tas Syd 1	Tas Syd 2
S.M. Small	6	4	27	7																
M.A. Taylor	3	8	9	5	72	—	12	8	35	—	22	71	15	3	29	0	18	2	144	3
D.R. Gilbert	13	—	9	4			10	10			17*	0	13	8	—					
P.L. Taylor	78	—	9	24*	—				1								46*	42*	31	—
M.E. Waugh	28	25	0	9	101*	—	5	6	114*	—	4	88	—	72	69	100*	95	1	116	—
S.R. Waugh	6	36	9	15					170	—							9	14	55	9*
M.D. O'Neill	1	16*	15	0	130*	—	20	0	36	—	9	70	18*	8	18	16	68	11		
G.R.J. Matthews	36	6*	47*	4	24	—	5	53	27	—	21	0	—	10	62	4	17	41	1	—
G.C. Dyer	16	—	0	5					0	—							9	7	25	—
G.F. Lawson	11	—	0	0	—		13	12	28	—	2	2	—	5	5	—	6	21*	14*	—
M.R. Whitney	0*	—	1	0	—		2*	2*	5*	—					5*	—	5	—	1	—
T.H. Bayliss					38	—	7	24									5	68	37	—
S.J. Rixon					—		11	0			12	28								
M.J. Bennett					—		6	2	7		5	8	5							
S.B. Smith					84		17	0	0	—	15	4	49	51	0	32				
J. Dyson											3	10	60*	28	17	19	1	3	5	11*
R.A. Jones											8	6*		1*						
P.A. Emery														18	11	28*				
G. Robertson															38	—				
S. Hookey																			16	44
Byes	3				4		4	1	1				1				2		4	
Leg-byes	2	1	4	7	6		3	6	7		2	7	2	3	10	4	5	3	11	1
Wides	2	1			1		1		3		1						9		4	
No-balls	1	1	9	3	7		3	4	4		8	5	6	2	7	3				
Total	206	98	139	83	467		115	131	438		129	300	150	219	279	206	295	213	460	72
Wickets	10	4	10	10	4		10	10	9		10	10	2	10	10	5	10	8	10	2
Result	W		L		W		L		Ab.		L		L		D		W		W	
Points	6		0		6		0		0		0		0		0		6		6	

Fielding Figures

18 – M.E. Waugh

16 – G.C. Dyer (ct 14/st 2) and M.A. Taylor (inc 1 as sub)

12 – G.R.J. Matthews

8 – S.J. Rixon (ct 7/st 1)

6 – S.R. Waugh

4 – P.L. Taylor, M.D. O'Neill, G.F. Lawson, T.H. Bayliss, P.A. Emery and D.R. Gilbert (inc 3 as sub)

3 – S.B. Smith and J. Dyson

2 – S.M. Small

1 – M.R. Whitney, R.A. Jones and M.J. Bennett (sub)

BOWLING

Match	G.F. Lawson	D.R. Gilbert	M.R. Whitney	P.L. Taylor	S.R. Waugh	G.R.J. Matthews	M.D. O'Neill
v. South Australia (Sydney) 13–15 November 1987	12–7–18–3 / 18.2–9–31–6	12–2–34–1 / 13–3–28–1	14.4–3–33–5 / 15–4–29–2	7–1–32–0 / 3–1–6–0	12–5–16–1 / 5–0–14–0	7–0–21–0 / 10–4–18–1	
v. Queensland (Newcastle) 27–9 November 1987	18–5–41–4 / 13–2–39–0	14–2–47–2 / 14–3–40–0	15–1–58–1 / 13–4–51–2	4–0–19–0 / 23–4–89–3	14–4–38–3 / 12–0–45–0	17–4–49–1	1–0–2–0
v. Tasmania (Devonport) 4–7 December 1987	16–4–22–3 / 36–12–72–5		16–4–31–2 / 27–3–89–2	15–8–19–3 / 16–2–41–0		9.1–5–10–2 / 19–10–29–0	1–0–1–0
v. Western Australia (Perth) 11–13 December 1987	23–6–60–2	14–2–55–1	18–3–40–1			26.5–6–49–5	
v. Victoria (Sydney) 18–21 December 1987	18–5–44–0		25–5–68–5	16–9–17–2		20–8–40–2	
v. Queensland (Brisbane) 1–4 January 1988	22–8–45–1 / 20–4–45–2	23–6–61–4 / 13–3–40–1				15–4–49–1 / 16.3–4–41–3	
v. South Australia (Adelaide) 22–5 January 1988	30.1–12–53–1 / 10–3–29–1	31–6–94–5 / 10–0–40–0				25–7–55–1 / 6–1–21–0	4–2–8–1
v. Victoria (Melbourne) 12–15 February 1988	25–3–79–2 / 9–4–20–3	23–4–91–0 / 3.4–0–11–0	24–5–71–0 / 9–3–23–0			49.1–19–97–6 / 18–3–52–1	5–0–15–0 / 11–1–38–0
v. Western Australia (Sydney) 24–7 February 1988	12–4–29–0 / 18–6–41–3		16–2–46–2 / 13.1–4–22–1	11.2–6–15–2 / 22–7–44–1	8–1–19–1 / 13–5–30–4	29–9–58–4 / 26–9–50–1	
v. Tasmania (Sydney) 2–5 March 1988	20–4–84–0 / 16–4–40–6		26–10–54–5 / 5–1–10–0	21–3–60–0 / 25–5–76–0	23.4–2–50–5 / 5–0–20–0	23–6–53–0 / 19–4–54–4	
Totals	336.3–102–792–42 *av.* 18.85	170.4–31–541–15 *av.* 36.06	236.5–52–625–28 *av.* 22.32	163.2–46–418–11 *av.* 38.00	92.4–17–232–14 *av.* 16.57	335.4–103–746–32 *av.* 23.31	22–3–64–1 *av.* 64.00

M	Inns	NOs	Runs	HS	Av
2	4	—	44	27	11.00
10	18	—	459	144	25.50
6	9	1	84	17*	10.50
6	7	3	231	78	57.75
10	16	3	833	116	64.07
5	9	1	323	170	40.37
9	16	3	436	130*	33.53
10	16	2	358	62	25.57
5	7	—	62	25	8.85
10	13	2	119	28	10.81
8	9	5	21	5*	5.25
4	6	—	179	68	29.83
3	4	—	51	28	12.75
5	6	—	33	8	5.50
6	10	—	252	84	25.20
5	10	2	157	60*	19.62
2	3	1	15	8	7.50
2	3	1	57	28*	28.50
1	1	—	38	38	38.00
1	2	—	60	44	30.00

held from 18 to 22 March, and after the New South Wales match at New Year had been won by 52 runs, it was a question of should the final 'be an all ticket match'.

The cocksure Queenslanders had every right to feel it was going to be their season after 61 futile years. For on Sunday 3 January 1988, the third highest crowd on record swarmed into the Gabba for a day of Shield cricket.

Put in to bat on a green pitch, Queensland's early batsmen fell to Dave Gilbert (4 for 61) and Mark Waugh (3 for 49) before Tazelaar with 56 and Trevor Hohns (55) – back after a short self-imposed retirement – saw the score to 278.

Carl Rackemann and Tazelaar powered their way through the New South Wales batting next day, Rackemann taking 2 for 26, which with a little luck could have been many more. The visitors fell for 129 and in turn had Queensland 2 for 0 after two overs.

Then Greg Ritchie put his head down and remained on 100 not out as the last wicket fell on 203. His 17th first-class century contained only 5 fours in a 5¼ hour stay at the crease.

Needing 353 to win in 553 minutes, New South Wales were 2 for 131 with 45 minutes left of the third day. Home acting-skipper Robbie Kerr then called up Carl Rackemann for his first bowl of the day, and the paceman came up trumps.

In six superb overs he took 3 for 12 and that was the beginning of the end for New South Wales. Although they reached 300, mainly due to 88 from the consistent Mark Waugh, Queensland were always going to win.

In Adelaide, the largest single-day crowd for nearly two decades saw the home side defeated by Western Australia by three wickets late on the fourth day.

Put in to bat on a perfect Adelaide Oval pitch, South Australia put on a poor performance to be dismissed for 158 just after tea on the first day. Western Australia did

M.E. Waugh	M.J. Bennett	R.A. Jones	G. Robertson	Byes	Leg-byes	Wides	No-balls	Total	Wkts
				4	13		7	171	10
					5		3	131	10
				1	6		6	210	10
2–0–8–0				1	21			345	6
10–2–28–0	4–0–19–0				5		8	134	10
7–4–5–1	22–5–49–2			1	8		14	295	10
2–0–11–0	14–6–33–1				8		18	256	10
	8–4–13–0			4	9			195	9
10–0–49–3	8–2–18–0	16–2–49–0		2	5	1	16	278	10
10–1–33–2	5–1–7–1	13–3–31–1		5	1		7	203	10
2–0–11–0	10–0–35–0	11–0–49–2		5	9		16	319	10
		6–1–21–1					2	113	3
			17–6–37–0		13		12	403	10
			14.3–3–62–1	6			1	212	5
				6	3			176	10
				5	9	4	2	201	10
3–0–13–0				7	6		4	327	10
							1	204	10
46–7–	71–18–	46–6–	31.3–9–						
158–6	174–4	150–4	99–1						
av. 26.33	av. 43.50	av. 37.50	av. 99.00						

Queensland 1987–8
First-Class Matches

BATTING

Matches:
- C1 = v. Victoria (Brisbane) 13–16 November 1987
- C2 = v. South Australia (Adelaide) 20–3 November 1987
- C3 = v. New South Wales (Newcastle) 27–9 November 1987
- C4 = v. Western Australia (Brisbane) 18–20 December 1987
- C5 = v. New South Wales (Brisbane) 1–4 January 1988
- C6 = v. Tasmania (Brisbane) 8–11 January 1988
- C7 = v. Western Australia (Perth) 15–18 January 1988
- C8 = v. South Australia (Brisbane) 6–9 February 1988
- C9 = v. Tasmania (Launceston) 24–7 February 1988
- C10 = v. Victoria (Melbourne) 2–5 March 1988

(Each cell shows both innings.)

	C1	C2	C3	C4	C5	C6	C7	C8	C9	C10
B.A. Courtice	1 2	13 7	0 9							
R.B. Kerr	2 21	91 63	0 107	102 31*	7 0	64 —	59 25	4 3	62 96	4 4
P.W. Anderson	1 0	16 4	36 18*	35 —	17 54	55 —	0 14			
G.M. Ritchie	19 12	30 55	64 0	2 —	4 100*	22 —	76 19		6 85	29 48
A.R. Border	168 35*	34 25	21 101	18 —				37 118*	47 17	33 12
G.S. Trimble	112 24	32 26	1 68*	15	67 18	1 —	2 30	57 27	138* 6	18 0
I.T. Botham	58 —	66 10	25 20	53	19 11	27 —	70 58	60 37	3 10	35 21
A.B. Henschell	0 20*	11 5	5 0	11	21 4	89 —	9 4	46 0		
C.J. McDermott	12	4 7*	18	0 —						
D. Tazelaar	16* —	0* 0*	24* —	43*	56 0	25 —	17 20	25 19	— 4	13 0
J.N. Maguire	2* —	1 —	3 —	10 —	0* 3	0* —	10 4	3 2	— 2	2 4
T.J. Barsby				2 50*	8 0	10 —	5 22	102 12	34 23	28 47
T.V. Hohns					55 0	14 —	32 23	0 —	16 22	17*
C.G. Rackemann					0 0	0 —	2* 10*	4* 4	0 0*	0
I.A. Healy								23 30	58* 22*	17 12
Byes	1	1 1	1 1	4	2 5	3		3 5	4	
Leg-byes	6 1	7 5	6 21	6 1	5 1	4	14 4	7 8	3 11	2 2
Wides	1	1 1	4	1	3	1		3	2 6	1
No-balls	6	11 1	6 17	6	16 7	7	7 4	11 6	6	20
Total	405 115	318 210	210 345	318 92	278 203	324	303 238	385 271	363 314	209 168
Wickets	9 5	10 8	10 6	10 0	10 10	10	10 10	10 10	10 5	10 10
Result	W	D	W	W	W	W	L	D	L	L
Points	6	0	6	6	6	6	0	2	0	0

Fielding Figures

- 27 – P.W. Anderson (ct 26/st 1)
- 18 – I.T. Botham
- 17 – I.A. Healy (ct 15/st 2)
- 15 – G.S. Trimble
- 13 – R.B. Kerr
- 9 – T.J. Barsby
- 6 – B.A. Courtice and G.M. Ritchie
- 5 – J.N. Maguire (inc 1 as sub)
- 4 – A.R. Border
- 3 – D. Tazelaar
- 2 – A.B. Henschell
- 1 – C.J. McDermott, C.G. Rackemann and T.V. Hohns

BOWLING

(Each cell shows both innings, separated by " / ".)

Match	C.J. McDermott	I.T. Botham	D. Tazelaar	J.N. Maguire	A.B. Henschell	A.R. Border	G.M. Ritchie
v. Victoria (Brisbane) 13–16 November 1987	20–3–65–5 / 26–2–78–2	19–6–35–1 / 18–4–42–2	16–4–33–2 / 28.2–8–70–3	12–3–25–0 / 13–8–17–0	20–4–64–1 / 29–11–71–3		
v. South Australia (Adelaide) 20–3 November 1987	29–5–107–0 / 1–0–3–0	28–10–57–3	28–5–79–1 / 2–1–6–0	24.5–1–60–5 / 2–0–11–0	35–12–78–1 / 20–1–84–3	8–0–60–0	8–0–44–0
v. New South Wales (Newcastle) 27–9 November 1987	21–7–56–3 / 11–1–54–7	6–2–12–3	16.3–3–37–3 / 10–2–22–3	16–5–30–1			
v. Western Australia (Brisbane) 18–20 December 1987	20–2–53–2 / 14–7–21–1	15–2–52–1 / 12–3–32–2	18.5–5–52–6 / 15–2–47–2	12–4–25–0 / 11.4–2–41–2	15–5–30–0 / 16–6–38–2		
v. New South Wales (Brisbane) 1–4 January 1988		11–7–12–1 / 17.2–4–61–3	15.1–3–33–3 / 23–6–64–2	19–2–56–3 / 11–2–44–0		4–1–12–0	
v. Tasmania (Brisbane) 8–11 January 1988		15–5–32–1 / 9–2–23–2	14–6–32–3 / 16.5–2–54–5	11–3–37–1 / 7–2–10–1			
v. Western Australia (Perth) 15–18 January 1988		27.3–3–89–2 / 28–8–51–2	7.3–1–31–0	17.4–4–70–3 / 13–2–40–0	7–2–26–0		
v. South Australia (Brisbane) 6–9 February 1988		13–3–47–0	18–3–51–0 / 3–0–23–0	13–2–41–0		27.2–10–56–3 / 27–7–101–4	
v. Tasmania (Launceston) 24–7 February 1988		23–8–67–1 / 13–3–41–3	19–1–94–1 / 6.1–0–22–1		28–3–78–1 / 22–4–81–2		
v. Victoria (Melbourne) 2–5 March 1988		17–2–53–1	31–13–55–5 / 32–10–87–2	20–7–55–1 / 39.5–10–89–5			
v. Western Australia (Perth) 18–22 March 1988	24–4–80–1 / 7–1–21–0	24–7–66–0 / 16–3–33–1	32–10–79–0 / 22.4–7–65–4				
Total	173–32–538–21 — av. 25.61	311.5–82–805–29 — av. 27.75	375–92–1036–46 — av. 22.52	293–64–810–25 — av. 32.40	200.2–59–560–17 — av. 32.94	9–0–64–0 — av. —	8–0–44–0 — av. —

a G.M. Wood absent injured

v. Western Australia (Perth) 18–22 March 1988		M	Inns	NOs	Runs	HS	Av
		3	6	—	32	13	5.33
46	2	11	21	1	793	107	39.65
		7	12	1	250	55	22.72
33	34	10	18	1	638	100*	37.52
66	6	8	15	2	738	168	56.76
15	3	11	20	2	660	138*	36.66
9	54	11	19	—	646	70	34.00
		8	14	1	225	89	17.30
8*	1	5	7	2	50	18	10.00
6	5	11	17	5	273	56	22.75
		10	14	3	46	10	4.18
48	21	8	15	1	412	102	29.42
14	59*	7	12	2	252	59*	25.20
0	8	7	12	4	28	10*	3.50
14	0	4	8	2	176	58*	29.33
9	9						
9	7						
8							
4	7						
289	216						
10	10						
L							
—							

C.G. Rackemann	T.V. Hohns	Byes	Leg-byes	Wides	No-balls	Total	Wkts
			4		10	226	9
			11		18	293	10
			6		15	387	10
			1		2	209	3
			4		9	139	10
			7		3	83	10
			5		12	217	10
		6	7		7	192	9a
15–4–26–2			2	1	8	129	10
20–4–54–4	20–4–57–1	1	7		5	300	10
14.5–3–51–4	12–5–12–1		9		6	173	10
11–0–37–1	11–6–20–1		3		7	147	10
28–6–56–4	21–2–67–1	1	8	1	8	348	10
30.2–5–65–4	10–3–19–0	10	9	1		194	7
20–4–58–1	45–13–100–5		11	2	12	364	10
4–0–15–0	26–2–102–3	5	1		1	247	8
33–4–121–2	39.5–6–115–5		6	1	6	481	10
4–0–33–0	33–7–107–2	1	5		3	290	8
25–12–47–2	13–5–35–1	1	10	3	9	256	10
31–15–72–2	16–3–68–0		12		4	328	10
30–7–69–5	19.5–7–35–2		15		12	344	10
14–4–29–0	4–1–6–0		8		1	162	5
280.1–68–	270.4–64–						
733–31	743–22						
av. 23.64	av. 33.77						

little better, gaining a 79-run first-innings lead, with Wayne Andrews (55) being the only player to pass the half-century mark.

Other than Andrew Hilditch, the highest South Australian second-innings score was 29 in a total of 328.

Opening the batting, Hilditch lasted until the score reached 291, being eighth out. He had scored a face-saving 166 in 397 minutes from 331 balls with 12 fours and shared half-century partnerships with Hookes, Phillips and Jolly.

Just after Hilditch completed his 10th first-class ton, so wicket-keeper Tim Zoehrer took his ninth dismissal of the match, still two short of equalling Rodney Marsh's record made a dozen seasons earlier.

Set 250 to win in 341 minutes, Western Australia lost 3 for 59 until Graeme Wood (82) and Kim Hughes (62) added 110 in exactly two hours. After that it was an easy canter to the finish.

The quite amazing resurgence in domestic cricket attendances continued four days later in Brisbane when Queensland took on Tasmania, humiliating them in 2½ days by an innings and four runs.

Put in to bat Queensland scored at three runs an over, making 324 with 89 from the talented Brett Henschell, 64 by Kerr and 55 from wicket-keeper Peter Anderson.

Only Peter Faulkner of the visiting attack showed any penetration, taking 3 for 66 from his two dozen overs.

In reply Tasmania made 173 (Rackemann 4 for 51) and 147 (Tazelaar 5 for 54), and started talk in certain circles as to whether they were good enough to stay in the competition.

In Perth, Victoria got what they really came for against Western Australia: a draw. In a dull match only three batsmen stood out: Victorian Davenell Whatmore, who scored a career-best 170 (after being dropped off three consecutive balls when 125), and Western Australia's Wood (150 not out) and Zoehrer (109). When the game was called off on the final day, the 11,485 fans had not really had their money's worth.

As Victoria left so Queensland arrived, with that man Botham in top form. The match was a total antithesis to what had gone on a few days earlier, as 29,194 spectators watched a superb game of cricket.

Western Australia dropped Greg Shipperd and brought in Jamie Brayshaw, son of the then Western Australia cricket manager Ian, for his début. Brayshaw junior repaid the faith in him by scoring 36 and 60 not out, hitting the winning runs half an hour before the scheduled close on the last day.

Queensland were asked to bat on a pitch which deteriorated all the time, being especially bad on the final day. Kerr (59) and Ritchie (76) added 121 for the second wicket, but it was Botham (70) who held the later order together. Terry Alderman bowled with guile and flair taking 4 for 87 until being forced to retire with a strained hamstring.

In reply to 303, Western Australia batted consistently with vice-captain Andrews (66) and captain Wood (61) keeping on top of the situation as they crept past Queensland for a 45-run first-innings lead.

Perth's second-highest crowd (in 156 Shield matches) saw an incident with the final ball of the second day's play.

South Australia 1987–8
First-Class Matches

BATTING

BATTING	v NSW (Sydney) 13–15 Nov 1987		v Queensland (Adelaide) 20–3 Nov 1987		v New Zealanders (Adelaide) 27–30 Nov 1987		v Victoria (Melbourne) 11–14 Dec 1987		v Western Australia (Adelaide) 1–4 Jan 1988		v Tasmania (Devonport) 15–18 Jan 1988		v NSW (Adelaide) 22–5 Jan 1988		v Queensland (Brisbane) 6–9 Feb 1988		v Tasmania (Adelaide) 18–21 Feb 1988		v Victoria (Adelaide) 24–7 Feb 1988	
G.A. Bishop	13	0	22	37	3	123	79	82*	19	2	22	—	67	26	100	34	101	—	19	8
A.M.J. Hilditch	57	16	56	91*	34	10	34	0	35	166	0	—	4	14	49	21	185	—	11	67
M.D. Haysman	0	33	60	—	43	43	0	29	16	6	47	—	0	10*						
D.W. Hookes	11	14	89	67	128	7	93	42*	4	29	132	—	82	9	112	26	112	—	60	65
W.B. Phillips	23	5	13	5	0	75	126	—	3	25	85	—	5	49*	36	53	67	—	3	24
P.R. Sleep	16	28	70	6*	6	25			38	15	1	—	58	—	4	52	57*	—	0	104*
D.F.G. O'Connor	3	9	22	—	13	42									35*	21	75	—	0	13
T.B.A. May	11	13	1	—	1		42*		2	8	8*		21*	—	0	5	3		2*	—
A.K. Zesers	11	0	4	—			6				8*				0	0*	5		15*	—
P.W. Gladigau	1	0	25	—	10	2*	11	—	13	3			0		3		15		25	17
I.R. Carmichael	1*	5*																		
S.P.G. George			4*	—	0*	—	0*	—	2	10	5*		2	—	0	—	1			
H.W.G. Smart					1															
D.S. Lehmann							10	—												
H.B. Jolly							65	—	9	28	19		41	—	0	13*	13		16	53
N.R. Plummer							23													
S.D.H. Parkinson									0*	17*										
J.K. Pyke													64	—	9				4	31*
C. Killen																				
Byes	4				7		1		3		8		5		5	8			4	4
Leg-byes	13	5	6	1	1	7	15	4	10	13	13		9	2	11	1	7		2	8
Wides						3			2	1	2				2		2		1	1
No-balls	7	3	15	2	2	3	3		5	2	18		16	3	12	1	12		7	7
Total	171	131	387	209	242	386	468	158	158	328	463		319	113	364	247	673		161	385
Wickets	10	10	10	3	10	7	10	2	10	10	9		10	3	10	8	10		9a	6
Result	L		D		W		L		L		W		W		D		D		D	
Points	0		2		—		0		0		6		6		0		2		0	

Fielding Figures
22 – W.B. Phillips (ct 18/st 4)
18 – D.W. Hookes
8 – A.M.J. Hilditch
7 – M.D. Haysman, D.F.G. O'Connor and P.W. Gladigau
6 – H.B. Jolly
5 – A.K. Zesers
4 – J.K. Pyke
3 – P.R. Sleep, S.P.G. George and G.A. Bishop
1 – T.B.A. May

a T.B.A. Moy retired hurt

BOWLING

	P.W. Gladigau	A.K. Zesers	P.R. Sleep	T.B.A. May	I.R. Carmichael	S.P.G. George	H.W.G. Smart
v. New South Wales (Sydney) 13–15 November 1987	21-6-48-5 / 10.4-1-35-1	15.5-9-17-2 / 15-5-28-3	19-3-70-2 / 9-4-33-0	17-3-47-1 / 1-0-1-0	7-2-19-0 / 1-0-1-0		
v. Queensland (Adelaide) 20–3 November 1987	21-9-50-1 / 15-0-57-1	24-16-33-0 / 13-3-24-1	45.5-9-110-3 / 19-3-53-3	32-15-55-4 / 21-4-46-3		20-2-62-2 / 3-0-24-0	
v. New Zealand (Adelaide) 27–30 November 1987	12-4-33-0 / 12-6-26-2		31-11-96-1 / 20-8-30-1	27-3-92-4 / 26-5-85-2		12-0-65-1 / 16-1-66-0	16-1-69-0 / 7-1-29-1
v. Victoria (Melbourne) 11–14 December 1987	30-9-57-2 / 12-0-47-1	48-20-85-1 / 22.1-0-121-0				28-4-81-4 / 10-1-48-0	
v. Western Australia (Adelaide) 1–4 January 1988	22-8-43-3 / 10.2-2-36-2	18.3-7-27-2 / 22-5-54-1	24-11-50-3 / 24-5-64-2			9-0-28-1 / 7-1-25-0	
v. Tasmania (Devonport) 15–18 January 1988		17.1-4-32-2 / 22-4-75-1	29-12-63-0			21-2-51-6 / 22.1-2-71-3	
v. New South Wales (Adelaide) 22–5 January 1988	7-1-36-1 / 15-2-39-2	7-2-13-0 / 25.5-12-42-3	3-0-12-0 / 25-5-78-3			10-0-50-1 / 7-1-25-0	
v. Queensland (Brisbane) 6–9 February 1988	24-5-99-1	32-12-62-2 / 27-9-69-2	28.1-5-91-4 / 14-2-44-1	12-1-44-0 / 37-9-78-2		13-1-78-1 / 5-0-30-1	
v. Tasmania (Adelaide) 18–21 February 1988	10.3-1-31-3 / 35-3-139-2	35-9-109-2	18-1-81-0	51-10-158-1		23-6-74-3	
v. Victoria (Adelaide) 24–7 February 1988	24-7-85-7 / 37-4-143-2	16-5-41-1 / 30-10-65-2	20-2-89-0	1-0-4-1			
v. Western Australia (Perth) 2–5 March 1988	24-6-80-1 / 7-2-20-1	32.5-12-86-4	14-3-59-0				
	349.3-76-1104-38 av. 29.05	423.2-140-983-29 av. 33.89	343-84-1023-23 av. 44.47	225-50-610-18 av. 33.88	7-2-19-0 av. —	206.1-21-778-23 av. 33.82	23-2-98-0 av. —

Western Australian batsman Tim Zoehrer swept off a bail with his hand after Carl Rackemann's final delivery, and following a concerted Queensland appeal for 'hit wicket', umpires Ric Evans and Peter McConnell rejected the claim – much to the relief of the crowd.

Batting a second time Queensland faltered until Ian Botham came in. Scoring 58 out of 90 in just over an hour, he had the 12,121 Sunday crowd roaring in appreciation.

However, it was Ken MacLeay's 5 for 99 which saw the visitors restricted to 236. With 192 needed, Western Australia were 3 for 153 and cruising until Carl Racke-mann added to his first innings 4 for 56, with 4 for 65 to send the score to 7 for 169 and some Western Australian concern. But young Brayshaw saw them home, with father Ian's chewed fingernails testimony to the tension.

Meanwhile in Tasmania it was the Dennis Lillee show. Although beaten by South Australia by an innings and 70 runs, the great man's inspiration permeated through to his new colleagues.

Tasmania's first innings was awful: 111 in three hours with no one to blame but themselves. The visitors had David Hookes (132) and Wayne Phillips (85) adding 187 in 218 minutes for the third wicket. Mike Haysman (46) and James Pyke (64) then saw the total to 9 for 463 before the declaration arrived.

Tasmania quickly fell to 5 for 71 until former South African tourists Mick Taylor and Peter Faulkner put on 188 in even time. Faulkner (57) became one of Pyke's five victims, but Taylor stayed until the end, being last man out. His 12th first-class century of 166 contained 19 fours and took slightly over 4½ hours.

South Australia's second victory in a week – and for the season – was due more to an inept New South Wales

Batting

v. Western Australia (Perth) 2–5 March 1988		M	Inns	NOs	Runs	HS	Av
21	55	11	20	1	833	123	43.84
13	59	11	20	1	922	185	48.52
		7	12	1	287	60	26.09
2	65	11	20	1	1149	132	60.47
13	59	11	19	1	669	126	37.16
34	9	10	17	3	523	104*	37.35
8	20	7	12	1	261	75	23.72
		6	9	2	78	42*	11.14
7	0*	10	14	5	87	21*	9.66
15	5	10	15	1	145	25	10.35
		1	2	2	6	5*	—
		8	9	4	24	10	4.80
		1	1	—	1	1	1.00
		1	1	—	10	10	10.00
18*	5	8	12	2	280	65	28.00
		2	2	—	62	39	31.00
		2	2	2	17	17*	—
0	41	4	6	1	149	64	29.80
0	0	1	2	—	0	0	0.00
1	3						
4	4						
2	1						
	5						
138	331						
10	10						
L							
0							

Bowling

M.D. Haysman	N.R. Plummer	H.B. Jolly	S.D.H. Parkinson	D.W. Hookes	J.K. Pyke	C. Killen	Byes	Leg-byes	Wides	No-balls	Total	Wkts
							3	2	2	1	206	10
								1	1	1	98	4
							1	7	1	11	318	10
							1	5	1	1	210	8
								5	1	6	360	7
6–1–26–0							3	2		4	267	6
12–2–36–1	28–9–69–0	3–0–10–0						7	1	1	345	8
	20–1–55–1						6	8	1		285	4
6–3–12–0			18–3–61–1				4	12	2	4	237	10
8–1–22–0			8–3–18–0	7–1–17–0			9	5	1		250	7
				8–3–11–1	11–3–15–1		1	1	4	10	111	10
				1–0–1–0	18–4–47–5			3	1	10	283	10
	6–2–14–0	2–0–9–0			15–5–37–0			2		6	150	2
					8–1–32–1		3			2	219	10
				2–1–1–0			3	7	3	11	385	10
		1–0–6–0					5	8		6	271	10
				5–0–22–2				9	1	5	592	10
					15–6–43–1		5	1	1		178	10
				4–0–11–0	35–3–136–1			11	3	3	455	5
					26–3–98–3	26–8–98–2	13	1		7	434	10
						6.5–3–15–2	1				36	3
32–7–96–1 av. 96.00	54–12–138–1 av. 138.00	6–0–25–0 —	26–6–79–1 av. 79.00	27–5–63–3 av. 21.00	128–25–408–12 av. 34.00	32.5–11–113–4 av. 28.25						

Tasmania 1987–8
First-Class Matches

BATTING — innings shown as *inn1 / inn2* under each match.

BATTING	WA (Perth) 13–16 Nov 1987	Vic (Melb) 20–3 Nov 1987	NSW (Devonport) 4–7 Dec 1987	NZ (Devonport) 18–21 Dec 1987	Qld (Brisbane) 8–11 Jan 1988	SA (Devonport) 15–18 Jan 1988	Sri Lankans (Hobart) 22–5 Jan 1988	Vic (Launceston) 29 Jan–1 Feb 1988	WA (Hobart) 6–9 Feb 1988	SA (Adelaide) 18–21 Feb 1988
D.C. Boon	22 / 69	24 / 22		44 / 101*					53 / 89	18 / —
N. Jelich	12 / 8		7 / 24	0 / 3						
G.A. Hughes	0 / 55	147 / 95	18 / 7	27 / 26	37 / 32	0 / 21	39 / —	45* / 13	4 / 6	32 / —
M.D. Taylor	4 / 24	10 / 59	0 / 19	85 / 1	35 / 28	1 / 166	5 / —	19 / 20	24 / 13	216 / —
D.J. Buckingham	20 / 5	35 / 11	31 / 112	5 / 13	4 / 8		71 / —	103* / 25	41 / 0	126 / —
B.F. Davison	8 / 7	40 / 20	41 / 25	30* / 23	13 / 4	20 / 6		33 / 16	59 / 0	55 / —
P.I. Faulkner	9 / 0*			46 / 10	6 / 4	4 / 19	57 / —	69* / 29	10 / 23	46 / —
R.E. Soule	39* / 0	22 / 16	2 / 45	17 / 6	0 / 16*	11 / 0	15* / —	— / 2	14 / 2	18 / —
T.J. Cooley	3 / —	10 / 0	0 / 17*	4 / 7*	0* / 1	2 / 0	— / —	— / 1*	3 / 7	30 / —
C.L. Broadby	4 / 5	12* / 23*	2 / 7							
T.D. Bower	1 / 1	4 / 0*	0* / 8	2 / —					16* / 0	10* / —
J. Cox		1 / 35	6 / 6							
A.J. de Winter		2 / 51	14 / 2		17 / 2	21 / 7				
B.A. Cruse				32 / 4	31 / 11					
S.L. Saunders						0 / 20				
E.J. Harris					15 / 11	17 / 0	56 / —		40 / 5	
R.J. Bennett						3 / 0				
R.D. Woolley						1 / 10	21 / —			
D.K. Lillee						0* / 2*	— / —	0 / 0	5* / 12	—
N. Courtney							38 / —	2 / 39	13 / 25	14 / —
C. Young								— / 1*		
K.R. Bradshaw										
Byes	2		4	1			1	2	7	1
Leg-byes	4 / 9	10 / 9	5 / 8	5 / 8	9 / 3	1 / 3	16	7 / 9	10 / 9	
Wides		/ 1	4 / 6			4 / 1	2		1	1
No-balls	7 / 5	3 / 3	8 / 14	8 / 6	6 / 7	10 / 10	7	7 / 3	5 / 2	5
Total	135 / 189	324 / 354	134 / 295	305 / 208	173 / 147	111 / 283	339	287 / 144	273 / 209	592
Wickets	10 / 9a	10 / 9	10 / 10	10 / 8	10 / 10	10 / 10	6	5 / 9	10 / 10	10
Result	L	D	L	D	L	L	D	D	L	D
Points	0	0	0	—	0	0	—	0	0	0

Fielding Figures

28 – R.E. Soule (ct 25/st 3)
8 – D.J. Buckingham, B.F. Davison and T.J. Cooley (inc 1 as sub)
7 – D.C. Boon
5 – G.A. Hughes, P.I. Faulkner and M.D. Taylor
3 – A.J. de Winter and B.A. Cruse
2 – C.L. Broady, D.K. Lillee, E.J. Harris and N. Courtney
1 – R.D. Woolley, R.J. Bennett, T.D. Bower and C. Young (sub)
a T.J. Cooley absent injured

BOWLING

BOWLING	T.J. Cooley	T.D. Bower	P.I. Faulkner	C.L. Broadby	G.A. Hughes	D.C. Boon	A.J. De Winter	B.A. Cruse
v. Western Australia (Perth) 13–16 November 1987	27–3–115–1	32–4–103–2	30–3–88–1	20–1–81–0	9–0–43–1	3–0–20–1		
v. Victoria (Melbourne) 20–2 November 1987	26–1–105–2	30–4–108–0		38–4–147–2	16–3–43–0		28–4–94–0	
v. New South Wales (Devonport) 4–7 December 1987	24–3–112–1	19–1–81–0		36.5–5–128–1	14–0–56–0		28–6–80–2	
v. New Zealanders (Devonport) 18–21 December 1987	26–4–96–0	31–4–98–1	33–11–77–3		14–2–59–1			17–1–68–1
	16.5–2–47–3	15–2–44–2	24–11–37–4					
v. Queensland (Brisbane) 8–11 January 1988	27–3–112–3		24–10–66–3				29.5–6–77–1	11–3–30–0
v. South Australia (Devonport) 15–18 January 1988	25–1–128–1		46.3–20–105–0		4–1–28–0		5.3–1–25–0	
v. Sri Lankans (Hobart) 22–5 January 1988	22.1–1–95–4		19–3–55–1		10–5–20–2			
v. Victoria (Launceston) 29 January–1 February 1988	21–2–97–2		26–4–75–2		17–4–50–1			
	3–0–16–0		6–1–25–0					
v. Western Australia (Hobart) 6–9 February 1988	18–3–67–0	21–1–70–3	26.1–8–69–3		18–1–70–2			
	10–2–53–1	13–0–49–1	10–1–38–2		14–2–56–0			
v. South Australia (Adelaide) 18–21 February 1988	38–2–137–2	6–0–26–0	51–15–136–0		41–11–100–1	10.4–4–25–1		
v. Queensland (Launceston) 24–7 February 1988			23–10–51–1	34–6–112–1	8–0–29–0			
				30–4–117–2				
v. New South Wales (Sydney) 2–5 March 1988	24–1–95–0		26–5–57–1	49.1–8–147–2	12–2–38–1		29–4–92–3	
			4–0–17–0	15–8–21–1	11.5–3–29–1			
Totals	308–28–1275–20	167–16–579–9	348.4–102–896–21	223–36–753–9	188.5–34–621–10	13.4–4–45–2	120.2–21–368–6	28–4–98–1
	av. 63.75	av. 64.33	av. 42.66	av. 83.66	av. 62.10	av. 22.50	av. 61.33	av. 98.00

v. Queensland (Launceston) 24-7 February 1988	v. New South Wales (Sydney) 2-5 March 1988			M	Inns	NOs	Runs	HS	Av
108	143	93	4	7	13	1	790	143	65.83
				3	6	—	54	24	9.00
71	56	7	16	12	22	1	754	147	35.90
89	18	81	86	12	22	—	1003	216	45.59
7	13	2	36	11	20	1	668	126	35.15
73	7	48	2	11	21	1	530	73	26.50
78*	1	26	20	10	18	3	512	78*	34.13
1	0	0	2	12	21	3	228	45	12.66
		13	4	11	17	4	102	30	7.84
9	42*	10*	0*	5	10	5	114	42*	22.80
				6	10	4	42	16*	7.00
		26	22	5	10	—	164	51	16.40
				2	4	—	78	32	19.50
				1	2	—	20	20	10.00
				4	7	—	144	56	20.57
				1	2	—	3	3	1.50
				2	3	—	32	21	10.66
18	—			6	7	3	37	18	9.25
14	1			5	8	—	146	39	18.25
0	—			3	2	1	1	1*	1.00
		4	7	1	2	—	11	7	5.50

	1	7	
6	5	6	4
1			
6	3	4	1
481	290	327	204
10	8	10	10
W		L	
6		0	

display than anything else. With the second day completely lost to rain, two declarations set up the result.

Batting first, Hookes led the way for South Australia hitting 82, Bishop 67 and Sleep 58 with the innings finishing on the third afternoon on 319. New South Wales then had another pair of South African tourists, Steve Smith (49) and John Dyson (60 not out) seeing them to 2 for 150 before Murray Bennett declared.

South Australia batted for 2¼ hours for 3 for 113 before they too declared, leaving New South Wales 390 minutes to score 283 for victory.

Only Smith (51) and a brilliant 72 from Mark Waugh – with 4 sixes and 7 fours – assisted New South Wales to 219 and defeat by 63 runs. After the match Bennett was deposed as New South Wales' acting captain, Geoff Lawson taking over the reins.

Tasmania now hosted two fixtures in 11 days at Launceston and the new TCA ground at Bellerive, Hobart.

In Launceston at the end of January, Victoria were the visitors. Opener Michael Quinn had been replaced by Gary Watts, who, after a four-year break, returned to Shield cricket with a career-best 176. With a hot northerly wind blowing dust, the Tasmanians fielded for all of the first day as the visitors piled on 4 for 332, carrying on to 8 for 409 the next morning before acting captain Simon Davis put a halt to the bowlers' misery.

Brian Davison then let the Tasmanian innings go on until late on the third day, declaring at 5 for 287, a deficit of 122. He allowed Danny Buckingham to bring up his century on his recall to the side.

Victoria scored quickly on the last morning, closing at 1 for 135, which set Tasmania to score 258 in 283 minutes for their first win of the season. At 4 for 128 a draw looked

E.J. Harris	D.K. Lillee	C. Young	N. Courtney	M.D. Taylor	B.F. Davison	D.J. Buckingham	K.R. Bradshaw	Byes	Leg-byes	Wides	No-balls	Total	Wkts
									11	2	5	461	6
									4	5	15	501	5
								4	6	1	7	467	4
									12		10	410	7
								5	10	1	4	143	10
18–7–32–2								3	4	3	7	324	10
21–2–57–4	45–10–99–4							8	13	2	18	463	9
5–0–26–0	24–9–58–1	12–4–42–2							7	6	14	303	10
11–1–27–0	28.5–2–92–3	9–0–57–0							11	1	14	409	8
	17–4–57–0	7–1–30–1						1	6		9	135	1
	32–11–48–2								10	1	7	334	10
	15.1–2–54–1								13		1	263	7
	55–7–165–4		7–0–44–2	3–0–15–0	3–0–10–0			8	7	2	12	673	10
	6.2–0–27–1	17.4–1–114–2	4–0–23–0					4	3	2	6	363	5
		23.5–0–120–6	8–0–32–0		9–3–18–0	7–1–16–0			11	2	20	314	10
							6–1–20–0		11	4		460	10
								4	1			72	2
55–10–142–6 av. 23.66	223.2–45–600–16 av. 37.50	69.3–6–363–11 av. 33.00	19–0–99–2 av. 49.50	3–0–15–0 —	12–3–28–0 —	7–1–16–0 —	6–1–20–0 —						

Victoria 1987–8
First-Class Matches

BATTING	v. Queensland (Brisbane) 13–16 November 1987		v. Tasmania (Melbourne) 20–3 November 1987		v. Western Australia (Melbourne) 27–30 November 1987		v. South Australia (Melbourne) 11–14 December 1987		v. New South Wales (Sydney) 18–21 December 1987		v. Western Australia (Perth) 8–11 January 1988		v. Tasmania (Launceston) 29 January–1 February 1988		v. Sri Lankans (Melbourne) 6–9 February 1988		v. New South Wales (Melbourne) 12–15 February 1988		v. South Australia (Adelaide) 24–7 February 1988	
D.F. Whatmore	51	11	24	—	127	—	69	46	31	—	170	51	52	71*	5	0	55	4	8	22
M.B. Quinn	5	41	36	—	81	—	13	—			8	4								
D.M. Jones	31	75	191	—	29	—			1						6	35			15	101
J.D. Siddons	28	44	5	—	0	—	64	124*	27	—	26	52	15	—	4	103	71	130	58	241*
P.W. Young	30	22	164*	—	93*	—	9	60	10	—	7	66*	35	—	0	9*	10	28*		
A.I.C. Dodemaide	45	14	37*	—	71*	—	2	9*	22	—					32	14*			3	3
D.A. Emerson	0	18	—																	
M.G.D. Dimattina	11	18	—		—		8	—	46*	—	26	10*	46	—	22	—	60	15	8	43*
R.J. Bright	8	20											4*	—						
D.J. Hickey	3*	1	—		—		10*	—			11	—					1	—	20	—
S.P. Davis	—	0*	—		—				2*		2*		—		3	—	1*	—	5*	—
M.G. Hughes			20						0		11				15		24			
P.W. Jackson					—				8		31		4		1		6		5	
I.D. Frazer							76	15	12		12	33								
W.G. Whiteside							84*	16	23		20	23	31	—			80	—	0	25
G.M. Watts													176	8	30	122	66	0	25	3
W.G. Ayres													20	40*			6	28		
P. Reiffel													—	—	6*	—	22	—		
Byes					2		6		4		6		1				6			
Leg-byes	4	11	4		9		7	8	9		5	11	11	6	8	8	13		5	11
Wides			5				1		1				1		2	1			1	3
No-balls	10	18	15		19		1				4		14	9	12	5	12	1	1	3
Total	226	293	501		431		345	285	195		333	256	409	135	146	297	403	212	178	455
Wickets	9	10	5		4		8	4	9		10	5	8	1	10	5	10	5	10	5
Result	L		D		D		W		Ab.		D		D		D		D		D	
Points	0		2		2		6		0		2		2		—		2		2	

Fielding Figures

33 – M.G. Dimattina (ct 30/st 3)	3 – M.B. Quinn and G.M. Watts
17 – P.W. Young	2 – D.J. Hickey, W.G. Whiteside, A.I.C. Dodemaide
15 – D.F. Whatmore	and W.G. Ayres (inc 1 as sub)
12 – D.M. Jones	1 – R.J. Bright, P.W. Jackson, I.D. Frazer,
10 – J.D. Siddons	M.G. Hughes and P. Reiffel
4 – S.P. Davis	

BOWLING	D.J. Hickey	S.P. Davis	A.I.C. Dodemaide	D.A. Emerson	D.M. Jones	R.J. Bright	M.G. Hughes	J.D. Siddons
v. Queensland (Brisbane) 13–16 November 1987	27–4–94–3 / 9–2–41–2	22–2–65–2 / 15–4–36–2	30–6–89–4 / 6–1–22–1	10–0–76–0 / 3–0–13–0	2–0–12–0 / 1.4–1–2–0	11–0–62–0		
v. Tasmania (Melbourne) 20–3 November 1987	24–3–88–2 / 20–2–72–3	12–3–27–0 / 23–6–48–1	19.4–2–43–5 / 21–5–79–0	24–3–90–0 / 22–5–47–2	14–6–23–0 / 7–1–19–0		20–6–43–2 / 21–5–68–1	2–0–5–0
v. Western Australia (Melbourne) 27–30 November 1987	27–3–100–2 / 9–2–29–0	16–5–35–1 / 11–4–22–0	11–3–26–1 / 11–2–45–0		5–0–9–0 / 13–3–28–1		28–6–55–3 / 13–5–30–0	
v. South Australia (Melbourne) 11–14 December 1987	24–2–104–0 / 11–0–45–1	28–5–70–4 / 9–1–36–0	37–7–112–3 / 7–0–36–0					
v. New South Wales (Sydney) 18–21 December 1987		35–4–121–0	45–9–114–5			12–2–26–0	10–2–22–1	
v. Western Australia (Perth) 8–11 January 1988	23–0–103–1	21–3–40–0					31–5–103–3	
v. Tasmania (Launceston) 29 January–1 February 1988		22–4–53–0 / 9–2–19–1				22–11–38–1 / 4–1–14–0		
v. Sri Lankans (Melbourne) 6–9 February 1988		20–8–50–5 / 24–6–57–3	11.5–5–17–1 / 22–9–48–1				19–3–56–1 / 27–3–83–1	
v. New South Wales (Melbourne) 6–9 February 1988	27–5–90–4 / 13–2–43–1	15–3–44–0 / 14–2–35–1						3–0–18–0
v. South Australia (Adelaide) 24–7 February 1988	8–0–43–1 / 17–2–90–0	6–2–19–1 / 10–0–37–0	19–7–37–4 / 33–7–75–2		8–3–16–0		15–4–52–1 / 31.2–5–91–3	
v. Queensland (Melbourne) 2–5 March 1988			16–3–59–1 / 5–0–21–2				16.3–4–43–4 / 14–4–59–2	
Totals	239–27–942–20 av. 47.10	312–64–814–21 av. 38.76	294.3–66–823–30 av. 27.43	59–8–226–2 av. 113.00	62.4–16–135–1 av. 135.00	37–12–114–1 av. 114.00	245.5–52–705–22 av. 32.04	5–0–23–0 av. —

a T.B.A. May retired hurt

v. Queensland (Melbourne) 2–5 March 1988		M	Inns	NOs	Runs	HS	Av
85	30	11	19	1	912	170	50.66
		5	7	—	188	81	26.85
13	20	7	11	—	517	191	47.00
9	76	11	18	2	1077	241*	67.31
		9	14	5	543	164*	60.33
20	0	8	13	4	272	71*	30.22
		2	2	—	18	18	9.00
16	25	11	14	3	354	60	32.18
		2	3	1	32	20	16.00
		7	6	2	46	20	11.50
		10	6	5	13	5*	13.00
4	8	7	7	—	82	24	11.71
6*	0	9	9	1	62	31	7.75
		3	5	—	148	76	29.60
16	15	7	11	1	333	84*	33.30
17	116	5	10	—	563	176	56.30
46	21	3	6	1	161	46	32.20
1	1*	4	4	2	30	22	15.00
1							
10	12						
3							
9	4						
256	328						
10	10						
	W						
6							

probable. Then five wickets fell for 15 runs with the wicket playing low, and it needed youngsters Claye Young and Troy Cooley to hold out for the final 5.2 overs.

Then to Bellerive Oval for yet another new Sheffield Shield venue, with Western Australia as opponents. Bowling against his old team on the first day, 38-year-old Dennis Lillee provided the crowd with a perfect example of line and length bowling. He finished with figures of 32-11-48-2: an excellent effort.

As Western Australia's score mounted up to 334, Geoff Marsh (86) and Wayne Andrews (57) provided the innings with its backbone. Tasmania's reply fell short by 61 – Davison a season-best 59, Chris Matthews 6 for 77 – which Western Australia extended to 324 before setting the home side a run-a-minute chase.

David Boon, back in the Tasmanian team following his successful international season, scored 89 out of 6 for 135 to show his superiority. But it was to no avail as defeat came with time running out.

South Australia had a good chance of defeating leaders Queensland in their early February match at the Gabba. But in the end the home team had the better of a draw after some very strange decisions by the visiting captain.

Asked to bat first, Queensland went on a run spree, chalking up 385 in quick time. Trevor Barsby scored 102 only after convincing the selectors he was fit enough to play, having had seven stitches put in a wound on his right hand. Barsby's third century came during a swashbuckling second-wicket stand of 163 with Glenn Trimble (57).

But the excitement the Saturday crowd had flocked to see came when Ian Botham crashed 60 in fractionally over an hour with 3 sixes and 7 fours. Whatever one says about

M.B. Quinn	P.W. Jackson	P.W. Young	W.G. Whiteside	P. Reiffel	D.F. Whatmore	G.M. Watts	Byes	Leg-byes	Wides	No-balls	Total	Wkts
							1	6	1	6	405	9
								1			115	5
								10	4	3	324	10
1–0–3–1							4	9	6	3	354	9
	34.3–12–55–3							11	2		291	10
	33–10–74–2	1–1–0–0					7	2			237	3
	40–8–137–3		10–1–30–0					15	3	3	468	10
	9–2–36–1						1	4			158	2
	53–14–128–3		4–0–19–0				1	7	3	4	438	9
	35.1–11–98–1		26–7–78–2					5	4	17	427	8
	27–7–87–2		17–7–36–0	24–8–47–2	4–0–17–0		2	7		7	287	5
	26–10–59–3		16–3–29–2	16–8–14–2	2–2–0–1			9		3	144	9
				15–4–30–2				4	4	3	157	10
	9–1–44–0	6–1–13–0		24–3–94–1		6–0–15–0		8	1	5	362	6
	30–11–68–2	2–0–6–0	1–0–4–1	25.3–6–57–2				10		7	279	10
	23–10–55–2		7–2–18–0	7.5–1–32–1	1–0–1–0			4		3	206	5
	1–0–4–1						4	2	1	7	161	9a
	32–15–53–1		5–0–11–0				4	8	1	7	385	6
	10–3–25–0			22–3–80–4				2	6		209	10
	8.3–2–24–2			12–3–62–3				2	1		168	10
1–0–	371.1–116–	9–2–	86–20–	146.2–36–	7–2–	6–0–						
3–1	947–26	19–0	225–5	416–17	18–1	15–0						
av. 3.00	av. 36.42	—	av. 45.00	av. 24.47	av. 18.00	—						

Western Australia 1987–8
First-Class Matches

BATTING

BATTING	v. Tasmania (Perth) 13–16 Nov 1987	v. New Zealanders (Perth) 20–2 Nov 1987	v. Victoria (Melbourne) 27–30 Nov 1987	v. New South Wales (Perth) 11–13 Dec 1987	v. Queensland (Brisbane) 18–20 Dec 1987	v. South Australia (Adelaide) 1–4 Jan 1988	v. Victoria (Perth) 8–11 Jan 1988	v. Queensland (Perth) 15–18 Jan 1988	v. Tasmania (Hobart) 6–9 Feb 1988	v. New South Wales (Sydney) 24–7 Feb 1988
G.R. Marsh	5 —	7 9	16 120*		4 8		.		86 13	4 82
M.R.J. Veletta	106 —	11 0	25 52		4 4				7 95	16 5
T.M. Moody	144 —	10 43	47 46	38 —	89 3	7 13	17 —	33 14	0 25	9 21
G.M. Wood	83 —	25 11	74 —	40 —	9* —	42 82	150* —	61 15	24 79	28 0
W.S. Andrews	72 —	32 1	4 2	9 —		55 19	50 —	66 39	57 23	46 7
K.H. MacLeay	22* —	20 0	28 —	2 —				38 9*	50* 0*	14 2
C.D. Matthews	6 —	8 19	36 —	4 —	45 33	24 15	20 —	16 9	29 12	27 40
P.A. Capes	5* —	1* 5	12 —	23	13 15	17 1*	2 —	13 —	9 —	0* 0
T.J. Zoehrer	—	7 8	28 8*	18 —	4 51	0 28*	109 —	16 0	39 2	23 5
S.J. Milosz	—	0 0*	7* —	0* —	2 1*	0* —	0* —			
B.A. Reid	—	5 9	1 —							
K.J. Hughes				76 —	22 3	21 62	7 —	0 0		
G. Shipperd				9 —		10 14	17 —			
T.M. Alderman				11 —	2 18	11 —	9	7* —	9 —	0 4
T.G. Breman					6 36					
M.W. McPhee						28 1	20*	44 28		
J.A. Brayshaw								36 60*		
T.G. Hogan									6 —	0 15*
A.D. Mullally										
Byes			7			6 4	9	1 10		6 5
Leg-byes	11	4	11 2	8	5	7 12	5 5	8 9	10 13	3 9
Wides	2		2			2 1	4	1 1	1	4
No-balls	5	5	8	18	12	7 4	17	8	7 1	2
Total	461	131 117	291 237	256	217 192	237 250	427	348 194	334 263	176 201
Wickets	6	10 10	10 3	10	10 9a	10 7	8	10 7	10 7	10 10
Result	W	L	D	W	L	W	D	W	W	L
Points	6	—	0	6	0	6	2	6	6	0

Fielding Figures

47 – T.J. Zoehrer (ct 44/st 3)
15 – M.R.J. Veletta
12 – W.S. Andrews
8 – T.M. Alderman and G.R. Marsh
7 – G.M. Wood and K.H. MacLeay
5 – C.D. Matthews
3 – S.J. Milosz, P.A. Capes, T.M. Moody and J. Brayshaw (inc 1 as sub)
2 – K.J. Hughes
1 – G. Shipperd and T.G. Hogan

a G.M. Wood absent injured

BOWLING

BOWLING	B.A. Reid	K.H. MacLeay	P.A. Capes	C.D. Matthews	S.J. Milosz	W.S. Andrews	T.M. Alderman	T.G. Breman
v. Tasmania (Perth) 13–16 November 1987	16–5–38–0 / 11–3–47–0	19–7–25–3 / 6–2–8–0	21–8–32–3 / 13–4–23–3	9–2–21–1 / 19–4–49–1	13–6–13–3 / 26.3–7–53–4			
v. New Zealanders (Perth) 20–2 November 1987	23–4–61–2	25–9–75–4	23–2–85–1	18–2–62–1	17–6–53–1	2–0–6–0		
v. Victoria (Melbourne) 27–30 November 1987	36–12–87–0	25–6–77–1	18–1–60–2	23–3–72–1	36–9–83–0	20–2–41–0		
v. New South Wales (Perth) 11–13 December 1987		8–3–18–1 / 4–1–10–0	7–2–20–1 / 11–3–23–2	15–4–39–3 / 16.4–2–56–6	1–0–1–0		13.5–1–35–5 / 22–6–31–2	
v. Queensland (Brisbane) 18–20 December 1987			13–3–30–1	25–3–69–3	16–4–60–1		31–6–70–3	17–0–83–2
v. South Australia (Adelaide) 1–4 January 1988			6–1–21–0	6–0–19–0	5–0–17–0		3–1–18–0	4–1–12–0
v. Victoria (Perth) 8–11 January 1988			19–4–46–2 / 34–4–86–2	21–4–41–4 / 26.4–2–79–3	4–2–4–1 / 20–1–61–0		27–11–57–2 / 29–10–67–4	
v. Queensland (Perth) 15–18 January 1988			34.1–16–61–2 / 22–5–56–3	31–3–107–4 / 16–3–60–1	27–9–67–1 / 28–10–74–0	7–4–9–0	38–11–93–2 / 19–8–40–0	
v. Tasmania (Hobart) 6–9 February 1988		22.5–5–48–1 / 24.3–4–99–5	35–3–87–4 / 18–3–68–3	21–2–67–1 / 13–1–43–2			32.3–7–87–4	
v. New South Wales (Sydney) 24–7 February 1988		16–4–33–2 / 6–3–13–0	19–2–74–1 / 8–1–49–0	34–9–77–6 / 14–1–44–1			16–4–35–0 / 21–9–45–2	
v. South Australia (Perth) 2–5 March 1988		20.5–3–47–3 / 19–8–35–2	24–7–66–2	21–5–71–2 / 13–3–35–2		12–0–45–1	33–11–67–3 / 16–8–22–1	
v. Queensland (Perth) 18–22 March 1988	14–6–34–5 / 21–5–48–0	9–4–21–1 / 22–3–88–2 / 27–10–53–1 / 17.2–6–40–2	31–11–79–4	32.5–7–101–8 / 27–9–52–1	10.2–2–34–2	5–1–16–0	15–2–44–2 / 23.4–5–80–3 / 26–10–62–0 / 28–4–91–6	
	121–35– / 315–7 / av. 45.00	271.3–78– / 690–28 / av. 24.64	325.1–69– / 887–32 / av. 27.71	443.3–82– / 1277–57 / av. 22.40	193.3–54– / 486–11 / av. 44.18	46–7– / 117–1 / av. 117.00	394–114– / 944–39 / av. 24.20	21–1– / 95–2 / av. 47.50

a T.J. Cooley absent injured

him, an 11,142 attendance showed the pulling power of a star.

In reply the South Australians had Bishop (100) and Hilditch (49) putting on 157 for the first wicket. Then David Hookes (112) scored a typically chancy century, and as soon as his three figures came up his irresponsibility cost his side first-innings points.

National selector Greg Chappell was scathing in his comments as Hookes hit two consecutive sixes off Henschell and was out two balls later going for a third. His team mates followed instructions as the last five wickets fell for 10 runs: Queensland gaining an unexpected 21-run advantage.

Allan Border starred in the second innings, remaining unbeaten on 118 out of 271. His 5-hour innings with 15 fours held his side up after three mini-collapses.

Needing 293 for victory, South Australia saw half-centuries from Wayne Phillips (53) and Peter Sleep (52) as they stuttered to 8 for 247.

When New South Wales visited Melbourne for their clash against Victoria, it was the first time fast bowlers (Lawson and Davis) had captained opposing sides since Dennis Lillee (Western Australia) and Jeff Thomson (Queensland) had fought out the 1983–4 Shield final.

Victoria won the toss and Davis had no hesitation in batting on a bare track, as he spent the rest of the first day, feet up, watching his side reach 5 for 288.

Whatmore (55) and Watts (66) put on 90 for the first wicket against on erratic New South Wales attack. Siddons (71) and Watts then plundered a hundred quick runs for the third wicket, after which Warren Whiteside (80) and Michael Dimattina (60) added 104 for the seventh. For New South Wales, off-spinner Greg Matthews took 6 for 97 as Victoria reached 403.

(Perth) 2–5 March 1988	v. Queensland (Perth)	18–22 March 1988	M	Inns	NOs	Runs	HS	Av
0	41	39	8	15	1	435	120*	31.07
13*	23	59	8	15	1	425	106	30.35
9			11	19	—	568	144	29.89
—	141	0	12	18	3	1050	186*	70.00
13*	71	20*	11	19	2	594	72	34.94
—	2	—	9	13	4	254	67	28.22
	2	—	12	18	—	409	64	22.72
			10	14	4	116	23	11.60
—	0	10*	12	19	3	376	109	23.50
			7	8	6	10	7*	5.00
—			4	4	—	40	25	10.00
	11	21	6	10	—	223	76	22.30
			3	4	—	50	17	12.50
—	0	—	9	11	1	88	18	8.80
			1	2	—	42	36	21.00
			3	5	1	121	44	30.25
0	24	4	3	6	1	144	60*	28.80
			2	3	1	21	15*	10.50
	2*	—	1	1	1	2	2*	—
1	15	8						
	12	1						
36	344	162						
3	10	5						
W		W						
6		—						

T.M. Moody	T.G. Hogan	J.A. Brayshaw	A.D. Mullally		Byes	Leg-byes	Wides	No-balls	Total	Wkts
					2	4		7	135	10
						9	1	5	189	9a
						2		17	344	9
					2	9		19	431	4
						3	1	3	115	10
					4	6		4	131	10
						6	4	17	318	10
					4	1		6	92	0
5–2–19–0						10	2	5	158	10
					3	13	1	2	328	10
						5		4	333	10
					6	11			256	5
6–0–24–0						14		7	303	10
						4	1	4	238	10
	16.1–4–37–1				7	10	1	5	273	10
	23.3–9–57–6				1			2	209	10
	10–1–37–0				2	5	9		295	10
	21–5–73–2					3			213	8
					1	4	2		138	10
		5–2–13–1			3	4	1	5	331	10
			17–2–55–1		9	9	8	4	289	10
			12–6–17–1		9	7		7	216	10
13–2–43–0	70.4–19–204–9	5–2–13–1	29–8–72–2							
—	av. 22.66	av. 13.00	av. 36.00							

It was Matthews the batsman who saved New South Wales from following-on with a well-compiled 62, as the last wicket pair got their side out of gaol. Only Mark Waugh (69) earlier in the innings had assisted New South Wales to 279.

In an unusual move on the third evening, the official scorers announced a seven-ball over which had to be read into the record. It started when New South Wales paceman Dave Gilbert suffered a recurrence of a thigh strain and left the field after bowling only four balls of his fourth over. Spinner Gavin Robertson completed the over, but was allowed to bowl three deliveries by umpire Bert Guy: so an official appendage was made to the sheets.

Poor old Bert Guy. He had a most controversial match. On the second morning he awarded a 'catch' to Mark Taylor, who did not appear to have control of the ball as he tried to simultaneously collect and throw it in the air from Whiteside's edge.

After other disputed decisions on the third day – moreso Mark Waugh's dismissal – Guy ruled against Geoff Lawson (5), who, when facing off-spinner Paul Jackson, launched a vicious off-drive which struck Gary Watts' foot at silly mid-off. The ball ricocheted over the wicket to silly mid-on where Peter Young accepted the catch.

Lawson's reaction was predictable.

Victoria batting a second time declared at 5 for 212 after Jamie Siddons recorded an amazing 130, the final 66 coming in just 47 minutes as he, along with Michael Dimattina and Peter Young, put on 103 runs.

New South Wales lost their way in response, getting to 5 for 206 fairly slowly, and the match was drawn but only after Mark Waugh had completed an unbeaten century.

Both Siddons and Waugh had now made three Shield centuries in eight matches. Who would be the first to the coveted 1,000 runs? Siddons had 693 runs at 53.33, and Waugh 621 at 62.10.

They are both gifted players and are the sign of Australia's new resurgence after a period in the doldrums.

Tasmania arrived in Adelaide in mid-February less three players, who finally turned up two hours before the start of play. Captain Brian Davison, his deputy Peter Faulkner, and Glenn Hughes had been in New Zealand playing for a Southland Invitation team, and had become stranded after a minor accident.

Davison won the toss, elected to bat, and sat back to enjoy the day. On a placid pitch the visitors lost three wickets for 80, and then had a record fourth-wicket partnership of 258 in four hours. And this from a team who had not won in its past 43 first-class matches!

Mick Taylor and Danny Buckingham tore into the South Australian attack aided by, as watching Australian team manager Bobby Simpson said: 'Some of the weirdest field placings I have ever seen.'

Buckingham fell shortly before stumps for 126, an innings which contained 17 fours and no little skill. Taylor next morning went on to a Shield-best score of 216 made in 7½ hours from 339 deliveries including 16 boundaries.

Davison, enjoying himself tremendously, made 55 and Faulkner 46 with Tasmania reaching 592, their highest score in first-class cricket.

At the end of their innings an exasperated South Australia captain, David Hookes, bowled five overs of 'donkey-drops', claiming 2 for 22. It was, however, not very nice to witness.

Glenn Bishop and Andrew Hilditch then put on a record first-wicket partnership of 199 before Bishop fell for 101, made from 169 balls. Hilditch was next to go, caught at second slip for 185 after adding 136 with Don O'Connor (75).

Hookes (112) and Wayne Phillips (67) then added 116 for the fourth wicket as South Australia recorded their second highest Shield total of 673. Peter Sleep, unbeaten on 57, remained a tantalizing one run short of 5,000 in Shield cricket.

Having taken 215 overs, South Australia left the match drawn. And the ultimate insult for the Tasmanians who did not have any points in the competition? A fine of 0.2 of a point for bowling slow over rates.

With all teams now having played eight matches, only two rounds were left. The Shield finalists were going to be Queensland and Western Australia: but at which venue?

The team finishing top had the home advantage and had to be beaten outright. Both sides were level with 32 points with all other factors equal. What possible confusion!

The penultimate round started on 24 February, with matches in Launceston, Sydney and Adelaide. In Launceston, Tasmania took on the mighty Queensland side. But Brian Davison was a canny captain and ran rings around Allan Border in what was described as 'a brilliant four days of ultimate leadership'.

Dead-beats no longer, and buoyed by Dennis Lillee's enthusiasm (well he was renting an old manse in Lord Street, Hobart) the Tasmanians struck gold.

Border, at first slip, dropped David Boon off the first ball of the day. Carl Rackemann was not amused. Boon was out – four hours later after cracking 108, his fourth century of the season, which also made him the first player to the 1,000 run mark.

With Glenn Hughes (71), the pair put on 126 for the first wicket before lunch. Mick Taylor contributed 89 as the visitors faltered. From an overnight 5 for 334, Davison (73) and Faulkner (78 not out) took the score to 481 half an hour after lunch on the second day. Only the greatly underrated leg-spinner Trevor Hohns with 5 for 115 from 40 overs caused any real concern to the batsmen.

At stumps Queensland were 5 for 200, of which Robbie Kerr had made 62. With Lillee and Faulkner unable to bowl, Davison had a problem. So on the third morning, disguising the injuries, Davison bowled his 'inexperienced' attack as a seeming gesture to make a game of the situation. Border responded by declaring at lunch at 5 for 363, so forfeiting two precious points for first-innings lead.

Glenn Trimble 138 and Ian Healey 58 both remained unbeaten, having added 163 in two hours. Davison then let his batsmen take over. David Boon made his second century of the match – 143 with a six and 23 fours to become only the third Tasmanian to achieve the feat.

Tasmania's 7 for 264 at stumps became 8 for 290 when a declaration came. Queensland now had to win the match. Attack or die: 409 runs from 89 overs in around 345 minutes.

With the two paceman out, Davison pulled the rabbit

from the hat. He opened the bowling himself, so nearly claiming both openers and recording acceptable figures of 9-3-18-0.

At 1 for 221 Queensland looked a good bet. Youngster Claye Young had opened with Davison, bowling badly and getting thrashed for 56 runs from his first two (yes, two!) overs, which contained 12 no-balls and a wide.

At lunch Dennis Lillee sat with Young and refused to let anyone else near them. Davison said later: 'He was bowling the biggest load of poop I've ever seen.'

The Lillee magic worked, for after the break Young bowled with confidence, taking six wickets as Tasmania recorded the shock win of the season by 94 runs. It was their first win since defeating New South Wales in Sydney in 1983–4.

In Sydney, Western Australia had New South Wales well under control after the first day. It was a struggle for Greg Dyer's boys as the four-pronged visiting pace attack sent down the required 96 overs without even conceding a no-ball, a rare occurrence in these times.

Mark Waugh (95) and Mark O'Neill (68) held out for a time as their side made 295.

The cocky Westerners then came down to earth with a bump as five New South Wales bowlers shared the spoils in gaining the Sydneysiders a completely unexpected 119-run lead.

A rushed third-day score of 8 for 213 declared left Western Australia to get 333 for victory on a very dodgy pitch. By stumps they were 2 for 18 and very lucky not to have lost more batsmen. Only a fighting 82 by Geoff Marsh delayed the inevitable on the final day, as Western Australia made 201 to lose by 131 runs.

In Adelaide 17 wickets fell on the first day on, unusually, an underprepared pitch. Curator Les Burdett explained that he had only two days for preparation since the finish of the Tasmania match, but the track would quickly right itself – as happened.

Dean Jones won the toss for Victoria and saw his team fall to Peter Gladigau's career-best bowling of 7 for 85. Only Jamie Siddons' fighting 58 made the 178 total more respectable.

South Australia then fell into a heap being dismissed early on the second day for 161, a disaster made worse by off-spinner Tim May fracturing a knuckle when batting.

Having got the two points for first-innings lead, Victoria stumbled to be 2 for 43. Then, in front of his family, who had travelled from the citrus-growing area of Robinvale in Northern Victoria, Jamie Siddons showed off his talents.

His unbeaten 241 was a classic. The footwork was perfection, the strokes had a classical grace to them, and his pivoting on the right leg made one purr in delight.

He shared in partnerships of 172 with Dean Jones (101 from 177 balls with a six and 9 fours), 104 with Warren Whiteside (25) and finally an unbeaten 102 with Michael Dimattina (43 not out). Siddons' innings took 424 minutes and came from 329 balls with a six and 31 fours. It was nearly perfection.

Jones declared at 5 for 455, leaving South Australia 512 minutes to score 473 to win or to hold out for a draw. To the surprise of many, the home side batted on and on, finishing with a most credible 6 for 385 and a deserved

draw. After a first-innings duck, Peter Sleep remained unbeaten on 104, his 11th first-class century.

So with one round to go, it was still tied at the top of the table. What would happen in the event of both teams finishing exactly equal? The answer was a confusing formula of wickets taken to runs scored: and the difference between Western Australia and Queensland? Just 0.008 or, in layman' terms, about 20 runs. It just could not be tighter.

Graeme Wood had an unforeseen advantage on 2 March. The matches in Sydney and Melbourne would start at 11 a.m. as normal. But Perth was three hours (in summertime) behind the eastern cities so Wood would have a breakdown of what Queensland were doing in Melbourne.

However, in Sydney the day was hot; David Boon continued on with his largely successful season scoring 93; Mick Taylor's revival continued with 81 and 'Davo' himself enjoyed an unbeaten 47 as Tasmania hit 6 for 276 – which eventually reached 327. For New South Wales, Mike Whitney (5 for 54) and Steve Waugh (5 for 50) shared the honours.

Then the two Marks struck again. Mark Taylor created his innings of 144 in 334 minutes, while Mark Waugh dashed to 116 in under half that time, their 142-run fourth-wicket stand taking just 113 minutes was delightful.

When it was too difficult to stem the tide, Davison juggled his inexperienced bowling attack, but to no avail as New South Wales reached 460. When David Boon fell for 4 (making him 1,287 runs for the season), bowler Greg Matthews danced a perfect Irish jig. A later explanation revealed it was his 100th Shield wicket.

When asked earlier in the season how he would have captained and coped with Matthews' on-field antics, the Greatest Living Australian had replied: 'I'd just have a quiet word in his ear.'

Tasmania on the final day fell to be dismissed for 204. The affable Mick Taylor made 86 to take him to 1,003 runs for a most successful return to domestic Australian cricket. Without too much effort New South Wales reached 2 for 72 and third spot on the Shield table.

In Melbourne, Allan Border won the toss and sent Victoria in to bat on a blazing hot day. Whatmore and Watts started with 52 in 56 minutes before Watts fell for 17 caught behind. As others fell around him, Davenell Whatmore made an attacking 85, and Jamie Siddons (9) just scraped past the 1,000 runs for the season mark.

But the controversial part of the day was the start of a bad month for Ian Botham. Umpires Robin Bailhache and Darrell Holt reported him for swearing, and Victorian Cricket Association executive director Ken Jacobs laid a charge of 'conduct detrimental to the game and crude and/or abusive language'.

Botham was later fined the maximum of $500 (£195) and warned by the Australian Cricket Board as to his future conduct.

Meanwhile, Victoria had been dismissed for 256, Dirk Tazelaar 5 for 55 from 31 good overs. Queensland's reply was to bat very cautiously to try and gain the all-important first-innings lead.

Bad news from Perth did nothing to spur them on and,

like on so many other occasions in recent years, Queensland fell at the final hurdle. They made 209 with Merv Hughes 4 for 43 and Paul Reiffel 4 for 80 bowling the bulk of the overs.

Victoria then went out to enjoy themselves.

Gary Watts scored yet another century, 116 off 264 balls with 11 fours, sharing partnerships of 66 with Whatmore (30) and 136 with Siddons (76).

Botham, having been hit in the pocket, was having treatment in the dressing room after pulling a number of back muscles, which left the Queensland bowling attack looking rather bare.

However, it was John Maguire (5 for 89) on the last morning who wrapped up Victoria for 328 with his off-cutters. Needing 376 to win Queensland inexplicably crumpled. Only a second-wicket stand of 73 between Greg Ritchie (48) and Trevor Barsby (47) was of any consequence as Victoria finished the season with a 207-run victory.

The 30th and final minor round match of the competition, in Perth, saw South Australia fall to pieces in the first three hours of play. Sent in on a seaming wicket, South Australia made 138 as the home pace attack ran riot, Bruce Reid taking 5 for 34 on his come-back after injury.

Western Australia did little better initially, being 5 for 37 then 6 for 88. But in an amazing turn-around the final four wickets put on 346!

The records fell as the partnerships grew. Captain Graeme Wood shared a seventh-wicket stand of 96 with Chris Matthews (64); a record eighth wicket of 160 in 145 minutes with Ken MacLeay (67) beating the 108 made by Rod Marsh and Les Varis against Queensland in 1972–3; 46 in 35 minutes with Terry Alderman (17) for the ninth; and 44 in 18 minutes with Reid (25) for the tenth. Western Australia reached 434, but the star was Graeme Wood, who recorded his 27th first-class century, his career-best score of 186 not out, and exhibited an innings of delightful drives, hooks and pulls in facing 318 deliveries of which 27 went to the boundary.

Wood also sent his Shield run tally to 5,257, having passed Rod Marsh (4,412) and Barry Shepherd (4,934) during the season, but still a fair way behind John Inverarity's Western Australian record of 6,888.

The South Australian side looked dejected. With Hookes' leadership just about at its end, the young team knew they were fighting a losing battle. On the third day Bishop (55) and Hilditch (59) put on 114 for the first wicket; Hookes (65), Phillips (59) and Pyke (41) all tried, but the visitors could only make 331.

Needing just 36 runs to win on the final morning, Western Australia had a scare when they lost three wickets for just 10 runs under an overcast sky, but they succeeded in recording an easy seven-wicket win.

The Shield final has already been described.

Looking at the season overall, there were far more pluses than minuses for the healthy future of Australian cricket.

The minuses mainly revolved around players aged 30 and over whose behaviour left a bad taste in the mouth.

The tail-end of Ian Chappell's 'Ugly Australians' still exists with some shocking acts of wanton vandalism occurring when certain teams were away from home.

Western Australia deserved to win the Shield. They might have lacked the glamour of Queensland but, once again, their long-standing youth policy paid off, with James Brayshaw, Alan Mullally and Peter Capes being the three youngsters to show the greatest promise. Chris Matthews took 57 wickets for the season at 22.40, with four Western Australian bowlers in the top ten averages.

Queensland were the team to watch for the early part of the season, especially when captained by Robbie Kerr. With Allan Border's enforced absence on national duty in a truncated season, Kerr scored 793 runs at 39.65 and led from the front. The return of bowlers Rackemann, Maguire and Hohns from the South African tours added to Queensland's power. But it was Ian Botham they flocked to see with home attendances nearly triple those of 1986–7.

How New South Wales claimed third spot is a mystery known only to them. Behind-the-scenes problems saw three captains used during the season: new skipper Greg Dyer, who took over on Dirk Wellham's sudden retirement at the beginning of the season, Murray Bennett and Geoff Lawson. Even coach Len Pascoe was requested to withdraw his mid-season resignation, which was then accepted three months later.

Blowing hot and cold all season, the players to emerge with dignity were batsmen Mark Waugh, rookie Steve Hookey – a most exciting young player, and Mark Taylor.

Fourth place for Victoria was a little unjust for they are beginning to emerge once again as a powerful unit. Wisely coached by Ian Redpath, the undoubted star is batsman Jamie Siddons, whose unbeaten 241 at Adelaide was the season's highest. Peter Young (average 60.33), Gary Watts (56.30) and veteran Davenell Whatmore (50.67) led the way. The bowling attack has not yet got the penetration Redpath is after, although off-spinner Paul Jackson did claim 26 victims.

South Australia has a problem. The team built up over the past two seasons would give most County Championship sides a very good run for their money. However, the erratic and uncommunicative captaincy of David Hookes will assure South Australia of a permanent fifth position until the selectors take the bit between their teeth.

The young player to impress most in 1987–8 was opening bowler Peter Gladigau. His 38 wickets for the year at 29.05 also saw a career-best return of 7 for 85 against Victoria.

Tasmania had a fairly poor season all told. It was an awful one until D.K. Lillee arrived to help, but then a few things started to go right. David Boon and Mick Taylor starred with the bat, and next season's captain Peter Faulkner bowled extremely well considering the situation.

To finish the season, Australia's youngsters won the Youth World Cup. The successes of the team were Williams, Berry, Scuderi, Parker, Law and Holdworth. Remember the names, for they are Australia's stars of the future.

Calm and Confusion

The season in New Zealand.
Shell Cup. Shell Trophy.
New Zealand *v.* England Test series
and One-Day Internationals.
Form charts.
First-class averages.
Review of the season by Don Cameron.

Pukekura Park, New Plymouth. Shell XI v. England XI.
(Simon Bruty/Allsport)

New Zealand's disappointing showing in the World Cup was not totally unexpected. The withdrawal of Hadlee added to the problems created by the retirement of Coney, Reid and Edgar, to whom Wellington granted a benefit in 1987–8, from international cricket. Enthusiasm remained undiminished, however, as New Zealand faced a period of reconstruction and looked to players like Franklin, Rutherford, Blain, Morrison and Watson to reach their full and exciting potential at international level. Stephen Boock's announcement that he was retiring from Test cricket came as a shock although he was later persuaded to change his mind and played against England.

The emphasis placed upon young and emerging players by Northern Districts and other associations augured well for the future. Northern granted a benefit match to Geoff Howarth in recognition of his services, and they accomplished the pre-season scoop when they signed Graeme Hick, the most exciting young batting talent in the world. Not to be outdone, Canterbury signed Michael Holding and had Lancashire's Dexter Fitton in reserve. Another English county player coaching in New Zealand during the season was Steve Rhodes.

Deprived of the services of Martin Crowe, who was with the national side in Australia and who had led them to such glories in 1987, Central Districts surprised many people by naming second-team skipper Ian Snook as captain for 1987–8. Snook had captained Central in the mid-seventies, but he had not played first-class cricket for six years and was 37 years old. Ian Smith left Central for Auckland and, restored to fitness, kept wicket for the New Zealand XI which beat Auckland by 97 runs in a warm-up match shortly before the side left for India and Pakistan.

The New Zealand season was once more logically organized, beginning with the Trans-Tasman one-day matches and Shell Cup and culminating with the Test series against England.

Continental Airlines One-Day Series

6 November 1987

at Western Springs

Victoria 113 for 9
Auckland 116 for 8

Auckland won by 2 wickets

8 November 1987

At Eden Park, Auckland

Auckland 203 for 8 (P.A. Horne 62)
Victoria 143 for 7

Auckland won by 60 runs

Vaughan Brown, who had moved from Canterbury because of business commitments, took the honours in the first game with two wickets and 28 not out, but only 500 people watched the day/night match.

The second match also provided scant entertainment, particularly as Snedden and Watson destroyed any hope of a serious challenge from Victoria with miserly opening spells.

Shell Cup

26 December 1987

at Eden Park, Auckland

Northern Districts 189 (B.A. Young 90, R. de Groen 4 for 16)
Auckland 150 (R.B. Reid 60, B.L. Cairns 4 for 35)

Northern Districts (2 pts) won by 39 runs

at Basin Reserve, Wellington

Wellington 222 for 6 (R.H. Vance 57, G.P. Burnett 56)
Central Districts 207 for 8 (R.J. Harden 58)

Wellington (2 pts) won by 15 runs

at Carisbrook, Dunedin

Otago 179 for 9
Canterbury 154 (P.W. Hills 4 for 23)

Otago (2 pts) won by 25 runs

Northern lost their first three batsmen, White, Crocker and Hick, for ducks and were 9 for 4. Newcomer Richard de Groen was the star for Auckland, but Brian Young, Man of the Match, and Chris Kuggeleijn added 95 for the sixth wicket. Lance Cairns, returning for the one-day tournament, dismissed the aggressive Richard Reid and the Auckland middle order collapsed to leave Northern surprisingly easy winners.

Richard Harden of Somerset. Harden did particularly well for Central Districts in the Shell Cup and was one of several English professionals working and playing in New Zealand. (George Herringshaw)

Robert Vance took the individual honours at Wellington, where he shared an opening stand of 106 with Bruce Edgar. Graham Burnett also batted well on his début, and, in spite of a good effort from Somerset's Richard Harden, Central were never in touch.

Recalled left-arm pace bowler Peter Hills gave Otago a surprise victory over Canterbury and took the individual award.

28 December 1987

at Blake Park, Tauranga

Central Districts 194 for 7 (I.R. Snook 52)
Northern Districts 76

Central Districts (2 pts) won by 118 runs

At Basin Reserve, Wellington

Canterbury 195 (P.E. McEwan 106)
Wellington 199 for 4 (B.A. Edgar 99 not out, G. R. Larsen 66)

Wellington (2 pts) won by 6 wickets

at Molyneux Park, Alexandra

Auckland 143 (P.W. Hills 4 for 26)
Otago 144 for 6 (B.R. Blair 56)

Otago (2 pts) won by 4 wickets

A reversal of first-round form saw Central overwhelm Northern, whose batting again collapsed. Gary Robertson's 37 and 3 for 21 gave him the individual award.

Paul McEwan hit a record one-day 106 for Canterbury, but surrendered the individual honours to Bruce Edgar, who shared a fourth-wicket stand of 142 with Gavin Larsen, a stand which was only two runs short of a record for any wicket in New Zealand one-day cricket.

With Hills again bowling well and Bruce Blair, Man of the Match, hitting fiercely, Otago completed their second win to level with Wellington. Neil Mallender's 3 for 9 in eight overs was a vital contribution to Otago's success.

30 December 1987

at Blake Park, Tauranga

Northern Districts 167 (B.L. Cairns 52)
Wellington 126 for 9

Northern Districts (2 pts) won by 41 runs

at Memorial Park, Motueka

Central Districts 198 for 9 (R.J. Harden 81, T.J. Wilson 4 for 39)
Otago 146

Central Districts (2 pts) won by 52 runs

at Lancaster Park, Canterbury

Auckland 119 (A.J. Hintz 4 for 24)
Canterbury 120 for 0 (D.A. Dempsey 85 not out)

Canterbury (2 pts) won by 10 wickets

Defeats for both Wellington and Otago left the competition with four teams level on points at the end of the third round and only Auckland out of contention. With Northern at 67 for 5, Lance Cairns hit Australian leg-spinner Bob Holland for 3 sixes in four balls and took his side to

Lance Cairns, retired from first-class cricket, but outstanding for Northern Districts with both bat and ball in the Shell Cup. (Adrian Murrell/Allsport)

167. He then took 2 for 14 in 10 overs to suggest that he might well have been of value in the World Cup had he been persuaded out of retirement.

Richard Harden's fine innings took the individual honours at Motueka while skipper Dave Dempsey and fellow opener David Boyle took Canterbury to victory with 17.1 of their allotted 50 overs unused.

1 January 1988

at Eden Park, Auckland

Central Districts 206 for 9 (A.T.R. Hellaby 5 for 38)
Auckland 207 for 6 (R.B. Reid 63)

Auckland (2 pts) won by 4 wickets

at Basin Reserve, Wellington

Otago 177 for 5 (S.J. McCullum 54, B.R. Blair 51 not out)
Wellington 173 for 8

Otago (2 pts) won by 2 wickets

at Dudley Park, Rangiora

Northern Districts 265 for 6 (G.A. Hick 100, B.L. Cairns 54)
Canterbury 200 (D.A. Dempsey 62)

Northern Districts (2 pts) won by 65 runs

The results of the fourth round of matches meant that the Shell Cup would be won by whoever was victorious in the final game at Molyneux Park. Central's chances evaporated when Richard Reid, cut on the cheek while fielding, began at a roaring pace and dominated a first-wicket stand of 79. Skipper Bill Fowler maintained the momentum with an innings of 49, and Steve Brown and Hellaby saw Auckland to victory with two overs to spare.

Wellington badly miscalculated against Otago, and, in spite of Edgar and McSweeney both getting into the forties and batting impressively, the home side never achieved the scoring rate required. Neil Mallender, who bowled his ten overs for 17 runs and the wickets of Vance and McSweeney took the individual award.

Hick's century and fifty off 26 balls from Lance Cairns took Northern to a total which Canterbury never looked likely to approach.

3 January 1988

at Eden Park, Auckland

Wellington 154 for 8
Auckland 158 for 4 (M.R. Pringle 50)

Auckland (2 pts) won by 6 wickets

at Pukekura Park, New Plymouth

Canterbury 223 for 7
Central Districts 185 (M.J. Greatbatch 67)

Canterbury (2 pts) won by 38 runs

at Molyneux Park, Alexandra

Northern Districts 183
Otago 185 for 8

Otago (2 pts) won by 2 wickets

Martin Pringle took the Man of the Match award at Eden Park and lost his place in the Shell Trophy side later the same day, while Michael Holding's economy earned the individual honour at Pukekura Park. The main interest centred on Alexandra, however, where Northern began well, but lost their way in the middle order when Derek Walker sent back Kuggeleijn, Cairns and Young, top scorer with 31. Steve Boock also made a vital contribution, bowling Hick for 18, and with Beard and Treiber both run out, Northern were all out on the second ball of the last over.

Otago started badly and were 66 for 6 when Walker was joined by Warren Lees. They added 55, and Lees and Mallender then put on 51. Cairns accounted for both Walker and Lees, 38 and 35 respectively, and when Hick began the last over Otago still needed 11 to win. Some powerful hitting and fierce running reduced the target to three off two balls, but John Wilson hit Hick's fifth

delivery straight for four to win the Shell Cup for Otago. Mallender finished on 30 not out.

Bruce Edgar with 220 runs was the leading run-getter in the competition, while Lance Cairns' 14 wickets placed him head of the bowlers. Both men have retired from international cricket. Tony Blain scored 105 runs for once out in three innings before he left with the New Zealand party for Australia.

Shell Trophy

5, 6 and 7 January 1988

at Seddon Park, Hamilton

Wellington 325 for 6 dec (T.D. Ritchie 102, R.H. Vance 85) and 193 for 3 dec (R.H. Vance 117 not out)
Northern Districts 217 (B.A. Young 69 not out, C.M. Kuggeleijn 60, D.J. White 58) and 302 for 5 (L.M. Crocker 99, G.E. Bradburn 58, G.A. Hick 64)

Northern Districts won by 5 wickets
Northern Districts 12 pts, Wellington 4 pts

at Pukekura Park, New Plymouth

Central Districts 266 for 8 dec (M.J. Greatbatch 93, S.W. Duff 70 not out, T.J. Wilson 5 for 82) and 283 for 6 dec (R.J. Harden 82, C.J. Smith 71, M.J. Greatbatch 53, T.J. Wilson 4 for 93)
Otago 240 (K.W. Martin 4 for 60) and 310 for 4 (K. Ibadulla 107, K.J. Burns 72)

Otago won by 6 wickets
Otago 12 pts, Central Districts 4 pts

Shell Cup – Final Table

	P	W	L	Pts
Otago	5	4	1	8
Northern Districts	5	3	2	6
Central Districts	5	2	3	4
Wellington	5	2	3	4
Auckland	5	2	3	4
Canterbury	5	2	3	4
(Placings decided on runs/wickets differential when points are level.)				

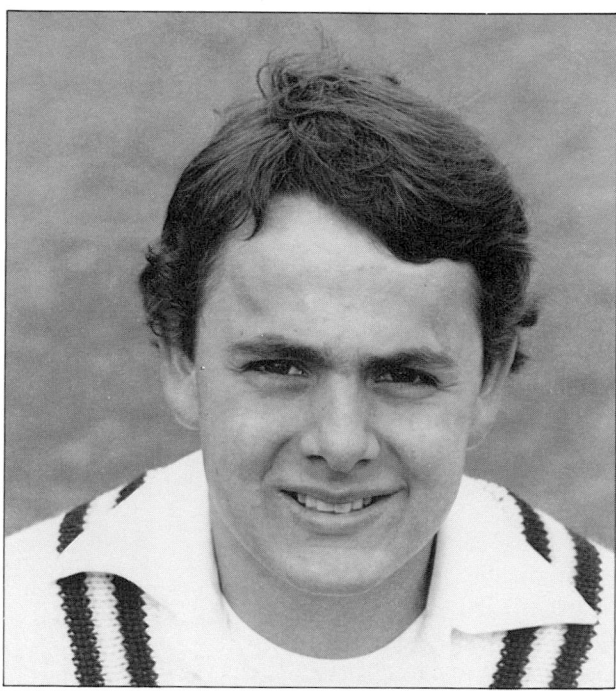

Robert Vance hit the two highest scores of his career and played with such consistency for Wellington that he won his first Test cap later in the season. (David Munden)

Trevor Franklin, courage and determination. Four centuries in the Shell Trophy won him back a Test place. (David Munden)

at Lancaster Park, Christchurch

Canterbury 309 for 8 dec (R.T. Latham 101, D.J. Boyle 56) and 34 for 1
Auckland 102 (M.A. Holding 5 for 29) and 240 (T.J. Franklin 106, W.P. Fowler 55)

Canterbury won by 9 wickets
Canterbury 16 pts, Auckland 0 pts

The New Zealand first-class competition opened with results in all three matches. The power of Graeme Hick was soon apparent as Northern Districts, trailing by 108 on the first innings, won a fine victory on the last afternoon. Bruce Edgar and Robert Vance began the match with a stand of 130, and Tim Ritchie hit his second first-class hundred to take Wellington to a formidable total. Northern slumped to 14 for 4 and were only saved from indignity by their middle order. Robert Vance reached the highest score of his career and set the home side to make 302. Lindsay Crocker and Grant Bradburn set them on the way with a stand of 111, and Hick and Crocker added 117 to make the task surprisingly easy.

The game at New Plymouth followed a similar pattern as Kassem Ibadulla and Kevin Burns put on 144 for the second wicket to prepare the way for Otago's win on the last day. Ibadulla reached a maiden first-class century.

The match at Lancaster Park was always in favour of the home side. Rod Latham received solid support as Canterbury passed the 300 mark, and Auckland were blasted out by Michael Holding. They fared better in their second innings, when Trevor Franklin batted with patience and

great courage. It was Franklin's first first-class match since his horrendous accident at Gatwick Airport sixteen months earlier, and his innings was widely welcomed as a sign of his complete rehabilitation.

9, 10 and 11 January 1988

at Basin Reserve, Wellington

Wellington 293 for 7 dec (B.A. Edgar 92, E.B. McSweeney 72, E.J. Gray 66) and 219 for 0 dec (R.H. Vance 107 not out, B.A. Edgar 103 not out)
Central Districts 237 for 9 dec (S.W. Duff 50, R.G. Holland 4 for 53) and 195 for 7 (S.J. Gill 53, R.G. Holland 4 for 84)

Match drawn
Wellington 4 pts, Central Districts 0 pts

at Lancaster Park, Christchurch

Northern Districts 229 (C.M. Kuggeleijn 87, B.G. Cooper 50) and 276 for 2 dec (G.A. Hick 113 not out, L.M. Crocker 66, G.E. Bradburn 52)
Canterbury 254 for 8 dec (J.G. Boyle 50) and 129 (B.J. Barrett 4 for 56)

Northern Districts won by 122 runs
Northern Districts 12 pts, Canterbury 4 pts

at Carisbrook, Dunedin

Auckland 286 (T.J. Franklin 120, S. Brown 69, S.L. Boock 4 for 85) and 137 (S.L. Boock 4 for 31, T.J. Wilson 4 for 48)
Otago 288 for 7 dec (R.N. Hoskin 101, W.K. Lees 53 not out) and 136 for 6 (W. Watson 4 for 49)

Otago won by 4 wickets
Otago 16 pts, Auckland 0 pts

Once again Northern Districts came from behind to win,

Kassem Ibadulla, a maiden first-class hundred, Otago v. Central Districts, 7 January. (Mike Powell/Allsport)

Auckland 1988
First-Class Matches

BATTING

BATTING	v. Canterbury (Canterbury) 5–7 January	v. Otago (Dunedin) 9–11 January	v. Wellington (Auckland) 13–15 January	v. Canterbury (Auckland) 25–7 January	v. Central Districts (Auckland) 29–31 January	v. Northern Districts (Auckland) 2–4 February	v. Wellington (Wellington) 6–8 February	v. Northern Districts (Hamilton) 10–12 February	M	Inns	NOs	Runs	HS	Av
R.B. Reid	4 22		87 6						2	4	—	119	87	29.75
T.J. Franklin	2	106 120	14 17	13 1	116 0	100	—	50	7	13	—	539	120	41.46
A.J. Hunt	0 5	6 5							3	6	—	28	6	4.66
M.J. Bradley			6* 0*	37* 11*					3	4	4	54	37*	
V.R. Brown	8 0	22 33	60 —						3	5	—	123	60	24.60
W.P. Fowler	15 55	15 43	2 0	56 29	30 2	9	—	29*	8	12	1	285	56	25.90
S.W. Brown	1 4	69 11	0 61	16 5	40 19*		7	—	7	11	1	233	69	23.30
A.T.R. Hellaby	36* 5	32 6							2	4	1	79	36*	26.33
P.J. Kelly	5 1	0 9	32* 27	11 11	10*	3		— —	7	10	2	109	32*	13.62
W. Watson	0 1	3 5	13* 12			1		—	5	7	1	35	13*	5.83
R.P. de Groen	3 11*	0 3	—	3*	0 25*			— —	5	7	3	45	25*	11.25
M. Bradley	6 13	2 0	0 0						3	6	—	21	13	3.50
M.R. Pringle			14 76	26 77	13	14		51*	6	7	1	271	77	45.16
P. Neutze			—	0					1	1	—	0	0	0.00
I.D. Fisher			14 9	0 0				—	3	4	—	23	14	5.75
P.A. Horne				30 14	31 43	66		61	4	6	—	245	66	40.83
D.K. Morrison				18 2	—	0*	— —		4	3	1	20	18	10.00
J.J. Crowe				125	0* 0				3	3	1	125	125	62.50
J.G. Bracewell				104		59			2	2	—	163	104	81.50
M.C. Snedden				16*		4	— —		3	2	1	20	16*	20.00
D.N. Patel					93			44	3	2	—	137	93	68.50
P.J. Hounsell							— — —		2					
I.D.S. Smith							— —		1					
J.F. Reid								112 —	1	1	—	112	112	112.00
S.R. Gillespie									1					

Extras / Match totals	v. Canterbury (Canterbury)	v. Otago	v. Wellington (Auckland)	v. Canterbury (Auckland)	v. Central Districts	v. Northern Districts (Auckland)	v. Wellington (Wellington)	v. Northern Districts (Hamilton)
Byes	4 4	9	4	4 9	1	4		4
Leg-byes	7 6	3	6 9	3 14	13 6	14		3
Wides	5	1	1		5			
No-balls	6 6	1 1	8 4	5	17 4	5		2
Total	102 240	286 137	253 224	204 329	400 174	322		313
Wickets	10 10	10 10	8 10	10 9	7 3	10		4
Result	L	L	D	W	W	W	Ab.	Ab.
Points	0	0	4	12	16	16		2

Fielding Figures
20 – P.J. Kelly (ct 18/st 2)
7 – S.W. Brown
5 – D.K. Morrison and J.J. Crowe
4 – J.G. Bracewell, W.P. Fowler and A.J. Hunt
3 – I.D. Fisher, M.R. Pringle, M. Bradley, S.R. Gillespie and P.J. Hounsell (as sub)
2 – V.R. Brown, M.J. Bradley, P.A. Horne, M.C. Snedden, W. Watson and T.J. Franklin
1 – A.T.R. Hellaby, R.P. de Groen, P. Neutze and R.B. Reid

BOWLING

BOWLING	W. Watson	R.P. de Groen	S.W. Brown	A.T.R. Hellaby	V.R. Brown	M.J. Bradley	P.S. Neutze	I.D. Fisher
v. Canterbury (Auckland) 5–7 January	38–10–86–3 4–0–24–1	33.1–9–82–1 4–0–9–0	20–4–56–2	15–4–33–1	20–6–37–1			
v. Otago (Dunedin) 9–11 January	28–8–60–0 20–7–49–4	22–3–83–3 15.1–3–51–2	12–3–58–2 2–0–11–0	4–0–28–0	9–0–20–1 8–2–19–0	11–1–25–1		
v. Wellington (Auckland) 13–15 January	22–7–55–2 11–5–23–1	18.1–3–71–4 10–3–27–2					8–3–20–0 20–0–75–0	27–6–58–3 14–2–37–4
v. Canterbury (Auckland) 25–7 January		16–2–72–1 7–2–17–1				8–0–38–0 9–2–40–2		17.2–3–56–2 5–0–15–1
v. Central Districts (Auckland) 29–31 January	19.2–6–55–6 10–0–47–1		8–4–14–0 4–1–19–0					
v. Northern Districts (Auckland) 2–4 February	12–4–14–4 10–0–40–0							
v. Wellington (Wellington) 6–8 February		14–2–57–0	19–8–34–0					
v. Northern Districts (Hamilton) 10–12 February			18–4–55–1			11–2–36–0		29–7–92–1
	174.2–47–453–22 av. 20.59	139.3–27–469–14 av. 33.50	83–24–247–5 av. 49.40	19–4–61–1 av. 61.00	37–8–76–2 av. 36.00	39–5–139–3 av. 46.33	28–3–95–0 av. —	92.2–18–258–11 av. 23.45

and once again they owed much to Graeme Hick. Skipper Chris Kuggeleijn resuscitated the Northern first innings, but the first two days of the match were generally lack-lustre, and a draw looked inevitable when the last day began with Northern on 35 for 0. Bradburn and Crocker extended their opening stand to 113 the next morning, and then came Hick with an explosive hundred in 78 minutes off 94 balls. Left to make 252 in 62 overs, Canterbury began promisingly enough, but Barrett, Kuggeleijn and Ward bowled well to bundle out the home side in under 40 overs annd take Northern to their second successive victory.

There was also a second victory for Otago, who were well served by Richard Hoskin and Warren Lees in batting, and by Stephen Boock in bowling. There was also some more impressive bowling from medium pacer Tim Wilson. Auckland began well enough with a stand of 146 between Steve Brown and Trevor Franklin, who gave further delight with his second century in succession, but thereafter the game moved steadily in favour of Otago. Watson and de Groen made the home side fight hard for victory on the last afternoon.

Wellington dominated the game at Basin Reserve, but they had to be content with excellent individual performances rather than a team victory. Edgar continued to celebrate his benefit year with two excellent innings, and he and Vance shared an unbeaten first-wicket stand of 219, Vance reaching his second hundred in the Trophy for the season. Ervin McSweeney had six dismissals behind the stumps.

Former Australian Test leg-break bowler Bob Holland performed splendidly for Wellington. (Adrian Murrell/Allsport)

13, 14 and 15 January 1988

at Eden Park No 2, Auckland

Auckland 253 for 8 dec (R.B. Reid 87, V.R. Brown 60, J.P. Millmow 4 for 63) and 224 (M.R. Pringle 76, S. Brown 61, R.G. Holland 7 for 69)
Wellington 225 (R.H. Vance 98, R. de Groen 4 for 71) and 217 for 8 (E.J. Gray 62, I.D. Fisher 4 for 37)

Match drawn
Auckland 4 pts, Wellington 0 pts

at Horton Park, Blenheim

Central Districts 294 for 3 dec (C.J. Smith 122, D.J. Guthardt 82 not out) and 246 for 8 dec (M.J. Greatbatch 149)

W.P. Fowler	D.K. Morrison	A.J. Hunt	M.C. Snedden	J.G. Bracewell	D.N. Patel	S.R. Gillespie	Byes	Leg-byes	Wides	No-balls	Total	Wkts
							1	14			309	8
							1				34	1
							2	12	1		288	7
							5	1	1	2	136	6
7–1–19–1								2			225	10
7–0–49–1								6		1	217	8
26–9–54–3	29–7–84–3	4–0–16–0					7	9	1	5	336	10
18.2–6–41–6	3–1–17–0							7			137	10
12–4–21–1	16–6–59–0		29–8–65–0	33–10–52–2				3	1	1	269	10
12–3–34–2	12.4–0–27–1		14–4–34–2		24–8–73–3		4	9			247	10
	4–2–15–1		16–6–31–5					4			64	10
8.5–2–26–1	13–2–44–2		21–5–42–4	18–6–64–3			8	9		13	233	10
8–3–15–0	3–1–5–0		21–9–30–0			16–3–34–1		6		5	181	1
33–8–105–1					20.3–4–59–2	24–6–81–1		4		11	432	6
132.1–36–	80.4–19	4–0–	101–32–	75–24–	36.3–7–	24–6–						
364–16	251–7	16–0	202–12	189–8	93–3	81–1						
av. 22.75	av. 35.85	—	av. 16.83	av. 23.62	av. 31.00	av. 81.00						

Canterbury 1988
First-Class Matches

BATTING

BATTING	v. Auckland (Canterbury) 5–7 Jan	v. Northern Districts (Christchurch) 9–11 Jan	v. Central Districts (Blenheim) 13–15 Jan	v. Otago (Christchurch) 17–19 Jan	v. Auckland (Auckland) 25–7 Jan	v. Wellington (Wellington) 29–31 Jan	v. Central Districts (Christchurch) 2–4 Feb	v. Otago (Dunedin) 6–8 Feb	M	Inns	NOs	Runs	HS	Av
J.G. Boyle	10	9* 50	15	11 0					3	6	1	95	50	19.00
D.A. Dempsey	22 19	11 35	39 12	16 38*	9 8	13 1	0 5	121 44	8	16	1	393	121	26.20
P.E. McEwan	35 5*	37 23	6 28	73 —	118 23	20 6	2 1	7 16	8	15	1	400	118	28.57
D.J. Boyle	56 —	29 23	11 31	0 —			27 1	60 17	6	10	—	255	60	25.50
R.T. Latham	101 —	16 4	98 29	17 —	5 23*	91 35	7 27	141* 14	8	14	2	608	141*	50.66
M.C. Bremner	15 —	35 4	20 17		0 3				4	7	—	94	35	13.42
M.W. Priest	7 —	2 16	20 9	50 —	13 1	2 8		7* 27*	7	12	2	162	50	16.20
L.K. Germon	37* —	22* 0	2* 20*	32* —	2 1	27 0	4 4	— 8*	8	13	6	159	37*	22.71
A.J. Hintz	11 —	0 2			62 0	0 1			4	7	—	76	62	10.85
M.A. Holding	— —	8* 0	0 4	0 —	1* 31	4* 0	0 14*		7	11	4	62	31	8.85
C.W.H. Lawrence	— —	— 0*	1 2	24 —	33 1	0 2	18* 14	— —	8	10	2	95	33	11.87
A.J. Nuttall			— 0						1	1	—	0	0	0.00
B.R. Hartland				0 13*	12 25		3 4	15 0	4	8	1	72	25	10.28
P.G. Kennedy				1 —	59 15	0 0			3	5	—	75	59	15.00
C.W. Flanagan				31 —			20 32	25 50	3	5	—	158	50	31.60
D.J. Hartshorn					0 2	38 14*	9 21	13 6	4	8	1	103	38	14.71
J.G. Wright								0 70	1	2	—	70	70	35.00
H. Richards									1					

	v. Auckland (C)	v. Northern Districts	v. Central Districts (Bln)	v. Otago (Ch)	v. Auckland (A)	v. Wellington	v. Central Districts (Ch)	v. Otago (Dun)
Byes	1 1	5 2	— 4	— 7	— 4	1 1	— 4	— —
Leg-byes	14 —	19 1	13 4	10 3	9 7	10 6	1 14	15 7
Wides		2 1		4 —	1 —	1 —		
No-balls		18 3	13 1	2 —	5 —	10 7	8 11	12 2
Total	309 34	254 129	234 157	264 54	336 137	220 84	100 218	420 191
Wickets	8 1	8 10	9 10	10 0	10 10	10 10	10 10	— 7
Result	W	L	L	D	L	L	L	D
Points	16	4	0	4	4	0	0	4

Fielding Figures
20 – L.K. Germon (ct 19/st 1)
9 – M.A. Holding
5 – R.T. Latham and B.R. Hartland
4 – M.W. Priest and C.W. Flanagan
3 – M.C. Bremner, D.J. Hartshorn and P.E. McEwan
2 – C.W.H. Lawrence
1 – D.A. Dempsey and D.J. Boyle

BOWLING

BOWLING	M.A. Holding	A.J. Hintz	C.W.H. Lawrence	M.W. Priest	D.A. Dempsey	R.T. Latham	D.J. Boyle	A.J. Nuttall
v. Auckland (Canterbury) 5–7 January	14.1–4–29–5	9–4–7–2	7–1–29–2	2.5–1–9–0	2.1–0–17–0			
	27–8–63–3	21–5–56–3	19–5–70–2	18–6–34–2		7–5–5–0	2–0–2–0	
v. Northern Districts (Christchurch) 9–11 January	27.1–10–36–2	22–6–51–3	23–7–50–3	21–6–63–1		9–1–20–0		
	15–4–36–0	0.2–0–1–0	11–0–46–0	18.4–3–66–2		18.3–0–93–0	7–2–28–0	
v. Central Districts (Blenheim) 13–15 January	22–9–37–0		17–2–66–0	40–10–95–3	40–0–20–0	3–0–16–0		22–8–44–0
	13–2–32–1		7–0–36–1	27–5–107–3				34–12–65–3
v. Otago (Christchurch) 17–19 January	35–19–52–7		22–6–59–0	18–7–27–0		6–2–8–0		
v. Auckland (Auckland) 25–7 January	23–9–33–2	5–0–17–0	11.5–2–33–3	16–4–62–2				
	32–6–77–6	8–2–18–0	18–5–40–1	36–10–85–2	3–2–3–0	1–0–4–0		
v. Wellington (Wellington) 29–31 January	25–10–59–1	11–1–52–0	18–4–56–1	16–6–21–3				
	4–2–6–0	4–1–22–0	5–1–22–1					
v. Central Districts (Christchurch) 2–4 February	8.3–2–11–0		16–4–43–4			14.3–1–41–2		
	13–5–17–2		17–3–64–0		3–0–13–0	6.5–0–27–0		
v. Otago (Dunedin) 6–8 February			14–1–36–2	19.5–3–63–5				
			7–0–34–0	27–7–100–5	9–1–26–0			
	258.5–90–488–29 av. 16.82	80.2–19–224–8 av. 28.00	212.5–41–684–20 av. 34.20	260.2–68–732–28 av. 26.14	21.1–3–79–0 —	65.5–9–214–2 av. 107.00	9–2–30–0 —	56–20–109–3 av. 36.33

Canterbury 234 for 9 dec (R.T. Latham 98) and 157

Central Districts won by 149 runs
Central Districts 16 pts, Canterbury 0 pts

at Molyneux Park, Alexandra

Northern Districts 118 (S.L. Boock 4 for 53) and 275 for 8 dec (G.A. Hick 90, D.J. White 68)
Otago 125 (K. Treiber 5 for 35) and 218 (D.J. Walker 54 not out, B.P. Ward 4 for 27, K. Treiber 4 for 60)

Northern Districts won by 50 runs
Northern Districts 12 pts, Otago 0 pts

Northern Districts won their third match in succession to lead the Shell Trophy, but once more they failed to collect first-innings points, a factor which was to prove decisive at the end of the season. On a treacherous pitch both sides struggled, but the second-innings aggression of White and Hick made it possible for Kuggeleijn to declare and leave Otago 82 overs in which to attempt to score 269. The left-arm pace of Treiber and the off-spin of Mark McKinnon, who had recently won a place in the side, proved too much for the home side. Hoskin, Walker and Lindsay offered stubborn resistance, but McKinnon bowled Boock with 5½ overs remaining to give his side a fine win.

Auckland gained their first points of the season in the drawn match against Wellington. Richard Reid hit a whirlwind 87, dominating an opening partnership of 91 with Franklin, who made 17. Vaughan Brown also batted well on the opening day before being withdrawn from the match to join the New Zealand side in Australia. He was replaced by Neutze, who bowled in both innings and batted in the second. Vance's rich vein of form continued, but he was caught and bowled two short of his hundred. Australian leg-spinner Bob Holland bowled magnificently in Auckland's second innings, and Wellington were left to make 253. The quick dismissal of Vance thwarted them, and they could never muster the four runs an over that were needed.

Career-best batting performances from Campbell

C.W. Flanagan	D.J. Hartshorn	H. Richards	Byes	Leg-byes	Wides	No-balls	Total	Wkts
			4	7	5	6	102	10
			4	6	1	6	240	10
			4	5	1	2	229	10
			2	4		6	276	2
			5	11		2	294	3
				6		1	246	8
20.2–6–51–3			5	19	2	3	221	10
	14–3–56–3			3			204	10
	27–5–79–0		9	14	5	5	329	9
	20–7–48–2		4	8	2	5	248	7
	2.5–0–7–0						57	1
13–3–35–1				8		5	138	9
9–2–35–0	3–0–19–0			7		1	182	2
7–2–17–0	29–8–119–2	14–2–44–0	5	8		3	292	10
9–2–27–2	15–2–55–2	6–0–21–0	1	7		3	271	9
58.2–15–	110.5–25–	20–2–						
165–6	383–9	65–0						
av. 27.50	*av. 42.55*	—						

Smith, Mark Greatbatch and new wicket-keeper Guthardt put Central Districts in total command over Canterbury.

17, 18 and 19 January 1988

at Albert Park, Te Awamutu

Central Districts 135 (B.J. Barrett 4 for 41) and 175 for 5 (S.P. Robertson 69)
Northern Districts 259 (B.A. Young 94, L.M. Crocker 65, T. McKenna 4 for 52)

Match drawn
Northern Districts 4 pts, Central Districts 0 pts

at Lancaster Park, Christchurch

Canterbury 264 (P.E. McEwan 73, M.W. Priest 50, N.A. Mallender 4 for 64) and 54 for 0
Otago 221 (D.J. Walker 77, M.A. Holding 7 for 52)

Match drawn
Canterbury 4 pts, Otago 0 pts

Rain ruined both Shell Trophy matches. There was no play on the last afternoon at Albert Park, where gale-force winds and rain swept the ground, with Northern Districts, thanks to Bryan Young's career-best 94, well poised for victory.

A last-wicket stand of 54 between Germon and Lawrence and magnificent bowling by Michael Holding gave Canterbury first-innings points at Christchurch, where there was no play at all on the last day.

18, 19 and 20 January 1988

at Basin Reserve, Wellington

Wellington 188 for 6 dec (G.P. Burnett 87 not out)
England XI 310 for 3 (B.C. Broad 100 retired hurt, M.W. Gatting 82, M.D. Moxon 62)

Match drawn

There was no play before lunch on the opening day and none at all on the second as England began their tour of New Zealand in unkind weather. In his third first-class innings, Graham Burnett batted securely for 330 minutes. A generous declaration allowed England batting practice on the last day. Broad and Moxon began with a stand of 171 in 198 minutes.

21 January 1988

at Basin Reserve, Wellington

Wellington 202 (G.P. Burnett 63, D.J. Capel 4 for 47)
England XI 203 for 2 (M.D. Moxon 59, C.W.J. Athey 50 not out)

England XI won by 8 wickets

A hastily arranged 50-over match which provided England with much-needed practice saw the visitors victorious with 25 balls to spare.

23, 24 and 25 January 1988

at Seddon Park, Hamilton

Northern Districts 242 for 4 dec (B.G. Cooper 116 not out, D.J. White 64) and 254 for 4 dec (G.A. Hick 146, D.J. White 80)

Central Districts 1988
First-Class Matches

BATTING

Match columns, left to right:
1. v. Otago (New Plymouth) 5–7 January
2. v. Wellington (Wellington) 9–11 January
3. v. Canterbury (Blenheim) 13–15 January
4. v. Northern Districts (Te Awamutu) 17–19 January
5. v. Wellington (Levin) 25–7 January
6. v. Auckland (Auckland) 29–31 January
7. v. Canterbury (Christchurch) 2–4 February
8. v. Northern Districts (Palmerston North) 6–8 February

	Otago (1)	Otago (2)	Wgtn (1)	Wgtn (2)	Cant‑B (1)	Cant‑B (2)	ND‑TA (1)	ND‑TA (2)	Levin (1)	Levin (2)	Auck (1)	Auck (2)	Cant‑C (1)	Cant‑C (2)	ND‑PN	M	Inns	NOs	Runs	HS	Av
C.J. Smith	31	71	42	15	122*	3	12	24	0	27	32	15	27	46*	63	8	15	2	530	122*	40.76
S.P. Robertson	13	16	31	13	36	1	8	69	30	40	36	7	1	9	94	8	15	—	404	94	26.93
M.J. Greatbatch	93	53	22	34	7	149	40	37	14	47	14	56	3	0		7	14	—	569	149	40.64
R.J. Harden	21	82	20	41	29	29	5	6	14	25	22	42	31	—	42	8	14	—	409	82	29.21
D.J. Guthardt	0	24	14	13	82*	16	21	0	12	18					3*	6	11	2	203	82*	22.55
S.W. Duff	70*	2	50	12*	—	7	15	29*	7	9			17*	—	20	7	11	4	238	70*	34.00
I.R. Snook	12	15*	8	—	0	1	0*	24	13	10	18				100*	7	11	3	201	100*	25.12
G.K. Robertson	2	7*	1	5	29	4	—	9	0*	44	15	6	—	—	—	8	11	2	122	44	13.55
D.A. Stirling	2	—							1		14	8	11	16		5	6	—	52	16	8.66
P.D. Unwin	3*	—	2*	—	5*											3	3	3	10	5*	—
K.W. Martin	—	—											0		—	3	1	—	0	0	0.00
S.J. Gill			22	53					15	8						2	4	—	98	53	24.50
G.R. Logan			0*	—	—	—	0	—			9*	0	0*	—	—	6	5	3	9	9*	4.50
T.M. McKenna					—	—	2*	—			14	4				3	3	1	20	14	10.00
G.W. Walton					5	—			0*	0	0	4*				3	5	2	9	5	3.00
T.E. Blain											75	62	10	—		2	3	—	147	75	49.00
M.D. Crowe													14	119*		1	2	1	133	119*	119.00
M.W. Douglas															5	1	1	—	5	5	5.00

Extras (in innings order):

- Byes: 4, 11, 5, 5, 4, 4, 4
- Leg‑byes: 7, 13, 5, 11, 6, 10, 5, 1, 6, 3, 9, 8, 7, 11
- Wides: 6, 2, 1, 1, 6
- No‑balls: 2, 9, 4, 2, 1, 10, 1, 3, 11, 1, 5, 1, 15

	Otago (1)	Otago (2)	Wgtn (1)	Wgtn (2)	Cant‑B (1)	Cant‑B (2)	ND‑TA (1)	ND‑TA (2)	Levin (1)	Levin (2)	Auck (1)	Auck (2)	Cant‑C (1)	Cant‑C (2)	ND‑PN
Total	266	283	237	195	294	246	135	175	131	222	269	247	138	182	359
Wickets	8	6	9	7	3	8	10	5	10	10	10	10	9	2	5

Results and points (per match):

Match	Result	Points
v. Otago	L	4
v. Wellington (Wgtn)	D	0
v. Canterbury (Blenheim)	W	16
v. Northern Districts (Te Awamutu)	D	0
v. Wellington (Levin)	L	0
v. Auckland	L	0
v. Canterbury (Christchurch)	W	16
v. Northern Districts (Palmerston N)	Ab.	2

Fielding Figures 16 – D.J. Guthardt (ct 14/st 2)
9 – C.J. Smith
5 – M.J. Greatbatch and T.E. Blain
4 – S.P. Robertson, G.K. Robertson and R.J. Harden
3 – K.W. Martin and I.R. Snook
2 – S.W. Duff, P.D. Unwin, G.R. Logan and D.A. Stirling

BOWLING

Match	G.K. Robertson	D.A. Stirling	K.W. Martin	R.J. Harden	P.D. Unwin	S.W. Duff	S.J. Gill	G.R. Logan
v. Otago (New Plymouth) 5–7 January	20.4–7–67–2 / 17–1–71–1	17–5–58–3 / 4–1–26–0	14–1–60–4 / 17–3–54–1	1–0–4–0	10–2–37–0	1–0–6–0 / 19–4–60–0		
v. Wellington (Wellington) 9–11 January	15–3–46–1 / 8–2–23–0			14–0–45–2	13–2–34–0 / 14–0–59–0	26–5–66–1 / 18–5–68–0	35–9–72–1 / 5–0–20–0	12.2–1–26–2 / 16–0–40–0
v. Canterbury (Blenheim) 13–15 January	20–3–55–1 / 15–4–37–3			5–0–22–0 / 5–2–7–2	4–0–20–0 / 12–2–27–1	17.3–0–25–3 / 22.2–10–30–3		22–8–63–2 / 11–1–26–0
v. Northern Districts (Te Awamutu) 17–19 January	25–10–38–1			3–1–11–0		5.3–1–24–1		25–10–67–1
v. Wellington (Levin) 25–7 January	28–6–86–3	21–1–101–0			2–0–17–0	11.2–1–45–1	19–1–80–0	
v. Auckland (Auckland) 29–31 January	22–4–86–2 / 15–3–41–1	15–3–66–1 / 11.3–2–44–0		1–0–18–0				25.2–8–77–1 / 10–1–43–2
v. Canterbury (Christchurch) 2–4 February	16–5–34–5 / 14–2–38–3	13–2–29–2 / 13–3–29–1	6–2–11–0 / 22–1–81–3			8–3–21–1		9–1–24–3 / 12.3–1–35–2
v. Northern Districts (Palmerston North) 6–8 February	8–3–13–0	8–3–27–1	19–2–76–5			21–7–65–2		4–1–10–0
Totals	223.4–53–635–23 av. 27.60	102.3–20–380–8 av. 47.50	78–9–282–13 av. 21.69	31–3–124–4 av. 31.00	72–7–261–3 av. 87.00	149.4–36–410–12 av. 34.16	59–10–172–1 av. 172.00	147.1–32–411–13 av. 31.61

England XI 203 for 2 dec (B.C. Broad 75, M.W. Gatting 54 not out) and 299 for 3 (R.T. Robinson 166, C.W.J. Athey 60)

England XI won by 7 wickets

Some violent batting adorned the match which was England's last in New Zealand before departing to Australia for the Bicentennial Test. Dilley began well with two wickets in his first five overs. Then Barry Cooper launched an attack on the bowling which brought him 15 fours in his innings and a hundred off 158 balls. He and White added 104 in 27 overs, and he and Kuggeleijn 78 off 21. Gatting declared in arrears, and Hick and White began their assault on the bowling on the second evening. Hick's mighty innings occupied only 152 minutes and he hit 7 sixes and 14 fours. Tim Robinson responded with 166 off 158 balls with 10 sixes and 13 fours, a glorious innings which set up an England victory.

25, 26 and 27 January 1988

at The Domain, Levin

Central Districts 131 and 222 (J.P. Millmow 4 for 48, E.J. Gray 4 for 63)
Wellington 435 for 5 dec (E.B. McSweeney 205 not out, G.R. Larsen 161)

Wellington won by an innings and 82 runs
Wellington 16 pts, Central Districts 0 pts

at Eden Park No 1, Auckland

Auckland 204 (W.P. Fowler 56) and 329 for 9 dec (T.J. Franklin 116, M.R. Pringle 77, M.A. Holding 6 for 77)
Canterbury 336 (P.E. McEwan 118, A.J. Hintz 62, P.G. Kennedy 59) and 137 (W.P. Fowler 6 for 41)

Auckland won by 60 runs
Auckland 12 pts, Canterbury 4 pts

Having bowled out Central Districts for 131, Wellington were struggling at 79 for 4 when Ervin McSweeney joined

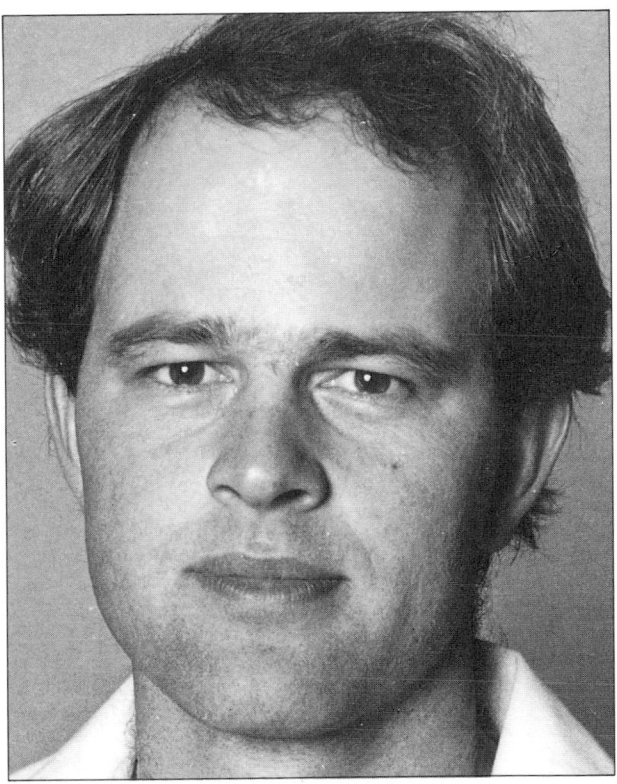

Ervin McSweeney, Wellington wicket-keeper, hit the highest score of his career, 205 not out v. Central Districts, 26 January, and shared a record fifth-wicket stand of 341 with Gavin Larsen. (Ross Setford)

Gavin Larsen. The pair added 341, which was the first triple-century stand for the fifth wicket in domestic cricket in New Zealand and beat the New Zealand record of 319

C.J. Smith	T.M. McKenna	S.P. Robertson	G.W. Walton		Byes	Leg-byes	Wides	No-balls	Total	Wkts
						8	4	16	240	10
					12	3		3	310	4
1–0–1–0						3		2	295	7
					2	7			219	0
	12–2–36–1					13		13	234	9
	5–1–21–0	2–0–5–1				4		1	157	10
	18–5–52–4	2–2–0–0	23–7–56–2			11		1	259	10
		2–0–12–0	28–5–84–1			10			435	5
	19–3–84–3	1–0–13–0	10–3–42–0		1	13		17	400	7
			7–0–40–0			6		4	174	3
					1	1		8	100	10
						14		11	218	10
						3			194	8
1–0–	54–11–	7–2–	68–15–							
1–0–	193–8	30–1	222–3							
	av. 24.12	av. 30.00	av. 74.00							

Northern Districts 1988
First-Class Matches

BATTING

BATTING	v. Wellington (Hamilton) 5–7 January		v. Canterbury (Christchurch) 9–11 January		v. Otago (Alexandra) 13–15 January		v. Central Districts (Te Awamutu) 17–19 January		v. England XI (Hamilton) 23–5 January		v. Otago (Hamilton) 29–31 January		v. Auckland (Auckland) 2–4 February		v. Central Districts (Palmerston North) 6–8 February		v. Auckland (Hamilton) 10–12 February	
L.M. Crocker	0	99	21	66	11	0	65	—	11	7	53	—	0	12	65	—	60	—
G.E. Bradburn	2	58	17	52	16	13	5	—	0	11	0	—	0	0	0	—		
G.A. Hick	0	64	7	113*	4	90	27	—	19	146	122	—	6	26	62	—	141	—
D.J. White	58	6	8	33*	8	68	14	—	64	80	31	—	15	4	18	—	77	—
B.G. Cooper	3	22	50	—	21	23	0	—	116*	—	88	—	12	37	0	—	43	—
C.M. Kuggeleijn	60	30*	87	—	12	6	2	—	27*	—	87	—	0	10			41	—
B.A. Young	69*	5*	0	—	34	38*	94	—	—	3*	25	—	16	0	41*	—	8*	—
D.A. Beard	7	—	9	—														
K. Treiber	8	—	16	—	0	18	6	—	—	—	22*	—	4	9	0	—	—	—
M.R. McKinnon	0	—	—	—	4	4*	0*	—	—	—	—	—	2	5	5*	—	—	—
B.J. Barrett	0	—	2	—	3	5	19	—	—	—	—	—	5*	25*	—	—	—	—
B.P. Ward			0*	—	1*	—												
S.A. Thomson							15	—			84	—	0	75	0	—	0*	—
B.T. Spragg															0	—	47	—
Byes	3	5	4	2	2	6			1	4	2			8				
Leg-byes	6	12	5	4	2	4	11		1	1	2		4	9	3		4	
Wides			1								1							
No-balls	1	1	2	6			1		3	2	3			13			11	
Total	217	302	229	276	118	275	259		242	254	520		64	233	194		432	
Wickets	10	5	10	2	10	10	10		4	4	10		10	10	8		6	
Result	W		W		W		D		L		D		L		Ab.		Ab.	
Points	12		12		12		4		—		4		0		2		2	

Fielding Figures
16 – B.A. Young
9 – G.A. Hick
7 – L.M. Crocker
5 – D.J. White and B.G. Cooper
4 – C.M. Kuggeleijn and G.E. Bradburn

3 – K. Treiber
2 – B.J. Barrett, S.A. Thomson and D.A. Beard (as sub)
1 – M.R. McKinnon, B.P. Ward and B.T. Spragg

BOWLING

	B.J. Barrett	K. Treiber	D.A. Beard	M.R. McKinnon	G.E. Bradburn	B.P. Ward	C.M. Kuggeleijn	G.A. Hick
v. Wellington (Hamilton)	19–3–76–1	29–4–99–2	23–7–52–3	15–5–52–0	8–1–30–0			
5–7 January	13–4–36–0	9.1–0–36–0	26–6–86–1	9–2–24–1	3–1–5–0			
v. Canterbury (Christchurch)	18–0–69–2	24–7–57–2	15–4–48–2		1–1–0–0	26–8–49–2	6–3–7–0	
9–11 January	15.2–2–56–4	3–0–19–1	4–1–19–0			10–3–24–2	7–3–8–3	
v. Otago (Alexandra)	11–1–30–2	18–6–35–5		12–2–26–2	3–1–5–1	9–2–24–0		
13–15 January	14–0–65–1	23–6–60–4		17.3–4–27–4	6–0–15–1			5–0–18–0
v. Central Districts (Te Awamutu)	16–2–41–4	17–3–39–1		16–6–17–1	12.5–6–9–2	8–2–21–0	6–5–1–0	
17–19 January	15–5–35–2	14–4–25–1		29–8–56–1	13–5–22–0			5–1–12–1
v. England XI (Hamilton)	16–3–48–0	14–1–54–0		22–8–60–1	2–1–5–0			
23–5 January	6–0–36–0	19–4–83–1		21–3–77–0	5–0–55–0		8–1–18–2	
v. Otago (Hamilton)	28–4–72–2	44.1–16–96–6		29–8–59–0	33–7–80–1		17–5–39–0	23–7–51–1
29–31 January								
v. Auckland (Auckland)	21–7–53–3	25–5–75–0		27.1–6–58–3	9–2–15–0		12–0–44–0	
2–4 February								
v. Central Districts (Palmerston North)		22–2–77–0		17–2–63–0	3–1–12–0	34–5–86–2		
6–8 February								
v. Auckland (Hamilton)	33–10–66–0	47.2–23–57–2		52–16–93–2			11–6–10–0	38–16–56–0
10–12 February								
	225.2–41–683–21	308.4–81–812–25	68–18–205–6	266.4–70–612–15	98.5–26–253–5	87–20–204–6	67–23–127–5	71–24–137–2
	av. 32.52	av. 32.48	av. 34.16	av. 40.80	av. 50.60	av. 34.00	av. 25.40	av. 68.50

M	Inns	NOs	Runs	HS	Av
9	14	—	470	99	33.57
8	13	—	174	58	13.38
9	14	1	827	146	63.61
9	14	1	484	80	37.23
9	12	1	415	116*	37.72
8	11	2	362	87	40.22
9	12	6	333	94	55.50
2	2	—	16	9	8.00
9	9	1	83	22*	10.37
8	7	3	20	5*	5.00
8	7	2	59	25*	11.80
3	2	2	1	1*	—
6	6	1	174	84	34.80
2	2	—	47	47	23.50

S.A. Thomson	L.M. Crocker	B.G. Cooper	Byes	Leg-byes	Wides	No-balls	Total	Wkts
				16	1	6	325	6
			3	3			193	3
			5	19	2	18	254	8
			2	1	1	3	129	10
			2	3	1	3	125	10
			2	10	6	5	218	10
				10	2	10	135	10
9–2–18–2			4	5		1	175	5
10–2–16–0			1	4	2	2	203	2
9–0–31–0								
6–2–11–0	1–0–5–0	0.3–0–6–0		8	1	6	299	3
19–7–42–0			5	13		14	457	10
25–8–59–3			4	14		5	322	10
25–1–110–2				11	6	15	359	5
11–1–24–0			4	3		2	313	4
114–23–311–7	1–0–5–0	0.3–0–6–0						
av. 44.42	—	—						

Bill Fowler, captain of Auckland, returned the best bowling figures of his career, 6 for 41, v. Canterbury, 27 January. (Michael King/Allsport)

by Rutherford and Gray against Close's XI at Scarborough in 1986. McSweeney hit the first double century of his career and Larsen hit a maiden first-class hundred. Thereafter Central Districts succumbed quietly to Millmow and Gray.

Trevor Franklin hit his third Shell Trophy century of the summer and helped bring about a remarkable reversal of fortune at Eden Park. McEwan's hundred and a ninth-wicket partnership of 75 between Hintz and Lawrence took Canterbury to a first-innings lead of 132, but this was wiped out when Pringle joined Franklin in a third-wicket stand of 170 when Auckland batted again. Canterbury were left to make a modest 197 and began confidently enough, but they collapsed before the spin bowling of Auckland skipper Bill Fowler, the former Derbyshire player, who returned the best figures of his career and gave his side a sensational victory. The last five Canterbury wickets fell for the addition of only 13 runs.

29, 30 and 31 January 1988

at Eden Park No 1, Auckland

Auckland 400 for 7 dec (J.J. Crowe 125, J.G. Bracewell 104) and 174 for 3 dec (T.J. Franklin 100)
Central Districts 269 (T.E. Blain 75, W. Watson 6 for 55) and 247 (T.E. Blain 62, M.J. Greatbatch 56)

Auckland won by 58 runs
Auckland 16 pts, Central Districts 0 pts

Otago 1988
First-Class Matches

Match column key:
- CD-NP = v. Central Districts (New Plymouth) 5–7 January
- Au-D = v. Auckland (Dunedin) 9–11 January
- ND-A = v. Northern Districts (Alexandra) 13–15 January
- Ca-C = v. Canterbury (Christchurch) 17–19 January
- ND-H = v. Northern Districts (Hamilton) 29–31 January
- We-O = v. Wellington (Oamaru) 2–4 February
- Ca-D = v. Canterbury (Dunedin) 6–8 February
- We-W = v. Wellington (Wellington) 10–12 February

BATTING

Batting	CD-NP (1)	CD-NP (2)	Au-D (1)	Au-D (2)	ND-A (1)	ND-A (2)	Ca-C (1)	Ca-C (2)	ND-H (1)	ND-H (2)	We-O (1)	We-O (2)	Ca-D (1)	Ca-D (2)	We-W (1)	We-W (2)	M	Inns	NOs	Runs	HS	Av
S.J. McCullum	6	27	42	0	0	1	16	—	15	—					46	14	6	10	—	167	46	16.70
K. Ibadulla	0	107	0	0	3	16											3	6	—	126	107	21.00
S.L. Boock	16	—	—	—	9*	1	1	13	—	—	—	—	2*	3*	—	—	8	7	3	45	16	11.25
K.J. Burns	48	72	0	34	6	44	1	—	136	—	112	8	20	21	0	18	8	14	—	520	136	37.14
B.R. Blair	34	26	28	9	8	1	5	—	29	—	19	20	86	55	29	64	8	14	—	413	86	29.50
R.N. Hoskin	46	38*	101	7	12	13	28	—	157	—	4*	12	14	1	61	105	8	14	2	599	157	49.91
D.J. Walker	20	22*	6	47	49	54*	77	—	15*	—	14*	43	2	65*	60	19	8	14	5	493	77	54.88
W.K. Lees	24*	—	53*	13*	—	6	—	0	—	—	112	23	20	68*	—		7	10	4	319	112	53.16
N.A. Mallender	10	—	21*	—	16	10	41*	—	4	—	—	16*					6	7	3	118	41*	29.50
T.J. Wilson	0	—	—	—	0	13	0	—	4	—	—	19*	19	13			7	8	1	68	19*	9.71
P.W. Hills	8	—					0				24	0	20*		3		5	6	1	55	24	11.00
J.K. Lindsay			22	17*	11	41	17	—	8	—	1	3	12	17	6	11*	7	12	2	166	41	16.60
K.J. McKnight					2	1											1	2	—	3	2	1.50
K.R. Rutherford									44	—	182	12	68	56	7	24	4	7	—	393	182	56.14
V.A. Johnson													6	9	3	—	2	3	—	18	9	6.00
Byes	12	2	5	2	2	5	5		3		5	1	2	1								
Leg-byes	8	3	12	1	3	10	19		13		8	9	8	7	5	10						
Wides	4			1	1	1	6		2													
No-balls	16	3		2	3	5	3		14		2	1	3	3	3	4						
Total	240	310	288	136	125	218	221		457		342	258	292	271	310	273						
Wickets	10	4	7	6	10	10	10		10		4	7	10	9	8	8						
Result	W		W		L		D		D		D		D		W							
Points	12		16		4		0		0		4		0		16							

Fielding Figures
- 17 – W.K. Lees (ct 13/st 4)
- 12 – S.J. McCullum (inc two as sub)
- 6 – D.J. Walker
- 5 – R.N. Hoskin
- 4 – B.R. Blair, N.A. Mallender and K.J. McKnight (ct 3/st 1)
- 3 – P.W. Hills and K.R. Rutherford
- 2 – S.L. Boock
- 1 – K.J. Burns and K. Ibadulla

BOWLING

Match	N.A. Mallender	P.W. Hills	T.J. Wilson	S.L. Boock	K. Ibadulla	J.K. Lindsay	B.R. Blair	V.A. Johnson
v. Central Districts (New Plymouth) 5–7 January	21.4-6-57-1 / 11-2-27-0	14-4-58-1 / 19-5-44-0	27-5-82-5 / 31-8-93-4	30-13-58-1 / 18-6-58-2	9-2-48-0			
v. Auckland (Dunedin) 9–11 January	29.2-10-55-3 / 14-1-47-2		25-5-81-1 / 14.2-3-48-4	49-20-85-4 / 15-7-31-4	6-3-16-0 / 1-0-4-0	4-1-10-0	9-1-30-2	
v. Northern Districts (Alexandra) 13–15 January	17-8-25-3 / 27-6-92-2		20-6-36-2 / 23-7-62-2	17-2-53-4 / 29-10-77-3				
v. Canterbury (Christchurch) 17–19 January	28-7-64-4 / 6-1-21-0	14-1-56-1 / 2-0-9-0	28.4-8-83-3 / 5-0-21-0	13-3-32-1		7-1-34-1 / 6-1-15-0		
v. Northern Districts (Hamilton) 29–31 January	27-3-81-2		28.2-3-122-2	50-11-158-3		20-2-114-0	11-2-41-1	
v. Wellington (Oamaru) 2–4 February	4.4-1-8-0	16-4-44-2 / 6-1-13-1	20-5-41-2 / 2-0-7-0	47.2-19-110-6 / 11-1-30-0		16-1-82-0 / 8-1-26-0	13-3-25-0	
v. Canterbury (Dunedin) 6–8 February		16-8-42-0	29-2-118-0 / 5-0-35-0	30-11-45-2 / 31-14-65-4		17-4-59-0 / 8-2-29-1	7-0-20-1	33-4-117-3 / 18-5-55-2
v. Wellington (Wellington) 10–12 February		16-4-47-1 / 10-3-33-0		33-16-61-3 / 22-9-32-4		26.2-5-110-5 / 14.3-4-48-5	3-0-24-0	13-3-43-0 / 2-0-13-0
Totals	185.4-45-477-17 *av. 28.05*	113-30-346-6 *av. 57.66*	258.2-51-829-25 *av. 33.16*	395.2-142-895-41 *av. 21.82*	16-5-68-0 *av. —*	126.5-22-527-12 *av. 43.91*	43-6-140-4 *av. 35.00*	66-12-228-5 *av. 45.60*

at Seddon Park, Hamilton

Northern Districts 520 for 8 dec (G.A. Hick 122, B.G. Cooper 88, C.M. Kuggeleijn 87, S. Thomson 84, L.M. Crocker 53)
Otago 457 (R.N. Hoskin 157, K.J. Burns 136, K. Treiber 6 for 96)

Match drawn
Northern Districts 4 pts, Otago 0 pts

at Basin Reserve, Wellington

Canterbury 220 (R.T. Latham 91, G.N. Cederwall 4 for 49) and 84 (J.P. Millmow 4 for 19)
Wellington 248 for 7 dec (B.A. Edgar 98, G.R. Larsen 55) and 57 for 1

Wellington won by 9 wickets
Wellington 16 pts, Canterbury 0 pts

The return of John Bracewell, Jeff Crowe and Willie Watson brought Auckland a resounding win over Central Districts. Put in to bat, Auckland reached 400 for 7 on the first day with Crowe and Bracewell hitting centuries. Bracewell's 104 was made in 89 minutes. The second day belonged to Watson, who returned the best figures of his career when he took 6 for 55. Only Tony Blain, returning from international duty, and Gary Robertson offered serious resistance. Trevor Franklin recorded his fourth century of the summer, and Bracewell, who won the individual award, was the main destroyer after Central, having reached 208 for 4, collapsed to 247 all out.

The wicket at Seddon Park continued to be a batsman's paradise. Another century from Hick and consistent batting after the early loss of Bradburn took Northern Districts to their highest total in first-class cricket, yet even so it looked as if Otago, 414 for 4 in the final session of the match, would take first-innings points. Karl Treiber brought about a remarkable collapse, and the last six wickets fell for 43 runs after Hoskin and Burns, who added 259 for the fourth wicket, had reached career-best scores.

Wellington took maximum points at Basin Reserve when Canterbury inexplicably collapsed to 84 all out

Willie Watson, treated in capricious manner by the New Zealand selectors, took a career best 6 for 55 for Auckland against Central Districts, 29–31 January. (Adrian Murrell/ Allsport)

against a varied attack in their second innings. The win took Wellington into second place behind Northern Districts, but it was still possible for any of the six associations to win the title.

2, 3 and 4 February 1988

at Eden Park No 2, Auckland

Northern Districts 64 (M.C. Snedden 5 for 31, W. Watson 4 for 14) and 233 (S. Thomson 75, M.C. Snedden 4 for 42)
Auckland 322 (D.N. Patel 93, P.A. Horne 66, J.G. Bracewell 59, T.J. Franklin 50)

Auckland won by an innings and 25 runs
Auckland 16 pts, Northern Districts 0 pts

at Lancaster Park, Christchurch

Canterbury 100 (G.K. Robertson 5 for 34) and 218 (J.G. Wright 70)
Central Districts 138 for 9 dec (C.W.H. Lawrence 4 for 43) and 182 for 2 (M.D. Crowe 119 not out)

Central Districts won by 8 wickets
Central Districts 16 pts, Canterbury 0 pts

	Byes	Leg-byes	Wides	No-balls	Total	Wkts
	4	7	6	2	266	8
		13			283	
	9		1	1	286	10
	4	3		1	137	10
	2	2			118	10
	6	4			275	8
	4	10	4	2	264	10
		3			54	0
	2	2	1	3	520	8
	4	13		6	327	10
					76	1
	4	15		2	420	6
		7		12	191	7
	1	7		2	293	9
	6	12		1	144	10

Wellington 1988
First-Class Matches

BATTING

	v. Northern Districts (Hamilton) 5–7 January		v. Central Districts (Wellington) 9–11 January		v. Auckland (Auckland) 13–15 January		v. England XI (Wellington) 18–20 January		v. Central Districts (Levin) 25–7 January		v. Canterbury (Wellington) 29–31 January		v. Otago (Oamaru) 2–4 February		v. Auckland (Wellington) 6–8 February		v. Otago (Wellington) 10–12 February	
B.A. Edgar	39	24	92	103*	28	16	10	—	28	—	98	33*	96	7	53	—	14	35
R.H. Vance	85	117*	16	107*	98	1			12	—			12	42*			121	27
G.R. Larsen	7	14	13	—	4	35	11	—	161	—	55	23*	2	—	35*	—	74	17
T.D. Ritchie	102*	23	16	—	14	23	0	—	0	—	18	—	30	—	—	—	11	2
E.J. Gray	10	9*	66*	—	12	62			9	—	1	—	37	—			38	28
E.B. McSweeney	48	—	72	—	17	7	10	—	205*	—	0	—	35	—			10	12
G.N. Cederwall	6	—	2	—	30	0	8*	—			21	0					8	2
I.W. Ormiston	5*	—	11	—			47	—			18*	—					6	2
S.J. Maguiness	—	—			6	43			10*	—								
R.G. Holland	—	—			2	—							7	—			—	0
J.P. Millmow	—	—			0*	11*					16*	—	1	—			0*	0
D.M. Molony																		
G.P. Burnett					12	12*	87*	—							82*	—		
A.J. Rohrs							4	—										
B.R. Williams									—	—								
F. Beyeler											2	—	43*	—			1	0*
A.H. Jones													26	27*				
E.J. Chatfield													15	—				
J.D. Milne																	—	—
Byes			3		2		3				4		4				1	6
Leg-byes	16	3	3	7	2	6	2		10		8		13		6		7	12
Wides	1										2							
No-balls	6		2				1	6			5		1	6	5		2	1
Total	325	193	293	219	225	217	188		435		248	57	327	76	181		293	144
Wickets	6	3	7	0	10	8	6		5		7	1	10	1	1		9	10
Result	L		D		D		D		W		W		D		Ab.		L	
Points	4		4		0		—		16		16		0		2		0	

Fielding Figures

19 – E.B. McSweeney (ct 15/st 4)
12 – G.R. Larsen
9 – T.D. Ritchie
7 – R.H. Vance and E.J. Gray
4 – I.W. Ormiston, S.J. Maguiness and B.A. Edgar
3 – R.G. Holland and A.H. Jones
2 – F. Beyeler and G.N. Cederwall
1 – J.P. Millmow, G.P. Burnett and B.R. Williams

BOWLING

	J.P. Millmow	G.N. Cederwall	R.G. Holland	E.J. Gray	S.J. Maguiness	I.W. Ormiston	D.M. Molony	G.R. Larsen
v. Northern Districts (Hamilton) 5–7 January	18–7–27–3	13–5–22–2	21–4–83–3	21–5–43–0	11–7–8–2	3–0–25–0		
	11.5–4–48–0	7–1–20–0	19–2–60–0	28–4–84–1		10–0–27–1		15–1–46–3
v. Central Districts (Wellington) 9–11 January	6–2–26–0	5–0–19–0	32–12–53–4	43–20–53–3		23–8–45–1	2–0–7–0	10–4–18–1
	8–2–21–0	2–0–7–0	22–6–84–4	22–9–74–2		1–0–4–0		
v. Auckland (Auckland) 13–15 January	25–10–63–4	21–4–67–0	12–4–42–1	5–2–14–1	25–8–40–0			9–1–21–2
	12–2–36–0	14–2–42–1	32.4–13–69–7	28–11–48–2	11–3–16–0			
v. England XI (Wellington) 18–20 January	16–3–41–1	16–2–65–0			14–4–38–0	20–1–74–0		8–2–37–0
v. Central Districts (Levin) 25–7 January	14–4–44–2	12.1–1–46–3	4–3–5–1		11–7–13–2			11–5–22–2
	16–4–48–4	17–4–52–2	12–4–28–0	30–9–63–4	13–7–16–0			3–1–5–0
v. Canterbury (Wellington) 29–31 January	18–5–50–3	20–8–49–4	21–11–32–0	16–7–17–0				3–1–6–0
	10–4–19–4	7–0–35–1	6.5–3–7–2	1–1–0–1				
v. Otago (Oamaru) 2–4 February	20–5–85–2		8–1–36–0	25–7–61–0				2–0–16–0
	13–2–31–2		9–1–53–1	17–2–65–1				3–0–11–0
v. Auckland (Wellington) 6–8 February								
v. Otago (Wellington) 10–12 February	16–4–56–1	3–0–14–0	22–7–81–5	28–9–61–1		6–1–19–0		5–1–17–0
	9–3–11–0	4–0–19–1	27.5–5–105–3	17–2–50–1		16–4–44–2		
	212.5–61– 606–26	141.1–27– 457–14	249.2–76– 738–31	281–88– 633–17	85–36– 131–4	79–14– 238–4	2–0– 7–0	69–16– 199–8
	av. 23.30	av. 32.64	av. 23.80	av. 37.23	av. 32.75	av. 59.50	—	av. 24.87

	M	Inns	NOs	Runs	HS	Av
	9	15	2	676	103*	52.00
	7	11	3	634	121	79.75
	9	13	2	451	161	41.00
	9	11	1	239	102*	23.90
	8	10	2	272	66*	34.00
	8	10	1	416	205*	46.22
	8	9	1	77	30	9.62
	7	6	2	89	47	22.25
	4	3	1	59	43	29.50
	7	3	—	9	7	3.00
	8	6	4	28	16*	14.00
	1					
	3	4	3	193	87*	193.00
	2	1		4	4	4.00
	1					
	4	4	2	46	43*	23.00
	1	2	1	53	27*	53.00
	1	1		15	15	15.00
	1					

at Centennial Park, Oamaru

Otago 342 for 4 dec (K.R. Rutherford 182, K.J. Burns 112) and 258 for 7 dec (W.K. Lees 112)
Wellington 327 (B.A. Edgar 96, S.L. Boock 6 for 110) and 76 for 1

Match drawn
Otago 4 pts, Wellington 0 pts

Auckland moved to the top of the table with an emphatic and surprise win over Northern Districts, who led the Trophy for most of the season. The visitors were destroyed on the first day after Jeff Crowe had won the toss and asked them to bat. Both openers were dismissed without a run scored, and Martin Snedden produced an inspired spell to rout Northern for 64. Watson gave him able support. Horne and Franklin strengthened Auckland's position with an opening stand of 124. Dipak Patel was run out for 93 in his first first-class innings of the season, and Bracewell hit a typical robust fifty before taking three wickets as Auckland completed a resounding victory in two days.

In Christchurch, Canterbury never totally recovered from losing four wickets for six runs on the opening morning. Gary Robertson was the arch destroyer of the middle order after Derek Stirling had made early inroads into the batting. Central struggled a little in their turn, Bill Lawrence bowling splendidly, but they still managed first-innings points. Eventually, Central needed to make 181 to win and lost two wickets for 14, but Martin Crowe, appearing in his only match of the season for the association, hit a glorious hundred and took his side to an excellent win.

Another returning international, Ken Rutherford, hit his highest score for Otago, who were put in to bat by Vance. Lindsay was out at 13, but Burns, with his second century in successive innings, and Rutherford added 254

B.A. Edgar	B.R. Williams	A.J. Rohrs	F. Beyeler	E.J. Chatfield	R.H. Vance	Byes	Leg-byes	Wides	No-balls	Total	Wkts
						3	6		1	217	10
						5	12		1	302	5
						11	5		9	237	9
0.4–0–0–1						5			4	195	7
							6		8	253	8
						4	9		4	224	10
	21–8–41–2	2–0–9–0					5	1	5	310	3
							1	1	3	131	10
						4	6		11	222	10
			15.2–6–52–3			4	10	1	10	220	10
			9–5–16–2			1	6		7	84	10
			14–1–67–0	34–6–69–2			8		2	342	4
			11–3–33–2	15–2–53–1		3	9		1	258	7
											Ab.
			18–5–55–1			2	5		3	310	8
2–0–15–0			3–1–11–0		1–0–7–0	1	10		4	273	8
2.4–0–15–1	21–8–41–2	2–0–9–0	70.2–21–234–8	49–8–122–3	1–0–7–0						
av. 15.00	*av.* 20.50	—	*av.* 29.25	*av.* 40.66	—						

One of New Zealand's exciting new pace bowlers, de Groen of Wellington. (Simon Bruty/Allsport)

for the second wicket, an Otago record. Stephen Boock then bowled Otago to a first-innings lead of 15, but a draw always looked certain in spite of Warren Lees' ferocious century, the fifth of his career.

6, 7 and 8 February 1988

at Basin Reserve, Wellington

Wellington 181 for 1 (G.P. Burnett 82 not out, B.A. Edgar 53)
v. Auckland

Match abandoned
Wellington 2 pts, Auckland 2 pts

at Fitzherbert Park, Palmerston North

Central Districts 359 for 5 dec (I.R. Snook 100 not out, S.P. Robertson 94, C.J. Smith 63)
Northern Districts 194 for 8 (L.M. Crocker 65, G.A. Hick 62, K.W. Martin 5 for 76)

Match abandoned
Central Districts 2 pts, Northern Districts 2 pts

at Carisbrook, Dunedin

Canterbury 420 for 6 dec (R.T. Latham 141 not out, D.A.

Dempsey 121, D.J. Boyle 69) and 191 for 7 dec (C.W. Flanagan 50, S.L. Boock 4 for 65)
Otago 292 (B.R. Blair 86, K.R. Rutherford 68, M.W. Priest 5 for 63) and 271 for 9 (D.J. Walker 65 not out, K.R. Rutherford 56, B.R. Blair 55, M.W. Priest 5 for 100)

Match drawn
Canterbury 4 pts, Otago 0 pts

Three hours' play on the second morning was all that was possible at Wellington. Graham Burnett again displayed fine talent and temperament.

There was no play on the third day at Palmerston North, where Ian Snook ended his come-back season with a century.

Centuries from opener David Dempsey and the very much in-form Rod Latham put Canterbury in a strong position in Dunedin, and their advantage was maintained through the spin of Mark Priest. Set to make 320, Otago scored at the required rate, but again lost wickets to Priest's left-arm bowling. The ninth wicket went down at 253, but Walker and Boock held out for nearly eight overs to save the game for Otago.

Canterbury's failure to win at Carisbrook meant that they were destined to finish bottom of the Shell Trophy table, but, of the other five teams, only Central Districts, who had also finished their programme, were unable to win the title. The competition seemed set for an exciting finish.

7, 8 and 9 February 1988

at Pukekura Park, New Plymouth

England XI 243 for 6 dec (R.T. Robinson 74) and 165 for 9 dec
Shell XI 139 (P.W. Jarvis 4 for 24) and 271 for 5 (A.H. Jones 72)

Shell XI won by 5 wickets

England returned from Australia to begin their tour in earnest but without the help of Neil Foster, whose knee trouble was to force him to return to England. Opposition for England before the first Test was provided by a select eleven which included Andrew Jones and Mark Greatbatch, who were in the New Zealand squad for the Test, and others, like skipper Robert Vance, Phil Horne, Tony Blain and all-rounder Chris Kuggeleijn, a surprising but inspired choice, who were very much in the selectors' minds. Watson, Millmow and Barrett exploited conditions well early in the match and England were 44 for 3 before Robinson and Fairbrother effected a recovery. The Shell XI batted limply, but Millmow, Barrett and Kuggeleijn struck back for the New Zealanders and Embury declared at lunch on the last day. Jones and Vance provided solidity, and Blain paced his innings admirably to bring the Shell XI victory with just under two overs to spare.

10, 11 and 12 February 1988

at Basin Reserve, Wellington

Otago 310 for 8 dec (W.K. Lees 68 not out, R.N. Hoskin 61, D.J. Walker 60, R.G. Holland 5 for 81) and 273 for 8 dec (R.N. Hoskin 105, B.R. Blair 64)

Wellington 293 for 9 dec (R.H. Vance 121, G.R. Larsen 74, J.K. Lindsay 5 for 110) and 114 (J.K. Lindsay 5 for 48, S.L. Boock 4 for 32)

Otago won by 147 runs
Otago 16 pts, Wellington 0 pts

at Seddon Park, Hamilton

Northern Districts 432 for 6 dec (G.A. Hick 141, D.J. White 77, L.M. Crocker 60)
Auckland 313 for 4 (J.F. Reid 112, P.A. Horne 61, M.R. Pringle 51 not out)

Match abandoned
Northern Districts 2 pts, Auckland 2 pts

What should have been an exciting and dramatic climax to the season transpired to be the lowest of farce. Auckland needed only to take first-innings points to be assured of the Trophy, but they were engaged at Seddon Park, where bowlers find it very hard to take wickets. Meanwhile, Otago, in fifth place before the final matches of the competition, were playing at Basin Reserve. They began badly, losing Burns and Rutherford for 9. Hoskin and Walker gave substance to the middle order, and some late blows from Warren Lees made a declaration possible. With Vance in mighty form and Larsen supporting him ably, Wellington reached 195 for 1, but Lindsay, who had never before taken five wickets in an innings and had captured only two wickets all season with his off-breaks, brought about a collapse in harness with Stephen Boock, and Otago claimed first-innings points, Vance declaring at the fall of the ninth wicket. Led by Hoskin and Blair, who shared a stand of 122, Otago now took charge of the match. Lees declared and left Wellington ample time in which to make 291. Vance and Edgar began promisingly with a stand of 68, but Boock dismissed them both, Larsen was run out, and Lindsay bettered the figures he had achieved in the first innings as he made the ball bite and turn. Otago took maximum points and moved two points ahead of Auckland at the top of the table.

There were no celebrations as Auckland were still engaged in their match with Northern Districts, who had built up a big total. The game had quickly been seen as a fight for first-innings points only. Crocker and Spragg put on 119 for the first wicket, Hick and White 170 for the third, and Kuggeleijn declared at 432 for 6. Brown left quickly when Auckland batted, but John Reid, returning to first-class cricket and awakening hope that he might return to Test cricket, showed all his old determination and concentration as Auckland ground towards the Northern score at 1.6 runs an over.

Under the rules of the competition, if sides finished level on points, the title would be decided on differentials, that is the average number of runs per wicket scored matched with the average runs per wicket conceded. Auckland officials concluded that they would win the Trophy if they reached 313 for 4, at which point the match was abandoned, but the scores that they had used to determine that Auckland would head Otago by 0.01 were incorrect (statistics are not a strong point in the reporting of cricket in New Zealand) and three days later it was announced that Otago had won the Trophy by 0.272.

The New Zealand Cricket Council comes out of the

	1st inns						
	P	W	L	D	lead	Ab	Pts
Otago (2)	8	3	1	4	4	–	52
Auckland (4)	8	3	2	1	3	2	52
Northern Districts (6)	8	3	1	2	2	2	48
Wellington (3)	8	2	2	3	4	1	42
Central Districts (1)	8	2	3	2	3	1	38
Canterbury (5)	8	1	5	2	5	–	32

Shell Trophy – Final Table (1987 positions in brackets)

whole affair very badly indeed, for they were unable to offer correct information on the last day of the Shell Trophy because they were too busy arranging the first Test match. Any governing body that so shamefully ignores its leading domestic competition does so at its peril.

Belatedly, congratulations should go to Warren Lees and Otago, who won both the Shell Trophy and the Shell Cup, a fine performance whatever the climax.

First Test Match
NEW ZEALAND v. ENGLAND

New Zealand omitted Greatbatch from their selected 12 and so Trevor Franklin returned to Test cricket. It was a well-deserved reward for one who had worked hard after having his leg broken in two places in an accident at Gatwick Airport at the close of the 1986 tour to England and who had, for a time, seemed destined never to play again. England gave a first Test cap to Paul Jarvis.

Jeff Crowe won the toss and asked England to bat first. The wicket was damp and green, and Hadlee was pounding the turf eager for the wicket which would make him the leading bowler in Test history. The initial glory belonged to Morrison, however, who had Moxon taken at short-leg off a simple lob when the batsman pushed forward uncertainly. Thereafter the day was dominated by the Nottinghamshire pair, Broad and Robinson. In 223 minutes they added 168, rarely looking troubled. Robinson batted with great confidence, and Broad, resolute and determined as ever, reached his sixth century in 10 overseas Tests. In all he hit 11 fours and faced 244 balls.

French is caught behind off Chatfield for 7. (Patrick Eagar)

ABOVE: *The New Zealand side for the first Test at Christchurch*. Back row – *Gren Alabaster (manager), M.C. Snedden, A.H. Jones, T.J. Franklin, M.J. Greatbatch and D.K. Morrison*. Front row – *I.D.S. Smith, M.D. Crowe, J.G. Wright, J.J. (capt.), R.J. Hadlee, E.J. Chatfield and J.G. Bracewell (David Munden)*
ABOVE RIGHT: *Lancaster Park, Christchurch. (David Munden)*
LEFT: *Graham Dilley produced the best performance of his Test career at Christchurch. Martin Crowe is caught at short leg by Moxon for 5. (Patrick Eagar)*
BELOW LEFT: *The luckless Jeff Crowe is caught by French off De Freitas. (Patrick Eagar)*

For Hadlee the day was a disaster. He seemed too tense to do himself justice, and after tea he retired from the scene with a torn calf muscle. It was not known at the time, but he had also retired from the series.

Chatfield bowled splendidly without luck, and Snedden, too, was often dangerous, but it was Morrison who raised New Zealand's hopes when he dismissed Robinson and Gatting in quick succession. Robinson was brilliantly caught behind the wicket one-handed on the leg-side, and Gatting slashed wildly to be well taken high at slip. Broad fell at 219, and England closed the day on 235 for 4.

The collapse which had begun after tea on the first day accelerated on the second as Morrison recorded his first five-wicket haul in Test cricket, and Chatfield's fine bowling received its just reward. Some swats by Dilley and

FIRST TEST MATCH – NEW ZEALAND v. ENGLAND
12, 13, 14, 16 and 17 February 1988 at Lancaster Park, Christchurch

ENGLAND

	FIRST INNINGS		SECOND INNINGS	
B.C. Broad	c Smith, b Snedden	114	c sub (Greatbatch), b Chatfield	20
M.D. Moxon	c Jones, b Morrison	1	c Jones, b Chatfield	27
R.T. Robinson	c Smith, b Morrison	70	c Wright, b Chatfield	2
M.W. Gatting†	c sub (Greatbatch), b Morrison	8	b Snedden	23
C.W.J. Athey	c sub (Greatbatch) b Morrison	22	c Smith, b Snedden	19
D.J. Capel	c Bracewell, b Chatfield	11	c M.D. Crowe, b Chatfield	0
J.E. Emburey	c Jones, b Morrison	42	run out	19
B.N. French*	c Smith, b Chatfield	7	c J.J. Crowe, b Snedden	3
P.A.J. De Freitas	c Morrison, b Chatfield	4	lbw, b Snedden	16
P.W. Jarvis	c Smith, b Chatfield	14	not out	10
G.R. Dilley	not out	7	c Jones, b Morrison	2
Extras	lb 11, w 1, nb 7	19	lb 7, nb 4	11
		319		**152**

	O	M	R	W	O	M	R	W
Hadlee	18	3	50	–				
Morrison	21.1	3	69	5	21.1	4	64	1
Chatfield	42	13	87	4	30	13	36	4
Snedden	33	9	86	1	23	8	45	4
Bracewell	6	1	16	–				

FALL OF WICKETS
1–7, 2–175, 3–187, 4–219, 5–237, 6–241, 7–248, 8–260, 9–285
1–32, 2–38, 3–55, 4–95, 5–96, 6–99, 7–118, 8–125, 9–147

NEW ZEALAND

	FIRST INNINGS		SECOND INNINGS	
J.G. Wright	c Moxon, b Dilley	10	lbw, b Dilley	23
T.J. Franklin	c Athey, b Dilley	10	lbw, b Dilley	12
A.H. Jones	c French, b Dilley	8	not out	54
M.D. Crowe	c Moxon, b Dilley	5	c French, b Jarvis	6
J.J. Crowe†	c French, b De Freitas	28	lbw, b De Freitas	0
J.G. Bracewell	c French, b Dilley	31	not out	20
R.J. Hadlee	c French, b Dilley	37		
I.D.S. Smith*	c Capel, b Jarvis	13		
M.C. Snedden	lbw, b De Freitas	0		
D.K. Morrison	b Jarvis	0		
E.J. Chatfield	not out	0		
Extras	b 2, lb 12, nb 12	26	b 6, lb 4, nb 5	15
		168	(for 4 wkts)	**130**

	O	M	R	W	O	M	R	W
De Freitas	22	6	39	2	19	6	26	1
Dilley	24.5	10	38	6	18	5	32	2
Capel	10	2	32	–	13	5	16	–
Jarvis	21	8	43	2	17	7	30	1
Emburey	4	3	2	–	10	4	16	–

FALL OF WICKETS
1–20, 2–25, 3–32, 4–40, 5–96, 6–131, 7–151, 8–155, 9–156
1–37, 2–43, 3–61, 4–78

Umpires: B.L. Aldridge & S.J. Woodward

Match drawn

Emburey for the last wicket took England past 300, which looked a good score on a wicket which was never likely to be easy. Rain had delayed the start for 42 minutes, and there was a further hold-up for bad light, but by the end of the day, New Zealand, 83 for 4, were in considerable trouble.

It was Graham Dilley who unsettled them with a spell of bowling that was quick and in which he moved the ball appreciably to trouble all batsmen. Wright was taken at short-leg, Franklin, who had been missed by Gatting, was held low at third slip, and Jones snicked high to the wicket-keeper. Most importantly for England, Martin Crowe was taken at short-leg.

Had England held all their catches, they might well have put New Zealand in a position of total despair, but the home side were allowed to hang on grimly. Bracewell checked the advance, and the injured Hadlee batted for three hours. Earlier, his skipper, Jeff Crowe, had extended his innings to 3½ hours, during which time he scored 28. Dilley finished with the best bowling figures of his Test career, and England lost Broad and Robinson before the close.

The first half of the fourth day's play was lost to the weather, and in what was left, England scored 97 runs and lost their last eight wickets. The outfield, like the batting, was slow, and it was pretty dour stuff watched by very few people. Chatfield's four wickets brought match figures of 8 for 123 in 72 overs and won him the individual award although the England captain was to make no disguise of the fact that he felt Broad should have had that honour.

John Bracewell is caught at short-leg by Moxon, and Dilley claims another wicket. (David Munden)

Bad light caused a stoppage on the last day, when New Zealand were intent only on survival. Wright batted for more than two hours and Franklin for nearly 1¾ hours, but the bravest innings came from Jones, who had his wrist broken by a ball from Dilley before he had scored, but batted for 199 minutes for 54 not out and saved the match.

It was not a memorable Test. Dilley bowled well, but he was fined on the last day when he swore after an appeal had been rejected. There was nothing unusual in this, but the microphone relayed Dilley's feelings to many listeners.

19, 20 and 21 February 1988

at Carisbrook Park, Dunedin

President's XI 181 for 7 dec (K.R. Rutherford 57, N.V. Radford 4 for 24) and 214 for 7 dec (R.T. Latham 58 not out)
England XI 236 for 7 dec (M.D. Moxon 117) and 163 for 2 (M.W. Gatting 97 not out)

England XI won by 8 wickets

England were aided by generous declarations in a match in which, for the most part, scoring was slow. Gatting hit boldly on the last day to give his side victory, and Radford bowled well enough to oust De Freitas from the Test side. Of the New Zealanders on trial, Rutherford, Young, Millmow and Latham were impressive.

Second Test Match
NEW ZEALAND v. ENGLAND

New Zealand began the second Test without their best bowler, Hadlee, and without Jones, the batsman who thrust himself to the fore as a player of character and quality, if not always of orthodoxy. Mark Greatbatch won his first Test cap, and Rutherford was brought back to the side. Fairbrother and Radford came into the England side.

The first day set the pattern of another grim match. Put in to bat, New Zealand reached 186 for 3 by the close. England dropped catches in abundance and followed their habit of showing their displeasure at the decisions of the umpires. Franklin fell to an in-cutter. Jeff Crowe edged to fourth slip, and brother Martin limply clouted to mid-wicket. Greatbatch began purposefully and was five not out at the end of the day, by which time John Wright had reached a highly commendable hundred.

Unfortunately he added only two to his score on the second morning before being caught behind off Dilley, who also accounted for Greatbatch and brought about a collapse as he took five wickets in an innings for the second Test in succession. Rutherford looked comfortable until he missed a straight ball, and it was left to Morrison and Chatfield to raise the 300 in a last-wicket stand of 22.

Broad was soon out, but Moxon and Robinson took the score to 97 by the end of the day. By the end of the third day, with eight wickets down, England led by one run. The second-wicket partnership had realized 108, and Gatting had joined Moxon in a partnership of 76, after which, Emburey's violations on the textbook apart, England had little to offer.

Having reached 98, Moxon was dropped at second slip

ABOVE: *The end of New Zealand centurion John Wright, caught by French off Dilley. (Patrick Eagar)*
ABOVE RIGHT: *A raucous appeal from Bracewell as Broad is taken at silly mid-off by Martin Crowe. (Patrick Eagar)*
RIGHT: *Martyn Moxon on his way to his highest Test innings, 99. (Patrick Eagar)*
BELOW RIGHT: *They shall not pass. New Zealand's new hero – Mark Greatbatch. (Simon Bruty/Allsport)*

off Chatfield, who sent down more than 31 overs and conceded only 37 runs, but the bowler got his reward when Moxon, numbed in sight of his hundred, edged to first slip and Jeff Crowe took the catch.

Generally, the play was mediocre, the umpiring drew adverse comments, and England once again did not hide their disapproval of some of the decisions. What honours there were went to the masterly Chatfield and to Moxon, whose tenacity and durability after several disappointments were two of the better features of England's winter excursions. He batted 349 minutes, faced 269 balls and hit 10 fours in his 99.

Wright and Franklin seemed to have determined the course of the match on the fourth day, when they put on 117 in 57 overs for New Zealand's first wicket. This was the first century opening stand by New Zealand against England since 1949, and there was delight that Trevor Franklin had notched his first Test half-century to add glow to a fine season. Suddenly, however, everything fell apart for New Zealand. Franklin was bowled by Dilley, and in the next over, Wright was caught behind off Radford. Jeff Crowe completely misread a ball from Dilley and was lbw. His run of miserable form was to cost him the captaincy and his Test place. Martin Crowe was also adjudged lbw, rather harshly it seemed, and Rutherford was beaten and bowled by Emburey. New Zealand closed on 154 for 5, a lead of 132, and the game had swung decidedly in favour of England.

The last day belonged to Mark Greatbatch. He batted all day for a maiden Test century which was founded on all that is good in international cricket – sound technique and

SECOND TEST MATCH – NEW ZEALAND v. ENGLAND
25, 26, 27, 28 and 29 February 1988 at Eden Park, Auckland

NEW ZEALAND

	FIRST INNINGS		SECOND INNINGS	
J.G. Wright	c French, b Dilley	103	(2) c French, b Radford	49
T.J. Franklin	b Jarvis	27	(1) b Dilley	62
J.J. Crowe†	c Capel, b Dilley	11	lbw, b Dilley	1
M.D. Crowe	c Capel, b Emburey	36	lbw, b Jarvis	26
M.J. Greatbatch	c French, b Dilley	11	not out	107
K.R. Rutherford	b Capel	29	b Emburey	2
J.G. Bracewell	c Moxon, b Dilley	9	(8) lbw, b Gatting	38
I.D.S. Smith*	c French, b Jarvis	23	(9) not out	23
M.C. Snedden	c Moxon, b Dilley	14	(7) c French, b Capel	20
D.K. Morrison	not out	14		
E.J. Chatfield	c French, b Capel	10		
Extras	b 1, lb 2, w 2, nb 9	14	b 8, lb 8, nb 6	22
		301	(for 7 wkts)	350

	O	M	R	W	O	M	R	W
Dilley	28	9	60	5	23	9	44	2
Jarvis	33	9	74	2	27	7	54	1
Radford	30	4	79	–	20	4	53	1
Capel	26.2	4	57	2	21	4	40	1
Emburey	17	7	28	1	57	24	91	1
Gatting					17	4	40	1
Fairbrother					2	–	9	–
Moxon					2	–	3	–

FALL OF WICKETS
1–77, 2–98, 3–169, 4– 191, 5–207, 6–219, 7–254, 8–262, 9–279
1–117, 2–119, 3–119, 4–150, 5–153, 6–232, 7–296

ENGLAND

	FIRST INNINGS	
B.C. Broad	c M.D. Crowe, b Bracewell	9
M.D. Moxon	c J.J. Crowe, b Chatfield	99
R.T. Robinson	c Morrison, b Bracewell	54
M.W. Gatting†	c Smith, b Morrison	42
N.H. Fairbrother	c Smith, b Chatfield	1
D.J. Capel	c Bracewell, b Morrison	5
J.E. Emburey	c Smith, b Chatfield	45
B.N. French*	c Franklin, b Bracewell	13
P.W. Jarvis	c Smith, b Snedden	10
N.V. Radford	b Chatfield	8
G.R. Dilley	not out	8
Extras	b 12, lb 12, nb 5	29
		323

	O	M	R	W
Morrison	32	7	95	2
Chatfield	31.1	15	37	4
Bracewell	39	8	88	3
Snedden	34	14	71	1
Rutherford	5	1	8	–

FALL OF WICKETS
1–27, 2–135, 3–211, 4–220, 5–222, 6–234, 7–267, 8–282, 9–308

Umpires: F.R. Goodall & R.L. McHarg
Match drawn

THIRD TEST MATCH – NEW ZEALAND v. ENGLAND
3, 4, 5, 6 and 7 March 1988 at Basin Reserve, Wellington

NEW ZEALAND

	FIRST INNINGS	
J.G. Wright†	c Fairbrother, b Capel	36
T.J. Franklin	lbw, b De Freitas	14
R.H. Vance	run out	47
M.D. Crowe	lbw, b Gatting	143
M.J. Greatbatch	c De Freitas, b Emburey	68
K.R. Rutherford	not out	107
J.G. Bracewell	c Fairbrother, b Capel	54
I.D.S. Smith*	not out	33
S.L. Boock		
D.K. Morrison		
E.J. Chatfield		
Extras	lb 10	10
	(for 6 wkts, dec)	512

	O	M	R	W
Dilley	11	1	36	–
De Freitas	50.1	21	110	1
Capel	39	7	129	2
Emburey	45.5	10	99	1
Hemmings	45	15	107	–
Gatting	6	1	21	1

FALL OF WICKETS
1–33, 2–79, 3–132, 4–287, 5–336, 6–470

ENGLAND

	FIRST INNINGS	
B.C. Broad	b Boock	61
M.D. Moxon	not out	81
R.T. Robinson	c Smith, b Chatfield	0
M.W. Gatting†	not out	33
N.H. Fairbrother		
D.J. Capel		
J.E. Emburey		
B.N. French*		
P.A.J. De Freitas		
E.E. Hemmings		
G.R. Dilley		
Extras	lb 6, nb 2	8
	(for 2 wkts)	183

	O	M	R	W
Morrison	6	–	41	–
Chatfield	23	10	38	1
Bracewell	23	9	44	–
Boock	26	9	53	1
Rutherford	1	–	1	–

FALL OF WICKETS
1–129, 2–132

Umpires: B.L. Aldridge & S.J. Woodward
Match drawn

temperament and unrelenting concentration. His large frame presented a barrier of defiance, and he exuded a confidence that, when the moment was ripe, he was capable of hitting the ball very hard. He was the fourth New Zealander to score a century on his Test début, the first for 15 years.

Snedden gave Greatbatch valuable assistance in helping to add 79 runs, which occupied the first 2¾ hours of the last day and ended England's hopes. The pitch had not helped. The scoring rate was 2.19 an over, and the 130 maiden overs bowled during the match meant, in effect, that more than one of the five days was sat through without a run being scored, a sobering thought. By the close, England had three substitutes on the field, and Greatbatch was in total command.

Third Test Match
NEW ZEALAND v. ENGLAND

There was a belief that the Basin Reserve pitch would help the spinners so New Zealand cajoled Stephen Boock out of his previously announced retirement from Test cricket and England brought in Eddie Hemmings. New Zealand also dropped Jeff Crowe, brought in Robert Vance for his first Test cap and gave the captaincy to John Wright, who won the toss and decided to bat first.

Franklin looked less happy than at Auckland and was lbw when he played across the line to a short ball from De Freitas. Wright had a miraculous escape when he nudged a ball from Capel onto his wicket only to see a bail rise in the air and fall back into the groove. He was finally out when he pulled the ball into the hands of Fairbrother. Vance, meanwhile, had produced an assured first innings in Test cricket, defending solidly and running between the wickets intelligently. Martin Crowe was less confident and was badly dropped at slip by Emburey, but, having escaped, he hit the ball with relish, once driving Hemmings for 3 fours in an over.

The English disease is not catching. Emburey drops Crowe off Capel. (David Munden)

A rare Test wicket for Mike Gatting. Martin Crowe is lbw for 143. (David Munden)

Vance was run out after batting for just over three hours when he found himself at the same end as Crowe, but he had done enough to suggest that New Zealand had found another batsman of calibre, albeit belatedly, for Vance is 32.

Crowe and the impressive Greatbatch took the score to 192 for 3 at the close of a dour first day in which England's out-cricket had been lacklustre and their catching deplorable.

On the second day, the England fielding reached a depth which one would have thought impossible five years ago. Catches tumbled, and much was fumbled. The bowling offered little and Dilley retired from the match with a knee injury. Crowe and Greatbatch took their stand to 155 before the bulky left-hander was deceived by Emburey, who had not bowled well, and skied the ball to cover. By then, Crowe had reached his ninth Test century and had regained his confidence after a lean spell. He was finally out when he played across the line rather casually to Gatting. His dismissal caused little stir, for Rutherford, shrugging off one of the most depressing starts that any man has had to a Test career, was producing some flowing drives and had reached 91 by the close, which came at 451 for 5. England were out of the match.

On the third morning, Rutherford reached an elegant and deserved maiden Test hundred, Bracewell completed a rugged fifty and Smith lashed 33 off 19 balls before Wright declared. England responded with a century open-

NEW ZEALAND v. ENGLAND – TEST MATCH AVERAGES

NEW ZEALAND BATTING

	M	Inns	NOs	Runs	HS	Av	100s	50s
M.J. Greatbatch	2	3	1	186	107*	93.00	1	1
K.R. Rutherford	2	3	1	138	107*	69.00	1	
I.D.S. Smith	3	4	2	92	33*	46.00		
J.G. Wright	3	5		221	103	44.20	1	
M.D. Crowe	3	5		216	143	43.20	1	
J.G. Bracewell	3	5	1	152	54	38.00		1
T.J. Franklin	3	5		125	62	25.00		1
D.K. Morrison	3	2	1	14	14*	14.00		
M.C. Snedden	2	3		34	20	11.33		
J.J. Crowe	2	4		40	28	10.00		
E.J. Chatfield	3	2	1	10	10	10.00		

Played in one Test: R.H. Vance 47; A.H. Jones 8 & 54*; R.J. Hadlee 37; S.L. Boock did not bat

NEW ZEALAND BOWLING

	Overs	Mds	Runs	Wkts	Av	Best	10/m 5/inns
E.J. Chatfield	126.1	51	198	13	15.23	4/36	
D.K. Morrison	80.2	14	269	8	33.62	5/69	1
M.C. Snedden	90	31	202	6	33.66	4/45	
J.G. Bracewell	68	18	148	3	49.33	3/88	
K.R. Rutherford	6	1	9	0	–		

Bowled in one innings: R.J. Hadlee 18–3–50–0; S.L. Boock 26–9–53–1

NEW ZEALAND FIELDING FIGURES

10 - I.D.S. Smith; 4 - A.H. Jones; 3 - M.J. Greatbatch (all as sub); 2 - M.D. Crowe, J.G. Bracewell, D.K. Morrison and J.J. Crowe; 1 - J.G. Wright and T.J. Franklin

ENGLAND BATTING

	M	Inns	NOs	Runs	HS	Av	100s	50s
M.D. Moxon	3	4	1	208	99	69.33		2
B.C. Broad	3	4		204	114	51.00	1	1
J.E. Emburey	3	3		106	45	35.33		
M.W. Gatting	3	4	1	106	42	35.33		
R.T. Robinson	3	4		126	70	31.50		2
G.R. Dilley	3	3	2	17	8*	17.00		
P.W. Jarvis	2	3	1	34	14	17.00		
P.A.J. De Freitas	2	2		20	16	10.00		
B.N. French	3	3		23	13	7.66		
D.J. Capel	3	3		16	11	5.33		

Played in two Tests: N.H. Fairbrother 1
Played in one Test: N.V. Radford 8; C.W.J. Athey 22 & 19; E.E. Hemmings did not bat

ENGLAND BOWLING

	Overs	Mds	Runs	Wkts	Av	Best	10/m 5/inns
G.R. Dilley	104.5	34	210	15	14.00	6/38	2
M.W. Gatting	23	5	61	2	30.50	1/21	
P.W. Jarvis	98	31	201	6	33.50	2/43	
P.A.J. De Freitas	91.1	33	175	4	43.75	2/39	
D.J. Capel	109.2	22	274	5	54.80	2/57	
J.E. Emburey	133.5	48	236	3	78.66	1/28	
N.V. Radford	50	8	132	1	132.00	1/53	

Bowled in one innings: E.E. Hemmings 45–15–107–0; N.H. Fairbrother 2–0–9–0; M.D. Moxon 2–0–3–0

ENGLAND FIELDING FIGURES

11 - B.N. French; 4 - M.D. Moxon; 3 - D.J. Capel; 2 - N.H. Fairbrother; 1 - P.A.J. De Freitas and C.W.J. Athey

A happy hundred for Ken Rutherford after a run of failures in Test cricket. (David Munden)

ing stand which was ended in the 50th over when Broad was caught in two minds against Boock and was bowled. Robinson was caught behind three overs later, and England ended the day on 183 for 2. It was also the end of the match. Two days of gale and rain absorbed the remainder. Few people seemed worried.

So ended a slow and tedious series. New Zealand had some cause for delight in the form of Greatbatch, Vance, Rutherford and Franklin; England had little. It was said that they were tired and jaded, which is a kind description of some of their cricket. One's sympathies lie with those who paid a considerable amount of money to travel to New Zealand to see three Tests which, in the words of one retired gentleman, 'It seemed that neither side wanted to win.'

First One-Day International
NEW ZEALAND v. ENGLAND

New Zealand gave international experience to Richard Reid, a quick scoring opener who had been injured for most of the season, and Chris Kuggeleijn, the all-rounder who had led Northern Districts with some success. Both were experienced men.

Gatting asked New Zealand to bat first, and Reid's stay was short. Crowe was unable to reproduce his Wellington form, and it was left to Wright and Greatbatch to get the innings moving. Wright was badly missed by French, who fumbled a stumping chance, but he was finally well caught

Chris Kuggeleijn – an excellent season as captain of Northern Districts and international recognition in the one-day series. (David Munden)

one-handed by Moxon as he and Greatbatch fell in quick succession. Rutherford and Kuggeleijn attempted to revive the innings, but the last five wickets fell for 16 runs, and England were faced with an easy task.

They began poorly, however, slipping to 114 for 4, Gatting having been caught on the boundary and Broad brilliantly run out by Crowe. England needed 91 from 21 overs, but Fairbrother and Capel, redeeming something from the tour, batted with panache and with five overs left only 19 runs were needed. Chatfield was restrictive as ever, and England found the final runs most difficult. When Fairbrother finished the game with a flourish there were only four balls remaining.

Emburey was first named as Man of the Match, but it was later stated that the award should have gone to Wright.

Second One-Day International
NEW ZEALAND v. ENGLAND

Rain delayed the start of the match and reduced it to one of 45 overs per innings. Put in to bat, New Zealand seemed to find the reduction in the number of overs

---

FIRST ONE-DAY INTERNATIONAL – NEW ZEALAND v. ENGLAND
9 March 1988 at Carisbrook Park, Dunedin

NEW ZEALAND				ENGLAND			
R.B. Reid	c Broad, b De Freitas		8	B.C. Broad	run out		33
J.G. Wright†	c Moxon, b Radford		70	M.D. Moxon	c Smith, b Chatfield		6
M.D. Crowe	b Jarvis		18	R.T. Robinson	lbw, b Snedden		17
M.J. Greatbatch	c Capel, b Emburey		28	M.W. Gatting†	c Kuggeleijn,		
K.R. Rutherford	c French, b Capel		13		b Rutherford		42
C.M. Kuggeleijn	c Gatting,			N.H. Fairbrother	not out		50
	b De Freitas		34	D.J. Capel	c Smith, b Chatfield		48
J.G. Bracewell	run out		7	J.E. Emburey	not out		2
I.D.S. Smith*	b Emburey		0	P.A.J. De Freitas			
M.C. Snedden	b Emburey		7	P.W. Jarvis			
W. Watson	not out		0	B.N. French*			
E.J. Chatfield	st French, b Emburey		0	N.V. Radford			
Extras	lb 13, w 5, nb 1		19	Extras	lb 6, w 2, nb 1		9
(49.4 overs)			204	(49.2 overs)	(for 5 wkts)		207

	O	M	R	W		O	M	R	W
De Freitas	10	1	26	2	Watson	10	2	46	–
Radford	10	–	47	1	Chatfield	10	2	15	2
Capel	10	1	45	1	Kuggeleijn	7	–	31	–
Jarvis	10	2	34	1	Snedden	10	1	46	1
Emburey	9.4	–	39	4	Bracewell	7.2	–	42	–
					Rutherford	5	–	21	1

FALL OF WICKETS
1–24, 2–50, 3–127, 4–140, 5–157, 6–188, 7–190, 8–204, 9–204

FALL OF WICKETS
1–28, 2–53, 3–69, 4–114, 5–192

Umpires: R.L. McHarg & G.C. Morris

Man of the Match: J.G. Wright

England won by 5 wickets

SECOND ONE-DAY INTERNATIONAL – NEW ZEALAND v. ENGLAND
12 March 1988 at Lancaster Park, Christchurch

NEW ZEALAND				ENGLAND			
R.B. Reid	c Broad, b Capel		8	B.C. Broad	c Rutherford, b Snedden		56
J.G. Wright†	c De Freitas, b Emburey		43	M.D. Moxon	c Kuggeleijn, b Watson		17
M.D. Crowe	c French, b De Freitas		2	R.T. Robinson	c Chatfield, b Rutherford		44
M.J. Greatbatch	run out		15	M.W. Gatting†	b Watson		33
K.R. Rutherford	run out		5	N.H. Fairbrother	not out		25
C.M. Kuggeleijn	b Emburey		40	D.J. Capel	not out		6
J.G. Bracewell	run out		43	J.E. Emburey			
I.D.S. Smith*	c Fairbrother, b Emburey		19	P.A.J. De Freitas			
M.C. Snedden	not out		1	B.N. French*			
W. Watson	not out		2	P.W. Jarvis			
E.J. Chatfield				N.V. Radford			
Extras	lb 5, w 3		8	Extras	lb 4, w 3		7
(45 overs)	(for 8 wkts)		186	(42.5 overs)	(for 4 wkts)		188

	O	M	R	W		O	M	R	W
De Freitas	9	–	53	1	Watson	9	1	31	2
Capel	9	3	27	1	Chatfield	7	–	32	–
Jarvis	9	–	33	–	Bracewell	5	–	28	–
Radford	9	–	30	–	Snedden	9	–	33	1
Emburey	9	1	38	3	Kuggeleijn	6	–	31	–
					Rutherford	6.5	–	29	1

FALL OF WICKETS
1–24, 2–26, 3–53, 4–68, 5–86, 6–149, 7–183, 8–183

FALL OF WICKETS
1–37, 2–112, 3–151, 4–167

Umpires: B.L. Aldridge & G.C. Morris

Man of the Match: B.C. Broad

England won by 6 wickets

THIRD ONE-DAY INTERNATIONAL – NEW ZEALAND v. ENGLAND
16 March 1988 at McLean Park, Napier

ENGLAND				NEW ZEALAND			
B.C. Broad	b Snedden		106	J.G. Wright†	c Robinson, b Emburey		101
C.W.J. Athey	run out		0	R.H. Vance	b De Freitas		5
R.T. Robinson	c Smith, b Snedden		36	A.H. Jones	b Jarvis		16
P.A.J. De Freitas	c Kuggeleijn, b Rutherford		23	M.J. Greatbatch	not out		64
M.W. Gatting†	b Rutherford		6	K.R. Rutherford	not out		27
N.H. Fairbrother	c and b Kuggeleijn		1	C.M. Kuggeleijn			
D.J. Capel	c Morrison, b Kuggeleijn		14	I.D.S. Smith*			
J.E. Emburey	c and b Snedden		15	M.C. Snedden			
P.W. Jarvis	not out		5	D.K. Morrison			
B.N. French*	b Chatfield		0	W. Watson			
N.V. Radford	c Rutherford, b Snedden		0	E.J. Chatfield			
Extras	lb 10, w 2, nb 1		13	Extras	lb 6, w 4		10
(47.3 overs)			219	(46.3 overs)	(for 3 wkts)		223

	O	M	R	W		O	M	R	W
Morrison	7	–	32	–	De Freitas	10	2	30	1
Watson	5	–	24	–	Capel	9	–	50	–
Chatfield	9	–	40	1	Radford	8	–	31	–
Snedden	8.3	–	34	4	Jarvis	9.3	1	45	1
Rutherford	10	–	39	2	Emburey	7	–	47	1
Kuggeleijn	8	–	40	2	Gatting	3	–	14	–

FALL OF WICKETS
1–1, 2–80, 3–114, 4–137, 5–142, 6–186, 7–205, 8–216, 9–218

FALL OF WICKETS
1–24, 2–62, 3–172

Umpires: F.R. Goodall & S.J. Woodward

Man of the Match: J.G. Wright

New Zealand won by 7 wickets

difficult to come to terms with and tried to hasten too soon. Capel bowled three maidens in succession to frustrate them further, and only Wright could find his touch. Crowe was caught behind although the umpire gave no signal as he was in doubt that the ball had carried, and Crowe walked when assured by French that he had caught the ball cleanly. Greatbatch was unluckily run out when backing up, and it was Kuggeleijn and Bracewell who were left to give the innings any substance and impetus.

The New Zealand bowling offered little threat, and England sauntered to their target with few mishaps and with 13 balls to spare.

Third One-Day International
NEW ZEALAND v. ENGLAND

New Zealand welcomed back Jones and brought Vance in for his first one-day international, but were without Martin Crowe, who was injured. Put in to bat, England made a disastrous start when Athey was run out without facing a ball. Broad stood resolute and reached his first century in limited-over international cricket when he swept Kuggeleijn for six. He also hit 9 fours in an innings which lasted five minutes under three hours. Robinson helped him to add 79, and De Freitas was promoted to give some early verve to the innings, but there was little else of note as New Zealand took wickets regularly, and Snedden finished with four wickets.

Without Crowe, it seemed that New Zealand might struggle to reach their target, but Wright continued his fine form and Greatbatch emphasized his arrival as an international cricketer, and the two left-handers added 109 in 19 overs as the England bowling and fielding fell apart. Emburey's first two overs cost 20 runs, but he dismissed Wright, who hit 15 fours, before Greatbatch and Kuggeleijn rushed New Zealand to victory with 21 balls to spare.

Fourth One-Day International
NEW ZEALAND v. ENGLAND

Belatedly, the contests between England and New Zealand came to life in a final rousing game. Hadlee and Crowe returned, and England struggled against some keen bowling and fielding after they had been put in. Hopes were revived by Gatting and Fairbrother, who added 75. Suddenly, a winning total looked possible, but the return of Chatfield blunted England's revival. He took wickets with the last two balls of the innings, and the catch with which Greatbatch dismissed French, airborne at square-leg, was among the most memorable one has seen in international cricket.

Again Wright led from the front. His spell as captain had enriched him as a player, and he and Jones began the New Zealand challenge with a partnership of 86. Wright was bowled behind his legs by Radford, and Jarvis put fresh heart into England with a fine, fast spell which

---

FOURTH ONE-DAY INTERNATIONAL – NEW ZEALAND v. ENGLAND
19 March 1988 at Eden Park, Auckland

ENGLAND				NEW ZEALAND			
B.C. Broad	b Snedden		12	J.G. Wright	b Radford		47
M.D. Moxon	b Watson		19	A.H. Jones	c Radford, b Jarvis		90
P.A.J. De Freitas	c M.D. Crowe, b Watson		6	M.D. Crowe	c French, b Jarvis		13
R.T. Robinson	c Kuggeleijn, b Rutherford		13	M.J. Greatbatch	c Radford, b Jarvis		5
M.W. Gatting	c Wright, b Watson		48	K.R. Rutherford	lbw, b Jarvis		0
N.H. Fairbrother	b Kuggeleijn		54	C.M. Kuggeleijn	b Capel		2
D.J. Capel	b Chatfield		25	R.J. Hadlee	not out		33
J.E. Emburey	b Chatfield		11	I.D.S. Smith	not out		1
P.W. Jarvis	run out		0	M.C. Snedden			
B.N. French	c Greatbatch, b Chatfield		2	W. Watson			
N.V. Radford	not out		0	E.J. Chatfield			
Extras	lb 12, w 5, nb 1		18	Extras	b 3, lb 12, w 5		20
(50 overs)			208	(49.2 overs)	(for 6 wkts)		211

	O	M	R	W		O	M	R	W
Hadlee	10	–	43	–	De Freitas	10	–	45	–
Watson	10	–	36	3	Capel	10	–	42	1
Snedden	10	2	30	1	Radford	10	2	32	1
Chatfield	10	2	31	3	Jarvis	9.2	1	33	4
Kuggeleijn	5	–	28	1	Emburey	10	–	44	–
Rutherford	5	–	28	1					

FALL OF WICKETS
1–33, 2–33, 3–41, 4–71, 5–146, 6–179, 7–197, 8–197, 9–208

FALL OF WICKETS
1–86, 2–115, 3–129, 4–129, 5–138, 6–199

Umpires: R.L. McHarg & S.J. Woodward

Man of the Match: A.H. Jones

New Zealand won by 4 wickets

Paul Jarvis enjoyed a fine one-day series, but this time his appeal against John Bracewell is unsuccessful. (Simon Bruty/Allsport)

brought him three wickets for six runs in four overs. Jones and Hadlee put New Zealand back on course with 61 off as many deliveries, Jones once again surprising with the power of his hitting.

Jones became Jarvis' fourth victim, but Hadlee hit Emburey for a huge six before hitting the winning boundary off the second ball of the last over. So New Zealand drew the series and ended on a note of joy and optimism. For England, a long, miserable winter was over. Much of it is best forgotten. Nothing was ever quite the same again from the time that Gatting played a reverse sweep to Border's first delivery in the World Cup Final, and that now seemed a very long time ago.

First-Class Averages

BATTING

	M	Inns	NOs	Runs	HS	Av	100s	50s
G.P. Burnett	3	4	3	193	87*	193.00		2
R.H. Vance	9	14	3	731	121	66.45	3	2
G.A. Hick	9	14	1	827	146	63.61	4	3
M.D. Crowe	4	7	1	349	143	58.16	2	
K.R. Rutherford	7	12	1	629	182	57.18	2	3
B.A. Young	10	14	7	384	94	54.85		2
W.K. Lees	7	10	4	319	112	53.16	1	
J.G. Bracewell	5	7	1	315	104	52.50	1	2
R.T. Latham	9	16	3	679	141*	52.23	2	3
B.A. Edgar	9	15	2	676	103*	52.00	1	4
R.N. Hoskin	8	14	2	599	157	49.91	3	1
A.H. Jones	3	6	2	199	72	49.75		2
T.E. Blain	3	5	1	196	75	49.00		2
D.J. Walker	9	16	5	536	77	48.72		4
E.B. McSweeney	9	12	2	459	205*	45.90	1	1
M.R. Pringle	6	7	1	271	77	45.16		3
M.J. Greatbatch	10	19	1	795	149	44.16	2	4
J.G. Wright	4	7		291	103	41.57	1	1
T.J. Franklin	10	16		664	120	41.50	4	2
G.R. Larsen	9	13	2	451	161	41.00	1	2
C.J. Smith	8	15	2	530	122*	40.76	1	2
C.M. Kuggeleijn	9	13	2	429	87	39.00		3
B.G. Cooper	9	12	1	415	116*	37.72	1	2
D.N. Patel	4	4		145	93	36.25		1
D.J. White	10	16	1	522	80	34.80		5
S. Thomson	6	6	1	174	84	34.80		2
K.J. Burns	9	16		550	136	34.37	2	1
S.W. Duff	7	11	4	238	70*	34.00		2
P.A. Horne	5	8		270	66	33.75		2
L.M. Crocker	9	14		470	99	33.57		6
E.J. Gray	9	12	3	293	66*	32.55		2
C.W. Flanagan	3	5		158	50	31.60		1
R.B. Reid	2	4		119	87	29.75		1
B.R. Blair	8	14		413	86	29.50		3
N.A. Mallender	6	7	3	118	41*	29.50		
R.J. Harden	8	14		409	82	29.21		1
P.E. McEwan	8	15	1	400	118	28.57	1	1
J.J. Crowe	5	7	1	165	125	27.50	1	
S.P. Robertson	8	15		404	94	26.93		2
D.A. Dempsey	8	16	1	393	121	26.20	1	
W.P. Fowler	8	12	1	285	56	25.90		2
D.J. Boyle	6	10		255	60	25.50		2
I.R. Snook	7	11	3	201	100*	25.12	1	
T.D. Ritchie	9	11	1	239	102*	23.90	1	
S.W. Brown	7	11	1	233	69	23.30		2
L.K. Germon	8	13	6	159	37*	22.71		
D.J. Guthardt	6	11	2	203	82*	22.55		1
V.R. Brown	4	6		127	60	21.16		1
K. Ibadulla	3	6		126	107	21.00	1	
S.J. McCullum	6	10		167	46	16.70		
J.K. Lindsay	7	12	2	166	41	16.60		
M.W. Priest	7	12	2	162	50	16.20		1
D.J. Hartshorn	4	8	1	103	38	14.71		
P.J. Kelly	7	10	2	109	32*	13.62		
G.K. Robertson	8	11	2	122	44	13.55		
G.E. Bradburn	8	13		174	58	13.38		1

(qualification – 100 runs, average 10.00) (J.F. Reid 112, one innings)

BOWLING

	Overs	Mds	Runs	Wkts	Av	Best	10/m	5/inns
M.A. Holding	258.5	90	468	29	16.82	7/52		3
E.J. Chatfield	175.1	59	320	16	20.00	4/36		
W. Watson	181.2	51	468	23	20.34	6/55		1
K.W. Martin	78	9	282	13	21.69	5/76		1
M.C. Snedden	191	63	404	18	22.44	5/31		1
S.L. Boock	421.1	151	946	42	22.57	6/110		1
W.P. Fowler	132.1	36	364	16	22.75	6/41		1
I.D. Fisher	92.2	18	258	11	23.45	4/37		
R.G. Holland	249.2	76	738	31	23.80	7/69		2
J.P. Millmow	264.5	69	776	31	25.03	4/19		
M.W. Priest	260.2	68	732	28	26.14	5/63	1	2
G.K. Robertson	223.4	53	635	23	27.60	5/34		1
N.A. Mallender	185.4	45	477	17	28.05	4/64		
J.G. Bracewell	143	42	337	11	30.63	3/64		
G.R. Logan	147.1	32	411	13	31.61	3/24		
K. Treiber	308.4	81	812	25	32.48	6/96		2
G.N. Cederwall	140.1	27	457	14	32.64	4/49		
B.J. Barrett	248.2	43	817	25	32.65	4/41		
S.W. Duff	149.4	36	410	12	34.16	3/25		
C.W.H. Lawrence	212.5	41	684	20	34.20	4/43		
D.K. Morrison	161	33	520	15	34.66	5/69		1
T.J. Wilson	293.3	58	957	27	35.44	5/82		1
R.P. de Groen	169.3	35	551	15	36.73	4/71		
E.J. Gray	289	88	663	17	39.00	4/63		
M.R. McKinnon	266.4	70	612	15	40.80	4/27		
J.K. Lindsay	126.5	22	527	12	43.91	5/48	1	2

(qualification – 10 wickets)

LEADING FIELDERS

24 - E.B. McSweeney (ct 20/st 4); 20 - L.K. Germon (ct 19/st 1) and P.J. Kelly (ct 18/st 2); 17 - W.K. Lees (ct 14/st 3) and B.A. Young; 16 - D.J. Guthardt (ct 14/st 2); 12 - G.R. Larsen; 11 - D.J. Walker; 10 - M.J. Greatbatch, S.J. McCullum and I.D.S. Smith

NEW ZEALAND 1987-8
by
DON CAMERON

If the New Zealand cricket side of 1987-8 could be depicted as a ship that had previously sailed a fairly smooth and successful course, then the events of last summer suggest that the deck crew should report for a refresher course at navigation school.

New Zealand cricket had a long and curious journey through the southern summer, and this after a conspicuously unsuccessful and disappointing World Cup in India.

From mid-November to late January they were in Australia, starting with great promise, going on the reefs with the loss of the first Test, almost coming back to win the third but losing the series, and then completing a losing and very undistinguished journey through the Benson and Hedges World Series Cup one-dayers, which Australia always looked likely to win, and duly did.

Then home to three Tests against a moderate England team, a series that produced flashes of drama on the field, but cricket of such modest quality that the easy forecast of three draws soon became a painful certainty.

There was a recovery in which New Zealand, after losing the first two one-day internationals against England, recovered well enough to square the tie at two-all. Then, as a quiet little prologue, New Zealand went to Sharjah, where they beat Sri Lanka twice, and lost twice to the eventual winners, India.

This left New Zealand with the following playing record: 6 Tests, 1 lost, 5 drawn; 18 one-day internationals, 8 won, 10 lost; 3 first-class matches, 2 won, 1 drawn, 1 lost.

Along the way no fewer than 24 players joined the crew, several of whom formed virtually a commuter party, moving to and from Australia with no great profit to the strength or morale of the side, but which must have pleased Air New Zealand no end.

Perhaps the celebrated case of Richard Hadlee's pursuit of the Test wicket-taking record rather typified the whole journey. Hadlee went to Australia with 355 wickets, 19 short of surpassing Ian Botham's 373. In his typical, and very accurate fashion, Hadlee suggested that he would pick up sufficient Test wickets in Australia to have him breaking the record on his home field of Lancaster Park in the first Test against England. He was devastatingly accurate. He had three wickets in the first Test, which Australia won by nine wickets, five in the second at Adelaide, and then came storming home with ten in the third, very nearly taking New Zealand to victory.

Hadlee has a well developed sense of the dramatic, but just failed to break the record and win a Test with one more wicket at Melbourne.

So Hadlee arrived at Lancaster Park level with Botham and the Christchurch faithful flocked along to see the great man duly take the record-breaking wicket on the first day.

They are still waiting. By tea on the first day Hadlee was not only wicket-less, but he had also discovered a calf muscle injury serious enough to keep him out of the rest of the first Test, and out of the second and third as well. It was the great deflationary exercise, kept constantly in front of the public because Hadlee is now a multi-media man, pouring out his thoughts almost daily through a newspaper column, radio programme and, after his injury, as a television commentator. The man was always present, even if the world record was not. It was all rather bizarre.

It may have produced a bonus. When arranging his contract with the New Zealand Cricket Council, which lasted some months before Hadlee decided not to attend the World Cup, Hadlee maintained that he preferred his health to tours of India or Pakistan.

Nine months or so after Hadlee did not break the record at Christchurch, New Zealand were due to play three Tests in a tour of India. Suddenly Hadlee let it be known that he might, after all, just be available for India. That record is a marvellous motivating thing.

But the whole yes-no, will-he, won't-he affair rather typified New Zealand's erratic course during the summer. There seemed to be two main efforts at the start of the Australian tour, the first to discard the disappointments of the World Cup, during which the players often suggested that Glenn Turner's cricket managership had been at fault, the second to launch a new campaign headed by Gren Alabaster as the cricket manager and supported by exceedingly effective and lively training sessions very much under the control of Martin Crowe and Ian Smith.

The effort seemed to work when the New Zealanders swept aside Western Australia, the Sheffield Shield champions, in a one-day warm-up and then in three days of what should have been a four-day game. The next match, against South Australia, was rather cast aside, New Zealand very much in control, but declarations opened the way for a South Australian win.

Then to the first Test, a patchy first New Zealand innings, a slightly better second, but Australia confident and dominant – and winning.

The New Zealanders regained ground in the high-scoring draw at Adelaide and very nearly won the third after a superb come-back on the last afternoon.

But by now the Perth shine was beginning to wear off. The practices which had been lively and fun at Perth became humdrum necessities. Captain Jeff Crowe, popular with his players but fallible at the crease, ran into a bad patch, and his confidence waned day by day. Evan Gray and Willie Watson were dispatched home, and Tony Blain and Stuart Gillespie promoted for the one-day matches. When John Bracewell, the remaining spinner, was injured, the selection reasoning became even more obscure.

Phil Horne, the opening batsman who had been injured, was posted home and Vaughan Brown, the off-spinner of modest international ability, brought to Australia. Then the selectors, on tour and at home, decided that Danny Morrison, the burgeoning young medium-fast bowler, would be better at home than trying to adapt to one-day methods, so he was dismissed and Watson returned.

Along the way Jeff Crowe's form did not improve, and, depending on the point of view, he was occasionally dropped, or rested.

While all this was going on Australia, who had lost the first one-dayer to New Zealand through a classic case of cricketing suicide, went sublimely along, always certain to reach the finals and, once there, just as certain to win against a side that had completely lost its way.

It was rather strange coming home to New Zealand after that expedition. In the past New Zealand's performances in Australia had always created high interest, and the live telecasts of the one-day internationals had been compulsive viewing which transformed about 99 per cent of New Zealanders into cricketing experts. This time, however, the home feeling seemed to be that the one-dayers had become, with New Zealand neither playing well nor winning, rather a bore.

Still, everyone perked up a little for the home series against what looked like a competent, but very manageable, England side. There was a touch of drama when the national selectors, after saying one day that Trevor Franklin, the former New Zealand opener, would not be considered since he had not fully recovered from the horrifying leg injury he received at Gatwick in 1986, decided two days later that Franklin would open the batting in the first Test. More of that later.

Then there was the heady drama that Hadlee, before his adoring public, would break Botham's record.

I suppose it was rather typical of the bathos of the summer that the lasting memory of the first Test was not provided by Franklin, nor by Hadlee, but by Graham Dilley, who, in the middle of one of his superior Test bowling performances, was fined for a very noisy expletive when his opinion did not coincide with the umpire's. The fact that the Test finished in a dawdling draw was lost amid the argument by the England manager Peter Lush that on-field microphones (placed in a stump at each end) should be removed, and the decision by the New Zealand Cricket Council and Television New Zealand, that the microphones would remain.

The second Test, at Auckland, was doomed to be a draw from the moment (a) that England let pass a slip chance from the first ball (this was very much par for the course) and (b) that the Eden Park pitch made survival a relatively simple task. This tedious draw presented a maiden Test century to Mark Greatbatch, a strong century to John Wright, a 99 to Martyn Moxon – and very little else. At least there were no electronic arguments afterwards.

The pitch for the third Test at the Basin Reserve in Wellington was as unyielding and unpromising as had been Eden Park. New Zealand laboured along to 512 for 6 wickets, Martin Crowe returning to form with 143 and Ken Rutherford, at long last, getting his first century from the middle of the batting order.

The pitch lasted, the sunshine did not, and there was blessed relief for the spectators, but alarm among the NZCC financial experts, when Wellington's rain removed the last two days.

So to the four one-dayers, and yet another brainstorm by the New Zealand selectors. Franklin, with his game leg, could not be considered for the hard-fielding exercises of one-day matches. After years of waiting in the wings, which had not pleased his father Bob Vance, chairman of the NZCC board, 31-year-old Robert Vance had been promoted to bat at number three in the third Test.

However, when it came to top-order batsmen for the one-day matches the selectors reached back and chose Richard Reid, a burly Aucklander, to partner Wright.

Reid, son of the famous New Zealand captain John, had been in and out of Auckland teams for two seasons. He was a renowned swatter of the ball in the right circumstances. He also has a sense of humour and when asked if his choice came out of the blue Reid quipped that the selection had come out of the red and yellow and green as well.

In the event Reid was not a success, out trying to hit early in the first two one-dayers, which England wrapped up efficiently. Andrew Jones, the success in Australia but injured in the first Test at Christchurch, came back for the third, Vance returned as an opening batsman, John Wright scored a brilliant hundred (surpassing one by Chris Broad) and New Zealand won handsomely, as they did in Auckland, England only 208, Jones scoring 90 as New Zealand won by six wickets.

Sharjah was something of an afterthought, New Zealand getting a lacing from India in the final, but time enough for Vance and Jones to produce long innings and further confirm their positions.

Stitched into this rather loose fabric was the continuing sad saga of Jeff Crowe as New Zealand captain. He had struggled for runs, his technique astray, in Australia. On return to New Zealand Crowe seemed to regain touch with a century for Auckland, but once back into the Tests the vultures reassembled above. After the second Test was finished Crowe was dropped for the third Test, and from the subsequent one-day matches.

At least the selectors showed some sense about this. Crowe was told before the team was announced that he would not be picked. It was done sensibly and sympathetically and what might have been a traumatic affair passed off fairly smoothly.

So by the end of the summer New Zealand had completed one of their less-distinguished seasons. They had not won a Test, but had preserved their 10-year record of not losing a series at home – mainly because England were not strong enough to press home from a winning position in the first Test at Christchurch.

England were almost as curious as New Zealand. They were pleasant company, from the friendly managership of Lush through the courteous captaincy of Mike Gatting to the forthright comments of Mickey Stewart.

There were touches of class from Broad, Tim Robinson and Moxon at the start of the innings, and until he became injured during the third Test Dilley had taken 15 wickets to give England a sharpish edge to their bowling.

However, they missed Neil Foster, home injured after the Bicentennial Test, and the supporting cast of Paul Jarvis, Philip De Freitas, Neal Radford and David Capel, while occasionally working well, never combined into an effective attack on the dull pitches they encountered in the Tests.

John Emburey was not as much a menace in the Tests as he was in the one-dayers, and all the time England were hampered by indifferent catching behind the wicket.

They were, too, perhaps too prone to rail against the fates – quite often a case of disputation not being matched by reputation.

Still they worked hard, they were pleasant company, and after the tribulations of Pakistan they seemed to enjoy even what was a frustratingly damp New Zealand summer.

It is an oddity that after all the disappointments and frustrations, prompted perhaps by too much theorizing by the selectors, New Zealand came out of the summer with considerable promise for the future.

The summer brought forwards the new players – Jones, Greatbatch, Danny Morrison and Robert Vance – as men of the future. It also produced Martin Snedden as a much more reliable seamer than before, and Willie Watson as the man almost ready to step into Ewen Chatfield's well-worn boots.

And it must be a mark of confidence that New Zealand were able to play almost all a home Test series without Hadlee and still manage to be at least competitive.

Of the new men Jones is by far the most interesting. He had been about the domestic scene for a good many years, an unglamorous labourer compared with the high-fliers like Martin Crowe, before he was taken on the aborted two-match tour of Sri Lanka in 1987. He made further progress during the World Cup and duly won a place in the first Test against Australia at the Gabba.

He survived 89 minutes for four in the first innings and, in a desperate second innings, managed 45 with so many exotic and erratic strokes that the Australian critics rather fell over themselves trying to describe what a thoroughly awful batsman Jones was.

At first sight they may have been right, but they were not aware of Jones' intense attitude, an enormous inner strength which on the surface produces only what seems a taciturn and lugubrious aspect. But the words from the Gabba had burned deep. In the next Test, at the Adelaide Oval, Jones scored 150 before he was run out, after 444 minutes' hard and honest toil.

Jones has all manner of habits and strokes which would not find a place in a coaching manual. He acquires runs, rather than demands them. He can squeeze and squirt ones and twos and, just when he seems on the point of infuriating the purists, can hit through the covers from the back foot with all the timing and savage power of the better West Indians.

Jones' Adelaide century was a landmark innings, for he had convinced himself he belonged in Test cricket, and could succeed. As he came through the members' area at the Oval after his magnificent innings he checked for a second or two, gave the nearby press-box a flick of his bat and the edge of his tongue – as if to suggest that beneath that cast-iron exterior there is a man of feeling.

And of courage. He scored 54 not out in 199 minutes to stifle England's chance of winning the first Test at Christchurch. Only afterwards was it discovered he had batted most of the time with a slight fracture of the wrist caused by a Dilley flier.

Jones may not be pretty to watch, perhaps something of a latter-day Bevan Congdon, but he has all the grit and gumption in the world and is on the brink of a long and solid Test career.

Greatbatch is a beefy, bouncy extrovert who came into the Auckland team as a youngster and was quickly, and probably accurately, regarded as being much too big for his boots. So he moved, as did Martin Crowe, to Central Districts and, in the 1986–7 summer had a glorious time picking up runs and centuries at one end while Crowe was producing a flood of runs at the other.

A summer around the Somerset club last season persuaded Greatbatch that work, as well as talent, were required to reach the top. He was delighted to win a place in the first Test squad against England, frustrated that he was 12th man, but did a lot of energetic fielding and took two very good catches.

He won a place in the second, vice Jones, and after a brief and rather loose 11 in the first innings, ground out a solid century in the second, satisfying his own sense of the dramatic with a century in his first Test.

Then followed 68 in the second Test, 64 not out in the one-day win at Napier, and some marvellously athletic fielding and catching in the fourth. Greatbatch is a much livelier man than Jones, but Greatbatch and Jones may, with Martin Crowe, become the solid middle of the New Zealand batting for a good many years.

Much to his father's dismay, Robert Vance had to wait a long time for his chance. As a not very imaginative captain of Wellington Vance gained a reputation for dourness, and away from the field he has a quiet rather than sparkling personality. Like Jones, Vance had to wait while rather more fashionable batsmen played for New Zealand.

When picked for his first Test, on his home ground at Wellington and batting number three, Vance was advised to play the rock, keep the strokes at home, survive. He did this most capably, 47 in three hours before being run out.

Then the selectors, after insisting on caution from Vance, left him out of the one-day matches (while they experimented with Reid) on the basis that Vance did not have the strokes for one-day matches. Vance was later to prove them wrong, his international place must be fairly secure, and the pity is that it took so long to arrive.

Morrison, a burly young man, caused a stir by taking four wickets in his first Test innings at the Gabba, and various people on both sides of the Tasman proclaimed a new Test bowler had arrived.

They are being a touch premature. Morrison is quickish, without being dynamically fast, and with his thick-set build is not likely to turn into a lithe speedster such as Malcolm Marshall. His future success, until he learns the arts of seam bowling, might well depend on the types of wickets he bowls on. He took eight wickets in three Tests in Australia, and five in the first innings of the first Test in New Zealand, yet rather fell away thereafter on flat pitches. Morrison is quick, strong, eager to learn, but at this stage must only be regarded as promising.

Franklin's return to international cricket is a tribute to his fortitude after his awful injury, which has reduced his mobility. Should his injured leg free up further next summer he must be on the Test short list, for New Zealand must start making plans to groom a replacement for the faithful Wright, whose time is running out, even if his form is not. Rutherford's improvement has come in direct relation to the selectors' acknowledgement that he is a middle-order batsman, and not an opener. This youngish man, with a full range of strokes, may be on the brink of a new career as the shot-maker at number six, especially if he is encouraged to work on his medium-pace bowling.

So New Zealand came out of their erratic summer in

John Wright. (Alan Cozzi)

tolerably good shape for a Test line-up of Wright and Vance, Jones, Martin Crowe, Greatbatch, Rutherford, Smith, Hadlee, Bracewell, Snedden, Chatfield, and perhaps Morrison, now looks rather better than any combination New Zealand might have found at the start of the season.

On the home front, with the New Zealand players absent for seven-eighths of the time, the Shell Trophy series produced a weird finish, very much in keeping with this curious season.

On the last day of the last match Otago came from behind to beat Wellington and join the leaders, Auckland, who were struggling along toward a first-innings lead over Northern Districts, which would have given them the title.

Should the Auckland–Northern Districts match not have produced a first-innings result, then the winner would have been decided on the basis of runs per wicket, for and against.

Going into the last day Auckland assembled all the season's scores, worked out Otago's position, and Auckland's. These told Auckland that should it reach a certain score for the loss of a certain number of wickets then Auckland would win the trophy, regardless of taking first-innings points from Northern Districts.

So Auckland reached their target score, and went away to celebrate the winning of the Trophy.

Unfortunately for them one very small piece of wrong evidence had been used (Wellington had lost 10 wickets in an innings against Otago while Auckland thought they had lost only 9). That very slight error changed the figures sufficiently for Otago to take the Trophy by some very small fraction of a point.

Unhappily, the NZCC and its executive director Graham Dowling, who should have been the fount of all knowledge, were busily engaged organizing the first England Test at Lancaster Park, and in any case the NZCC had not received by then the official scoresheets from which any calculations would have to be made.

So, three days after Auckland had begun their celebrations the NZCC released the news that Otago, and not Auckland, had won the Trophy.

It was, then, one of those seasons.

Next summer the plan is that if two teams finish level on points they will share the Trophy. At least everyone will understand that, at the right time.

Distant Voice in the Darkness

Cricket in South Africa. The Castle
Currie Cup. The Castle Bowl. Nissan
Shield. Benson and Hedges Trophy.
First-class averages.

*The South African side that faced the Australians in 1987. Injury or
retirement kept four of them, Page, Pollock, Kourie and McKenzie,
from the first-class scene in 1987–8.*
Back row, left to right: *D.J. Richardson, S.T. Jefferies,
B.M. McMillan, H.A. Page, A.J. Kourie, K. McKenzie and
B.J. Whitfield.*
Front row, left to right: *P.N. Kirsten, S.J. Cook, C.E.B. Rice
(captain), D. Carlstein (manager), R.G. Pollock and G.S. Le Roux.*
(C. Harte)

For only the second time in seven years the South African season offered no touring team. In an effort to place more emphasis on the senior competition, the Currie Cup, the South African Cricket Union decided to condense the fixtures into a period of seven weeks at the turn of the year. This was an attempt to improve the gates and to give the tournament as much exposure as possible. Coastal provinces were given four home games each and the inland associations only three. The SACU reasoned that holiday-makers would flock to the coastal resorts and help swell the attendances. Notable British television and radio commentators were invited to broadcast on the Cup matches in an effort to stimulate interest. Certainly there was a renewed interest in the Currie Cup and attendances improved, but the Benson and Hedges one-day matches still drew by far the largest crowds with the Nissan Shield knockout competition second.

The Currie Cup and Castle Bowl were divided into Northern and Southern sections with the winners of each competing in the final. Transvaal, Natal and Northern Transvaal comprised the Northern Section of the Currie Cup, and their 'B' sides, with Griqualand West, the Northern Section of the Castle Bowl. Eastern Province, Western Province and Orange Free State made the Southern Section of the Currie Cup, and the 'B' sides of the first two associations plus Boland and Border comprised the Southern Section of the Bowl.

In the Currie Cup each side played the other sides in its section twice and the teams from the other section once; in the Castle Bowl each side played each other in its section twice.

Cricket in South Africa. (C. Harte)

There were suggestions that the might of Transvaal would be threatened. Sylvester Clarke had moved to Orange Free State, who could also call upon Allan Lamb and Alvin Kallicharran. They were master-minded by Mike Procter. Eastern Province had the services of Wessels, McEwan, who had moved from Western province to his old home to take over the family farm, Australian fast bowler Rod McCurdy and Glamorgan and England paceman Greg Thomas. As usual, there was a large sprinkling of English professionals in both competitions; Barnett, Moles, Topley and Igglesden were among the more prominent. Neal Radford was only able to assist Transvaal in the weeks before leaving to join the England party in New Zealand.

Nissan Shield

Preliminary Round

3 October 1987

at SFW Ground, Stellenbosch

Griqualand West 186 for 6 (M.N. Kellow 88)
Boland 187 for 5

Boland won by 5 wickets

17 October 1987

at De Beers Country Club, Kimberley

Boland 265 for 8 (S. Nackerdien 78, K.J. Barnett 70, C.F. Spilhaus 50, P. MacLaren 4 for 59)
Griqualand West 197 for 9 (A.J. Moles 50)

Boland won by 68 runs

Boland disposed of Griqualand West with considerable ease, winning the first-leg match with seven balls to spare. The matches were of 55-over duration.

Benson and Hedges Trophy

14 October 1987

at Danie Craven Stadium, Stellenbosch

Eastern Province 214 for 5 (M.W. Rushmere 110 not out)
Impalas 205 for 9 (J.D. du Toit 51)

Eastern Province (2 pts) won by 9 runs

16 October 1987

at Centurion Park, Verwoerdburg

Northern Transvaal 299 for 5 (L.J. Barnard 86, R.F. Pienaar 83)
Western Province 220 (P.N. Kirsten 65, A.M. Ferriera 5 for 44)

Northern Transvaal (2 pts) won by 9 runs

21 October 1987

at Danie Craven Stadium, Stellenbosch

Impalas 250 for 7
Transvaal 222

Impalas (2 pts) won by 28 runs

at Centurion Park, Verwoerdburg

Eastern Province 244 for 6 (K.S. McEwan 62, M.W. Rushmere 55, K.C. Wessels 51)
Northern Transvaal 17 for 2

Match abandoned
Eastern Province 1 pt, Northern Transvaal 1 pt

The day/night 45-over competition began with a major surprise when Impalas beat Transvaal, who always maintained the right run rate but lost too many wickets. Steve Jones hit 47 off 32 balls with 6 fours and 2 sixes to give Impalas' innings a tremendous boost after five wickets had fallen for 155.

Roy Pienaar and Lee Barnard added 180 in 79 minutes for Northern Transvaal's second wicket against Western Province.

Nissan Shield

24 October 1987

at University Oval, Bloemfontein

Western Province 211 for 9 (P.N. Kirsten 52)
Orange Free State 212 for 8 (L.J. Wilkinson 65, P.R. Steyn 57)

Orange Free State (2 pts) won by 2 wickets

at SFW Ground, Stellenbosch

Eastern Province 195 for 8 (K.C. Wessels 51)
Boland 188 (J.D. du Toit 58, S.A. Jones 51, R.J. McCurdy 4 for 15)

Eastern Province (2 pts) won by 7 runs

The first round of matches in the qualifying leagues for the

Jimmy Cook, centuries in successive matches for Transvaal in the Nissan Shield and a consistent season as opening batsman for the Currie Cup winners. (Adrian Murrell/ Allsport)

Nissan Shield produced two close matches. Steyn and Wilkinson put on 115 for Orange Free State's first wicket, but three wickets fell for one run, and at 179 for 7 they looked doomed. Sylvester Clarke played a couple of lusty shots and Robert East, with van Zyl, kept his head and steered his side to victory with an over to spare.

Rod McCurdy's remarkable economic spell snatched a win for Eastern Province. Boland lost their last three wickets without adding a run.

Benson and Hedges Trophy

28 October 1987

at Harmony Ground, Virginia

Impalas 192 (L.J. Wilkinson 4 for 48)
Orange Free State 187 (L.J. Wilkinson 70, P.J.R. Steyn 52)

Impalas (2 pts) won by 5 runs

Impalas maintained their challenge in the Benson and Hedges Trophy with another unexpected win. Steyn and Wilkinson began the chase for 193 runs with a stand of 118, but panic caused five men to be run out and Impalas snatched a narrow victory.

27, 28 and 29 October 1987

at Kingsmead, Durban

South African Defence Force 186 for 5 dec and 265 (P.G. Amm 54, R.K. McGlashan 8 for 122)
Natal 197 for 5 dec (B.J. Whitfield 50) and 255 for 8 (A.C. Hudson 115 not out, T.R. Madsen 61, R.F. Pienaar 5 for 95)

Natal won by 2 wickets

The first-class season opened with the traditional fixture involving the Defence Force. Sporting declarations kept the game alive after rain had interrupted. In the Defence Force's second innings, Richard McGlashan took a career best 8 for 122. It was McGlashan's 13th first-class match and his leg-breaks had only once. before claimed five wickets in an innings. His match figures of 11 for 175 were also the best of his career. Chasing a target of 255 at nearly four an over, Natal were led to victory by opener Andrew Hudson, who hit a maiden first-class hundred.

Castle Bowl

30, 31 October and 1 November 1987

at Jan Smuts Stadium, Pietermaritzburg

Natal 'B' 258 for 9 dec (M.J. Pearse 69, G.W. Symmonds 4 for 37) and 187 for 2 dec (P.H. Rayner 100 not out)
Griqualand West 193 (A.D. Methven 57, A.J. Moles 50, M.R. Hobson 4 for 62) and 213 (I. Human 54, D.R. Hewson 50, M.R. Hobson 4 for 25)

Natal 'B' won by 39 runs
Natal 'B' 23 pts, Griqualand West 6 pts

The first match in the Castle Bowl produced a convincing win for Natal 'B'. Paul Rayner hit the third century of his career, and the medium pace of Hobson was effective in both innings.

Nissan Shield

31 October 1987

at Centurion Park, Verwoerdburg

Natal 251 for 6 (C.L. King 52 not out)
Northern Transvaal 252 for 6 (K.D. Verdoorn 102, N.T. Day 51)

Northern Transvaal (2 pts) won by 4 wickets

at Jan Smuts Ground, East London

Transvaal 262 for 5 (S.J. Cook 115)
Border 259 for 7 (I.L. Howell 64 not out, G.L. Hayes 62)

Transvaal (2 pts) won by 3 runs

Northern Transvaal, thanks to a splendid hundred from Kevin Verdoorn, his first in senior cricket, beat Natal with seven balls to spare. He and Day took the score from 116 for 4 to 229 before Day fell to Packer.

Border put up a very brave show against Transvaal, for whom Jim Cook hit an accomplished century. At 152 for 6, Border looked well beaten, but Hayes and Howell batted heroically to bring their side very close to a famous victory.

Benson and Hedges Trophy

4 November 1987

at Wanderers, Johannesburg

Eastern Province 297 for 4 (K.C. Wessels 81 not out)
Transvaal 163 (B.M. McMillan 75)

Eastern Province (2 pts) won by 44 runs

at University Oval, Bloemfontein

Northern Transvaal 201 for 6 (M.J.R. Rindel 56 not out)
Orange Free State 170 for 3 (L.J. Wilkinson 54)

Orange Free State (2 pts) won on faster scoring rate

Transvaal suffered their second defeat in the competition, and Steyn and Wilkinson put on 106 for Orange Free State's first wicket to launch their side on the way to success in the rain-affected match at Bloemfontein.

Castle Bowl

6, 7 and 8 November 1987

at Kemsley Park, Port Elizabeth

Border 211 (E.N. Trotman 68) and 246 (A.L. Wilmot 135, B.E. van der Vyver 5 for 82, C. Wulfsohn 4 for 69)
Eastern Province 'B' 142 (W.K. Watson 5 for 36) and 319 for 7 (A.V. Birrell 78 not out, J.W. Furstenburg 57, M.W. Pringle 50 not out)

Eastern Province 'B' won by 3 wickets
Eastern Province 'B' 20 pts, Border 7 pts

Eastern Province 'B' were outplayed for three-quarters of the match but forged a commendable victory over Border. Solid batting and a fine spell of bowling from the former Notts medium-pacer Watson put Border in a comfortable position. Another veteran, Anthony Wilmot, hit the 11th hundred of his distinguished career to make Border's position seemingly even more secure, but Eastern Province 'B' scored at three an over after the early loss of Armitage and batted with consistency and determination to reach a formidable target.

Nissan Shield

7 November 1987

at Wanderers, Johannesburg

Transvaal 277 for 4 (S.J. Cook 126, M. Yachad 106)
Orange Free State 250 for 9 (A.C. Storie 97)

Transvaal (2 pts) won by 27 runs

at SFW Ground, Stellenbosch

Natal 291 for 6 (R.M. Bentley 60, T.R. Madsen 51)
Boland 93

Natal (2 pts) won by 198 runs

A second victory for Transvaal in the Nissan Shield was brought about by a magnificent opening stand of 232 between Cook and Yachad. The stand was only nine runs short of the Nissan Shield first-wicket record.

Natal swept aside Boland to keep alive their hopes of qualifying for the semi-finals.

Don Topley – 10 wickets in a match for the first time, Griqualand West v. Transvaal 'B' 13–15 November. (Adrian Murrell/Allsport)

Benson and Hedges Trophy

11 November 1987

at Kingsmead, Durban

Natal v. impalas

Match abandoned

Castle Bowl

13, 14 and 15 November 1987

at De Beers Country Club, Kimberley

Griqualand West 202 (A.J. Moles 114, M. James 6 for 62) and 116
Transvaal 'B' 110 (T.D. Topley 5 for 50, P. McLaren 4 for 19) and 151 (T.D. Topley 5 for 81, G.W. Symmonds 4 for 47)

Griqualand West won by 57 runs
Griqualand West 21 pts, Transvaal 'B' 5 pts

13, 14 and 15 November 1987

at SFW Ground, Stellenbosch

Boland 195 (S.A. Jones 79, A.P. Igglesden 5 for 52) and 198 (A.P. Igglesden 5 for 61)
Western Province 'B' 199 (J.B. Commins 51, P.J. Newport 4 for 32) and 150

Boland won by 44 runs
Boland 21 pts, Western Province 'B' 6 pts

A century by Warwickshire's Andy Moles and 10 wickets in a match for the first time by Essex's Don Topley took Griqualand West to their first win of the season. They always seemed to have the better of Transvaal 'B' in spite of James' best bowling performance.

Kent's Alan Igglesden was another bowler to take 10 wickets in a match for the first time, but he ended on the losing side as Steve Jones urged his Boland side to victory with a typically aggressive performance.

Nissan Shield

14 November 1987

at Newlands, Cape Town

Western Province 282 for 6 (L. Seeff 100, P.N. Kirsten 62)
Border 114 (S.T. Jefferies 4 for 15)

Western Province (2 pts) won by 168 runs

at St George's Park, Port Elizabeth

Eastern Province 232 for 6 (M.W. Rushmere 106)
Northern Transvaal 226 for 9 (L.J. Barnard 106, R.F. Pienaar 77, R.J. McCurdy 4 for 42)

Eastern Province (2 pts) won by 6 runs

Western Province overwhelmed Border and, in doing so, assured that semi-final places would not be decided until the last round of matches. Seeff and Kirsten added 110 for the second wicket after Seeff had completely dominated an opening stand of 82 with Lazard, who was run out for 16. Steve Jefferies settled the match with a magnificent spell of bowling which reduced Border to 36 for 5. Jefferies took four of the wickets and finished with figures of 11–5–11–4.

Eastern Province recovered from the loss of Amm and Wessels for 22 with McEwan giving Rushmere, who hit his first Shield century, fine support. Callaghan and Shaw provided a late burst of quick scoring. Pienaar and Barnard, who also hit his first Shield century, put on 178 for Northern Transvaal's second wicket, but no other batsman reached double figures.

Benson and Hedges Trophy

18 November 1987

at Danie Craven Stadium, Stellenbosch

Western Province 272 for 7 (D.J. Cullinan 74, L. Seeff 50)
Impalas 201 (E.N. Trotman 66, C.R. Matthews 4 for 65)

Western Province (2 pts) won by 71 runs

Consistent batting was the foundation of Western Province's victory.

Simon Base had an outstanding season for Boland. His 35 wickets did much to help them win the Castle Bowl. His 6 for 28 against Border, 11–13 December, was a career-best bowling performance. (Tony Edenden)

Castle Bowl

20, 21 and 22 November 1987

at Centurion Park, Verwoedburg

Northern Transvaal 'B' 309 for 8 dec (P.J.A. Visagie 146 not out) and 40 for 3
Natal 'B' 104 and 244 (G.M. Walsh 113, P.L. Symcox 6 for 72)

Northern Transvaal 'B' won by 7 wickets
Northern Transvaal 'B' 23 pts, Natal 'B' 3 pts

20, 21 and 23 November 1987

at Uitenhage CC Ground, Uitenhage

Boland 312 (W.S. Truter 107, O. Henry 91)
Eastern Province 'B' 136 (P.J. Newport 4 for 36) and 161 (A.V. Birrell 61, O. Henry 5 for 41)

Boland won by an innings and 15 runs
Boland 22 pts, Eastern Province 'B' 3 pts

A maiden first-class century from skipper Peter Visagie put Northern Transvaal 'B' in a strong position after they

had lost their first four wickets for 71. A varied attack quickly disposed of Natal 'B' in just over 30 overs, but the visitors fought back after they had been forced to follow on, with Greg Walsh reaching the first hundred of his career. Pat Symcox's off-breaks plagued the rest of the visiting batsmen, but they came close to denying Northern Transvaal 'B', who had a late rush for the winning runs.

Boland were most impressive in beating Eastern Province 'B' and looked as if they would be strong contenders for the Bowl. Opener Truter's hundred and Omar Henry's late flourish provided the substance of the runs while the new ball attack of Phil Newport and Simon Base did well in both innings, reducing the home side to 28 for 4 after they had followed on. Henry's left-arm spin completed the victory.

Nissan Shield

21 November 1987

at University Oval, Bloemfontein

Orange Free State 259 for 7 (J.J. Strydom 70, A.C. Storie 54 not out)
Border 118

Orange Free State (2 pts) won by 141 runs

at Kingsmead, Durban

Natal 259 for 8 (R.M. Bentley 112, D. Bestall 71)
Eastern Province 263 for 5 (K.C. Wessels 98, D.J. Richardson 94)

Eastern Province (2 pts) won by 5 wickets

Eastern Province assured themselves of a place in the semi-finals when they beat Natal with two balls to spare, Callaghan and Shaw sharing an unbroken stand of 39, which brought victory after fine batting by Wessels and Richardson, who added 149 for the fourth wicket. It was hard on Rob Bentley, who had earlier hit his highest score in the Shield.

Orange Free State also looked likely to qualify by crushing Border, who were bowled out in 44.2 overs.

Benson and Hedges Trophy

25 November 1987

at Newlands, Cape Town

Natal 209 for 7 (M.B. Logan 110)
Western Province 210 for 3 (T.N. Lazard 88 not out, P.N. Kirsten 55)

Western Province (2 pts) won by 7 wickets

27 November 1987

at St George's Park, Port Elizabeth

Eastern Province 238 for 4 (M.W. Rushmere 121)
Orange Free State 165

Eastern Province (2 pts) won by 73 runs

Lazard carried his bat to take Western Province to victory with four balls to spare while Rushmere's century dominated the game at Port Elizabeth, where Orange Free State, a strong side on paper, were completely outplayed.

Castle Bowl

26, 27 and 28 November 1987

at R.J.E. Burt Oval, Constantia

Western Province 'B' 353 for 7 dec (G. Kirsten 163 not out, E.O. Simons 68) and 195 for 4 dec (F.B. Touzel 75 not out)
Border 278 for 7 dec (K.G. Bauermeister 74, B.M. Osborne 68, I.L. Howell 55 not out) and 221 for 7 (K.G. Bauermeister 72 not out)

Match drawn
Western Province 'B' 4 pts, Border 4 pts

at Kingsmead, Durban

Natal 'B' 301 for 8 dec (D.A. Scott 75, P.H. Rayner 57) and 41 for 1
Transvaal 'B' 387 (D.H. Howell 151, M.S. Venter 57, R.K. McGlashan 4 for 60)

Match drawn
Transvaal 'B' 6 pts, Natal 'B' 4 pts

A fifth-wicket stand of 129 between Simons and Kirsten, who hit a maiden first-class century, took Western Province 'B' to a big score, but on a placid wicket it was never likely that they would force a result.

David Howell, having played for both Western and Eastern Provinces, hit the highest score of his career in his second match for Transvaal 'B'. He and Venter put on 156 for the first wicket, but a docile pitch and interruptions for rain dashed any chance of a result.

Nissan Shield

28 November 1987

at Centurion Park, Verwoerdburg

Boland 176 (P.J. Newport 57, T. Bosch 4 for 20)
Northern Transvaal 177 for 6 (N.T. Day 72 not out)

Northern Transvaal (2 pts) won by 4 wickets

at Wanderers, Johannesburg

Transvaal 176
Western Province 177 for 5 (P.N. Kirsten 72)

Western Province (2 pts) won by 5 wickets

Having bowled out Boland with some ease, Northern Transvaal were in dreadful trouble at 32 for 5. Anton Ferreira helped Noel Day to add 64, and Rodney Ontong then hit ferociously to score 44 and, with Day, to take Northern Transvaal to victory and the semi-finals with 11 balls to spare.

The real excitement was at Johannesburg where, put in to bat, Transvaal slumped to 78 for 5, having lost McKen-

Pool A	P	W	L	Pts	R/R
Orange Free State	3	2	1	4	4.68
Western Province	3	2	1	4	4.336
Transvaal	3	2	1	4	4.333
Border	3	–	3	0	2.97

Pool B	P	W	L	Pts	R/R
Eastern Province	3	3	–	6	4.19
Northern Transvaal	3	2	1	4	4.008
Natal	3	1	2	2	4.89
Boland	3	–	3	0	2.76

zie retired hurt. Brian McMillan and McBride added 68, but the final total was still meagre. Transvaal had looked certain to qualify for the semi-finals, but Western Province, realizing that they could beat them for a place in the last four on a faster run rate, went for the runs quickly. Radford and Rice apart, the Transvaal bowlers were savaged, and Western reached their target in 44.3 overs so beating Transvaal by .003 for a place in the semi-finals.

Benson and Hedges Trophy

4 December 1987

at Wanderers, Johannesburg

Transvaal 249 for 2 (S.J. Cook 116, L.P. Vorster 53 not out, H.R. Fotheringham 52)
Northern Transvaal 253 for 5 (L.J. Barnard 71, R.C. Ontong 57 not out)

Northern Transvaal (2 pts) won by 5 wickets

A stand of 130 for the first wicket between Cook and Fotheringham, who then added 90 with Vorster, took Transvaal to a formidable total, but, on a perfect wicket, it proved insufficient as the visitors won with two balls to spare.

Castle Bowl

4, 5 and 6 December 1987

at Centurion Park, Verwoerdburg

Griqualand West 278 (A.J. Moles 111, G. Grobler 4 for 47) and 109 for 0 (A.J. Moles 61 not out)
Northern Transvaal 'B' 302 for 5 dec (A. Geringer 113, A. Da Costa 80)

Match drawn
Northern Transvaal 'B' 9 pts, Griqualand West 5 pts

Andy Moles, the Warwickshire batsman, shared two century opening partnerships and took two wickets for 24, but Northern Transvaal 'B' still had the better of a draw. Da Costa and Geringer put on 178 for the home side's third wicket before Moles dismissed them both, Geringer hit a maiden first-class hundred.

5, 7 and 8 December 1987

at St George's Park, Port Elizabeth

South African Universities 122 (R.J. McCurdy 6 for 11) and 267 (J.B. Commins 70, T.G. Shaw 4 for 68, J.G. Thomas 4 for 92)
Eastern Province 440 (K.S. McEwan 104, K.C. Wessels 69, D.J. Callaghan 58, D.J. Richardson 50, M.R. Hobson 4 for 97)

Eastern Province won by an innings and 51 runs

In the Universities annual first-class friendly match, the pace of Rod McCurdy, the Australian, proved too much for the students. Ken McEwan hit his only first-class hundred of the season as he and Wessels put on 120 for the third wicket.

Benson and Hedges Trophy

9 December 1987

at Wanderers, Johannesburg

Natal 160 (N.P. Daniels 63, B.M. McMillan 4 for 46)
Transvaal 163 for 9 (H.L. Alleyne 4 for 25)

Transvaal (2 pts) won by 1 wicket

11 December 1987

at Kingsmead, Durban

Northern Transvaal 126
Natal 129 for 5

Natal (2 pts) won by 5 wickets

12 December 1987

at St George's Park, Port Elizabeth

Western Province 145 (R.J. McCurdy 4 for 13)
Eastern Province 134

Western Province (2 pts) won by 11 runs

15 December 1987

at Newlands, Cape Town

Transvaal 224 for 8 (M. Yachad 72, G.S. le Roux 4 for 25)
Western Province 123 for 9

Transvaal (2 pts) won by 101 runs

In the last round of matches before a two-month break in the Benson and Hedges competition, Transvaal kept their hopes of qualifying for the semi-finals alive by beating both Natal and Western Province. The victory over Natal came with one wicket and four balls to spare. Australian Rod McCurdy bowled an inspired spell of nine overs against Western Province and still ended on the losing side.

Castle Bowl

11, 12 and 13 December 1987

at Cape Town CC, Plumstead

Eastern Province 'B' 179 (A. van Snyman 58) and 242 (B.E. van der Vyver 54)
Western Province 'B' 227 for 6 dec (G. Kirsten 80 not out) and 131 for 6 (M.W. Pringle 6 for 33)

Match drawn
Western Province 'B' 7 pts, Eastern Province 'B' 4 pts

at SFW Ground, Stellenbosch

Boland 71 (J.A. Carse 4 for 16) and 97 (G.L. Hayes 4 for 30)
Border 124 (S.J. Base 6 for 28, O. Henry 4 for 39) and 46 for 2

Border won by 8 wickets
Border 20 pts, Boland 5 pts

at De Beers Country Club, Kimberley

Griqualand West 359 (J.M. Arthur 123, A.D. Methven 63, C.S. Stirk 4 for 73) and 117 for 4
Natal 'B' 510 for 4 dec (A.C. Hudson 148, G.M. Walsh 138 not out, D.A. Scott 66 not out)

Match drawn
Natal 'B' 6 pts, Griqualand West 3 pts

Eastern Province 'B' barely scored at more than two an over in the match at Plumstead, where the wicket was slow. Needing 195 to win in 34 overs, the home side never looked likely to match the rate required and faltered as Wayne Pringle took a career best 6 for 33.

Having swept all before them in their first two matches, Boland suffered a rude shock at the hands of Border. Electing to bat when they won the toss, they found the wicket treacherous and were beaten inside two days in spite of a career best bowling performance by Simon Base.

In contrast, the match at Kimberley produced an abundance of runs. John Arthur hit a maiden first-class century, and there were career bests from Andrew Hudson and Greg Walsh. Inevitably, the game was drawn.

Castle Currie Cup

17, 18 and 19 December 1987

at University Oval, Bloemfontein

Eastern Province 268 for 7 dec (K.C. Wessels 101, D.J. Callaghan 70) and 280 (K.C. Wessels 130, P.G. Amm 60)
Orange Free State 517 for 8 dec (A.J. Lamb 294, J.J. Strydom 107, R.J. McCurdy 4 for 109) and 33 for 4

Orange Free State won by 6 wickets
Orange Free State 23 pts, Eastern Province 5 pts

19, 20 and 21 December 1987

at Wanderers, Johannesburg

Northern Transvaal 206 (L.J. Barnard 50, B.M. McMillan 5 for 39) and 251 (A.M. Ferreira 72, N.V. Radford 4 for 80)
Transvaal 192 (R.F. Pienaar 4 for 40) and 269 for 8 (C.E.B. Rice 73)

Transvaal won by 2 wickets
Transvaal 22 pts, Northern Transvaal 7 pts

at Kingsmead, Durban

Natal 266 (A.C. Hudson 72, D.B. Rundle 5 for 59) and 208 (T.R. Madsen 50, D.B. Rundle 6 for 37)
Western Province 396 for 8 dec (L. Seeff 125, T.N. Lazard 90) and 71 for 5 (T.J. Packer 4 for 40)

Match drawn
Western Province 7 pts, Natal 4 pts

The Currie Cup, South Africa's premier competition, could not have begun on a higher note. At Bloemfontein, Wessels won the toss, decided to bat and set a captain's example with 101 in 216 minutes with 15 fours. He declared shortly before the end of the first day, and the home side, 48 for 3, stuttered in reply. The fourth wicket went down at 119, and at this point, skipper Joubert Strydom joined Allan Lamb. In 342 minutes, they put on 355, a South African record for the fifth wicket. Lamb's 294 was made off as many deliveries and contained 5 sixes

The Currie Cup began in sensational fashion with Allan Lamb hitting 294 off as many deliveries for Orange Free State against Eastern Province, 18 December. (David Munden)

and 33 fours. His innings lasted for 394 minutes and his 294 was the fifth highest score to be recorded in first-class cricket in South Africa. Strydom declared with a lead of 249, but hopes of a quick victory were dashed by Wessels, who hit his second century of the match after Snyman and Rushmere had gone for 34. This remarkable match was to save its final drama for the last ball. Orange Free State had only four overs in which to score 32, and when the last ball of the fourth over arrived they were still five runs short. Sylvester Clarke promptly hit a six and won the match.

There was similar excitement at Johannesburg. Transvaal, needing 266 to win, were 50 for 3, but Clive Rice and Louis Vorster added 114. Five wickets fell for 24 runs, leaving Transvaal on 198 for 8 and Northern Transvaal with victory in their grasp. Two English county players, Bruce Roberts and Neal Radford, staged a dramatic recovery to win the match for the home side. Roberts hit 43 and Radford 31.

Western Province were thwarted by the weather. David Rundle took a career best with his off-breaks, and Terry Lazard and Lawrie Seeff put on 222 for the first wicket so that Kuiper was able to declare with a first-innings lead of

130. Rundle then bettered his first innings performance by taking 6 for 37 in 28.5 overs, and Western Province were left with 79 to make in 42 overs, but rain cost them 65 minutes play after they had reached 41 for 1, and 15 overs became their maximum. They hit bravely, but finished eight runs short.

Castle Bowl

19, 20 and 21 December 1987

at Centurion Park, Verwoerdburg

Transvaal 'B' 205 (B. McBride 68, M.S. Venter 57, G.L. Ackermann 5 for 36) and 260 for 9 dec (W. Kirsh 109, M.S. Venter 62, P.L. Symcox 7 for 93)
Northern Transvaal 'B' 210 (V.G. Cresswell 102, P.J.A. Visagie 54, M. James 5 for 68) and 167 (V.G. Cresswell 66, M. James 7 for 45)

Transvaal 'B' won by 89 runs
Transvaal 'B' 22 pts, Northern Transvaal 'B' 6 pts

26, 27 and 28 December 1987

at Jan Smuts Ground, East London

Border 325 for 9 dec (A.L. Wilmot 105, M.J.P. Ford 67, E.N. Trotman 54, A.J. McClement 4 for 78) and 246 for 5 (E.N. Trotman 101 not out, B.W. Lones 57)
Western Province 'B' 400 (M.H. Austen 121, K.J. Bridgens 79, G. Kirsten 56, I.L. Howell 6 for 89)

Match drawn
Western Province 'B' 7 pts, Border 5 pts

Wicket-keeper Vernon Cresswell's maiden first-class century helped Northern Transvaal 'B' to a small first-innings lead. Venter and Kirsh responded with an opening stand of 146, and McMillan was able to declare and ask the home side to score 256 to win. Few batsmen had been able to cope with the off-spin of Pat Symcox, who bettered his six-wicket performance of earlier in the season. James had plagued Northern in the first innings, and when they went in search of victory he tortured them even more, returning the best figures (innings and match) of his brief career and winning the game for Transvaal 'B'.

A batsman's paradise in East London precluded the possibility of a result but allowed three centuries to be scored, one of which, by Michael Austen, was a maiden first-class hundred. There was some magnificent bowling by Ian Howell, who took 6 for 89 in 50 overs, 14 of which were maidens.

Castle Currie Cup

26, 27 and 28 December 1987

at Wanderers, Johannesburg

Natal 176 (M.B. Logan 52, N.V. Radford 5 for 42, B.M. McMillan 4 for 35) and 83 (N.V. Radford 6 for 38)
Transvaal 193 (L.P. Vorster 64, M. Yachad 50, P.B. Clift 4 for 46) and 67 for 1

Transvaal won by 9 wickets
Transvaal 21 pts, Natal 6 pts

took Transvaal to 152 for 2, but 8 wickets fell for 41 runs, and Transvaal took only a 17-run first-innings lead. Natal lost five wickets in clearing those small arrears as Radford and Estwick destroyed the upper order. There was no effective recovery, and the home side ran out easy winners.

Mark Rushmere carried his bat through the innings at Port Elizabeth, the first Eastern Province player to do so for 30 years. His 136 took 379 minutes and included 12 fours. Barnard and du Preez countered with an opening stand of 189 after Pienaar had been forced to retire hurt at 16. Barnard declared and set Eastern Province to make 240 in 45 overs. Amm gave them a good start, but Ontong and Morris turned the match in favour of Northern Transvaal so that the home side were happy to escape with a draw.

The major performance came at Newlands. Having decided to bat first, Orange Free State were bundled out for 134, David Rundle's off-spin bemusing the middle order. Consistent batting took Western Province to a healthy lead, and Orange Free State began their second innings 189 runs in arrears. Whatever hopes they had of saving the game were quickly shattered by Steve Jefferies, the 28-year-old left-arm fast medium-pace bowler who became only the second player in South African cricket history to take all 10 wickets in an innings. The only man to have achieved the feat previously was Vogler in 1906–7, for Eastern Province against Griqualand West. Jefferies bowled East and had Clarke lbw, the other batsmen were caught. His final figures were: 23.5–7–59–10.

Only the second bowler in the history of South African cricket to take all 10 wickets in an innings. Stephen Jefferies, Western Province v. Orange Free State, 28 December. (David Munden)

at St George's Park, Port Elizabeth

Northern Transvaal 204 (K.D. Verdoorn 57, R.C. Ontong 56, R.L.S. Armitage 4 for 70) and 312 for 5 dec (L.J. Barnard 102, V.F. du Preez 79, N.T. Day 56 not out)
Eastern Province 277 (M.W. Rushmere 136 not out) and 205 for 8 (P.G. Amm 75)

Match drawn
Eastern Province 6 pts, Northern Transvaal 5 pts

at Newlands, Cape Town

Orange Free State 134 (D.B. Rundle 5 for 33) and 113 (S.T. Jefferies 10 for 59)
Western Province 323 for 9 (T.N. Lazard 69, P.N. Kirsten 51, L. Seeff 50, A.P. Kuiper 50)

Western Province won by an innings and 76 runs
Western Province 22 pts, Orange Free State 4 pts

Transvaal's second victory in as many matches placed them firmly at the top of the Northern Section of the Currie Cup. They had an emphatic victory in a low-scoring game at Wanderers. The combined medium pace of Neal Radford and Brian McMillan disposed of Natal after they had won the toss and elected to bat. Yachad and Vorster

1, 2 and 3 January 1988

at Kingsmead, Durban

Northern Transvaal 243 (V.F. du Preez 92 not out, T.J. Packer 6 for 67) and 170 (N.T. Day 57)
Natal 312 (P.H. Rayner 60, R.C. Ontong 6 for 70) and 102 for 0 (A.C. Hudson 70 not out)

Natal won by 10 wickets
Natal 22 pts, Northern Transvaal 6 pts

at St George's Park, Port Elizabeth

Orange Free State 297 (A.J. Lamb 88, L.J. Wilkinson 70) and 232 for 4 (A.J. Lamb 56 not out, A.C. Storie 53)
Eastern Province 433 (M.W. Rushmere 140, P.G. Amm 129, D.J. Richardson 65 not out, K.S. McEwan 58)

Match drawn
Eastern Province 6 pts, Orange Free State 4 pts

at Newlands, Cape Town

Western Province 157 and 246 (P.N. Kirsten 57, D.J. Cullinan 50, N.V. Radford 4 for 68)
Transvaal 370 for 6 dec (L.P. Vorster 174, B. Roberts 104) and 37 for 2

Transvaal won by 8 wickets
Transvaal 22 pts, Western Province 3 pts

Vernon du Preez emulated the feat of Mark Rushmere a few days earlier when he carried his bat through Northern Transvaal's innings at Durban. He was the only batsman to cope confidently with the medium pace of Trevor Packer, who returned career-best bowling figures. Rodney

Ontong bowled well for Northern, but Natal batted consistently in the later part of their innings after losing their first four wickets for 86 and took a first-innings lead of 69. Northern Transvaal lost four wickets in clearing these arrears, and Natal romped to victory when Whitfield and Hudson reached the target of 102 runs in under 24 overs.

Mark Rushmere confirmed the opinion that he was the best young batsman in South Africa with a second Currie Cup century of the season and the highest score of his career as he and Philip Amm, who also hit a career best, put on 278 for Eastern Province's first wicket against Orange Free State. One of the bowlers opposed to them was Mike Procter, who, at the age of 41, had been forced out of retirement to assist his side, which was depleted by injuries. Procter contrived to bowl 48 overs of off-breaks and took 3 for 144. The run-saturated match moved inevitably to a draw.

The traditional New Year meeting between Western Province and Transvaal went very much in favour of the eastern state. Radford, in his last game for Transvaal before joining the England party, joined with Estwick and McMillan to dispose of Western Province twice with efficiency. In their first innings, Transvaal lost Cook, Fotheringham and Yachad with only 27 scored, but Louis Vorster and Bruce Roberts added 233 for the fourth wicket. The 22-year-old left-handed Vorster hit 21 fours in the highest score of his career.

Castle Bowl

1, 2 and 3 January 1988

at Jan Smuts Ground, East London

Border 226 (B.M. Osborne 52, P.A. Rayment 4 for 55) and 337 for 4 dec (B.M. Osborne 86 not out, B.W. Lones 74, M.J.P. Ford 73, A.L. Wilmot 50)
Eastern Province 'B' 283 (M. Michau 51) and 176 for 9 (P. Barclay 59, I.L. Howell 4 for 52)

Match drawn
Eastern Province 'B' 7 pts, Border 4 pts

A dramatic finish saw Eastern Province set to make 281 and slump from 136 for 2 to 174 for 9. At this point, Katz, who had been forced to retire hurt in the first innings, came to the wicket to join Pringle. The pair withstood the final onslaught to force a draw.

8, 9 and 10 January 1988

at Wanderers, Johannesburg

Transvaal 'B' 219 (N.E. Wright 94, P.L. Symcox 4 for 39) and 247 for 5 dec (M.S. Venter 80, M.J. Mitchley 64 not out)
Northern Transvaal 'B' 290 for 6 dec (A. Geringer 73, G.J. Turner 78) and 22 for 0

Match drawn
Northern Transvaal 'B' 9 pts, Transvaal 'B' 4 pts

at R.J.E. Burt Oval, Constantia

Western Province 'B' 289 for 6 dec (J.J.E. Hardy 75, A. Plantema 66, J.B. Commins 63) and 186 for 9 dec
Boland 274 (S. Nackerdien 60, A.P. Igglesden 4 for 73) and 134 (A.P. Igglesden 4 for 57)

Louis Vorster began the New Year with a career best 174 for Transvaal against Western Province at Cape Town. (Adrian Murrell/Allsport)

Western Province 'B' won by 67 runs
Western Province 'B' 22 pts, Boland 4 pts

A rather dour game at Wanderers in which scoring never reached three runs an over ended predictably in a draw while at Constantia, Boland suffered another reverse. Plantema and Hardy gave substance to Western's innings with a second-wicket stand of 122. Boland batted consistently to bring the first innings almost to parity, but on a deteriorating wicket Boland were always likely to be struggling on the last day. Set to make 202 to win, they reached 51 for 1, but Igglesden, who had a fine match, and skipper During broke the resistance.

Castle Currie Cup

8, 9 and 10 January 1988

at Centurion Park, Verwoerdburg

Transvaal 587 for 6 dec (B. Roberts 174, S.J. Cook 159, C.E.B. Rice 150 not out) and 1 for 0
Northern Transvaal 411 (P.J.A. Visagie 164, V.F. du Preez 70, W.F. Morris 58, C.E.B. Rice 4 for 66)

Match drawn
Transvaal 7 pts, Northern Transvaal 5 pts

8, 9 and 11 January 1988

at University of OFS Ground, Bloemfontein

Orange Free State 248 (G.S. le Roux 4 for 60) and 226 for 9 dec (A.J. Lamb 101, R.J. East 58 not out)
Western Province 130 (S.T. Clarke 4 for 49) and 205 for 4 (D.J. Cullinan 95 not out, P.N. Kirsten 82)

Match drawn
Orange Free State 7 pts, Western Province 5 pts

9, 10 and 11 January 1988

at Jan Smuts Stadium, Pietermaritzburg

Eastern Province 310 for 8 dec (D.J. Callaghan 148) and 98 for 0 dec (P.G. Amm 62 not out)
Natal 154 for 7 dec (R.M. Bentley 51) and 257 for 6 (A.C. Hudson 58, P.H. Rayner 51)

Natal won by 4 wickets
Natal 19 pts, Eastern Province 5 pts

There was much money made and many runs scored at Verwoerdburg, where Clive Rice defended his decision to bat on by saying that, in doing so, he had virtually destroyed Northern Transvaal's chances of qualifying for the final ahead of Transvaal. Transvaal lost their first three wickets for 101 after they had won the toss, but Jimmy Cook and Bruce Roberts then added 248 in 191 minutes. Two more century stands followed, and Cook, Roberts and Rice all earned £2,900 for hitting 150 inside 300 balls. Piet Visagie's career best was to earn him a similar reward. Amazingly, these individual awards were worth more than the winning of the Currie Cup itself.

There were no such glittering prizes at Bloemfontein, where Jefferies, le Roux, Clarke and Donald made the ball fly all over the place on the first day when the highest score was Lamb's 39. The pace trio of Clarke, Donald and van Zyl reduced Western Province to 94 for 9, and it was only last-wicket heroics by Ryall and Rundle that took them to 130. With the wicket easing, Allan Lamb hit 101 in 217 minutes with 11 fours, and Strydom declared, setting the visitors the task of making 345 to win. At 19 for 3, Western Province looked to be sliding to defeat, but Kirsten and Cullinan added 181 and saved the game.

David Callaghan hit 2 sixes and 19 fours in a career best 148 made in 278 minutes and helped Eastern Province past 300. Natal laboured in reply, and Madsen declared 156 behind. Wessels made a generous declaration in an effort to force victory, but solid and consistent batting took Natal to their target with little fuss.

15, 16 and 17 January 1988

at St George's Park, Port Elizabeth

Transvaal 255 (R.V. Jennings 65 not out, A.L. Hobson 4 for 86) and 236 for 8 (H.R. Fotheringham 150 not out)
Eastern Province 257 (D.J. Richardson 72, R.O. Estwick 4 for 47) and 23 for 1

Match drawn
Eastern Province 7 pts, Transvaal 6 pts

at Newlands, Cape Town

Northern Transvaal 195 (N.T. Day 60, S.T. Jefferies 4 for 55) and 96 (S.T. Jefferies 5 for 48, A.P. Kuiper 4 for 12)

Western Province 120 (P.S. de Villiers 4 for 29, T. Bosch 4 for 38) and 173 for 4 (M.H. Austen 83)

Western Province won by 6 wickets
Western Province 20 pts, Northern Transvaal 6 pts

15, 16 and 18 January 1988

at University Oval, Bloemfontein

Orange Free State 301 (A.J. Lamb 133, S.T. Clarke 60) and 254 (A.J. Lamb 59)
Natal 333 (B.J. Whitfield 113, R.M. Bentley 67, C.J.P.G. van Zyl 4 for 40) and 222 for 7 (B.J. Whitfield 59)

Natal won by 3 wickets
Natal 22 pts, Orange Free State 7 pts

A game of fluctuating fortune at Port Elizabeth ended with Henry Fotheringham batting for 438 minutes to hit 150 not out with a six and 13 fours, thereby saving the match for Transvaal. Rice's declaration left Eastern Province 20 overs and 15 minutes in which to make 205, a gesture which they ignored.

A wicket of dubious quality at Newlands helped bowlers to thrive. Bosch and de Villiers bowled Northern Transvaal to a first-innings lead of 75, which looked as if it could be decisive, but Jefferies maintained his magnificent form and, with Kuiper's medium pace providing excellent support, Northern Transvaal were shot out for 96 in their second innings. Needing 172 to win, Western Province started uncomfortably, losing Lazard and Seef for 32, but Austen batted with dash and Kirsten finished with a flourish so that the match was over in two days.

Another century from Allan Lamb, 133 off 151 balls, and a hurricane 60 from Sylvester Clarke, who hit 3 sixes and 8 fours, gave Orange Free State a respectable total against Natal after they had lost their first four wickets for 47. Natal reached 198 for 2 thanks to Whitfield and Bentley, but van Zyl bowled an economical spell to limit Natal's lead. Packer, Clift and Bentley restricted the home side when they batted again, and Clift had Lamb caught when he again threatened to take charge. Natal were left with the task of scoring 221 in 54 overs to win the match, not easy in the conditions, but, after a fiery burst from Clarke, Whitfield and later Lister-James put them in sight of victory. The match was won when Chris Lister-James hit the penultimate ball of the last over for six. Mike Procter was the bowler.

Castle Bowl

15, 16 and 17 January 1988

at Kingsmead, Durban

Natal 'B' 303 for 9 dec (D. Norman 97) and 297 for 7 dec (C.S. Stirk 154, M.J. Pearse 53)
Northern Transvaal 'B' 321 for 8 dec (M.J. Rindel 157 not out) and 199 for 8 (V.G. Cresswell 53, M.D. Mellor 4 for 88)

Match drawn
Northern Transvaal 'B' 8 pts, Natal 'B' 7 pts

at Wanderers, Johannesburg

Griqualand West 121 (C.D. Mitchley 4 for 41) and 259 (J.M. Arthur 78, I.F. Mellett 54)

Transvaal 'B' 257 (M.S. Venter 131, N.E. Wright 56, D.G. Mills 4 for 34) and 53 for 3

Match drawn
Transvaal 'B' 8 pts, Griqualand West 6 pts

15, 16 and 18 January 1988

at SFW Ground, Stellenbosch

Eastern Province 'B' 188 (O. Henry 4 for 69) and 133 (M. Michau 76 not out, O. Henry 6 for 57)
Boland 245 (K.J. Barnett 73, R.L.S. Armitage 6 for 68) and 78 for 3 (K.J. Barnett 51 not out)

Boland won by 7 wickets
Boland 21 pts, Eastern Province 'B' 6 pts

Career-best batting performances by Norman, Stirk and Rindel highlighted a fine game at Durban. Craig Stirk's innings transformed the match, for Mellor was able to declare and ask Northern Transvaal 'B' to make 280 in 62 overs. They took the bait, but Mellor himself gnawed away at the middle order, and Northern were happy to escape defeat as Botha and Robinson played out time.

Transvaal 'B' had the better of the match at Wanderers in spite of losing the last nine wickets of their first innings for 57 runs after Mark Venter and Wright had put on 180 for the second wicket. The visitors batted with grim determination in the second innings, Arthur and Mellet laying a solid foundation with a stand of 117 for the second wicket, and Transvaal 'B' were left only 13 overs in which to make 124, a task which they found too daunting.

Boland ensured that they would be contesting the final when they outplayed Eastern Province 'B' in Stellenbosch. Marcelle Michau played a valiant innings, but the slow left-arm of Omar Henry proved to be a match-winner on a wicket which gave him some assistance.

Castle Currie Cup

22, 23 and 24 January 1988

at St George's Park, Port Elizabeth

Western Province 274 (T.N. Lazard 66, A.P. Kuiper 51, T.G. Shaw 6 for 112) and 91
Eastern Province 392 for 9 dec (M.W. Rushmere 136, K.S. McEwan 88, P.G. Amm 61, D.B. Rundle 4 for 96)

Eastern Province won by an innings and 27 runs
Eastern Province 19 pts, Western Province 2 pts

at Centurion Park, Verwoerdburg

Northern Transvaal 197 (V.F. du Preez 57, A.M. Ferreira 51, T.J. Packer 6 for 38) and 289 (M.J.R. Rindel 83 not out, C.M. Lister-James 4 for 53)
Natal 329 (G. Grobler 4 for 93) and 158 for 4

Natal won by 6 wickets
Natal 22 pts, Northern Transvaal 5 pts

at Wanderers, Johannesburg

Orange Free State 163 (R.J. East 58, R.O. Estwick 4 for 45, C.E.B. Rice 4 for 48) and 51 (R.O. Estwick 5 for 17)
Transvaal 130 (S.T. Clarke 7 for 48) and 85 for 1 (S.J. Cook 56 not out)

Transvaal won by 9 wickets
Transvaal 20 pts, Orange Free State 6 pts

Slow left-arm bowler Tim Shaw returned his best figures of the season as Western Province were bowled out after a dour display at St George's Park. Mark Rushmere and Philip Amm began Eastern's reply with a partnership of 146 which ended when Amm was stumped by Ryall off Jefferies. McEwan and Rushmere added 117 for the third wicket, and Eastern Province took a commanding lead. Batting again, Western Province reached 67 for 1 when disaster struck. Wickets tumbled to Hobson, Ferrant and Shaw, and the visitors were all out for 91 although the innings lasted for 66.3 overs. Shaw had 3 for 17 in 28.3 overs, 21 of them maidens, and Hobson's 3 for 19 came from 12 overs. Ferrant had figures of 17–8–22–2. The last nine wickets fell for the addition of only 24 runs.

Natal maintained pressure on Transvaal with a fine team performance at Centurion Park. Trevor Packer, his back injury now completely cured, bettered his career-best performance of earlier in the season as Northern were bowled out for 197. Natal batted consistently, only one man failing to reach double figures, and when Northern batted again, without the injured Ontong, they were again victims of team efficiency. Natal romped to victory with ease.

Natal's win made no impression on Transvaal's lead in the Northern Section, for the leaders swept aside Orange Free State in a sensational match at Wanderers. Put in to bat on a doubtful wicket, Orange Free State recovered from the depths of 46 for 6 to which Clive Rice and Estwick had sent them to reach 163 thanks to a hard-hit 58 from wicket-keeper Robert East. Transvaal struggled painfully in reply. They were 51 for 6 and 91 for 7, and only a courageous last-wicket stand of 39 between Gordon McMillan, 34 not out, and Estwick, 16, the only two batsmen to reach double figures, took them to 130. Sylvester Clarke was the bowler who had wrecked Transvaal, his former team. The fireworks were not yet over, however, for Rice and Estwick again tore the visitors apart. The first three batsmen failed to score, and five wickets were down for 7. There was no effective recovery, and Transvaal swept to a resounding victory over the side that they were most likely to meet in the Currie Cup final.

29, 30 and 31 January 1988

at Newlands, Cape Town

Western Province 454 for 9 dec (M.H. Austen 202 not out, T.N. Lazard 76, J.G. Thomas 4 for 122)
Eastern Province 292 (K.S. McEwan 97, G.S. le Roux 4 for 72) and 217 for 4 (D.J. Callaghan 72, K.S. McEwan 53 not out)

Match drawn
Western Province 8 pts, Eastern Province 5 pts

at Centurion Park, Verwoerdburg

Orange Free State 186 (W.F. Morris 4 for 37) and 204 (R.J. East 56, W.F. Morris 6 for 59)
Northern Transvaal 124 (A.A. Donald 4 for 39, S.T. Clarke 4 for 47) and 242 (L.J. Barnard 56, S.T. Clarke 5 for 48, C.J.P.G. van Zyl 4 for 41)

Clive Rice, 101 and match figures of 9 for 35, Transvaal v. Natal, 30 January–1 February. An inspiring captain and an all-rounder with no superior anywhere in the world. (George Herringshaw)

Orange Free State won by 24 runs
Orange Free State 21 pts, Northern Transvaal 5 pts

30, 31 January and 1 February 1988

at Kingsmead, Durban

Natal 97 (C.E.B. Rice 5 for 14) and 168 (M. James 5 for 55, C.E.B. Rice 4 for 21)
Transvaal 254 (C.E.B. Rice 101, P.B. Clift 5 for 53) and 14 for 0

Transvaal won by 10 wickets
Transvaal 22 pts, Natal 5 pts

A maiden first-class century by Michael Austen became a double hundred before Kuiper declared. Austen came to the wicket at 28 for 1 and shared century stands with Lazard and Kirsten for the second and fourth wickets. Western needed to force victory to reach the Currie Cup final, but they were denied by Ken McEwan, who played beautifully until le Roux knocked back his off stump. Eastern Province were compelled to follow on, and when Amm again went cheaply it looked as if the home side might achieve success. Three wickets went down for 90,

but McEwan and Callaghan added 126, and Western Province were thwarted. Their main adversary had been their ex-batsman Ken McEwan, who finished the season in his best form.

Orange Free State entered the Currie Cup final with a tense win over Northern Transvaal. The Free State were without Allan Lamb, who, with Sylvester Clarke, had given the side its substance during the season. It was Clarke who led the fight back against Northern Transvaal, hitting a brisk 39 after Willie Morris' left-arm spin had caused so much damage and then combining with Donald to cause the home side much discomfort and give Orange Free State an invaluable first-innings lead of 62. They battled throughout their second innings to build on that lead and put the game out of Northern's reach, but Morris again caused problems and it was only another late injection of runs from East which boosted the Free State. Set to make 267 to win, the home side were given a fine start by du Preez and skipper Barnard, who put on 104. Both fell at the same total, and Clarke quickly sent back Verdoorn while van Zyl accounted for Grobler. Clarke bowled Rindel, and Northern Transvaal had slumped to 132 for 5. Day, Geringer and Ferreira led the recovery, but Clarke and van Zyl always had the edge, and Orange Free State took the 15 points for victory and a place in the Currie Cup final although many would suggest that the new system had rather favoured them.

In the final they were to meet Transvaal who, inspired by some magnificent all-round cricket from Clive Rice, overwhelmed Natal. Rice took 5 for 14 in as many overs as Natal were routed, and then came to the wicket at 103 for 5 and hit 101 out of 151. He and James dismissed Natal cheaply when they batted again, Rice finishing with match figures of 9 for 35 on a wicket on which he had scored a century. He may be at the veteran stage, but he has no superior as an all-rounder anywhere in the world.

Castle Currie Cup – Final Tables							
Northern Section							
	P	W	L	D	Btg pts	Blg pts	Pts
Transvaal	7	5	–	2	12	33	120
Natal	7	4	2	1	8	30	98
Northern Transvaal	7	–	5	2	9	30	39
Southern Section							
Orange Free State	7	2	3	2	15	27	72
Western Province	7	2	2	3	9	28	67
Eastern Province	7	1	2	4	16	22	53

Castle Bowl

29, 30 and 31 January 1988

at Wanderers, Johannesburg

Natal 'B' (M.D. Tramontino 55, P.E. Smith 4 for 54) and 162 (M.D. Mellor 70, S. Elworthy 4 for 56)
Transvaal 'B' 333 (M.S. Venter 62, B. McBride 55, K.J. Kerr 53, M.R. Hobson 4 for 43) and 29 for 0

Transvaal 'B' won by 10 wickets
Transvaal 'B' 21 pts, Natal 'B' 6 pts

at De Beers Country Club, Kimberley

Griqualand West 338 for 4 dec (A.J. Moles 200 not out, J.M. Arthur 51) and 177 for 6 (I.F. Mellett 52, P.L. Symcox 4 for 43)
Northern Transvaal 'B' 248 (P.J.A. Visagie 55, T.D. Topley 4 for 62) and 184 for 9 (T.D. Topley 5 for 51)

Match drawn
Griqualand West 8 pts, Northern Transvaal 'B' 4 pts

at Old Grey Ground, Port Elizabeth

Western Province 'B' 150 (A.P. Plantema 69) and 263 (J.J.E. Hardy 71, R.L.S. Armitage 6 for 64)
Eastern Province 'B' 268 (P.I. Barclay 82, A.P. Igglesden 4 for 60) and 85 (E.O. Simons 4 for 35)

Western Province 'B' won by 60 runs
Western Province 'B' 18 pts, Eastern Province 'B' 6 pts

29, 30 January and 1 February 1988

at Jan Smuts Ground, East London

Boland 502 for 6 dec (S.A. Jones 209 not out, O. Henry 125)
Border 310 (B.W. Lones 139, M.J.P. Ford 64, S.J. Base 5 for 68) and 259 for 6 (E.N. Trotman 51)

Match drawn
Boland 4 pts, Border 4 pts

With Boland having already qualified for the final of the Castle Bowl the main interest centred on who would win the right to meet them. The final round of matches quickly produced an answer as Transvaal 'B', with an effective team performance, crushed Natal 'B' to confirm that they would head the Northern Section.

Elsewhere, it was individual performances that caught the attention. Andy Moles of Warwickshire hit the first double century of his career, but, in spite of Don Topley's fine bowling, Griqualand West could not quite snatch victory in Kimberley. Botha and Ackermann, Northern Transvaal 'B''s last pair, held out defiantly for half an hour to save the match.

Western Province 'B' brought about a remarkable reversal of fortune at Port Elizabeth. Trailing by 118 on the first innings, they were 129 for 5 in their second but the tail wagged manfully to set the home side 146 to win.

A career best 200 not out for Andy Moles, Griqualand West v. Northern Transvaal 'B', 29 January. (Ken Kelly)

Without the injured Katz, Eastern Province 'B' reached 67 for 3 and then collapsed to 85 all out against Igglesden, Simons and McClement.

The two left-handers, Stephen Jones and Omar Henry, celebrated Boland's excellent season with the highest scores of their careers and a sixth-wicket partnership of 259. Jones reached two hundred for the first time. Ford and Lones, a maiden first-class century, replied with an opening stand of 127, and Osborne helped Lones add 102 for the second wicket, after which Border fell apart and were forced to follow on. They had little difficulty in gaining a draw, however.

Castle Bowl Final
BOLAND v. TRANSVAAL 'B'

Boland, with three English county players in their side, beat Transvaal 'B' as comfortably as had been expected to take the Bowl for the second time in three years. They were soundly led and a balanced side who played as an effective team unit.

Castle Bowl – Final Tables

Northern Section

	P	W	L	D	Btg pts	Blg pts	Pts
Transvaal 'B'	6	2	1	3	13	23	66
Northern Transvaal 'B'	6	1	1	4	15	27	57
Griqualand West	6	1	1	4	10	24	49
Natal 'B'	6	1	2	3	13	21	49

Southern Section

	P	W	L	D	Btg pts	Blg pts	Pts
Boland	6	3	2	1	9	23	77
Western Province 'B'	6	2	1	3	10	24	64
Eastern Province 'B'	6	1	3	2	5	26	46
Border	6	1	1	4	11	18	44

Jones won the toss and decided to bat first. When Elworthy dismissed Lambrechts and Henry in the same over, reducing Boland to 170 for 6, Transvaal 'B' had their best chance of taking a firm grip on the game, but the left-handed Jacobus du Toit joined Phil Newport in a vital stand of 118. Newport made the highest score of his career, and after du Toit was dismissed at 318 Carl Spilhaus hit positively to take Boland to 367.

Against a varied attack Transvaal 'B' could make little headway, and they trailed by 199 runs on the first innings. Boland were soon adding to this, and when Jones finally declared after some brisk scoring the visitors faced the task of scoring 457 to win. There was never a remote possibility of Transvaal 'B' reaching this target, and Boland rightly claimed the Bowl for they had been the best side in the competition throughout the season.

Castle Currie Cup Final
TRANSVAAL v. ORANGE FREE STATE

Having won the Currie Cup four times in the previous five seasons and dominated the current competition since its beginning in December, Transvaal entered the final as firm favourites. Five days were allotted to the match, but

Brian McMillan took 3 for 18 and 3 for 7 in the Currie Cup Final and topped the first-class bowling averages. (Mark Leech)

CASTLE BOWL FINAL – BOLAND v. TRANSVAAL 'B'
5, 6, 7 and 8 February 1988 at SFW Ground, Stellenbosch

BOLAND

	FIRST INNINGS		SECOND INNINGS	
K. J. Barnett	b Smith	18	c Rule, b C. Mitchley	41
W. S. Truter	c M. Mitchley, b C. Mitchley	46	lbw, b Elworthy	20
S. Nackerdien	lbw, b Elworthy	21	not out	70
P.J. Newport	c Wright, b Smith	86	c Wright, b Booyens	18
S.A. Jones†	b C. Mitchley	6	lbw, b C. Mitchley	64
N.M. Lambrechts	lbw, b Elworthy	26		
O. Henry	c McBride, b Elworthy	0	not out	25
J.D. du Toit	c McBride, b C. Mitchley	89	(6) c Wright, b C. Mitchley	12
C.F. Spilhaus*	not out	44		
S.J. Base	b C. Mitchley	8		
P. Anker	lbw, b C. Mitchley	10		
Extras	b 1, lb 3, w 5, nb 4	13	lb 2, nb 5	7
		367	(for 5 wkts, dec)	257

	O	M	R	W	O	M	R	W
C.D. Mitchley	32.5	3	108	5	16	2	84	3
Smith	27	3	91	2	14	2	67	–
Elworthy	24	3	86	3	8	1	35	1
Booyens	17	6	40	–	13	4	31	1
Kerr	14	3	38	–	14	4	38	–

FALL OF WICKETS
1–31, 2–64, 3–117, 4–123, 5–170, 6–170, 7–288, 8–318, 9–332
1–64, 2–68, 3–99, 4–191, 5–223

TRANSVAAL 'B'

	FIRST INNINGS		SECOND INNINGS	
W. Kirsh	c Spilhaus, b Newport	2	c Anker, b Newport	1
M.S. Venter†	b du Toit	22	c Newport, b Base	16
N.E. Wright	b Newport	36	c and b Henry	16
K.J. Rule	c and b Henry	36	c Jones, b Anker	33
M.J. Mitchley	c Jones, b Anker	17	c and b Henry	6
S. Elworthy	c Spilhaus, b Henry	19	lbw, b Henry	6
B. McBride*	c Spilhaus, b Anker	4	c Spilhaus, b Base	30
K.J. Kerr	not out	20	not out	49
W. Booyens	c Lambrechts, b Henry	0	lbw, b Barnett	16
C.D. Mitchley	c Henry, b Anker	1	c Truter, b Anker	5
P.E. Smith	c Spilhaus, b Newport	2	c Spilhaus, b Anker	9
Extras	b 3, lb 3, w 2, nb 1	9	b 6, lb 6, nb 3	15
		168		197

	O	M	R	W	O	M	R	W
Base	10	3	27	–	14	4	37	2
Newport	13	4	20	3	13	2	41	1
du Toit	14	4	27	1				
Anker	23	6	48	3	20.5	13	19	3
Henry	14	3	40	3	23	5	71	3
Barnett	14				7	1	17	1

FALL OF WICKETS
1–9, 2–49, 3–83, 4–113, 5–126, 6–144, 7–144, 8–145, 9–146
1–6, 2–22, 3–67, 4–67, 5–69, 6–80, 7–108, 8–168, 9–179

Umpires: R.L. Symcox & H. de Bruin

Boland won by 259 runs

Transvaal needed less than four to emphasize that they continue to reign supreme in South African cricket.

Rice won the toss, asked Orange Free State to bat first, and he and the other medium-pace bowlers were soon among the wickets. Conditions were never easy, and Orange Free State, which included six players currently playing first-class cricket in England, were always struggling. The only impetus given to the innings was a stand of 68 for the ninth wicket between van Heerden and van Zyl.

Transvaal laboured a little in their turn, and Cook, Fotheringham, Yachad and the promising Vorster were back in the pavilion with only 80 scored, but Roberts and, inevitably, Rice added 83 to take the home side into the lead. Jennings and Estwick enjoyed a violent last-wicket stand of 74, and the game was practically out of sight for Orange Free State.

Worse followed. Both openers fell cheaply to Brian McMillan, and it was not until East came to the wicket that there was any hope of avoiding an innings defeat. Transvaal were forced to bat again, but the Cup had long since been won before Fotheringham hit Lamb for the winning four.

Benson and Hedges Trophy

17 February 1988

at Centurion Park, Verwoerdburg

Impalas 208 for 7
Northern Transvaal 208 for 9 (V.F. du Preez 62)

Impalas (2pts) won on losing fewer wickets with the scores level

24 February 1988

at Newlands, Cape Town

Western Province 244 for 4 (L. Seeff 82, M.H. Austen 54)
Orange Free State 153 for 9 (J.J. Strydom 55 not out)

Western Province (2 pts) won by 91 runs

at St George's Park, Port Elizabeth

Eastern Province 174 for 8 (T.J. Packer 4 for 28)
Natal 125 (M.K. van Vuuren 4 for 23)

Eastern Province (2 pts) won by 49 runs

With the first-class competitions at an end, the South African season moved to its close with the final stages of the one-day tournaments. Impalas made certain of a Benson and Hedges semi-final place with victory in a thrilling match at Centurion Park. Northern Transvaal's ninth wicket fell at 188, but de Villiers and Bosch took the score to 208, one run short of their target.

Western Province dismissed Orange Free State as contemptuously as Transvaal had done in the Currie Cup final. Austen and Seeff began with a partnership of 146,

CASTLE CURRIE CUP FINAL – TRANSVAAL v. ORANGE FREE STATE
11, 12, 13 and 14 February 1988 at Wanderers, Johannesburg

ORANGE FREE STATE

	FIRST INNINGS			SECOND INNINGS	
P.J.R. Steyn	b Estwick	12	lbw, b B. McMillan	2	
L.J. Wilkinson	c Jennings, b Estwick	30	c G. McMillan, b B. McMillan	0	
A.C. Storie	lbw, b Estwick	5	c G. McMillan, b Rice	9	
A.I. Kallicharran	b B. McMillan	7	c Fotheringham, b Estwick	10	
A.J. Lamb	lbw, b B. McMillan	8	c Vorster, b Estwick	33	
J.J. Strydom†	c Jennings, b G. McMillan	3	c Voster, b B. McMillan	1	
C.J. van Heerden	c Jennings, b B. McMillan	28	lbw, b G. McMillan	26	
R.J. East*	c Jennings, b Rice	0	not out	50	
S.T. Clarke	b Estwick	0	c Jennings, b Estwick	21	
C.J.P.G. van Zyl	c Cook, b Estwick	31	c Jennings, b Estwick	0	
A.A. Donald	not out	0	c Vorster, b Rice	10	
Extras	b 6, lb 9, w 3, nb 2	20	lb 2, w 1, nb 1	4	
		144		**166**	

	O	M	R	W	O	M	R	W
Estwick	26.5	12	47	4	17	3	63	4
Rice	27	14	38	2	22	6	57	2
Hooper	2	1	2	–	2	–	5	–
B. McMillan	17	7	18	3	9	4	7	3
G. McMillan	13	6	18	1	10	3	32	1
Roberts	4	1	6	–				

TRANSVAAL

	FIRST INNINGS			SECOND INNINGS	
S.J. Cook	c Kallicharran, b Clarke	11	not out	15	
H.R. Fotheringham	c Clarke, b Donald	1	not out	17	
M. Yachad	c East, b Donald	15			
L.P. Vorster	c Lamb, b Donald	36			
B. Roberts	c Clarke, b Van Zyl	64			
C.E.B. Rice†	c East, b Van Zyl	38			
B.M. McMillan	c East, b Van Zyl	1			
G.E. McMillan	c Clarke, b van Zyl	5			
R.V. Jennings*	c and b van Heerden	43			
J.J. Hooper	c East, b Donald	0			
R.O. Estwick	not out	43			
Extras	b 1, lb 11, w 5, nb 5	22	b 1, w 1	2	
		279	(for no wkt)	**34**	

	O	M	R	W	O	M	R	W
Clarke	25	6	55	1	1	1	0	–
Donald	31	5	83	4	4	–	14	–
van Zyl	28	6	71	4	4	1	15	–
van Heerden	19.4	4	52	1				
Kallicharran	3	–	6	–				
Lamb					1.5	1	4	–

FALL OF WICKETS
1–26, 2–50, 3–51, 4–65, 5–70, 6–70, 7–71, 8–76, 9–144
1–1, 2–3, 3–20, 4–49, 5–59, 6–64, 7–105, 8–109, 9–144

FALL OF WICKETS
1–16, 2–18, 3–65, 4–80, 5–163, 6–165, 7–183, 8–188, 9–205

Umpires: S.B. Lambson & L.J. Rautenbach

Transvaal won by 10 wickets

and Orange Free State were 96 for 7 before saved from total ignominy by some late hitting.

Eastern Province confirmed a semi-final place when their bowlers won a low-scoring match at Port Elizabeth.

Nissan Shield

Semi-Finals – First Leg

20 February 1988

at Centurion Park, Verwoerdburg

Northern Transvaal 239 for 9 (V.F. du Preez 91, N.T. Day 82, S.T. Clarke 6 for 31)
Orange Free State 130

Northern Transvaal won by 109 runs

at Newlands, Cape Town

Western Province 174
Eastern Province 178 for 9

Eastern Province won by 1 wicket

With a gap of nearly three months in between the qualifying rounds and the semi-final of the competition, the contestants in the Nissan Shield could be forgiven for forgetting who their opponents were. A third-wicket stand of 195 between du Preez and Day was the substance of Northern Transvaal's innings. Sylvester Clarke returned to destroy the later order, but his inspired spell could not bring victory. Allan Lamb's 31 was the top score for Orange Free State, who were bowled out in 44.5 overs.

The game at Newlands provided more excitement. Chasing 175 to win, Eastern Province were 97 for 5. Richardson and Shaw added 65, but four wickets fell for 10 runs so that when van Vuuren joined Rayment three runs were still needed. The scores were brought level and then van Vuuren hit Rundel for four to win the match.

Semi-Finals – Second Leg

27 February 1988

at St George's Park, Port Elizabeth

Western Province 244 for 5 (D.J. Cullinan 57, E.O. Simons 51 not out)
Eastern Province 248 for 6 (M.W. Rushmere 81, P.G. Amm 80)

Eastern Province won by 4 wickets

at Harmony Ground, Virginia

Orange Free State 216 (A.J. Lamb 71)
Northern Transvaal 202 (R.F. Pienaar 69)

Orange Free State won by 14 runs

There was some glorious batting at St George's Park, where Eric Simons, coming in when Western Province were limping a little at 158 for 5, hit 51 off 34 balls. He and Kuiper added 86 in the last eleven overs of the innings. It proved to be of no avail as Philip Amm and Mark Rushmere began Eastern's reply with a stand of 167 in 39 overs. They fell within two runs of each other, and there was an element of panic, but Wessels kept the score moving, and Shaw and van Vuuren took them to victory on the last ball of the match.

Orange Free State forced a third encounter when Lamb, East and Clarke helped them to recover from the shock of 26 for 3, and Clarke and Donald cut down Northern Transvaal when they looked likely to win.

Semi-Finals – Third Leg

28 February 1988

at Harmony Ground, Virginia

Northern Transvaal 170 for 5 (R.F. Pienaar 68)
Orange Free State 161 for 9

Northern Transvaal won by 9 runs

In a match reduced to 30 overs, the individual honours went to Roy Pienaar, who dominated an opening stand of 116 with du Preez. Morris then produced a remarkable spell of economic bowling which brought him 3 for 17 in 6 overs, a match-winning performance.

Nissan Shield Final
NORTHERN TRANSVAAL v. EASTERN PROVINCE

Wessels won the toss and asked Northern Transvaal to bat first in a match which, having been twice postponed, was reduced to 52 overs by the weather. There was an early mishap for Northern Transvaal when du Preeze was run out, but Roy Pienaar, who had played so well throughout the competition, and skipper Lee Barnard added 82 in what was the one stand of substance in the innings. An economic spell from slow left-arm bowler Tim Shaw frustrated the middle order, but some dash at the end of the innings took the home side to a respectable, although not daunting, 216.

Eastern Province began badly, with prolific run-scorers Amm and Rushmere both falling to the left-arm fast medium bowler Gerbrand Grobler. When Callaghan and McEwan came together, however, the whole complexion of the game changed. In a delightful display of stroke-making, they added 168 in 103 minutes and took Eastern Province to their first Nissan Shield triumph since 1976. The win was achieved with style and panache, and with 3.2 overs to spare.

Benson and Hedges Trophy

9 March 1988

at Harmony Ground, Virginia

Orange Free State 121
Transvaal 122 for 2 (H.R. Fotheringham 69 not out)

Transvaal (2 pts) won by 8 wickets

11 March 1988

at Kingsmead, Durban

Orange Free State 118 (H.L. Alleyne 4 for 35)
Natal 95 for 3

Natal (2 pts) won on faster scoring rate

Defeat in their last two matches ended Orange Free State's interest in the day/night competition. Transvaal won the game at Virginia with 3.4 overs to spare.

NISSAN SHIELD FINAL – NORTHERN TRANSVAAL v. EASTERN PROVINCE
13 March 1988 at Centurion Park, Verwoerdburg

NORTHERN TRANSVAAL

V.F. du Preez	run out	3
R.F. Pienaar	c McEwan, b van Vuuren	62
L.J. Barnardt†	c Rushmere, b Pringle	48
N.T. Day*	c Michau, b Callaghan	11
M.J.R. Rindel	c van Vuuren, b Rayment	37
A.M. Ferreira	run out	3
A. Geringer	b Thomas	10
P.L. Symcox	not out	12
W.F. Morris	not out	16
G. Grobler		
P.S. de Villiers		
Extras	lb 9, w 3, nb 2	14
(52 overs)	(for 7 wkts)	216

	O	M	R	W
Thomas	10	2	26	1
Rayment	10	–	58	1
Pringle	10	1	39	1
Shaw	10	–	28	–
van Vuuren	7	–	28	1
Callaghan	5	–	28	1

FALL OF WICKETS
1–4, 2–86, 3–108, 4–161, 5–170, 6–185, 7–199

EASTERN PROVINCE

P.G. Amm	c and b Grobler	2
M.W. Rushmere	c Barnard, b Grobler	7
K.C. Wessels†	c and b Morris	19
K.S. McEwan	not out	90
D.J. Callaghan	not out	92
M. Michau*		
T.G. Shaw		
J.G. Thomas		
P.A. Rayment		
M.K. van Vuuren		
M.W. Pringle		
Extras	b 4, lb 4	8
(48.4 overs)	(for 3 wkts)	218

	O	M	R	W
de Villiers	9	1	21	–
Grobler	8·	1	29	2
Pienaar	8.4	–	44	–
Ferreira	10	–	47	–
Morris	10	–	50	1
Symcox	3	–	19	–

FALL OF WICKETS
1–3, 2–18, 3–50

Umpires: J.W. Peacock & K.E. Liebenberg

Eastern Province won by 7 wickets

Qualifying League – Final Table

	P	W	L	N/R	Pts
Western Province	6	4	2		8
Transvaal	6	4	2		8
Eastern Province	6	4	1	1	8
Impalas	6	3	2	1	6
Natal	6	2	3	1	4
Northern Transvaal	6	1	4	1	2
Orange Free State	6	1	5		2

The first leg of the semi-finals produced two resounding victories. Inspired by Kirsten and Hardy, Western Province scored at 5.7 an over and then bowled out Impalas in 33.2 overs. Jefferies and le Roux destroyed the Impalas early order to leave them in a hopeless position at 22 for 6. Bravery from Bauermeister and McLaren took the score past a hundred. Callaghan played a lone hand for Eastern Province at Wanderers, and Jim Cook steered Transvaal to victory with 9.1 overs to spare.

Semi-Finals – First Leg

16 March 1988

at Danie Craven Stadium, Stellenbosch

Western Province 257 for 6 (P.N. Kirsten 93, J.J.E. Hardy 75 not out)
Impalas 114

Western Province won by 142 runs

15 March 1988

at Wanderers, Johannesburg

Eastern Province 171 (D.J. Callaghan 80, R.O. Estwick 4 for 23)
Transvaal 172 for 2 (S.J. Cook 85 not out)

Transvaal won by 8 wickets

Semi-Finals – Second Leg

18 March 1988

at Newlands, Cape Town

Western Province 185 for 9 (A.P. Kuiper 76, S.J. Base 4 for 37)
Impalas 137

Western Province won by 48 runs

at St George's Park, Port Elizabeth

Eastern Province 235 for 4 (M.W. Rushmere 70, P.G. Amm 54)
Transvaal 191

Eastern Province won by 44 runs

Western Province entered the final with another convincing win over Impalas although not before they suffered some shocks. Simon Base was in fine form, and the home side were struggling at 100 for 8 before Adrian Kuiper found a useful partner in Craig Matthews. They added 76.

BENSON AND HEDGES TROPHY FINAL – TRANSVAAL v. WESTERN PROVINCE
25 March 1988 at Wanderers, Johannesburg

TRANSVAAL

S.J. Cook	c Seeff, b Kuiper		24
H.R. Fotheringham	c Cullinan, b Jefferies		16
M. Yachad	c and b Kuiper		1
L.P. Vorster	c Ryall, b le Roux		41
B. Roberts	c Kirsten, b Kuiper		31
C.E.B. Rice†	c Ryall, b le Roux		0
B.M. McMillan	c Austen, b Matthews		25
R.V. Jennings*	c Cullinan, b Kuiper		14
C.D. Mitchley	c Ryall, b Matthews		7
N.V. Radford	not out		3
R.O. Estwick	run out		7
Extras	b 2, lb 11, w 6, nb 1		20
(44.3 overs)			189

WESTERN PROVINCE

M.H. Austen	c Jennings, b Radford		7
L. Seeff	run out		42
P.N. Kirsten	run out		64
D.J. Cullinan	c Jennings, b Mitchley		15
J.J.E. Hardy	not out		25
A.P. Kuiper†	c Jennings, b B.M. McMillan		13
G.S. le Roux	not out		5
E.O. Simons			
C.R. Matthews			
S.T. Jefferies			
R.J. Ryall*			
Extras	lb 12, w 4, nb 3		19
(44 overs)	(for 5 wkts)		190

	O	M	R	W
le Roux	8.3	–	27	2
Jefferies	9	–	26	1
Kuiper	9	2	28	4
Simons	5	–	26	–
C.R. Matthews	8	–	44	2
Kirsten	5	–	25	–

	O	M	R	W
Radford	9	–	44	1
Estwick	9	2	24	–
C.D. Mitchley	9	2	24	1
B.M. McMillan	9	–	66	1
Rice	8	–	20	–

FALL OF WICKETS
1–34, 2–42, 3–46, 4–118, 5–118, 6–135, 7–154, 8–176, 9–181

FALL OF WICKETS
1–11, 2–101, 3–138, 4–144, 5–168

Umpires: K.E. Liebenberg & S.B. Lambson

Western Province won by 5 wickets

Impalas could effect no such recovery and were bowled out in the 42nd over. Another scintillating opening partnership between Amm and Rushmere, who put on 114, gave Eastern Province a platform for victory over Transvaal. Dave Callaghan had another fine all-round match, hitting 39 not out and taking 3 for 27 with his medium pace.

Semi-Finals – Third Leg

19 March 1988

at St George's Park, Port Elizabeth

Eastern Province 208 (D.J. Callaghan 75 not out)
Transvaal 209 for 5 (S.J. Cook 94, L.P. Vorster 56)

Transvaal won by 5 wickets

In spite of another good opening partnership and a fine innings by David Callaghan, Eastern Province were beaten in the deciding match by Transvaal. Jimmy Cook and Louis Vorster added 109 for Transvaal's third wicket, and the visitors won with seven balls to spare.

Benson and Hedges Trophy Final
TRANSVAAL v. WESTERN PROVINCE

The contestants were the same as they had been the previous season, and the result was also the same as Western Province took the Trophy for the third year in succession. Put in to bat, Transvaal started soundly

enough, but lost their way when Adrian Kuiper brought himself into the attack and produced an excellent spell of medium-pace bowling which blunted Transvaal's attacking inclinations.

Radford, who had returned from the England tour of New Zealand, had Austen caught behind, but Seeff and Kirsten added 90, and the innings was so well paced that a comfortable win was achieved without heroics and with an over to spare.

First-Class Averages

BATTING

	M	Inns	NOs	Runs	HS	Av	100s	50s
A.J. Lamb	6	12	2	878	294	87.80	3	3
A.J. Moles	6	12	2	657	200*	65.70	3	2
G. Kirsten	6	11	4	424	163*	60.57	1	2
C.E.B. Rice	8	10	2	459	150*	57.37	2	1
M.W. Rushmere	8	14	3	576	140	52.36	3	
P.J.A. Visagie	8	13	2	543	164	49.36	2	2
S.A. Jones	7	12	2	487	209*	48.70	1	2
B. Roberts	10	13	1	568	174	47.33	2	1
K.S. McEwan	8	11	1	468	104	46.80	1	4
M.S. Venter	7	13	1	557	131	46.41	1	5
K.C. Wessels	8	12	1	504	130	45.81	2	1
V.G. Cresswell	6	9	1	363	102	45.37	1	2
D.A. Scott	4	6	1	223	86*	44.60		2
A.C. Hudson	9	17	2	649	148	43.26	2	3
M.H. Austen	9	16	1	642	202*	42.80	2	1
G.M. Walsh	6	10	2	339	138*	42.37	2	
M.J.R. Rindel	7	13	2	463	157*	42.09	1	1
P.G. Amm	9	15	1	571	129	40.78	1	5

First-Class Averages continued

	M	Inns	NOs	Runs	HS	Av	100s	50s
N.E. Wright	4	7		284	94	40.57		2
E.N. Trotman	6	12	2	402	101*	40.20	1	3
D.J. Callaghan	9	13		520	148	40.00	1	3
I.L. Howell	6	10	4	240	55*	40.00		2
P.N. Kirsten	7	12	2	398	82	39.80		3
A.L. Wilmot	6	12	1	435	135	39.54	2	1
A.P. Plantema	4	7		269	69	38.42		2
S.J. Cook	8	16	5	422	159	38.36	1	1
K.J. Barnett	6	11	1	383	73	38.30		2
K.G. Bauermeister	6	9	2	265	74	37.85		2
T.N. Lazard	7	11		416	90	37.81		4
B.M. Osborne	6	12	2	376	86*	37.60		3
C.S. Stirk	6	11	1	371	154	37.10	1	
M.J. Pearse	5	6		221	69	36.83		2
L.P. Vorster	8	11	1	368	174	36.80	1	1
J.M. Arthur	6	12	1	400	123	36.36	1	2
P.I. Barclay	3	6		215	82	35.83		2
D.H. Howell	5	8		286	151	35.75	1	
V.F. du Preez	7	13	1	423	92*	35.25		4
O. Henry	7	11	1	346	125	34.60	1	1
B.W. Lones	5	10		344	139	34.40	1	2
P.H. Rayner	8	15	2	442	100*	34.00	1	3
D.J. Richardson	8	11	2	291	72	32.33		3
C.A. Lowe	4	4		128	49	32.00		
P. McLaren	5	8	4	128	38*	32.00		
A. Geringer	7	12	1	349	113	31.72	1	1
B.J. Whitfield	8	16	1	452	113	30.13	1	2
N.T. Day	7	13	1	360	60	30.00		3
S. Nackerdien	4	7	1	180	70*	30.00		2
R.J. East	8	14	2	356	58*	29.66		4
M.B. Logan	8	15	1	415	52	29.64		1
J.D. du Toit	5	8		233	89	29.12		1
A.V. Birrell	6	12	1	320	78*	29.09		2
M.B. Minnaar	5	7	3	115	40*	28.75		
M. Michau	7	12	1	315	76*	28.63		2
J.J.E. Hardy	5	9		255	75	28.33		2
M.J.P. Ford	6	12		335	73	27.91		3
B. McBride	4	6		167	68	27.83		2
W.S. Truter	5	8		222	107	27.75	1	
D.J. Cullinan	7	12	2	275	95*	27.50		2
J.W. Lloyds	4	7		190	40	27.14		
L. Seeff	7	12		324	125	27.00	1	1
R.C. Ontong	6	10	2	215	56	26.87		1
B. van Onselen	2	4		106	42	26.50		
R.F. Pienaar	3	6	1	132	38	26.40		
A. van N. Snyman	5	9		237	58	26.33		1
L.J. Barnard	7	13		340	102	26.15	1	2
R.M. Bentley	7	13		338	67	26.00		2
I.F. Mellett	3	6		156	54	26.00		2
M.D. Tramontino	3	5		128	59	25.60		2
P.J. Newport	7	11		272	86	24.72		1
A.M. Ferreira	7	13		321	72	24.69		2
H.R. Fotheringham	8	16	4	294	150*	24.50	1	
T.R. Madsen	8	15	1	340	61	24.28		2
C. Wulfsohn	5	9	4	120	36	24.00		
D. Norman	5	7	1	143	97	23.83		1
F.B. Touzel	5	9	1	189	75*	23.62		1
A. da Costa	6	10		235	80	23.50		1
J. During	5	8	3	116	41*	23.20		
W. Kirsch	5	10	1	207	109	23.00	1	
E.O. Simons	7	12	2	228	68	22.80		1
C.M. Lister-James	8	14	4	227	45	22.70		
K.J. Bridgens	6	11		247	79	22.45		1
M.J. Mitchley	7	12	2	221	64*	22.10		1
G.J. Turner	6	10		220	58	22.00		1
K.J. Kerr	8	9	2	153	53	21.85		1
M. Yachad	7	12	3	195	50	21.66		1
A.D. Methven	5	8		173	63	21.62		2
J.B. Commins	7	13		280	70	21.53		3
A.P. Kuiper	7	12	2	214	51	21.40		2
D.R. Hewson	3	5		106	50	21.20		1
P.A. Amm	4	8		169	40	21.12		

	M	Inns	NOs	Runs	HS	Av	100s	50s
M.D. Mellor	6	11		230	70	20.90		2
T.D. Topley	6	10	2	167	47	20.87		
I. Human	6	8		166	54	20.75		1
N.P. Daniels	8	14	1	269	47	20.69		
D.B. Rundle	8	11	2	185	45	20.55		
P.L. Symcox	6	8	1	143	36	20.42		
G.E. McMillan	9	12	3	180	39	20.00		
G.P. Thomas	3	5		100	47	20.00		
R.V. Jennings	8	10	1	172	65*	19.11		1
M.W. Pringle	7	11	3	144	50*	18.00		1
B.E. van der Vyver	6	11		191	54	17.36		1
L.J. Wilkinson	9	18		311	70	17.27		1
P.A. Tullis	4	8		136	36	17.00		
J.J. Strydom	9	18	1	287	107	16.88	1	
J.W. Furstenburg	3	6		100	57	16.66		1
P.J.R. Steyn	8	16	1	239	49	15.93		
G.S. le Roux	7	10	2	126	47*	15.75		
S.T. Clarke	7	14	1	201	60	15.46		1
W.F. Morris	7	12		178	58	14.83		1
K.D. Verdoorn	7	13		188	57	14.46		1
T.G. Shaw	8	9	1	111	28	13.87		
C.J.P.G. van Zyl	8	14	5	123	37*	13.66		
G.L. Hayes	5	9		128	38	13.66		
C.J. van Heerden	5	10		136	30	13.60		
A.C. Storie	5	9		107	53	11.88		1
P.B. Clift	7	10	1	104	37	11.55		
G. Grobler	8	11		126	42	11.45		

(Qualification – 100 runs, average 10.00)

BOWLING

	Ovs	Mds	Runs	Wkts	Av	Best	10/m	5/inns
B.M. Mcmillan	100.1	36	178	19	9.36	5/39		1
N.V. Radford	109.5	20	313	24	13.04	6/38	1	2
R.J. McCurdy	55	11	173	12	14.41	6/11		1
S.J. Base	224	58	541	35	15.45	6/28		2
S.T. Clarke	231.4	58	504	32	15.75	7/48		2
R.O. Estwick	236.4	79	591	36	16.41	5/17		1
C.E.B. Rice	218.3	75	498	30	16.60	5/14		1
G.E. McMillan	134.5	50	248	14	17.71	3/23		
M. James	227.3	76	519	29	17.89	7/45	1	4
A.P. Igglesden	191.2	36	565	31	18.22	5/52	1	2
C.J.P.G. van Zyl	203	49	472	25	18.88	4/40		
P.J. Newport	170.2	31	448	23	19.47	4/32		
O. Henry	258.4	71	713	36	19.80	6/57	1	2
S. Elworthy	62.3	8	222	11	20.18	4/56		
C.D. Mitchley	181.1	44	513	25	20.52	5/108		1
P.B. Clift	208.4	58	474	23	20.60	5/53		1
D.J. Callaghan	94.1	19	248	12	20.66	2/16		
R.L.S. Armitage	265.1	89	560	27	20.74	6/64		2
P. Anker	200.5	65	345	16	21.56	3/19		
P. McLaren	137	33	346	16	21.62	4/19		
T.D. Topley	221.2	56	652	29	22.48	5/50	1	3
S.T. Jefferies	289.2	72	793	35	22.66	10/59	1	2
M.R. Hobson	147.5	16	502	22	22.81	4/25		
D.B. Rundle	268.1	76	628	27	23.25	6/37	1	3
R.F. Pienaar	65.5	8	233	10	23.30	5/95		1
P.L. Symcox	279.1	77	703	30	23.43	7/93		2
P.S. de Villiers	208.3	48	594	25	23.76	4/29		
A.J. McClement	124	38	334	14	23.85	4/77		
G.S. le Roux	201.1	38	505	21	24.04	4/60		
D.J. Ferrant	98	26	242	10	24.20	3/62		
I.L. Howell	247.5	81	510	21	24.28	6/89		1
J.A. Carse	100	18	292	12	24.33	4/31		
J.J. Hooper	102	27	270	11	24.54	3/50		
E.O. Simons	203.3	41	591	24	24.62	4/35		
W.K. Watson	161.3	43	444	18	24.66	5/36		1
T.J. Packer	219.3	30	823	33	24.93	6/38		2
W.F. Morris	208.4	48	609	24	25.37	6/59	1	2
R.K. McGlashan	222	46	636	25	25.44	8/122	1	1
M.W. Pringle	164	30	515	20	25.75	6/33		1
C. Wulfsohn	120	30	329	12	27.41	4/69		
H. Lindenberg	143.5	32	390	14	27.85	3/100		

First-Class Averages continued

BOWLING

	Ovs	Mds	Runs	Wkts	Av	Best	10/m	5/inns
R.M. Bentley	114.2	26	283	10	28.30	3/10		
G. Grobler	253.1	47	818	28	29.21	4/47		
J.G. Thomas	222.4	40	678	23	29.47	4/92		
P.E. Smith	215.2	49	621	21	29.57	4/54		
A.A. Donald	263.1	53	755	25	30.20	4/39		
C.M. Lister-James	151.1	25	487	16	30.43	4/53		
T.G. Shaw	406.4	146	835	27	30.92	6/112		1
M.D. Clare	143.3	27	361	11	32.81	3/54		
G.L. Ackermann	115.3	23	335	10	33.50	5/36		1
B.E. van der Vyver	123	25	379	11	34.45	5/82		1
G.L. Hayes	118.2	23	361	10	36.10	4/30		
A.L. Hobson	248	63	670	18	37.22	4/86		
G.W. Symmonds	151.5	25	465	12	38.75	4/37		
K.J. Kerr	174.4	52	484	12	40.33	2/9		

BOWLING

	Ovs	Mds	Runs	Wkts	Av	Best	10/m	5/inns
P.A. Rayment	250.5	51	709	17	41.70	4/55		
J.W. Lloyds	154	34	426	10	42.60	3/115		

(Qualification – 10 wickets)

LEADING FIELDERS

32 - R.V. Jennings; 27 - C.F. Spilhaus (ct 24/st 3); 25 - N.T. Day (ct 19/st 6); 24 - T.R. Madsen (ct 23/st 1); 23 - R.J. Ryall (ct 21/st 2); 20 - D.J. Richardson (ct 17/st 3) and V.G. Cresswell (ct 18/st 2); 19 - I. Human and R.J. East (ct 18/st 1); 14 - K.J. Bridgens (ct 12/st 2) and A. da Costa (ct 13/st 1); 13 - M.H. Austen, A.C. Hudson, M. Michau, M.J. Mitchley, M.J. Pearse and P.A. Tullis (ct 12/st 1); 11 - D.J. Callaghan, D.J. Cullinan, G. Kirsten, B. McBride, G.E. McMillan and E.N. Trotman (ct 10/st 1); 10 - H.R. Fotheringham and L.J. Wilkinson.

Bruce Roberts, Transvaal. (Allsport)

Ken McEwan, Eastern Province. (Ken Kelly)

Dignity and Repose

The season in India. Duleep Trophy.
Irani Cup. The West Indies tour.
Wills Trophy. Ranji Trophy.
First-class averages.

*Raman Lamba. An innings of 320 in the Duleep Trophy final, and the
only batsman to score a thousand runs in the Indian season. (Allsport)*

One of the fullest Indian seasons in history, which included the staging of the World Cup, began with the Duleep Trophy. With the top players on international duty, batsmen like Lamba, Gaekwad and Arun Lal were to make early claims for recognition for the Indian side which was to face West Indies after the World Cup.

Duleep Trophy

Quarter-Final

8, 9, 10 and 11 October 1987

at Barkatullah Stadium, Jodhpur

North Zone 536 (R. Lamba 197, K. Bhaskar Pillai 129, M. Nayyar 67) and 216 for 3 (K. Bhaskar Pillai 103 not out, A. Sharma 60)
East Zone 241 (J. Arun Lal 143)

North Zone won on first innings

The inevitable high scoring allowed North Zone to qualify for the semi-final by virtue of their first-innings lead. After Lamba and Nayyar had begun the match with a stand of 104 Lamba and Pillai added 262 for the third wicket. The 25-year-old Bhaskar Pillai hit his first century in the Duleep Trophy and completed his second century in the

second innings. Skipper Arun Lal was the only batsman to offer serious resistance from the East Zone.

Semi-Finals

15, 16, 17 and 18 October 1987

at Vidarbha Cricket Association Stadium, Nagpur

West Zone 676 for 8 dec (S.V. Manjrekar 278, A.D. Gaekwad 195) and 445 for 3 (L.S. Rajput 275, S.K. Kulkarni 80, M.D. Gunjal 63 not out)
Central Zone 360 (Padam Shastri 118, R.P. Singh 79, Suhail Ansari 53)

West Zone won on first innings

at Green Park, Kanpur

North Zone 334 (R. Lamba 114, Arshad Ayub 8 for 65) and 283 (R. Vinayak 88, Kirti Azad 52, B. Arun 4 for 68)
South Zone 177 and 291 (B. Arun 89, W.V. Raman 60)

North Zone won by 149 runs

A second-wicket stand of 288, a Duleep Trophy record, assured West Zone of a massive score and of a place in the final. S.V. Manjrekar hit his first century in the competition and the highest score of his career and drew the

---

DULEEP TROPHY FINAL – NORTH ZONE v. WEST ZONE
21, 22, 23, 25 and 26 October 1987 at Bhilai, Madhya Pradesh

WEST ZONE

	FIRST INNINGS		SECOND INNINGS	
A.D. Gaekwad†	run out	216	(7) c A. Sharma, b Talwar	4
L.S. Rajput	c Pillai, b Ghai	8	(1) c Pillai, b Talwar	83
S.V. Manjrekar	c Amarnath, b Ghai	8	c A. Sharma, b Talwar	40
S. Kalyani	c Ghai, b Madan Lal	20	c Nayyar, b Talwar	15
M.D. Gunjal	b Amarnath	19	not out	23
S. Keshwala	b Amarnath	60	c and b Talwar	8
S.K. Kulkarni*	b Talwar	42	(2) c sub, b A. Sharma	66
Azim Khan	c Nayyar, b A. Sharma	3	not out	24
A.K. Patel	c Madan Lal, b A. Sharma	26		
R.R. Kulkarni	c Talwar, b A. Sharma	1		
Rashid Patel	not out	3		
Extras	b 4, lb 4, w 6, nb 8	22	b 9, lb 7, nb 5	21
	penalty runs	16		
		444	(for 6 wkts)	284

	O	M	R	W	O	M	R	W
Madan Lal	26	6	76	1				
Ghai	21	3	82	2	12	–	68	–
S. Sharma	12	1	51	–	12	1	47	–
Amarnath	23	5	70	2				
Talwar	30	3	92	1	30	7	91	5
A. Sharma	22.1	6	30	3	29	10	62	1
Kirti Azad	6	–	19	–				

NORTH ZONE

	FIRST INNINGS	
M. Nayyar	lbw, b R.R. Kulkarni	66
R. Lamba	c Gunjal, b Azim Khan	320
M.B. Amarnath	c sub, b Azim Khan	32
K. Bhaskar Pillai	b R. Patel	64
A. Sharma	st S.K. Kulkarni, b R. Patel	4
R. Vinayak*	c S.K. Kulkarni, b Keshwala	23
Kirti Azad	c S.K. Kulkarni, b Rajput	7
U.S. Madan Lal†	c Rajput, b Gunjal	107
R.S. Ghai	lbw, b Keshwala	79
S. Sharma	not out	52
S. Talwar	c sub, b R. Patel	5
Extras	b 12, lb 5, w 4, nb 20	41
	penalty runs	68
		868

	O	M	R	W
R.R. Kulkarni	23	1	137	1
R. Patel	32	5	86	3
Keshwala	23	3	66	2
A.K. Patel	6	–	33	–
Azim Khan	39	3	149	2
Gaekwad	24	3	71	–
Rajput	22	1	104	1
Gunjal	18	1	84	1
Manjrekar	6	–	29	–
Kalyani	4	1	24	–

FALL OF WICKETS
1–38, 2–58, 3–119, 4–176, 5–295, 6–383, 7–394, 8–400, 9–403
1–38, 2–176, 3–205, 4–216, 5–230, 6–238

FALL OF WICKETS
1–176, 2–253, 3–399, 4–409, 5–463, 6–481, 7–618, 8–696, 9–787

Umpires: S.M. Basu & R.V. Ramani

Match drawn. North Zone took the Trophy on first-innings lead

attention of the Indian selectors, as did the veteran Gaekwad. Skipper Padam Shastri and R.P. Singh battled bravely, but the match ended with Rajput hitting his second double century in the Duleep Trophy, the highest score of his career, and sharing an opening partnership of 253 with Kulkarni.

At Kanpur, there was a result, a feat which has become rare in the Duleep Trophy. In spite of Lamba's second century, the highlight of the match was the bowling of Arshad Ayub, whose 8 for 65 was the second best return in the history of the competition. His match figures, 11 for 127, have been bettered on only five occasions. His magnificent effort was in vain, however, for South Zone offered little resistance to North's varied attack. Left to make 441 to win after North's tail had rallied spiritedly, South Zone slumped to 131 for 8, but they were saved from ignominy by a brisk stand of 127 between Arun and Raman.

Duleep Trophy Final
NORTH ZONE v. WEST ZONE

Yet another Duleep final was dominated by the batsmen and decided on the first innings. West Zone owed their large score to Gaekwad's first double century in the competition. It proved insufficient, however, as Raman

Lamba shared in three century partnerships and established a record with the first triple century in the competition. North Zone's 868 was the highest score ever recorded in the Duleep Trophy, and ten West Zone bowlers were used. As the match drifted to its inevitable end, Sarkar Talwar took five wickets with his off-breaks.

Irani Cup
HYDERABAD v. REST OF INDIA

Winning the toss, Hyderabad were happy to bat first, but they struggled against some impressive medium-pace bowling by Ghai. It was not until Narasimha Rao joined Qayyum at the fall of the fourth wicket that the innings gained substance, but the Ranji Trophy holders never fully took command of the bowling.

The representative side were given a sound start by Lamba and Arun Lal, and Manjrekar, too, played well. Arshad Ayub gnawed away at the middle order, however, and his fine bowling in this match, following his performance in the Duleep Trophy, earned him his first Test cap.

Sanjeeva Sharma and M.I. Singh revived the Rest's flagging fortunes with a ninth-wicket stand of 67, but Hyderabad took first-innings lead and, inevitably, the Cup, for the second innings again became little more than exhibition cricket.

IRANI CUP HYDERABAD v. REST OF INDIA
30, 31 October, 1, 3 and 4 November 1987

HYDERABAD

	FIRST INNINGS		SECOND INNINGS	
Abdul Azeem	c Kulkarni, b Ghai	5	run out	16
V. Mohan Raj	c Arun Lal, b Ghai	47	c Raman, b Singh	30
V. Manohar	c Yashpal, b S. Sharma	31		
K.A. Qayyum	b Ghai	106	lbw, b S. Sharma	18
V. Jaisimha	c and b Ghai	0	not out	92
M.V. Narasimha Rao†	run out	65	c Arun Lal, b Raman	22
Arshad Ayub	c Manjrekar, b Hirwani	19	c Lamba, b Hirwani	1
Ehtesham Ali Khan*	lbw, b S. Sharma	30	(3) b Hirwani	35
R. Yadav	c sub, b Ghai	18		
N.S. Yadav	c Manjrekar, b Singh	30	(8) not out	18
M.V. Ramana Murthy	not out	15		
Extras	lb 7, nb 16	23	b 7, lb 13, nb 4	24
	penalty runs	16		
		405	(for 6 wkts)	256

REST OF INDIA

	FIRST INNINGS	
R. Lamba	c and b Narasimha Rao	53
J. Arun Lal†	c Ehtesham, b Ayub	53
S.V. Manjrekar	c Narasimha Rao, b R. Yadav	59
K. Bhaskar Pillai	lbw, b N.S. Yadav	20
Yashpal Sharma	c sub, b Ayub	37
S.K. Kulkarni*	c Qayyum, Ayub	16
W.V. Raman	c sub, b Ayub	17
R.S. Ghai	c Ehtesham, b Ayub	0
Sanjeeva Sharma	b Ayub	50
M.I. Singh	b N.S. Yadav	39
N. Hirwani	not out	11
Extras	b 8, lb 6, nb 9	23
		378

	O	M	R	W	O	M	R	W
Ghai	26	5	117	5	8	–	43	1
S. Sharma	30	7	91	2	20.2	4	44	1
M.I. Singh	15.4	–	60	1	22	5	49	1
Hirwani	17	3	47	1	13	3	41	2
Arun Lal	1	1	0	–				
Raman	21	3	67	–	17	1	48	1
Yashpal Sharma					2	–	11	–

	O	M	R	W
R. Yadav	22	2	66	1
Ramana Murthy	12	–	41	–
N.S. Yadav	24.4	2	91	2
Arshad Ayub	41	10	105	6
Narasimha Rao	15	1	55	1
Qayyum	2	–	6	–

FALL OF WICKETS
1–11, 2–58, 3–99, 4–103, 5–205, 6–254, 7–320, 8–331, 9–354
1–45, 2–94, 3–94, 4–130, 5–192, 6–193

FALL OF WICKETS
1–103, 2–128, 3–171, 4–217, 5–246, 6–267, 7–271, 8–274, 9–341

Umpires: S. Banerjee & V.D. Gupte

Match drawn. Hyderabad took the cup on first-innings lead

14, 15 and 16 November 1987

at Hyderabad

Hyderabad v. West Indians

Match abandoned

The opening match of the West Indies tour was completely washed out so that the Ranji Trophy holders were unable to test their strength. This was not the only unease at the start of the tour, for the West Indians were unhappy with a schedule which, insanely, included eight one-day internationals. Agreement was finally reached with four Tests being played instead of five, but, following so quickly upon the World Cup, the tour failed to excite the interest of the Indian public.

Dilip Vengsarkar took over as captain of India and hit two centuries in three Tests before being injured. He was later in trouble with the Indian Board, who alleged his activities as a journalist were in breach of agreement. (Adrian Murrell/ Allsport)

20, 21 and 22 November 1987

at Sector 16 Stadium, Chandigarh

West Indians 550 for 9 dec (C.G. Greenidge 174 retired, I.V.A. Richards 138 retired, A.L. Logie 52, C.A. Walsh 50) and 237 for 6 dec (P.V. Simmons 72, N. Hirwani 6 for 100)
India Under-25 XI 228 (Sanjeeva Sharma 76, Jaspal Singh 70) and 41 for 1

Match drawn

A third-wicket partnership of 303 between Greenidge and Richards took the West Indies to a mammoth score. They then reduced the young Indian side to 73 for 7, only Bhaskar Pillai with 22 offering resistance. Jaspal Singh joined Sanjeeva Sharma in an eighth-wicket stand of 135, but the Indians still fell more than 300 short of the West Indian score. Richards did not enforce the follow-on, but the spin attack of Azim Khan and Hirwani pinned down the West Indians. Only Dujon seemed able to cope as leg-spinner Hirwani returned career-best bowling figures.

First Test Match
INDIA v. WEST INDIES

With Kapil Dev replaced by Vengsarkar as captain after the former's failure to win the World Cup for the second time, and Azharuddin, Amarnath and Sidhu missing through injury or illness, and Gavaskar having retired, India produced something of a new-look side. Success in domestic cricket brought a return to the national side for Lamba and Arun Lal and first caps for Manjrekar and Arshad Ayub. West Indies gave Winston Benjamin his Test début.

Vengsarkar won the toss and decided to bat. He could not have had a worse baptism as a Test captain. The third ball of the match accounted for Srikkanth, caught behind, and wickets fell at regular intervals. In just under 31 overs, India were all out for 75, their lowest score in a Test match in India. Fine swing bowling on a pitch of uneven bounce in an atmosphere that was heavy early on was the cause of India's downfall, although some reckless shots did not help their cause.

The West Indian bowling was fast, hostile and accurate. It was Winston Davis who did the early damage with three wickets in eleven overs, and eight of the Indians were caught in the arc between wicket-keeper and gully. The innings was finished by Patterson, who took three wickets in five balls in the last over to give him figures of 5 for 24, his best return in Test cricket.

Kapil Dev continued the dominance of the pace bowlers when he had Greenidge lbw in the first over of the West Indian innings with a ball that kept low. He soon accounted for Richardson, and with Chetan Sharma revelling in the conditions, West Indies were 29 for 6. Only Haynes, staunch and runless, had stood firm.

He was well supported by Benjamin, who became off-spinner Arshad Ayub's first Test victim, and later by Walsh. The first day ended with West Indies 118 for 8. The day had seen 18 wickets fall for 193 runs.

The innings lasted another fifteen minutes on the second morning, Haynes being last out. His defiant innings included 7 fours.

India again began disastrously, losing Srikkanth to a wretched shot, and Lamba, who offered no stroke, to successive deliveries. Arun Lal and Vengsarkar added 60 before Arun Lal hooked Walsh into the hands of long-leg. Vengsarkar was badly dropped by Dujon, but Shastri was taken at second slip. Manjrekar, son of the great Indian batsman of the 1950s, was hit over the left eye by a ball from Benjamin and forced to retire hurt, but Kapil Dev stayed with Vengsarkar until the close, which came at 210 for 5, Vengsarkar on 74.

The new Indian captain reached his 16th Test century on the third day and, once Kapil Dev's buccaneering innings had come to an end, he added 96 with More. Walsh, the most impressive of the West Indian bowlers, returned his best Test figures as India were out for 327, testimony to the improvement in the batting conditions and more resolution in the batting itself. West Indies lost both openers to Ayub and closed at 80 for 2.

Needing another 196 to win at the start of the fourth day, West Indies immediately lost night-watchman Davis, who followed contemporary fashion by showing his disagreement with the decision. Richardson was out after a careful innings, and the decisive stand between Richards and Logie then took place. Arshad Ayub had been accurate rather than spinning the ball venomously, but Richards launched an attack on him. He square cut and drove through the covers to the boundary and scored 53 of the last 73 needed for victory. It was a captain's innings, occupying 156 minutes. Richards' 21st Test hundred came off 102 balls and he hit 13 fours. What had been a close contest was suddenly decided by the genius of one man.

3, 4 and 5 December 1987

at Nehru Stadium, Pune

West Indians 576 for 7 dec (R.B. Richardson 147, R.A. Harper 82, E.A.E. Baptiste 75 not out, D.L. Haynes 70, C.G. Greenidge 58, A. Sharma 4 for 105)
North Zone 468 for 6 (R. Lamba 101, A. Sharma 99, M.B. Amarnath 71, Gursharan Singh 65)

Match drawn

Having led the West Indian run riot, Richie Richardson lapsed when he twice dropped Lamba, who went on to make 101 off 237 balls with 11 fours. Lamba shared a stand of 174 with Amarnath for the second wicket, but the most entertaining batting came from Gursharan Singh and Ajay Sharma, who put on 117 for the fourth wicket. Sharma had bowled his slow left-arm with great accuracy and batted well until giving Hooper a meek return catch when one short of his century.

First One-Day International
INDIA v. WEST INDIES

It was hard to follow some of Vengsarkar's reasoning in the way in which he handled his bowlers in the first one-day international. Kapil Dev had 1 for 13 in 7 overs, three overs unused of his quota, while Gaekwad, a surprise selection, bowled eight overs. The Indian attack, with Maninder and the other spinners Arshad Ayub and Shastri particularly effective, contained the West Indian

Courtney Walsh who returned his best Test match figures of 5 for 54 at both Delhi and Bombay. (Adrian Murrell/ Allsport)

batsmen, and it was not until Hooper and Benjamin added 65 for the eighth wicket that the tourists offered any prospect of a reasonable score.

India began disastrously against Patterson's pace and accuracy, but at 31 for 5, Kapil Dev strode to the wicket. He hit 11 fours and 2 sixes as he made 87 from 64 balls,

FIRST TEST MATCH – INDIA v. WEST INDIES
25, 26, 28 and 29 November 1987 at Ferozeshah Kotla, Delhi

INDIA

	FIRST INNINGS		SECOND INNINGS	
K. Srikkanth	c Dujon, b Patterson	0	c Harper, b Patterson	5
J. Arun Lal	c Greenidge, b Davis	20	c Benjamin, b Walsh	40
R. Lamba	b Davis	1	b Patterson	0
D.B. Vengsarkar†	c Harper, b Davis	10	c Greenidge, b Walsh	102
R.J. Shastri	c Richardson, b Benjamin	6	c Harper, b Patterson	4
S.V. Manjrekar	c Harper, b Patterson	5	retired hurt	10
R.N. Kapil Dev	c Dujon, b Walsh	7	lbw, b Benjamin	44
K.S. More*	not out	12	c Dujon, b Walsh	49
Arshad Ayub	c Harper, b Patterson	7	lbw, b Walsh	17
C.M. Sharma	c Richardson, b Patterson	0	b Walsh	24
Maninder Singh	b Patterson	0	not out	2
Extras	lb 1, w 3, nb 3	7	b 17, lb 7, w 5, nb 1	30
		75		327

	O	M	R	W	O	M	R	W
Patterson	8.5	1	24	5	29	6	100	3
Davis	11	2	20	3	20	3	60	–
Benjamin	7	–	17	1	23	3	76	1
Walsh	4	–	13	1	29.3	9	54	5
Harper					12	3	13	–

WEST INDIES

	FIRST INNINGS		SECOND INNINGS	
C.G. Greenidge	lbw, b Kapil Dev	0	lbw, b Arshad Ayub	33
D.L. Haynes	c Lamba, b Sharma	45	hit wkt, b Ayub	27
R.B. Richardson	lbw, b Kapil Dev	4	c Lamba, b Kapil Dev	31
I.V.A. Richards†	c More, b Sharma	9	(5) not out	109
A.L. Logie	lbw, b Sharma	4	(6) lbw, b Ayub	46
P.J.L. Dujon*	c Lamba, b Kapil Dev	5	(7) not out	12
R.A. Harper	run out	4		
W.W. Davis	c and b Sharma	6	(4) c sub (Pandit), b Arshad Ayub	1
W.K.M. Benjamin	b Arshad Ayub	19		
C.A. Walsh	c Lamba, b Sharma	16		
B.P. Patterson	not out	5		
Extras	b 3, lb 1, w 1, nb 5	10	b 1, lb 9, nb 7	17
		127	(for 5 wkts)	276

	O	M	R	W	O	M	R	W
Kapil Dev	18	8	41	3	20	8	44	1
Sharma	13.1	2	55	5	11	1	44	–
Maninder Singh	7	3	13	–	20	4	75	–
Arshad Ayub	9	4	14	1	25	4	72	4
Shastri					9	2	30	–
Arun Lal					0.3	–	1	–

FALL OF WICKETS

1–0, 2–7, 3–32, 4–42, 5–42, 6–52, 7–58, 8–75, 9–75
1–6, 2–6, 3–66, 4–82, 5–178, 6–274, 7–277, 8–318, 9–327

FALL OF WICKETS

1–0, 2–4, 3–13, 4–17, 5–25, 6–29, 7–49, 8–102, 9–122
1–62, 2–69, 3–81, 4–111, 5–203

Umpires: D.N. Dotiwala & V.K. Ramaswamy

West Indies won by 5 wickets

FIRST ONE-DAY INTERNATIONAL – INDIA v. WEST INDIES
8 December 1987 at Vidarbha Cricket Association Stadium, Nagpur

WEST INDIES

D.L. Haynes	run out	20
C.G. Greenidge	b Maninder Singh	36
R.B. Richardson	c Gaekwad, b Maninder Singh	11
I.V.A. Richards†	st More, b Maninder Singh	1
A.L. Logie	lbw, b Shastri	13
C.L. Hooper	not out	57
P.J.L. Dujon*	c Vengsarkar, b Shastri	4
R.A. Harper	st More, b Gaekwad	7
W.K.M. Benjamin	b Kapil Dev	31
C.A. Walsh	not out	3
B.P. Patterson		
Extras	lb 12, w 2, nb 6	20
(50 overs)	(for 8 wkts)	203

	O	M	R	W
Kapil Dev	7	–	13	1
Sharma	7	–	49	–
Maninder Singh	8	–	40	3
Arshad Ayub	10	–	26	–
Shastri	10	1	24	2
Gaekwad	8	–	39	1

FALL OF WICKETS

1–51, 2–71, 3–73, 4–81, 5–101, 6–107, 7–128, 8–193

INDIA

K. Srikkanth	c Richards, b Patterson	5
J. Arun Lal	b Patterson	7
A.D. Gaekwad	lbw, b Patterson	0
D.B. Vengsarkar†	c Richards, b Benjamin	8
C.S. Pandit	lbw, b Richards	6
R.J. Shastri	b Patterson	20
R.N. Kapil Dev	c Haynes, b Patterson	87
K.S. More*	c Haynes, b Patterson	33
Arshad Ayub	b Hooper	4
C.M. Sharma	lbw, b Walsh	2
Maninder Singh	not out	4
Extras	b 2, lb 7, w 3, nb 5	17
(44.4 overs)		193

	O	M	R	W
Patterson	9.4	–	29	6
Walsh	9	–	21	1
Richards	9	1	39	1
Benjamin	10	1	53	1
Hooper	7	–	42	1

FALL OF WICKETS

1–13, 2–13, 3–18, 4–31, 5–31, 6–144, 7–145, 8–150, 9–155

Umpires: Rajen Mehra & V. Vikram Raj

Man of the Match: B.P. Patterson

West Indies won by 10 runs

and he and Shastri added 113 for the sixth wicket. Indian hopes rose, but Patterson returned to dismiss them both, and in spite of some brave blows by More, India fell 10 short of the West Indian total.

Patterson's 6 for 29 was the fifth best return in a one-day international match.

<hr>

Second Test Match
INDIA v. WEST INDIES

<hr>

West Indies gave a first Test cap to Carl Hooper and brought in Butts for the injured Harper while India welcomed back Amarnath and Azharuddin. The first day was restricted to little over two hours' play by dark and drizzle, yet it was enlivened by an innings of 71 off 63 balls from Srikkanth, who hit a six and 11 fours and dominated an opening stand of 60 with Arun Lal, who made three.

There was no play at all on the second day, but Azharuddin and Vengsarkar began the third day brightly enough for India until Azharuddin was run out. Vengsarkar provided Butts with his first Test wicket when the off-spinner beat the Indian captain in the flight, and after that only Kapil Dev offered significant resistance.

West Indies reached 49 in the hour before the close and next morning only six had been added when Greenidge was given out caught at silly point, a decision which was hotly disputed. The West Indian innings was sustained by Richie Richardson, who batted for four hours, but he was responsible for running out Logie, who had faced one ball. Hooper batted with polish, and after Richardson was

seventh out, Butts, Davis and Patterson boosted the score with positive batting which took the innings into the last morning.

It now seemed that the match was meandering to a predictable draw, but the last hours were not without incident. Srikkanth batted with his customary panache although he enjoyed a little fortune. His 65 came off 78 balls and contained 10 fours. He was disdainful of Patterson's short-pitched bowling, but his colleagues suffered somewhat. Patterson had been incensed by the barrage of short-pitched bowling which Chetan Sharma had unleashed in the early overs of the day and which had gone unchecked by the umpires.

It was Patterson who gave West Indies a hint of victory when, bowling at a furious pace, he knocked out Srikkanth's middle stump, had Azharuddin taken at square-leg and dismissed Kapil Dev and More with successive deliveries. This reduced India to 132 for 7, and there was anger in the West Indian camp that their pacemen had been denied other valid wickets by the umpires. Richards later withheld comment, but suggested that his side had been very unlucky.

Vengsarkar, who received a terrible battering, and Ayub batted bravely to add 41, and this stand thwarted the West Indians.

18, 19 and 20 December 1987

<hr>

at Indira Priyadarshini Stadium, Visakhapatnam

West Indians 394 (P.J.L. Dujon 123, A.L. Logie 54, Ghopal

SECOND TEST MATCH – INDIA v. WEST INDIES
11, 12, 13, 15 and 16 December 1987 at Wankhede Stadium, Bombay

INDIA

	FIRST INNINGS		SECOND INNINGS	
K. Srikkanth	b Walsh	71	b Patterson	65
J. Arun Lal	c Richardson, b Walsh	3	c Greenidge, b Patterson	1
M.B. Amarnath	c Butts, b Walsh	1	c Richards, b Walsh	8
D.B. Vengsarkar†	st Dujon, b Butts	51	not out	40
M. Azharuddin	run out	34	c Davis, b Patterson	5
R.J. Shastri	c Richards, b Davis	0	c Butts, b Davis	5
R.N. Kapil Dev	c Greenidge, b Butts	47	c Dujon, b Patterson	5
K.S. More*	c Dujon, b Patterson	9	c Richards, b Patterson	0
Arshad Ayub	c Richardson, b Walsh	8	b Walsh	18
C.M. Sharma	not out	22	b Walsh	0
Maninder Singh	c Richards, b Walsh	0	c Richardson, b Walsh	0
Extras	b 4, lb 15, nb 16	35	b 1, lb 5, w 8, nb 12	26
		281		**173**

WEST INDIES

	FIRST INNINGS		SECOND INNINGS	
C.G. Greenidge	c Arun Lal, b Shastri	15	c Kapil Dev, b Sharma	2
D.L. Haynes	c sub (Pandit), b Shastri	58	not out	0
R.B. Richardson	lbw, b Sharma	89	not out	0
I.V.A. Richards†	b Maninder Singh	37		
A.L. Logie	run out	0		
C.L. Hooper	lbw, b Kapil Dev	37		
P.J.L. Dujon*	c and b Shastri	14		
C.G. Butts	c More, b Shastri	18		
W.W. Davis	c and b Sharma	30		
C.A. Walsh	c Srikkanth, b Sharma	5		
B.P. Patterson	not out	21		
Extras	lb 8, w 1, nb 4	13	lb 1, nb 1	2
		337	(for 1 wkt)	**4**

	O	M	R	W	O	M	R	W		O	M	R	W	O	M	R	W
Patterson	17	3	78	1	16	1	68	5	Kapil Dev	25	8	72	1	1	–	2	–
Davis	15	–	71	1	15	2	59	1	Sharma	13	1	64	3	1	–	1	1
Walsh	17.4	2	54	5	12	2	40	4	Arshad Ayub	20	1	54	–				
Butts	18	5	59	2	1	1	0	–	Maninder Singh	17	5	68	1				
									Shastri	28.3	9	71	4				

FALL OF WICKETS
1–60, 2–74, 3–85, 4–157, 5–162, 6–222, 7–241, 8–247, 9–271
1–16, 2–58, 3–105, 4–112, 5–126, 6–132, 7–132, 8–173, 9–173

FALL OF WICKETS
1–55, 2–99, 3–146, 4–146, 5–210, 6–258, 7–258, 8–300, 9–308
1–3

Umpires: R.B. Gupta & P.D. Reporter

Match drawn

Sharma 6 for 136, W.V. Raman 4 for 94)
Indian Cricket Board President's XI 93 (E.A.E. Baptiste 4 for 27) and 218 (W.V. Raman 51, E.A.E. Baptiste 7 for 70)

West Indians won by an innings and 83 runs

A side of promising young Indian cricketers led by Gaekwad was severely trounced by the tourists. Batting at number three and enjoying his first good knock for some months, Dujon gave an elegant and aggressive display after Richardson and Simmons had begun with a stand of 80 in 19 overs. Dujon and Logie added 102 for the third wicket. Baptiste had a fine game while Raman and Manjrekar showed up best of the young Indians.

Indian captain Vengsarkar faced an enquiry by the Indian Board for continuing to write newspaper articles in spite of the Board's regulation against doing so.

Second One-Day International
INDIA v. WEST INDIES

On a wicket which always gave assistance to the bowlers, Viv Richards played a defiant knock, and his stand of 69 with Logie was crucial in the context of a low-scoring match. Richards, scorning the dangers of the ball, which kept low, hit 41 off 52 balls. His innings was ended by Shastri, who blunted the West Indians' middle order.

India lost their openers cheaply, but they were rallied by Amarnath and Vengsarkar, who was out when he spooned a catch to mid-on. From that point only Kapil Dev gave India hope, but he was left partnerless.

Ravi Shastri took over as captain of India after Vengsarkar had been injured and led his side to victory at the first attempt in the Test at Madres. (Adrian Murrell/Allsport)

SECOND ONE-DAY INTERNATIONAL – INDIA v. WEST INDIES
23 December 1987 at Nehru Stadium, Gauhati

WEST INDIES			
D.L. Haynes	b Maninder Singh		17
P.V. Simmons	c Srikkanth, b Amarnath		34
R.B. Richardson	c More, b Amarnath		10
I.V.A. Richards†	st More, b Shastri		41
A.L. Logie	lbw, b Kapil Dev		34
C.L. Hooper	c Kapil Dev, b Shastri		2
R.A. Harper	not out		18
W.K.M. Benjamin	st More, b Shastri		4
P.J.L. Dujon*	not out		13
C.A. Walsh			
B.P. Patterson			
Extras	lb 12, w 2		14
(45 overs)	(for 7 wkts)		187

	O	M	R	W
Kapil Dev	9	1	47	1
Prabhakar	4	–	22	–
Maninder Singh	9	3	19	1
Amarnath	9	1	21	2
Shastri	9	–	30	3
Arshad Ayub	5	–	36	–

FALL OF WICKETS
1–40, 2–62, 3–74, 4–143, 5–145, 6–163, 7–170

INDIA			
K. Srikkanth	b Walsh		1
A.D. Gaekwad	b Benjamin		12
M.B. Amarnath	c Richardson, b Hooper		33
D.B. Vengsarkar†	c Harper, b Richards		24
M. Azharuddin	c and b Hooper		3
R.N. Kapil Dev	not out		22
R.J. Shastri	b Walsh		12
K.S. More*	c Dujon, b Patterson		1
M. Prabhakar	lbw, b Walsh		1
Arshad Ayub	run out		6
Maninder Singh	b Walsh		0
Extras	b 8, lb 8, w 4		20
(41.3 overs)			135

	O	M	R	W
Patterson	8	2	20	1
Walsh	7.3	2	16	4
Benjamin	5	1	15	1
Harper	9	–	21	–
Richards	8	–	37	1
Hooper	4	1	10	2

FALL OF WICKETS
1–9, 2–25, 3–83, 4–89, 5–89, 6–117, 7–118, 8–122, 9–134

Umpires: S.K. Ghosh & R.V. Ramani

Man of the Match: I.V.A. Richards

West Indies won by 52 runs

Gus Logie hit his second Test century in the match at Calcutta. (Adrian Murrell/Allsport)

A maiden Test century in only his second Test match for Carl Hooper. (Allsport)

Third Test Match
INDIA v. WEST INDIES

After the uncertainties of the wicket at Gauhati the Eden Gardens pitch offered a batsman's paradise, and several batsmen took advantage of the gift with which they were presented. The result, predictably, was a rather tedious draw.

At the end of the first day, West Indies were 263 for 2. Greenidge and Richardson added 147 for the second wicket, and Greenidge hit his 14th Test century. Richards reached fifty before the close, but both batsmen were out early on the second day. Greenidge hit 4 sixes and 14 fours.

What hopes India had of a quick breakthrough were thwarted by Hooper and Logie, who combined to add 169. Gus Logie hit 15 fours in what was his second Test hundred while Carl Hooper confirmed the wisdom of the praise which had been heaped upon him by good judges of the game when, in his second Test match, he completed an impressive century off 171 deliveries. He hit 3 sixes and 7 fours.

Richards declared when Hooper reached his hundred, and India took 20 runs from four overs of high pace before the close. Arun Lal went on to reach his highest Test score on the third day, and there was solid support from Amarnath. Sadly, there was another unsavoury incident when Richardson appeared to catch Azharuddin at second slip. The batsman stood his ground, and umpire Reporter consulted Gupta and ruled 'not out'. Richards engaged in

THIRD TEST MATCH – INDIA v. WEST INDIES
26, 27, 28, 30 and 31 December 1987 at Eden Gardens, Calcutta

WEST INDIES

	FIRST INNINGS		SECOND INNINGS	
C.G. Greenidge	c More, b Kapil Dev	141	c sub (S. Sharma), b Shastri	69
D.L. Haynes	c Srikkanth, b Kapil	5	c and b Shastri	47
R.B. Richardson	c Azharuddin, b Shastri	51	not out	8
I.V.A. Richards†	c Kapil Dev, b Sharma	68		
A.L. Logie	c and b Maninder Singh	101	(4) not out	20
C.L. Hooper	not out	100		
P.J.L. Dujon*	not out	40		
C.G. Butts				
C.A. Walsh				
W.W. Davis				
B.P. Patterson				
Extras	b 2, lb 12, nb 10	24	b 4, lb 2, nb 7	13
	(for 5 wkts, dec)	530	(for 2 wkts)	157

	O	M	R	W	O	M	R	W
Kapil Dev	28	6	103	2	10	2	19	–
Sharma	15.1	–	80	1	4	–	24	–
Maninder Singh	36.5	5	111	1	16	2	43	–
Arshad Ayub	46	5	146	–	14	5	34	–
Shastri	22	4	60	1	10	3	13	2
Amarnath	3.5	–	16	–	4	–	11	–
Srikkanth					3	–	7	–
Arun Lal					1	1	0	–

FALL OF WICKETS
1–13, 2–160, 3–284, 4–288, 5–457
1–114, 2–129

INDIA

	FIRST INNINGS	
K. Srikkanth	c Dujon, b Walsh	23
J. Arun Lal	lbw, b Walsh	93
M.B. Amarnath	b Davis	43
D.B. Vengsarkar†	retired hurt	102
M. Azharuddin	c Logie, b Walsh	60
R.J. Shastri	b Davis	47
R.N. Kapil Dev	lbw, b Davis	4
K.S. More*	c Richardson, b Richards	44
Arshad Ayub	c Richardson, b Patterson	57
C.M. Sharma	b Walsh	27
Maninder Singh	not out	1
Extras	b 12, lb 25, nb 27	64
		565

	O	M	R	W
Patterson	22.2	–	107	1
Walsh	29	3	136	4
Davis	27	3	84	3
Butts	50	13	122	–
Richards	24	6	39	1
Hooper	20	5	40	–

FALL OF WICKETS
1–56, 2–152, 3–201, 4–305, 5–403, 6–410, 7–505, 8–553, 9–565

Umpires: R. B. Gupta & P.D. Reporter

Match drawn

fierce debate and much arm waving, but neither captain nor umpire would comment after the match. India closed at 304 for 3.

Azharuddin was out the following morning without adding to his score, but Vengsarkar battled on to reach his 17th Test hundred. It contained 11 fours and was his eighth in his last 16 Tests. His innings ended sadly, a rising ball from Davis breaking a finger on his left hand and ending his participation in the series.

More, Shastri and Ayub added useful runs. India ended on 521 for 7, and the last day only confirmed what had long been known. Sixty-four extras seemed an exorbitant contribution to the Indian total.

the second wicket. The innings looked like disintegrating when four wickets fell for 10 runs, but Azharuddin and Shastri stopped the rot and added 54. Azharuddin hit 44 from 57 balls before being run out.

Kapil Dev and Sanjeeva Sharma troubled the West Indians with considerable movement in their opening spell, yet it was Maninder Singh who caused the breakthrough. In a wonderfully economic spell, he had Richards caught in the 18th over and then deceived Greenidge into looping a catch to mid-on. Hooper and Logie added 60, but Kapil Dev trapped Hooper and the last six wickets went down for 14 runs.

The game was watched by 85,000 people.

Third One-Day International
INDIA v. WEST INDIES

India beat West Indies in a one-day international in India for the first time when Ravi Shastri, captain in the absence of the injured Vengsarkar, relied on left-arm spin to tilt the game in favour of the home side.

India brought in three new caps, Raman, Ajay Sharma and Sanjeeva Sharma, but none of them was to make a particular mark in this match. Batting first, India quickly lost Srikkanth, but Arun Lal and Amarnath put on 128 for

Fourth One-Day International
INDIA v. WEST INDIES

A thrilling innings by Viv Richards reasserted West Indies' authority in the one-day series. Playing in his second international match, Raman gave India early hope with a good innings in which he had the luck to be missed three times, once by débutant wicket-keeper Williams. Azharuddin hit 24 runs off 26 balls before being smartly caught and bowled by Richards, but the Indians could be satisfied with their 221 from 43 overs. West Indies were fined

THIRD ONE-DAY INTERNATIONAL – INDIA v. WEST INDIES
2 January 1988 at Eden Gardens, Calcutta

INDIA				WEST INDIES			
K. Srikkanth	c Dujon, b Walsh		1	C.G. Creenidge	c Amarnath, b Maninder Singh		44
J. Arun Lal	c Greenidge, b Hooper		51	D.L. Haynes	lbw, b Kapil Dev		3
M.B. Amarnath	run out		70	R.B. Richardson	run out		28
Sanjeeva Sharma	c Richardson, b Richards		0	I.V.A. Richards†	c Arun Lal, b Maninder Singh		3
M. Azharuddin	run out		44	A.L. Logie	c Azharuddin, b Shastri		38
R.N. Kapil Dev	c Benjamin, b Richards		1	C.L. Hooper	lbw, b Kapil Dev		27
R.J. Shastri†	lbw, b Patterson		25	W.K.M. Benjamin	c and b Shastri		1
W.V. Raman	not out		8	P.J.L. Dujon*	run out		2
K.S. More*	not out		9	E.A.E. Baptiste	lbw, b Amarnath		6
Ajay Sharma				C.A. Walsh	c sub, b S. Sharma		2
Maninder Singh				B.P. Patterson	not out		3
Extras	lb 10, w 2, nb 1		13	Extras	lb 6, w 2, nb 1		9
(45 overs)	(for 7 wkts)		222	(41.5 overs)			166

	O	M	R	W		O	M	R	W
Patterson	9	–	36	1	Kapil Dev	7	1	20	2
Walsh	9	2	26	1	Sanjeeva Sharma	5.5	–	29	1
Baptiste	5	–	23	–	Amarnath	9	–	46	1
Benjamin	5	–	29	–	Maninder Singh	9	–	19	2
Richards	9	–	48	2	Shastri	9	1	31	2
Hooper	8	–	51	1	Ajay Sharma	2	–	15	–

FALL OF WICKETS
1–2, 2–130, 3–131, 4–138, 5–140, 6–194, 7–210

FALL OF WICKETS
1–12, 2–53, 3–65, 4–92, 5–152, 6–153, 7–153, 8–158, 9–162

Umpires: R.B. Gupta & P.D. Reporter

Man of the Match: M.B. Amarnath

India won by 56 runs

FOURTH ONE-DAY INTERNATIONAL – INDIA v. WEST INDIES
5 January 1988 at Rajkot

INDIA				WEST INDIES			
K. Srikkanth	c Williams, b Benjamin		32	D.L. Haynes	b Raman		49
J. Arun Lal	c Greenidge, b Patterson		10	R.B. Richardson	c Kapil Dev, b S. Sharma		27
W.V. Raman	c Baptiste, b Patterson		95	A.L. Logie	c S. Viswanath, b Arshad Ayub		12
M. Azharuddin	c and b Richards		24	I.V.A. Richards†	not out		110
R.N. Kapil Dev	c Logie, b Richards		22	C.L. Hooper	c Manjrekar, b Kapil Dev		12
R.J. Shastri†	c and b Hooper		7	E.A.E. Baptiste	not out		7
S. Viswanath*	c Baptiste, b Richards		1	W.K.M. Benjamin			
S.V. Manjrekar	not out		19	C.G. Greenidge			
Ajay Sharma	not out		2	D.A. Williams*			
Sanjeeva Sharma				C.A. Walsh			
Arshad Ayub				B.P. Patterson			
Extras	lb 8, nb 1		9	Extras	lb 7, w 1		8
(43 overs)	(for 7 wkts)		221	(40.1 overs)	(for 4 wkts)		225

	O	M	R	W		O	M	R	W
Patterson	8	1	49	2	Kapil Dev	8	1	22	1
Walsh	8	–	39	–	Sanjeeva Sharma	6	–	31	1
Benjamin	9	–	35	1	Ajay Sharma	3	–	12	–
Baptiste	9	1	40	–	Arshad Ayub	10	1	55	1
Hooper	1	–	8	1	Shastri	9	1	50	–
Richards	8	–	42	3	Raman	4	–	44	1
					Srikkanth	0.1	–	4	–

FALL OF WICKETS
1–34, 2–69, 3–119, 4–151, 5–173, 6–176, 7–214

FALL OF WICKETS
1–38, 2–77, 3–147, 4–191

Umpires: D.N. Dotiwala & S.B. Kulkarni

Man of the Match: I.V.A. Richards

West Indies won by 6 wickets

heavily for bowling three overs short of the minimum quota. Raman fell to Patterson in the last over of the innings. He had faced 123 balls and hit 6 fours.

West Indies began soundly enough, but they required a formidable 72 from the last 10 overs. Richards then took total command. He hit Shastri for 3 sixes in one over, and altogether hit 7 sixes, a record for a one-day international. His seventh six brought him his century, and it had taken just 75 balls. He also hit 7 fours, and his match-winning innings lasted 77 deliveries.

Fifth One-Day International
INDIA v. WEST INDIES

The wrangle over the tour itinerary continued and revolved around the status of this match. With the number of Tests reduced to four and the number of one-day internationals increased to eight, there was a belief that the game at Ahmedabad was a charity match. It was later decreed that it was an official international, but that it would not count in the current series of 'seven' internationals. It was a ruling that most chose to ignore.

With Haynes and Greenidge absent injured, West Indies struggled against some accurate bowling after Chetan Sharma had made an initial breakthrough. A fifth-wicket stand of 46 between Logie and Hooper helped

to revive West Indies somewhat, but Logie was caught in the deep field, and India were well pleased to have bowled the visitors out for under 200.

Srikkanth gave his side a pugnacious start with a six and 5 fours in his 53 off 72 balls, but neither Arun Lal nor Amarnath could show any sparkle. When Kapil Dev was run out a sense of panic gripped the Indian batting, and the last over arrived with the last pair needing to score six to win the match. Only three were managed, and West Indies were 4–1, or 3–1, up in the series.

Fourth Test Match
INDIA v. WEST INDIES

With Vengsarkar's left hand fractured, Ravi Shastri led India in the fourth and final Test match. An injury to Maninder Singh meant a first Test cap for Hirwani, the young and inexperienced leg-spinner, while Venkat Raman and Ajay Sharma also made their Test débuts. Simmons, who had done so well in the World Cup, played his first Test match for West Indies in place of the injured Greenidge.

Captaining in a Test for the first time, Shastri won the toss and India batted. They were soon in trouble. Srikkanth mis-timed a pull to be caught at mid-wicket after beginning at his usual brisk rate, and Amarnath edged

---

FIFTH ONE-DAY INTERNATIONAL – INDIA v. WEST INDIES
7 January 1988 at Motera, Ahmedabad

WEST INDIES			
R.B. Richardson	b C.M. Sharma		4
P.V. Simmons	lbw, b Kapil Dev		20
P.J.L. Dujon	c and b C.M. Sharma		11
I.V.A. Richards†	b Amarnath		17
A.L. Logie	c Srikkanth, b Arshad Ayub		30
C.L. Hooper	c Arun Lal, b Srikkanth		33
E.A.E. Baptiste	run out		31
W.K.M. Benjamin	b Arshad Ayub		5
D.A. Williams*	run out		1
W.W. Davis	b Kapil Dev		10
B.P. Patterson	not out		13
Extras	b 7, lb 10, w 1, nb 3		21
(48.3 overs)			196

INDIA			
K. Srikkanth	c Baptiste, b Richards		53
J. Arun Lal	c Williams, b Patterson		16
M.B. Amarnath	c Simmons, b Baptiste		21
W.V. Raman	c Williams, b Benjamin		14
R.N. Kapil Dev	run out		21
S.V. Manjrekar	c Richards, b Benjamin		0
R.J. Shastri†	b Davis		19
S. Viswanath*	b Patterson		7
C.M. Sharma	not out		16
Arshad Ayub	c Simmons, b Patterson		14
Sanjeeva Sharma	not out		1
Extras	b 1, lb 8, w 3		12
(50 overs)	(for 9 wkts)		194

	O	M	R	W
C.M. Sharma	5	–	31	2
Sanjeeva Sharma	5	1	24	–
Amarnath	10	1	28	1
Kapil Dev	8.3	–	21	2
Arshad Ayub	10	1	37	2
Shastri	3	–	23	–
Srikkanth	5	1	15	1

	O	M	R	W
Patterson	9	2	26	3
Davis	10	2	35	1
Benjamin	10	–	30	2
Baptiste	10	–	49	1
Richards	10	1	43	1
Hooper	1	–	2	–

FALL OF WICKETS
1–6, 2–28, 3–55, 4–65, 5–111, 6–163, 7–166, 8–168, 9–173

FALL OF WICKETS
1–26, 2–69, 3–98, 4–127, 5–127, 6–136, 7–160, 8–162, 9–191

Umpires: P.G. Pandit & R.V. Ramani

Man of the Match: K. Srikkanth

West Indies won by 2 runs

The remarkable hero of India. Hirwani, the young leg-spinner, who took 16 wickets on his Test début to bring about the defeat of West Indies at Madras. (P.M. Shirodkar)

A dazzling century from Kapil Dev set up India's chance of victory at Madras. (Adrian Murrell/Allsport)

Walsh to the wicket-keeper. Raman suffered the same fate against Davis, and India were 62 for 3. Azharuddin and Arun Lal showed sense and accomplishment to add 91, but they fell in quick succession to Hooper, and at 156 for 5, India were precariously placed on a wicket which had already begun to show signs of wear and of taking spin.

It was at this point that Kapil Dev joined Ajay Sharma and played an innings of blistering authority. Off 105 balls in two hours and twenty minutes, he reached his sixth Test hundred. Kapil Dev hit 17 fours and played a glittering array of shots to all parts of the ground. Ajay Sharma gave him most commendable support, hitting 5 fours in his 30 before falling to Viv Richards. India closed at 308 for 6, a strong position.

Kapil Dev added only five to his overnight score before falling to Walsh, but Shastri, More and Arshad Ayub conjured 69 runs for the last three wickets on a pitch which Jackie Hendricks, the West Indian manager, described as a mockery for a five-day Test.

Kapil Dev quickly removed Simmons, but it was the spinners who began to tantalize from the eighth over of the West Indian innings. Haynes was caught in the gully off Shastri, and Hirwani took his first Test wicket when, after Richardson and Richards had batted with sense and care, Richardson hit a long hop to backward point. Logie fell in exactly the same manner to an equally bad ball, but Hooper was trapped lbw, and West Indies ended the day on 147 for 5, 36 needed to avoid the follow-on, and Richards unbeaten on 62.

Whatever success Narendra Hirwani had enjoyed on the second day was nothing compared with the joy that was his on the third. He took the five remaining wickets to become only the fourth bowler in Test history to take eight wickets on his Test début; Albert Trott, Alf Valentine and Bob Massie were the first three. Richards was bowled and, as

Hirwani tossed the ball well up, Dujon and Butts fell to successive deliveries. Dujon was the first of More's six stumpings in the match, a Test record. Walsh hit Hirwani for a straight six before falling to the leg-spinner's combination with his wicket-keeper.

The follow-on was narrowly avoided, but it is unlikely that Shastri would have enforced it, for a confident India sought quick runs. They lost Srikkanth, Arun Lal and Amarnath quickly, all three to the pace bowlers. Raman and Azharuddin showed no fear, however, and played some scintillating strokes against the West Indian quick bowlers. Azharuddin should have been stumped off Richards and was finally caught at long-on, but he and Raman had added 87. Ajay Sharma joined his fellow débutant in the merriment, and India were 181 for 4 at the close, an impregnable position, with Raman 82 not out.

India's one disappointment in the match was that Raman failed to reach his century on the fourth morning, for his rich stroke play and enterprise had certainly made him worthy of the feat. Shastri declared with eight wickets down, leaving West Indies to make 416 to win and his bowlers the best part of two days to bowl them out.

After six perfunctory overs of medium pace, Hirwani was back in the attack. Simmons hit a full toss into the hands of mid-on, Haynes misread a googly and Richardson swept off-spinner Ayub to backward short-leg. Richards ballooned a ball behind the wicket-keeper and

A test wicket-keeping record for Kiran More. (Alan Cozzi)

Kapil Dev ran from second slip to take the catch. Hooper and Dujon were both bamboozled in the flight and stranded. However bad the pitch, the West Indian batting lacked sense and application. They had convinced themselves that the wicket was all against them and batted accordingly.

Logie used his feet more sensibly than his colleagues and hit 67 off 62 balls. Butts hit 3 sixes and helped give the score some respectability. Both fell to Hirwani, who added Davis, the last wicket to fall, to give himself match figures of 16 for 136, the best return by a bowler on his début in Test cricket. Bob Massie of Australia took 16 for 137 against England at Lord's in 1972. Raman bowled his first over in Test cricket and had Walsh stumped, and More's five stumpings in the innings constituted another Test record. Sixteen wickets for a leg-spinner and six stumpings for a wicket-keeper suggested a joyful reawakening to many who love the game.

The West Indians were bitter in their complaints about the wicket and the help it offered to the 19-year-old, bespectacled leg-spinner, but they needed to ponder, too, the fact that their off-spinner Butts had bowled eleven more overs in the match than Hirwani and had failed to take a wicket.

FOURTH TEST MATCH – INDIA v. WEST INDIES
11, 12, 13, 15 and 17 January 1988 at M.A. Chidambaram Stadium, Madras

INDIA

	FIRST INNINGS		SECOND INNINGS	
K. Srikkanth	c Davis, b Walsh	23	lbw, b Davis	17
J. Arun Lal	c Logie, b Hooper	69	lbw, b Walsh	1
M.B. Amarnath	c Dujon, b Walsh	3	(4) c Richardson, b Walsh	1
W.V. Raman	c Dujon, b Davis	9	(3) c Dujon, b Walsh	83
M. Azharuddin	c Haynes, b Hooper	47	c Davis, b Richards	39
Ajay Sharma	lbw, b Richards	30	lbw, b Patterson	23
R.N. Kapil Dev	c Richards, b Walsh	109	lbw, b Patterson	5
R.J. Shastri†	b Davis	23	not out	20
K.S. More*	b Davis	17	c Dujon, b Walsh	0
Arshad Ayub	not out	23	not out	3
N.D. Hirwani	c Richardson, b Davis	1		
Extras	b 15, lb 4, nb 9	28	b 8, lb 7, nb 10	25
		382	(for 8 wkts, dec)	217

WEST INDIES

	FIRST INNINGS		SECOND INNINGS	
D.L. Haynes	c Kapil Dev, b Shastri	13	lbw, b Hirwani	6
P.V. Simmons	c and b Kapil Dev	8	c Amarnath, b Hirwani	14
R.B. Richardson	c Azharuddin, b Hirwani	36	c Amarnath, b Arshad Ayub	7
I.V.A. Richards†	b Hirwani	68	c Kapil, b Hirwani	4
A.L. Logie	c Azharuddin, b Hirwani	12	st More, b Hirwani	67
C.L. Hooper	lbw, b Hirwani	2	st More, b Hirwani	8
P.J.L. Dujon*	st More, b Hirwani	24	st More, b Hirwani	2
C.G. Butts	c Raman, b Hirwani	0	c Sharma, b Hirwani	38
W.W. Davis	lbw, b Hirwani	1	st More, b Hirwani	7
C.A. Walsh	c More, b Hirwani	8	st More, b Raman	0
B.P. Patterson	not out	0	not out	0
Extras	b 8, lb 2, nb 2	12	b 4, lb 1, nb 2	7
		184		160

	O	M	R	W	O	M	R	W
Patterson	15	1	62	–	9	2	17	2
Walsh	27	3	85	3	16	5	55	4
Davis	18.1	–	76	4	6	–	20	1
Butts	24	4	62	–	21	1	62	–
Richards	8	1	36	1	18	4	28	1
Hooper	12	3	42	2	6	1	20	–

	O	M	R	W	O	M	R	W
Kapil Dev	7	–	20	1	4	3	8	–
Amarnath	3	–	8	–	2	–	7	–
Shastri	13	6	29	1	5	–	25	–
Arshad Ayub	28	10	47	–	14	5	33	1
Hirwani	18.3	3	61	8	15.2	3	75	8
Ajay Sharma	4	–	9	–	1	–	7	1
Raman								

FALL OF WICKETS
1–30, 2–38, 3–62, 4–153, 5–156, 6–269, 7–313, 8–342, 9–369
1–3, 2–36, 3–37, 4–124, 5–185, 6–185, 7–190, 8–194

FALL OF WICKETS
1–17, 2–37, 3–98, 4–128, 5–132, 6–163, 7–175, 8–175, 9–183
1–22, 2–24, 3–33, 4–41, 5–61, 6–79, 7–138, 8–153, 9–160

Umpires: R.B. Gupta & P.D. Reporter

India won by 255 runs

Sixth One-Day International
INDIA v. WEST INDIES

Choosing to bat first, India quickly lost Arun Lal, but Mohinder Amarnath settled to score his first century in a one-day international and to help his side to a substantial score. Amarnath's innings included a six and 5 fours and he saw India through a difficult period as four wickets fell for 76. The impetus to the innings came from Kapil Dev, who hit 45 off 44 balls in his typically swashbuckling style.

After the early departure of Haynes, West Indies appeared to be strolling to victory, reaching 126 for 1 in 30 overs. Then the unlikely medium pace of Srikkanth accounted for Simmons, Richardson and Richards, and the match became evenly poised. Logie played some courageous shots, but it was the calm and control of Carl Hooper that saw West Indies to victory with five balls to spare.

Seventh One-Day International
INDIA v. WEST INDIES

The calm and confidence which Carl Hooper had shown at Faridabad was translated into brilliance at Gwalior, where his 133 off 97 balls, his first century in a limited-over international, put West Indies in a commanding position. Sanjeeva Sharma struck an early blow for India when he bowled Haynes, and West Indies were uneasily placed at 65 for 3. Richards left at 103, and from that point, first

INDIA v. WEST INDIES – TEST MATCH AVERAGES

INDIA BATTING

	M	Inns	NOs	Runs	HS	Av	100s	50s
D.B. Vengsarkar	3	5	2	305	102*	101.66	2	1
M. Azharuddin	3	5		185	60	37.00		1
J. Arun Lal	4	7		227	93	32.42		2
R.N. Kapil Dev	4	7		221	109	31.57	1	
K. Srikkanth	4	7		204	71	29.14		2
A. Ayub	4	7	2	133	57	26.60		1
K.S. More	4	7	1	131	49	21.83		
C.M. Sharma	3	5	1	73	27	18.25		
R.J. Shastri	4	7	1	105	47	17.50		
M.B. Amarnath	3	5		56	43	11.20		
Maninder Singh	3	5	2	3	2*	1.00		

Played in one Test: R. Lamba 1 & 0; S.V. Manjrekar 5 & 10*; W.V. Raman 9 & 83; A. Sharma 30 & 23; N. Hirwani 1

INDIA BOWLING

	Overs	Mds	Runs	Wkts	Av	Best	10/m	5/inns
N. Hirwani	33.5	6	136	16	8.50	8/61	2	1
C.M. Sharma	57.2	4	268	10	26.80	5/55		1
R.J. Shastri	87.3	24	228	8	28.50	4/71		
R.N. Kapil Dev	113	35	309	8	38.62	3/41		
A. Ayub	156	34	400	6	66.66	4/72		
Maninder Singh	96.5	19	310	2	155.00	1/68		
J. Arun Lal	1.3	1	1	0	–			
M.B. Amarnath	12.5	–	42	0	–			

Bowled in one innings: K. Srikkanth 3-0-7-0; A. Sharma 4-0-9-0; W.V. Raman 1-0-7-1

INDIA FIELDING FIGURES

10 - K.S. More (ct 4/st 6); 5 - R.N. Kapil Dev; 4 - R. Lamba; 3 - M. Azharuddin; 2 - K. Srikkanth, R.J. Shastri, C.M. Sharma, M.B. Amarnath and C.S. Pandit (as sub); 1 - J. Arun Lal, Maninder Singh, W.V. Raman, A. Sharma, and Sanjeeva Sharma (as sub)

WEST INDIES BATTING

	M	Inns	NOs	Runs	HS	Av	100s	50s
I.V.A. Richards	4	6	1	295	109*	59.00	1	2
C.L. Hooper	3	4	1	147	100*	49.00	1	
C.G. Greenidge	3	6		260	141	43.33	1	1
A.L. Logie	4	7	1	250	101	41.66	1	1
R.B. Richardson	4	8	2	226	89	37.66		2
D.L. Haynes	4	8	1	201	58	28.71		1
P.J.L. Dujon	4	6	2	97	40*	24.55		
C.G. Butts	3	3		56	38	18.66		
W.W. Davis	4	5		45	30	9.00		
C.A. Walsh	4	4		29	16	7.25		

Played in four Tests: B.P. Patterson 5*, 21*, 0* & 0*
Played in one Test: R.A. Harper 4; W.K.M. Benjamin 19; P.V. Simmons 8 & 14

WEST INDIES BOWLING

	Overs	Mds	Runs	Wkts	Av	Best	10/m	5/inns
C.A. Walsh	137.1	24	437	26	16.80	5/54		2
B.P. Patterson	117.1	14	456	17	26.82	5/24		2
W.W. Davis	112.1	10	390	13	30.00	4/76		
I.V.A. Richards	50	11	103	3	34.33	1/28		
W.K.M. Benjamin	30	3	93	2	46.50	1/17		
C.L. Hooper	38	9	102	2	51.00	2/42		
C.G. Butts	114	24	305	2	152.50	2/59		

Bowled in one innings: R.A. Harper 12-3-13-0

WEST INDIES FIELDING FIGURES

11 - P.J.L. Dujon (ct 10/st 1); 9 - R.B. Richardson; 5 - I.V.A. Richards and R.A. Harper; 4 - C.G. Greenidge; 3 - W.W. Davis; 2 - A.L. Logie and C.G. Butts; 1 - D.L. Haynes and W.K.M. Benjamin

SIXTH ONE-DAY INTERNATIONAL – INDIA v. WEST INDIES
19 January 1988 at Mayur Stadium, Faridabad

INDIA			
K. Srikkanth	b Baptiste		28
J. Arun Lal	c Dujon, b Walsh		0
M.B. Amarnath	not out		100
W.V. Raman	b Benjamin		13
M.Azharuddin	b Baptiste		2
R.N. Kapil Dev	c Hooper,		
	b Benjamin		45
R.J. Shastri†	c Baptiste, b Davis		28
K.S. More*	not out		9
C.M. Sharma			
Maninder Singh			
Arshad Ayub			
Extras	lb 4, nb 1		5
(50 overs)	(for 6 wkts)		230

	O	M	R	W
Walsh	10	1	42	1
Davis	10	–	69	1
Benjamin	10	2	38	2
Baptiste	10	2	41	2
Richards	8	1	31	–
Hooper	2	–	5	–

FALL OF WICKETS
1–3, 2–50, 3–73, 4–76, 5–142, 6–213

WEST INDIES			
D.L. Haynes	b Kapil Dev		12
P.V. Simmons	c and b Srikkanth		67
R.B. Richardson	lbw, b Srikkanth		49
I.V.A. Richards†	c Arun Lal,		
	b Srikkanth		9
A.L. Logie	run out		29
C.L. Hooper	not out		39
P.J.L. Dujon*	st More, b Shastri		9
E.A.E. Baptiste	not out		3
C.A. Walsh			
W.K.M. Benjamin			
W.W. Davis			
Extras	b 1, lb 13		14
(49.1 overs)	(for 6 wkts)		231

	O	M	R	W
Kapil Dev	9	1	37	1
C.M. Sharma	5	–	25	–
Amarnath	6	–	14	1
Maninder Singh	9.1	–	55	–
Arshad Ayub	10	–	37	–
Shastri	4	–	24	1
Srikkanth	6	–	25	3

FALL OF WICKETS
1–18, 2–126, 3–144, 4–155, 5–192, 6–223

Umpires: S.K. Ghosh & V.K. Ramaswamy

Man of the Match: M.B. Armarnath

West Indies won by 4 wickets

SEVENTH ONE-DAY INTERNATIONAL – INDIA v. WEST INDIES
22 January 1988 at Roop Singh Stadium, Gwalior

WEST INDIES			
D.L. Haynes	b S. Sharma		5
P.V. Simmons	lbw, b Arshad Ayub		21
R.B. Richardson	c Arshad Ayub,		
	b Shastri		30
I.V.A. Richards†	c S. Sharma,		
	b Maninder Singh		33
A.L. Logie	c S. Sharma,		
	b Arshad Ayub		54
C.L. Hooper	not out		113
E.A.E. Baptiste	run out		4
W.K.M. Benjamin	not out		0
P.J.L. Dujon*			
C.A. Walsh			
B.P. Patterson			
Extras	b 2, lb 14, w 2		18
(50 overs)	(for 6 wkts)		278

	O	M	R	W
Sanjeeva Sharma	6	–	42	1
Amarnath	10	–	43	1
Arshad Ayub	9	1	36	2
Shastri	9	–	48	1
Hirwani	10	–	34	–
Raman	3	–	23	–
Kapil Dev	3	–	36	–

FALL OF WICKETS
1–8, 2–55, 3–65, 4–103, 5–211, 6–268

INDIA			
K. Srikkanth	c Baptiste, b Patterson		9
J. Arun Lal	b Patterson		0
M.B. Amarnath	c Dujon, b Patterson		3
W.V. Raman	c Dujon, b Walsh		1
M. Azharuddin	c Dujon, b Benjamin		23
R.N. Kapil Dev	b Baptiste		52
R.J. Shastri†	not out		73
K.S. More*	run out		10
Arshad Ayub	st Dujon, b Richards		12
Sanjeeva Sharma	c Haynes, b Richards		1
N.D. Hirwani	b Patterson		2
Extras	b 4, lb 8, w 4, nb 3		19
(41 overs)			205

	O	M	R	W
Patterson	8	–	29	4
Walsh	6	1	23	1
Benjamin	10	1	34	1
Baptiste	5	–	37	1
Richards	9	–	34	2
Hooper	2	–	27	–
Simmons	1	–	9	–

FALL OF WICKETS
1–1, 2–14, 3–14, 4–15, 5–88, 6–94, 7–117, 8–134, 9–152

Umpires: D.N. Dotiwala & S.B. Kulkarni

Man of the Match: C.L. Hooper

West Indies won by 73 runs

with the able assistance of Logie, Hooper dominated events.

India made a horrendous start and were out of contention, but Kapil Dev batted with customary panache, and Shastri hit a six and 11 fours in his unbeaten 73. When the ninth wicket fell India were 152, and Hirwani, playing his first one-day international, gave his skipper resolute assistance in a last-wicket stand of 53, which was ended when Patterson bowled Hirwani with the last ball of his eighth over.

Eighth One-Day International
INDIA v. WEST INDIES

Heavy early morning dew delayed the start of the final match of the West Indian tour and reduced the contest to 45 overs. Put in to bat, India had a lucky escape when Srikkanth was dropped at slip by Richardson in the opening over. It was a costly miss, for Srikkanth went on to hit 3 sixes and 10 fours in an innings of 101, his third century in one-day internationals. Amarnath gave him spirited support in a second-wicket stand of 127 by hitting 56 off 84 balls. Amarnath hit 1 six and 3 fours, but after his departure the Indian innings fell apart.

Mohinder Amarnath hit his first century in a one-day international at Faridabad and still ended on the losing side. (Adrian Murrell/Allsport)

EIGHTH ONE-DAY INTERNATIONAL – INDIA v. WEST INDIES
25 January 1988 at University Stadium, Trivandrum

INDIA			
K. Srikkanth	b Baptiste		101
R. Lamba	lbw, b Patterson		8
M.B. Amarnath	b Patterson		56
R.N. Kapil Dev	lbw, b Richards		1
R.J. Shastri†	st Williams,		
	b Richards		3
M. Azharuddin	c Baptiste, b Davis		36
K.S. More*	c Richards,		
	b Patterson		3
S.V. Manjrekar	not out		14
Sanjeeva Sharma	run out		2
Maninder Singh	not out		1
N.D. Hirwani			
Extras	b 2, lb 7, w 1, nb 4		14
(45 overs)	(for 8 wkts)		239

	O	M	R	W
Patterson	9	–	34	3
Davis	9	–	59	1
Benjamin	9	–	41	–
Baptiste	9	–	51	1
Richards	8	–	40	2
Hooper	1	–	5	–

FALL OF WICKETS
1-33, 2-160, 3-161, 4-167, 5-200, 6-203, 7-232, 8-234

WEST INDIES			
C.G. Greenidge	st c More,		
	b Maninder Singh		84
P.V. Simmons	not out		104
R.B. Richardson	not out		37
I.V.A. Richards†			
A.L. Logie			
C.L. Hooper			
E.A.E. Baptiste			
W.K.M. Benjamin			
D.A. Williams*			
W.W. Davis			
B.P. Patterson			
Extras	b 1, lb 12, w 1, nb 2		16
(42.5 overs)	(for 1 wkt)		241

	O	M	R	W
Kapil Dev	4	–	28	-
Sanjeeva Sharma	7.5	–	47	–
Amarnath	5	–	21	–
Maninder Singh	9	–	42	1
Hirwani	9	–	40	–
Shastri	2	–	24	–
Srikkanth	7	–	26	–

FALL OF WICKETS
1-164

Umpires: P.G. Pandit & V. Vikram Raju

Man of the Match: P.V. Simmons

West Indies won by 9 wickets

Needing to score at 5.33 an over to win the match, West Indies were given a furious start. Greenidge walloped 84 off 75 balls with 5 sixes and 4 fours. He was stumped as his century loomed, but Simmons went on to his first hundred in international cricket. He hit 4 sixes and as many fours, and his innings occupied only 129 balls so that West Indies swept to victory with 2.1 overs to spare. Their margin of victory emphasized their dominance of the one-day series, and their 7–1 margin in the eight internationals played pointed to the futility of so long a one-day series.

Wills Trophy
Quarter-Finals
2 February 1988

at Guwahati

Rajasthan 155 for 6
Wills XI 159 for 3 (M. Prabhakar 78 not out)

Wills XI won by 7 wickets

at Jamshedpur

Karnataka 202 for 7 (G.R. Viswanath 55)
Haryana 167

Karnataka won by 35 runs

4 February 1988

at Calcutta

Board President's XI 251 for 6 (W.V. Raman 100, S. Kalyani 99)
Bengal 232 for 8 (K. Dubey 68)

Board President's XI won by 19 runs

India's 50-over knockout competition saw the Wills XI win with 4.4 overs to spare and Karnataka brush aside Haryana and Kapil Dev with surprising ease. Carlton Sadanha batted brilliantly before being run out for 43, but the individual award went to the veteran Viswanath, who had announced that he was retiring from first-class cricket. Raman and Kalyani, who was run out for 99, put on 171 for the President's XI's third wicket against Bengal.

Semi-Finals
5 February 1988

at Cuttack

Board President's XI 264 for 5 (Ajay Sharma 71)
Bombay 217 for 6 (S.V. Manjrekar 58)

Board President's XI won by 47 runs

at Guwahati

Karnataka 214 for 9 (G.R. Viswanath 53)
Wills XI 186 (M. Prabhakar 54)

Karnataka won by 28 runs

An electrifying 71 by Ajay Sharma helped the President's XI to an impressive 264 in 46 overs. Bombay could never match the required run rate, and Ajay Sharma took 3 for 42 in 10 overs to clinch the Man-of-the-Match award. Gundappa Viswanath hit 53 off 87 balls in 57 minutes to

place Karnataka in a strong position. The Wills XI were given a good start by Nayyar, Lamba and Prabhakar, who added 54 to his 3 for 35 to take the individual award, but the remaining batsmen could not keep up the required run rate. There were three run outs, and Wills XI were all out in the 48th over.

Final
8 February 1988

at Calcutta

Board President's XI 248 for 5 (W.V. Raman 90 not out, S. Kalyani 77)
Karnataka 184 (P. Ramesh Rao 76, Ajay Sharma 5 for 35)

Board President's XI won by 64 runs

Once again Raman and Kalyani enjoyed a successful third-wicket partnership when they added 143 to put the President's XI in an impregnable position. The final total of 248 was reached in 47 overs. The loss of Saldanha at 2, and of Sashikant and Gundappa Viswanath at 51, left Karnataka struggling, and they were all out in 45.5 overs.

Ranji Trophy
North Zone
6, 7 and 8 October 1987

at Sher-i-Kashmir Stadium, Srinagar

Himachal Pradesh 118 and 239 (V. Sen 73, Inderjeet Singh 66, R.K. Gupta 6 for 38)
Jammu and Kashmir 431 for 7 dec (Vidya Bhaskar 125, Shahid Pervez 103, Akhtar Aijaz 56, Ashwini Gupta 50, Om Prakash 4 for 65)

Jammu and Kashmir won by an innings and 74 runs
Jammu and Kashmir 21 pts, Himachal Pradesh 2 pts

After striving for success for a quarter of a century, Jammu and Kashmir have made considerable advances in recent seasons. They emphasized their improvement by beginning the 1987–8 Ranji Trophy campaign with the first four hundred score in their history and a resounding victory. Put in to bat, Himachal Pradesh fared badly, and Jammu, with century stands for the third and sixth wickets, built up a lead which proved sufficient to give them an innings victory.

14, 15 and 16 November 1987

at Air Force Ground, Palam, Delhi

Jammu and Kashir 373 (Shahid Perves 92, Nirmal Singh 88, Vidya Bhaskar 71, Idris Gandroo 62, R.K. Verma 4 for 97) and 248 for 7 (Shahid Pervez 84, Vidya Bhaskar 52 not out)
Services 370 (Gauri Shankar 93, A.S. Bajwa 92, Bhaskar Ghosh 85, Idris Gandroo 5 for 48)

Match drawn
Services 13 pts, Jammu and Kashmir 13 pts

at Gandhi Ground, Amritsar

Punjab 451 for 6 dec (Dhruve Pandove 94, R.S. Ghai 97, Sapan Choprak 70, Raj Puri 61 not out)
Himachal Pradesh 142 and 153 (D. Chopra 5 for 37)

Punjab won by an innings and 156 runs
Punjab 22 pts, Himachal Pradesh 2 pts

Jammu effected a remarkable recovery in Delhi. Choosing to bat first, they lost their first three wickets for eight runs, and their first four, three of them to Verma, for 33 runs. Nirmal Singh and Bhaskar then added 107, and this was followed by a stand of 105 between Nirmal and Shahid Pervez. In reply, Services found their strength at the beginning of their innings, with Bajwa and Shankar adding 140 for the second wicket, but the last six wickets fell for six runs, and the capture of second-innings points was the only remaining interest.

Punjab swamped the weak Himachal Pradesh side. Chopra had eight wickets in the match, and Gursharan Singh took five catches in the second innings. The Punjab batting was consistent and brisk.

18, 19 and 20 November 1987

at Mohan Nagar

Jammu and Kashmir 204 (Ashwini Gupta 61, Maninder Singh 7 for 62) and 196 (Ravi Pandit 71, M. Prabhakar 4 for 52)
Delhi 458 (S.C. Khanna 143, Kirti Azad 96, Ajay Sharma 53, Narender Sharma 5 for 145)

Delhi won by an innings and 58 runs
Delhi 21 pts, Jammu and Kashmir 4 pts

19, 20 and 21 November 1987

at Nehru Stadium, Gurgaon

Himachal Pradesh 116 (R.N. Kapil Dev 4 for 38) and 178 (R.N. Kapil Dev 5 for 61)
Haryana 411 for 8 dec (R.N. Kapil Dev 87, Amarjeet Kaypee 79, R. Jolly 73, C.J. Sharma 55, R. Chadha 53, Shakti 5 for 123)

Haryana won by an innings and 117 runs
Haryana 24 pts, Himachal Pradesh 4 pts

The two strong associations entered the competition with resounding victories. Jammu lost their last eight wickets for 80 runs in the first innings and for 95 in the second while Delhi, having suffered the shock of having Lamba bowled by Pervez for one, plundered runs freely. Khanna shared in two century stands.

Like Delhi, Haryana fielded a very strong side and overwhelmed Himachal Pradesh after putting them in to bat. Kapil Dev and Chetan Sharma took 14 wickets in the match, and, recovering from 41 for 3, Haryana's batsmen scored quickly. Shakti Singh took 5 for 123 in 25 overs without bowling a maiden, figures indicative of Haryana's aggression.

23, 24 and 25 November 1987

at Vishkarma School Ground, Rothak

Surinder Khanna has put his days as a wicket-keeper behind him, but his 220 not out for Delhi against Himachal Pradesh was the first double century of his career. He and Nayyar put on 348 for the first wicket. (Adrian Murrell/ Allsport)

Jammu and Kashmir 231 (S. Chowdhary 67, Akhtar Aijaz 52, D. Sharma 6 for 76) and 302 for 8 (Ravi Pandit 119, Nirmal Singh 57, D. Sharma 5 for 101)
Haryana 489 for 8 dec (Amarjeet Kaypee 126, R. Chadha 123, R. Jolly 79, Yashpal Sharma 78)

Match drawn
Haryana 12 pts, Jammu and Kashmir 7 pts

at Roshanara Bagh, Delhi

Himachal Pardesh 128 (Vijay Sen 74, U.S. Madan Lal 4 for 37, M. Prabhakar 4 for 47) and 166 (Rajiv Nayyar 78)
Delhi 481 for 1 dec (S.C. Khanna 220 not out, M. Nayyar 184)

Delhi won by an innings and 187 runs
Delhi 23 pts, Himachal Pradesh 0 pts

These were two significant results. Both Haryana and Delhi were below full strength, but while Delhi managed a massive win, Haryana were held to a draw, and their chances of qualifying for the play-offs suffered in consequence. Eleven wickets from Deepak Sharma and stands of 193 between Amarjeet Kaypee and Yashpal Sharma for the fourth wicket and 200 for the sixth between Jolly and Chadha could not force victory for Haryana against Jammu, who were admirably served by Ravi Pandit and Nirmal Singh.

Remarkably, skipper Vijay Sen was the only batsman to reach double figures as Himachal crashed to Madan Lal and Prabhakar. Khanna, his wicket-keeping days seemingly over, hit the first double century of his career, and he and Nayyar opened the Delhi innings with a stand of 348. This was a record for Delhi and the fourth highest first-wicket stand in the history of the competition. Delhi, who scored their runs in 86 overs, completed victory on the second day.

27, 28 and 29 November 1987

at Air Force Ground, Palam, Delhi

Himachal Pradesh 169 (R.H. Khan 4 for 48) and 247 (Rajiv Nayyar 63, S.C. Sadangi 5 for 71)
Services 427 for 5 (A.K. Seth 120, B. Ghosh 95, A.S. Bajwa 64, K.M. Roshan 50)

Services won by an innings and 11 runs
Services 21 pts, Himachal Pradesh 1 pt

28, 29 and 30 November, 1987

at Ludhiana

Punjab 300 (R.S. Ghai 99, Ravi Pandit 4 for 42)
Jammu and Kashmir 81 (M.I. Singh 6 for 34, D. Chopra 4 for 22) and 139 (Z. Bhatt 50, D. Chopra 6 for 29)

Punjab won by an innings and 80 runs
Punjab 21 pts, Jammu and Kashmir 3 pts

Himachal Pradesh and Jammu and Kashmir both finished their programmes with innings defeats which condemned them to the bottom two places in the North Zone. Solid batting throughout the order took Services to a comfortable win while Punjab, put in to bat, fought doggedly to recover from 97 for 6. Skipper Ghai was again a hero, hitting 99 at number eight. It was the second match in succession in which he had got into the nineties, but he used his pace bowling little as spinners Chopra and M.I. Singh twice accounted for Jammu.

1, 2 and 3 December 1987

at Air Force Ground, Palam, Delhi

Services 171 (P. Jain 6 for 36) and 187 (Chinmoy Sharma 63 not out)
Delhi 356 for 8 dec (U.S. Madan Lal 80, S. Bharadwaj 77, A. Mahindra 54, M. Nayyar 52) and 3 for 0

Delhi won by 10 wickets
Delhi 17 pts, Services 2 pts

Although further weakened by national calls, Delhi brushed aside Services. Jain had nine wickets in the match.

5, 6 and 7 December 1987

at Ferozeshah Kotla Ground, Delhi

Haryana 333 (N. Goel 94, R. Ghadha 61, Aman Kumar 53 not out, S. Saini 4 for 73) and 164 for 8 (D. Sharma 59 not out, S. Saini 5 for 60)
Delhi 419 for 7 dec. (M. Nayyar 178, Kirti Azad 100, Yashpal Sharma 5 for 106)

Match drawn
Delhi 15 pts, Haryana 5 pts

Rajinder Singh Ghai, captain of Punjab, seemed to lose form with his medium-pace bowling, but hit 97 and 99 in successive matches. (Patrick Eagar)

6, 7 and 8 December 1987

at Burlton Park, Jullundur

Punjab 485 for 6 dec (A. Kapoor 170, Gursharan Singh 121, S. Chopra 72, R. Kalsi 59)
Services 269 (Chinmoy Sharma 101, A.S. Bajwa 60, D. Chopra 4 for 55) and 157 for 4 (A.K. Seth 102 not out)

Match drawn
Punjab 15 pts, Services 5 pts

Delhi's batting strength in depth gave them by far the better of the draw with Haryana and ensured them of a place in the quarter-finals. A second-wicket stand of 203 between Nayyar and Azad took them to a position of dominance which they never relinquished.

A fourth-wicket record stand of 271 by Kapoor and Gursharan Singh took Punjab to a strong position on the matting at Jullundur. Services were forced to follow on, but they saved the game with ease.

10, 11 and 12 December 1987

at Gandhi Ground, Amritsar

Punjab 207 (U.S. Madan Lal 4 for 49)
Delhi 164 for 4 (M. Prabhakar 51 not out)

Match drawn
Delhi 7 pts, Punjab 2 pts

11, 12 and 13 December 1987

at Mayur Stadium, Faridabad

Haryana 237 (R. Chadha 78, D. Sharma 50, Srinivasan 6 for 39) and 119 (Srinivasan 5 for 32)
Services 182 (Gauri Shankar 52) and 88 (D. Sharma 5 for 32, S. Talwar 4 for 24)

Haryana won by 86 runs
Haryana 17 pts, Services 9 pts

No play was possible on the third day at Amritsar when the important meeting between Delhi and Punjab was well balanced.

At Faridabad, the wicket was kind to the bowlers after the first few hours and disintegrated dangerously towards the close. Haryana won comfortably, having been given a sound start, but their batting could not muster as many points as they would have liked, and their chances of qualifying for the final stages of the tournament rested entirely on their showing in the last match.

15, 16 and 17 December 1987

at Mayur Stadium, Faridabad

Punjab 579 (Gursharan Singh 100, R.S. Ghai 83, Arun Sharma 80 not out, D. Chopra 74, A. Kapoor 75, Bhupinder Singh 56, S. Talwar 5 for 180, D. Sharma 5 for 259)
Haryana 139 for 3

Match drawn
Punjab 6 pts, Haryana 3 pts

Punjab qualified for the play-offs with two days' relentless batting. There were century partnerships for the fifth and eighth wickets and very few failures. Most praise should go to the Haryana spinners, Sarkar Talwar and Deepak Sharma, whose figures were:

72.3–12–180–5

and:

97–15–259–5.

They deserve commendation for perseverance and bravery under enemy fire.

North Zone Final Table

	P	W	L	D	Pts
Delhi	5	3	–	2	83
Punjab	5	2	–	3	69
Haryana	5	2	–	3	64
Services	5	1	2	2	50
Jammu and Kashmir	5	1	2	2	48
Himachal Pradesh	5	–	5	–	9

Central Zone

14, 15 and 16 November 1987

at Railways Stadium, Moradabad

Uttar Pradesh 238 (P.N.S. Rana 67, S. Takle 4 for 31, S. Jugade 4 for 48) and 268 for 8 dec (S.S. Khandkar 64, K.K. Sharma 63, S. Jugade 6 for 84)
Vidarbha 283 (P. Hingnikar 92, S. Gujar 63, K.K. Sharma 4 for 65) and 91 for 5

Match drawn
Vidarbha 14 pts, Uttar Pradesh 11 pts

Put in to bat on the matting at Moradabad, Uttar Pradesh were rallied from the depths of 97 for 7 by Rana and Ghopal Sharma, but a third-wicket stand of 161 between Hingnikar and Gujar assured Vidarbha of first-innings lead. Jugada claimed 10 wickets in the match, but Vidarbha could not force victory.

20, 21 and 22 November 1987

at Bhilwara

Vidarbha 285 (S. Phadkar 53, Ratan Singh 5 for 114) and 191 (S. Takle 55 not out, R. Rathore 4 for 33)
Rajasthan 311 (A. Asawa 128, D. Jain 51 not out, S. Jugade 5 for 97) and 170 for 2 (Dalbir Singh 91 not out)

Rajasthan won by 8 wickets
Rajasthan 20 pts, Vidarbha 8 pts

at Bhilai C.C., Bhilai

Madhya Pradesh 223 (K.K. Sharma 4 for 105) and 254 (A. Vijayavargiya 115, Ghopal Sharma 5 for 62)
Uttar Pradesh 265 (V.S. Yadav 100, R. Sapru 58, S. Lahore 6 for 83) and 128 for 5 (S.S. Khandkar 56)

Match drawn
Uttar Pradesh 13 pts, Madhya Pradesh 9 pts

Rajasthan won most convincingly in their opening match of the tournament. Vyas won the toss and asked Vidarbha to bat. They batted solidly down the order to reach 285. In contrast, Rajasthan struggled to 68 for 5, but Asawa and Mudkavi added 143, and with wicket-keeper Jain hitting 51 not out, they took a first-innings lead of 26. Vidarbha lost four wickets in clearing off the arrears, and at 69 for 8, they were in total disarray. Takle, Jugade, Sahastra-buddhe and 24 penalty runs boosted them, but Rajasthan, inspired by Dalbir Singh, scored at five an over to win the match.

Uttar Pradesh rarely scored above two an over at Bhilai until the fourth-innings slog, and a draw always looked likely.

27, 28 and 29 November 1987

at BHEL Sports Complex, Bhopal

Railways 408 for 6 dec (P. Amre 186 not out, K.B. Kala 74, Durga Prasad 59)
Madhya Pradesh 198 (S. Ansari 63, S. Valson 7 for 59) and 195 (A. Vijayvergiya 64, Durga Prasad 5 for 63)

Railways won by an innings and 15 runs
Railways 20 pts, Madhya Pradesh 2 pts

Sunil Valson, having moved from Delhi, destroyed Madhya Pradesh with a fine spell of bowling, the last eight wickets going down for 38 runs. Amre hit an excellent hundred, sharing century partnerships with Kala and Durga Prasad. Railways were always in total command.

4, 5 and 6 December 1987

at Birsinghpur

Uttar Pradesh 493 (V.S. Yadav 93, Ghopal Sharma 66, S. Chaturvedi 64, R.P. Singh 51, R. Sapru 50) and 24 for 2 dec
Railways 452 (K.B. Kala 203 not out, P. Bhatnagar 105, K. Bharatan 65, R.P. Singh 5 for 83) and 11 for 0

Match drawn
Railways 11 pts, Uttar Pradesh 10 pts

at Kota

Madhya Pradesh 234 (R. Talwar 54, P. Sunderam 7 for 75) and 318 (S. Lahore 89, C.P. Singh 69, P. Sunderam 6 for 99)
Rajasthan 316 (Padam Shastri 80, S. Mudkavi 73, A. Mudkavi 63, N.D. Hirwani 5 for 95) and 136 for 5

Match drawn
Rajasthan 16 pts, Madhya Pradesh 11 pts

Whereas Uttar Pradesh scored consistently throughout the order, Railways were reliant upon a fifth-wicket stand of 240 between Kala and Bhatnagar. The stand established a record for Railways and Kala hit the highest score of his career. With the first innings of both sides occupying nearly three days, the game was inevitably drawn.

Magnificent bowling by Sunderam and consistent batting put Rajasthan on top at Kota, but Madhya Pradesh held out doggedly in their second innings, and Rajasthan never looked like scoring 237 in 32 overs.

11, 12 and 13 December 1987

at Agra

Match abandoned
Railways 4 pts, Rajasthan 4 pts

at Vidarbha Cricket Association, Nagpur

Madhya Pradesh 493 for 8 dec (R. Talwar 199, A. Vijayavargiya 84, M. Satokar 51)
Vidarbha 306 (S. Phadkar 79, J. Vegud 6 for 138) and 202 for 2 (U. Phate 102 not out, P. Hingnikar 54)

Match drawn
Madhya Pradesh 14 pts, Vidarbha 8 pts

Vidarbha's poor showing at Nagpur left them almost without hope of qualifying for the final stage of the competition. Put in to bat, Madhya Pradesh moved to their large total with century stands for the first, fourth and seventh wickets. R. Talwar failed by one run to equal the highest score ever made for Madhya in the Ranji Trophy. Vidarbha stumbled to 208 for 8 and were boosted only by Gawate, Wasu and 36 penalty runs. They could not avoid the follow-on, however, and it was left to Phate and Hingnikar to restore some honour.

18, 19 and 20 December 1987

at Vidarbha Cricket Association, Nagpur

Railways 270 (N. Churi 56, K. Bharatan 53, H. Wasu 4 for 84) and 240 for 8 dec (N. Churi 58, Durga Prasad 55, H. Wasu 4 for 71)
Vidarbha 149 and 330 (S. Gujar 101, S. Phadkar 72, H. Joshi 4 for 64)

Railways won by 31 runs
Railways 19 pts, Vidarbha 8 pts

at Obera Sports Complex, Obera, Uttar Pradesh

Uttar Pradesh 357 (Indrapal Singh 76, P.N.S. Rana 71 not out, S. Vyas 6 for 82) and 64 for 0 dec
Rajasthan 219 (S. Mudkavi 60 not out, R.P. Singh 4 for 48) and 174 for 9 (Dalbir Singh 52, M. Ali 5 for 48)

Match drawn
Uttar Pradesh 16 pts, Rajasthan 7 pts

Railways won the Central Zone championship with a splendid win at Nagpur. Electing to bat first on a wicket that was never easy, Railways recovered from the shock of losing both openers for 0 and reached 270 with batting that was consistent in application. A varied attack then had the home side struggling, and Railways took a first-innings lead of 121. Again they batted with solidity rather than brilliance, and Vidarbha were left to make 362 to win, a daunting task. At 76 for 3, they looked without hope, but Gujar batted splendidly until being run out, and he and Phadkar added 89. It seemed for a time that the home side might achieve what had looked to be impossible, but they lost their way when four wickets fell for 23 runs, and a brave last-wicket stand was not quite enough.

Rajasthan paid a high price for their game against Railways being abandoned, for their failure to beat Uttar Pradesh left them in third place in the table and out of the pre-quarter-finals. Vyas adopted the policy of asking Uttar Pradesh to bat first when he won the toss, but although he himself bowled splendidly, the move was far from successful. Eventually, Rajasthan were asked to make 203 in 38 overs, but four overs short were bowled and even with the resultant 16 penalty runs, Rajasthan were short of their target and happy to settle for a draw.

Central Zone Final Table

	P	W	L	D	Ab.	Pts
Railways	4	2	–	1	1	54
Uttar Pradesh	4	–	–	4	–	50
Rajasthan	4	1	–	2	1	47
Vidarbha	4	–	2	2	–	38
Madhya Pradesh	4	–	1	3	–	36

South Zone

8, 9 and 10 November 1987

at Arlem Breweries Ground, Margao

Goa 183 (H. Angle 54 not out, N.S. Yadav 5 for 54, Arshad Ayub 4 for 51) and 299 (S. Dhuri 88, P. Revankar 73, M.V. Narasimha Rao 5 for 66)
Hyderabad 262 (J. Shetty 50, P. Kamat 5 for 47) and 84 for 7

Match drawn
Hyderabad 13 pts, Goa 11 pts

The opening match of the South Zone almost provided a sensation as Hyderabad, the Ranji Trophy holders, came close to being beaten by lowly Goa. They took a first-innings lead of 79, but a third-wicket partnership of 166 between Revankar and Dhuri edged the game in favour of Goa. In the mandatory 25 overs at the end of the third day, Hyderabad needed 221 to win. They lashed out for bonus points, but came close to losing the match.

12, 13 and 14 November 1987

at Panaji Gymkhana, Panaji

Goa 148 (Jayakumar 5 for 65, V. Hariharan 4 for 33) and 277 (H. Angle 77 not out, S. Kangralkar 51)
Kerala 239 (S. Pednekar 4 for 51) and 35 for 0

Match drawn
Kerala 12 pts, Goa 7 pts

Opting to bat on a perfect wicket, Goa were bundled out by Kerala's seamers in 169 minutes. It was the débutant Jayakumar who began the collapse. He started with a no-ball, but bowled Mayekar with his next delivery. He took wickets in his second and third overs of a dream début. By the end of the day, Kerala were 109 for 2 and in total command. Kerala were restricted by some accurate bowling from Vinod Korgaonkar and Sharad Pednekar on the second morning, but they still took a lead of 91. On the last day, a career-best innings from Angle, which lasted 230 minutes, thwarted Kerala.

22, 23 and 24 November 1987

at Chandrasekhar Patil Stadium, Gulbarga

Goa 164 (Sanath Kumar 5 for 37) and 314 (S. Kangralkar 108, S. Mahadevan 83, Sanath Kumar 7 for 81)
Karnataka 525 for 6 dec (B.P. Patel 144, R.M.H. Binny 101 not out, S.M.H. Kirmani 106, K. Jeshwant 71 not out)

Karnataka won by an innings and 47 runs
Karnataka 22 pts, Goa 3 pts

The might of Karnataka crushed Goa in decisive fashion. Karnataka took a first-innings lead with only three wickets down, and Kirmani, having surrendered the wicket-keeping job to Viswanath, skipper Binny and the prolific Brijesh Patel all scored centuries. Sanath Kumar bowled his side to an easy win and finished with match figures of 12 for 118.

5, 6 and 7 December 1987

at Gymkhana Ground, Hyderabad

Andhra 416 (J.K. Ghia 91, V. Chamundeswaranath 54) and 219 for 7 (G.A. Pratap Kumar 74)
Hyderabad 445 for 6 dec (Ehtesham Ali Khan 106 not out, K.A. Qayyum 76, M. Azharuddin 61, M.V. Narasimha Rao 64)

Match drawn
Hyderabad 14 pts, Andhra 9 pts

at Raichur

Karnataka 445 for 9 dec (B.P. Patel 124, R.M.H. Binny 78, K. Jeshwant 54 not out) and 263 for 6 dec (C. Saldanha 60)
Kerala 340 (S. Rajesh 70, S. Ramesh 69, S. Santosh 52, A.R. Bhat 5 for 126) and 6 for 0

Roger Binny faded from the international scene but led Karnataka into the play-off stage of the Ranki Trophy and produced some excellent innings. (Alan Cozzi)

Match drawn
Karnataka 15 pts, Kerala 11 pts

At Hyderabad, a placid pitch ensured the dominance of batsmen and a draw. Both sides had batting in depth, and Hyderabad were indebted to a sixth-wicket partnership of 127 between Ehtesham Ali Khan and Narasimha Rao for taking them to a position from which they could obtain a first-innings lead.

Brijesh Patel hit his second century in successive matches and Raghuram Bhat's slow left-arm bowling took Karnataka to a first-innings lead at Raichur.

12, 13 and 14 December 1987

at Little Flower School Ground, Salem

Kerala 170 (Robin Singh 5 for 44) and 113 (Robin Singh 6 for 28)
Tamil Nadu 186 (G. Jayakumar 5 for 62) and 101 for 3

Tamil Nadu won by 7 wickets
Tamil Nadu 17 pts, Kerala 6 pts

at the Railway Stadium, Visakhapatnam

Goa 303 (S. Shinde 57, P. Dhuri 57, B.S. Mangesh 5 for 72) and 214 for 9 dec (S. Krishnamohan 6 for 80)

Andhra 326 for 9 dec (M. Rehman 86, K. Kamaraju 61, J.K. Ghia 58, S. Pednekar 4 for 77) and 34 for 0

Match drawn
Andhra 17 pts, Goa 11 pts

at Gymkhana, Secunderabad

Hyderabad 417 (N.V. Narasimha Rao 81, K.A. Qayyum 76, Arun Paul 71, V. Jaisimha 59, K. Jeshwant 5 for 92, A.R. Bhat 4 for 138)
Karnataka 158 (N.S. Yadav 4 for 32, L.V. Raju 4 for 34) and 204 for 7

Match drawn
Hyderabad 15 pts, Karnataka 6 pts

Tamil Nadu made an impressive start to their season on the matting at Salem, which never helped the batsmen. V.B. Chandrasekhar's 45 not out in the second innings was the highest score of the match. Drizzle and bad light caused play to begin late on the second day, and, on the first day, the matting frequently needed nailing down, caused an uneven bounce and 15 wickets fell. Robin Singh exploited the position admirably with his intelligent medium pace, and Jayakumar bowled well for Kerala so that Tamil Nadu finished the first day on 93 for 5. They claimed a 16-run lead on the second day when 16 wickets fell, and closed on 31 for 1, moving to victory on the last morning.

By one of those paradoxes which plague Indian cricket, Andhra, who could only draw against Goa, took the same number of points as Tamil Nadu claimed for their win. Put in to bat, Goa confirmed their improved form with a consistent display, but débutant seam bowler Mangesh had fine figures of 5 for 72. Jugal Kishore Ghia boosted Andhra as they seemed to be flagging with 58 off 63 balls. More than two hours was lost on the last day and the game meandered to a draw.

Hyderabad ended the first day at Secunderabad on 313 for 5, and by the end of the second day, thanks to some top-class bowling, they were in an impregnable position, with Karnataka 143 for 8. Off-spinner Shivlal Yadav and left-arm spinner Venkatapathi Raju were the main destroyers, and when Karnataka were forced to follow on early on the last day a Hyderabad victory looked likely, but Brijesh Patel and Sadanand Viswanath batted with great determination to thwart Hyderabad.

19, 20 and 21 December 1987

at Police Parade Ground, Guntur

Andhra 116 (S. Vasudevan 4 for 11, B. Arun 4 for 62) and 159
Tamil Nadu 357 (D. Girish 87, U.R. Radhakrishnan 64, B.S. Mangesh 5 for 129, J.K. Ghia 4 for 110)

Tamil Nadu won by an innings and 82 runs
Tamil Nadu 23 pts, Andhra 3 pts

With their second win in as many matches Tamil Nadu looked set for a place in the later stages of the competition. Vasudevan gambled in putting Andhra in to bat and his gamble was justified when the home side was bowled out by lunch-time on the first day. V.B. Chandrasekhar and Radhakrishnan began Tamil's reply with a stand of 103, and, in spite of some more impressive bowling from

newcomer Mangesh, Tamil Nadu never lost their grip on the game. Laxman Sivaramakrishnan made the early breakthroughs when Andhra batted again. They ended the second day on 122 for 5 and were all out in 90 minutes on the last morning with Raman and Robin Singh sharing the remaining wickets.

27, 28 and 29 December 1987

at VOC Park, Erode

Tamil Nadu 458 for 8 dec (Robin Singh 107 not out, L. Sivaramakrishnan 104, W.V. Raman 86)
Goa 144 and 223

Tamil Nadu won by an innings and 91 runs
Tamil Nadu 23 pts, Goa 2 pts

Tamil Nadu overwhelmed Goa, ensuring themselves of a play-off place and condemning Goa to the wooden spoon. Laxman Sivaramakrishnan hit the second century of his career and had match figures of 5 for 79 while Robin Singh, the left-hander, hit a maiden first-class hundred.

2, 3 and 4 January 1988

at Nehru Stadium, Kottayam

Kerala 191 (T.C. Sudheesh 70, B.S. Mangesh 4 for 69) and 327 for 8 (Narayan Kutty 102, T.P. Ajit Kumar 58, S. Ramesh 53)
Andhra 384 (M. Rehman 115, Chamundeswaranath 80 not out, S. Santosh 4 for 87)

Match drawn
Andhra 13 pts, Kerala 7 pts

at Chidambaram Stadium, Madras

Tamil Nadu 411 (Robins Singh 101 not out, V.B. Chandrasekhar 83, D. Girish 54, V.P. Raju 5 for 93) and 64 for 1
Hyderabad 429 for 4 dec (J. Shetty 113, Abdul Azeem 93, V. Jaisimha 83 not out)

Match drawn
Hyderabad 11 pts, Tamil Nadu 7 pts

Having put Kerala in to bat and, with Rehman holding the batting together after early uncertainty and Chanundeswaranath providing the later panache, Andhra took a first-innings lead of 93, but failed to press home their advantage, being denied by a patient century from Kutty.

After three successive wins on batting wickets Tamil Nadu took on Hyderabad on grass. They won the toss and reached 300 for 6 on the opening day. On the second, Robin Singh reached his second century in succession, but Hyderabad ended the day on 110 for 0 so that a draw was already ordained. Jyothi Shetty reached his first Ranji Trophy hundred, and he and Abdul Azeem extended their stand to 217 on the last day. Hyderabad took a first-innings lead and kept in contention for a play-off place.

7, 8 and 9 January 1988

at Nehru Stadium, Kottayam

Kerala 161 (V.P. Raju 6 for 52) and 230 (Thomas Mathew 80, N.S. Yadav 5 for 73)
Hyderabad 309 (Arun Paul 79, Abdul Azeem 71, K.A. Qayyum 50, G. Jayakumar 4 for 102) and 85 for 1

Hyderabad won by 9 wickets
Hyderabad 16 pts, Kerala 5 pts

8, 9 and 10 January 1988

at Chinnaswamy Stadium, Bangalore

Karnataka 253 (M. Venkataramana 6 for 107) and 94 (S. Vasudevan 6 for 30)
Tamil Nadu 156 (A.R. Bhat 8 for 43) and 124 (A.R. Bhat 7 for 41)

Karnataka won by 67 runs
Karnataka 19 pts, Tamil Nadu 9 pts

Hyderabad kept alive their faint hopes of retaining the Ranji Trophy by beating Kerala. Veteran Narasimha Rao reached 200 Ranji Trophy wickets on the opening day, but it was the left-arm spinner Venkatapathy Raju who took the major honours as Kerala were all out by mid-afternoon. Hyderabad had levelled the scores for the loss of three wickets by the end of the day, and thanks to a last-wicket stand of 48 between Raju and Gevin Shurma passed 300 the next afternoon. Kerala refused to capitulate and were a stubborn 117 for 1 by the close. It was Shival Yadav who brought about a collapse on the last morning, and Kerala were all out shortly after lunch so that Hyderabad quickly hit off the runs needed for victory.

There was a fascinating encounter at Bangalore, when the young off-spinner Venkataramana bowled magnificently on the opening day. The sound temperament and technical expertise of Gundappa Viswanath helped Karnataka through a middle-order crisis, and by the end of the day they were very much back in the game as Tamil Nadu had slumped to 62 for 4. Bhat revelled on a turning wicket to take 8 for 43, the best figures of his career and of the season by any bowler, and Tamil Nadu trailed by 97 on the first innings. Skipper Vasudevan responded with a remarkable spell which helped shoot out Karnataka for 94. Chasing 192 to win, Tamil Nadu ended the penultimate day on 77 for 4. The game was in the balance, but Bhat and Surendra confirmed Karnataka's superiority with fine bowling on the last morning, which saw Tamil Nadu bowled out in 90 minutes. Bhat returned the best match analysis of his career and the best Ranji Trophy figures of the season.

17, 18 and 19 January 1988

at Kurnool

Karnataka 413 for 9 dec (B.P. Patel 100 not out, C. Saldanha 92, R.M.H. Binny 67, K. Jeshwant 58, J.K. Ghia 4 for 95) and 267 for 7 dec (S. Viswanath 83)
Andhra 290 (L.K. Adisheshu 75, S. Chamundeswaranath 76) and 42 for 1

Match drawn
Karnataka 16 pts, Andhra 11 pts

Needing eight points to move into second place and claim a place in the play-offs, Karnataka accomplished their task with few problems. Brijesh Patel hit his third century in five matches and shared a sixth-wicket stand of 115 with Jeshwant which assured Karnataka of a big score. It was a total that Andhra were never likely to match, and further

second-innings points put Karnataka in a most comfortable position.

South Zone Final Table					
	P	W	L	D	Pts
Tamil Nadu	5	3	1	1	79
Karnataka	5	2	–	3	78
Hyderabad	5	1	–	4	69
Andhra	5	–	1	4	53
Kerala	5	–	2	3	41
Goa	5	–	2	3	34

West Zone

22, 23 and 24 November 1987

at Municipal Ground, Rajkot

Saurashtra 272 (K. Chauhan 52, A. Petiwale 5 for 36) and 92 (Rashid Patel 5 for 33)
Baroda 364 (R. Parikh 130, K.S. Chavan 96, B. Radia 6 for 106) and 1 for 0

Baroda won by 10 wickets
Baroda 18 pts, Saurashtra 4 pts

at GNFC Ground, Narmadanagar, Broach

Gujarat 326 (D. Patel 63, P. Bhatt 62, B. Patel 61, B. Mistry 59, V.V. Oak 4 for 70) and 91 (S.J. Jadhav 5 for 18)
Maharashtra 241 (S.J. Kalyani 98, M.D. Gunjal 56) and 60 for 3

Match drawn
Gujarat 12 pts, Maharashtra 11 pts

Baroda outplayed Saurashtra in the opening match in the West Zone. Saurashtra struggled against a varied attack, but recovered bravely towards the end of their innings. Parikh and Chavan put Baroda completely on top with an opening stand of 226, and although six wickets fell for 32 runs, they recovered to take a first-innings lead of 92. It proved sufficient as Saurashtra collapsed before Rashid Patel and Pardeshi.

There was a similar collapse at Broach, but Maharashtra stumbled in an attempt to score 177 in 31 overs to win the match.

19, 20 and 21 December 1987

at Moti Baug, Baroda

Baroda 536 for 6 dec (K.S. Chavan 247, R. Parikh 137, M. Narula 50, S.V. Nayak 4 for 155)
Bombay 451 for 4 (S.S. Hattangadi 115, Iqbal Khan 95 not out, A. Sippy 91, C.S. Pandit 80)

Match drawn
Baroda 7 pts, Bombay 6 pts

at Nehru Stadium, Pune

Saurashtra 356 (S. Keshwala 130, Azim Khan 4 for 71) and 80 for 1 dec
Maharashtra 262 (S. Sugwekar 61, P.R. Pradhan 50, S. Keshwala 4 for 32) and 44 for 2

Match drawn
Saurashtra 12 pts, Maharashtra 8 pts

Bombay's entry into the Ranji Trophy, 1987–8, was greeted by Parikh and Chavan opening Baroda's innings with a stand of 242. Chavan hit the highest score of his career and the highest Ranji Trophy score of the season. There were three other century partnerships in this high-scoring game which left both sides shorter of points than they would have liked.

Saurashtra skipper Suresh Keshwala saved his side with a fine 130. He hit 20 fours and batted for three hours, facing 160 balls. He was missed twice, costly lapses for Maharashtra, and the visitors ended the first day on 273 for 8. The tail wagged strongly on the second morning and Keshwala made early strikes to leave Maharashtra 132 for 4 at the close. Débutant Shantanu Sugwekar hit a sparkling 61 to rally his side, but there was little support. Eventually, Maharashtra were left 13 mandatory overs in which to make 170. They succeeded in losing both openers to give Saurashtra another point.

25, 26 and 27 December 1987

at Moti Baug, Baroda

Baroda 305 (M. Narula 102, R. Parikh 57) and 263 for 3 dec (R. Parikh 74 not out, S.R. Gaekwad 65)
Gujarat 325 (S. Talati 79, B. Mistry 69, J. Zinto 62 not out, A.D. Gaekwad 4 for 73) and 94 for 2.

Match drawn
Baroda 16 pts, Gujarat 13 pts

at Wankhede Stadium, Bombay

Saurashtra 139 (A.K. Patel 50) and 416 for 6 (A. Pandya 198 not out, A.K. Patel 59, S. Keshwala 55)
Bombay 472 for 4 dec (S.S. Hattangadi 186, L.S. Rajput 150, V. Gohil 4 for 127)

Match drawn
Bombay 14 pts, Saurashtra 4 pts

Mukesh Narula was Baroda's saviour on Christmas Day with a dramatic century. Narula was on 54 and the score was 214 for 9 when Palkar joined him. They added 83, and Baroda took their fourth point when Gujarat conceded 8 penalty runs. Abhay Palkar, who was playing in only his second match, hit 33 not out and dismissed Pathak before the close. The Gujarat innings followed a pattern similar to Baroda's. It was last-wicket pair, Zinto and Thakkar, who added 68 to clinch first-innings lead. After losing Chavan first ball Baroda went for quick runs in their second innings, and Samarjeet Gaekwad hit 65 off 46 balls, but the declaration enabled Baroda to gain more points not to win the match.

Bombay took complete command of the match against Saurashtra on the opening day when they bowled out the visitors for 139, which included 24 penalty runs, and ended on 190 for 0. Hattangadi and Rajput, jettisoned by the Indian selectors, took their stand to 299, and Bombay led by 333 on the first innings. Bombay seemed certain of victory, but Atul Pandya batted throughout the last day, just under eight hours in all, to save the game and finish with the highest score of his career.

2, 3 and 4 January 1988

at Sardar Patel Stadium, Valsad

Bombay 293 (A. Sippy 111 not out, C.S. Pandit 61, J. Zinto 5 for 102) and 202 for 2 dec (L.S. Rajput 112 not out, S.K. Kulkarni 68)
Gujarat 169 and 244 (B. Patel 69, K.D. Mokashi 5 for 39, L.S. Rajput 4 for 64)

Bombay won by 82 runs
Bombay 18 pts, Gujarat 5 pts

at Nehru Stadium, Pune

Maharashtra 392 for 7 dec (R. Poonawala 146, S. Sugwekar 100 not out, S.J. Kalyani 62) and 203 for 7 dec
Baroda 254 (V.S. Wadkar 59, S.J. Jadhav 5 for 83) and 223 for 4 (T. Arothe 102 not out, A.D. Gaekwad 69 not out)

Match drawn
Maharashtra 17 pts, Baroda 12 pts

Alan Sippy held the Bombay first innings together with a not out 111 which included 3 sixes and 10 fours. Skipper Pandit hit 11 fours to give the innings a further boost, but there was a general lack of confidence in the rest of the Bombay batting. Joy Zinto finished with his best figures in the Ranji Trophy. Bombay took charge of the match on the second day. Gujarat collapsed before Mokashi, Rajput and Nayak, and Lalchand Rajput hit 4 sixes and 8 fours in an unbeaten 112. He and Sulakshan Kulkarni added 178 for the second wicket, and Bombay declared 326 runs ahead, leaving themselves the last day in which to bowl out Gujarat. This they duly did with the spinners taking the honours. Rajput had match figures of 7 for 68, and Mokashi 8 for 86.

In their final zonal match, Baroda were fortunate to survive against Maharashtra. Sparkling centuries by opener Riaz Poonawala and young Shantanu Sugwekar took Maharashtra to their fourth batting point as early as the 65th over. Baroda were saved from following on by Vinit Wadkar's 59. The rest of the Baroda batting crumbled before off-spinner Srikant Jadhav and leg-spinner Sunil Gudge, who took 3 for 34. Baroda were finally asked to make 342 in 59 overs to win, and they looked likely to lose when 4 wickets fell for 93, but Tushar Arothe, a 20-year-old left-hander, batted for more than three hours and faced 117 balls to hit his second Ranji Trophy hundred and, with Anshuman Gaekwad, his captain, added 130 and saved the game.

9, 10 and 11 January 1988

at Wankhede Stadium, Bombay

Bombay 467 (S.S. Hattangadi 118, L.S. Rajput 86, R.R. Kulkarni 50, S.J. Jadhav 4 for 103) and 11 for 1
Maharashtra 471 for 8 dec (M.D. Gunjal 120, S.J. Jadhav 71, N. Phadnis 70 not out, S.J. Kalyani 59, S. Sugwekar 50)

Match drawn
Maharashtra 9 pts, Bombay 8 pts

10, 11 and 12 January 1988

at Municipal Stadium, Rajkot

Saurashtra 445 (B. Jadeja 117, S. Tanna 89, A.K. Patel 59, S.

Keshwala 58, J. Zinto 4 for 120) and 15 for 0
Gujarat 327 (S. Talati 86)

Match drawn
Saurashtra 10 pts, Gujarat 7 pts

Hattangadi, who hit 3 sixes and 10 fours, and Rajput put on 158 for Bombay's first wicket and accelerated in the afternoon session after a sedate start. Batting on into the second day, Bombay killed any hope of a definite result, and once again the limitations of their bowling were exposed as Maharashtra plundered runs. Skipper Gunjal hit a century, but with bowling points scarce to the point of almost non-existence, Maharashtra could close the gap on Bombay to the extent of only one point, and Bombay waited on the outcome of the game at Rajkot to see if they had qualified for the quarter-finals.

They had no need to fear. Mammoth scoring again precluded any chance of a result, and Saurashtra were left to lament.

West Zone Final Table

	P	W	L	D	Pts
Baroda	4	1	–	3	53
Bombay	4	1	–	3	46
Maharashtra	4	–	–	4	45
Gujarat	4	–	1	3	37
Saurashtra	4	–	1	3	30

East Zone

5, 6 and 7 January 1988

at Hazaribagh

Bihar 349 (H. Gidwani 116, A. Hussain 81, A. Das 4 for 146)
Tripura 60 (K.V.P. Rao 4 for 6) and 145 (Sanjay Ranjan 5 for 39)

Bihar won by an innings and 144 runs
Bihar 24 pts, Tripura 3 pts

The opening match in the East Zone went according to prediction, lowly Tripura being crushed by Bihar, for whom Rao had match figures of 7 for 30 and for whom Gidwani and débutant Hussain shared a third-wicket stand of 164.

10, 11 and 12 January 1988

at Keenan Stadium, Jamshedpur

Bihar 170 (S.G. Chakraborty 4 for 42, N. Konwar 4 for 68) and 217 for 2 dec (H. Gidwani 101 not out)
Assam 72 (V. Venkatram 4 for 29) and 126 (K.V.P. Rao 4 for 31)

Bihar won by 189 runs
Bihar 15 pts, Assam 4 pts

11, 12 and 13 January 1988

at Barabatti Stadium, Cuttack

Orissa 369 for 8 dec (Avinash Khatua 84, Swapan Mitra 69, R. Biswal 57, P. Bose 53)

Tripura 134 (S. Mohapatra 6 for 23) and 84 (S. Mohapatra 7 for 40)

Orissa won by an innings and 151 runs
Orissa 24 pts, Tripura 2 pts

Bihar swept aside Assam as easily as they had swept aside Tripura and, in doing so, virtually assured themselves of a place in the play-offs.

It was the match at Cuttack which claimed the honours, however. On the second day, Sourajit Mohapatra, who was making his Ranji Trophy début, performed the hat-trick when he had Paul caught behind, Dutta lbw and Das caught behind off successive deliveries. He finished with 6 for 23 and, when Tripura followed on, took 7 for 40 to complete a remarkable début. The match was over after 28 minutes' play in the last morning.

15, 16 and 17 January 1988

at Veer Surendra Sai Stadium, Sambalpur

Orissa 236 (D. Mohanty 82, N. Konwar 6 for 84) and 216 for 8 dec (A. Khatua 56, S. Mitra 54, N. Konwar 4 for 71)
Assam 160 (R. Bora 80, M. Saudagar 8 for 64) and 136 (M. Saudagar 4 for 47)

Orissa won by 156 runs
Orissa 17 pts, Assam 7 pts

at Eden Gardens, Calcutta

Tripura 84 (D. Mukherjee 5 for 17, J. Singh 4 for 34) and 94 (D. Mukherjee 5 for 28, S. Singh 5 for 30)
Bengal 384 for 5 dec (K. Dubey 139, A.O. Malhotra 93, I.B. Roy 50)

Bengal won by an innings and 206 runs
Bengal 23 pts, Tripura 1 pt

Orissa moved ahead of Bihar when they gained a comfortable win over Assam. Saudagar became one of three bowlers to take eight wickets in an innings during the Ranji Trophy season and finished with match figures of 12 for 111. Naba Konwar again bowled splendidly for the ailing Assam side.

Bengal entered the Trophy with a crushing win over Tripura, the highest of the season in terms of runs. D. Mukherjee, J. Singh and S. Singh shared 20 wickets between them as Tripura twice failed to reach a hundred. Dubey and Malhotra put on 142 for Bengal's fourth wicket.

22, 23 and 24 January 1988

at Veer Surendra Sai Stadium, Sambalpur

Bihar 277 (S.S. Karim 106, S. Mohapatra 4 for 80) and 182 for 4 dec (P. Khanna 69, H. Gidwani 57 not out)
Orissa 226 and 137 for 6 (Amiya Roy 59 not out)

Match drawn
Bihar 16 pts, Orissa 10 pts

at Eden Gardens, Calcutta

Bengal 443 (I.B. Roy 110, S. Ganguly 107, J. Mukherjee 62) and 260 for 4 (K. Dubey 108, A.O. Malhotra 84)
Assam 254 (A. Bhattacharjee 5 for 62)

Match drawn
Bengal 16 pts, Assam 7 pts

Enjoying the better of a draw with Orissa, Bihar moved to the top of the East Zone table, encouraged by Bengal's failure to beat Assam. Wicket-keeper Karim boosted Bihar after five wickets had fallen for 87, and a varied attack gained them first-innings points. Set to make 234 in 38 overs, Orissa went for the runs, but could claim only two more batting points to Bihar's three bowling points.

Bengal won the toss, batted first and, thanks to a third-wicket stand of 200 between I.B. Roy and Dubey, amassed a large score, but Assam batted stubbornly in response and denied Bengal victory. Dubey, with his second century in as many matches, and Malhotra added 139 for the third wicket in Bengal's second innings.

27, 28 and 29 January 1988

at Mecon Stadium, Ranchi

Bihar 557 for 8 dec (A. Dayal 121, R. Arora 110 not out, V. Venkatram 79, P. Khanna 81, H. Gidwani 65)
Bengal 309 for 7 (K. Dubey 120, I.B. Roy 62, V. Venkatram 6 for 109)

Match drawn
Bihar 11 pts, Bengal 7 pts

A battle for points rather than for victory began with Khanna and Dayal sharing a stand of 163. Later Rajiv Arora and skipper Venkatram put on 164 for the seventh wicket. Venkatram bowled manfully when Bengal batted, but Dubey, three hundreds in three matches, put on 144 for the first wicket, and the match was stalemate.

Bengal's failure to extract more from this match left them in danger of failing to qualify for the knock-out stage of the competition. They trailed Orissa by five points with one match to play, and with Bihar already assured of reaching the final stages of the competition.

10, 11 and 12 February 1988

at Railway Stadium, Maligaon, Gauhati

Tripura 132 (I.M. Kakoti 8 for 63) and 189 (S. Paul 71, N. Konwar 5 for 45)
Assam 425 for 6 dec (R. Das 170, R. Bora 126, P. Datta 95)

Assam won by an innings and 104 runs
Assam 24 pts, Tripura 3 pts

Tripura's fourth innings defeat in as many matches in the Ranji Trophy confirmed the lowliness of their standard and raised questions as to their right to be judged first-class. Skipper S. Paul hit their only fifty of the season as Assam's batsmen and bowlers sharpened their averages. Rajkumar Das and Rajesh Bora added 166 for the third wicket, and Das and Datta 210 for the fourth, and Assam themselves had suffered two crushing defeats in their first two matches, which left no doubt as to Tripura's standing.

16, 17 and 18 February 1988

at Barabatti Stadium, Cuttack

Bengal 348 for 6 dec (J. Mukherjee 79, J. Arun Lal 74, I.B. Roy 71) and 313 (J. Arun Lal 75, S. Banerjee 53 not out, P. Agarwal 5 for 111)

Orissa 134 (D. Mohanty 51) and 43 for 3

Match drawn
Bengal 14 pts, Orissa 7 pts

The return of skipper Arun Lal, consistent batting after the loss of Dubey for 0 and sharp bowling gave Bengal the edge in the final and decisive match in the East Zone. Arun Lal and Indu Bhushan Roy added 154 after Dubey had been caught at slip in Praharaj's first over, and from then on Bengal were in charge of the match, taking eight bonus points in the first innings to Orissa's two and never relaxing their grip.

East Zone Final Table				
	P	W	L	D	Pts
Bihar	4	2	–	2	66
Bengal	4	1	–	3	60
Orissa	4	2	–	2	58
Assam	4	1	2	1	42
Tripura	4	–	4	–	9

Pre-Quarter-Finals

12, 13, 14 and 15 February 1988

at Dr Sampurnanda Stadium, Varanasi

Uttar Pradesh 301 (V.S. Yadav 95, S. Chaturvedi 57)
Baroda 7 for 0

Match abandoned
Uttar Pradesh won on toss of a coin

at Wankhede Stadium, Bombay

Bombay 408 (L.S. Rajput 139, S.V. Nayak 84, S.V. Manjrekar 80, K. Jeshwant 5 for 60) and 137 for 4 (S.V. Manjrekar 50 not out)
Karnataka 396 (C. Saldanha 144, B.P. Patel 91, K.D. Mokashi 4 for 71)

Match drawn
Bombay qualified for quarter-final on first-innings lead

Uttar Pradesh made 122 for 2 on a rain-interrupted first day, and their innings did not end until the end of the third day. The game was abandoned at 1.30 on the last day. In all, 904 minutes were lost to rain and bad light and to the lack of groundsmen to give the pitch correct attention. The farce was resolved by the toss of a coin.

A third hundred of the season on the opening day in Bombay by Lalchand Rajput put the home side in a respectable position. Rajput batted throughout the day to hit 110 out of 241 for 4. After three wickets had gone for 91, Manjrekar, who played a series of lovely shots through the covers, particularly off Bhat, helped Rajput to add 150 before being caught at silly point. Rajput was out on the second morning, but Karnataka had missed him twice by then and, indeed, they had spilled several other chances, too. The highlight of the second day was the reception given to Gundappa Viswanath, who was playing his last Ranji Trophy innings, but he was caught at cover by Deepak off the bowling of the veteran spinner Padmakar Shivalkar for 13. Shivalkar, at 47, is five years senior to

Viswanath. Karnataka closed on 84 for 3. By the end of the third day, the issue had still not been resolved, for Karnataka, 363 for 8, were still 45 runs behind. They had been magnificently served by young Carlton Saldanha, who batted for 427 minutes, faced 367 balls and looked like the natural successor to Sunil Gavaskar. He and Brijesh Patel took their fourth-wicket stand to 155 with Patel providing the panache. The score was 377 before Jeshwant, who had batted heroically for 45, edged Rajput to wicket-keeper Kulkarni. Bhat had batted for 110 minutes for 20 before off-spinner Kiran Mokashi bowled him to give Bombay the vital first-innings lead.

Quarter-Finals

27, 28, 29 February and 1 March 1988

at Karnail Singh Stadium, Delhi

Railways 483 for 4 dec (K.B. Kala 119 not out, Devindra Arora 113, P. Karkera 110, Yusuf Ali Khan 68) and 49 for 0
Bihar 320 (S.S. Karim 114)

Match drawn
Railways qualified for semi-final on first-innings lead

at Chandigarh

Bengal 414 for 6 dec (J. Arun Lal 205, I.B. Roy 54)
Punjab 391 for 4 (Gursharan Singh 132, D. Chopra 66, Ashwini Kapoor 73, N.S. Sidhu 66)

Match drawn
Punjab qualified for semi-final on quotient rule

at Chidambaram Stadium, Madras

Tamil Nadu 578 (V.B. Chandrasekhar 160, L. Sivaramakrishnan 124, W.V. Raman 98) and 493 for 8 dec (W.V. Raman 182, V. Sivaramakrishnan 68, K. Srikkanth 58, M.A.N. Ansari 4 for 171)
Uttar Pradesh 190 (M. Venkatarama 5 for 54) and 31 for 0

Match drawn
Tamil Nadu qualified for semi-final on first-innings lead

at Ferozeshah Kotla Ground, Delhi

Bombay 329 (R.J. Shastri 94, Sanjeeva Sharma 5 for 81) and 203 for 5
Delhi 508 (R. Lamba 242, Kirti Azad 51, R.S. Lele 6 for 130)

Match drawn
Delhi qualified for semi-final on first-innings lead

Prakesh Karkera's maiden century and his opening stand of 164 with Yusuf Ali Khan took Railways to a commanding position on the first day of their match with Bihar. There was no play on the second day because the covering provided had been totally inadequate to protect the pitch from rain. Significantly, the game at Ferozeshah Kotla a few miles away was only briefly curtailed. On the third day, Devinder Arora and Krishna Behari Kala took their fourth-wicket stand to 225 and Hyder Ali declared at 483 when Arora was caught and bowled by Avinash Kumar. Bihar lost four wickets before the close and were, in effect, out of the contest in spite of Saba Karim's last-day century.

Arun Lal, the Bengal captain, hit the fifth double century of his career and declared half an hour before tea

India's exciting discovery, all-rounder Venkat Raman. He won his first Test cap and batted and bowled with distinction. In the Ranji Trophy quarter-final at Madras he hit 98 and 198, his maiden first-class hundred, for Tamil Nadu against Uttar Pradesh. (P.M. Shirodkar)

on the third day. Punjab replied with some exhilarating batting by Sidhu and Ashwini Kapoor, and Gursharan Singh hit a career best on the last day, when only three wickets fell, so that Punjab passed into the semi-final on the quotient rule – number of runs scored divided by number of wickets fallen, 97.75 to 69.

The first day at Madras saw Tamil Nadu reach 379 for 4 and take a grip on the match which they were never to relax. V.B. Chandrasekhar outshone his skipper Srikkanth with an exciting display. He hit 25 fours and faced 222 balls in a 4¾ hour stay which gave him his first Ranji Trophy century. He and Raman added 204 for the second wicket. On the second day Tamil Nadu continued their rout of the Uttar Pradesh bowling to reach their highest score in the Ranji Trophy. Laxman Sivaramakrishnan reached the third century of his career, 124 out of 184. A fine spell of off-spin bowling by the young Venkataramana accounted for Uttar Pradesh on the third day, and the left-handed Raman hit a maiden century on the final day in celebration. He and V. Sivaramakrishnan added 135 in 127 minutes.

Ravi Shastri defied Delhi on the opening day at the Ferozeshah Kotla after Madan Lal and Sanjeeva Sharma had made early breakthroughs. Manjrekar's attractive stroke-play was ended when he was stumped off Maninder Singh, and the equally attractive Nayak was bowled by Sanjeeva Sharma, who was instrumental in bringing the Bombay innings to a close after 1½ hours on the second day. Delhi were in dreadful trouble when Rajendra Lele sent back Khanna and Bhaskar with only four scored, but Raman Lamba took total command, hitting the highest score ever made for Delhi in the Ranji Trophy and putting the game out of Bombay's reach.

Semi-Finals

11, 12, 13 and 14 March 1988

at Chidambaram Stadium, Madras

Tamil Nadu 601 (Robin Singh 152, V. Sivaramakrishnan 122, B. Arun 62, Bhupinder Singh 4 for 117, D. Chopra 4 for 160) and 157 for 6 (L. Sivaramakrishnan 52)

Punjab 416 (N.S. Sidhu 146, R.S. Ghai 88, Ashwini Kapoor 81, M. Venkataramana 4 for 172)

Match drawn
Tamil Nadu qualified for final on first-innings lead

at Karnail Stadium, Delhi

Delhi 230 for 5 dec (K. Bhaskar Pillai 74 not out)
Railways 140 for 3

Match drawn
Railways qualified for final on quotient rule

After early mishaps, which caused three wickets to fall before lunch on the first day, Tamil Nadu, who had seemed to fritter away the advantage of winning the toss, were revived by the two left-handers V. Sivaramakrishnan and Robin Singh. Venkatraman Sivaramakrishnan had been recalled to the side at the expense of younger players whom some thought should be playing, but the 36-year-old vindicated the selectors with his 10th Ranji Trophy century. He and Robin Singh continued their stand for the

---

RANJI TROPHY FINAL – TAMIL NADU v. RAILWAYS
25, 26, 27, 29 and 30 March 1988 at Chidambaram Stadium, Madras

RAILWAYS

	FIRST INNINGS		SECOND INNINGS	
P. Karkera	c Senthilnathan, b Arun	4	c V. Sivarmakrishnan, b L. Sivarakrishnan	48
Yusuf Ali Khan	lbw, b Vasudevan	87	c V. Sivaramakrishnan, b Vasudevan	12
N. Churi	c Vasudevan, b Venkataramana	112	c V. Sivaramakrishnan, b Vasudevan	34
D. Arora	c Senthilnathan, b Venkataramana	0	(5) c Robin Singh, b Vasudevan	17
K.B. Kala	lbw b Venkataramana	21	(4) b Vasudevan	38
P. Bhatnagar*	c L. Sivaramakrishnan, b Venkataramana	10	(8) c Girish b L. Sivarakrishnan	17
K. Durga Prasad	c L. Sivaramakrishnan, b Venkataramana	4	(7) lbw, b Vasudevan	28
K. Bharathan	c Chandrasekhar, b Vasudevan	27	(6) c Radharkrishnan, b Venkataramana	0
Hyder Ali†	c V. Sivaramakrishnan, b Venkataramana	10	(10) c Prakash, b Vasudevan	0
H. Joshi	not out	13	(9) not out	10
S. Valson	c V. Sivaramakrishnan, b Venkataramana	5	c Venkataramana, b Vasudevan	18
Extras	b 14, lb 8, nb 2	24	b 19, lb 4, nb 3	26
		317		**248**

TAMIL NADU

	FIRST INNINGS	
U.R. Radhakrishnan	st Bhatnagar, b Durga Prasad	30
V.B. Chandrasekhar	lbw, b Joshi	89
P.C. Prakash	c Yusuf Ali, b Hyder Ali	50
M. Senthilnathan	c Bhatnagar, b Bharathan	21
V. Sivaramakrishnan	c Bharathan, b Valson	94
Robin Singh	c Hyder Ali, b Churi	131
L. Sivaramakrishnan	c Bharathan, b Durga Prasad	101
B. Arun	c sub, b Bharathan	39
D. Girish*	c Bhatnagar, b Hyder Ali	55
S. Vasudevan†	c Karkera, b Hyder Ali	30
M. Venkataramana	not out	24
Extras	b 21, lb 10, nb 14	45
		709

	O	M	R	W	O	M	R	W
Arun	10	2	23	1	2	–	8	–
Robin Singh	7	1	20	–	1	–	8	–
Venkataramana	41.3	14	94	7	32	7	106	1
Vasudevan	47	9	113	2	37	12	59	7
L. Sivaramakrishnan	9	–	45	–	13	1	44	2

	O	M	R	W
Valson	19	4	75	1
Arora	5	–	24	–
Joshi	30	2	122	1
Bharathan	69	17	156	2
Durga Prasad	44	9	128	2
Hyder Ali	57	14	139	3
Churi	10	1	34	1

FALL OF WICKETS
1–8, 2–172, 3–173, 4–226, 5–242, 6–258, 7–267, 8–288, 9–312
1–36, 2–96, 3–104, 4–138, 5–143, 6–179, 7–219, 8–221, 9–221

FALL OF WICKETS
1–57, 2–172, 3–174, 4–220, 5–392, 6–484, 7–566, 8–578, 9–625

Umpires: M.G. Deshpande & B.A. Jamula

Tamil Nadu won by an innings and 144 runs

Navjot Singh Sidhu missed most of the season through injury but returned for the Ranji Trophy semi-final at Madras and hit a glorious 146 for Punjab, but it was not enough to win the game against Tamil Nadu. (Adrian Murrell/Allsport)

the first ball of the afternoon. They slipped to 82 for 3, and it was left to Bhaskar Pillai to resurrect the innings. Madan Lal had no option but to declare overnight and to bank on capturing wickets on the last day. There was no play before lunch because of more overnight rain and Karkera was dropped first ball, an expensive miss for the first wicket, which realized 64. Delhi's hopes rose when Yusuf Ali and Arora fell in quick succession, and, at 109 for 3, Railways were trailing. Their saviour was Naresh Churi, who batted 139 minutes and faced 142 balls for his 28 not out. The young left-hander defended stubbornly and showed admirable composure when Madan Lal crowded the bat for Kirti Azad's last over. Churi survived, and Railways quotient was 46.66 to Delhi's 46.

Ranji Trophy Final
TAMIL NADU v. RAILWAYS

Electing to bat first, Railways were again well served by Naresh Churi. Playing with more force than when circumstances dictated defence in the semi-final, he hit his first century of the season and shared a second-wicket stand of 164 with Yusuf Ali Khan, whose form had not matched that of the previous season. The hero, however, was the young Tamil Nadu off-spinner Venkataramana, who took seven of the last eight wickets to fall to claim the best figures of his career. He was to take one more wicket in the second innings to bring his total to 35 for the season, second only to Raghuram Bhat, a most praiseworthy performance.

From the time that Chandrasekhar and Prakash came together in a second-wicket stand of 115, there seemed

fifth wicket into the second day when Robin reached his third hundred of the season and the partnership reached 186 before V. Sivaramakrishnan's dismissal. Slow in the afternoon, Tamil Nadu were given late impetus by Arun, and they finally reached 601, their record score in the Ranji Trophy, with the help of 16 penalty runs. It was the second match in succession in which Tamil Nadu had passed their previous best score. Inspired by Navjot Singh Sidhu's 146, his highest first-class score, and a second-wicket stand of 197 between him and Ashwini Kapoor, Punjab looked as if they might achieve the improbable, particularly as Sidhu hit his runs off a mere 199 deliveries with 20 fours and 4 sixes and the partnership occupied only 210 minutes, but from 263 for 2 Punjab slumped to 313 for 6 by the close, and the last day was a perfunctory exercise.

For Delhi there was total desolation. The first two days' play were lost to rain, with covers again proving inadequate. On the third day, Delhi went to lunch at 71 for 0, but lost Lamba to veteran left-arm spinner Hyder Ali on

Laxman Sivaramakrishnan. His leg-spin bowling may have declined in effectiveness, but he hit three centuries for Tamil Nadu during the season, the last of them in the Ranji Trophy final. (Adrian Murrell/Allsport)

little doubt that Tamil Nadu would take a first-innings lead. What was not expected was that for the third match in succession they would better their highest score in first-class cricket. They moved into the lead with only four wickets down when Venkatraman Sivaramakrishnan again proved his worth and added 172 with Robin Singh, who hit his fourth century of the season. This was followed by Laxman Sivaramakrishnan's third, pugnacious century in the 1987–8 Ranji Trophy, a remarkable performance by one who had hit only one century before the start of the season. If Laxman Sivaramakrishnan's control of the leg-break seems temporarily to have deserted him, he has the compensation of an improvement in his batting which makes him an invaluable member of any side.

Tamil Nadu's massive score, the highest of the season, assured them of the Ranji Trophy, but they took the Trophy in fine style when they completed an innings victory on the last day. It was the only outright win in the final stages of the competition. The spinners dominated, and it was Vasudevan who took the honours with his best performance of the season.

Tamil Nadu's only previous appearance in the final had been in 1972–3 when they had lost to Bombay.

So ended a long, hard Indian season in which there were some bright moments and some tedious ones. Gursharan Singh established a Ranji Trophy record with 15 catches in the season for Punjab while Deepak Sharma of Haryana set up another record when he sent down 97 overs against Punjab at Faridabad.

As the Test series against West Indies showed, Indian cricket is in something of a transitional phase. New, exciting faces are appearing on the international scene – Hirwani, Raman, Sidhu. It is possible that they could soon be joined by players like Bhaskar Pillai, Churi and Saldanha.

First-Class Averages

BATTING

	M	Inns	NOs	Runs	HS	Av	100s	50s
S. Sugwekar (Maharashtra)	3	5	3	234	100*	117.00	1	2
S. Banerjee (Bengal)	4	4	3	106	53*	106.00		1
S.C. Khanna (Delhi)	5	5	1	408	220*	102.00	2	
D.B. Vengsarkar	3	5	2	305	102*	101.66	2	1
R.B. Parikh (Baroda)	5	8	3	443	137	88.60	2	2
K.B. Kala (Railways)	7	9	3	522	203*	87.00	2	1
R. Lamba (Delhi)	11	13		1097	320	84.38	5	1
V. Sivaramakrishnan (Tamil Nadu)	3	5	1	334	122	83.50	1	2
V. Bhaskar (Jammu & K.)	3	5	1	312	125	78.00	1	2
A.D. Gaekwad (Baroda)	7	10	2	617	216	77.12	2	1
Gursharan Singh (Punjab)	8	8	1	529	132*	75.57	3	1
Amarjeet Kaypee (Haryana)	5	6	2	301	126	75.25	1	1
B.P. Patel (Karnataka)	6	10	2	596	144	74.50	3	1
J. Mukherjee (Bengal)	5	6	2	291	79	72.75		2
H. Gidwani (Bihar)	6	8	2	432	116	72.00	2	2
A. Sippy (Bombay)	5	7	3	285	111*	71.25	1	1
A. Kapoor (Punjab)	6	6		417	170	69.50	1	3
Robin Singh (Tamil Nadu)	8	10	2	555	152	69.37	4	
S.V. Manjrekar (Bombay)	8	14	4	678	278	67.80	1	3
K.S. Chavan (Baroda)	5	8	2	403	247	67.16	1	1
L.S. Rajput (Bombay)	8	15	1	928	245	66.28	4	2
R. Das (Assam)	3	4		262	170	65.50	1	
M. Nayyar (Delhi)	8	12	2	653	184	65.30	2	3
J. Arun Lal (Bengal)	8	12		777	205	64.75	2	5
R.S. Ghai (Punjab)	11	12	2	517	99	64.62		5
N. Churi (Railways)	4	6	1	311	112	62.20	1	1
S.S. Hattangadi (Bombay)	6	9	1	497	186	62.12	3	
R. Talwar (Madhya P.)	4	7		424	199	60.57	1	1
R. Chadha (Haryana)	5	6		360	123	60.00	1	3
L. Sivaramakrishnan (Tamil Nadu)	8	11	2	531	124	59.00	3	1
K.B. Pillai (Delhi)	10	12	3	530	129	58.88	2	3
K. Jeshwant (Karnataka)	6	10	4	345	71*	57.50		3
A. Paul (Hyderabad)	3	3		171	79	57.00		2
I.B. Roy (Bengal)	5	7		398	110	56.85	1	4
A. Pandya (Saurashtra)	4	6	1	273	198	54.60	1	
S.S. Karim (Bihar)	5	7	1	327	114	54.50	2	
T. Arothe (Baroda)	5	5	1	215	102*	53.75	1	
W.V. Raman (Tamil Nadu)	8	13	1	637	182	53.08	1	5
S. Mudkavi (Rajasthan)	4	7	2	265	73	53.00		2
A. Asawa (Rajasthan)	3	5	1	210	128	52.50	1	
V. Jaisimha (Hyderabad)	6	8	2	308	92*	51.33		3
Aman Kumar (Haryana)	3	5	3	102	53*	51.00		1
M.D. Gunjal (Maharashtra)	6	10	2	405	120	50.62	1	2
Iqbal Khan (Bombay)	5	5	1	202	95*	50.50		1
S.S. Talati (Gujarat)	4	7	1	300	86*	50.00		2
M. Prabhakar (Delhi)	6	5	2	149	51*	49.66		1
K. Dubey (Bengal)	6	8		395	139	49.37	3	
S.V. Nayak (Bombay)	6	6	2	196	84	49.00		1
A. Vijayvergiya (Madhya P.)	4	7		342	115	48.25	1	2
M.F. Rehman (Andhra)	5	8	2	290	115	48.33	1	1
U. Phate (Vidarbha)	2	4	1	145	102*	48.33	1	
R. Bora (Assam)	4	6		288	126	48.00	1	1
A.O. Malhotra (Bengal)	5	7		332	93	47.42		2
A.K. Patel (Saurashtra)	5	6	1	237	59	47.40		3
M.V. Narasimha Rao (Hyderabad)	6	9	2	330	81	47.14		3
B. Jadeja (Suarashtra)	4	7	1	278	117	46.33	1	
D.S. Chopra (Punjab)	7	6	2	184	74	46.00		2
P. Bhatnagar (Railways)	5	7	2	230	105	46.00	1	1
V.B. Chandrasekhar (Tamil Nadu)	8	13	1	551	160	45.91	1	2
S.K. Sharma (Delhi)	7	8	2	275	76	45.83		3
L.K. Adisheshu (Andhra)	3	5	1	183	75	45.75		1
Ehtesham Ali Khan (Hyderabad)	5	5	1	183	106*	45.75	1	
H. Angle (Goa)	5	10	4	274	77*	45.66		2
Indrapal Singh (Uttar P.)	3	3		136	76	45.33		1
V. Chamundeswanath (Andhra)	5	7	1	268	80*	44.66		3
V.S. Wadkar (Baroda)	4	4	1	132	59	44.00		1
V.S. Yadav (Uttar P.)	6	11	2	394	100	43.77	1	2
J. Shetty (Hyderabad)	4	6	1	218	113	43.60	1	1
A.K. Seth (Services)	5	8	1	303	120	43.28	2	
S. Keshwala (Saurashtra)	6	9		389	130	43.22	1	3
P.N.S. Rana (Uttar P.)	6	9	4	215	71*	43.00		2
R. Poonawala (Maharashtra)	4	7	1	255	146	42.50	1	
U.S. Madan Lal (Delhi)	10	9	2	296	107	42.28	1	1
R. Vinayak (Delhi)	9	6	1	208	88	41.60		1

First-Class Averages continued

	M	Inns	NOs	Runs	HS	Av	100s	50s
Chimnoy Sharma (Services)	4	7	1	248	101	41.33	1	1
Ajay Sharma (Delhi)	11	14	2	494	99	41.16		3
M. Azharuddin (Hyderabad)	4	6		246	61	41.00		2
C. Saldanha (Karnataka)	7	13		531	144	40.84	1	2
S. Takle (Vidarbha)	4	6	2	160	55*	40.00		1
M.S. Narula (Baroda)	5	6		240	102	40.00	1	1
S. Mitra (Orissa)	4	7	1	239	69	39.83		2
Shahid Pervez (Jammu & K.)	5	9		358	103	39.77	1	2
Padam Shastri (Rajasthan)	4	7		277	118	39.57	1	1
R. Nayyar (Himachal P.)	2	4		156	78	39.00		2
Kirti Azad (Delhi)	9	9		350	100	38.88	1	3
R.N. Kapil Dev (Haryana)	5	8		308	109	38.50	1	1
U.R. Radhakrishnan (Tamil Nadu)	5	6		230	64	38.33		1
A.S. Bajwa (Services)	5	8		304	92	38.00		3
S.J. Phadkar (Vidarbha)	4	6		228	79	38.00		3
S. Gujar (Vidarbha)	4	8	1	262	101	37.42	1	1
A. Dayal (Bihar)	5	7		260	121	37.14	1	
Gauri Shankar (Services)	5	7	1	222	93	37.00		2
S.S. Khandekar (Uttar P.)	6	10		329	64	36.55		2
S.M.H. Kirmani (Karnataka)	5	8	1	254	106	36.28	1	
P. Bhatt (Gujarat)	4	7		254	62	36.28		1
N. Goel (Haryana)	4	6		216	94	36.00		1
S. Ansari (Madhya P.)	5	8		282	63	35.25		2
K.A. Qayyum (Hyderabad)	8	12		423	106	35.25	1	3
A. Hussain (Bihar)	5	6	1	176	81	35.20		1
P.S. Karkera (Railways)	5	7	1	211	110	35.16	1	
P. Khanna (Bihar)	5	7		242	81	34.57		2
R.M.H. Binny (Karnataka)	6	10	1	310	101*	34.44	1	2
S. Chopra (Punjab)	7	6		206	72	34.33		2
S. Ramesh (Kerala)	5	8	1	240	69	34.28		2
Bhaskar Ghosh (Services)	5	8		274	95	34.25		2
R. Jolly (Haryana)	5	6	1	171	79*	34.20		2
R. Pandit (Jammu & K.)	5	9		304	119	33.77	1	1
Abdul Azeem (Hyderabad)	7	11	1	336	93	33.60		3
D. Girish (Tamil Nadu)	7	10	1	301	87	33.44		3
C.P. Singh (Madhya P.)	4	7		231	69	33.00		1
S.J. Kalyani (Maharashtra)	6	11	1	327	98	32.70		3
K. Srikkanth (Tamil Nadu)	6	10		322	71	32.20		3
Deepak Sharma (Haryana)	5	7	1	192	59*	32.00		2
Dalbir Singh (Rajasthan)	3	6	1	160	91*	32.00		2
N. Kutty (Kerala)	5	10	2	255	102	31.87	1	
P.B. Hingnikar (Vidarbha)	4	8		255	92	31.87		2
A. Khatwa (Orissa)	4	7	1	190	84	31.66		2
R. Sapru (Uttar P.)	7	8		251	58	31.37		2
P.C. Prakash (Tamil Nadu)	8	13	1	376	50	31.33		1
T.C. Sudeesh (Kerala)	5	8	1	218	70	31.14		1
S.K. Ganguly (Bengal)	4	4		124	107	31.00	1	
Yusuf Ali Khan (Railways)	7	9		278	87	30.88		2
S. Tanna (Saurashtra)	4	8	2	185	89	30.83		1
C.S. Pandit (Bombay)	7	9		276	80	30.66		2
B.K. Patel (Gujarat)	4	6		184	69	30.66		2
S. Paul (Tripura)	4	8		245	71	30.62		1
S.K. Kulkarni (Bombay)	10	16	1	457	80	30.46		3
J.K. Ghia (Andhra)	5	7		213	91	30.42		2
K. Bharatan (Railways)	5	5		151	65	30.20		2
D. Arora (Railways)	4	6		177	113	29.50	1	
V. Sen (Himachal P.)	5	10		291	74	29.10		2
B. Radia (Saurashtra)	4	6	2	116	42*	29.00		
R. Kalsi (Punjab)	7	7		202	59	28.85		1
M. Kakoti (Assam)	4	5	1	114	46	28.50		
B. Arun (Tamil Nadu)	9	14	1	370	89	28.46		2
R.J. Shastri (Bombay)	5	8	1	199	94	28.42		1
Durga Prasad (Railways)	6	7	1	169	59	28.16		1
D. Mohanty (Orissa)	4	7		197	82	28.14		2
B.H. Mistry (Gujarat)	3	6	1	140	69	28.00		2
S. Chaturvedi (Uttar P.)	6	8		222	64	27.75		2
J.J. Zinto (Gujarat)	4	6	2	111	62*	27.75		1
T.P. Ajit Kumar (Kerala)	3	4		110	58	27.50		1
Nirmal Singh (Jammu & K.)	5	9		247	88	27.44		2
T. Mathew (Kerala)	5	10	2	219	80	27.37		1
A. Bhattacharjee (Bengal)	6	7	3	107	33*	26.75		
Ghopal Sharma (Uttar P.)	5	7	1	159	66	26.50		1
Yashpal Sharma (Haryana P.)	6	7		185	78	26.42		1
Inderjeet Singh (Himachal P.)	5	10		260	66	26.00		1
C.J. Sharma (Haryana)	4	6	1	128	55	25.60		1
H. Praharaj (Orissa)	4	6	1	127	40*	25.40		
Ashfaq Rahim Khan (Andhra)	5	9	1	201	91	25.12		1
K.K. Sharma (Uttar P.)	7	10	2	201	53	25.12		1
G.R. Viswanath (Karnataka)	4	6		149	41	24.83		
S. Kangtalkar (Goa)	5	10		242	108	24.20	1	1
A.V. Mudkavi (Rajasthan)	3	6		145	63	24.16		1
M. Venkataramana (Tamil Nadu)	8	10	5	120	48	24.00		
G.A. Pratap Kumar (Andhra)	3	5		120	74	24.00		1
M.B. Amarnath (Delhi)	9	12		287	71	23.91		1
A. Roy (Orissa)	3	6	1	119	59*	23.80		1
D. Bangera (Goa)	5	10	1	213	44*	23.66		
V. Venkatram (Bihar)	6	6		142	79	23.66		1
A. Akhtar (Jammu & K.)	5	9		212	56	23.55		2
R.P. Singh (Uttar P.)	7	9	1	186	79	23.25		2
S. Viswanath (Karnataka)	8	14		295	83	22.69		1
S.J. Jadhav (Maharashtra)	4	6	1	113	71	22.60		1
V. Mohan Raj (Hyderabad)	3	5		113	47	22.60		
P. Dutta (Assam)	4	6		135	95	22.50		1
K. Chauhan (Saurashtra)	4	7		156	52	22.28		1
S. Dhuri (Goa)	5	10		222	88	22.20		2
S. Mahadevan (Goa)	5	10		221	83	22.10		1
K.S. More (Baroda)	5	7	1	131	49	21.83		
P.R. Pradhan (Maharashtra)	4	7		150	50	21.42		1
M. Inder Singh (Punjab)	11	9	2	149	39	21.28		
K.V.S.D. Kamaraju (Andhra)	5	7		148	61	21.14		1
A. Gupta (Jammu & K.)	5	9		190	61	21.11		2
K.B. Ramamurthy (Andhra)	5	7	1	126	39*	21.00		
Azim Khan (Maharashtra)	6	8	2	125	32*	20.83		
R. Krishna Mohan (Andhra)	5	7		103	25*	20.60		
P. Ramesh Rao (Karnataka)	5	8		159	43	19.87		
C. Sudharkar Rao (Services)	4	7	1	119	44	19.83		

First-Class Averages continued

	M	Inns	NOs	Runs	HS	Av	100s	50s
S. Lahore (Madhya P.)	4	7		135	89	19.28		1
M. Satokar (Madhya P.)	4	7	1	114	51	19.00		1
D.T. Patel (Gujarat)	4	6		114	63	19.00		1
S. Santosh (Kerala)	5	8		150	52	18.75		1
Arshad Ayub (Hyderabad)	7	12	2	186	57	18.60		1
S. Pednekar (Goa)	5	10	2	148	44	18.50		
S. Chowdhary (Tripura)	4	8	1	129	49	18.42		
S. Shinde (Goa)	4	8		146	57	18.25		1
S. Rajesh (Kerala)	5	8		145	70	18.12		1
S. Chowdhary (Jammu & K.)	4	7		125	67	17.85		1
V. Hariharan (Kerala)	5	8	2	101	35*	16.83		
P. Revankar (Goa)	4	8		129	73	16.12		1
Raj Kumar (Himachal P.)	4	8		128	49	16.00		
Idris Gundroo (Jammu & K.)	5	9	2	106	62	15.14		1
M.R. Srinivasa Prasad (Karnataka)	5	9		128	32	14.22		
M. Jayaram (Kerala)	5	8		107	37	13.37		
S. Vasudevan (Tamil Nadu)	8	9	1	101	30	12.62		
V. Korgaonkar (Goa)	5	10	1	112	29*	12.44		

(Qualification – 100 runs, average 10.00)

Also scored 100 runs: P. Amre (Railways) 186* & 9; R. Arora (Bihar) 110* & 0; N.S. Sidhu (Punjab) 146 & 66; D. Pandove (Punjab) 94 & 13 (each played in two matches)
Arun Sharma (Punjab) 80* & 25 (played in three matches)

BOWLING

	Overs	Mds	Runs	Wkts	Av	Best	10/m	5/inns
K.V.P. Rao (Bihar)	53.1	17	111	13	8.53	4/6		
D. Mukherjee (Bengal)	43.3	7	109	10	10.90	5/17	1	2
Srinivasan (Services)	54.4	16	145	11	13.18	6/39	1	2
R. Venkatapathi (Hyderabad)	121.3	38	276	20	13.80	6/52		2
M. Saudagar (Orissa)	111	15	309	19	16.26	8/64	1	1
P. Jain (Delhi)	152	49	303	18	16.83	6/36		1
D.S. Chopra (Punjab)	275.3	87	546	32	17.06	6/29	1	2
Satynder Singh (Bengal)	76.4	19	190	11	17.27	5/30		1
M.Kakoti (Assam)	65.5	10	228	13	17.53	8/63		1
Sanath Kumar (Karnataka)	113.5	27	319	18	17.72	7/81	1	2
Robin Singh (Tamil Nadu)	92.4	14	309	17	18.17	6/28		2
P. Sundaram (Rajasthan)	72.5	14	255	14	18.21	7/75	1	2
Ajay Sharma (Delhi)	153.2	35	361	18	20.05	4/105		
K.D. Mokashi (Bombay)	130.4	38	324	16	20.25	5/39		1
M. Venkataramana (Tamil Nadu)	239.1	55	716	35	20.45	7/94		3
L. Sivaramakrishnan (Tamil Nadu)	78.4	9	288	13	22.15	3/43		
S. Vasudevan (Tamil Nadu)	265.4	78	600	27	22.22	7/59		2
A.R. Bhat (Karnataka)	286.4	63	780	35	22.28	8/43	1	3
S.C. Sadangi (Services)	92.2	17	291	13	22.38	5/71		1
S. Mahapatra (Orissa)	121.3	12	410	18	22.77	7/40	1	2
K. Jeshwant (Karnataka)	108.5	18	319	14	22.78	5/60		2
S. Pednekar (Goa)	61.3	6	298	13	22.92	4/51		
S.V. Jugade (Vidarbha)	110.4	15	415	18	23.05	6/84	1	2
S. Jadhav (Maharashtra)	140.4	17	418	18	23.22	5/18		2
N. Konwar (Assam)	177	19	592	25	23.68	6/84	1	2
R.N. Kapil Dev (Haryana)	143.5	45	408	17	24.00	5/61		1
Deepak Sharma (Haryana)	238.3	42	628	26	24.15	6/76	1	4
N.D. Hirwani (Madhya P.)	267.1	31	923	38	24.28	8/61	1	4
S. Valson (Railways)	128.2	15	469	19	24.68	7/59		1

	Overs	Mds	Runs	Wkts	Av	Best	10/m	5/inns
Idris Gundroo (Jammu & K.)	68	7	276	11	25.09	5/48		1
C.J. Sharma (Haryana)	80.5	6	383	15	25.53	5/55		1
K.G. Jayakumar (Kerala)	146.5	24	618	24	25.75	5/62		2
B.S. Mangesh (Andhra)	194	47	541	21	25.76	5/72		2
N.S. Yadav (Hyderabad)	286.4	65	727	28	25.96	5/54		2
Arshad Ayub (Hyderabad)	278.4	61	712	27	26.37	8/65	1	2
B. Arun (Tamil Nadu)	155	28	609	23	26.47	4/62		
L.S. Rajput (Bombay)	89.1	15	294	11	26.72	4/64		
V. Venkatram (Bihar)	191	27	538	20	26.90	6/109		1
R. Pandit (Jammu & K.)	70.1	9	275	10	27.50	4/42		
R. Patel (Madhya P.)	101	18	310	11	28.18	3/91		
U.S. Madan Lal (Delhi)	217.2	35	656	23	28.52	4/37		
S. Talwar (Haryana)	300.2	55	856	30	28.53	5/91		2
Durga Prasad (Railways)	147	36	373	13	28.69	5/63		1
Ghopal Sharma (Uttar P.)	144.2	28	410	14	29.28	6/136		2
M.A. Ansari (Uttar P.)	209.1	42	560	19	29.47	5/48		1
A.D. Gaekwad (Baroda)	141.5	22	385	13	29.61	4/73		
Rashid Patel (Baroda)	151.2	20	566	19	29.78	5/33		1
R.P. Singh (Uttar P.)	190.2	21	728	24	30.33	5/83		1
M.V. Narasimha Rao (Hyderabad)	137.5	18	428	14	30.57	5/66		1
S. Takle (Vidarbha)	111.4	21	401	13	30.84	4/31		
M. Inder Singh (Punjab)	344.3	82	833	27	30.85	6/34		1
Kirti Azad (Delhi)	131.4	35	340	11	30.90	3/28		
J.J. Zinto (Gujarat)	152.1	29	469	15	31.26	5/102		1
S. Santosh (Kerala)	128	25	407	13	31.30	4/87		
K.K. Sharma (Uttar P.)	182.1	19	721	23	31.34	4/65		
A. Bhattacharjee (Bengal)	196.1	45	474	15	31.60	5/62		1
M. Prabhakar (Delhi)	115	22	412	13	31.69	4/47		
Raviknat Gupta (Jammu & K.)	172.5	28	455	14	32.50	6/38		1
V. Hariharan (Kerala)	148.3	26	521	16	32.56	4/33		
P. Kamath (Goa)	94.5	9	326	10	32.60	5/47		1
B. Radia (Saurashtra)	113.5	20	331	10	33.10	6/106		1
H. Joshi (Railways)	160	34	535	16	33.43	4.76		
S.G. Chakraborty (Assam)	119.4	19	370	10	37.00	4/42		
S. Krishna Mohan (Andhra)	130	15	482	13	37.07	6/80		1
K. Bharatan (Railways)	161.5	35	414	11	37.63	3/30		
J.K. Ghia (Andhra)	212	47	586	15	39.06	4/95		
B. Ghosh (Services)	170.4	28	471	12	39.25	3/28		
D.V. Pardeshi (Baroda)	171	48	401	10	40.10	3/16		
S.K. Sharma (Delhi)	184.4	31	644	16	40.25	5/81		1
Randhir Singh (Bihar)	171	30	487	12	40.58	3/55		
W.V. Raman (Tamil Nadu)	122	20	408	10	40.80	4/94		
Abhijit Das (Tripura)	117	9	412	10	41.20	4/146		
Maninder Singh (Delhi)	216.5	56	551	13	42.38	7/62		1
S.C. Gudge (Maharashtra)	125.2	7	435	10	43.50	3/34		
Azim Khan (Maharashtra)	204.5	45	627	13	48.23	4/71		
R.S. Ghai (Punjab)	234.1	28	970	20	48.50	5/117		1
Ratan Singh (Rajasthan)	183.3	24	661	13	50.84	5/114		1
S.V. Nayak (Bombay)	192.3	34	638	11	58.00	4/155		

(Qualification – 10 wickets)

LEADING FIELDERS

17 - R. Vinayak (Delhi) (ct 12/st 5) and P.B. Hingnikar (Hyderabad) (ct 14/st 3); 16 - P.L. Bose (Orissa) (ct 14/st 2) and S. Viswanath (Karnataka) (ct 11/st 5); 15 - Gursharan Singh (Punjab); 14 - Ehtesham Ali Khan (Hyderabad) (ct 13/st 1), C.S. Pandit (Bombay) (ct 13/st 1) and D. Girish (Tamil Nadu); 13 - K.S. More (ct 6/st 7); 12 - P. Khanna (Bihar) and M.S. Patel (Baroda) (ct 11/st 1); 11 - Ajay Sharma (Delhi); 10 - D. Bangera (Goa) (ct 9/st 1), R. Lamba (Delhi), B.K. Patel (Gujarat) (ct 8/st 2), Robin Singh (Tamil Nadu) and V. Yadav (Haryana)

'Discord, Dispute, Disarray'

The season in Pakistan. The Wills Cup.
England *v.* Pakistan, One-Day
International and Test series. BCCP
Patron's Trophy. Quaid-e-Azam
Trophy. First-class averages.

Dispute and discord. Shakoor Rana, Mike Gatting and Peter Lush.
(Adrian Murrell/Allsport)

With the World Cup and the England tour dominating, Pakistan domestic cricket was once more pushed into the shadows. Indeed, the PACO Pentagular tournament was not played so great was the pressure from international commitments. The season began with the national one-day competition, the Wills Cup, which was played before the Reliance World Cup.

Wills Cup

Pool A

8 September 1987

at National Stadium, Karachi

Karachi 217 for 8 (Saleem Yousuf 62)
PIA 219 for 3 (Rizwan-uz-Zaman 105)

PIA (4 pts) won by 7 wickets

at Niaz Stadium, Hyderabad

United Bank 180 for 8
HBFC 159 for 9 (Shahid Saeed 75)

United Bank (4 pts) won by 21 runs

9 September 1987

at National Stadium, Karachi

Muslim Commercial Bank 206 (Salahuddin 65, Ijaz Faqih 53, Zahid Ahmed 4 for 35)
PIA 207 for 5 (Feroze Mehdi 76)

PIA (4 pts) won by 5 wickets

at Niaz Stadium, Hyderabad

PACO 194 for 9 (Farukh Raza 55, Umar Rasheed 53)
HBFC 195 for 5 (Saadat Ali 52)

HBFC (4 pts) won by 5 wickets

10 September 1987

at National Stadium, Karachi

United Bank 208 for 9
Karachi 149

United Bank (4 pts) won by 59 runs

at Niaz Stadium, Hyderabad

PACO 133 for 9
PIA 134 for 4 (Zahid Ahmed 55 not out)

PIA (4 pts) won by 6 wickets

11 September 1987

at National Stadium, Karachi

United Bank 199 for 7 (Saifullah 67)
PIA 153 (Rizwan-uz-Zaman 55, Tauseef Ahmed 4 for 27)

United Bank (4 pts) won by 46 runs

at Niaz Stadium, Hyderabad

Muslim Commercial Bank 180 for 9 (Nadeem Yousuf 58, Umar Rasheed 4 for 25)
PACO 183 for 6 (Zahoor Elahi 68, Tahir Mahmood 50 not out)

PACO (4 pts) won by 4 wickets

12 September 1987

at National Stadium, Karachi

Karachi 251 for 5 (Basit Ali 91, Sajid Khan 68)
PACO 228 for 9 (Shahid Anwar 86, Yahya Toor 53)

Karachi (4 pts) won by 23 runs

at Niaz Stadium, Hyderabad

United Bank 182 for 9 (Mahmood Rasheed 50 not out)
Muslim Commercial Bank 103 for 9

United Bank (4 pts) won by 79 runs

13 September 1987

at Niaz Stadium, Hyderabad

Muslim Commercial Bank 176 for 9 (Salahuddin 52 not out)
HBFC 149

Muslim Commercial Bank (4 pts) won by 27 runs

at National Stadium, Karachi

United Bank 227 for 6 (Ashraf Ali 83 not out)
PACO 173 for 9 (Masood Anwar 4 for 40)

United Bank (4 pts) won by 54 runs

14 September 1987

at Niaz Stadium, Hyderabad

PIA 201 for 7 (Asif Mujtaba 67, Zahid Ahmed 54)
HBFC 146 (Zahid Ahmed 4 for 14)

PIA (4 pts) won by 55 runs

at National Stadium, Karachi

Karachi 216 for 9 (Saleem Yousuf 63)
Muslim Commercial Bank 181 (Anwar-ul-Haq 56)

Karachi (4 pts) won by 35 runs

15 September 1987

at National Stadium, Karachi

Karachi 279 for 8 (Saleem Yousuf 91, Raees Ahmed 73, Shahid Saeed 4 for 25)
HBFC 213 for 8 (Saadat Ali 55, Sagheer Abbas 55, Shakeel Sajjad 4 for 47)

Karachi (4 pts) won by 66 runs

Pool A – Final Table

	P	W	L	Pts	R/R
United Bank	5	5	–	20	4.00
PIA	5	4	1	16	4.00
Karachi	5	3	2	12	4.53
PACO	5	1	4	4	3.66
HBFC	5	1	4	4	3.60
Muslim Commercial Bank	5	1	4	4	3.46

The weather was far kinder than in the previous season, and every match in Pool A was played without curtailment to the full quota of 50 overs.

Saleem Yousuf had an outstanding series with the bat although, inevitably, it was Rizwan-uz-Zaman who hit the only century in this group. The player of the group, however, was all-rounder Zahid Ahmed of Pakistan International Airlines. He won three Man-of-the-Match awards in five matches and, against Muslim Commercial Bank in Karachi, he performed the first hat trick ever to be performed in the competition.

Pool B

8 September 1987

at Qaddafi Stadium, Lahore

Lahore 229 (Babar Zaman 74, Asif Faridi 4 for 49)
ADBP 233 for 3 (Masood Anwar 72, Najeeb Wajid 69)

ADBP (4 pts) won by 7 wickets

at Pindi Club Ground, Rawalpindi

Habib Bank 283 for 7 (Ijaz Ahmed 110, Javed Miandad 59)
Rawalpindi 169 for 6 (Mujahid Hameed 56 not out, Shahid Javed 51)

Habib Bank (4 pts) won by 114 runs

9 September 1987

at Qaddafi Stadium, Lahore

Lahore 210 for 8 (Babar Zaman 110 not out)
WAPDA 124

Lahore (4 pts) won by 86 runs

at Municipal Stadium, Gujranwala

National Bank 97 (Manzoor Elahi 4 for 32)
ADBP 101 for 8

ADBP (4 pts) won by 2 wickets

10 September 1987

at Qaddafi Stadium, Lahore

Habib Bank 317 for 3 (Saleem Malik 115, Ijaz Ahmed 69, Anwar Miandad 54 not out, Agha Zahis 53)
Lahore 235 for 9 (Rameez Raja 67, Abdul Qadir 4 for 34)

Habib Bank (4 pts) won by 82 runs

at Pindi Club Ground, Rawalpindi

WAPDA 134 for 8 (Zahid Umar 73)
Rawalpindi 90

WAPDA (4 pts) won by 44 runs

11 September 1987

at Municipal Stadium, Gujranwala

WAPDA 204 for 8 (Zahid Umar 73)
ADBP 205 for 7 (Masood Anwar 59)

ADBP (4 pts) won by 3 wickets

at Qaddafi Stadium, Lahore

National Bank 114 for 9
Habib Bank 115 for 2

Habib Bank (4 pts) won by 8 wickets

Manzoor Elahi, ADBP, fine all-round cricket in the Wills One-Day Competition. (Adrian Murrell/Allsport)

12 September 1987

at Iqbal Stadium, Faisalabad

ADBP 231
Habib Bank 235 for 3 (Saleem Malik 102 not out, Javed Miandad 57 not out)

Habib Bank (4 pts) won by 7 wickets

at Pindi Club Ground, Rawalpindi

Rawalpindi 217 for 7 (Sajjad Ahmed 84 not out)
National Bank 172 (Asad Rauf 53, Mohammad Riaz 4 for 27)

Rawalpindi (4 pts) won by 45 runs

13 September 1987

at Qaddafi Stadium, Lahore

National Bank 239 for 7 (Saeed Azad 67, Ameer Akbar 63)
Lahore 241 for 0 (Rameez Raja 122 not out, Saleem Raza 109 not out)

Lahore (4 pts) won by 10 wickets

14 September 1987

at Qaddafi Stadium, Lahore

WAPDA 182 for 6 (Ali Bahadur 50)
Habib Bank 184 for 3 (Agha Zahid 76 not out, Javed Miandad 62 not out)

Habib Bank (4 pts) won by 7 wickets

at Pindi Club Ground, Rawalpindi

ADBP 270 for 6 (Atif Rauf 76 not out, Ghaffar Kazmi 63)
Rawalpindi 201 for 9 (Mujahid Hameed 57, Khatib Rizwan 4 for 35)

ADBP (4 pts) won by 69 runs

15 September 1987

at Qaddafi Stadium, Lahore

WAPDA 208 for 7 (Munawwar 57 not out)
National Bank 207

WAPDA (4 pts) won by 1 run

at Pindi Club Ground, Rawalpindi

Lahore 163 (Rameez Raja 60)
Rawalpindi 166 for 8 (Nadeem Abbasi 57)

Rawalpindi (4 pts) won by 2 wickets

Pool B – Final Table					
	P	W	L	Pts	R/R
Habib Bank	5	5	–	20	5.38
ADBP	5	4	1	16	4.60
Lahore	5	2	3	8	4.66
WAPDA	5	2	3	8	3.87
Rawalpindi	5	2	3	8	3.67
National Bank	5	–	5	0	4.16

There were some splendid batting performances in the second group, and Rameez Raja and Saleem Raza established a new first-wicket record for the competition when they shared an unbroken stand of 241 for Lahore against National Bank at the Qaddafi Stadium. Saleem Malik hit two centuries for Habib Bank, and his 115 against Lahore came off only 86 balls and included 2 sixes and 16 fours. Manzoor Elahi, Abdul Qadir, Ijaz Ahmed and Babar played consistently well.

Semi-Finals

18 September 1987

at National Stadium, Karachi

United Bank 208 for 7 (Ali Zia 66, Mansoor Akhtar 54)
ADBP 149

United Bank won by 59 runs
(Man of the Match: Ali Zia)

at Shahi Bagh Stadium, Peshawar

Habib Bank 222 for 7 (Aamer Sohail 67 not out)
PIA 224 for 6 (Shoaib Mohammad 67, Asif Mohammad 65)

PIA won by 4 wickets
(Man of the Match: Wasim Akram)

United Bank batted with a degree of consistency and bowled with accuracy to reach the final with some ease. ADBP began their innings well enough, reaching 48 before the first wicket fell, but five wickets went down for 44 runs, and there was no effective recovery.

In the other semi-final, Habib Bank lost three wickets, including Ijaz Ahmed and Saleem Malik, for 38 runs, but

Aamer Sohail and Javed Miandad shared a fifth-wicket stand of 53, and they reached a commendable 222. Rizwan fell early, but Shoaib and Asif Mohammad added 126 for the second wicket. Asif Mujtaba was run out for one, but Wasim Akram hit lustily to give the innings a necessary momentum. He was stumped for 42, but he had dealt some telling blows off Abdul Qadir, and PIA won with 15 balls to spare. Earlier Wasim had accounted for both openers.

Wills Cup Final
PAKISTAN INTERNATIONAL AIRLINES v. UNITED BANK

The two top teams from Pool A qualified for the final, and, as United Bank had been victorious when the sides met in the qualifying competition a fortnight earlier and were unbeaten in the tournament, they started as favourites. They suffered an early disaster when Kamal Merchant was hit and forced to retire hurt, and Mudassar was caught with only eight scored. Kamal was not only a reliable opening batsman, but a vital member of the United Bank attack, so the blow was doubly felt.

United Bank, who had been put in to bat, were revived by Mansoor Akhtar, Ali Zia and Saeed Anwar, but the repairs took time, and when the later batsmen tried to force the pace, as was necessary, they floundered, and the final score of 206 looked insufficient for victory.

It looked massive, however, when Sikhander Bakht and Saleem Jaffer and some unwise running saw PIA plunge to 26 for 4. Aamer Malik and Zahid Ahmed rescued their side with a stand of 109. Anil Dalpat played sensibly for 28, and Wasim Haider provided just the blows that were needed to make victory a formality.

Javed Miandad was named batsman of the tournament while the bowling prize went to Zahid Ahmed, the wicket-keeping award to Ashraf Ali and the fielding medal to Aamer Malik, who won the Man-of-the-Match award in the final.

There were misgivings about England's tour of Pakistan from the start, but few imagined the disasters and damage that lay ahead when the party assembled at the beginning of November. The excitement and clamour of the World Cup had scarcely died down before the round of Tests and one-day internationals began again. England were rejuvenated by the arrival of Capel, Nick Cook, French, Russell, Fairbrother and Dilley, for three separate parties had been selected for England's winter programme, although as England had been struggling for success for some time, it seemed ambitious to suggest that they could field three sides of international standard. The first disquieting note of the tour was the poor standard of the practice facilities that were made available to the tourists, and, perhaps, in analysing the events a few weeks later, one should always consider the attitude that seemed to apply towards the England party from the outset.

14, 15 and 16 November 1987

at Pindi Club Ground, Rawalpindi

England XI 385 (R.T. Robinson 118, C.W.J. Athey 101 retired hurt, D.J. Capel 67)

WILLS CUP FINAL – PAKISTAN INTERNATIONAL AIRLINES v. UNITED BANK
25 September 1987 at Qaddafi Stadium, Lahore

UNITED BANK				PIA			
Mudassar Nazar	c Asif Mohammad, b Rashid Khan	4		Rizwan-uz-Zaman	c Ashraf Ali, b Sikhander	1	
Kamal Merchant	retired hurt	0		Shoaib Mohammad†	c Ashraf Ali, b Sikhander	9	
Mansoor Akhtar	c Anil Dalpat, b Wasim Haider	45		Asif Mohammad	c Sikhander, b Saleem Jaffer	9	
Ali Zia	c Asif Mohammad, b Zahid Ahmed	64		Asif Mujtaba	run out	1	
Saeed Anwar	c Asif Mujtaba, b Zahid Ahmed	51		Zahid Ahmed	c Sikhander, b Mudassar	46	
Mahmood Rasheed	b Wasim Akram	3		Aamer Malik	c sub (Saifullah), b Tauseef	67	
Ashraf Ali*	lbw, b Wasim Akram	13		Anil Dalpat*	b Masood Anwar	28	
Masood Anwar	c Asif Mujtaba, b Rizwan	5		Wasim Akram	run out	2	
Tauseef Ahmed	not out	1		Wasim Haider	not out	25	
Sikhander Bakht†	run out	0		Rashid Khan	not out	9	
Saleem Jaffer	not out	0		Feroze Mehdi			
Extras	lb 9, w 9, nb 2	20		Extras	b1, lb 6, w 6, nb 2	15	
(49 overs)	(for 8 wkts)	206		(47.4 overs)	(for 8 wkts)	212	

	O	M	R	W		O	M	R	W
Wasim Akram	9	1	32	2	Sikhander Bakht	8	2	17	1
Rashid Khan	7	2	21	1	Saleem Jaffer	9	1	34	2
Asif Mohammad	9	1	34	–	Mudassar Nazar	10	–	43	1
Wasim Haider	7	–	24	1	Masood Anwar	4.4	–	45	1
Zahid Ahmed	10	–	50	2	Tauseef Ahmed	10	–	37	1
Shoaib Mohammad	1	–	8	–	Saeed Anwar	6	1	29	–
Asif Mujtaba	3	–	16	–					
Rizwan-uz-Zaman	3	–	12	1					

FALL OF WICKETS
1–8, 2–77, 3–165, 4–179, 5–199, 6–203, 7–205, 8–206

FALL OF WICKETS
1–2, 2–17, 3–19, 4–26, 5–135, 6–155, 7–165, 8–200

Umpires: Khizar Hayat & Mahboob Shah

PIA won by 2 wickets

BCCP President's XI 318 for 8 (Asif Mujtaba 157, Asif Mohammad 56, E.E. Hemmings 4 for 70)

Match drawn

The first day of the tour saw England reach 274 for 3 with Robinson and Athey sharing a second-wicket stand of 154. Athey completed his hundred on the second day and retired hurt. From that point it was downhill all the way for the tourists, who suffered more than seven hours in the field. Asif Mujtaba gave further evidence that he possesses the ability to become one of the world's great batsmen.

First One-Day International
PAKISTAN v. ENGLAND

There is a Greek fable that tells of a countryman who had a goose that laid golden eggs and that, greedy to become rich more quickly and to get the whole stock of eggs at once, the countryman killed the goose, but rather than finding himself rich, he found that he had lost everything. There was a time when the fable was known by every schoolboy and schoolgirl, but it is unknown, seemingly, to those who administer and schedule international cricket. If they know the fable, they have not heeded its warning, for how else, in the wake of a highly successful and emotionally exhausting World Cup competition, could they

Rawalpindi. BCCP President's XI v the English tourists. (Adrian Murrell/Allsport)

FIRST ONE-DAY INTERNATIONAL – PAKISTAN v. ENGLAND
18 November 1987 at Qaddafi Stadium, Lahore

PAKISTAN			
Rameez Raja	c Gatting, b Capel		38
Shoaib Mohammad	c French, b Foster		11
Saleem Malik	run out		30
Ijaz Ahmed	c Gooch, b Hemmings		17
Mudassar Nazar	c Fairbrother, b Foster		10
Saleem Yousuf*	c French, b Hemmings		22
Manzoor Elahi	b Emburey		14
Wasim Akram	b Emburey		5
Abdul Qadir†	run out		7
Zahid Ahmed	c and b Emburey		0
Saleem Jaffer	not out		2
Extras	b 1, lb 5, w 2, nb 2		10
(41.3 overs)			166

	O	M	R	W
De Freitas	7	1	19	–
Foster	8	1	37	2
Capel	9	–	43	1
Emburey	8.3	2	17	3
Hemmings	9	1	44	2

FALL OF WICKETS
1–25, 2–62, 3–96, 4–102, 5–132, 6–138, 7–154, 8–163, 9–163

ENGLAND			
G.A. Gooch	b Abdul Qadir		43
B.C. Broad	c Manzoor Elahi, b Wasim Akram		1
M.W. Gatting†	lbw, b Abdul Qadir		16
C.W.J. Athey	lbw, b Wasim Akram		20
D.J. Capel	run out		8
N.H. Fairbrother	b Zahid Ahmed		25
J.E. Emburey	c Ijaz Ahmed, b Zahid Ahmed		4
P.A.J. De Freitas	not out		14
N.A. Foster	lbw, b Wasim Akram		0
B.N. French*	not out		7
E.E. Hemmings			
Extras	b 13, lb 10, w 4, nb 2		29
(44.3 overs)	(for 8 wkts)		167

	O	M	R	W
Wasim Akram	9	–	25	3
Saleem Jaffer	3	–	18	–
Mudassar Nazar	9	1	19	–
Manzoor Elahi	2	–	12	–
Abdul Qadir	8.3	2	32	2
Zahid Ahmed	9	1	24	2
Shoaib Mohammad	4	–	14	–

FALL OF WICKETS
1–5, 2–61, 3–74, 4–89, 5–120, 6–127, 7–137, 8–140

Umpires: Shakeel Khan & Shakoor Rana

Man of the Match: J.E. Emburey

England won by 2 wickets

SECOND ONE-DAY INTERNATIONAL – PAKISTAN v. ENGLAND
20 November 1987 at National Stadium, Karachi

ENGLAND			
G.A. Gooch	st Zulqarnain, b Abdul Qadir		142
B.C. Broad	c Manzoor Elahi, b Abdul Qadir		22
M.W. Gatting†	run out		21
N.H. Fairbrother	b Zahid Ahmed		2
D.J. Capel	not out		50
J.E. Emburey	c Manzoor Elahi, b Abdul Qadir		1
P.A.J. De Freitas	b Mohsin Kamal		0
N.A. Foster	not out		5
C.W.J. Athey			
B.N. French*			
E.E. Hemmings			
Extras	b 3, lb 9, w 6, nb 2		20
(44 overs)	(for 6 wkts)		263

	O	M	R	W
Wasim Akram	4	1	9	–
Mohsin Kamal	9	–	57	1
Manzoor Elahi	3	–	19	–
Zahid Ahmed	7	–	37	1
Asif Mujtaba	3	–	25	–
Abdul Qadir	8	–	30	3
Saleem Malik	5	–	32	–
Shoaib Mohammad	5	–	42	–

FALL OF WICKETS
1–70, 2–135, 3–140, 4–249, 5–251, 6–251

PAKISTAN			
Rameez Raja	obstructing the field		99
Shoaib Mohammad	run out		37
Saleem Malik	c Fairbrother, b Foster		35
Manzoor Elahi	run out		17
Abdul Qadir†	c Broad, b Foster		0
Ijaz Ahmed	c Athey, b Emburey		26
Wasim Akram	c Foster, b Emburey		9
Asif Mujtaba	b Capel		0
Zahid Ahmed	not out		3
Zulqarnain*			
Mohsin Kamal			
Extras	lb 7, w 7		14
(44 overs)	(for 8 wkts)		240

	O	M	R	W
De Freitas	9	1	35	–
Foster	9	–	47	2
Capel	8	1	41	1
Hemmings	9	–	45	–
Emburey	9	–	65	2

FALL OF WICKETS
1–77, 2–138, 3–172, 4–172, 5–214, 6–228, 7–230, 8–240

Umpires: Khizar Hayat & Mahboob Shah

Man of the Match: G.A. Gooch

England won by 23 runs

arrange three one-day internationals as the prelude to the Test series. This, surely, was a recipe for disaster, and so it proved.

Javed Miandad, named as successor to Imran as captain of Pakistan, decided to forgo the series, thereby showing his wisdom, and saved himself for the Test matches. Abdul Qadir took over the leadership of the home country, for whom Zahid Ahmed made his international début.

Qadir elected to bat first when he won the toss, but the batting proved to be rather pedestrian against some accurate bowling, Emburey and De Freitas excelling. Abdul Qadir hit the only six of the innings before being run out by Capel's direct throw. Gooch hit 61 in 15 overs, including 3 successive fours off Qadir, before he was bowled next ball. Gatting and Athey were more ponderous, and it was left to Fairbrother, 25 off 36 balls, to take England within sight of victory. Eventually it was the exuberance of De Freitas, who hit Qadir for a massive six, that gave England a stuttering win.

Saleem Yousuf in aggressive mood in the one-day international in Lahore. He sustained an injury in the match which was to keep him out of the rest of the series. (Adrian Murrell/Allsport)

Second One-Day International
PAKISTAN v. ENGLAND

Gooch's sixth and highest hundred in one-day internationals was the highlight of the second match, which, like the first, aroused little interest. Gooch hit 14 fours and batted for 183 minutes, facing 134 balls for his 142. He batted with a sense of calm and contentment which had not been with him in England for most of 1987. David Capel gave spirited support with 61 off 40 balls, including 3 sixes. He and Gooch added 109 in 13 overs.

Needing to score at six runs an over, Pakistan began well. Rameez and Shoiab put on 77 in 19 overs, and

---

THIRD ONE-DAY INTERNATIONAL – PAKISTAN v. ENGLAND
22 November 1987 at Shahi Bagh Stadium, Peshawar

ENGLAND					PAKISTAN			
G.A. Gooch	c Zulqarnain, b Mudassar		57		Rameez Raja	lbw, b Foster		5
B.C. Broad	b Shakeel Khan		66		Shoaib Mohammad	retired hurt		6
M.W. Gatting†	c Manzoor Elahi, b Abdul Qadir		53		Saleem Malik	b Cook		52
D.J. Capel	st Zulqarnain, b Tauseef Ahmed		25		Ijaz Ahmed	c Russell, b Cook		15
J.E. Emburey	run out		3		Mudassar Nazar	b Capel		1
P.A.J. De Freitas	c Shoaib, b Abdul Qadir		3		Manzoor Elahi	c Gooch, b Emburey		21
C.W.J. Athey	st Zulqarnain, b Abdul Qadir		6		Abdul Qadir†	c Russell, b De Freitas		21
N.H. Fairbrother	run out		1		Zulqarnain*	c Russell, b De Freitas		0
N.A. Foster	not out		2		Mohsin Kamal	b Foster		5
R.C. Russell*	not out		2		Tauseef Ahmed	not out		0
N.G.B. Cook					Shakeel Khan	b Foster		0
Extras	b 1, lb 7, w 5, nb 5		18		Extras	lb 3, w 3, nb 6		12
(45 overs)	(for 8 wkts)		236		(31.5 overs)			138

	O	M	R	W
Moshin Kamal	9	–	37	–
Shakeel Khan	9	–	50	1
Mudassar Nazar	9	–	33	1
Tauseef Ahmed	9	–	59	1
Abdul Qadir	9	–	49	3

	O	M	R	W
De Freitas	7	–	31	2
Foster	6.5	–	20	3
Cook	6	1	18	2
Capel	9	–	44	1
Emburey	3	–	22	1

FALL OF WICKETS
1–101, 2–168, 3–214, 4–221, 5–221, 6–231, 7–232, 8–234

FALL OF WICKETS
1–11, 2–34, 3–43, 4–78, 5–122, 6–126, 7–138, 8–138, 9–138

Umpires: Amanullah Khan & Javed Akhtar

Man of the Match: N.A. Foster

England won by 98 runs

Rameez and Saleem Malik 62 in 10. Ijaz hit fiercely, but once Wasim Akram was out, Pakistan's hopes of victory vanished.

Twenty-nine were needed from the last over, but the only interest was whether or not Rameez would reach his hundred. He needed two from the last ball, which he clipped to square leg. He ran one and the ball was returned to French by the time he had begun his second. French rolled the ball down the wicket, and Rameez, in fun one feels, intercepted it with his bat. England appealed, and he was given out 'obstructing the field'.

In the first match, when Saleem Yousuf had dislocated a thumb, an injury that was to keep him out of the Test series, England had refused Pakistan permission to bring on a specialist wicket-keeper as substitute. The appeal against Rameez hardly seemed necessary, and although none complained at the time, it set the tone of the relationships between the two sides for much of the remainder of the tour.

Third One-Day International
PAKISTAN v. ENGLAND

International débuts for 'Jack' Russell, long overdue, and Shakil Khan were the most significant features of a match which saw Pakistan play rather dispiritedly. England built on a firm foundation and lost wickets quickly only in the final mad rush, three falling in the last over.

Pakistan were never in touch, and a bruised shoulder sustained by Gatting was England's only worry.

First Test Match
PAKISTAN v. ENGLAND

The Test series began against a darkening backdrop. The England team had shown obvious unrest over the standard of umpiring in the one-day internationals while Sarfraz

Gooch is bowled by Abdul Qadir's googly, the first of the great leg-spinner's nine wickets, first Test, Lahore. (Adrian Murrell/Allsport)

Neil Foster restores some sanity to the England batting in the first Test. (Adrian Murrell/Allsport)

Nawaz, the former Northants and Pakistan quick bowler, had launched a violent attack on Bird and Shepherd, the English umpires, accusing them of incompetence, or worse, in the way that they had handled the World Cup semi-final between Pakistan and Australia. He, and others, believed that decisions they had given against Pakistan, notably Dean Jones, not out, and Imran Khan, out, had cost the home country the match and that both decisions were bad ones.

The wicket at Lahore had twice been used in World Cup matches in the three weeks before the first Test match, and Pakistan, sensing spin, recalled Iqbal Qasim and played three spinners. Gatting, who was delighted to win the toss, opted for a more balanced attack with Cook partnering Emburey in the spin department.

Gooch and Broad started very quietly against Wasim Akram and Mudassar Nazar, but the 10 overs of seam were a lull before a storm of slow bowling. After 45 minutes Abdul Qadir bowled his first over, the 11th of the match. In his third over, he deceived Gooch with a googly. The batsman played back and lost his off stump.

Robinson's limitations had become increasingly obvious since the beginning of the World Cup and now he plunged gropingly forward until he pushed at a wider leg-break and

Mudassar Nazar hits a four and French and Emburey follow the flight of the ball as Robinson leaps for his life. (Adrian Murrell/Allsport)

was caught behind. Two balls later, Gatting was out. He played a wretched and reckless sweep at a ball pitched on off stump, missed and was given out lbw. Some, not all, believed that the ball would have missed off stump. Gatting did, and he remained too long at the crease, showing obvious dissent. One thing is certain, for the shot he played, whether he was out or not, Gatting deserved to be.

Athey was out in the same manner as Gatting although he had little reason to feel aggrieved, and England were 44 for 4 at lunch. Five overs into the afternoon, Tauseef had Capel taken at silly mid-off, bat and pad, although the England camp, with some justification, believed it to be only pad.

De Freitas played with some restraint before trying to pull and missing, and Emburey was bowled off his pads. Throughout these traumas Broad had batted with the utmost resolution. He played straight, never lost concentration and picked up his runs with nudges and taps. He had just completed a thousand runs in Test cricket when he popped a catch to silly mid-off. At 94 for 8, England were sinking fast.

That they did not sink altogether was due to Foster and French, who decided to give the ball a welt. Foster went down the wicket and hit Qadir high over mid-wicket for six, Qasim was hit for 10 off two balls, and the ninth-wicket stand raised 57 in 18 overs. The last wicket added 24 before Cook edged Qadir to slip to give the leg-spinner his ninth wicket for 56 runs. This was his best return in Test cricket, and the best performance by any bowler against England in a Test match. He had perplexed all the England batsmen with a display of spin bowling that, in variety and intelligent deception, can never have been bettered. His two types of googly supplement an accurately controlled and flighted leg-break, a flipper and a top-spinner which leave batsmen constantly at odds with themselves. He was immeasurably superior to any other cricketer in the match, and when the events which sullied

the game are, hopefully, long forgotten his performance will continue to shine bright.

Pakistan were 13 for 0 at the close, and next morning, Mudassar and Rameez, thriving on some wayward bowling by Foster and De Freitas early on, took their stand to 71 in 70 minutes. De Freitas was particularly erratic, and his first four overs cost 28 runs, including three no-balls. Emburey brought some calm when he spun successive deliveries from outside off stump to bowl Rameez and Saleem Malik, but Javed and Mudassar engaged in a vital stand against bowling which never suggested potency nor threatened.

Javed started shakily, but was soon smothering, flicking and cutting so that on a pitch which was dead Pakistan conjured three runs an over, a very healthy rate of scoring. Javed was dropped by French, who had a very bad game behind the stumps. Gooch also put down a chance. Capel did not bowl and most of the bowling looked innocuous. Javed and Mudassar added 142 before Javed drove on the up to extra cover.

Mudassar reached his 10th Test century in his 100th Test innings, a most valuable and praiseworthy effort. He is never a brisk scorer, but he is not a dull batsman, he has too much character for that. His 120 came off 257 balls and included 18 fours. He fell to the second new ball when Foster forced him back on his stumps. Pakistan closed at 277 for 4.

A breezy innings from Wasim Akram and some batting from Abdul Qadir which suggested his right to be considered an all-rounder were the sparks of the third day's earlier part, but the Pakistan innings ended on a note of controversy. Qadir moved down the wicket to Cook, missed and French took the bails off. Qadir was quickly given out stumped by umpire Shakeel Khan although it was apparent that French had missed the wicket at his first attempt and that Qadir had regained his crease by the time

England look aggrieved, but Javed Miandad trots through for a run as he and Mudassar add 142 for the third wicket, first Test. (Adrian Murrell/Allsport)

the bails were removed. Qadir turned to the umpire in supplication. Gatting roared with laughter at the protest, and the players left the field in some altercation.

The England innings started well enough, but, at 23, came the incident that was to sour the rest of the winter. Iqbal Qasim spun a ball past Broad's bat. Ashraf Ali

Abdul Qadir All-Rounder. (Adrian Murrell/Allsport)

caught it, and he and the close fielders leapt in appeal. Shakeel Khan immediately raised his finger. Broad spread his arms wide in indication that he had not touched the ball, shook his head in disagreement and refused to leave the wicket. He was there for more than half a minute before Gooch walked down the pitch to him and ushered him back to the pavilion.

It is possible that Broad saw his dismissal as the culmination of a long line of injustices, most of which had been suffered at the hands of English umpires in the previous summer. That may be, but he was very wrong in his action, and the fault did not end there.

Peter Lush, the tour manager, made a statement. He condemned Broad's action and said that the player had been reprimanded, but he was neither fined nor punished in any way. Lush went on to say that the incident was a culmination of frustrations that had been built up over the first three days of the match. He added that he thought that for the benefit of the game Test cricket should be handled by neutral umpires. Pakistan had advocated this some years earlier, but the TCCB was opposed to the idea.

The failure of the England management and captain to respond positively to Broad's breach of acceptable conduct was the gravest of errors. Whatever the circumstances, whatever the provocation, cricket operates on the well-understood principle that the umpire's decision is final, and his decision must be accepted without comment

FIRST TEST MATCH – PAKISTAN v. ENGLAND
25, 26, 27 and 28 November 1987 at Qaddafi Stadium, Lahore

ENGLAND

	FIRST INNINGS		SECOND INNINGS	
G.A. Gooch	b Abdul Qadir	12	c Ashraf Ali, b Iqbal	15
B.C. Broad	c Asif, b Qadir	41	c Ashraf Ali, b Iqbal	13
R.T. Robinson	c Ashraf Ali, b Qadir	6	lbw, b Abdul Qadir	1
M.W. Gatting†	lbw, b Abdul Qadir	0	lbw, b Abdul Qadir	23
C.W.J. Athey	lbw, b Abdul Qadir	5	c Ashraf Ali, b Tauseef	2
D.J. Capel	c Asif, b Tauseef	0	(7) c Javed, b Qadir	0
P.A.J. De Freitas	lbw, b Abdul Qadir	5	(8) c Tauseef, b Iqbal	15
J.E. Emburey	b Abdul Qadir	0	(9) not out	38
N.A. Foster	lbw, b Abul Qadir	39	(10) c sub (Akram Raza), b Tauseef	1
B.N. French*	not out	38	(6) lbw, b Abdul Qadir	9
N.G.B. Cook	c Javed, b Abdul Qadir	10	b Tauseef Ahmed	5
Extras	b 4, lb 14, nb 1	19	b 4, lb 4	8
		175		130

	O	M	R	W	O	M	R	W
Wasim Akram	14	4	32	–	2	–	6	–
Mudassar Nazar	5	3	9	–	1	–	4	–
Abdul Qadir	37	13	56	9	36	14	45	4
Tauseef Ahmed	23	9	38	1	20.2	7	28	3
Iqbal Qasim	4	–	22	–	20	10	39	3

PAKISTAN

	FIRST INNINGS	
Mudassar Nazar	lbw, Foster	120
Rameez Raja	b Emburey	35
Saleem Malik	b Emburey	0
Javed Miandad†	c Gooch, b Cook	65
Ijaz Ahmed	b De Freitas	44
Asif Mujtaba	b Foster	7
Ashraf Ali*	b Emburey	7
Wasim Akram	c Broad, b Cook	40
Abdul Qadir	st French, b Cook	38
Iqbal Qasim	run out	1
Tauseef Ahmed	not out	5
Extras	b 18, lb 8, nb 4	30
		392

	O	M	R	W
De Freitas	29	7	84	1
Foster	23	6	58	2
Emburey	48	16	109	3
Cook	31	10	87	3
Capel	3	–	28	–

FALL OF WICKETS
1–22, 2–36, 3–36, 4–44, 5–55, 6–70, 7–81, 8–94, 9–151
1–23, 2–24, 3–38, 4–43, 5–66, 6–70, 7–73, 8–105, 9–116

FALL OF WICKETS
1–71, 2–71, 3–213, 4–272, 5–290, 6–301, 7–328, 8–360, 9–370

Umpires: Amanullah Khan & Shakeel Khan

Pakistan won by an innings and 87 runs

ABOVE: *The moment the tour turned sour. Ashraf Ali and his colleagues leap in appeal. Broad stands his ground. (Adrian Murrell/Allsport)*

RIGHT: *Gatting, lbw to Abdul Qadir. Ashraf Ali is again excited. (Adrian Murrell/Allsport)*

or dissent. When the acceptance of that principle breaks down then cricket itself will cease to exist.

There was a time when cricket led the world in standards of behaviour and in the way in which the game was disciplined and conducted. In Pakistan, November 1987, that leadership was surrendered. Cricket must now learn from golf and rugby in how laws are applied and decisions are accepted. The way back may not be as easy as it seems.

The conflict in Pakistan had its roots deep in events of the past decade when Pakistan themselves believe that they have been treated with a sort of colonial contempt by the TCCB, particularly with regard to the handling of their justifiable queries regarding the standing of English umpires in matches against them. They still believe that David Constant cost them the Test series in 1982. They resent what they see as the arrogance that only in England is the game run and judged properly. In short, the atmosphere was sour before this unhappy series began, nor were matters improved by the instant clamour to bring home the English party because they were being cheated. Human error and fallibility are not to be confused with dishonesty.

Robinson was lbw to a huge googly. Gooch was adjudged caught behind as Broad had been, and he accepted the decision ruefully. Athey was caught off his glove. England closed at 47 for 4, and the next day they succumbed to the inevitable with Abdul Qadir taking three more wickets.

There were more decisions which the English camp felt were unfair, and the entire England party, players and management, was absent from the post-match presentation ceremony. This was a disgraceful discourtesy.

There was more than one county chairman and county secretary who believed that Broad should have been sent home for his display of dissent, and in taking the course that they did, the England management lost the chance of asserting dignity, authority and diplomacy. The error was further compounded by Gatting's post-match statement when he said, 'The bad decisions went against us by 10–1. I've never seen it so blatant over here. To put an inexperienced umpire into the first Test on a turning pitch, and without even first informing us, smacks of something.'

His frankness was, to say the least, unwise, and there were many professionals in England, some of whom had played Test cricket in the Indian subcontinent, who were appalled by the attitudes that were being adopted, so bereft of tact were they. England lost more than a Test match at Lahore.

2, 3 and 4 December 1987

at Zafar Ali Stadium, Sahiwal

England XI 279 (R.T. Robinson 51, Mushtaq Ahmed 6 for 81) and 222 for 5 dec (R.T. Robinson 76, N.H. Fairbrother 66)
Punjab Chief Minister's XI 215 (Zahoor Elahi 62) and 21 for 3

Match drawn

A 17-year-old leg-spinner, Mushtaq Ahmed, returned the best figures of his embryo career and on the opening day gave more evidence of England's vulnerability to leg-spin bowling.

Iqbal Qasim – a successful domestic season and surprisingly, and again successfully, recalled to the Test side. (Adrian Murrell/Allsport)

Second Test Match
PAKISTAN v. ENGLAND

The wounds of the first Test had not healed when the second began in Faisalabad. Indeed, there were those who believed that the Pakistan Cricket Board were being deliberately provocative in naming Shakoor Rana as one of the umpires for the match at Faisalabad, for he was a man with a record which suggested an unhappy relationship with touring sides.

Hemmings for De Freitas was the only change in the England side, which was very hard on Russell, whom one felt should have replaced French. Pakistan made two changes. Aamer Malik won his first cap at the expense of Wasim Akram, who had a fever, and Shoaib Mohammad came in for Asif Mujtaba. One would question this last selection, for Asif is a young man of outstanding talent who needs encouragement and confidence.

Gatting won the toss and was happy to bat on a wicket which looked as if it would crumble before the end of the five days. The Pakistan opening attack was gentle and brief, and the spinners were soon in action. Gooch and Broad gave their side a solid start, and the partnership was broken only when Gooch was given out caught bat and pad although his bat seemed far from the ball. In exemplary manner, Gooch left the wicket with an air of dignified resignation. Athey, too, seemed to have the worst of a decision, but since the World Cup Athey had looked pained at every decision he received. Gatting, on the other hand, survived a confident appeal for lbw against Iqbal Qasim and seemed fortunate to do so. His response was to play a belligerent innings which put the spinners firmly in their place and gave England the advantage.

Gatting was at his pugnacious best. In two hours, off 81 balls, he hit 79 and 14 times struck the ball to the fence. While he provided the aggression, Broad played with a soundness which gave the England innings backbone. He reached his fourth Test hundred with his 13th boundary in the penultimate over of the day, and England finished happily on 254 for 4.

On the second morning, in less than 26 overs, the last six England wickets fell for the addition of only 38 runs. Iqbal

SECOND TEST MATCH – PAKISTAN v. ENGLAND
7, 8, 9, 11 and 12 December 1987 at Iqbal Stadium, Faisalabad

ENGLAND

	FIRST INNINGS		SECOND INNINGS	
G.A. Gooch	c Aamer, b Iqbal	28	lbw, b Abdul Qadir	65
B.C. Broad	b Tauseef Ahmed	116	st Ashraf, b Qadir	14
C.W.J. Athey	c Aamer, b Qadir	27	b Mudassar	20
M.W. Gatting†	b Abdul Qadir	79	c Qadir, b Iqbal	8
R.T. Robinson	c Ashraf, b Qadir	2	(8) not out	7
N.G.B. Cook	c Ashaf, b Iqbal	2		
D.J. Capel	c Aamer, b Qadir	1	lbw, b Iqbal	2
J.E. Emburey	st Ashraf, b Iqbal	15	(5) not out	10
N.A. Foster	c Aamer, b Iqbal	0	(6) c Javed, b Qadir	0
B.N. French*	st Ashraf, b Iqbal	2		
E.E. Hemmings	not out	1		
Extras	b 10, lb 5, w 1, nb 3	19	b 1, lb 9, nb 1	11
		292	(for 6 wkts, dec)	137

PAKISTAN

	FIRST INNINGS		SECOND INNINGS	
Mudassar Nazar	c French, b Foster	1	b Cook	4
Rameez Raja	c Gooch, b Foster	12	not out	13
Saleem Malik	b Cook	60	not out	28
Javed Miandad†	b Emburey	19		
Ijaz Ahmed	c Robinson, b Emburey	11		
Shoaib Mohammad	b Emburey	0		
Aamer Malik	c French, b Foster	5		
Ashraf Ali*	c French, b Foster	4		
Abdul Qadir	c Gooch, b Cook	38		
Iqbal Qasim	lbw, b Hemmings	24		
Tauseef Ahmed	not out	5		
Extras	lb 5, nb 7	12	b 4, lb 1, nb 1	6
		191	(for 1 wkt)	51

	O	M	R	W	O	M	R	W
Aamer Malik	5	–	19	–	3	–	20	–
Mudassar Nazar	3	–	8	–	12	1	33	1
Abdul Qadir	42	7	105	4	15	3	45	3
Tauseef Ahmed	28	9	62	1				
Iqbal Qasim	35.2	7	83	5	10	2	29	2
Shoaib Mohammad	1	1	0	–				

	O	M	R	W	O	M	R	W
Foster	18	4	43	4	3	–	4	–
Capel	7	1	23	–				
Hemmings	18	5	35	1	7	3	16	–
Emburey	21	8	49	3	2	–	3	–
Cook	20.3	10	37	2	9	3	15	1
Gooch					2	1	4	–
Broad					1	–	4	–

FALL OF WICKETS
1–73, 2–124, 3–241, 4–249, 5–258, 6–259, 7–288, 8–288, 9–288
1–47, 2–102, 3–107, 4–115, 5–115, 6–120

FALL OF WICKETS
1–11, 2–22, 3–58, 4–77, 5–77, 6–115, 7–122, 8–123, 9–175
1–15

Umpires: Khizar Hayat & Shakoor Rana

Match drawn

Qasim's left-arm spin gained the greatest reward, but the events of the second day served most to underline the merit of the innings played by Gatting and Broad. The Notts left-hander was ninth out, having batted nearly seven hours for his 116.

England gained a bonus when Foster picked up two wickets. Mudassar was taken low down by French, and Rameez was beautifully taken at second slip. Saleem was dropped by Gatting off Capel, but Emburey accounted for Javed and then for Ijaz and Shoaib with successive deliveries. There was altercation between Athey and the umpire Shakoor Rana when Robinson had an appeal for a catch disallowed, and Gatting made it loudly obvious that he believed that different standards were being applied to the two sides by the umpires.

Saleem battled bravely for Pakistan on a wicket that was offering more and more assistance to the spinners, and he was facing Hemmings in what would have been the penultimate over of the day when Gatting gestured that he wanted square leg up to save the single and leave Aamer to face the last over. The gesture was made behind his back, but Gatting had first informed Saleem of what he was doing. Seeing the gesture, umpire Rana called 'dead ball' and remonstrated with Gatting. A heated argument took place. Gatting said that he was accused of cheating. Rana insists that Gatting swore at him. Gatting stated that Rana swore first. The tedious events which followed were a disgrace to the game and those who were the participants and need occupy us little. On the third day, Shakoor Rana refused to take the field without a written apology. There was a state of impasse. Raman Subba Row and A.C. Smith flew from England in an attempt to save the tour and to restore some semblance of diplomatic relations. Eventually, Gatting gave a written apology, and, a day having been lost, the game was resumed, but with neither interest nor any hope of a result. This was the saddest of all Test matches.

Third Test Match
PAKISTAN v. ENGLAND

Controversy continued in that Pakistan initially named Shakeel Khan as one of the umpires for the final Test of the series, but, after protest, Khizar Hayat was brought in to partner Mahboob Shah. Indisputably, these are Pakistan's two best umpires, and two of the best in the world, but one must question why, in 1987, when Pakistan had protested so vehemently from the start of the tour that they did not want David Constant to stand in any of the Tests against them, the TCCB provocatively appointed him as one of three umpires who stood in two of the five Tests.

England were without Foster and Jarvis, who were unfit, Foster's knee injury necessitating an operation, and neither Capel nor Emburey were fully fit when they took the field. Robinson and Hemmings were omitted, and

Fairbrother and Dilley made their first appearances of the series. De Freitas returned after injury.

Gatting won the toss and was happy to bat first, not so happy about what was soon to happen. Gooch was caught at the wicket off Wasim Akram, who bowled a fine opening burst, the umpires debating whether or not the ball carried to the keeper, and Broad was lbw offering no stroke to an in-swinger. Athey lost his middle stump to a googly first ball after lunch, and Gatting, heaving to leg, played on. Fairbrother, inevitably, fell to a short pitched ball, and by mid-afternoon, England were 85 for 6, De Freitas also having fallen to Abdul Qadir, who had produced a spell of 3 for 6 in six overs and managed an argument with a spectator.

Sanity was restored by Capel and Emburey. Capel showed great resolve, and Emburey batted with his urban rustic charm. He reached fifty with a six off Abdul Qadir, and, in all, batted for 164 minutes, hitting 8 fours as well as his six. He and Capel added 114 in 41 overs. Capel was unbeaten at the close, which came with England on 222 for 7.

Capel and French were not separated on the second morning until the last ball before lunch, when French was very well caught, left-handed at slip by Javed. French had batted well and had hit Saleem Jaffer for six as well as hitting 3 fours.

When Nick Cook was lbw to Abdul Qadir without offering a stroke Capel was on 97, and only Dilley remained to offer him support towards his maiden Test hundred, but it was not to be. Capel himself was deceived by a Qadir googly and bowled for 98.

Mudassar went quickly, but Rameez and Saleem scored at a furious rate, and Pakistan were 100 for 1 off 25 overs. Then four wickets fell quickly. Javed offered no shot and was leg before. Ijaz was run out third ball. Rameez gave himself room to cut and clipped the ball to the wicket-keeper.

Pakistan's revival came on the third day when, after being 146 for 6, they were well served by Aamer Malik, playing only his second Test, and by Abdul Qadir, in particular. They were aided by some quite dreadful bowling with the second new ball by Dilley and De Freitas, who conceded 49 runs off nine overs, and by some lax fielding. Qadir was dropped at second slip when eight, and Cook failed to accept a return catch from Aamer Malik, who was then on 72. Wasim Akram had already hit 2 sixes and 3 fours before Abdul Qadir joined Aamer.

Having bamboozled England with the ball, Qadir now set about them with the bat, hitting 4 sixes and 6 fours in his highest Test score, 61, which occupied 132 minutes. He was finally yorked by David Capel, the Northamptonshire all-rounder's first Test wicket. Pakistan ended the day on 345 for 8, with Aamer Malik 91 not out.

He richly deserved a century for his stay of nearly seven

THIRD TEST MATCH – PAKISTAN v. ENGLAND
16, 17, 18, 20 and 21 December 1987 at National Stadium, Karachi

ENGLAND

	FIRST INNINGS		SECOND INNINGS	
G.A. Gooch	c Ashraf Ali, b Wasim	12	b Mudassar	93
B.C. Broad	lbw, b Wasim Akram	7	lbw, b Abdul Qadir	13
C.W.J. Athey	b Abdul Qadir	26	c Ashraf, b Jaffer	12
M.W. Gatting†	b Abdul Qadir	18	lbw, b Saleem Jaffer	0
N.H. Fairbrother	c sub (Asif Mujtaba), b Jaffer	3	c sub (Asif Mujtaba), b Qadir	1
D.J. Capel	b Abdul Qadir	98	c Iqbal, b Qadir	24
P.A.J. De Freitas	b Abdul Qadir	12	(9) lbw, b Qadir	6
J.E. Emburey	c Qadir, b Jaffer	70	(7) not out	74
B.N. French*	c Javed, b Malik	31	(8) lbw, b Jaffer	0
N.G.B. Cook	lbw, b Abdul Qadir	2	b Abdul Qadir	14
G.R. Dilley	not out	0	not out	0
Extras	lb 8, w 1, nb 6	15	b 9, lb 5, w 1, nb 6	21
		294	(for 9 wkts)	258

PAKISTAN

	FIRST INNINGS	
Mudassar Nazar	lbw, b De Freitas	6
Rameez Raja	c French, b Cook	50
Saleem Malik	c Gatting, b De Frietas	55
Javed Miandad†	lbw, b Emburey	4
Ijaz Ahmed	run out	0
Aamer Malik	not out	98
Ashraf Ali	c French, b Dilley	12
Wasim Akram	c French, b De Freitas	37
Abdul Qadir	b Capel	61
Iqbal Qasim	c French, b De Freitas	11
Saleem Jaffer	lbw, b De Freitas	0
Extras	lb 11, nb 8	19
		353

	O	M	R	W	O	M	R	W
Wasim Akram	24.1	3	64	2				
Saleem Jaffer	23.5	6	74	2	42	9	79	3
Abdul Qadir	49.4	15	88	5	55	16	98	5
Iqbal Qasim	18	4	51	–	27	10	44	–
Mudassar Nazar	1	1	0		4	3	2	1
Saleem Malik	5	2	9	1	7	2	14	–
Aamer Malik					2	–	7	–

	O	M	R	W
Dilley	21	2	102	1
De Freitas	23.5	3	86	5
Emburey	53	24	90	1
Cook	33	12	56	1
Capel	3	–	8	1

FALL OF WICKETS
1–20, 2–41, 3–55, 4–72, 5–72, 6–85, 7–199, 8–274, 9–291
1–34, 2–54, 3–54, 4–61, 5–115, 6–175, 7–176, 8–187, 9–246

FALL OF WICKETS
1–18, 2–105, 3–110, 4–110, 5–122, 6–146, 7–222, 8–316, 9–349

Umpires: Khizar Hayat & Mahboob Shah

Match drawn

PAKISTAN v. ENGLAND – TEST MATCH AVERAGES

PAKISTAN BATTING

	M	Inns	NOs	Runs	HS	Av	100s	50s
Aamer Malik	2	2	1	103	98*	103.00		1
Saleem Malik	3	4	1	143	60	47.66		2
Abdul Qadir	3	3		137	61	45.66		1
Wasim Akram	2	2		77	40	38.50		
Rameez Raja	3	4	1	110	50	36.66		1
Mudassar Nazar	3	4		131	120	32.75	1	
Javed Miandad	3	3		88	65	29.33		1
Ijaz Ahmed	3	3		55	44	18.33		
Iqbal Qasim	3	3		36	24	12.00		
Ashraf Ali	3	3		23	12	7.66		

Played in two Tests: Tauseef Ahmed 5* & 5*
Played in one Test: Asif Mujtaba 7; Saleem Jaffer 0; Shoaib Mohammad 0

PAKISTAN BOWLING

	Overs	Mds	Runs	Wkts	Av	Best	10/m	5/inns
Abdul Qadir	234.4	68	437	30	14.56	9/56	2	3
Saleem Malik	12	4	23	1	23.00	1/9		
Tauseef Ahmed	71.2	25	128	5	25.60	3/28		
Iqbal Qasim	114.2	33	268	10	26.80	5/83		1
Mudassar Nazar	26	8	56	2	28.00	1/2		
Saleem Jaffer	65.5	15	153	5	30.60	3/79		
Wasim Akram	40.1	7	102	2	51.00	2/64		
Aamer Malik	10	–	46	0	–			

Bowled in one innings: Shoaib Mohammad 1–1–0–0

PAKISTAN FIELDING FIGURES

11 – Ashraf Ali (ct 8/st 3); 4 – Javed Miandad, Aamer Malik and Asif Mujtaba (two as sub); 2 – Abdul Qadir; 1 – Iqbal Qasim, Tauseef Ahmed and sub (Akram Raza)

ENGLAND BATTING

	M	Inns	NOs	Runs	HS	Av	100s	50s
J.E. Emburey	3	6	3	207	74*	69.00		2
G.A. Gooch	3	6		225	93	37.50		2
B.C. Broad	3	6		204	116	34.00	1	
M.W. Gatting	3	6		128	79	21.33		1
D.J. Capel	3	6		125	98	20.83		1
B.N. French	3	5	1	80	38*	20.00		
C.W.J. Athey	3	6		92	27	15.33		
N.A. Foster	2	4		40	39	10.00		
P.A.J. De Freitas	2	4		38	15	9.50		
N.G.B. Cook	3	5		33	14	6.60		
R.T. Robinson	2	4	1	16	7*	5.33		

Played in one test: N.H. Fairbrother 3 & 1; G.R. Dilley 0* & 0*; E.E. Hemmings 1*

ENGLAND BOWLING

	Overs	Mds	Runs	Wkts	Av	Best	10/m	5/inns
N.A. Foster	44	10	104	6	17.33	4/42		
N.G.B. Cook	93.3	35	195	7	27.86	3/87		
P.A.J. De Freitas	52.5	10	170	6	28.33	5/86		1
J.E. Emburey	124	48	251	7	35.85	3/49		
E.E. Hemmings	25	8	51	1	51.00	1/35		
D.J. Capel	13	1	59	1	59.00	1/8		

Bowled in one innings: G.R. Dilley 21–2–102–1; G.A. Gooch 2–1–4–0; B.C. Broad 1–0–4–0

ENGLAND FIELDING FIGURES

8 – B.N. French (ct 7/st 1); 3 – G.A. Gooch; 1 – B.C. Broad, M.W. Gatting and R.T. Robinson

hours, but De Freitas quickly took the last two wickets on the fourth morning to finish with his first five-wicket return in Test cricket and to leave Aamer unbeaten on 98.

England ended the day at 150 for 5, of which Gooch had made an unbeaten 79. Defeat seemed likely, but what was worse was that Broad, Athey and Gatting had all sought to question the decisions which were given against them. None of their complaints seemed justified and were, in any case, indefensible. One despaired for the future of the game if the attitudes of the England captain were to shape it.

On the last day, Abdul Qadir brought his total of wickets for the series to 30, an outstanding achievement by a brilliant bowler. Gooch and the redoubtable Emburey saved the game for England, and Nick Cook, too, stood firm for 2¼ hours.

It was later announced that every member of the England party was to receive £1000 bonus, usually given for 'good' behaviour, but was seen in this instance by many as being a bribe or a condition for having played out the series. It was a ridiculous award and a shame on those who awarded it. There were grave failings on the Pakistani side and there were injustices, but to condone the behaviour of some of the England players was to do the greatest disservice to the game of cricket.

BCCP Patron's Trophy

As in 1986–87, the 39 teams belonging to associations and

departments played in groups on a league basis with 12 sides from the eight groups qualifying for the knock-out stage of the competition which, unlike the preliminary part of the Trophy, was deemed to be first class. These 12 sides were also to be the teams who would be allowed to compete in the Quaid-e-Azam Trophy, Pakistan's senior competition. In favour of the Patron's Trophy was the fact that it was the only Pakistan domestic competition in which the leading players were able to participate. Of the Test side, only Imran Khan, Mudassar Nazar and the injured Wasim Akram did not appear in any of the matches, but the public response remained poor.

The qualifying leagues were not without their problems. Pakistan Education Boards failed to arrive for any of their matches in Group A, and the Pakistan Army failed to turn up for any of their matches in Group C. PNSC lodged a complaint in Group D, where Combined Universities had conceded the match against PACO when they refused to take the field on the second morning in protest against the behaviour of their own coach. PNSC's protest was upheld, and all points scored by and against Combined Universities were discounted. This put PNSC in second place in the group, and meant that Railways, like PACO, would not qualify for the Quaid-e-Azam Trophy.

Pre-Quarter Finals

24, 25 and 26 January 1988

at National Stadium, Karachi

Ijaz Ahmed – stirring cricket for Habib Bank in the BCCP Patron's Trophy, and for Pakistan. (Simon Bruty/Allsport)

PNSC 221 (Sajjad Akbar 72, Azeem Hafees 69) and 263 for 6 dec (Rameez Raja 102)
PIA 237 for 5 dec (Asif Mujtaba 98 not out) and 173 (Asif Mohammad 52, Sajjad Akbar 5 for 59)

PNSC won by 74 runs

at Bakhtiari Youth Centre Ground, Karachi

Multan 200 (Zakir Hussain 100) and 239 for 9 dec (Inzaman-ul-Haq 106)
Karachi Blues 223 for 6 dec (Zafar Ali 53) and 217 for 3 (Raees Ahmed 97, Sajid Khan 52 not out)

Karachi Blues won by 7 wickets

at LCCA Ground, Lahore

Lahore City 'A' 214 (Rizwan Qazi 52, Raja Sarfraz 5 for 73) and 257 for 7 dec (Wasim Ali 106, Rizwan Qazi 51)
Rawalpindi 227 for 4 (Jamal Siddiqi 74, Nadeem Abbasi 55) and 248 for 1 (Nadeem Abbasi 120 not out, Jamal Siddiqi 99 not out)

Rawalpindi won by 9 wickets

at Jinnah Stadium, Sialkot

Habib Bank 278 for 5 (Ijaz Ahmed 59) and 299 (Akram Raza 112, Kazim Mehdi 4 for 86)
HBFC 190 (Waheed Niazi 4 for 67) and 70 for 5

Match drawn – Habib Bank qualified on first-innings lead

In spite of winning the toss and batting first, PNSC trailed by 16 runs on the first innings to PIA, who were brilliantly served by Asif Mujtaba, playing with exciting freedom. His innings was countered by Rameez Raja, who shared a second-wicket stand of 121 with Qaiser Rasheed and declared, leaving PIA to make 248 to win. They passed 100 with only two wickets down, but their last seven wickets fell for 18 runs.

Multan batsmen Zakir Hussain and Inzaman-ul-Haq received little support, and Karachi Blues were always on top. Sajid Khan and Raees Ahmed began the Blues' second innings with a partnership of 132.

Rawalpindi overwhelmed Lahore City 'A'. Needing 245 to win, they lost Mohammad Akram at three, but Nadeem Abbasi and Jamal Siddiqi shared an unbroken partnership of 245.

There was no play before lunch on the opening day at Sialkot, where Habib Bank's large first-innings score was always likely to prove decisive in difficult conditions.

Quarter-Finals

28, 29 and 30 January 1988

at National Stadium, Karachi

Muslim Commercial Bank 263 for 7 (Babar Basharat 115, Salahuddin 72) and 323 (Babar Basharat 61, Ilyas Khan 61, Raees Ahmed 5 for 96)
Karachi Blues 206 (Raees Ahmed 64, Mohiuddin Khan 6 for 79) and 172 for 4 (Zafar Ahmed 62 not out)

Match drawn – Muslim Commercial Bank entered semi-final by virtue of first-innings lead

at LCCA Ground, Lahore

Rawalpindi 240 for 8 (Mujahid Hameed 56) and 278 for 8 dec (Mujahid Hameed 81, Zafar Abbasi 50, Sikhander Bakht 4 for 71)
United Bank 243 for 9 (Moin-ul-Atiq 66, Ashraf Ali 55, Raja Sarfraz 4 for 91) and 175 for 1 (Moin-ul-Atiq 102 not out)

Match drawn – United Bank entered semi-final by virtue of first-innings lead

at Qaddafi Stadium, Lahore

ADBP 203 (Raja Afaq 65, Mohsin Kamal 4 for 101, Abdullah Khan 4 for 49) and 361 (Atif Rauf 99, Ghaffar Kazmi 63, Mohsin Kamal 5 for 117)
PNSC 193 (Qasim Shera 4 for 32) and 332 (Farukh Baru 86, Mahmood Hamid 75)

ABPD won by 39 runs

at Jinnah Stadium, Sialkot

National Bank 135 for 8 (Nadeem Ghauri 6 for 39) and 83 for 1 (Sajid Ali 65)
Habib Bank 288 for 8 (Aamer Sohail 125)

National Bank conceded the match

Having chosen to bat on winning the toss, Muslim Commercial Bank lost three wickets for 52, but a stand of 152 between Babar Basharat and Salahuddin took them to a strong position, and their 263 for 7 off 65 overs always looked certain to be good enough for first-innings lead. So it proved, and when MCB batted again they adopted a policy of what we have, we hold. Karachi Blues captured nine wickets for 250, which still gave them a chance of victory, but Ilyas Khan, at number ten, hit a violent 61 as the last wicket realized 73, and the game was out of Karachi Blues' reach.

United Bank, too, won their place in the semi-final on first-innings lead, but they just squeezed through. Rawalpindi made 240 for 8 in 65 overs, and United Bank's ninth wicket went down at 224. Skipper Sikhander Bakht joined Masood Anwar to add 19 priceless runs, but it was not until the 65th over that they nudged into the lead. Rawalpindi never scored quickly enough in their second innings to give themselves a chance of victory, and Moin-ul-Atiq's century came when the game was dead and occasional bowlers in operation.

The only outright winners in the quarter-finals were ADBP, who recovered from a dreadful start to beat PNSC. Having been put in to bat, ADBP lost seven wickets for 81 runs. Raja Afaq and Qasim Shera added 107, and it was Qasim Shera, with his medium pace, who troubled PNSC most after Zakir Khan had made the early breakthroughs. With the wicket having lost its spite, ADBP moved to a massive score which was founded on the 99-run stand for the fifth wicket between Mansoor Rana and Atif Rauf and some fine later hitting by Ghaffar Kazmi. PNSC were left with the daunting task of scoring 372 to win at more than eight runs an over. In spite of Farukh Bari's excellent knock, they lost seven wickets for 169 at which point Mahmood Hamid came to the wicket and hit a whirlwind 75. Aided mostly by Amin Lakhani, he took PNSC to within 40 of their target before dying bravely.

At Sialkot, wet conditions delayed the start for more than two hours, and, put in to bat, National Bank struggled painfully on a difficult wicket. With conditions eased, Habib Bank took a first-innings lead of 153, thanks mainly to a fine century by Aamer Sohail. With no hope of forcing a result, National Bank conceded the match before the start of play on the final day.

Semi-Finals

2, 3, 4 and 5 February 1988

at National Stadium, Karachi

Habib Bank 378 for 6 (Agha Zahid 162, Ijaz Ahmed 125) and 568 (Aamer Sohail 112, Agha Zahid 108, Ijaz Ahmed 93, Tahir Rashid 86 not out)
Muslim Commercial Bank 180 (Naved Anjum 4 for 56) and 244 for 2 (Anwar-ul-Haq 102 not out, Asif Ali 102 not out)

Match drawn – Habib Bank qualified for final by virtue of first-innings lead

at LCCA Ground, Lahore

United Bank 314 (Mansoor Akhtar 132) and 421 (Moin-ul-Atiq 157, Shafiq Ahmed 88, Khatib Rizwan 4 for 109)
ADBP 186 and 201 (Masood Anwar 4 for 41)

United Bank won by 348 runs

For the semi-finals, matches were extended to four days, and the first-innings duration to 85 overs. Javed Miandad had no hesitation in batting first when he won the toss in Karachi, and his opening batsmen, Agha Zahid and Ijaz Ahmed, virtually won the match with an opening stand of 227. Saleem Malik and Javed himself plundered late runs, and Habib Bank reached a formidable 378 for 6. MCB came nowhere near matching this score, and by the end of the second day, which came with Habib Bank on 144 for 1 in their second innings, the game was out of their reach. Agha Zahid and Ijaz Ahmed had again begun with a century partnership, 133, but the stand was totally dominated by Ijaz, who scored 93 before being lbw to Nadeem Yousuf. Agha and Aamer took their second-wicket stand to 139 on the third day, and both batsmen completed hundreds, for Agha Zahid it was the second of the match. Some hard hitting by wicket-keeper Tahir Rasheed took Habib's innings into the last morning, and MCB were left to score 767 to win. Anwar-ul-Haq and Asif Ali shared an unbroken stand of 181 and reached centuries against some generous bowling.

An elegantly accomplished innings of 132 by Mansoor Akhtar lifted United Bank from the depths of 42 for 3 to 314 all out in the 85th over. This was a score that ADBP were unable to match as they plunged to 18 for 4 and continued to flounder against a varied attack. A magnificent innings of 157 by Moin-ul-Atiq, who shared a third-wicket stand of 164 with skipper Shafiq Ahmed, put United Bank in an impregnable position, and Masood Anwar ended ADBP's resistance as United Bank sailed into the final.

BCCP Patron's Trophy Final
HABIB BANK v. UNITED BANK

Play began half an hour late because of rain, and Javed asked United Bank to bat first when he won the toss. There was no immediate breakthrough, but, at 37, Moin-ul-Atiq, who had batted splendidly throughout the tournament, edged a ball from fast medium pacer Naved Anjum to Javed at slip. Naved struck again when he dismissed Saifullah and Shafiq Ahmed at the same score, and when three wickets fell for four runs United Bank, 78 for 6, were in total disarray. The experienced tail, with three players in the last four who had tasted Test cricket, wagged strongly, but Habib Bank were batting by the end of the first day and closed at 38 for the loss of Agha.

Aamer Sohail was out early on the second morning, but Ijaz and Saleem Malik gave a foretaste of the quality of batting to come. Javed was at his brilliant best and stroked his side to a lead of 90 on the first innings.

Having failed in the first innings, the 24-year-old Moin-ul-Atiq redeemed himself with a magnificent century and confirmed his selection for the party to tour West Indies. Apart from Shafiq Ahmed, he received little substantial support, and United Bank's second innings ended before lunch on the fourth morning. This left Habib Bank the best part of two days in which to score 247 to win the match.

Agha and Ijaz gave them a sound start, but there was a minor crisis when three wickets fell for 32 runs. Saleem

BCCP PATRON'S TROPHY FINAL – HABIB BANK v. UNITED BANK
8, 9, 10 and 11 February 1988 at Qaddafi Stadium, Lahore

UNITED BANK

	FIRST INNINGS		SECOND INNINGS	
Saifullah	lbw, b Naved Anjum	34	c Tahir, b Nadeem	8
Moin-ul-Atiq	c Javed, b Naved Anjum	10	c Saleem, b Waheed	134
Mansoor Akhtar	c Tahir, b Naved Anjum	14	c Tahir, b Abdul Qadir	34
Shafiq Ahmed†	c Ijaz, b Naved Anjum	0	run out	51
Ali Zia	b Abdul Qadir	9	c Tahir, b Naved Anjum	32
Ashraf Ali*	c Tahir, b Waheed	27	lbw, b Waheed	26
Kamal Merchant	b Naved Anjum	0	b Abdul Qadir	11
Tauseef Ahmed	c Tahir, b Waheed	34	lbw, b Abdul Qadir	0
Masood Anwar	c Saleem, b Qadir	34	c Javed, b Waheed	4
Sikhander Bakht	b Waheed	36	not out	13
Saleem Jaffer	not out	10	b Qadir	9
Extras	b 9, lb 7, w 1, nb 5	22	lb 8, nb 6	14
		230		336

	O	M	R	W	O	M	R	W
Waheed Niazi	21	5	56	3	20	2	80	3
Naved Anjum	22	5	74	5	18	4	62	1
Abdul Qadir	20.4	3	83	2	34.5	9	121	4
Nadeem Ghauri	1	–	1	–	25	9	41	1
Saleem Malik					4	–	13	–
Agha Zahid					3	1	11	–

HABIB BANK

	FIRST INNINGS		SECOND INNINGS	
Agha Zahid	c Ashraf Ali, b Saleem	16	c sub (Mahmood Rasheed), b Tauseef	32
Ijaz Ahmed	b Sikhander	62	b Tauseef Ahmed	35
Aamer Sohail	c Ali Zia, b Saleem	6	c sub (Mahmood Rasheed), b Tauseef	9
Saleem Malik	run out	32	st Ashraf, b Tauseef	95
Javed Miandad†	not out	144	not out	48
Anwar Miandad	st Ashraf, b Kamal	1		
Naved Anjum	b Kamal Merchant	15		
Tahir Rasheed*	b Kamal Merchant	14		
Abdul Qadir	run out	6	(6) not out	19
Nadeem Ghauri	not out	3		
Waheed Niazi				
Extras	b 4, lb 8, nb 9	21	lb 5, nb 7	12
(85 overs)	(for 8 wkts)	320	(for 4 wkts)	250

	O	M	R	W	O	M	R	W
Sikhander Bakht	15	–	63	1	5	–	23	–
Saleem Jaffer	12	–	59	2	4	1	29	–
Ali Zia	2	–	13	–				
Tauseef Ahmed	21	1	67	–	28	4	112	4
Kamal Merchant	25	2	55	3	7	2	18	–
Masood Anwar	10	–	51	–	23	2	59	–
Moin-ul-Atiq					0.1	–	4	–

FALL OF WICKETS
1–37, 2–59, 3–59, 4–74, 5–78, 6–78, 7–113, 8–147, 9–205
1–38, 2–98, 3–186, 4–246, 5–286, 6–305, 7–305, 8–309, 9–315

FALL OF WICKETS
1–22, 2–55, 3–104, 4–137, 5–153, 6–190, 7–260, 8–272
1–62, 2–83, 3–94, 4–220

Umpires: Khalid Aziz & Shakeel Khan

Habib Bank won by 6 wickets

Malik, however, was at his most exciting, and with Javed playing an anchor role, 126 were added for the fourth wicket. Saleem was stumped with victory in sight, but Abdul Qadir came in to play some lusty blows, and Habib Bank had won by six wickets with more than a day to spare. It was their first triumph in the Patron's Trophy for 10 years.

Quaid-e-Azam Trophy Championship

Once again the senior Pakistan domestic competition suffered in the absence of the country's leading players. The national side was preparing for the tour of the West Indies, and teams were even deprived of their leading young players who were in training for the Youth World Cup tournament in Australia.

The fixture congestion caused by the World Cup and the England tour meant that it was impossible to play the Quaid-e-Azam on a single-league basis as was customary as this would have meant 78 matches, so the participants were divided into two groups with the top two in each group meeting in the semi-finals. Twelve teams had qualified from the BCCP Patron's Trophy, but the new BCCP chief, Lt-Gen Zahid Ali Akbar, allowed Railways to be included as the 13th side on account of their long service to Pakistan cricket and because they had missed qualification through the cancellation of points won in matches against

Combined Universities in Group D. Railways were added to Group B, which gave that group seven teams as opposed to six in Group A.

15, 16, 17 and 18 February 1988

at National Stadium, Karachi

Habib Bank 277 for 6 (Azhar Khan 73 not out, Sajjad Akbar 5 for 31) and 298 for 3 dec (Shaukat Mirza 100 not out, Agha Zahid 69, Azhar Khan 67 not out)
PNSC 144 (Waheed Niazi 5 for 53) and 314 for 9 (Qaiser Rasheed 99, Mahmood Hamid 113 not out, Nadeem Ghauri 7 for 100)

Match drawn
Habib Bank 10 pts, PNSC 3 pts

at Bahawal Stadium, Bahawalpur

PIA 297 (Rizwan-uz-Zaman 53, Asif Mujtaba 51, Ilyas Khan 4 for 42, Farrukh Zaman 4 for 120) and 81 for 3
Muslim Commercial Bank 104 (Asif Mujtaba 6 for 25, Tanvir Ali 4 for 33) and 272 (Asad Mahmood 88, Salahuddin 59, Anwar-ul-Haq 51)

PIA won by 7 wickets
PIA 18 pts, Muslim Commercial Bank 4 pts

at Montgomery Biscuit Factory Ground, Sahiwal

Karachi 276 for 9 (Nazir Shah 100, Zafar Ahmed 76) and 313 for 6 dec (Sajid Khan 100, Zafar Ali 74)

Multan 167 (Raees Ahmed 6 for 51) and 110 (Zahid Ahmed 4 for 36, Raees Ahmed 4 for 53)

Karachi won by 312 runs
Karachi 18 pts, Multan 5 pts

at Bagh-e-Jinnah Ground, Lahore

Lahore v. National Bank

Match abandoned
Lahore 5 pts, National Bank 5 pts

at Iqbal Stadium, Faisalabad

ADBP 375 for 6 (Masood Anwar 144, Manzoor Elahi 103, Sabih Azhar 59)
HBFC 210 (Raja Afaq 7 for 62) and 119 (Raja Afaq 5 for 47, Khatib Rizwan 4 for 44)
ADBP won by an innings and 46 runs

ADBP 18 pts, HBFC 6 pts

at Pindi Club Ground, Rawalpindi

United Bank 279 for 9 (Ashraf Ali 80 not out, Shakeel Ahmed 5 for 102) and 354 for 3 dec (Saifullah 175 not out, Mansoor Akhtar 60 not out, Shafiq Ahmed 58)
Rawalpindi 127 (Masood Anwar 7 for 53) and 215 (Nadeem Abbasi 88, Masood Anwar 7 for 77)

United Bank won by 291 runs
United Bank 18 pts, Rawalpindi 4 pts

In Group A, a tenacious innings by Mahmood Hamid saved PNSC from defeat at the hands of Habib Bank after they had been set 432 to win and had lost eight wickets for 254. The match was marred by the collapse of umpire Tahir, who suffered a severe heart attack on the last day.

At Nahawalpur, PIA beat MCB by 7 wickets with more than a day to spare. The Bank's first-innings collapse was brought about by a career-best bowling performance from Asif Mujtaba, better known as a batsman, who took 6 for 25 with his left-arm spin.

Karachi were too strong for Multan in Sahiwal. Nasir Shah and skipper Zafar Ahmed put on 139 for Karachi's fifth wicket, and Sajid Khan and Zafar Ali added 154 for the second wicket in the second innings after Karachi had taken a first-innings lead of 109. They eventually won early on the last day with leg-spinner Raees Ahmed returning match figures of 10 for 104.

The two matches in Group B were very one-sided. ADBP ran to a massive score with Masood Anwar, right-handed batsman, 28 years old, and Manzoor Elahi hitting centuries. New skipper Raja Afaq took 12 for 109 with his off-breaks, and ADBP won by an innings.

In Rawalpindi, Saifullah hit 3 sixes and 18 fours in his magnificent 175 not out, which helped United Bank to set Rawalpindi 507 to win. The task was obviously well beyond them, and Masood Anwar, left-handed batsman, slow left-arm bowler, 20 years old, returned match figures of 14 for 130 to play the crucial role in his side's victory.

20, 21, 22 and 23 February 1988

at National Stadium, Karachi

Karachi 162 (Nasir Shah 75, Waheed Niazi 6 for 57) and 336 (Sajid Khan 131, Zafar Ahmed 103, Nadeem Ghauri 6 for 113)
Habib Bank 250 for 9 (Irfan Habib 4 for 57) and 252 for 3 (Aamer Sohail 90, Shaukat Mirza 66 not out, Arshad Pervez 58)

Habib Bank won by 7 wickets
Habib Bank 18 pts, Karachi 5 pts

at Bahawal Stadium, Bahawalpur

Muslim Commercial Bank 187 (Ilyas Khan 63, Azeem Hafees 4 for 50, Sajjad Akbar 4 for 53) and 161
PNSC 154 (Farrukh Zaman 6 for 78, Ilyas Khan 4 for 44) and 181 (Nasir Wasti 81 not out, Salahuddin 5 for 47)

Muslim Commercial Bank won by 13 runs
Muslim Commercial Bank 16 pts, PNSC 5 pts

at Montgomery Biscuit Factory, Sahiwal

PIA 351 for 7 (Feroze Mehdi 163 not out, Zahid Ahmed 80)
Multan 126 (Iqbal Sikander 4 for 36) and 214 (Mohammad Zahid 110)

PIA won by an innings and 11 runs
PIA 18 pts, Multan 4 pts

at Municipal Stadium, Gujranwala

National Bank 200 (Khatib Rizwan 4 for 50) and 205 for 6
ADBP 230 (Atif Rauf 59)

Match drawn
ADBP 9 pts, National Bank 7 pts

at Bagh-e-Jinnah Ground, Lahore

United Bank 306 for 6 (Mahmood Rasheed 104, Ali Zia 55)
Lahore 95 (Masood Anwar 6 for 29) and 119 (Masood Anwar 5 for 39)

United Bank won by an innings and 92 runs
United Bank 18 pts, Lahore 3 pts

at Pindi Club, Rawalpindi

HBFC 261 for 6 (Tariq Alam 93, Sagheer Abbas 52) and 22 for 2
Rawalpindi 192 (Kazim Mehdi 5 for 59)

Match drawn
HBFC 10 pts, Rawalpindi 5 pts

PIA notched up their second victory in Group A when they beat Multan by an innings inside three days. Feroze Mehdi played a fine knock, but the chief honours went to the Multan opener Mohammad Zahid who hit a century on his first-class début.

Habib Bank were also victorious in Group A in spite of centuries from Karachi's Sajid Khan and Zafar Ahmed, who shared a fourth-wicket partnership of 215. Waheed Niazi's pace bowling was again impressive.

In a low-scoring game in Bahawalpur, Muslim Commercial Bank just got the better of PNSC. There was a heroic innings from Nasir Wasti, who came in at 33 for 2 and was not out on 81 with his side just 14 runs short of victory.

In Group B, there was no play at all on the second day at Gujranwala so that a draw became inevitable although the loss of more than a day's play did not prevent United Bank from beating Lahore. The young left-arm spinner, Masood Anwar, again proved the match-winner with 11 for 68.

There was no play on the first two days at Rawalpindi and again a draw was inevitable.

25, 26, 27 and 28 February 1988

at National Stadium, Karachi

PIA 305 for 7 (Anil Dalpat 51) and 312 for 8 dec (Rizwan-uz-Zaman 113, Asif Mujtaba 102 not out, Zahid Ahmed 58, Akhtar Munir 4 for 96)
Karachi 181 (Zafar Ali 51) and 291 (Nasir Shah 118, Zafar Ahmed 59, Iqbal Sikander 6 for 118)

PIA won by 145 runs
PIA 18 pts, Karachi 6 pts

at Bahawal Stadium, Bahawalpur

Muslim Commercial Bank 155 (Nadeem Ghauri 5 for 56) and 171 (Altaf Sheikh 92 not out, Nadeem Ghauri 5 for 61)
Habib Bank 322 for 6 (Anwar Miandad 101 not out, Azhar Khan 57) and 5 for 0

Habib Bank won by 10 wickets
Habib Bank 18 pts, Muslim Commercial Bank 4 pts

at Montgomery Biscuit Factory Ground, Sahiwal

Multan 204 (Sajid Waheed 76) and 257 (Amin Lakhari 7 for 94)
PNSC 325 for 4 (Abdullah Khan 155 not out, Farukh Bari 71, Nasir Wasti 56 not out) and 138 for 3 (Farukh Bari 54, Nasir Wasti 53 not out)

PNSC won by 7 wickets
PNSC 18 pts, Multan 5 pts

at Municipal Stadium, Gujranwala

Lahore 250 (Hammad Khan 88 not out) and 229 for 8 (Saleem Raza 71, Qasim Shera 4 for 19)
ADBP 360 (Manzoor Elahi 87, Atif Rauf 86, Babar Zaman 6 for 119)

Match drawn
ADBP 10 pts, Lahore 8 pts

at Iqbal Stadium, Faisalabad

United Bank 293 (Mansoor Akhtar 116, Sajid Bashir 50, Kazmi Mehdi 5 for 79) and 231 for 9 dec (Saifullah 61, Shafiq Ahmed 54)
HBFC 150 and 160

United Bank won by 214 runs
United Bank 18 pts, HBFC 5 pts

at Pindi Club Ground, Rawalpindi

Railways 146 (Iqbal Qasim 5 for 56, Hafeez-ur-Rehman 5 for 57) and 134 (Hafeez-ur-Rehman 4 for 35)
National Bank 257 (Saeed Azad 96, Sajid Ali 63, Mohammad Nazir 8 for 99) and 24 for 0

National Bank won by 10 wickets
National Bank 18 pts, Railways 4 pts

PIA assured themselves of qualification for the semi-finals with their third win in as many matches in Group A. Their batsmen put them in a commanding position, Rizwan and Asif Mujtaba putting on 130 for the third wicket in the second innings. Karachi's veteran left-hander Nasir Shah hit a valiant hundred, but he could not save his side from defeat.

Habib Bank looked likely to join PIA in the semi-finals when they overwhelmed Muslim Commercial Bank in three days. MCB lost their last eight wickets for 33 runs, and Habib Bank built up a big lead thanks to an excellent century from Anwar Miandad, but it was the bowling of

Nadeem Ghauri which was the decisive factor in Habib's victory. His spin twice proved too much for MCB.

PNSC won their first victory when they beat the weak Multan side, opener Abdullah Khan batting throughout the 85 overs for 155.

In Group B, ADBP took first-innings points in the match at Gujranwala, which was badly affected by rain and poor light. United Bank crushed HBFC. They were given a splendid start by the technically accomplished Mansoor Akhtar, and a fine team performance assured them of a place in the semi-final. Railways first game in the competition proved disastrous. In spite of a wonderful, career-best bowling performance by former Test off-spinner Mohammad Nazir, 42 years old, they were beaten in two days by National Bank.

1, 2, 3 and 4 March 1988

at National Stadium, Karachi

PNSC 254 (Qaiser Rasheed 78, Abdullah Khan 61, Iqbal Sikander 6 for 50) and 335 (Nasir Wasti 108, Abdullah Khan 57, Iqbal Sikander 6 for 114)
PIA 301 for 5 (Rizwan-uz-Zaman 133 not out, Wasim Haider 57, Amin Lakharni 4 for 155) and 289 for 7 (Rizwan-uz-Zaman 81, Zahid Ahmed 68, Wasim Haider 52 not out)

PIA won by 3 wickets
PIA 18 pts, PNSC 7 pts

2, 3, 4 and 5 March 1988

at Bakhtiari Youth Centre Ground, Karachi

Muslim Commercial Bank 254 for 6 (Anwar-ul-Haq 85, Ijaz Faqih 55) and 126 (Nadeem Khan 5 for 62, Akhtar Munir 4 for 27)
Karachi 155 (Raees Ahmed 79, Ijaz Faqih 6 for 72) and 120 (Ijaz Faqih 5 for 47, Farukh Zaman 5 for 62)

Muslim Commercial Bank won by 105 runs
Muslim Commercial Bank 18 pts, Karachi 4 pts

at Montgomery Biscuit Factory Ground, Sahiwal

Multan 185 (Tariq Chrishty 50, Nadeem Ghauri 5 for 47, Waheed Niazi 4 for 53) and 273 (Mohammad Zahid 86, Saleem Sajjad 66, Nadeem Ghauri 6 for 85)
Habib Bank 365 for 6 (Aamer Sohail 110, Azhar Khan 65) and 95 for 1

Habib Bank won by 9 wickets
Habib Bank 18 pts, Multan 5 pts

at Qaddafi Stadium, Lahore

National Bank 293 (Sajid Ali 100, Ameer Akbar 53, Masood Anwar 5 for 121, Kamal Merchant 4 for 74) and 296 for 9 dec (Shahid Tanvir 67, Sajid Ali 53)
United Bank 299 for 9 (Shafiq Ahmed 75, Saifullah 58, Kamal Merchant 50 not out) and 154 for 5

Match drawn
United Bank 10 pts, National Bank 8 pts

at Iqbal Stadium, Faisalabad

HBFC 231 (Saleem Taj 81, Mohammad Nazir 7 for 66) and 82 (Mohammad Nazir 6 for 24)
Railways 180 (Kazim Mehdi 4 for 44, Ali Ahmed 4 for 69) and 103 (Kazim Mehdi 5 for 48, Sohail Khan 4 for 13)

HBFC won by 30 runs
HBFC 17 pts, Railways 6 pts

at Pindi Club Ground, Rawalpindi

ADBP 276 (Ghaffar Kazmi 67, Mansoor Rana 50, Raja Sarfraz 5 for 92) and 214 (Raja Afaq 60 not out, Raja Sarfraz 5 for 68)
Rawalpindi 133 (Khatib Rizwan 7 for 52) and 212 (Khatib Rizwan 4 for 63, Raja Afaq 4 for 70)

ADBP won by 145 runs
ADBP 18 pts, Rawalpindi 4 pts

PIA maintained their hundred per cent record by beating PNSC in Karachi, but they had a very close game. They seemed well in command when Rizwan-uz-Zaman completed yet another century to complement Iqbal Sikander's fine spell of leg-break bowling, which had destroyed PNSC's middle order. Led by Nasir Wasti, PNSC fought back splendidly, and PIA were left to make 289 to win, not an easy task. They were 219 for 5, but Wasim Haider played a sensible innings and, in spite of losing two wickets on 287, PIA won with three wickets to spare.

Muslim Commercial Bank beat Karachi in three days, with Ijaz Faqih, later to be called to join the Pakistan side in the Caribbean, giving a fine all-round display. Habib Bank crushed lowly Multan to confirm their place in the semi-finals.

With more matches to play, the position in Group B was less clear, but although United Bank were held to a draw in Lahore, they still seemed certain to be one of the four semi-finalists. Once again, the young left-arm spinner Masood Anwar had a fine match, taking 8 for 207.

ADBP climbed into second place with a resounding win over Rawalpindi, the left-arm bowling of Khatib Rizwan proving decisive. Another magnificent bowling performance by Railways' skipper Mohammad Nazir was nullified by some woefully weak batting, and his side was beaten in three days by HBFC.

6, 7, 8 and 9 March 1988

at Aga Khan Gymkhana Ground, Karachi

PNSC 254 for 8 (Qaiser Rasheed 82, Raees Ahmed 4 for 99) and 170 (Sajjad Akbar 51, Nadeem Khan 5 for 58)
Karachi 174 (Sajjad Akbar 9 for 59) and 186 (Sajjad Akbar 6 for 53)

PNSC won by 64 runs
PNSC 18 pts, Karachi 5 pts

7, 8, 9 and 10 March 1988

at National Stadium, Karachi

PIA 245 for 9 (Hammad Butt 63 not out, Asif Mujtaba 57, Nadeem Ghauri 4 for 94) and 280 for 7 dec (Zahid Ahmed 116 not out, Rizwan-uz-Zaman 57)
Habib Bank 317 for 4 (Aamer Sohail 114, Shaukat Mirza 108 not out)

Match drawn
Habib Bank 10 pts, PIA 5 pts

at Montgomery Biscuit Factory Ground, Sahiwal

Muslim Commercial Bank 306 (Salahuddin 103 not out) and 212 for 5 (Asad Mahmood 50)

Asif Mujtaba, a young cricketer of immense talent. (Adrian Murrell/Allsport)

Multan 251 (Tariq Chrishty 58, Tariq Mahboob 57, Farrukh Zaman 4 for 74)

Match drawn
Muslim Commercial Bank 10 pts, Multan 8 pts

PNSC's off-spinner Sajjad Akbar dominated the last round of matches in Group A by taking 9 for 59 in the first innings against Karachi and returning match figures of 15 for 122. His 9 for 59 was the best performance in the competition and was bettered only by Abdul Qadir's performance against England during the course of the season.

Group A – Final Table					
	P	W	L	D	Pts
PIA	5	4	–	1	77
Habib Bank	5	3	–	2	74
Muslim Commercial Bank	5	2	2	1	52
PNSC	5	2	2	1	51
Karachi	5	1	4	–	38
Multan	5	–	4	1	27

There was no play possible on the fourth day in Sahiwal where Salahuddin continued his impressive batting form, and the match at the National Stadium was called off 70 minutes after lunch on the final day when it was realized that no result could be achieved and that both sides had already qualified for the semi-finals. Aamer Sohail and Shaukat Mirza shared a third-wicket stand of 167 for Habib Bank.

8, 9, 10 and 11 March 1988

at Qaddafi Stadium, Lahore

ADBP 288 for 8 (Bilal Ahmed 65, Atif Rauf 69, Masood Anwar 5 for 86)
United Bank 122 for 4

Match drawn
ADBP 6 pts, United Bank 4 pts

at Iqbal Stadium, Faisalabad

National Bank 199 (Ali Ahmed 5 for 77) and 69 for 3
HBFC 254 for 9 (Sagheer Abbas 82 not out)

Match drawn
HBFC 10 pts, National Bank 6 pts

at Bagh-e-Jinnah Ground, Lahore

Lahore 56 for 1
v. Railways

Match abandoned
No points

Only 20.3 overs were possible at the Bag-e-Jinnah ground while there was no play on the third and fourth day in the other match in Lahore. Rain also marred the game in Faisalabad.

14, 15, 16 and 17 March 1988

at Pindi Club Ground, Rawalpindi

National Bank 159 (Tahir Shah 81, Raja Sarfraz 5 for 68, Mohammad Arif Snr 4 for 43) and 216 for 4 dec (Saleem Pervez 72)
Rawalpindi 113 (Iqbal Qasim 6 for 40) and 255 for 9 (Nadeem Abbasi 64, Iqbal Qasim 4 for 100)

Match drawn
National Bank 7 pts, Rawalpindi 4 pts

at Bagh-e-Jinnah Ground, Lahore

Lahore 112 (Shahzad Ilyas 4 for 30, Mohinder Kumar 4 for 50) and 155 (Haroon Rasheed 51, Ali Ahmed 5 for 49)
HBFC 301 for 5 (Saleem Taj 120, Sagheer Abbas 51 not out)

HBFC won by an innings and 34 runs
HBFC 18 pts, Lahore 3 pts

at Qaddafi Stadium, Lahore

Railways 134 (Shakeel Ahmed 58, Khatib Rizwan 4 for 30) and 295 (Abid Sarwar 110, Musleh-ud-Din 56, Khatib Rizwan 5 for 103)
ADBP 264 (Ghaffar Kazmi 98, Manzoor Elahi 64, Qaiser Hussain 4 for 82) and 166 for 1 (Masood Anwar 79 not out, Ghaffar Kazmi 71 not out)

ADBP won by 9 wickets
ADBP 18 pts, Railways 4 pts

A Railways side without skipper Nazir, who was playing

for a veterans side against the visiting Indians, was no match for ADBP, for whom Ghaffar Kazmi excelled, and was beaten in three days. HBFC also won in three days, easily disposing of Lahore.

The contest in Rawalpindi proved to be a much more exciting affair. Iqbal Qasim bowled splendidly for National Bank, but the home side, set to score 263 in 150 minutes plus 20 overs, reached 255 for 9 when the game ended.

20, 21, 22 and 23 March 1988

at Qaddafi Stadium, Lahore

United Bank 370 for 7 (Shafiq Ahmed 155 not out, Ali Zia 112, Musleh-ud-Din 4 for 76) and 262 for 3 dec (Mahmood Rasheed 84 not out, Ali Zia 103)
Railways 230 for 9 and 371 (Pervez Shah 136, Wasif Butt 50, Kamal Merchant 4 for 41)

United Bank won by 31 runs
United Bank 18 pts, Railways 7 pts

at Pindi Club Ground, Rawalpindi

Lahore 314 (Shahid Nawaz 100, Rizwan Qazi 63, Babar Zaman 54, Shakeel Ahmed 4 for 118, Raja Sarfraz 4 for 119) and 435 for 8 dec (Hammad Khan 111, Rizwan Qazi 68, Khamran Khan 61)
Rawalpindi 309 for 8 (Mujahid Hameed 79, Nadeem Abbasi 70, Sajjad Ahmed 55 not out) and 224 for 3 (Nadeem Abbasi 103, Shahid Javed 101 not out)

Match drawn
Lahore 10 pts, Rawalpindi 8 pts

Already assured of a place in the semi-finals, United Bank were closely run by Railways, who rallied splendidly in their second innings, thanks to a maiden century by all-rounder Pervez Shah, but were still beaten for the fourth time in the competition. Skipper Shafiq Ahmed hit a fine unbeaten 155 for United Bank, but their real hero was Ali Zia, who, for the second time in his career, hit a century in each innings.

There was a run feast in Rawalpindi although both sides' interest in the tournament had long since ended. Of the four centuries scored in the game, the one that gave the most encouragement was the one by Shahid Nawaz, who had just returned from the Youth World Cup in Australia.

26, 27, 28 and 29 March 1988

at Pindi Club Ground, Rawalpindi

Rawalpindi 204 for 7 (Nadeem Abbasi 63, Jamal Siddiqi 62, Sajid Bokhari 4 for 96) and 208 for 6 dec (Nadeem Abbasi 55, Shahid Javed 55)
Railways 144 (Raja Sarfraz 6 for 29) and 88 for 1

Match drawn
Rawalpindi 9 pts, Railways 4 pts

The last match in Group B between the bottom two sides in the group ended in a draw after interruptions by rain. There was no play on the first day, and Railways looked in a good position as they ended the second day on 50 for 0, but they collapsed against the left-arm spin of Raja Sarfraz. Eventually, Railways were set to make 269 in 150 minutes plus 20 overs, but, limply, they made no attempt to get the runs.

Group B – Final Table

	P	W	L	D	Pts
United Bank	6	4	–	2	86
ADBP	6	3	–	3	79
HBFC	6	2	2	2	66
National Bank	6	1	–	5	51
Rawalpindi	6	–	2	4	34
Lahore	6	–	2	4	29
Railways	6	–	4	2	25

Semi-Finals

1, 2, 3 and 4 April 1988

at Aga Khan Gymkhana Ground, Karachi

PIA 238 (Nasir Khan 62, Asif Mujtaba 54, Khatib Rizwan 7 for 84) and 554 for 7 (Zahid Ahmed 179, Iqbal Sikander 107 not out, Nasir Khan 64, Asif Mujtaba 53)
ADBP 183 (Mansoor Rana 58, Zulfiqar Ali 4 for 32, Wasim Haider 5 for 74)

Match drawn
PIA entered final on first-innings lead

at Qaddafi Stadium, Lahore

United Bank 250 (Saifullah 55, Kamal Merchant 80, Nadeem Ghauri 4 for 71) and 284 (Saifullah 56, Ali Zia 55)
Habib Bank 265 for 6 (Arshad Pervez 118 not out, Masood Anwar 4 for 152) and 207 (Azhar Khan 64, Masood Anwar 6 for 54)

United Bank won by 62 runs

Leading by 55 runs on the first innings, PIA preferred to take no chances and batted for most of the last two days, content to enter the final on their first-innings superiority. Nasir Khan, younger brother of PIA skipper Rashid Khan, played two good innings and shared an important third-wicket stand of 104 with Asif Mujtaba in the face of some excellent slow left-arm bowling by the veteran Khatib Rizwan. Youthful pace bowlers Zulfiqar Ali and Wasim Haider had ADBP in trouble, and the only batsman to offer real resistance was Mansoor Rana, the 25-year-old son of umpire Shakoor Rana. PIA's second innings was dominated by a brilliant innings from Zahid Ahmed, who hit a career-best 179 in just over six hours. He hit 14 fours and shared a fine seventh-wicket stand of 254 in 231 minutes with Iqbal Sikander, who hit the second century of his career.

Skipper Arshad Pervez hit an excellent 118 not out to

QUAID-E-AZAM TROPHY FINAL – PAKISTAN INTERNATIONAL AIRLINES v. UNITED BANK

7, 8 and 9 April 1988 at Qaddafi Stadium, Lahore

PIA

	FIRST INNINGS		SECOND INNINGS	
Rizwan-uz-Zaman	c Ali Zia, b Sikander	4	c Ali Zia, b Sikander	25
Nasir Khan	lbw, b Ali Zia	29	c Arif, b Mushtaq	37
Hammad Butt	c Mushtaq, b Sikander	112	c sub (Shahid Butt), b Sikander	4
Asif Mujtaba	not out	122	c Ashraf, b Sikander	16
Zahid Ahmed	c Ali Zia, b Sikander	32	c Ashraf, b Sikander	2
Wasim Haider	b Kamal Merchant	38	(9) not out	45
Anil Dalpat*	c Ashraf, b Sajid	0	lbw, b Masood Anwar	25
Rashid Khan†	c Mansoor, b Sikander	6	(10) c and b Masood	15
Iqbal Sikander	b Sikander Bakht	4	(8) c Ashraf, b Sikander	11
Asif Mohammad			(6) c Saifullah, b Masood	20
Zulfiqar Ali			lbw, b Mushtaq	0
Extras	b 11, lb 3, w 1, nb 7	22	lb 9, nb 3	12
	(85 overs)	369	(for 8 wkts)	212

	O	M	R	W	O	M	R	W
Sikhander Bakht	23	4	107	5	19	3	88	5
Sajid Bashir	12	2	49	1	7	2	29	–
Masood Anwar	17	3	67	–	23	10	27	3
Ali Zia	12	2	28	1	4	3	2	–
Kamal Merchant	18	2	80	1	2	1	1	–
Mushtaq Ahmed	3	–	24	–	15.5	3	56	2

FALL OF WICKETS
1–22, 2–48, 3–196, 4–250, 5–340, 6–349, 7–364, 8–369,
1–35, 2–47, 3–75, 4–79, 5–105, 6–139, 7–148, 8–153, 9–191

UNITED BANK

	FIRST INNINGS		SECOND INNINGS	
Saifullah	c Rizwan, b Zulfiqar	12	b Zulfiqar Ali	2
Arif-ud-Din	lbw, b Rashid Khan	8	c sub (Faisal Qureshi), b Wasim	24
Mansoor Akhtar	c Anil, b Zulfiqar	10	c Asif Mujtaba, b Wasim	67
Shafiq Ahmed†	c sub (Shahid Mohammad), b Rashid Khan	28	c Anil, b Wasim	7
Ali Zia	lbw, b Zulfiqar Ali	2	c Asif Mujtaba, b Wasim	3
Ashraf Ali*	b Wasim Haider	10	c Nasir, b Wasim	19
Kamal Merchant	c Anil, b Zulfiqar	3	c Anil, b Rashid	19
Sikhander Bakht	c Hammad, b Rashid	15	c Nasir, b Rashid	9
Masood Anwar	c Anil, b Wasim	0	c Anil, b Rashid	2
Sajid Bashir	not out	0	run out	2
Mushtaq Ahmed	c Anil, b Zulfiqar	4	not out	0
Extras	lb 4, nb 1	5	b 5, lb 2, w 1, nb 13	21
		97		175

	O	M	R	W	O	M	R	W
Rashid Khan	11	–	39	3	15.5	–	63	3
Zulfiqar Ali	9.5	–	52	5	11	2	35	1
Wasim Haider	2	2	2	2	15	–	66	5
Iqbal Sikander					4	2	4	–

FALL OF WICKETS
1–13, 2–24, 3–34, 4–51, 5–65, 6–70, 7–91, 8–91, 9–91
1–11, 2–82, 3–101, 4–109, 5–136, 6–160, 7–166, 8–169, 9–175

Umpires: Khalid Aziz & Mian Aslam

PIA won by 309 runs

Rashid Khan led PIA to triumph in the Quaid-e-Azam Trophy. (George Herringshaw/ASP)

give Habib Bank a first-innings lead of 12, but United Bank fought back through Saifullah, Ali Zia and Masood Anwar, who made a very valuable 42 not out. The young spinner then destroyed Habib Bank to return match figures of 10 for 206 and give his side a place in the final. Only Azhar Khan, with 13 fours in a fiery 64, offered hope for the losers.

Quaid-e-Azam Trophy Final
PAKISTAN INTERNATIONAL AIRLINES v. UNITED BANK

The final of Pakistan's premier competition proved to be alarmingly and surprisingly one-sided and two days of the allotted five were unused. United Bank, runners-up in all the major domestic competitions in 1986–7 and runners-up in the BCCP Patron's Trophy earlier in the season, began as firm favourites, but Shafiq Ahmed erred when he won the toss and asked PIA to bat on what appeared to be a perfect wicket. He could point to quick success when both PIA openers were dismissed, but the two left-handers, Hammad Butt and the highly talented Asif Mujtaba, added 138. Hammad's 112 came off 154 balls and included 2 sixes and 18 fours, and he gave the innings just the early impetus that it needed to reach a good score in the allotted 85 overs. Zahid Ahmed and Wasim Haider also provided panache while Asif Mujtaba held the innings together. He

batted for 269 minutes and faced 183 balls for his 122 not out, which included a six and 9 fours.

What followed was incomprehensible as United Bank were bowled out in 22.5 overs for 97. The three-pronged PIA pace attack of Rashid Khan, Zulfiqar Ali, fresh from the Youth World Cup in Australia, and Wasim Haider, proved devastating, but Rashid decided not to impose the follow-on, and by the end of the second day, at 149 for 7, PIA had a lead of 421. Wasim Haider ended the innings with a flourish on the third morning, hitting 6 fours in his unbeaten 45. Sikhander Bakht, 30 years old, but still on the verge of the national side, finished with admirable match figures of 10 for 195.

United Bank needed 485 to win in 2½ days, but apart from a spirited innings by the ever-elegant Mansoor Akhtar, they never looked likely to survive a day. Wasim Haider claimed five wickets and a special award, and United Bank were once again the bridesmaids.

Zahid Ahmed was named as batsman of the tournament, and Masood Anwar, inevitably, was deemed the best bowler in the competition. Asif Mujtaba won the all-rounder's prize, the wicket-keeping award went to Anil Dalpat, and three players, Ghaffar Kazmi, Mahmood Rasheed and Arshad Pervez, won fielding prizes.

So a rather discordant season came to an end, but the dispute and discord should not hide the fact that a great deal of exciting cricketing talent is emerging in Pakistan.

First-Class Averages

BATTING

	M	Inns	NOs	Runs	HS	Av	100s	50s
Moin-ul-Atiq (UB)	4	8	1	528	157	75.42	3	1
Azhar Khan (HB)	6	9	3	425	73*	70.83		5
Asif Mujtaba (PIA)	10	17	3	840	157	60.00	3	5
Javed Miandad (HB)	6	8	2	358	144*	59.66	1	1
Nasir Khan (PIA)	4	6	2	227	64	56.75		2
Tahir Rasheed (HB)	10	11	6	275	86*	55.00		
Nadeem Abbasi (Rp)	8	15	1	769	120*	54.92	2	6
Zahid Ahmed (PIA)	9	15	1	767	179	54.78	2	3
Shaukat Mirza (HB)	7	11	3	424	108*	53.00	2	1
Nasir Wasti (PNSC)	6	11	3	417	108	52.12	1	3
Aamer Sohail (HB)	10	17	2	763	125	50.86	4	1
Rizwan-uz-Zaman (PIA)	7	14	1	661	133*	50.84	2	3
Ijaz Ahmed (HB)	7	10		493	125	49.30	1	3
Saleem Taj (HBFC)	5	7	1	288	120	48.00	1	1
Saleem Malik (HB)	7	10	2	381	95	47.62		3
Rameez Raja (PNSC)	5	8	1	305	102	43.57	1	1
Mansoor Akhtar (UB)	10	18	3	649	132	43.26	2	2
Shafiq Ahmed (UB)	10	17	1	690	155*	43.12	1	5
Agha Zahid (HB)	9	16		679	162	42.43	2	1
Feroze Mehdi (PIA)	5	8	1	295	163*	42.14	1	
Mohammad Zahid (M)	4	7		295	110	42.14	1	1
Sajid Ali (NB)	6	12	1	457	100	41.54	1	3
Pervez Shah (Rly)	6	9	2	288	136	41.14	1	
Atif Rauf (ADBP)	9	12	1	449	99	40.81		4
Rizwan Qazi (L)	6	10	1	364	68	40.44		4
Abdullah Khan (PNSC)	7	14	1	520	155*	40.00	1	2
Nasir Shah (K)	5	10		382	118	38.20	2	1
Ghaffar Kazmi (ADBP)	9	13	1	455	98	37.91		4
Mahmood Hamid (PNSC)	6	10	1	339	113*	37.66	1	1
Sajid Khan (K)	7	14	1	489	131	37.61	2	1
Anwar-ul-Haq (M CB)	7	14	1	487	102*	37.46	1	2
Arshad Pervez (HB)	8	13	2	403	118*	36.63	1	1
Zafar Ahmed (K)	7	12	2	364	103	36.40	1	3
Masood Anwar (ADBP)	9	13	1	435	144	36.25	1	1
Mujahid Hameed (Rp)	7	12	2	356	81	35.60		3
Saifullah (UB)	11	20	1	673	175*	35.42	1	4

	M	Inns	NOs	Runs	HS	Av	100s	50s
Qaiser Rasheed (PNSC)	7	14	1	445	99	34.23		3
Hammad Butt (PIA)	7	11	1	341	112	34.10	1	1
Salahuddin (M CB)	7	13	2	372	103*	33.81	1	2
Anwar Miandad (HB)	11	16	4	402	101*	33.50	1	
Hammad Khan (L)	6	10	2	267	111	33.37	1	
Shahid Tanvir (NB)	6	10	2	265	67	33.12		1
Manzoor Elahi (ADBP)	9	12		394	103	32.83	1	2
Wasim Haider (PIA)	8	13	4	293	57	32.55		2
Raees Ahmed (K)	6	12		390	97	32.50		3
Ali Zia (UB)	10	17	1	513	112	32.06	2	
Tahir Shah (NB)	6	10	3	222	81	31.71		1
Tariq Alam (HBFC)	7	9		281	93	31.22		1
Mansoor Rana (ADBP)	9	12		371	58	30.91		2
Akram Raza (HB)	10	11	3	236	112	29.50	1	
Asif Mohammad (PIA)	5	7		206	56	29.42		2
Abid Sarwar (Rly)	6	10	1	258	110	28.66	1	
Zakir Hussain (M)	6	11		315	100	28.63	1	
Raja Afaq (ADBP)	9	11	2	251	65	27.88		2
Ashraf Ali (UB)	13	17	2	417	80*	27.80		2
Shahid Javed (Rp)	8	14	2	333	101*	27.75	1	1
Altaf Sheikh (M CB)	5	10	1	243	92*	27.00		1
Jamal Siddiqi (Rp)	8	15	1	373	99*	26.64		3
Farrukh Bari (PNSC)	7	14	1	341	86	26.23		3
Ameer Akbar (NB)	6	9		235	53	26.11		1
Sagheer Abbas (HBFC)	7	11	2	234	82*	26.00		3
Asad Mahmood (M CB)	7	14		358	88	25.57		2
Sajid Waheed (M)	6	11		277	76	25.18		1
Mahmood Rasheed (UB)	7	12	1	271	104	24.63	1	1
Zafar Ali (K)	7	14	1	313	74	24.07		3
Sajjad Akbar (PNSC)	8	14	2	281	72	23.41		2
Sikhander Bakht (UB)	8	12	3	210	36	23.33		
Bilal Ahmed (ADBP)	7	11		256	65	23.27		1
Raja Sarfraz (Rp)	8	12	3	209	34*	23.22		
Saleem Raza (L)	7	12		268	71	22.33		1
Munir-ul-Haq (HBFC)	7	12	1	241	46	21.90		
Kamal Merchant (UB)	10	12	1	240	80	21.81		2
Masood Anwar (UB)	11	15	4	240	42*	21.81		
Anil Dalpat (PIA)	9	16	4	259	51	21.58		1
Mohammad Arif Snr (Rp)	8	12	1	235	49	21.36		
Ilyas Khan (M CB)	7	11	1	203	63	20.30		2

(Qualification – 200 runs, average 20.00)

BOWLING

	Overs	Mds	Runs	Wkts	Av	Best	10/m	5/inns
Mohammad Nazir (Rly)	162.1	39	329	27	12.18	8/99	1	3
Shahzad Ilyas (HBFC)	68.2	13	209	13	16.07	4/30		
Shahid Butt (UB)	77.1	27	163	10	16.30	3/64		
Zulfiqar Ali (PIA)	68.5	8	265	16	16.56	5/52		1
Nadeem Ghauri (HB)	492	166	1097	65	16.87	7/100	2	7
Abdul Qadir (HB)	293.1	81	648	36	18.00	9/56	2	3
Ijaz Faqih (M CB)	95.1	15	235	13	18.07	6/72	1	2
Tanvir Ali (PIA)	90.3	26	216	11	19.63	4/33		
Iqbal Qasim (NB)	312.5	79	769	39	19.71	6/40	1	3
Masood Anwar (UB)	522.3	130	1343	67	20.04	7/53	3	7
Khatib Rizwan (ADBP)	389	89	1004	50	20.08	7/52	1	3
Mohinder Kumar (HBFC)	102.2	24	324	16	20.25	4/50		
Iqbal Sikander (PIA)	227	33	615	30	20.50	6/50	1	3
Kazim Mehdi (HBFC)	179.2	36	580	28	20.71	5/48		3

	Overs	Mds	Runs	Wkts	Av	Best	10/m	5/inns
Sajjad Akbar (PNSC)	425.2	121	958	46	20.82	9/59	1	4
Abdullah Khan (PNSC)	103.4	24	251	11	22.81	4/49		
Raees Ahmed (K)	210.4	39	626	26	24.07	6/51	1	2
Wasim Haider (PIA)	137.3	10	537	22	24.40	5/66		2
Raja Afaq (ADBP)	374.2	87	980	40	24.50	7/62	1	2
Kamal Merchant (UB)	222.4	58	540	22	24.54	4/41		
Asif Mujtaba (PIA)	122.4	22	320	13	24.61	6/25		1
Raja Sarfraz (Rp)	430.2	83	1246	50	24.92	6/29	1	5
Rashid Khan (PIA)	122.5	10	450	18	25.00	3/39		
Zahid Ahmed (PIA)	181.4	46	362	14	25.85	3/26		
Farrukh Ahmed (M CB)	277	44	809	31	26.09	6/78		2
Waheed Niazi (HB)	314.4	47	1080	40	27.00	6/57		2
Naved Anjum (HB)	87	17	301	11	27.36	5/74		1
Sikhander Bakht (UB)	184.2	26	743	27	27.51	5/88	1	2
Mushtaq Ahmed (UB)	134	28	442	16	27.62	6/81		1
Sohail Khan (HBFC)	95	15	333	12	27.75	4/13		
Mohammad Arif Snr (Rp)	107.1	21	309	11	28.09	4/43		
Hafeez-ur-Rehman (NB)	143	22	453	16	28.31	5/57		1
Qasim Shera (ADBP)	130.4	22	435	16	28.31	4/49		
Ali Ahmed (HBFC)	225	40	712	25	28.48	5/49		2
Nadeem Iqbal (M)	107	13	376	13	28.92	3/46		
Barkatullah (NB)	73	6	294	10	29.40	3/45		
Ali Zia (UB)	131.1	35	354	12	29.50	3/41		
Tahir Shah (NB)	96	20	295	10	29.50	3/47		
Ilyas Khan (M CB)	173.4	26	536	18	29.77	4/42		
Nadeem Khan (K)	256.5	42	715	24	29.79	5/58		2
Azeem Hafeez (PNSC)	192	36	634	21	30.19	4/50		
Manzoor Elahi (ADBP)	173	33	517	16	32.31	3/32		
Akram Raza (HB)	438	126	970	29	33.44	3/60		
Mohsin Kamal (PNSC)	131.1	15	536	16	33.50	5/117		1
Tauseef Ahmed (UB)	207.3	49	545	16	34.06	4/112		
Sajid Bashir (UB)	178	34	617	18	34.27	3/43		
Mohiuddin Khan (M CB)	129.1	15	481	14	34.35	6/79		1
Amin Lakharni (PNSC)	270.1	55	760	21	36.19	7/94		1
Akhtar Munir (K)	169	21	537	14	38.35	4/27		
Shakeel Ahmed (Rp)	315.3	51	993	23	43.17	5/102		1
Sajid Bokhari (R)	150	25	443	10	44.30	4/96		
Abubakar Siddiq (M)	185	25	634	11	57.63	3/41		
Mohammad Afzal (M)	179.1	19	636	11	57.81	3/32		

(Qualification – 10 wickets)

LEADING FIELDERS

40 – Ashraf Ali (UB) (ct 32/st 8); 34 – Tahir Rasheed (HB) (ct 27/st 7); 28 – Anil Dalpat (PIA) (ct 23/st 5); 23 – Asmat Baig (K) (ct 15/st 8); 19 – Wasim Arif (HBFC) (ct 14/st 5); 18 – Pervez-ul-Hasan (PNSC) (ct 13/st 5); 17 – Sajid Abbasi (MCB) (ct 14/st 3); 16 – Bilal Ahmed (ADBP) (ct 13/st 3); 15 – Maqsood Kundi (ADBP) (ct 12/st 3); Mohammad Jamil (NB) (ct 12/st 3); Zulqarnain (Rly) (ct 9/st 6); and Ghaffar Kazmi (ADBP); 14 – Saifullah (UB) (ct 13/st 1); 13 – Mohammad Arif Snr (Rp); 12 – Arshard Pervez (HB); 11 – Mahmood Rasheed (UB); 10 – Dildar Malik (M) (ct 9/st 1) and Manzoor Elahi (UB)

Abbreviations of team names: ADBP Agricultural Development Bank of Pakistan; HB – Habib Bank; HBFC – House Building Finance Corporation; K – Karachi; L – Lahore; M – Multan; MCB – Muslim Commercial Bank; NB – National Bank; PIA – Pakistan International Airlines; PNSC – Pakistan National Shipping Corporation; Rly – Railways; Rp – Rawalpindi; UB – United Bank.

SECTION G
Time to Consider

The season in Zimbabwe.
Tours by New South Wales and by
Sri Lanka 'B'.
First-class averages.
Facts and figures supplied by
John R. Ward.

Andy Pycroft. A century against New South Wales.
(Ken Kelly)

In an attempt to provide the national side with match practice before the World Cup, cricket in Zimbabwe began earlier than it had ever done before, the first week in September. As they had done 18 months previously, New South Wales provided the opposition, but this time with a full strength side. As Zimbabwe had been beaten by the first New South Wales side, it was clear that the stronger team which arrived in 1988 would prove very difficult to beat. In the event, the visitors took the one-day series by five matches to one, but, on the slow wickets prepared, were unable to force victory in the three-day matches. The limitations of the Zimbabwe side were obvious, and Dirk Wellham, who led the New South Wales side and announced his retirement from first-class cricket just after the end of the tour, commented that he was playing against the same players that he had played against five years earlier when he captained the Young Australian side. Whitney was also in that side, and he is the only player to have toured Zimbabwe three times.

5 September 1987

at Harare Sports Club

Zimbabwe 162 (P.W.E. Rawson 57 not out)
New South Wales 163 for 4 (M.E. Waugh 93 not out)

New South Wales won by 6 wickets

In spite of conceding 22 wides, New South Wales bowled

Dirk Wellham led New South Wales on their tour of Zimbabwe and then announced his retirement from first-class cricket. (Adrian Murrell/Allsport)

Zimbabwe out in 48.4 overs. They lost Small and Taylor for 24, but Bayliss and Mark Waugh added 61, and Waugh finished the game in remarkable fashion, hitting the first five balls of an over from off-spinner Meman for sixes. Meman's figures were 2.5–0–56–0.

6 September 1987

at Harare Sports Club

Zimbabwe 172 for 9 (A.H. Omarshah 50, R.J. Tucker 4 for 30)
New South Wales 176 for 4 (G.C. Dyer 52 not out)

New South Wales won by 6 wickets

The Sunday proved to be no luckier for Zimbabwe than the Saturday had been. Again put in to bat, they lost both openers for three, but did manage to last the 50 overs, with considerable effort coming from the tail. Meman finished on 38 not out. He also bowled his 10 overs for 36 runs and the wicket of Mark Taylor, but New South Wales were never troubled.

8, 9, 10 September 1987

at Harare Sports Club

Zimbabwe 325 (A.J. Pycroft 104, G.A. Paterson 59) and 106 for 5
New South Wales 404 (P.L. Taylor 105 not out, G.R.J. Matthews 72, M.E. Waugh 61, E.A. Brandes 4 for 143)

Match drawn

For the first of the first-class matches, Zimbabwe were considerably weakened by the loss of the injured Traicos and of Rawson, who could not obtain leave from his employers. Brown and Arnott gave Zimbabwe a solid start, but the honours went to Andy Pycroft, who hit 104 off 162 balls, with 14 fours. It was his first first-class century for five years. Grant Paterson, badly out of form, dropped down to number six and scored a dour fifty. Charlie Lock, from Mutare, making his first-class début, had Small caught for four, and Mark Taylor also went cheaply, but there was consistent batting from that point. Peter Taylor, coming in at number nine, hit 105 not out off 106 balls. This innings, his maiden first-class century, contained 3 sixes and 14 fours. Zimbabwe batted again on the third afternoon with a very grim determination.

12 September 1987

at Bulawayo Athletic Club

New South Wales 201 for 6 (D.M. Wellham 57)
Zimbabwe 202 for 4 (R.D. Brown 71)

Zimbabwe won by 6 wickets

A stand of 87 for the second wicket between Robin Brown and Ali Omarshah was the basis of Zimbabwe's victory, which came with 4.3 overs to spare. The visitors batted in a rather lethargic manner.

13 September 1987

at Bulawayo Athletic Club

New South Wales 243 for 8 (M.D. O'Neill 66)
Zimbabwe 239 (D.L. Houghton 67)

New South Wales won by 4 runs

An eighth wicket stand of 65 between Gavin Robertson and Geoff Lawson gave the New South Wales innings a necessary boost. In reply, Zimbabwe batted with great determination, and Dave Houghton hit splendidly to make victory a possibility. When the last pair, Jarvis and Duers, came together, however, 19 were needed. With the aid of scampered leg-byes, they scored 14 before Gilbert bowled Duers with three balls remaining.

16 September 1987

at Mutare Sports Club

Zimbabwe 186 (W.R. James 57, M.R. Whitney 4 for 13)
New South Wales 190 for 6 (D.M. Wellham 57 not out, T.H. Bayliss 53)

New South Wales won by 4 wickets

A useful innings from Wayne James could not provide the Zimbabwe innings with a necessary impetus, and the later batsmen, Rawson and Butchart, failed against Lawson and Whitney. Although they lost 4 wickets for 77, New South Wales were never really pressed, and Bayliss and Wellham added 78.

19, 21 and 22 September 1987

at Harare Sports Club

New South Wales 231 for 4 dec (S.M. Small 78) and 238 for 5 dec (P.L. Taylor 71, A.J. Traicos 4 for 77)
Zimbabwe 169 for 4 dec (A.J. Pycroft 57 not out, D.L. Houghton 54) and 161 for 5

Match drawn

Both captains made every effort to obtain a result, but the deadness of the wicket ensured that only 18 wickets fell in three full days' play. The match saw the return of Kevin Curran, who, after protracted negotiations between the Zimbabwe Cricket Union and the government, was allowed to retain his dual nationality and play for Zimbabwe. Unfortunately, as in the World Cup which followed, he was unable to bowl, sending down but one over in the second innings. Traicos bowled 39 overs in succession in the first innings. Small and Mark Taylor began the match with a stand of 123.

20 September 1987

at Harare Sports Club

Zimbabwe 222 for 7 (A.H. Omarshah 98)
New South Wales 225 for 3 (T.H. Bayliss 104 not out, M.A. Taylor 52)

New South Wales won by 7 wickets

Ali Omarshah completed a fine series with a magnificent innings of 98. New South Wales countered with a Trevor Bayliss century. His innings lasted 127 balls and included 3 sixes and 5 fours. New South Wales won with 3.2 overs to spare.

Omarshah's good form was reflected to some extent in the World Cup, where he bowled well, but Curran never found his form, and, like Arnott and Rawson, never seemed fully fit. Pycroft gave substance to the middle order, and Houghton played one glorious innings and was always looking for runs. Traicos, the oldest man in the competition, scarcely bowled a loose ball, but the failure to win a game in the World Cup only emphasised what had been realised after the matches with New South Wales, that the time had come for reconstruction and for thoughts to be on the next I.C.C. Trophy and World Cup rather than on former glories.

There was further disappointment for cricket-lovers in Zimbabwe when it was learned that the Sri Lankan side to tour the country in March was not to be the Test side that had been promised, but a 'B' side. Yet another disappointment followed when an invitation to the Australians to send a full Test team for three weeks in April to replace the cancelled tour by the Sri Lankans was rejected. There is a feeling that Zimbabwe is not receiving sufficient positive encouragement from most of the Test-playing countries and that Zimbabwe needs more experience at the top level than the full member countries seem prepared to give.

As it transpired, the Sri Lanka 'B' side provided much stronger opposition than had been anticipated. They displayed a thoroughly professional and dedicated approach to the tour, spending several weeks in preparation before the tour actually started. They were most efficiently managed by a former captain, Michael Tissera, and were a group of very fit and enthusiastic young men, ably led by Roy Dias, who was on his second trip to Zimbabwe. His deputy was Karnain, who had appeared in 15 one-day internationals but in only two first-class matches, which is a not uncommon record for a Sri Lankan.

Tillekeratne, one of the most exciting of the world's young players, batted inconsistently, although he played some outstanding innings, but his fielding was of the highest possible level, and it is doubtful if he has a superior anywhere in the world.

Ashley de Silva was a solid opening batsman and capable wicket-keeper. There were several useful pace bowlers, of whom Wijegunewardena was the most impressive, but the mainstay of the attack was the left-arm spinner Roger Wijesuriya. The outstanding player of the tour, however, was the all-rounder Athula Samarasekera, who dominated the Zimbabwe bowling with greater consistency than any other batsman since independence. He scored 868 runs on the tour and was only twice dismissed for less than fifty. He is a powerful conventional hitter of the ball who scored at a rate of nearly six runs an over. The 26-year-old 'Big Sam' was also a very useful medium-pace bowler who invariably took on the responsibility of bowling the final over in the one-day matches. He was the Colossus of the tour, but his performances hid what was really a weakness in the depth of both batting and bowling for Sri Lanka.

The Zimbabwe approach was less disciplined and less enthusiastic than it should have been, for many of the senior players were obviously disappointed that they were not to face a full-strength Sri Lankan side. The selectors had a difficult task after the World Cup failures, and there was a sensation on the eve of the tour when it was announced that Kevin Curran would not be selected for the opening matches. No official reason was given, but it was rumoured that his attitude in India had not been satisfactory. He also had a long-standing quarrel with the

Zimbabwe Cricket Union over his contract. In effect, he did not appear against the Sri Lankans, and his career in Zimbabwe, so recently renewed, may well have come to an end.

Others of the World Cup squad who were dropped from the side were Robin Brown and Babu Meman, both of whom were nearing the veteran stage and were omitted in the interests of team-building, and Paterson and Butchart. Again it was rumoured that their attitude in India had not been all that was desired, and one can see no other reason for omitting such a highly talented one-day cricketer as Butchart for any other reason. On a happier note, two young players, Darrel Goodwin, in style and approach not unlike Colin Milburn, and Trevor Penney, who did a splendid job when entrusted with the difficult task of captaining the ICC Associates team in the World Youth Cup in Australia, were two young players who found a place in the Zimbabwe first team, and they acquitted themselves well.

13 March 1988

at Harare Sports Club

Young Zimbabwe 105
Sri Lanka 'B' 109 for 1

Sri Lanka 'B' won by 9 wickets

A mainly inexperienced Zimbabwe side offered little opposition to the tourists as they strolled to victory with 11.1 of their 50 overs to spare.

15, 16 and 17 March 1988

at Harare South Country Club

Sri Lanka 'B' 282 for 3 dec (R.L. Dias 86, H.P. Tillekeratne 76 not out, D.S.G. Bulankulame 67, M.A.R. Samarasekera 52) and 204 for 4 dec (M.A.R. Samarasekera 71, D. Dolphin 4 for 78)
Country Districts 226 (A. Elliott 85, N.L.K. Ratnayake 4 for 33) and 26 for 1

Match drawn

This match did not have first-class status. Dias batted into the second day before declaring, and Country Districts slumped to 122 for 7. Alan Elliott roused them with some powerful hitting. Left to make 261 in 38 overs, Country Districts were 26 for 1 in 10.1 when rain ended the match.

19 March 1988

at Harare Sports Club

Sri Lanka 'B' 253 for 4 (M.A.R. Samarasekera 146, A.M. de Silva 54)
Young Zimbabwe 158 for 9

FIRST ONE-DAY INTERNATIONAL – ZIMBABWE v. SRI LANKA 'B'
20 March 1988 at Harare Sports Club

SRI LANKA 'B'			
D.C. Wickremasinghe	c W.R. James, b Rawson	0	
M.A.R. Samarasekera	run out	2	
A.M. de Silva*	c Traicos, b Omarshah	6	
R.L. Dias†	c W.R. James, b Brandes	3	
B.R. Jurangpathy	c Traicos, b Brandes	1	
H.P. Tillekeratne	c Waller, b Duers	58	
U.S.H. Karnain	lbw, b Houghton	15	
R.G.C.E. Wijesuriya	not out	24	
K.I.W. Wijegunewardena	b Brandes	2	
M.A.W.R. Madurasinghe	run out	0	
A.K. Kuruppuarachchi	not out	0	
Extras	b 3, lb 7, w 17, nb 7	34	
(50 overs)	(for 9 wkts)	145	

ZIMBABWE			
A.H. Omarshah	c Wickremasinghe, b Kuruppuarachchi	18	
C.D. James	c Wickremasinghe, b Wijegunewardena	0	
A.C. Waller	b Wijegunewardena	5	
A.J. Pycroft	c Wijegunewardena, b Kuruppuarachchi	5	
D.L. Houghton	st de Silva, b Wijesuriya	25	
K.J. Arnott	c and b Wijesuriya	12	
W.R. James*	c de Silva, b Wijesuriya	9	
P.W.E. Rawson	c de Silva, b Samarasekera	23	
E.A. Brandes	c Wickremasinghe, b Samarasekera	35	
A.J. Traicos†	run out	7	
K.G. Duers	not out	0	
Extras	lb 2, w 4	6	
(50 overs)		145	

	O	M	R	W
Rawson	10	1	12	1
Brandes	10	–	37	3
Duers	10	2	18	1
Traicos	10	1	18	–
Omarshah	6	–	33	1
Houghton	2	–	9	1
Pycroft	2	–	8	–

	O	M	R	W
Wijegunewardena	10	1	37	2
Kuruppuarachchi	10	2	34	2
Samarasekera	10	2	23	2
Wijesuriya	10	4	14	3
Madurasinghe	8	2	26	–
Karnain	1	–	4	–
Jurangpathy	1	–	5	–

FALL OF WICKETS
1–0, 2–4, 3–9, 4–12, 5–39, 6–95, 7–139, 8–144, 9–144

FALL OF WICKETS
1–1, 2–13, 3–29, 4–39, 5–70, 6–75, 7–81, 8–137, 9–144

Umpires: K. Kanjee & R. Jackson

Sri Lanka 'B' won by virtue of losing fewer wickets

Ashley de Silva, a capable wicket-keeper and solid opening batsman for the Sri Lanka 'B' side. (Michael King/Allsport)

Sri Lanka 'B' won by 95 runs

The tourists opened with stands of 106 and 119, and outclassed the Young Zimbabwe side.

First One-Day International
ZIMBABWE v. SRI LANKA 'B'

The Zimbabwe bowlers were in fine form. Rawson accounted for Wickremasinghe before a run was scored, and the dangerous Samarasekera was brilliantly run out by Arnott. Four men were out for 12, and a fifth for 39. Tillekeratne batted with great maturity and was aided by Karnain and Wijesuriya, but the great lapse from Zimbabwe's point of view was the bowling of Omarshah, so capable in the World Cup, who sent down eight wides and was totally unable to find direction so that his quota had to be completed by the occasional bowlers, Houghton and Pycroft.

In spite of conceding 34 extras, Zimbabwe were thought to have little problem in reaching a target of 146, but the Sri Lankans bowled tightly and fielded tigerishly. Zimbabwe, with a hint of self-destruction, lost seven wickets for 81 runs before Rawson and Brandes hit powerfully.

SECOND ONE-DAY INTERNATIONAL – ZIMBABWE v. SRI LANKA 'B'
26 March 1988 at Bulawayo Athletic Club

SRI LANKA 'B'			
D.C. Wickremasinghe	c Pycroft, b Jarvis		16
A.M. de Silva*	c Waller, b Traicos		59
M.A.R. Samarasekera	b Duers		95
R.L. Dias†	run out		6
H.P. Tillekeratne	c James, b Brandes		4
B.R. Jurangpathy	not out		19
U.S.H. Karnain	not out		17
D.S.G. Bulankulame			
R.G.C.W. Wijesuriya			
M.A.W.R. Madurasinghe			
A.K. Kuruppuarachchi			
Extras	lb 8, w 2		10
(50 overs)	(for 5 wkts)		226

ZIMBABWE			
W.R. James*	c Jurangpathy, b Wijesuriya		12
C.G. Goodwin	c Dias, b Karnain		0
D.L. Houghton	c Jurangpathy, b Madurasinghe		60
A.J. Pycroft	c Bulankulame, b Madurasinghe		27
A.C. Waller	c Dias, b Jurangpathy		28
E.A. Brandes	c Madurasinghe, b Samarasekera		51
P.W.E. Rawson	not out		40
T.L. Penney	lbw, b Samarasekera		0
A.J. Traicos†	run out		2
M.P. Jarvis	not out		0
K.G. Duers			
Extras	lb 3, w 5		8
(49.2 overs)	(for 8 wkts)		228

	O	M	R	W
Brandes	10	2	27	1
Jarvis	10	1	28	1
Rawson	10	–	58	–
Duers	10	–	58	1
Traicos	10	–	47	1

	O	M	R	W
Kuruppuarachchi	9	1	48	–
Karnain	10	–	42	1
Samarasekera	8.2	–	33	2
Wijesuriya	10	–	37	1
Madurasinghe	9	1	36	2
Jurangpathy	3	–	29	1

FALL OF WICKETS
1–37, 2–163, 3–181, 4–185, 5–189

FALL OF WICKETS
1–0, 2–65, 3–88, 4–129, 5–133, 6–215, 7–216, 8–224

Umpires: R. Jackson & E. Gilmour

Zimbabwe won by 2 wickets

The Sri Lankan fielding began to wilt, but with two runs needed for victory, Brandes attempted to hit a six and was brilliantly caught on the boundary.

In the final over, Traicos ran a single to level the scores, and, faced, by the last ball of the match, Duers was beaten outside the off stump. Traicos attempted to steal a single to win the match, but the wicket-keeper hit the wicket with a direct throw and Sri Lanka 'B' took the match by virtue of having lost fewer wickets with the scores level.

22, 23 and 24 March 1988

at Harare Sports Club

Zimbabwe 'B' 108 and 244 (D.L. Houghton 126, M.V. Deshapriya 4 for 60)
Sri Lanka 'B' 356 for 5 dec (A.M. de Silva 76, D.C. Wickremasinghe 69, H.P. Tillekeratne 61 not out, B.R. Jurangpathy 60)

Sri Lanka 'B' won by an innings and 4 runs

This match was awarded first-class status. An inexperienced Zimbabwe side, led by David Houghton, were well beaten. Goodwin, 33, and Penney, 47 not out, were the only batsmen to show resistance in the first innings. Sri Lanka 'B' scored consistently after Wickremasinghe and de Silva had put on 122 for the first wicket. Houghton scored the highest score of his career in the second innings, but the tourists won with an hour to spare.

Second One-Day International
ZIMBABWE v. SRI LANKA 'B'

Sri Lanka 'B''s innings was built around a second-wicket partnership of 126 between de Silva and Samarasekera, but both were dismissed just as the final onslaught on the bowling was needed so that the visitors' final total fell short of what might have been expected.

Darrell Goodwin was out in the second over of Zimbabwe's innings, but Houghton assumed responsibility and led a spirited recovery. Nevertheless, with five men out for 133, Zimbabwe were behind the required run rate. Rawson and Brandes came together in a thrilling stand. Brandes hit 51 off 28 balls with 5 sixes and 2 fours while Rawson, who also faced 28 deliveries, stood resolute as wickets went down at the other end. With four balls of the match remaining, Rawson hit Samarasekera for four to give Zimbabwe victory.

Third One-Day International
ZIMBABWE v. SRI LANKA 'B'

The third one-day international, played the day after the tense second encounter, produced another exciting finish. Zimbabwe batted first and again started uncertainly, but they were revived by Andy Waller, who hit a dashing 67. Penney also batted encouragingly, and Peter Rawson hit

---

THIRD ONE–DAY INTERNATIONAL – ZIMBABWE v. SRI LANKA 'B'
27 March 1988 at Bulawayo Athletic Club

ZIMBABWE			
W.R. James*	c Madurasinghe, b Karnain	3
D.G. Goodwin	run out	9
D.L. Houghton	c and b Madurasinghe	30
A.J. Pycroft	c Wijesuriya, b Samarasekera	22
E.A. Brandes	c Kuruppuarachchi, b Wijesuriya	10
A.C. Waller	b Samarasekera	67
T.L. Penney	c Kuruppuarachchi, b Samarasekera	25
P.W.E. Rawson	not out	33
D.B. Lake	not out	1
A.J. Traicos†		
M.P. Jarvis		
Extras	b 2, lb 9, w 8	19
(50 overs)	(for 7 wkts)	219

SRI LANKA 'B'			
A.M. de Silva*	c and b Traicos	28
D.S.G. Bulankulame	run out	44
M.A.R. Samarasekera	c Rawson, b Traicos	61
R.L. Dias†	b Brandes	22
B.R. Jurangpathy	run out	10
H.P. Tillekeratne	c Houghton, b Lake	3
U.S.H. Karnain	not out	22
R.G.C.E. Wijesuriya	b Rawson	0
M.A.W.R. Madurasinghe	run out	0
M.V. Deshapriya	b Brandes	4
A.K. Kuruppuarachchi	b Brandes	0
Extras	b 1, lb 6, w 8	15
(50 overs)		211

	O	M	R	W
Kuruppuarachchi	10	–	31	–
Karnain	10	–	48	1
Madurasinghe	9	–	40	1
Samarasekera	10	2	54	3
Wijesuriya	10	–	30	1
Jurangpathy	1	–	5	–

	O	M	R	W
Brandes	10	2	30	3
Jarvis	10	–	39	–
Lake	10	–	51	1
Traicos	10	–	45	2
Rawson	10	–	39	1

FALL OF WICKETS
1–4, 2–25, 3–71, 4–77, 5–89, 6–177, 7–186

FALL OF WICKETS
1–59, 2–105, 3–163, 4–166, 5–177, 6–182, 7–195, 8–211, 9–211

Umpires: R. Jackson & E. Gilmour

Zimbabwe won by 8 runs

33 off 14 balls with 3 sixes and a four.

Sri Lanka 'B' batted consistently well in reply, and with Samarasekera in full flight and the score at 163 for 2, they seemed to be certain of victory. Traicos dismissed Samarasekera, however, and accurate bowling and keen fielding frustrated the Sri Lankans so that when the last over began nine runs were needed for victory with two wickets standing. Unfortunately for the tourists Karnain was stranded at the non-striker's end as Brandes clean bowled both Deshapriya and Kuruppuarachchi to give the game to Zimbabwe.

30 March 1988

at Mutare Sports Club

Sri Lanka 'B' 284 for 5 (R.L. Dias 59, M.A.R. Samarasekera 50)
Zimbabwe 271 (D.L. Houghton 104, K.J. Arnott 70)

Sri Lanka 'B' won by 13 runs

A 50-over match in which Sri Lanka 'B' batted consistently and the Zimbabwe side was strengthened by the inclusion of Arnott, Houghton, Omarshah and Butchart always saw the tourists with a slight edge. Arnott and Houghton shared a third-wicket stand of 178. Houghton's century came off 84 balls with 4 sixes and 11 fours, but the rest offered little and Zimbabwe 'B' were all out in 49 overs.

First International Match
ZIMBABWE v. SRI LANKA 'B'

With the Harare pitch noted for its placidity and a draw the most probable result before a ball had even been bowled, the public showed little interest in the first of the two three-day international matches.

Dias won the toss and decided to bat first, but the tourists quickly lost both openers. Dias and Samarasekera denied Zimbabwe further advance with a stand of 107. Samarasekera looked set for another century, but he was brilliantly caught in the gully by Traicos, a veteran but still superbly fit and athletic.

The Sri Lankan middle order batted solidly, and the first day ended with the visitors on 251 for 9. Eleven more runs were added on the second morning so that the total of 262 was not too daunting for Zimbabwe to face, but the home side began uneasily, and it was left to Darrell Goodwin, playing his first three-day match for the senior side, to hold the innings together. His application contrasted sharply to that of Pycroft and Houghton, who perished to shots unworthy of players of their standing. Goodwin batted with admirable self-discipline until being trapped into giving a catch while attempting his favourite lofted drive.

Goodwin found an excellent partner in Rawson, who is

FIRST INTERNATIONAL MATCH – ZIMBABWE v. SRI LANKA 'B'
1, 2 and 4 April 1988 at Harare Sports Club

SRI LANKA 'B'

	FIRST INNINGS		SECOND INNINGS	
D.C. Wickremasinghe	c Rawson, b Brandes	6	c Pycroft, b Jarvis	8
A.M. de Silva*	c Goodwin, b Jarvis	1	c sub (Penney), b Duers	31
M.A.R. Samarasekera	c Traicos, b Brandes	77	(6) lbw, b Jarvis	0
R.L. Dias†	c Rawson, b Traicos	39	c Traicos, b Jarvis	27
B.R. Jurangpathy	c Duers, b Brandes	46	(7) c Goodwin, b Traicos	11
H.P. Tillekeratne	run out	15	(5) not out	38
S.K. Ranasinghe	lbw, b Brandes	27	(3) c Arnott, b Duers	14
U.S.H. Karnain	c Jarvis, b Rawson	35	not out	0
R.G.C.E. Wijesuriya	b Brandes	5		
A.K. Kuruppuarachchi	lbw, b Jarvis	1		
M.V. Deshapriya	not out	6		
Extras	lb 2, nb 2	4	lb 8, nb 1	9
		262	(for 6 wkts)	138

ZIMBABWE

	FIRST INNINGS	
K.J. Arnott	c and b Karnain	5
D.G. Goodwin	c Jurangpathy, b Wijesuriya	66
W.R. James*	c Samarasekera, b Wijesuriya	11
A.J. Pycroft	st de Silva, b Wijesuriya	10
D.L. Houghton	c Samarasekera, b Wijesuriya	4
A.C. Waller	c Samarasekera, b Wijesuriya	17
P.W.E. Rawson	not out	72
E.A. Brandes	c Tillekeratne, b Wijesuriya	4
A.J. Traicos†	st de Silva, b Deshapriya	26
M.P. Jarvis	not out	8
E.G. Duers		
Extras	lb 5, w 1	6
	(for 8 wkts, dec)	229

	O	M	R	W	O	M	R	W
Brandes	25	5	76	5				
Jarvis	18	7	37	2	17	5	31	2
Rawson	16.2	3	48	1	14	4	26	–
Duers	18	5	49	–	20	6	47	2
Traicos	23	9	50	1	17	5	26	1

	O	M	R	W
Kuruppuarachchi	5	1	16	–
Karnain	8	2	13	1
Ranasinghe	4	–	11	–
Wijesuriya	32	2	102	6
Deshapriya	16	–	50	1
Jurangpathy	15	2	32	–

FALL OF WICKETS
1–2, 2–12, 3–119, 4–125, 5–146, 6–211, 7–218, 8–236, 9–237
1–13, 2–49, 3–82, 4–99, 5–101, 6–130

FALL OF WICKETS
1–13, 2–44, 3–55, 4–60, 5–93, 6–145, 7–154, 8–219

Umpires: I.D. Robinson & D.C. Moore-Gordon

Match drawn

a much better batsman against pace than against spin, yet in this particular innings, Rawson faced only the spinners and batted resolutely, sharing stands of 52 with Goodwin and 65 with Traicos. Zimbabwe declared 33 runs in arrears in an attempt to capture a wicket before the close, but Sri Lanka 'B' ended at 13 without loss.

They had to struggle for runs next morning as Jarvis, Rawson and Duers extracted some life from the pitch, but Zimbabwe were handicapped by the absence of Brandes, who had suffered a groin strain. He had bowled particularly well in the first innings.

Any hopes of a result being manufactured were lost when rain prevented play for 71 minutes either side of lunch.

Fourth One-Day International
ZIMBABWE v. SRI LANKA 'B'

Played on the Sunday in the middle of the first three-day international, the fourth one-day international was the only match of the series which did not provide an exciting finish. Andy Pycroft was the only one of the earlier Zimbabwe batsmen to play a substantial innings after a solid start from Houghton and Goodwin. The home side lapsed to 125 for 6, and once again it was Peter Rawson who roused them.

The achievements of the Zimbabwe batsmen were put into perspective by the innings of Samarasekera, who

The scourge of Zimbabwe – Athula Samarasekera. (Michael King/Allsport)

came in at 43 for 1 and hit 111 off 98 balls as he dominated an unfinished stand of 187 with de Silva. Samarasekera hit 2 sixes and 10 fours and treated all bowlers with savage contempt as he swept his side to victory with 3.2 overs to spare.

Second International Match
ZIMBABWE v. SRI LANKA 'B'

Zimbabwe were weakened by the absence of Pycroft, for personal reasons, and by Duers and Waller, for business reasons. Bruk-Jackson made his first-class début and his first appearance in the Zimbabwe national side.

Dias won the toss and asked Zimbabwe to bat first. They responded with their most consistent batting performance of the season although the run rate was slow. Arnott was the backbone of the innings and a big score looked possible, but towards the end of the first day quick runs were sought, and several batsmen perished in the attempt to score briskly. Tillekeratne took three good catches in quick succession, and the catch with which he accounted for Jarvis can rarely have been bettered. The batsman hit an enormous skier towards the third-man boundary, and Tillekeratne turned and raced back from

---

FOURTH ONE-DAY INTERNATIONAL – ZIMBABWE v. SRI LANKA 'B'
3 April 1988 at Harare Sports Club

ZIMBABWE				SRI LANKA 'B'			
D.L. Houghton*	c Tillekeratne, b Samarasekera	26		A.M. de Silva*	not out		87
D.G. Goodwin	c Bulankulame, b N.L.K. Ratnayake	19		D.S.G. Bulankulame	c Traicos, b Brandes		22
A.H. Omarshah	c Dias, b Karnain	9		M.A.R. Samarasekera	not out		111
A.J. Pycroft	b Tillekeratne	69		R.L. Dias†			
A.C. Waller	c de Silva, b Samarasekera	9		B.R. Jurangpathy			
T.L. Penney	lbw, b Wijesuriya	14		H.P. Tillekeratne			
E.A. Brandes	c de Silva, b Ranasinghe	7		S.K. Ranasinghe			
P.W.E. Rawson	not out	48		U.S.H. Karnain			
D.B. Lake	c Tillekeratne, b Karnain	5		R.G.C.E. Wijesuriya			
A.J. Traicos†				N.L.K. Ratnayake			
M.P. Jarvis				A.K. Kuruppuarachchi			
Extras	lb 11, w 9, nb 1	21		Extras	lb 4, w 5, nb 1		10
(50 overs)	(for 8 wkts)	227		(46.4 overs)	(for 1 wkt)		230

	O	M	R	W		O	M	R	W
Kuruppuarachchi	4	–	21	–	Rawson	8.4	2	42	–
N.L.K. Ratnayake	6	–	39	1	Jarvis	8	1	36	–
Samarasekera	10	1	31	2	Lake	10	1	46	–
Karnain	9	–	42	2	Brandes	10	1	53	1
Wijesuriya	10	1	31	1	Traicos	10	–	49	–
Ranasinghe	9	–	34	1					
Tillekeratne	2	–	18	1					

FALL OF WICKETS
1–35, 2–63, 3–71, 4–93, 5–116, 6–125, 7–196, 8–227

FALL OF WICKETS
1–43

Umpires: K. Kanjee & R. Jackson

Sri Lanka 'B' won by 9 wickets

SECOND INTERNATIONAL MATCH – ZIMBABWE v. SRI LANKA 'B'
6, 7 and 8 April 1988 at Harare Sports Club

ZIMBABWE

	FIRST INNINGS			SECOND INNINGS	
K.J. Arnott	c Bulankulame, b Ranasinghe	64		not out	40
D.G. Goodwin	b Wijesuriya	23		b Samarasekera	10
G.K. Bruk-Jackson	c de Silva, b Wijesuriya	10		c Wickremasinghe, b Kuruppuarachchi	33
D.L. Houghton	c Bulankulame, b Wijesuriya	40		c and b Kuruppuarachchi	0
T.L. Penney	c Samarasekera, b Ratnayake	19		not out	67
A.H. Omarshah	b Wijesuriya	16			
P.W.E. Rawson	c Ranasinghe, b Kuruppuarachchi	34			
E.A. Brandes	c Tillekeratne, b Ranasinghe	0			
W.R. James*	c Tillekeratne, b Ratnayake	9			
M.P. Jarvis	c Tillekeratne, b Ratnayake	1			
A.J. Traicos†	not out	0			
Extras	b 3, lb 8, nb 4	23		b 5, lb 4, w 1, nb 4	14
		231		(for 3 wkts)	**164**

SRI LANKA 'B'

	FIRST INNINGS	
A.M. de Silva	c Brandes, b Traicos	16
D.S.G. Bulankulame	c Arnott, b Traicos	18
M.A.R. Samarasekera	lbw, b Traicos	79
R.L. Dias†	c and b Rawson	18
H.P. Tillekeratne	not out	128
S.K. Ranasinghe	c Arnott, b Brandes	2
A.G.D. Wickremasinghe*	not out	103
R.G.C.E. Wijesuriya		
M.V. Deshapriya		
N.L.K. Ratnayake		
A.K. Kuruppuarachchi		
Extras	b 10, lb 3, w 2, nb 1	16
	(for 5 wkts, dec)	**380**

	O	M	R	W	O	M	R	W
Kuruppuarachchi	10	1	27	1	14	3	34	2
N.L.K. Ratnayake	22.2	8	44	3				
Samarasekera	4	–	21	–	7	1	20	1
Wijesuriya	32	8	83	4	21	5	33	–
Ranasinghe	15	5	21	2	6	2	19	–
Deshapriya	8	1	24	–	10	–	30	–
Tillekeratne					5	1	8	–
Dias					1	–	11	–

	O	M	R	W
Brandes	33	7	115	1
Jarvis	23	4	90	–
Traicos	38	12	76	3
Rawson	17	2	76	1
Omarshah	4	1	10	–

FALL OF WICKETS
1–37, 2–71, 3–130, 4–155, 5–173, 6–203, 7–204, 8–230, 9–231
1–14, 2–56, 3–56

FALL OF WICKETS
1–37, 2–42, 3–123, 4–139, 5–163

Umpires: I.D. Robinson & R. Jackson

Match drawn

gully to take the ball cleanly while still running at full tilt towards the boundary as the ball came down over his shoulder.

Zimbabwe were all out just before the end of the first day, and the visitors began their innings on the second morning, soon losing both openers to the off-spin of Traicos. The arrival of Samarasekera changed the complexion of the match. He hit 79 off 70 balls before playing across a straight ball from Traicos. His dismissal left Sri Lanka 'B' at 163 for 5 and the game nicely poised, but when Tillekeratne and wicket-keeper Gamini Wickremasinghe, who is unrelated to the opening batsman of the same name and who had had few opportunities on the tour, came together they put the game completely out of Zimbabwe's reach. Both reached centuries, and Tillekeratne faced 204 balls while Wickremasinghe faced 208 balls. Their unbroken partnership of 217, which extended into the third morning, was the highest sixth-wicket stand for a first-class match in Zimbabwe. It was a remarkable achievement.

Zimbabwe began their second innings 149 runs in arrears with only a draw to play for. Arnott set the pattern with 40 not out, which was accumulated from 17 deliveries. The pleasing aspect of the last afternoon was Trevor Penney's 67 not out in what was his maiden first-class match for the senior team. He batted with confidence and, after a slow start, played some pleasing strokes.

So the match ended in a draw. It was the 20th successive first-class match played by Zimbabwe in which they have failed to record a victory.

Fifth One-Day International
ZIMBABWE v. SRI LANKA 'B'

With the one-day series level at two matches each, the final match of the Sri Lankan's tour had an added interest, and it produced another exciting climax.

Once more Samarasekera was the outstanding performer. Coming in with the score at 12 for 1, he hit 94 off 108 balls. He and Dias added 81 for the third wicket, but Tillekeratne and Jurangpathy went quickly, and when the final surge for runs was needed over the closing overs of the innings there was inadequate support for Ranasinghe.

Zimbabwe began well, but they lost momentum after

Still keen and able, an intelligent leader and Zimbabwe's best bowler, John Traicos. (Ken Kelly)

Houghton had chopped a ball from Samarasekera into his stumps. Goodwin was impressive, but the run rate needed climbed to eight an over. Brandes improved the situation, but when Rawson ran himself out the cause looked lost. From the last 10 overs, 84 runs had been needed. Young Trevor Penney played finely, but he was torn between the need to stay at the crease and the need to score off every ball.

From the last over 14 were needed. Arnott was caught in the covers, and, after two fine blows, Jarvis was bowled. This left Traicos to face the last ball of the match and to be faced with the position of having to hit it for six to win the game and the series. Amid great tension, he drove powerfully, but Samarasekera, the bowler, got his hands to the ball above his head although he could not hold the catch.

The Zimbabwe team lined up to congratulate the Sri Lankans as they left the field, a nice gesture which confirmed that they had recovered their reputation for good sportsmanship, which had been tarnished the previous season when Pakistan 'B' were the visitors. The Sri Lankans, like New South Wales earlier in the year, were well led and strongly managed. They played hard but sportsmanlike cricket.

There is, perhaps, a need to assess the position of some of Zimbabwe's senior players. Traicos is still an accurate off-break bowler and excellent fielder in the gully and has

---

FIFTH ONE-DAY INTERNATIONAL – ZIMBABWE v. SRI LANKA 'B'
10 April 1988 at Harare Sports Club

SRI LANKA 'B'				ZIMBABWE			
A.M. de Silva*	b Brandes	10		D.L. Houghton*	b Samarasekera	27
D.S.G. Bulankulame	c Waller, b Duers	8		D.G. Goodwin	c Dias, b Wijesuriya	54
M.A.R. Samarasekera	b Duers	94		A.J. Pycroft	c de Silva,	
R.L. Dias†	c and b Jarvis	34			b Samarasekera	5
H.P. Tillekeratne	c Houghton, b Jarvis	0		A.C. Waller	c Jurangpathy,	
B.R. Jurangpathy	b Jarvis	6			b Wijesuriya	24
S.K. Ranasinghe	not out	46		T.L. Penney	not out	44
U.S.H. Karnain	lbw, b Brandes	3		E.A. Brandes	c Bulankulame,	
R.G.C.E. Wijesuriya	not out	6			b Ranasinghe	32
M.A.W.R.				P.W.E. Rawson	run out	2
Madurasinghe				K.J. Arnott	c Dias,	
A.K. Kuruppuarachchi					b Samarasekera	9
Extras	b 3, lb 5, w 3	11		M.P. Jarvis	b Samarasekera	4
				A.J. Traicos†	not out	0
(50 overs)	(for 7 wkts)	218		K.G. Duers		
				Extras	b 2, lb 6, w 4	12
				(50 overs)	(for 8 wkts)	213

	O	M	R	W		O	M	R	W
Brandes	10	1	23	2	Kuruppuarachchi	7	–	31	–
Jarvis	10	1	31	3	Karnain	6	–	27	–
Rawson	10	1	44	–	Samarasekera	10	–	44	4
Duers	10	–	69	2	Madurasinghe	10	–	26	–
Traicos	10	–	43	–	Wijesuriya	9	–	39	2
					Ranasinghe	8	–	38	1

FALL OF WICKETS
1-12, 2-32, 3-113, 4-113, 5-133, 6-180, 7-198

FALL OF WICKETS
1-65, 2-79, 3-98, 4-128, 5-179, 6-188, 7-209, 8-213

Umpires: R. Jackson & K. Kanjee

Sri Lanka 'B' won by 5 runs

shown no indication of wanting to retire for two or three years yet. Pycroft's batting seems to have been damaged by the one-day game, but he played well against New South Wales. Houghton, whose wicket-keeping was sorely missed, was too prone to waste his talents. He needs discrimination and self-discipline to ensure that he produces more innings like his memorable century in the Reliance World Cup. Rawson is no longer the fiery spearhead of Zimbabwe's attack, but the aggression and determination that was once a mark of his bowling seems now to appear in his batting, and he can claim to be his country's most reliable batsman.

The most encouraging sign, apart from the form of Goodwin and Penney, was the advent of the black pace bowler Elton Dube, who was one of Zimbabwe's representatives in the ICC Associates team in the World Youth Cup in Australia. If he can develop his undoubted potential, he could prove an inspiration to other black cricketers of Zimbabwe and the country's cricketing future would be assured.

First-Class Averages

BATTING

	M	Inns	NOs	Runs	HS	Av	100s	50s
T.L. Penney	2	4	2	142	67*	71.00		1
G.A. Paterson	1	2	1	61	59	61.00		1
A.J. Pycroft	3	5	1	234	104	58.50	1	1
K.J. Arnott	3	4	1	135	64	45.00		1
D.G. Goodwin	3	5		172	66	34.40		1
A.C. Waller	3	4	1	103	39*	34.33		
R.D. Brown	2	4	1	91	46	30.33		
D.L. Houghton	5	9		262	126	29.11	1	1
W.R. James	3	4		61	27	15.25		
A.H. Omarshah	3	5		53	23	10.60		

(Qualification – 50 runs, average 10.00)

BOWLING

	Overs	Mds	Runs	Wkts	Av	Best	10/m	5/inns
A.J. Traicos	140.5	43	306	10	30.60	4/77		
M.P. Jarvis	48	16	158	4	39.50	2/31		
E.A. Brandes	128.5	26	448	10	44.80	5/76		1
P.W.E. Rawson	71.3	14	218	4	54.50	2/64		

(Qualification – 4 wickets)

LEADING FIELDERS

6 - D.L. Houghton (ct 5/st 1); 4 - P.W.E. Rawson; 3 - K.J. Arnott and A.J. Traicos

Limited Season

The three-nations Sharjah Cup – India,
New Zealand and Sri Lanka at the
Sharjah Cricket Association Stadium,
United Arab Emirates.

Arivinda de Silva (Sri Lanka). (Adrian Murrell/Allsport)

The Reliance World Cup in October and November meant that Sharjah was able to stage only one international tournament in 1987–8, and the relentless programme of Test cricket meant that the tournament itself was restricted to three nations, India, Sri Lanka and New Zealand, all others being engaged or exhausted.

Sharjah Cup – Match One
INDIA v. SRI LANKA

The Sharjah Cricket Stadium maintained its tradition of providing thrilling finishes in the opening match of the competition. Madugalle won the toss and asked India to bat first. Srikkanth and Sidhu threatened a big stand, but Ratnayeke bowled Sidhu, and Amarnath was run out to give Sri Lanka the advantage. The Sri Lankans fielded splendidly and bowled with admirable control. Their most effective bowler was Aravinda de Silva, whose medium pace accounted for Raman and Kapil Dev when both were looking dangerous. The young all-rounder also bowled most economically and conceded only 28 runs in his nine overs so that Sri Lanka could be well pleased in having restricted India to 219.

On a perfect wicket, this was a moderate score, but Sri Lanka made a poor start in their quest for victory, losing Kuruppu and Gurusinha at 14. It was Aravinda de Silva

who revived them. He and Mahanama joined in an exciting partnership of 137 which took Sri Lanka to within 69 runs of victory, but both fell to the outstanding leg-spin bowling of Hirwani within seven runs of each other. Now wickets tumbled as a mixture of panic and inexperience saw the later Sri Lankan batsmen throw away a match which should have been theirs.

Sharjah Cup – Match Two
INDIA v. NEW ZEALAND

India reached the final of the competition with an emphatic win over New Zealand, who fielded poorly. Richard Hadlee played in Sharjah for the first time and gave a creditable all-round performance, but it was the teamwork of the Indians that triumphed. They lost Srikkanth and Raman for two after they had been put in to bat, but Sidhu and Amarnath added 158 for the third wicket, and Amarnath hit the third century to be made at Sharjah. Azharuddin and Shastri plundered well, and India's 267 was the highest score made in a Sharjah tournament.

There never seemed a remote chance of New Zealand reaching their target. Hirwani followed his excellent bowling in the opening match with another outstanding performance, and Kiran More became the first wicket-keeper to claim five dismissals in an international match in

---

SHARJAH CUP – MATCH ONE – INDIA v. SRI LANKA
25 March 1988 at Sharjah Cricket Association Stadium

INDIA				SRI LANKA			
K. Srikkanth	c Mahanama, b Ramanayake	32		R.S. Mahanama	b Hirwani	51	
N.S. Sidhu	b J.R. Ratnayeke	17		D.S.B.P. Kuruppu	c Shastri, b Sharma	6	
M.B. Amarnath	run out	1		A.P. Gurusinha	run out	0	
W.V. Raman	c Madugalle, b de Silva	21		P.A. de Silva	b Hirwani	88	
M. Azharuddin	b Ramanayake	7		A. Ranatunga	c Azharuddin, b Shastri	8	
R.N. Kapil Dev	c Madugalle, b de Silva	48		R.S. Madugalle†	st More, b Shastri	11	
R.J. Shastri†	c Mahanama, b J.R. Ratnayeke	26		R.G. de Alwis*	c Srikkanth, b Kapil Dev	2	
K.S. More*	run out	9		J.R. Ratnayeke	run out	4	
Arshad Ayub	not out	31		G.F. Labrooy	run out	0	
C.J. Sharma	not out	12		C.P. Ramanayake	run out	11	
N. Hirwani				S.D. Anurasiri	not out	3	
Extras	b 1, lb 7, w 2, nb 5	15		Extras	b 3, lb 10, w 3, nb 1	17	
(50 overs)	(for 8 wkts)	219		(49.2 overs)		201	

	O	M	R	W		O	M	R	W
J.R. Ratnayeke	10	–	34	2	Kapil Dev	9.2	2	26	1
Labrooy	9	–	41	–	Sharma	6	3	19	1
Ramanayake	7	–	37	2	Amarnath	6	–	26	–
Anurasiri	10	–	44	–	Shastri	8	–	40	2
P.A. de Silva	9	2	28	2	Hirwani	10	1	40	2
Ranatunga	5	–	27	–	Arshad Ayub	10	–	37	–

FALL OF WICKETS
1–31, 2–32, 3–63, 4–71, 5–125, 6–140, 7–152, 8–198

FALL OF WICKETS
1–14, 2–14, 3–151, 4–158, 5–177, 6–180, 7–181, 8–182, 9–190

Umpires: Khizar Hayat & Mahboob Shah

Man of the Match: P.A. de Silva

India won by 18 runs

Sharjah. All the honours went to India, and the New Zealanders did not come out of the match well, not least because of some of the comments that were attributed to them.

Sharjah Cup – Match Three
NEW ZEALAND v. SRI LANKA

The third match in the tournament was, in effect, an irrelevance. Having won their two matches, India had reached the final while Sri Lanka and New Zealand, now meeting in the qualifying league, were destined to meet in the semi-final for the right to play India.

Sri Lanka won the toss and asked New Zealand to bat first. Wright fell without a run on the board, but Vance and Jones added 94 before Vance was unnecessarily run out. Jones and Rutherford then added 103. Jones took the individual award for his 85 off 98 balls and his 2 sixes and 4 fours, but it was Rutherford who provided the greater aggression as he hit eight boundaries in his 65 which came off 58 balls. He fell to E.A.R. de Silva, who thereby captured his first wicket in a one-day international.

Dipak Patel, on his recall to the New Zealand side, batted well and was to complete an excellent all-round performance with a fine spell of bowling. His 27 came off only 30 deliveries, and his 3 for 22 represented his best

bowling performance in an international.

Kuruppu and Gurusinha gave Sri Lanka a good start, but thereafter there was little heart in the batting, a lack of fight which has become all too prominent in Sri Lankan cricket.

Sharjah Cup – Final League Table

	P	W	L	Pts	R/R
India	2	2	–	4	4.86
New Zealand	2	1	1	2	4.52
Sri Lanka	2	–	2	0	3.90

Sharjah Cup – Semi-Final
NEW ZEALAND v. SRI LANKA

Wright decided to bat first when he won the toss, and he and Robert Vance had fifty on the board in 12.1 overs. Wright was out at 76, the highest opening stand in the competition, but Vance shared another good partnership of 70 with Jones. The Wellington skipper reached his highest score in a one-day international and was unlucky to be run out just four short of his century as runs were

---

SHARJAH CUP – MATCH TWO – INDIA v. NEW ZEALAND
27 March 1988 at Sharjah Cricket Association Stadium

INDIA				NEW ZEALAND			
K. Srikkanth	b Watson	1		J.G. Wright†	c More, b Kapil Dev	19	
N.S. Sidhu	c Rutherford, b Watson	88		R.H. Vance	c More, b Arshad Ayub	42	
W.V. Raman	c Greatbatch, b Hadlee	1		A.H. Jones	c and b Azharuddin	6	
M.B. Amarnath	not out	102		M.J. Greatbatch	c More, b Hirwani	45	
R.N. Kapil Dev	c Kuggeleijn, b Hadlee	5		K.R. Rutherford	c sub, b Hirwani	3	
M. Azharuddin	run out	29		I.D.S. Smith*	b Hirwani	17	
R.J. Shastri†	c Smith, b Hadlee	29		C.M. Kuggeleijn	st More, b Hirwani	3	
K.S. More*	not out	3		R.J. Hadlee	not out	35	
Arshad Ayub				D.K. Morrison	st More, b Arshad Ayub	6	
C.J. Sharma				W. Watson	not out	4	
N. Hirwani				E.J. Chatfield			
Extras	lb 4, w 4, nb 1	9		Extras	b 1, lb 6, w 6, nb 1	14	
(50 overs)	(for 6 wkts)	267		(50 overs)	(for 8 wkts)	194	

	O	M	R	W
Hadlee	10	–	54	3
Watson	10	2	36	2
Morrison	10	–	45	–
Chatfield	10	–	57	–
Rutherford	5	–	38	–
Kuggeleijn	5	–	33	–

	O	M	R	W
Kapil Dev	10	2	30	1
Sharma	7	–	28	1
Azharuddin	4	–	15	1
Shastri	8	1	29	–
Hirwani	10	–	43	4
Arshad Ayub	10	1	41	2
Raman	1	–	1	–

FALL OF WICKETS
1–1, 2–4, 3–162, 4–167, 5–212, 6–260

FALL OF WICKETS
1–32, 2–46, 3–118, 4–120, 5–124, 6–139, 7–144, 8–175

Umpires: Khizar Hayat & Mahboob Shah

Man of the Match: M.B. Amarnath

India won by 73 runs

SHARJAH CUP – MATCH THREE – SRI LANKA v. NEW ZEALAND
29 March 1988 at Sharjah Cricket Association Stadium

NEW ZEALAND			
J.G. Wright†	c Kuruppu, b J.R. Ratnayeke		0
R.H. Vance	run out		45
A.H. Jones	run out		85
K.R. Rutherford	st Kuruppu, b E.A.R. de Silva		65
D.N. Patel	run out		27
M.J. Greatbatch	c Kaluperuma, b J.R. Ratnayeke		15
T.E. Blain*	run out		6
C.M. Kuggeleijn	not out		7
D.K. Morrison	run out		0
W. Watson	not out		2
E.J. Chatfield			
Extras	lb 4, w 2		6
(50 overs)	(for 8 wkts)		258

	O	M	R	W
J.R. Ratnayeke	10	–	33	2
Labrooy	7	–	41	–
Anurasiri	10	–	49	–
E.A.R. de Silva	10	–	42	1
Ranatunga	8	–	44	–
P.A. de Silva	4	–	31	–
Amalean	1	–	14	–

SRI LANKA			
D.S.B.P. Kuruppu*	run out		46
A.P. Gurusinha	c Vance, b Watson		27
R.S. Madugalle†	c Jones, b Kuggeleijn		15
P.A. de Silva	c Blain, b Rutherford		1
A. Ranatunga	b Kuggeleijn		6
J.R. Ratnayeke	c Blain, b Patel		25
S.M.S. Kaluperuma	lbw, b Patel		7
E.A.R. de Silva	c Jones, b Patel		4
G.F. Labrooy	b Morrison		5
S.D. Anurasiri	not out		5
K.N. Amalean	run out		6
Extras	lb 3, w 8, nb 1		12
(42.5 overs)			159

	O	M	R	W
Morrison	8	–	36	1
Chatfield	8	–	24	–
Watson	5	–	19	1
Kuggeleijn	10	2	32	2
Rutherford	5	–	23	1
Patel	6.5	–	22	3

FALL OF WICKETS
1–0, 2–94, 3–197, 4–201, 5–223, 6–248, 7–248, 8–249

FALL OF WICKETS
1–50, 2–93, 3–96, 4–96, 5–111, 6–124, 7–140, 8–142, 9–150

Umpires: Khizar Hayat & Mahboob Shah

Man of the Match: A.H. Jones

New Zealand won by 99 runs

SHARJAH CUP – SEMI-FINAL – SRI LANKA v. NEW ZEALAND
31 March 1988 at Sharjah Cricket Association Stadium

NEW ZEALAND			
R.H. Vance	run out		96
J.G. Wright†	st de Alwis, b P.A. de Silva		45
A.H. Jones	b Ranatunga		33
M.J. Greatbatch	run out		12
K.R. Rutherford	c Gurusinha, b E.A.R. de Silva		9
R.J. Hadlee	c Ratnayeke, b E.A.R. de Silva		14
D.N. Patel	lbw, b E.A.R. de Silva		0
C.M. Kuggeleijn	not out		24
T.E. Blain*	not out		6
W. Watson			
E.J. Chatfield			
Extras	b 1, lb 5, w 4		10
(50 overs)	(for 7 wkts)		249

	O	M	R	W
J.R. Ratnayeke	8	–	27	–
Labrooy	10	–	65	–
P.A. de Silva	10	1	41	1
Ranatunga	10	–	43	1
Anurasiri	4	–	29	–
E.A.R. de Silva	8	–	38	3

SRI LANKA			
R.S. Mahanama	c Rutherford, b Patel		43
D.S.B.P. Kuruppu	c Vance, b Watson		0
A.P. Gurusinha	lbw, b Hadlee		60
P.A. de Silva	c and b Kuggeleijn		1
A. Ranatunga	b Patel		2
R.S. Madugalle†	run out		25
J.R. Ratnayeke	c Greatbatch, b Watson		31
R.G. de Alwis*	not out		16
E.A.R. de Silva	b Chatfield		10
G.F. Labrooy	b Watson		1
S.D. Anurasiri	not out		3
Extras	lb 12, w 1, nb 1		14
(50 overs)	(for 9 wkts)		206

	O	M	R	W
Hadlee	10	1	25	1
Watson	9	1	37	3
Chatfield	10	–	48	1
Kuggeleijn	10	–	37	1
Patel	10	–	45	2
Jones	1	–	2	–

FALL OF WICKETS
1–76, 2–146, 3–180, 4–199, 5–204, 6–204, 7–230

FALL OF WICKETS
1–0, 2–90, 3–92, 4–95, 5–115, 6–158, 7–174, 8–192, 9–196

Umpires: Khizar Hayat & Mahboob Shah

Man of the Match: R.H. Vance

New Zealand won by 43 runs

Dipak Patel was recalled by New Zealand and played some of his best all-round cricket at international level. (George Herringshaw)

being plundered and wickets were tumbling in the late-innings frenzy. Having tasted blood in the previous match, E.A.R. de Silva took 3 for 38, a commendable performance.

Chasing a target of five runs an over, Sri Lanka lost Kuruppu for 0, but Mahanama and Gurusinha added 90 in a solid stand which raised hopes. Then wickets began to fall, and even a brave stand by Ratnayeke and Madugalle could not stop the inevitable.

Sri Lanka suffered their eighth consecutive defeat in Sharjah. They had won their opening match, against Pakistan in 1984, since when they had known nothing but defeat. Their poor showing in the World Cup and in Australia indicated that desperate remedies are urgently needed, and surely a domestic first-class competition must be the priority.

Tony Blain kept wicket well and batted with elegance when given the opportunity in both Australia and Sharjah but remains in the shadow of Ian Smith. (Adrian Murrell/ Allsport)

Sharjah Cup Final
INDIA v. NEW ZEALAND

Choosing to bat first after winning the toss, India were so restricted by the accuracy of the New Zealand attack and the keenness of the fielding that after 27 overs they had made only 87 for 4. The hundred went up five overs later, but there was no suggestion that they would reach a big score. Sidhu had started briskly, but Hadlee, Watson and Chatfield conceded only 33 in a 15-over period. Amarnath was unable to lift the rate, but he was able to stay put until the arrival of Shastri, and together they added 72. Armanath hit 58 off 71 balls with a six and 3 fours, but it was the advent of Shastri which transformed the match. He hit the first ball he received for a towering six, and when he was joined by Kapil Dev the ball flew in all directions.

Shastri hit 72 from 68 deliveries, with 3 sixes and 3 fours, and passed 2,000 runs in one-day international cricket. Kapil Dev was even more violent with 2 fours and 2 sixes as he hit 49 off 26 balls. His 2 sixes were off successive balls in the last over of the innings, which was bowled by Chatfield and which produced 18 runs. In the last nine overs, India scored 100 runs and at one point 50 came in 3.3 overs. None of the New Zealand bowlers was spared. Hadlee's last five overs cost him 41 runs while Chatfield's last six cost 51 and Morrison's last four, 33.

A shell-shocked New Zealand side soon lost Vance to Sanjeeva Sharma, who had replaced Chetan Sharma in the Indian side. Wright batted with elegance and composure and hit 5 fours before attempting an impossible run. Greatbatch, benefiting from being twice dropped, sug-

gested temporary aggression, and Smith hit 40 off 33 balls, but wickets fell and the cause always looked lost. In fact, New Zealand needed only 56 from the last ten overs, a by no means impossible task if they had other than Morrison, Watson and Chatfield left to make them. It was Hirwani who had destroyed the middle order and given the match to India.

The young leg-spinner was named Man of the Series for his remarkable 10 wickets for 129 runs in three matches, and he received not only 2,500 American dollars as part of the award, but a gift of Dhs 10,000 from the Sindhi community in the United Arab Emirates. India, New Zealand and Sri Lanka all went home very much richer, and there were large donations to the two beneficiaries, Lala and Mohinder Amarnath, while Richard Hadlee was presented with 20,000 American dollars in recognition of his 373 Test wickets.

Pakistan were sorely missed, for this was the first tournament to be played in Sharjah in which they have not competed, but still the attendances were large. New Zealand very much missed Martin Crowe, who had remained in New Zealand to attend the wedding of brother Jeff, but India dominated even without the banned Dilip Vengsarkar.

SHARJAH CUP FINAL – INDIA v. NEW ZEALAND
1 April 1988 at Sharjah Cricket Association Stadium

INDIA				NEW ZEALAND			
K. Srikkanth	b Chatfield		14	R.H. Vance	c More, b S.K. Sharma		3
N.S. Sidhu	c Hadlee, b Patel		33	J.G. Wright†	run out		55
W.V. Raman	b Kuggeleijn		7	A.H. Jones	lbw, b Amarnath		15
M.B. Amarnath	c Greatbatch, b Morrison		58	M.J. Greatbatch	c Kapil Dev, b Hirwani		47
M. Azharuddin	run out		6	D.N. Patel	c Shastri, b Hirwani		1
R.J. Shastri†	b Hadlee		72	R.J. Hadlee	c Arshad Ayub, b Hirwani		3
R.N. Kapil Dev	not out		49	C.M. Kuggeleijn	c Srikkanth, b Hirwani		7
K.S. More*	c Morrison, b Chatfield		5	I.D.S. Smith*	c S.K. Sharma, b Raman		40
Arshad Ayub	not out		0	D.K. Morrison	b Kapil Dev		7
S.K. Sharma				W. Watson	b Shastri		10
N. Hirwani				E.J. Chatfield	not out		1
Extras	b 1, lb 3, w 2		6	Extras	lb 7, w 2		9
(50 overs)	(for 7 wkts)		250	(45.3 overs)			198

	O	M	R	W		O	M	R	W
Hadlee	10	–	49	1	Kapil Dev	7.3	2	14	1
Watson	7	2	37	–	S.K. Sharma	6	–	21	1
Chatfield	10	–	57	2	Shastri	9	–	25	1
Kuggeleijn	10	–	38	1	Amarnath	2	–	14	1
Patel	9	–	32	1	Hirwani	10	–	46	4
Morrison	4	–	33	1	Arshad Ayub	9	–	48	–
					Raman	2	–	23	1

FALL OF WICKETS
1–28, 2–49, 3–70, 4–82, 5–154, 6–227, 7–232

FALL OF WICKETS
1–15, 2–60, 3–92, 4–94, 5–94, 6–113, 7–160, 8–182, 9–196

Umpires: Khizar Hayat & Mahboob Shah

Man of the Match: R.J. Shastri

India won by 52 runs

Clash of Giants

The season in West Indies.
Red Stripe Cup.
West Indies *v.* Pakistan, Test series
and One-Day International series.
First-class averages.
Form charts.

Curtley Ambrose – 35 wickets in the Red Stripe Cup – a new record for West Indian domestic competition. (ASP)

After 22 years of sponsorship of West Indies domestic competition Shell withdrew and were replaced by Red Stripe, 'the Great Jamaican Beer'. The new sponsors revitalized the tournament, marketing soundly and vigorously, so that public interest was awakened after the economic restrictions of the previous season. Most marked was the advance of several young players, a happy state of affairs for West Indies, who had been somewhat worried at an apparent dearth of talent in recent seasons.

Guystac Trophy

30, 31 October, 1 and 2 November 1987

at Camo, Ayangana, Georgetown, Guyana

Demarara 284 (M.A. Harper 85, D.I. Harper 70, R. Doodnauth 5 for 83) and 77 for 4
Berbice 216 (S. Dhaniram 72, C.G. Butts 5 for 56)

Match drawn

The only first-class match played before Christmas was marred by bad weather. Mark Hooper confirmed his promise of the previous season with a good innings.

Red Stripe Cup

22, 23, 24 and 25 January 1988

at Guaracara Park, Point-à-Pierre, Trinidad

Leeward Islands 147 (I.R. Bishop 4 for 23) and 195 (K.L.T. Arthurton 69, R. Nanan 4 for 32, I.R. Bishop 4 for 42)
Trinidad and Tobago 171 and 172 for 8

Trinidad and Tobago won by 2 wickets
Trinidad and Tobago 16 pts, Leeward Islands 0 pts

The sensation of the opening match of the Red Stripe Cup was fast bowler Ian Bishop. He had played in two matches the previous season without making any impact, but he opened the new competition with a furious spell of bowling which, in conjunction with Tony Gray, reduced the visitors to 33 for 5 on the opening morning. Conditions were never easy for batsmen, and Trinidad were happy to take a first-innings lead of 24. Bishop and off-break bowler Nanan, seven wickets in the match, again troubled Leeward, but Keith Arthurton played a mature and delightful innings, and Trinidad were left to make 172 to win. At 148 for 7, the game was in the balance, but Gray and Joseph added 22, and Bishop came in to make the winning runs. Ranjie Nanan's 48 and 5 not out and 7 for 56 earned him the individual award.

29, 30, 31 January and 1 Feburary 1988

at Queen's Park Oval, Port-of-Spain, Trinidad

Barbados 250 (M.D. Marshall 71, R. Dhanraj 4 for 67) and 205 (C.A. Best 77, A.H. Gray 4 for 54)
Trinidad and Tobago 292 (B.C. Lara 92)

Match drawn
Trinidad and Tobago 8 pts, Barbados 4 pts

Another West Indian fast bowler emerges. Ian Bishop, 4 for 23 in the opening Red Stripe Cup match and a highly successful season for Trinidad. (Alan Cozzi)

at Albion Complex, Berbice, Guyana

Guyana 260 (C. Burnett 50) and 242 (C. Burnett 52, R.C. Haynes 4 for 51)
Jamaica 358 (R.C. Haynes 87, W.W. Lewis 85) and 148 for 1 (W.W. Lewis 72 not out, D.S. Morgan 57)

Jamaica won by 9 wickets
Jamaica 16 pts, Guyana 0 pts

at Recreation Ground, St John's, Antigua

Windward Islands 244 (D. Joseph 70) and 233 for 8 dec (D. Telemaque 71)
Leeward Islands 238 (R.M. Otto 59, L. Harris 52) and 95 for 2

Match drawn
Windward Islands 8 pts, Leeward Islands 4 pts

Rain interrupted the game at Queen's Park Oval, where Trinidad were in a strong position. Brian Lara, a diminutive left-handed batsman, 18 years old, played most impressively for the home side.

Jamaica gained a most important away victory and owed much to a fine all-round performance from Robert Haynes, the left-handed batsman and leg-break and googly bowler. He captured the first three wickets and shared a second-wicket stand of 147 with Wayne Lewis, who played two fine innings. Jamaica romped to victory at five runs an over.

Tony Gray, conspicuous in Trinidad's early season success, but could not find his way back into the Test side. (Mark Leech)

Windward Islands gained what were to be their only points of the season in the drawn match with Leeward Islands, for whom Curtley Ambrose took three wickets to add to the six he had taken in the opening match. Ambrose had been called for throwing by Test umpire Cumberbatch in the game in Trinidad, but he went through the rest of the season unscathed.

4, 5, 6 and 7 February 1988

at Queen's Park, St George's, Grenada

Barbados 279 (T.R.O. Payne 127, A.L. Grant 75, D.J. Collymore 4 for 72) and 241 for 7 dec (M.D. Marshall 55 not out, T.R.O. Payne 53)
Windward Islands 154 (D.J. Collymore 52 not out, M.D. Marshall 5 for 55) and 222 (L.C. Sebastien 55, M.D. Marshall 4 for 54, J. Garner 4 for 59)

Barbados won by 122 runs
Barbados 16 pts, Windward Islands 0 pts

5, 6, 7 and 8 February 1988

at Hampton Court, Essequibo, Guyana

Guyana 178 for 2 (C.B. Lambert 103 not out, R. Seeram 56 not out)
v. Trinidad and Tobago

Match drawn
Guyana 4 pts, Trinidad and Tobago 4 pts

6, 7, 8 and 9 February 1988

at Warner Park, Basseterre, St Kitts

Leeward Islands 186 (R.C. Haynes 6 for 85) and 401 for 3 dec (E.A.E. Baptiste 99, A.L. Kelly 79, K.L.T. Arthurton 77 not out, R.M. Otto 74 not out)
Jamaica 96 (E.L.C. Ambrose 5 for 40, W.K.M. Benjamin 5 for 50) and 186 (E.L.C. Ambrose 4 for 52)

Leeward Islands won by 305 runs
Leeward Islands 16 pts, Jamaica 0 pts

Thelston Payne hit the fifth century of his career and shared a fourth-wicket stand of 147 with Adrian Grant after Barbados had lost their first three wickets for seven runs to set Barbados on their way to victory over Windward Islands. It was veteran Test bowlers Garner and Marshall who twice destroyed the home side, returning match figures of 7 for 98 and 9 for 109 respectively. Payne continued his dominance of the match with five catches behind the stumps in Windward's first innings and two in the second.

There was no play possible on the first three days at Hampton Court, where Clayton Lambert and Ravi Seeram shared an unbroken third-wicket stand of 156, which was dominated by Lambert.

Thelston Payne displayed outstanding form with the bat for Barbados. (George Herringshaw)

Barbados 1988
First-Class Matches

BATTING

	v. Trinidad & Tobago (Port-of-Spain) 29 Jan.–1 Feb.		v. Windward Islands (St George's) 4–7 February		v. Guyana (Bridgetown) 13–16 February		v. Jamaica (Kingston) 20–3 February		v. Leeward Islands (Bridgetown) 26–9 February	
C.A. Best	15	77	2	5	98	—	1	54	53	23
A.S. Gilkes	15	20	0	17						
R.I.C. Holder	33	25	0	5						
P.J. Alleyne	0	0			10	—			6	3
T.R.O. Payne	31	20	127	53	92	—	82	8	11	37
A.L. Grant	10	32*	75	21	8	—	43	24	4	6
M.D. Marshall	71	2	16	55*	77	—	1	8	56	12
H. Springer	0	0*	9*	—	—	—	0	18*	17*	14*
J. Garner	29	0	8	17	62	—	2	18	0	1
V.S. Greene	16	2	1	—	0*	—				
W.E. Reid	6*	9	0	31						
L.N. Reifer			23	10						
C.G. Greenidge					41	36*	4	70	18	46
D.L. Haynes					64	33*	20	7	39	35
V. Walcott					—	—	1	1	1	11
T.A. Hunte							12	0		
G.L. Linton							3*	0	1	7
Byes	2	9	1	5	5		4	6	13	
Leg-byes	8	4	5	8	10		4	9	5	3
Wides	7					2			1	
No-balls	7	5	12	14	7		4	4	18	10
Total	250	205	279	241	474	71	181	227	243	208
Wickets	10	9	10	7	8	0	10	10	10	10
Result	D		W		W		L		L	
Points	4		16		16		0		0	

Fielding Figures
15 – T.R.O. Payne (ct 14/st 1)
5 – M.D. Marshall
4 – C.A. Best and H. Springer
3 – V.S. Greene, A.L. Grant and subs
1 – P.J. Alleyne, J. Garner and V. Walcott

BOWLING

	J. Garner	M.D. Marshall	V.S. Greene	H. Springer	W.E. Reid	C.A. Best	A.L. Grant	V. Walcott	G.L. Linton
v. Trinidad & Tobago (Port-of-Spain) 29 Jan.–1 Feb.	24–3–71–3	24–2–60–2	14–4–31–0	24–5–61–1	14–1–42–3	5–1–17–1			
v. Windward Islands (St George's) 4–7 February	15–3–39–3	19–5–55–5	11–3–35–2	8–2–16–0	1–0–6–0				
	21–8–59–4	24–7–54–4	12–1–25–0	19–5–32–2	16–4–34–0		1–1–0–0		
v. Guyana (Bridgetown) 13–16 February	11–1–36–1	17–2–67–3	8–2–22–1	19–2–63–4				13–0–41–1	
	19–4–64–4	20.1–1–67–3	8–1–32–0	13–1–58–0			1–0–7–0	19–4–63–1	
v. Jamaica (Kingston) 20–3 February	16.4–2–39–4	18–8–59–1		10–1–37–2				13–1–48–0	21–5–58–2
	19–3–47–1	15.4–6–24–5		15–4–19–1				14–2–33–1	28–6–59–2
v. Leeward Islands (Bridgetown) 26–9 February	22.1–1–95–3	21–1–80–4		15–0–52–1				17–0–78–0	25–2–86–1
	1–1–0–0			2–0–5–0			4–0–26–0		1–0–14–0
	148.5–26–	158.5–32–	53–11–	125–20–	31–5–	5–1–	2–1–	80–7–	75–13–
	450–23	466–27	145–3	343–11	82–3	17–1	7–0	289–3	217–5
	av. 19.56	*av.* 17.25	*av.* 48.33	*av.* 31.18	*av.* 27.33	*av.* 17.00	—	*av.* 96.33	*av.* 43.40

a S. Dhaniram absent injured
b G.J.F. Ferris absent injured

	M	Inns	Nos	Runs	HS	Av
	5	9	—	328	98	36.44
	2	4	—	52	20	13.00
	2	4	—	63	33	15.75
	3	5	—	19	10	3.80
	5	9	—	461	127	51.22
	5	9	1	223	75	27.87
	5	9	1	298	77	37.25
	5	7	5	58	18*	29.00
	5	9	—	137	62	15.22
	3	4	1	19	16	6.33
	2	4	1	46	31	15.33
	1	2	—	33	23	16.50
	3	6	1	215	70	43.00
	3	6	1	198	64	39.60
	3	4	—	14	11	3.50
	1	2	—	12	12	6.00
	2	4	1	11	7	3.66

	Byes	Leg-byes	Wides	No-balls	Total	Wkts
	5	5		27	292	10
	1	2		9	154	10
	8	10	1	10	222	10
	1	3		14	233	10
	6	12		18	309	9a
	14	8	2	8	263	10
	10	6	1	4	198	10
	10	5	1	9	406	9b
			2	1	47	0

Robert Haynes produced the best bowling performance of his career and, seemingly, put Jamaica in a strong position against Leeward Islands, who lost their last six wickets for 63 runs. The game was completely transformed, however, by Curtley Ambrose and Winston Benjamin, who bowled out the visitors before lunch on the second day. Some splendidly consistent and aggressive batting then took Leeward Islands to a massive total. Kelly and Baptiste added 113 for the second wicket, and the exciting Arthurton and Otto shared an unbroken partnership of 148 for the fourth wicket. The sharp lift of Ambrose again proved too much for Jamaica, and the home side won by a huge margin. The achievement of Ambrose was all the more remarkable when one considered that in his two previous matches prior to 1988, he had taken 4 wickets for 140 runs.

13, 14, 15 and 16 February 1988

at Sabina Park, Kingston, Jamaica

Windward Islands 236 (D. Joseph 109, C.A. Walsh 5 for 45) and 233
Jamaica 505 for 5 dec (W.W. Lewis 132, P.J.L. Dujon 108, D.S. Morgan 101 not out)

Jamaica won by an innings and 36 runs
Jamaica 16 pts, Windward Islands 0 pts

at Kensington Oval, Bridgetown, Barbados

Guyana 233 (H. Springer 4 for 63) and 309 (R. Seeram 87, C. Burnett 63, J. Garner 4 for 64)
Barbados 474 for 8 dec (C.A. Best 98, T.R.O. Payne 92, M.D. Marshall 77, D.L. Haynes 64, J. Garner 62) and 71 for 0

Barbados won by 10 wickets
Barbados 16 pts, Guyana 0 pts

Welcoming back their Test players, Walsh, Patterson, Dujon and Holding, who had been in New Zealand, Jamaica completely overwhelmed Windward Islands. Having lost two wickets for eight runs, Windward were held together by Darnley Joseph, who hit a maiden first-class century, but the last five wickets fell for 25 runs. Lewis and Morgan put on 145 for Jamaica's first wicket, at which point Morgan, on 65, was forced to retire hurt. He returned at 417 for 3 and became the third Jamaican to complete a hundred in the match. Windward began promisingly enough in their second innings, but their middle order fell apart and they never looked like saving the game.

Barbados moved four points clear of Jamaica at the top of the table when they beat Guyana with ease. Marshall, Garner and Springer proved too much of a handful for the visitors, and the powerful Barbadian batting built up an impregnable score. Payne was again in splendid form and added 168 with Best, and Marshall and Garner hit furiously before the declaration.

19, 20, 21 and 22 February 1988

at Windsor Park, Roseau, Dominican Republic

Trinidad and Tobago 201 (P.V. Simmons 64) and 146
Windward Islands 172 (D.J. Collymore 87 not out, A.H. Gray 4 for 56) and 101 (L.D. John 53, R. Nanan 5 for 31, G. Mahabir 4 for 30)

Guyana 1988
First-Class Matches

BATTING

	v. Jamaica (Albion) 29 Jan.–1 Feb.		v. Trinidad & Tobago (Essequibo) 5–8 February		v. Barbados (Bridgetown) 13–16 February		v. Leeward Islands (St John's) 19–22 February		v. Windward Islands (Albion) 26–9 February	
C.B. Lambert	39	27	103*	—	39	59	40	43	162	36*
S. Dhaniram	30	45	2	—	31	—				
A.F.D. Jackman	32	8								
M.A. Harper	21	10					21	0		
R. Seeram	31	14	56*	—	39	87	0	40	119	38*
C. Burnett	50	52	—	—	38	63	15	10	0	—
G.E. Charles	0	17	—	—	6	20	7	11	3	—
M.R. Pydanna	0	17	—	—	9	20	0*	2		
S. Matthews	28*	7	—		25*	4	0	4	0	—
J. Angus	4	3*								
C.V. Solomon	4	5	—	—						
A.A. Lyght			4	—						
C.G. Butts			—	—	8	16	16	2	3	—
D.I. Harper			—	—	1	0	11	52*	3	—
A.F. Sattaur					16	4				
B.St A. Browne					3	0*	2	1	0*	—
J.I. Simpson						4		51	0	4
R.A. Harper									29	—
S. Mohammed									47	—
Byes	5	17	6		1	6	8	2	8	
Leg-byes	6	11	3		3	12	6	2	10	3
Wides	2		1				4			
No-balls	8	9	3		14	18	6	12	11	
Total	260	242	178		233	309	140	232	395	85
Wickets	10	10	2		10	9†	10	10	10	1
Result	L		D		L		L		W	
Points	0		4		0		0		16	

Fielding Figures

4 – C.B. Lambert and R. Seeram
3 – M.R. Pydanna and S. Mohammed (ct 2/st 1)
2 – C.G. Butts, M.A. Harper and R.A. Harper
1 – C. Burnett, G.E. Charles, J.I. Simpson and S. Matthews

†S. Dhaniram absent injured

BOWLING

	C.V. Solomon	G.E. Charles	C. Burnett	S. Matthews	J. Angus	S. Dhaniram	B.St A. Browne	C.G. Butts	C.B. Lambert
v. Jamaica (Albion) 29 Jan.–1 Feb.	14–2–66–3 5–0–24–0	24–7–63–2 5–0–19–0	25–12–38–1 8–0–37–0	33–5–100–3 4–0–22–0	28–7–62–0 6–0–38–0	0.4–0–3–0			
v. Trinidad & Tobago (Essequibo) 5–8 February									
v. Barbados (Bridgetown) 13–16 February		30–0–99–0 3–0–32–0	9–0–41–0	31.3–1–115–2			25–1–83–2 4–0–26–0	49–13–121–3	1.5–0–11–0
v. Leeward Islands (St John's) 19–22 February		21.4–2–97–5	10–0–37–0	27–4–84–0			24–0–95–3	33–5–83–2	
v. Windward Islands (Albion) 26–9 February		17–3–48–5 15–2–72–2	4–1–14–0	5.2–1–10–0 16–2–51–1			11–0–44–1 13–0–47–2	9–3–40–1 27–5–64–1	
	19–2– 90–3 av. 30.00	115.4–14– 430–14 av. 30.71	56–13– 167–1 av. 167.00	116.5–13– 382–6 av. 63.66	34–7– 100–0 —	0.4–0– 3–0 —	77–1– 295–8 av. 36.87	118–26– 308–7 av. 44.00	1.5–0– 11–0 —

M	Inns	Nos	Runs	HS	Av
5	9	2	548	162	78.28
3	4	—	108	45	27.00
1	2	—	40	32	20.00
2	4	—	52	21	13.00
5	9	2	424	119	60.57
5	7	—	228	63	32.57
5	7	—	64	20	9.14
4	6	1	48	20	9.60
5	7	2	68	28*	13.60
1	2	1	7	4	7.00
2	2	—	9	5	4.50
1	1	—	4	4	4.00
4	5	—	45	16	9.00
4	5	1	67	52*	16.75
1	2	—	20	16	10.00
3	5	2	6	3	2.00
2	4	—	59	51	14.75
1	1	—	29	29	29.00
1	1	—	47	47	47.00

D.I. Harper	R.A. Harper	Byes	Leg-byes	Wides	No-balls	Total	Wkts
		20	9	2	2	358	10
		4	1	1		148	1
							Ab.
		5	10		7	474	8
1-0-2-0				2		71	0
		1	11	1	5	408	10
	9-2-27-1	4	4			177	10
	14.3-1-33-2	12	4		1	297	10
1-0-	23.3-3-						
2-0	60-3						
—	av. 20.00						

Still a fine cricketer for Barbados with bat and ball – Joel Garner. (Adrian Murrell/Allsport)

Trinidad and Tobago won by 74 runs
Trinidad and Tobago 16 pts, Windward Islands 0 pts

at Recreation Ground, St John's, Antigua

Guyana 140 (E.L.C. Ambrose 7 for 61) and 232 (D.I. Harper 52 not out, J.I. Simpson 51, E.L.C. Ambrose 5 for 67)
Leeward Islands 408 (K.L.T. Arthurton 122, I.V.A. Richards 119, L. Harris 63, G.E. Charles 5 for 97)

Leeward Islands won by an innings and 36 runs
Leeward Islands 16 pts, Guyana 0 pts

at Sabina Park, Kingston, Jamaica

Jamaica 263 (J. Garner 4 for 39) and 198 (M.C. Neita 55, M.D. Marshall 5 for 24)
Barbados 181 (T.R.O. Payne 82, M.A. Tucker 6 for 38) and 227 (C.G. Greenidge 70, C.A. Best 54, M.A. Tucker 5 for 66)

Jamaica won by 59 runs
Jamaica 16 pts, Barbados 0 pts

The penultimate round of matches in the Red Stripe Cup

Jamaica 1988
First-Class Matches

BATTING

BATTING	v. Guyana (Albion) 29 Jan.–1 Feb.		v. Leeward Islands (Basseterre) 6–9 February		v. Windward Islands (Kingston) 13–16 February		v. Barbados (Kingston) 20–3 February		v. Trinidad & Tobago (Kingston) 26–9 February	
D.S. Morgan	11	57			101*	—	3	16	18	—
W.W. Lewis	85	72*	23	13	132	—	49	10	44	—
R.C. Haynes	87	13*	23	17	36	—	30	20	10	—
M.C. Neita	22	—	1	34	58	—	16	55	45	—
C.A. Davidson	21	—	9	10	3*	—	28	24	55	—
J.C. Adams	34	—	2	0						
M.A. Tucker	43	—	6	23	—		0	15	18	—
A.G. Daley	2	—	10	32					23	—
P.A. Francis	9	—	0	0						
N.O. Perry	4*	—	8*	9						
K.W. McLeod	7	—	0	1*						
N. Kennedy			3	27*						
G. Powell					8	—				
P.J.L. Dujon					108	—	37	16	80	—
M.A. Holding					—	—	24	6*		
C.A. Walsh					—	—	29	8	24	—
B.P. Patterson					—	—	15*	0	3*	—
F.A. Cunningham							0	7	3	—
C.St G. O'Connor										
S. Gordon										
G.A. Heron										
D.C. Dixon										
T. Samuels										
E.L. Wilson										
L.O. Cunningham										
Byes	20	4	5	8	22		14	10	17	
Leg-byes	9	1	1	6	15		8	6	33	
Wides	2	1					2	1		
No-balls	2		5	6	22		8	4	5	
Total	358	148	96	186	505		263	198	378	
Wickets	10	1	10	9†	5		10	10	10	
Result	W		L		W		W		D	
Points	16		0		16		16		8	

Fielding Figures

7 – P.J.L. Dujon

5 – D.S. Morgan

3 – P.A. Francis (ct 1/st 2), A.G. Daley, M.A. Tucker, C.A. Davidson, M.C. Neita and subs

2 – N.O. Perry

1 – N. Kennedy, J.C. Adams, C.A. Walsh, R.C. Haynes and W.W. Lewis

†N. Kennedy retired hurt

BOWLING

BOWLING	K.W. McLeod	A.G. Daley	N.O. Perry	R.C. Haynes	M.A. Tucker	J.C. Adams	M.C. Neita	B.P. Patterson
v. Guyana (Albion) 29 Jan.–1 Feb.	9–2–32–0	17–6–56–2	18–3–51–0	34–8–56–3	20–6–42–3	5–1–12–1		
	8–0–39–0	24–3–59–2	14–6–28–1	26–8–51–4	17–7–15–1		10–3–22–1	
v. Leeward Islands (Basseterre) 6–9 February	7–0–21–0	13–3–34–2	13–5–22–0	34.3–11–85–6	15–8–21–1			
	14–1–57–0	31–3–100–1	21–6–48–0	34–6–99–1	7–2–14–0		16–1–61–1	
v. Windward Islands (Kingston) 13–16 February				30–7–71–0	14–2–32–0			12–2–43–3
				22–8–52–1	12–3–26–3			16.2–3–59–3
v. Barbados (Kingston) 20–3 February				7–2–25–0	15.1–5–38–6			10–1–51–1
				6–1–10–0	27–7–66–5			16–4–42–2
v. Trinidad & Tobago (Kingston) 26–9 February		5–0–37–1		19.1–5–53–6	10–2–33–0			11–4–32–1
		26–6–66–3		28.2–5–62–1	6–3–11–1			15–3–54–0
v. Lancashire (Kingston) 5–7 April		27.3–2–103–6						
	38–3– 149–0	143.3–23– 455–17	66–20– 149–1	241–61– 564–22	143.1–45– 298–20	5–1– 12–1	26–4– 83–2	80.2–17– 281–10
	—	av. 26.76	av. 149.00	av. 25.63	av. 14.90	av. 12.00	av. 41.50	av. 28.10

a G.A. Heron 17–2–36–0

v. Lancashire (Kingston) 5–7 April		M	Inns	Nos	Runs	HS	Av
		4	6	1	206	101*	41.20
71	9	6	10	1	508	132	56.44
		5	8	1	236	87	33.71
		5	7	—	231	58	33.00
4	23	6	9	1	177	55	22.12
		2	3	—	36	34	12.00
		5	6	—	105	43	17.50
30	0	4	6	—	97	32	16.50
36	0*	3	5	1	45	36	11.25
		2	3	2	21	9	21.00
		2	3	1	8	7	4.00
		1	2	1	30	27*	30.00
		1	1	—	8	8	8.00
		3	4	—	241	108	60.25
		2	2	1	30	24	30.00
		3	3	—	61	29	20.33
		3	3	2	18	15*	18.00
		2	3	—	10	7	3.33
36	9	1	2	—	45	36	22.50
3	12	1	2	—	15	12	7.50
0	12*	1	2	1	12	12*	12.00
10	2	1	2	—	12	10	6.00
5	—	1	1	—	5	5	5.00
17*	—	1	1	1	17	17*	—
46	35	1	2	—	81	46	40.50
6							
6	1						
1							
1							
272	103						
10	7						
D	—						

provided some tense struggles, outstanding performances and controversial incidents.

Trinidad had the better of a low-scoring match at Roseau where the slow pitch was typical of many in the Caribbean. Indeed, Malcolm Marshall threatened to bowl leg-breaks if wickets in Barbados could not be made with more pace. The spinners, Nanan, off-breaks, and Mahabir, leg-breaks, were ultimately responsible for Trinidad's victory as Windward, 54 without loss, collapsed to 101 all out.

The magnificent bowling of Curtley Ambrose, 9 of whose 12 wickets were clean bowled, gave Leeward Islands a resounding victory over Guyana. Ambrose bowled unchanged in the first innings, and his 12 for 128 brought him to within three of Winston Davis' record 33 wickets in the Shell Shield. Keith Arthurton, the young pretender, and Viv Richards, the old master, combined in a fourth-wicket stand of 153 which gave substance and panache to the Leeward innings. They looked the best balanced and strongest side in the tournament, but their indifferent start to the season had made their chances of winning the title slim.

It looked as if the championship would go to the winners of the game at Sabina Park, and the tension in this match led to argument and dissension. Garner captured two early wickets for the visitors, but consistently solid batting thereafter took Jamaica to 263 after rain interruptions. Payne and Grant threatened to take a grip on the game for Barbados, who reached 156 for 3, but Holding broke the stand, and Marlon Tucket, the Jamaican captain, who had an outstanding match, took three quick wickets. From 170 for 4, Barbados collapsed to 181 all out, and Jamaica had grabbed first-innings points and a most valuable lead of 82 runs. Marshall, who was captain of Barbados for the first time in 1988, brought his side back into contention with some glorious bowling which brought him 5 for 24 in 15.4 overs. Needing 287 to win, Barbados lost Haynes at 20 when he was adjudged lbw to Patterson. It seemed to

C.A. Walsh	M.A. Holding	D.S. Morgan	F.A. Cunningham	T. Samuels	E.L. Wilson	D.C. Dixon	C.A. Davidson	Byes	Leg-byes	Wides	No-balls	Total	Wkts
								5	6	2	8	260	10
								17	11		9	242	10
									3		1	186	10
15.5–5–45–5	12–3–29–2							15	7	1	12	401	3
15–4–40–0	11–2–32–3							9	7	1	5	236	10
9–3–19–2	10–1–40–1							14	10		1	233	10
19.2–2–55–2	12–2–39–1							4	4		4	181	10
19–1–66–2								6	9		4	227	10
16–4–61–3		6–0–24–0	1–0–3–0					1	6		14	228	10
				19–1–69–0	42–7–89–3	14–3–32–0	10–0–33–1	11	8	1	12	300	9
								18	10	1	12	390	10a
94.1–19–	45–8–	6–0–	1–0–	19–1–	42–7–	14–3–	10–0–						
286–14	140–7	24–0	3–0	69–0	89–3	32–0	33–1						
av. 20.42	av. 20.00	—	—	—	av. 29.66	—	av. 33.00						

Leeward Islands 1988
First-Class Matches

BATTING

BATTING	v. Trinidad & Tobago (Pointe-à-Pierre) 22–5 January		v. Windward Islands (Antigua) 29 Jan.–1 Feb.		v. Jamaica (Basseterre) 6–9 February		v. Guyana (St John's) 19–22 February		v. Barbados (Bridgetown) 26–9 February	
A.L. Kelly	16	8	5	11	23	79	18	—	2	30*
L.L. Lawrence	7	21	16	2						
K.L.T. Arthurton	3	69	1	34*	28	77*	122	—	46	—
R.M. Otto	2	24	59	38*	0	74*	24	—	0	—
V.A. Eddy	0	2	25	—	38*	—				
L. Harris	49	24	52	—	16	—	63		0	—
N.C. Guishard	28	20	13	—	3	—			24	—
T.A. Merrick	0	2	33*	—						
E.T. Willett	14*	9	5	—	0	—	0	—		
E.L.C. Ambrose	1	2	2	—	19	—	6*	—	2*	—
G.J.F. Ferris	10	0*	5	—			13	—	—	—
H. Walsh					41	37				
E.A.E. Baptiste					14	99	18	—	58	—
W.K.M. Benjamin					0	—	4	—	3	—
R.B. Richardson							3	—	176	14*
I.V.A. Richards							119		70	—
Byes	2	4	5	2		15	1		10	
Leg-byes	10	6	2	3	3	7	11		5	2
Wides	3	1	2			1	1		1	
No-balls	2	3	13	5	1	12	5		9	1
Total	147	195	238	95	186	401	408		406	47
Wickets	10	10	10	2	10	3	10		9†	0
Result	L		D		W		W		W	
Points	0		4		16		16		16	

Fielding Figures

15 – L. Harris (ct 13/st 2)
5 – R.M. Otto and subs
4 – K.L.T. Arthurton and E.T. Willett
3 – N.C. Guishard, H. Walsh and R.B. Richardson
2 – V.A. Eddy, T.A. Merrick, A.L. Kelly, E.L.C. Ambrose and I.V.A. Richards
1 – W.K.M. Benjamin

†G.J.F. Ferris absent injured

BOWLING

BOWLING	T.A. Merrick	G.J.F. Ferris	E.L.C. Ambrose	N.C. Guishard	E.T. Willett	V.A. Eddy	W.K.M. Benjamin	E.A.E. Baptiste	I.V.A. Richards
v. Trinidad & Tobago (Pointe-à-Pierre) 22–5 January	18–4–45–2	12–3–28–1	20–8–37–3	21–4–31–2	14–5–22–2				
	13.3–2–31–0	12–1–33–1	20–1–43–3	14–3–22–1	16–2–31–2				
v. Windward Islands (Antigua) 29 Jan.–1 Feb.	15.2–4–59–3	14–0–51–1	22–5–53–1	15–6–29–1	23–6–48–3				
	20–5–53–0	18–4–43–2	24–2–54–2	14–2–27–0	21.2–7–42–3	3–0–6–1			
v. Jamaica (Basseterre) 6–9 February			15–3–40–5				15.4–2–50–5		
			20–7–52–4	8–2–21–0	15.4–3–54–2		15–3–34–1	6–1–11–0	
v. Guyana (St John's) 19–22 February		8.4–0–40–1	15–0–61–7				7–3–25–0		
		9–1–33–1	17.2–2–67–5		11–3–49–0		17–2–52–2	9–2–25–1	2–0–2–0
v. Barbados (Bridgetown) 26–9 February		6–0–47–1	21–4–66–3		7.3–2–27–2		14–5–26–2	14–2–41–1	13–4–18–1
			16–2–65–2	12.2–2–39–3			15–6–53–4	12–1–48–1	
	66.5–15– 188–5 av. 37.60	79.4–9– 275–8 av. 34.27	190.2–34– 538–35 av. 15.37	91.5–21– 196–9 av. 21.77	101–26– 246–12 av. 20.50	3–0– 6–1 av. 6.00	83.4–21– 240–14 av. 17.14	41–6– 125–3 av. 41.66	15–4– 20–1 av. 20.00

a N. Kennedy retired hurt

M	Inns	Nos	Runs	HS	Av
5	9	1	192	79	24.00
2	4	—	46	21	11.50
5	8	2	380	122	63.33
5	8	2	221	74*	36.83
3	4	1	65	38*	21.66
5	6	—	204	63	34.00
4	5	—	88	28	17.60
2	3	1	35	33*	17.50
4	5	1	28	14*	7.00
5	6	2	32	19	8.00
4	4	1	28	13	9.33
1	2	—	78	41	39.00
3	4	—	189	99	47.25
3	3	—	7	4	2.33
2	3	1	193	176	96.50
2	2	—	189	119	94.50

Byes	Leg-byes	Wides	No-balls	Total	Wkts
5	3		12	171	10
5	7	1	10	172	8
		4	6	244	10
5	3	4	8	233	8
5	1		5	96	10
8	6		6	186	9a
8	6	4	6	140	10
2	2		12	232	10
13	5	1	18	243	10
		3	10	208	10

many that Desmond Haynes had hit the ball, and he knocked the stumps over angrily in protest at the decision. He was given a suspended fine by the Jamaican Board. Greenidge and Best added 94 before Best was also given out lbw, another decision which was contested. Barbados then lost wickets steadily, and at one time, five wickets fell for 29 runs, so that Jamaica ran out comfortable winners. Marshall was fined £135 for alleging in a newspaper interview that the umpiring was biased, and he called for neutral umpires in future inter-island matches. He later apologized to a disciplinary committee. Winston Davis, the Windward Islands captain, had suffered suspension over his reaction to umpiring decisions.

26, 27, 28 and 29 February 1988

at Kensington Oval, Bridgetown, Barbados

Barbados 243 (M.D. Marshall 56, C.A. Best 53) and 208 (W.K.M. Benjamin 5 for 53)
Leeward Islands 406 (R.B. Richardson 176, I.V.A. Richards 70, E.A.E. Baptiste 58, M.D. Marshall 4 for 80) and 47 for 0

Leeward Islands won by 10 wickets
Leeward Islands 16 pts, Barbados 0 pts

at Albion Sports Complex, Berbice, Guyana

Windward Islands 177 (G.E. Charles 5 for 48) and 297 (L.C. Sebastien 116)
Guyana 395 (C.B. Lambert 162, R. Seeram 119) and 85 for 1

Guyana won by 9 wickets
Guyana 16 pts, Windward Islands 0 pts

at Sabina Park, Kingston, Jamaica

Trinidad and Tobago 228 (K.A. Williams 77, R.C. Haynes 6 for 53) and 300 for 9 (H.A. Gomes 66)
Jamaica 378 (P.J.L. Dujon 80, C.A. Davidson 55)

Match Drawn
Jamaica 8 pts, Trinidad and Tobago 4 pts

The strength of Leeward Islands was ably demonstrated in the final round of matches in the Red Stripe Cup when they triumphed in Barbados and clinched the runners-up spot in the league. Curtley Ambrose took five wickets in the match to establish a new record in West Indian domestic competition, 35 wickets at 15.51 runs each, and Richie Richardson played a mighty innings which placed his side in a commanding position.

Guyana also had their record-breaker. Having bowled out Windward Islands for 177, they lost Simpson at 14, but Lambert and Seeram, both of whom hit career bests, put on 221 for the second wicket. A brave century by Sebastien meant that Guyana had to bat again and score 80 to win. With the scores level, Clayton Lambert hit John for six to win the match and to bring his aggregate of runs in the competition to 548, three more than the Guyanese record set up by Roy Fredericks in 1975.

When the last round of matches began Jamaica held a four-point lead over Trinidad and needed only to take first-innings' lead and draw the last match to take the title. This is precisely what they accomplished. Robert Haynes bettered his career-best bowling performance of a few days earlier, and Trinidad were bowled out for 228. Dujon batted with great composure, and Jamaica passed Trini-

Trinidad and Tobago 1988
First-Class Matches

BATTING	v. Leeward Islands (Pointe-à-Pierre) 22–5 January		v. Barbados (Port-of-Spain) 29 Jan.–1 Feb.		v. Guyana (Essequibo) 5–8 February		v. Windward Islands (Roseau) 19–22 February		v. Jamaica (Kingston) 26–9 February	
C.R. Rampersad	8	26	4	—						
C.G. Yorke	12	4	23	—	—	—	4	1	7	5
A. Rajah	22	31	0	—	—	—	7	15	12	10
H.A. Gomes	2	33	36	—	—	—	0	13	15	66
B.C. Lara	14	22	92	—	—	—				
D.I. Mohammed	0	1								
R. Nanan	48	5*	46*	—	—	—	0	0	0	2
A.H. Gray	26	15	15	—	—	—	10	9	8	47
H. Joseph	2	10	13	—	—	—				
I.R. Bishop	17*	2*	6	—	—	—	0	4*	1*	19*
A. Dwarika	0	—								
K.A. Williams			19		—		33	9	77	43
R. Dhanraj			1		—					
P.V. Simmons					—		64	45	25	7
D. Williams					—		44*	36	16	24
A.L. Logie							22	0	46	45
G. Mahabir							0	2	0	—
Byes	5	5	5						1	11
Leg-byes	3	7	5				3	7	6	8
Wides		1					1			1
No-balls	12	10	27				13	5	14	12
Total	171	172	292				201	146	228	300
Wickets	10	8	10				10	10	10	9
Result	W		D		Ab.		W		D	
Points	16		8		4		16		4	

Fielding Figures

6 – C.R. Rampersad and B.C. Lara
5 – D. Williams (ct 4/st 1)
4 – A. Rajah and A.L. Logie (ct 3/st 1)
2 – D.I. Mohammed and K.A. Williams
1 – H.A. Gomes, P.V. Simmons, R. Nanan, I.R. Bishop and C.G. Yorke

BOWLING	A.H. Gray	I.R. Bishop	R. Nanan	H. Joseph	A. Dwarika	R. Dhanraj	B.C. Lara	P.V. Simmons
v. Leeward Islands (Pointe-à-Pierre) 22–5 January	9–1–36–2	8.3–3–23–4	11–5–24–3	11–1–43–1	1–0–9–0			
	12–2–51–0	14–2–42–4	25–9–32–4	12–3–31–1	5–1–29–0			
v. Barbados (Port-of-Spain) 29 Jan.–1 Feb.	16–2–50–1	13–1–48–3	27–9–41–2	12–3–34–0		25.2–4–67–4		
	15–1–54–4	16–2–32–1	38–14–39–2	14–3–25–0		16–4–42–1		
v. Guyana (Essequibo) 5–8 February	7–0–34–1	7–2–14–1	5–1–15–0	12–0–43–0		12–1–49–0	1.5–0–14–0	
v. Windward Islands (Roseau) 19–22 February	21–3–56–4	5.1–0–23–3	31–6–22–1					4–0–9–0
	4–0–13–0	6.2–0–18–1	20–8–31–5					
v. Jamaica (Kingston) 26–9 February	24–5–55–2	26–2–60–2	39–10–99–3					7–0–25–1
	108–14–	96–12–	196–62–	61–10–	6–1–	53.2–9–	1.5–0–	11–0–
	349–14	260–19	303–20	176–2	38–0	158–5	14–0	34–1
	av. 24.92	av. 13.68	av. 15.15	av. 88.00	—	av. 31.60	—	av. 34.00

M	Inns	Nos	Runs	HS	Av
2	3	—	38	26	12.66
5	7	—	56	23	8.00
5	7	—	97	31	13.85
5	7	—	165	66	23.57
3	3	—	128	92	42.66
1	2	—	1	1	0.50
5	7	2	101	48	20.20
5	7	—	130	47	18.57
3	3	—	25	13	8.33
5	7	5	49	19*	24.50
1	1	—	0	0	0.00
3	5	—	181	77	36.20
2	1	—	1	1	0.50
3	4	—	141	64	35.25
3	4	1	120	44*	40.00
2	4	—	113	46	28.25
2	3	—	2	2	0.66

G. Mahabir	H.A. Gomes	Byes	Leg-byes	Wides	No-balls	Total	Wkts
		2	10	3	2	147	10
		4	6	1	3	195	10
		2	8	7	7	250	10
		9	4		5	205	9
		6	3	1	3	178	2
23–3–55–2	1–1–0–0	2	5	2	1	172	10
17–4–30–4		6	3			101	10
29.3–3–87–2	1–0–2–0	17	33		5	378	10
69.3–10–	2–1–						
172–8	2–0						
av. 21.50	—						

Red Stripe Cup – Final Table

	P	W	L	D	Nr	Pts
Jamaica	5	3	1	1		56
Leeward Islands	5	3	1	1		52
Trinidad and Tobago	5	2	–	2	1	48
Barbados	5	2	2	1		36
Guyana	5	1	3	–	1	20
Windward Islands	5	–	4	1		8

dad's total for the loss of only four wickets before the end of the second day. They batted on until mid-afternoon on the third day, effectively killing the game. Trinidad were forced to settle for a draw, and Jamaica were the Red Stripe Cup winners. It was only their second win in 23 years of domestic competition.

Barbados gained some consolation a fortnight later when Vibert Greene hit two runs off the last ball of the match, bowled by Courtenay Walsh, to win his side the Geddes Grant/Harrison Line one-day final.

6, 7, 8 and 9 March 1988

at Sabina Park, Kingston, Jamaica

Pakistanis 332 (Saleem Malik 86, Javed Miandad 63, C.L. Hooper 4 for 72) and 271 (Javed Miandad 111)
West Indian Cricket Board President's XI 311 (C.L. Hooper 67, Saleem Jaffer 6 for 67) and 50 for 1

Match drawn

Imran Khan came out of his short retirement from international cricket to lead Pakistan on their tour of West Indies. In Pakistan, and in most other cricket-playing countries, the meeting between West Indies and Pakistan was seen as being for the unofficial championship of the world. The Pakistan side was managed by Intikhab Alam and included Haafiz Shahid, Moin-ul-Atiq and Naved Anjum, untried at the top level, and welcomed back Saleem Yousuf after injury. Surprisingly, no place was found for Asif Mujtaba. The opening match of the tour saw Mudassar Nazar forced to retire hurt with concussion after being hit on the helmet by a ball from Ian Bishop. A strong President's XI, captained by Roger Harper, were set to make 293 in 40 minutes plus 20 overs, a task which they declined. Hooper, Arthurton and Benjamin were the most impressive of the young West Indian players vying for Test places. The tourists missed several catches and were also shown to be in need of Abdul Qadir, who was receiving treatment for kidney problems. Javed Miandad scored a patient century against an attack which was weak in spin bowling.

First One-Day International
WEST INDIES v. PAKISTAN

Having put West Indies in to bat, Imran Khan marked his return to international cricket by dismissing Haynes in his opening over and the hard-hitting Simmons in his third. West Indies, who were without Greenidge and Marshall, both injured, were revived by Gus Logie and Richie Richardson, whose stand of 187 was the highest for any wicket in one-day internationals between West Indies and

Windward Islands 1988
First-Class Matches

BATTING

BATTING	v. Leeward Islands (Antigua) 29 Jan.–1 Feb.		v. Barbados (St George's) 4–7 February		v. Jamaica (Kingston) 13–16 February		v. Trinidad & Tobago (Roseau) 19–22 February		v. Guyana (Albion) 26–9 February	
L.D. John	18	3	4	30	0	29	2	53	46	11
D. Telemaque	24	71	13	7						
D. Joseph	70	30	18	6	109	32	0	14	20	9
J.D. Charles	23	6	20	40	0	17	19	1	0	28
L.C. Sebastien	8	26	0	55	14	48	27	3	4	116
D.J. Collymore	3	35	52*	4	44	2	87*	2	6	27
K. Williams	18	1							21	26
T.Z. Kentish	17	21	0	18	7	7	4	4	5	9
J.R. Murray	29	20*	0	6	26	31*	2	4	47	7
W.L. Thomas	23	—			0*	0	6	0		
J.T. Etienne	1*	—	27	8*	0	20	8	7*	15*	7
S.L. Mahon			5	17	4	13	0	0		
W.W. Davis			3	2	10	9	7	4	0	16*
J. Pierre									5	24
Byes		5	1	8	9	14	2	6	4	12
Leg-byes	4	3	2	10	7	10	5	3	4	4
Wides			4		1	1		2		
No-balls	6	8	9	10	5	1	1			1
Total	244	233	154	222	236	233	172	101	177	297
Wickets	10	8	10	10	10	10	10	10	10	10
Result	D		L		L		L		L	
Points	8		0		0		0		0	

Fielding Figures
7 – J.R. Murray (ct 6/st 1)
4 – J.D. Charles and D. Joseph
3 – L.C. Sebastien, L.D. John and T.Z. Kentish
2 – S.L. Mahon
1 – W.L. Thomas, D. Telemaque, J. Pierre and sub

BOWLING

BOWLING	D.J. Collymore	W.L. Thomas	K. Williams	T.Z. Kentish	J.T. Etienne	J.D. Charles	W.W. Davis	L.D. John
v. Leeward Islands (Antigua) 29 Jan.–1 Feb.	19–3–41–1	12–2–33–2	12–1–35–1	30–6–65–2	24–7–57–3			
	5–0–24–1	3–0–19–1	4–0–13–0	6–1–11–0	8–2–18–0	4–2–5–0		
v. Barbados (St George's) 4–7 February	21–2–72–4			19–2–36–1	23–6–59–1	6–0–21–0	29.4–4–85–3	
	20–4–47–3			18–3–37–0	14–1–64–3		23–3–80–1	
v. Jamaica (Kingston) 13–16 February	25–2–69–0		24–1–115–1		23–1–79–0	1–0–8–0	27–2–92–0	
v. Trinidad & Tobago (Roseau) 19–22 February	19–5–48–2	7–0–26–1		23–7–57–3	4–0–18–0		17–2–49–3	
	6–2–11–1	5–0–34–2		20–3–47–2	18–6–31–3		9.4–2–16–2	
v. Guyana (Albion) 26–9 February	18–1–88–3		13.1–0–44–2	30–6–74–2	38–4–120–2		16–1–47–0	
	7–0–22–1		2–0–8–0		2–0–12–0	1–0–4–0	8–1–26–0	0.3–0–6–0
	140–19–	51–3–	31.1–1–	169–29–	166–33–	12–2–	130.2–15–	0.3–0–
	422–16	227–7	100–3	406–10	484–15	50–0	395–9	6–0
	av. 26.37	av. 32.42	av. 33.33	av. 40.60	av. 32.26	—	av. 43.88	—

M	Inns	Nos	Runs	HS	Av
5	10	—	196	53	19.60
2	4	—	115	71	28.75
5	10	—	308	109	30.80
5	10	—	154	40	15.40
5	10	—	301	116	30.10
5	10	2	262	87*	32.75
2	4	—	66	26	16.50
5	10	—	92	21	9.20
5	10	2	172	47	21.50
3	5	1	29	23	7.25
5	9	4	93	27	18.60
3	6	—	39	17	6.50
4	8	1	51	16*	7.28
1	2	—	29	24	14.50

Byes	Leg-byes	Wides	No-balls	Total	Wkts
5	2	2	13	238	10
2	3		5	95	2
1	5		12	279	10
5	8		14	241	7
22	15		22	505	5
	3	1	13	201	10
	7		5	146	10
8	10		11	395	10
	3			85	1

Two centuries against the Pakistan tourists, exciting batting for Leeward Islands and a place in the party to tour England – Keith Arthurton. (David Munden)

Pakistan. Logie reached his first hundred in limited-over international matches and hit 10 fours. Richardson's 84 came off 125 balls and included a six and 3 fours. The third-wicket stand lasted for 36 overs.

Curtley Ambrose, who had won the position of Marshall's replacement on the strength of his fine showing in the Red Stripe Cup, made a sensational début in international cricket. Rameez Raja attempted to pull his third ball and had his leg stump uprooted. With the third ball of his second over Ambrose clipped Shoaib's off stump. The tall fast bowler later removed both Javed and Imran, and Pakistan never looked like matching the required run rate in spite of some energetic batting by Ijaz Ahmed against some rather loose off-spin from Hooper and Richards.

Second One-Day International
WEST INDIES v. PAKISTAN

West Indies lost the services of Viv Richards, who missed the rest of the one-day series and the first Test through illness. Gordon Greenidge returned to the side and took over the captaincy while Pakistan welcomed back Wasim Akram and gave pace bowler Haafiz Shahid his first taste of international cricket.

FIRST ONE-DAY INTERNATIONAL – WEST INDIES v. PAKISTAN
12 March 1988 at Sabina Park, Kingston, Jamaica

WEST INDIES					PAKISTAN			
D.L. Haynes		b Imran Khan	0		Rameez Raja		b Ambrose	5
P.V. Simmons		c Rameez Raja,			Shoiab Mohammad		b Ambrose	3
		b Imran Khan	15		Saleem Malik		b Walsh	20
R.B. Richardson		b Saleem Jaffer	84		Javed Miandad		c Richards,	
A.L. Logie		not out	109				b Ambrose	47
I.V.A. Richards†		b Imran Khan	15		Ijaz Ahmed		run out	39
C.L. Hooper		not out	1		Imran Khan†		b Ambrose	7
P.J.L. Dujon*					Naved Anjum		not out	17
W.K.M. Benjamin					Saleem Yousuf*		c Logie, b Patterson	10
C.A. Walsh					Zakir Khan		not out	11
B.P. Patterson					Tauseef Ahmed			
E.L.C. Ambrose					Saleem Jaffer			
Extras		b 3, lb 10, w 1, nb 3	17		Extras		b 10, lb 12, w 9, nb 4	35
(46 overs)		(for 4 wkts)	241		(46 overs)		(for 7 wkts)	194

	O	M	R	W		O	M	R	W
Imran Khan	8	1	36	3	Patterson	10	2	21	1
Saleem Jaffer	10	1	55	1	Ambrose	10	1	39	4
Naved Anjum	10	1	37	–	Walsh	10	1	37	1
Zakir Khan	10	–	54	–	Benjamin	10	1	34	–
Tauseef Ahmed	5	–	28	–	Richards	5	1	30	–
Shoaib Mohammad	3	–	18	–	Hooper	1	–	11	–

FALL OF WICKETS
1–0, 2–25, 3–212, 4–236

FALL OF WICKETS
1–7, 2–8, 3–55, 4–131, 5–145, 6–146, 7–163

Umpires: D. Sang Hue & J. Gayle

Man of the Match: A. L. Logie

West Indies won by 47 runs

Ambrose again broke the back of the Pakistan batting. He bowled a full length and made the ball rear alarmingly and swing late. Winston Benjamin bowled his 10 overs in one disciplined spell and thwarted any attempt at recovery by the visitors. Imran played a restrained innings, and Saleem Yousuf and Wasim Akram shone briefly, but Pakistan had no prospect of reaching a total that would trouble the West Indians.

Simmons dominated an opening partnership of 86 in 19 overs, hitting 9 fours before edging a ball into his stumps, and this opening stand allowed West Indies to canter to victory with ease.

Third One-Day International
WEST INDIES v. PAKISTAN

Abdul Qadir made his first appearance of the tour although it was apparent that he was still far from fit. Aamer Malik appeared in his first one-day international.

Desmond Haynes returned to the West Indian side and scored the highest of his 10 centuries in one-day internationals. His hundred came off 132 balls and he hit a six and 14 fours. He and Richardson shared a second-wicket stand of 142 in 26 overs, Richardson's 78 coming off 76 balls and including 12 fours. Haynes, on 85, was involved in an unusual incident. He hobbled after being struck on the knee by a ball from Saleem Jaffer and was given out lbw on appeal, but he protested that he had hit the ball, and Imran withdrew the appeal so that Haynes could continue his innings. He went on to steer West Indies to their highest score in 36 one-day internationals against Pakistan.

Desmond Haynes, 142 not out in the second one-day international at Port-of-Spain, the highest of his ten centuries in limited-over international matches. (ASP)

SECOND ONE-DAY INTERNATIONAL – WEST INDIES v. PAKISTAN
15 March 1988 at Recreation Ground, St John's, Antigua

PAKISTAN			
Mudassar Nazar	b Ambrose		4
Rameez Raja	c Hooper, b Patterson		14
Saleem Malik	c Greenidge, b Ambrose		0
Javed Miandad	c Dujon, b Benjamin		24
Ijaz Ahmed	c Simmons, b Benjamin		6
Imran Khan†	c and b Ambrose		53
Naved Anjum	b Benjamin		2
Saleem Yousuf*	run out		24
Wasim Akram	c Simmons, b Ambrose		18
Haafiz Shahid	not out		7
Saleem Jaffer	not out		2
Extras	lb 2, w 7, nb 3		12
(46 overs)	(for 9 wkts)		166

	O	M	R	W
Patterson	8	–	37	1
Labrooy	10	2	35	4
Benjamin	10	1	27	3
Walsh	10	1	25	–
Hooper	8	–	40	–

FALL OF WICKETS
1–20, 2–21, 3–24, 4–40, 5–72, 6–78, 7–118, 8–153, 9–162

WEST INDIES			
C. G. Greenidge†	c Imran Khan, b Haafiz Shahid		35
P.V. Simmons	b Mudassar Nazar		54
R.B. Richardson	c Javed Miandad, b Mudassar		12
C.A. Best	lbw, b Imran Khan		17
A.L. Logie	c Ijaz Ahmed, b Imran Khan		8
C.L. Hooper	not out		21
P.J.L. Dujon*	not out		11
W.K.M. Benjamin			
C.A. Walsh			
B.P. Patterson			
E.L.C. Ambrose			
Extras	lb 1, w 3, nb 5		9
(37.1 overs)	(for 5 wkts)		167

	O	M	R	W
Imran Khan	7	1	38	2
Wasim Akram	6	1	21	–
Saleem Jaffer	8.1	–	36	–
Haafiz Shahid	9	–	41	1
Mudassar Nazar	7	1	30	2

FALL OF WICKETS
1–86, 2–104, 3–106, 4–123, 5–144

Umpires: L. Barker & P. Whyte

Man of the Match: W.K.M. Benjamin

West Indies won by 5 wickets

THIRD ONE-DAY INTERNATIONAL – WEST INDIES v. PAKISTAN
18 March 1988 at Queen's Park Oval, Port-of-Spain, Trinidad

WEST INDIES			
D.L. Haynes	not out		142
P.V. Simmons	c Saleem Malik, b Naved Anjum		12
R.B. Richardson	c Abdul Qadir, b Saleem Jaffer		78
C.G. Greenidge†	c and b Saleem Malik		27
A.L. Logie	c Saleem Yousuf, b Imran Khan		9
C.L. Hooper	not out		27
P.J.L. Dujon*			
W.K.M. Benjamin			
C.A. Walsh			
B.P. Patterson			
E.L.C. Ambrose			
Extras	b 4, lb 12, w 4		20
(47 overs)	(for 4 wkts)		315

	O	M	R	W
Imran Khan	8	–	48	1
Naved Anjum	9	–	56	1
Saleem Jaffer	9	–	58	1
Abdul Qadir	10	–	64	–
Mudassar Nazar	4	–	32	–
Saleem Malik	7	–	41	1

FALL OF WICKETS
1–28, 2–180, 3–236, 4–270

PAKISTAN			
Mudassar Nazar	c Dujon, b Benjamin		33
Rameez Raja	b Benjamin		47
Saleem Yousuf*	c Ambrose, b Walsh		8
Aamer Malik	run out		12
Javed Miandad	c Ambrose, b Hooper		17
Saleem Malik	c and b Ambrose		85
Imran Khan†	c Hooper, b Patterson		20
Ijaz Ahmed	c sub (A.H. Gray), b Patterson		9
Naved Anjum	c Walsh, b Patterson		7
Abdul Qadir	c Dujon, b Ambrose		2
Saleem Jaffer	not out		1
Extras	b 4, lb 5, w 11, nb 4		24
(43.3 overs)			265

	O	M	R	W
Patterson	10	–	77	3
Ambrose	8.3	–	30	2
Walsh	8	1	43	1
Benjamin	10	–	64	2
Hooper	7	–	42	1

FALL OF WICKETS
1–70, 2–80, 3–106, 4–111, 5–188, 6–242, 7–248, 8–260, 9–260

Umpires: C. Cumberbatch & Mohammed Hosein

Man of the Match: D.L. Haynes

West Indies won by 50 runs

Pakistan were given a romping start by Mudassar and Rameez, who put on 70 in 14 overs, and Saleem Malik took up the challenge with 85 off 55 balls. He hit a six and 10 fours. He found little support, however, as the home side stuck to their task and fielded and caught well.

Fourth One-Day International
WEST INDIES v. PAKISTAN

Moin-ul-Atiq was introduced to international cricket and was soon in action as Pakistan chose to bat when they won the toss. He shared an opening partnership of 109 with Rameez Raja, who hit a six and 10 fours in his 71 made off 65 balls. Moin-ul-Atiq batted most promisingly and hit 4 fours in his 115-minute stay, which gave him a share of a first-wicket one-day international record stand for Pakistan against West Indies. Javed maintained the pace of scoring with 3 sixes and 2 fours in his 49-ball innings, and Pakistan reached their highest one-day score in an international with West Indies.

It served them little. Greenidge led a violent assault on the tourists' bowling, hitting 3 sixes and 7 fours in his 66, which came off 51 deliveries. He and Simmons put on 112 in 13.3 overs of massive stroke-play. Richardson was more sedate as he hit a six and 6 fours in his 79 not out, which came from 87 balls. West Indies reached their target with 17 balls to spare after a day which had seen 11 sixes and 42 fours give huge entertainment to a large crowd.

24, 25, 26 and 27 March 1988

at Bourda, Georgetown, Guyana

Pakistanis 495 for 9 dec (Shoaib Mohammad 208 not out, Aamer Malik 51) and 230 for 4 dec (Mudassar Nazar 72)
West Indian Cricket Board XI 341 (K.L.T. Arthurton 132, Imran Khan 4 for 75, Saleem Malik 4 for 101) and 90 for 4

Match drawn

Shoaib Mohammad became the first Pakistani batsman to score a double century in the West Indies since his father, Hanif, in 1957–8. He also became only the second batsman to hit a double century on the occasion of his first-class début in the Caribbean, 'Patsy' Hendren being the first. Shoaib's innings, which lasted 8½ hours, was cautious and chanceless. He hit a five and 25 fours. The Board XI began uneasily against Imran, but the left-handed Keith Arthurton played a fine innings to enhance his chances of selection for the tour of England. When Saleem Yousuf was injured, Aamer Malik took over behind the stumps and caught three and stumped three batsmen. With Tauseef Ahmed nursing an injured shoulder, Pakistan called for their perennial replacement, Ijaz Faqih, to be flown to join the party.

Fifth One-Day International
WEST INDIES v. PAKISTAN

West Indies won their 10th one-day international match in

FOURTH ONE-DAY INTERNATIONAL – WEST INDIES v. PAKISTAN
20 March 1988 at Queen's Park Oval, Port-of-Spain, Trinidad

PAKISTAN					WEST INDIES			
Rameez Raja	c Greenidge, b Patterson		71		C.G. Greenidge†	b Haafiz Shahid		66
Moin-ul-Atiq	c Greenidge, b Gray		46		P.V. Simmons	c Saleem Yousuf, b Haafiz Shahid		49
Saleem Malik	b Gray		26		R.B. Richardson	not out		79
Javed Miandad	c Richardson, b Patterson		59		A.L. Logie	c and b Saleem Malik		29
Imran Khan†	c sub (D. Williams), b Benjamin		16		C.A. Best	not out		32
Ijaz Ahmed	c Gray, b Patterson		19		C.L. Hooper			
Saleem Yousuf*	not out		8		P.J.L. Dujon*			
Haafiz Shahid	not out		2		W.K.M. Benjamin			
Shoaib Mohammad					A.H. Gray			
Abdul Qadir					C.A. Walsh			
Zakir Khan					B.P. Patterson			
Extras	b 3, lb 15, w 1, nb 5		24		Extras	b 4, lb 7, w 3, nb 3		17
(43 overs)	(for 6 wkts)		271		(40.1 overs)	(for 3 wkts)		272

	O	M	R	W
Patterson	9	–	77	3
Walsh	9	–	43	–
Gray	10	–	45	2
Benjamin	8	–	58	1
Hooper	7	–	30	–

	O	M	R	W
Imran Khan	8	–	76	–
Zakir Khan	6	–	49	–
Abdul Qadir	10	–	42	–
Haafiz Shahid	9.1	1	56	2
Saleem Malik	4	–	23	1
Shoaib Mohammad	3	–	15	–

FALL OF WICKETS
1–109, 2–139, 3–160, 4–194, 5–256, 6–256

FALL OF WICKETS
1–112, 2–149, 3–207

Umpires: G.T. Browne & C.E. Cumberbatch

Man of the Match: C.G. Greenidge

West Indies won by 7 wickets

Shoaib Mohammad emulated his father, Hanif, in scoring a double century in the West Indies. (Allsport)

succession to win the series by 5–0, and Pakistan suffered their 10th defeat in a row, the sequence beginning when they lost the last of the qualifying matches in the Reliance World Cup.

Rameez Raja hit 67 cultured runs off 79 balls, and Javed Miandad hit his sixth hundred in one-day internationals, the first by a Pakistani against West Indies, but even these efforts could not prevent West Indies from sweeping to a comfortable victory. Javed hit 10 fours in his century, which came off 99 balls. He and Imran added 66 in 12 overs.

West Indies replied in cavalier fashion. Simmons was again full of daring strokes and hit 79 off 74 balls with 2 sixes, a five and 11 fours. Richardson gave able support as West Indies won with six overs to spare.

The return of Marshall after injury and their dominance in the one-day series gave West Indies optimism and encouragement for the Test series.

First Test Match
WEST INDIES v. PAKISTAN

Malcolm Marshall was forced to withdraw from the West Indian side with a knee injury so that, in effect, the home team were without their best batsman and best bowler for

---

FIFTH ONE-DAY INTERNATIONAL – WEST INDIES v. PAKISTAN
30 March 1988 at Bourda, Georgetown, Guyana

PAKISTAN				WEST INDIES			
Rameez Raja	b Gray		67	D.L. Haynes	c Saleem Malik, b Wasim Akram		9
Shoaib Mohammad	c Dujon, b Marshall		0	P.V. Simmons	b Imran Khan		79
Aamer Malik*	run out		6	R.B. Richardson	c Ijaz Ahmed, b Imran Khan		68
Javed Miandad	not out		100	P.J.L. Dujon*	not out		18
Saleem Malik	c Benjamin, b Gray		0	C.G. Greenidge†	not out		26
Imran Khan†	run out		17	A.L. Logie			
Ijaz Ahmed	b Walsh		10	C.L. Hooper			
Wasim Akram	c Haynes, b Gray		0	M.D. Marshall			
Ijaz Faqih	not out		6	W.K.M. Benjamin			
Abdul Qadir				C.A. Walsh			
Saleem Jaffer				A.H. Gray			
Extras	b 3, lb 7, nb 5		15	Extras	b 9, lb 13, w 1, nb 2		25
(43 overs)	(for 7 wkts)		221	(37 overs)	(for 3 wkts)		225

	O	M	R	W		O	M	R	W
Marshall	10	2	41	1	Imran Khan	8	1	58	2
Walsh	10	2	50	1	Wasim Akram	9	–	48	1
Gray	10	–	43	3	Abdul Qadir	7	1	23	–
Benjamin	7	–	32	–	Saleem Jaffer	6	–	46	–
Hooper	6	–	45	–	Ijaz Faqih	7	–	28	–

FALL OF WICKETS
1–1, 2–41, 3–94, 4–94, 5–160, 6–183, 7–184

FALL OF WICKETS
1–15, 2–172, 3–182

Umpires: D. Archer & C. Duncan

Man of the Match: Javed Miandad

West Indies won by 7 wickets

the crucial first Test of the series. Curtley Ambrose made his Test début as replacement for Marshall.

Greenidge, leading West Indies for the first time in a Test match, won the toss and batted first. There was early success for Pakistan when Haynes edged an Imran out-swinger to the wicket-keeper in the third over. Simmons played with a greater caution than in the one-day matches, but he was still eager to play his shots. He was bowled by Ijaz Faqih's first ball of the match when he played down the wrong line. Abdul Qadir troubled both Richardson and Greenidge, but they added 54 in under an hour. The stand was ended when Wasim Akram was reintroduced. Greenidge was caught in the gully at the second attempt off a fierce cut.

Runs had come briskly, and by tea West Indies were 219 for 4. The course of the game turned dramatically in the last session. Abdul Qadir had Logie lbw with a flipper to end a good knock, and Imran Khan produced an inspired spell of 4 for 29 in nine overs. There was a last-wicket stand of 34 in 45 minutes between Patterson and Ambrose, but Imran returned to bowl Patterson in the last over of the day, which had gone triumphantly in favour of Pakistan and their captain.

One of the most frightening features of the second day was the West Indian over rate, which was little over 11 an hour, a tedium which could destroy Test cricket. A contributory factor to the lethargy was the plethora of no-balls sent down by the West Indian pacemen.

Rameez Raja was out quickly to an injudicious shot. He attempted a pull in Patterson's third over and skied the ball to gully. Ambrose yorked Mudassar to claim his first Test wicket, and Shoaib was caught at slip off the persistent Walsh. There was much short-pitched bowling, which allowed the batsmen to watch as the ball sailed harmlessly over their heads, and Benjamin was warned for bowling too many short-pitched deliveries.

It was a dour, disciplined fourth-wicket stand between Javed Miandad and Saleem Malik which enabled Pakistan to maintain the grip on the game which Imran's bowling had given them. Saleem batted 166 minutes for his 27, but, in the context of the match, with the wicket wearing rapidly, it was an invaluable knock. No praise can be too high for Javed, who controlled his natural aggression to play the innings which his side required of him. He ended the second day on 96 not out, and Pakistan, 249 for 4, were optimistic.

The optimism was well founded, for on the third day, they moved to a first-innings lead of 143 and captured the wicket of Haynes before the close. Javed recorded his first century against West Indies and, in all, batted for 405 minutes and faced 234 deliveries. He hit 12 fours. Having seen Pakistan into the lead, he and Ijaz Ahmed fell in successive overs. Saleem Yousuf, as so often before, ensured that the tail would wag, dominating a seventh-wicket stand of 64 with Imran with some aggressive batting. That Pakistan led by as many as 143 was due to a great extent to a record for a Test match of 71 extras, which included 38 no-balls. Welsh sent down 14, Ambrose 12, Patterson nine and Benjamin three.

Pakistan were thankful for the rest day which allowed Imran to receive treatment for an infected foot. It was

A reluctant return to Test cricket, but a masterly performance of fast bowling and leadership; Imran Khan, 11 for 121, and victory for Pakistan in the first Test. (Allsport)

apparent that he was still handicapped when play resumed, but he had scented a famous victory and was eager to lead his team to triumph. It was Abdul Qadir who made the all-important breakthrough when he bowled Simmons, off stump with a top-spinner, in the third over of the day. Ten runs later he had Richardson caught behind and West Indies were in deep trouble. Logie and Green-idge countered with an aggressive stand of 65 in an hour. Imran ended the partnership when a sharp leg-cutter took the edge of Logie's bat for Saleem Yousuf, who was keeping wicket with a damaged finger, to take a diving catch.

Greenidge was in flamboyant mood when more caution might have been advisable, but, in the penultimate over before lunch, he attempted to cover drive Imran and dragged the ball onto his stumps. The Pakistan captain missed a straightforward caught and bowled offered by Dujon immediately after lunch, but he made amends with an inspired bowling change. With Hooper and Dujon proving obdurate, Imran called upon Shoaib to bowl his occasional off-breaks. Dujon immediately drove a catch into the covers and Benjamin edged the next ball to slip. Hooper was deceived by the incomparable Qadir, and Imran dismissed Walsh and Patterson.

Needing 30 to win, Pakistan lost Mudassar without a run scored, but they romped to victory in 22 balls with more than a day to spare. It was West Indies first home defeat for 10 years, and it was the first time for 12 years that they had lost two Test matches in succession.

Imran Khan, 11 for 121, was named Man of the Match, and his countrymen were thankful that the late President Zia had persuaded one of the greatest all-rounders that the game has known to return to the Test arena for at least one more series.

9, 10, 11 and 12 April 1988

at Mindoo Phillip Park, Castries, St Lucia

Pakistanis 447 (Ijaz Ahmed 84, Rameez Raja 82, Wasim Akram 56 not out, Saleem Malik 53, Ijaz Faqih 51) and 173 (Rameez Raja 65)
West Indies Under-23 250 (K.L.T. Arthurton 124, J.C. Adams 51 not out) and 159 (Abdul Qadir 6 for 42)

Pakistanis won by 211 runs

A second century against the tourists by Keith Arthurton was the sole consolation for the West Indian selectors, who saw their under-23 side outplayed for most of the match. Ijaz Ahmed hit a six and 10 fours in a fine knock, which was the highlight of a consistent first innings by the Pakistanis. A stand of 120 for the fifth wicket saved the home side from ignominy and gained plaudits for Arthurton and Adams. As Arthurton had already taken 3 for 14,

his place in the side to tour England was assured, but he was the only batsman to offer resistance as Qadir bewildered the young West Indians on the last day.

Second Test Match
WEST INDIES v. PAKISTAN

Richards and Marshall returned to bring the West Indies to full strength. Pakistan were unchanged.

Imran won the toss and asked West Indies to bat first on a pitch which had spots of damp and under heavy cloud. His decision proved correct. With the last ball of the opening over he had Greenidge caught at short-leg off bat-pad. Within the hour Wasim Akram trapped Haynes lbw. The left-arm pace bowler accounted for Richardson just after lunch, and Abdul Qadir quickly dismissed Logie and Hooper so that West Indies slumped to 89 for 5 in the early afternoon. Richards and Dujon adopted a positive approach in an attempt to repair the damage and added 58 in 13 overs. Imran ended the stand when he had Dujon caught behind, and 10 runs later, Richards, who had hit 49 off 43 balls with 8 fours, tried to pull against the spin and was caught at slip off Qadir. Imran and Qadir quickly finished the innings.

Pakistan's dreams of a big first-innings lead were soon

FIRST TEST MATCH – WEST INDIES v. PAKISTAN
2, 3, 4 and 6 April 1988 at Bourda, Georgetown, Guyana

WEST INDIES

	FIRST INNINGS		SECOND INNINGS	
D.L. Hyanes	c Yousuf, b Imran	1	b Ijaz Faqih	5
P.V. Simmons	b Ijaz Faqih	16	b Qadir	11
R.B. Richardson	c Shoaib, b Imran	75	c Yousuf, b Qadir	16
C.G. Greenidge†	c Malik, b Wasim	17	b Imran	43
A.L. Logie	lbw, b Qadir	80	c Yousuf, b Imran	24
C.L. Hooper	c Wasim, b Imran	33	c Malik, b Qadir	30
P.J.L. Dujon*	lbw, b Imran	15	c Imran, b Shoaib	11
W.K.M. Benjamin	lbw, b Imran	2	c Javed, b Shoaib	0
C.A. Walsh	b Imran	7	c Yousuf, b Imran	14
E.L.C. Ambrose	not out	25	not out	1
B.P. Patterson	b Imran	10	b Imran	0
Extras	b 2, lb 3, nb 6	11	b 4, lb 8, nb	17
		292		172

PAKISTAN

	FIRST INNINGS		SECOND INNINGS	
Mudassar Nazar	b Ambrose	29	lbw, b Patterson	0
Rameez Raja	c Haynes, b Patterson	5	not out	18
Shoaib Mohammad	c Greenidge, b Walsh	46	not out	13
Javed Miandad	b Patterson	114		
Saleem Mallik	c Greenidge, b Patterson	27		
Ijaz Ahmed	c Haynes, b Ambrose	31		
Imran Khan†	c Simmons, b Benjamin	24		
Saleem Yousuf*	lbw, b Walsh	62		
Ijaz Faqih	b Hooper	5		
Abdul Qadir	b Walsh	19		
Wasim Akram	not out	2		
Extras	b 21, lb 8, w 4, nb 38	71	nb 1	1
		435	(for 1 wkt)	32

	O	M	R	W	O	M	R	W
Imran Khan	22.4	2	80	7	14.4	–	41	4
Wasim Akram	14	5	41	1	6	1	7	–
Ijaz Faqih	14	–	60	1	15	4	38	1
Abdul Qadir	24	2	91	1	25	5	66	3
Saleem Malik	1	–	6	–				
Mudassar Nazar	5	2	9	–				
Shoaib Mohammad					2	–	8	2

	O	M	R	W	O	M	R	W
Patterson	24	2	82	3	2	–	19	1
Ambrose	28	5	108	2	1.4	–	13	–
Walsh	27	4	80	3				
Benjamin	31	3	99	1				
Hooper	12	–	37	1				

FALL OF WICKETS
1–7, 2–41, 3–95, 4–144, 5–220, 6–244, 7–248, 8–249, 9–258
1–18, 2–34, 3–44, 4–109, 5–120, 6–145, 7–145, 8–166, 9–172

FALL OF WICKETS
1–20, 2–57, 3–127, 4–217, 5–297, 6–300, 7–364, 8–383, 9–423
1–0

Umpires: D.M. Archer & L.H. Barker

Pakistan won by 9 wickets

dispelled as Marshall dismissed both openers and Benjamin bowled Javed Miandad to leave the visitors tottering on 55 for 5 at the end of the first day, which had seen 15 wickets fall while 229 runs were scored.

Ijaz Ahmed and Imran Khan were soon out on the second morning, but Saleem Malik batted with great application and, finding a reliable partner in Saleem Yousuf, added 94 for the eighth wicket. Saleem Malik was ninth out when he pushed defensively at a ball that turned and was caught at short-leg. A spirited last-wicket stand between Abdul Qadir and Wasim Akram took Pakistan into the lead. Qadir hit Hooper for a straight six.

Haynes was out to the second ball of West Indies' second innings, and Imran dismissed Greenidge and Logie before the close, which came with West Indies on 78 for 3 and Pakistan very much in control. That control was wrested from them on the third day when West Indies scored 251 runs for the loss of five more wickets.

The day belonged to Viv Richards, who hit his 22nd Test century and shared stands of 94 with Hooper and 97 with Dujon. His innings was all the more commendable in that he was troubled throughout by cramp and bouts of nausea. He survived a confident appeal for lbw by Imran when 25, and some altercation followed the rejection of the appeal. Richards reached his hundred off 134 balls in 232 minutes. It contained 10 fours. Abdul Qadir bowled Marshall shortly before the close to claim his 200th Test wicket in his 53rd Test. Only Imran Khan of other Pakistan Test bowlers has reached this mark.

Dujon completed his fifth Test century on the fourth morning and, aided by Benjamin and Walsh, cajoled 90 runs from the last two wickets, a most significant contribution.

Shortly before lunch on the fourth day, Pakistan began their mighty task of trying to score 372 to win the match. They began brightly enough with Rameez Raja in exciting form, but Marshall got rid of Rameez, and Benjamin dismissed Mudassar and Shoaib to plunge Pakistan from 60 for 0 to 67 for 3. Javed Miandad and Saleem Malik played out the rest of the day in sedate and cautious fashion.

When the last day began Pakistan were 107 for 3, with Javed 19 not out. The score moved to 153 before Saleem Malik, who had done so much to help repair early damage, was lbw to Walsh. Unfortunately for Pakistan, Imran Khan did not last long, but Javed found an excellent partner in Ijaz Ahmed. The young Pakistan batsman was given a torrid time by the West Indian pacemen, but Javed

SECOND TEST MATCH – WEST INDIES v. PAKISTAN
14, 15, 16, 17 and 19 April 1988 at Queen's Park Oval, Port-of-Spain, Trinidad

WEST INDIES

	FIRST INNINGS		SECOND INNINGS	
C.G. Greenidge	c Ijaz Ahmed, b Imran	1	(2) c Richards, b Imran Khan	29
D.L. Haynes	lbw, Wasim Akram	17	c Ijaz Ahmed, b Imran	0
R.B. Richardson	c Qadir, b Wasim	42	c Saleem Yousuf, b Imran	40
A.L. Logie	c Javed, b Qadir	18	b Imran Khan	1
I.V.A. Richards†	c Javed, b Qadir	49	lbw, b Wasim Akram	123
C.L. Hooper	c Yousuf, b Qadir	0	c Ijaz Ahmed, b Imran	26
P.J.L. Dujon*	c Yousuf, b Imran	24	not out	106
M.D. Marshall	not out	10	b Abdul Qadir	2
E.L.C. Ambrose	lbw, b Imran Khan	4	lbw, b Abdul Qadir	9
W.K.M. Benjamin	b Abdul Qadir	0	lbw, b Abdul Qadir	16
C.A. Walsh	b Imran Khan	5	st Yousuf, b Qadir	12
Extras	lb 2, nb 2	4	b 9, lb 14, nb 4	27
		174		391

PAKISTAN

	FIRST INNINGS		SECOND INNINGS	
Rameez Raja	c Richardson, b Marshall	1	(2) c Richards, b Marshall	44
Mudassar Nazar	c Haynes, b Marshall	14	(1) c Dujon, b Benjamin	13
Shoaib Mohammad	c Richards, b Ambrose	12	b Benjamin	0
Javed Miandad	b Benjamin	18	c Richards, b Ambrose	102
Ijaz Faqih	c Richards, b Benjamin	0	(10) not out	10
Saleem Malik	c Logie, b Hooper	66	(5) lbw, b Walsh	30
Ijaz Ahmed	c Logie, b Benjamin	3	st Dujon, b Richards	43
Imran Khan†	c Logie, b Marshall	4	(6) c Dujon, b Benjamin	1
Saleem Yousuf*	c Dujon, b Marshall	39	(8) lbw, b Richards	35
Wasim Akram	run out	7	(9) c Richardson, b Marshall	2
Abdul Qadir	not out	17	not out	0
Extras	b 1, lb 4, nb 8	13	b 17, lb 17, w 2, nb 25	61
		194	(for 9 wkts)	341

	O	M	R	W	O	M	R	W
Imran Khan	16.3	2	38	4	45	9	115	5
Wasim Akram	14	4	35	2	25	4	75	1
Ijaz Faqih	3	–	13	–	4	–	22	–
Mudassar Nazar	1	–	3	–				
Abdul Qadir	19	2	83	4	47.4	6	148	4
Shoaib Mohammad					3	–	8	–

	O	M	R	W	O	M	R	W
Marshall	20	4	55	4	30	4	85	2
Ambrose	14	3	44	1	30	7	62	1
Walsh	8	–	23	–	29	8	52	1
Benjamin	8	–	32	3	32	9	73	3
Hooper	9.1	1	35	1	4	1	18	–
Richards					4	1	17	2

FALL OF WICKETS
1–2, 2–25, 3–80, 4–89, 5–89, 6–147, 7–157, 8–166, 9–167
1–1, 2–54, 3–66, 4–81, 5–175, 6–272, 7–284, 8–301, 9–357

FALL OF WICKETS
1–3, 2–25, 3–46, 4–49, 5–50, 6–62, 7–68, 8–162, 9–170
1–60, 2–62, 3–67, 4–153, 5–169, 6–282, 7–288, 8–311, 9–341

Umpires: L.H. Barker & C.E. Cumberbatch

Match drawn

nursed him through the early stages of his innings and suddenly a Pakistan victory became a possibility. With 20 overs remaining, Pakistan needed 85 to win, but Ijaz's brave innings was ended when he was stumped off Richards, and Javed's mighty knock was brought to an end by Ambrose. Javed had completed his second century in consecutive Tests against West Indies. His innings lasted for 427 minutes, and he faced 240 balls, taking his side from a state of disarray to a point from which victory could be glimpsed. He gave a chanceless display and played one of the great innings in Pakistan Test history.

The quick loss of Wasim Akram forced Pakistan to turn their thoughts from victory to achieving a draw, and this seemed to be easily accomplished until, with the first ball of the last over of the match, Viv Richards trapped Saleem Yousuf lbw. Abdul Qadir, already a hero for his eight wickets in the game, now proved himself the hero with the bat, defying Richards and the close set field for the last five, dramatic balls of the match.

So ended a memorable Test worthy of that name, unlike so many that had been played in other parts of the world in recent months.

Third Test Match
WEST INDIES v. PAKISTAN

Pakistan made two changes for the final Test match, bringing in Saleem Jaffer and Aamer Malik for Ijaz Faqih and Ijaz Ahmed. Saleem Yousuf was injured while batting in the first innings, and Aamer Malik kept wicket throughout the match.

Put in to bat, Pakistan began briskly. Rameez Raja played some delightful shots before being deceived by a slower ball from Benjamin and spooning the ball into the covers in the last over before lunch, which Pakistan took at 99 for 2. Javed and Shoaib batted authoritatively in the early part of the afternoon, but Marshall caught the edge of Javed's bat with a leg-cutter and brought a ball back sharply to bowl Saleem Malik. In the last over before tea, Shoaib, having batted with good sense until that point, cut recklessly at Ambrose and was caught in the gully. Aamer Malik and Imran Khan were out in quick succession in the last session, but Saleem Yousuf and Wasim Akram hit out boldly, although never unwisely, to score 50 in five overs. The stand was worth 67 when Saleem, attempting to hook a Marshall bouncer, was hit in the face and suffered a badly broken nose. Wasim Akram continued to hit boldly, taking 18 in one over from Walsh before becoming another Marshall victim. Pakistan were all out just before the close.

By tea on the second day, West Indies were 153 for 3 with Richards in flowing mood and Haynes, who batted 286 minutes for his 48, providing the anchor. In an after-tea spell, Wasim Akram, who bowled at his fastest, dismissed Richards, and Mudassar accounted for Haynes and Logie with successive deliveries. West Indies ended the day on 226 for 8.

The next morning Marshall and Benjamin hit 57 in 10 overs to nullify much of Wasim Akram's good work of the day before, and West Indies seized the advantage when

Elegant batting and wicket-keeping in the second Test in Trinidad by Jeff Dujon. (ASP)

Logie took a spectacular diving catch at square-leg to dismiss the dangerous Rameez. Shoaib and Mudassar took the score to 100, but then the innings fell apart. Spin accounted for both Hooper and Shoaib, and when Marshall had Javed caught behind and Saleem Malik and Aamer Malik were out shortly after, Pakistan were in deep trouble. Saleem was obviously disturbed by an incident with Marshall when he complained to Richards about the bowler's language and attitude. Pakistan closed at 177 for 6.

Imran Khan batted well on the fourth morning and was ably supported by the most courageous Saleem Yousuf, who was dropped first ball by Richards. Again West Indies started badly, and at the end of the day they were 154 for 5, but with Richards one of the not out batsmen they still seemed likely to score the 266 that they needed for victory. Within 35 minutes on the last morning, however, both Richards and Ambrose were out, and when Marshall fell to Wasim Akram for 15, West Indies were 207 for 8, and Pakistan were in sight of success. Dujon and Benjamin met the situation with a combination of aggression and good sense, and the tension mounted. Pakistan felt somewhat aggrieved when several confident appeals were rejected, and Abdul Qadir, the main sufferer, reacted angrily to the jibes of a spectator and crossed the boundary line and became involved in a scuffle, a very sad incident.

Benjamin, who was only in the side because of Pat-

THIRD TEST MATCH – WEST INDIES v. PAKISTAN
22, 23, 24, 26 and 27 April 1988 at Kensington Oval, Bridgetown, Barbados

PAKISTAN

Batsman	FIRST INNINGS		SECOND INNINGS	
Mudassar Nazar	b Ambrose	18	(2) c Greenidge, b Hooper	41
Rameez Raja	c Greenidge, b Benjamin	54	(1) c Logie, b Marshall	4
Shoaib Mohammad	c Greenidge, b Ambrose	54	c and b Richards	64
Javed Miandad	c Richardson, b Marshall	14	c Dujon, b Marshall	34
Saleem Malik	b Marshall	15	lbw, b Benjamin	9
Aamer Malik	c Hooper, b Benjamin	32	c Logie, b Marshall	2
Imran Khan†	c Dujon, b Benjamin	18	not out	43
Saleem Yousuf*	retired hurt	32	(9) c Richards, b Benjamin	28
Wasim Akram	c Benjamin, b Marshall	38	(8) lbw, b Marshall	0
Abdul Qadir	c Walsh, b Marshall	17	c Greenidge, b Marshall	2
Saleem Jaffer	not out	1	b Ambrose	4
Extras	lb 7, nb 9	16	b 3, lb 14, nb 14	31
		309		**262**

	O	M	R	W	O	M	R	W
Marshall	18.4	3	79	4	23	3	65	5
Ambrose	14	2	64	2	20.5	3	74	1
Benjamin	14	3	52	3	15	1	37	2
Walsh	10	1	53	–	12	1	22	–
Hooper	12	3	35	–	10	1	39	1
Richards	6	–	19	–	7	3	8	1

FALL OF WICKETS
1–46, 2–99, 3–128, 4–155, 5–186, 6–215, 7–218, 8–297, 9–309
1–6, 2–100, 3–153, 4–165, 5–167, 6–169, 7–182, 8–234, 9–245

WEST INDIES

Batsman	FIRST INNINGS		SECOND INNINGS	
C.G. Greenidge	lbw, b Imran Khan	10	c Shoaib, b Saleem Jaffer	35
D.L. Haynes	c Aamer, b Mudassar	48	c Saleem Malik, b Wasim	4
R.B. Richardson	c Aamer, b Wasim	3	st Aamer, b Qadir	64
C.L. Hooper	b Wasim Akram	54	run out	13
I.V.A. Richards†	c Mudassar, b Wasim	67	b Wasim Akram	39
A.L. Logie	c Javed, b Mudassar	0	b Abdul Qadir	3
P.J.L. Dujon*	run out	0	(8) not out	29
M.D. Marshall	c Aamer, b Imran	48	(9) lbw, b Wasim Akram	15
E.L.C. Ambrose	lbw, b Imran Khan	7	(7) c Saleem Jaffer, b Wasim Akram	1
W.K.M. Benjamin	run out	31	not out	40
C.A. Walsh	not out	14		
Extras	b 5, lb 11, nb 8	24	b 9, lb 6, nb 10	25
		306	(for 8 wkts)	**268**

	O	M	R	W	O	M	R	W
Imran Khan	25	3	108	3	6	–	34	–
Wasim Akram	27	1	88	3	31	7	73	4
Abdul Qadir	15	1	35	–	32	5	115	2
Saleem Jaffer	7	1	35	–	5	–	25	1
Mudassar Nazar	10	4	24	2				
Shoaib Mohammad					3	1	6	–

FALL OF WICKETS
1–18, 2–21, 3–100, 4–198, 5–198, 6–199, 7–201, 8–225, 9–283
1–21, 2–78, 3–118, 4–128, 5–150, 6–159, 7–180, 8–207

Umpires: D.M. Archer & L.H. Barker

West Indies won by 2 wickets

TEST MATCH AVERAGES – WEST INDIES v. PAKISTAN

WEST INDIES BATTING

	M	Inns	NOs	Runs	HS	Av	100s	50s
I.V.A. Richards	2	4		278	123	69.50	1	1
P.J.L. Dujon	3	6	2	185	106*	46.25	1	
R.B. Richardson	3	6		240	75	40.00		2
C.L. Hooper	3	6		156	54	26.00		1
M.D. Marshall	2	4	1	75	48	25.00		
C.G. Greenidge	3	6		135	43	22.50		
A.L. Logie	3	6		126	80	21.00		1
W.K.M. Benjamin	3	6	1	89	40*	17.80		
C.A. Walsh	3	5	1	52	14*	13.00		
D.L. Haynes	3	6		75	48	12.50		
E.L.C. Ambrose	3	6	2	47	25*	11.75		

Played in one Test: P.V. Simmons 16 & 11; B.P. Patterson 10 & 0

WEST INDIES BOWLING

	Overs	Mds	Runs	Wkts	Av	Best	10/m	5/inns
I.V.A. Richards	17	4	44	3	14.66	2/17		
M.D. Marshall	91.4	14	284	15	18.93	5/65		1
W.K.M. Benjamin	100	16	293	12	24.41	3/32		
B.P. Patterson	26	2	101	4	25.25	3/82		
E.L.C. Ambrose	108.3	20	365	7	52.14	2/64		
C.L. Hooper	47.1	6	164	3	54.66	1/35		
C.A. Walsh	86	14	230	4	57.50	3/80		

WEST INDIES FIELDING FIGURES
6 - I.V.A. Richards, C.G. Greenidge and P.J.L. Dujon (ct 5/st 1); 5 - A.L. Logie; 3 - R.B. Richardson and D.L. Haynes; 1 - C.L. Hooper, W.K.M. Benjamin, C.A. Walsh and P.V. Simmons

PAKISTAN BATTING

	M	Inns	NOs	Runs	HS	Av	100s	50s
Javed Miandad	3	5		282	114	56.40	2	
Saleem Yousuf	3	5	1	196	62	49.00		1
Shoaib Mohammad	3	6	1	189	64	37.80		2
Saleem Malik	3	5		147	66	29.40		1
Ijaz Ahmed	2	3		77	43	25.66		
Rameez Raja	3	6	1	126	54	25.20		
Imran Khan	3	5	1	90	43*	22.50		
Mudassar Nazar	3	6		115	41	19.16		
Abdul Qadir	3	5	2	55	19	18.33		
Wasim Akram	3	5	1	49	38	12.25		
Ijaz Faqih	2	3		15	10*	7.50		

Played in one Test: Aamer Malik 32 & 2; Saleem Jaffer 1* & 4

PAKISTAN BOWLING

	Overs	Mds	Runs	Wkts	Av	Best	10/m	5/inns
Shoaib Mohammad	8	1	22	2	11.00	2/8		
Mudassar Nazar	16	6	36	2	18.00	2/24		
Imran Khan	129.5	16	416	23	18.08	7/80	1	2
Wasim Akram	117	22	319	11	29.00	4/73		
Abdul Qadir	162.4	21	538	14	38.42	4/83		
Saleem Jaffer	12	1	60	1	60.00	1/25		
Ijaz Faqih	36	4	133	2	66.50	1/38		

Bowled in one innings: Saleek Malik 1-0-6-0

PAKISTAN FIELDING FIGURES
8 - Saleem Yousuf (ct 7/st 1); 4 - Javed Miandad and Aamer Malik (ct 3/st 1); 3 - Ijaz Ahmed & Saleem Malik; 2 - Shoaib Mohammad; 1 - Imran Khan, Wasim Akram, Saleem Jaffer, Mudassar Nazar, Abdul Qadir and sub (Naved Anjum)

The hero of West Indies' triumph in the final Test – Winston Benjamin. (Adrian Murrell/Allsport)

terson's injury, twice lofted Abdul Qadir for six and won the match when he hit the leg-spinner for four. He and Dujon received heroes' receptions.

The cricket throughout the series was of a very high order, and no other Test series in recent series can compare with it. Imran, returning for the most challenging task of his career, was quite magnificent and Javed Mian-dad must now stand on a par with Richards. Imran insisted that this would definitely mark the end of his career at international level, but Pakistan live in hope that he will change his mind. As a team, they have no superior in the world at present.

5, 6 and 7 April 1988

at Sabina Park, Kingston, Jamaica

Jamaica 272 (W.W. Lewis 71, I. Folley 4 for 73) and 103 for 7
Lancashire 390 (N.H. Fairbrother 106, A.N. Hayhurst 83, G.D. Mendis 71, A.G. Daley 6 for 103)

Match drawn

In the middle of the Pakistan tour, Lancashire made a short visit to the Caribbean and had much the better of a draw with a weakened Jamaican side. Fairbrother and Hayhurst put on 146 for the sixth wicket. Bad light ended play early on the last day.

Trintoc Cup

20, 21, 22 and 23 May 1988

at Guaracara Park, Point-à-Pierre, Trinidad

South Trinidad 278 (S. Ragoonath 90, D. Deyal 57, D.V. St Hilaire 4 for 64) and 132 for 8 dec
North Trinidad 149 (R.J. Bishop 59, R. Nanan 5 for 26) and 220 for 6 (R.J. Bishop 65)

Match drawn

There was no play on the third day of the Trintoc (formerly Beaumont) Cup, and the match ended evenly poised. Deyal and Ragoonath began the game with a partnership of 138.

First-Class Averages

BATTING

	M	Inns	NOs	Runs	HS	Av	100s	50s
I.V.A. Richards	4	6		467	123	77.83	2	2
K.L.T. Arthurton	8	13	2	685	132	62.27	3	2
C.B. Lambert	7	12	2	604	162	60.40	2	1
W.W. Lewis	7	12	2	584	132	58.40	1	3
R.B. Richardson	5	9	1	433	176	54.12	1	1
P.J.L. Dujon	6	10	2	425	108	53.12	2	1
R. Seeram	7	13	3	504	119	50.40	1	2
E.A.E. Baptiste	3	4		189	99	47.25		2
T.R.O. Payne	6	11		465	127	42.27	1	3
D.S. Morgan	5	8	1	260	101*	37.14	1	1
R.M. Otto	5	8	2	221	74*	36.83		2
C.A. Best	6	11	1	351	98	35.10		4
L. Harris	5	6		204	63	34.00		2
M.D. Marshall	7	13	2	373	77	33.90		4
R.C. Haynes	5	8	1	236	87	33.71		1
P.V. Simmons	6	9	1	268	64	33.50		1
K.A. Williams	4	7		233	77	33.28		1
M.C. Neita	5	7		231	58	33.00		2
C. Burnett	5	7		228	63	32.57		3
D.J. Collymore	6	11	2	287	87*	31.88		2
C.L. Hooper	4	7		223	67	31.85		2
C.G. Greenidge	6	12	1	350	70	31.81		1
D. Joseph	5	10		308	109	30.80	1	1
L.C. Sebastien	5	10		301	116	30.10	1	1
D. Telemaque	2	4		115	71	28.75		1
A.L. Grant	5	9	1	223	75	27.87		1
D.I. Harper	5	6	1	137	70	27.40		2
D. Williams	5	6	1	136	44*	27.20		
H.A. Gomes	6	9	1	205	66	25.62		1
D.L. Haynes	6	12	1	273	64	24.81		1
B.C. Lara	5	7		171	92	24.42		1
M.A. Harper	3	6		146	85	24.33		1
A.L. Kelly	5	9	1	192	79	24.00		1
A.L. Logie	5	10		239	80	23.90		1
S. Dhaniram	6	9		203	72	22.55		1
C.A. Davidson	6	9	1	177	55	22.12		1
L.D. John	5	10		196	53	19.60		1
A.H. Gray	7	9		165	47	18.33		
C.G. Butts	6	7		125	48	17.85		
M.A. Tucker	5	6		105	43	17.50		
J.R. Murray	6	12	2	174	47	17.40		
C.A. Walsh	6	8	1	113	29	16.14		
R. Nanan	6	9	2	108	48	15.42		

First-Class Averages continued

J.D. Charles	5	10	154	40	15.40	
J. Garner	5	9	137	62	15.22	1
W.K.M. Benjamin	7	10 1	115	41*	12.77	

(Qualification: 100 runs, average 10.00)

R.J. Bishop played in one match – 65 & 59

BOWLING

	Overs	Mds	Runs	Wkts	Av	Best	10/m	5/inns
R. Nanan	226.4	77	386	26	14.84	5/26		2
M.A. Tucker	143.1	45	298	20	14.90	6/38	1	2
M.D. Marshall	250.3	46	750	42	17.85	5/24		3
J. Garner	148.5	26	450	23	19.56	4/39		
E.T. Willett	101	26	246	12	20.50	3/42		
W.K.M. Benjamin	217.4	48	631	30	21.03	5/50		1
E.L.C. Ambrose	298.5	52	903	42	21.50	7/61	1	3
I.R. Bishop	207.4	28	661	27	24.48	4/23		
R.C. Haynes	241	61	564	22	25.63	6/53		2
A.G. Daley	143.3	23	455	17	26.76	6/103		1
B.P. Patterson	106.3	18	382	14	27.28	3/43		

	Overs	Mds	Runs	Wkts	Av	Best		
C.A. Walsh	180.1	34	516	18	28.66	5/45		1
D.J. Collymore	164	23	495	17	29.11	4/72		
G.E. Charles	115.4	14	430	14	30.71	5/48		2
R.A. Harper	132.2	19	340	11	30.90	3/60		
H. Springer	125	20	343	11	31.18	4/63		
J.T. Etienne	166	33	484	15	32.26	3/31		
A.H. Gray	181	25	557	17	32.76	4/54		
C.G. Butts	211	49	537	15	35.80	5/56		1
R. Dhanraj	116.2	17	363	10	36.30	4/67		
T.Z. Kentish	169	29	406	10	40.60	3/57		
B. St A. Browne	133	4	501	12	41.75	3/95		

(Qualification – 10 wickets)

LEADING FIELDERS

15 - L. Harris (ct 13/st 2) and T.R.O. Payne (ct 14/st 1); 13 - P.J.L. Dujon (ct 12/st1); 11 - J.R. Murray (ct 9/st 2); 9 - A.L. Logie (ct 8/st 1); 8 – B.C. Lara and I.V.A. Richards; 7 - C.B. Lambert and D. Williams (ct 6/st 1); 6 - C.R. Rampersan, C.A. Best, R. Seeram, R.M. Otto and R.B. Richardson.

A Summer of Captains

The season in England. Benson and Hedges Cup.
Britannic Assurance County Championship.
Refuge Assurance League and Cup.
NatWest Bank Trophy. Tilcon Trophy. Four Counties Tournament.
Cornhill Test Matches, England *v.* West Indies, England *v.* Sri Lanka.
Texaco Trophy, England *v.* West Indies, England *v.* Sri Lanka.
Form charts. First-class averages. Review of the season.
In Defence of One-Day Cricket by Chris Cowdrey.
World Rankings, Ted Dexter talks to Brian Scovell of the *Daily Mail*.

Save the Oval. By means of hard work, enthusiasm, generous donation and sponsorship, it seemed that by the end of the 1988 season, The Oval, one of the world's great cricket grounds, would be saved. (Michael King/Allsport)

Botham emulated Hannibal and crossed The Alps. Unlike Hannibal, he was in search of neither conquest nor personal glory. His giant task was undertaken to raise money for leukaemia research. This was, indeed, Botham the Dr Jekyll. Mr Hyde had struck in Australia, and Botham's brief career with Queensland was at an end because of unsavoury activities on the aeroplane that was flying the Queensland side to Perth for the Sheffield Shield final. It had not been the only unhappy event of the winter, and English cricket, tainted by happenings in Pakistan and Australia and by dullness in New Zealand, began the season under a cloud. The cloud was not lifted by the announcement that Broad and Dilley had won large monetary prizes for their performances on tour. The prizes, it was emphasized, were for achievements with bat and ball, not for attitudes or behaviour.

An upheaval at Warwickshire had led to some public blood-letting and to the loss of some very good men from the Warwickshire committee. There were also rumblings at Sussex, where Paul Parker became captain and John Jameson arrived as coach. Dynamic new secretary Nigel Bett faced a difficult task, but he has the energy and the drive capable of overcoming the many difficulties that the south coast county presents to any who would wish to bring it into the twentieth century. There was new energy, too, at Glamorgan, where Tony Lewis took over as chairman of the cricket committee. The Welsh county faced an immediate problem when they lost Simon Base to Derbyshire. Glamorgan complained that the player had given a verbal agreement that he would sign a contract that had been presented to him, and a subsequent TCCB enquiry ruled that Base should be barred from playing for Derbyshire until July. In fact, he did assist them in the opening match at Cambridge.

More serious was the news of the threat to The Oval. The Surrey Club had planned extensive redevelopment and had worked towards raising a million pounds to pay for the project, believing that the government would honour a promise to supply funds as the redevelopment would bring new jobs and wealth to an area where they were much needed. The government failed to meet the promise given, and the Surrey Club, faced with the closure of a noble and historic ground, had to set about the difficult task of raising more money so that work on the ground could begin in September 1988. Indeed, several clouds hung over cricket in England as the new season approached.

There was the round of dinners and lunches and launches, and old acquaintances and new friends were met. When it began to rain steadily one knew that the season had arrived.

16, 17 and 18 April

at Lord's

Nottinghamshire 298 for 3 dec (R.T. Robinson 129, P. Johnson 61 not out) and 139 for 2 dec (P. Johnson 59 not out)
MCC 159 for 7 dec (G.A. Hick 61) and 222 for 5 (G. Fowler 73)

Match drawn

at Cambridge

Cambridge University 86 (A.E. Warner 4 for 22) and 106
Derbyshire 406 for 5 dec (P.D. Bowler 155 not out, K.J. Barnett 151, S.C. Goldsmith 55)

Derbyshire won by an innings and 214 runs

16, 18 and 19 April

at Oxford

Oxford University 98 (P.A.J. De Freitas 4 for 15, C.C. Lewis 4 for 48) and 68 (C.C. Lewis 6 for 22)
Leicestershire 319 for 6 dec (N.E. Briers 80, L. Potter 54 not out, J.J. Whitaker 53)

Leicestershire won by an innings and 153 runs

Broad and Robinson began the season with a stand of 116, but, in spite of declarations, the rain was the only winner at Lord's. Hick took the eye with some glorious shots in the gloom, and Robinson and Barnett hit the first centuries of the season, both coming to their hundreds on the Sunday. Barnett hit the highest score of his career, and a century on his début for Derbyshire by Peter Bowler, formerly with Leicestershire; and a bright fifty from another new recruit, Goldsmith from Kent, gave credibility to Barnett's prophecy that his side would win one of the four titles. Bowler and Barnett put on 238 for the first wicket, and the county crushed the University, for whom

A career-best 155 for Peter Bowler on the occasion of his début for Derbyshire against Cambridge University, 16–17 April. (George Herringshaw/ASP)

Atherton and Fenton impressed. Like Derbyshire, Leicestershire sharpened their teeth on moderate University opposition.

20, 21 and 22 April

at Cambridge

Cambridge University 78 (G.J. Parsons 7 for 16)
Warwickshire 405 for 2 (M. Asif Din 158 not out, A.I. Kallicharran 117 not out, A.J. Moles 95)

Match drawn

at Oxford

Oxford University 137 and 95 (N.G.B. Cook 4 for 32)
Northamptonshire 389 for 5 dec (A.J. Lamb 101 retired hurt, R.J. Bailey 101, N.A. Stanley 66)

Northamptonshire won by an innings and 157 runs

There was no play on the third day at Fenner's where Gordon Parsons returned an amazing career best of 7 for 16 in 16 overs on the first morning, and Asif Din reached the highest score of his career, sharing stands of 175 for the second wicket with Moles and an unbroken 216 with Kallicharran for the third. Allan Lamb and Robert Bailey hit centuries at Oxford and shared a third-wicket stand of 180 while Neil Stanley hit 66 on his début at Oxford, where the home side was again overwhelmed.

21, 22, 23 and 25 April

at Derby

Derbyshire 324 (B.J.M. Maher 121 not out, C.C. Lewis 5 for 73) and 331 for 8 dec (J.G. Wright 84, R.J. Finney 52 not out)
Leicestershire 482 for 8 dec. (J.J. Whitaker 145, L. Potter 107, N.E. Briers 90)

Match drawn
Leicestershire 7 pts, Derbyshire 4 pts

at Chelmsford

Kent 400 for 7 dec (M.R. Benson 110, N.R. Taylor 94) and 384 (G.R. Cowdrey 145, S.A. Marsh 120, C.S. Cowdrey 54, J.H. Childs 5 for 113)
Essex 616 (G.A. Gooch 275, D.R. Pringle 128, K.W.R. Fletcher 58, R.P. Davis 5 for 132) and 170 for 2 (G.A. Gooch 73, A.R. Border 55 not out)

Essex won by 8 wickets
Essex 21 pts, Kent 4 pts

at Bristol

Glamorgan 372 for 9 dec (M.P. Maynard 126, G.C. Holmes 117, T.M. Alderman 4 for 70) and 296 for 8 dec (H. Morris 84, M.P. Maynard 68, M.W. Alleyne 4 for 48)
Gloucestershire 341 for 7 dec (C.W.J. Athey 123, J.W. Lloyds 68, P. Bainbridge 52, A.W. Stovold 52) and 329 for 4 (C.W.J. Athey 88 not out, A.J. Wright 87, M.W. Alleyne 56)

Gloucestershire won by 6 wickets
Gloucestershire 21 pts, Glamorgan 5 pts

at Southampton

Surrey 246 (C.J. Richards 61, C.A. Connor 4 for 71) and 47 for 1
Hampshire 81 (N.H. Peters 4 for 47) and 198 (S.T. Jefferies 60, I.A. Greig 6 for 56)

Surrey won by 9 wickets
Surrey 22 pts, Hampshire 4 pts

at Old Trafford

Worcestershire 409 for 7 dec (G.A. Hick 212) and 29 for 0
Lancashire 101 (R.K. Illingworth 5 for 46) and 336 (M. Watkinson 68, J. Simmons 57 not out, N.H. Fairbrother 56, G. Fowler 50, R.K. Illingworth 5 for 107, G.A. Hick 4 for 138)

Worcestershire won by 10 wickets
Worcestershire 23 pts, Lancashire 1 pt

at Lord's

Middlesex 199 (R.O. Butcher 73, J.E. Emburey 61, K.E. Cooper 5 for 52) and 505 for 5 dec (M.W. Gatting 210, K.R. Brown 131 not out, J.D. Carr 106)
Nottinghamshire 308 (M. Newell 80, B.C. Broad 68, F.D. Stephenson 63, A.R.C. Fraser 6 for 75) and 155 (P. Johnson 60, A.R.C. Fraser 4 for 42)

Middlesex won by 241 runs
Middlesex 19 pts, Nottinghamshire 7 pts

at Hove

Somerset 142 (A.C.S. Pigott 4 for 55) and 333 (N.D. Burns 133 not out, A.M. Babington 4 for 66)
Sussex 266 (P.W.G. Parker 101 not out, D.J. Foster 4 for 67) and 213 for 3 (P.W.G. Parker 71 not out)

Sussex won by 7 wickets
Sussex 23 pts, Somerset 4 pts

County Championship matches of four days' duration were played in England for the first time. There was general pleasure on their outcome by those who administer the game although the paying customers were more sceptical. Surrey needed only two days in which to beat Hampshire. Put in to bat, Surrey were 39 for 4 in spite of Hampshire dropping catches in profusion, but Jack Richards played positive cricket and helped his side rally to 246, Greig and Medlycott making very useful contributions. Left with 16 overs in which to bat out the first day, Hampshire lost Terry, Chris Smith and Nicholas for 44, and on the second morning their decline quickened as Nick Peters, on his first-class début, took 4 for 47. Mark Feltham finished off the innings with 3 for 6 in 16 balls, and Hampshire had to follow on. Ian Greig led his side splendidly and bowled finely. He was well supported in the field, and Hampshire were wallowing at 43 for 5 and 118 for 8. Steve Jefferies and Tim Tremlett added 74, but they could not stay the Surrey victory for long.

Derbyshire, 58 for 5, were rallied by Bernard Maher, batting at number seven since the arrival of Bowler, but Leicestershire built up a big score, with Whitaker and Potter adding 199 for the fifth wicket. Derbyshire batted through the last day for a draw.

In spite of four days being allocated to the game, the match at Chelmsford ended in a run chase. Benson and Taylor began with an accomplished stand of 208, but Essex were 279 for 3 in 77 overs by the end of the second day. Gooch and Pringle both reached the highest scores of their careers on the Saturday as they extended their fourth-wicket stand to 254. Gooch's 275 came off 399 balls and included 4 sixes and 27 fours. Pringle batted with a runner in the latter part of his innings because of a groin strain.

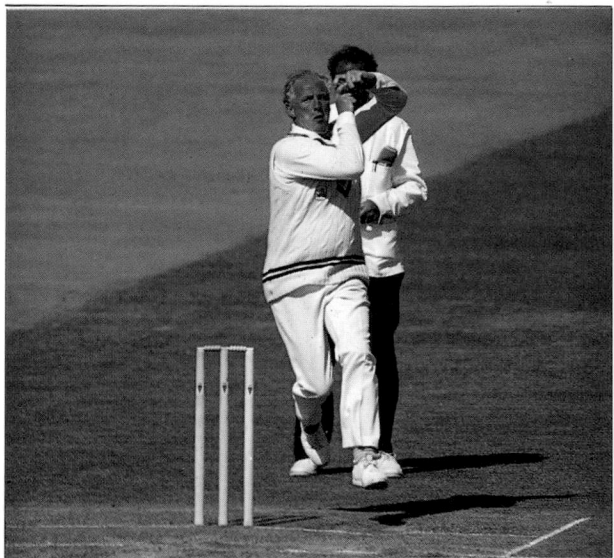

Norman Gifford, Warwickshire, begins his 29th season in first-class cricket. (Ken Kelly)

Essex passed 600 and Kent, 76 for 4, looked well beaten by the close. Chris Cowdrey rallied them on the Monday, but the exciting partnership came from Graham Cowdrey and Steve Marsh, who added 222 for the seventh wicket, both batsmen reaching the highest scores of their careers. Childs bowled a splendid 45-over stint for Essex, who were left to make 169 in 25 overs. Gooch was again in majestic form. He and Border added 97 for the second wicket, and victory came with 3.4 overs to spare. In fairness to Kent, it should be said that neither Igglesden nor Penn could bowl in Essex's second innings due to injury.

There was an equally exciting finish at Bristol, where Maynard hit 126 in just over three hours and Holmes hit a career best. Athey steered the home county to near parity, and Morris' declaration asked Gloucestershire to make 328 in 78 overs. Wright and Alleyne laid the foundation for success with a second-wicket stand of 120 in 33 overs. Athey, Lloyds and Curran played some crisp shots and ran eagerly between the wickets, and victory came with 17 balls to spare.

An innings of 212 in 345 minutes by Graeme Hick dominated the Worcestershire innings at Old Trafford. He hit 4 sixes and 25 fours and mocked a wicket which was giving encouragement to the bowlers. He and Phil Neale added 202 for the fourth wicket, Neale hitting 40 in 4½ hours. In contrast, Lancashire succumbed meekly to the spin of Richard Illingworth. Following on, they batted with more solidity, but it took a last-wicket stand of 87 between Simmons and Folley to save an innings defeat. Illingworth, who bowled 59 overs, and Hick, with 4 for 138 from 44 overs of off-breaks, toiled manfully, and Worcestershire moved to an easy win.

Middlesex made a remarkable recovery at Lord's. They trailed by 109 on the first innings, but John Carr and Mike Gatting wiped this out in a third-wicket stand of 161.

Gatting and Keith Brown then added 264 for the fourth wicket, Gatting reaching his double century in the last session and Brown claiming a first championship hundred. Notts were left to make 397 to win in just over a day, but Angus Fraser added to his career-best bowling performance of the first innings with four more wickets, which brought him 10 wickets in a match for the first time and enabled Middlesex to win comfortably.

Paul Parker led by example at Hove. His elegant century took Sussex to a first-innings lead of 124. Somerset were saved from indignity by wicket-keeper Neil Burns, who hit the highest score of his career after his side had been rocking at 66 for 5. It was a brave effort, but it could not prevent Green, Parker and Colin Wells stroking Sussex to a heartening victory.

Refuge Assurance League

24 April

at Derby

Leicestershire 168
Derbyshire 171 for 3 (K.J. Barnett 77 not out)

Derbyshire (4 pts) won by 7 wickets

at Chelmsford

Kent 201 for 8 (S.G. Hinks 55)
Essex 202 for 1 (G.A. Gooch 90, B.R. Hardie 78 not out)

Essex (4 pts) won by 9 wickets

at Bristol

Glamorgan 176 for 6 (R.J. Shastri 84 not out)
Gloucestershire 177 for 5 (C.W.J. Athey 67)

Gloucestershire (4 pts) won by 5 wickets

Sussex v. Somerset at Hove, 21 April. Colin Wells drives through the off side as Felton and Harden look on apprehensively. (Steve Lindsell)

at Southampton

Surrey 236 for 9 (D.M. Smith 75, A.J. Stewart 53)
Hampshire 214 for 5 (D.R. Turner 103 not out)

Surrey (4 pts) won by 22 runs

at Old Trafford

Worcestershire 172 for 8 (S.J. O'Shaughnessy 50)
Lancashire 176 for 3

Lancashire (4 pts) won by 7 wickets

at Lord's

Nottinghamshire 165 for 7
Middlesex 166 for 6

Middlesex (4 pts) won by 4 wickets

at Hove

Somerset 191 for 6 (R.J. Harden 52)
Sussex 195 for 5 (P.W.G. Parker 90)

Sussex (4 pts) won by 5 wickets

The first round of Sunday league matches produced nothing sensational, and only Lancashire reversed the result of the Britannic Assurance County Championship match then in progress. Gooch and Hardie put on 145 for the Essex first wicket as Kent again suffered, and Parker played another fine innings for Sussex. Hampshire lost Tremlett with injury, and David Turner's century could not halt Surrey. Shastri and O'Shaughnessy, against his old county, joined Turner with a brave innings that proved unavailing.

Neil Burns, an immaculate wicket-keeper pressing strongly for representative honours, hit 133 not out for Somerset against Sussex at Hove but still finished on the losing side. (Adrian Murrell/Allsport)

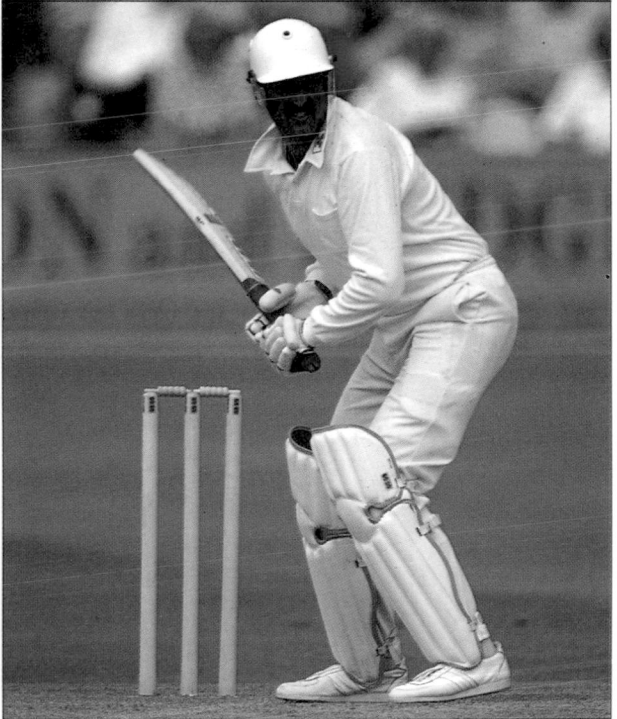

A mighty start to the season for Graham Gooch, 275 and 73, Essex v. Kent at Chelmsford. (George Herringshaw/ ASP)

Ten wickets in a match for the first time for Angus Fraser, Middlesex v. Notts, 21–5 April, heralded an outstanding season for the pace bowler. (David Munden)

The Refuge Assurance League had an added interest in its new format in that not only would it produce a champion, but the top four sides were to play off on a knock-out basis for the Refuge Assurance Cup.

Benson and Hedges Cup

26 April

at Chelmsford

Surrey 143 (T.D. Topley 4 for 22)
Essex 144 for 2 (P.J. Prichard 68 not out)

Essex (2 pts) won by 8 wickets
(Gold Award – T.D. Topley)

at Trent Bridge

Minor Counties 133 (K. Saxelby 5 for 21, F.D. Stephenson 4 for 14)
Nottinghamshire 137 for 2 (B.C. Broad 52)

Nottinghamshire (2 pts) won by 8 wickets
(Gold Award – K. Saxelby)

at Glasgow (Hamilton Crescent)

Scotland 148 for 9
Derbyshire 149 for 3 (K.J. Barnett 66)

Derbyshire (2 pts) won by 7 wickets
(Gold Award – K.J. Barnett)

at Taunton

Somerset 197 for 8 (N.A. Felton 50)
Hampshire 201 for 5 (M.C.J. Nicholas 72)

Hampshire (2 pts) won by 5 wickets
(Gold Award – S.T. Jefferies)

at Hove

Sussex 207 for 7 (A.P. Wells 53)
Kent 208 for 3 (S.G. Hinks 78 not out)

Kent (2 pts) won by 7 wickets
(Gold Award – S.G. Hinks)

26 and 27 April

at Bristol

Gloucestershire 242 for 7 (C.W.J. Athey 82)
Combined Universities 182 (M.P. Speight 83, M.W. Alleyne 5 for 27)

Gloucestershire (2 pts) won by 60 runs
(Gold Award – C.W.J. Athey)

at Leicester

Leicestershire 213 for 8 (P. Willey 59, T.J. Boon 53, T.E. Jesty 5 for 39)
Lancashire 167 (T.E. Jesty 57, P.A.J. De Freitas 4 for 27)

Leicestershire (2 pts) won by 46 runs
(Gold Award – T.E. Jesty)

at Leeds

Yorkshire 173 for 1 (M.D. Moxon 82 not out, A.A. Metcalfe 70)
v Northamptonshire

Match abandoned
Yorkshire 1 pt, Northamptonshire 1 pt

Gold Award Winner Don Topley dances with delight as he captures the wicket of Ian Greig, Essex v. Surrey, Benson and Hedges Cup, 26 April. (Gray Mortimore/Allsport)

The first round of zonal matches in the Benson and Hedges Cup produced some fine cricket but few surprises. Essex brushed aside Surrey with unexpected ease and owed much to Don Topley, who exploited the conditions well to send back Clinton, Lynch, Greig and Clarke and win his first Gold Award. Surrey reached 61 for 1 and then lost three wickets for four runs and their hold on the match. Essex took nine good catches and East stumped Smith at the second attempt so that the quality of their cricket was altogether superior to that of Surrey, who were very disappointing. Essex lost Hardie in the second over, but still won with 15.1 overs to spare.

Kevin Saxelby took his first Gold Award as Notts trounced the Minor Counties, and Kim Barnett steered Derbyshire to victory in Glasgow in spite of fine all-round cricket from Clive Rice. Kent beat Sussex with 5.4 overs in hand, and Gloucestershire won comfortably enough at Bristol although the Combined Universities showed they were a much stronger side than in the days when Oxford and Cambridge supplied all the players.

The match at Bristol was one of three which was marred by the weather. Another was at Leicester, where Lancashire, chasing 214, finished the first day on 46 for 6 from 19 overs. Trevor Jesty followed splendid bowling with heroic batting on the Wednesday, but he could not prevent a Leicestershire victory. Like Jesty, Steve Jefferies took the

Gold Award in his first Benson and Hedges game for his new county.

Yorkshire, the cup holders, began in the manner in which they had played the 1987 competition with Moxon and Metcalfe sharing an opening stand of 166, but then came the rain and abandonment.

Monte Lynch hit 15 fours in his first hundred of the season, and Ian Greig returned his best bowling figures for Surrey. Frost, making his first-class début, bowled impressively. Again Atherton stood head and shoulders above the other undergraduates.

28, 29 and 30 April

at Cambridge

Surrey 310 for 3 dec (M.A. Lynch 103 not out, G.S. Clinton 74, D.M. Ward 53 not out) and 166 for 3 dec (I.A. Greig 67)
Cambridge University 176 (I.A. Greig 6 for 34) and 203 (M.A. Atherton 100 not out, M. Frost 4 for 56, K.T. Medlycott 4 for 76)

Surrey won by 97 runs

28, 29, 30 April and 2 May

at Cardiff

Glamorgan 543 for 8 dec (R.J. Shastri 157, M.P. Maynard 122, G.C. Holmes 108)
Somerset 267 (N.D. Burns 66, S.R. Waugh 53, J.G. Thomas 4 for 74) and 100 for 0 (N.A. Felton 64 not out)

Match drawn
Glamorgan 8 pts, Somerset 4 pts

Combined Universities 1988
Benson and Hedges Cup

BATTING	v. Gloucestershire (Bristol) 26 & 27 April	v. Somerset (Oxford) 4 May	v. Glamorgan (Cardiff) 12 May	v. Hampshire (Cambridge) 14 May	Runs
P.A.C. Bail	0	1	13	18	32
T. O'Gorman	14	39	43	12	108
M.A. Atherton	0	29	17	38	84
N. Hussain	44	4	76*	2	126
J.C.M. Atkinson	24	5	6		35
M.P. Speight	83	17	8	20	128
T.M. Barry	6	6		8	20
G. Harding	0			3	3
M. Smith	0	1	3	1	5
J. Boiling	3	2*	9*	2*	16
N.C.W. Fenton	0*	0	—	1*	1
M. Hickson		4	10		14
M.J. Kilborn			10	14	24
Byes			4		
Leg-byes	4	3	12	8	
Wides	2	1	5	2	
No-balls	2		2	1	
Total	182	112	218	130	
Wickets	10	10	8	9	
Result	L	L	L	L	
Points	0	0	0	0	

Fielding Figures 4 – M.A. Atherton and J. Boiling
3 – N. Hussain and M.P. Speight
1 – J.C.M. Atkinson, N. Smith and P.A.C. Bail

BOWLING	N.C.W. Fenton	M. Smith	T.M. Barry	G. Harding	J. Boiling	M.A. Atherton	M. Hickson	J.C.M. Atkinson	M.J. Kilborn
v. Gloucestershire (Bristol) 26 & 27 April	11-0-31-1	11-2-45-0	10-0-52-3	11-0-54-1	11-0-44-2	1-0-8-0			
v. Somerset (Oxford) 4 May	9-1-26-1	8-0-49-4	8-0-50-1		8-0-27-1		8-1-27-1		
v. Glamorgan (Cardiff) 12 May	11-0-44-3	10-0-59-1			11-2-51-0		11-0-64-0	7-0-46-0	5-0-29-0
v. Hampshire (Cambridge) 14 May	9-2-21-1	7-1-36-0		4-0-19-0	9.1-0-48-2				
Wickets	6	5	4	1	5	0	1	0	0

at Bristol

Sussex 324 (A.P. Wells 69, T.M. Alderman 5 for 75) and 116 for 4 (P.W.G. Parker 55 not out)
Gloucestershire 252 (A.W. Stovold 136, R.A. Bunting 5 for 86)

Match drawn
Sussex 7 pts, Gloucestershire 5 pts

at Canterbury

Kent 230 (S.J. Andrew 4 for 52, S.T. Jefferies 4 for 80) and 99 (K.D. James 4 for 22)
Hampshire 170 (C.S. Cowdrey 5 for 46) and 160 for 3 (M.C.J. Nicholas 74, C.L. Smith 62)

Hampshire won by 7 wickets
Hampshire 21 pts, Kent 6 pts

at Old Trafford

Warwickshire 155 (P.A. Smith 68, C.D. Matthews 4 for 47) and 297 (G.C. Small 70, T.A. Lloyd 64, P.J.W. Allott 5 for 65)
Lancashire 217 (W.K. Hegg 76, G.C. Small 5 for 60, T.A. Merrick 5 for 67) and 83 for 1

Match drawn
Lancashire 6 pts, Warwickshire 5 pts

at Leicester

Northamptonshire 176 (A.J. Lamb 54, J.P. Agnew 6 for 66) and 100 (P.A.J. De Freitas 5 for 40, J.P. Agnew 5 for 56)
Leicestershire 327 (P.A.J. De Freitas 66, N.E. Briers 63, P. Willey 56, W.W. Davis 4 for 115)

Leicestershire won by an innings and 51 runs
Leicestershire 23 pts, Northamptonshire 4 pts

at Lord's

Middlesex 263 (J.D. Carr 66, D.R. Pringle 4 for 90) and 275 for 8 dec (J.E. Emburey 76 not out, W.N. Slack 65, T.D. Topley 5 for 94)
Essex 187 (A.W. Lilley 52, N.F. Williams 6 for 42) and 175 (N.G. Cowans 4 for 45)

Middlesex won by 176 runs
Middlesex 23 pts, Essex 5 pts

at Worcester

Worcestershire 290 (G.A. Hick 86, K.E. Cooper 5 for 75, F.D. Stephenson 4 for 99) and 92 for 4
Nottinghamshire 132 (B.C. Broad 53, N.V. Radford 5 for 55, G.R. Dilley 4 for 37) and 248 (D.W. Randall 69, G.R. Dilley 5 for 80)

Rodney Bunting started his career for Sussex with two five-wicket hauls, but weather was the winner in the game at Bristol at the end of April. (Neil Simpson/ASP)

Worcestershire won by 6 wickets
Worcestershire 23 pts, Nottinghamshire 4 pts

at Leeds

Yorkshire 161 (M.D. Moxon 79, D.E. Malcolm 4 for 36) and 192 (P.G. Newman 8 for 29)
Derbyshire 170 (S.C. Goldsmith 51 not out, P.W. Jarvis 5 for 49) and 184 for 5 (K.J. Barnett 52)

Derbyshire won by 5 wickets
Derbyshire 21 pts, Yorkshire 5 pts

The idea of four-day county championship matches was mocked in the second series of games when four of the encounters were over in three days so leaving Bank Holiday crowds and county secretaries with a blank day when they could have expected lucrative cricket. At Canterbury, Kent were enlivened by Chris Cowdrey and Danny Kelleher, whose 43 not out was a career-best batting performance. Chris Cowdrey also bowled well and returned his best figures as he took his side to a first-innings lead of 60. From that point Kent's fortunes declined. The Hampshire seamers bowled them out for 99, and Chris Smith and Mark Nicholas shared a second-wicket stand of 120 to move Hampshire to a comfortable win inside three days.

Leicestershire also triumphed in three days with Jonathan Agnew taking 11 for 122 in the match to prompt the

	Byes	Leg-byes	Wides	No-balls	Total	Wkts
		8	8		242	7
	1	2	7	4	182	9
	2	7	6	1	302	6
			7	2	131	3

selectors. He and De Freitas bowled unchanged in the second innings to shoot out Northants in 31.1 overs. Consistent application had been the key to Leicestershire's first-innings lead of 151 with Briers and Willey putting on 76 for the second wicket and Agnew hitting 38 at number ten.

Worcestershire gave further indication of their strength as championship challengers when they took little over two days to beat the reigning champions, Nottinghamshire. Hick was again the backbone of the batting, and pace bowlers Radford and Dilley encountered little

resistance on a pitch which always encouraged the bowlers.

Paul Newman produced by far the best bowling performance of his career, a remarkable 8 for 29, as Derbyshire became the fourth side to win in three days. Yorkshire were struggling from the start against the Derbyshire pace attack, in which Holding and Malcolm were outstanding. Martyn Moxon offered lone resistance with his accomplished 79. No other batsman reached double figures. Derbyshire's batsmen found the conditions equally hard against Jarvis and Sidebottom, and only a

Minor Counties 1988
Benson and Hedges Cup

BATTING	v. Nottinghamshire (Trent Bridge) 26 April	v. Worcestershire (Old Heath) 3 & 4 May	v. Northamptonshire (Darlington) 10 May	v. Yorkshire (Leeds) 12 May	Runs
D.W. Varey	5				5
C.J. Stockdale	9		25	21	55
R.D.V. Knight	18			38	56
S.P. Henderson	6				6
S.G. Plumb	21		16	1	38
G.R.J. Roope	18		1	39	58
M.A. Garnham	0		11	13*	24
S. Turner	2				2
S. Greensword	21		20	2*	43
A.J. Webster	12		4	—	16
S. Edwards	2*				2
J.P. Addison			2		2
P.R. Oliver			31	48	79
S. Burrow			20	28	48
R.A. Evans			3*	—	3
R.N. Busby			9	—	9
Byes			1	6	
Leg-byes	12		9	5	
Wides	6		4	2	
No-balls	1		2	3	
Total	133		158	206	
Wickets	10		10	6	
Result	L	Ab.	L	L	
Points	0	1	0	0	

Fielding Figures   2 – G.R.J. Roope and M.A. Garnham (st 2)
1 – R.A. Evans

BOWLING	A.J. Webster	S. Turner	S. Edwards	S.G. Plumb	R.D.V. Knight	R.N. Busby	R.A. Evans	S. Greensword	S. Burrow
v. Nottinghamshire (Trent Bridge) 26 April	5–0–19–0	6–0–21–0	4–1–23–0	9–0–34–1	7–0–36–1				
v. Worcestershire (Old Heath) 3 & 4 May									
v. Northampton (Darlington) 10 May	11–1–43–2			10–1–43–1		7–1–19–0	11–5–21–0	7–0–26–0	9–0–43–1
v. Yorkshire (Leeds) 12 May	11–0–42–0			1–0–6–0	10–1–38–1	8–1–43–1	11–0–44–1	11–3–28–1	
Wickets	2	0	0	2	2	1	1	1	1

Paul Newman took 8 for 29 as Derbyshire beat Yorkshire in three days at the end of April. (Oli Tennent/Allsport)

brave knock by Goldsmith took them to a narrow first-innings lead. It was then that Newman struck. A fourth-wicket stand of 76 between Love and Robinson after three wickets had gone for eight and an eighth-wicket stand of 68 between Sidebottom and Peter Hartley were the only respites in an otherwise constant fall of Yorkshire wickets. Derbyshire needed 184 to win, and Barnett gave them a sound start. When the middle order began to creak Goldsmith again batted well, and there were no more alarms.

Middlesex took four days to beat Essex on a pitch of uneven bounce and regular movement off the seam. Carr again impressed with his elegance, and Neil Williams, injury free at last, took six wickets in a championship innings for the first time to give his side a first-innings lead of 76. Essex clawed their way back into the game on the Saturday by taking five wickets for 132 runs, but John Emburey laid about him in characteristic fashion and put the game out of Essex's reach. There was some defiant batting on the last day, but Cowans, Fraser, Hughes and Williams proved too formidable an attack to withstand for long.

Rain ruined Lancashire's chances of victory after a fine spell of bowling by Paul Allott had put them on top. Lancashire were 82 for 7 in their first innings and were revived by Warren Hegg and the Australian Chris Matthews, who was assisting the county until the arrival of Wasim Akram. Gladstone Small hit a career-best 70 to rally Warwickshire, but rain was the eventual winner.

Glamorgan batted for two days to reach their highest score at Sophia Gardens. Maynard hit his second century in as many matches, as did Holmes. Maynard's 122 included a six and 17 fours, and he and Shastri added 216 for the fourth wicket. Shastri reached his second century for the county and his highest score for them. Greg Thomas generated a lively pace and was instrumental in forcing Somerset to follow on, but, aided by rain, they had no difficulty in saving the match.

There was no play on the last day at Bristol, where Andy Stovold hit a sparkling 136 to revivify a flagging Gloucestershire and Rodney Bunting returned the best figures of a travelling career.

	Byes	Leg-byes	Wides	No-balls	Total	Wkts
	1	3	1	3	137	2
						Ab.
	1	6	5		202	6
	5	2		1	208	4

Refuge Assurance League

1 May

at Cardiff

Somerset 134 for 5
Glamorgan 138 for 2 (R.J. Shastri 53 not out)

Glamorgan (4 pts) won by 8 wickets

at Bristol

Sussex 69 for 5
Gloucestershire 71 for 3

Gloucestershire (4 pts) won by 7 wickets

at Canterbury

Hampshire 215 for 9 (C.L. Smith 70, D.R. Turner 54)

Kent 218 for 8 (N.R. Taylor 68)

Kent (4 pts) won by 2 wickets

at Old Trafford

Warwickshire 212 for 5 (A.I. Kallicharran 63)
Lancashire 144 for 9 (G.C. Small 4 for 44)

Lancashire (4 pts) won on faster scoring rate

at Leicester

Leicestershire 173 for 8
Northamptonshire 112

Leicestershire (4 pts) won by 48 runs

at Lord's

Middlesex 198 for 8
Essex 172

Middlesex (4 pts) won by 26 runs

at Worcester

Worcestershire 169 for 7 (D.B. d'Oliveira 54 not out)
Nottinghamshire 157 for 5

Worcestershire (4 pts) won by 12 runs

at Leeds

Derbyshire 157

Scotland 1988
Limited-Over Matches

BATTING	v. Derbyshire (Glasgow) 26 April (B&H)	v. Leicestershire (Glasgow) 3 & 4 May (B&H)	v. Warwickshire (Edgbaston) 10 May (B&H)	v. Lancashire (Old Trafford) 12 & 13 May (B&H)	v. Glamorgan (Edinburgh) 22 June (NW)	Runs
I.L. Phillip	3		51	20	0	74
K. Scott	0		30	34		64
R.G. Swan	13		1	60*	9	83
C.E.B. Rice	32		56	—	6	94
D.B. Pauline	42		7			49
M.J. Smith	20		19*	4*	17	60
J.W. Govan	12				0	12
P.G. Duthie	5*		—	—		5
D. Fleming	4		—	—	0	4
E.J. McIntyre	6		—	—	6*	12
C.L. Parfitt	—		—	—	9*	9
G.B.J. McGurk			2*	33	36	71
J.E. Ker			—	1		1
B.M.W. Patterson				5		5
Byes				1		
Leg-byes	8		13	2	5	
Wides	2		1	9		
No-balls	1		5			
Total	148		185	163	94	
Wickets	9		5	3	10	
Result	L	Ab.	L	L	L	
Points	0	1	0	0	—	

Fielding Figures   5 – C.E.B. Rice
3 – R.G. Swan
2 – E.J. McIntyre and D. Fleming
1 – J.W. Govan, K. Scott, G.B.J. McGurk and I.L. Phillip

BOWLING	C.E.B. Rice	P.G. Duthie	J.W. Govan	C.L. Parfitt	E.J. McIntyre	D.B. Pauline	J.E. Ker
v. Derbyshire (Glasgow) 26 April (B&H)	9–1–31–0	7–1–28–0	7–1–31–0	11–3–27–2	11–3–23–1		
v. Leicestershire (Glasgow) 3 & 4 May (B&H)							
v. Warwickshire (Edgbaston) 10 May (B&H)	11–3–58–2	11–1–75–1		11–0–54–0	11–0–64–1	11–0–50–0	
v. Lancashire (Old Trafford) 12 & 13 May (B&H)	11–0–59–1	11–0–96–0		11–1–30–0	11–0–44–1		11–1–77–2
v. Glamorgan (Edinburgh) 22 June (NW)	12–2–29–4		12–3–29–2	11.2–5–11–2	12–1–50–0		12–3–36–2
Wickets	7	1	2	4	3	—	4

Yorkshire 36 for 3

Match abandoned
Yorkshire 2 pts, Derbyshire 2 pts

Rain caused abandonment at Headingley and reduction of overs elsewhere. A 16-over contest at Cardiff saw Glamorgan, thanks to Ravi Shastri, win off the last ball while the game at Bristol was reduced to a 10-over slog and the home side won with five balls to spare. Lancashire were fortunate that their target was reduced to one of reasonable proportions, 144 in 25 overs, and they won with three balls to spare. The outstanding Sunday performance came in the uninterrupted game at Canterbury. Chris Smith and David Turner added 94 for Hampshire's fourth wicket, which helped the visitors to a commendable 215. Kent struggled in reply, losing seven wickets for 116 runs, before Neil Taylor, batting at number seven, was joined by Richard Ellison. They added a record 93 in eight overs, and Kent won with a ball to spare.

Benson and Hedges Cup

3 May

at Southampton

Glamorgan 157 for 9 (R.J. Shastri 55)
Hampshire 158 for 0 (V.P. Terry 80 not out, C.L. Smith 70 not out)

Hampshire (2 pts) won by 10 wickets
(Gold Award – V.P. Terry)

3 and 4 May

at Derby

Warwickshire 233 for 5 (M. Asif Din 67 not out)
v Derbyshire

Match abandoned
Derbyshire 1 pt, Warwickshire 1 pt

at Lord's

Sussex 182 for 9 (Imran Khan 77, N.J. Lenham 55)
Middlesex 183 for 5 (J.D. Carr 62, M.W. Gatting 56 not out)

Middlesex (2 pts) won by 5 wickets
(Gold Award – M.W. Gatting)

Two exciting centuries at the start of the season and an England cap in August – Matthew Maynard, Glamorgan. (Simon Bruty/Allsport)

at Trent Bridge

Yorkshire 8 for 0
v Nottinghamshire

Match abandoned
Nottinghamshire 1 pt, Yorkshire 1 pt

at The Oval

Kent 245 for 8 (N.R. Taylor 137)
Surrey 249 for 1 (G.S. Clinton 121 not out, A.J. Stewart 57 not out, D.M. Smith 55)

Surrey (2 pts) won by 9 wickets
(Gold Award – G.S. Clinton)

4 May

at Oxford

Somerset 182 for 9 (S.R. Waugh 79, M. Smith 4 for 49)
Combined Universities 112 for 9 (A.N. Jones 4 for 19)

Somerset (2 pts) won by 70 runs
(Gold Award – S.R. Waugh)

at Cradley Heath

Minor Counties v Worcestershire

Match abandoned
Minor Counties 1 pt, Worcestershire 1 pt

	Byes	Leg-byes	Wides	No-balls	Total	Wkts
	3	6	1	1	149	3
						Ab.
	1	6	4		308	4
	6	5		4	317	5
	15	9	6		179	10

Dennis Lillee takes his first wicket for Northamptonshire. Andy Stovold is bowled for four, Northampton, 6 May. (David Munden)

at Glasgow (Titwood)

Scotland v Leicestershire 1 pt

Match abandoned
Scotland 1pt, Leicestershire 1pt

The cruellest of weather ravaged the second round of matches in the Benson and Hedges Cup. Only four of the eight matches could be completed and of those the one at Oxford was reduced to 40 overs. In miserable gloom at Lord's, the Sussex innings was ended by a hat trick from Angus Fraser. It was the ninth hat trick in the history of the competition. On the second day Carr confirmed the good impression that he had created in the near dark of Tuesday evening, and Gatting stroked Middlesex to victory with 7.1 overs to spare.

Hampshire were the other side to complete their second win and the only side to win on the Tuesday. They routed Glamorgan by 10 wickets with eight overs to spare. It was the first time that Hampshire had won a Benson and Hedges Cup match by 10 wickets.

There were two outstanding innings at The Oval. Neil Taylor, following his Sunday triumph, hit his highest Benson and Hedges score, his 137 coming off 146 balls. He steered Kent to a good score although after his dismissal they could make only 46 from the last 10 overs. Surrey were splendidly served by openers Smith and Clinton, who put on 136 in 36 overs. Smith was bowled by Ellison, but Clinton and Stewart took Surrey to victory on the Wednesday with 11 balls to spare. Clinton's innings was the highest by a Surrey batsman in the Benson and Hedges Cup.

5, 6, 7 and 9 May

at Chesterfield

Derbyshire 218 (K.J. Barnett 52, T.D. Topley 7 for 75) and 340 (P. D. Bowler 159 not out, S.C. Goldsmith 52, T.D. Topley 5 for 104)
Essex 374 (A.R. Border 169 not out, G.A. Gooch 86, J.P. Stephenson 74, M.A. Holding 4 for 74) and 111 for 9 (G.A. Gooch 56)

Match drawn
Essex 8 pts, Derbyshire 3 pts

at Leicester

Kent 121 (N.R. Taylor 67 not out, J.P. Agnew 6 for 37) and 128 (P.A.J. De Freitas 4 for 52)
Leicestershire 296 (T.J. Boon 131, P.A.J. De Freitas 60, H.L. Alleyne 5 for 54, R.M. Ellison 4 for 90)

Leicestershire won by an innings and 47 runs
Leicestershire 23 pts, Kent 3 pts

at Northampton

Northamptonshire 206 (R.J. Bailey 66, T.M. Alderman 4 for 52) and 216 (R.G. Williams 51, T.M. Alderman 4 for 52)
Gloucestershire 172 (A. Walker 4 for 50) and 201 (D.K. Lillee 6 for 68)

Northamptonshire won by 49 runs
Northamptonshire 22 pts, Gloucestershire 5 pts

at Trent Bridge

Lancashire 221 (N.H. Fairbrother 101, K.E. Cooper 5 for 60) and 289 (G.D. Mendis 87, D.P. Hughes 62)
Nottinghamshire 223 (F.D. Stephenson 79, I. Folley 4 for 79) and 236 (R.T. Robinson 115, I. Folley 5 for 89)

Lancashire won by 51 runs
Lancashire 22 pts, Nottinghamshire 6 pts

at Taunton

Worcestershire 628 for 7 dec (G.A. Hick 405 not out, S.J. Rhodes 56)
Somerset 222 (P.J. Newport 4 for 59, N.V. Radford 4 for 77) and 192 (M.D. Crowe 53, P.J. Newport 6 for 50)

Worcestershire won by an innings and 214 runs
Worcestershire 23 pts, Somerset 4 pts

at The Oval

Middlesex 207 (M.W. Gatting 52) and 216 (M.W. Gatting 79, K.T. Medlycott 5 for 82)
Surrey 97 and 178 (M.A. Lynch 73, N.G. Cowans 4 for 20)

Middlesex won by 148 runs
Middlesex 22 pts, Surrey 4 pts

at Edgbaston

Yorkshire 194 (D.L. Bairstow 68, P. Carrick 64, G.C. Small 5 for 29, D.A. Reeve 4 for 50) and 175 (G.C. Small 5 for 55, T.A. Merrick 4 for 77)

Warwickshire 235 (G.W. Humpage 80) and 135 for 3 (M. Asif Din 62 not out)

Warwickshire won by 7 wickets
Warwickshire 22 pts, Yorkshire 5 pts

Once again three of the scheduled four-day matches were completed inside three days, but the third round of matches in the Britannic Assurance County Championship were dominated by one man. On the first day at Taunton, Worcestershire recovered from the depths of 132 for 5 to close at 312 without further loss. Graeme Hick finished the day on 179 not out. Next morning, he and Steven Rhodes extended their sixth-wicket stand to 265, a county record. Rhodes batted for 5½ hours and scored 56. At lunch, Hick was 257, and in the afternoon he cut loose. Richard Illingworth joined him in an unbroken eighth-wicket partnership of 177, another county record. Hick reached 300 with 2 sixes in three balls off Rose, and he then moved to his fourth hundred off another 58 balls. He brought his number of sixes to 10, and, on 399, he pulled Dredge over the mid-wicket boundary for his 11th. Neale declared, leaving Hick on 405 not out, the second highest score ever recorded in first-class cricket in England, beaten only by Archie MacLaren's 424 scored on the same ground 93 years earlier. Hick batted for 9¼ hours and hit 35 fours as well as his 11 sixes. His runs were made out of 550 scored while he was at the wicket. He brought his total of first-class runs for the season to 815 so making it highly possible that he could reach the coveted thousand by the end of May. To add to their woe Somerset lost Roebuck to the second ball of their innings, but they held out until the Monday when Worcestershire duly completed an innings victory. Newport had match figures of 10 for 109.

Middlesex maintained their pace at the top by beating Surrey in three days. It was a remarkable performance in that Middlesex were shot out by the Surrey seamers on the first day, but they countered with their own pace attack demolished Surrey for 97. When Middlesex batted again a third-wicket stand of 168 between Gatting and Brown gave substance to their innings. There was a late flourish by Emburey, and Surrey were left to make 327 to win. They never looked like doing it. Only Lynch and Greig offered real resistance, and Middlesex won by 148 runs a match in which the highest score of the four innings had been 216.

Warwickshire were also three-day winners. Yorkshire's first innings relied entirely upon a sixth-wicket stand of 106 by Bairstow and Carrick. Warwickshire recovered from the unease of 50 for 4 through some positive batting from Humpage and Paul Smith. Once again Small, aided by Merrick, proved too quick for Yorkshire, and Asif Din batted pleasantly as Warwickshire moved to victory on Saturday afternoon.

The third side to win in three days was Leicestershire, who overwhelmed a Kent side depleted by injuries. Neil Taylor bravely carried his bat through Kent's first innings as Agnew laid waste the rest of the Kent batting. In difficult, though easing, conditions, Tim Boon showed commendable application as he hit his first century for two seasons and rescued his side from 96 for 5. De Freitas and Lewis brought some panache towards the end of the innings to complement Boon's long vigil, and Agnew and Ferris reduced Kent to 17 for 3 in their second innings before the end of the second day. There was no recovery on the Saturday.

The only side unable to force a victory was Essex, who, having commanded the game at Chesterfield for the best part of the four days, were lucky to escape defeat in the end. Rain restricted play on the first day, and Don Topley completed the best bowling performance of his career on the second. Allan Border played brilliantly to take Essex from 12 for 2 and, sharing century stands with Gooch and Stephenson, he led them to a first-innings lead of 156. Peter Bowler batted dourly to hit the highest score of his career in his second century of the season. He received admirable assistance from Derbyshire's other newcomer, Goldsmith, and the home side held out until Monday afternoon although they had been only 15 runs ahead with five wickets standing. Topley took 10 wickets in a match for the second time, the first in England, and his 12 for 179 was a career best. Essex were left to make 185 in 60 overs, but it was left to Gooch and, ultimately, Topley to save them from an embarrassing defeat.

There were two centuries at Trent Bridge and some hard hitting from Franklyn Stephenson, but Gehan Mendis' 87 was an invaluable knock as, with David Hughes, he revived Lancashire's flagging fortunes and enabled Ian Folley to spin them to victory on the last day.

Dennis Lillee, the great Australian fast bowler, played his first game for Northamptonshire, but he watched the first innings' honours go to his countryman Terry Alderman. Lillee bowled Stovold to claim his first county wicket, and Walker took 4 for 50 to snatch a surprise lead of 34 for the home side. Alderman again struck, and Gloucestershire were left to make 251 to win. They ended Saturday's play on 103 for 2, victory looking a formality, but, on the Monday, in 16 overs either side of lunch, Lillee took five wickets to add to the one he had taken on Saturday evening, and Northants won their first championship victory of the season by 49 runs. Lillee captured the last four Gloucestershire wickets.

5, 6 and 7 May

---

at Cambridge

Glamorgan 368 for 5 dec (A.R. Butcher 166, G.C. Holmes 79, P.A. Cottey 68) and 232 for 4 (P.A. Cottey 92, J.A. Hopkins 68)
Cambridge University 278

Match drawn

at Oxford

Hampshire 370 for 7 dec (R.A. Smith 118, D.R. Turner 76) and 130 for 7 dec (R.A. Smith 54 not out)
Oxford University 118 (S.J.W. Andrew 5 for 36) and 206 for 6

Match drawn

Alan Butcher hit three sixes and 17 fours at Fenner's before he retired. He shared century stands with Holmes and Cottey who, in the second innings, hit a career best. Cambridge batted with consistent solidity.

In the Parks, Robin Smith hit his first century of the season, and the University showed pleasing determination in their second innings.

Graeme Hick lifts the ball into the crowd for one of his 11 sixes as he raced to 405 not out, the second highest score ever recorded in first-class cricket in England. Neil Burns looks on in wonder. (Allsport)

7, 9 and 10 May

at Hove

West Indians 561 for 9 dec (R.A. Harper 217 not out, I.V.A. Richards 128, E.L.C. Ambrose 59, R.A. Bunting 5 for 161) and 305 for 5 dec (D.L. Haynes 158, R.B. Richardson 82)
Sussex 252 (P.W.G. Parker 89, I.L. Bishop 4 for 55)

Match drawn

The West Indian tour began at Hove with an abundance of runs. At 94 for 5 on the Saturday, the tourists were in some difficulties, but Viv Richards and Roger Harper added 227 in 187 minutes to restore perspective as to the strength of the West Indian batting. On the Monday, Harper took his score to 217 in 396 minutes with 25 fours

before the declaration. Ian Bishop, the young pace bowler, was impressive, and there was already much talk as to which county would win the contest to engage him for the 1989 season. Essex started as early favourites. Paul Parker again showed that captaincy has only enhanced his batting qualities, but he could not save his side from trailing by 309 on the first innings. Richards, however, opted for batting practice rather than attempt to win the game, which ended dully.

8 May

at Arundel

West Indians 201 for 5 (A.L. Logie 53, C.L. Hooper 52, D.L. Haynes 50)
Lavinia, Duchess of Norfolk's XI 135 for 5 (Imran Khan 56 not out)

West Indians won by 66 runs

A 40-over match watched by a large crowd who were luckier with the weather than people elsewhere revealed the strength of the West Indians. Marshall was particularly impressive, taking 3 for 7 in his six overs. Arthurton batted pleasantly enough to suggest that he would be challenging strongly for a Test place. Five recently retired players aged 40 or more, Stuart Turner, Amiss, Underwood, Pocock and Radley, were in the Duchess' side.

Refuge Assurance League

8 May

at Derby

Essex 201 for 5 (B.R. Hardie 64, G.A. Gooch 54)
Derbyshire 142 (T.D. Topley 5 for 25)

Essex (4 pts) won by 59 runs

at Southampton

Hampshire 212 for 5 (M.C.J. Nicholas 63 not out)
Glamorgan 152 for 8

Glamorgan (4 pts) won by 60 runs

at Leicester

Leicestershire v. Kent

Match abandoned
Leicestershire 2 pts, Kent 2 pts

at Northampton

Gloucestershire 169 for 7 (C.W.J. Athey 51)
Northamptonshire 172 for 9 (A.J. Lamb 59)

Northamptonshire (4 pts) won by 1 wicket

at Trent Bridge

Nottinghamshire 202 for 7 (D.W. Randall 54)
Lancashire 208 for 8 (N.H. Fairbrother 116 not out)

Lancashire (4 pts) won by 2 wickets

at Taunton

Somerset 145 for 8
Worcestershire 148 for 3 (T.S. Curtis 63)

Worcestershire (4 pts) won by 7 wickets

at The Oval

Surrey 200 (D.M. Smith 54, N.F. Williams 4 for 39)
Middlesex 31 for 3

Match abandoned
Surrey 2 pts, Middlesex 2 pts

at Edgbaston

Yorkshire 208 for 7
Warwickshire 181 for 8 (A.J. Moles 79)

Yorkshire (4 pts) won by 27 runs

A full round of Sunday league matches ended with Lancashire as the only county with three wins in as many games. They owed their victory at Trent Bridge to a remarkable innings by Neil Fairbrother, who hit 116 off 97 balls and, spectacularly, clouted the last ball of the match for six to give his side a two-wicket victory. Middlesex failed to win for the first time in the season, and, indeed, the rain at The Oval may well have saved them from defeat. David Smith and Monte Lynch shared a third-wicket partnership of 92 for Surrey. Essex trounced Derbyshire to move into third

Beauty and excitement. The West Indians at Arundel, 8 May. (Adrian Murrell/Allsport)

place. The most reliable of opening partnerships, Gooch and Hardie, started with a stand of 87, and Don Topley, enjoying a run of consistent success, added his best bowling figures in the Sunday league to the career-best figures in first-class cricket he had achieved the day before. Gloucestershire, level with Essex, lost a rather bizarre game at Northampton. Chasing a meagre 170, the home side appeared to be in total command when Larkins and Lamb took the score from 19 for 1 to 126 before being separated. Wickets then tumbled. Russell held three catches and stumped Lamb off David Graveney, who produced six varied and enigmatic overs. When Jarvis began the last over Northamptonshire were 165 for 7. Ripley was run out and Nick Cook came in, clumped a two over mid-off and was out next ball when he tried to repeat the shot. Walker came in to face the last ball with two needed to win. He edged it for four.

Benson and Hedges Cup

10 May

at Southampton

Hampshire 205 for 9
Gloucestershire 207 for 4 (P. Bainbridge 96)

Gloucestershire (2 pts) won by 6 wickets
(Gold Award – P. Bainbridge)

at Liverpool

Lancashire 257 for 7 (M. Watkinson 70 not out, G.D. Mendis 55, G. Fowler 50)
Derbyshire 258 for 5 (K.J. Barnett 85, P.D. Bowler 64)

Derbyshire (2 pts) won by 5 wickets

at Taunton

Somerset 228 for 4 (S.R. Waugh 75 not out, J.J.E. Hardy 60)
Glamorgan 229 for 4 (M.P. Maynard 71, A.R. Butcher 57)

Glamorgan (2 pts) won by 6 wickets
(Gold Award – M.P. Maynard)

Cambridge University 1988
First-Class Matches

BATTING

BATTING	v. Derbyshire (Cambridge) 16–18 April	v. Warwickshire (Cambridge) 20–2 April	v. Surrey (Cambridge) 28–30 April	v. Glamorgan (Cambridge) 5–7 May	v. Essex (Cambridge) 18–20 May	v. Middlesex (Cambridge) 21–3 May	v. Yorkshire (Cambridge) 11–13 June	v. Surrey (The Oval) 15–17 June	v. Oxford University (Lord's) 2–4 July	M	Inns	NOs	Runs	HS	Av
P.A.C. Bail	7 44	4 —	27 13	7 —						4	6	—	102	44	17.00
A.M. Hooper	3 2	0 —								2	3	—	5	3	1.66
M.A. Atherton	44 3	11 —	46 100*	16 —	84 9	151* —	75 35	86 5		8	13	2	665	151*	60.45
J.M. Tremellen	1 8	18 —	0 7	33 —	21 22		2	2 15	2	7	12	—	131	33	10.91
J.C.M. Atkinson	0 25	0 —	11 35	42 —		5 26	15 3	73 22		7	12	—	257	73	21.41
S.J. Noyes	6 2	0 —	10 17	33 —	33 3	1 24*	0 1	38 2		8	14	1	170	38	13.07
R.J. Turner	2* 3	27 —	23 7	17 —	0 6	24 16	0 15	9 6		8	14	1	155	27	11.92
R.J. Hart	0 1						0 6	— 0*		3	5	1	7	6	1.75
J.N. Perry	6 4	14* —	2 0	7 —		— —	7 7	— 26		7	9	1	73	26	9.12
G.A. Pointer	0 5	0 —	0 7	17 —	16 18*		15 13	12* 11		7	12	2	114	18*	11.40
N.C.W. Fenton	1 0*	1 —		0	0* 2	— —	0 0*	— 0		7	9	3	4	2	0.66
R. Bate		0 —	28 0	45 —	6 9	1 12*	28* 29	2 0		7	12	2	160	45	16.00
S.D. Heath			12 1	33* —	8 16	6 —		13 11		5	8	1	100	33*	14.28
A.M.G. Scott				1* 0	0 0	8 —				3	5	1	9	8	2.25
R. Heap					0 15					1	2	—	15	15	7.50
R.A. Pyman					3 0	4 —				2	3	—	7	4	2.33
A.K. Golding						18* —				1	1	1	18	18*	—
J.M.C. Stenner								10 13		1	2	—	23	13	11.50
Byes	2 2		4 2	6	6 3	10 '8		3 1							
Leg-byes	6 2		3 5	12	8 5	5 4	4	8 9							
Wides	2 1		4	1	3 2	2		1							
No-balls	6 4	3	5 9	9		11 2		7 1							
Total	86 106	78	176 203	278	188 121	237 90	156 135	266 86							
Wickets	10 10	10	10 10	10	10 10	7 2	10 10	7 10							
Result	L	D	L	D	L	D	L	L	Ab.						

Fielding Figures
10 – R.J. Turner (ct 9/st 1) and M.A. Atherton
5 – J.C.M. Atkinson
3 – J.M. Tremellen and J.N. Perry
2 – S.D. Heath, A.K. Golding, R.A. Pyman and R. Heap
1 – N.C.W. Fenton, P.A.C. Bail and R. Bate

BOWLING

BOWLING	N.C.W. Fenton	G.A. Pointer	J.N. Perry	R.J. Hart	M.A. Atherton	P.A.C. Bail	J.C.M. Atkinson	A.M.G. Scott	A.K. Golding
v. Derbyshire (Cambridge) 16–18 April	35.4–4–102–3	19–3–55–0	22–4–84–1	25–1–94–0	26–5–59–1				
v. Warwickshire (Cambridge) 20–2 April	39–7–118–2	28–2–91–0	30–8–84–0		9–1–54–0	2–0–15–0	5–0–26–0		
v. Surrey (Cambridge) 28–30 April		25–4–89–0 / 7–1–33–0	20–3–62–0 / 8–4–21–0		19–1–56–1 / 5.3–0–20–1		3–1–8–0 / 7–0–43–1	20–5–77–2 / 12–2–46–1	
v. Glamorgan (Cambridge) 5–7 May	34–12–66–1 / 7–2–14–0	18.1–4–58–0 / 21–3–73–1	27–4–100–1 / 16–2–43–2		30–4–97–0 / 21.3–0–66–1	7–1–36–1 / 5–0–20–0	1–0–4–0 / 1–0–5–0		
v. Essex (Cambridge) 18–20 May	28–5–78–4 / 8–0–41–0	19–1–87–1 / 7–2–20–1			12.5–2–43–1 / 14–3–39–0			31–8–80–2 / 8–1–41–0	
v. Middlesex (Cambridge) 21–3 May	28–10–72–2 / 22–5–64–4		14–2–42–0 / 12–2–25–2		10–0–38–2 / 4–2–5–0			27–7–66–4 / 22–3–75–2	16–7–37–0 / 7–4–6–0
v. Yorkshire (Cambridge) 11–13 June	25–8–65–3 / 4–0–12–0	10.4–2–31–3 / 4–0–17–0	25–8–61–0 / 1–0–2–0	30–9–66–4	8–0–18–0 / 0.3–0–4–0				
v. Surrey (The Oval) 15–17 June	22–8–45–0 / 18–4–49–2	17–1–70–0 / 9–1–39–1	25–4–72–3 / 11–3–47–1	12–1–71–0	11–0–37–0 / 8–1–29–0				
v. Oxford University (Lord's) 2–4 July									
	270.4–65– 726–21 av. 34.57	184.5–24– 663–7 av. 94.71	211–44– 643–10 av. 64.30	67–11– 231–4 av. 57.75	179.2–19– 565–7 av. 80.71	14–1– 71–1 av. 71.00	17–1– 86–1 av. 86.00	120–26– 385–11 av. 35.00	23–11– 43–0 —

at Darlington

Northamptonshire 202 for 6 (W. Larkins 70, R.J. Bailey 57)
Minor Counties 158

Northamptonshire (2 pts) won by 44 runs
(Gold Award – R. Evans)

at The Oval

Middlesex 224 for 9 (M.W. Gatting 72)
Surrey 223 for 5 (D.M. Smith 85, M.A. Lynch 63 not out)

Middlesex (2 pts) won by 1 run
(Gold Award – M.A. Lynch)

at Edgbaston

Warwickshire 308 for 4 (M. Asif Din 107, T.A. Lloyd 93, A.I. Kallicharran 90 not out)
Scotland 185 for 5 (C.E.B. Rice 56, I.L. Phillip 51)

Warwickshire (2 pts) won by 123 runs
(Gold Award – A.I. Kallicharran)

10 and 11 May

at Canterbury

Essex 282 for 7 (G.A. Gooch 120 not out, B.R. Hardie 51)
Kent 283 for 4 (M.R. Benson 113, N.R. Taylor 87)

Kent (2 pts) won by 6 wickets
(Gold Award – M.R. Benson)

at Worcester

Worcestershire 198 for 9
Nottinghamshire 202 for 9 (D.W. Randall 69)

Nottinghamshire (2 pts) won by 1 wicket
(Gold Award – D.W. Randall)

After three rounds of the Benson and Hedges Cup no one county was certain of a place in the quarter-finals. Hampshire, who had romped to victory in their first two games, were brought down to earth by Gloucestershire.

J.M. Tremellen	Byes	Leg-byes	Wides	No-balls	Total	Wkts
	4	8	5	4	406	5
	5	12	4	5	405	2
	8	10	1	3	310	3
		3			166	3
	3	4	6	2	368	5
	5	6	3		232	4
	2	9	10		299	8
		4	2		145	1
	2	5	1	4	262	10
	17	3	4		195	8
	3	7	1	4	251	10
	4	2			41	0
	6	8		2	309	3
5–0–13–1		15	1		192	6
						Ab.
5–0– 13–1 *av.* 13.00						

Put in to bat, Hampshire lost three wickets to Graveney, the third the last ball before lunch, and were 114 for 4 at the interval. Nicholas and James injected some life into the innings, but the final total was still a disappointment. Gloucestershire lost Stovold and Wright with only 20 scored, but Phil Bainbridge and Bill Athey put on 105 in 29 overs. Athey was superbly run out by Scott, but Curran hit lustily, and Bainbridge took his score to 96 off 139 balls with 9 fours before falling to a diving catch at cover by Chris Smith. Lloyds and Curran managed the last ten runs with ease.

Lancashire's interest in the competition ended with defeat at Liverpool. They were without Trevor Jesty, who had been taken ill during the county championship match a few days earlier, but an opening stand of 106 between Mendis and Fowler put them in good heart. Thereafter they lost their way, and 18 overs realized only 64 runs before Watkinson hit 70 off 80 balls and helped to score 50 from the last seven overs. Barnett and Bowler began Derbyshire's challenge with 140 in 37 overs, and when the visitors looked likely to fall behind the required run rate Holding joined Morris and hit 2 fours and a six in an over by Watkinson and 2 sixes off Allott to take Derbyshire to victory with eight balls to spare.

Glamorgan kept in contention with a win at Taunton, where, in glorious weather, Matthew Maynard played another dazzling innings and enabled his side to win with 10 balls to spare. Northamptonshire moved into second place in Zone B with a hard-earned victory at Darlington, where off-spinner Evans took the Gold Award for an economic spell which conceded only 21 runs from his 11 overs.

Warwickshire reached their highest score in the competition. Alvin Kallicharran followed a second-wicket stand of 138 between Asif Din and Andy Lloyd with an unbeaten 90 in just over an hour.

There was a wonderful game at The Oval. Put in to bat, Middlesex were 134 for 3 from 36 overs at lunch and looked set for a big score, but Gatting fell to Bullen and a hostile spell from Sylvester Clarke blunted the middle order. It was only an excellent 32 not out by Keith Brown that took the score to 224.

This seemed to be a target within the compass of the Surrey batsmen, but the Middlesex seam attack was hostile and accurate. Clinton and Smith began sensibly, and Alec Stewart was soon in flowing mood. At tea, he was on 43 and Surrey were 105 for 1 from 35 overs. The task of scoring at six an over against the Middlesex bowlers proved an arduous one, however, and Surrey fell well behind the required run rate. They were revived by Monte Lynch, who played a heroic innings, but he could not manage the six off the last over that were needed.

Gooch batted dominantly at Canterbury and there was a gem of an innings from Fletcher to boost the run rate late in the innings, but, undeterred, Kent romped to a fine victory with five balls to spare. The game went into a second day and Kent's victory was founded on a splendid opening partnership of 180 in 39 overs between Benson and Taylor.

The other match to go into the second day was at Worcester. Put in to bat on an uncertain wicket, Worces-

Oxford University 1988
First-Class Matches

BATTING

Player	v. Leicestershire (Oxford) 16–19 April	v. Northamptonshire (Oxford) 20–2 April	v. Hampshire (Oxford) 5–7 May	v. Kent (Oxford) 18–20 May	v. Lancashire (Oxford) 21–4 May	v. Gloucestershire (Oxford) 1–3 June	v. Nottinghamshire (Oxford) 15–17 June	v. Cambridge University (Lord's) 2–4 July	M	Inns	Nos	Runs	HS	Av
D.A. Hagan	9, 18	43	36, 0	42, 33	6*, 30	59, 10	16*, 4	—	7	13	2	306	59	27.81
R.E. Morris	1, 1	21	5, 8	1, 0	2				4	8	—	39	21	4.87
M.J. Kilborn	48, 8	7	6, 30	40, 51	3, 32	45, 1	78, 2	—	7	13	—	351	78	27.00
G.D. Reynolds	7, 13	1	1, 14	29*, 69	—, 3		10, —	—	6	9	1	147	69	18.37
N.H. Green	9, —								1	1	—	9	9	9.00
A.N.S. Hampton	0, 7	12	2, 0	1					3	6	—	22	12	3.66
S.D. Weale	8, 12	14	10, 0	7, 21	—, 40		—, 24	—	6	9	—	136	40	15.11
I.M. Henderson	1, 0	9	6, 18		0, —		—, 21*	—	5	7	1	55	21*	9.16
P.G. Edwards	5*, 1	9	8*, 8*	—, 0	1				5	7	3	32	9	8.00
J.D. Nuttall	1, 2*	0		0, 35		—	—, 14*		5	6	2	52	35	13.00
M.R. Sygrove	4, 1	0*	8, 0	8*	—	6*	2		7	8	3	29	8*	5.80
S.A. Almaer		4	9, 16	36, 24	3, 16	67, 35	21, 25	—	6	11	—	256	67	23.27
D.A. Polkinghorne			12, 45*	9, —			6		3	4	1	72	45*	24.00
M.A. Crawley				0, 10*	6, 14*	8, —	98, 41		4	7	2	177	98	35.40
T. Jack					29, 5	23, —			2	3	—	57	29	19.00
M.E.O. Brown					47, 6*	2, —	0*, 16		3	5	2	71	47	23.66
A.M. Searle						2, —			1	1	—	2	2	2.00
M. Heppel						14*, —			1	1	1	14	14*	—
J.E.B. Cope						—	—		1					

Extras:
- Byes: 1, 3, 1, 5, 1, 6, 4
- Leg-byes: Leics 3, 2 | North 2 | Hants 3, 4 | Kent 4, 9 | Lancs 2, 12 | Glos 13, 2 | Notts 5, 4
- Wides: 1, 1, 1, 2, 1, 4
- No-balls: 2, 2, 11, 1, 7, 12, 6, 4, 8, 1

	v. Leics	v. North	v. Hants	v. Kent	v. Lancs	v. Glos	v. Notts	v. Camb
Total	98, 68	137	95, 118	206, 277	28, 230	213, 117	228, 162	—
Wickets	10, 9†	10	10, 10	6, 10	3, 10	4, 9††	3, 7	—
Result	L	L	D	D	D	D	D	Ab.

Fielding Figures
6 – G.D. Reynolds
5 – M.J. Kilborn
3 – D.A. Hagan and S.D. Weale
2 – J.D. Nuttall, S.A. Almaer, M.A. Crawley and P.G. Edwards
1 – N.H. Green, R.E. Morris, I.M. Henderson, D.A. Polkinghorne, J.E.B. Cope, T. Jack and M.E.O. Brown

† N.H. Green absent hurt
†† J.D. Nuttall absent hurt

BOWLING

Match	I.M. Henderson	J.D. Nuttall	P.G. Edwards	M.R. Sygrove	S.D. Weale	D.A. Hagan	M.J. Kilborn	M.A. Crawley	M. Heppel
v. Leicestershire (Oxford) 16–19 April	7–0–35–0	13–1–70–0	31–7–74–2	23–4–91–3	15–5–40–1				
v. Northamptonshire (Oxford) 20–2 April	34–8–104–3	23–5–59–1	23–3–85–0	16–3–57–0	35–13–66–1	1–0–4–0	1–0–7–0		
v. Hampshire (Oxford) 5–7 May	13–2–66–1		25–4–88–3; 15–4–33–1	23.4–3–95–3; 11–1–35–2	31–4–101–0; 6–0–24–1	2–0–17–0	11–5–37–3		
v. Kent (Oxford) 18–20 May		24–2–105–2; 6–1–23–0	30–9–129–1; 11.3–2–35–1	21–4–76–0; 12–3–39–1	34–3–188–0; 6–1–21–0		7–1–33–0	11–1–41–0	
v. Lancashire (Oxford) 21–4 May	3–0–19–0		36–14–116–1	33–7–113–3	35–6–130–3		4–0–27–0	8–3–19–0	
v. Gloucestershire (Oxford) 1–3 June		20–5–64–2		19–4–91–2; 13–2–79–1			4.5–0–18–0; 12–2–59–2	6–0–25–0; 1–0–2–0	14–0–74–0
v. Nottinghamshire (Oxford) 15–17 June	14–0–92–1	25–5–77–1; 5–1–12–1		32–2–112–2; 12–1–60–1	30–9–74–2; 8–0–37–0		2–0–4–0	10–3–37–0; 2–0–12–0	
v. Cambridge University (Lord's) 2–4 July									
Totals	71–10–316–5 av. 63.20	116–20–410–7 av. 58.57	171.3–43–560–9 av. 62.22	215.4–34–848–18 av. 47.11	200–41–681–8 av. 85.12	3–0–21–0 av. —	41.5–8–185–5 av. 37.00	38–7–136–0 av. —	14–0–74–0 av. —

tershire suffered the early loss of Curtis and Hick, their two most prolific batsmen, and at 104 for 6, they were in deep trouble. It was stability by Rhodes, some good shots from d'Oliveira and a late flourish from Radford and Dilley that took the home side to 198 for 9, commendable in the circumstances. A second-wicket stand of 74 between Broad and Randall gave substance to the Nottinghamshire innings, but when bad light ended play they were 124 for 3, 75 still needed from 18.2 overs. Tight bowling, good fielding and necessary haste reduced Notts to 169 for 8, but Eddie Hemmings found a good partner in Kevin Cooper and they added 18. Five runs were needed from the last over, bowled by Ian Botham, and three were scrambled before Cooper was bowled. Pick, batting with a broken hand that was to keep him out of the game for some weeks, snicked a single off the fifth ball to level the scores, and Hemmings clubbed the last ball of the match to the boundary.

12 May

at Southampton

West Indians 279 for 5 (C.G. Greenidge 103, C.L. Hooper 56, P.V. Simmons 55)
Hampshire 186 for 6

West Indians won by 93 runs

Greenidge hit 8 sixes in his innings which set up victory for the tourists in the 50-over match.

Benson and Hedges Cup

12 May

at Chelmsford

Sussex 217 for 6 (P.W.G. Parker 64, A.M. Green 53)
Essex 218 for 8 (D.R. Pringle 51, B.R. Hardie 51)

Essex (2 pts) won by 2 wickets
(Gold Award – D.R. Pringle)

at Cardiff

Glamorgan 302 for 6 (M.P. Maynard 115, G.C. Holmes 59 not out, J.A. Hopkins 50)
Combined Universities 218 for 8 (N. Hussain 76 not out, J. Derrick 4 for 53)

Glamorgan (2 pts) won by 84 runs
(Gold Award – M.P. Maynard)

at Bristol

Somerset 227 for 6 (J.J.E. Hardy 70 not out, J.G. Wyatt 55)
Gloucestershire 228 for 4 (A.W. Stovold 78, A.J. Wright 66)

Gloucestershire (2 pts) won by 6 wickets
(Gold Award – A.W. Stovold)

at Canterbury

Kent 206 for 8 (M.R. Benson 61, J.E. Emburey 4 for 42)
Middlesex 207 for 4 (M.W. Gatting 68)

Middlesex (2 pts) won by 6 wickets

at Old Trafford

Lancashire 317 for 5 (N.H. Fairbrother 116 not out, G. Fowler 66, G.D. Mendis 61)
Scotland 166 for 3 (R.G. Swan 60)

Lancashire (2 pts) won by 154 runs
(Gold Award – N.H. Fairbrother)

at Leicester

Leicestershire 196 for 9 (D.I. Gower 53, T.A. Merrick 4 for 24)
Warwickshire 187 (A.I. Kallicharran 79, G.J.F. Ferris 5 for 28)

Leicestershire (2 pts) won by 9 runs
(Gold Award – G.J.F. Ferris)

at Northampton

Worcestershire 256 for 8 (T.S. Curtis 52)
Northamptonshire 131 (N.V. Radford 4 for 25)

Worcestershire (2 pts) won by 125 runs
(Gold Award – G.A. Hick)

at Leeds

Minor Counties 206 for 6
Yorkshire 208 for 4 (M.D. Moxon 83)

Yorkshire (2 pts) won by 6 wickets
(Gold Award – M.D. Moxon)

Middlesex became the first side to be guaranteed a place in the quarter-finals when they beat Kent with considerable ease at Canterbury. Emburey stifled the Kent innings after they had reached 142 for 2 from 38 overs at lunch. Carr and Slack gave Middlesex a good start, and Gatting provided the clout which took Middlesex to victory with 10.3 over and six wickets to spare, a very large margin.

In the same group, Essex ended Sussex's interest in the competition, but made hard work of beating a moderate team. Put in to bat, Sussex scored only 44 from the first 22 overs. Parker and Alan Wells gave the innings some sense of urgency, but Imran was held back, and the final score of 217 for 6 looked unlikely to cause Essex any problems on a wicket of easy pace. Gooch and Hardie started in characteristic fashion, putting on 49 for the first wicket, but then the home side lost their way as Kimber dismissed both openers and Border, Babington had Prichard lbw for 0 and Fletcher fell to Imran. Five men were out for 137 before

A.M. Searle	Byes	Leg-byes	Wides	No-balls	Total	Wkts
	3	6		10	319	6
	2	5	1	7	389	5
		3		10	370	7
		1		2	130	7
	3	5			539	3
	6	3	1	1	168	2
	1	4	2	5	429	7
17–2–76–0	4	8		4	360	4
		1	1	1	141	3
	3	6	11	12	405	7
		2			123	2
						Ab.
17–2–76–0						

Pringle and Lilley batted with energy and audacity to add 64. Parker erred in removing the economic Standing from the attack and giving three unproductive overs to Lenham, and Essex won with a ball to spare.

Yorkshire won their first game after two abandonments, and in the much publicized meeting between Botham and Lillee in the same group, the honours went decidedly in favour of Curtis, Hick, Botham, Radford and Worcestershire. Lillee took three wickets, including that of Botham, but they cost 61 runs.

Stovold and Wright put on 137 for Gloucestershire's first wicket against Somerset and helped their side to a comfortable win while Glamorgan revived their hopes of qualifying for the quarter-finals from the same group with their highest score in the Benson and Hedges Cup. Maynard reached a century off 75 balls, hitting Atherton for 16 in one over. Fenton, formerly of Durham University, bowled an excellent spell for the Universities, taking 3 for 44 in his 11 overs, while Nasser Hussain, Durham University and Essex, again showed his class as a batsman.

There was an exciting game at Leicester, where Gower hit 53 off 69 balls and the home side reached 114 for 1. They were restricted in the final search for quick runs by Merrick, who took four wickets, and by Humpage, who took five catches behind the stumps. Needing 197 to win, Warwickshire seemed well placed when Kallicharran hit 79 off 112 balls. They needed only 79 off the last 20 overs and had eight wickets in hand, but, incredibly, they lost their last seven wickets in eight overs for 36 runs and lost by nine runs. The West Indian pace bowler Ferris did most of the damage. In the same group, Lancashire beat Scotland with ease in a match that spilled into a second day. Neil Fairbrother hit his third century in four innings in three different competitions as Lancashire reached their highest score in the Benson and Hedges Cup.

14 May

at Cambridge

Combined Universities 130 for 9
Hampshire 131 for 3 (V.P. Terry 68)

Hampshire (2 pts) won by 7 wickets
(Gold Award – V.P. Terry)

at Derby

Leicestershire 186 for 5 (P.A.J. De Freitas 57)
Derbyshire 190 for 4 (K.J. Barnett 71, P.D. Bowler 55)

Derbyshire (2 pts) won by 6 wickets
(Gold Award – K.J. Barnett)

at Swansea

Gloucestershire 101
Glamorgan 106 for 5

Glamorgan (2 pts) won by 5 wickets
(Gold Award – R.C. Ontong)

at Lord's

Middlesex 236 for 9 (R.O. Butcher 75)
Essex 237 for 5 (A.R. Border 75 not out, G.A. Gooch 57)

Essex (2 pts) won by 5 wickets
(Gold Award – A.R. Border)

at Northampton

Northamptonshire 226 for 8 (R.J. Bailey 89, R.G. Williams 75)
Nottinghamshire 214 (D.J. Wild 4 for 32)

Northamptonshire (2 pts) won by 12 runs
(Gold Award – D.J. Wild)

at Hove

Sussex 198 for 9
Surrey 156

Sussex (2 pts) won by 42 runs
(Gold Award – I.J. Gould)

at Edgbaston

Warwickshire 249 (A.J. Moles 68)
Lancashire 160

Warwickshire (2 pts) won by 89 runs
(Gold Award – A.R.K. Pierson)

at Worcester

Worcestershire 227 for 6 (P.A. Neale 91)
Yorkshire 172 (K. Sharp 75, I.T. Botham 5 for 41)

Worcestershire (2 pts) won by 55 runs
(Gold Award – P.A. Neale)

Rarely has the last round of zonal matches in the Benson and Hedges Cup begun with so many issues undecided. In Group A, Leicestershire had looked likely to qualify, but they were beaten by Derbyshire. Leicestershire made a wretched start. They lost Tim Boon, who had his wrist broken by a ball from Devon Malcolm, and lost both Willey and Gower to be 76 for 4 off 30 overs. De Freitas and Potter added 93 in 22 overs to leave the Leicestershire bowlers some hope, but that evaporated when Barnett and Bowler, a very useful acquisition, put on 114 for Derbyshire's first wicket. Then the home side slipped in their run-chase, and when Goldsmith was bowled at 161, 27 runs were required from just over three overs. Michael Holding was sent in and he hit the first ball from Ferris for four. His 17 came off seven balls, and he hit the fourth ball of the last over through the covers for the winning boundary. Leicestershire's defeat allowed Warwickshire, winners against Lancashire, to claim the other qualifying place from Zone A. Moles, Lloyd, Asif Din and Kallicharran all batted well, and Adrian Pierson claimed his first Gold Award for his 3 for 34 in 11 overs of off-breaks.

In Group B, both of the 1987 finalists, Yorkshire and Northamptonshire, were eliminated. Nottinghamshire lost narrowly at Northampton, but they scored quickly enough to edge into second spot on a faster run rate. Worcestershire, inspired by Phil Neale, recovered from the trauma of 41 for 3 to reach 227. This proved too good for Yorkshire, whose batting looked very brittle. The substance of the Worcestershire innings came from a record sixth-wicket stand of 121 between Neale and Rhodes. Ian Botham took five wickets and became the sixth bowler to reach 100 wickets in the Benson and Hedges Cup.

Middlesex suffered their first defeat of the season in any competition when Essex won at Lord's. Carr had given Middlesex a good start, but Gatting could not get into his stride and although Butcher provided substance, he never achieved fluency. Nevertheless, Middlesex's accurate seam attack looked to have the measure of Essex. Hardie was completely out of touch and Gooch could not find the boundary with his customary regularity. Prichard was quickly run out and hopes were fading when Pringle and Border suddenly launched an assault on the Middlesex bowling which produced 105 in 20 overs. Border hit Fraser for a huge six into the Warner Stand, and, although Fletcher was soon out, Lilley pulled Cowans to the boundary to give Essex victory with a ball to spare. Remarkably, it also gave them first place in the group. Elsewhere, Surrey had died magnificently. Knowing that their only hope of qualifying for the quarter-finals was on run rate, they attempted to score 199 to beat Sussex in 22 overs. They failed bravely. They were all out for 156, made at more than seven an over.

Hampshire reached the quarter-finals by beating Combined Universities as expected, but Glamorgan claimed top place in the group and so qualified for the later stages of the competition for the first time in nine seasons. It was a very close encounter. Gloucestershire entered the last round with maximum points, but, having been put in to bat, were bowled out for a meagre 101, ruinous to their run rate. Glamorgan slumped to 52 for 5 in reply before Holmes and Ontong, who had already taken 2 for 11 in six overs, came together and took them to victory in the 44th over.

Matthew Cleal, an impressive début for Somerset against West Indians at Taunton, 16 May. (Neal Simpson/ASP)

Benson and Hedges Cup – Zonal Tables Final Positions

	P	W	L	N/R	Pts	R/R
Group A						
Derbyshire	4	3	–	1	7	64.89
Warwickshire	4	2	1	1	5	75.15
Leicestershire	4	2	1	1	5	60.10
Lancashire	4	1	3	–	2	68.25
Scotland	4	–	3	1	1	50.10
Group B						
Worcestershire	4	2	1	1	5	68.78
Nottinghamshire	4	2	1	1	5	65.36
Northamptonshire	4	2	1	1	5	56.46
Yorkshire	4	1	1	2	4	59.19
Minor Counties	4	–	3	1	1	50.20
Group C						
Essex	4	3	1	–	6	72.15
Middlesex	4	3	1	–	6	70.01
Kent	4	2	2	–	4	73.53
Sussex	4	1	3	–	2	60.90
Surrey	4	1	3	–	2	58.89
Group D						
Glamorgan	4	3	1	–	6	63.36
Hampshire	4	3	1	–	6	62.61
Gloucestershire	4	3	1	–	6	60.94
Somerset	4	1	3	–	2	67.47
Combined Universities	4	–	4	–	–	48.63

15, 16 and 17 May

at Taunton

Somerset 113 (E.L.C. Ambrose 4 for 27, W.K.M. Benjamin 4 for 34) and 146
West Indians 251 (R.A. Harper 53 not out, C.L. Hooper 54, D.L. Haynes 50, M.W. Cleal 4 for 41) and 12 for 0

West Indians won by 10 wickets

The West Indians brushed aside Somerset in two days. Even with both Crowe and Waugh in the side, the Somerset batting looked very fragile against the West Indian pace bowlers. The one bright spot for Somerset was the performance of 18-year-old Matthew Cleal, a medium-pace bowler, who took four wickets on his début.

Refuge Assurance League

15 May

at Chelmsford

Essex 214 for 7 (B.R. Hardie 87, G.A. Gooch 50)
Northamptonshire 190 for 5 (R.G. Williams 55)

Essex (4 pts) won by 24 runs

at Southampton

Middlesex 189 for 8 (J.F. Sykes 57, S.J.W. Andrew 4 for 50)
Hampshire 160 for 8 (D.R. Turner 61)

Middlesex (4 pts) won by 29 runs

at Canterbury

Lancashire 169 (C. Penn 4 for 22)
Kent 172 for 3 (N.R. Taylor 85)

Kent (4 pts) won by 7 wickets

at Trent Bridge

Nottinghamshire 208 for 7 (R.T. Robinson 50)

Gloucestershire 209 for 8

Gloucestershire (4 pts) won by 2 wickets

at Hove

Sussex 154 for 7
Surrey 155 for 3

Surrey (4 pts) won by 7 wickets

at Edgbaston

Warwickshire 142 for 9
Glamorgan 143 for 0 (H. Morris 72 not out, J.A. Hopkins 55 not out)

Glamorgan (4 pts) won by 10 wickets

at Worcester

Yorkshire 223 for 5 (M.D. Moxon 79)
Worcestershire 224 for 5 (G.A. Hick 111, T.S. Curtis 53)

Worcestershire (4 pts) won by 5 wickets

Fine weather meant that seven Sunday league matches were played without interruption. Middlesex went clear at the top of the table and owed much to Sykes and Williams, who added 65 for the seventh wicket. Hampshire could never score freely against the tight Middlesex attack. Kent inflicted the first Sunday defeat of the season on Lancashire. Taylor took them to victory with five overs to spare. Gooch and Hardie began Essex's innings with a partnership of 113, Pringle took three wickets and Northants made a total hash of an attempt to chase 215. Surrey showed their all-round strength as they beat Sussex with four overs to spare, and Gloucestershire held on to joint second place when Graveney and Greene put on 25 for the ninth wicket and scored the winning run against Notts with one ball of the match remaining. Glamorgan overwhelmed Warwickshire, Morris and Hopkins taking them to victory with 10 wickets and four overs to spare. Curtis and Hick shared a second-wicket stand of 87, and Hick then dominated a third-wicket stand of 97 with d'Oliveira. Hick hit his first Sunday league century and reached a thousand runs in all cricket for the summer.

Asif Din, a disciplined century for Warwickshire against Northamptonshire. (Adrian Murrell/Allsport)

Wish

Middlesex County Cricket Club

every success

for the coming season.

Try Construction Group
Cowley, Uxbridge, Middlesex UB8 2AL.
Telephone (0895) 51222. Telex 934164
Fax (0895) 59090

17, 18, 19 and 20 May

at Northampton

Warwickshire 415 (M. Asif Din 131, D.A. Reeve 103, W.W. Davis 6 for 141) and 112 (W.W. Davis 4 for 44)
Northamptonshire 170 (R.J. Bailey 76) and 363 (R.J. Bailey 60, D.J. Wild 58)

Northamptonshire won by 6 runs
Northamptonshire 19 pts, Warwickshire 7 pts

18, 19 and 20 May

at Bournemouth

Hampshire 217 (R.C. Ontong 4 for 47) and 259 for 2 dec (M.C.J. Nicholas 132 not out, R.A. Smith 87 not out)
Glamorgan 276 (R.C. Ontong 60 not out) and 177 for 8 (R.J. Maru 4 for 70)

Match drawn
Glamorgan 7 pts, Hampshire 6 pts

at Leicester

Leicestershire 114 (N.F. Williams 5 for 46) and 265 (D.I. Gower 74, J.J. Whitaker 55, N.F. Williams 4 for 60)
Middlesex 329 (J.D. Carr 144, K.R. Brown 58, J.P. Agnew 6 for 67) and 52 for 2

Middlesex won by 8 wickets
Middlesex 24 pts, Leicestershire 4 pts

at Trent Bridge

Gloucestershire 254 (A.W. Stovold 84, F.D. Stephenson 4 for 80) and 80 for 4
Nottinghamshire 97 (D.V. Lawrence 4 for 36) and 234 (D.W. Randall 58, D.V. Lawrence 5 for 73)

Gloucestershire won by 6 wickets
Gloucestershire 23 pts, Nottinghamshire 4 pts

at Worcester

Worcestershire 240 (T.S. Curtis 70, G.J. Lord 64, D.J. Foster 4 for 46) and 119
Somerset 327 (M.D. Crowe 132, J.J.E. Hardy 70, P.J. Newport 4 for 97) and 33 for 1

Somerset won by 9 wickets
Somerset 24 pts, Worcestershire 6 pts

at Cambridge

Essex 298 for 8 dec (P.J. Prichard 97, I.L. Pont 68, N.C.W. Fenton 4 for 78) and 145 for 1 dec (J.P. Stephenson 79 not out, D.E. East 55)
Cambridge University 188 (M.A. Atherton 84, J.H. Childs 5 for 36) and 121 (J.H. Childs 4 for 25, I.L. Pont 4 for 58)

Essex won by 135 runs

at Oxford

Kent 539 for 3 dec (C.J. Tavare 138 not out, S.G. Hinks 138, R.F. Pienaar 127, C.S. Cowdrey 124 not out) and 168 for 2 dec (S.A. Marsh 100 not out)
Oxford University 277 (G.D. Reynolds 69, M.J. Kilborn 51, M.D. Harman 55) and 28 for 3

Match drawn

Worcestershire suffered their first championship defeat of the season and with it the loss of Ian Botham, who, it was announced, was to undergo surgery on his spine. The surprise winners at New Road were Somerset, ravaged by Worcestershire at Taunton a fortnight earlier and with only a win over Combined Universities in the Benson and Hedges Cup to cherish before this match. Worcestershire began well enough when Curtis and Lord put on 131 in under three hours for the first wicket. Collapse followed with Foster taking the main honours after Rose and Marks had made the initial breakthroughs. Martin Crowe played his first substantial innings of the season, sharing stands of 75 with Hardy and 102 with Wyatt and enabling Somerset to take a first-innings lead of 87. On a wearing wicket it proved conclusive. Worcestershire, with Botham unable to bat, floundered against the Somerset seam attack, and Somerset scored the 33 runs that they needed to win the match for the loss of Roebuck.

Middlesex maintained their hundred per cent record and went clear at the top of the table by beating Leicestershire with ease. Neil Williams, again in impressive form, spearheaded the Middlesex attack as Leicestershire were shot out for 114. John Carr hit a six and 19 fours as he and Keith Brown took Middlesex to 212 before the fall of the first wicket. The innings had begun dramatically, however, when Wilf Slack, having scored four, collapsed and was taken to hospital with a blood disorder. Leicestershire also suffered a casualty, losing wicket-keeper Whitticase after he had been struck in the face. Even without Whitticase, Leicestershire batted with much more resolution in their second innings, but their last six wickets went down for 47 runs and Middlesex took maximum points 45 minutes after lunch on the last day.

Offerings from very occasional bowlers enabled Nicholas and Robin Smith to add 190 for Hampshire's third wicket in their second innings. Nicholas' declaration left Glamorgan to make 201 in 38 overs. They reached the last 20 overs with nine wickets in hand and 124 needed, but collapse set in and six wickets fell while only 39 runs were scored so that Glamorgan were happy to settle for a draw.

The fast bowling of David Lawrence was a vital factor in Gloucestershire's win at Trent Bridge. In their second innings, Notts reached 193 for 4, but Lawrence brought about a reversal of fortune with four quick wickets, which saw the home side lose their last six wickets for 41 runs.

The most remarkable events occurred in the four-day game at Northampton. Batting first, Warwickshire reached 320 for 7 at the end of the opening day. Asif Din had provided the backbone of the innings with a disciplined century after an uncertain start, and Dermot Reeve was on 75 not out. Reeve duly completed his first century for his new county on the second morning, and Northants were then routed by Merrick and Paul Smith, who picked up the wickets of Bailey, Nick Cook and Brown in six overs for eight runs. Following on 245 runs in arrears, the home side were eight wickets down and led by only 23 runs when they batted again, but Ripley and Davis put on 89 for the ninth wicket and eventually Warwickshire were left to score 119 to win. As the home side had just scored 363, there seemed little cause to worry about the state of the wicket, but Lloyd was caught at slip, Moles and Kallicharran were lbw and Humpage stabbed a return catch to

Gordon Greenidge is bowled by Gladstone Small, first Texaco Trophy match, Edgbaston. (Adrian Murrell/ Allsport)

Davis so that at lunch on the last day, Warwickshire were 38 for 4. Reeve and Asif Din came together at 51 for 5 and added 47 so that when Asif Din was caught at mid-wicket Warwickshire needed only 21 to win with four wickets standing, but three wickets fell for six runs. Parsons and Gifford put on seven, but Gifford was caught at slip, although not in his opinion, by Larkins off Williams, and Northants had won an amazing victory by six runs. This was the first time they had won after being asked to follow on since 1906.

Essex gave first-class débuts to Pook, Seymour and Ilott at Cambridge, but relied on Prichard and Childs to win them the match. Kent enjoyed batting practice, where, among five centuries, Hinks hit a career best.

Texaco Trophy

First Texaco One-Day International
ENGLAND v. WEST INDIES

From their party of 14, England omitted Athey, Hemmings and Radford and gave a first international appearance to Monte Lynch, a surprise selection. West Indies were without Haynes, and Patterson and Benjamin were also unavailable for selection through injury.

Gatting won the toss and asked West Indies to bat first. Phil Simmons began in violent mood. He hit 22 off 16 balls before, overconfident, he attempted a lofted drive off Dilley and was caught on the boundary fence. It was the advent of Small which brought about the most significant change in the match, however. With his fourth ball he beat Greenidge's hurried defensive shot and bowled him. Viv Richards was at his most swaggering. He hit Dilley for three consecutive fours and then slashed Small to point where Emburey took a low, fine catch. Richardson was lazily beaten by the accurate Pringle, and West Indies were 72 for 4.

Logie and Hooper did their best to repair the damage with a stand of 97 in 30 overs, and Carl Hooper looked particularly elegant and impressive, but the innings gathered little momentum, and in the last 12 overs, the last five wickets went down for the addition of only 48 runs.

Faced with a modest 217, England were given the soundest of starts by Gooch and Broad, who put on 70 in 67 minutes. When Marshall joined the attack prospects looked brighter for West Indies. He had Broad very well caught at slip and imposed a control on the batsmen which Walsh had not managed. It was Ambrose who struck the vital blow, however, when he had Gooch taken at slip off a ball that lifted sharply. Sadly, Lynch was run out when, after facing two balls, he was eager for a run and was sent back by Gatting and beaten by Richardson's throw to the bowler from square-leg.

Lamb was bowled when he tried to give himself room to hit against Hooper's gentle off-breaks. Pringle, vindicating the selectors' faith in him, joined Gatting in an unbroken stand of 66 in 13 overs, which took England to victory with two overs to spare.

The individual award went to Gladstone Small, whose bowling had turned the match in England's favour.

FIRST TEXACO ONE-DAY INTERNATIONAL – ENGLAND v. WEST INDIES
19 May 1988 at Edgbaston, Birmingham

WEST INDIES			
C.G. Greenidge	b Small		18
P.V. Simmons	c Lamb, b Dilley		22
R.B. Richardson	lbw, b Pringle		11
I.V.A. Richards†	c Emburey, b Small		13
A.L. Logie	c Downton, b Small		51
C.L. Hooper	c Emburey, b Small		51
P.J.L. Dujon*	run out		27
R.A. Harper	b Emburey		4
M.D. Marshall	c Lamb, b De Freitas		6
E.L.C. Ambrose	b Emburey		1
C.A. Walsh	not out		2
Extras	lb 2, w 3, nb 6		11
(55 overs)			217

ENGLAND		
G.A. Gooch	c Harper, b Ambrose	43
B.C. Broad	c Greenidge, b Marshall	35
M.W. Gatting†	not out	82
M.A. Lynch	run out	0
A.J. Lamb	b Hooper	11
D.R. Pringle	not out	23
P.R. Downton*		
J.E. Emburey		
P.A.J. De Freitas		
G.C. Small		
G.R. Dilley		
Extras	b 2, lb 10, w 7, nb 6	25
(53 overs)	(for 4 wkts)	219

	O	M	R	W
De Freitas	11	2	45	1
Dilley	11	–	64	1
Small	11	–	31	4
Pringle	11	5	26	1
Emburey	11	1	49	2

	O	M	R	W
Ambrose	11	1	39	1
Walsh	11	1	50	–
Richards	7	1	29	–
Marshall	11	1	32	1
Harper	7	–	33	–
Hooper	6	–	24	1

FALL OF WICKETS
1–34, 2–50, 3–66, 4–72, 5–169, 6–180, 7–195, 8–209, 9–212

FALL OF WICKETS
1–70, 2–119, 3–121, 4–153

Umpires: J. Birkenshaw & B.J. Meyer

Man of the Match: G.C. Small

England won by 6 wickets

An unhappy international début. Monte Lynch is run out for nought. (David Munden)

Second Texaco One-Day International
ENGLAND v. WEST INDIES

England fielded the side that had won at Edgbaston while West Indies introduced Ian Bishop to international cricket at the expense of the out of form Harper.

Richards won the toss and asked England to bat first on a wicket that was not ideal for a one-day game. It encouraged movement off the seam and produced the occasional high bounce so that it was, in fact, to the liking of the West Indian pacemen. Gooch and Broad gave a falsely encouraging start when they scored 17 from the first three overs, but Walsh and Ambrose imposed tight restrictions thereafter, and Marshall and the most impressive Bishop beat the bat consistently. Broad fell to a fine catch off the inside edge by Dujon, and Gatting was well taken in the gully. Lynch, patently nervous, was lbw to Marshall, whose rhythmic approach to the wicket purred with elegance and menace. Lamb surprisingly fell to Simmons when he swatted at the medium pacer. At lunch, England were 83 for 4 from 31 overs. Gooch, 32 not out, was the hope for the afternoon.

It was not to be, for the opener fell to the first ball after the break, the seemingly innocuous Simmons having him caught in the gully. That a batsman of Gooch's stature and temperament, ever eager to hit the ball, had taken 31 overs to score 32 was indicative of the wicket.

Richards erred in overbowling himself and Simmons and thereby underbowling Marshall. Salvation for England came in the form of Downton and Pringle, who added 66 off 81 balls. Pringle exacted revenge for past indignities by hitting Richards for six.

De Freitas almost immediately cut a ball back to bowl the dangerous Simmons, and with Dilley in top gear, the

---

SECOND TEXACO ONE-DAY INTERNATIONAL – ENGLAND v. WEST INDIES
21 May 1988 at Headingley, Leeds

ENGLAND				WEST INDIES			
G.A. Gooch	c Greenidge, b Simmons	32		C.G. Greenidge	c Downton, b Small	21
B.C. Broad	c Dujon, b Ambrose	13		P.V. Simmons	b De Freitas	1
M.W. Gatting†	c Richards, b Marshall	18		R.B. Richardson	c Downton, b Dilley	1
M.A. Lynch	lbw, b Marshall	2		I.V.A. Richards†	b Small	31
A.J. Lamb	c Dujon, b Simmons	2		A.L. Logie	c Lynch, b Dilley	8
D.R. Pringle	c Dujon, b Walsh	39		C.L. Hooper	lbw, b Pringle	12
P.R. Downton*	c Dujon, b Bishop	30		P.J.L. Dujon*	b Pringle	12
J.E. Emburey	c Ambrose, b Bishop	8		M.D. Marshall	c Downton, b Gooch	1
P.A.J. De Freitas	not out	15		E.L.C. Ambrose	c Downton, b Pringle	23
G.C. Small	not out	7		C.A. Walsh	b Emburey	18
G.R. Dilley				I.R. Bishop	not out	2
Extras	b 3, lb 1, w 3, nb 13	20		Extras	lb 3, w 3, nb 3	9
(55 overs)	(for 8 wkts)	186		(46.3 overs)		139

	O	M	R	W		O	M	R	W
Walsh	11	–	39	1	Dilley	11	–	45	2
Ambrose	7	2	19	1	De Freitas	9	2	29	1
Marshall	9	1	29	2	Small	9	2	11	2
Bishop	11	1	32	2	Pringle	11	–	30	3
Simmons	9	2	30	2	Gooch	3	–	12	1
Richards	8	–	33	–	Emburey	3.3	–	9	1

FALL OF WICKETS
1–29, 2–64, 3–72, 4–80, 5–83, 6–149, 7–154, 8–169

FALL OF WICKETS
1–2, 2–11, 3–38, 4–67, 5–67, 6–83, 7–84, 8–104, 9–132

Umpires: D.J. Constant & D.R. Shepherd

Man of the Match: D.R. Pringle

England won by 47 runs

take a dour, long look at the bowling in preparation for the Test series. They welcomed Haynes back and had Benjamin in for Ambrose. Radford replaced the injured Dilley in the England side.

The most memorable shot of the first day was a four off the back foot through the covers by Hooper. The rest of the time was mostly dominated by the bowlers. On the Tuesday morning, however, Dujon and Marshall hit 53 from the remaining five overs. Marshall's 41 included sixes off Small and Emburey, who came in for some very rough treatment before claiming Marshall with the last ball of the innings.

Gooch and Broad, knowledge of the West Indian bowlers uppermost in their minds, took 31 overs to put on 71 for the first wicket. Gooch was stumped when he lost his balance, and Bishop returned to dismiss both Broad and Lynch, but Gatting revitalised the innings as he and Lamb added 56 in only six overs to take England to their third victory in the series.

Gatting and Marshall were named as players of the series for their respective sides. England looked forward to the Test series a little more refreshed.

___

21, 23 and 24 May

at Swansea

Derbyshire 453 (J.E. Morris 175, J.G. Wright 79, S.R. Barwick 4 for 130)
Glamorgan 89 for 0

Match drawn
Derbyshire 4 pts, Glamorgan 2 pts

England attack looked menacing. Dilley removed Richardson, and West Indies were struggling. Greenidge could not time his square cut, and eventually he touched Small to the wicket-keeper. Small also induced Richards to play on, and England were rampant.

Pringle, who took the individual honours, followed his fine batting with an equally fine spell of bowling. Hooper and Dujon were beaten by excellent deliveries, and Ambrose was cut down when he threatened recovery. Only briefly, during a ninth-wicket stand, was England's supremacy ever in doubt. The triumph was total, and the Texaco Trophy went to England with one match still to be played.

___

Third Texaco One-Day International
ENGLAND v. WEST INDIES

___

It was predictable that the third one-day international in the Texaco Trophy series would be something of an anti-climax. The weather was miserable, and West Indies ended the first day on 125 for 6 from 50 overs. When they were not running themselves out they were attempting to

Haynes is run out by Pringle in the third Texaco Trophy match. De Freitas looks on. (Adrian Murrell/Allsport)

THIRD TEXACO ONE-DAY INTERNATIONAL – ENGLAND v. WEST INDIES
23 and 24 May 1988 at Lord's

WEST INDIES			
C.G. Greenidge	c De Freitas, b Emburey		39
D.L. Haynes	run out		10
R.B. Richardson	c Downton, b Pringle		13
I.V.A. Richards†	c Emburey, b De Freitas		9
A.L. Logie	run out		0
C.L. Hooper	run out		12
P.J.L. Dujon*	not out		30
M.D. Marshall	b Emburey		41
W.K.M. Benjamin			
C.A. Walsh			
I.R. Bishop			
Extras	b 2, lb 10, w 12		24
(55 overs)	(for 7 wkts)		178

	O	M	R	W
De Freitas	11	5	20	1
Radford	11	2	29	–
Small	10	1	34	–
Pringle	11	4	27	1
Emburey	10	1	53	2
Gooch	2	1	3	–

FALL OF WICKETS
1–40, 2–75, 3–79, 4–79, 5–95, 6–111, 7–178

ENGLAND			
G.A. Gooch	st Dujon, b Hooper		28
B.C. Broad	b Bishop		34
M.W. Gatting†	not out		40
M.A. Lynch	b Bishop		6
A.J. Lamb	not out		30
D.R. Pringle			
P.R. Downton*			
J.E. Emburey			
P.A.J. De Freitas			
G.C. Small			
G.R. Dilley			
Extras	b 6, lb 17, w 5, nb 14		42
(50 overs)	(for 3 wkts)		180

	O	M	R	W
Marshall	9	2	21	–
Walsh	11	5	11	–
Bishop	11	1	33	2
Benjamin	9	–	38	–
Hooper	10	–	54	1

FALL OF WICKETS
1–71, 2–108, 3–124

Umpires: H.D. Bird & N.T. Plews

Man of the Match: P.A.J. De Freitas

England won by 7 wickets

---

at Canterbury

Yorkshire 244 (A.A. Metcalfe 67, K. Sharp 57) and 133 (C. Penn 6 for 66)
Kent 274 (R.F. Pienaar 144, S.G. Hinks 66, C. Shaw 4 for 56, P.W. Jarvis 4 for 75) and 104 for 7 (P.W. Jarvis 6 for 40)

Kent won by 3 wickets
Kent 22 pts, Yorkshire 3 pts

at Leicester

Worcestershire 291 (P.A. Neale 72, T.S. Curtis 57, G.J.F. Ferris 5 for 47) and 222 for 7 dec (T.S. Curtis 78, R.K. Illingworth 60)
Leicestershire 280 for 5 dec (J.J. Whitaker 100 not out) and 99 for 5

Match drawn
Leicestershire 7 pts, Worcestershire 5 pts

at Trent Bridge

Nottinghamshire 270 (D.W. Randall 64, F.D. Stephenson 63, A.C.S. Pigott 5 for 46, C.M. Wells 4 for 59) and 150 (A.C.S. Pigott 4 for 40)
Sussex 182 (A.P. Wells 74, A.M. Green 54, K.E. Cooper 5 for 41) and 171

Nottinghamshire won by 67 runs
Nottinghamshire 23 pts, Sussex 5 pts

at The Oval

Northamptonshire 298 for 5 dec (A. Fordham 125, D.J. Capel 81) and 174 for 3 dec (D.J. Capel 83 not out)
Surrey 215 for 6 dec (C.J. Richards 85, D.M. Ward 51 not out, G.S. Clinton 50) and 188 for 7 (N.G.B. Cook 4 for 68)

Match drawn
Northamptonshire 5 pts, Surrey 4 pts

at Edgbaston

Essex 166 (T.A. Merrick 4 for 39) and 247 (A.R. Border 112, K.W.R. Fletcher 57)
Warwickshire 160 (T.D. Topley 4 for 57) and 254 for 5 (T.A. Lloyd 86)

Warwickshire won by 5 wickets
Warwickshire 21 pts, Essex 5 pts

at Cambridge

Middlesex 262 (S.P. Hughes 53, R.O. Butcher 52, A.M.G. Scott 4 for 56) and 195 for 8 dec (M.C.W. Fenton 4 for 64)
Cambridge University 237 for 7 dec (M.A. Atherton 151 not out, S.P. Hughes 4 for 39) and 90 for 2

Match drawn

at Oxford

Oxford University 230 and 213 for 4 (S.A. Almaer 67, D.A. Hagan 59)
Lancashire 429 for 7 dec (G.D. Mendis 139, T.E. Jesty 63, D.P. Hughes 57 not out)

Match drawn

Worcestershire were unable to take advantage of Middlesex's non-involvement in the county championship and remained eight points behind the leaders when they drew with third place Leicestershire. Worcestershire found batting hard on the first day when, after an opening stand of 103 between Curtis and Lord, they lost four wickets for 38 runs. Phil Neale revived them, but they batted on until Monday morning when they lost their last three wickets to Ferris in six balls. Gower was in good form for Leicestershire after a sound opening stand by Cobb and Briers, and Whitaker hit his second century of the season in 159 minutes. It included 10 fours. On the last morning, having been 29 for 4, Worcestershire were given a glimpse of victory by Curtis and Illingworth, who put on 97 in 39 overs. Neale set Leicestershire the task of scoring 234 in two hours, but they were 47 for 3 at the start of the last 20 overs and any hope of an exciting finish was gone.

Meanwhile Middlesex were the victims of a magnificent 151 not out by Mike Atherton and were pleased to draw with their weakened side. Lancashire gained necessary batting practice against Oxford, with Mendis to the fore, and the University acquitted themselves creditably.

Nottinghamshire, the reigning champions, gained their first win of the season. Some violent blows from Stephenson and a good knock from Randall brought a stand of 110 after five first-innings wickets had gone for 147. Sussex closed the first day at 19 for 4, two of the victims being night-watchmen, and they immediately became 19 for 5 on the Monday morning. Alan Wells and Green, who had stood fast through the disasters, added 68, and Colin Wells helped his brother add 49. Nevertheless, Sussex trailed by 88 on the first innings, a sorry position on a wicket which was deteriorating and which was likely to aid Cooper and Stephenson. The task of making 239 to win in the fourth innings proved to be far too much after Saxelby had made early breakthroughs.

With Geoff Cook recovering from a broken jaw, Larkins led Northants at The Oval in what proved to be a rather dour encounter. The acting captain was out early after Greig had asked the visitors to bat first, but Alan Fordham batted throughout the day, six hours, 35 minutes, for 125, his maiden first-class century. David Capel hit 81 in 79 minutes to enliven the day, but it was left to Ian Greig to keep the game alive when he declared 83 behind on the Monday evening after a rain-interrupted day. Eventually asked to make 258 at more than five an over, Surrey approached the task positively, but lost their way against an accurate spell by Nick Cook.

Allan Border was forced to retire hurt at Edgbaston after being struck by a ball from Tony Merrick, but he returned on the Monday to hit a wonderfully courageous 112 on a fiery wicket. Warwickshire needed to make 254 on the final day to win a match that had been very much in favour of the bowlers. Moles and Lloyd gave them a fine start with a partnership of 106, and Lloyd then added 70 with Asif Din. It formed the basis of a surprisingly easy win on a wicket on which seam bowlers and left-handed batsmen had taken the honours.

There was little excitement at Swansea, where Derbyshire, 356 for 6 on the first day, batted on for 90 minutes on the Monday, Morris taking his score to 175. As the weather was threatening, it was hard to understand Barnett's reasoning. In the event, a dull game was mercifully put to sleep on the last afternoon when Tony Cottey had reached his best score in the championship, 49 not out.

Kent and Yorkshire met at Canterbury as the bottom

two sides in the championship. Choosing to bat first, Yorkshire reached 174 for 2 and then lost their eight wickets for 70 runs. Taylor was caught behind off Sidebottom on the Saturday evening, and night-watchman Davis was soon out on the Monday, but Pienaar and Hinks added 168. Pienaar hit a six and 11 fours and batted most pleasantly for five hours, 40 minutes, enabling Kent to take a first-innings lead of 30. Richard Ellison, 3 for 41 and looking closer and closer to full fitness, and Chris Penn, with a career-best 6 for 66, bowled Yorkshire out shortly after lunch for 133. The bowling was good, but the Yorkshire batting was dreadful. Kent themselves found the task of scoring 104 harder than they had anticipated. The wicket assisted the seam bowlers, and the Yorkshire bowling, spearheaded by Jarvis, was infinitely better than their batting. Hinks and Tavare gave what little substance there was to the Kent innings, and the home side won their first championship match of the season with three wickets and 14 overs to spare. Yorkshire's third successive defeat represented their worst start to a first-class season.

Refuge Assurance League

22 May

at Newport

Glamorgan 199 for 8 (J.A. Hopkins 60)
Derbyshire 174 (K.J. Barnett 90 not out)

Glamorgan (4 pts) won by 25 runs

at Canterbury

Yorkshire 159 for 6
Kent 116 (S.D. Fletcher 4 for 11)

Yorkshire (4 pts) won by 43 runs

at Leicester

Leicestershire 197 for 9 (D.I. Gower 50, A.P. Pridgeon 4 for 36)
Worcestershire 201 for 6 (G.A. Hick 66, T.S. Curtis 50)

Worcestershire (4 pts) won by 4 wickets

at Trent Bridge

Sussex 152 for 8
Nottinghamshire 156 for 4 (J.D. Birch 65 not out)

Nottinghamshire (4 pts) won by 6 wickets

at The Oval

Northamptonshire 133
Surrey 137 for 3 (I.A. Greig 56 not out)

Surrey (4 pts) won by 7 wickets

at Edgbaston

Essex 130 (D.A. Reeve 5 for 23)
Warwickshire 133 for 4

Warwickshire (4 pts) won by 6 wickets

Surrey moved level with Middlesex at the top of the Refuge Assurance League when they beat Northants with two overs to spare. They owed much to skipper Ian Greig, who took 3 for 20 and followed it with an innings of 56 not out in a stand of 105 with David Ward. Glamorgan had an inspired day in the field to beat Derbyshire and leave Kim Barnett unbeaten on 90. Curtis and Rhodes began Worcestershire's innings at Grace Road with a stand of 83. There was then a middle-order collapse, but Hick, limping from a thigh strain, hit a six and 6 fours and kept Worcestershire in contention to retain their title. Dermot Reeve produced his best Sunday bowling figures as Warwickshire beat Essex with surprising ease, and Fletcher his best Sunday bowling figures as Yorkshire demolished Kent.

Michael Atherton, a brilliant 151 not out for Cambridge University against Middlesex, 23 May. (Steve Lindsell)

25, 26 and 27 May

at Bristol

West Indians 257 (P.V. Simmons 53 retired hurt, V.S. Greene 5 for 53) and 233 (I.V.A. Richards 63)
Gloucestershire 140 (B.P. Patterson 5 for 39, M.D. Marshall 4 for 14) and 98 for 1 (A.J. Wright 50 not out)

Match drawn

All else in this match, which was badly affected by rain, was overshadowed by the injury to Phil Simmons. He was hit behind the left ear by a ball from David Lawrence and taken to hospital for an emergency operation to remove a blood clot on the brain.

Benson and Hedges Cup

Quarter Finals

25 May

at Chelmsford

Warwickshire 219 for 7 (T.A. Lloyd 87)
Essex 223 for 1 (G.A. Gooch 117 not out, B.R. Hardie 53)

Essex won by 9 wickets
(Gold Award – G.A. Gooch)

25 and 26 May

at Derby

Middlesex 110 (D.E. Malcolm 5 for 27)
Derbyshire 111 for 1 (K.J. Barnett 69 not out)

Derbyshire won by 9 wickets
(Gold Award – D.E. Malcolm)

26 May

at Cardiff

Nottinghamshire 220 for 8 (R.T. Robinson 60)
Glamorgan 223 for 4 (M.P. Maynard 108, J.A. Hopkins 81)

Glamorgan won by 6 wickets
(Gold Award – M.P. Maynard)

26 and 27 May

at Worcester

Worcestershire 169 (M.J. Weston 50, S.T. Jefferies 4 for 34)
Hampshire 170 for 7 (R.A. Smith 87 not out)

Hampshire won by 3 wickets
(Gold Award – R.A. Smith)

Only the match at Chelmsford could be completed on the scheduled day. No play was possible on the Wednesday at Cardiff and Worcester, and the game at Derby saw only 52 overs bowled. This was a match where winning the toss proved all decisive. Barnett had no hesitation in asking Middlesex to bat first on a pitch which gave much assistance to the Derbyshire seam attack. Holding had Carr lbw with the fourth ball of the match. The West Indian paceman dismissed Gatting in a similar manner in his third over and Butcher hit a low catch to cover second ball. At 8 for 3, Middlesex were in despair, and, in spite of Brown's 32 off 21 overs, there was no effective recovery. Devon Malcolm took the last four wickets as only eight were scored. By the close, Derbyshire were 33 for 0 off eight overs, and next morning, with the wicket drier and easier, they strolled to victory with 24.3 overs to spare.

Having lost Moles and Asif Din for 36, Warwickshire were revived by Lloyd and Kallicharran, who added 68, but just as it seemed that Alvin Kallicharran would play a major innings, he turned the ball gently into the hands of backward square-leg. The bowler was Foster, who was playing his first significant match of the season and came through well. Lloyd remained steadfast until the 54th over, when he fell to Pringle, but, apart from a brief

Robin Smith played a memorable innings on a difficult wicket to win the Gold Award as Hampshire beat Worcestershire in the quarter-final of the Benson and Hedges Cup at Worcester. (Neal Simpson/ASP)

splutter by Reeve, there was no impetus to the Warwickshire innings. Warwickshire had begun the match without the injured Small, now their attack was further weakened when Reeve sustained an injury while batting which was to prevent him from bowling. The Essex openers were completely untroubled by a seven-man attack. Hardie and Gooch started slowly, but batted with ever-increasing momentum so that when Hardie was caught behind off an Asif Din leg-break just before tea the partnership had realized 157 in 35 overs, and the game was as good as won. Prichard came in to play a series of elegant boundaries, and the massive Gooch continued his dominance with his seventh Benson and Hedges Cup century and his record 14th Gold Award so that Essex had no need of 7.4 of their overs.

Robinson and Broad began Notts' innings at Cardiff with a stand of 108 in 25 overs, but their colleagues could muster only another 112 from the last 30 overs, and the initiative was lost. Glamorgan were disturbed by the loss of Butcher and Morris for 32, but Hopkins and Maynard added 187 in 35 overs. Maynard hit a six and 7 fours in his 108, which came off 117 balls. Glamorgan romped to victory with 5.4 overs to spare.

Play was not possible until just before five o'clock on the Thursday at Worcester. Hampshire won the toss and Worcestershire were asked to bat first on an untrustworthy wicket. Jefferies soon beat Lord's defensive push, and Connor bowled Curtis, but the prize wicket fell to Ayling, who, with his third ball in the competition, had Hick finely caught by the running Jefferies off a top edge. Neale and O'Shaughnessy put on 36 in 14 overs, but both were out before the end of the day when Worcestershire were 111 for 5 off 42 overs. Weston reached a brave fifty the next morning and 69 with Rhodes, but Jefferies returned to finish off the innings, and Worcestershire had only a meagre total to defend. They fashioned a wonderful match on a dreadful pitch. Hampshire were reduced to 84 for 6, but Robin Smith, who had had a poor season, stood resolute while all about him fell. He and Jefferies added 30, and Cowley proved the ideal partner in an unbroken stand which took Hampshire to victory with 11 balls to spare.

28, 29 and 30 May

---

at Worcester

Worcestershire 321 for 3 dec (G.A. Hick 172, T.S. Curtis 82)
West Indians 170 for 5 (D.L. Haynes 71, I.V.A. Richards 50)

Match drawn

28, 30 and 31 May

---

at Derby

Derbyshire 143 (P.D. Bowler 50, F.D. Stephenson 6 for 44) and 159 for 7 (P.D. Bowler 84, F.D. Stephenson 6 for 59)
Nottinghamshire 184 (O.H. Mortenson 5 for 24)

Match drawn
Nottinghamshire 5 pts, Derbyshire 4 pts

at Chelmsford

Essex 302 (G.A. Gooch 139) and 45 for 0 dec
Surrey 22 for 0 dec and 130 (D.R. Pringle 6 for 39)

Essex won by 195 runs
Essex 20 pts, Surrey 4 pts

at Swansea

Glamorgan v Gloucestershire

Match abandoned
No points

at Old Trafford

Lancashire 329 for 9 dec (Wasim Akram 116 not out, M. Watkinson 52) and 145 (G.D. Rose 4 for 39)
Somerset 273 for 5 dec (M.D. Crowe 136 not out) and 202 for 8 (M.D. Crowe 80, J. Simmons 4 for 58)

Somerset won by 2 wickets
Somerset 22 pts, Lancashire 5 pts

at Lord's

Middlesex 261 (J.D. Carr 76, Imran Khan 5 for 50)
Sussex 49 for 2

Match drawn
Sussex 4 pts, Middlesex 3 pts

Graeme Hick raises his bat in joy as he completes a thousand runs in first-class cricket before the end of May, Worcestershire v. West Indians. (Mark Leech)

at Northampton

Northamptonshire 327 for 8 dec (D.J. Capel 75, A.J. Lamb 70, R.J. Bailey 55) and 62 for 6
Leicestershire 143 (D.J. Capel 4 for 40) and 264 (R.A. Cobb 64, A. Walker 4 for 59)

Match drawn
Northamptonshire 8 pts, Leicestershire 2 pts

at Middlesbrough

Hampshire 130 (A. Sidebottom 5 for 30) and 149 for 4 (C.L. Smith 88 not out)
Yorkshire 239

Match drawn
Yorkshire 6 pts, Hampshire 4 pts

Rain hampered all matches. There was no play at all at Swansea, none after the first day at Lord's although those present on the Tuesday would suggest that a greater willingness on the part of the captains could have provided some, and no play on the Monday at Chelmsford. The weather could not dampen the spirits at Worcester, however, where on Saturday 28 May Graeme Hick hit 172 against the touring West Indians and so became the eighth player in the history of the game to score a thousand runs before the end of May. He began the day 153 runs short of the target and was forced to work hard for his runs on a pitch that was never easy and against bowling that was always sharp. He was soon at the wicket, for Lord was bowled by Ambrose for 0, and hit 22 fours as he and Tim Curtis put on 284. Hick was out on the Sunday without addition to his overnight score. Louis Vorster made an interesting first appearance for Worcestershire, and the West Indians ended the match with batting practice.

Franklyn Stephenson routed Derbyshire on a seam bowler's dream wicket, and Nottinghamshire appeared to be in a strong position when they closed at 124 for 4 on the Saturday, but Ole Mortensen, in his first first-class game of the season after injury, took five wickets, including a spectacular caught and bowled to dismiss Cooper, to bring Derbyshire back into the game on the Monday. Rain ruined the game on the last day, but not before Stephenson had brought his match figures to 12 for 103 and Chris Scott, holding a regular place as wicket-keeper because Bruce French had undergone surgery and was out for the season, brought his number of catches in the match to 10 and so equalled the county record.

An effortless century by Graham Gooch, who dominated an opening partnership of 138 in 34 overs with Brian Hardie, seemed to have set Essex on the way to a big score at Chelmsford, but the middle order fell apart against Medlycott, and it was left to Miller and Childs to conjure a last-wicket stand of 38 which just brought the fourth batting point. No play on the Monday brought declarations on the last day and a target of 326 in a minimum of 90 overs for Surrey. After an opening stand of 42 it was a target they never had the remotest chance of reaching. Pringle took three wickets in 25 balls without conceding a run, and Miller bowled Clinton so that Surrey slipped to 48 for 4. Ably supported by Miller, Pringle went on to return his best figures of the season and inflict a crushing defeat on Surrey.

Rain and Chris Smith helped Hampshire to survive at

Franklyn Stephenson routed Derbyshire, 28–31 May. Succeeding Hadlee at Nottinghamshire, Stephenson became the most prolific wicket-taker in the country and was the first bowler to take a hundred wickets. (Neal Simpson/ASP)

Acklam Park, Middlesbrough, while interruptions and injury thwarted Northants. Consistent batting from the first six in the order took Northants to a commanding position on the opening day, and the position was strengthened when Walker, Capel and Wild bowled out Leicestershire for 143. Following on, the visitors closed at 117 for the loss of Briers and Gower.

Northants had also suffered a loss, however, for Dennis Lillee had been carried off in considerable pain with an ankle injury. Four stoppages for rain and brave resistance from Briers, Lewis and Agnew, who had risen from his sick bed to bat, reduced the home side's chances of winning, and they were left eight overs in which to score 81 on a wicket which was not conducive to run-making. Bailey, Lamb and Capel clouted courageously, but the task was too great.

At Old Trafford, Wasim Akram, coming in at 127 for 5, hit a maiden first-class century, beginning cautiously and blossoming into fruitful aggression. Martin Crowe brought respite to injury-stricken Somerset with an accomplished century on the second day. Marks, leading Somerset in the absence of Roebuck, declared 56 runs in arrears and was rewarded when Rose dismissed Jesty and Folley with successive deliveries. Lancashire had lost Fowler through injury, and they lost wickets regularly on the final morning so that Somerset were left to make 202 in 55 overs. At 46 for 4, their hopes seemed to have vanished, but Martin Crowe played another masterly innings. He and Marks shared an exhilarating partnership of 82, and Burns and Cleal gave the New Zealander useful support, but, with 13 needed from 12 balls, Crowe was bowled by Simmons. Mallender, batting with a runner, and Rose, positive in approach, took Somerset to victory with four balls to spare.

Refuge Assurance League

29 May

---

at Derby

Nottinghamshire 158 for 7 (D.W. Randall 59, M.A. Holding 4 for 22)
Derbyshire 93 for 1 (J.E. Morris 50 not out)

Derbyshire (4 pts) won on faster scoring rate

at Chelmsford

Essex 138 for 8 (A.H. Gray 4 for 56)
Surrey 139 for 2 (C.J. Richards 105 not out)

Surrey (4 pts) won by 8 wickets

at Bristol

Gloucestershire v Warwickshire

Match abandoned
Gloucestershire 2 pts, Warwickshire 2 pts

at Old Trafford

Lancashire 214 for 7 (A.N. Hayhurst 84, G.J.F. Ferris 4 for 24)
Leicestershire 99 for 1

Lancashire (4 pts) won on faster scoring rate

at Lord's

Middlesex 213 for 5 (R.O. Butcher 77, M.W. Gatting 51)
Sussex 160 for 7

Middlesex (4 pts) won by 53 runs

at Northampton

Kent 143 for 3
v Northamptonshire

Match abandoned
Kent 2 pts, Northamptonshire 2 pts

at Middlesbrough

Yorkshire 141 for 3
Hampshire 90 for 3

Hampshire (4 pts) won on faster scoring rate

Uncertain weather reduced the number of overs played and brought down targets, but the two matches involving the top sides were more fortunate than others. In a 38-over game at Lord's, Middlesex had no problem in disposing of Sussex, and at Chelmsford, in a match reduced to 32

Jack Richards hit a violent century off 94 balls as Surrey beat Essex by eight wickets in the Sunday league match at Chelmsford. Richards finished with 105 not out in an innings of 139 for 2. (Adrian Murrell/Allsport)

Adrian Jones, 7 for 30, Somerset against Hampshire, the best bowling performance of his career, 2 June. (Stuart D. Franklin/ASP)

Nottinghamshire were bowled out for 65 by Kent at Dartford, 1 June. Kevin Saxelby becomes Richard Davis' fourth victim, bowled middle stump. (Tom Morris)

overs, Surrey made surprisingly easy work of beating Essex. They had the best possible start when skipper Ian Greig dismissed Gooch and Hardie with only 12 on the board. Essex would have been in total disarray but for some late hitting by Lilley, East and Miller. Surrey coasted to victory, reaching their target of 139 with 5.3 overs to spare. Jack Richards played a remarkable innings, hitting 2 sixes and 11 fours as he reached a century off 94 balls. He scored 106 out of 139, the next top scoring being 11 leg-byes.

1, 2 and 3 June

at Southampton

Somerset 308 (S.R. Waugh 115 not out, C.A. Connor 4 for 89)
Hampshire 156 (A.N. Jones 7 for 30) and 336 for 4 (V.P. Terry 106, D.R. Turner 100 not out, J.R. Ayling 66 not out)

Match drawn
Somerset 6 pts, Hampshire 4 pts

at Dartford

Nottinghamshire 65 (R.P. Davis 4 for 12) and 357 (P. Pollard 142, R.T. Robinson 56, R.M. Ellison 7 for 75)

Kent 312 for 9 dec (R.F. Pienaar 53, M.R. Benson 52, R.M. Ellison 50 not out, C.L. Cairns 4 for 70) and 111 for 8 (K.E. Cooper 5 for 61)

Kent won by 8 wickets
Kent 23 pts, Nottinghamshire 3 pts

at Northampton

Yorkshire 155 (W.W. Davis 5 for 54) and 228 for 9 dec
Northamptonshire 130 (C. Shaw 4 for 50) and 192 for 7 (R.J. Bailey 72)

Match drawn
Yorkshire 5 pts, Northamptonshire 4 pts

at The Oval

Surrey 467 for 5 dec (D.M. Smith 131, C.J. Richards 102 not out, M.A. Lynch 93, D.M. Ward 66)
Sussex 188 (I.J. Gould 82, I.A. Greig 4 for 44) and 268 (C.M. Wells 109 retired hurt)

Surrey won by an innings and 11 runs
Surrey 24 pts, Sussex 2 pts

at Worcester

Lancashire 189 (Wasim Akram 55, P.J. Newport 6 for 51) and 147 (S.M. McEwan 4 for 43)
Worcestershire 119 (P.J.W. Allott 4 for 29, M. Watkinson 4 for 37) and 118 for 6 (P.J.W. Allott 4 for 43)

Match drawn
Lancashire 5 pts, Worcestershire 4 pts

at Oxford

Gloucestershire 360 for 4 dec (P. Bainbridge 119, J.W. Lloyds 102 not out, I.P. Butcher 75) and 141 for 3 dec (R.C. Russell 69, D.J. Thomas 57 not out)
Oxford University 117 (P. Bainbridge 5 for 33)

Match drawn

Having tasted victory in their previous match against Yorkshire, Kent moved further up the Britannic Assurance County Championship table with their second win of the season, a remarkable one over Notts. The reigning champions were bowled out shortly after lunch on the first day for the season's lowest total, 65. It was a lamentable batting display against a varied attack, and no blame could be attached to the pitch. The Kent innings was a stop-start affair. Three wickets fell for 73 before Tavare and Benson added 79, after which three wickets fell for 9 runs. The second day saw Marsh, Ellison and Penn advance the total by 137, enabling Chris Cowdrey to declare with a lead of 247. Robinson and Pollard began Nottinghamshire's second innings with a partnership of 122. Paul Pollard reached the first century of his young career the next day and batted for nearly eight hours, hitting 11 fours. It was a most commendable effort. Richard Ellison gave more evidence of his return to full fitness with a splendid bowling performance in which he ended the Notts' innings with a spell of 4 for 9 to finish with the best bowling figures of his career, 7 for 75. Kent needed 111 in 24 overs to win, and some accurate seam bowling by Cooper and Saxelby, not always well supported in the field, and an element of panic on the part of the batsmen, gave the task a sense of drama. The last over arrived with ten runs still needed and only two wickets standing, but Chris Cowdrey was at the crease, and he took his side to victory with a ball to spare. Chris Cairns, son of Lance Cairns, the former New Zealand Test player, made his first-class début in place of the injured Stephenson and bowled well for Notts on the first day.

Steve Waugh marked his 23rd birthday with a delightful innings of 115 not out for Somerset at Southampton, and Adrian Jones followed this with the best bowling performance of his career so that Hampshire were forced to follow on, but Terry, Turner and Ayling, a consistently impressive young all-rounder, took them to safety.

Surrey plundered runs at The Oval, scoring 467 for 5 at four an over on the opening day. The gem of several fine innings was Jack Richards' 102 with a six and 15 fours. Sussex wilted in reply, but, inspired by Colin Wells, showed more resource in their second innings, which was ended shortly after Wells had been forced to retire hurt after being hit on the hand.

Wickets tumbled at New Road, where the wicket was becoming notorious, and in the end heavy showers saved Worcestershire from what looked likely to be defeat. Rain also brought an abrupt end at Northampton, where the wicket also came in for criticism and where the home side were chasing a target of 254 in four hours.

TOP: *Gooch plays on and England lose their first wicket. (Adrian Murrell/Allsport)*

ABOVE: *Broad follows in the same manner. (Adrian Murrell/Allsport)*

First Test Match
ENGLAND v. WEST INDIES

Not surprisingly the England selectors chose the old guard for the first Test match against West Indies. The side was basically that which had acquitted itself competently and unfussily in the Texaco Trophy matches. Foster and Small were unfit and could not be considered, and Downton had played so well in the one-day games that it was hard to leave him out although Russell and Rhodes were two who were certainly superior wicket-keepers.

From the selected 13, Hemmings and Thomas were omitted. Gatting won the toss, and Gooch and Broad opened and batted into the afternoon, putting on 125 in 174 minutes.

All appeared to be going smoothly for England when Marshall, having assessed how best to exploit the conditions and the wicket, suddenly began to trouble both batsmen. Gooch was beaten, dropped at slip and finally bowled off an inside edge by an in-swinger. He had hit 8 fours and looked in fine form.

West Indies now moved onto the attack. Logie was moved in to short-leg and almost immediately caught Gatting off bat and thigh. Broad had battled valiantly for four hours when, in the last over before tea, he, like Gooch, was bowled off the inside edge. The last ball of the over was delayed until after tea, and it accounted for Lamb, lbw playing round his front pad.

Gower had watched these catastrophes with great patience, but, having been dropped by Greenidge off Ambrose, he succumbed to the same bowler as he swatted lazily and all too familiarly at a widish delivery.

Thankfully, Pringle batted with confidence and good sense, and he and Downton took England to 220 for 5 at the close of a day which had begun with so much promise.

England were soon out on the second morning. Pringle had not added to his overnight score when he played across an in-swinger and was bowled. Marshall switched to bowling round the wicket at Emburey and immediately exploited the batsman's fallible technique, slanting the ball across him to have him caught behind fourth ball. Ambrose quickly took the last three wickets and, in doing so, displayed considerable pace and a devastating yorker. His 4 for 53 represented the best return of his short Test career, and he was clapped from the field by his team mates.

The whole of the afternoon session was lost to rain, but

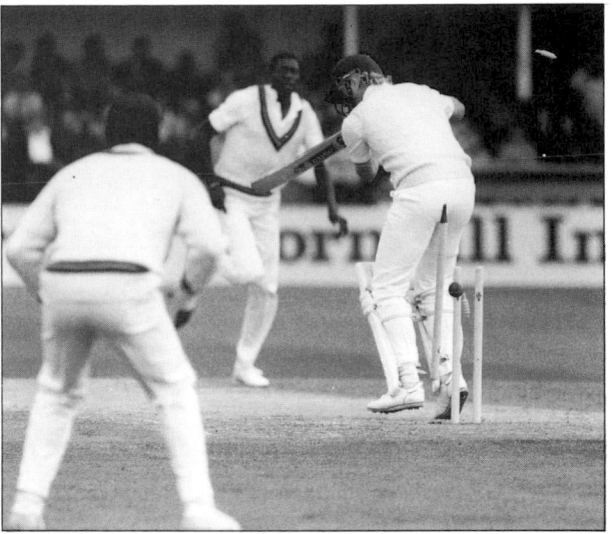

Dilley is bowled by Curtley Ambrose, who took a Test-match best 4 for 53. (Adrian Murrell/Allsport)

West Indies had moved into an ominously strong position by the close. Dilley and De Freitas were rather wasteful, but Jarvis and Pringle soon found a nagging length. Jarvis had Greenidge dropped at slip by Emburey, but justice

FIRST CORNHILL TEST MATCH – ENGLAND v. WEST INDIES
2, 3, 4, 6 and 7 June 1988 at Trent Bridge, Nottingham

ENGLAND

	FIRST INNINGS			SECOND INNINGS	
G.A. Gooch	b Marshall	73		c Dujon, b Patterson	146
B.C. Broad	b Marshall	54		c Dujon, b Ambrose	16
M.W. Gatting†	c Logie, b Marshall	5		b Marshall	29
D.I. Gower	c Dujon, b Ambrose	18		not out	88
A.J. Lamb	lbw, b Marshall	0		not out	6
D.R. Pringle	b Marshall	39			
P.R. Downton*	not out	16			
J.E. Emburey	c Dujon, b Marshall	0			
P.A.J. De Freitas	b Ambrose	3			
P.W. Jarvis	b Ambrose	6			
G.R. Dilley	b Ambrose	2			
Extras	lb 3, w 5, nb 11	29		lb 10, nb 6	16
		245		(for 3 wkts)	301

WEST INDIES

	FIRST INNINGS	
C.G. Greenidge	c Downton, b Jarvis	25
D.L. Haynes	c Downton, b Jarvis	60
R.B. Richardson	c Gatting, b Emburey	17
I.V.A. Richards†	c Gooch, b De Freitas	80
C.L. Hooper	c Downton, b De Freitas	84
A.L. Logie	c Gooch, b Pringle	20
P.J.L. Dujon*	c and b Dilley	16
M.D. Marshall	b Emburey	72
C.E.L. Ambrose	run out	43
C.A. Walsh	not out	3
B.P. Patterson		
Extras	b 6, lb 8, nb 14	28
	(for 9 wkts, dec)	448

	O	M	R	W	O	M	R	W		O	M	R	W
Marshall	30	4	69	6	13	4	23	1	Dilley	34	5	101	1
Patterson	16	2	49	–	24	6	69	1	De Freitas	27	5	93	2
Ambrose	26	10	53	4	23	4	56	1	Jarvis	18.1	1	63	2
Walsh	20	4	39	–	25	5	84	–	Pringle	34	11	82	1
Hooper	8	1	20	–	14	1	33	–	Emburey	16	4	95	2
Richards	1	–	2	–	9	1	26	–					

FALL OF WICKETS
1–125, 2–141, 3–161, 4–161, 5–186, 6–223, 7–223, 8–235, 9–243
1–39, 2–116, 3–277

FALL OF WICKETS
1–54, 2–84, 3–159, 4–231, 5–271, 6–309, 7–334, 8–425, 9–448

Umpires: H.D. Bird & J. Birkenshaw

Match drawn

TOP: *A deserved wicket for Paul Jarvis as he has Haynes caught behind by Downton. (Adrian Murrell/Allsport)*

ABOVE: *Richie Richardson is brilliantly caught at short-leg by Gatting off Emburey. Paul Downton is the third Middlesex player in the picture. (Adrian Murrell/Allsport)*

was done five balls later when Greenidge cut at a ball that lifted and Downton took the catch which gave Jarvis his first Test wicket. Emburey found some turn in the wicket and quickly had Richardson taken at short-leg, but Viv Richards hit 5 fours, scoring 22 off 23 balls before the close, 126 for 2, and West Indies looking very powerful.

Only six balls were possible on the Saturday morning, and the afternoon, too, was fractured so that an early tea was taken, but even then the dark clouds persisted. In what play was possible Richards played a scorching innings, continuing from where he had left off on the Friday evening. He launched a violent attack on Emburey,

who was hit for 37 in three overs and forced to retire. Emburey's figures at the end of the day were 1 for 62 off 7 overs. Richards' 80 came off 97 balls, and he was ruthless on anything that was not on the perfect length, and on much that was. He and Haynes lifted the whole tempo of the match with 75 from 13 overs.

Haynes was caught off his glove. The ball lifted awkwardly and, falling forward, Downton took a good catch. Richards finally fell to De Freitas, Gooch holding a very fast edge at slip. Undaunted, Logie and Hooper added 33 from six overs before the close.

Although Pringle took a deserved wicket when he had Logie taken at second slip and Dilley had a less deserved success when Dujon cross-batted an extraordinary return catch, West Indies moved to a position of total authority on the Monday. Hooper suggested a calm control and elegance of style that looks certain to dominate Test cricket in the near future. He suddenly lost his timing, however, and fell to a lifting ball from De Freitas in the second over after lunch.

His dismissal did not end West Indies' dominance as Marshall and Ambrose joined in a stand of 91 in which the England attack was savaged mercilessly. If Ambrose's strokes were limited, Marshall's were not. He added to the lustre of his bowling performance with a thrilling innings. In the space of four balls, he hit Emburey for 2 consecutive sixes and smashed Pringle high over the boundary. When, finally, he chanced his arm once too often against the suffering Emburey he and Ambrose were within eight runs of the West Indian eighth-wicket record. There were more flourishes from Ambrose, and Richards declared leaving England to negotiate the last 2¼ hours. There were some alarms, and Broad hung out his bat rather tamely to be caught behind, but England ended on 67 for 1, 136 in arrears and a day in which to save the game.

That they did so was due mainly to Gooch, who batted for 416 minutes, faced 303 balls and hit 15 fours with a cool and cultured authority which heartened England and gave hope for the series. There was, too, a hint of the old Gower. He produced glimpses of former fluency and languid charm, and he played with great sense after Marshall had bowled Gatting. He, like England, must have been relieved, however, when Man-of-the-Match Marshall left the field with a rib injury soon after lunch.

4, 6 and 7 June

at Cardiff

Glamorgan 369 for 7 dec (R.C. Ontong 120 not out, J.A. Hopkins 61, A.R. Butcher 52, J. Derrick 50 not out) and 152 for 7 dec
Kent 252 for 2 dec (N.R. Taylor 112 not out, S.G. Hinks 72, M.R. Benson 54) and 271 for 6 (C.J. Tavare 129 not out)

Kent won by 5 wickets
Kent 21 pts, Glamorgan 1 pt

at Liverpool

Hampshire 320 for 6 dec (J.R. Ayling 88 not out, V.P. Terry 74) and 186 for 5 dec (C.L. Smith 124 not out)
Lancashire 251 for 5 dec (A.N. Hayhurst 80, N.H. Fairbrother

69) and 259 for 6 (M. Watkinson 73 not out, T.E. Jesty 60)

Lancashire won by 4 wickets
Lancashire 21 pts, Hampshire 5 pts

at Lord's

Worcestershire 333 for 8 dec (T.S. Curtis 108, G.A. Hick 78) and 0 for 0 dec
Middlesex 0 for 0 dec and 124 (P.J. Newport 8 for 52)

Worcestershire won by 209 runs
Worcestershire 19 pts, Middlesex 3 pts

at Taunton

Somerset 215 (W.W. Davis 5 for 92) and 178 (J.G. Wyatt 69, W.W. Davis 4 for 54)
Northamptonshire 260 (R.J. Bailey 59, R.G. Williams 55) and 134 for 3 (W. Larkins 81 not out)

Northamptonshire won by 7 wickets
Northamptonshire 23 pts, Somerset 6 pts

at Horsham

Sussex 272 (N.J. Lenham 62, R.I. Alikhan 56, D.E. Malcolm 5 for 52) and 155 (O.H. Mortensen 4 for 57)
Derbyshire 250 (K.J. Barnett 67, P.D. Bowler 62, A.C.S. Pigott 4 for 60) and 178 for 9 (J.E. Morris 71)

Derbyshire won by 1 wicket
Derbyshire 22 pts, Sussex 1 pt

at Edgbaston

Warwickshire 300 for 8 dec (A.C. Storie 68, G.W. Humpage 58, C.L. Cairns 4 for 89) and 111 for 4 dec
Nottinghamshire 206 for 6 dec (D.W. Randall 69 not out) and 44 (G.C. Small 7 for 15)

Warwickshire won by 161 runs
Warwickshire 22 pts, Nottinghamshire 5 pts

at Harrogate

Yorkshire 142 (P.E. Robinson 58, K.T. Medlycott 4 for 19) and 310 for 6 dec (J.D. Love 93 not out, A.A. Metcalf 87)
Surrey 342 for 4 dec (G.S. Clinton 101, C.J. Richards 60 not out, K.T. Medlycott 54 not out)

Match drawn
Surrey 8 pts, Yorkshire 1 pt

A career-best 7 for 15 for Gladstone Small as Warwickshire bowled out Notts for 44, Edgbaston, 7 June. (Ken Kelly)

Martin Bicknell, still troubled by a back injury, Feltham and, especially, Ian Greig reduced Yorkshire to 18 for 5 on the opening morning at Harrogate. Rain and Robinson helped a revival before Medlycott finished off the innings. Surrey were badly hit by injuries, the most serious of which was the loss of Stewart with a broken thumb, but Clinton batted soundly, the middle order was consistent and Richards and Medlycott finished the second day with a partnership of 79 in 13 overs. On the last day, Love ended a very lean spell when he played a major part in saving the game for Yorkshire. Clinton bowled the last over of the match to him, and he hit 2 huge sixes, losing the ball on both occasions, so that Carrick felt it better to declare with two balls of the match remaining and Love on 93 not out.

Nottinghamshire, like Surrey, were hit by injury, but they were also shattered by Gladstone Small's best bowling performance in first-class cricket. Rain badly hindered play on the first day, but Warwickshire batted with exuberance on the Monday, declaring as soon as the fourth batting point was reached. Notts ended the day on

146 for 5 and with skipper Tim Robinson out of the game for some weeks with a damaged knuckle. With French already in hospital, this was a serious blow to the county defending two titles. In order to keep the game alive, Notts declared 94 runs behind and were then set to make 206 in 49 overs. Lloyd's declaration seemed to set Notts a none too difficult task, but it was soon apparent that a side lacking in confidence were on their way to their sixth defeat in eight games. Bowling unchanged, Small took 7 for 15 in 11.2 overs. Notts were out for the lowest score of the season in 87 minutes. They had one hero, Mike Newell, who carried his bat throughout the innings for 10.

There was a far closer contest at Horsham, where Sussex batted into the second day against Derbyshire, who, thanks to a late surge by Barnett and Warner, scored at a brisker rate and captured two Sussex wickets before the close. Mortensen bowled well on the last day, and Derbyshire were left to make 178 in 50 overs. The wicket aided the bowlers, but Morris batted bravely after Wright and Roberts had gone for 12. Leg-spinner Clarke bowled Mortensen in the penultimate over so that Malcolm and Sharma faced the last over with four needed. Two singles left Sharma facing Pigott's last ball, and the batsman flayed furiously to send the ball whistling past slip for the two winning runs.

There was a less dramatic finish at Taunton although the

Phil Newport, a devastating 8 for 52 to take Worcestershire to a vital victory over Middlesex, 4–7 June. (David Munden)

career-best 8 for 52 on a wicket which gave him no undue encouragement.

As Worcestershire took over first place, Kent moved into fourth position in the championship with their third win in succession. Glamorgan batted tediously on the opening day. At the 100-over mark, they were 197 for 6, but Ontong and Derrick added 116 in 22 overs after Morris had decided to bat on for 85 minutes on the Monday. The Kent approach was more positive. Benson and Taylor began with a partnership of 88, and when Hinks was out after adding 164 with Taylor, Cowdrey declared, 117 runs behind. The Kent spinners, Harman and Davis, bowled well on the last morning and suggested that Kent's task of scoring 280 in 2¼ hours plus 20 overs would be a formidable one. It looked impossible when Benson, Taylor and Hinks were out for 29, but Tavare and Pienaar defended stoutly, and Tavare and Chris Cowdrey put on 110 in 21 overs to give a glimpse of victory, which was finally achieved with 14 balls to spare. Tavare's masterly innings included a six and 14 fours, and he batted for 187 minutes.

events of the second day, when 20 wickets fell and Northants, in search of 134 to win, lost three wickets to Adrian Jones for 15 runs.

Declarations to compensate for some rather slow Hampshire batting on the opening day at Liverpool resulted in an interesting finish. Hughes ended the Lancashire first innings 69 runs in arrears, but immediately captured three Hampshire wickets for 10 runs on the second evening. Chris Smith survived and later prospered when occasional bowlers entered the attack to encourage a declaration. Eventually, Lancashire were asked to make 256 in 135 minutes plus 20 overs. Victory came with 14 balls to spare. Jesty and Watkinson batted well, but both were dropped by Nicholas, the Hampshire skipper.

The championship had new leaders as a result of Worcestershire beating Middlesex at Lord's. There was no play on the first day, and a rather tedious second day saw Curtis and Lord begin proceedings with a stand of 46 which occupied 80 minutes, and Curtis take more than six hours for his century. There was some sparkle from Hick, but the Middlesex over rate extended the game beyond seven o'clock. The forfeiture of Middlesex's first innings and Worcestershire's second left the home side to do on the last day what the visitors had done on the second. It proved a forlorn hope as the championship leaders were 4 for 3 and 15 for 4 and were finally bowled out for 124 at ten minutes past three on a sunny afternoon. Rhodes took four catches behind the stumps, but the hero of the day was Phil Newport, who bowled magnificently to take a

Refuge Assurance League

5 June

at Merthyr Tydfil

Glamorgan 134 (C.S. Cowdrey 4 for 20)
Kent 135 for 5 (N.R. Taylor 62)

Kent (4 pts) won by 5 wickets

at Old Trafford

Hampshire 196 for 6 (R.A. Smith 51)
Lancashire 197 for 4 (N.H. Fairbrother 57 not out)

Lancashire (4 pts) won by 6 wickets

at Lord's

Middlesex 237 (J.D. Carr 69)
Worcestershire 192 for 8

Middlesex (4 pts) won by 45 runs

at Taunton

Northamptonshire 211 (R.J. Bailey 78)
Somerset 212 for 8 (S.R. Waugh 109 not out)

Somerset (4 pts) won by 2 wickets

at Horsham

Derbyshire 213 for 8 (B. Roberts 59, K.J. Barnett 50)
Sussex 208 for 8 (P.W.G. Parker 80)

Derbyshire (4 pts) won by 5 runs

at Edgbaston

Warwickshire 184 for 9 (D.A. Reeve 69)
Nottinghamshire 155 for 7

Nottinghamshire (4 pts) won by 3 wickets

at Leeds

Surrey 212 for 8 (A.J. Stewart 60)
Yorkshire 216 for 6 (A.A. Metcalf 79, D. Byas 69 not out)

Yorkshire (4 pts) won by 6 wickets

A violent innings by David Byas, who hit 5 sixes and 3 fours in his 69 off 47 balls brought about a surprise defeat for Surrey and allowed Middlesex to go clear at the top of the Sunday league table. Lancashire moved into second place by beating Hampshire with two balls to spare. Another side to win on the fourth ball of the last over was Somerset. They owed their victory to Steve Waugh, who hit his second century in four days and proved himself a more than adequate replacement for Martin Crowe, whose back injury had forced him to return to New Zealand. The win over Northants was Somerset's first Sunday league win of the season. They remained level at the bottom with Sussex, beaten in spite of Parker's fine knock.

8, 9 and 10 June

at Old Trafford

West Indians 287 for 5 dec (D.L. Haynes 93, C.G. Greenidge 63, K.L.T. Arthurton 60)
Lancashire 238 for 6 (G.D. Mendis 59)

Match drawn

The match was badly affected by rain.

Benson and Hedges Cup

Semi-Finals

8 and 9 June

at Chelmsford

Essex 238 for 6
Hampshire 239 for 3 (V.P. Terry 109, C.L. Smith 56)

Hampshire won by 7 wickets
(Gold Award – V.P. Terry)

8 and 10 June

at Swansea

Derbyshire 217 for 8
Glamorgan 203 (M.A. Holding 5 for 31)

The Benson and Hedges Cup Semi-Final Glamorgan v. Derbyshire at Swansea. (Adrian Murrell/Allsport)

Gold Award winner at Chelmsford – Paul Terry. (Allsport)

Derbyshire won by 14 runs
(Gold Award – M.A. Holding)

The eagerly awaited semi-final of the Benson and Hedges Cup at Chelmsford proved to be something of a disappointment. The game spluttered on several occasions but never caught fire. Put in to bat, Essex began slowly but soon forced the pace so that they moved sweetly to 88 at four runs an over. At this point Hardie was lbw to a grotesque shot off an equally grotesque, short, low ball. Four runs later, Gooch, who had hit 7 fours, was bowled by Ayling as he played across the line. Hardie, one of Cowley's two victims, made 40, Gooch 41. Their scores epitomized the Essex innings, promise without fulfilment. Prichard, at number three, was without form and confidence, and when he skied a top edge off Cowley Essex were 125 for 3 at three runs an over. Pringle went quickly, and Border was never quite in touch, nor quite sure of what his approach should be. It was left to Fletcher and Lilley to add 59 from eight overs in the closing stages and to Foster to hit the day's first six off the last ball of the innings.

Essex had preferred to play five seamers, using Topley in place of Miller and, presumably, not contemplating playing Childs. Hampshire had chosen Cowley, and his off-breaks, bowled flat, had proved to be economical and rewarding. Foster alone seemed to trouble the Hampshire openers in the initial stages, but once his first spell was at an end, they began to score freely. They put on 118 in 33 overs before the patient Chris Smith was caught behind driving at Gooch. It was Essex's only success of the day as bad light and rain caused the match to move into a second

Peter Bowler is the victim of a fine leg-side stumping by Colin Metson. (Adrian Murrell/Allsport)

day with Hampshire, 192 for 1 from 46 overs, poised for victory.

In fact, play could not begin until 5.00 p.m. on the Thursday. David Turner, who had batted with controlled urgency, was quickly out, only five having been added to the overnight score, but Paul Terry and Robin Smith played with exuberance to quash any slim hopes Essex may have nurtured. Terry's fine innings came to an end in the 54th over, but Robin Smith took Hampshire to their first Lord's final later the same over. It was a success well deserved by a side and supporters who had waited long and patiently with dignity and good humour.

At Swansea, Derbyshire were put in to bat in grey weather and made to work hard for their runs. Barnett and Bowler started briskly enough, but 11 overs of off-breaks from Ontong, mostly pitched on leg stump, frustrated them. He conceded only 19 runs. Morris and Roberts both fell to Derrick as they threatened to cut loose, and the medium pacer also had the advantage of Bowler's wicket, a fine leg-side stumping by Metson. The Derbyshire innings was swollen by an unforgivable 13 wides and by a last-over slog of 15 by Newman.

In the circumstances, Derbyshire must have been well

satisfied by their 217, but it shrank in size when Butcher and Hopkins began Glamorgan's reply with 58 in 18 overs. Hopkins chopped on to an off-break from Bowler, Butcher was lbw to Mortensen and Morris chased a wide ball from Holding. There was great faith in Maynard, however, who was striking the ball cleanly, but he met with disaster. Playing back to a lifting ball from Holding, he had his helmet dislodged. It fell back onto the stumps knocking off a bail. The game was abandoned in the gloom at 7.30 p.m., Glamorgan 130 for 5, and not restarted until 3.00 p.m. on the Friday.

The home side needed 88 off 12 overs, and Ontong and Holmes, the not-out batsmen, punished the wayward Warner, but Newman returned to have Holmes caught first ball. Derrick was bowled by Holding, who began the last over with Glamorgan needing 15 to win. He had Metson caught with his first ball and Thomas with his second and the game was over.

The Glamorgan tragedy. Matthew Maynard's helmet falls onto his wicket as he plays a ball from Michael Holding. (Adrian Murrell/Allsport)

Tilcon Trophy

8 June

at Harrogate

Warwickshire 152 for 8
Gloucestershire 150 for 6

Warwickshire won by 2 runs

9 June

at Harrogate

Yorkshire 283 for 9 (A.A. Metcalfe 81, N.G.B. Cook 4 for 52)
Northamptonshire 155 (R.J. Bailey 50)

Yorkshire won by 128 runs

Final

10 June

at Harrogate

Warwickshire 159 for 9 (A.C. Storie 59, S.D. Fletcher 4 for 38)
Yorkshire 160 for 8 (A.A. Metcalfe 89)

Yorkshire won by 2 wickets

Yorkshire won the Tilcon Trophy for the first time since 1978 to bring some consolation to an unhappy season.

11, 12 and 13 June

at Northampton

West Indians 288 (D.L. Haynes 72) and 345 for 8 dec (K.L.T. Arthurton 121, C.L. Hooper 74, D. Williams 51)
Northamptonshire 232 (N.A. Stanley 55, C.A. Walsh 5 for 49)

Match drawn

at Cambridge

Cambridge University 156 (M.A. Atherton 75, P. Carrick 4 for 42) and 135 (S.D. Fletcher 4 for 35)
Yorkshire 251 (D. Byas 69, A.A. Metcalfe 52, R.J. Hart 4 for 66) and 41 for 0

Yorkshire won by 10 wickets

at Downpatrick

Ireland 138 (M.F. Cohen 51, N. Maxwell 4 for 15) and 345 for 9 dec (S.J.S. Warke 64, A. Masood 57, M.F. Cohen 55, J. Simmons 4 for 77)
MCC 217 (S. Ducat 53) and 206 for 7 (A.J.T. Miller 94)

Match drawn

11, 13 and 14 June

at Derby

Derbyshire 329 (K.J. Barnett 175, B. Roberts 69, K.M. Curran 6 for 103) and 182 (S.C. Goldsmith 63, K.M. Curran 6 for 59)
Gloucestershire 308 for 5 dec (A.J. Wright 136, P. Bainbridge 75) and 204 for 6

Gloucestershire won by 4 wickets
Gloucestershire 24 pts, Derbyshire 6 pts

Roy Pienaar. Fine all-round cricket helped Kent to their fourth successive win. Middlesex were the victims at Tunbridge Wells, 11–14 June. (Tom Morris)

at Ilford

Sussex 155 (G. Miller 5 for 76) and 134 (N.A. Foster 5 for 61)
Essex 462 for 8 dec (A.R. Border 161, G.A. Gooch 113, P.J. Prichard 80, T.D. Topley 56 not out)

Essex won by an innings and 173 runs
Essex 24 pts, Sussex 3 pts

at Tunbridge Wells

Middlesex 92 (C.S. Cowdrey 4 for 16, C. Penn 4 for 36) and 272 (M.W. Gatting 76, P.R. Downton 74, R.F. Pienaar 5 for 27)
Kent 110 (A.R.C. Fraser 4 for 30) and 255 for 4 (M.R. Benson 110, R.F. Pienaar 58 not out, N.R. Taylor 52)

Kent won by 6 wickets
Kent 20 pts, Middlesex 4 pts

at Trent Bridge

Nottinghamshire 178 (D.W. Randall 67, J.G. Thomas 6 for 68) and 230 (F.D. Stephenson 65, J. Derrick 4 for 67, S.R. Barwick 4 for 93)
Glamorgan 91 (F.D. Stephenson 5 for 42) and 175 (A.R. Butcher 65)

Nottinghamshire won by 142 runs
Nottinghamshire 21 pts, Glamorgan 4 pts

at Bath

Warwickshire 315 for 9 dec (T.A. Lloyd 151, G.D. Rose 6 for 47) and 209 (V.J. Marks 4 for 75)
Somerset 284 for 3 dec (S.R. Waugh 103 not out, J.J.E. Hardy 81) and 215 for 9 (S.R. Waugh 79, J.G. Wyatt 59, G.C. Small 4 for 32)

Match drawn
Somerset 4 pts, Warwickshire 4 pts

at The Oval

Surrey 179 (G.S. Clinton 59, P.A.J. De Freitas 5 for 43) and 291 for 8 dec (K.T. Medlycott 71, D.M. Smith 59, P.A.J. De Freitas 4 for 114)
Leicestershire 255 for 7 dec (R.A. Cobb 65) and 38 for 2

Match drawn
Leicestershire 7 pts, Surrey 4 pts

at Worcester

Worcestershire 397 for 7 dec (G.A. Hick 177, T.S. Curtis 131) and 17 for 0
Hampshire 203 (S.T. Jefferies 53, P.J. Newport 5 for 61) and 210 (C.L. Smith 87, G.R. Dilley 5 for 65)

Worcestershire won by 10 wickets
Worcestershire 24 pts, Hampshire 3 pts

Another sparkling innings from Graeme Hick, who hit 177 off 223 balls as he and Curtis added 276 for the second wicket, kept Worcestershire firmly on top of the Britannic Assurance County Championship. There is no greater sight in cricket at the present time than Hick in flow at New Road. He dismisses balls from his presence with an elegance of style that never violates the aesthetic. He and the Worcester ground merge in beauty. Yet in eulogizing over Hick, one is apt to forget the contribution of Tim Curtis, who batted until Monday morning. He is not regal as Hick is regal, but he has qualities of concentration, determination and correctness of style which are in themselves a delight to behold. Once Hick and Curtis had put Worcestershire in an unassailable position, the Worcestershire seamers took command. There was second innings bravery from Chris Smith, but Hampshire were handicapped by an injury to Nigel Cowley and never looked like saving the game.

Middlesex, meanwhile, continued to slide. Put in to bat on a damp wicket at Tunbridge Wells, they were bowled out for 92 by Ellison, Chris Cowdrey and Penn. Kent fared almost as badly. They lost seven wickets for 55, and only the late efforts of Marsh, Ellison and Penn took them to a first-innings lead of 18. Middlesex were batting again before the end of the first day, and on the Monday, with the wicket dry, they reached 272, thanks mainly to middle-order substance from Gatting, Downton and Emburey. Pienaar, splendidly supported behind the stumps by Marsh, a wicket-keeper of high quality, returned his best figures in the championship, and Kent had more than a day in which to score 255 to win. They finished strongly on 46 for 0. Benson and Taylor extended their opening stand to 98, and although Tavare and Hinks went quickly, Benson defied Emburey and Cowans to reach his second championship hundred of the season and make victory possible. Roy Pienaar also batted most sensibly at a vital time, proving his worth as an all-rounder of great sub-

Another fine all-rounder, Kevin Curran, took 12 wickets and hit a decisive 40 not out in Gloucestershire's win over Derbyshire, 11–14 June. (Steve Lindsell)

stance, and Kent moved into second place with their fourth win in succession.

Northamptonshire were engaged against the West Indians, for whom Keith Arthurton scored a delightful century and furthered his claim for a place in the Test team. Northants maintained fourth position in the championship table while Essex moved into fifth spot with a resounding win over Sussex at Ilford. Sussex were demolished by Miller and Childs on the opening day and Gooch raced to 113 off 58 overs before the close, by which time Essex were already 42 ahead. He was out without addition on the Monday, his stand with Prichard having realized 160, but Allan Border dominated the rest of the innings, hitting his first century in front of an Essex crowd. Sussex were 77 for 5 at the end of the second day, and it took only 90 minutes for Essex to complete victory on the last morning. Neil Foster showed a happy return to fitness.

Yorkshire won their first first-class match of the season when they beat Cambridge University, but they dropped again to bottom place in the championship when Glamorgan took four points on the opening day at Trent Bridge. Nottinghamshire were bowled out for 178 with Greg Thomas taking a career-best 6 for 68. Glamorgan fared even worse in reply against the formidable pace combination of Stephenson and Cooper. Stephenson emphasized Notts' superiority when he hit 12 fours in a brisk 65 as the home side batted again and set Glamorgan 318 to win. They were 9 for 2 at the end of the second day and slumped to 38 for 5 before Alan Butcher saved honour if not the match.

Gloucestershire maintained their title challenge with a fine win at Derby. Kim Barnett and Bruce Roberts shared a second-wicket stand of 185 on the opening day, which was dominated by the Derbyshire captain. He reached a century before lunch and hit a career-best 175 off 200 balls in under four hours as his side reached 329 at four an over. The visitors' reply was totally professional. Wright and Bainbridge added 113 in 29 overs for the fourth wicket, and Graveney was able to declare and allow Alderman to capture three wickets before the end of the second day. It was Kevin Curran who was the ultimate hero, however, as he refound form and fitness as an all-rounder to bring his match figures to a career-best 12 for 162 and then hit 40 not out as he and Russell took Gloucestershire to victory after they had been a precarious 123 for 6 when searching for 204 to win.

There was an exciting finish at Bath where Somerset, needing 241 in 48 overs to beat Warwickshire and having been given a splendid start by Waugh, Hardy and Wyatt, were thankful to hold on at 215 for 9. Warwickshire skipper Andy Lloyd held sway on the first day, but his first century of the season, 151 in 324 minutes with a six and 13 fours, was matched by the brilliant Steve Waugh. Another to draw comfort from the match was recently capped Graham Rose, who took six first-innings Warwickshire wickets.

De Freitas found good form as Surrey were shot out at The Oval, but Leicestershire's batsmen failed to sparkle or, ultimately, to respond to Greig's challenge. Leicestershire were also rather listless in the field, and the bright spot of the match was the form of Thorpe, making his début for Surrey and claiming Gower as his first wicket.

Refuge Assurance League

12 June

at Heanor

Gloucestershire 258 for 8 (P. Bainbridge 63, C.W.J. Athey 55)
Derbyshire 216 (B. Roberts 53)

Gloucestershire (4 pts) won by 42 runs

at Ilford

Sussex 204 for 6 (A.M. Green 57)
Essex 204 for 9 (A.R. Border 77)

Match tied
Essex 2 pts, Sussex 2 pts

at Trent Bridge

Glamorgan 198 for 4 (M.P. Maynard 75, R.J. Shastri 52 not out)
Nottinghamshire 193 for 7 (B.C. Broad 61)

Glamorgan (4 pts) won by 5 runs

at Bath

Warwickshire 202 for 8

Somerset 170 (S.R. Waugh 68)

Warwickshire (4 pts) won by 32 runs

at The Oval

Leicestershire 158 for 8
Surrey 159 for 6 (Zahid Sadiq 53)

Surrey (4 pts) won by 4 wickets

at Worcester

Worcestershire 196 for 7 (T.S. Curtis 88)
Hampshire 45 (M.J. Weston 4 for 11)

Worcestershire (4 pts) won by 151 runs

Surrey drew level with Middlesex at the top of the Sunday League table when they beat Leicestershire with four balls to spare. Gloucestershire maintained their challenge with some heavy scoring at Heanor. Mark Alleyne had a fine all-round match, hitting 49 not out at the close of his side's innings and taking three early wickets for 36 runs. Hampshire dissolved for 45 at Worcester, while leg-break bowler Clarke played a prominent part in earning Sussex a tie at Ilford.

15, 16 and 17 June

at Ilford

Gloucestershire 370 (C.W.J. Athey 76, R.C. Russell 64) and 69 for 2
Essex 188 (A.W. Lilley 80 not out, T.M. Alderman 6 for 41) and 249 (D.E. East 134, D.V. Lawrence 7 for 85)

Gloucestershire won by 8 wickets
Gloucestershire 24 pts, Essex 4 pts

at Basingstoke

Hampshire 136 (A.R.C. Fraser 5 for 34, N.G. Cowans 4 for 33) and 312 for 9 dec (D.R. Turner 150 not out, A.R.C. Fraser 6 for 68)
Middlesex 149 (C.A. Connor 4 for 61) and 186 for 4 (M.W. Gatting 104)

Match drawn
Hampshire 4 pts, Middlesex 4 pts

at Tunbridge Wells

Lancashire 199 (C.S. Cowdrey 4 for 36, R.F. Pienaar 4 for 77) and 203 (C. Penn 5 for 60)
Kent 252 (C.J. Tavare 63, P.J.W. Allott 6 for 86) and 154 for 5

Kent won by 5 wickets
Kent 23 pts, Lancashire 5 pts

at Leicester

Leicestershire 313 for 7 dec (L. Potter 96, J.J. Whitaker 68) and 164 (N.E. Briers 59, J. Derrick 6 for 54)
Glamorgan 246 (J.A. Hopkins 71, R.C. Ontong 66 not out, G.J.F. Ferris 4 for 51) and 71 for 2

Match drawn
Leicestershire 8 pts, Glamorgan 5 pts

at Bath

Sussex 320 for 6 dec (R.I. Alikhan 98, I.J. Gould 69 not out, A.P. Wells 64) and 206 for 3 dec (P.W.G. Parker 101 not out)

Somerset 276 for 6 dec (S.R. Waugh 137) and 250 for 7 (S.R. Waugh 85)

Match drawn
Somerset 13 pts, Sussex 4 pts

at Leeds

Yorkshire 163 (D. Byas 57, A.A. Donald 5 for 57) and 123 (T.A. Munton 4 for 35, A.A. Donald 4 for 36)
Warwickshire 81 (C. Shaw 4 for 17) and 206 for 3 (M. Asif Din 77)

Warwickshire won by 7 wickets
Warwickshire 20 pts, Yorkshire 5 pts

at Oxford

Nottinghamshire 405 for 7 dec (J.D. Birch 114 not out, P. Johnson 104) and 123 for 2 dec (P. Johnson 58 not out, D.J.R. Martindale 52 not out)
Oxford University 228 for 3 dec (M.A. Crawley 98, M.J. Kilborn 78) and 162 for 7

Match drawn

at The Oval

Surrey 309 for 3 dec (P.D. Atkins 114 not out, G.P. Thorpe 100 not out, D.J. Bicknell 62) and 192 for 6 dec (Zahid Sadiq 64, C.K. Bullen 56)
Cambridge University 266 for 7 dec (M.A. Atherton 86, J.C.M. Atkinson 73, C.K. Bullen 4 for 56) and 86 (M.P. Bicknell 9 for 45)

Surrey won by 149 runs

The Kent success continued. Medium-pace bowling supported by dynamic fielding accounted for Lancashire on the first day after Chris Cowdrey had elected to field when he won the toss. Cowdrey himself bowled splendidly and Pienaar again gave evidence of his all-round value. Kent lost Benson through injury, but he returned on the second day and played an important part in Kent securing a first-innings lead of 53. The main honours, however, went to Tavare and Chris Cowdrey, who batted for nearly 1¾ hours in difficult conditions. Allott bowled outstandingly well, but Kent captured five wickets for 90 before the end of the second day to put them well on top. They took Jesty's wicket very quickly on the final day, but Lancashire's tail wagged hard before Penn completed the job. Benson and Taylor gave the Kent second innings a sound start, and after a few misgivings the Cowdrey brothers took Kent to their fifth victory in succession and to within five points of Worcestershire.

Gloucestershire moved into fourth place with a resounding win over Essex. Gloucestershire batted into the second day with 'Jack' Russell providing the late boost to the innings. Essex wilted before Alderman, who exploited conditions favourable to seam bowling in a way which few can match. Forced to follow on, Essex were crushed by the pace of David Lawrence, who took four wickets in nine balls in one spell. An innings victory for the visitors looked certain, but David East played a violently heroic knock, hitting 5 sixes and 19 fours before being

caught at long-on for 134 made off 113 balls. His effort proved to be in vain as Gloucestershire won by eight wickets, and it was also learned that he had chipped a bone in his finger while keeping wicket, an injury which was to keep him out of the game for three weeks.

Middlesex lost more ground. Seventeen wickets fell on the first day at Basingstoke with Angus Fraser again displaying his considerable advance as a pace bowler. Cardigan Connor, another improved bowler, struck back for Hampshire, who surrendered a slender lead on the first innings. David Turner put the home side on top with a skilful and confident 150 off 294 balls while Angus Fraser returned the best figures of his career and claimed 11 wickets in the match. Asked to make 300 from a minimum of 71 overs, Middlesex showed no inclination whatsoever to attempt the task, and Gatting reached a century which was little more than batting practice.

Leicestershire and Glamorgan played out a rather dour draw on a wicket which was a test of technique, but Somerset and Sussex fashioned considerable excitement at Bath. The game began grimly enough as Alikhan batted for six hours to score 98 and Sussex spent the first day reaching 286 for 6. Ian Gould enlivened matters on the second morning, but Steve Waugh took the honours with a graceful century full of exciting shots. Parker followed suit on the last morning, his second century of the season coming in under three hours. He declared on reaching his hundred and asked Somerset to make 251 in 172 minutes. There was little sign early on that Somerset would approach their target. They were particularly troubled by leg-spinner Clarke, but Waugh and Marks thrashed 86 in 12 overs for the fourth wicket to take the score to 200 and put Somerset on course for victory. The quick dismissals of Burns and Rose tilted the game back in favour of Sussex, and Pringle and Mallender came together with 19 needed from 11 balls. The last ball arrived with three wanted, but they could only scramble a two to third man to level the scores and give Somerset eight points for being the side batting second with the scores level.

Having bowled out Warwickshire for 81 in the first innings, Yorkshire still contrived to lose at Headingley where Asif Din steered his side to victory after Lloyd and Moles had given them a fine start with a stand of 93. With several players unwell, Notts still managed to score heavily in The Parks, but Oxford University countered bravely, Kilborn and Crawley adding 120 for the second wicket.

Surrey blooded young players at The Oval. Atkins hit a hundred on his first-class début and Thorpe a hundred in 122 minutes in what was his second first-class game. Martin Bicknell, having missed much of the season with back trouble, routed Cambridge in the second innings, returning 9 for 45, the best of his career and the best of the season.

David East, the Essex wicket-keeper, sustained a broken finger in the match with Gloucestershire at Ilford, but hit an exhilarating 134. (Tony Edenden)

Second Cornhill Test Match
ENGLAND v. WEST INDIES

The prelude to the second Test of the series came close to dwarfing the match itself. Allegations as to Gatting's behaviour in a Leicestershire hotel on the Monday evening of the first Test at Trent Bridge were made in the popular press, nor was the England captain the only one accused of sexual indiscretion. The Test and County Cricket Board and the selectors took the only course open to them in depriving Gatting of the captaincy. His position had been in jeopardy since the incidents in Pakistan, and he had violated his contract with the TCCB in allowing a book to be published under his name in which one chapter (appearing under the name of his 'ghost') dealt with the Pakistan tour. The TCCB, which is simply the voice of the 17 counties, and the selectors were roundly abused in many quarters for their dismissal of Gatting, and one was saddened by the level of journalism to which even an eminent newspaper like the *Guardian* descended upon this occasion.

Cricket has attracted large amounts of money from sponsors and donors (much of which has gone into the pockets of top players) because, unlike soccer, it offers a clean, family image. That image needs to be jealously preserved for the good of the game and all those connected with it in whatever capacity. Cornhill Insurance made their position quite plain in their press statement issued on the eve of the Lord's Test: 'No one with the interests of England's cricket at heart can take pleasure from what has happened from the first Cornhill Test, at Trent Bridge. Certainly not the sponsors, who must be as concerned as the TCCB about the image the game projects at the highest level. They support the Board in its efforts and determination to maintain standards of behaviour both on and off the field.'

Gatting asked not to be considered for the second Test and was replaced by Moxon. John Emburey took over the captaincy. In doing so, he realized a well-publicized ambition although the realization came in circumstances different from what he would have wished. Small replaced De Freitas in the attack. West Indies were unchanged.

Richards won the toss and chose to bat. There was nothing to suggest that he had chosen wrongly, for the sun was shining from a blue sky, and it was not until the West Indian innings was in progress that cloud and haze moved in to assist the bowler and encourage extravagant swing.

Gus Logie joyously hits West Indies to safety. (Adrian Murrell/Allsport)

For three quarters of an hour there was nothing to suggest the drama that was to come. Then, at 11.42, with the score on 21, Haynes turned an in-swinger from Dilley off his legs, very much bat and a little pad, to Moxon at short-leg, who took a good catch, left-handed close to the ground. Twenty-five minutes later, Greenidge edged an out-swinger and Downton took a fine, diving catch in front of first slip. Two overs later, Richardson steered the ball to Emburey at third slip and left with his captain's angry words ringing in his ears. In the same over, the 17th, Hooper drove through the covers for three to bring up the fifty, but West Indian joy was short-lived, for the three proved to be Hooper's only scoring shot as he offered Downton a straightforward catch off Small in the next over. Downton claimed a greater prize in Dilley's next over when Richards jabbed at an away swinger and the wicket-keeper moved in front of first slip to take the catch without falling. In 49 minutes, within the space of ten overs, West Indies had lost five wickets, the cream of their batting, for the addition of 33 runs. The position could have been even worse, for, in Dilley's next over, Pringle failed to move quickly enough to a slip chance offered by Logie and the ball went for four. West Indies lunched at 66 for 5 from 25 overs. Dilley was a national hero, and England had enjoyed their best day in the field for nearly two years. A capacity crowd was ecstatic.

If the morning belonged to England, the afternoon belonged to West Indies. Logie had been seen as a

SECOND CORNHILL TEST MATCH – ENGLAND *v.* WEST INDIES
16, 17, 18, 20 and 21 June 1988 at Lord's

WEST INDIES

	FIRST INNINGS		SECOND INNINGS	
C.G. Greenidge	c Downton, b Dilley	22	c Emburey, b Dilley	103
D.L. Haynes	c Moxon, b Dilley	12	c Downton, b Dilley	5
R.B. Richardson	c Emburey, b Dilley	5	lbw, b Pringle	26
I.V.A. Richards†	c Downton, b Dilley	6	b Pringle	72
C.L. Hooper	c Downton, b Small	3	c Downton, b Jarvis	11
A.L. Logie	c Emburey, b Small	81	not out	95
P.J.L. Dujon*	b Emburey	53	b Jarvis	52
M.D. Marshall	c Gooch, b Dilley	11	b Jarvis	6
E.L.C. Ambrose	c Gower, b Small	0	b Dilley	0
C.A. Walsh	not out	9	b Dilley	0
B.P. Patterson	b Small	0	c Downton, b Jarvis	2
Extras	lb 6, nb 1	7	lb 19, w 1, nb 5	25
		209		**397**

ENGLAND

	FIRST INNINGS		SECOND INNINGS	
G.A. Gooch	b Marshall	44	lbw, b Marshall	16
B.C. Broad	lbw, b Marshall	0	c Dujon, b Marshall	1
M.D. Moxon	c Richards, b Ambrose	26	run out	14
D.I. Gower	c sub (Arthurton), b Walsh	46	c Richardson, b Patterson	1
A.J. Lamb	lbw, b Marshall	10	run out	113
D.R. Pringle	c Dujon, b Walsh	1	lbw, b Walsh	0
P.R. Downton*	lbw, b Marshall	11	lbw, b Marshall	27
J.E. Emburey†	b Patterson	7	b Ambrose	30
G.C. Small	not out	5	c Richards, b Marshall	7
P.W. Jarvis	c Haynes, b Marshall	7	not out	29
G.R. Dilley	b Marshall	0	c Richardson, b Patterson	28
Extras	lb 6, nb 2	8	b 5, lb 20, w 2, nb 14	41
		165		**307**

	O	M	R	W	O	M	R	W
Dilley	23	6	55	5	27	6	73	4
Jarvis	13	2	47	–	26	3	107	4
Small	18	5	64	4	19	1	76	–
Pringle	7	3	20	–	21	4	60	2
Emburey	6	2	17	1	15	1	62	–

	O	M	R	W	O	M	R	W
Marshall	18	5	32	6	25	5	60	4
Patterson	13	3	52	1	21.5	2	100	2
Ambrose	12	1	39	1	20	1	75	1
Walsh	16	6	36	2	20	4	47	1

FALL OF WICKETS
1–21, 2–40, 3–47, 4–50, 5–54, 6–184, 7–199, 8–199, 9–199
1–32, 2–115, 3–198, 4–226, 5–240, 6–371, 7–379, 8–380, 9–384

FALL OF WICKETS
1–13, 2–58, 3–112, 4–129, 5–134, 6–140, 7–153, 8–157, 9–165
1–27, 2–29, 3–31, 4–104, 5–105, 6–161, 7–212, 8–232, 9–254

Umpires: K.E. Palmer & D.R. Shepherd

West Indies won by 134 runs

ABOVE: *Marshall appeals and Lamb is lbw. These two players made significant contributions to a fine Test match. (Adrian Murrell/Allsport)*

TOP RIGHT: *Greenidge in full flow. (Adrian Murrell/ Allsport)*

RIGHT: *Richards is bowled by Pringle. (Adrian Murrell/ Allsport)*

vulnerable spot in the West Indian armour, as is any batsman whose primary concern is to score runs and to play shots, but he rescued West Indies with some glorious cricket, ably assisted by the elegant and aggressive Dujon. Logie hit Small for 2 fours in the 34th over to put the hundred up. Chances were offered, but not taken, and the cricket was consistently energetic and enthralling. By tea, the stand had realized 130 when Dujon played half forward to Emburey and was bowled off the inside edge.

In an hour after tea, the last four wickets went down for 25 runs. Logie's glorious innings, containing 14 fours and lasting three hours, ended in anti-climax when he slashed to point. Marshall was taken at slip. Ambrose clipped the ball off his legs for Gower to take dramatically, and Walsh, having been ludicrously dropped off a skier by Lamb, watched as Patterson was bowled to give Small his fourth, rather fortunate, wicket. To have dismissed West Indies for 209 on the first day was glory indeed for England, but had they held their catches, England would have been in an even stronger position.

Gooch savaged 3 fours when England began their reply in gathering gloom, but Broad was given out leg before to Marshall. Broad left the wicket muttering at the decision, and was castigated by the press for his mouthings, to himself. This incident was to prove costly to Broad at a later date, but one must sympathize with the player who was the victim of television coverage and the close-up rather than anything else. England closed at 20 for 1.

Gooch and Moxon had almost survived the first hour of the second day when Moxon was caught at first slip. Gower started at a rush, 16 from eight balls, and looked at his very best. At 112 for 2, England seemed on the verge of greatness, but the light was snuffed out. Gower, having dominated the stand with Gooch, hit tamely to mid-wicket. Gooch, his vigil having lasted for 3¼ hours, was bowled by Marshall. Pringle was caught down the leg side, and Lamb was leg before. Emburey flattered briefly and was bowled. The last three England wickets went to Marshall in 11 balls, and the euphoria of Thursday had turned to dismay.

That dismay turned to greater despair on the Saturday as Greenidge moved to centre stage to dominate the bowling with an innings of fluency, composure and correctness which never failed to thrill. In a third-wicket stand of 83, he and Richards treated the crowd to an array of brilliant strokes. Richards edged on to Pringle, the best of the England bowlers, but not before he had hit Small for 4 fours off successive deliveries and threatened general mayhem to the England attack. Greenidge was eventually caught at first slip, and Hooper had already been caught behind, but Logie and Dujon finished the day with a flurry of shots that suggested the first innings had only been an appetizer. The day ended with Logie on 69, Dujon on 45, and West Indies 354 for 5, the game out of England's reach.

Jarvis, persevering rather than penetrative, brought the West Indian innings to a close after 11 overs of the fourth morning. Logie and Dujon had taken their stand to 131 when Jarvis bowled Dujon, and the ebullient Logie was

One of the features of the series was the acrobatic wicket-keeping of Jeff Dujon. Pringle is caught down the leg side. (Adrian Murrell/Allsport)

left 95 not out when Patterson offered a catch behind.

To achieve a miracle and win the match, England needed a big innings from one of their first four batsmen and a major contribution from another. As it was, Gooch, Broad and Gower were out with only 31 scored. Lamb met hostility with aggression, and he found a good ally in Moxon, who opted for defence. They added 73 before Moxon insanely ran himself out. Pringle, too high at number six, was lbw for nought, but Downton and Emburey assisted bravely and belligerently before succumbing to Marshall and Ambrose. Emburey was particularly unlucky, being bowled off a full toss which hit him on the hand and fell onto the stumps. England ended the day alive, 214 for 7, Lamb 99.

Lamb's fine innings ended on the last morning when he ran himself out in trying to keep the strike. He had battled for 338 minutes, faced 212 balls and hit 15 fours in his 113, his first Test century in four years and a very fine one. There was a violent last-wicket partnership between Dilley and Jarvis which ended when Dilley edged to slip. Richards left the field with his arm around Marshall, whose bowling had been a decisive factor in the match. England had promised so much and had been beaten by 134 runs, a bitter disappointment.

Gus Logie, rightly, was named Man of the Match for his two excellent innings.

18, 20 and 21 June

at Derby

Worcestershire 367 (P.A. Neale 125, S.J. Rhodes 108, P.G. Newman 4 for 108) and 200 for 3 dec (T.S. Curtis 76, G.J. Lord 53)
Derbyshire 322 for 9 dec (B.J.M. Maher 76 not out, B. Roberts 65) and 115 for 4

Match drawn
Worcestershire 7 pts, Derbyshire 6 pts

at Southampton

Nottinghamshire 197 (C.A. Connor 5 for 70) and 359 (P. Johnson 140, M. Newell 80, R.J. Maru 4 for 132)

Hampshire 389 (C.L. Smith 117, D.R. Turner 75, N.G. Cowley 55, E.E. Hemmings 4 for 96) and 45 for 5

Match drawn
Hampshire 7 pts, Nottinghamshire 3 pts

at Old Trafford

Lancashire 329 for 6 dec (G.D. Mendis 151, N.H. Fairbrother 54) and 257 for 7 dec (D.P. Hughes 55, N.H. Fairbrother 54, D.V. Lawrence 5 for 54)
Gloucestershire 256 for 2 dec (P.W. Romaines 101 not out, C.W.J. Athey 72 not out) and 296 for 9 (A.W. Stovold 72, C.W.J. Athey 58, J. Simmons 5 for 81)

Match drawn
Gloucestershire 5 pts, Lancashire 4 pts

at Leicester

Sussex 159 (Imran Khan 55, P.A.J. De Freitas 5 for 38) and 210 (A.C.S. Pigott 56, J.P. Agnew 4 for 70)
Leicestershire 309 (P. Willey 130, P. Hepworth 51, A.C.S. Pigott 6 for 100) and 61 for 2

Leicestershire won by 8 wickets
Leicestershire 23 pts, Sussex 4 pts

Stuart Fletcher, 8 for 58 for Yorkshire against Essex. 18–21 June, and still on the losing side. (Stuart D. Franklin/ASP)

at Luton

Northamptonshire 338 (D.J. Capel 92, N.A. Stanley 62, A.R.C. Fraser 4 for 58) and 235 for 5 dec (G. Cook 124 not out)
Middlesex 277 (R.O. Butcher 61, M.W. Gatting 54, W.W. Davis 5 for 54, N.G.B. Cook 4 for 61) and 234 for 6 (W.N. Slack 54)

Match drawn
Northamptonshire 8 pts, Middlesex 6 pts

at Edgbaston

Kent 327 (C.J. Tavare 103, C.S. Cowdrey 78)
Warwickshire 107 (A.J. Moles 67 not out) and 174 (M. Asif Din 52)

Kent won by an innings and 46 runs
Kent 23 pts, Warwickshire 2 pts

at Sheffield

Yorkshire 133 (N.A. Foster 6 for 53) and 113 (N.A. Foster 4 for 33)
Essex 158 (P.J. Prichard 54, S.D. Fletcher 8 for 58) and 89 for 1

Essex won by 9 wickets
Essex 21 pts, Yorkshire 4 pts

It took both Essex and Kent only two days to win their matches. Essex's win at Sheffield was a remarkable affair. Put in to bat on a wicket which always encouraged the seamers, Yorkshire were bowled out in 54.1 overs. Essex lost seven wickets by the end of the first day, which they ended just two runs ahead. Topley, Brown, making his championship début, and Childs took the first-innings lead to a valuable 25 on the Monday morning. Stuart Fletcher finished with 8 for 58, the best performance of his career, and the best performance by a Yorkshire bowler for eight years. Sadly, the batsmen could not match his performance, and Yorkshire again succumbed in 46.3 overs to the Essex seam attack, spearheaded by Foster, who proved he was back to his best after injury. Essex had no difficulty in hitting off the runs at four an over after Stephenson had fallen at 25. Prichard played two fine innings, showing

Steven Rhodes allied his excellent wicket-keeping to some fine batting and a maiden first-class century against Derbyshire, 18–21 June. (Alan Cozzi)

admirable technique and temperament in difficult conditions.

Kent were fortunate in that Warwickshire lost Kallicharran, who broke a finger fielding on the first day, and Reeve, who broke a thumb practising on the Sunday. Nothing, however, should detract from another fine performance by Kent, whose sixth win in succession took them to the top of the championship. Put in to bat, they played with great resolution. Tavare batted with all his old determination, holding the innings together after early mishaps and sharing a sixth-wicket partnership of 169 with the energetic and resourceful Chris Cowdrey. Batting two short, Warwickshire were twice shot out on the Monday by the Kent seam attack, which was backed, as ever, by dynamic fielding and catching.

Worcestershire surrendered first place when they could only manage a draw at Derby. They were 126 for 5 on the opening day when Rhodes joined Neale. They added 206. Both batsmen reached centuries, for Rhodes it was the first of his career. It occupied 154 minutes and included a six and 7 fours and awakened again the debate as to why he now seemed to be excluded from the reckoning as a Test player. Derbyshire batted with unusual energy in reply after losing both openers for 32. The tail wagged very strongly, but the game petered to a tame draw.

Chris Cowdrey. His inspiring leadership and example took Kent to the top of the Championship in June. (Tom Morris)

Sound captaincy and consistent batting. Phil Neale of Worcestershire. (Allsport)

Mendis batted faultlessly on the opening day to reach 151 and take Lancashire to maximum batting points, but on the second day he was forced to retire hurt after being hit on the elbow by the fiery Lawrence. Gloucestershire declared 73 runs behind with Romaines and Athey sharing an unbeaten third-wicket partnership of 157. Romaines reached an impressive first century of the season. Hughes and Fairbrother revived Lancashire on the last morning, and Hughes was able to set Gloucestershire the stiff task of scoring 331 in 67 overs. The visitors went for the runs zestfully and, with five overs remaining, were 49 short with three wickets standing, but Simmons proved too much of a handful, and Russell played out the last 20 balls for a draw.

Refuge Assurance League

19 June

at Knypersley

Worcestershire 280 for 9 (P.A. Neale 91, M.J. Weston 72)
Derbyshire 211 (S.M. McEwan 4 for 37)

Worcestershire (4 pts) won by 69 runs

at Basingstoke

Hampshire 206 for 7 (D.R. Turner 79)
Nottinghamshire 201 for 5 (P. Johnson 82, J.D. Birch 54)

Hampshire (4 pts) won by 5 runs

at Old Trafford

Gloucestershire 206 for 4 (P.W. Romaines 78 not out)
Lancashire 209 for 9 (G.D. Mendis 50, V.S. Greene 4 for 25)

Lancashire (4 pts) won by 1 wicket

at Leicester

Sussex 182 for 4 (P.W.G. Parker 78)
Leicestershire 179 for 7

Sussex (4 pts) won by 3 runs

at Luton

Northamptonshire 200 for 8 (W. Larkins 65)
Middlesex 201 for 2 (M.W. Gatting 105 not out, W.N. Slack 65)

Middlesex (4 pts) won by 8 wickets

at Bath

Somerset 233 for 9 (J.G. Wyatt 77, P.M. Roebuck 64, S.T. Clarke 4 for 38)
Surrey 216 for 9

Somerset (4 pts) won by 17 runs

at Edgbaston

Warwickshire 180 for 6 (T.A. Lloyd 66, G.W. Humpage 53)
Kent 185 for 6 (C.S. Cowdrey 63 not out, G.R. Cowdrey 53)

Kent (4 pts) won by 4 wickets

at Sheffield

Essex 174 for 9 (B.R. Hardie 59, S.D. Fletcher 4 for 28)
Yorkshire 178 for 6 (A.A. Metcalfe 79, K. Sharp 52)

Yorkshire (4 pts) won by 4 wickets

Like Warwickshire, Sussex were hard hit by injuries. Alan Wells was hit on the hand on the opening day and could not bat in the second innings, in which both Green and Lenham were forced to retire hurt after being hit in a similar manner. For Leicestershire, Hepworth, in his second county match, hit 51 and shared a fifth-wicket partnership of 148 with the durable Willey after four wickets had fallen for 27. The Leicestershire tails supported Willey's first century of the season well and the home side won comfortably on the last morning.

Middlesex continued to lose ground. They trailed Northamptonshire by 61 on the first innings, and then suffered as Geoff Cook, returning after a five-week absence through injury, reached a century off 193 balls with 13 fours. In search of 297 in 64 overs, Middlesex began positively, but they slipped to 191 for 6 with 10 overs remaining, at which point Roseberry and Hughes settled for a draw.

Johnson hit his highest score, 140, for Notts against Hampshire and shared a partnership of 211 in 64 overs with Newell for the third wicket and so saved Notts from defeat at Southampton after Chris Smith and David Turner had put Hampshire in a strong position. Hampshire were badly served in the field and eventually found the task of scoring 168 in 20 overs way beyond them.

There was some fine cricket at Old Trafford. Gehan

While Middlesex maintained their Sunday form with a resounding victory over Northants based on a second-wicket stand of 154 between Slack and Gatting, Surrey lost ground with a surprising defeat at Bath. Roebuck was in good form for Somerset, and he shared stands of 54 with Hardy and 60 with Wyatt for the first and second wickets. Burns gave the later part of the innings a boost until he became one of Clarke's victims. The last ball of the Somerset innings saw Clarke run out Marks backing up, but Greig withdrew the appeal and Clarke bowled Mallender instead. While it has always been considered unsporting to run out a batsman backing up, it must be considered equally unsporting to try to steal runs in limited-over cricket in particular. In spite of a good knock by Ian Greig, Surrey could not match the required run rate. Lancashire moved into second place when Ian Austin hit the fourth ball of the last over against Gloucestershire for four. Lancashire had lost three wickets in Greene's last over and needed 61 from the last 10 overs. Kent and Yorkshire, Stuart Fletcher again to the fore, enhanced their chances with comfortable victories while Worcestershire won a high-scoring game on the small and attractive Knypersley ground. Weston and Neale added 123 for the fifth wicket. Weston's 72 came off 44 balls, but he, like other Worcestershire batsmen, was aided by poor fielding and inept field-placing.

NatWest Bank Trophy

Round One

22 June

at Finchampstead

Berkshire 105
Yorkshire 109 for 0 (A.A. Metcalf 74 not out)

Yorkshire won by 10 wickets
(Man of the Match – S.D. Fletcher)

at Boughton Hall, Chester

Northamptonshire 161 (G. Cook 53 not out)
Cheshire 164 for 9

Cheshire won by 1 wicket
(Man of the Match – B. Wood)

at Torquay

Nottinghamshire 302 for 3 (D.W. Randall 149 not out, J.D. Birch 55 not out)
Devon 238 for 6 (P.A. Brown 67 not out, R.G. Twose 56)

Nottinghamshire won by 64 runs
(Man of the Match – D.W. Randall)

at Darlington

Somerset 240 for 7 (J.J.E. Hardy 100)
Durham 206 for 8 (B.L. Cairns 54)

Somerset won by 34 runs
(Man of the Match – J.J.E. Hardy)

at Chelmsford

Essex 386 for 5 (D.R. Pringle 80 not out, B.R. Hardie 77, P.J. Prichard 77, G.A. Gooch 70)
Wiltshire 95

Essex won by 291 runs
(Man of the Match – D. R. Pringle)

at Bristol

Ireland 186 (M.F. Cohen 66, T.M. Alderman 5 for 34)
Gloucestershire 190 for 1 (A.W. Stovold 104 not out, A.J. Wright 55)

Gloucestershire won by 9 wickets
(Man of the Match – A.W. Stovold)

at Canterbury

Buckinghamshire 113
Kent 115 for 2 (S.G. Hinks 64 not out)

Kent won by 8 wickets
(Man of the Match – R.F. Pienaar)

at Old Trafford

Lancashire 305 (N.H. Fairbrother 80 not out, G.D. Mendis 64)
Lincolnshire 147 (Wasim Akram 4 for 27)

Lancashire won by 158 runs
(Man of the Match – N.H. Fairbrother)

at Leicester

Leicestershire 255 for 9 (D.I. Gower 99)
Suffolk 168 for 6

Leicestershire won by 87 runs
(Man of the Match – D.I. Gower)

Still entertaining. Derek Randall, Notts, a century in the first round of the NatWest Bank Trophy. (Stuart D. Franklin/ASP)

at Lord's

Hertfordshire 142 for 7
Middlesex 143 for 2 (M.W. Gatting 80 not out)

Middlesex won by 8 wickets
(*Man of the Match* – P.C.R. Tufnell)

at Myreside, Edinburgh

Glamorgan 179 (C.E.B. Rice 4 for 29)
Scotland 94 (R.J. Shastri 5 for 13)

Glamorgan won by 85 runs
(*Man of the Match* – R.J. Shastri)

at St George's, Telford

Hampshire 294 for 5 (C.L. Smith 117, V.P. Terry 83)
Shropshire 208 for 7 (J.B.R. Jones 83)

Hampshire won by 86 runs
(*Man of the Match* – C.L. Smith)

at Burton-upon-Trent

Surrey 285 for 9 (A.J. Stewart 54, C.J. Richards 50)

David Banks performed admirably for Staffordshire in the NatWest Bank Trophy and was offered a contract by Warwickshire in mid-season. (David Munden)

Staffordshire 230 for 8 (D.A. Banks 62 not out, J. Waterhouse 52, S.T. Clarke 4 for 27)

Surrey won by 55 runs
(*Man of the Match* – D.A. Banks)

at Hove

Sussex 134 (A.C.S. Pigott 53, M.A. Holding 8 for 21)
Derbyshire 135 for 4

Derbyshire won by 6 wickets
(*Man of the Match* – M.A. Holding)

at Edgbaston

Warwickshire 240 for 8 (T.A. Lloyd 121)
Cambridgeshire 173 for 6 (M.A. Garnham 110)

Warwickshire won by 67 runs
(*Man of the Match* – M.A. Garnham)

at Worcester

Worcestershire 336 for 5 (G.A. Hick 138, P.A. Neale 98)
Cumberland 228 for 8 (C.J. Stockdale 51)

Worcestershire won by 108 runs
(*Man of the Match* – G.A. Hick)

The first round of the NatWest Bank Trophy produced its customary offering of sacrificial lambs. Nottinghamshire

Michael Garnham hit a century for Cambridgeshire in the first round of the NatWest Bank Trophy and was recalled to play one first-class game for Leicestershire when Whitticase was injured. (Adrian Murrell/Allsport)

Michael Holding, a world-record 8 for 21 in a one-day game, Derbyshire v. Sussex at Hove. (David Munden)

and Essex made their highest scores in the competition. Randall set up a Notts' record with his 149 not out, and Shastri set up a bowling record for Glamorgan, for whom Morris equalled the tournament record with four catches in the field. Stuart Fletcher continued his run of success with 3 for 20 and the individual award at Finchampstead, and another bowler, slow left-arm spinner Phil Tufnell, took the honours at Lord's. David Banks, once of Worcestershire, hit 62 not out, took 2 for 49 and held a catch to trouble Surrey at Burton-upon-Trent. His performance attracted the attention of Warwickshire, who offered him a contract and brought him back to first-class cricket. The outstanding events, however, were at Chester and Hove.

At Hove, Paul Parker elected to bat when he won the toss and must have regretted his decision as Michael Holding dismissed the Sussex captain, Standing, and Imran Khan in his first 12 deliveries. Alikhan and the Wells brothers were accounted for in Holding's seventh and eighth overs to reduce Sussex to 27 for 6. Purposeful aggression by Pigott and Moores revived Sussex spirits, but Holding returned to claim Pigott and Clarke, who also batted sensibly, and to finish with a world record for limited-over cricket of 8 for 21, nine of which were no-balls. Derbyshire lost four wickets for 79, but Maher and Morris took them to victory with nearly 31 overs to spare.

Equally sensational were the happenings at Boughton Hall, where Cheshire beat the 1987 finalists Northamptonshire by one wicket and with one ball to spare. Put in to

bat, Northamptonshire began soundly enough when Larkins and Geoff Cook put on 31, but although Cook stayed at the wicket and played with great caution, only Allan Lamb of the other batsmen hinted at playing an innings. Lamb fell to Cheshire skipper Neil O'Brien, and Barry Wood, formerly of Yorkshire, Lancashire, Derbyshire and England, dismissed Capel and Williams in quick succession. Cook remained a spectator as his side were tumbled out in 55.2 overs and he carried his bat, having managed three fours off the 114 balls he faced. Barry Wood gave Cheshire an encouraging start when he clipped Davis' first ball through mid-wicket for four and he went on to score 40 before being run out by Wild, who also threw down Hitchmough's wicket. It seemed that Cheshire would lose their way, but Neil O'Brien took them to within sight of victory. Nevertheless, when the last pair, Fox and John O'Brien, came together 12 runs were still needed. The last over arrived with six required. One was scrambled, and on the fifth ball of Walker's over, Fox edged to the third-man boundary for the winning runs.

23 and 24 June

at Cambridge

West Indians 355 for 9 dec (D. Williams 84, K.L.T. Arthurton 70, A.L. Logie 57, C.L. Hooper 51, J.N. Perry 4 for 82)
Oxbridge 38 (I.R. Bishop 4 for 12) and 145 (W.K.M. Benjamin 4 for 18)

West Indians won by an innings and 172 runs

25, 26 and 27 June

at Canterbury

West Indians 275 (C.L. Hooper 87, R.A. Harper 56 not out)
Kent 81 (R.A. Harper 4 for 10) and 151 (D.J.M. Kelleher 51, I.R. Bishop 6 for 39)

West Indians won by an innings and 43 runs

A very inexperienced Kent side was beaten inside two days. Seven Kent first-team players were unfit, and their replacements found Ian Bishop very hard to deal with. Bishop had match figures of 7 for 63.

25, 27 and 28 June

at Chelmsford

Middlesex 259 (M.W. Gatting 67, N.F. Williams 63 not out, J.H. Childs 4 for 52, N.A. Foster 4 for 64) and 66 for 3
Essex 296 (A.W. Lilley 61, B.R. Hardie 58, A.R.C. Fraser 5 for 59)

Match drawn
Essex 7 pts, Middlesex 5 pts

at Swansea

Lancashire 155 (R.J. Shastri 4 for 41) and 163 (G.D. Mendis 65 not out, R.J. Shastri 7 for 49)
Glamorgan 199 (J. Simmons 5 for 53) and 47 (I. Folley 6 for 20, J. Simmons 4 for 9)

Lancashire won by 72 runs
Lancashire 21 pts, Glamorgan 5 pts

Ian Folley – 6 for 20 for Lancashire as they bowled out Glamorgan for 47, 28 June. (Mark Leech)

at Gloucester

Leicestershire 189 (N.E. Briers 53, K.M. Curran 4 for 55) and 177 (N.E. Briers 51, K.M. Curran 7 for 54)
Gloucestershire 142 (P.A.J. De Freitas 5 for 41) and 144 (J.P. Agnew 6 for 39, P.A.J. De Freitas 4 for 63)

Leicestershire won by 80 runs
Leicestershire 21 pts, Gloucestershire 4 pts

at Trent Bridge

Nottinghamshire 143 (D.J. Wild 4 for 18) and 275 (J.D. Birch 75)
Northamptonshire 105 (K.E. Cooper 4 for 25) and 122 (F.D. Stephenson 7 for 56)

Nottinghamshire won by 191 runs
Nottinghamshire 20 pts, Northamptonshire 4 pts

at The Oval

Derbyshire 329 for 9 dec (P.D. Bowler 158) and 171 for 1 dec (B.J.M. Maher 75, P.D. Bowler 57 not out)
Surrey 250 for 8 dec (C.J. Richards 77, M.A. Lynch 56, A.E. Warner 4 for 36) and 47 for 1

Match drawn
Derbyshire 6 pts, Surrey 5 pts

at Hove

Sussex 299 (R.I. Alikhan 71, N.J. Falkner 55, P. Carrick 4 for 71) and 105 (P.W. Jarvis 4 for 21, A. Sidebottom 4 for 47)

Yorkshire 219 (A.M. Babington 4 for 66) and 188 for 7 (M.D. Moxon 61)

Yorkshire won by 3 wickets
Yorkshire 22 pts, Sussex 7 pts

At the end of the second day at Swansea, Glamorgan seemed poised for their first championship victory of the season. They led by 44 on the first innings and, in spite of Gehan Mendis' magnificent effort in carrying his bat through Lancashire's second innings, they bowled out the visitors for 163 with Ravi Shastri taking 7 for 49, his best performance for Glamorgan. Fourteen of the fifteen wickets that fell on the second day were taken by spinners, and when John Derrick played on to Jack Simmons he became the veteran off-spinner's 1000th first-class victim. So Glamorgan had a day in which to score 120, but the wicket, which had encouraged spin from the start, was now treacherous. Folley and Simmons grabbed their chance. No Glamorgan batsman was able to show the diligent technique that Mendis had displayed. From 24 without loss, Glamorgan collapsed to 47 all out in 89 minutes, 23.5 overs.

Rain badly hit the game between Essex and Middlesex, only 23.1 overs in three sessions being possible on the last day, but the game at The Oval was drawn, not only due to bad weather, but also because of some rather tedious play by Derbyshire, who, inevitably, batted into the second day. Bowler again proved his worth with an innings of 158 which occupied all the first day and some of the second morning and which was punctuated by much playing and missing and several chances which were not accepted. Clarke was particularly unlucky. Surrey, lacking Stewart, who had an injured thumb, attempted to keep the game alive, but it was dying from the first day. Derbyshire were without Barnett and Mortensen and gave a first-class début to Chris Adams, who batted with welcome aggression and fielded with zest, a very promising cricketer.

Sixteen wickets fell on the first day at Gloucester, where the pace bowlers enjoyed themselves. The home side trailed by 42 on the first inning, and, in spite of Kevin Curran's career-best 7 for 54 and match analysis of 11 for 109, they were always struggling. Set to make 225, they ground their way to 95 for 3, but De Freitas and Agnew took over and the last seven wickets fell for 49 runs.

On a Trent Bridge wicket which earned censure from Geoff Cook, Nottinghamshire beat Northamptonshire by 191 runs although neither side reached 150 in their first innings. The Notts heroes were skipper John Birch and West Indian Franklyn Stephenson, who lashed 132 for the fifth wicket in the second innings and made victory possible. Cooper and Stephenson bowled unchanged throughout the second innings, Stephenson taking a career-best 7 for 56 and reaching 61 wickets for the season, the same number as Cooper.

An opening partnership of 91 between Alikhan and Falkner gave Sussex an encouraging start against Yorkshire, and Colin Wells and Babington bowled them to a first-innings lead of 80. The Sussex batsmen lost their way dreadfully against the Yorkshire seamers, Jarvis, Sidebottom and Fletcher, on the last morning, and the visitors were left to make 186 off 57 overs. At 72 for 5, Yorkshire looked beaten, but Carrick, 43, joined Moxon in a crucial partnership of 70. Leg-spinner Clarke accounted for Moxon, and Carrick was bowled by Babington, but Sidebottom batted with great resolution and, with Jarvis, took Yorkshire to their first championship win of the season.

Refuge Assurance League

26 June

at Pontypridd

Glamorgan 163 for 9 (A.N. Hayhurst 4 for 37)
Lancashire 28 for 3

Match abandoned
Glamorgan 2 pts, Lancashire 2 pts

at Gloucester

Gloucestershire 202 for 9 (P.W. Romaines 67, P.A.J. De Freitas 4 for 33)
Leicestershire 139 (N.E. Briers 54, K.M. Curran 5 for 15)

Gloucestershire (4 pts) won by 63 runs

at Bournemouth

Hampshire 172 for 7
Essex 101 for 2

Essex (4 pts) won on faster scoring rate

at Lord's

Somerset 247 for 5 (S.R. Waugh 140 not out, R.J. Bartlett 50)
Middlesex 220 for 9 (K.R. Brown 102, N.A. Mallender 4 for 31)

Somerset (4 pts) won by 27 runs

at Trent Bridge

Nottinghamshire 220 for 3 (B.C. Broad 96 not out, M. Newell 58)
Northamptonshire 223 for 3 (A.J. Lamb 79, R.J. Bailey 75)

Northamptonshire (4 pts) won by 7 wickets

at The Oval

Surrey 225 for 4 (M.A. Lynch 50)
Derbyshire 225 for 8 (K.J. Barnett 72)

Match tied
Surrey 2 pts, Derbyshire 2 pts

at Hove

Yorkshire 176 for 8
Sussex 177 for 3 (C.M. Wells 57 not out, P.W.G. Parker 54)

Sussex (4 pts) won by 7 wickets

Surrey's uncertain Sunday form continued when they tied with Derbyshire. In spite of three men being run out, Surrey reached a creditable 225, and Derbyshire looked beaten when they needed 70 off the last seven overs and 21 off the last two. The last ball, bowled by Clarke, arrived with two needed, and Maher and Newman scrambled a bye to level the scores. Steve Waugh's might continued as he helped inflict the first Sunday league defeat of the season on Middlesex. He hit a hundred off 92 balls, added 141 for the fourth wicket with Bartlett and ended on 140 not out. Middlesex slumped to 74 for 6, but Keith Brown hit his first century in the competition and added 132 with Neil Williams to ensure that Middlesex died bravely. Kevin Curran continued his weekend of bowling glory to take Gloucestershire into fourth place while Chris Broad hit 96 not out and shared an opening stand of 129 with Newell to give heart to the England selectors. Lamb gave them further heart by adding 148 with Bailey and taking Northamptonshire to victory.

25 June

at Londonderry

Worcestershire 200 (S.J. O'Shaughnessy 68, S.J. Halliday 4 for 57)
Ireland 152 for 7 (R.K. Illingworth 5 for 40, D.B. d'Oliveira 4 for 9)

Worcestershire won by 48 runs

26 June

at Dublin (Malahide)

Worcestershire 286 for 8 (P.J. Newport 55, S.J. O'Shaughnessy 52, G.A. Hick 51)
Ireland 171 for 9

Worcestershire won by 115 runs

29, 30 June and 1 July

at Gloucester

Gloucestershire 307 for 9 dec (R.C. Russell 72, J.R. Ayling 4 for 57) and 248 (R.C. Russell 69, S.T. Jefferies 8 for 97)
Hampshire 315 for 4 dec (R.A. Smith 141 not out, R.J. Maru 74, D.R. Turner 64 not out) and 226 for 6 (C.L. Smith 94)

Match drawn
Hampshire 8 pts, Gloucestershire 5 pts

at Canterbury

Essex 330 (A.R. Border 168) and 82 for 1 dec
Kent 231 (N.R. Taylor 77, T.R. Ward 70, G. Miller 4 for 95)

Match drawn
Essex 7 pts, Kent 4 pts

at Lord's

Yorkshire 187 and 80 for 4
Midddlesex 388 (W.N. Slack 144, J.F. Sykes 86, C. Shaw 4 for 54, S.D. Fletcher 4 for 108)

Match drawn
Middlesex 8 pts, Yorkshire 4 pts

at Taunton

Glamorgan 252 for 8 dec (G.C. Holmes 100 not out, D.J. Foster 4 for 72) and 247 for 7 dec (G.C. Holmes 107, M.P. Maynard 53 retired hurt)
Somerset 243 for 2 dec (P.M. Roebuck 112 not out, S.R. Waugh 101 not out)

Match drawn
Somerset 5 pts, Glamorgan 3 pts

at Nuneaton

Warwickshire 234 (A.J. Moles 115, A.N. Hayhurst 4 for 45) and 129 (M. Watkinson 6 for 43)
Lancashire 213 (T.A. Munton 4 for 55) and 152 for 4 (G.D. Mendis 56 not out)

Lancashire won by 6 wickets
Lancashire 22 pts, Warwickshire 6 pts

Bad weather blighted the chances of a result at most venues. Allan Border transformed the Essex innings at Canterbury, at one time they were 117 for 5, with his fourth century of the summer. Fletcher helped him in a partnership of 124. Taylor and Ward began Kent's reply with a stand of 109, but Pringle took three wickets in five balls without a run being scored to rock Kent, and Miller put Essex on top. Rain was the final arbiter.

Rain also had the last say at Lord's. The Middlesex seamers disposed of Yorkshire in 61 overs, and Slack hit 144 off 251 balls, his first century of the summer, to put the home side on top. Sykes hit a brisk, entertaining championship best and added 144 with Slack for the sixth wicket at five an over. Yorkshire were in desperate straits on the last day when rain saved them. Wayne Daniel had returned for this match after back injury, but he retired after bowling one over in the second innings with Achilles tendon trouble.

Batsmen enjoyed themselves at Gloucester in the main, but the home county were indebted to two excellent innings from Jack Russell for staving off defeat. Steve Jefferies recorded his best figures in English cricket when

Geoff Holmes – a century in each innings for Glamorgan against Somerset at Taunton, 29 June–1 July (Adrian Murrell/Allsport

he took 8 for 97 in Gloucestershire's second innings, and both the Smith brothers batted well. Chris Smith made a valiant effort to lead Hampshire to victory, but they finished 15 runs short in their attempt to make 241 off 49 overs.

There were centuries galore at Taunton, but the match ended in a dull draw. Geoff Holmes hit a century in each innings, bringing his total of centuries for the season to four, and, with the help of rain, Shastri and Maynard, who retired after being hit on the finger, he helped to save Glamorgan. On the second day, Roebuck and Waugh shared an unbroken third-wicket stand of 179. Both batsmen reached accomplished hundreds, and Waugh completed a thousand runs in all competitions during the month of June.

The only result achieved was at Nuneaton. Andy Moles hit his first championship hundred of the season on the opening day, but Hayhurst bowled Lancashire back into the game as five wickets fell with the score on 222. The wickets went down in the space of 14 deliveries. Munton, ever improving, was still able to bowl Warwickshire to a slim first-innings lead, but their batting collapsed for a second time, with Watkinson, Wasim Akram and Allott doing the damage. Needing 151 to win, Lancashire, guided by the reliable Mendis, swept to victory with 30 overs to spare.

Third Cornhill Test Match
ENGLAND v. WEST INDIES

Almost a third of the first day's play was lost to rain, but there was still ample time for West Indies to inflict most grievous wounds upon England, although some might say that many of the wounds were self-inflicted. England dropped Broad, although he was in the party of 13, brought in Capel for Pringle, recalled Gatting, had De Freitas back for the injured Small and gave a first Test cap to John Childs, the slow left-arm bowler. He had not been the original choice, Nick Cook having been chosen, but Cook was injured, and there was general delight at the selection of Childs, the best spin bowler in England for the past three seasons, not always used or encouraged to the full, and one of the nicest of men. West Indies brought in Harper for Haynes, who was injured, and preferred Benjamin to Patterson.

Emburey was delighted to win the toss and to bat first although the conditions proved to be not so amiable as had been hoped. For 33 minutes all seemed well although Moxon was runless, and it was the frailty of the Yorkshireman's technique that was the first to be exposed. Pushing indecisively forward to Marshall, he was bowled through a gap between bat and pad. Gatting came in to a reception which seemed to be based on the mistaken impression that he was a martyr. He was soon on his way back in silence after, bewilderingly and nightmarishly, offering no stroke to Marshall. Gower hit 2 fours and then flicked lazily at a ball outside off stump and was caught at third slip. Lamb joined Gooch in sound defence, but with the respite of lunch looming, Gooch played an inexplicably wild shot to a ball wide outside the off-stump and was given out caught behind although it seemed that he had not, in fact, made contact.

Capel offered eight overs of correct defence into the afternoon, but never looked like scoring a run and was finally bowled by a violent break back. Lamb's defiance was ended when he square cut into the hands of gully, and then there was a stoppage after which Emburey was cramped by a shortish ball and caught behind. Downton went as Lamb had done, and De Freitas also offered Greenidge catching practice. Dilley and Childs added 12 for the last wicket, and then the most wretched batting performance one had witnessed by an England side was over, but the day's misery was not. Three overs remained of the day. Dilley bowled the first, Emburey the second. Emburey turned his first delivery appreciably. Richardson attempted to sweep and gloved the ball, but Downton moved forward too late to it. In the last over, Greenidge edged Dilley waist high to slip and Gooch dropped the catch.

Momentarily, on the second day, England's hopes flickered. Richardson began with a flourish and then dragged on to Dilley. Hooper looked cultured and compassed and then offered no stroke to a ball from Childs which went straight on and trapped him palpably leg

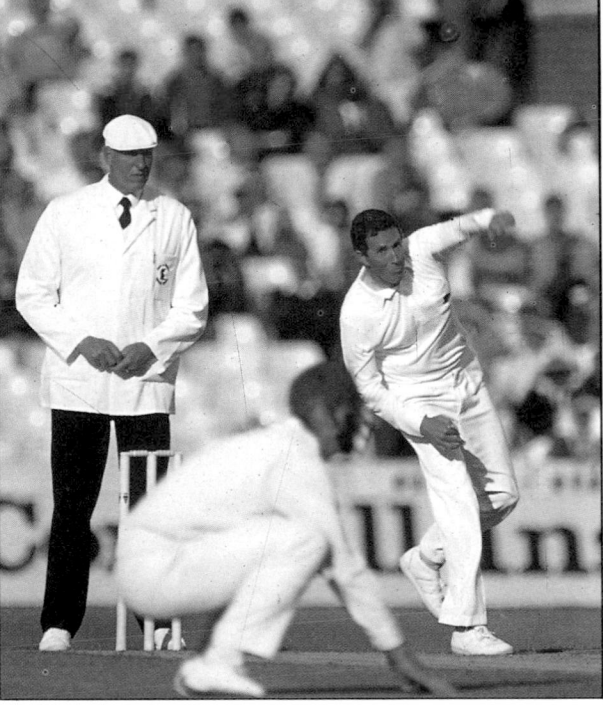

England débutant John Childs. (Adrian Murrell/Allsport)

THIRD CORNHILL TEST MATCH – ENGLAND v. WEST INDIES
30 June, 1, 2, 4 and 5 July 1988 at Old Trafford, Manchester

ENGLAND

	FIRST INNINGS		SECOND INNINGS	
G.A. Gooch	c Dujon, b Benjamin	27	lbw, b Marshall	1
M.D. Moxon	b Marshall	0	c Richards, b Benjamin	15
M.W. Gatting	lbw, b Marshall	0	c Richardson, b Marshall	4
D.I. Gower	c Harper, b Walsh	9	c Richardson, b Marshall	34
A.J. Lamb	c Greenidge, b Ambrose	33	c Logie, b Ambrose	9
D.J. Capel	b Benjamin	1	c sub (Arthurton), b Marshall	0
P.R. Downton*	c Greenidge, b Walsh	24	c Harper, b Marshall	6
J.E. Emburey†	c Dujon, b Walsh	1	c Logie, b Ambrose	8
P.A.J. De Freitas	c Greenidge, b Ambrose	15	c Harper, b Marshall	0
G.R. Dilley	c Harper, b Walsh	14	b Marshall	4
J.H. Childs	not out	2	not out	0
Extras	lb 4, nb 5	9	b 1, lb 10, nb 1	12
		135		93

	O	M	R	W	O	M	R	W
Marshall	12	5	19	2	15.4	5	22	7
Ambrose	17	5	35	2	16	4	36	2
Walsh	18.2	4	46	4	4	1	10	–
Benjamin	13	4	31	2	4	1	6	1
Harper					2	1	4	–
Hooper					1	–	4	–

FALL OF WICKETS
1–12, 2–14, 3–33, 4–55, 5–61, 6–94, 7–98, 8–113, 9–123
1–6, 2–22, 3–36, 4–73, 5–73, 6–73, 7–87, 8–87, 9–93

WEST INDIES

	FIRST INNINGS	
C.G. Greenidge	lbw, b De Freitas	45
R.B. Richardson	b Dilley	23
C.L. Hooper	lbw, b Childs	15
I.V.A. Richards†	b Capel	47
A.L. Logie	lbw, b Dilley	39
P.J.L. Dujon*	c Capel, b Dilley	67
R.A. Harper	b Dilley	74
M.D. Marshall	not out	43
E.L.C. Ambrose	not out	7
W.K.M. Benjamin		
C.A. Walsh		
Extras	lb 21, nb 3	24
	(for 7 wkts, dec)	384

	O	M	R	W
Dilley	28.1	4	99	4
Emburey	25	7	54	–
De Freitas	35	5	81	1
Capel	12	2	38	1
Childs	40	12	91	1

FALL OF WICKETS
1–35, 2–77, 3–101, 4–175, 5–187, 6–281, 7–373

Umpires: D.J. Constant & N.T. Plews

West Indies won by an innings and 156 runs

before wicket. It was well deserved by Childs. He bowled quite admirably throughout the day, not always to wisely set fields, spun the ball appreciably and was unlucky not to get a better reward. His first ball to Richards spat, turned and lifted viciously, and once the great man, aiming to hit Childs over long-on for six, hit him just over long-off. He kissed his bat in thanks, but this was no consolation to Childs, who had still conceded a six when he might have expected a wicket.

Richards, in truth, was not at his best, and he was unwell, but he still made 47 off 71 balls before playing on to Capel. Greenidge grafted 2½ hours for his 45, and although no West Indian batsman was able to build a big score, they were all willing to show admirable determination to come to terms with the conditions and work for their runs with an assurance based on technical competence. Five wickets were down for 187, but Dujon and Harper took the score to 242 by the close. They were

Fatal edge. Gower taken at slip off Marshall. (Adrian Murrell/Allsport)

The Glory of Dujon. (Adrian Murrell/Allsport)

The end of De Freitas. (Adrian Murrell/Allsport)

patient and correct, and for England, in spite of some courageous bowling, the signs were ominous.

Only 3¼ hours' play was possible on the Saturday and during that time England captured the wicket of Dujon, well caught by Capel running in from mid-on, and West Indies advanced to 357, Harper 61, Marshall 37.

No play was possible before lunch on the fourth day. Harper's excellent innings was ended by a Dilley yorker, and Richards declared shortly afterwards. The England second innings had a fractured start because of light and weather interruptions, but Gooch was a grievous loss, lbw to the fourth ball of Marshall's second over. Gatting, whose record against West Indies is very poor, was caught at third slip of what was, in fact, a straight ball, and Benjamin's first ball accounted for Moxon. Stiff, bat away from body, Moxon offered the ball to a grateful first slip. It was a dreadful spectacle. Gower played with some flourish, and the day closed with England 60 for 3, hoping for rain.

The rain did come after an hour on the last day, but by then, England's innngs, one of abject poverty which reached depths lower than had been seen in the first innings, was over. There was an encouragingly positive start, but, in the fourth over, Gower flicked again and gave Richards a catch at slip. Capel was taken at silly mid-off, and Lamb and Emburey were caught at short-leg where Logie was a perpetual threat. Downton and De Freitas, second ball, were taken in a similar manner, pushing the bat away from the body and offering a catch to third slip. Marshall flattened Dilley's off stump, and the game was over. Marshall had finished with 7 for 22, the best figures of his Test career, and a heavy depression had settled upon English cricket.

2, 3 and 4 July

at Lord's

Oxford University v. Cambridge University

Match abandoned

A SUMMER OF CAPTAINS/333

A moment of joy for England. Richards is bowled by David Capel. (Pascal Rondeau/Allsport)

2, 4 and 5 July

at Derby

Middlesex 138 (A. Needham 66 not out, O.H. Mortensen 6 for 35) and 40 for 0
Derbyshire 0 for 0 dec

Match drawn
Derbyshire 4 pts, Middlesex 0 pts

at Northampton

Northamptonshire 147 (Wasim Akram 7 for 53) and 134 for 2 (A. Fordham 50 not out)
Lancashire 250 for 7 dec (G. Fowler 78)

Match drawn
Lancashire 7 pts, Northamptonshire 3 pts

at Taunton

Essex 258 for 7 dec (D.R. Pringle 75, B.R. Hardie 50) and 0 for 0 dec
Somerset 0 for 0 dec and 85 for 2

Match drawn
Somerset 3 pts, Essex 3 pts

at The Oval

Warwickshire 74 (N.H. Peters 6 for 31, S.T. Clarke 4 for 40) and 116 (N.H. Peters 4 for 36, S.T. Clarke 4 for 40)
Surrey 233 for 6 dec (M.A. Lynch 63, D.M. Ward 62 not out, T.A. Munton 5 for 50)

Surrey won by an innings and 44 runs
Surrey 22 pts, Warwickshire 2 pts

at Hastings

Sussex 71 (C. Penn 5 for 29, D.J. M. Kelleher 4 for 24) and 322 (P.W.G. Parker 117, M.P. Speight 50)
Kent 288 (C.J. Tavare 95, C.M. Wells 4 for 94) and 106 for 6 (M.R. Benson 54)

Kent won by 4 wickets
Kent 23 pts, Sussex 4 pts

at Worcester

Gloucestershire 332 for 4 dec (C.W.J. Athey 91 not out, A.J. Wright 69, P.W. Romaines 59) and 0 for 0 dec
Worcestershire 0 for 0 dec and 233 for 6 (M.J. Weston 65)

Match drawn
Gloucestershire 4 pts, Worcestershire 1 pt

at Leeds

Leicestershire 253 (P. Willey 104, P. Carrick 5 for 46) and 0 for 0 dec
Yorkshire 0 for 0 dec and 256 for 6 (J.D. Love 68, R.J. Blakey 51, G.J.F. Ferris 4 for 74)

Yorkshire won by 4 wickets
Yorkshire 19 pts, Leicestershire 2 pts

Rain again ravaged first-class cricket. Collusions and forfeitures could bring no results at Taunton, Worcester or Derby, where Ole Mortensen produced another fine spell of bowling to rout Middlesex. At Northampton, Wasim Akram displayed his best bowling form to put Lancashire on top, but rain was again the only winner. Peter Willey completed a typically defiant hundred for Leicestershire against Yorkshire when all about him were falling, but the home side benefited from the last-day manipulations and reached their target of 254 in 68 overs with nine balls and four wickets to spare. They owed much to Jim Love, recalled to the side after being omitted for three matches due to loss of form, who hit a commanding 68 and shared a stand of 81 in 15 overs with Neil Hartley for the sixth wicket.

Nick Peters. Ten wickets in a match for the first time, Surrey v. Warwickshire, 2 July. (Tom Morris)

Humpage is caught by Richards off Peters for 1 as Surrey bowl Warwickshire out for 74, 2 July. Lynch and Ian Greig are at slip. (Tom Morris)

Surrey, in need of a championship win, destroyed a limp Warwickshire side at The Oval. Clarke and Peters, who took a career-best 6 for 31, bowled unchanged and shot out the visitors just after lunch on the opening day. Surrey lost no time in taking the lead, and Lynch's 63 off 74 balls and some fine hitting by Ward and Richards on the last morning compensated for the total loss of the second day. Clarke and Peters then went into action again, and Warwickshire subsided without a fight. Peters took 10 wickets in a match for the first time.

The only other side to force a win was, inevitably, Kent, who moved 37 points clear at the top of the table over Worcestershire, who had a game in hand. Kent had claimed six points by Saturday evening. Chris Penn, ably supported by Ellison and the impressive Kelleher, bowled wonderfully well and Sussex batted woefully weakly to be all out shortly after lunch. Kent showed that the wicket held no terrors, and Chris Tavare steered them to an emphatic lead before he was run out for 95, a sacrifice for quick runs after play was not able to start until 2.00 p.m. on the Monday. Paul Parker batted with elegant defiance to hold Kent at bay on the last day, and he completed the 34th century of his career, which has only one Test appearance to show for 13 years of charm and endeavour. There was an encouraging maiden fifty from Speight, but again Kent bowled accurately and caught thrillingly and Sussex were bowled out just before tea. This left Kent 35 overs in which to make 106, a modest target, but Sussex fielded tigerishly, Clarke, in particular, bowled his leg-breaks well, and the championship leaders showed signs of frailty under pressure. Benson calmed the nerves, but it was left to Penn to flick the only ball he received to the fine leg boundary to win the match with five balls to spare.

Sadly, the 144th Varsity match was abandoned without a ball being bowled.

Refuge Assurance League

3 July

at Repton School

Derbyshire 130 (S.C. Goldsmith 61)
Middlesex 32 for 0

Match abandoned
Derbyshire 2 pts, Middlesex 2 pts

at Canterbury

Kent v. Nottinghamshire

Match abandoned
Kent 2 pts, Nottinghamshire 2 pts

at Tring

Northamptonshire v. Lancashire

Match abandoned
Northamptonshire 2 pts, Lanchashire 2 pts

at Taunton

Somerset v. Essex

Match abandoned
Somerset 2 pts, Essex 2 pts

at The Oval

Surrey v. Warwickshire

Match abandoned
Surrey 2 pts, Warwickshire 2 pts

at Hereford

Worcestershire v. Gloucestershire

Match abandoned
Worcestershire 2 pts, Gloucestershire 2 pts

at Hull

Leicestershire 172 for 3 (L. Potter 66 not out)
Yorkshire 173 for 4 (K. Sharp 56)

Yorkshire (4 pts) won by 6 wickets

In the only match which survived the rain, Sharp and Robinson added 80 for Yorkshire's second wicket and provided the basis of their side's victory over bottom-of-the-table Leicestershire.

NatWest Bank Trophy

Round Two

6 July

at Canterbury

Warwickshire 144
Kent 148 for 3 (R.F. Pienaar 58 not out)

Kent won by 7 wickets
(Man of the Match: R.F. Pienaar)

ABOVE: *NatWest Bank Trophy second round at Canterbury, Thorne is stumped by Marsh off Graham Cowdrey for 20. (Tom Morris)*

RIGHT: *John O'Brien, Cheshire hero. A hat-trick against Derbyshire. (David Munden)*

6 and 7 July

at Chelmsford

Essex 141 (G.A. Gooch 71)
Surrey 142 for 7

Surrey won by 3 wickets
(Man of the Match: G. A. Gooch)

at Cardiff

Glamorgan 246 for 5 (A.R. Butcher 80)
Lancashire 215 (J. Derrick 4 for 57)

Glamorgan won by 31 runs
(Man of the Match: A.R. Butcher)

at Southampton

Somerset 227 for 7 (R.J. Bartlett 85)
Hampshire 229 for 5 (C.L. Smith 99 not out)

Hampshire won by 5 wickets
(Man of the Match: C.L. Smith)

at Leicester

Gloucestershire 273 for 5 (P. Bainbridge 89, C.W.J. Athey 62, K.M. Curran 58 not out)
Leicestershire 200 (C.C. Lewis 53)

Gloucestershire won by 73 runs
(Man of the Match: K.M. Curran)

at Trent Bridge

Worcestershire 283 for 5 (T.S. Curtis 120, G.A. Hick 105)
Nottinghamshire 74 for 3

Worcestershire won on faster scoring rate
(Man of the Match: T.S. Curtis)

6, 7 and 8 July

at Leeds

Middlesex 225 for 7 (M.W. Gatting 74, C. Shaw 4 for 29)

Yorkshire 188 (J.D. Love 67, A.R.C. Fraser 4 for 34)

Middlesex won by 37 runs
(Man of the Match: M.W. Gatting)

6 and 8 July

at Boughton Hall, Chester

Derbyshire 190 (B. Roberts 57, A. Fox 4 for 24, J.F.M. O'Brien 4 for 40)
Cheshire 103 (O.H. Mortensen 5 for 15)

Derbyshire won by 87 runs
(Man of the Match: O.H. Mortensen)

The unrelenting rain took all matches bar the one at Canterbury into a second day. Kent brushed aside Warwickshire with contemptuous ease. Chris Cowdrey won the toss and asked the visitors to bat. Kent had immediate success when Penn trapped Moles lbw without a run on the board, and when Storie fell to Ellison at 11 Warwickshire were in deep trouble and never effectively recovered. There was an early shock for Kent when Benson was bowled by Merrick for one, but Taylor was durable and Pienaar followed his economic 1 for 25 with a fluent fifty which won him the individual award and Kent the match.

Essex had a disastrous match against Surrey. At 30, Brian Hardie had his left arm broken by a ball from Sylvester Clarke and two balls later Prichard had his stumps wrecked by the same bowler. Border tried to break the shackles and hit Peters over cover, but Lynch plucked the ball out of the air. Pringle was hit on the hand and then caught at the wicket, and Lilley and Fletcher were both lbw. Miller was caught behind off Greig, and Essex were 77 for 6, and Hardie out of cricket for four weeks. Foster and Gooch added 28, but the return of Clarke accounted for Foster. East swotted effectively, but Gooch's fine innings came to an end when he was very well caught by Greig at mid-on off Bullen. The innings ended when East skied a return catch to Clarke. Surrey lost Clinton before the close, but they should never have been in any doubt about their success although they did contrive to make very hard work of it on the second day.

A third-wicket stand of 111 between Athey and Bainbridge put Gloucestershire in a very strong position at Leicester, and the home side were never in touch when they went in search of 274 and were bowled out in 47.2 overs. Curran had a good all-round match, taking 3 for 31 and hitting 58 not out in 49 minutes.

There was little play on the Wednesday at Trent Bridge and none at all on the Friday when the game was called off, but Worcestershire had looked sure winners from the moment that Hick and Curtis came together and added 186 in 36 overs. It was a partnership that was punctuated by rain, but not even the weather could diminish the quality of the batting, which was of the highest order.

Chris Smith took Hampshire to victory over Somerset with an over to spare and always had control of affairs at Southampton although, having pulled a hamstring, he had the help of a runner for much of his innings. The runner was Paul Terry, and his eagerness to play a part in events caused an altercation, for the opposing captain, Peter Roebuck, suggested that he was jumping the gun, beginning his run before a shot had been made. Robin Smith ran and hit furiously, and although two wickets fell at 180 and 117 were needed from the last 20 overs, Hampshire won with comparative ease after Steve Jefferies had hit 31 off 23 balls.

Lancashire won the toss and asked Glamorgan to bat first at Cardiff, but, in spite of the quick capture of Hopkins' wicket, it was a decision they must have regretted. Alan Butcher and Hugh Morris put on 108 in 36 overs, and this was followed by some good running and clean hitting by the remaining batsmen. Holmes and Shastri hit 55 in nine overs. Lancashire lost Mendis before the end of the first day, and they never looked like approaching the Glamorgan score on the second, their innings being boosted towards the close by Allott and Hayhurst. John Derrick produced a fine spell of bowling and was awarded his county cap.

Gatting and Downton added 119 in 31 overs to provide the substance of Middlesex's innings at Headingley. The Yorkshire reply was spread over two days, and they ended the first of them on 59 for 4 from 25 overs, a seemingly lost position. On the Friday, Love and Bairstow took their fifth-wicket partnership to 94 from 27 overs, but when Love was out 76 were needed from 10 overs, and the batting subsided against Fraser, who was continuing to thrive in all forms of cricket. Sadly for Middlesex, they lost Neil Williams with injury.

On Wednesday evening, Cheshire stood at 78 for 3 from 34.5 overs, and, having bowled out Derbyshire for 190, looked to have a great chance of victory. Mudassar had bowled Barnett with the fifth ball of his first over. Bowler and Roberts had added 109. Morris helped take the score on to 171, and then left-arm spinner John O'Brien caught and bowled Morris, had Goldsmith caught behind by Neil Smith and had Malcolm taken in the deep to perform the first hat trick by a Minor Counties player in the history of the 60-over competition. After a soggy Thursday without play, the game restarted at 4.30 p.m. on the Friday, and

Derbyshire found their own bowling hero in Ole Mortensen, the great Dane, who took four more wickets to add to that of Varey, whom he had caught and bowled on the first day, and ended the game by catching Blackburn on the boundary. It took Derbyshire only 57 minutes to complete their victory, but the delay cost them much in their preparations for the Benson and Hedges Cup Final.

Benson and Hedges Cup Final
HAMPSHIRE v. DERBYSHIRE

The rain relented for the season's great mid-term highlight, the Benson and Hedges Cup Final. The occasion had an added lustre in that Hampshire had never before appeared in a Lord's final, but one was sorry that Marshall and Greenidge, who had done so much for the county, and Tim Tremlett, through injury, were not to be part of the celebrations. There was a worry for Hampshire in that Chris Smith had been injured in the NatWest Bank Trophy tie with Somerset, but he declared himself fit on the morning of the match. Derbyshire did not arrive in London until late on the Friday evening because of their delayed cup tie at Chester.

Mark Nicholas won the toss and asked Derbyshire to bat first, for the heavy cloud and early moisture were likely to give help to the seam bowlers. So it proved, and, in effect, the game was decided within the first hour of play.

The Derbyshire openers received a rapturous welcome, and there were ecstasies when both Barnett and Bowler hit

Gold Award winner Steve Jefferies, who virtually decided the match in the first hour. (Adrian Murrell/Allsport)

boundaries, but the joy was short lived. The last ball of the sixth over, Jefferies' third from the Pavilion End, proved a devastating blow for Derbyshire as Barnett was bowled off his pads. He is so large a part of the Derbyshire batting that his departure sends a shiver of uncertainty through the side.

For the first ball of Jefferies' next over, Nicholas moved himself to short-leg, and Bowler obligingly steered a catch into his hands. Roberts gave a re-run of the shot four balls later. Nor was Jefferies done yet, for with the first ball of his next over he trapped Goldsmith lbw with an in swinger. The South African left-arm medium-pacer was enjoying himself immensely; Derbyshire were not. In the first hour of play they lost their first four wickets for 37 runs in 13 overs.

Morris and Maher had begun to effect some sort of a recovery when, in the 27th over, Maher played a grotesque cross-batted shot to Ayling and was bowled. Hopes now rested with Holding. He hit a four and roused Derbyshire spirits, but Nigel Cowley had replaced Jefferies and begun a beautiful spell of limited-over bowling, maintaining a nagging line and length on the leg stump. Holding attempted to hit him over the Pavilion, but the ball soared high into the air and there, standing in front of the Pavilion steps, was David Turner with one of the safest pair of hands English cricket has known. The ball seemed long in the air, but Turner's eyes never left it. His hands were sure, and Derbyshire were 80 for 6. With lunch looming, Holding's shot had a touch of lunacy about it. So did Morris' running in the 37th over. He had batted with purpose, and Derbyshire needed runs rather than quick runs, particularly as Cowley's marvellous spell was nearly at an end, but Morris turned the ball square on the leg side and attempted an insane second run. Cowley's throw to Parks was straight and true.

Newman and Warner provided temporary respite from the clatter of wickets, but Jefferies returned to complete his memorable day with his fifth wicket. Connor had not been at his best early on, and now he bowled three wides in succession to Newman, but a word of encouragement from Nicholas seemed to settle him and his plague of wides was ended with the wickets of Newman and Malcolm off consecutive deliveries.

Hampshire had conceded 12 wides and three no-balls, failed to hold four catches in the slip area, none of them difficult, and had still bowled Derbyshire out for the lowest score in a Benson and Hedges Final, or, indeed, in any Lord's final.

Malcolm looked briefly brisk from the Pavilion End and had Terry taken at second slip in the fourth over, but he seemed to lose heart and direction. Holding was well below par, and Mortensen provided the only consistent fire, his unquenchable enthusiasm, as always, lusting after a wicket every delivery. He did have Chris Smith caught behind in the 17th over, but Hampshire were already on their way to victory by then.

Robin Smith came in to play the innings of the day, and one which was to prove very important to him. The crowd, starved of quality batting, warmed to him, and seven times he crashed the ball to the boundary as he hit 38 off 27 balls. He fell to quite the most remarkable catch one has

TOP: *Roberts is caught at short-leg, one of two catches in an over for Mark Nicholas. (Adrian Murrell/Allsport)*
ABOVE: *John Morris, a belated sign of sense and aggression for Derbyshire. (Adrian Murrell/Allsport)*
BELOW: *Nigel Cowley is congratulated by his team mates after running out Morris. Cowley's economic spell of off-break bowling was decisive in the destruction of the Derbyshire batting. (Adrian Murrell/Allsport)*

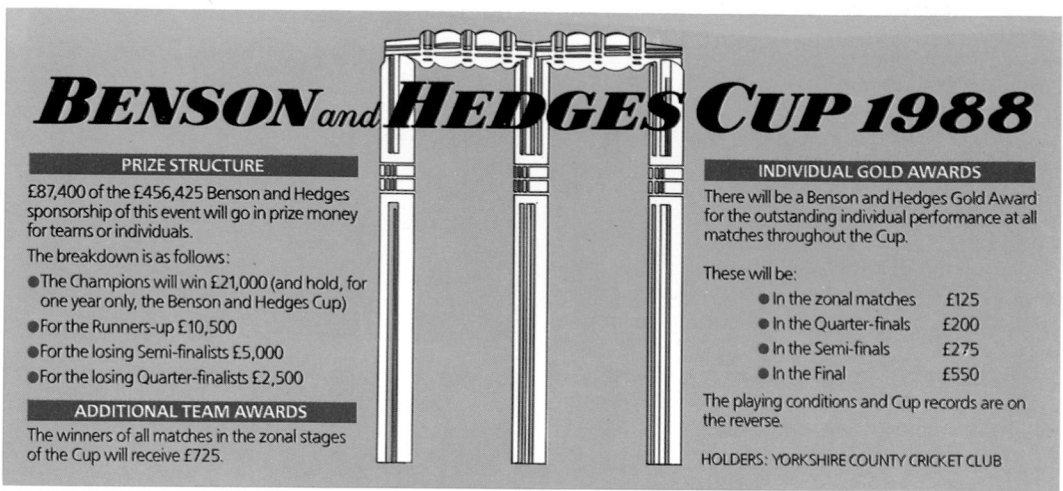

BENSON and HEDGES CUP 1988

PRIZE STRUCTURE

£87,400 of the £456,425 Benson and Hedges sponsorship of this event will go in prize money for teams or individuals.

The breakdown is as follows:

- The Champions will win £21,000 (and hold, for one year only, the Benson and Hedges Cup)
- For the Runners-up £10,500
- For the losing Semi-finalists £5,000
- For the losing Quarter-finalists £2,500

ADDITIONAL TEAM AWARDS

The winners of all matches in the zonal stages of the Cup will receive £725.

INDIVIDUAL GOLD AWARDS

There will be a Benson and Hedges Gold Award for the outstanding individual performance at all matches throughout the Cup.

These will be:

In the zonal matches	£125
In the Quarter-finals	£200
In the Semi-finals	£275
In the Final	£550

The playing conditions and Cup records are on the reverse.

HOLDERS: YORKSHIRE COUNTY CRICKET CLUB

MARYLEBONE CRICKET CLUB

20p

FINAL

DERBYSHIRE v. HAMPSHIRE

at Lord's Ground, Saturday, July 9th 1988

Any alterations to teams will be announced over the public address system

20p

DERBYSHIRE

†1 K. J. Barnett	b Jefferies		13
2 P. D. Bowler	c Nicholas b Jefferies		4
3 B. Roberts	c Nicholas b Jefferies		0
4 J. E. Morris	run out		42
5 S. C. Goldsmith	l b w b Jefferies		0
*6 B. J. M. Maher	b Ayling		8
7 M. A. Holding	c Turner b Cowley		7
8 P. G. Newman	b Connor		10
9 A. E. Warner	b Jefferies		4
10 O. H. Mortensen	not out		0
11 D. E. Malcolm	b Connor		0
	B , l-b 14, w 12, n-b 3,		29
	Total...		117

FALL OF THE WICKETS
1...27 2...28 3...29 4...32 5...71 6...80 7...101 8...114 9...117 10...117

Bowling Analysis	O.	M.	R.	W.	Wd.	N-b
Connor	7.3	1	27	2	7	...
Jefferies	10	3	3	5	1	3
Andrew	9	0	0	0	4	...
Ayling	9	2		1	...	...
Cowley	11			1	...	...
	...	...		...	...	...
	...	...		...	...	...

HAMPSHIRE

1 V. P. Terry	c Roberts b Malcolm		2
2 C. L. Smith	c Maher b Mortensen		20
†3 M. C. J. Nicholas	not out		35
4 R. A. Smith	c Goldsmith b Warner		38
5 D. R. Turner	not out		7
6 J. R. Ayling			
7 S. T. Jefferies			
*8 R. J. Parks			
9 N. G. Cowley			
10 C. A. Connor			
11 S. J. W. Andrew			
	B , l-b 8, w 3, n-b 5,		16
	Total...		118

FALL OF THE WICKETS
1...10 2...44 3...90 4... 5... 6... 7... 8... 9... 10...

Bowling Analysis	O.	M.	R.	W.	Wd.	N-b
Holding	11	2	36	0	1	2
Malcolm	7	2	25	1	1	...
Newman	3	1	11	0	...	...
Mortensen	5	1	19	1	1	...
Warner	5.5	0	19	1	...	3
	...	...	...	...	...	...
	...	...	...	...	...	...

† Captain   * Wicket-keeper
Umpires—D. J. Constant & N. T. Plews
Scorers—V. H. Isaacs, S. W. Tacey & E. Solomon

Toss won by—Hampshire who elected to field
RESULT—Hampshire won by 7 wickets

The playing conditions for the Benson & Hedges Cup Competition are printed on the back of this score card.

Total runs scored at end of each over :—

Derbyshire	1	2	3	4	5	6	7	8	9	10	11	12	13	14	15	16	17	18	19	20
	21	22	23	24	25	26	27	28	29	30	31	32	33	34	35	36	37	38	39	40
	41	42	43	44	45	46	47	48	49	50	51	52	53	54	55					

Hampshire	1	2	3	4	5	6	7	8	9	10	11	12	13	14	15	16	17	18	19	20
	21	22	23	24	25	26	27	28	29	30	31	32	33	34	35	36	37	38	39	40
	41	42	43	44	45	46	47	48	49	50	51	52	53	54	55					

Reproduced by kind permission of MCC

Mark Nicholas and his side enjoy their first success in a Lord's final. (Adrian Murrell/Allsport)

seen at Lord's, and certainly the best thing in Derbyshire's day. Smith mis-hooked, the ball flying fast and high over Maher's head. Goldsmith was fielding at fine leg, and he raced some 50 yards to dive and hold the ball as he fell just inside the boundary rope. Percy Chapman in his youth could not have done better.

It had come too late to alter the course of the game, and it was right that David Turner, long and faithful servant and very fine cricketer, should be at the wicket when the game was won. Nicholas had been confident and composed in all that he did, and he, with Turner, steered Hampshire quietly and effectively to the brink of a crushing victory. It came when Warner bowled a no-ball which just about summed up Derbyshire's day.

---

9 and 10 July

at Trowbridge

West Indians 358 for 5 dec (C.L. Hooper 140 not out, A.L. Logie 100)
Minor Counties 18 for 1

Match abandoned

Refuge Assurance League

10 July

at Chelmsford

Essex 204 (A.R. Border 73)
Glamorgan 206 for 4 (R.J. Shastri 60 not out, J.A. Hopkins 50)

Glamorgan (4 pts) won by 6 wickets

at Southampton

Hampshire 157 for 5 (R.A. Smith 57)
Gloucestershire 106 for 2

Gloucestershire (4 pts) won on faster scoring rate

at Canterbury

Kent 187 for 5 (C.S. Cowdrey 61 not out)
Middlesex 191 for 8 (R.F. Pienaar 4 for 34)

Middlesex (4 pts) won by 2 wickets

at Old Trafford

Somerset 190 for 7 (R.J. Bartlett 55)
Lancashire 184 for 8 (N.H. Fairbrother 51 not out)

Somerset (4 pts) won by 6 runs

at Northampton

Northamptonshire v. Yorkshire

Match abandoned
Northamptonshire 2 pts, Yorkshire 2 pts

at Trent Bridge

Nottinghamshire v. Leicestershire

Match abandoned
Nottinghamshire 2 pts, Leicestershire 2 pts

at The Oval

Worcestershire 205 for 9 (T.S. Curtis 97)
Surrey 166

Worcestershire (4 pts) won by 39 runs

at Hove

Sussex 157 for 5 (P.W.G. Parker 52, Imran Khan 50)
Warwickshire 149 for 7

Sussex (4 pts) won by 8 runs

An astounding win by Middlesex at Canterbury took them four points clear at the top of the Refuge Assurance League. Chasing a target of 188, Middlesex looked well beaten at 141 for 8 in the 36th over, but Simon Hughes and Angus Fraser hit 50 in four overs to win the match, Fraser finishing with 30. Meanwhile Lancashire were beaten at home for the first time in six matches, Surrey again slipped when Tim Curtis hit his fifth Sunday league fifty of the season to maintain Worcestershire's challenge to hold on to their title, and Gloucestershire spoiled Hampshire's triumphant return to Southampton. The day began badly for Hampshire when Mark Nicholas collided with Gloucestershire wicket-keeper Jack Russell and broke his nose.

13, 14 and 15 July

at Southend

Derbyshire 336 (K.J. Barnett 99, J.G. Wright 82, J.E. Morris 56, N.A. Foster 6 for 96) and 136
Essex 300 for 5 dec (A.R. Border 85 not out, G.A. Gooch 53) and 175 for 1 (J.P. Stephenson 78 not out, P.J. Prichard 65 not out)

Essex won by 9 wickets
Essex 22 pts, Derbyshire 5 pts

at Bristol

Northamptonshire 349 for 5 (W. Larkins 134, A.J. Lamb 117) and 0 for 0 dec
Gloucestershire 0 for 0 dec and 348 (C.W.J. Athey 168 not out, P.W. Romaines 55, P. Bainbridge 55, W.W. Davis 6 for 92)

Northamptonshire won by 1 run
Northamptonshire 20 pts, Gloucestershire 2 pts

Kevin Cooper. A formidable partnership with Stephenson for Nottinghamshire. (Adrian Murrell/Allsport)

at Old Trafford

Lancashire 304 for 8 dec (M. Watkinson 85 not out, G. Fowler 75, P.M. Such 4 for 81) and 119 for 2 dec (G.D. Mendis 51)
Leicestershire 173 for 6 dec (D.I. Gower 96) and 133 for 9 (I. Folley 4 for 41)

Match drawn
Lancashire 5 pts, Leicestershire 4 pts

at Trent Bridge

Nottinghamshire 173 (D.W. Randall 50, A.R.C. Fraser 5 for 43)
Middlesex 133 (F.D. Stephenson 6 for 45, K.E. Cooper 4 for 34)

Nottinghamshire won by 40 runs
Nottinghamshire 12 pts, Middlesex 0 pts

at Guildford

Surrey 301 for 2 dec (D.M. Smith 157 not out, A.J. Stewart 72) and 122 for 3 dec
Hampshire 125 for 4 dec (M.C.J. Nicholas 57 not out) and 299 for 2 (V.P. Terry 126 not out, M.C.J. Nicholas 97)

Hampshire won by 8 wickets
Hampshire 16 pts, Surrey 5 pts

at Edgbaston

Worcestershire 130 (T.A. Munton 6 for 21) and 14 for 0
Warwickshire 250 for 9 dec (M.J. Weston 4 for 24)

Match drawn
Warwickshire 7 pts, Worcestershire 4 pts

at Swansea

West Indians 302 for 3 dec (P.J.L. Dujon 141) and 67 for 1
Glamorgan 180 for 5 dec (J.A. Hopkins 87)

Match drawn

The July monsoons continued unabated in most areas. The game at Trent Bridge was reduced to a one-innings affair, and Middlesex, their early season championship form a distant memory fared badly against Cooper and Stephenson on their own track. Tim Munton returned the best bowling figures of his career, confirming his great advance throughout the season and blunting Worcestershire's championship hopes, in the match at Edgbaston, where there was no play on the second day.

There was no play on the opening day in the tourists' match at Swansea, where Dujon displayed his power and elegance and John Hopkins his grit and determination, nor at Bristol. The game at Bristol developed into a most exhilarating encounter. On the second day, when play began, Wayne Larkins hit his first century of the season, and he and Allan Lamb added 105 for the third wicket. Lamb reached his hundred off 86 balls, the fastest of the season, and Geoff Cook, who had partnered Larkins in an opening stand of 106, declared early on the last day. Both sides forfeited an innings so that Gloucestershire were left most of the final day in which to score 350 at just over 3½ an over. Winston Davis accounted for Stovold and Wright for 19, but Romaines and Athey took the score to 114 before Romaines became Davis' third victim. Bainbridge, a county player of the best quality, helped Athey continue the assault in a stand of 100. Nick Cook ended the partnership when he bowled Bainbridge, and Davis quickly accounted for Curran and Lloyds. Nick Cook then lured Russell into being stumped, and Gloucestershire had lost four wickets for 27 runs and with them, it seemed, the match. But Athey remained, and Graveney played a captain's role in a stand of 50. Lawrence stayed until 24 were needed, and when Nick Cook began the last over 15 runs were wanted for a Gloucestershire victory. Athey drove the first ball for four, the next for two and hit the fourth low over mid-wicket for six. The fifth ball was driven to long-off for an easy single or a risky two. The batsmen gambled on the second of these alternatives and Alderman was run out by Walker's throw giving Northants victory by one run.

There was not quite such a sensational finish at Old Trafford. Watkinson revitalized the Lancashire first innings, 144 runs coming in the final session of the first day. David Gower graced what little play was possible on the second, and Leicestershire were asked to make 251 on a wicket which encouraged spin. Jack Simmons made early inroads and Ian Folley took four wickets in 12 balls to move Lancashire close to victory. Whitticase and Agnew resisted until six overs remained, and Whitticase's brave 27 spanned as many overs. He was out to the fourth ball of the last over, but Such survived the remaining two.

Hampshire were somewhat fortunate winners at Guildford in that they were totally outplayed for the first two days. In 46 overs on the first day, Surrey hit 181 for 1, Smith 101. Greig declared at lunch on the second day, Surrey's 301 having come from 77 overs. Hampshire lost four wickets before the rain returned. More brisk hitting on the last morning led to another Surrey declaration, but Greig appeared to be over-generous, and Hampshire, hitherto not in the game, strolled to victory with 5.1 overs to spare. Paul Terry played his first significant innings of the season, Nicholas again batted well, and an inexperienced Surrey attack showed that it badly missed Sylvester Clarke.

Derbyshire began soundly at Southend. John Wright, on one of his all too rare appearances, played an innings of delight and after another brief flourish from Morris, Kim Barnett batted with power and authority to reach 99 before being caught behind. Derbyshire batted on until the second morning, and Foster confirmed that he was ready for an England recall with six wickets. In contrast to Derbyshire's batting, Essex romped to 300 at nearly four an over. Gooch and Border were in powerful mood, but Nasser Hussain took the eye with an impressive 47 before running himself out. Derbyshire were soon in trouble, closing at 55 for 3, and they continued to bat quite dreadfully on the last day so that Stephenson and Prichard, two young Essex batsmen, were able to demonstrate the art of elegant and forceful play in a second-wicket partnership of 135 that took Essex to victory and, surprisingly, to second place in the championship.

16, 17 and 18 July

at Derby

Derbyshire 308 for 6 dec (J.E. Morris 79, K.J. Barnett 73, P.D. Bowler 61) and 0 for 0 dec
Northamptonshire 0 for 0 dec and 164 (O.H. Mortensen 5 for 28)

Derbyshire won by 144 runs
Derbyshire 20 pts, Northamptonshire 2 pts

at Leicester

West Indians 370 (C.G. Greenidge 75, C.L. Hooper 62, P.J.L. Dujon 51)
Leicestershire 90 (W.K.M. Benjamin 4 for 20, B.P. Patterson 4 for 44) and 103 for 6

Match drawn

16, 18 and 19 July

at Southend

Essex 346 for 7 dec (G.A. Gooch 96, N. Hussain 80 not out, G. Miller 77, J.P. Stephenson 55, J. Simmons 4 for 83) and 169 for 9 dec (J.P. Stephenson 84 not out, P.J.W. Allott 6 for 59)
Lancashire 227 (G. Fowler 104, T.E. Jesty 73, J.H. Childs 4 for 63) and 289 for 6 (N.H. Fairbrother 111, M. Watkinson 70)

Lancashire won by 4 wickets
Lancashire 20 pts, Essex 7 pts

at Bristol

Gloucestershire 168 (C.W.J. Athey 56, N.A. Mallender 4 for 47) and 119 (V.J. Marks 4 for 25)
Somerset 195 (T.M. Alderman 4 for 75) and 93 for 2 (J.J.E. Hardy 52 not out)

Somerset won by 8 wickets
Somerset 21 pts, Gloucestershire 5 pts

at Lord's

Middlesex 420 for 3 dec (M.W. Gatting 180, W.N. Slack 163 not out) and 191 for 1 dec (W.N. Slack 105 not out)
Glamorgan 298 for 4 dec (H. Morris 87, A.R. Butcher 83, M.P.

Maynard 71) and 265 for 8 (M.P. Maynard 64, G.C. Holmes 50, A. Needham 5 for 125)

Match drawn
Middlesex 5 pts, Glamorgan 4 pts

at Trent Bridge

Worcestershire 159 (N.V. Radford 65, R.K. Illingworth 58, F.D. Stephenson 5 for 52, K.E. Cooper 4 for 40) and 199 (G.A. Hick 76)
Nottinghamshire 135 (G.R. Dilley 5 for 46, N.V. Radford 5 for 67) and 226 for 4 (R.T. Robinson 107 not out)

Nottinghamshire won by 6 wickets
Nottinghamshire 20 pts, Worcestershire 5 pts

at Guildford

Kent 324 for 9 dec (R.F. Pienaar 88, T.R. Ward 72, K.T. Medlycott 4 for 80) and 288 for 8 dec (N.R. Taylor 114, M.R. Benson 66, K.T. Medlycott 6 for 112)
Surrey 303 for 7 dec (D.M. Ward 70 not out, A.J. Stewart 56) and 168 for 7 (G.S. Clinton 71 not out, C. Penn 4 for 41)

Match drawn
Surrey 8 pts, Kent 7 pts

at Edgbaston

Hampshire 122 (T.A. Merrick 6 for 40) and 157 (T.A. Merrick 4 for 29)
Warwickshire 300 for 3 dec (T.A. Lloyd 160 not out, A.J. Moles 60)

Warwickshire won by an innings and 21 runs
Warwickshire 24 pts, Hampshire 1 pt

Guildford's Golden Jubilee of county cricket was at last rewarded with a day of sunshine on the second day of the Surrey–Kent match. Drizzle had interrupted the first day, but it had not prevented the championship leaders from claiming four batting points, mainly because Ward and Pienaar were willing to punish any loose bowling, and because Chris Penn hit fiercely towards the end of the innings. Surrey moved briskly to 303 for 7 in 77.3 overs on the Monday in spite of losing David Smith with an injured back. There was a bright knock from Alec Stewart, still seeking his best form, but it was David Ward, sound in defence, punishing in attack, who was the backbone of the innings. Benson and Taylor scored at a run a minute in the last hour of the second day, and they took their stand to 133 on the last morning. Taylor completed a fine hundred and, in all, batted for 224 minutes and hit 17 fours. Keith Medlycott bowled his left-arm spin effectively and finished with match figures of 10 for 192. Chris Cowdrey asked Surrey to make 310 off 53 overs, but wickets fell regularly and it was only the stability of Clinton and the courage of Smith who came in at number nine that saved the game.

Kent's failure to win mattered little for both Worcestershire and Essex were beaten. On the notorious Trent Bridge wicket, Worcestershire were 39 for 8 on the first day. A splendid revival was brought about by Illingworth and Radford, who added 113 in a positive manner. On the Monday, 20 wickets fell. Like Worcestershire, Notts were saved from humiliation by their ninth-wicket pair. Scott and Cooper added 76 after their side had been 47 for 8. Hick then played a brilliant innings of 76 from 111 balls, and Notts were left with the daunting task of scoring 244 on the final day on a wicket on which Stephenson, Cooper,

Radford and Dilley had so far taken 29 wickets for 400 runs, and a spinner did not bowl an over until more than 200 had been sent down by the seamers. The final day produced an amazing twist in fortune as Tim Robinson played with calm authority to take his side to an improbable victory. He was ably supported by Birch and Randall and Newell, but Robinson's 30th first-class century was the dominant feature of the match and earned his side a surprising victory which kept alive their championship hopes.

At Southend, Lancashire achieved an equal reversal of fortune. Gooch and Stephenson got Essex off to a brisk start with a 104-run partnership, but Simmons checked the home side, who were not aided when Border ran himself out first ball. Hussain and Miller halted the slide, at first slowly accumulating runs and then scoring more briskly. They added 149, and Hussain reached his highest first-class score. Lancashire reached 109 for the loss of Mendis on the Monday, but Childs caught and bowled Jesty on the stroke of lunch, and he, Foster and Miller brought about Lancashire's decline in the afternoon after Fowler had reached a solid century. Stephenson and Prichard apart, Essex stumbled in their effort to score brisk runs in their second innings. Allott bowled an admirable line and length, and Gooch's declaration left Lancashire to make 289 at approximately four an over. Three wickets fell at 32, but there was inadequate support for Childs. Fairbrother batted superbly, and Watkinson and Hughes gave all the aid that was needed to take Lancashire to an excellent victory and move them level with Worcestershire in third place.

Weather meant the forfeitures of innings at Derby where Mortensen, in top form, bowled the home county to victory on the last day and revived some of their sagging spirits after recent happenings.

Warwickshire also regained some lost joy by overwhelming Hampshire. Only 17 overs were possible on the Saturday, but Merrick bowled unchanged to turn Hampshire's 63 for 4 to 122 all out on the Monday. Skipper Andy Lloyd, missed several times in the slips, dominated an opening stand of 203 with Andy Moles and steered his side to 300 for 3 in 70 overs. Hampshire were soon in trouble again, but resolute batting by the Smith brothers delayed Warwickshire's victory until just before tea on the last day.

Wilf Slack hit a century in each innings at Lord's, and he and Gatting shared a third-wicket stand of 184 on the first day when runs came at four an over. Undeterred, Glamorgan batted spiritedly in reply, but, after Slack's second not out hundred, when in search of 314, they stumbled against a long spell of off-spin from Andy Needham. Revived by Maynard and Holmes, they were well worthy of a draw.

At Bristol, there were only 3.4 overs on the first day, during which Gloucestershire lost Wright and Stovold. Mallender and Jones continued to have the better of the batsmen on the Monday, and only Athey and Curran offered serious resistance. Alderman and Curran proved as difficult for Somerset to handle as Jones and Mallender had been for Gloucestershire, and the visitors ended the day two runs in arrears with two wickets standing. Somerset gained an unexpected bonus on the last morning, however, when Jones hit a sprightly career-best 38 to give his side an unexpected and invaluable 27-run lead. Gloucestershire collapsed for a second time although this time the main destroyers were Marks and Rose. Needing 93 on a deteriorating pitch, Somerset were taken to the brink of victory by Hardy and Roebuck, who put on 89 for the first wicket.

The West Indians decided not to take the last 20 overs at Leicester although it is likely that they would have claimed a win. They batted consistently, bowled aggressively and fielded well. Laurie Potter was unbeaten in both Leicestershire innings.

Tony Merrick, a highly successful opening bowler for Warwickshire. His season included a match-winning performance, 10 for 69 against Hampshire, 16–19 July. (Ken Kelly)

Refuge Assurance League

17 July

at Southend

Lancashire 170 for 9 (N.A. Foster 4 for 25)
Essex 171 for 4 (A.R. Border 72 not out)

Essex (4 pts) won by 6 wickets

at Bristol

Somerset 184 for 9
Gloucestershire 188 for 3 (P. Bainbridge 73 not out)

Gloucestershire (4 pts) won by 7 wickets

at Lord's

Middlesex *v.* **Glamorgan**

Match abandoned
Middlesex 2 pts, Glamorgan 2 pts

at Trent Bridge

Nottinghamshire 125 for 8
Yorkshire 126 for 3

Yorkshire (4 pts) won by 7 wickets

at The Oval

Kent 183 for 9 (R.F. Pienaar 84, I.A. Greig 5 for 30)
Surrey 187 for 5 (M.A. Lynch 67 not out)

Surrey (4 pts) won by 5 wickets

at Edgbaston

Warwickshire 207 for 6 (G.W. Humpage 56)
Hampshire 96

Warwickshire (4 pts) won by 111 runs

With Middlesex's game abandoned, Surrey gained a necessary victory in order to keep in touch at the top of the Refuge Assurance League. Ian Greig had a fine all-round match. He snatched two early Kent wickets and returned to capture three more after Pienaar had rallied Kent. Then he came in to hit a brisk 30 and help Monte Lynch to take Surrey to victory with seven balls to spare. Gloucestershire maintained their challenge with a comfortable win over Somerset; Bainbridge and Curran were in excellent form. Yorkshire drew level with Lancashire, who were well beaten at Southend.

17, 18 and 19 July

at Dublin

Ireland 307 for 6 dec (S. Warke 83, M.F. Cohen 75, A. Lewis 53 not out) and 223 for 7 dec (A. Lewis 54, D. Vincent 52 not out)
Wales 259 (D.A. Francis 85, A. Puddie 59, A. Nelson 4 for 68, H. Milling 4 for 71) and 233 for 9 (D.A. Francis 69, C. Elward 67, G. Harrison 4 for 72)

Match drawn

20, 21 and 22 July

at Cardiff

Glamorgan 246 (G.C. Holmes 79, R.J. Shastri 52) and 278 for 4 dec (A.R. Butcher 93, M.P. Maynard 72 not out, H. Morris 51)
Warwickshire 255 (M. Asif Din 65, S.L. Watkin 4 for 66) and 32 for 1

Match drawn
Warwickshire 7 pts, Glamorgan 5 pts

at Portsmouth

Hampshire 201 (M.C.J. Nicholas 66, J.K. Lever 4 for 61, T.D. Topley 4 for 88) and 214 for 1 dec (C.L. Smith 103 not out, M.C.J. Nicholas 102 not out)
Essex 203 for 7 dec (A.R. Border 55, P.J. Bakker 5 for 54) and 117 for 3 (A.W. Lilley 53 not out)

Match drawn
Essex 6 pts, Hampshire 5 pts

at Southport

Surrey 253 (P.D. Atkins 99, A.J. Stewart 73, Wasim Akram 5 for 58) and 158 for 7 dec

Kim Barnett, a career-best 239 not out for Derbyshire at Leicester, 17 July. (David Munden)

Lancashire 140 (Wasim Akram 58, I.A. Greig 4 for 26) and 271 for 9 (Wasim Akram 98, N.H. Fairbrother 64)

Match drawn
Lancashire 12 pts, Surrey 7 pts

at Leicester

Derbyshire 429 for 6 dec (K.J. Barnett 239 not out) and 125 for 5 dec
Leicestershire 254 for 3 dec (N.E. Briers 125 not out, T.J. Boon 70) and 183 for 8 (N.E. Briers 60)

Match drawn
Derbyshire 5 pts, Leicestershire 4 pts

at Northampton

Northamptonshire 329 (D.J. Wild 75, R.G. Williams 71, R.J. Bailey 63, C. Penn 5 for 82) and 226 for 3 dec (W. Larkins 112 not out, A. Fordham 52)
Kent 268 for 7 dec (R.F. Pienaar 74 not out, M.R. Benson 65, R.G. Williams 5 for 86) and 288 for 9 (T.R. Ward 59, N.G.B. Cook 5 for 105, R.G. Williams 4 for 113)

Kent won by 1 wicket
Kent 22 pts, Northamptonshire 7 pts

at Hove

Gloucestershire 276 (A.W. Stovold 63, R.C. Russell 50, A.J. Wright 50, R.A. Bunting 4 for 59) and 141 for 5 dec (A.W. Stovold 77)
Sussex 161 for 6 dec (A.P. Wells 69 not out, D.V. Lawrence 4 for 38) and 174 for 7 (A.P. Wells 54)

Match drawn
Sussex 5 pts, Gloucestershire 5 pts

Two wicket-keepers who had outstanding seasons: Philip Whitticase of Leicestershire (Steve Lindsell)

. . . and Chris Scott of Nottinghamshire, who was a more than adequate understudy for Bruce French. (Stuart D. Franklin/ASP)

at Worcester

Worcestershire 358 for 7 dec (G.A. Hick 198, P.J. Newport 77) and 215 for 4 dec (G.J. Lord 85, P. Bent 50)
Yorkshire 302 for 6 dec (P.E. Robinson 51) and 248 (M.D. Moxon 106, N.V. Radford 4 for 60, R.K. Illingworth 4 for 82)

Worcestershire won by 21 runs
Worcestershire 22 pts, Yorkshire 7 pts

20 and 21 July

at Oxton

League Cricket Conference 147 for 8 dec and 120 for 4
Sri Lankans 138 for 3 dec (M.A.R. Samarasekera 74)

Match abandoned

Again matches were severely hit by rain. The last afternoon was lost at Cardiff, where Warwickshire had been set a challenging target and where Watkin returned the best figures of a short career. At Portsmouth, Essex seized the initiative on the first day when Hampshire were bowled out cheaply by Lever and Topley. The Dutch pace bowler Bakker bowled finely to take five wickets and suggest that he should have a regular place in the side, and, to

compensate for the loss of so much play to rain, Fletcher declared with a two-run lead and fed Chris Smith and Mark Nicholas some generous bowling so that Hampshire could score runs quickly and declare. This they did, but just as Lilley had begun to strike the ball confidently for Essex, the rain returned.

With the press clamouring for his inclusion in the England side, some, bewilderingly, as captain, Kim Barnett chose his own way of reminding the selectors of his prowess by hitting the first double century of his career. As has become an inevitability with the Derbyshire captain, he batted on until the second day, and it is hard to understand why a cricketer who is such an entertaining and aggressive batsman is such a cautious captain. Briers reached an accomplished century and declared Leicestershire's innings closed when they still trailed Derbyshire by 175 runs. The visitors then scored briskly and set Leicestershire the task of making 301 in 64 overs. This was a stiff task and never looked likely to be attained, and the match ended with Leicestershire resisting in the gloom.

There was a similar tale at Hove, where Sussex were left to make 257 off 59 overs. Lenham and Falkner began well enough, and Alan Wells batted resolutely, but Sussex lost their way and must have been quite gratified that bad light and rain aided them to a draw.

Southport's one county match of the season (this lovely club was a victim of the four-day venture) provided a spectacular finish and an absorbing match in which Wasim Akram was the outstanding performer. Paul Atkins, in his first championship match, was lbw to Watkinson for 99. He and Alec Stewart put on 152 for the second wicket, and Surrey were 213 before their third wicket fell. At 222, Wasim Akram took the first hat trick of his career when he had Greig lbw and then wrecked the stumps of both Medlycott and Feltham. In all, Wasim had a spell of 5 for 15 in 10 overs, and Surrey lost their last eight wickets for 40 runs. Surrey's lead began to look massive on the second day when Lancashire collapsed to 59 for 6, but Wasim hit a lively fifty, the follow-on was saved and Surrey's first-innings lead was restricted to 113. Alec Stewart, deputizing behind the stumps for Jack Richards, took six catches. On the last day, some enterprising hitting by Surrey allowed Greig to declare and ask Lancashire to make 272 in 70 overs. At 129 for 5, Lancashire appeared to have no hope of victory, but Wasim Akram played a remarkable innings, hitting 98 off 78 balls. He hit 9 fours and was caught on the boundary in the last over while attempting to hit his fifth six. Simmons hit a four, and he received two balls with the scores level, but the veteran off-spinner could connect with neither, and Hegg was run out off the last ball in a vain attempt to steal the winning run.

Worcestershire reasserted their championship challenge in a thrilling match against Yorkshire. Again, the imperious and delightful Graeme Hick drove, cut and pulled his way to a massive score. His 198 came off 227 balls, and 27 times he sent the ball to the boundary. Neale was able to declare in the 99th over with 356 on the board. Hick was most splendidly supported by Phil Newport, and the pair put on 205, a Worcestershire record for the seventh wicket. Without suggesting the same flair, Yorkshire batted competently and consistently on the second day to take four batting bonus points. Lord and Bent gave Worcestershire's second-innings search for quick runs an enterprising start with a stand of 102, and Neale asked Yorkshire to make 270 in 68 overs. Martyn Moxon batted for 60 overs to hit Yorkshire's first century of the season before he became one of Illingworth's four victims. The left-arm spinner bowled a long, intelligent and important spell. Yorkshire needed 31 from four overs when Hartley skied a catch which Illingworth, the bowler, took in the area of mid-on. In the previous over, Radford had dismissed both Carrick and Sidebottom, and when Swallow was run out attempting an impossible run Worcestershire had won with 13 balls to spare.

The spirit of Kent, however, remained unquenchable, even without their inspiring captain. Northamptonshire dominated the first day's play with some rich batting, and Tavare declared when his side were within 61 runs of the Northants total. Larkins completed a fluent century in 2¾ hours after Northants had been 15 for 2 in their second innings, and Geoff Cook asked Kent to make 288 in 63 overs. Faced almost entirely by spin, Kent showed the character which had taken them to the top of the table as nearly every batsman made a useful contribution with

none dominating. Ward hit a vigorous 59 in 79 minutes, and when quick runs were needed Graham Cowdrey hit 3 sixes and 4 fours in his 49 off 41 balls. Marsh nursed the final assault, sprinting between the wickets with Penn and then Kelleher, who hit Nick Cook for six and four in the penultimate over before being caught off Williams in the last, but Marsh was still there to take Kent to victory with a wicket and two balls to spare. Credit is due to Geoff Cook, who persisted with spin and came close to snatching victory for his side.

There were noises off the field at Trent Bridge where Tim Robinson stated he would give up the captaincy because he did not have the support of some of the senior Notts players. He was persuaded to continue, but Chris Broad was dropped for two matches as a disciplinary measure. It had been a bad six months for the likeable left-hander.

Fourth Cornhill Test Match
ENGLAND v. WEST INDIES

England made an attempt to revitalize their Test side by bringing in some new faces for the fourth Test match. Chris Cowdrey was named as captain for the last two matches of the series. This was a bold and wise move. There had not been too much joy among the senior England players for some time, and the appointment of Cowdrey brought a new sense of dynamism and, above all, the feeling that at the top was a man who enthused about playing the game of cricket. There were doubts as to his quality as a player of international standing, but what England needed was inspirational leadership of the sort that Cowdrey had provided for Kent. In the field, he was outstanding, and England at Old Trafford had been a sorry sight in the field. One had sympathy for Emburey, who was a far better captain tactically than Gatting, but who had inherited the England captaincy at a time when his own form was poor and the England side in need of an injection of new blood.

Other changes in the England side saw Tim Curtis called in for his first Test cap, an honour he well deserved, Foster and Pringle recalled, and Robin Smith given a first Test outing. Smith's record in the season hardly warranted his selection, but he is a positive, attractive batsman of undoubted quality, and this, again, was a wise move on the part of the selectors, who were seeking boldness of spirit. There were also recalls for Athey and Richards although one was less enthusiastic about these two choices. Athey had failed to suggest that he was a Test player in a long, extended run in the side, and Richards, quite simply, was not the best wicket-keeper in the country. He was scoring runs heavily, but Russell was also scoring consistently and he had no superior as a keeper.

West Indies were without Richardson, who had damaged a finger nail while taking a catch at Old Trafford, and Greenidge, who had been troubled by a mystery virus. Keith Arthurton was given a first Test cap, and his form on the tour had earned it.

On the morning of the match, England decided to make Childs 12th man, which left them with a very thin attack.

ABOVE LEFT: *Gooch is caught behind off Marshall. (Adrian Murrell/Allsport)*

LEFT: *The end of Tim Curtis' first Test innings, lbw to Benjamin for 12. (David Munden)*

ABOVE: *David Gower's 100th Test match fails to bring joy. He is caught behind off Benjamin. The Headingley Test was also an historic occasion for Ken Kelly, the doyen of cricket photographers, for it marked 50 years to the day since he first photographed a Test match – England v. Australia on the same ground in 1938. It was also to mark his last attendance at a Test before his retirement. He was made an honorary life member of the Cricket Writers' Club, and his work will continue to be used in* Benson and Hedges Cricket Year. *(Ken Kelly)*

Richards won the toss and asked England to bat first on a wicket that looked good. Play began 50 minutes late because of heavy overnight rain, but after one over, the players left the field and did not return for another two hours because water had seeped from a drain to ruin the bowler's run up at one end. This was as bizarre as it was incomprehensible, and the whole affair led one to wonder how much longer a paying public will suffer the varieties of contempt that are offered them.

Play finally began at 2.30 p.m., and the West Indies claimed their first scalp half an hour later when Gooch faintly edged a ball from Marshall which pitched on off stump and moved away late. Curtis batted solidly for 1½ hours and hinted that he could provide the concrete that England's batting needs before he fell to Benjamin. Gower came in to thunderous applause in his 100th Test match and played a few handsome shots and one thrilling four before he was not quite in line to a ball from Benjamin and his attempted drive became an edge to the keeper. Athey had begun with signs of confidence, but he had now stagnated. Ambrose returned to trap him lbw on

the back foot. England were 80 for 4, and the new order was very much on trial.

Robin Smith might have been caught at short-leg by Logie, a difficult chance, but he survived, and he and Lamb played some encouraging shots. They took the fight to the enemy. Lamb hit 45 off 60 balls and found the boundary seven times. Three times Smith went down on one knee and crashed the ball thrillingly through the off-side field. Bad light ended play early, by which time Lamb and Smith had added 57, and England were in joyful mood.

Smith and Lamb continued on the second day as they had finished the first. They took their stand to 103 when Lamb pushed a ball into the covers and ran. It was apparent as he reached the other end that he was in great pain. He was helped from the field with a torn calf muscle. This was the crucial event of the match. The West Indian attack had begun to look jaded, now it found second wind. Almost immediately, Robin Smith edged to the keeper. Chris Cowdrey was given a torrid time as the pressure was put on him, and then he was adjudged lbw. Pringle

RIGHT: *England's moment of agony – Allan Lamb is injured. (Ken Kelly)*

received a beast of a ball which took the edge on its way to the wicket-keeper, and Richards, looking way out of his depth, had his stumps scattered by Ambrose. Foster and Dilley flourished briefly until Dilley, flat-footed, steered Ambrose to slip, and from 183 for 4, England had declined to 201 all out.

By the end of the day, however, they had clawed their way back into the game. Dujon, the emergency opener, drove loosely to cover, and in a nine-over spell before tea, Foster trapped Hooper lbw and had Richards caught at square-leg. Richards had looked in mighty mood and had hit 20 off 18 balls when he pulled Foster to square-leg, where Curtis dived low to his right to take a magnificent two-handed catch.

Haynes stayed for 40 overs before he played lazily at a straight ball from Pringle and was leg before. Logie was vehement in attack and hit eight fours in his 44 off 51 balls, but Pringle deceived him with an intelligent and well-disguised slower ball, and the batsman lofted gently to mid-on. West Indies were 157 for 5 at the end of play, and the game was in the balance.

Robin Smith is caught behind off Ambrose and the England decline has begun. (Ken Kelly)

Play was only possible during the afternoon session on the Saturday, and during that time England kept in touch with West Indies as they had done at no other time in the series save, briefly, in the first Test. It was Pringle, whose selection had been much criticized, who struck for England, having Arthurton caught behind just as he looked dangerous, Marshall spectacularly taken at slip and trapping Ambrose lbw. Foster bowled quite splendidly without any luck whatsoever, and he had Harper badly missed off his bowling by Athey at slip. The ball went at waist height between first and second slip and Athey, at second slip a few paces ahead of Cowdrey at first, moved to his left to take the catch and then withdrew his hands so obscuring Cowdrey and not laying a hand on the ball. Harper had another fortunate let off when he survived a confident appeal for lbw, and he ended the day on 31, with Benjamin on 7, and West Indies 238 for 8.

England needed an early breakthrough on the Monday morning, and they got it when Benjamin responded slowly to a call from Harper and was run out by substitute Fairbrother's throw. The last-wicket stand between Walsh and Harper was frustrating, however, and West Indies had a lead of 74 by the time Harper skied Foster into the covers. England had virtually managed on three bowlers, and that they were able to do this was due to the fractured nature of the West Indian innings, interrupted as it was by rain.

Gooch began England's reply in authoritative fashion, and he and Curtis looked like wiping off the arrears when Curtis was bowled by a ball of full length from Ambrose. England had just moved ahead and there were hopes of a declaration and setting West Endies a target when Gooch

LEFT: *Arthurton pulls Foster to leg. (Ken Kelly)*
BELOW LEFT: *Winston Benjamin runs himself out. (Adrian Murrell/Allsport)*

was caught at second slip driving at a widish ball from Marshall. Gower clipped Marshall off his legs to reach 7,000 runs in Test cricket, and then he flicked a ball going down the leg side into the keeper's gloves. As he left the field, one wondered if we had seen the last of Gower at Test level. If we have, it is to be pitied, for here was one of the loveliest sights in international cricket.

Athey offered a straightforward catch to Dujon, and three wickets had gone down for five runs. Smith and Cowdrey battled grimly until tea, but after the break Smith was given out lbw and Cowdrey got cramped up and played horribly across a ball from Walsh. Richards again looked out of his depth, Pringle played lazily and Foster sliced to slip. Lamb batted for 87 minutes on one leg with Smith as runner. He hit three cracking fours before his defiant, courageous innings ended when he was caught behind. England's dreams had vanished in under three hours, and West Indies needed only 65 to win. They scored 27 of them by the close, and the remainder came inside half an hour on the last morning. For the best part of four days, England had matched them, and then found themselves beaten by 10 wickets because of another miserable batting collapse.

It should be said, however, that they were not well served by fortune in this match. The injury to Lamb came at a crucial time, and next time the standard of umpiring in

FOURTH CORNHILL TEST MATCH – ENGLAND *v.* WEST INDIES
21, 22, 23, 25 and 26 July 1988 at Headingley, Leeds

ENGLAND

	FIRST INNINGS		SECOND INNINGS	
G.A. Gooch	c Dujon, b Marshall	9	c Hooper, b Walsh	50
T.S. Curtis	lbw, b Benjamin	12	b Ambrose	12
C.W.J. Athey	lbw, b Ambrose	16	c Dujon, b Walsh	11
D.I. Gower	c Dujon, b Benjamin	13	c Dujon, b Marshall	2
A.J. Lamb	retired hurt	64	(8) c Dujon, b Ambrose	19
R.A. Smith	c Dujon, b Ambrose	38	(5) lbw, b Marshall	11
C.S. Cowdrey†	lbw, b Marshall	0	(6) b Walsh	5
C.J. Richards*	b Ambrose	2	(7) b Ambrose	8
D.R. Pringle	c Dujon, b Marshall	0	b Benjamin	3
N.A. Foster	not out	8	c Hooper, b Benjamin	0
G.R. Dilley	c Hooper, b Ambrose	8	not out	2
Extras	b 1, lb 18, w 6, nb 6	31	b 3, lb 8, nb 4	15
		201		**138**

	O	M	R	W	O	M	R	W
Marshall	23	8	55	3	17	4	47	2
Ambrose	25.1	8	58	4	19.5	4	40	3
Benjamin	9	2	27	2	5	4	2	2
Walsh	12	4	42	–	20	9	38	3

FALL OF WICKETS
1–14, 2–43, 3–58, 4–80, 5–183, 6–183, 7–185, 8–185, 9–201
1–56, 2–80, 3–85, 4–85, 5–105, 6–105, 7–127, 8–132, 9–132

WEST INDIES

	FIRST INNINGS		SECOND INNINGS	
D.L. Haynes	lbw, b Pringle	54	not out	25
P.J.L. Dujon*	c Smith, b Dilley	13	not out	40
C.L. Hooper	lbw, b Foster	19		
I.V.A. Richards†	c Curtis, b Foster	18		
A.L. Logie	c Foster, b Pringle	44		
K.L.T. Arthurton	c Richards, b Pringle	27		
R.A. Harper	c Gower, b Foster	56		
M.D. Marshall	c Gooch, b Pringle	3		
E.L.C. Ambrose	lbw, b Pringle	8		
W.K.M. Benjamin	run out	9		
C.A. Walsh	not out	9		
Extras	lb 15	15	lb 2	2
		275	(for no wkt)	**67**

	O	M	R	W	O	M	R	W
Dilley	20	5	59	1	4	–	16	–
Foster	32.2	6	98	3	7	1	36	–
Pringle	27	7	95	5				
Cowdrey	2	–	8	–	3.3	–	13	–

FALL OF WICKETS
1–15, 2–61, 3–97, 4–137, 5–156, 6–194, 7–210, 8–222, 9–245

Umpires: H.D. Bird & D.R. Shepherd

West Indies won by 10 wickets

Athey moves in front of Cowdrey and a chance is lost. (David Munden)

Pakistan is criticized, people would do well to ponder some of the decisions that were made in this match. Cowdrey, Smith and Hooper were three who might feel aggrieved while Harper could consider himself doubly fortunate.

23, 25 and 26 July

at Cardiff

Yorkshire 322 for 9 dec (P.E. Robinson 63, J.D. Love 52) and 0 for 0 dec
Glamorgan 20 for 1 dec and 179 for 4 (M.P. Maynard 60 not out)

Match drawn
Glamorgan 2 pts, Yorkshire 2 pts

at Portsmouth

Hampshire 251 for 7 dec (D.R. Turner 62, C.L. Smith 53) and 0 for 0 dec
Derbyshire 45 for 1 dec and 182 for 7 (B.J.M. Maher 62, R.J. Maru 5 for 69)

Match drawn
Hampshire 3 pts, Derbyshire 3 pts

at Folkestone

Worcestershire 238 (P.A. Neale 108 not out, R.M. Ellison 6 for 99) and 81 for 2
Kent 152 (P.J. Newport 4 for 50)

Match drawn
Worcestershire 6 pts, Kent 5 pts

at Leicester

Leicestershire 300 for 9 dec (N.E. Briers 119, P. Whitticase 50 not out) and 129 for 1 (N.E. Briers 63 not out)
Essex 200 for 3 dec (P.J. Prichard 71 not out, A.R. Border 65 not out)

Match drawn
Essex 6 pts, Leicestershire 5 pts

at Lord's

Surrey 334 for 9 dec (G.S. Clinton 100, D.M. Ward 57, J.E. Emburey 6 for 94) and 0 for 0 dec
Middlesex 28 for 0 dec and 185 for 3 (J.D. Carr 97 not out, M.W. Gatting 55)

Match drawn
Surrey 3 pts, Middlesex 2 pts

at Northampton

Sussex 118 (W.W. Davis 7 for 52) and 287 for 8 dec (C.M. Wells 62, N.J. Lenham 52)
Northamptonshire 233 (R.J. Bailey 127 not out)

Match drawn
Northamptonshire 6 pts, Sussex 4 pts

at Taunton

Nottinghamshire 211 (P. Johnson 73, R.T. Robinson 50, V.J. Marks 5 for 73) and 103 (V.J. Marks 5 for 43)
Somerset 167 (F.D. Stephenson 4 for 41, E.E. Hemmings 4 for 50) and 27 for 1

Match drawn
Nottinghamshire 6 pts, Somerset 5 pts

at Edgbaston

Warwickshire 212 for 7 dec (D.A. Banks 61, M. Asif Din 59)
Sri Lankans 225 for 3 (P.A. de Silva 117 not out, S.A.R. Silva 62)

Match drawn

The rain was the victor in every match as one of the wettest Julys on record moved to its close. The top of the table clash at Folkestone saw Phil Neale lead his side back from the depths of 71 for 6 with a valiant century which was completed on the Monday when there was only four hours' play. Kent succumbed on the last day on a wicket which was aiding the bowlers, but time ran out for any spectacular finish to be achieved.

There was no play on the opening day at Cardiff, Portsmouth or Edgbaston. At Portsmouth, Derbyshire made a bold attempt to score 207 in 52 overs on a doubtful wicket, but eventually were thankful to draw. Yorkshire batted dourly but consistently at Cardiff, and rain accounted for 17 overs on the last day so that, in spite of Maynard's fourth half-century in five innings, the game petered out to a draw. The opening first-class match of Sri Lanka's tour was enlivened by an innings of 117 off 149 balls by Aravinda de Silva. He hit 3 sixes and 21 fours. Wicket-keeper Amal Silva hit 62 in just over three hours and the pair added 137 for the third wicket.

Leicestershire omitted De Freitas as a disciplinary measure against the attitude that they said he had been adopting. Nigel Briers hit a century, and Essex raced to 200 through an unbroken partnership of 111 between Border and Prichard, who outscored his eminent partner. Fletcher declared 100 runs in arrears, but rain destroyed any hope of an exciting finish.

It was the same story at Lord's, where Clinton played with his usual calm after a first day consisting of four overs. Middlesex had a fright when Slack suffered another fainting fit in their brief first innings, but he was later deemed to be well. John Carr batted in stylish and exciting form as Middlesex chased 307 in just under four hours on a pitch which was still in good condition, but rain ended the chances of an enthralling end to the game.

Somerset's hopes were blighted by rain at Taunton, where Vic Marks took 10 for 116 in the match. Twenty wickets fell on the second day, two of them, Johnson and Millns, to off-spinner Harvey Trump, who was making his first-class début.

Winston Davis took a career-best 7 for 52 for Northants against Sussex, and Robert Bailey hit a glorious century, which immediately had people clamouring for his inclusion in the England side, but Colin Wells and rain saved Sussex from defeat.

Refuge Assurance League

24 July

at Cardiff

Glamorgan 160 for 4 (M.P. Maynard 63, R.J. Shastri 50 not out)
Yorkshire 145 for 7 (J. Derrick 4 for 36)

Glamorgan (4 pts) won by 15 runs

at Portsmouth

Derbyshire 133 (P.J. Bakker 5 for 26)
Hampshire 134 for 6

Hampshire (4 pts) won by 4 wickets

at Folkestone

Kent 191 for 5 (M.R. Benson 66)
Worcestershire 192 for 3 (D.A. Leatherdale 62 not out)

Worcestershire (4 pts) won by 7 wickets

at Leicester

Essex 133 (C.C. Lewis 4 for 13)
Leicestershire 137 for 2 (L. Potter 66 not out)

Leicestershire (4 pts) won by 8 wickets

at Lord's

Warwickshire 184 for 8
Middlesex 187 for 4 (W.N. Slack 77 not out)

Middlesex (4 pts) won by 6 wickets

at Northampton

Sussex 152 for 6
Northamptonshire 153 for 5 (D.J. Capel 83)

Northamptonshire (4 pts) won by 5 wickets

at Taunton

Nottinghamshire 162 for 9 (D.W. Randall 68)
Somerset 163 for 1 (G.D. Rose 93 not out)

Somerset (4 pts) won by 9 wickets

Middlesex and Worcestershire maintained their strong position in the Refuge Assurance League with comfortable victories. Worcestershire's recruit from Yorkshire, David Leatherdale, hit his first Sunday league fifty in what

Dutchman Paul-Jan Bakker won a regular place in the Hampshire side and performed with distinction. (Neal Simpson/ASP)

was only his third match. He and Neale added 110 in 15 overs to take their side to victory. Maynard was again in sparkling form, and Shastri hit 50 off 68 balls as Glamorgan scored at a rate which Yorkshire could not match. Dutch pace bowler Bakker again showed his worth in a low-scoring game at Portsmouth while Graham Rose, tried as opener, hit a Sunday league best of 93 off 99 balls as Somerset trounced Notts by nine wickets with 9.3 overs to spare.

NatWest Bank Trophy

Quarter-Finals

27 July

at Derby

Derbyshire 191
Hampshire 193 for 6 (V.P. Terry 67)

Hampshire won by 4 wickets
(Man of the Match: V.P. Terry)

at Lord's

Kent 195
Middlesex 199 for 5 (R.O. Butcher 64)

Middlesex won by 5 wickets
(Man of the Match: R.O. Butcher)

LEFT: *Three England captains of 1988 in one frame. Emburey, Gatting and Chris Cowdrey, Middlesex v. Kent, NatWest Bank Trophy Quarter-Final. (Adrian Murrell/ Allsport)*
BELOW LEFT: *Chris Penn narrowly avoids being run out in the NatWest Bank Quarter-Final at Lord's. Paul Downton breaks the wicket. (Tom Morris)*

at The Oval

Glamorgan 235 for 6 (M.P. Maynard 64, R.J. Shastri 59 not out)
Surrey 236 for 6 (P.D. Atkins 82, M.A. Lynch 61)

Surrey won by 4 wickets
(Man of the Match: P.D. Atkins)

at Worcester

Gloucestershire 185 (K.M. Curran 53)
Worcestershire 189 for 6

Worcestershire won by 4 wickets
(Man of the Match: P.A. Neale)

Derbyshire appeared to meet no other county but Hampshire in July, and just as Hampshire had thwarted them in the Benson and Hedges Cup so they thwarted them in the NatWest Trophy. Put in to bat, Derbyshire suggested that they would build an innings only during a second-wicket stand of 49 between Barnett and Maher. The first 13 overs had produced 25 runs before Bowler was

caught behind off James. Barnett and Maher batted for another 20 overs before Barnett's inevitable frustration caused him to hit Jefferies high to Robin Smith at cover. Maher tried to hold the innings together, but none of the later stroke-makers stayed long enough to make an impact. Faced with a target of 192, Hampshire were given a sound start by Terry and Chris Smith who put on 67 in 25 overs. Ole Mortensen sent back Nicholas, Robin Smith and Jefferies in successive overs to raise Derbyshire's hopes, but Ayling and James kept their heads and took their side to victory with 16 balls to spare. Terry took the individual award, but Hampshire's victory was essentially a team effort. Cowley had again bowled with great economy, and the bowlers had been well supported in the field. Chris Smith took a fine running catch to dismiss the dangerous Roberts.

Gatting also asked Kent to bat first at Lord's and was well rewarded when Benson and Ward were out with only eight scored. To make matters worse for the visitors, Neil Taylor was bogged down for 19 overs, during which time he made seven. Tavare and Pienaar brought the first ray of light to the Kent innings with a stand of 55 in 12 overs, but Pienaar was bowled attempting a reverse sweep and Chris Cowdrey was caught behind pushing forward at Needham. There were late, useful contributions from Graham Cowdrey, Marsh and Ellison, but Middlesex remained satisfied with their work in the field. Ellison quickly had Slack caught behind. Penn bowled Carr, and Pienaar dismissed both Needham and Gatting so that Middlesex were 79 for 4 and a little worried, but Butcher and Brown added 76 in 19 overs and made a victory a formality.

Ian Greig asked Glamorgan to bat first at The Oval, and his bowlers, Clarke and Martin Bicknell, kept a stranglehold on the visiting batsmen. In the 10th over, Hopkins was caught behind off Bicknell with the score at 14, and when Todd, deputizing for the injured Morris, was bowled by Peters three overs later only 10 more runs had been added. Butcher attempted to increase the run rate, but unwisely he hit the accurate Greig to square-leg, where Atkins judged a good catch. Holmes became Greig's second victim, falling to a very fine catch by Bullen, and at lunch, Glamorgan were staggering at 95 for 4 from 36 overs, meagre fare for a good wicket. Matthew Maynard increased the tempo in the afternoon. He hit 6 fours and made 64 off 89 balls before impetuosity won the day and he drove the admirable Bullen into the hands of Bicknell at long-on. Shastri, Ontong and Thomas plundered 81 from the last 10 overs, 55 coming from the last five. Bicknell looked spent, and Lynch bowled the last over, conceding 13 runs, but Glamorgan's 235 always looked likely to be some fifty runs short of a winning score. Clinton was an early victim of Barwick's, but Stewart

West Indians in England, 1988
First-Class Matches

BATTING	v. Sussex (Hove) 7–10 May		v. Somerset (Taunton) 14–16 May		v. Gloucestershire (Bristol) 25–7 May		v. Worcestershire (Worcester) 28–30 May		First Test Match (Trent Bridge) 2–7 June		v. Lancashire (Old Trafford) 8–10 June		v. Northamptonshire (Northampton) 11–13 June		Second Test Match (Lord's) 16–21 June		v. Kent (Canterbury) 25–7 June		Third Test Match (Old Trafford) 30 June–5 July		v. Glamorgan (Swansea) 13–15 July		v. Leicestershire (Leicester) 16–18 July		Fourth Test Match (Leeds) 21–6 July	
C.G. Greenidge	15	2	22	4*			2	—	25	—	67	—			22	103			45	—			75	—		
D.L. Haynes	36	158	50	8*	19	22	71	—	60	—	93	—	72	22	12	5	10	—			14	28*	16	—	54	25*
R.B. Richardson	20	82	26	—	2	10	5	—	17	—	16	—	42	0	5	26	5	—	23	—						
C.L. Hooper	7	34	54	—			7	—	84	—			0	74	3	11	87	—	15	—	49	18*	62	—	19	—
A.L. Logie	3	10*			38	25	29*	—	20	—	0	—	23	10	81	95*	39	—					18	—	44	—
I.V.A. Richards	128	—			10	63	50	—	80	—			39	6	6	72	7	—	47	—	23*	—	0	—	18	—
R.A. Harper	217*	—	53*	—							0*	—	44	5	56*	—			74	—			47	—	56	—
W.K.M. Benjamin	10	1*	8	—							—	—	1*	21*			16	—					19	—	9	—
D. Williams	28	5			20	17					—	—	44	51			13	—								
I.R. Bishop	9*	—			7	11*	—	—	—	—	—	—					23	—								
E.L.C. Ambrose	59	—	12	—	25	25	—	—	43	—			1	14*	0	0	18	—	7*	—			18	—	8	—
K.L.T. Arthurton			1	—	10	4					60	—	3	121			22	—			45*	—	3	—	27	—
P.J.L. Dujon			5	—			4*	—	16	—	35*	—			53	52	10	—	67	—	141	16	51	—	13	40*
M.D. Marshall			9	—	46	23			72	—					11	6					43*	—			3	—
C.A. Walsh			4	—			—	—	3*	—			1	—	9*	0									9*	—
P.V. Simmons					53*	—																				
B.P. Patterson					5*	14									0	2							23*	—		
Byes	9	1				4			6		5		4	6							10					
Leg-byes	4	6	5		4	5			8		5		10	13	6	19	6		21		12	1	16		15	2
Wides	7					1					2		1		1	1					3		2			
No-balls	9	6	2		17	10	2		14		4		3	2	1	5	1		3		5	4	20			
Total	561	305	251	12	257	233	170		448		287		288	345	209	397	275		384		302	67	370		275	67
Wickets	9	5	10	10	9†	9	5		9		5		10	8	10	10	10		7		3	1	10		10	0
Result	D		W		D		D		D		D		W		W		W		W		D		D		W	

Fielding Figures:
32 – P.J.L. Dujon
20 – R.A. Harper
12 – D. Williams (ct 11/st 1)
10 – I.V.A. Richards, C.L. Hooper and subs
9 – A.L. Logie
8 – R.B. Richardson and K.L.T. Arthurton
6 – C.G. Greenidge, W.K.M. Benjamin and D.L. Haynes
3 – M.D. Marshall
1 – E.L.C. Ambrose, I.R. Bishop and B.P. Patterson
† P.V. Simmons retired hurt, absent hurt

scored freely, and when Lynch joined Atkins he seemed intent on ending the game as soon as possible. In 20 overs, they added 102. Lynch hit a six and 9 fours and gave Butcher, Glamorgan's acting captain, many headaches as to how to manipulate his bowling resources. On Lynch's departure, Ward kept the momentum going until lazily running himself out. Richards' stay was brief, but Greig put bat to ball in positive fashion, and by the time Atkins' excellent innings came to an end Surrey were only seven runs short of victory. Bullen scampered the winning run with three overs to spare.

Like the other losers of the toss, Gloucestershire were asked to bat first at Worcester. Wright went cheaply, but Stovold and Romaines repaired the damage. It was the spin of Illingworth and Hick which turned the game in favour of Worcestershire, and when Dilley was brought back to account for Alleyne and Russell Gloucestershire had slumped from 54 for 1 to 113 for 7. Curran and Graveney asserted themselves bravely, but 185 did not seem a daunting score. After Alderman had bowled, Curtis Graveney came into the attack and O'Shaughnessy and Hick had to fight hard for runs. The Gloucestershire skipper finally dismissed them both, and when Leatherdale was brilliantly caught second ball by Athey the home side were 86 for 4, and the game in the balance. Neale and Weston righted matters with a stand of 74, and although Rhodes went cheaply, Worcestershire won with 13 balls to spare. Neale's innings of 45 and his handling of the Worcestershire side made him an obvious recipient of the individual award.

27 July

at Osterley

Indian Gymkhana 88
Sri Lankans 89 for 1

Sri Lankans won by 9 wickets

27, 28 and 29 July

at Trent Bridge

West Indians 362 (C.G. Greenidge 101, I.V.A. Richards 75, A.L. Logie 53, C.L. Cairns 4 for 82) and 17 for 0
Nottinghamshire 247 (C.W. Scott 63 not out, F.D. Stephenson 56)

Match drawn

Greenidge proved his return to full health with a century on the first day of a match marred by rain. Notts fielded

v. Nottinghamshire (Trent Bridge) 27-9 July		v. Essex (Chelmsford) 30 July-1 August		Fifth Test Match (The Oval) 4-8 August		M	Inns	Nos	Runs	HS	Av
101	—	81	111	10	77	11	16	1	762	111	50.66
		14	35	2	77*	14	23	4	903	158	47.52
						10	14	—	279	82	19.92
3	—	34	30	11	23	14	20	1	625	87	32.89
53	—	13	—	47	38*	13	18	4	586	95*	41.85
75	—			0	—	13	16	1	624	128	41.60
28	—	6	19	17	—	12	13	5	622	217*	77.75
17*	—			0	—	10	10	4	102	21*	17.00
2	1*	1	—			8	10	1	182	51	20.22
6	—	0	—			8	6	2	56	23	14.00
		31	—		17*	13	15	3	278	59	23.16
24	—	101*	78*			10	13	3	499	121	49.90
18	16*			64	—	12	16	4	601	141	50.08
		76	—	0	—	9	10	1	289	76	32.11
				5	—	9	7	3	31	9*	7.75
						1	1	1	53	53*	—
16	—	0	—								
		4			2						
10	3	5		7	3						
2	3		1								
7	11	2		2	6						
362	17	378	280	183	226						
10	0	10	3	10	2						
D		D		W							

three overseas players, West Indian Franklyn Stephenson, New Zealander Chris Cairns, who again showed precocious all-round ability, and South African David Callaghan.

28 July

at Jesmond

England XI v. Rest of the World XI

Match abandoned

29 July

at Jesmond

England XI 233 for 8 (N.H. Fairbrother 81, Javed Miandad 4 for 10)
Rest of World XI 231 for 8 (Saleem Malik 67)

England XI won by 2 runs

at Arundel

Lavinia, Duchess of Norfolk's XI 214 for 3 (G.S. Clinton 107, P.W.G. Parker 50)
Sri Lankans 23 for 0

Match abandoned

30, 31 July and 1 August

at Chelmsford

West Indians 378 (K.L.T. Arthurton 101 not out, C.G. Greenidge 81, M.D. Marshall 76) and 280 for 3 dec (C.G. Greenidge 111, K.L.T. Arthurton 78 not out)
Essex 250 for 9 dec (A.W. Lilley 68, G.A. Gooch 56, P.J. Prichard 52 not out, I.R. Bishop 5 for 49) and 113 for 5 (G.A. Gooch 67 not out)

Match drawn

30 July, 1 and 2 August

at Derby

Derbyshire 166 (J.E. Morris 54 not out, T.A. Merrick 6 for 29) and 428 for 7 dec (J.G. Wright 154 not out, S.C. Goldsmith 84, B. Roberts 60)
Warwickshire 285 (M. Asif Din 52, G.W. Humpage 52, A.J. Moles 50 not out, D.E. Malcolm 6 for 68)

Match drawn
Warwickshire 7 pts, Derbyshire 5 pts

at Cheltenham

Surrey 312 (G.S. Clinton 102, K.M. Curran 4 for 62, T.M. Alderman 4 for 81) and 115 (D.V. Lawrence 7 for 47)
Gloucestershire 163 for 9 (K.M. Curran 52, S.T. Clarke 5 for 44) and 243 (K.M. Curran 101, S.T. Clarke 6 for 63)

Surrey won by 21 runs
Surrey 24 pts, Gloucestershire 5 pts

at Canterbury

Somerset 452 for 4 dec (S.R. Waugh 161, R.J. Bartlett 102 not out, P.M. Roebuck 68, N.J. Pringle 54)
Kent 121 (H.R.J. Trump 4 for 17) and 185 (G.R. Cowdrey 65 not out, N.A. Mallender 5 for 12)

Somerset won by an innings and 146 runs
Somerset 23 pts, Kent 1 pt

at Worksop

Leicestershire 257 (P.A.J. De Freitas 113, J.J. Whitaker 61, F.D. Stephenson 6 for 66) and 200 for 7 (D.I. Gower 72 not out)
Nottinghamshire 367 for 8 dec (D.W. Randall 134, F.D. Stephenson 57, J.P. Agnew 6 for 117)

Match drawn
Nottinghamshire 8 pts, Leicestershire 6 pts

at Eastbourne

Glamorgan 283 (R.C. Ontong 89, M.P. Maynard 68, H. Morris 56, A.C.S. Pigott 4 for 82) and 227 for 6 dec (H. Morris 63, R.J. Shastri 54 not out)
Sussex 265 (A.C.S. Pigott 52, A.P. Wells 50, S.L. Watkin 5 for 89) and 115 for 3

Match drawn
Sussex 7 pts, Glamorgan 7 pts

at Worcester

Worcestershire 363 for 6 dec (G.A. Hick 132, M.A. Robinson 4 for 102)
Northamptonshire 191 (D.J. Capel 70, N.V. Radford 7 for 73) and 205 for 4 (D.J. Capel 51 not out)

Match drawn
Worcestershire 8 pts, Northamptonshire 3 pts

BOWLING	E.L.C. Ambrose	I.R. Bishop	W.K.M. Benjamin	R.A. Harper	I.V.A. Richards	C.L. Hooper	M.D. Marshall	C.A. Walsh
v. Sussex (Hove) 7–10 May	14-4-42-1	14-1-55-4	15-4-38-2	10-3-24-0	8-1-22-0	16.5-2-61-3		
v. Somerset (Taunton) 14–16 May	13-3-27-4 8-1-26-2		13-5-34-4 4-0-11-2	14-5-26-0		7.2-1-25-2	8.4-3-23-2	8-0-28-0 10-4-21-1
v. Gloucestershire (Bristol) 25–7 May	6-0-18-0 5-0-20-0	6-0-25-0 5-1-23-0			7-2-24-0 2-0-7-0		4.5-1-14-4 3-0-5-0	
v. Worcestershire (Worcester) 28–30 May	19-4-59-1	13-2-32-0			9-1-33-0	14-1-46-0		22-4-78-0
First Test Match (Trent Bridge) 2–7 June	26-10-53-4 23-4-56-1				1-0-2-0 9-1-26-0	8-1-20-0 14-1-33-0	30-4-69-6 13-4-23-1	20-4-39-0 25-5-84-0
v. Lancashire (Old Trafford) 8–10 June		14-1-61-2	15-2-39-1	29-10-57-1				
v. Northamptonshire (Northampton) 11–13 June	14-6-23-0		19.2-4-44-3	25-7-58-0		12-4-35-2		22-3-49-5
Second Test Match (Lord's) 16–21 June	12-1-39-1 20-1-75-1						18-5-32-6 25-5-60-4	16-6-36-2 20-4-47-1
v. Kent (Canterbury) 25–7 June	8-3-6-2 7-3-11-1	11-3-24-1 15-3-39-6	7-2-23-3 8-5-14-0	10.5-7-10-4 20.5-6-51-3		2-1-1-0		
Third Test Match (Old Trafford) 30 June–5 July	17-5-35-2 16-4-36-2		13-4-31-2 4-1-6-1	2-1-4-0		1-0-4-0	12-5-19-2 15.4-5-22-7	18.2-4-46-4 4-1-10-1
v. Glamorgan (Swansea) 13–15 July		20-6-56-2		8-2-12-2			6-3-15-0	13-4-34-0
v. Leicestershire (Leicester) 16–18 July	10-2-19-2 12-3-19-0		7.5-1-20-4 10-3-24-1	2-1-1-0 13-6-23-1	5-2-7-1	2-1-1-0		
Fourth Test Match (Leeds) 21–6 July	25.1-8-58-4 19.5-4-40-3		9-2-27-2 5-4-2-2				23-8-55-3 17-4-47-2	12-4-42-0 20-9-38-3
v. Nottinghamshire (Trent Bridge) 27–9 July		12-7-11-0	17-1-69-1	31-11-87-3	4.4-3-1-2	5-2-5-0		
v. Essex (Chelmsford) 30 July–1 August	10-1-18-0	22-5-49-5 10-1-31-1		17.5-0-68-2 9-1-41-0		15-0-58-0 8-1-14-2	7-0-22-0	
Fifth Test Match (The Oval) 4–8 August	20-6-31-3 24.1-10-50-1		14-2-33-1 22-4-52-4	21-7-50-3 6-3-9-2		1-1-0-0	24.3-3-64-3 25-6-52-1	10-1-21-0 12-5-21-2
	329.1-83- 761-35 av. 21.74	142-30- 406-21 av. 19.33	183.1-44- 467-33 av. 14.15	229.3-70- 531-21 av. 25.28	45.4-10- 122-3 av. 40.66	106.1-16- 303-9 av. 33.66	232.2-56- 553-42 av. 13.16	232.2-58- 594-18 av. 33.00

at Leeds

Lancashire 154 (G.D. Mendis 58, A. Sidebottom 4 for 32) and 156 (S.D. Fletcher 4 for 36)
Yorkshire 293 (J.D. Love 77, A. Sidebottom 55, P.J.W. Allott 5 for 85) and 18 for 0

Yorkshire won by 10 wickets
Yorkshire 23 pts, Lancashire 5 pts

at Lord's

Middlesex 324 (J.F. Sykes 88) and 185 for 2 dec (K.R. Brown 107 not out)
Sri Lankans 265 (A. Ranatunga 84) and 80 for 3

Match drawn

The West Indian tourists won no friends at Chelmsford. They batted attractively on the opening day, when Arthurton scored an accomplished hundred and shared a sixth-wicket stand of 110 with Marshall. A solid innings from Gooch, an enterprising knock from Lilley and an elegant piece of batting by Prichard provided Essex with a good reply, and Gooch declared behind. By lunch on the last day, West Indians had a lead of 317 and Greenidge had completed his century with a six off the last ball before the break. Greenidge, however, did not declare, killing the game and showing total contempt for the paying public. If

matches against the tourists are to mean anything and are to continue to make a profit for all concerned, they will need to be treated with more concern than they were by the West Indians. Their attitude in this game was indefensible.

There was a rumpus of a different kind at Worcester. Another glorious Hick hundred dominated the first day, and Neale declared his innings closed after a further six overs' batting on the Monday. A magnificent spell of bowling by Radford then saw Northants demolished in 65.1 overs, but both sides took the field for the second innings. Neale insisted that he had indicated that Northants must follow on, which seemed the obvious course, while Geoff Cook asserted that he had not been informed that his side was to follow on. Twenty-two players were on the field until 7.25 p.m., by which time a ruling had been received from the TCCB that Northants should follow on. It was decided that play should be abandoned for the day and that four overs should be added to the last day. Northants ground out their anger at two runs an over on the Tuesday and stated that they would be taking the matter further and asking that the match should be replayed. As Worcestershire took only 8 points instead of the 24 that they had hoped for in order to narrow the gap

B.P. Patterson	K.L.T. Arthurton	R.B. Richardson	Byes	Leg-byes	Wides	No-balls	Total	Wkts
			5	5	4	4	252	10
				1		8	113	10
			1	5		3	146	10
8-0-39-5	3-1-2-0		8	10		24	140	10
5-0-20-0		4-0-22-0		1		12	98	1
19.1-6-59-2			1	13	2	26	321	3
16-2-49-0				13	5	11	245	10
24-6-69-1				10		6	301	3
12-2-34-1	10-3-31-1			16	5	21	238	6
			6	17	4	8	232	10
13-3-52-1				6		2	165	10
21.5-2-100-2			5	20	2	14	307	10
			11	7			81	10
	2-0-25-0		4	6		1	151	10
				4		5	135	10
			1	10		1	93	10
19-6-35-1			20	8	5	10	180	5
16-1-44-4			4	2		11	90	10
10-1-29-3						4	103	6
			1	18	6	6	201	9
			3	8		4	138	10
15-3-45-3	10-3-21-0		5	3		5	247	10
11-1-33-2				2	1	10	250	9
6-0-24-0	2.1-1-1-2		1	1		6	113	5
				6		15	205	10
			3	15		15	202	10
196-33–	27.1-8–	4-0–						
632-25	80-3	22-0–						
av. 25.28	av. 26.66	—						

The destroyer of Kent – Steve Waugh of Somerset. (Neal Simpson/ASP)

between them and Kent, it is likely that they might have been happy to have a replay.

Worcestershire did gain some ground on Kent, who lost their first Championship match since May. They lost rather badly to Somerset at Canterbury. The visitors just failed to clinch a fourth batting point on the Saturday when Steve Waugh continued in his mighty form with his fifth century of the summer in first-class cricket. He passed 1000 runs for the season. Richard Bartlett reached a fine maiden Championship century on the Monday, and Kent were then bowled out for 121. Jones and Mallender made early inroads into the Kent batting and Harvey Trump finished the innings with his remarkably mature off-break bowling. Forced to follow on, Kent were 109 for 5 at the close and, in spite of Graham Cowdrey's brave and positive knock, were well beaten on the last morning. That was not the end of their woe. Chris Cowdrey was hit on the foot by a ball from Jones. Although no break was revealed, he was in great discomfort and batted number eleven in the second innings when he was bowled for 0. His injury forced him to withdraw from the England side.

Equally unfortunate was Kim Barnett of Derbyshire. He was one of Tony Merrick's hat-trick victims on the first day when Derbyshire lost their last seven wickets for five runs as Merrick produced a devastating spell of 6 for 0 in ten Balls. Warwickshire's innings also came to an abrupt end as Devon Malcolm took 4 for 0 in seven balls and finished with a career-best 6 for 68. The last five Warwickshire wickets went down for three runs, but they still led by 119 on the first innings. John Wright retired with a damaged knee when his score was on 24 and Derbyshire were fighting to save the game, but he returned on the last day after splendid work by Goldsmith and Roberts and hit a match-saving 154 not out. Norman Gifford proved that age is no hindrance to stamina by bowling 50 overs and taking 3 for 125.

Yorkshire took only two days to win the Roses match at Headingley. Lancashire were always struggling against the Yorkshire seamers on the opening day, but the home side were not without their troubles against Paul Allott in spite of Love's 77. It was a seventh-wicket stand of 78 in 24 overs between Carrick and Sidebottom which put Yorkshire on top. Sidebottom followed this with two wickets in his second over when Lancashire batted again. Fowler and Fairbrother batted with grim determination, but although an innings defeat was avoided, Lancashire could offer Yorkshire only a meagre target and were beaten inside two days.

Sussex and Glamorgan were engaged in a bottom-of-the-table struggle at Eastbourne, and Sussex showed the greater urgency although a result never looked likely.

Having been dropped for his attitude towards playing

Sri Lankans in England, 1988
First-Class Matches

Column key (match venues/dates):
W = v. Warwickshire (Edgbaston) 23–6 July · M = v. Middlesex (Lord's) 30 July–2 Aug. · N = v. Nottinghamshire (Trent Bridge) 6–8 August · Y = v. Yorkshire (Leeds) 10–12 August · Su = v. Surrey (The Oval) 13–15 August · G = v. Gloucestershire (Bristol) 17–19 August · H = v. Hampshire (Southampton) 20–2 August · T = Test Match (Lord's) 25–30 August · D = v. Derbyshire (Derby) 31 Aug.–2 Sept. (1)/(2) = innings

BATTING

BATTING	W(1)	W(2)	M(1)	M(2)	N(1)	N(2)	Y(1)	Y(2)	Su(1)	Su(2)	G(1)	G(2)	H(1)	H(2)	T(1)	T(2)	D(1)	D(2)	M	Inns	Nos	Runs	HS	Av
R.S. Mahanama	6	—	40	18	8	37*					12	46*	12	—					5	8	2	179	46*	29.83
S.A.R. Silva	62	—	42	13	3	1	112	3*	3	24			3	19	1	16	36	—	8	14	1	338	112	26.00
M.A.R. Samarasekera	21	—	17	11	0	28	40	4*	104	1	53	—	0	40*	0	57	25	—	9	15	2	401	104	30.84
R.S. Madugalle	11*	—	3	—	72	77	48	—	44	22			97	—	3	20	6*	—	8	11	2	403	97	44.77
A. Ranatunga	—		84	—			27	—	9	0*	4	—	39	—	5	78	25	—	8	9	1	271	84	33.87
P.A. de Silva	117*	—	5	22*							13	65*	14	—	3	18	76		6	9	3	333	117*	55.50
L.R.D. Mendis	—		10	12*	24	1	20*		0	124	39	—	0	—	21	56	55	—	9	12	2	362	124	36.20
J.R. Ratnayeke	—		2	—	17*	35	—		5	15*	60*	—	41	45*	59*	32			8	10	5	311	60*	62.20
G.F. Labrooy	—				—		—		18	—			4	—	42	9*	—		7	4	1	73	42	24.33
H.C.P. Ramanayake	—		18	—							—	—			0	2			4	3	—	20	18	6.66
B. Rajadurai	—	—									—	—							2					
W.R. Madurasinghe			30	—	—		8*	—	3	1*			27	—	4	2			6	7	2	75	30	15.00
S.D. Anurasiri	4*	—																	3	1	1	4	4*	—
D.S.B.P. Kuruppu					158	4	19	0	5	87	39				46	25	55*	—	6	10	1	438	158	48.66
H.P. Tillekeratne					5	32			22	7	50*	—					5	—	5	6	1	121	50*	24.20
F.S. Ahangama									0*				3*				—		5	2	2	3	3*	—
Byes			2	2	2		9		4	4			12			1								
Leg-byes	3		2	2	9	5	9		2	10	10	1	14	1	7	8	3							
Wides					4				3	1			1				1							
No-balls	5		6		9	12	3		2	4	13		1	2	8		10							
Total	225		265	80	307	244	287	7	219	300	285	112	280	106	194	331	297							
Wickets	3		10	3	7	7	5	1	10	6	6	0	10	1	10	10	6							
Result	D		D		D		D		D		D		D		L		D							

Fielding Figures
15 – S.A.R. Silva
5 – M.A.R. Samarasekera
4 – R.S. Madugalle and H.P. Tillekeratne
3 – A. Ranatunga and P.A. de Silva
2 – G.F. Labrooy, L.R.D. Mendis,
   W.R. Madurasinghe and
   D.S.B.P. Kuruppu (ct 1/st 1)
1 – R.S. Mahanama, F.S. Ahangama,
   S.D. Anurasiri and J.R. Ratnayeke

BOWLING

BOWLING	J.R. Ratnayeke	G.F. Labrooy	M.A.R. Samarasekera	H.C.P. Ramanayake	B. Rajadurai	A. Ranatunga	S.D. Anurasiri	W.R. Madurasinghe
v. Warwickshire (Edgbaston) 23–6 July	14–4–26–1	13–4–45–3	9–0–32–0	13–2–36–2	11–1–28–1	4–0–25–0		
v. Middlesex (Lord's) 30 July–2 Aug.	24.5–6–77–3 / 19–0–66–1		21–2–77–3 / 9–0–29–1	23–3–81–2 / 5–0–36–0		2–1–5–0 / 8–2–12–0	13–0–53–0 / 10–4–17–0	9–1–19–2 / 4–0–23–0
v. Nottinghamshire (Trent Bridge) 6–8 August	17–4–53–0 / 7–1–16–0	20–2–57–1 / 7–0–38–0	12–1–36–0 / 1–0–5–0					29.2–14–50–3 / 6–1–20–0
v. Yorkshire (Leeds) 10–12 August	16–1–61–1 / 21–5–47–3	13–0–71–0 / 16.5–1–61–6	5–1–21–0			4–0–12–0		26–6–61–0 / 2–0–11–0
v. Surrey (The Oval) 13–15 August	20–2–59–1	29–6–86–4	15.4–4–31–3					13–5–21–0
v. Gloucestershire (Bristol) 17–19 August	23–5–59–2			19–3–76–1	9–2–37–0	6–1–30–0	12–3–38–0	
v. Hampshire (Southampton) 20–2 August	19–2–66–1 / 12–2–34–0	18–4–68–1 / 17–1–52–0	15–0–53–0			9–0–35–0 / 3–0–14–0		21–1–75–0 / 18.2–3–55–1
Test Match (Lord's) 25–30 August	32–3–107–2 / 7–1–16–0	40–7–119–4 / 9–0–24–0	22–5–66–1 / 10–0–38–2	27.2–3–86–2		6–3–6–1 / 8.4–4–14–1		16–4–41–0
v. Derbyshire (Derby) 31 Aug.–2 Sept.		19–5–44–1	8–1–18–0				27–9–67–2	
	231.5–36–687–15 *av. 45.80*	201.5–30–665–20 *av. 33.25*	127.4–14–406–10 *av. 40.60*	87.2–11–315–7 *av. 45.00*	20–3–65–1 *av. 65.00*	50.4–11–153–2 *av. 76.50*	62–16–175–2 *av. 77.50*	144.4–35–376–6 *av. 62.66*

for his county, Phillip De Freitas came back with a vengeance. He hit 100 off 82 balls in 95 minutes, the quickest century of the season. His innings included 6 sixes and 12 fours, and he helped lift Leicestershire from 98 for 5 to 257 all out. Nottinghamshire, with Broad back in the side, took a first-innings lead of 110 thanks to Derek Randall's first century of the season. Leicestershire earned a draw because of David Gower's last-day 72 not out, some missed chances by Robinson and his Notts fielders, and rain.

The opening match of the Cheltenham Festival produced a wonderful game of cricket. Put in to bat, Surrey were held together by Clinton, who scored his second century in a week although hampered by a thigh strain which caused him to bat with a runner for much of the time. Lynch, Ward, who was hit on the head and retired for a while, and Richards all contributed brisk runs, and Surrey reached 312 in 90.2 overs. By the end of the day, they seemed to have taken a complete grip on the match, for Stovold, Wright and Bainbridge were out with only 12 scored. There were more problems for Gloucestershire on the second day when Athey had a knuckle broken by a ball from Clarke. Romaines and Curran revived their sagging spirits with some aggressive batting, but Clarke reappeared to take four wickets in 17 balls to reduce Gloucestershire to 162 for 9. Athey bravely returned and stayed as Alderman scored the run that saved the follow-on. The game then took an amazing twist as David Lawrence, fast and hostile, returned the best bowling figures of his career, 7 for 47, and Surrey were shot out for 115. But for the positive approach of Ian Greig, 35, they would have fared even worse. Gloucestershire closed, early because of a bright, low sun, at 55 for 0 and had the last day to score the remaining 210 that they needed for victory. A spell of four

wickets in 19 balls by Sylvester Clarke took the heart out of the Gloucestershire batting on the last morning. At lunch, they were 132 for 8, and with Athey unable to bat, defeat seemed imminent. Alderman played commendably, however, and with Kevin Curran at last rediscovering his batting form, an amazing 111 were added for the ninth wicket. The pair held out for 2½ hours between lunch and tea, and Curran had just completed a memorable hundred and a historic victory had just become a possibility when, in the last over before tea, Curran played back to a short ball from Clarke and pushed the ball into the hands of gully.

At Lord's, the Sri Lankan tourists, the Cinderellas of international cricket, had Middlesex at 64 for 4 on the first day. Jamie Sykes hit well for 88, and Sri Lanka wilted a little in field and showed the limitations of their attack. Arjuna Ranatunga showed his class when the tourists batted, and the whole side showed more zest in the field when Middlesex batted again and Keith Brown hit his first hundred since the opening game of the season.

F.S. Ahangama	H.P. Tillekeratne	P.A. de Silva	Byes	Leg-byes	Wides	No-balls	Total	Wkts
			6	14		7	212	7
				12	1	16	324	10
				2		7	185	2
17–5–41–1	2–0–7–0			6	2	17	250	5
6–2–19–0			1	2		5	101	0
16.1–2–51–4	2–0–14–0		1	5		4	297	5
11–4–23–1			2	8	3	7	152	10
13–3–36–2			1	8	2	6	242	10
				6		7	246	3
11.1–2–55–1		1–0–10–0		6	1	5	368	3
6–1–26–1			4			3	185	3
			1	3	2	17	429	10
				8	2	4	100	3
19–3–70–2	5–1–14–1	13–5–32–1		2	1	11	247	7
99.2–22–	9–1–	14–5–						
321–12	35–1	42–1						
av. 26.75	av. 35.00	av. 42.00						

Refuge Assurance League

31 July

at Derby

Warwickshire 210 for 3 (D.A. Thorne 59 not out, D.A. Banks 51 not out)
Derbyshire 202 for 5 (K.J. Barnett 74)

Warwickshire (4 pts) won by 8 runs

at Cheltenham

Gloucestershire 228 for 5 (C.W.J. Athey 50)
Surrey 164 for 2 (M.A. Lynch 85 not out, C.J. Richards 72 not out)

Surrey (4 pts) won on faster scoring rate

at Canterbury

Somerset 125
Kent 126 for 3

Kent (4 pts) won by 7 wickets

at Leicester

Leicestershire 130 (J.J. Whitaker 51)
v. Middlesex

Match abandoned
Leicestershire 2 pts, Middlesex 2 pts

at Eastbourne

Glamorgan 194 for 8 (M.P. Maynard 92 not out, A.R. Clarke 4 for 24)
Sussex 194 for 4 (I.J. Gould 59 not out)

Match tied
Sussex 2 pts, Glamorgan 2 pts

at Worcester

Northamptonshire 123 for 6
Worcestershire 124 for 4

Worcestershire (4 pts) won by 6 wickets

at Scarborough

Yorkshire 208 for 8 (A.A. Metcalfe 69)
Lancashire 209 for 8 (P. Carrick 4 for 40)

Lancashire (4 pts) won by 2 wickets

Kim Barnett's misfortune, to which we made reference earlier, was that, having been selected for England, he sustained a hand injury while fielding which was to force him to withdraw from the side. Derbyshire's interest in the Sunday league also ended when Warwickshire beat them by eight runs. With Middlesex's game abandoned, Worcestershire, Lancashire and Surrey kept up the pressure with good wins. Gloucestershire hit 228 in 35 overs at Cheltenham, but rain reduced Surrey's target to 164 in 25 overs. The task looked impossible when they were 6 for 2, but Richards and Lynch put on 158, and Surrey won with 3.4 overs to spare. Matthew Maynard celebrated his England selection with 92 not out off 104 balls, but leg-spinner Clarke claimed praise with four wickets. Sussex, who were without Imran, who had failed to arrive in time, needed 10 from the last over, and eventually Pigott scrambled two off the last ball to give them their second Sunday tie of the season.

3, 4 and 5 August

at Cheltenham

Gloucestershire 356 for 8 dec (P. Bainbridge 119, P.W. Romaines 99, A.W. Stovold 52, D.A. Reeve 4 for 71) and 234 for 7 dec (P. Bainbridge 70, P.W. Romaines 50)
Warwickshire 307 for 7 dec (M. Asif Din 84, D.A. Thorne 64, P.A. Smith 50 not out) and 191 for 8 (G.J. Parsons 52, D.V. Lawrence 4 for 71)

Match drawn
Gloucestershire 7 pts, Warwickshire 6 pts

at Canterbury

Kent 327 (R.F. Pienaar 128, J.P. Agnew 7 for 61) and 140 for 6 dec
Leicestershire 247 (D.I. Gower 90, C. Penn 5 for 68) and 203 for 7 (M.D. Harman 5 for 68)

Match drawn
Kent 8 pts, Leicestershire 5 pts

at Northampton

Northamptonshire 283 (R.G. Williams 119, M.R. Gouldstone 71, G. Miller 4 for 36) and 89 (T.D. Topley 5 for 38)
Essex 238 (A.R. Border 110 not out) and 135 for 6

Essex won by 4 wickets
Essex 22 pts, Northamptonshire 7 pts

at Weston-super-Mare

Surrey 148 (N.A. Mallender 4 for 22) and 159 (V.J. Marks 5 for 41)
Somerset 159 (K.T. Medlycott 5 for 55, I.A. Greig 4 for 40) and 110 for 5 (K.T. Medlycott 5 for 33)

Somerset won by 5 wickets
Somerset 21 pts, Surrey 4 pts

at Eastbourne

Sussex 279 (A.R. Clarke 68, A.P. Wells 56, J.R. Ayling 4 for 57) and 225 for 5 dec (P.W.G. Parker 104 not out)

Hampshire 253 for 6 dec (J.R. Ayling 86, V.P. Terry 53) and 207 for 7 (R.J. Scott 58, V.P. Terry 50 not out, A.R. Clarke 5 for 60)

Match drawn
Hampshire 7 pts, Sussex 5 pts

at Sheffield

Yorkshire 337 (P.E. Robinson 129 not out, J.D. Love 69, E.E. Hemmings 4 for 73) and 119 afor 0 dec (M.D. Moxon 64 not out, A.A. Metcalfe 51 not out)
Nottinghamshire 195 (P. Johnson 124, P.J. Hartley 5 for 85) and 198 for 5 (R.T. Robinson 67, S.D. Fletcher 4 for 48)

Match drawn
Yorkshire 8 pts, Nottinghamshire 5 pts

3 August

at Swansea

Rest of World XI 255 for 9 (M.J. Greatbatch 95, D.M. Jones 89)
Glamorgan 208 (Maninder Singh 4 for 52)

Rest of World XI won by 47 runs

4 and 5 August

at Sleaford

Sri Lankans 224 for 4 dec (S.A.R. Silva 76, D.S.B.P. Kuruppu 52) and 240 for 4 dec (R.S. Mahanama 92, S.A.R. Silva 53)
Minor Counties 184 for 5 dec (S.G. Plumb 59) and 234 for 7 (S.G. Plumb 108, H.C.P. Ramanayake 4 for 80)

Match drawn

With Worcestershire idle, Kent had a chance to extend their lead at the top of the Britannic Assurance County Championship, but they were thwarted by a graceful Ladies' Day innings from David Gower and a fine match ended with honours even. Roy Pienaar hit his third century of the season to put Kent in a strong position on the opening day, and they looked to be well on top before Gower held Leicestershire together and restricted Kent's first-innings lead to 80. Eventually, Leicestershire were asked to make 221 to win, and Tavare kept the target ever before them as he bowled nothing but the spin of Harman and Davis after the first eight overs. Gower and Whitaker, in a stand of 84, gave the visitors a glimpse of victory, but three wickets fell for 28 runs, and Leicestershire were happy to draw.

Essex took advantage of Kent's failure to win and Worcestershire's rest days to move into second place in the table, 27 points behind the leaders. On a wicket of uncertain quality, Northamptonshire were rescued from disaster by Richard Williams and Mark Gouldstone. Williams, in spite of straining ligaments in his right knee and being forced to call upon the services of a runner for the later stages of his innings, hit a fiercely competitive century. Essex finished the first day disastrously on 48 for 4, but they, too, found their hero on the second day when Allan Border, ably supported by young Nasser Hussain, played a match-saving innings. He batted for five hours, meeting the variances of the pitch with his impeccable technique so that Essex surrendered a lead of only 45 runs on the first innings. Topley and Miller then routed North-

England v. West Indies – The Fifth Test. (Adrian Murrell/Allsport)

ants, but Essex were still left with a none too easy task of scoring 135 to win. Some early swashbuckling from emergency opener David East and the technical assurance and concentration of the veteran Fletcher and the young Prichard took them to victory.

Gloucestershire could not quite force victory at Cheltenham, where the bat dominated for most of the game, while the two Robinsons, one on each side, had good reason to be pleased with the game at Sheffield, which also ended in a draw. Phil Robinson hit a career-best 129 not out for Yorkshire, but this was matched by Paul Johnson's remarkable hundred for Notts. Broad and Tim Robinson began Notts' second innings with a partnership of 119, a reminder of past glories.

Lowly Sussex came close to beating Hampshire, one above them in the table at 15th, through the efforts of Paul Parker, out of whom captaincy has brought the best – he hit his fourth majestic century of the season – and leg-spinner Andy Clarke, who hit 68 off 94 balls, a career best, and followed it with 5 for 60, also a career best.

At Weston-super-Mare, the bowlers had a happy time. Greig and Medlycott bowled Surrey back into contention after they had been shot out for 148, and it was these two who adopted the positive approach when Surrey batted again, an example their colleagues failed to follow. At the close of the second day, Medlycott took 4 for 4 in four overs to give his side a chance of victory after opening bowlers Peters, Feltham and Martin Bicknell had been wasteful, but Roebuck and Burns kept their heads to steer their side to victory on the last morning.

Fifth Cornhill Test Match
ENGLAND v. WEST INDIES

England could not have had a more disheartening run up to the final Test against West Indies. Injury forced the withdrawal of skipper Chris Cowdrey, batsmen Barnett and Lamb and opening bowler Dilley, although Dilley wanted to play for Worcestershire at Kidderminster on the Saturday and had bowled in such a manner in the fourth Test as to suggest that his interest in international cricket was waning. Robert Bailey and Matthew Maynard, much forwarded by the press, came into the side as batsmen. David Capel was recalled, and De Freitas, recently dropped by his county for his attitude to the game, was, embarrassingly, named as replacement for Dilley. Incomprehensibly, he was then preferred to Small, an original choice, on the morning of the match.

Gooch had become the fourth England captain of the summer, and he won the toss, batted and promptly cut the second ball of the match, bowled by Marshall, for four. Ambrose swung the ball prodigiously, but mostly down the leg side, and when Gooch repeated his shot of the opening over the day looked bright for England. Then the runs dried up, and the last ball of the eighth over popped unexpectedly at Gooch, who could only fend it gently into

Tim Curtis hooks to the boundary. (Adrian Murrell/Allsport)

Foster traps Haynes. (Adrian Murrell/Allsport)

the hands of short-leg. With two inexperienced batsmen, Curtis and Bailey, together, England faced a tense period, but Curtis pulled the second and third balls of the 11th for four in regal manner, and even Marshall looked less menacing. Bailey got off the mark with a push into the covers, and by lunch, in spite of Curtis being crowded by a silly mid-off and overs from Harper and Hooper, England were 56 for 1 from 29 overs, Curtis 21, Bailey 20.

Nine overs into the afternoon, Curtis was caught behind off Benjamin, but Robin Smith asserted himself immediately with a violent hook for four and a drive to long-on for three. The hundred was passed in the 44th over, and then things began to fall apart. Bailey looked set for a big innings when he wafted vaguely at Ambrose and was caught by Dujon. After frenetically facing six balls during which he should have been both run out and caught, Maynard was caught by Dujon after a juggling act.

Gooch is taken at short-leg. (Adrian Murrell/Allsport)

Capel did not look capable of a big Test innings, and so it proved. Roger Harper had now joined the attack, bowling his off-breaks with an action which one former Test cricketer insisted should never make him capable of taking a Test wicket. He found the edge of Capel's bat, and Dujon was again exultant. Richards had looked neither as good a wicket-keeper nor as good a batsman as his predecessor Downton in the Test at Headingley, and he again proved to be well out of his depth, lobbing to short-leg. A bewildered Pringle flicked Marshall to Dujon, and De Freitas perished bat/pad. Smith's doughty 3½-hour innings was ended by a Marshall lifter, and England's bright morning had faded to evening gloom at 203 for 9.

After one clout by Foster, the England innings ended in the first over of the second morning. The home side's spirits were soon roused by Foster, however, who had an indecisive Haynes caught behind, just, captured an arrogant Greenidge who slogged to mid-on, and saw Richards taken at short-leg without scoring. Hooper hit one amazing six over extra cover which suggested the extraordinary talent of this young batsman, of whom we had not seen the best on the tour before he edged to first slip. A tired Foster retired with the brave figures of 4 for 41 from 10 overs. Logie and Dujon began their usual repair job. Neither De Freitas nor Capel posed a threat, and it was the returning Foster who ended the stand of 69 in 93 minutes when he had Logie taken at slip.

Dujon had played another delightfully aggressive innings before he shuffled across his crease and was lbw to Pringle, and Childs, who did not bowl until the 48th over, deceived Marshall with a beautiful ball and gratefully accepted the return catch. Harper moved the match from the sublime to the ridiculous as he attempted a second run with Ambrose static. He turned to regain his ground, but with wicket already broken, Pringle plucked a stump from the earth, and Harper was run out although whether or not Pringle really obeyed the letter of the law was debatable. Pringle bowled Benjamin first ball and had Walsh very

Man of the Series – Malcolm Marshall. (Adrian Murrell/ Allsport)

well taken at mid-off after the quick bowler had attempted to hit him out of the ground. England, wonderfully, led by 22 runs although why neither side had made 350 on the best wicket of the series remains a mystery.

Gooch and Curtis began the England second innings with a purposefulness which hinted at authority. They put on 50 before Curtis fell to Marshall, who had established a new West Indian record for the series in the first over of the day and now passed Trueman's record as the highest wicket-taker on either side during a series. The great drama was supplied by Benjamin, however, who yorked Bailey and gave Smith a torrid four deliveries before trapping him lbw with a ball that swung in to him. England closed on 64 for 3, a little chastened.

Gooch was England's hope on the Saturday, yet the fourth-wicket partnership was dominated by night-watchman Foster, who was intent on lashing the ball in all directions while his captain played the sleeping partner. Foster finally hooked Benjamin, a most valuable cricketer, to Logie and England were 108 for 4. Maynard hit his first Test boundary, but looked too raw a recruit for an

---

FIFTH CORNHILL TEST MATCH – ENGLAND v. WEST INDIES
4, 5, 6 and 8 August 1988 at The Oval, Kennington

ENGLAND

	FIRST INNINGS		SECOND INNINGS	
G.A. Gooch†	c Logie, b Ambrose	9	c Greenidge, b Ambrose	84
T.S. Curtis	c Dujon, b Benjamin	30	lbw, b Marshall	
R.J. Bailey	c Dujon, b Ambrose	43	b Benjamin	3
R.A. Smith	c Harper, b Marshall	57	lbw, b Benjamin	0
M.P. Maynard	c Dujon, b Ambrose	3	(6) c and b Benjamin	10
D.J. Capel	c Marshall, b Harper	16	(7) lbw, b Walsh	12
C.J. Richards*	c Logie, b Harper	0	(8) c Dujon, b Walsh	3
D.R. Pringle	c Dujon, b Marshall	1	(9) b Harper	8
P.A.J. De Freitas	c Haynes, b Harper	18	(10) c Haynes, b Harper	0
N.A. Foster	c sub (Arthurton), b Marshall	7	(5) c Logie, b Benjamin	34
J.H. Childs	not out	0	not out	0
Extras	lb 6, nb 15	21	b 3, lb 15, nb 15	33
		205		**202**

WEST INDIES

	FIRST INNINGS		SECOND INNINGS	
C.G. Greenidge	c De Freitas, b Foster	10	c Richards, b Childs	77
D.L. Haynes	c Richards, b Foster	2	not out	77
C.L. Hooper	c Gooch, b Foster	11	b Foster	23
I.V.A. Richards†	c Curtis, b Foster	0		
A.L. Logie	c Gooch, b Foster	47	(4) not out	38
P.J.L. Dujon*	lbw, b Pringle	64		
R.A. Harper	run out	17		
M.D. Marshall	c and b Childs	0		
E.L.C. Ambrose	not out	17		
W.K.M. Benjamin	b Pringle	0		
C.A. Walsh	c De Freitas, b Pringle	5		
Extras	lb 7, w 1, nb 2	10	b 2, lb 3, nb 6	11
		183	(for 2 wkts)	**226**

	O	M	R	W	O	M	R	W
Marshall	24.3	3	64	3	25	6	52	1
Ambrose	20	6	31	3	24.1	10	50	1
Walsh	10	1	21	–	12	5	21	2
Benjamin	14	2	33	1	22	4	52	4
Harper	21	7	50	3	6	3	9	2
Hooper	1	1	0	–				

	O	M	R	W	O	M	R	W
Foster	16	2	64	5	18	3	52	1
De Freitas	13	4	33	–	17	4	46	–
Pringle	17	4	45	3	13	4	24	–
Capel	7	–	21	–	3	–	20	–
Childs	6	1	13	1	40	16	79	1

FALL OF WICKETS
1–12, 2–77, 3–116, 4–121, 5–160, 6–160, 7–165, 8–196, 9–198
1–50, 2–55, 3–55, 4–108, 5–125, 6–139, 7–157, 8–175, 9–177

FALL OF WICKETS
1–9, 2–16, 3–16, 4–57, 5–126, 6–155, 7–156, 8–167, 9–168
1–131, 2–162

Umpires: H.D. Bird & K.E. Palmer

West Indies won by 8 wickets

TEST MATCH AVERAGES – ENGLAND v. WEST INDIES

ENGLAND BATTING

	M	Inns	NOs	Runs	HS	Av	100s	50s
G.A. Gooch	5	10		459	146	45.90	1	3
A.J. Lamb	4	8	2	254	113	42.33	1	1
D.I. Gower	4	8	1	211	88*	30.14		1
R.A. Smith	2	4		106	57	26.50		1
P.R. Downton	3	5	1	84	27	21.00		
P.W. Jarvis	2	3	1	42	29*	21.00		
B.C. Broad	2	4		71	54	17.75		1
T.S. Curtis	2	4		69	30	17.25		
N.A. Foster	2	4	1	49	34	16.33		
M.D. Moxon	2	4		55	26	13.75		
G.R. Dilley	4	7	1	58	28	9.67		
M.W. Gatting	2	4		38	29	9.50		
J.E. Emburey	3	5		46	30	9.20		
D.R. Pringle	4	7		52	39	7.42		
D.J. Capel	2	4		29	16	7.25		
P.A.J. De Freitas	3	5		36	18	7.20		
C.J. Richards	2	4		13	8	3.25		

Played in two Tests: J.H. Childs 2*, 0*, 0* & 0*
Played in one Test: G.C. Small 5* & 7; C.W.J. Athey 16 & 11; C.S. Cowdrey 0 & 5; R.J. Bailey 43 & 3; M.P. Maynard 3 & 10

WEST INDIES BATTING

	M	Inns	NOs	Runs	HS	Av	100s	50s
A.L. Logie	5	7	2	364	95*	72.80		2
P.J.L. Dujon	5	7	1	305	67	50.83		4
R.A. Harper	3	3		147	74	49.00		2
C.G. Greenidge	4	6		282	103	47.00	1	1
D.L. Haynes	4	7	2	235	77*	47.00		3
I.V.A. Richards	5	6		223	80	37.16		2
M.D. Marshall	5	6	1	135	72	27.00		1
C.L. Hooper	5	7		166	84	23.71		1
E.L.C. Ambrose	5	6	2	75	43	18.75		
R.B. Richardson	3	4		71	26	17.75		
C.A. Walsh	5	5	3	26	9*	13.00		
W.K.M. Benjamin	3	2		9	9	4.50		
B.P. Patterson	2	2		2	2	1.00		

Played in one Test: K.L.T. Arthurton 27

ENGLAND BOWLING

	Overs	Mds	Runs	Wkts	Av	Best	10/m	5/inns
G.R. Dilley	136.1	26	403	15	26.86	5/55		1
N.A. Foster	73.2	12	250	9	27.77	5/64		1
D.R. Pringle	119	33	326	11	29.63	5/95		1
G.C. Small	37.5	6	140	4	35.00	4/64		
P.W. Jarvis	57.1	6	217	6	36.16	4/107		
J.H. Childs	86	29	183	3	61.00	1/13		
J.E. Emburey	62	14	228	3	76.00	2/95		
D.J. Capel	22	2	79	1	79.00	1/38		
P.A.J. De Freitas	92	16	253	3	84.33	2/93		
C.S. Cowdrey	5.3	–	21	–	–			

WEST INDIES BOWLING

	Overs	Mds	Runs	Wkts	Av	Best	10/m	5/inns
W.K.M. Benjamin	67	17	151	12	12.58	4/52		
R.A. Harper	29	11	63	5	12.60	3/50		
M.D. Marshall	203.1	49	443	35	12.65	7/22	1	3
E.L.C. Ambrose	203.1	53	473	22	21.50	4/53		
C.A. Walsh	157.2	43	384	12	32.00	4/46		
B.P. Patterson	76.5	13	270	4	67.50	2/100		
I.V.A. Richards	10	1	28	–	–			
C.L. Hooper	24	2	57	–	–			

ENGLAND FIELDING FIGURES

9 – P.R. Downtown; 6 – G.A. Gooch; 3 – J.E. Emburey and C.J. Richards; 2 – D.I. Gower, T.S. Curtis and P.A.J. De Freitas; 1 – M.D. Moxon, M.W. Gatting, G.R. Dilley, D.J. Capel, R.A. Smith and N.A. Foster

WEST INDIES FIELDING FIGURES

20 – P.J.L. Dujon; 6 – A.L. Logie; 5 – R.A. Harper; 4 – I.V.A. Richards and C.G. Greenidge; 3 – R.B. Richardson, D.L. Haynes, C.L. Hooper and sub (K.L.T. Arthurton); 1 – M.D. Marshall and W.K.N. Benjamin

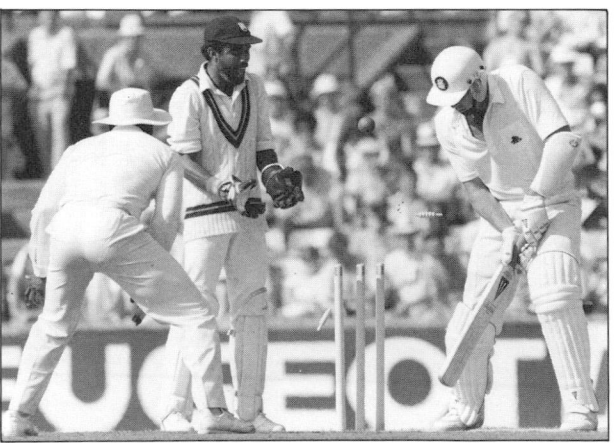

Pringle falls to Harper. (Adrian Murrell/Allsport)

England side as yet, and the afternoon session saw only 47 runs scored for the loss of Capel and Richards. It was grim stuff, but Gooch had taken upon himself the mantle of

captaincy and opted for survival rather than assertion. Many would have liked to have seen him choose the latter, but it is hard to fault the man for such a courageous and determined knock, particularly as he watched Pringle and De Freitas fall to dreadful shots.

Childs played manfully to help Gooch add 25 for the last wicket before Gooch was out after 430 minutes and 240 deliveries faced. West Indies needed 225 to win and were given a bonus by some quite awful new-ball bowling which allowed them to move to 71 for 0 off 24 overs by the close, only Childs offering a restraint on the scoring. Greenidge raced to 53, and England had lost Gooch with a damaged finger. Pringle became England's fifth captain of the summer.

Childs should have bowled from the start on the Monday, but he did not. He alone posed a threat to the West Indians and sent down maiden after maiden. There was a half chance to the wicket-keeper, but the opening stand was not broken until the first ball after lunch, when Childs found the rough outside leg stump and Greenidge spooned the ball up. Foster later bowled the aggressive Hooper, but West Indies claimed their 14th win in 15 Tests against England at 4.18 p.m. on the fourth day. As at Headingley, England had glimpsed a winning position at the half-way mark and had ended well beaten. Emotionally, all concerned with and for English cricket were exhausted.

Dujon was named Man of the Match, Gooch and Marshall Men of the Series. The indelible memory is of the silky smoothness of the great West Indian fast bowler who has no superior anywhere in the world, of his pace generated from the economy of his rhythm and of his constant menace.

6, 7 and 8 August

at Trent Bridge

Sri Lankans 307 for 7 dec (D.S.B.P. Kuruppu 158, R.S. Madugalle 72) and 244 for 7 dec (R.S. Madugalle 77)
Nottinghamshire 250 for 5 dec (B.C. Broad 73, R.J. Evans 50 not out) and 101 for 0 (P. Pollard 62 not out)

Match drawn

6, 8 and 9 August

at Swansea

Surrey 297 (D.M. Ward 126) and 171 for 9 dec (S.R. Barwick 5 for 37, R.C. Ontong 4 for 38)
Glamorgan 262 (A.R. Butcher 54, H. Morris 51, P.A. Cottey 50, K.T. Medlycott 5 for 122) and 98 for 3 (A.R. Butcher 65 not out)

Match drawn
Surrey 6 pts, Glamorgan 5 pts

at Cheltenham

Yorkshire 367 for 8 dec (D. Byas 112, P. Carrick 81) and 104 for 4
Gloucestershire 214 (A. Sidebottom 5 for 34) and 404 for 6 dec (P. Bainbridge 169, K.M. Curran 98)

Match drawn
Yorkshire 8 pts, Gloucestershire 5 pts

at Old Trafford

Lancashire 235 (M. Watkinson 50, A.R.C. Fraser 4 for 37) and 142 (N.G. Cowans 5 for 48, J.E. Emburey 4 for 26)
Middlesex 305 (P.R. Downton 120) and 73 for 0

Middlesex won by 10 wickets
Middlesex 22 pts, Lancashire 6 pts

at Leicester

Leicestershire 298 (P. Willey 98, S.T. Jefferies 5 for 126) and 212 for 4 dec (J.J. Whitaker 87 not out, P. Willey 56)
Hampshire 260 for 8 dec (K.D. James 77) and 233 for 9 (C.L. Smith 68, L.B. Taylor 6 for 49)

Match drawn
Leicestershire 7 pts, Hampshire 6 pts

at Weston-super-Mare

Derbyshire 324 (R.J. Sharma 80, B. Roberts 62) and 222 for 4 dec (J.E. Morris 59 not out, J.G. Wright 59)
Somerset 281 for 8 dec (R.J. Bartlett 66, J.J.E. Hardy 60) and 82 (A.E. Warner 4 for 37, D.E. Malcolm 4 for 43)

Derbyshire won by 183 runs
Derbyshire 22 pts, Somerset 5 pts

at Edgbaston

Northamptonshire 261 (M.R. Gouldstone 50, T.A. Merrick 4 for 85) and 98 (T.A. Merrick 5 for 26)
Warwickshire 278 (T.A. Lloyd 121, W.W. Davis 5 for 76) and 82 for 4

Warwickshire won by 6 wickets
Warwickshire 23 pts, Northamptonshire 7 pts

at Kidderminster

Sussex 146 (I.J. Gould 60, P.J. Newport 5 for 62) and 237 (A.P. Wells 65, A.C.S. Pigott 55, P.J. Newport 4 for 66)
Worcestershire 370 (P.A. Neale 167, M.J. Weston 94, A.M. Babington 4 for 83) and 14 for 1

Worcestershire won by 9 wickets
Worcestershire 24 pts, Sussex 2 pts

Worcestershire took the advantage of Kent and Essex being without fixtures to overwhelm Sussex and reclaim second place in the Championship, just eleven points adrift of Kent. Sussex gave a miserable batting display on the Saturday morning, only Ian Gould playing with any positivity on a wicket which held no terrors. Worcestershire were batting by early afternoon and although the wiles of Parker as captain and Babington as bowler quickly accounted for Hick, the home side were well in the lead by the close. On the Monday, Neale and Weston took their fifth-wicket stand to 181 before Weston edged leg-spinner Clarke to the keeper. Neale reached the highest score of his career so emulating another Worcestershire captain, Don Kenyon, who made his highest score at Kidderminster. By the end of the day, Worcestershire were poised for victory, and the match was over after 75 minutes on the third morning.

To the amazement of many, Warwickshire found themselves in fourth place after beating Northants on an Edgbaston wicket which was giving cause for concern. Moles had a thumb broken on the first day and Larkins sustained badly bruised ribs. Andy Lloyd asked Northants to bat first, and he justified his decision with a courageous four-hour innings of 121 on a second day on which 19 wickets fell. Warwickshire won 23 minutes after lunch on the last day, but the scoring of 82 was no easy task and they owed much to a gritty innings of 31 not out by Asif Din.

In spite of the meagreness of Somerset's second-innings total, the pitch at Weston-super-Mare had presented few terrors, and it was a lack of application that caused the home side to collapse against the Derbyshire seamers. Roebuck was unable to bat through injury.

Middlesex revived early-season memories as they brushed aside Lancashire. Paul Downton played with admirable resolution to steer his side to a commanding position after four wickets had fallen for 60, and Emburey complemented the pace bowling of Cowans and Fraser as Lancashire batted poorly in their second innings, and Middlesex won shortly after lunch on the last day, their first Championship victory since 20 May.

Surrey and Glamorgan played a rather tedious draw at Swansea while Gloucestershire, having been forced to follow on by Yorkshire, regained the initiative and finished with honour. David Byas, the young left-hander, hit a maiden century for Yorkshire, but Gloucestershire countered in their second innings when Phil Bainbridge hit a career-best 169 and added 218 for the third wicket with Curran. Set to make 252 in 47 overs, Yorkshire quickly lost their way and settled for a draw.

There was a more exciting finish at Leicester, where Gower asked Hampshire to make 251 in 50 overs. Chris Smith, Terry and Turner got the visitors off to a good start, but Les Taylor took three wickets in nine balls to bring about a slump. Scott and Ayling rallied Hampshire with 50 in eight overs, but the Leicestershire seamers again broke through, and Hampshire finished 18 runs and Leicestershire one wicket short.

Refuge Assurance League

7 August

at Ebbw Vale

Glamorgan 197 for 7 (H. Morris 51)
Surrey 189 (J.G. Thomas 4 for 31)

Glamorgan (4 pts) won by 8 runs

at Cheltenham

Yorkshire 191 for 8
Gloucestershire 193 for 7 (P.J. Hartley 4 for 27)

Gloucestershire (4 pts) won by 3 wickets

at Blackpool

Lancashire 207 (G.D. Mendis 86)
Middlesex 155 (J.E. Emburey 50, M. Watkinson 4 for 17)

Lancashire (4 pts) won by 52 runs

at Leicester

Hampshire 240 for 5 (D.R. Turner 51)
Leicestershire 177 for 7 (L. Potter 52)

Hampshire (4 pts) won by 63 runs

at Weston-super-Mare

Derbyshire 174 for 8
Somerset 172 for 9 (V.J. Marks 80)

Derbyshire (4 pts) won by 2 runs

at Edgbaston

Warwickshire 184 for 8 (M. Asif Din 93 not out)
Northamptonshire 186 for 5 (D.J. Wild 74 not out)

Northamptonshire (4 pts) won by 5 wickets

at Worcester

Sussex 165 for 9 (P.W.G. Parker 74 not out, G.A. Hick 4 for 42)
Worcestershire 166 for 2 (G.A. Hick 52 not out, D.A. Leatherdale 51 not out)

Worcestershire (4 pts) won by 8 wickets

Middlesex were beaten in the Sunday league for only the second time in the season, but it was a crucial defeat for they lost to close challengers Lancashire. Gehan Mendis gave Lancashire a fine start, and Middlesex never recovered from the loss of their first five wickets for 26 runs. Worcestershire and Gloucestershire kept up their pressure with good wins, but Surrey lost their way in

several senses when they went down to Glamorgan. They restricted the home side to 197 at Ebbw Vale, and at 184 for 7, with Medlycott and Feltham striking well, they were in sight of victory, but three wickets went down for five runs. Sylvester Clarke and Monte Lynch were not in the Surrey side, having lost their way to Ebbw Vale from Swansea. Clarke was later disciplined and fined a week's wages. Somerset conjured a greater disaster than Surrey, losing five wickets in 10 balls for nine runs to go down to Derbyshire by two runs. Vic Marks had earlier hit 80 off 117 balls, his highest Sunday League score.

10, 11 and 12 August

at Leeds

Yorkshire 297 for 5 dec (M.D. Moxon 132, K. Sharp 128, F.S. Ahangama 4 for 51) and 152 (R.J. Blakey 85 not out, G.F. Labrooy 6 for 61)
Sri Lankans 287 for 5 dec (S.A.R. Silva 112) and 7 for 1

Match drawn

Following their creditable performance against Notts when Kuruppu had hit a bustling century, the Sri Lankan tourists gave Yorkshire something of a fright at Headingley. Moxon and Sharp shared a second-wicket stand of 237 at a brisk pace on the opening day, but Amal Silva had brought the tourists to parity on the second. Then Graeme Labrooy wrought havoc in the Yorkshire batting to reduce them to 78 for 7 before Blakey restored order and rain brought an early finish. Blakey was to retain his place as Yorkshire's wicket-keeper even when Bairstow was passed fit again after this match.

NatWest Bank Trophy

Semi-Finals

10 August

at The Oval

Middlesex 258 for 7 (R.O. Butcher 65, W.N. Slack 56)
Surrey 188 (A.J. Stewart 107 not out, N.G. Cowans 4 for 45)

Middlesex won by 70 runs
(Man of the Match: R.O. Butcher)

at Worcester

Worcestershire 268 (T.S. Curtis 74, S.J. O'Shaughnessy 62)
Hampshire 239 (V.P. Terry 80, G.A. Hick 4 for 54)

Worcestershire won by 29 runs
(Man of the Match: T.S. Curtis)

Middlesex travelled to The Oval in the knowledge that, in five previous meetings with Surrey at The Oval in the 60-over competition, they had always ended as losers. They betrayed no sign of nerves, however, and Gatting had no hesitation in deciding to bat when he won the toss. Carr took three off Clarke's first ball; Slack four off the second. Martin Bicknell's first ball was despatched for four so that 11 had come from the first seven balls. Such a heady rate of scoring had to end, and in the fifth over, Carr touched Clarke down the leg side where Richards held a fine, low catch. The first wicket had fallen at 17, and

Needham tried to hustle the score along although he was not at his best with his timing. With the score on 63 in the 23rd over, Bullen's first, seemingly frustrated, Needham clouted the ball into the hands of mid-wicket. Surrey would have taken a firm grip on the game had Feltham held on to a chance that Gatting offered to cover off Greig two overs later. It was not to be the last chance to go begging off the Surrey skipper, who bowled admirably and finished with 0 for 52, four chances missed, while Clarke bowled without either endeavour or passion to finish with 3 for 49, two in one over when the slog was on. The Gatting miss did not prove to be as costly as it might have done, for in the 30th over, the score on 99, Gatting cut Greig to Bullen and ran. He changed his mind and began to run back to his crease so that we had the sight of Slack and Gatting racing towards one wicket. Richards had stood back indolently, seemingly uninterested, but Bullen hit the stumps with a gentle throw just as the wicket-keeper roused from his slumbers. Gatting was given out although most thought that Slack was ahead in the sprint for the crease. It was quite dreadful cricket all round. Only Bullen escaped with honour. Butcher now played the innings that gave Middlesex the ascendancy, hitting 65 off 80 balls with a six and 7 fours. He was out in the 51st over to leave his side at 189 for 5. Downton played a gem of an innings, 40 off 36 balls, and Middlesex reached a commendable 258.

Surrey began bleakly. Runs were at a premium, and Atkins was caught behind in the second over. Clinton could not get going, and only a generous sprinkling of wides from Hughes was an encouragement to the home side. Lynch was restricted by an injured knee, but just as he seemed to find his touch he missed a straight ball from Carr, pressed into service because of the vagaries of Hughes, and was bowled. Ward suffered a similar fate two overs later and when Richards was bowled by Cowans and Greig run out when he was sent back by Stewart Surrey's hopes were at an end. Alec Stewart continued to bat most pleasingly, and he reached a delightful century, but never at any time did it look as if it would become a match-winning one.

Mark Nicholas' decision to field first at Worcester proved to be an unwise one. Curtis and O'Shaughnessy began the Worcestershire innings with a stand of 148 in 40 overs. Such a foundation was sure to give a formidable total, and although Worcestershire lost seven wickets in 25 balls for 24 runs at the close of their innings, they still reached 268, Hick and Leatherdale having added a quick-fire 49 from seven overs.

Terry played an anchor role of 80 from 141 balls and added 98 for the second wicket with David Turner, which kept Hampshire in contention, but the loss of three wickets, including that of Robin Smith, in 10 balls undid all the good work. Hampshire scorned three offers of bad light, but they could never regain momentum and, like the day, they ended in gloom, beaten by 29 runs.

13, 14 and 15 August

at The Oval

Sri Lankans 219 (M.A.R. Samarasekera 104) and 300 for 6 dec

(L.R.D. Mendis 124, D.S.B.P. Kuruppu 87)
Surrey 242 (C.K. Bullen 59 not out, K.T. Medlycott 51, G.F. Labrooy 4 for 86)

Match drawn

13, 15 and 16 August

at Chesterfield

Derbyshire 262 (B. Roberts 58, P.D. Bowler 53, C. Penn 4 for 43) and 317 for 6 dec (S.C. Goldsmith 89, P.D. Bowler 84, T.J.G. O'Gorman 78)
Kent 466 for 8 dec (C.J. Tavare 119, C.S. Cowdrey 108, R.F. Pienaar 52)

Match drawn
Kent 8 pts, Derbyshire 6 pts

at Colchester

Essex 347 for 9 dec (A.R. Border 130 not out, K.E. Cooper 4 for 114) and 226 for 6 dec (G.A. Gooch 90)
Nottinghamshire 300 for 6 dec (D.W. Randall 76 not out, R.T. Robinson 63) and 274 for 8 (R.T. Robinson 134 not out, J.D. Birch 75)

Nottinghamshire won by 2 wickets
Nottinghamshire 24 pts, Essex 6 pts

at Abergavenny

Glamorgan 298 for 9 dec (J.G. Thomas 100 not out) and 242 for 3 dec (M.P. Maynard 108 not out, P.A. Cottey 59)
Worcestershire 200 for 5 dec (G.J. Lord 56) and 344 for 5 (G.A. Hick 159, T.S. Curtis 86, P.A. Neale 51)

Worcestershire won by 5 wickets
Worcestershire 22 pts, Glamorgan 5 pts

at Bournemouth

Hampshire 239 (V.P. Terry 82, C.L. Smith 59) and 164 for 9 dec (D.R. Turner 51, M.A. Robinson 4 for 38)
Northamptonshire 205 (G. Cook 50) and 108 for 7 (T.M. Tremlett 4 for 19)

Match drawn
Hampshire 6 pts, Northamptonshire 6 pts

at Lord's

Gloucestershire 268 (K.M. Curran 142) and 161 (J.E. Emburey 6 for 24)
Middlesex 261 for 8 dec (J.E. Emburey 82, W.N. Slack 56, M.W. Gatting 51) and 169 for 1 (M.W. Gatting 93 not out, J.D. Carr 58 not out)

Middlesex won by 9 wickets
Middlesex 22 pts, Gloucestershire 6 pts

at Hove

Lancashire 337 for 6 dec (M.A. Atherton 152, I.D. Austin 57 not out) and 111 for 2 (G.D. Mendis 53)
Sussex 172 (C.M. Wells 68) and 275 (P. Moores 97 not out, A.N. Hayhurst 4 for 78)

Lancashire won by 8 wickets
Lancashire 24 pts, Sussex 3 pts

at Edgbaston

Warwickshire 181 (P.A.J. De Freitas 5 for 74) and 173
Leicestershire 206 (P.A.J. De Freitas 55, T.A. Merrick 6 for 64) and 149 for 9 (N.E. Briers 54)

Leicestershire won by 1 wicket
Leicestershire 22 pts, Warwickshire 5 pts

at Scarborough

Yorkshire 369 for 3 dec (A.A. Metcalfe 98, D. Byas 98, M.D. Moxon 81, P.E. Robinson 81 not out) and 182 for 7 dec (P.E. Robinson 53)
Somerset 270 for 8 dec (J.J.E. Hardy 97, G.D. Rose 69 not out, P. Carrick 4 for 77) and 241 for 9 (N.A. Felton 61, S.D. Fletcher 4 for 40, P. Carrick 4 for 95)

Match drawn
Yorkshire 7 pts, Somerset 3 pts

For two days, Kent held the advantage at Chesterfield. The Derbyshire innings occupied a shortened first day, and on the Monday, Tavare and Chris Cowdrey scored sparkling hundreds. Tavare reached his century off 115 balls while Chris Cowdrey's hundred came off as many deliveries. They savaged the Derbyshire attack, and the erratic Malcolm, whose control had been lacking all summer, conceded 131 runs in 17 overs. A lead of 204 put Kent in healthy mood, but Bowler and O'Gorman began Derbyshire's second innings with a stand of 168. Steve Goldsmith, against his old county, then played a most disciplined innings as Derbyshire batted throughout the last day and saved the game.

Kent's failure to win cost them the leadership of the Britannic Assurance County Championship as Worcestershire won a memorably thrilling victory at Abergavenny. A shortened first day saw Glamorgan reach 192 for 7, and on the Monday, Greg Thomas reached a maiden first-class century with some powerful hitting. Having been 92 for 6, Glamorgan were well pleased with their 298 for 9 declared. Neale declared as soon as his side had claimed a second batting point, for he had to keep alive a hope of victory. Maynard hit a century before lunch on the last morning, but he was aided by some friendly bowling, Neale being anxious to force a declaration. It came, and Worcestershire were asked to make 341 in 72 overs. Lord went quickly, but Hick and Curtis began to score briskly and sensibly. At tea, Worcestershire were 125 for 1 with two hours remaining. Hick launched an assault on the bowling after the interval, but Curtis was out when his partnership with Hick had realized 192 in 49 overs. Hick became the first player to reach two thousand runs for the season, and Neale hit cleanly so that 72 were needed from the last 10 overs. Neale and Hick added 100 in 49 minutes, and although both were out, Weston hit 13 in the penultimate over to make victory certain.

Essex lost a glorious opportunity to maintain pressure when they lost to Notts at Colchester. Border's hundred seemed to have put them in a strong position, but Robinson and Randall proved obdurate, and the last day was reached with the usual slog, and declaration the only option. Gooch was power and majesty, Lilley and Pringle plundered well, and Notts were asked to make 274 in the last two sessions. Pringle and Foster captured the first four wickets for 39, and an Essex victory seemed assured. Robinson, however, played a captain's innings, a knock of eloquence and character. He was ably supported by Birch, and the last over arrived with Robinson facing and six runs needed, two wickets to fall. Aided by a dropped catch and some wild throwing, Robinson scored the runs, the last two coming from the final ball. The failure to bowl Topley and some strange field-placings by Gooch certainly helped Notts in their quest.

There was an equally exciting finish at Edgbaston, where Jonathan Agnew, enjoying another marvellous season with the ball, hit the last ball for a single and a Leicestershire victory by one wicket. There was also high drama at Scarborough, where Yorkshire's first four batsman each passed eighty on the opening day. Somerset kept in contention, but, needing 282 to win, they reached the last over on 241 for 7. Stuart Fletcher bowled Mallender and had Trump lbw with the first two deliveries, but Adrian Jones survived the last four to save the match.

Middlesex kept up their recently returned form with an exhilarating win over Gloucestershire in spite of Curran's glorious career best on the opening day. John Emburey showed a complete regain of confidence with bat and ball.

Tim Tremlett was another, happily, to show a return to form after a season plagued by injury, but Northants survived at Bournemouth.

Following recent traumas, Lancashire swamped Sussex and were indebted to Atherton's first century for the county, the highest score of his career. Moores did as much for Sussex, but failed to find sufficient support.

The Sri Lankans showed some graceful and attractive batting at The Oval, but still lacked the capacity to win.

Refuge Assurance League

14 August

at Chesterfield

Derbyshire 184 for 8
Kent 186 for 4 (C.J. Tavare 82 not out)

Kent (4 pts) won by 6 wickets

at Colchester

Essex 236 for 6 (M.E. Waugh 103)
Nottinghamshire 159 for 9 (T.D. Topley 6 for 33)

Essex (4 pts) won by 77 runs

at Swansea

Glamorgan 81 for 5
Worcestershire 85 for 3

Worcestershire (4 pts) won by 7 wickets

at Bournemouth

Northamptonshire 94 for 6
Hampshire 97 for 2

Hampshire (4 pts) won by 8 wickets

at Lord's

Middlesex 203 for 8 (W.N. Slack 53)
Gloucestershire 168 for 6

Middlesex (4 pts) won on faster scoring rate

at Hove

Sussex 218 for 5 (C.M. Wells 85, A.P. Wells 51)

Lancashire 219 for 5 (M. Watkinson 58, G.D. Mendis 51)

Lancashire (4 pts) won by 5 wickets

at Edgbaston

Leicestershire 109 (D.A. Reeve 4 for 17)
Warwickshire 110 for 3

Warwickshire (4 pts) won by 7 wickets

at Scarborough

Somerset 235 for 6 (J.G. Wyatt 89)
Yorkshire 233 for 9 (M.D. Moxon 68, P.E. Robinson 51)

Somerset (4 pts) won by 2 runs

Middlesex's win over Gloucestershire kept them at the top of the Sunday league, and with only two matches remaining, the top four looked assured of places in the Refuge Assurance Cup, although Surrey, Glamorgan and Kent still cherished hopes. Glamorgan lost a vital contest to the confident Worcestershire side, the match being reduced to 11 overs, while Lancashire won a fine victory at Hove with two balls to spare. Essex provided the two outstanding individual performances of the day as Mark Waugh, on his début for the county as replacement for Allan Border, hit 103 off 94 balls and Don Topley returned the remarkable Sunday best figures of 6 for 33.

17, 18 and 19 August

---

at Chesterfield

Yorkshire 301 (A.A. Metcalfe 115, A. Sidebottom 51 not out, D.E. Malcolm 4 for 78) and 25 for 0 dec
Derbyshire 83 for 3 dec (K.J. Barnett 64) and 218 for 6 (K.J. Barnett 109)

Match drawn
Yorkshire 5 pts, Derbyshire 4 pts

at Colchester

Glamorgan 192 (D.R. Pringle 6 for 51) and 291 for 7 dec (R.C. Ontong 83 not out, A.R. Butcher 66)
Essex 211 (G.A. Gooch 65, S.L. Watkin 4 for 56) and 272 for 9 (G.A. Gooch 72, D.R. Pringle 54, G.C. Holmes 5 for 38)

Match drawn
Essex 14 pts, Glamorgan 5 pts

at Bournemouth

Kent 240 (S.A. Marsh 50, J.R. Ayling 4 for 62) and 140 for 4 dec
Hampshire 139 (A.P. Igglesden 5 for 40) and 150 (A.P. Igglesden 5 for 51, R.M. Ellison 4 for 29)

Kent won by 91 runs
Kent 22 pts, Hampshire 4 pts

at Lytham

Nottinghamshire 272 and 0 for 0 dec
Lancashire 0 for 0 dec and 121 (F.D. Stephenson 5 for 25, K.E. Cooper 4 for 42)

Nottinghamshire won by 151 runs
Nottinghamshire 19 pts, Lancashire 4 pts

at Uxbridge

Somerset 275 (N.A. Felton 88, S.R. Waugh 83, P.C.R. Tufnell 4

Cricket at Colchester where the crowd enjoyed an eventful week. (Allsport)

for 88) and 232 for 4 dec (S.R. Waugh 112 not out)
Middlesex 255 for 8 dec (K.R. Brown 73) and 149 for 6

Match drawn
Middlesex 6 pts, Somerset 6 pts

at The Oval

Worcestershire 303 (T.S. Curtis 86) and 251 for 5 dec (G.A. Hick 127)
Surrey 302 for 7 dec (C.J. Richards 87, A.J. Stewart 77, K.T. Medlycott 77 not out) and 5 for 0

Match drawn
Surrey 6 pts, Worcestershire 6 pts

at Hove

Sussex 300 for 6 dec (A.P. Wells 120, P.W.G. Parker 79) and 259 for 3 dec (A.P. Wells 74 not out, I.J. Gould 69 not out, P.W.G. Parker 61)
Warwickshire 303 for 8 dec (M. Asif Din 84, G.A. Tedstone 50, A.C.S. Pigott 4 for 96) and 96 (R.A. Bunting 5 for 44)

Sussex won by 160 runs
Sussex 22 pts, Warwickshire 7 pts

at Bristol

Sri Lankans 285 for 6 dec (J.R. Ratnayeke 60 not out, M.A.R. Samarasekera 53, H.P. Tillekeratne 50 not out) and 112 for 0 (P.A. de Silva 65 not out)
Gloucestershire 246 for 3 dec (A.J. Wright 137, P.W. Romaines 62)

Match drawn

The rain returned to hinder progress in the County Championship matches. Ashley Metcalfe hit a welcome century for Yorkshire at Chesterfield, but there was so little play on the second day that freak declarations had to be made to keep the game alive. Eventually, Derbyshire were asked to make 244, and Barnett's 109 off 134 balls set them on their way, but after he was bowled by Fletcher the runs dried up and both sides settled for a draw.

Kent beat the weather and Hampshire to return to the top of the table. The consistent team effort which had been the finest quality of their cricket since May saw them reach 240 on a none too easy wicket on the opening day, with the impressive Marsh making a particularly valuable contribution. Four Hampshire wickets were captured for 45 before the close, but the second day was heavily hampered by rain. Kent plundered quick runs on the last morning, and Cowdrey declared 10 minutes before lunch. The Kent drive and enthusiasm was then apparent as Cowdrey's dynamic leadership, excellent fielding and wicket-keeping, and tight, attacking bowling took them to success. Igglesden had a fine match with figures of 10 for 91, but it was good to see Ellison, sorely missed by England, performing as of old.

Meanwhile, Worcestershire had a poor first day at The Oval, batting laboriously against a keen Surrey side. Indeed, Surrey had by far the best of the first two days. They batted with zest, passing 300 in 78.5 overs. On the Friday morning, Hick added to his other glories with the fastest century of the season, his eighth century of the summer coming off only 79 balls. Then rain ended any hope of a result.

Forfeitures of innings and the bowling of Stephenson, who moved to 99 wickets for the season, and Cooper gave Notts the match at Lytham after a black second day, and the Sri Lankans were also badly affected at Bristol, where batting practice again became the only course of action. Wright was most impressive for the home side in a century which stretched over the three days.

Sussex won their second match of the season in splendid style against Warwickshire. Paul Parker and Alan Wells shared a third-wicket stand of 175 on the opening day, and the same two batsmen and Ian Gould were again in fine form in the second innings after Warwickshire had achieved parity on the first innings. Bunting and Pigott then routed the visitors on the last afternoon to give Sussex their first success since the first match of the season.

Steve Waugh played two fine innings for Somerset in his last game for the county before leaving for Australia's tour of Pakistan, but the game with a Middlesex side troubled by injury was drawn. No praise can be too high for Waugh's contribution to the English summer. He delighted wherever he went, quietly unassuming, but always plundering runs in a charming manner.

The game involving third-place Essex ended in total confusion. Pringle claimed his second six-wicket haul of the week, but Essex could only manage a disappointing first innings lead of 19, losing their last seven wickets for 62 runs. Glamorgan· began their second innings with a bounce, lost their way and then regained it through Rodney Ontong so that Morris was able to set Essex 273 to win. Gooch, Lilley and Border gave the run chase just the start that was needed, but Essex tottered as Geoff Holmes returned the best figures of his career. The last over was reached with seven needed, and Pringle, who batted quite splendidly, and Childs at the wicket. Pringle was run out on the last ball of the match as he attempted the winning run. The scores had finished level, and as Essex's last man, Miller, had taken no part in the match and was not on the ground through illness, many thought the match a tie, but as Essex had lost only nine wickets, it was deemed a draw, much to the chagrin of Glamorgan. It brought to an end a fine week at Colchester when both matches had been decided on the last ball.

20, 21 and 22 August

at Southampton

Hampshire 368 for 3 dec (V.P. Terry 190, R.A. Smith 104 not out, M.C.J. Nicholas 57) and 185 for 2 (R.J. Scott 107 not out)
Sri Lankans 280 (R.S. Madugalle 97, K.D. James 5 for 80) and 106 for 1

Match drawn

at Dumfries

Scotland 396 (B.M.W. Patterson 100, R.G. Swann 77, G.B.J. McGurk 63, A.N. Nelson 4 for 100)
Ireland 168 (J.W. Govan 4 for 38) and 185 (M.P. Rea 53, J.W. Govan 5 for 54)

Scotland won by an innings and 43 runs

20, 22 and 23 August

at Bristol

Kent 301 for 5 dec (M.R. Benson 70, R.F. Pienaar 51, G.R. Cowdrey 50) and 184 for 7 dec (M.R. Benson 58, M.W. Pooley 4 for 80)
Gloucestershire 259 for 7 dec (K.B.K. Ibadulla 77, P. Bainbridge 55) and 161 for 7 (P.W. Romaines 61, R.M. Ellison 5 for 46)

Match drawn
Kent 7 pts, Gloucestershire 5 pts

at Old Trafford

Lancashire 197 (I.D. Austin 64, F.A. Griffith 4 for 47) and 220 for 1 dec (M.A. Atherton 115 not out, N.H. Fairbrother 50 not out)
Derbyshire 157 for 3 dec (J.G. Wright 82, P.D. Bowler 51 not out) and 142 for 8 (J.E. Morris 86 not out, M. Watkinson 6 for 50)

Match drawn
Derbyshire 5 pts, Lancashire 2 pts

at Hinckley

Somerset 164 (J.G. Wyatt 57, J.P. Agnew 5 for 51) and 170 (V.J. Marks 50, G.J.F. Ferris 4 for 36)
Leicestershire 233 (P. Whitticase 71, L. Potter 52) and 103 for 3

Leicestershire won by 7 wickets
Leicestershire 22 pts, Somerset 5 pts

at Uxbridge

Warwickshire 212 (T.A. Lloyd 101, N.G. Cowans 6 for 49) and 158 (N.G. Cowans 4 for 48)
Middlesex 274 (J.E. Emburey 102, G.C. Small 5 for 74) and 97 for 3

Middlesex won by 7 wickets
Middlesex 23 pts, Warwickshire 6 pts

at Wellingborough

Glamorgan 220 (G.C. Holmes 83, A. Walker 5 for 64) and 157 (M.A. Robinson 4 for 19)
Northamptonshire 201 for 3 dec (G. Cook 75, W. Larkins 67) and 178 for 3 (A.J. Lamb 104 not out)

Northamptonshire won by 7 wickets
Northamptonshire 22 pts, Glamorgan 3 pts

at Trent Bridge

Nottinghamshire 144 (M.P. Bicknell 4 for 34, M.A. Feltham 4 for 43) and 131 (S.T. Clarke 6 for 52)
Surrey 269 (C.J. Richards 80, A.J. Stewart 76) and 10 for 1

Surrey won by 9 wickets
Surrey 23 pts, Nottinghamshire 4 pts

at Worcester

Essex 262 for 9 dec (G.A. Gooch 72, D.R. Pringle 63, P.J. Newport 5 for 70) and 182 (P.J. Prichard 80, P.J. Newport 4 for 56)
Worcestershire 150 (N.A. Foster 6 for 67) and 217 (N.A. Foster 4 for 61)

Essex won by 77 runs
Essex 23 pts, Worcestershire 4 pts

The crucial top-of-the-table clash at Worcester ended in murky conditions and victory for Essex. Uncertain weather troubled the match throughout, and Essex, with Gooch again prominent, made the best of a limited first day. Pringle hit well at the close, and Foster routed Worcestershire on the Monday. The home side struck back through some fine bowling by Newport, and Essex were 77 for 6, the game slipping from them, in their second innings. Paul Prichard then played a masterly innings on a difficult wicket, and Worcestershire were left to make 295 to win, a most formidable task in the circumstances. Early success for Foster, and Hick taken at short-leg by Lilley off Pringle, put Essex well on top. When the gloom descended Childs was called upon and dismissed the dangerous Neale, but it was Foster who bowled Essex to victory with 22 balls to spare.

Kent were thwarted by bad light at Bristol, but their positive approach to the game nearly snatched victory and won them seven points, which increased their lead at the top of the table. Only 67 overs were possible on the opening day, but Kent had reached four bonus points by lunchtime on the Monday. Ibadulla, with his best score in county cricket, held them up on the second afternoon, but Chris Cowdrey judged his declaration beautifully on the last day, setting Gloucestershire the tempting target of 227. At 45 for 4, the home side were losing interest in the chase, but Kent cleverly kept the game open before bringing back Harman and Ellison to capture three more wickets. Then, with four overs remaining, the gloom brought the game to an end.

Andy Lloyd hit another brave century for Warwickshire, but Emburey's improvization and Cowans' 10 for 97 turned the game in favour of Middlesex. The aggression of Wayne Larkins and Allan Lamb proved decisive for Northamptonshire against Glamorgan, and Morris saved the game for Derbyshire against Lancashire, for whom the highly exciting Atherton hit a second century and Watkinson bowled superbly to come close to winning the match.

A career-best batting performance by wicket-keeper Phil Whitticase, who had performed outstandingly behind the stumps for Leicestershire throughout the season, brought victory over Somerset. Both sides had their problems in that Roebuck was to resign the Somerset captaincy and was obviously not well pleased with events while Leicestershire and De Freitas were to part company.

Alan Igglesden returned from injury to play a decisive part in Kent's victory over Hampshire at Bournemouth. (Sporting Pictures UK Ltd)

The all-rounder later joined Lancashire, where, one hopes, he will be able to acquire a maturity of attitude that has eluded him at Leicester.

Surrey, with pacemen Martin Bicknell, Feltham and the chastened Clarke to the fore, took little over two days to beat Nottinghamshire at Trent Bridge. The home side's one consolation was that Franklyn Stephenson became the first bowler to take a hundred wickets in the season.

Paul Terry and Richard Scott hit career-best scores for Hampshire against the Sri Lankans, who entered the Test match without a win and with a reputation for being unable to bowl sides out.

Refuge Assurance League

21 August

at Moreton-in-Marsh

Gloucestershire 269 for 8 (A.J. Wright 81, P. Bainbridge 81)
Kent 189

Gloucestershire (4 pts) won by 80 runs

at Old Trafford

Lancashire 200 for 7 (A.N. Hayhurst 77)
Derbyshire 198 (M.A. Holding 53)

Lancashire (4 pts) won by 2 runs

at Leicester

Somerset 175 for 5 (R.J. Bartlett 50)
Leicestershire 143 for 8

Leicestershire (4 pts) won on faster scoring rate

at Wellingborough

Northamptonshire 171 for 8 (D.J. Wild 54)
Glamorgan 172 for 4 (R.J. Shastri 57 not out)

Glamorgan (4 pts) won by 6 wickets

at Trent Bridge

Nottinghamshire 233 for 4 (R.T. Robinson 100, D.W. Randall 60)
Surrey 160 for 9 (F.D. Stephenson 4 for 23)

Nottinghamshire (4 pts) won on faster scoring rate

at Worcester

Worcestershire 179 for 4 (G.A. Hick 59, P.A. Neale 54 not out)
Essex 161 (A.P. Pridgeon 4 for 36)

Worcestershire (4 pts) won by 18 runs

The penultimate round of matches in the Refuge Assurance League saw Worcestershire gain a comfortable win over Essex and go top of the table, seeming assured of retaining their title. Lancashire made certain of a place in the top four when Base was run out on the fifth ball of the last over to leave Derbyshire two runs adrift at Old Trafford. Gloucestershire overwhelmed Kent to keep hold

Kim Barnett catches Kuruppu. (Adrian Murrell/Allsport)

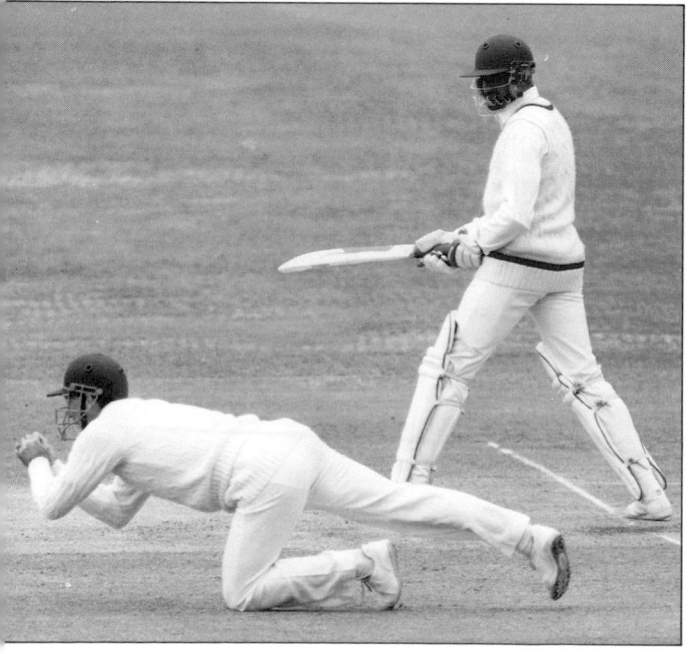

of fourth place. They were well served by Wright and Bainbridge, who shared a second-wicket stand of 166 in 24 overs. Surrey's hopes of a Cup place ended when they lost to bottom-of-the-table Notts at Trent Bridge. Tim Robinson hit a century for the home side, and darkening, damp weather left Surrey to make 164 in 28 overs, which, with Stephenson taking four wickets at the close, they just failed to do. Glamorgan alone kept alive their chances of dislodging Gloucestershire when they romped to victory at Wellingborough with 15 balls to spare.

Cornhill Test Match
ENGLAND v. SRI LANKA

While one had had sympathy for the selectors throughout the season and felt that the criticism levelled against them much of the time had been unjustified, it became difficult to support them in some of their choices for the Test against Sri Lanka. Chris Cowdrey had been chosen to lead the side in the last two Tests against West Indies. The reason for his selection had been to bring a sense of rejuvenation and joy to the England side. At Headingley, he had been forced to operate with three bowlers and had lost his most successful batsman with injury at a key time. For 3½ days England had matched West Indies, only to fall at the last and to suffer some dreadful umpiring decisions on the way. Cowdrey had been forced to withdraw from The Oval Test through injury and Gooch had taken over. The game had followed a very similar pattern to the previous Test. Now Gooch was named as captain against Sri Lanka and was, what amounted to, bribed with the captaincy if he would tour India. This appeared to be a complete reversal of the selectors' policy of revitalization when they appointed Cowdrey, whose failings at international level were known before he was appointed captain so were, presumably, no barrier then nor should be now. Seemingly, nothing had been learned from the defeats inflicted upon us by Pakistan and West Indies.

It was also hard to reconcile oneself to the recall of Robinson. He had proved all too fallible against quality bowling, and it was difficult to justify his inclusion against the moderate Sri Lankan attack when others had been asked to face the flak of the West Indians. Lawrence, Russell and Newport won first Test caps. Emburey was brought back as spinner, and Lamb returned after injury. Kim Barnett took the field as an England player for the first time, having been forced to withdraw from The Oval Test with a hand injury. Maynard was dropped, for he had not looked to be ready for Test cricket, as were Bailey and Curtis, both of whom looked deserving of another chance. The Sri Lankans were unable to consider Mahanama because of injury.

Gooch won the toss and asked Sri Lanka to bat first. He was soon rewarded as the Sri Lankan batting of which much had been expected fell apart. Silva soon edged to Russell who, surprisingly, had a very ragged time behind the stumps on his Test début. Kuruppu plundered 17 from Newport's first two overs, but Samarasekera was unable to get off the mark and, in desperation, flashed at Foster and

Samarasekera is lbw to Emburey. (Adrian Murrell/ Allsport)

was caught behind. Kuruppu, having hit 46 out of 52, was taken at slip to give Newport his first Test wicket, and the Worcestershire all-rounder accounted for De Silva in the same manner. Madugalle and Ranatunga failed, and at 63 for 6, the contest was virtually at an end. There was a very spirited stand by Mendis and Ratnayeke, who lashed the ball in all directions after lunch, but it ended sadly when Mendis splayed his feet and slashed at Lawrence to be caught at third man. Lawrence deserved the wicket, having had Silva dropped by Russell early on. Madurasinghe and Ramanayake looked lost at sea, but Labrooy dominated a brave last-wicket stand of 64, which constituted a record for Sri Lanka. Pringle ended the innings when he trapped Labrooy, who had hit his highest Test score, with a slower ball.

England lost Robinson to a poor shot before the close, 47 for 1, but the next day a somnolent Gooch was adjudged lbw just as he was threatening to assert himself. One commentator remarked that Constant gave the deci-sion because he was getting bored. In truth, it was a very poor day's cricket; second-rate bowling, backed by third-rate fielding and wicket-keeping, was met by mediocre batting. Night-watchman Russell, profiting from missed chances, batted into the afternoon for his highest score in first-class cricket. Having been kept out of the side

---

CORNHILL TEST MATCH – ENGLAND *v.* SRI LANKA
25, 26, 27, 29 and 30 August 1988 at Lord's

SRI LANKA

	FIRST INNINGS		SECOND INNINGS	
D.S.B.P. Kuruppu	c Gooch, b Newport	46	c Barnett, b Foster	25
S.A.R. Silva*	c Russell, b Foster	1	c Russell, b Newport	16
M.A.R. Samarasekera	c Russell, b Foster	0	lbw, b Emburey	57
P.A. de Silva	c Gooch, b Newport	3	lbw, b Lawrence	18
R.S. Madugalle†	lbw, b Foster	3	b Foster	20
A. Ranatunga	lbw, b Newport	5	b Newport	78
L.R.D. Mendis	c Smith, b Lawrence	21	lbw, b Pringle	56
J.R. Ratnayeke	not out	59	c Lamb, b Lawrence	32
W.R. Madurasinghe	run out	4	b Newport	2
H.C.P. Ramanayake	lbw, b Pringle	0	(11) c Gooch, b Newport	2
G.F. Labrooy	lbw, b Pringle	42	(10) not out	9
Extras	b 1, lb 7, nb 2	10	lb 8, nb 8	16
		194		**331**

ENGLAND

	FIRST INNINGS		SECOND INNINGS	
G.A. Gooch†	lbw, b Ratnayeke	75	c Silva, b Samarasekera	36
R.T. Robinson	c Samarasekera, b Ratnayeke	19	not out	34
R.C. Russell*	c Samarasekera, b Labrooy	94		
K.J. Barnett	c Ranatunga, b Labrooy	66	(3) c Silva, b Samarasekera	0
A.J. Lamb	b Labrooy	63	(4) c de Silva, b Ranatunga	8
R.A. Smith	b Ranatunga	31	(5) not out	14
D.R. Pringle	c Silva, b Labrooy	14		
J.E. Emburey	c de Silva, b Samarasekera	0		
P.J. Newport	c de Silva, b Ramanayake	26		
N.A. Foster	not out	14		
D.V. Lawrence	c Mendis, b Ramanayake	4		
Extras	b 1, lb 3, w 3, nb 17	23	lb 8, w 2, nb 4	14
		429	(for 3 wkts)	**100**

	O	M	R	W	O	M	R	W
Foster	21	5	51	3	33	10	98	2
Lawrence	15	4	37	1	21	5	74	2
Newport	21	4	77	3	26.3	7	87	4
Pringle	6.5	1	17	2	11	2	30	1
Emburey	2	1	4	–	18	9	34	1

	O	M	R	W	O	M	R	W
Ratnayeke	32	3	107	2	7	1	16	–
Labrooy	40	7	119	4	9	–	24	–
Ramanayake	27.2	3	86	2				
Madurasinghe	16	4	41	–				
Samarasekera	22	5	66	1	10	–	38	2
Ranatunga	6	3	6	1	8.4	4	14	1

FALL OF WICKETS
1–7, 2–44, 3–52, 4–53, 5–61, 6–63, 7–122, 8–127, 9–130
1–43, 2–51, 3–96, 4–145, 5–147, 6–251, 7–309, 8–311, 9–323

FALL OF WICKETS
1–40, 2–171, 3–233, 4–320, 5–358, 6–373, 7–378, 8–383, 9–420
1–73, 2–73, 3–82

Umpires: D.J. Constant & J.W. Holder

England won by 7 wickets

LEFT: *Test débutant David Lawrence. (Adrian Murrell/ Allsport)*
BELOW LEFT: *Graeme Labrooy, who bowled finely to record his best performance in Test cricket. (Adrian Murrell/ Allsport)*

because of doubts about his quality as a batsman, he had proved a point on his Test début, and he looked sure of reaching a century when nerves gripped him and he slashed into the hands of cover. Lamb played a few fine shots before the close and the bouncy Barnett reached fifty in his first Test.

Sri Lanka came back well on the Saturday and restricted England to another 151 for the loss of their last seven wickets. Labrooy, with a nice, easy action, was particularly impressive and added a Test best bowling performance to his highest Test score. Sri Lanka lost both openers before the close, which came at 92 for 2, but showed altogether more heart.

This was confirmed on the Monday when Samarasekera reached a fifty of charm and panache. Ranatunga and Mendis added 104 in a stand of joyful cricket and some exquisite shots. England were left just over a day in which to score 97. Phil Newport added to his first-innings tally with four more wickets and a general impression of good seam bowling.

There were hiccups on the last morning. Gooch and Barnett were caught behind within the space of three balls, and Lamb lofted lazily to mid-wicket. At lunch-time the scores were level, and the game dragged into the afternoon when, four balls after the break, England won their first Test match in the last 19 attempts.

Sri Lanka had shown great charm after the first two days, but, having been elevated to Test status, they are burdened by the fact that nobody seems willing to play Test cricket against them. They deserve far more encouragement and fuller series than they are getting.

England's victory was welcome, but one would still place only Sri Lanka below them in world rankings, which, one suggests, should be:

1. Pakistan
2. West Indies
3. India
4. Australia
5. New Zealand
6. England
7. Sri Lanka

England might be level with New Zealand, and Australia with India, but the top two are quite clear.

25, 26, 27 and 29 August

at Neath

Leicestershire 314 (J.J. Whitaker 126, L. Potter 66, S. Bastien 5 for 90)
Glamorgan 11 for 2

Match drawn
Leicestershire 3 pts, Glamorgan 1 pt

Paul Parker played a vital part in Sussex's victory over Kent at Maidstone and enjoyed an excellent season with the bat. (George Herringshaw/ASP)

at Maidstone

Sussex 184 (A.P. Igglesden 4 for 53) and 359 (P.W.G. Parker 124, N.J. Lenham 74, I.J. Gould 50, C. Penn 4 for 100, A.P. Igglesden 4 for 105)
Kent 233 (R.F. Pienaar 72, C.M. Wells 4 for 43) and 247 (C.J. Tavare 97, G.R. Cowdrey 50, A.C.S. Pigott 4 for 86)

Sussex won by 63 runs
Sussex 21 pts, Kent 6 pts

at Northampton

Northamptonshire 193 (R.J. Bailey 51, O.H. Mortensen 6 for 40) and 362 for 9 dec (R.J. Bailey 110, G. Cook 69)
Derbyshire 260 (B. Roberts 71) and 172 for 8

Match drawn
Derbyshire 7 pts, Northamptonshire 5 pts

at Taunton

Hampshire 321 (D.R. Turner 93) and 135 for 9 dec (G.D. Rose 4 for 47, A.N. Jones 4 for 77)
Somerset 202 and 149 for 3 (N.A. Felton 57, J.J.E. Hardy 50)

Match drawn
Hampshire 7 pts, Somerset 5 pts

at The Oval

Lancashire 84 (M.A. Feltham 5 for 45, S.T. Clarke 4 for 29) and 246 (G. Fowler 97, S.T. Clarke 6 for 60)
Surrey 331 (M.A. Lynch 103, A.J. Stewart 70, I.D. Austin 5 for 79)

Surrey won by an innings and 1 run
Surrey 24 pts, Lancashire 4 pts

at Worcester

Warwickshire 198 (G.R. Dilley 4 for 53) and 318 for 7 dec (D.A. Thorne 76, A.I. Kallicharran 60)
Worcestershire 281 (M.J. Weston 95 not out, G.A. Hick 75, G.C. Small 5 for 95)

Match drawn
Worcestershire 7 pts, Warwickshire 5 pts

at Leeds

Yorkshire 463 for 3 dec (A.A. Metcalfe 216 not out, P.E. Robinson 88, J.D. Love 70 not out, M.D. Moxon 57) and 185 for 0 dec (M.D. Moxon 89 not out, A.A. Metcalfe 78 not out)
Middlesex 315 for 6 dec (W.N. Slack 75, M.A. Ramprakash 78 not out, M.A. Roseberry 67, P. Carrick 4 for 67) and 322 for 9 (W.N. Slack 83, A. Needham 53)

Match drawn
Yorkshire 4 pts, Middlesex 4 pts

Neither Kent nor Worcestershire could draw much comfort from the first of the final rounds of four-day matches with which the Britannic Assurance County Championship came to a close. Kent began well enough in dismissing Sussex for 184, but they failed to build a substantial lead, and when the visitors batted again they were splendidly served by Parker and Lenham, and later by Gould. Parker, enjoying the best of seasons, hit his second century of the Championship against Kent, who were left to score 311 to win. They could not have had a worse start, losing four wickets for 17 runs, two of them to controversial decisions. Tavare and Graham Cowdrey battled bravely, adding 96, and there were valuable contributions from Marsh and Penn, but Ellison had a broken left hand, and when Tavare was bowled by Bunting for 97 the cause was lost.

As it transpired, Kent surrendered only one point of their lead, for rain badly affected the game at Worcester, where there was no play on the Saturday and an early end on the Monday. Worcestershire took a first-innings lead of 83, but then had difficulty in dismissing Thorne and Kallicharran, returning to the side after a long absence through injury.

There was no play at all after the second day at Neath, but the Leicestershire innings had produced a century by one of England's forgotten hopefuls, James Whitaker, and five wickets for Steve Bastien on his first-class début. Bastien, a medium pace bowler, is another graduate of the Haringey Cricket School. He was ably supported by wicket-keeper Colin Metson, who equalled the Glamorgan record with six catches.

Rain deflated the game at Taunton, where Somerset battled back well through Jones and Rose and where Felton and Hardy had given them a fine start in their quest for 255 to win.

Having been placed in a good position by Mortensen's

Derbyshire CCC
Limited-Over Matches

BATTING

BATTING	v. Leicestershire (Derby) 24 April (RA)	v. Scotland (Glasgow) 26 April (B&H)	v. Yorkshire (Leeds) 1 May (RA)	v. Warwickshire (Derby) 3 & 4 May (B&H)	v. Essex (Derby) 8 May (RA)	v. Lancashire (Liverpool) 10 May (B&H)	v. Leicestershire (Derby) 14 May (B&H)	v. Glamorgan (Newport) 22 May (RA)	v. Middlesex (Derby) 25 & 26 May (B&H)	v. Nottinghamshire (Derby) 29 May (RA)	v. Sussex (Horsham) 5 June (RA)	v. Glamorgan (Swansea) 8 June (B&H)	v. Gloucestershire (Heanor) 12 June (RA)	v. Worcestershire (Knypersley) 19 June (RA)	v. Sussex (Hove) 22 June (NW)	v. Surrey (The Oval) 26 June (RA)	v. Middlesex (Repton) 3 July (RA)	v. Cheshire (Chester) 6–8 July (NW)
K.J. Barnett	77*	66	26	—	1	85	71	90*	69*	38	50	43	33	30	49	72	6	1
P.D. Bowler	32	19	4	—	7	64	55	5	26	—	9	23	28	4	6	25	0	46
B. Roberts	47*	7	18	—	8	0	29*	0	4*	0*	59	44	53	32	9	26	14	57
J.E. Morris	—	19*	16	—	39	48*	9	5	—	50*	43	19	0	47	43*	1	0	41
S.C. Goldsmith	—	27*	40	—	7	12	0	1	—	—	11	25	14	19	3	21	61	8
B.J.M. Maher	—	—	5	—	27*	1	—	4	—	—	16*	1	0	36*	21*	23*	9	4
P.G. Newman	—	—	27*	—	8	—	—	6	—	—	1*	15*	7	1	—	0*	15	3
A.E. Warner	—	—	0	—	11	—	—	11	—	—	0	13	14	16	—	7	5	
R.J. Finney	—			—			—	15										
M.A. Holding	—	—	1	—	14	35*	17*	19	—	—	6	15	21	3	—	40	1	1
O.H. Mortensen	—	—	0	—	2	—	—	5	—	—	—	—	1*	—	—	—	0*	0*
F.A. Griffith			8															
M. Jean-Jacques					7									13	—	—		
D.E. Malcolm					—		—			—		0*						0
R.J. Sharma											5		30	0		—	0	4
S.J. Base																	0	
J.G. Wright																		
T.J.G. O'Gorman																		
Byes	2	3			1		1	2	4		1					3	2	8
Leg-byes	7	6	9		3	6	4	5	9	1	8	4	10	6	1	5	6	8
Wides	4	1	2		8	6	1	7			4	13	5	4	2	2	11	8
No-balls	2	1	1				4		1		1	1						1
Total	171	149	157		142	258	190	174	111	93	213	217	216	211	135	225	130	190
Wickets	1	3	10		10	5	4	10	1	1	8	8	10	10	4	8	10	10
Result	W	W	Ab.	Ab.	L	W	W	L	W	W	W	W	L	L	W	Tie	Ab.	W
Points	4	2	2	1	0	2	2	0	—	4	4	—	0	0	—	2	2	—

Fielding Figures

33 – B.J.M. Maher (ct 31/st 2)	5 – O.H. Mortensen and S.J. Base
13 – B. Roberts	4 – J.E. Morris and P.D. Bowler
12 – S.C. Goldsmith	2 – P.G. Newman and J.G. Wright
8 – M.A. Holding	1 – M. Jean-Jacques and sub
6 – A.E. Warner, R.J. Sharma and K.J. Barnett	

BOWLING

BOWLING	P.G. Newman	O.H. Mortensen	R.J. Finney	A.E. Warner	M.A. Holding	P.D. Bowler	F.A. Griffith	M. Jean-Jacques
v. Leicestershire (Derby) 24 April (RA)	8–1–23–1	8–0–34–2	4–0–16–0	5.3–0–21–3	7–0–38–1	5–0–29–2		
v. Scotland (Glasgow) 26 April (B&H)	11–2–21–2	11–2–31–1		11–1–37–2	11–2–22–3	11–3–29–0		
v. Yorkshire (Leeds) 1 May (RA)	3–0–6–1	6–1–14–2						3–0–15–0
v. Warwickshire (Derby) 3 & 4 May (B&H)	11–0–33–0	11–0–39–1	1–0–5–1	11–2–48–1	11–1–59–1	10–0–33–1		
v. Essex (Derby) 8 May (RA)	8–1–30–3	8–0–35–0		8–0–38–0	8–1–43–1	2–0–8–0		6–0–35–0
v. Lancashire (Liverpool) 10 May (B&H)	11–0–52–0	11–0–50–0			11–0–52–3	11–1–49–1		
v. Leicestershire (Derby) 14 May (B&H)	11–1–33–1		5–0–18–0	8–1–33–1	11–1–34–2	11–2–30–1		
v. Glamorgan (Newport) 22 May (RA)	8–0–31–2	8–0–38–0		7–0–40–1	8–1–30–2	4–1–16–1		
v. Middlesex (Derby) 25 & 26 May (B&H)	9–2–13–1			8–1–25–0	9–3–13–3	6–2–18–1		
v. Nottinghamshire (Derby) 29 May (RA)	7–0–38–0	8–0–29–1		8–0–42–1	7–0–22–4	4–0–18–0		
v. Sussex (Horsham) 5 June (RA)	8–1–34–2	8–1–18–2		8–1–37–1	8–0–43–1			
v. Glamorgan (Swansea) 8 & 10 June (B&H)	8–0–36–1	11–0–28–1		11–1–52–1	10.2–1–31–5	3–0–15–1		
v. Gloucestershire (Heanor) 12 June (RA)	8–0–29–1	6–0–24–0		8–0–82–1	8–0–40–1			
v. Worcestershire (Knypersley) 19 June (RA)	8–0–63–1			8–1–34–3	8–0–46–1			8–0–52–1
v. Sussex (Hove) 22 June (NW)	9–4–15–2			8–2–27–0	10.1–2–21–8			10–0–46–
v. Surrey (The Oval) 26 June (RA)	8–1–35–0			8–0–61–1	8–1–30–0			8–0–42–0
v. Middlesex (Repton) 3 July (RA)	2–0–11–0	5–1–10–0		3.2–0–9–0				
v. Cheshire (Chester) 6–8 July (NW)	8.5–2–19–2	12–4–15–5			8–4–8–1		3–0–14–0	
v. Hampshire (Lord's) 9 July (B&H)	3–1–11–0	5–1–19–1			5.5–0–19–1	11–2–36–0		
v. Hampshire (Portsmouth) 24 July (RA)	7–0–26–1	8–2–19–1			3.5–0–13–0	2–0–16–0		
v. Hampshire (Derby) 27 July (NW)	12–2–34–0	10.2–5–35–3			12–2–38–1	12–2–31–1		
v. Warwickshire (Derby) 31 July (RA)	8–0–65–0	5–0–19–0				7–0–48–0	8–0–37–0	
v. Somerset (Weston-super-Mare) 7 August (RA)	8–0–27–1	8–3–22–0		8–0–35–2				
v. Kent (Chesterfield) 14 August (RA)		8–2–15–1		7–0–38–0	6.3–0–45–0		8–0–50–1	
v. Lancashire (Old Trafford) 21 August (RA)				8–0–68–1	8–1–35–0	3–0–19–1	1–0–8–0	
v. Northamptonshire (Northampton) 28 August (RA)				8–0–60–1	8–0–35–3	5–0–31–0		8–2–27–2
Wickets	22	21	1	25	41	8	3	1

bowling, Derbyshire then had to rely on the Dane to save them from defeat. Robert Bailey had helped wipe out Derbyshire's first-innings lead of 67 although he was aided by the fact that Mortensen had injured his back and was unable to bowl in the second innings. Derbyshire were asked to make 296 in 71 overs, but they were soon in trouble against a varied attack, and Mortensen and Frank Griffith, playing only his third first-class innings, batted through 15 overs to save the game.

Surrey once again disdained the idea of four-day cricket and beat Lancashire by an innings early on the third day. Clarke and Feltham routed the visitors on the first morning, and Lynch and Stewart then engaged in a third-wicket

English Counties Form Charts

The statistics of all limited-over cricket matches are given on pages 374–411. The games covered are:

Refuge Assurance League and Cup (RA)
Tilcon Trophy (TT)
Benson and Hedges (B&H)
Four Counties Tournament (FC)
National Westminster Bank Trophy (NW)

Once again averages are not produced as it is felt that they have little relevance in limited-over cricket where batsmen often sacrifice wickets for quick runs and bowlers are ordered to contain rather than capture wickets.

In the batting tables a blank indicates that a batsman did not *play* in a game, a dash (—) that he did not *bat*.

Batting

v. Hampshire (Lord's) 9 July (B&H)	v. Hampshire (Portsmouth) 24 July (RA)	v. Hampshire (Derby) 27 July (NW)	v. Warwickshire (Derby) 31 July (RA)	v. Somerset (Weston-super-Mare) 7 August (RA)	v. Kent (Chesterfield) 14 August (RA)	v. Lancashire (Old Trafford) 21 August (RA)	v. Northamptonshire (Northampton) 28 August (RA)	Runs
13	1	32	74				3	930
4	33	13	—	21	42	44	38	548
0	1	21	4	25	40*	37	3	538
42	32	16	37	34	20	2	65	628
0	26	10	22*	6	23	5	43	384
8	13	44	27	6	6	20	1*	272
10	0*	15	—	9*				117
4	1	9		18	0	16*	4	129
								15
7	14	0			2	53	10	259
0*	0	0*	—	—	—			8
			4*		9	8	0	29
								20
0		0						0
				33	30	0	23*	125
	3		—	—	1*	0	—	4
			15	4				19
							14	14
				1			2	5
14	5	23	7	15	8	8	10	
12	2	7	9	2	3		10	
3	2	1	2	1			1	
117	133	191	202	174	184	198	227	
10	10	10	5	8	8	10	8	
L	L	L	L	W	L	L	W	
—	0	—	0	4	0	0	4	

Bowling

D.E. Malcolm	B. Roberts	R.J. Sharma	S.C. Goldsmith	S.J. Base	K.J. Barnett	Byes	Leg-byes	Wides	No-balls	Total	Wkts
							7	3		168	10
							8	2	1	148	9
							1			36	3
							16	9	4	233	5
						4	8	3	2	201	5
11–1–40–1							14	10		257	7
9–0–32–0							6	4	4	186	5
	5–0–28–1						16	4	1	199	8
9–0–27–5	5–1–12–0						2	5		110	10
							9	3		158	7
	5–0–53–2	3–0–13–0					10	4	1	208	8
11–1–25–1							16	11	1	203	10
	6–1–55–3	4–0–19–1					9	10		258	8
	4–0–35–3	2–0–20–0	2–0–23–0				7	5	4	280	9
	3–0–5–0	6–1–16–0					4	7	13	134	10
	4–0–25–1	4–0–26–0				1	5	5		225	4
							2	2		32	0
10–2–24–0		7–1–17–1				1	5	4	1	103	10
7–2–25–1							8	3	5	118	3
				7–1–30–1		2	3	4	1	134	6
11–1–48–1							7	4		193	6
	4–0–15–1			8–1–20–2		1	5		2	210	3
	2–0–10–2	6–1–35–3		8–0–33–0		1	9	4		172	9
				8–0–30–2			8	6	2	186	4
		8–2–22–1		8–0–21–2	4–0–22–0		5	4	2	200	7
		3–0–30–3		8–1–32–1			7	3	2	222	10
9	16	6	0	8	0						

Essex CCC
Limited-Over Matches, 1988

BATTING

BATTING	v. Kent (Chelmsford) 24 April (RA)	v. Surrey (Chelmsford) 26 April (B&H)	v. Middlesex (Lord's) 1 May (RA)	v. Derbyshire (Derby) 8 May (RA)	v. Kent (Canterbury) 10 & 11 May (B&H)	v. Sussex (Chelmsford) 12 May (B&H)	v. Middlesex (Lord's) 14 May (B&H)	v. Northamptonshire (Chelmsford) 15 May (RA)	v. Warwickshire (Edgbaston) 22 May (RA)	v. Warwickshire (Chelmsford) 25 May (B&H)	v. Surrey (Chelmsford) 29 May (RA)	v. Hampshire (Chelmsford) 8 & 9 June (B&H)	v. Sussex (Ilford) 12 June (RA)	v. Yorkshire (Sheffield) 19 June (RA)	v. Wiltshire (Chelmsford) 22 June (NW)	v. Hampshire (Bournemouth) 26 June (RA)	v. Somerset (Taunton) 3 July (RA)	v. Surrey (Chelmsford) 6 & 7 July (NW)
G.A. Gooch	90	43	33	54	120*	20	57	50		117*	1	41	4		70	16		71
B.R. Hardie	78*	0	5	64	51	51	36	87	10	53	5	40	39	59	77	32		11*
A.R. Border	26*	19*	5		12	29	75*	5	9	—	30	38	77	0	35	44*		1
P.J. Prichard	—	68*	10	18	8	0	7	15	7	30*	0	14	3	9	77			0
A.W. Lilley	—	—		29*	7	28	4*	8	14	—	38*	29	23	6	7	—		1
K.W.R. Fletcher				0	11	38	6	4	9	1	—	21	40*	14				0
G. Miller			3	—	0*	1*		7*	20	—	16*	14		29	—	—		9
D.E. East				9	—	12	5	—	10*	1	—	14	—	24				20
T.D. Topley			23	—		6*			9*	—	—	1	0		—	—		
J.K. Lever			0				1			—	3*	5*			—	—		1*
I.L. Pont	—	29*					—		12					36				
D.R. Pringle		—	40	0	5	51	40	7		—	6	4	0		80*	8*		6
J.P. Stephenson				8*										2	31*	—		
N.A. Foster									40	—		9*		1*				12
J.H. Childs												1*						
N. Hussain														4				
A.D. Brown															1*	—	—	
M.E. Waugh																		
Byes		4		4	1			1		2	1		7		1			
Leg-byes	7	5	6	8	13	15	6	12	4	10	4	12	5	16	5	1		1
Wides		5	7	3	10	4	7	2	2	5	1	7	3	6	3	1		6
No-balls	1		2	2	5	2	1	1		6		3		1				2
Total	202	144	172	201	282	218	237	214	130	223	138	238	204	174	386	102		141
Wickets	1	2	10	5	7	8	5	7	10	1	8	6	9	9	5	2		9†
Result	W	W	L	W	L	W	W	W	L	W	L	L	Tie	L	W	W	Ab.	L
Points	4	2	0	4	0	2	2	4	0	—	0	—	2	0	—	4	2	—

Fielding Figures
25 – D.E. East (ct 21/st 4)
15 – A.R. Border
9 – G. Miller
8 – J.K. Lever, D.R. Pringle and G.A. Gooch

6 – J.P. Stephenson
5 – B.R. Hardie
4 – K.W.R. Fletcher and P.J. Prichard
3 – T.D. Topley and N. Hussain

2 – A.D. Brown and M.E. Waugh
1 – A.W. Lilley, N.A. Foster, J.H. Childs and I.L. Pont

† B.R. Hardie retired hurt

BOWLING

BOWLING	J.K. Lever	I.L. Pont	T.D. Topley	G. Miller	G.A. Gooch	D.R. Pringle	A.R. Border	N.A. Foster
v. Kent (Chelmsford) 24 April (RA)	8–0–43–1	8–0–41–1	8–0–46–3	8–2–29–2		8–1–34–1		
v. Surrey (Chelmsford) 26 April (B&H)	9.1–1–22–3			11–2–22–4	11–2–29–1	10–2–37–1	11–1–29–1	
v. Middlesex (Lord's) 1 May (RA)	7–0–29–0	7–0–42–2	6–0–29–0	7–0–34–3	7–0–49–2			
v. Derbyshire (Derby) 8 May (RA)	6–0–15–0		7.4–0–25–5	8–0–44–2	7–0–36–0	6–0–19–2		
v. Kent (Canterbury) 10 & 11 May (B&H)	10.1–3–36–0		11–0–41–2	4–0–38–0	11–0–59–1	11–1–46–1	7–0–48–0	
v. Sussex (Chelmsford) 12 May (B&H)	11–2–45–1		11–0–50–1	11–1–35–1	11–1–33–0	11–1–43–2		
v. Middlesex (Lord's) 14 May (B&H)	11–1–25–1	7–0–44–0	11–0–53–3		11–2–44–3	11–2–30–2		4–0–22–0
v. Northamptonshire (Chelmsford) 15 May (RA)	8–0–43–1		8–1–41–0		8–1–22–0	8–0–43–1	8–0–31–3	
v. Warwickshire (Edgbaston) 22 May (RA)	6–0–31–0	5.5–0–29–0	5–2–16–0		8–0–12–2		4–0–16–1	7–0–26–0
v. Warwickshire (Chelmsford) 25 May (B&H)	11–1–58–1				11–3–22–0	11–2–30–1	11–0–56–3	11–2–38–1
v. Surrey (Chelmsford) 29 May (RA)	6.3–0–18–1				3–0–25–0	4–0–31–0	5–0–28–1	8–0–26–0
v. Hampshire (Chelmsford) 8 & 9 June (B&H)	10–1–36–0		11–0–56–0		11–0–46–1	10.4–0–56–1		11–4–30–1
v. Sussex (Ilford) 12 June (RA)	8–1–34–2		8–0–35–0			8–0–38–2		
v. Yorkshire (Sheffield) 19 June (RA)	8–0–28–0	7–0–33–2	8–0–41–2		8–1–37–1			
v. Wiltshire (Chelmsford) 22 June (NW)	8–2–17–1		9–1–17–1		8.3–2–23–3	9–3–19–2	7–2–9–1	
v. Hampshire (Bournemouth) 26 June (RA)	8–0–36–1		4–0–21–1	8–1–36–0	6–0–29–1	8–0–40–3		
v. Somerset (Taunton) 3 July (RA)								
v. Surrey (Chelmsford) 6 & 7 July (NW)	9–4–15–2				12–2–21–1	8–0–21–1	7.5–0–26–0	12–0–51–3
v. Glamorgan (Chelmsford) 10 July (RA)	8–0–41–0		7.2–0–42–1		8–0–55–2			8–0–18–1
v. Lancashire (Southend) 17 July (RA)	8–0–54–1			8–1–18–2	8–1–32–0			8–1–25–4
v. Leicestershire (Leicester) 24 July (RA)	6–1–23–0	8–0–32–0	7–0–23–1		8–1–23–1	8–1–27–2	7.4–1–23–0	
v. Nottinghamshire (Colchester) 14 August (RA)			8–0–33–6	8–1–36–0		5–0–33–0	7–0–18–0	7–1–15–0
v. Worcestershire (Worcester) 21 August (RA)			7–0–37–0			7–0–26–1	7–0–34–1	
v. Gloucestershire (Chelmsford) 28 August (RA)	6–0–22–1	4.3–0–19–1	5–0–17–1					
v. Lancashire (Scarborough) 4 September (FC)	9–1–35–2	9–0–58–2	10–1–39–3	10–1–30–2				
v. Yorkshire (Scarborough) 6 September (FC)	6–2–12–0	6–1–14–0	7–1–18–3	8.5–0–28–4				
Wickets	19	8	37	25	19	24	1	10

v. Glamorgan (Chelmsford) 10 July (RA)	v. Lancashire (Southend) 17 July (RA)	v. Leicestershire (Leicester) 24 July (RA)	v. Nottinghamshire (Colchester) 14 August (RA)	v. Worcestershire (Worcester) 21 August (RA)	v. Gloucestershire (Chelmsford) 28 August (RA)	v. Lancashire (Scarborough) 4 September (FC)	v. Yorkshire (Scarborough) 6 September (FC)	Runs
12	7		2	32				840
				47	7	42	9	803
73	72*	3						553
10	22	10	36	14	8	45	41	452
5	31	22	11	4	26	111	4	408
2	10*	24	—		12			192
	—	31	—			—	14*	130
23*	—	2	29*	2	5	5	10	171
0		3	—	1	6	0	6*	55
1	—	2*			0	—	—	13
		6			15	3*	13	114
			8	8				263
8		0		22*	4	26	50	151
1	—		0*					63
				1	2*			4
38	22	14	30	0		—	0	108
								1
			103	12	5	2	36	158
3			1	2	3		2	
18	5	14	11	13	7	13	13	
8	1	1	4	2	2	3	8	
2	1	1	1	1				
204	171	133	236	161	102	250	206	
10	4	10	6	10	10	7	8	
L	W	L	W	L	L	W	W	
0	4	0	4	0	0	—	—	

stand of 182 in 46 overs of savagery on the Lancashire bowlers. Lynch's 103 included a six and 18 fours. Fowler resisted bravely for Lancashire, but Clarke, revitalized since being disciplined, took another six wickets to bring his match figures to 10 for 89 and to bring victory to Surrey.

Ashley Metcalfe hit the highest score of his career, became the first Yorkshire batsman to a thousand runs and helped his county to their highest score for 35 years. He shared an opening stand of 134 with Moxon and a third-wicket stand of 203 with Robinson, who had become the most reliable of the Yorkshire batsmen, but the first day was tedium in the extreme as Yorkshire ground to 215 for 2 at little more than two runs an over. Love enlivened matters on the second day with 70 off 86 balls. Gatting declared as soon as the follow-on had been avoided, and Carrick finally asked Middlesex to make 334 to win. This was a daunting target, but Slack, Needham, Gatting and Ramprakash made it seem possible, and with eight overs left and six wickets in hand, Middlesex needed only 49 to win. The loss of five wickets for 28 runs blunted the challenge, and Middlesex had a fright when Cowans brushed a ball from Carrick which had lodged in his pad onto his wicket without dislodging a bail. Yorkshire could not separate the last pair, and Middlesex ended 12 short of their target.

J.H. Childs	J.P. Stephenson	M.E. Waugh	A.W. Lilley
8-0-44-1			
	8-1-35-0		
	8-0-42-0		
	0.2-0-4-0		
		4-0-16-2	1-0-3-0
8-1-29-1	2-0-11-1	5-1-28-0	
6-1-14-2		4-0-24-0	
		3-0-10-0	
		7-1-38-1	
	7-1-14-2	5-0-20-0	
4	3	3	0

Byes	Leg-byes	Wides	No-balls	Total	Wkts
1	7	7		201	8
	4			143	10
5	10	10	3	198	8
	3	8		142	10
	15	7		283	4
	11	8		217	6
3	15	6	2	236	9
	10	1	1	190	5
	3	3	6	133	4
	15	7	2	219	7
	11			139	2
	15	6	1	239	3
1	17	2		204	6
	4	2	1	178	6
	10	1	1	95	10
	10		1	172	7
					Ab.
4	4	4		142	7
2	6	5		206	4
	14	1	2	170	9
1	8	3	3	137	2
	5			159	9
	14		1	179	4
2	7	2		105	5
3	10	6		223	10
	6		1	112	10

Glamorgan CCC
Limited-Over Matches, 1988

BATTING

BATTING	v. Gloucestershire (Bristol) 24 April (RA)	v. Somerset (Cardiff) 1 May (RA)	v. Hampshire (Southampton) 3 May (B&H)	v. Hampshire (Southampton) 8 May (RA)	v. Somerset (Taunton) 10 May (B&H)	v. Combined Universities (Cardiff) 12 May (B&H)	v. Gloucestershire (Swansea) 14 May (B&H)	v. Warwickshire (Edgbaston) 15 May (RA)	v. Derbyshire (Newport) 22 May (RA)	v. Nottinghamshire (Cardiff) 26 May (B&H)	v. Kent (Merthyr Tydfil) 5 June (RA)	v. Derbyshire (Swansea) 8 June (B&H)	v. Nottinghamshire (Trent Bridge) 12 June (RA)	v. Scotland (Edinburgh) 22 June (NW)	v. Lancashire (Pontypridd) 26 June (RA)	v. Lancashire (Cardiff) 6 & 7 July (NW)	v. Essex (Chelmsford) 10 July (RA)
J.A. Hopkins	8		8	40*	22	50		55*	60	81	8	18	2	12	26	0	50
H. Morris	37	—			5	15	11	72*	10	9	23	3	16	17	22	39	22
M.P. Maynard	1	27	4	24	71	115	15	—		108	1	22	75	35	3	22	9
A.R. Butcher	2	—	14	0	57	12	0	—	34*	1	34	31		47		80	5*
R.J.Shastri	84*	53*	55	31	39*	0	7	—	26	0*	2	16	52*	11	19	33*	60*
G.C. Holmes	18	43	18	17	19*	59*	29*	—	15	4*	17	28		15	15	38	47
R.C. Ontong	7	—	0	13	—	19	24*	—	0*	—	7	26	—	8	29	—	—
J.G. Thomas	0*	9*	14	3	—	16*	—	—	5	—	2	18	2*	0	25	10*	—
J. Derrick	—	—		6	—	—	—	—	10	—	15	4	—	4	3	—	—
C.P. Metson	—	—	11	0*	—	—	—	—	9*	—	2	9	—	0	5	—	—
S.R. Barwick	—	—	3*	—	—	—	—	—	—	—	4*	0*	—	0*	3*	—	—
S.L. Watkin		—	4*												1*		
P.A. Cottey			15	4			14						—				
P.A. Todd									9				38				
P.D. North																	
Byes	4	1	1			2	1	2		2	2			15			2
Leg-byes	9		4	8	13	7		5	16	12	6	16	9	9	11	14	6
Wides	4	5	2	5	1	6	2	6	4		10	11	4	6	1	9	5
No-balls	2		4	1	2	1	3	3	1	6	1	1				1	
Total	176	138	157	152	229	302	106	143	199	223	134	203	198	179	163	246	206
Wickets	6	2	9	8	4	6	5	0	8	4	10	10	4	10	9	5	4
Result	L	W	L	L	W	W	W	W	W	W	L	L	W	W	Ab.	W	W
Points	0	4	0	0	2	2	2	4	4	—	0	—	4	—	2	—	4

Fielding Figures 32 – C.P. Metson (ct 25/st 7)
11 – H. Morris
8 – R.J. Shastri
5 – J. Derrick
4 – R.C. Ontong, M.P. Maynard and P.A. Todd
3 – S.R. Barwick, P.A. Cottey, J.A. Hopkins and G.C. Holmes
2 – A.R. Butcher
1 – J.G. Thomas

BOWLING

BOWLING	J.G. Thomas	S.R. Barwick	R.C. Ontong	J. Derrick	R.J. Shastri	G.C. Holmes	S.L. Watkin
v. Gloucestershire (Bristol) 24 April (RA)	8–2–23–1	6–0–32–1	7–0–31–0	8–0–39–1	4–0–23–0	6–1–20–2	
v. Somerset (Cardiff) 1 May (RA)	4–0–25–1	3–0–27–0		1–0–13–0	3–0–19–2	3–0–25–1	2–0–16–0
v. Hampshire (Southampton) 3 May (B&H)	9–1–25–0	10–1–18–0	5–0–20–0		8–0–29–0	3–0–11–0	3–0–25–0
v. Hampshire (Southampton) 8 May (RA)	8–0–48–1	8–1–29–2	8–0–43–0		8–0–33–2	3–0–24–0	
v. Somerset (Taunton) 10 May (B&H)	11–1–40–2	11–2–57–0	11–1–47–0	11–1–27–2	11–0–52–0		
v. Combined Universities (Cardiff) 12 May (B&H)	5–1–6–0	6–2–21–0	11–2–43–1	11–3–53–4	11–2–24–1	9–1–41–1	
v. Gloucestershire (Swansea) 14 May (B&H)	8.4–4–22–2	11–4–10–2	6–2–11–2	11–6–12–2	9–2–17–1	5–0–16–0	
v. Warwickshire (Edgbaston) 15 May (RA)	8–1–20–1	8–0–32–1	8–1–22–2	8–0–23–2	5–0–26–1	3–0–10–1	
v. Derbyshire (Newport) 22 May (RA)	7–1–27–2	6–0–19–1	8–2–29–1	8–1–41–1	8–0–34–2	2.2–0–18–2	
v. Nottinghamshire (Cardiff) 26 May (B&H)	11–1–34–2	11–1–46–1	11–1–34–0	11–0–39–2	11–0–51–1		
v. Kent (Merthyr Tydfil) 5 June (RA)	7–2–17–0	8–2–10–1	2–0–18–0	8–1–21–2	7–0–42–1	6–0–24–1	
v. Derbyshire (Swansea) 8 June (B&H)	11–0–54–1	11–3–45–3	11–1–19–0	11–0–52–3	11–2–42–0		
v. Nottinghamshire (Trent Bridge) 12 June (RA)	8–0–40–1	8–0–46–2	8–1–18–0	8–0–41–1	8–0–33–2		
v. Scotland (Edinburgh) 22 June (NW)	6–0–14–1	10.2–3–23–2	12–0–27–1	6–2–12–1	11–2–13–5		
v. Lancashire (Pontypridd) 26 June (RA)	4–0–15–0	4–0–8–3					
v. Lancashire (Cardiff) 6 & 7 July (NW)	10.5–1–39–1	11–5–22–1	12–0–31–1	12–1–57–4	12–0–52–3		
v. Essex (Chelmsford) 10 July (RA)	8–0–40–1	8–0–38–3	8–1–39–1	8–0–27–0	8–1–39–1		
v. Middlesex (Lord's) 17 July (RA)							
v. Yorkshire (Cardiff) 24 July (RA)		8–0–34–1	5–0–34–0	8–1–36–4			7–1–19–2
v. Surrey (The Oval) 27 July (NW)	12–1–44–1	12–1–40–1	8–0–42–1	12–1–47–1	8–0–38–0	5–0–17–1	
v. Sussex (Eastbourne) 31 July (RA)	7–0–33–0	8–0–31–1	8–1–23–1	8–0–41–1	5–0–31–0	4–0–24–0	
v. Surrey (Ebbw Vale) 7 August (RA)	6.2–1–31–4	7–2–18–1	8–1–29–1	3–0–25–1	2–0–14–0	5–0–30–1	8–0–28–2
v. Worcestershire (Swansea) 14 August (RA)	2–0–13–1	2–0–13–0	3–0–17–1	2–0–23–1		0.1–0–4–0	1–0–13–0
v. Northamptonshire (Wellingborough) 21 August (RA)	7–1–30–2			5–0–23–1	7–0–31–0	6–0–24–0	8–1–28–2
v. Leicestershire (Llanelli) 28 August (RA)	2.1–0–10–0	3–0–21–0		1–0–5–0	2–0–14–0	1–0–8–0	3–0–17–1
Wickets	25	27	13	34	22	10	7

Batting

v. Middlesex (Lord's) 17 July (RA)	v. Yorkshire (Cardiff) 24 July (RA)	v. Surrey (The Oval) 27 July (NW)	v. Sussex (Eastbourne) 31 July (RA)	v. Surrey (Ebbw Vale) 7 August (RA)	v. Worcestershire (Swansea) 14 August (RA)	v. Northamptonshire (Wellingborough) 21 August (RA)	v. Leicestershire (Llanelli) 28 August (RA)	Runs
21	3	33	12	9	10		28	556
2	8	51	4*		32		7	405
63	64	92*		11		44	4	810
11*	26	0	27			7*	2	390
50*	59*	31	18	18	57*		12	733
13	15	33	28*		9		3	483
—	40	2	35	1				211
12*	1	2	7	—			13	139
—	—	0*	0*	—	—			42
—	—	7*	10*	—			3*	56
—	—	—	—	—				10
—	—	—	—	—				5
								33
								49
0	2							—

	1							
11	8	4	3	1	5	3		
2	7	1	6	2	8	2		

160	235	194	197	81	172	77		
4	6	8	7	5	4	7		
W	L	Tie	W	L	W	L		
2	4	—	2	4	0	4	0	

Ab.

Bowling

A.R. Butcher	M.P. Maynard	H. Morris	P.D. North
7-2-19-0	2-0-6-0		
5-0-25-0			
		2-0-14-1	
			7-2-20-3
0	0	1	3

Byes	Leg-byes	Wides	No-balls	Total	Wkts
	9	4		177	5
1	8	3		134	5
	5		3	158	0
1	9	4	2	212	5
1	4	1		228	4
4	12	5	2	218	8
4	9	3	1	101	10
	9	4	1	142	9
1	5	7		174	10
4	12	6	1	220	8
	3	1		135	5
1	4	13	1	217	8
	15	3	1	193	7
	5			94	10
	5		2	28	3
11	3	10	3	215	10
3	18	8	2	204	10
					Ab.
7	15	1		145	7
	8	10	3	236	6
	11	8	3	194	4
5	9	5		189	10
	2	4		85	3
3	12	6		171	8
	3	2		78	2

Refuge Assurance League

28 August

at Chelmsford

Essex 102
Gloucestershire 105 for 5

Gloucestershire (4 pts) won by 5 wickets

at Llanelli

Glamorgan 77 for 7
Leicestershire 78 for 2

Leicestershire (4 pts) won by 8 wickets

at Maidstone

Sussex 125 for 8
Kent 126 for 6

Kent (4 pts) won by 4 wickets

at Northampton

Derbyshire 227 for 8 (J.E. Morris 65)
Northamptonshire 222 for 8 (D.J. Wild 91)

Derbyshire (4 pts) won by 5 runs

at Taunton

Hampshire 207 for 5 (V.P. Terry 77)
Somerset 145 (J.G. Wyatt 72, P.J. Bakker 4 for 15)

Hampshire (4 pts) won by 62 runs

at The Oval

Lancashire 181 for 5 (G. Fowler 70)
Surrey 182 for 4 (C.J. Richards 71)

Surrey (4 pts) won by 6 wickets

National Westminster Bank Trophy 1988

The County winning the Trophy will receive a prize of £21,000, the losing Finalist £10,500, the losing Semi-finalists £5,000 each and the losing Quarter-finalists £2,500 each.

MARYLEBONE CRICKET CLUB

NatWest Bank Trophy Final

20p   20p

MIDDLESEX v. WORCESTERSHIRE

at Lord's Ground, †Saturday, September 3rd, 1988

MIDDLESEX

1 J. D. Carr	c Rhodes b Dilley	1
2 W. N. Slack	b Dilley	14
3 A. Needham	b Dilley	6
‡4 M. W. Gatting	run out	0
5 R. O. Butcher	run out	24
6 M. R. Ramprakash	c Radford b Dilley	56
7 J. E. Emburey	b Dilley	35
*8 P. R. Downton	not out	8
9 S. P. Hughes	not out	0
10 A. R. C. Fraser		
11 N. G. Cowans		
B 4, l-b 5, w 7, n-b 2,		18
	Total..	162

FALL OF THE WICKETS

1...3 2...21 3...21 4...25 5...64 6...149 7...159 8... 9... 10...

Bowling Analysis	O.	M.	R.	W.	Wd.	N-b
Dilley	12	3	29	5	2	...
Radford	11.3	3	37	0	...	1
Illingworth	12	4	24	0	...	...
Newport	10	1	20	0	...	1
Weston	2	0	9	0	1	...
Hick	5	0	19	0	4	...
O'Shaughnessy	3	0	15	0	..	..

WORCESTERSHIRE

1 T. S. Curtis	b Fraser	4
2 S. J. O'Shaughnessy	c Downton b Cowans	1
3 G. A. Hick	b Fraser	4
4 D. A. Leatherdale	b Needham	29
‡5 P. A. Neale	b Hughes	64
6 M. J. Weston	c Downton b Fraser	31
*7 S. J. Rhodes	c Emburey b Hughes	1
8 P. J. Newport	b Hughes	4
9 N. V. Radford	b Hughes	5
10 R. K. Illingworth	not out	6
11 G. R. Dilley	not out	2
B , l-b 7, w 1, n-b 2,		10
	Total..	161

FALL OF THE WICKETS

1.. 5 2...9 3 ..9 4...71 5.. 137 6.. 140 7...145 8...148 9...153 10...

Bowling Analysis	O.	M.	R.	W.	Wd.	N-b
Cowans	12	6	23	1	...	...
Fraser	12	5	36	3	...	...
Carr	4	1	9	0	1	...
Hughes	8	0	30	4	...	2
Needham	12	1	25	1	...	...
Emburey	12	3	31	0	...	...

Any alterations to teams will be announced over the public address system

RULES—1 The Match will consist of one innings per side and each innings is limited to 60 overs.

2 No one bowler may bowl more than 12 overs in an innings.

3 Hours of play : 10.30 a.m. to 7.10 p.m. In certain circumstances the Umpires may order extra time.

Luncheon Interval 12.45 p.m.—1.25 p.m.   Tea Interval will be 20 minutes and will normally be taken at 4.30 p.m.

‡Captain   * Wicket-keeper

Umpires—H. D. Bird & D. R. Shepherd   Scorers—H. P. H. Sharp, J. W. Sewter & E. Solomon

†This match is intended to be completed in one day, but three days have been allocated in case of weather interference.

Middlesex won the toss and elected to field

Middlesex won by 3 wickets

Total runs scored at end of each over:

First Innings	1	2	3	4	5	6	7	8	9	10	11	12	13	14	15	16	17	18	19	20
	21	22	23	24	25	26	27	28	29	30	31	32	33	34	35	36	37	38	39	40
	41	42	43	44	45	46	47	48	49	50	51	52	53	54	55	56	57	58	59	60

Second Innings	1	2	3	4	5	6	7	8	9	10	11	12	13	14	15	16	17	18	19	20
	21	22	23	24	25	26	27	28	29	30	31	32	33	34	35	36	37	38	39	40
	41	42	43	44	45	46	47	48	49	50	51	52	53	54	55	56	57	58	59	60

Today's Adjudicator is Geoffrey Boycott (Yorkshire and England)

'Man of the Match' Award

In each match in the National Westminster Bank Trophy a 'Man of the Match' was given a medal, a tie and a cheque. In the first round the cheque was for £100. In the second round £125, Quarter-Finals £200, the Semi-Finals £275 and £550 in the Final. The selection was made by a team of Test cricketers, one at each game.

The panel was as follows: David Allen (Gloucestershire), Trevor Bailey (Essex), Alec Bedser (Surrey), Freddie Brown (Northamptonshire), Basil D'Oliveira (Worcestershire), Godfrey Evans (Kent), Farokh Engineer (Lancashire), Don Kenyon (Worcestershire), Colin Milburn (Northamptonshire), Arthur Milton (Gloucestershire), Jim Parks (Sussex), Geoff Pullar (Lancashire), Phil Sharpe (Yorkshire), Reg Simpson (Nottinghamshire), Brian Statham (Lancashire), Roy Tattersall (Lancashire), Fred Titmus (Middlesex), Cyril Washbrook (Lancashire).

Reproduced by kind permission of MCC (Full match report on pp. 393–6.)

Worcestershire win the Refuge Assurance Sunday League. Phil Neale holds the trophy among his happy team mates. (Adrian Murrell/Allsport)

at Worcester

Warwickshire 82 (N.V. Radford 4 for 14)
Worcestershire 83 for 0

Worcestershire (4 pts) won by 10 wickets

at Leeds

Middelesex 150 for 9 (M.A. Ramprakash 51, S.D. Fletcher 4 for 37)
Yorkshire 143 for 6

Yorkshire (4 pts) won on faster scoring rate

Worcestershire retained their Refuge Assurance League title when they swamped a listless Warwickshire side by 10 wickets. The Worcestershire attack held the Warwickshire batting by the throat for 36 overs, only young Holloway offering resistance, and Curtis and O'Shaughnessy hit off the runs in 27.1 overs of intelligent application. Glamorgan failed in a 13-over game at Llanelli so that the top four

remained unscathed although Gloucestershire, victors over Essex, leaped above Middlesex and Lancashire, both beaten, to claim second place and a home tie in the Refuge Assurance Cup. Surrey scored a fine victory over Lancashire in a match reduced to 31 overs. Richards, Lynch and Greig batted splendidly and made their supporters ponder what could have been achieved had their side found consistency.

Refuge Assurance League – Final Table

	P	W	L	N/R	Pts	R/R
Worcestershire (1)	16	12	3		1	50
Gloucestershire (3)	16	10	4		2	44
Lancashire (9)	16	10	4		2	44
Middlesex (10)	16	9	3			44
Surrey (7)	16	8	5	1	2	38
Glamorgan (14)	16	8	5	1	2	38
Kent (6)	16	7	6		3	34
Yorkshire (12)	16	7	7		2	32
Hampshire (7)	16	7	8		1	30
Warwickshire (17)	16	6	8		2	28
Essex (14)	16	6	8	1	1	28
Somerset (4)	16	6	9		1	26
Derbyshire (5)	16	5	8	1	2	26
Northamptonshire (10)	16	4	9		3	22
Sussex (14)	16	4	9	2	1	22
Leicestershire (12)	16	4	9		3	22
Nottinghamshire (2)	16	3	11		2	16

(1987 positions in brackets)

The top four sides qualified for the Refuge Assurance Cup.

Middlesex v. Worcestershire, Lord's on NatWest Final day. The scoreboard shows Middlesex at 24 for 4. (Ken Kelly)

Gloucestershire CCC
Limited-Over Matches, 1988

BATTING

BATTING	v. Glamorgan (Bristol) 24 April (RA)	v. Combined Universities (Bristol) 26 April (B&H)	v. Sussex (Bristol) 1 May (RA)	v. Northamptonshire (Northampton) 8 May (RA)	v. Hampshire (Southampton) 10 May (B&H)	v. Somerset (Bristol) 12 May (B&H)	v. Glamorgan (Swansea) 14 May (B&H)	v. Nottinghamshire (Trent Bridge) 15 May (RA)	v. Warwickshire (Bristol) 29 May (RA)	v. Warwickshire (Harrogate) 8 June (TT)	v. Derbyshire (Heanor) 12 June (RA)	v. Lancashire (Old Trafford) 19 June (RA)	v. Ireland (Bristol) 22 June (NW)	v. Leicestershire (Gloucester) 26 June (RA)	v. Worcestershire (Hereford) 3 July (RA)	v. Leicestershire (Leicester) 6 & 7 July (NW)	v. Hampshire (Southampton) 10 July (RA)
A.W. Stovold	41	42		27	13	78	0	2		49	7	9	104*	23		11	43*
C.W.J. Athey	67	82	32*	51	37	27*	31	48		4	55	26	—	12		62	31
K.M. Curran	34*	1	2	16	32*	30	0	2		11	20		—	8		58*	13*
J.W. Lloyds	13	20	2	1	7*	8*	1			25*	8		—	4			
P.W. Romaines	8		27	5				25		1	78*	18*	67			20	
M.W. Alleyne	0	9	—	32			2	45			49*	37*		13		2*	
D.J. Thomas	1*	12*	—														
R.C. Russell	—		—	0*			11	17		—	20			0		—	—
V.S. Greene	—			7*				21*		0	2*			6*			
D.A. Graveney	—	2*		—			5*	4*									
K.B.S. Jarvis	—			—				—			—			1*			
A.J. Wright		11			1	66	9	11			14	20	55	12		9	
P. Bainbridge		47	4*	17	96	6	11	17		36	63	21	—	37		89	0
A.J. Brassington		—															
T.M. Alderman		—		—			8				—					—	
M.W. Pooley																	
D.V. Lawrence							6			6							
Byes			2				4				1						4
Leg-byes	9	8		11	14	3	9	9		10	9	14	6	14		15	12
Wides	4	8		1	5	3	3	6		4	10		7	2		5	1
No-balls			2	1	2	7	1	2		4		1	3			2	2
Total	177	242	71	169	207	228	101	209		150	258	206	190	202		273	106
Wickets	5	7	3	7	4	4	10	8		6	8	4	1	9		5	2
Result	W	W	W	L	W	W	L	W	Ab.	L	W	L	W	W	Ab.	W	W
Points	4	2	4	0	2	2	0	4	2	—	4	0	—	4	2	—	4

Fielding Figures

25 – R.C. Russell (ct 23/st 2)	5 – A.W. Stovold
12 – C.W.J. Athey	4 – T.M. Alderman, P.W. Romaines, K.M. Curran and K.B.S. Jarvis
9 – M.W. Alleyne	3 – J.W. Lloyds
8 – V.S. Greene	2 – D.V. Lawrence and P. Bainbridge
7 – A.J. Wright	1 – A.J. Brassington
6 – D.A. Graveney	

BOWLING

BOWLING	K.B.S. Jarvis	V.S. Greene	K.M. Curran	D.J. Thomas	M.W. Alleyne	T.M. Alderman	P. Bainbridge
v. Glamorgan (Bristol) 24 April (RA)	8-0-18-2	8-2-42-2	8-1-32-1	8-0-33-0	8-0-38-1		
v. Combined Universities (Bristol) 26 April (B&H)		6-0-24-1		8-0-45-0	9.1-2-27-5	7-2-14-2	10-1-34-1
v. Sussex (Bristol) 1 May (RA)	2-0-11-0	2-0-14-0	2-0-17-1		2-0-12-1		2-0-9-1
v. Northamptonshire (Northampton) 8 May (RA)	8-1-30-2	8-1-22-2	8-0-27-2		4-0-19-0		6-1-37-0
v. Hampshire (Southampton) 10 May (B&H)			11-2-34-1		7-0-23-0	11-2-38-2	6-1-27-1
v. Somerset (Bristol) 12 May (B&H)			11-2-42-2		10-0-35-1	11-1-57-1	11-3-29-1
v. Glamorgan (Swansea) 14 May (B&H)			11-2-27-2		2-1-9-0	11-2-24-2	8-0-23-0
v. Nottinghamshire (Trent Bridge) 15 May (RA)	8-0-48-0		8-0-42-2	8-0-23-1	8-0-44-1		8-0-43-3
v. Warwickshire (Bristol) 29 May (RA)							
v. Warwickshire (Harrogate) 8 June (TT)	2-0-13-2	4-0-27-1	4-0-28-2			4-0-31-0	2-0-23-1
v. Derbyshire (Heanor) 12 June (RA)	8-0-47-0	6-0-27-0	6.5-0-54-3		8-1-36-3		8-0-42-2
v. Lancashire (Old Trafford) 19 June (RA)	8-0-36-3	8-0-25-4			8-1-47-1		7.4-0-56-0
v. Ireland (Bristol) 22 June (NW)			12-1-35-0			11.5-0-34-5	12-2-42-2
v. Leicestershire (Gloucester) 26 June (RA)	8-1-16-1	6-1-19-0	6.1-1-15-5		8-0-37-2		8-0-41-2
v. Worcestershire (Hereford) 3 July (RA)							
v. Leicestershire (Leicester) 6 & 7 July (NW)			7-1-31-3		6-1-37-0	10.2-2-47-2	12-3-19-1
v. Hampshire (Southampton) 10 July (RA)	8-0-27-1	8-0-46-0	8-0-33-1		8-0-32-2		8-2-14-0
v. Somerset (Bristol) 17 July (RA)	8-1-28-3	8-0-38-2	8-0-39-0		8-0-33-2		8-0-27-1
v. Worcestershire (Worcester) 27 July (NW)			10.5-0-48-1			12-4-46-2	11-2-24-0
v. Surrey (Cheltenham) 31 July (RA)	7-1-58-1	6-0-28-1	5.2-0-42-0				3-0-33-0
v. Yorkshire (Cheltenham) 7 August (RA)	8-2-27-3	7-0-35-1	8-1-43-0	4-0-23-0			8-1-28-1
v. Middlesex (Lord's) 14 August (RA)	8-1-38-0	8-0-48-0	8-0-31-2				8-0-30-2
v. Kent (Moreton-in-Marsh) 21 August (RA)	5-0-22-1	7-0-16-2	6.1-0-24-3				8-0-47-2
v. Essex (Chelmsford) 28 August (RA)	5-0-14-2	6-0-13-3	6-0-25-0				5-0-21-3
v. Yorkshire (Scarborough) 5 September (FC)	10-0-66-2	8.4-1-24-2	10-4-20-3				
v. Lancashire (Bristol) 7 September (RA)	8-1-17-1	8-3-16-2	4-0-15-1			4-0-17-0	7.5-0-33-0
Wickets	24	24	35	0	19	16	23

Batting

	17 July (RA) v. Worcestershire (Worcester)	27 July (NW) v. Surrey (Cheltenham)	31 July (RA) v. Yorkshire (Cheltenham)	7 August (RA) v. Middlesex (Lord's)	14 August (RA) v. Kent (Moreton-in-Marsh)	21 August (RA) v. Essex (Chelmsford)	28 August (RA) v. Yorkshire (Scarborough)	5 September (FC) v. Lancashire (Bristol); 7 September (RA)	Runs
	48	28		24	4	12	4	40	619
	11	50					6	0	671
	53	13	7	32	12	30*	6	9	430
			18						107
*	18	21	15	6	42	32	2	15	414
	0	21*	25*	24*	1	9*	9		278
			29			4	4	15	65
	4	—	28	2	21			1	104
			11*	5*	11	—	13	2	78
	22	—	—	—	1*	—	1	3*	38
		—	—	—	—		4	4*	9
	2	49*	36	46	81	4	28	10	464
*	12	38	7	17	81	3		4	679
									—
	0								8
				1*	—	23*			24
	2*								14
	5		4			2	5		
	5	4	13	7	3	7	4	6	
	3	4		5	8	2	2	8	
					3		1		
	185	228	193	168	269	105	112	117	
	10	5	7	6	8	5	10	9	
	L	L	W	L	W	W	L	L	
	—	0	4	0	4	4	—	—	

Bowling

D.A. Graveney	D.V. Lawrence	M.W. Pooley	Byes	Leg-byes	Wides	No-balls	Total	Wkts
			4	9	4	2	176	6
11–2–34–0				4	2	2	182	10
			6				69	5
6–1–20–1			2	15	13	1	172	9
9–0–35–3	11–1–36–2			12	2	2	205	9
8–1–29–1	4–0–24–0		1	10	3		227	6
2.3–1–7–0	11–5–15–1		1		2	3	106	5
				8	14	1	208	7 Ab.
	4–0–26–1			4	5		152	8
				10	5		216	10
8–1–37–0				8	2		209	9
12–1–33–0	12–2–25–1		4	13	5	3	186	10
				10	6		139	10 Ab.
5–0–36–1	7–0–24–1			6	4	1	200	9a
			5		3	1	157	5
			1	18	4		184	9
12–5–23–3	12–2–33–0		6	9	2	1	189	6
				3	2	1	164	2
5–0–24–1				11	2	4	191	8
	8–0–40–2			16	2		203	8
7–0–45–2	3–0–20–0			15	6		189	10
		5–0–19–1	3	7	2		102	10
10–1–37–2	9–1–24–1		2	12	1		185	10
8–1–18–1				5	9	2	121	7
15	6	4						

a J.P. Agnew absent hurt

30, 31 August, 1 and 2 September

at Southampton

Hampshire 113 (K.M. Curran 4 for 24) and 150 (K.M. Curran 6 for 58)
Gloucestershire 138 (K.D. James 5 for 25, C.A. Connor 4 for 43) and 128 for 5

Gloucestershire won by 5 wickets
Gloucestershire 20 pts, Hampshire 4 pts

at Old Trafford

Yorkshire 224 (P.J. Hartley 127, P.J.W. Allott 5 for 70) and 171 for 8 (J.D. Fitton 6 for 59)
Lancashire 218 (A.N. Hayhurst 57, P. Carrick 5 for 62, P.A. Booth 5 for 98)

Match drawn
Lancashire 6 pts, Yorkshire 6 pts

at Leicester

Leicestershire 332 for 9 dec (D.I. Gower 146, L. Potter 85, F.D. Stephenson 4 for 107)
Nottinghamshire 133 (G.J.F. Ferris 5 for 49) and 258 for 7 (D.W. Randall 90 not out, P. Johnson 74, B.C. Broad 52)

Match drawn
Leicestershire 7 pts, Nottinghamshire 3 pts

at The Oval

Surrey 362 (A.J. Stewart 133, D.J. Bicknell 50, D.M. Ward 50, I.L. Pont 5 for 103)
Essex 257 for 6 (G.A. Gooch 123)

Match drawn
Surrey 6 pts, Essex 6 pts

at Hove

Middlesex 471 for 9 dec (R.O. Butcher 134, J.E. Emburey 73 not out, M.R. Ramprakash 66, A.C.S. Pigott 4 for 139) and 8 for 1 dec
Sussex 320 (C.M. Wells 86 not out, A.M. Green 52)

Match drawn
Middlesex 5 pts, Sussex 3 pts

at Edgbaston

Glamorgan 272 (J.G. Thomas 110, M.P. Maynard 63, G.C. Small 6 for 79, A.A. Donald 4 for 59) and 136 (G.C. Small 6 for 42)
Warwickshire 215 (A.I. Kallicharran 63, S.L. Watkin 8 for 59) and 189 (G.C. Small 69, J.G. Thomas 6 for 70, J. Derrick 4 for 47)

Glamorgan won by 4 runs
Glamorgan 23 pts, Warwickshire 6 pts

31 August, 1 and 2 September

at Derby

Sri Lankans 297 for 6 dec (P.A. de Silva 76, L.R.D. Mendis 55, D.S.B.P. Kuruppu 55)
Derbyshire 247 for 7 dec, (S.C. Goldsmith 60, B.J.M. Maher 54)

Match drawn

at Scarborough

Rest of World XI 143 and 198 for 4 dec (S. Hookey 90)

Hampshire CCC
Limited-Over Matches, 1988

BATTING

	v. Surrey (Southampton) 24 April (RA)	v. Somerset (Taunton) 26 April (B&H)	v. Kent (Canterbury) 1 May (RA)	v. Glamorgan (Southampton) 3 May (B&H)	v. Glamorgan (Southampton) 8 May (RA)	v. Gloucestershire (Southampton) 10 May (B&H)	v. West Indians (Southampton) 12 May	v. Combined Universities (Cambridge) 14 May (B&H)	v. Middlesex (Southampton) 15 May (RA)	v. Worcestershire (Worcester) 26 & 27 May (B&H)	v. Yorkshire (Middlesbrough) 29 May (RA)	v. Lancashire (Old Trafford) 5 June (RA)	v. Essex (Chelmsford) 8 & 9 June (B&H)	v. Worcestershire (Worcester) 12 June (RA)	v. Nottinghamshire (Basingstoke) 19 June (RA)	v. Shropshire (Telford) 22 June (NW)
R.A. Smith	6	8	18	—	28	2	37	8	12	87*	15	51	20*	0	46	40
V.P. Terry	43	47	15	80*				68*	0	5	14	3	109	20	2	83
M.C.J. Nicholas	2	72	9	—	63*	48	9	18	11	5	19	3	1*	0	14	—
D.R. Turner	103*	3	54		43	29	47	14	61	11	27*	34	31	3	79	0
C.L. Smith	10	13	70	70*	44	18	18	14*	13	10	8*	20	56	1	0	117
S.T. Jefferies	39	—	5	—	12*	1	10*	—	4	7		21*				39
N.G. Cowley	1*	—	0	—		7	—		11	18*	—			3*	19*	1*
T.M. Tremlett	—															
R.J. Parks	—	23*	4*	—	3	9	13*	—	35*	1				0	10*	—
K.D. James	—	21*	14	—	3	25	16	—	0			24*		5	8	—
C.A. Connor	—	—	2	—		5*	—	—	4*	—	—	—		5	—	—
S.J.W. Andrew		—	1*	—		4*	—	—							—	
J.R. Ayling								—		1		30		0	10	1*
R.J. Scott						41	12									
P.J. Bakker													6*			
R.J. Maru																
A.N. Aymes																
Byes					1			4	4	2					1	1
Leg-byes	10	10	14	5	9	12	4	7	3	8	4	8	15		9	5
Wides		3	3		4	2	9	2	1	12		2	6	1	7	7
No-balls		1	6	3	2	2	11		1	1	1		1		1	1
Total	214	201	215	158	212	205	186	131	160	170	90	196	239	45	206	294
Wickets	5	5	9	0	5	9	6	3	8	7	3	6	3	9†	7	5
Result	L	W	L	W	W	L	L	W	L	W	W	L	W	L	W	W
Points	0	2	0	2	4	0	—	2	0	0	4	0	0	0	4	—

Fielding Figures

37 – R.J. Parks (ct 33/st 4)
19 – R.A. Smith
10 – M.C.J. Nicholas
8 – V.P. Terry
6 – C.L. Smith

5 – K.D. James and S.T. Jefferies
4 – N.G. Cowley
3 – J.R. Ayling
2 – D.R. Turner
1 – S.J.W. Andrew, T.M. Tremlett, R.J. Maru and P.J. Bakker

† N.G. Cowley retired hurt

BOWLING

	S.T. Jefferies	T.M. Tremlett	C.A. Connor	K.D. James	N.G. Cowley	M.C.J. Nicholas	S.J.W. Andrew
v. Surrey (Southampton) 24 April (RA)	8-2-26-1	7-0-48-3	7-0-40-2	8-0-46-1	3-0-23-0	6-0-46-1	
v. Somerset (Taunton) 26 April (B&H)	11-0-44-3		11-3-32-1	11-1-37-2	11-4-28-0		11-1-47-2
v. Kent (Canterbury) 1 May (RA)	8-1-31-2		7.5-0-48-1	8-1-23-1	7-0-53-2	1-0-16-0	8-0-31-1
v. Glamorgan (Southampton) 3 May (B&H)	11-0-36-2		11-2-28-2	11-2-31-3	11-3-31-0		11-0-26-2
v. Glamorgan (Southampton) 8 May (RA)	4-0-8-1		6-2-11-1	8-0-31-2	8-0-31-2		6-0-22-0
v. Gloucestershire (Southampton) 10 May (B&H)	11-0-55-1		10.5-1-38-2	10-1-41-0	11-3-13-0		11-0-46-0
v. West Indians (Southampton) 12 May	10-0-44-1		10-2-67-2	10-1-51-0	10-0-61-2		10-0-46-0
v. Combined Universities (Cambridge) 14 May (B&H)	11-2-28-2		11-4-16-1	11-1-35-0	11-2-23-1		11-4-20-3
v. Middlesex (Southampton) 15 May (RA)	8-0-48-1		8-1-29-1	8-0-28-1	8-0-27-1		8-0-50-4
v. Worcestershire (Worcester) 26 & 27 May (B&H)	10.2-0-34-4		11-1-33-2		11-1-23-0		11-0-33-2
v. Yorkshire (Middlesbrough) 29 May (RA)	6-0-30-2		5.3-1-15-0		8-0-35-1		6-0-26-0
v. Lancashire (Old Trafford) 5 June (RA)	8-1-37-2		8-2-32-0	7.4-0-51-0			8-0-43-0
v. Essex (Chelmsford) 8 June (B&H)	11-0-63-1		11-1-41-2		11-0-31-2		11-2-48-0
v. Worcestershire (Worcester) 12 June (RA)			8-0-44-3	8-0-33-2	8-0-41-0		
v. Nottinghamshire (Basingstoke) 19 June (RA)			8-2-33-2	8-1-33-1	8-0-49-1		8-0-44-0
v. Shropshire (Telford) 22 June (NW)	12-1-40-2		10-3-20-0		12-0-39-0	1-0-3-0	12-1-32-0
v. Essex (Bournemouth) 26 June (RA)	6.5-0-22-1		6-0-42-1		1-0-9-0		2-0-12-0
v. Sussex (Hastings) 3 July (RA)							
v. Somerset (Southampton) 6 & 7 July (NW)	12-0-65-2		12-1-42-1		12-3-38-0		12-2-37-2
v. Derbyshire (Lord's) 9 July (B&H)	10-3-13-5		7.3-1-27-2		11-2-17-1		9-0-25-0
v. Gloucestershire (Southampton) 10 July (RA)	3-0-13-0	2-0-8-0	4-0-6-0	4-0-15-0	7-1-32-2		
v. Warwickshire (Edgbaston) 17 July (RA)	8-0-36-3		8-0-46-2	8-1-28-0	8-1-38-1		
v. Derbyshire (Portsmouth) 24 July (RA)	7-2-11-1	8-0-35-1		8-0-20-0			
v. Derbyshire (Derby) 27 July (NW)	12-1-32-1			12-2-37-2	12-2-21-1		
v. Leicestershire (Leicester) 7 August (RA)	4-0-15-0			6-0-31-0	8-0-31-1	1-0-4-0	
v. Worcestershire (Worcester) 10 August (NW)	12-0-67-3			11-1-45-1	12-0-47-1		
v. Northamptonshire (Bournemouth) 14 August (RA)		2-0-6-0			5-0-10-2		
v. Somerset (Taunton) 28 August (RA)			6-1-15-0	8-1-24-2	8-0-54-1		
Wickets	41	6	26	18	20	1	16

Batting

v. Essex (Bournemouth) 26 June (RA)	v. Sussex (Hastings) 3 July (RA)	v. Somerset (Southampton) 6 & 7 July (NW)	v. Derbyshire (Lord's) 9 July (B&H)	v. Gloucestershire (Southampton) 10 July (RA)	v. Warwickshire (Edgbaston) 17 July (RA)	v. Derbyshire (Portsmouth) 24 July (RA)	v. Derbyshire (Derby) 27 July (NW)	v. Leicestershire (Leicester) 7 August (RA)	v. Worcestershire (Worcester) 10 August (NW)	v. Northamptonshire (Bournemouth) 14 August (RA)	v. Somerset (Taunton) 28 August (RA)	Runs
41	36	38	57	22		38		1	21			632
40	9	2	31	0	23	67	40	80	20	77		878
31	32	35*	0*	7	9	31	18	20	—	36		493
13	0	7*	5	16	0	7	51	35	47*	37		757
19*	99*	20		1	0	23	47	29	4*	28*		752
14	31	—	15*	0	30	5	18*	8				259
3	1*	—	16*	0	—		1	—	—			81
			—	8	—		—		—			8
—			—	15	—	—	—	18*	—			131
			0		15*	4*	—	12	—	2*		149
—	—	—		5*								21
—	—	—										5
0	—	—	24	3	41*	7*	34	25	—	11		187
					6					4		63
					—	—	—	2	—	—		8
					—							—
					—							—

Byes	Leg-byes	Wides	No-balls	Total	Wkts	Result	Points

Essex	Sussex	Somerset	Derbyshire (Lord's)	Gloucestershire	Warwickshire	Derbyshire (Portsmouth)	Derbyshire (Derby)	Leicestershire	Worcestershire	Northamptonshire	Somerset (Taunton)
(Byes)		4	5	3	2		11			4	
(Leg-byes) 10		11	8	12	3	7	10	2	4	4	
(Wides) 1		5	3	3	4	4	8	6	1	4	
(No-balls)		1	5	1	1	1		3			
Total 172		229	118	157	96	134	193	240	239	97	207
Wkts 7		5	3	5	10	6	6	5	10	2	5
Result L	Ab.	W	W	L	L	W	W	W	L	W	W
0	2	—	—	0	0	4	—	4	—	4	4

Bowling

J.R. Ayling	P.J. Bakker	C.L. Smith	R.J. Maru	Byes	Leg-byes	Wides	No-balls	Total	Wkts
					7	1		236	9
					9	7	1	197	8
				4	12	11	4	218	8
				1	4	2	4	157	9
8–0–31–3					8	5	1	152	8
					14	5	2	207	4
					10	7		279	5
					8	2	1	130	9
11–3–36–1				1	6	8	1	189	8
6–1–33–0				1	9	13	4	169	10
8–0–28–1					2	2		141	3
11–2–42–1					6	2	1	197	4
8–0–37–0	8–0–39–1			1	12	7	3	238	6
					2			196	7
8–0–32–1				1	9	7	5	201	5
11–5–26–0		2–0–24–2		2	22	3	3	208	7
2–0–16–0					1	1		102	Ab.
12–2–35–2					10	2	3	227	7
9–2–21–1					14	12	3	117	10
6–1–16–0				4	12	1	2	106	2
7–0–35–0				3	21	7	3	207	6
8–0–36–2	7.5–1–26–5				5	2	2	133	10
12–2–42–1	11.5–1–36–2				23	7	1	191	10
7–0–38–2	6–0–20–0		8–0–30–3		8	4	1	177	7
12–0–51–2	11.5–2–34–3	1–0–3–0		1	20	5	5	268	10
5–0–29–1	8–0–44–2				5	1		94	6
8–0–31–2	5.4–1–15–4			1	5	2		145	10
20	**17**	**2**	**3**						

Kent CCC
Limited-Over Matches, 1988

BATTING

	v. Essex (Chelmsford) 24 April (RA)	v. Sussex (Hove) 26 April (B&H)	v. Hampshire (Canterbury) 1 May (RA)	v. Surrey (The Oval) 3 & 4 May (B&H)	v. Leicestershire (Leicester) 8 May (RA)	v. Essex (Canterbury) 10 & 11 May (B&H)	v. Middlesex (Canterbury) 12 May (B&H)	v. Lancashire (Canterbury) 15 May (RA)	v. Yorkshire (Canterbury) 22 May (RA)	v. Northamptonshire (Northampton) 29 May (RA)	v. Glamorgan (Merthyr Tydfil) 5 June (RA)	v. Warwickshire (Edgbaston) 19 June (RA)	v. Buckinghamshire (Canterbury) 22 June (NW)	v. Nottinghamshire (Canterbury) 3 July (RA)	v. Warwickshire (Canterbury) 6 July (NW)	v. Middlesex (Canterbury) 10 July (RA)
M.R. Benson	9	14	44	6		113	61	11			4	0	38		1	
R.F. Pienaar	6		2					—	13	38	11*	3	—		58*	34
C.J. Tavare	23	31	3	26		16	15	17	3	40*	25	10	6*			8
C.S. Cowdrey	11	40*	12	4		21*	6	10*	9	14*	14	63*	—			61*
S.G. Hinks	55	78*	8	4		2	28	36*	32	11	1	23	64*		8*	6
G.R. Cowdrey	45	—	9	11				—	1	—	14*	53	—			22*
N.R. Taylor	7	31	68	137		87	38	85	12	29	62	13	5		41	22
S.A. Marsh	9	—	4	17			3	—	5	—	—	—				
R.M. Ellison	14*	—	34*	17		22*	10	—	3			7*	—		—	—
D.J.M. Kelleher	7*	—														
R.P. Davis	—	—	—	0*		—	—		0						—	—
H.L. Alleyne		—	—			—	8*									
C. Penn			3*	5*		—	3	—	8	—	—					
V.J. Wells						—	15*	—	10*	—	—					
T.R. Ward															34	25
M.D. Harman																
M.V. Fleming																
D.J. Sabine																
Byes	1	2	4										2			
Leg-byes	7	5	12	13		15	16	10	13	4	3	9	2		2	7
Wides	7	1	11	5		7	2	2	6	7	1	2			1	1
No-balls		6	4				1	1	1						3	1
Total	201	208	218	245		283	206	172	116	143	135	185	115		148	187
Wickets	8	3	8	8		4	8	3	10	3	5	6	2		3	5
Result	L	W	W	L	Ab.	W	L	W	L	Ab.	W	W	W	Ab.	W	L
Points	0	2	4	0	2	2	0	4	0	2	4	4	—	2	—	0

Fielding Figures
34 – S.A. Marsh (ct 27/st 7)
9 – G.R. Cowdrey and R.P. Davis
5 – S.G. Hinks, C.S. Cowdrey, N.R. Taylor and R.F. Pienaar
4 – C.J. Tavare
3 – R.M. Ellison
2 – M.R. Benson and H.L. Alleyne
1 – C. Penn, T.R. Ward and V.J. Wells

BOWLING

	D.J.M. Kelleher	R.M. Ellison	R.F. Pienaar	R.P. Davis	C.S. Cowdrey	G.R. Cowdrey	H.L. Alleyne
v. Essex (Chelmsford) 24 April (RA)	6–0–31–0	8–0–40–0	4–0–23–0	7.3–1–41–1	6–0–42–0	5–0–18–0	
v. Sussex (Hove) 26 April (B&H)	11–2–43–1	11–3–30–0		10–1–33–2	10–1–40–2	4–2–6–1	9–0–43–1
v. Hampshire (Canterbury) 1 May (RA)		8–2–29–1	7–0–49–1	8–2–36–3	8–0–39–2	1–0–9–0	
v. Surrey (The Oval) 3 & 4 May (B&H)		10–1–44–1		10.1–0–63–0	11–2–38–0	2–0–11–0	10–2–39–0
v. Leicestershire (Leicester) 8 May (RA)							
v. Essex (Canterbury) 10 May (B&H)		11–0–58–2		8–1–40–0	11–0–50–2		11–0–62–1
v. Middlesex (Canterbury) 12 May (B&H)		9.3–0–39–1		11–0–43–0	9–0–38–1		6–0–40–0
v. Lancashire (Canterbury) 14 May (RA)		8–0–27–2	8–0–48–0	2–0–12–0	8–0–34–2	6–0–21–2	
v. Yorkshire (Canterbury) 22 May (RA)		8–2–34–1	8–0–22–2		8–2–16–0	4–0–18–0	
v. Northamptonshire (Northampton) 29 May (RA)							
v. Glamorgan (Merthyr Tydfil) 5 June (RA)		8–1–37–2	8–1–20–2	8–0–21–1	6.4–1–20–4	3–0–13–0	
v. Warwickshire (Edgbaston) 19 June (RA)		8–0–35–0	5–0–29–0	8–0–27–2	4–0–17–0	8–0–32–2	
v. Buckinghamshire (Canterbury) 22 June (NW)		7–1–15–0	12–2–19–3	7–2–19–3	8–0–16–1	12–7–20–2	
v. Nottinghamshire (Canterbury) 3 July (RA)							
v. Warwickshire (Canterbury) 6 July (NW)		10–2–18–1	12–3–25–1	4.3–1–11–1	10–1–31–0	7–0–19–2	
v. Middlesex (Canterbury) 10 July (RA)		7.3–0–33–1	8–0–34–4	4–0–19–0	8–0–25–0	5–0–22–1	
v. Surrey (The Oval) 17 July (RA)		8–0–36–0	8–0–38–2	2.5–0–9–0	7–0–34–0	5–0–37–1	
v. Worcestershire (Folkestone) 24 July (RA)	7–1–27–2	7–0–45–1	5–0–30–0	8–2–16–0		3–0–23–0	
v. Middlesex (Lord's) 27 July (NW)		11.5–1–53–1	11–0–46–2	7–0–33–0	8–0–27–0	3–0–10–0	
v. Somerset (Canterbury) 31 July (RA)	5–1–18–0			8–1–23–1	5–0–27–2	8–1–13–2	6.2–0–19–2
v. Derbyshire (Chesterfield) 14 August (RA)		5–0–40–1		8–0–22–2	7–0–40–0	8–0–20–2	8–0–34–3
v. Gloucestershire (Moreton-in-Marsh) 21 August (RA)		6–1–22–0		8–0–50–1	7–0–55–1	5–0–39–1	8–0–42–2
v. Sussex (Maidstone) 28 August (RA)				3–0–19–3	1–0–7–1	4–1–16–1	
Wickets	3	15	17	20	18	17	9

MCC 137 for 2 dec (W. Larkins 51) and 172 (R.J. Bartlett 56, W. Larkins 52, B.L. Cairns 4 for 11)

Rest of World XI won by 32 runs

v. Surrey (The Oval) 17 July (RA)	v. Worcestershire (Folkestone) 24 July (RA)	v. Middlesex (Lord's) 27 July (NW)	v. Somerset (Canterbury) 31 July (RA)	v. Derbyshire (Chesterfield) 14 August (RA)	v. Gloucestershire (Moreton-in-Marsh) 21 August (RA)	v. Sussex (Maidstone) 28 August (RA)	Runs
	66	7		8	3		385
84	9	34				44	336
9	34*	49	30*	82*	6		433
6		10	46	20	30	9	396
16			0*	4	25	33*	434
3	6	25	—	50*	22	7	268
1	20	7	21	—	22	10	718
7*	—	24*	—	6	9	0	84
44	37*	21		—	18		227
—							7
—	—	0	—	—	0	—	0
				—	25		33
2	—	0		—			21
				—			25
0	5	1	20		6		91
				8*			8
					3*		3
							—
1	11						
6		7	4	8	15	4	
4	3	9	2	6	6	9	
		1	3	2		1	
183	191	195	126	186	189	126	
9	5	10	3	4	10	6	
L	L	L	W	W	L	W	
0	0	—	4	4	0	4	

A second century for Greg Thomas as Glamorgan gain their first win of the season, 2 September. (Simon Bruty/ Allsport)

C. Penn	V.J. Wells	M.D. Harman	D.J. Sabine	M.V. Fleming	Byes	Leg-byes	Wides	No-balls	Total	Wkts
						7		1	202	1
						12	3	7	207	7
8–0–39–1						14	3	6	215	9
10–0–46–0						8	8		249	1
										Ab.
11–1–40–2	3–0–18–0				1	13	10	5	282	7
5–0–26–1	4–1–15–0				2	4	4	3	207	4
7.1–0–22–4					1	4	5		169	10
8–0–39–2	4–0–14–1					16	8		159	6
										Ab.
	6–0–15–1				2	6	10	1	134	10
7–0–30–1						10	7		180	6
10–1–22–0						2	13	2	113	10
										Ab.
12–3–30–3					2	8	2		144	10
7–0–46–0						12	8	1	191	8
8–0–20–2						13	9	1	187	5
8–0–41–0					1	9	2	1	192	3
10–2–25–2						5	7		199	5
	7–1–17–3					8			125	10
4–0–20–0						8	3		184	8
		6–0–58–2				3	8	3	269	8
	5–0–22–2		5–0–19–0	5–0–34–1	1	7			125	8
18	7	2	0	1						

Lancashire CCC
Limited-Over Matches, 1988

BATTING

BATTING	v. Worcestershire (Old Trafford) 24 April (RA)	v. Leicestershire (Leicester) 26 & 27 April (B&H)	v. Warwickshire (Old Trafford) 1 May (RA)	v. Nottinghamshire (Trent Bridge) 8 May (RA)	v. Derbyshire (Liverpool) 10 May (B&H)	v. Scotland (Old Trafford) 12 & 13 May (B&H)	v. Warwickshire (Edgbaston) 14 May (B&H)	v. Kent (Canterbury) 15 May (RA)	v. Leicestershire (Old Trafford) 29 May (RA)	v. Hampshire (Old Trafford) 5 June (RA)	v. Gloucestershire (Old Trafford) 19 June (RA)	v. Lincolnshire (Old Trafford) 22 June (NW)	v. Glamorgan (Pontypridd) 26 June (RA)	v. Northamptonshire (Tring) 3 July (RA)	v. Glamorgan (Cardiff) 6 & 7 July (NW)	v. Somerset (Old Trafford) 10 July (RA)	v. Essex (Southend) 17 July (RA)
G.D. Mendis	42	1	1	4	55	61	39	19	0	48	50	64	1		4	4	16
G. Fowler	43	0	14	26	50	66	10	0		14	38	6			35	5	14
T.E. Jesty	33	57	9					10	2	39	37	14*			0	41	0
N.H. Fairbrother	40*	0	5	116*		116*	27	6	43	57*	15	80*	0		35	51*	7
M. Watkinson	4*	0	6	16	70*	18	14	48	30	40	24	2	0*		9	2	49
D.P. Hughes	—	12	2	4	7	19	15	5	6	7*	6	23			18	3	27
W.K. Hegg	—	11	7	—			1	1	—		3*	6			20	0*	9*
P.J.W. Allott	—	6	43	11	0*	14*	0	30	3	—	2	0			14	15	3
C.D. Matthews	—	43	1*														
J. Simmons	—	31*	20*	1*			8*	2*	—		0	0			6	—	1*
A.N. Hayhurst	—	3	24	2	12		0	4	84	34	27	35			38*	37	20
I.D. Austin				4	9	—	20	20	1*	—	19*						
Wasim Akram				13	23	8	11	24	21*	—		14			9	12	7
J. Abrahams					7												
D.J. Makinson																	
I. Folley																	
A.J. Murphy																	
Byes				2		6		1							11	5	
Leg-byes	4		8	8	14	5	1	4	6	6	8	4	5		3	3	14
Wides	8	3	3		10		14	5	8	2	2	2			10	6	1
No-balls	2		1	1		4		2	1				2		3		2
Total	176	167	144	208	257	317	160	169	214	197	209	305	28		215	184	170
Wickets	3	10	9	8	7	5	10	10	7	4	9	10	3		10	8	9
Result	W	L	W	W	L	W	L	L	W	W	W	W	Ab.	Ab.	L	L	L
Points	4	0	4	4	0	2	0	0	4	4	4	—	2	2	—	0	0

Fielding Figures
- 29 – W.K. Hegg (ct 27/st 2)
- 11 – J. Simmons
- 9 – M. Watkinson
- 7 – D.P. Hughes
- 4 – G.D. Mendis, G. Fowler and N.H. Fairbrother
- 3 – T.E. Jesty and Wasim Akram
- 2 – P.J.W. Allott and I.D. Austin
- 1 – I. Folley and A.N. Hayhurst

BOWLING

BOWLING	P.J.W. Allott	C.D. Matthews	M. Watkinson	A.N. Hayhurst	J. Simmons	T.E. Jesty	Wasim Akram	I.D. Austin
v. Worcestershire (Old Trafford) 24 April (RA)	8–1–24–1	8–0–44–2	8–0–33–2	8–0–30–0	8–1–30–0			
v. Leicestershire (Leicester) 26 April (B&H)	11–4–19–2	5–0–17–0	10–0–48–1	8–1–27–0	10–0–55–0	11–0–39–5		
v. Warwickshire (Old Trafford) 1 May (RA)	7–0–21–0	6.1–0–27–1	8–0–46–1	8–0–59–1	8–0–47–1			
v. Nottinghamshire (Trent Bridge) 8 May (RA)	8–0–32–1		4–0–33–0	6–0–28–2	6–1–30–1		8–1–37–2	8–0–34–1
v. Derbyshire (Liverpool) 10 May (B&H)	10–1–42–2		6–0–45–0	7–0–33–0	11–2–41–2		10.4–0–45–0	9–0–45–1
v. Scotland (Old Trafford) 12 & 13 May (B&H)	9–5–15–1		11–1–38–0	7–1–29–1	7–2–26–0		9–0–27–0	10–3–17–1
v. Warwickshire (Edgbaston) 14 May (B&H)	11–0–57–3		11–1–35–0	2–0–11–1	11–0–50–1		11–1–37–3	9–0–50–0
v. Kent (Canterbury) 15 May (RA)	6–0–11–0		8–0–36–0	4–0–36–0	3–0–20–0		6–0–31–1	8–0–28–2
v. Leicestershire (Old Trafford) 29 May (RA)	8–1–26–0		3–0–19–0		3–0–21–0		4.3–0–16–1	4–1–13–0
v. Hampshire (Old Trafford) 5 June (RA)	8–0–43–0		8–0–36–2		8–0–42–0		8–0–33–2	8–1–34–2
v. Gloucestershire (Old Trafford) 19 June (RA)	8–0–38–1		8–0–38–0	8–0–50–0	8–0–29–1			8–0–37–1
v. Lincolnshire (Old Trafford) 22 June (NW)	9–2–24–1		12–2–37–1	11–2–24–2	9–1–27–2		12–2–27–4	
v. Glamorgan (Pontypridd) 26 June (RA)	8–0–28–0		8–1–22–3	6–0–37–4	7–0–28–1	1–0–5–0	8–0–32–1	
v. Northamptonshire (Tring) 3 July (RA)								
v. Glamorgan (Cardiff) 6 & 7 July (NW)	9–1–21–1		12–0–61–1	8–1–29–0	12–2–35–1	11–1–48–0		8–0–38–0
v. Somerset (Old Trafford) 10 July (RA)	7–0–28–1		7–0–36–1	6–0–39–1	7–0–42–1		7–1–24–3	
v. Essex (Southend) 17 July (RA)	8–2–26–0		7.1–1–41–2	7–1–34–0	8–0–43–2		8–0–22–0	
v. Yorkshire (Scarborough) 31 July (RA)			8–0–57–0	8–1–36–1	8–1–35–2		8–1–30–2	8–0–35–3
v. Middlesex (Blackpool) 7 August (RA)	7–0–19–2		7.4–2–17–4	7–0–50–0	8–1–36–2			8–0–27–1
v. Sussex (Hove) 14 August (RA)	7–0–26–0		8–1–41–2	2–0–18–0	7–0–38–0		8–0–39–2	8–0–46–0
v. Derbyshire (Old Trafford) 21 August (RA)	7.5–1–21–1		8–1–33–0	8–0–55–1	8–0–45–2			8–1–34–3
v. Surrey (The Oval) 28 August (RA)	5.2–0–31–0		6–0–49–0	6–0–24–0	7–0–29–2			6–0–42–0
v. Essex (Scarborough) 4 September (FC)		8–0–62–2	10–1–45–1					
v. Gloucestershire (Bristol) 7 September (RA)	8–4–14–2		8–0–29–1	8–0–24–1	8–1–14–3			8–0–30–1
v. Worcestershire (Edgbaston) 18 September (RA)	6–2–10–1		6–2–10–1	8–0–46–4	8–0–22–1			7.5–0–51–1
Wickets	20	5	23	19	25	5	21	19

A round of four-day Championship matches began on an uneasy note of controversy. Both Essex and Middlesex started their matches with ten players, for they had included Gooch and Emburey in their sides although both were still engaged in the Test match at Lord's which did not end until after lunch. When Gooch took the field at The Oval his arrival was greeted with a cluster of photographers and television cameras which, as one Surrey member commented with justification, detracted from the magnificent innings played by Alec Stewart, who hit a six and 21 fours in his first Championship hundred of the season. Gooch later dominated the Essex innings to complete a powerful century, but rain robbed Surrey of their last hope of winning the title and did not enhance Essex's chances either.

Emburey did not have to take the field until the second day at Hove, when he continued with his good batting form, but the earlier honours had gone to Roland Butcher, at his bubbling best, and young Mark Ramprakash. Colin Wells saved Sussex from a difficult position and rain was again the only winner.

There was no play on the last day at Old Trafford, where, in the initial stages, there was some extraordinary cricket. Television coverage demanded a 10.30 start, which must have made Carrick hesitate to bat first when he won the toss, but bat he did, and Yorkshire found themselves at 37 for 6 when Peter Hartley joined his captain. Hartley remained at the wicket for 248 minutes and hit a six and 11 fours in his maiden first-class century which changed the complexion of the game. Lancashire then found runs as difficult to score as Yorkshire had done and fell to the combined left-arm spin of Booth, a career best, and Carrick. Batting a second time, Yorkshire were

v. Yorkshire (Scarborough) 31 July (RA)	v. Middlesex (Blackpool) 7 August (RA)	v. Sussex (Hove) 14 August (RA)	v. Derbyshire (Old Trafford) 21 August (RA)	v. Surrey (The Oval) 28 August (RA)	v. Essex (Scarborough) 4 September (FC)	v. Gloucestershire (Bristol) 7 September (RA)	v. Worcestershire (Edgbaston) 18 September (RA)	Runs
9	86	51	9	5	46	1	0	616
24	16	34	13	70		19	26	523
7	28		31	18*	36	0	59	421
46	6	3	5	22	2	18	38	738
19	41	58	1	9	9	18*	42*	529
34	0	16*	1*	—		4	—	209
—	0	—	—	—	33	—	—	91
	0	—	11*	—		16*	—	168
				1				45
0*	9*	—	—	—		—	—	78
20	11	27	77	44	32	26	1	558
10*	1	—	41	6*		3	6*	140
29		20*						191
					33			40
					9			9
					2*			2
					1			1
					3		4	
8	4	7	5	4	10	5	12	
3	3	3	4	3	6	9	13	
2		2		2			2	
209	207	219	200	181	223	121	201	
8	10	5	7	5	10	7	5	
W	W	W	W	L	L	W	W	
4	4	4	4	0	—	—	—	

D.P. Hughes	A.J. Murphy	D.J. Makinson	I. Folley	Byes	Leg-byes	Wides	No-balls	Total	Wkts
				1	10			172	8
				2	6	9		213	8
					12	2		212	5
					8			202	7
				1	6	6		258	5
2–0–8–0				1	2	9		163	3
					9	9		249	10
					10	2	1	172	3
					4	7		99	1
					8	2		196	6
					14		1	206	4
					8	10	1	147	10
					11	1		163	9
									Ab.
					14	9	1	246	5
				5	16	2		190	7
					5	1	1	171	4
					15	4	1	208	8
				1	5	1		155	10
					10	3	4	218	5
				2	8			198	10
					7		2	182	4
8–1–34–1	10–1–38–1	10–1–27–2	4–0–31–0		13	3		250	7
					6	8		117	9
					10	4		149	10
1	1	2	0						

Leicestershire CCC
Limited-Over Matches, 1988

BATTING

	v. Derbyshire (Derby) 24 April (RA)	v. Lancashire (Leicester) 26 & 27 April (B&H)	v. Northamptonshire (Leicester) 1 May (RA)	v. Scotland (Glasgow) 3 & 4 May (B&H)	v. Kent (Leicester) 8 May (RA)	v. Warwickshire (Leicester) 12 May (B&H)	v. Derbyshire (Derby) 14 May (B&H)	v. Worcestershire (Leicester) 22 May (RA)	v. Lancashire (Old Trafford) 29 May (RA)	v. Surrey (The Oval) 12 June (RA)	v. Sussex (Leicester) 19 June (RA)	v. Suffolk (Leicester) 22 June (NW)	v. Gloucestershire (Gloucester) 26 June (RA)	v. Yorkshire (Hull) 3 July (RA)	v. Gloucestershire (Leicester) 6 & 7 July (NW)	v. Nottinghamshire (Trent Bridge) 10 July (RA)
L. Potter	2	19	49			10	37*	5	51	41	10	22	1	66*	22	
N.E. Briers	42	1	7			44	5	2	36*	29	48	42	54	22	16	
D.I. Gower	5	14	14			53	15	50	1*	2		99	0		28	
J.J. Whitaker	4		13			16	7	31	—	24	13	14	11	12	0	
P. Willey	27	59	2			2	37	43	—	2		15	21	23	7	
T.J. Boon	22	53				37	6*									
P.A.J. De Freitas	37	1	1			4	57		—	19	3	7	1		11	
C.C. Lewis	14*	2	40			13*	8*	5	—		4	10	1	28*	53	
P. Whitticase	1	4	19*			2	—			0	—	5*	9	—	23	
J.P. Agnew	3	5*	16			3		8*		18*	0*	1	4		—	
L.B. Taylor	1	—	5*					1	—			—			—	
J.D.R. Benson		37*						19	—	13	35					
G.J.F. Ferris			—			1*	—	13*		1*	0*	—	5*		1*	
M.A. Garnham								0								
L. Tennant										—						
P. Hepworth											38		16	—		
R.A. Cobb												14			28	
P.M. Such																
Byes		2				1						2				
Leg-byes	7	6	3			7	6	9	4	6	24	15	10	13	6	
Wides	3	9	3			1	4	9	7	2	3	8	6	8	4	
No-balls		1	1			2	4	2		1	1	1			1	
Total	168	213	173			196	186	197	99	158	179	255	139	172	200†	
Wickets	10	8	8			9	5	9	1	8	7	9	10	3	9†	
Result	L	W	W	Ab.	Ab.	W	L	L	L	L	L	W	L	L	L	Ab.
Points	0	2	4	1	2	2	0	0	0	0	0	—	0	0	—	2

Fielding Figures
23 – P. Whitticase
6 – P. Willey
3 – L.B. Taylor, N.E. Briers, P.A.J. De Freitas, D.I. Gower and C.C. Lewis
2 – L. Tennant
1 – J.P. Agnew, G.J.F. Ferris, P.M. Such, J.J. Whitaker and T.J. Boon

† J.P. Agnew absent hurt

BOWLING

	J.P. Agnew	P.A.J. De Freitas	C.C. Lewis	P. Willey	L.B. Taylor	G.J.F. Ferris	L. Potter
v. Derbyshire (Derby) 24 April (RA)	8–0–26–0	7.3–1–22–0	8–0–39–0	8–0–29–0	8–0–46–1		
v. Lancashire (Leicester) 26 & 27 April (B&H)	9–1–42–0	9–0–27–4	9–0–41–3	9.5–1–34–2	5–0–23–1		
v. Northamptonshire (Leicester) 1 May (RA)	8–0–32–3	5–1–11–0	6–0–16–0		6.5–0–20–3	7–0–30–2	
v. Scotland (Glasgow) 3 May (B&H)							
v. Kent (Leicester) 8 May (RA)							
v. Warwickshire (Leicester) 12 May (B&H)	11–1–49–1	10–1–27–2	11–1–39–1	11–1–41–1		11–2–28–5	
v. Derbyshire (Derby) 14 May (B&H)	5–0–22–0	9.4–0–39–1	8–1–29–0	11–0–26–1		10–1–42–1	11–1–28–0
v. Worcestershire (Leicester) 22 May (RA)	8–1–37–1		7.4–0–40–0	6–2–20–3	8–0–42–0	8–0–36–2	2–0–11–0
v. Lancashire (Old Trafford) 29 May (RA)		8–0–41–0	8–0–40–0	8–0–33–0	7–0–53–1	7–1–24–4	2–0–17–1
v. Surrey (The Oval) 12 June (RA)	8–1–34–1	7.2–1–24–1		8–0–35–3		8–2–30–1	
v. Sussex (Leicester) 19 June (RA)	8–0–38–0	8–0–43–0	8–1–26–2		8–0–38–1	8–0–30–1	
v. Suffolk (Leicester) 22 June (NW)	7–1–25–0	8–1–14–1	12–1–32–2	12–1–24–0		6–0–28–1	12–4–31–1
v. Gloucestershire (Gloucester) 26 June (RA)	8–0–24–2	8–0–33–4	8–0–46–2	8–0–40–0		8–0–45–1	
v. Yorkshire (Hull) 3 July (RA)	6–1–21–1		5–0–29–0	8–0–28–0	8–0–30–2	7.4–1–28–0	3–0–22–0
v. Gloucestershire (Leicester) 6 & 7 July (NW)	12–2–37–1	12–0–37–0	12–1–54–2	12–0–68–0		12–2–62–1	
v. Nottinghamshire (Trent Bridge) 10 July (RA)							
v. Essex (Leicester) 24 July (RA)	8–2–15–1		8–0–13–4	8–1–24–0	8–0–31–3		
v. Middlesex (Leicester) 31 July (RA)							
v. Hampshire (Leicester) 7 August (RA)				8–0–27–1	8–0–55–1	8–0–34–1	1–0–4–0
v. Warwickshire (Edgbaston) 14 August (RA)	7.1–1–29–1	6–0–22–0		6–1–16–0	4–0–20–1		
v. Somerset (Leicester) 21 August (RA)	8–0–34–2	7–0–37–0		8–0–46–0	6–0–24–1		
v. Glamorgan (Llanelli) 28 August (RA)	3–0–13–2			2–0–18–0	3–0–20–1	3–0–9–3	
Wickets	16	13	16	11	16	23	2

v. Essex (Leicester) 24 July (RA)	v. Middlesex (Leicester) 31 July (RA)	v. Hampshire (Leicester) 7 August (RA)	v. Warwickshire (Edgbaston) 14 August (RA)	v. Somerset (Leicester) 21 August (RA)	v. Glamorgan (Llanelli) 28 August (RA)	Runs
66*	19	52	0	0	4	476
26	0	32	8	30	37*	481
	15	4	30	1	2	333
25*	51	0	13	11	30*	275
5	4	16	7	18	—	288
—	11	11				140
	8		1	4		154
—						178
	1		0	21	—	85
	10		9	19*	—	96
	1	—	2*	—	—	10
		42*		10		156
		2			—	23
						0
—	1*	5*	5	17*	—	28
—			15			69
						42
—						—
1	1			1		
8	5	8	9	10	3	
3	3	4	10	1	2	
3		1				
137	130	177	109	143	78	
2	10	7	10	8	2	
W	Ab.	L	L	W	W	
4	2	0	0	4	4	

in dire trouble against young off-spinner Dexter Fitton, who also had the best bowling performance of his career, and then came the rain.

With Kevin Curran taking 10 for 82 in a low-scoring match, Gloucestershire did beat the conditions and Hampshire at Southampton while David Gower's first hundred of the summer and Ferris' bowling were nullified by the rain at Leicester after Notts had been forced to follow on.

Sri Lanka's first-class matches ended without a win and in bitterly cold and damp weather at Derby, but there was brightness for Glamorgan at Edgbaston. They were 41 for 5 before being rallied by Maynard and Greg Thomas, who showed that his maiden century of a fortnight earlier had been no fluke by hitting a most assured 110. He was very well assisted by Bastien who, in his first Championship innings, hit 36 not out and shared a last-wicket stand of 83. On the second day, Steve Watkin, the young medium pacer, crowned an excellent season by taking a fine career-best 8 for 59 and bowling Glamorgan to a first-innings lead of 57. Gladstone Small responded by tearing the heart out of the Glamorgan batting to bring him match figures of 12 for 142 and his side a chance of success. Warwickshire needed 194 to win, and when Thomas and Derrick reduced them to 107 for 9 it seemed that Glamorgan must claim their first win of the season. Small and Gifford had other ideas, and with strong hitting and bold running they took Warwickshire nearer and nearer to their target. With seven needed Butcher recalled Thomas. Small hit him through mid-wicket for two, but was lbw when he tried to repeat the shot, and Glamorgan had their first Championship win of the season.

L. Tennant	J.J. Whitaker	D.I. Gower	P.M. Such		Byes	Leg-byes	Wides	No-balls	Total	Wkts
					2	7	4	2	171	1
							3		167	10
						3	5	3	112	10
									Ab.	Ab.
						3	4		187	10
						4	1	4	190	4
						15	7	2	201	6
						6	8	2	214	7
8–1–27–0					1	8	2	2	159	6
						7	4	9	182	4
	2–0–4–0	1–0–4–0			1	5	5	3	168	6
						14	2	3	202	9
					15		2	1	173	3
						15	5	2	273	5
									Ab.	
8–0–36–1						14	1	1	133	10
									Ab.	
8–0–46–0			7–0–53–2		11	10	8	3	240	5
8–2–18–1						5	2		110	3
8–0–29–2						5	2	2	175	5
2–0–14–1						3	2		77	7
5	0	0	2							

Middlesex CCC
Limited-Over Matches, 1988

BATTING

	v. Nottinghamshire (Lord's) 24 April (RA)	v. Essex (Lord's) 1 May (RA)	v. Sussex (Lord's) 3 & 4 May (B&H)	v. Surrey (The Oval) 8 May (RA)	v. Surrey (The Oval) 10 May (B&H)	v. Kent (Canterbury) 12 May (B&H)	v. Essex (Lord's) 14 May (B&H)	v. Hampshire (Southampton) 15 May (RA)	v. Derbyshire (Derby) 25 & 26 May (B&H)	v. Sussex (Lord's) 29 May (RA)	v. Worcestershire (Lord's) 5 June (RA)	v. Northamptonshire (Luton) 19 June (RA)	v. Hertfordshire (Lord's) 22 June (NW)	v. Somerset (Lord's) 26 June (RA)	v. Derbyshire (Repton) 3 July (RA)	v. Yorkshire (Leeds) 6–8 July (NW)	v. Kent (Canterbury) 10 July (RA)	v. Glamorgan (Lord's) 17 July (RA)
J.D. Carr	8		62	0	0	35	29	30	0	21	69	9	42	1	15*	7		
M.W. Gatting	0	28	56*	6	72	68	38		5	51		105*	80*	33		74	18	
P.R. Downton	49	14	2*	1	28	6*	6	7	9	27				5		43	7	
R.O. Butcher	0	30	5	13*	49	36	75	7	0	77	47	17*	13*	2		—	11	
J.E. Emburey	47	16	—	—	9	2*	17	12	18	18				2		16	15	
K.R. Brown	10	27	7	—	32*	—	2	14	32	11*	21			102		11	14	
J.F. Sykes	33*	0						57	24	2*	4*						9	
N.F. Williams		14*	—	—	3	—	3	28*	12					43		8*		
A.R.C. Fraser	—	0*	13	—	0	—	13*	—	1*					0*		—	30*	
S.P. Hughes					1		0	3*	2					3*		3*	18*	
N.G. Cowans		0			1*		4*	3	0					0				
W.N. Slack		41	16	9*	8	47	23	12				65	0	12	13*	5	12	
A. Needham											39				—	30	36	
M.A. Roseberry											13	—						
N.R.C. MacLaurin											15*	—						
P.C.R. Tufnell															—			
I.J.F. Hutchinson																—		
M.R. Ramprakash																		
Byes		5			2	2	3	1			1			1		4		
Leg-byes	6	10		1	11	4	15	6	2	4	11	3	4	12	2	17	12	
Wides	1	10	16	1	8	4	6	8	5	1	15	1	4	4	2	3	8	
No-balls	1	3	6		3	2	1			1	2	1		1		4	1	
Total	166	198	183	31	224	207	236	189	110	213	237	201	143	220	32	225	191	
Wickets	6	8	5	3	9	4	9	8	10	5	5	2	2	9	0	7	8	
Result	W	W	W	Ab.	W	W	L	W	L	W	W	W	W	L	Ab.	W	W	Ab.
Points	4	4	2	2	2	2	0	4	0	4	4	4	—	0	2	—	4	2

Fielding Figures
26 – P.R. Downton (ct 24/st 2)
1 – K.R. Brown (ct 15/st 1)
9 – J.E. Emburey and R.O. Butcher
7 – M.W. Gatting
6 – J.F. Sykes
5 – J.D. Carr

4 – A. Needham and A.R.C. Fraser
3 – P.C.R. Tufnell, W.N. Slack and N.G. Cowans
1 – N.F. Williams, S.P. Hughes, N.R.C. MacLaurin and sub

BOWLING

	N.G. Cowans	A.R.C. Fraser	N.F. Williams	J.E. Emburey	J.F. Sykes	S.P. Hughes	M.W. Gatting	K.R. Brown
v. Nottinghamshire (Lord's) 24 April (RA)	4-0-21-0	8-0-23-2	8-0-28-3	7-0-25-0	6-1-22-1	7-0-34-0		
v. Essex (Lord's) 1 May (RA)	7-0-29-3	7-0-24-0	6-0-30-3	7-0-45-1		6.3-0-38-2		
v. Sussex (Lord's) 3 & 4 May (B&H)	11-3-28-1	11-3-39-3	11-2-21-2	11-0-58-1		11-2-29-1		
v. Surrey (The Oval) 8 May (RA)	6-1-24-1	8-1-21-1	8-0-39-4	8-0-35-1		8-0-43-2	2-0-22-0	
v. Surrey (The Oval) 10 May (B&H)	11-1-30-0	11-1-57-1	11-1-42-1	11-2-29-0		11-1-55-2		
v. Kent (Canterbury) 12 May (B&H)	11-0-21-2	11-3-33-1	11-0-45-0	11-1-42-4		11-2-49-1		
v. Essex (Lord's) 14 May (B&H)	10.5-0-44-0	11-1-54-0	11-0-57-0	10-0-37-1		11-0-39-3		
v. Hampshire (Southampton) 15 May (RA)	8-0-33-1	8-1-19-3	2-0-18-0	8-1-22-1	6-0-29-1	8-0-32-2		
v. Derbyshire (Derby) 25 & 26 May (B&H)	4-1-12-0	10-2-27-1	4-0-21-0	3-0-14-0		4-0-16-0	4.3-1-10-0	1-1-0-0
v. Sussex (Lord's) 29 May (RA)	6-0-23-0	7-0-18-1	8-0-33-2	8-1-30-2	2-0-8-0	7-0-33-1		
v. Worcestershire (Lord's) 5 June (RA)	8-1-28-2	8-0-50-0	8-0-37-0		8-0-41-1	8-0-26-3		
v. Northamptonshire (Luton) 19 June (RA)		8-1-21-2	7-1-19-1		5-0-38-2	8-1-58-2	4-0-29-1	
v. Hertfordshire (Lord's) 22 June (NW)		12-3-25-1	11-3-22-2	12-6-15-1		8-2-16-0	5-2-14-0	
v. Somerset (Lord's) 26 June (RA)	8-0-42-0	8-0-48-2	8-1-38-3	8-0-43-0		8-0-72-0		
v. Derbyshire (Repton) 3 July (RA)	7-1-12-2	8-2-8-3			6.1-0-26-2	8-0-29-2		
v. Yorkshire (Leeds) 6–8 July (NW)	11-1-29-2	12-2-34-4	1.1-1-2-0	12-0-49-1		10-0-33-2	5.5-0-17-0	
v. Kent (Canterbury) 10 July (RA)	5-1-11-0	7-2-34-0		8-1-36-1	7-1-32-1	7-0-43-1		
v. Glamorgan (Lord's) 17 July (RA)								
v. Warwickshire (Lord's) 24 July (RA)	4-0-22-0	8-0-30-3		8-0-31-3		6-0-32-1		
v. Kent (Lord's) 27 July (NW)	10-2-32-2	12-3-20-2		11.3-1-44-1		9-0-39-1	5-0-17-1	
v. Leicestershire (Leicester) 31 July (RA)	5-0-22-1	6-0-17-1		3-0-15-3		3-0-19-1	4-0-26-0	
v. Lancashire (Blackpool) 7 August (RA)	6-0-24-0	8-1-27-2		8-0-41-1		8-0-43-3		
v. Surrey (The Oval) 10 August (NW)	12-0-45-4	10.4-3-29-2		11-2-40-0		6-0-26-0		
v. Gloucestershire (Lord's) 14 August (RA)	8-0-27-1	6-0-24-1		8-0-31-2	4-0-28-0	8-0-51-1		
v. Yorkshire (Leeds) 28 August (RA)	8-1-24-0	8-1-19-1				6.5-0-37-3		
v. Worcestershire (Lord's) 3 September (NW)	12-6-23-1	12-5-36-3		12-3-31-0		8-0-30-4		
v. Worcestershire (Worcester) 7 September (RA)	8-2-18-1	7.4-2-26-0		8-1-37-1		7-1-40-1		
Wickets	24	40	21	25	8	39	2	0

v. Warwickshire (Lord's) 24 July (RA)	v. Kent (Lord's) 27 July (NW)	v. Leicestershire (Leicester) 31 July (RA)	v. Lancashire (Blackpool) 7 August (RA)	v. Surrey (The Oval) 10 August (NW)	v. Gloucestershire (Lord's) 14 August (RA)	v. Yorkshire (Leeds) 28 August (RA)	v. Worcestershire (Lord's) 3 September (NW)	v. Worcestershire (Worcester) 7 September (RA)	Runs
16			2	8	37	0	1	17	409
37	24	—	3	18	10	11	0	9	746
—	18*	—	32	40	36*		8*	30*	368
30	64	—	21	65	14		24	14	614
4*	—	—	50	10*	6		35	6	283
7	37*	—	0	20	2	5			354
					5	21			155
									122
—	—	—	0	—	9*	2	—	0	68
—	—	—	16*	4*	13	12*	0*	5	80
			10			0*		23*	41
77*	1	—	11	56	53	15	14	7	497
15	27	—	3	24		7	6	2	189
						10			23
									15
—									—
									—
						51	56	11	118
				1	1			4	
16	5		5	5	16	12	5	14	
1	7		1	7	2	4	7	6	
						2		2	
187	199		155	258	203	150	162	146	
4	5		10	7	8	9	7	9	
W	W	Ab.	L	W	W	L	W	L	
4	—	2	0	—	4	0	—	—	

An early disaster for Worcestershire. Curtis is bowled by Fraser. (Ken Kelly)

National Westminster Bank Trophy Final
MIDDLESEX v. WORCESTERSHIRE

Middlesex made a cruel decision when they selected their side for the NatWest Final. They omitted Keith Brown, who had played in every one-day game of the season and in all but two first-class matches, and included Mark Ramprakash, two days short of his 19th birthday, in his place. On form, and as it transpired in performance, it was a wise decision. Gatting won the toss and asked Worces-

P.C.R. Tufnell	W.N. Slack	J.D. Carr	A. Needham	Byes	Leg-byes	Wides	No-balls	Total	Wkts
				2	10	4		165	7
					6	7	2	172	10
					7	6	1	182	9
				1	15	4	5	200	10
				4	6	1	3	223	5
					16	2	1	206	8
					6	7	1	237	5
				4	3	1	1	160	8
				2	9		1	111	1
				3	12	5	1	160	7
				2	8	7	1	192	8
8–1–30–0					5	6		200	8
12–4–29–3				2	19	5	2	142	7
		3–0–25–0	4–0–9–1		4	3	3	247	5
		6–0–20–1		2	6	11		130	10
			6–1–24–2		4	10	5	188	10
					7	1	1	187	5
									Ab.
6–0–32–1			8–0–22–0	2	13	4		184	8
			12–1–36–1		7	9	1	195	10
			6–0–25–0	1	5	3		130	10
		5–0–30–1	5–0–38–2		4	3	2	207	10
		5–0–19–2	12–1–23–1		6	8	1	188	10
					7	5		168	6
		5–0–23–1	7–0–33–1	1	6	2	2	143	6
		4–1–9–0	12–1–25–1		7	1	2	161	9
		8–2–22–0			4	8	1	147	3
4	0	5	9						

Northamptonshire CCC
Limited-Over Matches, 1988

BATTING

BATTING	v. Yorkshire (Leeds) 26 & 27 April (B&H)	v. Leicestershire (Leicester) 1 May (RA)	v. Gloucestershire (Northampton) 8 May (RA)	v. Minor Counties (Darlington) 10 May (B&H)	v. Worcestershire (Northampton) 12 May (B&H)	v. Nottinghamshire (Northampton) 14 May (B&H)	v. Essex (Chelmsford) 15 May (RA)	v. Surrey (The Oval) 22 May (RA)	v. Kent (Northampton) 29 May (RA)	v. Somerset (Taunton) 5 June (RA)	v. Yorkshire (Harrogate) 9 June (TT)	v. Middlesex (Luton) 19 June (RA)	v. Cheshire (Chester) 22 June (NW)	v. Nottinghamshire (Trent Bridge) 26 June (RA)	v. Lancashire (Tring) 3 July (RA)	v. Yorkshire (Northampton) 10 July (RA)
G. Cook	—	8	5	18	0*							26	53*	—		
W. Larkins	—	0	37	70	0	5	37	40	—	42	24	65	19	32		
R.J. Bailey	—	17	9	57	22	89	20	5	—	78	50	24	7	75		
A.J. Lamb	—	26	59	19	6	8	16		—				27	79		
R.G. Williams	—	9	0	10*	9	75	55	18	—	7		0	3	12*		
N. Stanley	—	12	14*	5		8	—	2				4				
D. Ripley	—	12	1	4*	30	4*	—	12		9*	0	11*	1			
N.G.B. Cook	—	13*	2	—	8	1*	—	11		4	11*	0*	9	—		
S.J. Brown	—															
W.W. Davis	—	0	2			8	6*	9		12	11	34	2			
A. Walker	—	4	4*	—	0*	—	—	1*	—				7			
M.A. Robinson	—	0								0	3					
D.J. Capel		8	7	25	23	38	12		—	18	16	22	4	2*		
D.K. Lillee			—	7												
D.J. Wild					0	1	6*	2		11	1	3	11			
A. Fordham								14	—	0	30					
M.R. Gouldstone										7	1					
D.S. Hoffman												2				
W. Noon																
Byes		2	1	1	2					2	2		4			
Leg-byes	3	15	6	9		10	3			14	2	5	3	12		
Wides	5	13	5	6	1	1	4			3	2	6	9	11		
No-balls	3	1		8	1	1				4			2			
Total	112	172	202	131	226	190	133			211	155	200	161	223		
Wickets	10		9	6	9†	8	5	10		10	10	8	10	3		
Result	Ab.	L	W	W	L	W	L	L	Ab.	L	L	L	L	W	Ab.	Ab.
Points	1	0	4	2	0	2	0	0	2	0	0	—	0	4	2	2

Fielding Figures
17 – D. Ripley (ct 13/st 4)
7 – G. Cook and D.J. Capel
6 – R.J. Bailey
4 – D.J. Wild, W. Larkins and A. Walker
3 – N.G.B. Cook and N. Stanley
2 – A.J. Lamb, D.K. Lillee and W. Noon
1 – A. Fordham, M.R. Gouldstone and R.G. Williams

† G. Cook retired hurt

BOWLING

BOWLING	W.W. Davis	S.J. Brown	R.G. Williams	N.G.B. Cook	W. Larkins	A. Walker	M.A. Robinson	D.J. Capel
v. Yorkshire (Leeds) 26 & 27 April (B&H)	8–1–37–0	7–0–33–0	2–0–7–0	7–0–31–0	7–0–31–0	6.2–0–29–1		
v. Leicestershire (Leicester) 1 May (RA)	8–0–47–1		8–0–28–1	8–1–19–2		8–0–41–2	8–0–35–1	
v. Gloucestershire (Northampton) 8 May (RA)	8–0–41–1		4–0–10–2	8–1–28–1	8–0–31–0	8–0–32–2		4–0–16–
v. Minor Counties (Darlington) 10 May (B&H)			11–1–27–3	11–4–21–2		8–2–21–2		11–2–35
v. Worcestershire (Northampton) 12 May (B&H)			7–1–21–0	8–2–17–1		11–0–59–1		10–0–39
v. Nottinghamshire (Northampton) 14 May (B&H)	11–0–40–2		5–0–20–0	11–0–34–0		11–2–34–2		9–0–33
v. Essex (Chelmsford) 15 May (RA)	8–0–37–0		4–0–31–2	8–0–29–1		4–0–29–1		8–0–36
v. Surrey (The Oval) 22 May (RA)	8–1–22–0		3–0–21–0	3–0–20–0	2–0–9–0	7–2–28–1		8–0–16
v. Kent (Northampton) 29 May (RA)	2–0–18–1			4–0–34–2		2–0–22–0		4–0–27
v. Somerset (Taunton) 5 June (RA)	8–1–28–1		8–0–65–2	4–0–18–0			5.4–0–37–0	6–0–29
v. Yorkshire (Harrogate) 9 June (TT)	8–1–18–0			9–0–52–4			11–3–46–0	
v. Middlesex (Luton) 19 June (RA)	8–1–29–1		2–0–15–0	7.5–0–51–0		5–0–32–0		6–1–26–
v. Cheshire (Chester) 22 June (NW)	12–1–48–1		5–2–10–1	10–1–20–1		11.5–2–37–1		12–3–28
v. Nottinghamshire (Trent Bridge) 26 June (RA)	8–2–40–0			8–0–47–0	2–0–11–0	8–0–60–3		8–0–22–
v. Lancashire (Tring) 3 July (RA)								
v. Yorkshire (Northampton) 10 July (RA)								
v. Sussex (Northampton) 24 July (RA)			6–0–22–1	8–1–21–0		8–0–33–1		8–0–31–
v. Worcestershire (Worcester) 31 July (RA)		5–0–25–2				6–0–21–1		6–0–30–
v. Warwickshire (Edgbaston) 7 August (RA)		8–0–46–1		8–0–20–0		8–1–35–1		
v. Hampshire (Bournemouth) 14 August (RA)		5–0–26–1		3.4–0–19–1		4–0–17–0		
v. Glamorgan (Wellingborough) 21 August (RA)		7.3–0–36–1		8–1–24–0		8–0–33–1	8–0–41–1	
v. Derbyshire (Northampton) 28 August (RA)	8–0–43–2	8–0–44–1		8–0–40–2		8–0–33–2		
Wickets	10	6	12	17	0	21	2	9

v. Sussex (Northampton) 24 July (RA)	v. Worcestershire (Worcester) 31 July (RA)	v. Warwickshire (Edgbaston) 7 August (RA)	v. Hampshire (Bournemouth) 14 August (RA)	v. Glamorgan (Wellingborough) 21 August (RA)	v. Derbyshire (Northampton) 28 August (RA)	Runs
8	21	8	37	7	43	234
1	9	11	3	3	9	407
3	5		12	19	24	516
			35			275
22	16					236
1*	14*	18				78
		24*	2*	20		130
				5*	—	64
				1		1
					16*	90
—	—	—	—		1	17
				—		3
83	25				10	293
—				6*		13
18*	7	74*	0	54	91	279
		30	23			97
		6	11	0	10	35
						2
	9*				6	15
				3		
11	10	10	5	12	7	
6	6	5	1	6	3	
	1				2	
153	123	186	94	171	222	
5	6	5	6	8	8	
W	L	W	L	L	L	
4	0	4	0	0	0	

Phil Neale is bowled. (Adrian Murrell/Allsport)

tershire to bat first on a damp pitch at a heavy 10.30 in the morning. It was a decisive toss to win.

Curtis was bowled by a magnificent ball from Fraser which pitched on leg stump and knocked back the off. O'Shaughnessy edged a widish ball to Downton, and Hick, whom so many had come to see and who had a dreadful day, hit one classical cover drive for four off a half-volley and then missed a straight ball. The first 12 overs produced only four scoring strokes, and Worcestershire were 9 for 3.

Leatherdale, a highly confident and capable young man, played perkily and Neale, who had been ill on the eve of the match, batted with customary determination in an attempt to resuscitate the Worcestershire innings. Middle-

D.K. Lillee	R.J. Bailey	N. Stanley	A.J. Lamb	D.J. Wild	D.S. Hoffman	G. Cook	Byes	Leg-byes	Wides	No-balls	Total	Wkts
								5	5	7	173	1
								3	3	1	173	8
								11	1	1	169	7
9–2–23–1	3–0–7–0	1–0–3–1	1–0–11–1				1	9	4	2	158	10
11–0–61–3				8–0–34–1			7	18	12	2	256	8
				8–0–32–4			4	17	4	3	214	10
				8–0–39–2			1	12	2	1	214	7
				7–2–12–0				9	3		137	3
				4–0–38–0				4	7		143	3
				8–0–28–3				7	3	1	212	8
	7–0–35–1			9–0–51–2	11–0–71–2			10	1		283	9
				8–1–45–1				3	1	1	201	2
				9–3–12–1			1	7		4	163	9
				6–0–31–0			5	4	7		220	3
												Ab.
												Ab.
7–0–18–1				3–0–18–1			9		2	1	152	6
6–0–21–0				5–0–19–0				8	5	1	124	4
8–0–38–3				8–1–41–2				4	2	1	184	8
6–0–31–0								4		1	97	2
8–2–21–1				6–0–45–1				5	8		172	4
				7–0–48–0		1–0–4–0	5	10	10	1	227	8
9	1	1	1	18	2	0						

sex raced through their overs in an attempt to keep the pressure on Worcestershire, and Leatherdale and Neal were confronted by the perplexity of evaporating overs and approaching lunch. Feeling the urge to score runs, Leatherdale, who batted with sense and aggression, hit at Needham in the last over before lunch and was bowled. The break came at 71 for 4 off 42 overs.

Weston helped Neale to add 66, but the stand was necessarily convalescent rather than virulent. Weston fell to the splendid Fraser, and Neale's brave knock was ended by Hughes, who profited as batsmen swung for quick runs.

Middlesex should never have had any fears about making 162 to win on a day that had defied forecast and remained fine and eventually warm, but Dilley bowled a lively, accurate and aggressive spell to move one away from Carr and force both Slack and Needham to nudge into their stumps. Even worse for Middlesex was that Gatting was run out without facing a ball when Slack drove to mid-off and the skipper trotted gently down the wicket, bat in air. At 28 for 4, Middlesex faced an embarrassing defeat although, with Emburey at seven and Downton at eight, they had a batting line-up which would be the envy of many. Butcher was stroking the ball with confidence when he charged down the wicket as Ramprakash stayed put and was run out. The score was 64 for 5 and the game was very much in the balance. It quickly tilted in favour of Middlesex.

Ramprakash, totally assured, was batting with a liquidity that was eminently pleasing to the eye, and Emburey, totally professional, was the perfect foil. In 24 overs of purposeful cricket, they added 85 and virtually took the game out of Worcestershire's reach before Dilley returned and bowled Emburey and had Ramprakash taken at long-leg after his first loose shot. Dilley's was a fine and brave performance, but Neale crowded the slip area and the batsmen far too late as Downton stroked his side to victory with five overs unused.

Boycott named Ramprakash as Man of the Match. Presumably, sponsors pay old players considerable sums of money to act as adjudicators and are entitled to expect something in return. Six or eight words, two of which were dominated, and no mention of Fraser or Cowans hardly seemed to justify payment.

Man of the Match Mark Ramprakash. (Adrian Murrell/Allsport)

Texaco Trophy
ENGLAND v. SRI LANKA

The unexpectedly bright and sunny weather drew a much larger crowd to The Oval than had been expected. They were rewarded by a most entertaining match. England recalled Vic Marks to international cricket, used none of the Middlesex or Worcestershire players and made Lawrence 12th man. Gooch won the toss and asked Sri Lanka to bat first.

They began purposefully and sensibly enough, but Small bowled Samarasekera just as he was looking set, and Gooch, who bowled very impressively, defeated de Silva. Kuruppu was striking the ball sweetly, but he became Gooch's second victim, and once more Sri Lanka had been cut short just as they looked to be moving into top gear. Mendis and Ranatunga added 69 off 14 overs of enterprising and attractive batting before Ranatunga was run out. Mendis hit 60 off 65 balls and put on 46 in eight overs with Madugalle, but Mendis strained a thigh muscle, called for a runner and was immediately bowled by Small as he slogged wildly. That was in the 46th over, just as the late

Middlesex again – Gatting holds the NatWest Bank Trophy. (Gray Mortimore/Allsport)

Tillekeratne just makes his ground. (Adrian Murrell/Allsport)

TEXACO TROPHY – ENGLAND *v.* SRI LANKA
4 September 1988 at The Oval, Kennington

SRI LANKA			
D.S.B.P. Kuruppu*	lbw, b Gooch	38
M.A.R. Samarasekera	b Small	10
P.A. de Silva	b Gooch	16
A. Ranatunga	run out	37
L.R.D. Mendis	b Small	60
R.S. Madugalle†	c Foster, b Pringle	17
J.R. Ratnayeke	c Pringle, b Small	19
H.P. Tillekeratne	not out	15
G.F. Labrooy	not out	10
W.R. Madurasinghe		
S.D. Anurasiri		
Extras	b 1, lb 10, w 8, nb 1	20
(55 overs)	(for 7 wkts)	242

ENGLAND			
G.A. Gooch	c de Silva, b Labrooy	7
R.T. Robinson	lbw, b Ratnayeke	13
K.J. Barnett	run out	84
A.J. Lamb	c sub (Rajadurai), b Labrooy	66
R.A. Smith	c Kuruppu, b Labrooy	9
R.J. Bailey	not out	43
D.R. Pringle	not out	19
V.J. Marks		
N.A. Foster		
R.C. Russell		
G.C. Small		
Extras	w 3, nb 1	4
(52.4 overs)	(for 5 wkts)	245

	O	M	R	W
Foster	11	–	47	–
Small	11	1	44	3
Gooch	11	1	35	2
Pringle	11	–	46	1
Marks	11	–	59	–

	O	M	R	W
Ratnayeke	9.4	3	37	1
Labrooy	10	–	40	3
Samarasekera	11	–	52	–
Ranatunga	11	–	42	–
Anurasiri	6	–	31	–
de Silva	2	–	19	–
Madurasinghe	3	–	24	–

FALL OF WICKETS
1–21, 2–54, 3–75, 4–144, 5–190, 6–193, 7–224

FALL OF WICKETS
1–9, 2–22, 3–140, 4–154, 5–213

Umpires: J.W. Holder & K.E. Palmer

England won by 5 wickets

REFUGE ASSURANCE CUP FINAL – WORCESTERSHIRE *v.* LANCASHIRE
18 September 1988 at Edgbaston, Birmingham

LANCASHIRE			
G.D. Mendis	b Weston	0
G. Fowler	c Neale, b Pridgeon	26
A.N. Hayhurst	st Rhodes, b Weston	1
N.H. Fairbrother	c Radford, b Newport	38
T.E. Jesty	b Radford	59
M. Watkinson	not out	42
I.D. Austin	not out	6
D.P. Hughes†		
P.J.W. Allott		
J. Simmons		
W.K. Hegg*		
Extras	b 4, lb 12, w 13	29
(40 overs)	(for 5 wkts)	201

WORCESTERSHIRE			
T.S. Curtis	c Hegg, b Hayhurst	32
S.J. O'Shaughnessy	c Mendis, b Allott	4
G.A. Hick	b Watkinson	2
D.A. Leatherdale	b Simmons	30
P.A. Neale†	c Watkinson, b Austin	42
M.J. Weston	c Hegg, b Hayhurst	1
S.J. Rhodes*	c Hughes, b Hayhurst	20
P.J. Newport	c Hegg, b Austin	2
N.V. Radford	c Hegg, b Hayhurst	0
R.K. Illingworth	c Hegg, b Austin	0
A.P. Pridgeon	not out	2
Extras	1b 10, w 4	14
(35.5 overs)		149

	O	M	R	W
Weston	8	–	19	2
Newport	8	–	40	1
Radford	8	–	44	1
Pridgeon	8	1	48	1
Illingworth	8	–	34	–

	O	M	R	W
Watkinson	6	2	10	1
Allott	6	2	10	1
Austin	7.5	–	51	3
Simmons	8	–	22	1
Hayhurst	8	–	46	4

FALL OF WICKETS
1–1, 2–4, 3–69, 4–113, 5–194

FALL OF WICKETS
1–19, 2–24, 3–75, 4–79, 5–90, 6–134, 7–145, 8–146

Umpires: J. Birkenshaw & J.W. Holder

Man of the Match: M. Watkinson

Lancashire won by 52 runs

(Refuge Assurance Cup Final report begins on page 425)

Nottinghamshire CCC
Limited-Over Matches, 1988

BATTING

BATTING	v. Middlesex (Lord's) 24 Apr (RA)	v. Minor Counties (TB) 26 Apr (B&H)	v. Worcestershire (Worcester) 1 May (RA)	v. Yorkshire (TB) 3 & 4 May (B&H)	v. Lancashire (TB) 8 May (RA)	v. Worcestershire (Worcester) 10 & 11 May (B&H)	v. Northamptonshire (Northampton) 14 May (B&H)	v. Gloucestershire (TB) 15 May (RA)	v. Sussex (TB) 22 May (RA)	v. Glamorgan (Cardiff) 26 May (B&H)	v. Derbyshire (Derby) 29 May (RA)	v. Warwickshire (Edgbaston) 5 June (RA)	v. Glamorgan (TB) 12 June (RA)	v. Hampshire (Basingstoke) 19 June (RA)	v. Devon (Torquay) 22 June (NW)	v. Northamptonshire (TB) 26 June (RA)
B.C. Broad	18	52	35	—	1	27	22	43		45	20		61		27	96*
R.T. Robinson	40	24	20	—	23	2	47	50	18	60	25	22				
P. Johnson	2	22*	3	—	21	9	30	33	15	37			14	82	16	17
D.W. Randall	12	—	20	—	54	69	5	27	18	23	59	35	12	19*	149*	32
J.D. Birch	35*	—	41*	—	14	15	14	19	65*	4	4	18	30	54	55*	1*
F.D. Stephenson	12	—	8	—	43	2	9	0	8*	10	7		0	1	—	—
B.N. French	23	—	17*	—	18											
K.P. Evans	6		—		8*	18	31*	11	—	11	1*	4*	0*	—	—	—
R.A. Pick	1*	—	—	—		1*										
K.E. Cooper	—	—	—	—		9	4	—	—	2*	—					
K. Saxelby	—						1		—	—						—
M. Newell		31*											23	44	3	35
E.E. Hemmings		—			12*	21*	5	2*		0	4	0*	3	2*	—	—
C.W. Scott						5	18	—	—	5*	1*	—				—
P. Pollard									25		25	17		18		
C.D. Fraser-Darling										—		9	10*			
C.L. Cairns												4				
M.K. Bore																
D.J. Millns																—
D.J.R. Martindale																
R.J. Evans																
G.W. Mike																
Byes	2	1	2			4		2	4		1		1			5
Leg-byes	10	3	9		8	5	17	8	4	12	9	16	15	9	13	4
Wides	4	1				6	4	14	1	6	3	4	3	7	7	7
No-balls		3	2		13	3	1	1		1		2	1	5		
Total	165	137	157		202	202	214	208	156	220	158	155	193	201	302	220
Wickets	7	2	5		7	9	10	7	4	8	7	7	7	5	3	3
Result	L	W	W	Ab.	L	W	L	L	W	L	L	L	L	L	W	L
Points	0	2	4	1	0	2	0	0	4	—	0	0	0	0	—	0

Fielding Figures

13 – C.W. Scott
12 – P. Johnson
8 – B.N. French
6 – M. Newell
5 – K.E. Cooper, K.P. Evans, E.E. Hemmings and J.D. Birch
4 – F.D. Stephenson and R.T. Robinson
3 – D.W. Randall
1 – R.A. Pick, C.L. Cairns, M.K. Bore, B.C. Broad, G.W. Mike and P. Pollard

BOWLING

BOWLING	R.A. Pick	K.E. Cooper	F.D. Stephenson	K.P. Evans	K. Saxelby	E.E. Hemmings	C.D. Fraser-Darling	J.D. Birch
v. Middlesex (Lord's) 24 April (RA)	8-0-46-0	8-1-22-2	7.1-1-23-1	8-0-32-2	7-0-37-0			
v. Minor Counties (Trent Bridge) 26 April (B&H)	11-2-41-1	11-4-28-0	10.2-2-14-4		11-4-21-5	11-2-17-0		
v. Worcestershire (Worcester) 1 May (RA)	6-0-58-1	7-1-32-2	8-0-35-2			6-0-37-2		
v. Yorkshire (Trent Bridge) 3 & 4 May (B&H)	1-0-6-0		2-1-2-0					
v. Lancashire (Trent Bridge) 8 May (RA)	8-0-30-1	8-0-39-2	8-0-50-1	8-0-53-1		8-0-26-1		
v. Worcestershire (Worcester) 10 & 11 May (B&H)	11-1-48-1	11-0-55-2	11-3-31-1	11-1-36-3		11-2-16-1		
v. Northamptonshire (Northampton) 14 May (B&H)		11-2-36-2	11-0-39-1	11-1-45-1	11-1-58-1	11-1-46-1		
v. Gloucestershire (Trent Bridge) 15 May (RA)		8-2-27-2	7.5-0-37-3	8-0-30-2	8-0-60-1	8-0-46-0		
v. Sussex (Trent Bridge) 22 May (RA)		8-0-19-1	8-1-33-3	6-0-20-0	8-1-18-2	8-1-18-2	7-0-40-1	3-0-17-1
v. Glamorgan (Cardiff) 26 May (B&H)		9-2-20-2	9-0-27-0	9.2-0-57-1	9-0-46-0	11-0-51-0		2-1-8-1
v. Derbyshire (Derby) 29 May (RA)		4-0-22-0	5-1-20-1	2-0-15-0	3-0-20-0	2-0-11-0		
v. Warwickshire (Edgbaston) 5 June (RA)				8-0-25-2		8-0-29-0	8-0-34-2	3-0-26-3
v. Glamorgan (Trent Bridge) 12 June (RA)		8-0-36-0	8-2-17-2	8-1-23-1		8-1-33-0	5-0-46-0	3-0-34-1
v. Hampshire (Basingstoke) 19 June (RA)		8-1-35-2	8-1-46-1	8-0-37-1	8-0-38-3	8-0-40-0		
v. Devon (Torquay) 22 June (NW)		12-3-25-1	10-5-24-2	11-1-48-2	12-0-48-0	12-3-38-1		
v. Northamptonshire (Trent Bridge) 26 June (RA)			8-0-36-1	8-0-33-1	7.4-0-48-0	8-0-39-0		
v. Kent (Canterbury) 3 July (RA)								
v. Worcestershire (Trent Bridge) 6–8 July (NW)		12-0-50-1	12-2-50-1	12-2-42-0	12-0-68-2	12-0-67-1		
v. Leicestershire (Trent Bridge) 10 July (RA)								
v. Yorkshire (Trent Bridge) 17 July (RA)		6-0-17-1	6-1-13-1	3.1-0-28-0	4-0-28-0			
v. Somerset (Taunton) 24 July (RA)		6-0-19-0	6-1-31-0	5.3-0-30-0	7-0-39-0			
v. Essex (Colchester) 14 August (RA)		8-0-39-1	8-0-54-1	8-1-26-3			8-0-48-0	
v. Surrey (Trent Bridge) 21 August (RA)			8-3-23-4	8-0-63-2			4-0-23-3	
Wickets	4	21	31	22	14	7	6	6

Russell in action in the Texaco Trophy match at The Oval. (Adrian Murrell/Allsport)

surge was needed, but, in fact, the last 9½ overs produced only 49 runs. Another 20 would have been a winning total.

There was soon joy for Sri Lanka when England batted, for Gooch clipped to square-leg. Robinson, whose presence in the side remained a mystery, survived a violent appeal for lbw, but next ball a similar appeal was upheld. Lamb immediately injected energy into the proceedings. He dominated a stand of 118 in 25 overs with Barnett, hitting 66 off 71 balls before clipping Labrooy to square-leg as Gooch had done. Sri Lanka's main weakness was in their fifth bowler. Madugalle used de Silva, an occasional bowler, before the off-spinner Madurasinghe, who bowled only three overs and, like Anurasiri, the left-arm spinner, was brought into the attack too late.

Smith went quickly, to his own obvious disgust and disagreement, and Barnett ran himself out after three

Batting

v. Kent (Canterbury) 3 July (RA)	v. Worcestershire (Trent Bridge) 6–8 July (NW)	v. Leicestershire (Trent Bridge) 10 July (RA)	v. Yorkshire (Trent Bridge) 17 July (RA)	v. Somerset (Taunton) 24 July (RA)	v. Essex (Colchester) 14 August (RA)	v. Surrey (Trent Bridge) 21 August (RA)	Runs
	2		19		11		479
	30		15	4	49	100	529
	29		5	3		19	357
	4*		44	68	0	60	710
	1*		3		21	2*	396
	—		1	14	41*	12*	168
						—	58
							2
	—		11	0	2	—	103
	—		0	1	3*		19
	—		2*	2*			5
				8	9	30	241
							49
	—		13*	9			51
							85
				10	—		29
							4
							—
	—			0*		—	0
				39			39
					7	—	7
					0		0
				10			
	3			8	5	6	
	3		3		1	4	
	2			1	4		
	74		125	162	159	233	
	3		8	9	9	4	
Ab.	L	Ab.	L	L	L	W	
2	—	2	0	0	0	4	

Bowling

C.L. Cairns	M.K. Bore	D.W. Randall	P. Johnson	M. Newell	D.J. Millns	G.W. Mike	Byes	Leg-byes	Wides	No-balls	Total	Wkts
								6	1	1	166	6
								12	6	1	133	10
								7	3		169	7
											8	0
							2	8		1	208	8
							3	9	9	10	198	9
							2		1	1	226	8
								9	6	2	209	8
							1	4	4	1	152	8
							2	12	6		223	4
							4	1			93	1
5–1–30–0	8–0–30–1						1	9	4	1	184	9
								9	4		198	4
							1	9	7	1	206	7
		1–0–20–0	1–0–11–0	1–0–10–0				14	2	1	238	6
					7–0–55–1			12	11		223	3
												Ab.
							2	6	3		285	5
												Ab.
					6–0–31–1			9	2		126	3
					6–0–37–1			7	1		163	1
						8–1–57–1	1	11	4	1	236	6
					4–0–22–0	4–0–24–0		5	1		160	9
0	1	0	0	0	3	1						

Somerset CCC
Limited-Over Matches, 1988

BATTING

BATTING	v. Sussex (Hove) 24 April (RA)	v. Hampshire (Taunton) 26 April (B&H)	v. Glamorgan (Cardiff) 1 May (RA)	v. Combined Universities (Oxford) 4 May (B&H)	v. Worcestershire (Taunton) 8 May (RA)	v. Glamorgan (Taunton) 10 May (B&H)	v. Gloucestershire (Bristol) 12 May (B&H)	v. Northamptonshire (Taunton) 5 June (RA)	v. Warwickshire (Bath) 12 June (RA)	v. Surrey (Bath) 19 June (RA)	v. Durham (Darlington) 22 June (NW)	v. Middlesex (Lord's) 26 June (RA)	v. Essex (Taunton) 3 July (RA)	v. Hampshire (Southampton) 6 & 7 July (NW)	v. Lancashire (Old Trafford) 10 July (RA)	v. Gloucestershire (Bristol) 17 July (RA)
N.A. Felton	0	50	8	9		13	10									
P.M. Roebuck	10	42	31	4	18					64	47	31		22	13	14
J.J.E. Hardy	45	8	0	34	21	60	70*	1	14	15	100	1		12	25	10
R.J. Harden	52	7	15	13	4	30	19									
N.D. Burns	6	5	—	2	6	—	—	2	17	30	1*	—		18	1*	34
V.J. Marks	27	9	—	15	25	—	16	16	7	12*	21	8*		45*	20	2
G.D. Rose	29*	22*	38*	6	10	—	18	19	14	2	8	6		3	2	15
G.V. Palmer	14*	14	1*	5*	25*	—	1*	0	4	1	17	—		10*	4*	3
N.A. Mallender	—	16*	—	0	23*	—	—			—		0		—	—	10*
A.N. Jones	—	—	—	1*	—			16*	2	—	—	—		—	—	—
D.J. Foster	—							—	0*							
S.R. Waugh		7	29	79		75*		109*	68	11	21	140*		0	37	30
J.G. Wyatt					2	44	55	11	4	77	8	1				
M.D. Crowe					2		24									
R.J. Bartlett								25	26	10	6*	50		85	55	28
C.H. Dredge								2	5							
N.J. Pringle														17	10	15
J.C.M. Atkinson																
H.R.J. Trump																
M.W. Cleal																
Byes	5		1	1	1	1	1			2					5	1
Leg-byes		9	8	2	5	4	10	7	4	9	1	4		10	16	18
Wides	2	7	3	7	3	1	3	3	4	2	4	3		2	2	4
No-balls	1	1		4				1	1	4	3	3				
Total	191	197	134	182	145	228	227	212	170	233	240	247		227	190	184
Wickets	6	8	5	9	8	4	6	8	10	9	7	5		7	7	9
Result	L	L	L	W	L	L	L	W	L	W	W	W	Ab.	L	W	L
Points	0	0	0	2	0	0	0	4	0	4	—	4	2	—	4	0

Fielding Figures

24 – N.D. Burns (ct 21/st 3)
9 – R.J. Bartlett
8 – G.D. Rose
6 – P.M. Roebuck, S.R. Waugh and J.G. Wyatt
5 – J.J.E. Hardy

4 – V.J. Marks
3 – C.H. Dredge and G.V. Palmer
2 – N.A. Mallender and A.N. Jones
1 – N.A. Felton, M.D. Crowe and N.J. Pringle

BOWLING

BOWLING	A.N. Jones	N.A. Mallender	G.V. Palmer	V.J. Marks	D.J. Foster	G.D. Rose	S.R. Waugh	C.H. Dredge
v. Sussex (Hove) 24 April (RA)	8–0–41–2	7–0–29–0	3–0–15–0	8–0–27–1	5–0–31–1	8–0–40–1		
v. Hampshire (Taunton) 26 April (B&H)	10–0–33–1	10–3–20–1	5–0–14–1	10.5–1–42–0		11–1–47–1	7–0–35–0	
v. Glamorgan (Cardiff) 1 May (RA)	3–0–27–0	4–0–41–1	3–0–26–1			3–0–23–0	3–0–20–0	
v. Combined Universities (Oxford) 4 May (B&H)	9–1–19–4		6.3–0–17–1	5–2–9–2	5–0–19–0	8–0–29–0	5–1–16–2	
v. Worcestershire (Taunton) 8 May (RA)	6–0–34–0	7–3–11–1	6.3–0–45–1	8–2–23–1		8–0–26–0		
v. Glamorgan (Taunton) 10 May (B&H)	8–0–55–0	11–2–28–0	10.2–0–50–0	11–1–39–1		11–2–32–3	2–0–12–0	
v. Gloucestershire (Bristol) 12 May (B&H)		9.4–0–36–1	8–1–40–0	9–0–42–0	11–0–57–1	11–0–50–1		
v. Northamptonshire (Taunton) 5 June (RA)		6–0–53–2	6.4–0–37–3	8–1–36–2	3–0–14–0	8–0–37–1		8–1–18–0
v. Warwickshire (Bath) 12 June (RA)		7–0–41–1	6–1–27–3	8–0–35–1	6–0–18–1	8–0–41–2		5–0–18–0
v. Surrey (Bath) 19 June (RA)	7–0–40–1	8–0–38–1	2–0–17–2	8–1–31–2		7–0–55–1	8–0–27–1	
v. Durham (Darlington) 22 June (NW)	5–0–41–0	11–1–35–2	12–3–24–3	12–3–24–0		9–3–27–0	11–3–45–2	
v. Middlesex (Lord's) 26 June (RA)	7–0–56–1	8–1–31–4	8–0–41–0	8–1–26–0		7–0–34–3	2–0–20–0	
v. Essex (Taunton) 3 July (RA)								
v. Hampshire (Southampton) 6 & 7 July (NW)	11–4–37–0	12–0–41–0	1–0–8–0	12–3–31–1		12–0–46–2	11–0–51–2	
v. Lancashire (Old Trafford) 10 July (RA)	5–0–21–1	7–0–35–1	4–0–30–1	7–0–26–2		4–0–17–1	7–0–47–1	
v. Gloucestershire (Bristol) 17 July (RA)	8–0–43–2	7–0–32–1	4.5–0–23–0	8–0–42–0		8–0–30–0		
v. Nottinghamshire (Taunton) 24 July (RA)		8–0–41–2	2–0–19–0	6–0–29–1	8–0–28–3	8–1–21–2		8–1–14–0
v. Kent (Canterbury) 31 July (RA)		5–0–10–1		6–1–29–0	7–1–32–0	5–0–13–1		6.4–0–38–
v. Derbyshire (Weston-super-Mare) 7 August (RA)	8–0–31–3	8–0–43–2		8–2–8–2				8–1–28–0
v. Yorkshire (Scarborough) 14 August (RA)	8–0–46–3	8–2–30–1		7–0–50–2			7–0–42–1	8–0–40–2
v. Leicestershire (Leicester) 21 August (RA)	4–0–28–0	5.5–0–35–1		6–0–19–3		8–0–33–2		8–0–17–2
v. Hampshire (Taunton) 28 August (RA)	8–1–47–2	8–0–34–1		8–0–39–0		8–0–42–1		8–0–37–1
Wickets	23	22	17	19	6	23	8	6

v. Nottinghamshire (Taunton) 24 July (RA)	v. Kent (Canterbury) 31 July (RA)	v. Derbyshire (Weston-super-Mare) 7 August (RA)	v. Yorkshire (Scarborough) 14 August (RA)	v. Leicestershire (Leicester) 21 August (RA)	v. Hampshire (Taunton) 28 August (RA)	Runs
						90
35	1	28		—	3	363
			30	40	0	486
			32	6		178
—	9	0	22	16*	5	174
—	2	80	11*	14*	4	334
93*	38		10	11	17	361
						99
—	5	3	5*	—	0	62
		2*	—	—	7*	28
—	2*					2
—	39	33	38			716
		2	89	3	72	368
						26
27*	2	0	23	50	23	410
	13	—	—	—	0	20
		9				51
—	2					2
	4					4
		1	—			1
		1	2		1	
7	8	9	3	5	5	
1		4	1	2	2	
			1	2		
163	125	172	235	175	145	
1	10	9	6	5	10	
W	L	L	W	L	L	
4	0	0	4	0	0	

N.J. Pringle	M.W. Cleal	Byes	Leg-byes	Wides	No-balls	Total	Wkts
		2	10	5	2	195	5
			10	3	1	201	5
		1		5		138	2
				3	1	112	10
				9	3	148	3
			13	1	2	229	4
			3	3	7	228	4
		2	14	3	4	211	10
		1	21	1		202	8
		1	7	7	2	216	9
		1	9	9	1	206	8
			12	4	1	220	9
							Ab.
		4	11	5	1	229	5
2–0–10–0		5	3	6		184	8
			5	3		185	3
		10			4	162	9
			4	2	3	126	3
	8–0–49–0		15	2	1	174	8
	2–0–17–0		8	2		233	9
		1	10	1		143	8
		4	4	4		207	5
0	0						

hours and 143 balls. He had played a bright and important innings without ever asserting himself in the way that he can, but it was, after all, only his second international match and he had passed fifty in both. This time, he was to be named England's Man of the Match; Mendis took the Sri Lankan award.

Bailey and Pringle each hit a six, and both batted with supreme confidence and flair to take England to victory with 14 balls to spare. It made a joyful end to a summer which had not been all joy by any means.

3 September

at Scarborough

Yorkshire 265 for 4 (D. Byas 111 not out, M.D. Moxon 63, P.E. Robinson 60)
Rest of World XI 258 for 9 (D.K. Lillee 51 not out)

Yorkshire won by 7 runs

Four Counties Competition

4 September

at Scarborough

Essex 250 for 7 (A.W. Lilley 111)
Lancashire 223

Essex won by 27 runs

5 September

Yorkshire 185
Gloucestershire 112

Yorkshire won by 73 runs

6 September

Essex 206 for 8 (J.P. Stephenson 50)
Yorkshire 112 (G. Miller 4 for 28)

Essex won by 94 runs

Essex took the first Four Counties Knock-Out competition, which replaced the former Asda tournament. The matches were of 50-over duration. Lilley and Stephenson took individual awards for Essex, for whom Topley bowled particularly well.

Refuge Assurance Cup

Semi-Finals

7 September

at Bristol

Gloucestershire 117 for 9
Lancashire 121 for 7

Lancashire won by 3 wickets
(Man of the Match: P.J.W. Allott)

at Worcester

Middlesex 146 for 9 (N.V. Radford 4 for 23)
Worcestershire 147 for 3 (G.A. Hick 74 not out)

Surrey CCC
Limited-Over Matches, 1988

BATTING

BATTING	v. Hampshire (Southampton) a24 April (RA)	v. Essex (Chelmsford) 26 April (B&H)	v. Kent (The Oval) 3 & 4 May (B&H)	v. Middlesex (The Oval) 8 May (RA)	v. Middlesex (The Oval) 10 May (B&H)	v. Sussex (Hove) 14 May (B&H)	v. Sussex (Hove) 15 May (RA)	v. Northamptonshire (The Oval) 22 May (RA)	v. Essex (Chelmsford) 29 May (RA)	v. Yorkshire (Leeds) 5 June (RA)	v. Leicestershire (The Oval) 12 June (RA)	v. Somerset (Bath) 19 June (RA)	v. Staffordshire (Burton-on-Trent) 22 June (NW)	v. Derbyshire (The Oval) 26 June (RA)	v. Warwickshire (The Oval) 3 July (RA)	v. Essex (Chelmsford) 6 & 7 July (NW)
C.J. Richards	30	19	—	0	1*	3	5	1	105*	18	4	29	50	24		30*
D.M. Smith	75	29	55	54	85	18	33	15	7	33	16	17	44			5
A.J. Stewart	53	21	57*	33	49	23	46	15	7	60			54			31
M.A. Lynch	25	23	—	48	63*	46	31*		8*	4	12	28	48	50		17
D.M. Ward	8	2	—	1	3	7	27*	38*		22	23	34	2	48*		0
Zahid Sadiq	0			18			—	—	—	23	53	7		10		
I.A. Greig	5	8	—	17*	0	0	—	56*	—	9	2	29	22	35*		1
C.K. Bullen	11	21	—	0	—	4*	—	—	—	21*	7*	1	0	—		22
M.A. Feltham	18	1	—	2	—	2	—	—	—	11	—	20*	16*	—		7*
S.T. Clarke	2*	4	—		32		—	—	—	0*	—	8	1	—		—
N.H. Peters	1*	1*	—	0	—											—
G.S. Clinton		10	121*		8	14										17
M.P. Bicknell				2						—		9*	1*	—		
K.T. Medlycott									—		29*	17		—		
A.H. Gray									—							
P.D. Atkins																
D.J. Bicknell																
G.P. Thorpe																
J.D. Robinson																
Byes				1	4	2				6	1	1	1	1		4
Leg-byes	7	4	8	15	6	4	5	9	11		8	7	9	5		4
Wides	1		8	4	1	1	7	3	1		1	2	7	5		4
No-balls				5	3		1				4	2	2	2		
Total	236	143	249	200	223	156	155	137	139	211	159	216	285	225		142
Wickets	9	10	1	10	5	10	3	3	2	8	6	9	9	4		7
Result	W	L	W	Ab.	L	L	W	W	W	L	W	L	W	Tie	Ab.	W
Points	4	0	2	2	0	0	4	4	4	0	4	0	—	2	2	—

Fielding Figures
23 – C.J. Richards (ct 20/st 3)   5 – M.P. Bicknell and I.A. Greig
16 – C.K. Bullen   4 – D.M. Smith
8 – S.T. Clarke and D.M. Ward   3 – G.S. Clinton
7 – M.A. Lynch and Zahid Sadiq   2 – M.A. Feltham
6 – A.J. Stewart   1 – N.H. Peters, P.D. Atkins and D.J. Bicknell

BOWLING

BOWLING	N.H. Peters	I.A. Greig	M.A. Feltham	C.K. Bullen	S.T. Clarke	M.A. Lynch	M.P. Bicknell	A.H. Gray
v. Hampshire (Southampton) 24 April (RA)	8–1–22–1	8–0–27–2	8–0–57–1	8–0–51–1	7–0–47–0			
v. Essex (Chelmsford) 26 April (B&H)	8–1–24–1	6–1–33–0	8–1–22–0	7.5–1–33–0	10–1–23–1			
v. Kent (The Oval) 3 & 4 May (B&H)	11–0–44–1	11–2–24–3	11–1–42–2	5–0–48–0	11–3–32–2	6–0–42–0		
v. Middlesex (The Oval) 8 May (RA)	4.5–0–16–2	4–0–14–1						
v. Middlesex (The Oval) 10 May (B&H)	11–2–33–1	11–3–31–1	11–0–54–1	11–0–55–2	11–1–38–2			
v. Sussex (Hove) 14 May (B&H)		11–1–33–2	11–0–35–3	11–0–46–0	11–1–27–1		11–1–46–2	
v. Sussex (Hove) 15 May (RA)		8–0–35–1	8–1–24–0	8–0–30–2	8–0–34–1		8–0–28–2	
v. Northamptonshire (The Oval) 22 May (RA)		8–1–20–3	8–0–38–1	8–1–23–1	7.4–0–25–2		8–0–24–2	
v. Essex (Chelmsford) 29 May (RA)		8–0–43–2	8–0–20–0				8–1–14–2	8–0–56–4
v. Yorkshire (Leeds) 5 June (RA)		6.3–0–44–0	8–0–60–1	8–0–57–3	7–0–17–1		8–0–28–1	
v. Leicestershire (The Oval) 12 June (RA)		8–1–38–1	8–0–37–1	8–1–27–3	8–0–23–2		8–0–27–0	
v. Somerset (Bath) 19 June (RA)		8–0–47–2	8–0–53–1	8–0–54–1	8–2–38–4		8–0–32–1	
v. Staffordshire (Burton-on-Trent) 22 June (NW)		10–4–28–1	12–1–59–1	12–2–39–1	12–0–27–4	6–0–25–0	8–2–36–0	
v. Derbyshire (The Oval) 26 June (RA)		8–0–46–2	8–0–45–1	8–0–48–2	8–0–46–1		8–0–32–1	
v. Warwickshire (The Oval) 3 July (RA)								
v. Essex (Chelmsford) 6 & 7 July (NW)	9–2–28–2	7–2–19–2	12–1–43–1	8–1–21–1	9–1–29–3			
v. Worcestershire (The Oval) 10 July (RA)	8–0–34–1	8–0–51–3		8–0–38–1	8–0–28–2		8–0–47–0	
v. Kent (The Oval) 17 July (RA)		8–1–30–5	8–0–33–0	8–0–59–2	8–0–43–0		8–3–11–1	
v. Glamorgan (The Oval) 27 July (NW)	12–1–50–1	12–0–48–2		12–0–29–1	12–0–36–1	1–0–13–0	11–0–50–1	
v. Gloucestershire (Cheltenham) 31 July (RA)	5–0–38–2	7–0–38–1	7–0–46–1	2–0–20–0			7–0–31–1	
v. Glamorgan (Ebbw Vale) 7 August (RA)	5–0–20–0	8–0–44–2	7–0–36–2	8–0–26–2				
v. Middlesex (The Oval) 10 August (NW)		12–0–52–0	12–3–58–0	12–0–55–2	12–1–49–3		12–0–38–1	
v. Nottinghamshire (Trent Bridge) 21 August (RA)		8–0–48–2	1.4–0–7–0	7–0–39–1	8–0–50–0		8–0–36–0	
v. Lancashire (The Oval) 28 August (RA)		4–0–15–1	6–0–52–2	7–0–31–0		1–0–12–0	5–0–15–0	
Wickets	12	39	19	26	30	0	15	4

a B.R. Hardie retired hurt

v. Worcestershire (The Oval) 10 July (RA)	v. Kent (The Oval) 17 July (RA)	v. Glamorgan (The Oval) 27 July (NW)	v. Gloucestershire (Cheltenham) 31 July (RA)	v. Glamorgan (Ebbw Vale) 7 August (RA)	v. Middlesex (The Oval) 10 August (NW)	v. Nottinghamshire (Trent Bridge) 21 August (RA)	v. Lancashire (The Oval) 28 August (RA)	Runs
17	6	4	72*		10	41	71	540
32								518
33	26	22	0	34	107*	25	7	703
17	67*	61	85*		15	9	43*	700
0	6	27	—	1	4	2	6	261
10	13		—	20				154
16	30*	13*	—	9	9	21	29*	311
19	—	3*	—	1	7	23	—	140
	—	—	1	19	0	4*		101
2*	—	—	—		3	12*		64
0	—	—	4*					6
	16	3			17		17	300
1	—	—			1	1	—	15
				34		2	—	82
		82			2	0		84
					31			31
					15			15
						14	—	14
				5				
14	13	8	3	9	6	5	7	
2	9	10	2	5	8	1		
3	1	3	1		1		2	
166	187	236	164	189	188	160	182	
10	5	6	2	10	10	9	4	
L	W	W	W	L	L	L	W	
0	4	—	4	0	—	0	4	

G.P. Thorpe	K.T. Medlycott	J.D. Robinson	Byes	Leg-byes	Wides	No-balls	Total	Wkts
				10			214	5
			4	5	5		144	2
				13	5		245	8
				1	1		31	3
			2	11	8		224	9
				11	7	2	198	9
				3	1	1	154	7
				3	4		133	10
			1	4	1		138	8
				10	3		216	6
				6	2	1	158	8
				9	2		233	9
			4	12	5	2	230	8
			3	5	2		225	8
								Ab.
				1	6	2	141	9a
			1	6	2	1	205	9
			1	6	4		183	9
			1	8	7		235	6
				4	4		228	5
4-1-25-0	8-0-43-1			3	6		197	7
			1	5	7		258	7
		7.2-1-47-0		6	4		233	4
	6-0-29-2	2-0-23-0		4	3		181	5
0	3	0						

Worcestershire won by 7 wickets
(*Man of the Match:* G.A. Hick)

The top four teams in the Refuge Assurance League competed for the Refuge Assurance Cup, and the semi-finals produced two tense matches. At Bristol, Gloucestershire, put in to bat, struggled against a Lancashire attack which was able to move the ball appreciably. Gloucestershire's embarrassment would have been greater had not Stovold, who made 40 and stayed 26 overs, been dropped off Allott at slip when 10. The Lancashire bowlers allowed their opponents no respite, for Simmons' spell of eight overs cost only 14 runs and gave him the wickets of Stovold, Romaines and Wright. Needing a moderate 118 to win, Lancashire struggled in their turn. They wanted only 41 from the last 13 overs with eight wickets in hand, but lost Fairbrother, Jesty and Hayhurst in the space of seven balls with the score stuck on 77. Austin and Hughes fell shortly after, and, having reduced Lancashire to 99 for 7, the home side had every chance of victory. Lancashire found a hero in Paul Allott, however, who joined Watkinson and batted in a positive manner. He hit the penultimate ball of the match for four to bring his side victory.

There was a dour struggle at Worcester, where Middlesex, having been put in, were soon in trouble. All the Worcestershire bowlers bowled well, but it was Radford who tore the heart out of the Middlesex innings and Illingworth who frustrated them when they looked to break free. The highest stand of the Middlesex innings came unexpectedly for the last wicket when Cowans joined Downton to add 36. Worcestershire soon lost Rhodes, and Curtis top-edged Emburey to square-leg after a defensive vigil on a wicket which denied stroke-

David Leatherdale — a brave and bold innings to take Worcestershire into the final of the Refuge Assurance Cup. (Adrian Murrell/Allsport)

Sussex CCC
Limited-Over Matches, 1988

BATTING

BATTING	Somerset (Hove) 24 Apr (RA)	Kent (Hove) 26 Apr (B&H)	Gloucs (Bristol) 1 May (RA)	Middlesex (Lord's) 3&4 May (B&H)	Essex (Chelmsf'd) 12 May (B&H)	Surrey (Hove) 14 May (B&H)	Surrey (Hove) 15 May (RA)	Notts (Trent Br.) 22 May (RA)	Middlesex (Lord's) 29 May (RA)	Derbys (Horsham) 5 June (RA)	Essex (Ilford) 12 June (RA)	Leics (Leicester) 19 June (RA)	Derbys (Hove) 22 June (NW)	Yorks (Hove) 26 June (RA)	Hants (Hastings) 3 July (RA)	Warwicks (Hove) 10 July (RA)
I.J. Gould	0	19	6	1	14	37	5	12	26	2	27					
N.J. Lenham	33	8	—	55	1*	22	39	4*	12*	18*	—	—				
P.W.G. Parker	90	10	12	3	64	0	13	1		80	10	78	0	54		52
C.M. Wells	1	1	12	8	10	26	47	47	25		36*	22*	0	57*		0
A.P. Wells	15	53	25	8	38	26	6	19	6	2	27		0	22		4
A.M. Green	22*	24	1*	7	53	29	19	9	13	2	57	24				
S.J.S. Kimber	15*	9	1*	15	—	2*	—	3	14*	15	—	—	0	—		—
A.R. Clarke	—												24	—		—
M.W. Pringle	—	19*														
A.M. Babington		—	—			4*	—	—	—	—			0*	—		
D.K. Standing	—	42*	—	0*	—	1	—	4*	—			4				
R.A. Bunting		—	—	0						—						
Imran Khan		6	71		3*	30	0	10	30	0	19	15	0	15		50
N.J. Falkner					15											10
A.C.S. Pigott						1	20*			5	40	4	22	53	15*	16*
P. Moores								33		8	34	4*	1*	20	—	3*
R.I. Alikhan											0*		—	9	—	
M.P. Speight															—	
Byes	2		6					1	3		1					14
Leg-byes	10	12		7	11	11	3	4	12	10	17	7	4	11		3
Wides	5	3	6	8	7	1	4	5	4		2	4	7	2		
No-balls	2	7	1		2	1	1	1	1		9	13	1			5
Total	195	207	69	182	217	198	154	152	160	208	204	182	134	177		157
Wickets	5	7	5	9	6	9	7	8	7	8	6	4	10	3		5
Result	W	L	L	L	L	W	L	L	L	L	Tie	W	L	W	Ab.	W
Points	4	0	0	0	0	2	0	0	0	0	2	4	—	4	2	4

Fielding Figures

13 – I.J. Gould (ct 12/st 1)
10 – P.W.G. Parker
9 – P. Moores (ct 7/st 2)
5 – A.C.S. Pigott
3 – C.M. Wells, S.J.S. Kimber,
    A.M. Green, A.M. Babington and A.R. Clarke
2 – D.K. Standing, A.P. Wells, Imran Khan and N.J. Faulkner
1 – N.J. Lenham, R.I. Alikhan, M.P. Speight
    and R.A. Bunting

BOWLING

BOWLING	A.M. Babington	M.W. Pringle	S.J.S. Kimber	A.R. Clarke	N.J. Lenham	D.K. Standing	R.A. Bunting	A.P. Wells
v. Somerset (Hove) 24 April (RA)	8–2–31–0	8–0–37–3	7–1–32–0	4–1–18–0	8–0–31–1	5–0–37–2		
v. Kent (Hove) 26 April (B&H)	11–0–43–0	9–2–33–1	11–1–42–1		2–0–18–0	4–1–17–0	11–0–36–1	1–0–9–0
v. Gloucestershire (Bristol) 1 May (RA)	2–0–14–1		1.1–0–17–0			2–0–21–0	2–0–8–2	
v. Middlesex (Lord's) 3 & 4 May (B&H)	11–0–48–1		10–2–34–1		4–0–17–1		11–0–52–2	0.5–0–6–0
v. Essex (Chelmsford) 12 May (B&H)	9–0–35–1		11–1–36–3		3–0–11–0	9.5–0–27–1		
v. Surrey (Hove) 14 May (B&H)	6–0–29–4					4–0–29–2		
v. Surrey (Hove) 15 May (RA)	3–0–10–0		8–0–31–0			2–0–13–0		
v. Nottinghamshire (Trent Bridge) 22 May (RA)	6–0–18–1		6–0–28–0		4–0–16–1	8–0–36–1		
v. Middlesex (Lord's) 29 May (RA)	8–0–47–2		8–0–37–0					
v. Derbyshire (Horsham) 5 June (RA)	8–1–33–1		8–0–49–1					
v. Essex (Ilford) 12 June (RA)			8–0–41–1	8–0–32–3				
v. Leicestershire (Leicester) 19 June (RA)			7–0–35–3	8–1–26–1			2–0–18–0	
v. Derbyshire (Hove) 22 June (NW)	6–0–32–1							
v. Yorkshire (Hove) 26 June (RA)	6–0–19–0		4–0–24–1	6–0–34–2				
v. Hampshire (Hastings) 3 July (RA)								
v. Warwickshire (Hove) 10 July (RA)	2–0–11–0		7–0–31–1	7–2–22–2				
v. Northamptonshire (Northampton) 24 July (RA)	6–0–15–1		4–0–12–0	6–0–27–1				
v. Glamorgan (Eastbourne) 31 July (RA)	8–0–48–0		8–1–50–0	8–1–24–4				
v. Worcestershire (Worcester) 7 August (RA)	8–0–37–0	1.4–0–9–0	7–0–31–0	5–0–36–1				
v. Lancashire (Hove) 14 August (RA)	8–0–51–0		8–0–50–2	7.4–1–32–1				
v. Kent (Maidstone) 28 August (RA)	5–0–19–1		3–0–28–0	5–1–16–2			4–0–23–0	
Wickets	14	4	14	17	3	6	5	0

v. Northamptonshire (Northampton) 24 July (RA)	v. Glamorgan (Eastbourne) 31 July (RA)	v. Worcestershire (Worcester) 7 August (RA)	v. Lancashire (Hove) 14 August (RA)	v. Kent (Maidstone) 28 August (RA)	Runs
9	59*	7	8	6	238
18			4*		214
10	42	74*	4	6	603
27	2	8	85	8	422
32	31	14	51	40	419
				8	268
—	—	5	—	2*	81
—	—	0	—	7	31
		11			30
—	—	—	—	—	4
					51
				5*	5
45*					294
2					27
3*	20*	20	12*		231
—		1	—	4	128
					9
12	—	7	37	31	87
9				1	
	11	12	10	7	
2	8	6	3		
1	3		4		
152	194	165	218	125	
6	4	9	5	8	
L	Tie	L	L	L	
0	2	0	0	0	

play. Leatherdale mocked the difficulties of the earlier batsman with an innings of 41 in a partnership of 66 in 11 overs with Hick, who was very much the junior partner. By the time Leatherdale was bowled, Worcestershire were only six short of victory, which came with eight balls to spare. Hick's durability on an untrustworthy pitch won him the individual award, but Leatherdale's knock was the one to remember.

8 September

at Scarborough

Yorkshire 158 for 7
The Yorkshiremen 162 for 2 (J.J. Whitaker 58 not out, G. Cook 56 not out)

The Yorkshiremen won by 8 wickets

9, 10, 11 and 12 September

at Chelmsford

Essex 592 for 8 dec (N. Hussain 165 not out, J.P. Stephenson 99, M.E. Waugh 86, D.E. East 66, P.J. Prichard 59, P. Willey 4 for 153)
Leicestershire 268 (D.I. Gower 172, J.H. Childs 5 for 88) and 241 (T.J. Boon 63 not out, L.B. Taylor 60, J.H. Childs 6 for 92)

Essex won by an innings and 83 runs
Essex 24 pts, Leicestershire 5 pts

at Cardiff

Glamorgan 259 (A.R. Butcher 74, P.A. Cottey 73, M.P. Maynard 50) and 243 (M.P. Maynard 71, A.R. Butcher 56, C.A. Connor 4 for 61)
Hampshire 126 (J.G. Thomas 4 for 67) and 370 for 8 (V.P. Terry 66, R.A. Smith 65, J.R. Ayling 54 not out)

Hampshire won by 2 wickets
Hampshire 19 pts, Glamorgan 7 pts

P.W.G. Parker	Imran Khan	C.M. Wells	A.C.S. Pigott	R.I. Alikhan	A.M. Green	Byes	Leg-byes	Wides	No-balls	Total	Wkts
						5		2	1	191	6
0.2–0–3–0						2	5	1	6	208	3
	2–0–9–0					2			2	71	3
		11–1–26–0						16	6	183	5
		11–1–43–1	11–0–51–2				15	4	2	218	8
		5.4–0–43–3	5–0–35–1	1–0–14–0		2	4	1		156	10
	8–2–27–1	8–0–31–0	7–0–38–2				5	7	1	155	3
0.1–0–4–0	8–2–22–1	6–0–26–0				2	4	1		156	4
	8–1–37–1	6–0–52–1	8–0–36–1				4	1	1	213	5
	8–0–33–2		8–0–48–3	8–0–42–0			8	4	1	213	8
	8–0–50–1	8–0–35–0	8–0–34–3			7	5	5		204	9
	7–0–38–0	8–3–11–1	8–1–27–1				24	3	1	179	7
	10.1–1–49–1	6–0–19–1	7–1–34–1				1	2	1	135	4
	8–0–24–0	8–0–25–2	8–0–42–3				8	3	1	176	8
											Ab.
	8–3–21–2	8–1–11–0	8–0–44–1			1	8	4		149	7
	7.3–0–24–1	8–3–25–1	8–0–39–1				11	6		153	5
		8–0–23–1	8–0–45–2				4	1		194	8
		8–1–21–1	3–0–23–0				9	3		166	2
		8–2–28–0	8–0–51–1				7	3		219	5
		3–0–20–0			2.4–1–16–3		4	9	1	126	6
0	14	11	19	0	3						

Warwickshire CCC
Limited-Over Matches, 1988

BATTING

BATTING	v. Lancashire (Old Trafford) 1 May (RA)	v. Derbyshire (Derby) 3 & 4 May (B&H)	v. Yorkshire (Edgbaston) 8 May (RA)	v. Scotland (Edgbaston) 10 May (B&H)	v. Leicestershire (Leicester) 12 May (B&H)	v. Lancashire (Edgbaston) 14 May (B&H)	v. Glamorgan (Edgbaston) 15 May (RA)	v. Essex (Edgbaston) 22 May (RA)	v. Essex (Chelmsford) 25 May (B&H)	v. Gloucestershire (Bristol) 29 May (RA)	v. Nottinghamshire (Edgbaston) 5 June (RA)	v. Gloucestershire (Harrogate) 8 June (TT)	v. Yorkshire (Harrogate) 10 June (TT)	v. Somerset (Bath) 12 June (RA)	v. Kent (Edgbaston) 19 June (RA)	v. Cambridgeshire (Edgbaston) 22 June (NW)	v. Surrey (The Oval) 3 July (RA)
T.A. Lloyd	11	36	17	93	1	31	15	21	87		30	28	18	40	66	121	
G.W. Humpage	46	13	4		11	14	19	26	14		0	19	13	16	53	2	
A.I. Kallicharran	63	2	32	90*	79	45	10	31*	42								
A.J. Moles	7	34	79	6	33	68	27	21	7		15			13	5	25	
P.A. Smith	48	43	13	0	0	17	0	14*	16		32	18	19	29	8	6	
M. Asif Din	17*	67*	5	107	40	27	12	8	5		10	31	1	36	7	25	
D.A. Reeve	6*	9*	21	1*	1	18	4	—	20*		69	35*	17	31			
G.C. Small	—	—	1*	—	1	2	1				4		8				
T.A. Merrick	—	—	2	—	8	6	19		0		4				3	13	
N. Gifford	—	—		—		0		—	—		2*	—	1*	0*	—	3*	
A.R.K. Pierson	—					3*	5*	—	4*								
G.J. Parsons		—	4*	—	3			16*				9	8			15*	
G.A. Tedstone				—													
T.A. Munton					3*			—			0*	—	3*		—	—	
N.M.K. Smith											3			2	—		
A.C. Storie												2	59			1	
J. Benjamin												1	1				
A.A. Donald												0	12	0*			
S.J. Green															10*	1	
D.A. Thorne															11*		
D.A. Banks																	
P.C.L. Holloway																	
S.D. Myles																	
Byes				1							1			1	1	11	
Leg-byes	12	16	3	6	3	9	9	3	15		9	4		21	10	10	
Wides	2	9		4	4	9	4	3	7		4	5	4	4	7	6	
No-balls		4					1	6	2		1			2	1	1	
Total	212	233	181	308	187	249	142	133	219		194	152	159	202	180	240	
Wickets	5	5	8	4	10	10	9	4	7		9	8	9	8	6	8	
Result	L	Ab.	L	W	L	W	L	W	L	Ab.	W	W	L	W	L	W	Ab.
Points	0	1	0	2	0	2	0	4	—	2	4	—	—	4	0	—	2

Fielding Figures
24 – G.W. Humpage (ct 22/st 2)
6 – D.A. Reeve
4 – P.A. Smith, T.A. Lloyd and G.A. Tedstone (ct 2/st 2)
3 – A.R.K. Pierson and A.J. Moles
2 – T.A. Merrick, G.C. Small, G.J. Parsons, T.A. Munton, D.A. Thorne, M. Asif Din and N.M.K. Smith
1 – A.C. Storie, J. Benjamin, A.A. Donald and P.C.L. Holloway

BOWLING

BOWLING	G.C. Small	T.A. Merrick	N. Gifford	D.A. Reeve	G.J. Parsons	P.A. Smith	M. Asif Din	A.J. Moles
v. Lancashire (Old Trafford) 1 May (RA)	8-0-44-4	7.3-0-41-1	5-0-22-2	4-0-29-0				
v. Derbyshire (Derby) 3 & 4 May (B&H)								
v. Yorkshire (Edgbaston) 8 May (RA)	8-1-25-1	8-1-32-2	8-0-51-1	8-0-42-2	6-1-23-0	2-0-21-1		
v. Scotland (Edgbaston) 10 May (B&H)	6-0-15-0	8-1-17-0	11-5-23-3	6-1-17-0	7-0-28-0	10-0-45-0	5-0-16-0	2-0-11-1
v. Leicestershire (Leicester) 12 May (B&H)	11-3-38-0	11-3-24-4		11-0-45-1	11-1-39-2			
v. Lancashire (Edgbaston) 14 May (B&H)	9-0-26-0	8-1-27-1	10.5-0-36-3	9-1-36-1				
v. Glamorgan (Edgbaston) 15 May (RA)	8-1-23-0	8-0-24-0		8-0-37-0	2-0-12-0	2-0-15-0		
v. Essex (Edgbaston) 22 May (RA)		6.2-2-16-2	7-1-29-1	7-1-23-5		6-2-20-0		
v. Essex (Chelmsford) 25 May (B&H)		11-2-27-0	7-1-33-0			5.2-0-38-0	4-0-26-1	4-0-20-0
v. Gloucestershire (Bristol) 29 May (RA)								
v. Nottinghamshire (Edgbaston) 5 June (RA)	8-0-38-0	8-0-30-1	8-1-23-3	8-0-37-1				
v. Gloucestershire (Harrogate) 8 June (TT)			4-0-33-0	2-0-16-0	4-0-39-2	2-0-23-0		
v. Yorkshire (Harrogate) 10 June (TT)			3-0-14-0	5-0-21-2	7-0-25-0	1.1-0-5-1	2-1-1-2	
v. Somerset (Bath) 12 June (RA)	8-0-40-2		5-0-28-1		7.2-1-26-2	3-0-25-1		
v. Kent (Edgbaston) 19 June (RA)		8-2-32-2	8-0-31-1			8-0-43-2		4-0-32-0
v. Cambridgeshire (Edgbaston) 22 June (NW)			9-6-3-1	12-0-27-1	12-0-35-0	12-0-54-2	3-1-3-1	
v. Surrey (The Oval) 3 July (RA)								
v. Kent (Canterbury) 6 July (NW)	10-1-32-0	12-1-36-2		3-2-2-0		9-3-19-1	5-0-16-0	
v. Sussex (Hove) 10 July (RA)	8-0-29-1	8-1-28-1		8-0-40-1		8-0-38-0		
v. Hampshire (Edgbaston) 17 July (RA)	3.3-1-6-3	5-1-8-1		3-0-6-1		8-1-26-3		
v. Middlesex (Lord's) 24 July (RA)	8-0-46-0			7.2-1-16-1				
v. Derbyshire (Derby) 31 July (RA)	8-0-26-3			8-0-48-0			5-0-17-1	
v. Northamptonshire (Edgbaston) 7 August (RA)	8-0-40-2			7.5-0-38-1	8-0-38-0			
v. Leicestershire (Edgbaston) 14 August (RA)	6-0-24-0	8-2-21-1		6-1-17-4				
v. Worcestershire (Worcester) 28 August (RA)	5-1-5-0						4.1-1-14-0	
Wickets	16	19	16	22	4	12	4	1

v. Kent (Canterbury) 6 July (NW)	v. Sussex (Hove)	v. Hampshire 10 July (RA)	(Edgbaston) 17 July (RA)	v. Middlesex (Lord's) 24 July (RA)	v. Derbyshire (Derby) 31 July (RA)	v. Northamptonshire (Edgbaston) 7 August (RA)	v. Leicestershire (Edgbaston) 14 August (RA)	v. Worcestershire (Worcester) 28 August (RA)	Runs
38	1		13	34	29	0	16	2	748
11			56	36	25	18	28		424
								0	394
0									340
5	1		9		—			11	289
28	34		29	5	38	93*	0	16	641
13	23		36*	10	—	1	24*		339
12	8		1*	13	—	5	—	0	56
2	—		—				—		57
									6
			—	5*	—	2*	—	6	25
						5			60
									—
0*	—		—	—		—		6*	18
	0								5
3									65
									2
			18*	—				7	37
			0			1			12
20	33*		2	29	59*	20	35*	2	211
	29		27	15	51*			6	128
	7*							13	20
					32		—		32
2	1		3	2	1			2	
8	8		21	13	5	4	5	7	
2	4		7	4		2	2	3	
			3			2	1	1	
144	149		207	184	210	184	110	82	
10	7		6	8	3	8	3	10	
L	L		W	L	W	L	W	L	
—	0		4	0	4	0	4	0	

at Bristol

Worcestershire 404 (G.A. Hick 121, P.A. Neale 102 not out, D.A. Graveney 8 for 127) and 199 (G.J. Lord 101, D.A. Graveney 6 for 38)
Gloucestershire 262 (P. Bainbridge 124, R.K. Illingworth 5 for 69) and 227 (K.M. Curran 57, R.K. Illingworth 5 for 63, G.A. Hick 4 for 114)

Worcestershire won by 114 runs
Worcestershire 23 pts, Gloucestershire 6 pts

at Lord's

Middlesex 290 (J.D. Carr 92, R.O. Butcher 59, M.R. Ramprakash 54, R.M. Ellison 4 for 49) and 351 (W.N. Slack 80, J.D. Carr 60, P.R. Downton 59 not out, C. Penn 7 for 70)
Kent 412 (G.R. Cowdrey 86, M.R. Benson 81, C.J. Tavare 78, N.G. Cowans 5 for 105) and 129 for 9 (A.R.C. Fraser 5 for 27)

Match drawn
Kent 7 pts, Middlesex 5 pts

at Trent Bridge

Derbyshire 347 (J.E. Morris 106, B. Roberts 62, P.D. Bowler 50, F.D. Stephenson 5 for 91) and 226 (F.D. Stephenson 4 for 76)
Nottinghamshire 614 (D.W. Randall 237, M. Newell 105, F.D. Stephenson 83, K.P. Evans 54, S.J. Base 4 for 123)

Nottinghamshire won by an innings and 41 runs
Nottinghamshire 22 pts, Derbyshire 4 pts

at Hove

Surrey 553 (G.S. Clinton 158, A.J. Stewart 119, M.A. Feltham 74, D.M. Ward 56, A.R. Clarke 5 for 133)
Sussex 229 (A.M. Green 68, K.T. Medlycott 4 for 53) and 205 (A.M. Green 53, K.T. Medlycott 8 for 52)

Surrey won by an innings and 119 runs
Surrey 24 pts, Sussex 3 pts

T.A. Munton	A.R.K. Pierson	A.A. Donald	J. Benjamin	N.M.K. Smith	Byes	Leg-byes	Wides	No-balls	Total	Wkts
						8	3	1	144	9
										Ab.
						8			202	7
						13	1	5	185	5
11–0–42–1					1	7	1	2	196	9
	11–1–34–3					1	14		160	10
	8–0–25–0				2	5	6	3	143	0
8–2–17–1	2–0–21–0					4	2		130	6
11–0–37–0	5–0–30–0				2	10	5	6	223	1
										Ab.
8–2–10–1					1	16	4	2	155	7
		4–0–10–0	4–0–18–2		1	10	4	4	150	6
6–0–35–1		11–3–23–2	5–0–27–0		1	8	3	2	160	8
8–2–17–1		7–2–30–1				4	4	1	170	10
7–3–17–1				4–0–19–0	2	9	2		185	6
12–1–42–0					2	7	1	2	173	6
										Ab.
9.4–2–41–0						2	1	3	148	3
8–2–8–1					14		3	5	157	5
8–1–22–2	5–0–13–0				3	12	3	1	96	10
8–1–29–0	7–0–49–0	8–0–31–1				16	1		187	4
7–0–36–0	4–0–16–0	8–0–51–0			1	7	9	2	202	5
8–0–38–1	8–0–22–0					10	5		186	5
8–1–17–2	7.2–2–21–3					9	10		109	10
5–0–9–0	8–0–30–0	5–0–21–0				4	1		83	0
12	6	4	2	0						

Worcestershire CCC
Limited-Over Matches, 1988

BATTING	v. Lancashire (Old Trafford) 24 April (RA)	v. Nottinghamshire (Worcester) 1 May (RA)	v. Minor Counties (Old Heath) 3 & 4 May (B&H)	v. Somerset (Taunton) 8 May (RA)	v. Nottinghamshire (Worcester) 10 & 11 May (B&H)	v. Northamptonshire (Northampton) 12 May (B&H)	v. Yorkshire (Worcester) 14 May (B&H)	v. Yorkshire (Worcester) 15 May (RA)	v. Leicestershire (Leicester) 22 May (RA)	v. Hampshire (Worcester) 26 & 27 May (B&H)	v. Middlesex (Lord's) 5 June (RA)	v. Hampshire (Worcester) 12 June (RA)	v. Derbyshire (Knypersley) 19 June (RA)	v. Cumberland (Worcester) 22 June (NW)	v. Gloucestershire (Hereford) 3 July (RA)	v. Nottinghamshire (Trent Bridge) 6–8 July (NW)
T.S. Curtis	1	45		63	0	52	5	53	50	3	41	88	2	40		120
I.T. Botham	39	22		10	4	43	7	9								
G.A. Hick	9	19		29	20	47	14	111	66	6	22	11	18	138		105
D.B. d'Oliveira	7	54*		24*	35	34	28	24		12	29	0	0			
P.A. Neale	31			10*	8	7	91	14*	9	26	8	15	91	98		12
S.J. O'Shaughnessy	50	6		—			8	1*	0	12	26		21			17
S.J. Rhodes	16	2*		—	21	10	43*	1	25	16	10	10	36	2*		2*
P.J. Newport	5	1		—	6	9	11*		0*	4	10*	1	1		—	—
N.V. Radford	3*	1		—	37*	6*	—	—		9*	3	12*	21*		—	—
R.K. Illingworth	0*			—	7*				—		0*					
G.R. Dilley	—			16		—					9				—	—
M.J. Weston		9							14*	50	42	28	72	45*		12
A.P. Pridgeon		—			5*	—	—		—		1	—	2*		—	
G.J. Lord				15		2					6			0		
D.A. Leatherdale									13							6*
S.M. McEwan										—	0*		0			
P. Bent																
Byes	1			3	7	2				1	2			1		2
Leg-byes	10	7		9	9	18	9	9	15	9	8	2	7	8		6
Wides		3		3	9	12	6	2	7	13	7		5	4		3
No-balls					10	2	3		2	4	1		4			
Total	172	169		148	198	256	227	224	201	169	192	196	280	336		285
Wickets	8	7		3	9	8	6	5	6	10	8	7	9	5		5
Result	L	L	Ab.	W	L	W	W	W	W	L	L	W	W	W	Ab.	W
Points	0	0	1	4	0	2	2	4	4	—	0	4	4	—	2	—

Fielding Figures

46 – S.J. Rhodes (ct 41/st 5)	6 – T.S. Curtis and S.J. O'Shaughnessy	2 – D.A. Leatherdale and D.B. d'Oliveira
10 – P.A. Neale	5 – M.J. Weston and A.P. Pridgeon	1 – I.T. Botham, G.R. Dilley and G.J. Lord
9 – N.V. Radford	4 – R.K. Illingworth	
7 – G.A. Hick	3 – P. Bent	

BOWLING	G.R. Dilley	P.J. Newport	R.K. Illingworth	N.V. Radford	I.T. Botham	S.J. O'Shaughnessy	A.P. Pridgeon
v. Lancashire (Old Trafford) 24 April (RA)	8–0–30–0	8–0–33–0	6.2–0–37–1	4–0–22–0	8–0–36–2	2–0–14–0	
v. Nottinghamshire (Worcester) 1 May (RA)	5–0–26–0			4–0–26–2	7.4–0–50–1		8–0–44–2
v. Minor Counties (Old Heath) 3 & 4 May (B&H)							
v. Somerset (Taunton) 8 May (RA)		8–0–35–2	8–0–29–1	8–0–31–1	8–2–32–2		8–1–12–2
v. Nottinghamshire (Worcester) 10 & 11 May (B&H)	11–0–40–1	11–1–29–1		11–1–45–2	11–1–48–2		11–1–35–1
v. Northamptonshire (Northampton) 12 May (B&H)	8.3–2–32–2	6–1–18–1	6–0–27–0	11–1–25–4	6–1–11–1		
v. Yorkshire (Worcester) 14 May (B&H)	9–3–10–1	11–1–42–1		10–1–39–1	11–2–41–5		11–1–34–1
v. Yorkshire (Worcester) 15 May (RA)	8–0–52–0	8–0–31–3		8–0–39–0	5–0–39–0		8–0–19–1
v. Leicestershire (Leicester) 22 May (RA)		8–0–49–1	8–0–43–1				8–1–36–4
v. Hampshire (Worcester) 26 & 27 May (B&H)	11–1–36–2	11–0–40–1		11–3–29–3		1–0–4–0	11–4–22–0
v. Middlesex (Lord's) 5 June (RA)		8–0–46–2		8–0–58–2		3–0–18–1	6–0–19–0
v. Hampshire (Worcester) 12 June (RA)	6–2–8–1			6–0–22–1			3.4–1–4–2
v. Derbyshire (Knypersley) 19 June (RA)		4.4–0–21–1		6–0–28–1		5–0–40–0	8–0–43–2
v. Cumberland (Worcester) 22 June (NW)	6–1–15–0	10–0–35–1		6–0–25–1			10–1–35–1
v. Gloucestershire (Hereford) 3 July (RA)							
v. Nottinghamshire (Trent Bridge) 6–8 July (NW)	5–2–16–1	4–0–20–1		5–0–20–0			
v. Surrey (The Oval) 10 July (RA)	7–0–36–1	5.2–0–17–1	3–0–19–1		8–0–26–2	8–0–26–2	
v. Kent (Folkestone) 24 July (RA)		6–0–20–0	8–0–34–0	8–0–44–0		2–0–13–1	8–0–39–3
v. Gloucestershire (Worcester) 27 July (NW)	12–1–30–3	12–2–34–0	12–0–28–2	12–0–55–2			
v. Northamptonshire (Worcester) 31 July (RA)		6–0–19–1		6–0–29–1		5–0–28–0	6–0–27–2
v. Sussex (Worcester) 7 August (RA)		5–0–12–2	8–0–24–1	7–0–30–1			5–0–22–0
v. Hampshire (Worcester) 10 August (NW)	11–2–50–2	12–1–37–2	12–2–44–0	7–0–24–0			
v. Glamorgan (Swansea) 14 August (RA)		1–0–10–0	3–0–22–0			2–0–12–2	2–0–11–2
v. Essex (Worcester) 21 August (RA)		5–0–20–0	3.3–0–17–2	7–0–29–3			7–0–36–4
v. Warwickshire (Worcester) 28 August (RA)	7–2–10–1		7–1–12–0		7–2–14–4		7–1–15–2
v. Middlesex (Lord's) 3 September (NW)	12–3–29–5	10–1–20–0	12–4–24–0	11.3–3–37–0		3–0–15–0	
v. Middlesex (Worcester) 7 September (RA)	8–0–29–0			8–0–29–3	8–1–23–4		8–2–23–0
v. Lancashire (Edgbaston) 18 September (RA)		8–0–40–1	8–0–34–0	8–0–41–1			8–1–48–1
Wickets	20	22	12	36	13	6	30

a G. Cook retired hurt   b N.G. Cowley retired hurt

v. Surrey (The Oval) 10 July (RA)	v. Kent (Folkestone) 24 July (RA)	v. Gloucestershire (Worcester) 27 July (NW)	v. Northamptonshire (Worcester) 31 July (RA)	v. Sussex (Worcester) 7 August (RA)	v. Hampshire (Worcester) 10 August (NW)	v. Glamorgan (Swansea) 14 August (RA)	v. Essex (Worcester) 21 August (RA)	v. Warwickshire (Worcester) 28 August (RA)	v. Middlesex (Lord's) 3 September (NW)	v. Middlesex (Worcester) 7 September (RA)	v. Lancashire (Edgbaston) 18 September (RA)	Runs
97		11	8		74	—	21	35*	4	17	32	862
												134
29	22	18	23	52*	31	42*	59	—	4	74*	2	971
						1	18	—		—		266
19	41*	45	37*	—	9	8	54*	—	64	1*	42	740
25	41	42	33	15	62	25	2	43*	1		4	434
8	—	6	—	—	9	—	—	—	1	1	20	239
10	—	10*	—	—	1	—	—	—	4		2	75
4*	—	—	—	—	3	—	—	—	5	—	0	104
0	—	—	—	—	2*	—	—	—	6*	—	0	15
—		—	—	—	1	—	—	—	2*	—		28
1	—	39*	9*	—	2	3*	10*	—	31	—	1	368
—		—	—	—					—		2*	10
												23
2	62*	0	0	51*	43				29	41	30	277
					—							0
	13				36							49

v. Surrey	v. Kent	v. Gloucs	v. Northants	v. Sussex	v. Hampshire	v. Glamorgan	v. Essex	v. Warwicks	v. Middlesex (Lord's)	v. Middlesex (Worc)	v. Lancashire
1	1	6			1						
6	9	9	8	9	20	2	14	4	7	4	10
2	2	2	5	3	5	4		1	1	8	4
1	1	1	1		5		1			2	1
205	192	189	124	166	268	85	179	83	161	147	149
9	3	6	4	2	10	3	4	0	9	3	10
W	W	W	W	W	W	W	W	W	L	W	L
4	4	—	4	4	—	4	4	4	—		—

G.A. Hick	M.J. Weston	S.M. McEwan	T.S. Curtis	D.B. d'Oliveira	Byes	Leg-byes	Wides	No-balls	Total	Wkts
						4	8	2	176	3
					2	9		2	157	5
										Ab.
					1	5	3		145	8
						5	6	13	202	9
3–0–8–0					1	9	6	8	131	9a
						6	6		172	10
3–0–30–1						13	3	1	223	5
	8–0–28–1	8–0–32–2				9	9	2	197	9
	8.1–0–27–1				4	8	12	1	170	7
3–0–26–0	8–0–25–0	4–0–33–0			1	11	15	2	237	5
	8–2–11–4						1	1	45	9b
	5–0–36–1	8–0–37–4				6	4		211	10
12–1–37–2	12–1–53–2		2–1–6–1	2–0–12–0	8	2	7	1	228	8
										Ab.
1–0–1–0	5.3–2–14–0					3	3	2	74	3
	8–1–28–1					14	2	3	166	10
	8–0–30–0				11		3		191	5
12–2–22–2	2–1–6–0				5	5	3		185	10
	6–1–10–2					10	6	1	123	6
7–0–42–4	8–0–23–0					12	6		165	9
11.3–0–54–4	5–0–28–2					2	6		239	10
2–0–11–1		1–0–14–0				1	2		81	5
5–0–23–0	7–0–21–0				2	13	2	1	161	10
	8–1–22–2				2	7	3	1	82	10
5–0–19–0	2–0–9–0				4	5	7	2	162	7
	8–0–28–1					14	6	2	146	9
	8–0–19–2				4	12	13		201	5
14	19	6	1	0						

Yorkshire CCC
Limited-Over Matches, 1988

BATTING

	v. Northamptonshire (Leeds) 26 & 27 April (B&H)	v. Derbyshire (Leeds) 1 May (RA)	v. Nottinghamshire (Trent Bridge) 3 & 4 May (B&H)	v. Warwickshire (Edgbaston) 8 May (RA)	v. Minor Counties (Leeds) 12 May (B&H)	v. Worcestershire (Worcester) 14 May (B&H)	v. Worcestershire (Worcester) 15 May (RA)	v. Kent (Canterbury) 22 May (RA)	v. Hampshire (Middlesbrough) 29 May (RA)	v. Surrey (Leeds) 5 June (RA)	v. Northamptonshire (Harrogate) 9 June (TT)	v. Warwickshire (Harrogate) 10 June (TT)	v. Essex (Sheffield) 19 June (RA)	v. Berkshire (Finchampstead) 22 June (NW)	v. Sussex (Hove) 26 June (RA)	v. Leicestershire (Hull) 3 July (RA)
M.D. Moxon	82*	1	3*	41	83	7	79	0	44	3	33	17		33*	30	
A.A. Metcalfe	70	—	5*	27	21	8	23	8	19	79	81	89	79	74*	4	20
R.J. Blakey	—	12*	—		9					2	0	7				
P.E. Robinson	—	11*	—	30	34	6	45*	2	35*	20	32	20	19	—	1	47
J.D. Love	4*	9	—	43	45*	17	5									2*
D.L. Bairstow	—	2	—	4	8*	13	5	7	22*				0		1	—
A. Sidebottom	—	—	—	—	—	2	—	6*		—			—		6	
P.J. Hartley	—	—	—	21*	—	12			—				4*			
P.W. Jarvis	—	—	—	—				—			0					
C. Shaw	—	—	—	—		4*	—		—		2*	4*	—	—	8*	—
S.D. Fletcher	—	—	—	—		1	—	—	—		—		—		—	—
S.N. Hartley		—		20			38*	30		8	20	5	15*		43*	9
P. Carrick				3	—	15	—	38*	—	4*	44*	0	0		15	—
K. Sharp						75	11	44	17	18	25	3	52	—	10	56
D. Byas										69*			2	—	46	21*
I.G. Swallow											13	1	—			
S.J. Dennis											22	0*				
C.S. Pickles																
P.J. Berry																
Byes					5								1			15
Leg-byes	5	1		14	2	6	13	16	2	10	10	8	4	2	8	
Wides	5			5		6	3	8	2	3	1	3	2		3	2
No-balls	7			1			1					2		1		1
Total	173	36	8	208	208	172	223	159	141	216	283	160	178	109	176	173
Wickets	1	3	0	7	4	10	5	6	3	6	9	8	6	0	8	4
Result	Ab.	Ab.	Ab.	W	W	L	L	W	L	W	W	W	W	W	L	W
Points	1	2	1	4	2	0	0	4	0	4	—	—	4	—	0	4

Fielding Figures
23 – D.L. Bairstow (ct 22/st 1)
14 – P.E. Robinson
10 – R.J. Blakey
9 – A.A. Metcalfe
6 – M.D. Moxon
5 – K. Sharp and S.N. Hartley
4 – J.D. Love, S.D. Fletcher and C. Shaw
3 – P. Carrick
2 – P.J. Hartley, A. Sidebottom, D. Byas, S.J. Dennis and P.J. Berry
1 – I. Swallow, P.W. Jarvis and sub

BOWLING

	C. Shaw	A. Sidebottom	S.N. Hartley	S.D. Fletcher	M.D. Moxon	P.J. Hartley	P.W. Jarvis	P. Carrick
v. Northamptonshire (Leeds) 26 & 27 April (B&H)								
v. Derbyshire (Leeds) 1 May (RA)	6–0–25–0	7–0–33–2	5–0–29–1	6–1–18–3	1–0–4–0	6–0–39–1		
v. Nottinghamshire (Trent Bridge) 3 & 4 May (B&H)								
v. Warwickshire (Edgbaston) 8 May (RA)	8–1–17–1			8–0–36–2		8–0–52–1	8–0–41–2	8–0–32–
v. Minor Counties (Leeds) 12 May (B&H)	11–3–30–2	11–1–23–0			1–0–6–1	11–1–55–2	10–1–43–1	11–0–38
v. Worcestershire (Worcester) 14 May (B&H)	11–3–30–0	11–4–32–0		11–1–55–3	9–1–17–1	11–2–72–2		2–0–10–
v. Worcestershire (Worcester) 15 May (RA)	7.1–0–27–2	8–0–36–2		8–0–58–0	8–0–60–0			8–0–34–
v. Kent (Canterbury) 22 May (RA)	8–0–24–3	6–1–14–1		6.4–0–11–4	3–0–9–1		8–2–27–0	5–0–18–
v. Hampshire (Middlesbrough) 29 May (RA)	1–0–5–0	8–1–32–0		2–0–11–0			8–0–36–3	
v. Surrey (Leeds) 5 June (RA)	8–0–35–2	8–0–49–1	8–0–39–3	8–0–40–1	4–0–20–0			4–1–23–
v. Northamptonshire (Harrogate) 9 June (TT)	7.3–2–21–3	6–0–25–1				5–0–18–2	6–2–13–1	
v. Warwickshire (Harrogate) 10 June (TT)	10–5–25–3		3–0–13–0	10–0–38–4				10–4–14–
v. Essex (Sheffield) 19 June (RA)	8–0–39–3	8–1–13–0	4–0–27–0	8–0–28–4		8–2–34–2		4–0–17–
v. Berkshire (Finchampstead) 22 June (NW)	12–5–20–1	12–3–22–2		10.1–2–20–3			11–1–18–2	12–4–23
v. Sussex (Hove) 26 June (RA)	8–2–46–0	7.2–0–22–1	4–0–10–1	8–0–34–0	5–0–22–0			7–0–32–
v. Leicestershire (Hull) 3 July (RA)	8–0–23–1	8–0–35–0	7–0–28–0	8–2–33–1				8–0–26–
v. Middlesex (Leeds) 6–8 July (NW)	12–4–29–4	12–1–29–1	2–0–12–0	12–0–51–0		12–0–37–2		10–1–46
v. Northamptonshire (Northampton) 10 July (RA)								
v. Nottinghamshire (Trent Bridge) 17 July (RA)	5–0–30–1	5–0–22–0		6–0–27–3		6–0–22–0		6–0–16–
v. Glamorgan (Cardiff) 24 July (RA)	6–0–36–2	6–2–26–1		8–0–48–0				8–1–39–
v. Lancashire (Scarborough) 31 July (RA)	8–0–29–1	8–0–45–1		8–0–42–0		7–0–45–2		8–0–40–
v. Gloucestershire (Cheltenham) 7 August (RA)	8–0–21–1	8–0–41–0		7–0–41–1		8–1–27–4		8–0–46–
v. Somerset (Scarborough) 14 August (RA)	8–1–40–1	8–0–45–0		8–0–37–2	3–0–18–0	5–0–40–0		8–0–50–
v. Middlesex (Leeds) 28 August (RA)	8–3–13–1			8–0–37–4	3–0–20–0	8–0–29–1		5–0–20–
v. Rest of World XI (Scarborough) 3 September	6–2–16–1			6–2–26–3		5–0–32–1		10–3–47–
v. Gloucestershire (Scarborough) 5 September (FC)						5–1–5–1		10–2–30–
v. Essex (Scarborough) 6 September (FC)						10–1–43–2		10–2–33–
Wickets	33	12	6	38	5	21	9	20

v. Middlesex (Leeds) 6-8 July (NW)	v. Northamptonshire (Northampton) 10 July (RA)	v. Nottinghamshire (Trent Bridge) 17 July (RA)	v. Glamorgan (Cardiff) 24 July (RA)	v. Lancashire (Scarborough) 31 July (RA)	v. Gloucestershire (Cheltenham) 7 August (RA)	v. Somerset (Scarborough) 14 August (RA)	v. Middlesex (Leeds) 28 August (RA)	v. Rest of World XI (Scarborough) 3 September	v. Gloucestershire (Scarborough) 5 September (FC)	v. Essex (Scarborough) 6 September (FC)	Runs
9					68	21	63	15	31		663
0		5	0	69	33	2	10	7	47	15	795
				40*	25	13*	0*				108
		41	49	7	4	51	25	60	9	7	555
67		19*	3	5	3		5	0	1	16	244
36		—	6	0					16	0	120
10			6*	10	3	1			16		44
5*		—		0	2	11	—	—	16	8	79
											0
1		—	—	4*	7*	13*	—	—			43
2		—	—	—	—	2*	—	—			5
4			2	14	28						236
14		—	4*	38*	41	21	8	—	35	9	289
21		41	30			29			17	6	455
		9*	22	41	13	0	43	111*			377
											14
								—	6*	2	30
							7*		8	11	26
									0	0*	0
		7					1	5	2		
4		9	15	15	11	8	6	10	12	6	
10		2	1	4	2	2	2	6	1	1	
5				1	4		2	3			
188		126	145	208	191	233	143	265	185	112	
10		3	7	8	8	9	6	4	10	10	
L	Ab.	W	L	L	L	L	W	W	W	L	
—	2	4	0	0	0	0	4	—	—	—	

S.J. Dennis	I.G. Swallow	J.D. Love	C.S. Pickles	A.A. Metcalfe	P.E. Robinson	P.J. Berry	Byes	Leg-byes	Wides	No-balls	Total	Wkts
												Ab.
								9	2	1	157	10
												Ab.
								3			181	8
							6	5	2	3	206	6
							2	9	6	3	227	6
								9	2		224	5
								13	6	1	116	10
							2	4		1	90	3
6–1–32–2	10–0–42–1							6	1	4	212	8
11–4–38–1	11–1–30–1						2	2	2		155	10
							1		4	2	159	9
								16	6	1	174	9
							1	1	1		105	10
		1–0–14–0						11	2	1	177	3
								13	8		172	3
							4	17	3	4	225	7
												Ab.
								8	3	1	125	8
								11	2		160	4
								8	3		209	8
							4	13			193	7
			8–2–19–2				2	3	1	1	235	6
								12	4		150	9
8–1–21–1		10–1–61–1		4–0–30–1	1–0–7–0		6	12	4	3	258	9
7.2–1–9–2		2–0–7–0	10–3–22–2			10–1–30–1	5	4	2	1	112	10
10–1–41–1			10–1–37–2			10–1–37–1	2	13	8		206	8
7	2	1	6	1	0	2						

Derbyshire CCC
First-Class Matches, 1988

Batting — each match cell shows 1st innings / 2nd innings scores. A blank indicates the batsman did not play; a dash (—) that he did not bat.

BATTING	v. Cambridge Univ. (Cambridge) 16–18 April	v. Leicestershire (Derby) 21–5 April	v. Yorkshire (Leeds) 28 April–2 May	v. Essex (Chesterfield) 5–9 May	v. Glamorgan (Swansea) 21–4 May	v. Nottinghamshire (Derby) 28–31 May	v. Sussex (Horsham) 4–7 June	v. Gloucestershire (Derby) 11–14 June	v. Worcestershire (Derby) 18–21 June	v. Surrey (The Oval) 25–8 June	v. Middlesex (Derby) 2–5 July	v. Essex (Southend) 13–15 July	v. Northamptonshire (Derby) 16–18 July	v. Leicestershire (Leicester) 20–2 July
K.J. Barnett	151 —	38 21	14 52	52 23	0 —	2 19	67 12	175 5	22 —		—	99 10	73 —	239* 16
P.D. Bowler	155* —	30 40	37 28	42 159*	10 —	50 84	62 29	0 23	5 18	158 57*	—	11 1	61 —	20 5
B. Roberts	0 —	0 42	11 23	31 14	0 —	0 19	28 1	69 24	65 2	39 30*	—	6 17	0 —	33 16
J.E. Morris	16 —	4 6	19 6	22 18	175 —	24 1	0 71	3 28	46 32*	18 —	—	56 36	79 —	18 42
S.C. Goldsmith	55 —	0 44	51* 42	22 52	25 —	3 27	0 9	5 63	30 16	4 —	—	47 15	25* —	45 40*
B.J.M. Maher	— —	121* 15	0 13*	4 13	14 —	13 2	38 28	3 0	76* 5*	1 75		2 0	48 —	14 5
R.J. Finney		33 52*	10 2*		45 —									
P.G. Newman		26 9*	8 —	5 18	24 —	0 3*			39 —	23* —		6 8	— —	0 0*
S.J. Base	8 —									21 —		4* 7		
A.E. Warner	— —	39 9	0 —	9* 3	22* —	16 0	26* 0	22 5		8	—	11 6		28* —
D.E. Malcolm	— —	22 —	0 —	12 7	19 —	5 —	0 5*	17 1			—	0 0*		
J.G. Wright		6 84	9 —		79 —	18 0*				12 34	—	82 34	5 —	
M.A. Holding				3 12				16 9			—			
M. Jean-Jacques				5 0					0 —	0 —				
O.H. Mortensen						0* —	2 2	1* 0*	1* —					
R. Sharma							0 16*	3 10		12 —		34 —		
C.J. Adams										21 —				
T.J.G. O'Gorman														
F.A. Griffith														
Byes	4		4 3	2 1	12	4 2	4	1 4	4 4	3		2 1	3	
Leg-byes	8	4 7	3 15	4 10	13	8 1	8 2	2 2	5 4	10 8		9 1	9	9 1
Wides	5	1 2		4	6		2	5 1		2		1	2	3
No-balls	4		4	5 10	9	1	4 3	7 7	5	8 1		8	3	20
Total	406	324 331	170 184	218 340	453	143 159	250 178	329 182	322 115	329 171	0	336 136	308 0	429 125
Wickets	5	10 8	10 5	10 10	10	10 7	10 9	10 10	9 4	9 1	0	10 10	6 0	6 1
Result	W	D	W	D	D	D	W	L	D	D	D	L	W	D
Points	—	4	21	3	4	4	22	6	6	6	4	5	20	5

Fielding Figures:
61 – B.J.M. Maher (ct 60/st 1)
16 – K.J. Barnett and S.C. Goldsmith
15 – B. Roberts
13 – P.D. Bowler
7 – M.A. Holding
6 – J.E. Morris and O.H. Mortensen
5 – T.J.G. O'Gorman and R. Sharma
4 – A.E. Warner
3 – S.J. Base

English Counties Form Charts

The statistics of all first-class matches are given on pages 412–79. The games covered are:

Britannic Assurance County Championship
Matches against touring and representative sides

In the batting table a blank indicates that a batsman did not *play* in a game, a dash (—) that he did not *bat*. A dash (—) is placed in the batting averages if a player had 2 innings or less, and in the bowling figures if no wicket was taken.

at Edgbaston

Somerset 372 (V.J. Marks 68, R.J. Bartlett 67, R.J. Harden 63) and 185 for 6 dec
Warwickshire 257 (P.A. Smith 84 not out) and 290 for 9 (T.A. Lloyd 69, A.J. Moles 64, G.C. Small 56 not out, D.A. Thorne 54)

Match drawn
Somerset 6 pts, Warwickshire 4 pts

at Scarborough

Yorkshire 320 (M.D. Moxon 86, A.A. Metcalfe 56, R.G. Williams 4 for 80) and 397 for 6 dec (M.D. Moxon 191, D. Byas 72)
Northamptonshire 464 (G. Cook 203, A.J. Lamb 76, D.J. Capel 69, P.A. Booth 4 for 132)

Match drawn
Northamptonshire 7 pts, Yorkshire 5 pts

The penultimate round of matches in the Britannic Assurance County Championship produced some excellent cricket and assured that the championship itself would not be decided until the last days of the season, one of the most dramatic finishes in the history of the competition.

	Ports. (i)	(ii)	Warwicks (i)	(ii)	Som. (i)	(ii)	Kent (i)	(ii)	Yorks (i)	(ii)	Lancs OT (i)	(ii)	N'hants (i)	(ii)	Sri Lankans (i)	(ii)	Notts (i)	(ii)	Lancs D (i)	(ii)	M	Inns	NOs	Runs	HS	Av
		18*	0	—					64	109							19	45	157	55	18	28	2	1557	239*	59.88
	9*	29	3	33	27	34	53	84	3	26	51*	1	10	42	7	—	50	11	23	134	24	42	5	1725	159*	46.62
		8	9	60	62	16*	58	15	—	17*	—	1	71	6	16	—	62	3	27	18*	24	39	4	919	71	26.25
		30	54*	31	24	59*	1	0	0*	7	—	86*	45	0	25	—	106	16			23	37	5	1204	175	37.62
		13	0	84	37	22	33	89	—	17	4*	4	0	36	60	—	30	6	5	11	24	39	4	1071	89	30.60
	1*	62	39	18	0	30	22	13	10*	—	—	0	24	25	54	—	33	37	92	24	24	39	6	974	121*	29.51
																					4	5	2	142	52*	47.33
		0*	0	0	5	—									13*	—					16	19	6	187	39	14.38
			0	11*													4	15	0	10	9	10	3	59	15	8.42
			1		45	—	0	4*	—	1*	17	20	6	2							19	25	6	300	45	15.78
		—	0	—	0	—	6	—	—	—			0	—			1*	6*	0	18*	20	21	5	119	22	7.43
	3	7	48	154*	31	59					82	10	28	28			12	4	30*	—	11	20	1	815	154*	42.89
							7	—	—	9											11	12	2	129	30*	12.90
																					4	4	—	5	5	1.25
		—	0	15	6*	—	3*	—							13*	3*	40*	—			12	12	8	46	15	11.50
					80	—	43	16*							—	0	3	41	17	—	10	14	3	315	80	28.63
																					1	1	—	21	21	21.00
							27	78	4	16			5	12	0	—			8	2	5	9	—	152	78	16.88
									—	15			37	5*	18	—	10	19	1	—	5	7	1	105	37	17.50

Bowling / wickets:

	Ports.		Warwicks		Som.		Kent		Yorks		Lancs OT		N'hants		Sri L.		Notts		Lancs D	
					4		3								2		2	5	1	8
			13	10	8	3	4	1	4	7	7		8	5	2		8	9	6	9
					6		3	1					4	1			4			
			1	3	4	1	2	10	2	7	3	5	11	4	11	7	5	6	5	

Team totals:

	Ports.		Warwicks		Som.		Kent		Yorks		Lancs OT		N'hants		Sri L.		Notts		Lancs D	
		182	166	428	324	222	262	317	83	216	157	142	260	172	247		347	226	373	294
		7	10	7	10	4	10	6	3	6	3	8	10	8	7		10	10	10	6
	D		D		W		D		D		D		D		D		L		D	
	3		5		22		6		4		5		7		—		4		5	

2 – M. Jean-Jacques and F.A. Griffith
1 – P.G. Newman, C.J. Adams, D.E. Malcolm, J.G. Wright and sub

Both Surrey and Essex won in three days. Surrey's big score at Hove was founded on a second-wicket partnership of 187 between Clinton and Stewart. Both made centuries, and for Stewart it was the second in succession, but like his county, he had found his best form just a week too late to win honours. Ward, Feltham, Greig and Medlycott all hit well, and for Keith Medlycott, in particular, the game became a memorable one. He bowled his left-arm spin with admirable control and returned figures of 4 for 53 and 8 for 52, the best performance of his career. He had developed strongly during the season and should soon be pushing for an England place.

The holder of the England place that Medlycott aspires to, John Childs, played a decisive part in Essex's victory over Leicestershire, taking 11 for 180 in the match. John Stephenson gave Essex a fine start and looked to be sure to reach a maiden first-class hundred until he had an attack of nerves in the nineties. Mark Waugh and Paul Prichard also batted excitingly, but the gem of the innings came from Nasser Hussain, who did reach a maiden first-class hundred and hit 102 of his 165 not out before lunch on the second day. David East gave him violent support. Nor were the glories yet finished, for David Gower, again opening the innings, delighted with his second hundred in successive matches before becoming one of Childs' victims. In spite of dropping several catches off Childs' bowling, Essex contrived to capture 16 wickets on the third day to win by an innings. Some of the Leicestershire batting was very limp, but Ferris countered Childs by batting left-handed and Foster and Pringle by batting right, much to the amusement of his team mates. He was eventually stumped, and Les Taylor then arrived to hit the first fifty of his career. In all, he hit 6 sixes, 3 in succession off Miller, before being caught at long-on off Childs.

Essex's win took them to within four points of Kent, who were cruelly treated by the weather and who failed bravely to beat Middlesex. Kent bowled the home side out on the first day, catching well and maintaining accuracy and aggression as their bowling virtues. Benson, solidly, Tavare, at times brilliantly until run out by Graham Cowdrey, and the culprit himself took Kent to a good lead, and Middlesex ended the third day on 230 for 5, Penn having taken three quick wickets after Slack and Carr had begun with a stand of 151. Gatting was out first ball of the last day, and Fraser followed shortly after, but Embury and Downton proved obdurate. Penn, who

Derbyshire CCC
First-Class Matches, 1988

BOWLING	P.G. Newman	D.E. Malcolm	S.J. Base	A.E. Warner	R.J. Finney	K.J. Barnett	P.D. Bowler	M.A. Holding	B. Roberts
v. Cambridge University (Cambridge) 16–18 April	11–5–12–1 7–1–13–1	14–6–21–3 6.1–2–13–3	8–3–20–2 2–1–1–1	18–11–22–4 11–1–38–3	7–5–3–0 7–2–34–1	3–2–3–1			
v. Leicestershire (Derby) 21–5 April	33–7–105–3	21–1–103–0		38–11–95–2	42–8–117–0		22–3–54–1		
v. Yorkshire (Leeds) 28 April–2 May	15–3–34–0 16.5–5–29–8	12.3–3–36–4 11–0–42–0		19–6–35–2 19–5–45–1				15–6–23–3 16–3–67–1	9–1–28–1
v. Essex (Chesterfield) 5–9 May	28–10–59–1 11–2–21–1	22–5–63–2 18–5–33–3		19–2–67–0 16–5–19–3			6–0–38–0	24–1–74–4 14–4–28–1	5–1–13–0
v. Glamorgan (Swansea) 21–4 May	9–1–22–0	11–3–23–0		8–3–9–0	3–0–14–0				7–2–16–0
v. Nottinghamshire (Derby) 28–31 May	10–1–32–0	20–6–54–3		7–2–17–0				21–6–49–2	
v. Sussex (Horsham) 4–7 June		19–5–52–5 14–6–19–2		20.2–6–42–2 19.2–4–52–3		17–2–69–2	6–0–20–0		5–2–14–0 9–6–6–0
v. Gloucestershire (Derby) 11–14 June		15–2–53–1 11–4–27–2		15–2–47–0 12–0–46–1		4–0–15–1 4–1–12–0	6–0–24–1	22–3–55–1 16–3–56–0	10–1–45–1
v. Worcestershire (Derby) 18–21 June	36–12–108–4 5.2–1–22–0						17–0–63–2		24–3–68–2
v. Surrey (The Oval) 25–8 June	19–5–51–1 2–0–7–0			16–6–36–4			7–3–20–0	18–2–63–2	
v. Middlesex (Derby) 2–5 July	19.1–3–53–2	11–6–10–0		5–0–14–0		6–1–16–0	5–0–24–0	2–0–4–0	3–0–12–1
v. Essex (Southend) 13–15 July	16–2–41–2 6–1–18–0	14–1–58–0 9–1–44–0	18–1–99–0 9–1–28–0	12–2–30–2 11–7–19–1		6.5–0–18–0 2.3–0–9–0	13–2–49–0 15–2–47–0		
v. Northamptonshire (Derby) 16–18 July	20.1–7–57–3		14–1–46–2	12–2–30–0					
v. Leicestershire (Leicester) 20–2 July	8–2–23–0 13–0–71–2	11–1–60–0 8–0–28–0		8–2–24–0 5–0–17–0		19–5–39–2 11–4–15–2	16–4–33–0 6–4–4–0	10–2–35–1 13–4–33–3	
v. Hampshire (Portsmouth) 23–6 July	14–3–37–2	19–3–64–2		15–4–35–1		29.2–8–74–1	7–1–21–0		
v. Warwickshire (Derby) 30 July–2 Aug.	13.2–2–41–2	18–4–68–6	21–4–79–1				4–0–27–0		1–0–6–0
v. Somerset (Weston-s-Mare) 6–9 August	12–3–46–1	17.3–4–63–3 12–1–43–4		13–4–42–1 13–2–37–4			5–1–13–1		
v. Kent (Chesterfield) 13–16 August		17–3–131–0		21–0–92–2			16–6–57–1	19–0–77–1	9–0–56–1
v. Yorkshire (Chesterfield) 17–19 August		23–5–78–4	23–0–86–2	18.2–6–48–3		2–0–10–0	1.5–0–15–0	23–5–81–1	
v. Lancashire (Old Trafford) 20–3 August		20–4–62–1 3–0–17–0	13–2–43–2 4–0–26–0	23–5–40–2 4–0–20–0			8–1–56–1		
v. Northamptonshire (Northampton) 25–9 August		20–1–83–1 37–6–109–3		11–0–42–2 36–6–91–1			9–1–12–0		11–4–17–2
v. Sri Lankans (Derby) 31 Aug.–2 Sept.	15–5–48–1		20–4–60–2						4–1–7–1
v. Nottinghamshire (Trent Bridge) 9–12 September		31–2–146–2	33–3–123–4			15.3–1–44–2		27–3–95–1	
v. Lancashire (Derby) 14–17 September		21–2–69–2 2–1–4–0	19–0–74–4 11–0–50–2			13–3–27–0 28–10–63–3		25.1–3–48–2 14–4–39–1	6–1–19–0
	339.5–81– 950–35 av. 27.14	488.1–93– 1676–56 av. 29.92	195–20– 735–22 av. 33.40	445–104– 1151–44 av. 26.15	59–15– 168–1 av. 168.00	161.37– 414–14 av. 29.57	169.5–28– 577–7 av. 82.42	279.1–49– 827–24 av. 34.45	103–22– 307–9 av. 34.11

a P.M. Roebuck absent hurt

M. Jean-Jacques	O.H. Mortensen	R. Sharma	S.C. Goldsmith	F.A. Griffith	J.E. Morris	Byes	Leg-byes	Wides	No-balls	Total	Wkts
						2	6	2	6	86	10
						2	2	1	4	106	10
							8		6	482	8
						3	2	2	4	161	10
							9	4	3	192	10
19.4–5–49–3						1	10	8	8	374	10
1–1–0–0						10			1	111	9
						4	1	1	4	89	0
	16.2–7–24–5						8	7	2	184	10
	22–8–32–1	14–3–32–0				1	10	2	12	272	10
	20–4–57–4	5–1–15–0				1	5	3	2	155	10
	6–1–11–0	19–9–54–0				1	3		3	308	5
	13–3–36–2	10–2–18–1					9	1	3	204	6
34.3–4–106–3	3–2–1–1	19–7–43–0	19–6–27–0			1	13	2		367	10
5–0–11–0		17–1–65–1	6–1–28–0			2	9		1	200	3
16–2–77–1		3.5–0–12–0				1	10	2	1	250	8
8–2–19–1							1			47	1
	21–8–35–6					1	9	6		138	10
										40	0
							5	2	18	300	5
							10		5	175	1
										0	0
	18–8–28–5						3		6	164	10
	15–3–33–0					4	3	1	7	254	3
	8–3–6–0					3	6		6	183	8
	12–5–15–1					2	3	2	6	251	7
										0	0
	19–0–60–1						4	3	4	285	10
	16–5–44–0	15–2–63–1					10		1	281	8
		0.2–0–0–1					2	2	5	82	9a
	18–3–42–2						11		5	466	8
						4	4	1	18	301	10
										25	0
		0.1–0–0–1		9–1–47–4		1	4	3	14	197	10
		10–2–30–0	5–1–24–0	5–0–24–0	5.1–0–19–0	2	2	2	9	220	1
	26.1–13–40–6			5–0–23–1			5	1	1	193	10
			13–0–46–0	33.3–12–67–2		6	14	6	6	362	9
17–2–66–1		10–2–34–0		19–3–79–1			3	1	10	297	6
		44–3–129–1		12–2–54–0		10	13		12	614	10
		30–7–66–0		16–2–53–2		5	7		20	368	10
		21–10–32–1				7			6	195	7
101.1–16–328–9 *av.* 36.44	233.3–73–464–34 *av.* 13.64	218.2–49–593–7 *av.* 84.71	43–8–125–0 —	99.3–20–347–10 *av.* 34.70	5.1–0–19–0 —						

Essex CCC
First-Class Matches, 1988

BATTING	v. Kent (Chelmsford) 21–5 April		v. Middlesex (Lord's) 28 April–2 May		v. Derbyshire (Chesterfield) 5–9 May		v. Cambridge Univ. (Cambridge) 18–20 May		v. Warwickshire (Edgbaston) 21–4 May		v. Surrey (Chelmsford) 28–31 May		v. Sussex (Ilford) 11–14 June		v. Gloucestershire (Ilford) 15–17 June		v. Yorkshire (Sheffield) 18–21 June		v. Middlesex (Chelmsford) 25–8 June		v. Kent (Canterbury) 29 June–1 July		v. Somerset (Taunton) 2–5 July		v. Derbyshire (Southend) 13–15 July		v. Lancashire (Southend) 16–19 July	
G.A. Gooch	275	73	43	12	85	56					139	—	113						29	—					53	17	96	2
B.R. Hardie	20	22	6	5	1	5	24	—	2	4	36	—	17		16	36	3	33*	58	—	4	35*	50	—				
P.J. Prichard	0	15*	16	25	2	11	97	—	29	0	0	—	80		6	2	54	39*	34	—	45	—	23	—	28	65*	4	44
A.R. Border	31	55*	30	19	169*	0			4*	112	4	—	161		14	0	39	—	20	—	168	—	1	—	85*	—	0	10
D.R. Pringle	128	—	6	20							7	—	1						0	—	13	—	75	—			—	7
K.W.R. Fletcher	58	—	14	9	0	3			7	57	9	—	—								36	—	35*	—				
D.E. East	29	—	1	20	0	1	13	55	15	9	21	—	13		0	134											0*	0
T.D. Topley	1	—	1	7	5	5*			16	1	17	15*	56*		44	20	17*	—										
G. Miller	16	—					32	—			39*	—	17		6	24	1	—	47	—	16	—	15*	—	9*	—	77	1
J.K. Lever	13*	—	0	20	4	0			6	5					0	0	1	—	0	—	1	—						
J.H. Childs	7	—	0*	1*			—	—	2*	0*	13	—			0	1*	4	—	0	—								
A.W. Lilley			52	18	1	8	0	5*	0	22					80*	0	13	—	61	—	10	—	25	—	37		16	2
J.P. Stephenson					74	11	5	79*	32	3					1	15	12	9			0	43	9	—	16	78*	55	84*
I.L. Pont					6	0*	68	—	29	16	0	25*																
R.N. Pook							6	—																				
A.C. Seymour							33*	—																				
M.C. Ilott							—	—																				
N.A. Foster															0		3	10	1	—	22	—	21	—			11	3
A.D. Brown																	2	—	6*	—	2*	0*	3	—				
N. Hussain																									47	—	80*	14
M.E. Waugh																												
Byes	6	1		2	1	10	2		1		6						5		1		1		1					
Leg-byes	24	4	13	11	10		9	4	12	12	9	3	4		11	3	3	4	16		7	4	11		5	10	5	2
Wides	1				8		10	2		1	1								1		1				2			
No-balls	7		5	6	8	1			11	5	1	2			7	4	2	4	2		5		10		18	5	2	
Total	616	170	187	175	374	111	299	145	166	247	302	45	462		188	249	158	89	296		330	82	258	0	300	175	346	169
Wickets	10	2	10	10	10	9	8	1	9†	10	10	0	8		10	10	10	1	10		10	1	7	0	5	1	7	9
Result	W		L		D		W		L		W		W		L		W		D		D		D		W		L	
Points	21		5		8		—		5		20		24		4		21		7		7		3		22		7	

Fielding Figures
66 – D.E. East (ct 60/st 6)   19 – G.A. Gooch   12 – P.J. Prichard
27 – A.R. Border   16 – A.W. Lilley   11 – A.D. Brown (ct 9/st 2)
22 – G. Miller   13 – J.P. Stephenson   9 – B.R. Hardie and K.W.R. Fletcher

bowled quite magnificently, had Emburey lbw and Cowans brilliantly caught by Tavare so that Middlesex were nine wickets down and only 183 runs ahead. Rain cost Kent 20 valuable overs, and, worse, Tufnell, with a career-best 20, and Downton shared a last-wicket stand of 46 which cost them 17 more. Their final target was 230 off 29 overs, impossible even by one-day rules. They went for the runs, however, and briefly suggested that they might accomplish the miracle, but the very fine bowling of Gus Fraser, in particular, proved too much for them, and they had to hang on for a draw.

The news of the cancellation of England's tour to India had tended to capture the headlines, and the dismissal of David Graveney as captain of Gloucestershire became the main talking point at Bristol, where Worcestershire won comfortably to take a vital one-point lead over Kent into the final round of matches. Hick produced another sparkling hundred for Worcestershire on the opening day, and skipper Phil Neale again proved resolute when his side threatened to throw away their advantage. Neale's contribution to Worcestershire's success in 1988 was immense. He was almost overshadowed by Graveney, who, in spite of a knee injury, took 8 for 127 in a sustained spell of left-arm spin. Bainbridge threatened to thwart the title contenders with a highly professional century, but Richard Illingworth, after a shaky start, found his line to turn the game in Worcestershire's favour. The home side just avoided the follow-on, but Worcestershire crumbled before Graveney's spin again and were only saved from humiliation by a truly splendid innings from Lord. Graveney's 14 for 165 was the best match return of the season, but he left the field after this outstanding performance to learn that he had been sacked. A man of such dignity and purpose deserves better than this. In spite of some blows by Russell and Lawrence, Gloucestershire never looked like avoiding defeat, and Worcestershire moved to the top of the table. Graveney was given a standing ovation when he came to the wicket and was applauded by the Worcestershire players.

Another to receive applause was Norman Gifford, who ended his long and distinguished career by playing out the last balls to save Warwickshire, 11 runs short of their target, from defeat by Somerset.

Geoff Cook hit a career best at Scarborough, where there was a run feast, rain and not much else. Derbyshire were overwhelmed by Notts, for whom Cooper reached a

v. Hampshire (Portsmouth) 20–2 July		v. Leicestershire (Leicester) 23–6 July		v. West Indians (Chelmsford) 30 July–1 Aug.		v. Northamptonshire (Northampton) 3–5 August		v. Nottinghamshire (Colchester) 13–16 August		v. Glamorgan (Colchester) 17–19 August		v. Worcestershire (Worcester) 20–3 August		v. Surrey (The Oval) 30 Aug.–2 Sept.		v. Leicestershire (Chelmsford) 9–12 September		v. Northamptonshire (Chelmsford) 14–17 September		M	Inns	Nos	Runs	HS	Av
				56	67*			36	90	65	72	72	14	123	—	23	—	35	108	15	25	1	1754	275	73.08
														0*	—					13	20	3	377	58	22.17
5	0	71*	—	52*	2	21	44*	32	33*	43	13	13	80	33	—	59	—	27	55*	24	39	8	1202	97	38.77
55	9	65*	—	32	0*	110*	0	130*	11	1	23	34	1			12	—	12	—	20	32	8	1393	169*	58.04
				1	3			12	31	3	54	63	2							14	19	—	450	128	23.68†
45*	—					1	20							9*	—					12	14	3	303	58	27.54
—	10	41	—	5	16	17	34	43	2	39*	5	16	0	40	—	66	—	24	—	20	30	2	669	134	23.89
3	—			2	0	2	—	0	—	2	1	5*	15*	—	—					16	22	6	235	56*	14.68
19	—	1	—	16	—	0	4*	10	—	—	—					17	—	10	—	19	21	4	377	77	22.17
						3	—													13	13	1	53	20	4.41
		—	—					25*	—	0	4*	—	11			3*	—			18	15	8	71	25*	10.14
35	53*	9	—	68	—	4	0	29	42	41	45	9	2	4	—	21	—	48	43	21	33	3	803	80*	26.76
4	34*					5	14	3	0	4	31	20	10	2	—	99	—	38	1	18	31	4	791	99	29.29
				5	—															8	8	2	149	68	24.83
																				1	1	—	6	6	6.00
				6	—															1	1	1	33	33*	—
																				2	1	—	6	6	6.00
								0	5*	3	5	0	16			6*	—	2	—	13	16	2	108	22	7.71
																				4	5	3	13	6*	6.50
19	—	—	—	0	17	45	1					4	25			165*	—	52	17*	9	13	3	486	165*	48.60
														29	—	86	—	35	28	3	4	—	178	86	44.50
8				1				1		2	6	1	6	1	1	2		8	10						
8	10	2		2	1	5	13	10	4	3	11	21	3	8		9		14	13						
1		3		1		1		5		1				1		1		2							
2		8		10	6	18	4	10	2	5	2	4	2	7		25		4							
03	117	200		250	113	238	135	347	226	211	272	262	182	257		592		312	275						
7	3	2		9	5	10	6	9	6	9‡	9	9	10	6		8		10	4						
D		D		D		W		L		D		W		D		W		W							
6		6		—		22		6		14		23		6		24		21							

8 – T.D. Topley
7 – N.A. Foster
5 – D.R. Pringle, J.H. Childs and N. Hussain
3 – R.N. Pook
2 – J.K. Lever, I.L. Pont and M.E. Waugh
† A.R. Border retired hurt
‡ G. Miller absent ill

hundred wickets for the season. Derek Randall also reached a thousand runs, and in spectacular style. He hit the highest score of his career, 237, and shared a fourth-wicket partnership of 345 with Newell, who was awarded his county cap, as was wicket-keeper Scott, who had performed so ably as French's deputy. Randall batted for five hours and hit 36 fours. The joy of watching the man play cricket does not diminish with the years.

Glamorgan confirmed their bottom of the table status by outplaying Hampshire for three days, dropping catches on the fourth and losing by two wickets to Hampshire.

14, 15, 16 and 17 September

at Derby

Derbyshire 373 (K.J. Barnett 157, B.J.M. Maher 92) and 294 for 6 dec (P.D. Bowler 134, K.J. Barnett 55)
Lancashire 368 (G. Fowler 172, A.N. Hayhurst 107, S.J. Base 4 for 74) and 195 for 7 (G.D. Mendis 60)

Match drawn
Derbyshire 5 pts, Lancashire 5 pts

at Chelmsford

Northamptonshire 340 (A.J. Lamb 155, N.A. Foster 4 for 106) and 243 for 8 dec (A. Fordham 70, R.G. Williams 63 not out, J.H. Childs 4 for 87)
Essex 312 (N. Hussain 52, N.G.B. Cook 6 for 56) and 275 for 4 (G.A. Gooch 108, P.J. Prichard 55 not out)

Essex won by 6 wickets
Essex 21 pts, Northamptonshire 7 pts

at Southampton

Sussex 278 (C.M. Wells 92, K.D. James 5 for 70) and 240 (M.P. Speight 58, C.L. Smith 5 for 69)
Hampshire 222 (C.L. Smith 59, A.M. Green 6 for 62) and 298 for 6 (R.A. Smith 119, R.J. Scott 56)

Hampshire won by 4 wickets
Hampshire 22 pts, Sussex 5 pts

at Canterbury

Kent 354 (S.G. Hinks 92, C.J. Tavare 60, M.A. Feltham 5 for 124)
Surrey 109 (A.P. Igglesden 6 for 34) and 179 (C. Penn 4 for 44)

Essex CCC
First-Class Matches, 1988

BOWLING	J.K. Lever	D.R. Pringle	T.D. Topley	G.A. Gooch	J.H. Childs	G. Miller	A.R. Border	I.L. Pont
v. Kent (Chelmsford) 21–5 April	33–11–62–2 19–4–85–1	37–7–77–1	39–6–124–3 21.2–5–57–3	9–3–19–1	24–6–65–0 45–16–113–5	7–1–30–0 28–6–95–1	3–1–6–0 4–0–21–0	
v. Middlesex (Lord's) 28 April–2 May	23–8–47–3 19–3–47–1	22.4–3–90–4 20–2–67–2	17–2–74–1 23–1–94–5	17–4–38–2 20–1–63–0	4–2–4–0			
v. Derbyshire (Chesterfield) 5–9 May	27–11–45–0 33.3–2–103–3		26.3–6–75–7 45–11–104–5	10–2–29–2 14–5–29–1		2–0–3–0		14–2–60–1 27–0–93–1
v. Cambridge University (Cambridge) 18–20 May					18.2–7–36–5 14.1–6–25–4	25–4–43–2 7–1–7–0		18–8–30–1 20–3–58–4
v. Warwickshire (Edgbaston) 21–4 May	16–5–32–3 15–4–48–1		18.1–1–57–4 22.1–4–71–1		10–3–21–0			17–1–65–3 20–1–104–3
v. Surrey (Chelmsford) 28–31 May		2–1–4–0 16–4–39–6	8–0–27–1		4–1–6–0	3–1–10–0 23–8–47–3		4–2–2–0 6–0–15–0
v. Sussex (Ilford) 11–14 June		6–1–16–0 18–7–41–2	3–0–9–1		23.1–9–46–3 4–3–4–0	22–4–76–5 6.2–2–11–2		
v. Gloucestershire (Ilford) 15–17 June	23–5–84–2 2–0–12–0		19–2–59–2		18–6–54–0 8–1–24–1	24.1–7–44–3 4.3–0–23–1		
v. Yorkshire (Sheffield) 18–21 June	17–4–30–3 15.3–3–41–3		13–1–39–1 15–2–38–3		2–1–4–0			
v. Middlesex (Chelmsford) 25–8 June	18–3–64–1 8–1–23–2	20–4–49–1 3.1–0–7–0		5–1–19–0	21.1–7–52–4	2–0–9–0		
v. Kent (Canterbury) 29 June–1 July	16–3–38–1	15–4–42–3				39–12–95–4		
v. Somerset (Taunton) 2–5 July	6–2–13–1	4–1–10–0				7–1–9–0		
v. Derbyshire (Southend) 13–15 July	22–4–72–1 7.4–1–18–3			14–5–33–2	28–7–64–1 21–7–62–3	22–8–46–0 5–2–7–1		
v. Lancashire (Southend) 16–19 July		11–2–48–0 10–0–38–1		8–3–15–0	29.4–8–63–4 28.1–8–79–3	20–5–42–3 23–3–91–1	8–3–16–0	
v. Hampshire (Portsmouth) 20–2 July	24–4–61–4 8–3–14–1		28–2–88–4 7–1–16–0			3–0–7–1		10–4–26–0
v. Leicestershire (Leicester) 23–6 July	26.4–2–75–3 11–0–32–0		29–5–100–3 17–3–54–0			2–1–8–0 1–1–0–0		20–1–86–2 11–1–37–1
v. West Indians (Chelmsford) 30 July–1 Aug.		19–2–64–1 7–2–24–1	24.3–3–91–3 14–3–52–0	9–1–35–0 8–1–24–1	14–3–46–1 17–3–53–0	16–5–57–1 10–0–45–1	8–1–39–0	17–3–78–3 7–0–38–0
v. Northamptonshire (Northampton) 3–5 August	21.4–3–60–3 11–2–14–1		32–6–100–3 21.1–8–38–5			19–7–36–4 19–9–36–3		
v. Nottinghamshire (Colchester) 13–16 August		15–3–40–1 19–1–82–6	11–1–41–0		18.2–2–61–1 15–2–59–0	21–2–74–2 14–2–36–0	1–1–0–0	
v. Glamorgan (Colchester) 17–19 August		21.4–7–51–6 16–6–30–0	14–1–48–1 18–2–63–1	12–7–17–0 8–2–21–1	9–6–17–2 40–17–91–3		5–0–20–1	
v. Worcestershire (Worcester) 20–3 August		17–5–32–1 25–6–74–3	12–2–44–3 14–4–31–2	3–1–17–0	1–0–1–0 7–3–9–1		5–3–8–0	
v. Surrey (The Oval) 30 Aug.–2 Sept.			26.5–5–70–3	1–1–0–0	19–6–41–0			29–4–103–5
v. Leicestershire (Chelmsford) 9–12 September		7–0–41–0 13–2–54–1		3–1–7–0	39.2–11–88–5 23.3–4–92–6	29–10–48–1 5–0–31–0		
v. Northamptonshire (Chelmsford) 14–17 September		22–3–69–2 12–2–30–1		5–1–18–0 6–0–17–0	31–14–55–3 33–11–87–4	16–1–57–0 10–2–33–0		
	422.4–88– 1120–43 av. 26.04	378.3–75– 1119–43 av. 26.02	538.4–87– 1664–65 av. 25.60	152–39– 401–10 av. 40.10	569.5–180– 1422–59 av. 24.10	433–105– 1153–39 av. 29.56	36–9– 113–1 av. 113.00	220–30– 795–24 av. 33.12

M.C. Ilott	J.P. Stephenson	N.A. Foster	A.W. Lilley	N. Hussain	P.J. Prichard	M.E. Waugh	Byes	Leg-byes	Wides	No-balls	Total	Wkts
							2	15	1	5	400	7
							3	10			384	10
							4	6	1	11	263	10
								4	1	9	275	8
							2	4		5	218	10
							1	10		10	340	10
22–11–40–1	12–4–25–1						6	8	3		188	10
12–3–23–2							3	5	2	11	121	10
								6	1	5	160	10
							1	9	4	8	254	5
											22	0
								2		6	130	10
		8–3–12–1					4	1			155	10
		23–5–61–5					1	7			134	10
	3–0–14–0	26–4–99–3					4	12	4	2	370	10
		6–1–9–0						1			69	2
		22.1–7–53–6					2	5		7	133	10
		16–6–33–4						1		6	113	10
		22–5–64–4					1	1		1	259	10
		12–2–36–1									66	3
		24.2–8–51–2					1	4			231	10
											0	0
		18–3–48–0						5			85	2
	3–0–14–0	29–7–96–6					2	9	1		336	10
		22–4–47–3					1	1			136	10
		19–3–47–3						12	1	1	227	10
		12–1–54–0						11			289	6
	5.2–3–10–1						4	5	1	5	201	10
	1–0–5–0		11–0–119–0	9–0–47–0	1–0–7–0		5	1		3	214	1
	11–3–26–0							5	4	9	300	9
								6			129	1
							4	3	3	11	378	10
								5		2	280	3
15–1–48–0	7–1–25–0						2	12		4	283	10
							1				89	10
		24–4–78–2						6		6	300	6
		20–2–88–2					3	6		3	274	8
		20–5–52–1					2	5		7	192	10
		16–4–56–0					5	5		4	291	7
		22.4–5–67–6					1	5		2	150	10
		22.2–3–61–4						17			217	10
22–5–66–2						12–0–75–0		7	2	3	362	10
		18–4–73–3					1	10	1		268	10
		14–3–64–3									241	10
	7–0–27–1	33.4–4–106–4						8		8	340	10
		21–2–68–3					2	6		2	243	8
49–15–	71.2–16–	471.1–95–	11–0–	9–0–	1–0–	12–0–						
111–3	212–5	1423–66	119–0	47–0	7–0	75–0						
av. 37.00	*av. 42.40*	*av. 21.56*	—	—	—	—						

Glamorgan CCC
First-Class Matches, 1988

BATTING	v. Gloucestershire (Bristol) 21–5 April		v. Somerset (Cardiff) 28 April–2 May		v. Cambridge Univ. (Cambridge) 5–7 May		v. Hampshire (Bournemouth) 18–20 May		v. Derbyshire (Swansea) 21–4 May		v. Gloucestershire (Swansea) 28–31 May		v. Kent (Cardiff) 4–7 June		v. Nottinghamshire (Trent Bridge) 11–14 June		v. Leicestershire (Leicester) 15–17 June		v. Lancashire (Swansea) 25–8 June		v. Somerset (Taunton) 29 June–1 July		v. West Indians (Swansea) 13–15 July		v. Middlesex (Lord's) 16–19 July		v. Warwickshire (Cardiff) 20–2 July	
A.R. Butcher	16	4	48	—	166	—	34	19					52	8	27	65	6	23*	36	16	4	2	18	—	83	9	47	93
J.A. Hopkins	1	27	42	—	11	68	1	47	30*	—			61	5	10	1	71	7	8	7	36	0	87	—	2	7	0	5
H. Morris	26	84	6	—			39	37					0	38	25	1	1	15	7	1	11	24	12	—	87	15	21	51
M.P. Maynard	126	68	122	—	19	47	39	23					1	5	0	10	6	13*	40	10	0	53*	12	—	71	64	0	72*
G.C. Holmes	117	36	108	—	79	—	12	7					34	10					18	1	100*	107	8*	—	5*	50	79	—
R.C. Ontong	11	9	5	—			60*	9					120*	12*	5	25	66*	—	3	3	17	12*	0	—	—	37	6	23*
J. Derrick	12	6			10*	7	4	0					50*	—	0	4*	0	—	0	0	0	0			—	13	7	—
J.G. Thomas	31	35*	2	—			2	19					14	10*	0	14	24	—	14	0			0*	—				
C.P. Metson	5*	1*	31*	—	—	4*	32	2*					—	48	1	3	27	—	2	4*	17	1			—	19*	20	—
C.J.P.G. van Zyl	5	2					11	7*									5	—										
S.R. Barwick	—	—					30	—					—	—			0	1										
S.L. Watkin			7*	—	—	—													0*	0	15*	3*			—	0*	1	—
R.J. Shastri			157	—					—				20	5	1	36					41	0	20	30	35*	34	52	15
P.A. Cottey					68	92			49*	—					12*	4	18	—										
P.D. North																									—	—		
S. Monkhouse																											0*	
M.J. Cann																												
S.R. Bastien																												
P.G.P. Roebuck																												
Byes	1	5			3	5	5		4				11	3	1		1	4	8	4	1		20		4			8
Leg-byes	7	9	3		4	6	2	4	1				5	2	9	5	8	3	21	1	14	7	8		6	15	2	5
Wides		1			6	3	5		1						3		1	3	3		1	3	5		1		1	3
No-balls	14	9	12		2			3	4				1	3	1	4	10	3	1		16	5	10		4	2	10	3
Total	372	296	543		368	232	276	177	89				369	152	91	175	246	71	199	47	252	247	180		298	265	246	278
Wickets	9	8	8		5	4	10	8	0				7	7	10	10	10	2	10	10	8	7	5		4	8	10	4
Result	L		D		D		D		D		Ab		L		L		D		L		D		D		D		D	
Points	5		8				7		2		0		1		4		5		5		3		—		4		5	

Fielding Figures
60 – C.P. Metson (ct 52/st 8)   13 – A.R. Butcher   7 – R.C. Ontong
22 – M.P. Maynard   10 – J. Derrick   6 – G.C. Holmes
15 – H. Morris   9 – J.A. Hopkins   5 – J.G. Thomas and R.J. Shastri

Kent won by an innings and 66 runs
Kent 24 pts, Surrey 4 pts

at Trent Bridge
Yorkshire 380 (P.E. Robinson 98, A.A. Metcalfe 74, M.D. Moxon 68, F.D. Stephenson 4 for 105) and 340 for 7 dec (D.L. Bairstow 94 not out, P.E. Robinson 80, F.D. Stephenson 7 for 117)
Nottinghamshire 296 (F.D. Stephenson 111, P. Johnson 59, A. Sidebottom 7 for 89) and 297 (F.D. Stephenson 117, D.W. Randall 59, S.D. Fletcher 6 for 74)

Yorkshire won by 127 runs
Yorkshire 24 pts, Nottinghamshire 5 pts

at Taunton
Somerset 277 (R.J. Harden 78, N.D. Burns 56, V.J. Marks 50) and 214 (N.A. Felton 127, R.J. Harden 52, T.M. Alderman 8 for 59)
Gloucestershire 335 (A.W. Stovold 133, P. Bainbridge 57, A.J. Wright 52, V.J. Marks 7 for 118) and 157 for 6 (K.M. Curran 51 not out)

Gloucestershire won by 4 wickets
Gloucestershire 21 pts, Somerset 6 pts

at Worcester
Glamorgan 244 (M.P. Maynard 69, N.V. Radford 4 for 84) and 103 (P.J. Newport 5 for 23)
Worcestershire 423 (G.A. Hick 197)

Worcestershire won by an innings and 76 runs
Worcestershire 24 pts, Glamorgan 4 pts

Mid-way through Friday afternoon, the third day of the last four-day match of the season, Worcestershire became Britannic Assurance County Champions when Bastien skied a ball from Illingworth, the slow left-arm spinner whose bowling in the last weeks of the season had done much to help win the title, and the enthusiastic young Leatherdale took the catch. Had Worcestershire, one point ahead when the last round of matches began, been allowed to choose their opponents for this deciding game, they would surely have chosen bottom of the table Glamorgan. The Welshmen performed doggedly enough on the opening day, but a suspect middle order was never likely to deny Worcestershire's all-round attack the four bowling bonus points that they sought. The second day belonged, inevitably, to Graeme Hick, who, dropped at slip on 41, hit his 10th century of the summer in character-

v. Yorkshire (Cardiff) 23–6 July		v. Sussex (Eastbourne) 30 July–2 Aug.		v. Surrey (Swansea) 6–9 August		v. Worcester (Abergavenny) 13–16 August		v. Essex (Colchester) 17–19 August		v. Northamptonshire (Wellingborough) 20–3 August		v. Leicestershire (Neath) 25–9 August		v. Warwickshire (Edgbaston) 30 Aug.–2 Sept.		v. Hampshire (Cardiff) 9–12 September		v. Worcestershire (Worcester) 14–17 September		M	Inns	Nos	Runs	HS	Av
4	0	0	0	54	65*	15	41	17	66	7	40	1	—	11	11	74	56	35	9	23	40	2	1282	166	33.73
																				13	23	1	534	87	24.27
5*	44	56	63	51	19*	24	3	22	31	8	2	1*	—							19	33	3	830	87	27.66
—	60*	68	27	10	108*	1	17*	26	0	22	8	1*	—	63	36	50	71	69	19	21	38	6	1439	126	44.96
—	4*	89	42	16	—	43	—	34	83*	83	4					6	0	6	33	20	32	4	999	117	35.67
—	—	1	—	19*	—			15	16*	13	5			4	21	0	1	21*	0	17	25	8	734	120*	43.17
	8	21	8*	100*	—			9	19	10	7			110	0	0	26	40	0	21	28	6	229	50*	10.40
—	—	3	7	23	—	43	—	3	7	3	1			19	1	21*	2	1	0	16	26	5	515	110	24.52
		2*	—	7	—	0*	—													23	30	8	351	48	15.95
																				4	5	1	30	11	7.50
—	—	6	—	1	—	23	—	0	—	1	20			0	5	8	11*	1	13*	13	7	2	40	30	8.00
	8	19	54*	50	2	14	—													16	19	7	115	23	9.58
7*	45			50	2	8	59	1	47	2	30	8	—	1	3	73	8	13	5	12	19	2	575	157	33.82
								15*	—	41*	19*			7	21	0	4			13	23	3	605	92	30.25
																				7	7	3	107	41*	26.75
—	—			0	—					7	6			6	22			28	9	3	1	1	0	0*	—
														36*	2*	0	4	5	10	6	7	—	78	28	11.14
																0	46	13	1	4	6	2	57	36*	14.25
																				2	4	—	60	46	15.00

4	8			4				4		2	5	4				2		12		2	1
8		3	3			10	2	1	3	5	5	8	9			11	1	12	1	4	1
		3	1				1	1	3								3				2
	2	4	3	9	2	6	5	7	4	11	6			4	4	3	4	6

20	179	283	227	262	98	298	242	192	291	220	157	11		272	136	259	234	244	103
1	4	10	6	10	3	9	3	10	7	10	10	2		10	10	10	10	10	10
D		D		D		L		D		L		D		W		L		L	
2		7		5		5		5		3		1		23		7		4	

4 – M.J. Cann and P.A. Cottey
3 – Subs
2 – P.D. North and S.R. Barwick
1 – P.G.P. Roebuck, S.L. Watkin, S.R. Bastien and C.J.P.G. van Zyl

istic regal style and swept his side to maximum batting points. A lunatic had attempted to vandalize the pitch before the start of the third day and an hour was lost as ground staff removed deposits of industrial soap. Worcestershire ended their innings at lunch-time, and Glamorgan's second innings occupied under 36 overs as the weakest side in the Championship crumbled before Newport and his colleagues, who, as always, were intelligently marshalled by Phil Neale.

Worcestershire well deserved the title, yet one had to commiserate with Kent, who had been deprived of a bowling point against Warwickshire when two batsmen were unfit to bat, and who had led the table so bravely for much of the season. They began at whirlwind pace against Surrey with Hinks in flowing form out shortly after lunch at a time when 400 in the day looked probable. As it was, it was left to a valiant last-wicket stand of 82 between Ellison and Igglesden, who hit a career-best 41, to take Kent past 300 and gain a fourth batting point. Igglesden then produced the best bowling performance of his career and Surrey twice disintegrated after reaching 100 with apparent ease. They had some excuse in that they lost Greig, who was hit in the face when batting, but they offered little resistance to Kent's exuberant cricket. Kent's fielding was of its usual high standard, and Chris Cowdrey's leadership was electric.

Essex confirmed third place with Gooch finishing the season as he had begun it in majestic form, and Childs and Foster bowling well. The unlucky Nick Cook bowled admirably for Northants, for whom Allan Lamb played an exciting innings to close the season.

In what was presumably his last game as captain of Gloucestershire, David Graveney led his side to victory. There was a fine innings from Andy Stovold, and Terry Alderman bowled outstandingly. Kevin Curran hit 51 not out on a difficult wicket on the last day to win the game and to reach a thousand runs for the season in the process. The saddest story from this match was that of Nigel Felton, who hit 127 on the third day, having learned the evening before that he was not to be offered another contract by the club.

Kim Barnett and Peter Bowler ended seasons of great personal achievement with fine and contrasting centuries at Derby, where Graeme Fowler hit his highest score of the season and Andy Hayhurst the first century of his career in a drawn match.

Glamorgan CCC
First-Class Matches, 1988

BOWLING	J.G. Thomas	C.J.P.G. van Zyl	S.R. Barwick	J. Derrick	R.C. Ontong	G.C. Holmes	A.R. Butcher	S.L. Watkin	M.P. Maynard
v. Gloucestershire (Bristol) 21–5 April	22–5–78–2 / 13–0–72–1	26–10–72–1 / 16.1–2–63–0	24–7–73–0 / 12–1–48–0	24.1–5–65–3 / 11–1–51–0	11–4–35–0 / 4–0–14–0	6–2–11–1 / 17–0–73–1	2–0–4–1		
v. Somerset (Cardiff) 28 April–2 May	24.2–6–74–4 / 4–0–14–0		26–6–74–3 / 5–2–11–0		9–4–8–1 / 9–3–12–0	3–0–9–0 / 5–1–19–0	10–1–28–2 / 2–0–6–0	19–4–59–0 / 7–3–8–0	2–0–5–0 / 3–2–8–0
v. Cambridge University (Cambridge) 5–7 May		15–3–48–1		14–8–40–1		5–3–5–0	5–2–8–0	22–4–76–2	
v. Hampshire (Bournemouth) 18–20 May	20–2–70–2 / 9–1–29–1	13–5–20–1 / 15–4–36–0	16–3–40–1 / 11–5–24–0	16–10–23–1 / 14–5–35–1	20.2–7–47–4 / 11–1–30–0		2–2–0–0		
v. Derbyshire (Swansea) 21–4 May	7–2–16–2		41–12–130–4	38.2–7–116–3	20–7–71–0	9–1–27–0	9–2–27–0		
v. Gloucestershire (Swansea) 28–31 May									
v. Kent (Cardiff) 4–7 June	13–1–37–0 / 14–2–43–2		15–5–31–0 / 10–0–43–2	4–2–10–0	20–1–80–0 / 14–0–65–0		7–2–25–0 / 4–0–25–0		
v. Nottinghamshire (Trent Bridge) 11–14 June	22.2–6–68–6 / 15–1–57–1		26–11–31–2 / 30–7–93–4	14–5–24–2 / 27.5–8–67–4	7–2–17–0				
v. Leicestershire (Leicester) 15–17 June	19–3–73–2 / 10–4–26–1	18–4–67–0 / 11–2–33–0	24–8–58–1 / 22–5–49–3	20–6–57–1 / 18.3–6–54–6	17–4–41–3		1–0–7–0		
v. Lancashire (Swansea) 25–8 June	11–3–41–2 / 2–0–7–0				18–5–51–2 / 40–11–82–3			8–1–16–2 / 4–0–8–0	
v. Somerset (Taunton) 29 June–1 July			17–2–51–1	14–2–58–1	3.2–0–20–0			20–3–57–0	
v. West Indians (Swansea) 13–15 July	14–2–52–0 / 8–0–35–1		20–9–37–0 / 5–1–13–0	18–5–49–1 / 4–2–4–0	19–6–50–2		2–0–18–0		
v. Middlesex (Lord's) 16–19 July			16–6–34–1	23–1–98–1 / 17–3–45–1	21–1–91–0 / 11.3–5–28–0	15–2–61–1 / 11–0–46–0		17–4–54–0 / 14–2–53–0	
v. Warwickshire (Cardiff) 20–2 July				22–3–52–3	7–1–22–0	4–2–14–0		31–11–66–4 / 4.3–0–15–1	
v. Yorkshire (Cardiff) 23–6 July				34–8–90–2	18–7–32–0		4–0–32–1	31–12–47–3	
v. Sussex (Eastbourne) 30 July–2 Aug.	10–2–26–1		20–4–57–1 / 3–1–3–0	8–3–19–0 / 1–0–12–0	6–2–9–0 / 8–3–12–0			28–5–89–5 / 15–4–53–2	
v. Surrey (Swansea) 6–9 August			22.5–9–44–3 / 17–3–37–5	11–1–43–0	24–8–53–2 / 15–4–38–4			26–9–69–2 / 15–0–49–0	
v. Worcestershire (Abergavenny) 13–16 August	11–0–62–1 / 13–1–69–1		12–4–22–1 / 14–1–61–0		19–3–69–2 / 12–0–43–0	5–0–17–1 / 14.2–1–68–2		15–6–28–0 / 18–2–90–2	
v. Essex (Colchester) 17–19 August	14–2–61–1 / 7–0–48–0			8–1–29–0 / 6–0–23–0	18–5–37–1 / 13–0–71–2		7–0–38–5	23–3–56–4 / 12–0–55–1	
v. Northamptonshire (Wellingborough) 20–3 August	10–0–39–0 / 14–2–44–2			16.5–3–57–1 / 16.4–4–55–1		6–1–14–0	2–1–9–1	14–4–33–1 / 15–4–36–0	
v. Leicestershire (Neath) 25–9 August				23–9–47–1		12–1–42–0	4–0–9–0	37–10–86–3	
v. Warwickshire (Edgbaston) 30 Aug.–2 Sept.	15–4–54–0 / 16.4–0–70–6			20–6–48–1 / 21–6–47–4		2–1–1–0		31–10–59–8 / 17–2–55–0	
v. Hampshire (Cardiff) 9–12 September	20–3–67–4 / 28–6–69–2			8.1–3–6–2 / 36.4–8–96–3				15–5–28–3 / 35–11–87–2	
v. Worcestershire (Worcester) 14–17 September	36–4–130–3			32–7–91–3				34–8–91–1	
	422.2–62–1531–48 av. 31.89	114.1–30–339–3 av. 113.00	408.5–112–1064–32 av. 33.25	542.1–136–1511–47 av. 32.14	395.1–94–1128–26 av. 43.38	121.2–15–445–11 av. 40.45	54–10–198–5 av. 39.60	527.3–127–1423–46 av. 30.93	5–2–13–0 —

a G. Miller absent ill

R.J. Shastri	S. Monkhouse	P.D. North	J.A. Hopkins	H. Morris	M.J. Cann	S.R. Bastien	Byes	Leg-byes	Wides	No-balls	Total	Wkts
							1	6		15	341	7
								4		10	329	4
6–2–14–0							6	4		1	267	10
							4	4		4	100	0
	23–9–37–3	26–13–46–2					6	12	1	9	278	10
							2	15		2	217	10
			5–1–46–0	4.3–0–58–0			1			2	259	2
9–2–41–0							12	13	6	9	453	10
												Ab.
23.4–2–59–2							4	6		4	252	2
21.4–6–89–1								6			271	6
15–6–30–0							4	4	2	3	178	10
2–1–4–0								9	3	2	230	10
							4	6	1	1	313	7
								2	1	1	164	10
21.1–7–41–4								6		3	155	10
45.1–22–49–7							5	12		2	163	10
15–0–49–0							5	3		4	243	2
		16–3–74–0					10	12	3	5	302	3
		6–4–14–0						1		5	67	1
11–0–66–0							2	14		2	420	3
4–1–11–0							3	5		1	191	1
9–2–15–0	24–4–72–1						3	11		10	255	8
	4–0–15–0							2		1	32	1
17–5–37–0	16–4–31–1				6–0–43–2		1	9	2	10	322	9
											0	0
24–7–58–2								7	1	4	265	10
14–2–26–1								9			115	3
40–11–80–3								8	4	4	297	10
26.4–12–40–0							4	3			171	9
							1	1		6	200	5
								13	2	2	344	5
		10.5–3–24–3					1	3	1	5	211	9
		4–0–20–0					6	11		2	272	9a
		9–0–46–0						3	1	4	201	3
		10–1–38–0					1	4			178	3
		17–4–35–1				28.1–4–90–5	1	4	1	5	314	10
		2–2–0–0				23–11–37–1	8	8	3	2	215	10
						6–1–11–0	4	2		1	189	10
						10–3–19–1	1	5		10	126	10
		12–2–32–1				27–11–67–0		19	4	11	370	8
					8–2–20–2	25–5–65–1	5	21	2	6	423	10
304.2–88–709–20 *av.* 35.45	67–17–155–5 *av.* 31.00	112.5–32–329–7 *av.* 47.00	5–1–46–0 —	4.3–0–58–0 —	14–2–63–4 *av.* 15.75	119.1–35–289–8 *av.* 36.12						

Gloucestershire CCC
First-Class Matches, 1988

BATTING	v. Glamorgan (Bristol) 21–5 April		v. Sussex (Bristol) 28 April–2 May		v. Northamptonshire (Northampton) 5–9 May		v. Nottinghamshire (Trent Bridge) 18–20 May		v. West Indians (Bristol) 25–7 May		v. Glamorgan (Swansea) 28–31 May		v. Oxford University (Oxford) 1–3 June		v. Derbyshire (Derby) 11–14 June		v. Essex (Ilford) 15–17 June		v. Lancashire (Old Trafford) 18–21 June		v. Leicestershire (Gloucester) 25–8 June		v. Hampshire (Gloucester) 29 June–1 July		v. Worcestershire (Worcester) 2–5 July		v. Northamptonshire (Bristol) 13–15 July	
A.W. Stovold	52	10	136	—	4	40	84	28							37	1	15	28	32	72	23	6	25	37	42	—	—	0
A.J. Wright	0	87	1	—	36	48	5	3	49	50*			—	9	136	13	42	19	36	14	5	34	13	16	69	—	—	7
M.W. Alleyne	0	56	2	—			12	—	8	—			36	—					—	21								
C.W.J. Athey	123	88*	0	—	27	40									18	47	76	9*	72*	58	35	41	23	22	91*	—	—	168*
P. Bainbridge	52	—	49	—	9	2			4	11*	2	—	119	—	75	12	37	—	—	48	5	30	43	8	38	—	—	55
K.M. Curran	1	32*	20	—			41	13									8*	40*	21	—	29	0	48	16	5*	—	—	1
J.W. Lloyds	68	42	8	—	2	0	0	14*	0	—			102*	—	0*	12	32	—	—	12	6	9	30	10			—	0
R.C. Russell	23*	—			29	10	29	—	19	—			11*	69	—	36*	64	—	—	13*	1	4	72	69			—	4
D.A. Graveney			—	9	20	1*	20*	—	4*	—							47	—	—	0	8	7					—	17
D.V. Lawrence			—	9	10	23	27	—	4	—							10	—	—	1*	8	0	24	13			—	6
T.M. Alderman			2*	—	3*	14	11	—									1*	—			2*	0*	1*	33			—	5
A.J. Brassington			1	—																								
P.W. Romaines					6	7			2	31*			1	0	27	30	3	12*	101*	46	10	6	0	4	59	—	—	55
D.J. Thomas					7	3			10	—			—	57*														
I.P. Butcher							11	8	0	4			75	—														
V.S. Greene									0	—									—	2								
M.W. Pooley															—	3*												
K.B.S. Jarvis													—	—											—	1*		
K.B.K. Ibadulla																												
M.J.C. Ball																												
Byes	1		2		4	7			8				4		1		4			11	1	4	6					9
Leg-byes	6	4	7		12	6	8	2	10	1			8	1	3	9	12	1	3	2	11	7	18					9
Wides							1						1		1		4		1		1		2	1				1
No-balls	15	10	6		3		1	1	24	12			4	1	3	3	2				5	1	9	11	10			11
Total	341	329	252		172	201	254	80	140	98			360	141	308	204	370	69	256	296	142	144	307	248	332	0	0	348
Wickets	7	4	10		10	10	10	4	10	1			4	3	5	6	10	2	2	9	10	10	9	10	4	0	0	10
Result	W		D		L		W		D		Ab.		D		W		W		D		L		D		D		L	
Points	21		5		5		23		—		0		—		24		24		5		4		5		4		2	

Fielding Figures
63 – R.C. Russell (ct 51/st 12)
19 – C.W.J. Athey
18 – J.W. Lloyds
16 – M.W. Alleyne (ct 15/st 1)
15 – K.M. Curran
14 – A.W. Stovold and A.J. Wright
13 – P.W. Romaines
12 – T.M. Alderman
9 – P. Bainbridge

Britannic Assurance County Championship – Final Table (1987 positions in brackets)

	P	W	L	D	Bonus pts Bt	Bl	Pts
Worcestershire (9)	22	10	3	9	55	75	290
Kent (14)	22	10	5	7	57	72	289
Essex (12)	22	9	5	8	61	69	282
Surrey (4)	22	7	5	10	57	72	241
Nottinghamshire (1)	22	8	8	6	31	74	229
Warwickshire (15)	22	6	8	8	48	74	218
Middlesex (16)	22	7	3	12	49	54	215
Leicestershire (3)	22	6	3	13	56	63	215
Lancashire (2)	22	6	7	9	45	63	212
Gloucestershire (10)	22	6	7	9	52	59	207
Somerset (11)	22	5	6	11	48	65	201
Northamptonshire (7)	22	5	7	10	48	71	199
Yorkshire (8)	22	4	6	12	48	65	177
Derbyshire (6)	22	4	3	15	53	54	171
Hampshire (5)	22	4	6	12	33	69	166
Sussex (17)	22	3	11	8	37	65	150
Glamorgan (13)	22	1	8	13	42	53	111

Lancashire, Somerset and Essex totals include 8 points for being the side batting 2nd in a match where the scores finished level. Nottinghamshire's total includes 12 points for a win in a 1-innings match.

There were career-best bowling performances by two occasional off-break bowlers at Southampton, Chris Smith and Allan Green, but it was Robin Smith's aggressive hundred that won the game for Hampshire, who had trailed by 56 on the first innings.

At Trent Bridge, the season ended in spectacular fashion. David Bairstow, recalled to the Yorkshire side, claimed his 1000th first-class victim behind the stumps for Yorkshire, and then hit 94 not out before Carrick declared at the end of the third day. Franklyn Stephenson, who hit his first century of the season, took all seven wickets to fall in Yorkshire's second innings to give him match figures of 11 for 222. Set to make 425 to win, the home side were never in contention, but Stephenson hit his second century of the match, 117 off 119 balls with two sixes and 20 fours. This was the first time since George Hirst performed the

Nasser Hussain hit a maiden first-class century, Essex v. Leicestershire at Chelmsford, and kept alive championship hopes. (Sporting Pictures UK Ltd)

v. Somerset (Bristol) 16–19 July		v. Sussex (Hove) 20–2 July		v. Surrey (Cheltenham) 30 July–2 Aug.		v. Warwickshire (Cheltenham) 3–5 August		v. Yorkshire (Cheltenham) 6–9 August		v. Middlesex (Lord's) 13–16 August		v. Sri Lankans (Bristol) 17–19 August		v. Kent (Bristol) 20–3 August		v. Hampshire (Southampton) 30 Aug.–2 Sept.		v. Worcestershire (Bristol) 9–12 September		v. Somerset (Taunton) 14–17 September		M	Inns	Nos	Runs	HS	Av
3	29	63	77	5	46	52	16*	49	30*	1	33			14	12	21	18	4	0	133	18	21	39	2	1296	136	35.02
0	0	50	—	1	27	9	0	33	34	40	43	137	—	22	5	19	0	39	39	52	26	24	42	1	1268	137	30.92
4	6	6	0	10	8	15	21	19	30	0	14	32*	—					0	—			14	21	1	300	56	15.00
56	18			25*	—																	12	20	6	1037	168*	74.07
4	13	11	2	3	0	119	70	1	169	2	3			55	8	47	19	124	27	57	1	23	38	1	1334	169	36.05
39	11	27	42*	52	101	5	2	10	98	142	33			0	4	19	28*	8	57	1	51*	19	34	7	1005	142	37.22
		0	0															47	1	22	16	16	24	3	433	102*	20.61
8	9	50	11*	4	5	4*	41	29	1	13	13	—		34*	34			1	41	1	5	22	33	7	757	72	29.11
22	4	3	—	13	5		3*	7*	—	16	0	—		—	2*	3	—	2*	4*	14*	—	23	24	9	231	47	15.40
11	2*	3	—	4	0	10	0	4	—	1*	0	—		—	—			6	29	16	—	21	25	3	221	29	10.04
1*	0	4*	—	1*	43*	—	—	0	—	2	0*	—		—	—	0	—	7	0	5	—	20	22	11	135	43*	12.27
																						1	1	—	1	1	1.00
7	19	36	2	33	2	99	50	35	4	1	17	62	—	42	61	7	33	0	20	7	18	21	39	3	955	101*	26.52
																						3	4	1	77	57*	25.66
												0	—									4	6	—	98	75	16.50
												—	—									3	2		2	2	1.00
						11	25*	10	25*	38	1	—	—	3	15*	9*	8	1	0			8	13	5	149	38	18.62
																						3	1	1	1	1*	—
												2*	—	77	14	0	10*			9	12*	4	7	3	124	77	31.00
												—	—			2	—					2	1	—	2	2	2.00

v. Somerset		v. Sussex		v. Surrey		v. Warwickshire		v. Yorkshire		v. Middlesex		v. Sri Lankans		v. Kent		v. Hampshire		v. Worcestershire		v. Somerset	
			3	6		4			2		1			3	3			1	3	5	2
7	5	15	4	5	3	22	4	8	7	6	1	6		4	2	1	8	9	2	9	8
		8			1	2		1	1						1		2				
6	3			1	2	4	2	8	3	6	2	7		5		10	2	13	4	4	
68	119	276	141	163	243	356	234	214	404	268	161	246		259	161	138	128	262	227	335	157
10	10	10	5	9	9†	8	7	10	6	10	10	3		7	7	10	5	10	10	10	6
L		D		L		D		D		L		D		D		W		L		W	
5		5		5		7		5		6		—		5		20		6		21	

6 – D.A. Graveney
3 – M.W. Pooley and D.V. Lawrence
2 – I.P. Butcher and A.J. Brassington (ct 1/st 1)

1 – D.J. Thomas, V.S. Greene, K.B.K. Ibadulla and sub
† C.W.J. Athey absent hurt

feat in 1906 that a player has taken 10 wickets and scored a century in each innings of a match. The only other cricketer to accomplish the feat was Bosanquet in 1905. Stephenson's second century also took him past a thousand runs for the season so that he completed the 'double'. No man was more deserving of the title of 'Britannic Assurance Championship Player of the Year'.

Whatever had happened at Test level, some good cricket was played by the counties, and certainly there is more joy, humour and entertainment here than one sees elsewhere. Cricket's cry should be 'Support Your Local County', for that is the place to start.

Refuge Assurance Cup Final
WORCESTERSHIRE v. LANCASHIRE

The last day of the season was celebrated by a fine Sunday, a full house at Edgbaston and the first final of the Refuge Assurance Cup. Neale won the toss and asked Lancashire to bat first. He was immediately rewarded. Weston bowled Mendis with the second legitimate ball of the match, and Hayhurst was stumped off the same bowler so that Lancashire were 4 for 2 in the third over. Without ever being

Gloucestershire CCC
First-Class Matches, 1988

BOWLING	D.V. Lawrence	T.M. Alderman	P. Bainbridge	K.M. Curran	D.A. Graveney	M.W. Alleyne	J.W. Lloyds	D.J. Thomas	V.S. Greene
v. Glamorgan (Bristol) 21–5 April	31–4–94–2 27–6–76–1	31–9–70–4 23–7–56–1	16–3–59–0	12–2–49–0 14–1–45–1	23–10–44–1 7–2–16–0	8–1–28–1 18–7–48–4	7–1–20–1 14–3–41–0		
v. Sussex (Bristol) 28 April–2 May	20–5–55–0 8–2–29–1	31–9–75–5 10–1–23–1	14–3–49–0 6–0–16–0	17–2–50–2 7–2–19–0	26–7–50–3 8–5–6–2	2–0–9–0 6–2–17–0	12–4–22–0 4–3–3–0		
v. Northamptonshire (Northampton) 5–9 May	16–3–54–3 18–2–59–1	24–7–52–4 22–6–52–4	15–1–40–1 10–3–27–0		15–6–22–1 22–11–32–3		2–1–6–0	11–3–27–1 13.4–2–39–2	
v. Nottinghamshire (Trent Bridge) 18–20 May	14–2–36–4 17.5–1–73–5	10–4–26–2 22–6–48–2	2–0–13–0 9–2–23–0	5.1–1–17–2 19–6–36–2	17–5–37–1	4–1–12–0			
v. West Indians (Bristol) 25–7 May	18–0–87–1 13–0–61–3		14–1–61–0 13–1–47–0		2.3–2–0–1		2–1–6–1 9–1–22–2	14–3–46–2 10–0–57–2	22–8–53–5 12–5–37–1
v. Glamorgan (Swansea) 28–31 May									
v. Oxford University (Oxford) 1–3 June			12.2–2–33–5		25–9–35–3		14–3–33–1	5–1–5–0	
v. Derbyshire (Derby) 11–14 June	18–2–80–2 16–4–38–1	19–2–81–2 13–2–45–3	12–3–37–0	26.1–3–103–6 14.3–2–59–6	7–3–25–0 11–2–23–0		2–0–11–0		
v. Essex (Ilford) 15–17 June	19–6–58–1 17.5–4–85–7	19–6–41–6 20–2–84–3	2–0–9–0	16–4–28–3 10–0–68–0	4–0–7–0		10–0–43–0		
v. Lancashire (Old Trafford) 18–21 June	16–5–50–2 20–4–54–5		13–2–49–1 20–4–59–0		26–4–57–1 18–5–51–1	13–0–44–1 5–0–30–0	19–4–66–1 13–0–48–1		18–3–49–0
v. Leicestershire (Gloucester) 25–8 June	24–4–67–3 14–3–34–2	17.2–6–35–1 15–3–40–1	10–3–21–0 20–8–41–0	25–8–55–4 17.2–4–54–7					
v. Hampshire (Gloucester) 29 June–1 July	9–2–45–3 14.4–1–47–2	12–4–34–0 8–2–18–1	10–2–21–0 1–0–6–0	8–3–26–0 11–2–50–2			30–5–91–1 10–0–58–0		
v. Worcestershire (Worcester) 2–5 July	13–2–59–0	11–2–38–2		5–3–6–2	20–2–70–2		13.3–0–56–0		
v. Northamptonshire (Bristol) 13–15 July	12–2–76–0	16–2–68–1	15–2–79–0	23–3–80–2	16–6–38–2				
v. Somerset (Bristol) 16–19 July	11.1–3–30–2 6–1–38–0	23–4–75–4 9–1–19–0	11–3–16–1	17–2–64–3 3.1–1–12–1	6–4–2–0 7–2–18–1				
v. Sussex (Hove) 20–2 July	13–2–38–4 11–1–48–3	13.2–3–36–0	8.4–2–31–0 11–1–49–2	7–0–32–0 10.4–1–48–1	8–4–15–2 11–3–23–1				
v. Surrey (Cheltenham) 30 July–2 Aug.	21–3–85–2 14.5–0–47–7	20–1–81–4 8–1–42–2	12–2–40–0	23.2–6–62–4 6–1–24–1	12–1–37–0				
v. Warwickshire (Cheltenham) 3–5 August	14–1–56–1 21–3–71–4	18–2–62–3 7.5–2–20–1	4–0–29–0	20–5–82–2 10–1–47–1	17.3–5–50–1 16–6–36–1				
v. Yorkshire (Cheltenham) 6–9 August	13–3–43–1 6–0–17–0	18–5–52–3 12–3–37–3	13–2–58–1	7–0–50–0 6–2–10–0	25.4–6–71–1 6–2–11–0	5–0–18–0			
v. Middlesex (Lord's) 13–16 August	14–0–72–2 8–2–30–0	16–3–46–1 7–2–18–1	1–0–3–0	16–2–65–3 8–2–33–0	14–2–63–2 11.3–0–65–0				
v. Sri Lankans (Bristol) 17–19 August					19–5–37–0 4–0–13–0	7–2–21–0			12–2–29–2 5–1–12–0
v. Kent (Bristol) 20–3 August	13–2–54–1 4–1–7–0	23–6–72–0	15–1–85–3	10–3–19–0 3–1–10–0	26.1–8–65–2				
v. Hampshire (Southampton) 30 Aug.–2 Sept.		12–3–27–0 16.1–2–38–1	9–2–20–2 10–5–10–1	17–8–24–4 20–5–58–6	9.1–1–22–3 10–4–15–0				
v. Worcestershire (Bristol) 9–12 September	22–2–75–0 12–2–45–2	23–5–66–1 11–1–31–0	9–4–14–0		57.3–14–127–8 30.2–11–38–6		25–5–89–1 32–5–84–2		
v. Somerset (Taunton) 14–17 September	20–4–75–3 11–0–37–0	12–4–44–0 27.2–7–59–8	4–0–9–0		46–16–66–3 29–6–66–1		12–4–30–1 9–2–28–1		
	611.2–94– 2185–81 *av.* 26.97	600–135– 1711–75 *av.* 22.81	324–62– 1054–17 *av.* 62.00	414.2–86– 1385–65 *av.* 21.30	613.2–179– 1353–53 *av.* 22.52	68–13– 227–6 *av.* 37.83	239.3–42– 757–13 *av.* 58.23	53.4–9– 174–7 *av.* 24.85	69–19– 180–8 *av.* 22.50

a P.V. Simmons retired hurt, absent hurt   b J.D. Nuttall absent hurt

M.W. Pooley	K.B.S. Jarvis	C.W.J. Athey	P.W. Romaines	M.J.C. Ball	K.B.K. Ibadulla	R.C. Russell	Byes	Leg-byes	Wides	No-balls	Total	Wkts
							1	7		14	372	9
							5	9	1	9	296	8
							4	10		18	324	10
								3		10	116	4
							5		1	9	206	10
								7		4	216	10
								5	2	1	97	10
								5	2	4	234	10
								4	1	17	257	9
							4	5		10	233	9a
												Ab.
1–0–3–0	5–2–6–0							2		8	117	9b
							1	2	5	7	329	10
							4	2	1	7	182	10
								11		7	188	10
								3		4	249	10
		1–0–3–0	0.1–0–6–0				4	10	1	5	329	6
							2	4		8	257	7
								11	7	6	189	10
							1	7		7	177	10
	18–1–72–0	3–0–15–0					1	10		4	315	4
	4–0–32–1						6	9		6	226	6
											0	0
							3	1		5	233	6
		1–0–2–0					1	5	1	8	349	5
											0	0
							1	7		5	195	10
							4	2		8	93	2
							4	5	1	1	161	6
								6		3	174	7
								7		1	312	10
							2		1	4	115	10
7–1–22–0							4	2		7	307	7
6–1–9–1							4	4		3	191	8
19–7–56–2							8	11	1	1	367	8
9–1–26–0							1	2		2	104	4
3–0–4–0								8		5	261	8
3–1–8–0							4	11		3	169	1
18–5–52–2	15–2–48–0			29–5–88–1				10	1	4	285	6
5–0–18–0	5–2–7–0				8–0–49–0	1–0–12–0		1			112	0
18–2–54–2					8–3–30–0			7	1	7	301	5
15.4–2–80–4							2			1	184	7
8–4–10–1							5	5	2	2	113	10
12–5–26–1				5–3–2–1				1		10	150	10
5–1–16–0							3	14		5	404	10
								1	3	2	199	10
					12.2–2–43–3		5	5		8	277	10
					6–1–21–0			3		4	214	10
129.4–30–	47–7–	5–0–	0.1–0–	34–8–	34.2–6–	1–0–						
384–13	165–1	20–0	6–0	90–2	143–3	12–0						
av. 29.53	av. 165.00	—	—	av. 45.00	av. 47.66	—						

Hampshire CCC
First-Class Matches, 1988

BATTING

	v. Surrey (Southampton) 21–5 April	v. Kent (Canterbury) 28 April–2 May	v. Oxford University (Oxford) 5–7 May	v. Glamorgan (Bournemouth) 18–20 May	v. Yorkshire (Middlesbrough) 28–31 May	v. Somerset (Southampton) 1–3 June	v. Lancashire (Liverpool) 4–7 June	v. Worcestershire (Worcester) 11–14 June	v. Middlesex (Basingstoke) 15–17 June	v. Nottinghamshire (Southampton) 18–21 June	v. Gloucestershire (Gloucester) 29 June–1 July	v. Surrey (Guildford) 13–15 July	v. Warwickshire (Edgbaston) 16–19 July	v. Essex (Portsmouth) 20–2 July
V.P. Terry	4 49	1 2		13 8	2 8	5 106	74 0	14 24	0 6	23 1*	4 10	4 126*	26 5	6 —
C.L. Smith	3 9	30 62		0 29	5 88*	11 47	24 124*	4 87	8 19	117 16	9 94	16 44	21 46	27 103*
M.C.J. Nicholas	18 0	18 74	40 19	45 132*	8 7	47 0	31 10	23 13	39 48	2 5	— 19	57* 97	3 0	66 102*
R.A. Smith	21 8	23 9*	118 54*	20 87*	36 1	7 13	29 18	45 4	33 18	20 8	141* 2	3 17*	14 32	
R.J. Maru	4 9	0 —	— 0	37 —	0 —	13 —	— 0		0 27	5 —	74 3*		2 0	5 —
D.R. Turner	7 1	31 6*	76 7*	38 —	30 20	0 100*	11 13	3 15	0 150*	75 7	64* 40	30 —	1 22	6 —
K.D. James	0 2	26 —	42 15								15 0			
R.J. Parks	12* 14	33 —	23 5		13 18*	0 —	11 —	22 13		7 0	24 0*		3 2	18 —
S.T. Jefferies	8 60	4 —		39 —	14 —	39 —	39* 19*	53 24			— 29*		13 14	6 —
T.M. Tremlett	3 38												15 4*	28 —
C.A. Connor	0 0*	0 —		0 —	5 —	22* —	— —	1 0	5 1	18 —	8 —	— —	7* 0	24 —
S.J.W. Andrew		0* —		4* —	1* —	6 —	— —	2 4*	12* 4*	8* —				
R.J. Scott			1 11											0 0
J.R. Ayling			41 3	0 —		0 66*	88* —	13 1	0 12	12 4	— 8	7* —	7 26	
N.G. Cowley			16* 13		10 —			10* —		55 —				
A.D. Mullally			— —											
P.J. Bakker														0* —
T.C. Middleton														
A.N. Aymes														
Byes		2		2 1	1	1	2 1	6	4 5	6 3	1 6			4 5
Leg-byes	4 1	1 5	3 1	15	2 2	5 2	11	10 7	6 16	15 1	10 9	2 5	3 2	5 1
Wides	3 1	1 1		2 2	4 4	1	1	1	6	3 6		4 6	2 1	1
No-balls	4 6		1	10 2	2 2			3 6	7 6	5		6 10	5 3	5 3
Total	91 198	170 160	370 130	217 259	130 149	156 336	320 186	203 210	136 312	389 45	315 226	125 299	122 157	210 214
Wickets	10 10	10 3	7 7	10 2	10 4	10 4	6 5	10 9†	10 9	10 5	4 6	4 2	10 10	10 1
Result	L	W	D	D	D	D	L	L	D	D	D	W	L	D
Points	4	21	—	6	4	4	4	3	4	7	8	16	1	5

Fielding Figures

73 – R.J. Parks (ct 63/st 10)	18 – M.C.J. Nicholas	10 – R.J. Scott
33 – V.P. Terry	15 – R.A. Smith	5 – D.R. Turner and J.R. Ayling
31 – R.J. Maru	13 – C.L. Smith	4 – S.T. Jefferies

commanding, Fowler and Fairbrother repaired the damage. They added 65, and Fowler's 26 occupied 62 balls, but their caution paved the way for the glorious onslaught that was to come. Jesty, who should have been run out for one, but who batted quite beautifully, and Watkinson put on 81 in 9 overs of exhilarating batting. The Worcestershire bowling erred, and the fielding wilted. A score of around 150 had once looked a dream; the total of 201 looked unbeatable. So it proved.

O'Shaughnessy was well caught by Mendis, and Hick once again failed in a final, bowled by Watkinson as he attempted to cut a ball too close to him after a frustratingly barren period. Curtis was out as he tried to force the pace, the first of five catches to the wicket-keeper, but Leatherdale breathed hope until beaten on the back foot by the wily Simmons. Neale played some fine shots on the off, but was caught by Watkinson at deep mid-wicket as he

Keith Medlycott – a career-best bowling performance as Surrey beat Sussex. (Simon Bruty/Allsport)

v. Derbyshire (Portsmouth) 23–6 July		v. Sussex (Eastbourne) 3–5 August		v. Leicestershire (Leicester) 6–9 August		v. Northamptonshire (Bournemouth) 13–16 August		v. Kent (Bournemouth) 17–19 August		v. Sri Lankans (Southampton) 20–2 August		v. Somerset (Taunton) 25–9 August		v. Gloucestershire (Southampton) 30 Aug.–2 Sept.		v. Glamorgan (Cardiff) 9–12 September		v. Sussex (Southampton) 14–17 September		M	Inns	Nos	Runs	HS	Av
20	—	53	50*	0	39	82	24	20	4	190	—	17	7	18	14	21	66	25	11	23	43	3	1182	190	29.55
53	—	5	27	28	68	59	6	5	0			2	0	0	46	0	34	59	1	22	43	3	1436	124*	35.90
4	—	20	17	3	6	5	15	13	15	57	—	35	10	10	0	21	47	31	30	24	45	3	1262	132*	30.04
				34*	1*	11*	1	34	16	104*	23*					0	65	41	119	18	36	7	1211	141*	41.75
								0	5			13	19*	6	2	3	28	0	—	23	29	5	302	74	12.58
62	—	45	0	30	32	27	51	2	14			93	13	1	17	40*	24			22	40	6	1204	150*	35.41
		17*	12	77	10	13	1	9	3	—	25	2	2	11	13	0	1	14	22*	12	22	2	320	77	16.00
0	—		11*	38*	4	4	31*	9	3			38	11	12	0	0	12	22*	5*	23	35	8	420	38*	15.55
45*	—	11*	22	15	8															14	19	5	462	60	33.00
6*	—					6	2	2	7											7	10	2	111	38	13.87
												9	21	7	0	1	5*	1	—	18	22	4	135	24	7.50
																				11	9	7	41	12*	20.50
0	—	5	58	2	41					—	107*	40	5	28	13			7	56	9	16	1	374	107*	24.93
48	—	86	2	5	9	5	10	23	11			49	24	6	21	17	54*	9	44	19	33	4	711	88*	24.51
								21	43*											6	7	3	168	55	42.00
																				1					—
—	—		5*	1	0*			0*	16			0*	8*	0*	13*	7	—			10	11	8	50	16	16.66
												5	23							1	2	—	28	23	14.00
																				1					—

2		1		2		1			9		4	1	5	5		1		6	5
3		6	6	9	5	5	4	4	3	6		11	6	5	1	5	19	4	5
2		2		3		2		1	4	1		1		2					4
6		2	2	14	5	6	3	5		5	3	11	3	2	10	10	11	3	
251	0	253	207	260	233	239	164	139	150	368	185	321	135	113	150	126	370	222	298
7	0	6	7	8	9	10	9	10	10	3	2	10	9	10	10	10	8	9‡	6
D		D		D		D		L		D		D		L		W		W	
3		7		7		6		4		—		7		4		19		22	

3 – T.M. Tremlett, A.N. Aymes and K.D. James
2 – C.A. Connor and sub
1 – N.G. Cowley, P.J. Bakker, S.J.W. Andrew and A.D. Mullally

† N.G. Cowley absent hurt
‡ P.J. Bakker absent hurt

A magnificent bowling performance rewarded by dismissal – David Graveney, captain of Gloucestershire. (Steve Lindsell)

attempted a massive hit. Rhodes promised briefly, but Hayhurst, bowling wide outside the off stump, claimed him and had Radford caught behind first ball so that Worcestershire had to be content with two trophies and Lancashire recalled past glories with a resounding win.

Mike Watkinson, who hit ferociously, bowled Hick and caught Neale, was named Man of the Match, but if one has delight for any man in particular it is for Trevor Jesty. Fortune has not treated him well. Three years ago at Surrey, he played one of the finest innings one has seen in the semi-final of the NatWest Bank Trophy against Lancashire, yet his side was narrowly beaten and his disappointment at again failing to reach a final after so many years of endeavour was intense. Perhaps, the Refuge Assurance Cup triumph and his part in it has been some recompense.

Hampshire CCC
First-Class Matches, 1988

BOWLING	S.T. Jefferies	C.A. Connor	T.M. Tremlett	K.D. James	R.J. Maru	R.A. Smith	S.J.W. Andrew	M.C.J. Nicholas	A.D. Mullally
v. Surrey (Southampton) 21–5 April	21.6–6–64–3 3–0–23–0	27–7–71–4 3–0–14–0	13–2–41–2	16–4–35–1	13–4–26–0	0.1–0–4–0			
v. Kent (Canterbury) 28 April–2 May	20.5–1–80–4 13–4–29–0	14–3–46–0 18–8–23–3		17–6–31–1 11.5–2–22–4	13–7–17–0 4–3–1–0		19–6–52–4 10–3–21–3	2–1–1–0	
v. Oxford University (Oxford) 5–7 May				10–6–15–3 13–6–15–1	8–6–4–0 37–15–72–2		16.2–4–36–5 19–4–48–0	1–0–1–0	12–1–44–0 8–4–8–0
v. Glamorgan (Bournemouth) 18–20 May	14.2–3–59–2 4–0–22–0	32–9–67–3 9.5–1–36–1			14–3–47–0 15–5–70–4		17–3–58–2		
v. Yorkshire (Middlesbrough) 28–31 May	13–5–30–0	21–2–63–2			20–7–45–2		19–5–46–3		
v. Somerset (Southampton) 1–3 June	33–8–93–2	34–3–89–4			11–1–23–0		18–5–44–1		
v. Lancashire (Liverpool) 4–7 June	19–6–34–1 11–0–54–1	11–1–49–1 11.4–0–60–2			34.1–13–79–2 21–3–106–3		14–1–52–1 4–1–16–0		
v. Worcestershire (Worcester) 11–14 June	15–0–59–0	19–5–66–3				1–0–9–0	26.3–8–78–2	6–1–23–0	
v. Middlesex (Basingstoke) 15–17 June		21.5–4–61–4 14–4–36–1		4–0–14–0 6–1–21–0	4–1–5–0 21–8–57–2	1–0–14–0	18–10–24–2 15–6–25–1		
v. Nottinghamshire (Southampton) 18–21 June		22–5–70–5 17–4–48–1			12–3–27–0 43–10–132–4		18–2–54–3 20–3–53–2	1–0–2–0	
v. Gloucestershire (Gloucester) 29 June–1 July	20–2–76–1 28–3–97–8	19–4–76–1 9.3–1–26–2			12.4–2–31–1 31–9–76–0		14–5–50–2 4–2–25–0		
v. Surrey (Guildford) 13–15 July	5–0–38–0 8–0–37–2	19–2–57–1 6–0–20–0			24–3–85–1 8.4–1–33–0		15–0–77–0 2–0–6–0		
v. Warwickshire (Edgbaston) 16–19 July	17–1–60–0	18–1–72–0	14–2–44–0		12–3–44–2			5–0–25–0	
v. Essex (Portsmouth) 20–2 July	24.4–4–59–0 10–2–37–2	7.2–1–20–1	12.3–3–44–1 6–1–17–0		11–7–5–0 4–1–11–0				
v. Derbyshire (Portsmouth) 23–6 July	3–0–12–0 5.4–0–26–0		6–4–13–0 4–0–15–0		20–2–69–5				
v. Sussex (Eastbourne) 3–5 August	30–4–79–3 6–0–22–0			11–4–36–0 22–4–67–2	14–8–22–1 16–2–46–1			1–0–5–0	
v. Leicestershire (Leicester) 6–9 August	30.3–3–126–5			12–4–25–0	31–7–69–3 23–5–49–0			18–1–58–1	
v. Northamptonshire (Bournemouth) 13–16 August		15–5–24–2 7–2–19–4		19–3–46–1 3–1–7–0	22–8–38–2 20.4–9–35–0	3–1–7–0			
v. Kent (Bournemouth) 17–19 August			17–8–32–2 11–2–32–2		20–4–57–1 2–0–9–0				
v. Sri Lankans (Southampton) 20–2 August		18.4–3–42–2 6–3–4–0	17–4–43–1 3–2–2–0	21–3–80–5 4–2–14–0	22–8–46–2 12–1–52–1	1–0–1–0			
v. Somerset (Taunton) 25–9 August		15–4–52–1 9–2–33–1		24–7–46–3 11–3–22–0	10–3–16–2 10.5–0–42–0				
v. Gloucestershire (Southampton) 30 Aug.–2 Sept.		13–1–43–4 9.4–0–40–1		12–3–25–5 8–0–24–0	5–1–10–0 5–0–6–0				
v. Glamorgan (Cardiff) 9–12 September		18–4–56–3 23–7–61–4		23–5–54–3 15–3–58–1	29–9–66–3 15.3–4–48–2				
v. Sussex (Southampton) 14–17 September		16–2–48–0 13–0–48–0		25–4–70–4 11–1–36–1	25.3–8–49–3 24–7–67–1				
	355.1–52– 1216–34 av. 35.76	495.3–91– 1497–55 av. 27.21	125.3–35– 326–14 av. 23.28	298.5–72– 763–35 av. 21.80	701–201– 1792–50 av. 35.84	6.1–1– 35–0 —	268.5–68– 765–31 av. 24.67	34–3– 115–1 av. 115.00	20–5– 52–0 —

J.R. Ayling	N.G. Cowley	C.L. Smith	D.R. Turner	P.J. Bakker	R.J. Scott	T.C. Middleton	Byes	Leg-byes	Wides	No-balls	Total	Wkts
							1	8		2	246	10
								6			47	1
								3		10	230	10
							2	1	1	6	99	10
13–8–14–2	2–2–0–0						1	4		7	118	10
10–5–19–0	31–12–39–3							4	1		206	6
20–6–38–3							5	2	5		276	10
9–1–45–3								4		3	177	8
	16.5–3–49–3							6		12	239	10
24.4–8–46–3							4	9	2	5	308	10
8–2–27–0		1–0–1–0					2	7	2	8	251	5
		7–0–20–0					1	2	1	4	259	6
25–1–68–1	30–5–86–1						4	13	2	1	397	7
			0.2–0–8–0								17	0
12–1–39–3		1–0–2–0						4		10	149	10
7–1–22–0		2–0–9–0						2	1	6	186	4
19–5–39–1	1.1–1–0–1							7	1	4	197	10
16–5–24–2	27.1–7–67–1	3–0–16–0					4	13		10	359	10
23–5–57–4							6	11	2	9	307	9
12–4–17–0								7	1	1	248	10
14–3–34–0								10		8	301	2
8–2–24–1								2		5	122	3
7–2–27–1							5	23		6	300	3
				20–5–54–5	3–1–5–0		8	8		2	203	7
				13–1–42–1				10	1		117	3
3.3–1–13–1				5–2–7–0					1	1	45	1
8–0–38–0				14–6–21–2				13		1	182	7
22.3–4–57–4				26–8–70–2			5	10	1	8	279	10
9–2–25–0				16–3–43–2	2.3–0–13–0			4	1	8	225	5
14–4–34–0				13–5–35–1			4	5		6	298	10
8–1–26–1		13–0–50–0		12–2–21–2				8			212	4
16.2–5–35–2				27–7–50–3			8	4		4	205	10
5–2–12–3		3–1–4–0		10–6–18–0			5	1			108	7
21.3–2–62–4	21–6–44–2			19–7–40–1				5			240	10
8–1–30–1				10.5–0–64–1				5			140	4
	12–4–29–0				6–1–14–0		12	14	1	13	280	10
	16–7–23–0					1–0–9–0		1		1	106	1
16–4–32–2				21.3–4–37–2	4–1–8–0			11		2	202	10
7–0–20–1				8–2–19–0			4	9		3	149	3
9–1–22–1				14–5–37–0				1		10	138	10
11–0–35–1				11–5–15–3				8	2	2	128	5
17–6–32–0				17–5–27–0			12	12		3	259	10
7–2–25–0				20–8–41–3				1		4	234	10
16.4–3–48–1				16.2–4–29–2	4–0–26–0		3	5		1	278	10
5–0–12–1		19–0–69–5					3	5			240	10
432.1–97– 1098–47 av. 23.36	157.1–47– 337–11 av. 30.63	49–1– 171–5 av. 34.20	0.2–0– 8–0 —	293.4–85– 670–30 av. 22.33	19.3–3– 66–0 —	1–0– 9–0 —						

Kent CCC
First-Class Matches, 1988

BATTING

BATTING	v. Essex (Chelmsford) 21–5 April		v. Hampshire (Canterbury) 28 April–2 May		v. Leicestershire (Leicester) 5–9 May		v. Oxford University (Oxford) 18–20 May		v. Yorkshire (Canterbury) 21–4 May		v. Nottinghamshire (Dartford) 1–3 June		v. Glamorgan (Cardiff) 4–7 June		v. Middlesex (Tunbridge Wells) 11–14 June		v. Lancashire (Tunbridge Wells) 15–17 June		v. Warwickshire (Edgbaston) 18–21 June		v. West Indians (Canterbury) 25–7 June		v. Essex (Canterbury) 29 June–1 July		v. Sussex (Hastings) 2–5 July		v. Surrey (Guildford) 16–19 July	
M.R. Benson	110	13	8	18	5	1			—	5*	52	16	54	5	10	110	48	38	37		—				0	54	24	66
N.R. Taylor	94	24	27	0	67*	2	—	10*	13	18	2	5	112*	6	0	52	25	17	6				77		21	5	7	114
S.G. Hinks	35	10	34	7	1	5	138	—	66	34	7	8	72	17	4	4	16	24	27		1	14	0					
C.J. Tavare	13	0			4	13	138*	—	18	21	42	4	—	129*	2	15	63	4	103				0		95		34	0
C.S. Cowdrey	48	54	48	12	0	16	124*	—	1	2	0	35*	—	49	16	7*	37	18*	78				43*		8	9	4	0
G.R. Cowdrey	35	145	0	10	0	—	4	18					—	6	4	—	6	20*	4		9	9	13		21	5	28	26
S.A. Marsh	7	120	9	0	15	26	—	100*	13	4	49	14	—	19*	23	—	5	—	4				0		21	5	1	11
C. Penn	25*	1			2	19*	—	29	0	0*	40	0*			15*	—	8	—	2				1		24*	4*	31*	2*
R.P. Davis	10*	1	16	23	2	10	—	—	2	—	0	—			0	—	4	—	2*		10*	2*	2		4	—	5*	—
H.L. Alleyne	—	0*	9	0	7	0															2	6						
A.P. Igglesden	—	3																										
T.R. Ward			11	2																	8	9	70		27	10	72	32
D.J.M. Kelleher			43*	0																	13	51			20	—		
M.D. Harman			12	17*					1	—			—	6			0*	—			7	2						
R.M. Ellison					6	27	—	—	4*	11	50*	3	—	—	17	—			5				0		20	8*	12	2*
R.F. Pienaar							127	—	144	0	53	14	—	34	16	58*	19	21	19		0	31	20		37	9	88	5
V.J. Wells																					0	6						
D.J. Sabine																					7	1						
P. Farbrace																					6	9						
Byes	2	3		2	1		3	6		4	5		4		3			6			11	4	1		1		1	16
Leg-byes	15	10	3	1	1	3	5	3	4	5	9	5	6	6		6	13	8	16		7	6	4		6	2	11	3
Wides	1			1	6	1		1	6								2		9						3			1
No-balls	5		10	6	4	5		1	2		3	1	4			3	6	4	9		1				1		6	10
Total	400	384	230	99	121	128	539	168	274	104	312	111	252	271	110	255	252	154	327		81	151	231		288	106	324	288
Wickets	7	10	10	10	10	9†	3	2	9‡	7	9	8	2	6	10	4	10	5	10		10	10	10		10	6	9	8
Result	L		L		L		D		W		W		W		W		W		W		L		D		W		D	
Points	4		6		3		—		22		23		21		20		23		23				4		23		7	

Fielding Figures

61 – S.A. Marsh (ct 56/st 5)	17 – N.R. Taylor	10 – G.R. Cowdrey and T.R. Ward
33 – C.S. Cowdrey	13 – M.R. Benson	8 – M.D. Harman
28 – C.J. Tavare	12 – S.G. Hinks and R.P. Davis	7 – C. Penn and R.M. Ellison

First-Class Averages

BATTING

	M	Inns	NOs	Runs	HS	Av	100s	50s		M	Inns	NOs	Runs	HS	Av	100s	50s
G.A. Hick	24	37	2	2713	405*	77.51	10	5	M.D. Moxon	21	39	3	1485	191	41.25	3	8
S.R. Waugh	15	24	6	1314	161	73.00	6	4	R.A. Smith	21	42	8	1356	141*	39.88	4	4
C.W.J. Athey	13	22	6	1064	168*	66.50	2	6	P.A. Neale	21	31	5	1036	167	39.84	4	2
G.A. Gooch	21	37	1	2324	275	64.55	6	15	M.A. Lynch	21	29	4	996	103*	39.84	2	4
M.D. Crowe	5	9	1	487	136*	60.87	2	2	G.P. Thorpe	3	6	2	158	100*	39.50	1	
A.R. Border	20	32	8	1393	169*	58.04	6	4	T.S. Curtis	22	38	4	1337	131	39.32	2	7
K.J. Barnett	19	30	2	1623	239*	57.96	5	8	D.W. Randall	21	37	4	1285	237	38.96	2	9
A.J. Lamb	16	27	5	1163	155	52.86	5	5	P.W.G. Parker	21	40	5	1359	124	38.82	5	5
M.A. Atherton	16	27	4	1121	152*	48.73	4	3	P.J. Prichard	24	39	8	1202	97	38.77		9
N. Hussain	9	13	3	486	165*	48.60	1	2	D.I. Gower	22	38	4	1318	172	38.76	2	5
D.M. Smith	11	18	5	630	157*	48.46	2	1	R.T. Robinson	21	35	4	1194	134*	38.51	4	4
M.W. Gatting	20	33	2	1469	210	47.38	3	9	M. Asif Din	23	41	4	1425	158*	38.51	2	8
R.J. Finney	4	5	2	142	52*	47.33		1	A.A. Metcalfe	22	40	5	1320	216*	37.71	2	8
M.R. Ramprakash	9	13	4	421	68*	46.77		3	J.E. Morris	23	37	5	1204	175	37.62	2	6
P.D. Bowler	24	42	5	1725	159*	46.62	4	9	K.M. Curran	19	34	7	1005	142	37.22	2	2
W.N. Slack	19	32	5	1228	163*	45.48	3	6	R.F. Pienaar	21	35	2	1228	144	37.21	3	7
M.E. Waugh	3	4		178	86	44.50		1	T.A. Lloyd	24	43	3	1448	160*	36.20	4	3
G.S. Clinton	18	29	5	1054	158	43.91	4	4	R.J. Bailey	24	42	2	1448	127*	36.20	3	8
R.C. Ontong	17	25	8	734	120*	43.17	1	4	P. Bainbridge	23	38	1	1334	169	36.05	4	6
J.G. Wright	11	20	1	815	154*	42.89	1	5	J.J. Whitaker	23	39	5	1223	145	35.97	3	5
C.J. Tavare	22	36	2	1429	138*	42.02	4	5	C.L. Smith	22	43	3	1436	124*	35.90	3	8
N.G. Cowley	6	7	3	168	55	42.00		1	G.D. Mendis	24	42	4	1364	151*	35.89	2	8
C.J. Richards	20	25	4	874	102*	41.61	1	6	P.D. Atkins	6	11	1	357	114	35.70	1	1
M.P. Maynard	23	42	6	1485	126	41.25	3	11	G.C. Holmes	20	32	4	999	117	35.67	4	4

	v. Northamptonshire (Northampton) 20–2 July		v. Worcestershire (Folkestone) 23–6 July		v. Somerset (Canterbury) 30 July–2 Aug.		v. Leicestershire (Canterbury) 3–5 August		v. Derbyshire (Chesterfield) 13–16 August		v. Hampshire (Bournemouth) 17–19 August		v. Gloucestershire (Bristol) 20–3 August		v. Sussex (Maidstone) 25–9 August		v. Middlesex (Lord's) 9–12 September		v. Surrey (Canterbury) 14–17 September		M	Inns	Nos	Runs	HS	Av
	65	30	28	—	6	12	44	15	30	—	19	33	70	58	30	0	81	25	7	—	21	37	1	1227	110	34.08
	0	17	40	—	3	18	13	22	5	—	29	15	41	8	10	0	20	23	92	—	21	37	3	925	114	27.20
									35	—			26*	44					92	—	16	27	1	764	138	29.38
	40	37	14	—	33	24	36	17	119	—	29	42	35	13	46	97	78	11	60	—	22	36	2	1429	138*	42.02
							8	0	108	—			3	37*	8*	2	37	5	9	—	20	34	7	838	124*	31.03
	35	49	7	—	12	65*	32	35*			11	0*	50	17	0	50	86	10	34	—	20	33	4	830	145	28.62
	5	38*	8	—	0	17	30*	—	39	—	50	—	5*	25*	0	28	21	1	0	—	23	35	6	713	120	24.58
	9*	10	16	—	18	11	1	7*	22*	—	10	—			16	34	30	30	19	—	20	31	12	436	40	22.94
	—	0*	5*	—	17*	0	0	—	—	—	—	—									19	21	8	115	23	8.84
																					4	7	1	24	9	4.00
									22*	—	13	—	—	—	—	—	1	5	17	1*	7	8	2	103	41	17.16
	23	59	1	—	17	1	0	12											8	—	10	17	—	362	72	21.29
	—	17	6	—																	5	7	1	150	43*	25.00
							4	—			4*						1*	12	14*	0*	12	13	6	80	17*	11.42
	2	13	14	—	0	14	19	1	18	—	20	—	—	—	33	0*	6	3	38*	—	20	27	6	346	50*	16.47
	74*	5	6	—	6	10	128	23	52	—	47	8	51	14	72	6	4	2	25	—	21	35	2	1228	144	37.21
																					1	2	—	6	6	3.00
																					1	2	—	8	7	4.00
																					1	2	—	15	9	7.50

	N'hants		Worcs		Som		Leics		Derbys		Hants		Glos		Sussex		Middx		Surrey	
	5				5		2	3					2				7		8	
	6	13	5		1	2	10	3	11		5	5	7		10	6	17	11	6	
			1			1					1		4	3					1	
	4		1			5	8	2	5				7	1			4	1	6	

	N'hants		Som	Leics		Derbys		Hants		Glos		Sussex		Middx		Surrey	
	68	288	152	121	185	327	140	466	240	140	301	184	233	247	412	129	354
	7	9	10	10	10	10	6	8	10	4	5	7	10	10	10	9	10
	W		D		L		D	D		W		D		L		D	W
	22		5		1		8	8		22		7		6		7	24

5 – R.F. Pienaar
4 – Subs
2 – P. Farbrace and D.J.M. Kelleher

1 – V.J. Wells, D.J. Sabine and A.P. Igglesden

† G.R. Cowdrey absent hurt
‡ M.R. Benson absent hurt

First-Class Averages continued

BATTING

	M	Inns	NOs	Runs	HS	Av	100s	50s		M	Inns	NOs	Runs	HS	Av	100s	50s
P. Johnson	24	42	3	1389	140	35.61	3	7	Wasim Akram	10	18	2	496	116*	31.00	1	3
D.R. Turner	22	40	6	1204	150*	35.41	2	6	A.J. Wright	24	42	1	1268	137	30.92	2	5
M.A. Crawley	4	7	2	177	98	35.40		1	I.D. Austin	6	9	2	216	64	30.85		2
J.D. Carr	24	43	6	1297	144	35.05	2	7	G. Fowler	21	38	1	1134	172	30.64	2	5
A.W. Stovold	21	39	2	1296	136	35.02	2	6	N.H. Fairbrother	23	41	4	1134	111	30.64	2	6
A.P. Wells	23	42	5	1286	120	34.75	1	9	R.O. Butcher	19	29	3	796	134	30.61	1	4
A.J. Stewart	22	32	3	1006	133	34.68	2	6	S.C. Goldsmith	24	39	4	1071	89	30.60		7
N.E. Briers	24	41	2	1335	125*	34.23	2	9	P.A. Cottey	13	23	3	605	92	30.25		5
M.R. Benson	21	37	1	1227	110	34.08	2	8	P. Carrick	23	34	7	815	81	30.18		2
R.J. Shastri	12	19	2	575	157	33.82	1	2	A.I. Kallicharran	9	15	1	418	117*	29.85	1	2
A.R. Butcher	23	40	2	1282	166	33.73	1	9	M.C.J. Nicholas	25	47	2	1301	132*	29.56	2	5
R.G. Williams	20	34	9	842	119	33.68	1	4	V.P. Terry	23	43	3	1182	190	29.55	3	5
D.J. Capel	21	36	5	1040	92	33.54		7	B.J.M. Maher	24	39	6	974	121*	29.51	1	5
A.J. Moles	18	31	2	968	115	33.37	1	5	R.J. Harden	6	11	1	295	78	29.50		3
P.J. Hartley	13	17	6	364	127*	33.09	1		S.G. Hinks	16	27	1	764	138	29.38	1	3
S.T. Jefferies	14	19	5	462	60	33.00		2	G. Cook	18	30	1	850	203	29.31	2	3
L. Potter	23	34	7	885	107	32.77	1	5	J.P. Stephenson	18	31	4	791	99	29.29		6
A. Needham	8	12	3	293	66*	32.55		2	J.E. Emburey	20	27	4	673	102	29.26	1	4
I.J. Gould	19	31	4	875	82*	32.40		6	F.D. Stephenson	22	35		1018	117	29.08	2	7
P.R. Downton	18	24	5	614	120	32.31	1	2	C.S. Cowdrey	21	36	7	843	124*	29.06	2	2
P.E. Robinson	24	40	3	1173	129*	31.70	1	8	J.D. Love	18	28	2	751	93*	28.88		6
D.M. Ward	25	36	6	942	126	31.40	1	8	T.E. Jesty	15	27	3	693	73	28.87		3
R.C. Russell	24	36	8	870	94	31.07		6	N.A. Felton	14	27	2	720	127	28.80	1	4
K.B.K. Ibadulla	4	7	3	124	77	31.00		1	R. Sharma	10	14	3	315	80	28.63		1

(continued on page 436)

Kent CCC
First-Class Matches, 1988

BOWLING	A.P. Igglesden	H.L. Alleyne	C. Penn	C.S. Cowdrey	R.P. Davis	G.R. Cowdrey	D.J.M. Kelleher	M.D. Harman	M.R. Benson
v. Essex (Chelmsford) 21–5 April	13–2–57–0	20–2–80–1 6–0–40–0	41–7–160–3	31–3–93–1 7–0–59–1	39.5–8–132–5 4.2–0–34–1	17–1–64–0 4–0–32–0			
v. Hampshire (Canterbury) 28 April–2 May		20–6–58–3 10–0–28–1		24.2–10–46–5 13–2–27–0	11–5–22–1 21–7–40–0	10–1–27–0 4–1–21–0	6–3–7–0	8–3–7–0 12–3–35–1	0.3–0–4–0
v. Leicestershire (Leicester) 5–9 May		18.3–5–54–5	23–7–66–0	23–7–56–1	14–4–23–0				
v. Oxford University (Oxford) 18–20 May			17–2–71–1	1–0–6–0	24–11–56–2			27–10–55–5	
v. Yorkshire (Canterbury) 21–4 May			20–7–55–2 24–6–66–6	14–5–30–0	16–3–23–2 9–4–11–1			19–6–37–2 4–2–7–0	
v. Nottinghamshire (Dartford) 1–3 June			10–4–23–3 9–1–41–0	7–3–9–2 12–6–15–0	14–8–12–4 56–23–106–2			1–0–1–0 29–6–72–1	
v. Glamorgan (Cardiff) 4–7 June				24–6–66–2 6–1–19–0	36–11–94–2 13–5–32–3	15–8–20–1		20–5–51–1 6–1–24–2	
v. Middlesex (Tunbridge Wells) 11–14 June			13–3–36–4 21–6–61–0	11.2–5–16–4 22–6–59–2	14–5–33–0				
v. Lancashire (Tunbridge Wells) 15–17 June			21–6–68–1 22.5–7–60–5	11.1–2–36–4 13–1–41–2	4–1–16–1				
v. Warwickshire (Edgbaston) 18–21 June			12.5–4–32–3 17.4–3–55–2	10–1–31–2 10–2–48–3		3–2–5–1			
v. West Indians (Canterbury) 25–7 June		20–4–62–2			9.4–3–20–2	5–1–14–1	22–5–41–2	1–0–1–0	
v. Essex (Canterbury) 29 June–1 July			27–9–69–1	16–6–45–0	17–4–55–3 10–4–19–1	5–1–20–0 5–0–31–0			
v. Sussex (Hastings) 2–5 July			12–3–29–5 24–2–106–1	13–4–29–2	24.4–10–41–2		13–6–24–4 11–4–18–1		
v. Surrey (Guildford) 16–19 July			5–0–40–0 11–0–41–4	12–1–66–1 2–0–9–0	26.3–7–96–1 19–8–36–2	4–2–14–1			
v. Northamptonshire (Northampton) 20–2 July			30.5–7–82–5 10–2–38–1		27–7–73–1 12–2–47–0	7.4–0–53–1	21–4–58–1 12–1–57–1		
v. Worcestershire (Folkestone) 23–6 July			25–5–74–3 5–1–9–0		14–3–32–0 14–5–29–0	2–0–5–0	3–0–6–0 6–0–18–0		
v. Somerset (Canterbury) 30 July–2 Aug.			30–3–107–2	29–11–81–1	38–7–114–0	10–1–54–0			
v. Leicestershire (Canterbury) 3–5 August			23–7–68–5 6–2–10–0		24–8–53–0 28–6–101–2			22–9–36–2 24.4–5–68–5	
v. Derbyshire (Chesterfield) 13–16 August	21–4–47–3 20–3–85–1		24.4–12–43–4 14–1–56–0	5–1–14–0 6–2–19–0	3–0–8–0 20–8–51–0				
v. Hampshire (Bournemouth) 17–19 August	20–7–40–5 13.2–2–51–5		14–2–40–2 8–2–27–0	7–0–22–1				4–1–9–1 6–2–9–0	
v. Gloucestershire (Bristol) 20–3 August	14–2–54–2 4–0–15–0			3–0–38–0		2–0–5–1		20–7–48–3 14–7–31–2	3–0–35–0
v. Sussex (Maidstone) 25–9 August	19–5–53–4 30.2–4–105–4		20.5–1–53–2 31–9–100–4	10–1–28–1 10–2–30–0				1–1–0–0 15–5–40–0	
v. Middlesex (Lord's) 9–12 September	22–3–86–3 33.5–9–117–2		15.3–2–52–1 30–5–70–7	6–2–15–1 11–1–19–1				14–6–27–0 19–7–35–0	
v. Surrey (Canterbury) 14–17 September	11–3–34–6 13–2–61–2		12–3–37–0 15–2–44–4	6–0–20–1 10–1–28–1					
	234.3–46– 805–37 av. 21.75	94.3–17– 322–12 av. 26.83	646.1–143– 1989–81 av. 24.55	385.5–92– 1120–39 av. 28.71	563–177– 1409–38 av. 37.07	93.4–18– 365–6 av. 60.83	94–23– 229–9 av. 25.44	266.4–86– 593–25 av. 23.72	3.3–0– 39–0 —

a D.A. Reeve and A.I. Kallicharran absent hurt   b I.A. Greig retired hurt, absent hurt

R.M. Ellison	R.F. Pienaar	D.J. Sabine	V.J. Wells	T.R. Ward	N.R. Taylor	S.G. Hinks	Byes	Leg-byes	Wides	No-balls	Total	Wkts
							6	24	1	7	616	10
							1	4			170	2
							2	1	1		170	10
								5	1	1	160	3
24–7–90–4								7	4	4	296	10
24–12–36–1	14–3–39–1						5	9	1	12	277	10
8–3–9–1	8–4–17–2							2	2		28	3
24–9–55–2	10–2–40–1						1	3	2		244	10
18.4–3–41–3								8		2	133	10
13–5–17–1								3			65	10
40.2–14–75–7	7–0–24–0						16	8		4	357	10
27–9–69–0	20–3–53–1						11	5		1	369	7
12–1–53–1	10–3–19–1						3	2	3	3	152	7
8–1–15–2	6–1–21–0							4	3	4	92	10
23–4–89–3	16.1–7–27–5							3	1	3	272	10
	21–6–77–4							2		1	199	10
	26–7–96–3							6	1	1	203	10
12–2–38–2								1	1	3	107	8
14–3–56–3	5–1–14–0							1	7		174	8[a]
	14–2–51–1	10–4–29–0	14–4–51–1					6	1	1	275	10
21–6–47–2	23.3–5–86–3						1	7	1	5	330	10
	7–2–23–0			4–1–4–0	2–1–1–0			4			82	1
9–5–15–1								3		5	71	10
31–10–78–2	17–4–38–2							12		10	322	10
20–5–47–3	10–2–31–1							9	1	9	303	7
10–3–37–0	10.4–2–41–0							4	3	4	168	7
19–5–59–2	13–3–48–0							9		5	329	10
9–4–23–0							2	6	1	4	226	3
29.2–6–99–6	8–4–16–1							11	2	2	238	10
4–2–13–2	5–0–6–0							1			81	2
8–3–14–0	18–1–75–1						3	4		1	452	4
17.4–4–47–2	13–2–32–0						4	7	1	1	247	10
2–0–14–0							3	7	1		203	7
18–4–89–2	19–3–57–1							4	3	2	262	10
13–3–53–0	18–7–40–3			6–3–6–1				7	1	10	317	6
14.3–5–32–2	7–4–14–0							4	1	5	139	10
9–0–29–4							9	3	4		150	10
19–5–66–0	17–5–41–1						3	4		5	259	7
16–5–46–5	2–1–1–0					2–0–28–0	3	2	1		161	7
16–5–34–1	10–4–13–2						2	1	4	6	184	10
8–0–28–0	25–8–45–2						1	10	1	4	359	10
17–5–49–4	17–2–56–0						4	1	2	5	290	10
27–7–80–0	5–1–16–0						8	6	1	11	351	10
8–4–16–1							2			13	109	9
10.1–2–39–2	2–0–5–0						2		1	10	179	9[b]
603.4–171– 1697–71 av. 23.90	404.2–99– 1162–36 av. 32.27	10–4– 29–0 —	14–4– 51–1 av. 51.00	4–1– 4–0 —	8–4– 7–1 av. 7.00	2–0– 28–0 —						

Lancashire CCC
First-Class Matches, 1988

BATTING

Each match cell shows the player's scores (1st innings / 2nd innings).

BATTING	v. Worcestershire (Old Trafford) 21–5 April	v. Warwickshire (Old Trafford) 28 April–2 May	v. Nottinghamshire (Trent Bridge) 5–9 May	v. Oxford University (Oxford) 21–4 May	v. Somerset (Old Trafford) 28–31 May	v. Worcestershire (Worcester) 1–3 June	v. Hampshire (Liverpool) 4–7 June	v. West Indians (Old Trafford) 8–10 June	v. Kent (Tunbridge Wells) 15–17 June	v. Gloucestershire (Old Trafford) 18–21 June	v. Glamorgan (Swansea) 25–8 June	v. Warwickshire (Nuneaton) 29 June–1 July	v. Northamptonshire (Northampton) 2–5 July	v. Leicestershire (Old Trafford) 13–15 July
G. Fowler	0 50	6 23	2 6		8 —				10 8	17 23	13 21	31 5	78 —	75 15
G.D. Mendis	3 19	10 41*	33 87	139 —	36 28	17 15	22 17	59 —	38 16	151 26*	13 65*	27 56*	34 —	25 51
T.E. Jesty	13 12	2 17*	4 26*	63 —	15 5	48 32	8 60	43 —	47 29		37 7	12 38	39 —	14 44*
N.H. Fairbrother	10 56	0 —	101 49		0 36	2 24	69 13	44* —	4 12	54 54	8 6	46 30	1 —	43 3*
M. Watkinson	6 68	19 —	22 6	30 —	52 3	4 21	6 73*	4	18 4	0 0	9 5	11 4*	12 —	85* —
D.P. Hughes	3 20	13 —	2 62	57* —	42 4	1 18	— 17		17 4	22 55	7 14	23* —	45* —	9 —
W.K. Hegg	8 0	76 —	11 8	42 —	10 30*	5 6	1* —	19 —	25 12	— 27*	6 0	13 —	3 —	0 —
P.J.W. Allott	7 1	15 —	4 25		18 13	14 19	— 31*		11 24		25 19	2 —	5* —	6 —
I. Folley	0* 30	3* —	5* 0	12* —	4* 0	— —	— —	— —	0* 4		4* 1		— —	— —
J. Simmons	32 57*	20 —	21 0*	27 —	23 0	1* 1*	— —		10 49*	— —	14 6	2 —	— —	27* —
C.D. Matthews	7 0	31 —												
Wasim Akram			7 0		116* 13	55 4	46* 7		16 33		10 0	22 —	5 —	
J. Abrahams				39 —			9 1	9 —						
A.N. Hayhurst				8 —		8 1	80 33	7 —		21* 5		1 1		4 —
D.J. Makinson				— —										
A.J. Murphy				— —				— —						
J.D. Fitton								11* —						
N.J. Speak										35 10				
I.D. Austin										9* 43				
M.A. Atherton														
G.D. Lloyd														
Byes	4 6	4	4 7	1		4	2 1			4 2	5	5	8	5 5
Leg-byes	4 4	8 1	2 11	4	2 3	8 4	7 2	16	2 6	10 4	6 12	12 6	6	4 1
Wides		3	4 1	2		1 2	4	5		1	1	4 4		1
No-balls	4 10	6	1 2	5	2 4	9 1	8 4	21	1 1	5 8	3 2	7 3	13	7
Total	101 336	217 83	221 289	429	329 145	189 147	251 259	238	199 203	329 257	155 163	213 152	250	304 119
Wickets	10 10	10 1	10 9†	7	9 9‡	10 10	5 6	6	10 10	6 7	10 10	10 4	7	8 2
Results	L	D	W	D	L	D	W	D	L	D	W	W	D	D
Points	1	6	22	—	5	5	21	—	5	4	21	22	7	5

Fielding Figures

60 – W.K. Hegg (ct 52/st 8)	15 – M. Watkinson	10 – G.D. Mendis	5 – M.A. Atherton
25 – D.P. Hughes	13 – P.J.W. Allott	9 – N.H. Fairbrother	3 – T.E. Jesty
19 – G. Fowler	12 – J. Simmons	6 – I. Folley	

First-Class Averages continued

BATTING

	M	Inns	NOs	Runs	HS	Av	100s	50s
G.R. Cowdrey	20	33	4	830	145	28.62	1	4
P.M. Roebuck	12	19	3	454	112*	28.37	1	1
K.R. Brown	21	34	5	822	131*	28.34	2	2
D.A. Hagan	7	13	2	306	59	27.81		1
G.J. Lord	20	33	2	862	101	27.80	1	4
A. Fordham	16	29	6	637	125*	27.69	1	3
H. Morris	19	33	3	830	87	27.66		6
K.W.R. Fletcher	12	14	3	303	58	27.54		2
A. Sidebottom	18	24	5	517	55	27.21		2
N.R. Taylor	21	37	3	925	114	27.20	2	4
M.J. Weston	18	24	5	514	95*	27.05		3
M.J. Kilborn	7	13		351	78	27.00		2
A.W. Lilley	21	33	3	803	80*	26.76		5
P. Pollard	9	17	1	428	142	26.75	1	1
P.D. North	7	7	3	107	41*	26.75		
P.W. Romaines	21	39	3	955	101*	26.52	1	6
N.A. Stanley	8	12	2	263	66	26.30		3
P.J. Newport	22	25	8	447	77*	26.29		1
B. Roberts	24	39	4	919	71	26.25		7
W. Larkins	23	41	2	1024	134	26.25	2	4
N.D. Burns	23	34	7	708	133*	26.22	1	2
S.J. Rhodes	23	33	10	597	108	25.95	1	1
J.J.E. Hardy	22	39	3	927	97	25.75		6
A.C.S. Pigott	20	34	8	668	56	25.69		3
B.C. Broad	20	34		872	73	25.64		5
R.J. Bartlett	19	31	3	707	102*	25.25	1	3
G.C. Small	20	29	7	554	70	25.18		3
P. Willey	24	40	1	978	130	25.07	2	3
D.J.M. Kelleher	5	7	1	150	51	25.00		1
R.J. Scott	9	16	1	374	107*	24.93	1	2
I.L. Pont	8	8	2	149	68	24.83		1
V.J. Marks	23	31	2	719	68	24.79		3
D. Byas	14	25	1	592	112	24.66	1	4
S.A. Marsh	23	35	6	713	120	24.58	2	1
C.M. Wells	24	41	4	908	109*	24.54	1	4
J.G. Thomas	16	26	5	515	110	24.52	2	
J.R. Ayling	19	33	4	711	88*	24.51		4
N.J. Lenham	18	32	2	733	74	24.43		3
D.A. Banks	7	9	1	195	61	24.37		1
J.F. Sykes	9	13	1	292	88	24.33		2
J.A. Hopkins	13	23	1	534	87	24.27		4
R.A. Cobb	11	20	2	432	65	24.00		2
D.E. East	20	30	2	669	134	23.89	1	2
A.M. Green	16	29	2	639	68	23.66		4
D.A. Thorne	15	25	1	566	76	23.58		4
P.A. Smith	16	27	4	542	84*	23.56		3
A.N. Hayhurst	14	23	2	492	107	23.42	1	2
S.A. Almaer	6	11		256	67	23.27		1

v. Essex (Southend) 16–19 July		v. Surrey (Southport) 20–2 July		v. Yorkshire (Leeds) 30 July–2 Aug.		v. Middlesex (Old Trafford) 6–9 August		v. Sussex (Hove) 13–16 August		v. Nottinghamshire (Lytham) 17–19 August		v. Derbyshire (Old Trafford) 20–3 August		v. Surrey (The Oval) 25–9 August		v. Yorkshire (Old Trafford) 30 Aug–2 Sept.		v. Derbyshire (Derby) 14–17 September		M	Inns	Nos	Runs	HS	Av
104	17	19	12	0	24	12	2	26	35*	—	17	38	40	20	97	16	—	172	19	20	36	1	1061	172	30.31
0	13	9	22	58	0	30	9	14	53	—	3	14	—	29	0	16	—	6	60	24	42	4	1364	151	35.89
73	0	1	4																	15	27	3	693	73	28.87
23	111	0	64	15	43	19	15	18	0*	—	31	15	50*	0	44	21	—	0	0	23	41	4	1134	111	30.64
1	70	19	28	20	11	50	34	18	—	—	4	8	—	1	0	0	—	6	27*	24	39	4	759	85*	21.68
0	45	0	12	3	5	0	2	0	—	—	3	2	—	9	6*	0	—			22	34	4	522	62	17.40
4	—	8	0	13*	31	21	41	—	—	—	2	7	—	6	0	8	—	2	22*	24	34	5	467	76	16.10
4	8*	11	17	1	0	5	14	—	—	—	3	0	—			6*	—			19	28	4	308	31*	12.83
0*	—	4*	—			3*	3*	—	—	—	1*	17*	—			10	—	1*	—	19	20	14	102	30	17.00
3	—	2	6*	18	7*	0	11	—	—	—	5	5	—	2*	13					21	27	9	362	57*	20.11
																				3	3	—	38	31	12.66
		58	98			0	6													10	18	2	496	116*	31.00
																				3	4	—	58	39	14.50
1	14*			1	3	37	0	30	—					9	17	57	—	107	47	14	23	2	492	107	23.42
																				1					—
														0	0	3	—			4	3	—	3	3	1.00
																36	—			2	2	1	47	36	47.00
																				1	2	—	45	35	22.50
								57*	—	—	39	64	—	0	4			0	0	6	9	2	216	64	30.85
				13	0	42	4	152*	15	—	0	5	115*	3	49	34	—	17	7	8	14	2	456	152*	38.00
																		22	0	1	2	—	22	22	11.00
				6		10	4	1				1	2	2	7	2		5	7						
12	11	5	8	10	13	3	3	16	2	6		4	2			7		7							
1				1	1							3	2	1											
1		4		1	6	3		2	3	7		14	9	2	1	4		20	6						
227	289	140	271	154	156	235	142	337	111	0	121	197	220	84	246	218		368	195						
10	6	10	9	10	10	10	10	6	2	0	10	10	1	10	10	10		10	7						
W		D		L		L		W		L		D		L		D		D							
20		12		5		6		24		4		2		4		6		5							

2 – Wasim Akram, N.J. Speak, A.N. Hayhurst, A.J. Murphy and J. Abrahams
1 – G.D. Lloyd and D.J. Makinson

† T.E. Jesty retired ill
‡ G. Fowler absent hurt

First-Class Averages continued

BATTING

Name	M	Inns	NOs	Runs	HS	Av	100s	50s		Name	M	Inns	NOs	Runs	HS	Av	100s	50s
J.G. Wyatt	15	26	1	578	69	23.12		3		M.A. Roseberry	14	21	3	386	67	21.44		1
K.T. Medlycott	23	28	4	554	77*	23.08		4		J.C.M. Atkinson	7	12		257	73	21.41		1
T.J. Boon	15	23	1	505	131	22.95	1	2		P. Whitticase	23	32	10	469	71	21.31		2
C. Penn	20	31	12	436	40	22.94				A. Walker	18	20	10	213	40*	21.30		
M.A. Feltham	22	25	9	367	74	22.93		1		T.R. Ward	10	17		362	72	21.29		3
R.I. Alikhan	10	19		429	98	22.57		3		C.C. Lewis	16	23	4	400	40	21.05		
K. Sharp	12	19		428	128	22.52	1	1		D.L. Bairstow	14	23	3	416	94*	20.80		2
Zahid Sadiq	4	6		135	64	22.50		1		I.G. Swallow	11	19	2	352	48*	20.70		
R.K. Illingworth	23	22	4	404	60	22.44		2		N.F. Williams	8	11	2	186	63*	20.66		1
R.J. Blakey	16	24	4	446	85*	22.30		2		J.W. Lloyds	16	24	3	433	102*	20.61	1	1
N.V. Radford	18	15	6	200	65	22.22		1		W.W. Davis	15	18	3	306	43	20.40		
P. Bent	3	6	1	111	50	22.20		1		K.P. Evans	15	24	4	406	54	20.30		1
N.J. Pringle	8	15	4	244	54	22.18		1		G.D. Rose	20	25	6	385	69*	20.26		1
B.R. Hardie	13	20	3	377	58	22.17		2		J. Simmons	21	27	9	362	57*	20.11		1
J.D. Birch	24	39	4	776	114*	22.17	1	2		D.J.R. Martindale	9	14	1	261	52*	20.07		1
G. Miller	19	21	4	377	77	22.17		1		S.P. Hughes	18	21	5	321	53	20.06		
P. Hepworth	4	6		132	51	22.00		1		M.P. Speight	7	13		258	58	19.84		2
M. Newell	20	37	3	740	105	21.76	1	2		I.A. Greig	23	28	1	529	67	19.59		1
C.K. Bullen	12	14	2	261	59*	21.75		2		G.J. Parsons	10	13	4	174	52	19.33		1
M.R. Gouldstone	7	12	1	239	71	21.72		2		D.R. Pringle	19	27		516	128	19.11	1	3
M. Watkinson	24	39	4	759	85*	21.68		6		D.J. Bicknell	11	19	1	343	62	19.05		2
D.A. Reeve	16	23	3	431	103	21.55	1			G.A. Tedstone	4	8		151	50	18.87		1
P.A.J. De Freitas	17	25	1	517	113	21.54	1	3		M.W. Pooley	8	13	5	149	38	18.62		
Imran Khan	5	7	1	129	55	21.50		1		G.D. Reynolds	6	9	1	147	69	18.37		1

(continued on page 440)

Lancashire CCC
First-Class Matches, 1988

BOWLING	C.D. Matthews	P.J.W. Allott	M. Watkinson	I. Folley	J. Simmons	T.E. Jesty	Wasim Akram	A.J. Murphy	D.J. Makinson
v. Worcestershire (Old Trafford) 21–5 April	24–7–78–1	26–10–44–0	13–4–37–0	38–8–116–3 8.3–5–10–0	43–9–113–3	9–4–11–0			
v. Warwickshire (Old Trafford) 28 April–2 May	15–3–47–4 21–6–52–0	18–6–33–3 32.5–7–65–5	18–6–37–1 23–4–48–0	10–2–19–1 26–11–57–2	3.5–3–0–1 44–18–61–2	3–0–16–0			
v. Nottinghamshire (Trent Bridge) 5–9 May		12–5–21–1 8–3–10–0	12–4–20–0 6–2–10–0	24–5–79–4 24–6–89–5	22–7–53–2 30.4–6–66–3		17–4–34–3 16–5–50–2		
v. Oxford University (Oxford) 21–4 May			15–1–47–1 13–1–32–0	20–7–43–2 20–9–34–2	16–3–33–2 28–6–58–1			17.4–5–45–3 12–1–31–0	15–9–28–1 12–5–22–0
v. Somerset (Old Trafford) 28–31 May		16–6–47–0 12–0–39–2	25–3–66–1 7–0–32–0	5–0–38–0	30–4–94–2 13–0–58–4		15–5–27–2 22.2–7–66–1		
v. Worcestershire (Worcester) 1–3 June		20.3–10–29–4 20.3–5–43–4	20–6–37–4 20–8–31–2		1–0–9–0		9–2–25–0 7–2–11–0		
v. Hampshire (Liverpool) 4–7 June		21–8–31–0 8–4–12–1	13–4–32–1 8–5–7–0	39–7–103–1 23–8–56–3	25–4–82–2 9–5–11–1		18–5–41–0 4–0–16–0		
v. West Indians (Old Trafford) 8–10 June	17.2–2–48–2		19–2–68–1	27–10–60–1				24–5–58–0	
v. Kent (Tunbridge Wells) 15–17 June		36.3–9–86–6 23–8–56–2	27–6–76–2 20.3–3–69–3	7–0–21–0	8–2–33–1		27–9–44–1		
v. Gloucestershire (Old Trafford) 18–21 June			16–4–65–1 8–1–29–1	23–5–44–0 23–0–128–2	14–3–35–0 26–5–81–5				
v. Glamorgan (Swansea) 25–8 June		9–2–18–2 3–0–8–0		30–10–68–2 9–4–20–6	31.1–14–53–5 8.5–4–9–4		21–10–31–1 3–1–5–0		
v. Warwickshire (Nuneaton) 29 June–1 July		24–6–59–3 12.3–1–40–2	18–2–52–0 25–8–43–6		3–0–7–1	4–1–8–0	19–4–48–2 21–5–43–2		
v. Northamptonshire (Northampton) 2–5 July		10.4–1–22–2 5–1–18–0	13–3–36–1 8–1–30–1	3–1–8–0 11–3–22–1	11–5–13–0 9–1–25–0	6–4–13–0	25–6–53–7 12–3–24–0		
v. Leicestershire (Old Trafford) 13–15 July		12–3–32–1 10–4–35–1	12–3–40–1 3–0–11–0	10–4–25–2 27–11–41–4	22–5–66–2 28–12–42–4				
v. Essex (Southend) 16–19 July		16–2–46–0 20–4–59–6	20–7–55–0 6–1–28–0	25–5–96–1 5–1–11–0	34–7–83–4 16–2–69–3				
v. Surrey (Southport) 20–2 July		15–4–33–0 22.4–8–52–2	25–8–54–3 10–1–42–1	16–5–44–0	16–3–45–1	3–1–8–0	27.2–6–58–5 13–0–58–3		
v. Yorkshire (Leeds) 30 July–2 Aug.		32–7–85–5	27–5–100–0		5.3–0–12–1		15–2–32–2		
v. Middlesex (Old Trafford) 6–9 August		16.2–1–43–2 3–1–5–0	13–4–31–1 3–0–8–0	20–3–68–3	37–6–120–1 10–4–24–0				
v. Sussex (Hove) 13–16 August		23–9–61–3 23–7–58–2	23–6–60–3 21–4–69–2		2–1–6–0 8–1–17–0				
v. Nottinghamshire (Lytham) 17–19 August		27.5–7–62–3	18–3–53–1	17–3–53–2	24–4–56–2				
v. Derbyshire (Old Trafford) 20–3 August		7–0–24–0 7–2–19–0	12–2–50–0 17–6–50–6	8–0–27–1 9–4–17–0	10–1–35–2 21–7–39–2				
v. Surrey (The Oval) 25–9 August			25–7–57–3		19–7–40–2			19–2–73–0	
v. Yorkshire (Old Trafford) 30 Aug.–2 Sept.		29–8–70–5 8–3–13–0	20–6–60–2 3–2–1–0	19–6–52–2 20–6–38–2					
v. Derbyshire (Derby) 14–17 September			28–6–70–2 14–4–36–1	31–9–103–3 37–10–91–2				19.1–3–70–3 9–2–41–0	
	77.2–18–225–7 av. 32.14	590.2–162–1378–67 av. 20.56	647.3–153–1779–52 av. 34.21	614.3–168–1681–57 av. 29.49	629–159–1548–63 av. 24.57	25–10–56–0 —	291.4–76–666–31 av. 21.48	100.5–18–318–6 av. 53.00	27–14–50–1 av. 50.00

A.N. Hayhurst	G.D. Mendis	N.H. Fairbrother	J.D. Fitton	I.D. Austin	M.A. Atherton	Byes	Leg-byes	Wides	No-balls	Total	Wkts
							21	1	1	409	7
							8			29	0
							3		2	155	10
						9	5	1	1	297	10
						7	9		2	223	10
						3	8	1	4	236	10
12–5–21–1						1	12	1	6	230	10
10–5–14–1	4–1–9–0						13		4	213	4
							1		4	273	5
							7			202	8
14–4–25–2						1	2		1	119	10
3–0–22–0							2			118	6
8–1–18–1						2	11			320	6
	8–0–35–0	7.3–0–48–0				1			1	186	5
			16–3–43–0			5	5	2	4	287	5
							13	2	6	252	10
							8		4	154	5
14–1–53–0				12.2–2–45–1		11	3	1		256	2
4–0–26–0				6–2–23–0			9			296	9
						8	21		1	199	10
						4	1			47	10
17.3–2–45–4						2	13	3	2	234	10
							3	2	3	129	10
						5	10	1		147	10
							2		3	134	2
						7	3		4	173	6
						3	1			133	9
16–4–61–1							5		2	346	7
							2			169	9
						1	10		2	253	10
						2	4	1	3	158	7
14–3–49–1							15			293	10
3–1–7–0		2.4–0–11–0								18	0
					17–5–32–3	3	8		2	305	10
					10–2–36–0				1	73	0
8–3–22–0				11–5–20–3			3		5	172	10
20–2–78–4				15.5–5–40–2	3–0–8–0		5		3	275	10
				15–5–42–2			6			272	10
										0	0
				4–1–21–0					3	157	3
					9.5–4–17–0				5	142	8
14–3–52–0				23–4–79–5	3–1–18–0	5	7		1	331	10
2–1–2–0			11–4–18–1		5–0–18–0		4		1	224	10
			31–9–59–6		17–2–56–0		4			171	8
19–4–56–2				20–7–41–0	11–4–26–0	1	6		6	373	10
3–2–2–0				30–12–56–2	14–5–51–1	8	9		5	294	6
181.3–41–553–17 av. 32.52	12–1–44–0 —	10.1–0–59–0 —	58–16–120–7 av.17.14	137.1–43–367–15 av. 24.46	89.5–23–262–4 av. 65.50						

Leicestershire CCC
First-Class Matches, 1988

Each opponent column shows the two innings scores (first innings, second innings); "—" indicates no second innings.

BATTING	v. Oxford University (Oxford) 16–19 April	v. Derbyshire (Derby) 21–5 April	v. Northamptonshire (Leicester) 28 April–2 May	v. Kent (Leicester) 5–9 May	v. Middlesex (Leicester) 18–20 May	v. Worcestershire (Leicester) 21–4 May	v. Northamptonshire (Northampton) 28–31 May	v. Surrey (The Oval) 11–14 June	v. Glamorgan (Leicester) 15–17 June	v. Sussex (Leicester) 18–21 June	v. Gloucestershire (Gloucester) 25–8 June	v. Yorkshire (Leeds) 2–5 July	v. Lancashire (Old Trafford) 13–15 July	v. West Indians (Leicester) 16–18 July
N.E. Briers	80 —	90 —	63 —	21 —	20 35	23 8	23 10	49 2	7 59	12 12	53 51	5 —	2 37	4 20
T.J. Boon	43 —	31 —	22 —	131 —										2 1
D.I. Gower	26 —	14 —	7 —	1 —	6 74	46 12	20 38	3 19*			10 7		96 23	3 21
P. Willey	8 —	34 —	56 —	4 —	27 0	23 14	21 27	10 6	42 0	130 6	12 23	104 —	40 6	3 21
J.J. Whitaker	53 —	145 —		7 —	13 55	100* 24	4 25	40 11*	68 43	0 17*	8 0	8 —	1 0	8 2
L. Potter	54* —	107 —	2 —	9 —	2 39*	15 6	5 27	13 —	96 23	1 —	35 0	10 —	4 29	16* 19*
P.A.J. De Freitas	0 —	17 —	66 —	60 —			14 2	30 —		34 —	7 21		10* 0	1 22
C.C. Lewis	36* —	1 —	8 —	40 —	1 5	35* 29*	20 29		26* 9	23 —	12 2	35 —	27 0	
P. Whitticase		8* —	14* —	6 —	0 —		2 0	9* —	10* 0	21* —	10 13	0 —	4* 27	2 14*
P.M. Such	— —					— —							0*	2 —
L.B. Taylor	— —	— —	7 —		4 8	— —	— —		— 0*			4 —		0 —
J.P. Agnew		21* —	38 —	2 —	3* 1	— —	— 23	18* —	5 12	22 —	11 4*	0 —	— 2	8 —
J.D.R. Benson			3											
G.J.F. Ferris				0* —	0 12	— —	— —	5* 2*	5	3 —	8* 0	8* —		— 0*
R.A. Cobb					31 14	22 6*	20 64	65 —	15 8	1 22*	7 33	38 —	2 5	
M.A. Garnham							— —							
P. Hepworth										32 1	51 —		35 —	
L. Tennant														
Byes	3				1 1	4	4	1	4	2 4	1		7 3	4
Leg-byes	6	8	14	7	10	7	6 5	10	6 2	3	11 7	5	3 1	2
Wides				4		2		4	1 1	1		7	1	
No-balls	10	6	27	4	6 11	5		3 6	3	1 1	5	6 7	8 4	11 4
Total	319	482	327	296	114 265	280 99	143 264	255 38	313 164	309 61	189 177	253 0	173 133	90 103
Wickets	6	8	10	10	10 9†	5 5	9‡ 10	7 2	7 10	10 2	10 10	10 0	6 9	10 6
Result	W	D	W	W	L	D	D	D	D	W	W	L	D	D
Points	—	7	23	23	4	5	2	7	8	23	21	2	4	—

Fielding Figures

75 – P. Whitticase (ct 71/st 4)	13 – L. Potter	8 – T.J. Boon	3 – Subs
16 – J.J. Whitaker	12 – P. Willey	6 – P.A.J. De Freitas	2 – M.A. Garnham and J.P. Agnew
14 – D.I. Gower and N.E. Briers	10 – R.A. Cobb and C.C. Lewis	4 – L.B. Taylor	1 – G.J.F. Ferris

First-Class Averages continued

BATTING

	M	Inns	NOs	Runs	HS	Av	100s	50s		M	Inns	NOs	Runs	HS	Av	100s	50s
D.A. Leatherdale	10	15	1	255	34*	18.21			D.A. Graveney	23	24	9	231	47	15.40		
P. Moores	14	24	2	395	97*	17.95		1	S.D. Weale	6	9		136	40	15.11		
F.A. Griffith	5	7	1	105	37	17.50			M.W. Alleyne	14	21	1	300	56	15.00		1
D.P. Hughes	22	34	4	522	62	17.40		3	M.W. Pringle	5	7		104	35	14.85		
A.P. Igglesden	7	8	2	103	41	17.16			T.D. Topley	16	22	6	235	56*	14.68		1
A.C. Storie	9	17	2	255	68	17.00		1	P.G. Newman	16	19	6	187	39	14.38		
P.A.C. Bail	4	6		102	44	17.00			S.D. Heath	5	8	1	100	33*	14.28		
I. Folley	19	20	14	102	30	17.00			T.A. Merrick	16	21	3	256	34	14.22		
C.W. Scott	19	27	6	356	63*	16.95		1	A.R. Clarke	21	32	8	337	68	14.04		1
T.J.G. O'Gorman	5	9		152	78	16.88		1	T.M. Tremlett	7	10	2	111	38	13.87		
D. Ripley	25	33	6	451	49	16.70			B.N. French	7	11	1	135	28	13.50		
N.J. Falkner	7	14		232	55	16.57		1	D.K. Lillee	8	11	2	120	22	13.33		
R.M. Ellison	20	27	6	346	50*	16.47		1	D.B. d'Oliveira	8	11	1	132	37	13.20		
G.W. Humpage	17	26	1	411	80	16.44		3	S.J. Noyes	8	14	1	170	38	13.07		
E.E. Hemmings	17	25	10	245	31*	16.33			C. Shaw	21	25	12	170	31	13.07		
D.J. Wild	18	27	1	423	75	16.26		2	M.A. Holding	11	12	2	129	30*	12.90		
W.K. Hegg	24	34	5	467	76	16.10		1	J.P. Agnew	24	29	8	271	38	12.90		
R. Bate	7	12	2	160	45	16.00			P.J.W. Allott	19	28	4	308	31*	12.83		
K.D. James	12	22	2	320	77	16.00		1	R.J. Maru	23	29	5	302	74	12.58		1
C.P. Metson	23	30	8	351	48	15.95			A.R.C. Fraser	23	27	9	223	41	12.38		
S.D. Myles	4	7		111	39	15.85			T.M. Alderman	20	22	11	135	43*	12.27		
A.E. Warner	19	25	6	300	45	15.78			N.A. Mallender	17	20	7	158	44	12.15		
S.T. Clarke	12	10	1	141	28	15.66			R.J. Turner	8	14	1	155	27	11.92		
R.J. Parks	23	35	8	420	38*	15.55			G.J.F. Ferris	18	20	8	139	36*	11.58		

v. Derbyshire (Leicester) 20–2 July		v. Essex (Leicester) 23–6 July		v. Nottinghamshire (Worksop) 30 July–2 Aug.		v. Kent (Canterbury) 3–5 August		v. Hampshire (Leicester) 6–9 August		v. Warwickshire (Edgbaston) 13–16 August		v. Somerset (Hinckley) 20–3 August		v. Glamorgan (Neath) 25–9 August		v. Nottinghamshire (Leicester) 30 Aug.–2 Sept.		v. Essex (Chelmsford) 9–12 September		M	Inns	Nos	Runs	HS	Av
25*	60	119	63*	24	34	17	20	28	23	0	54	22	19	6	—	4	—	6	25	24	41	2	1335	125*	34.23
70	5	2	—	8	21	0	33	2	2	2	0	13	19	9	—	15	—	11	63*	15	23	1	505	131	22.95
				4	72*	90	43	10	13	20	20	10	29*	39	—	146	—	172	37	18	30	3	1107	172	41.00
13*	7	6	—	0	1	39	16	98	56	37	3	10	22	28	—	1	—	11	13	24	40	1	978	130	25.07
12	22	12	—	61	36	36	48	28	87*	27	36	22	10*	126	—	5	—	30	1	23	39	5	1223	145	35.97
—	41*	10	—	9	9	30*	14	26	23*	6	2	52	—	66	—	85	—			23	34	7	885	107	32.77
—	6			113	1					55	9	13	—							14	20	1	481	113	25.31
—	0	18	—											39	—	5	0			16	23	4	400	40	21.05
—	16	50*	40*	0	5	19	11*	34	—	35	8	71	—	6	—	15	—	10	9	23	32	10	469	71	21.31
				6	—	0	—	1	—					0*	—					8	6	2	9	6	2.25
		0*	—	6*	—	0	—	6	—	14*	2	0*	—	0	—	—	—	0*	60	17	16	6	111	60	11.10
—	0*	18	—	10	9*	0	3	14	—	0	5*	0	—	21	—	15*	—	2	4	23	29	8	271	38	12.90
																				1	1	—	3	3	3.00
—	—	18	—			3	4*	36*	—			8	—	2	—	0	—	0	25	18	20	8	139	36*	11.58
19	11	29	20																	11	20	2	432	65	24.00
																				1					
												3	0*					9	4	4	6	—	132	51	22.00
																				1	2	1	3	3	3.00

4	3				1	4	3	4		2	4	4		1				1	
3	6	5	6	11	10	7	7	5	8	5	4	2	2	4		6		10	1
1		4				1	1			1		1						1	
7	6	9		5	1	1		6				6	2	5		1			

54	183	300	129	257	200	247	203	298	212	206	149	233	103	314		332		268	241
3	8	9	1	10	7	10	7	10	4	10	9	10	3	10		9		10	10
L		D		D		D		D		W		W		D		D		L	
4		5		6		5		6		22		22		3		7		5	

† P. Whitticase absent hurt
‡ J.P. Agnew absent ill

First-Class Averages continued

BATTING

	M	Inns	NOs	Runs	HS	Av	100s	50s
G.A. Pointer	7	12	2	114	18*	11.40		
G.R. Dilley	13	15	2	147	36	11.30		
K.E. Cooper	24	34	9	282	39	11.28		
L.B. Taylor	17	16	6	111	60	11.10		1
J.M. Tremellen	7	12		131	33	10.91		
J. Derrick	21	28	6	229	50*	10.40		1
N.A. Foster	16	21	4	171	34	10.05		
A.N. Jones	20	21	8	130	36*	10.00		

(Qualification – 100 runs, average 10.00)
(B.M.W. Patterson 100 in one innings)

BOWLING

	Overs	Mds	Runs	Wkts	Av	Best	10/m	5/inns
O.H. Mortensen	233.3	73	464	34	13.64	6/35		4
S.T. Clarke	396.4	108	913	63	14.49	6/52	2	4
N.F. Williams	178.3	33	511	30	17.03	6/42		2
P.W. Jarvis	233.2	52	651	37	17.59	6/40	1	2
N.G. Cowans	491.5	123	1290	71	18.16	6/49	1	3
F.D. Stephenson	819.1	196	2289	125	18.31	7/56	3	10
G.J. Parsons	228	69	553	29	19.06	7/16		1

	Overs	Mds	Runs	Wkts	Av	Best	10/m	5/inns
A.R.C. Fraser	697.1	195	1550	80	19.37	6/68	2	6
P.J. Newport	600.3	127	1844	93	19.82	8/52	1	7
G.C. Small	628.1	170	1605	80	20.06	7/15	2	8
A.A. Donald	180.4	40	534	26	20.53	5/57		1
P.J.W. Allott	590.2	162	1378	67	20.56	6/59		5
A. Sidebottom	512.2	135	1303	63	20.68	7/89		3
N.A. Mallender	433.3	111	1037	50	20.74	5/12		1
K.M. Curran	414.2	86	1385	65	21.30	7/54	3	4
Wasim Akram	291.4	76	666	31	21.48	7/53		2
K.E. Cooper	816	220	2179	101	21.57	5/41		5
A.P. Igglesden	234.3	46	805	37	21.75	6/34	1	3
K.D. James	298.5	72	763	35	21.80	5/25		2
R.K. Illingworth	597.4	189	1274	58	21.96	5/46	2	4
W.W. Davis	537.2	92	1614	73	22.10	7/52	2	7
T.A. Merrick	468.3	105	1437	65	22.10	6/29	1	5
S.D. Fletcher	412	66	1308	59	22.16	8/58		2
G.J.F. Ferris	452.1	82	1380	62	22.25	5/447		2
P.J. Bakker	293.4	85	670	30	22.33	5/54		1
G.R. Dilley	387.1	70	1098	49	22.40	5/46		4
D.A. Graveney	613.2	99	1353	53	22.52	8/127	1	2
T.A. Munton	425.1	126	1047	46	22.76	6/21		2
N.A. Foster	598.3	122	1822	80	22.77	6/53	2	5
T.M. Alderman	600	135	1711	75	22.81	8/59		3
M.A. Robinson	402.4	85	1055	46	22.93	4/19		

(continued on page 443)

Leicestershire CCC
First-Class Matches, 1988

BOWLING	P.A.J. De Freitas	L.B. Taylor	C.C. Lewis	P.M. Such	J.P. Agnew	P. Willey	L. Potter	G.J.F. Ferris	L. Tennant
v. Oxford University (Oxford) 16–19 April	22–13–15–4 8–4–18–1	10–3–32–2 9–5–16–0	19.2–4–48–4 13–5–22–6	8.5–2–9–2					
v. Derbyshire (Derby) 21–5 April	30–7–94–0 39–14–93–3 ·	20–4–78–2 17–5–43–1	26.5–5–73–5 30–7–109–1		27–9–57–2 6–3–8–0	15–8–11–1 43–17–62–3	1–0–7–0 5–2–9–0		
v. Northamptonshire (Leicester) 28 April–2 May	12–3–22–1 16–5–40–5	3–1–4–0	22–5–75–3		20.3–3–66–6 15.1–2–56–5				
v. Kent (Leicester) 5–9 May	8–2–14–0 18–4–52–4		10–2–37–2 4.2–0–24–1		13.2–1–37–6 18–4–45–3			10–1–31–2 5–1–4–1	
v. Middlesex (Leicester) 18–20 May		18–3–58–1 6.3–1–20–1	17–1–72–1		24–6–67–6 2–0–2–0	10–1–26–0	2–0–6–0	23–3–90–1 7–0–22–1	
v. Worcestershire (Leicester) 21–4 May		23–6–53–3 5–1–17–0	23–3–65–1 23–3–60–2		30–10–73–0 21–5–36–2	15–5–35–1 13–4–25–0	16–3–32–2	21.2–6–47–5 18–4–36–1	
v. Northamptonshire (Northampton) 28–31 May	26–6–65–1 4–0–27–2		27–4–86–2		24–5–86–0	14–4–53–3	1–0–1–0	18–7–25–2 4–0–32–3	
v. Surrey (The Oval) 11–14 June	21.3–7–43–5 30–3–114–4			10–2–20–1 6–2–5–0	27–8–63–1 20–3–88–3	5–1–6–0	3–2–9–0	16–3–43–3 21–4–54–1	
v. Glamorgan (Leicester) 15–17 June		9–2–31–0 2–1–3–0	23–7–55–3 5.1–1–22–1		36–8–94–3 9–4–16–0	1–0–6–0		26.4–9–51–4 9–0–23–1	
v. Sussex (Leicester) 18–21 June	13.3–1–38–5 15–2–38–0		12–7–16–0 11–5–20–1		15–3–50–3 19.1–3–70–4		13–8–9–0	14–2–41–2 18–2–65–1	
v. Gloucestershire (Gloucester) 25–8 June	14.3–5–41–5 20–2–63–4		14–3–46–2 8–1–23–0		9–3–15–0 20.2–6–39–6			9–0–36–3 4–0–13–0	
v. Yorkshire (Leeds) 2–5 July		12–0–46–2	15–2–43–0		20–4–78–0			19.3–4–74–4	
v. Lancashire (Old Trafford) 13–15 July	22–6–67–1			29–4–81–4 20–0–66–1	15–2–53–0 3–1–5–0	24–9–42–2 14–5–26–0	6–2–14–1	17–3–52–1 3–2–2–0	
v. West Indians (Leicester) 16–18 July	23–3–81–2	22–4–69–2	17–6–38–1		29–3–114–2	8–2–28–1	5.3–1–24–2		
v. Derbyshire (Leicester) 20–2 July	22–5–81–0		9–0–34–0 16–4–43–2		31–8–122–2 12–2–36–1	35–11–75–1	21–5–42–1 7.1–2–42–2	17–2–66–2 3–2–3–0	
v. Essex (Leicester) 23–6 July		12–2–42–0	4–1–14–0		15.2–3–43–2	16–4–44–0	1–0–4–0	8–0–51–1	
v. Nottinghamshire (Worksop) 30 July–2 Aug.	19–3–62–2	6–1–30–0		12–4–34–0	28–2–117–6	10–1–49–0	11–1–74–0		
v. Kent (Canterbury) 3–5 August		19–6–53–1		17–4–47–0 7–1–25–2	28.4–8–61–7 17–3–55–0	25–7–61–1 4–0–12–1	5–0–16–0	21–4–77–1 13–3–42–3	
v. Hampshire (Leicester) 6–9 August		15–5–48–2 11–0–49–6		7–2–29–0 7–1–24–0	25.3–3–63–2 16–1–79–3	26–11–51–0 3–0–24–0		24–5–58–3 13–3–52–0	
v. Warwickshire (Edgbaston) 13–16 August	32–5–74–5 19–6–52–2	14–5–19–4 18–6–48–3			29.2–7–62–1 18.4–3–65–3	9–6–3–0	1–0–4–0		6–1–19–0 1–1–0–1
v. Somerset (Hinckley) 20–3 August	17–4–57–3 14–1–51–2	8–0–25–0 17–4–30–1			19–7–51–5 12.5–2–34–2	6–3–10–1		11–2–19–2 16–2–36–4	
v. Glamorgan (Neath) 25–9 August					2–1–2–0			3–1–9–2	
v. Nottinghamshire (Leicester) 30 Aug.–2 Sept.		8–3–16–2 21–2–57–1	4–1–9–0 16–2–67–3		19–4–59–3 19–7–64–1	2–1–1–0		15.4–4–49–5 15–1–60–2	
v. Essex (Chelmsford) 9–12 September		19–2–80–1	22–4–109–1		31–2–122–0	43–6–153–4		29–2–117–1	
	465.3–111– 1302–61 av. 21.34	324.3–72– 967–35 av. 27.62	391.4–83– 1210–42 av. 28.80	123.5–22– 340–10 av. 34.00	747.5–159– 2253–90 av. 25.03	341–106– 803–19 av. 42.26	98.4–26– 293–8 av. 36.62	452.1–82– 1380–62 av. 22.25	7–2– 19–1 av. 19.00

a N.H. Green absent hurt   b G.R. Cowdrey absent hurt   c W.N. Slack retired ill

Byes	Leg-byes	Wides	No-balls	Total	Wkts
	3		2	98	10
1	2		2	68	9a
		4	1	324	10
		7	2	331	8
		9	2	176	10
		4		100	10
1	1	6	4	121	10
	3	1	5	128	9b
8	8		22	329	9c
1	1		3	52	2
5	13	8	22	291	10
2	14		5	222	7
	11	1	5	327	8
	3	1	1	62	6
4	6		3	179	10
4	11	1	13	291	8
1	8	3	10	246	10
4	3	3	3	71	2
4	10		15	159	10
	8		18	210	7d
1	3	1	5	142	10
4	2		1	144	10
				0	0
	15	3	12	256	6
5	4		7	304	8
5	1			119	2
	16	2	20	370	10
	9	3	20	429	6
	1			125	5
	2	3	8	200	2
	1		6	367	8
2	10		8	327	10
3	3		2	140	6
2	9	3	14	260	8
	7	2	6	181	10
	1		4	173	10
	12	1	11	164	10
	9	3	12	170	10
			11		2
			7	133	10
3	6		4	258	7
2	9	2	25	592	8

d A.M. Green and N.J. Lenham retired hurt; A.P. Wells absent hurt

First-Class Averages continued

BOWLING

	Overs	Mds	Runs	Wkts	Av	Best	10/m	5/inns
T.M. Tremlett	125.3	35	326	14	23.28	4/19		
I.A. Greig	402.3	83	1143	49	23.32	6/34		2
J.R. Ayling	432.2	97	1098	47	23.36	4/57		
P.A. Smith	164.3	20	540	23	23.47	3/7		
M.D. Harman	266.4	86	593	25	23.72	5/55		2
Imran Khan	116.3	27	310	13	23.84	5/50		1
R.M. Ellison	603.4	171	1697	71	23.90	7/75		3
N.G.B. Cook	768.2	264	1635	68	24.04	6/56		2
K.T. Medlycott	593.1	159	1660	69	24.05	8/52	3	6
P.A.J. De Freitas	557.3	127	1555	64	24.29	5/38		5
I.D. Austin	137.1	43	367	15	24.46	5/79		1
C. Penn	646.1	143	1989	81	24.55	7/70		6
J. Simmons	629	159	1548	63	24.57	5/53		2
S.J.W. Andrew	268.5	68	765	31	24.67	5/36		1
N.V. Radford	570.5	101	1770	71	24.92	7/73		3
J.P. Agnew	783.5	166	2367	93	25.45	7/61	1	8
A. Walker	465.5	98	1380	54	25.55	5/64		1
T.D. Topley	538.4	87	1664	65	25.60	7/75	1	4
C.L. Cairns	109	16	384	15	25.60	4/70		
J.H. Childs	655.5	209	1605	62	25.88	6/92	1	4
J.K. Lever	422.4	88	1120	43	26.04	4/61		
A.E. Warner	445	104	1151	44	26.15	4/22		
D.R. Pringle	515.2	111	1492	57	26.17	6/39		4
J.E. Emburey	671.5	215	1543	58	26.60	6/24		2
M.J. Weston	124	31	320	12	26.66	4/24		
G.D. Rose	504.5	116	1527	57	26.78	6/47		1
H.L. Alleyne	94.3	17	322	12	26.83	5/54		1
P.G. Newman	339.5	81	950	35	27.14	8/29		1
C.A. Connor	495.3	91	1497	55	27.21	5/70		1
D.V. Lawrence	647.2	103	2296	84	27.33	7/47		4
L.B. Taylor	324.3	72	967	35	27.62	6/49		1
N.H. Peters	278.2	50	954	34	28.05	6/31		1
A.C.S. Pigott	624	109	2078	74	28.08	6/100		2
C.K. Bullen	107.1	25	316	11	28.72	4/56		
C.C. Lewis	391.4	83	1210	42	28.80	6/22		2
H.R.J. Trump	270	74	696	24	29.00	4/17		
M.W. Cleal	168	25	582	20	29.10	4/41		
V.J. Marks	862.5	222	2214	76	29.13	7/118	1	5
C.S. Cowdrey	391.2	92	1141	39	29.25	5/46		1
I. Folley	614.3	168	1681	57	29.49	6/20		2
M.W. Pooley	129.4	30	384	13	29.53	4/80		
G. Miller	433	105	1153	39	29.56	5/76		1
K.J. Barnett	161.1	37	414	14	29.57	3/63		
R.G. Williams	331	72	980	33	29.69	5/86		1
D.E. Malcolm	488.1	93	1676	56	29.92	6/68		2
M.A. Feltham	584.1	135	1679	56	29.98	5/45		2
A.N. Jones	512	85	1658	55	30.14	7/30		1
M.P. Bicknell	516.2	136	1511	50	30.22	9/45		1
G.A. Hick	204	43	642	21	30.57	4/114		
N.G. Cowley	157.1	47	337	11	30.63	3/39		
S.L. Watkin	527.3	127	1423	46	30.93	8/59		2
P. Carrick	593	179	1551	50	31.02	5/46		2
E.E. Hemmings	508.5	139	1312	42	31.23	4/50		
D.A. Reeve	292	71	750	24	31.25	4/50		
D.J. Wild	187.5	37	563	18	31.27	4/18		
N. Gifford	425.1	121	976	31	31.48	3/66		
A.P. Pridgeon	266.3	58	662	21	31.52	3/68		
J.G. Thomas	422.2	62	1531	48	31.89	6/68		2
R.A. Bunting	400	69	1320	41	32.19	5/44		3
R.F. Pienaar	404.2	99	1162	36	32.27	5/27		1
A.N. Hayhurst	181.3	41	553	17	32.52	4/45		
M. Frost	99.5	23	326	10	32.60	4/56		
P.A. Booth	135.4	35	361	11	32.81	5/98		1
J. Derrick	542.1	138	1511	46	32.84	6/54		1
C. Shaw	507.5	110	1522	46	33.08	4/17		
I.L. Pont	220	30	795	24	33.12	5/103		1
A.M. Babington	554.5	110	1628	49	33.22	4/66		
S.R. Barwick	408.5	112	1064	32	33.25	5/37		1
S.J. Base	195	20	735	22	33.40	4/74		
P.M. Such	123.5	22	340	10	34.00	4/81		
C.M. Wells	534.4	119	1469	43	34.16	4/43		
M. Watkinson	647.3	153	1779	52	34.21	6/43		2

(continued on page 444)

Middlesex CCC
First-Class Matches, 1988

BATTING (paired columns are 1st / 2nd innings)

Batting	Notts (Lord's) 21–5 Apr		Essex (Lord's) 28 Apr–2 May		Surrey (Oval) 5–9 May		Leics (Leicester) 18–20 May		Camb U (Cambridge) 21–3 May		Sussex (Lord's) 28–31 May		Worcs (Lord's) 4–7 Jun		Kent (Tun. Wells) 11–14 Jun		Hants (Basingstoke) 15–17 Jun		Northants (Luton) 18–21 Jun		Essex (Chelmsford) 25–8 Jun		Yorks (Lord's) 29 Jun–1 Jul		Derby (Derby) 2–5 Jul		Notts (Trent Bridge) 13–15 Jul	
J.D. Carr	16	106	66	5	0	7	144	36*	38	5	76	—	—	0	0	6	8	6	21	15	29	14	30	—	12	23*	4	—
P.R. Downton	0	24	39	35	32	12					19	—			6	74					27	7*					0	—
M.W. Gatting	7	210	0	16	52	79					31	—			20	76	18	104	54	34	67	—					7	—
K.R. Brown	14	131*	13	20	6	41	58	0	0	30	14	—	—	31	25	13	10	2*	0	33	12	9	39	—	12	—	21	—
R.O. Butcher	73	4	22	19	29	3	5	—	52	20	30	—	—	0	9	7	24	17*	61	17	6	23*	22	—	17	—		
M.A. Roseberry	0	—					24	3*	2	16	11	—	—	1					9	42*			0	—	5	—		
J.E. Emburey	61	12*	18	76*	9	41					1	—			4	39					7	0*					12	—
A.R.C. Fraser	7	4	14*	7*	5	6*	2	—			13	—	—	0	8*	7*	16	—	4*	—	17	—	7	—	0	—	0*	—
S.P. Hughes	4*	—	19	16	25*	2	19	—	53	12	8	—	—	20			34	—	28	22*			18*	—	1	—	3	—
N.G. Cowans	6	—	1	—	6	5	17*	—			2	—	—	2*	0	0	0*	—			4	—	2	—	0	—	4	—
W.W. Daniel	0	—																					0					
W.N. Slack			5	65	21	11	4*	—			34*	—	—	5	0	28	19	42	44	54	23	13	144	—	4	—	46	—
N.F. Williams			44	2	8	1	1	—					—	32	0	9			0	6	19	—	63*	—	2	—		
J.F. Sykes							1	8	37	3			—	16					4	—			86	—	2	—		
M.C.W. Olley							16	—	6	27*																		
N.R.C. MacLaurin									2	35																		
A. Needham									44	18			—	6											66*	17*	5	—
A.G.J. Fraser									14	5*																		
P.C.R. Tufnell									2*	—					9	6	2	—	0	—	1	—			3	—		
I.J.F. Hutchinson																	25	13					7	—	3	—		
M.R. Ramprakash																											0	—
A.A. Barnett																												
Byes	4	11	4		4		8	1	2	17	6			2					6	1	1		9		1			
Leg-byes	7		6	4	4	8	8	1	5	3	7		7		4	3	4	2	1	1	1		10		9		15	
Wides			1	1	4		1	4	1				1		3	1	1		1	1	1		1		6		16	
No-balls		3	11	9	2		22	3	4		8		1		4	3	10	6	5		1		13					
Total	199	505	263	275	207	216	329	52	262	195	261		0	124	92	272	149	186	277	234	259	66	388		138	40	133	
Wickets	10	5	10	8	10	10	9†	2	10	8	10		0	10	10	10	10	4	10	6	10	3	10		10	0	10	
Result	W		W		W		W		D		D		L		L		D		D		D		D		D		L	
Points	19		23		22		24		—		3		3		4		4		8		5		8		0		0	

Fielding Figures
36 – P.R. Downton (ct 31/st 5) 20 – J.E. Emburey 10 – W.N. Slack
32 – K.R. Brown 15 – R.O. Butcher 9 – M.W.C. Olley
21 – J.D. Carr 14 – M.W. Gatting 5 – M.A. Roseberry, N.G. Cowans, P.C.R. Tufnell and A. Needham

---

First-Class Averages continued

BOWLING

	Overs	Mds	Runs	Wkts	Av	Best	10/m	5/inns
M.A. Holding	279.1	49	827	24	34.45	4/74		
N.C.W. Fenton	271.4	65	726	21	34.57	4/64		
F.A. Griffith	99.3	20	347	10	34.70	4/47		
A.M.G. Scott	120	26	385	11	35.00	4/66		
D.J. Capel	436.1	76	1451	41	35.39	4/40		
R.J. Shastri	304.2	91	709	20	35.45	7/49	1	1
S.T. Jefferies	355.1	52	1216	34	35.76	8/97		2
R.J. Maru	701	201	1792	50	35.84	5/69		1
P.J. Hartley	307.3	32	1213	34	35.85	5/85		1
D.J. Millns	179	22	683	19	35.94	3/37		
D.K. Lillee	245	45	778	21	37.04	6/68		1
R.P. Davis	563	177	1409	38	37.07	5/132		1
D.J. Foster	299.3	46	1044	28	37.28	4/46		
A.R. Clarke	618	156	1650	44	37.50	5/60		2
K.P. Evans	258.5	49	829	22	37.68	3/22		
A.M. Green	151.5	50	392	10	39.20	6/82		2
G.A. Gooch	152	39	401	10	41.10	2/29		
G.C. Holmes	121.2	15	445	11	40.45	5/38		1
P. Willey	341	106	803	19	42.26	4/153		
P.C.R. Tufnell	433.2	119	1058	25	42.32	4/88		
R.C. Ontong	395.1	94	1128	26	43.38	4/38		
S.P. Hughes	441.3	84	1258	27	46.59	4/39		
M.R. Sygrove	215.4	34	848	18	47.11	3/91		
K. Saxelby	245.2	42	837	17	49.23	3/21		
J.W. Lloyds	239.3	42	757	13	58.23	2/22		
P. Bainbridge	324	62	1054	17	62.00	5/33		1
J.N. Perry	211	44	643	10	64.30	3/72		
M.A. Atherton	269.1	42	827	11	75.18	3/32		

(Qualification – 10 wickets)

LEADING FIELDERS

87 – D. Ripley (ct 80/st 7); 78 – S.J. Rhodes (ct 70/st 8); 75 – P. Whitticase (ct 71/st 4); 73 – R.J. Parks (ct 63/st 10); 68 – R.C. Russell (ct 56/st 12); 66 – D.E. East (ct 60/st 6); 64 – C.J. Richards (ct 63/st 1); 61 – B.J.M. Maher (ct 60/st 1) and S.A. Marsh (ct 56/st 5); 60 – W.K. Hegg (ct 52/st 8) and C.P. Metson (ct 52/st 8); 59 – N.D. Burns (ct 57/st 2); 57 – G.W. Humpage (ct 56/st 1); 51 – C.W. Scott (ct 49/st 2); 45 – P.R. Downton (ct 40/st 5); 39 – D.L. Bairstow (ct 38/st 1); 33 – V.P. Terry, C.S. Cowdrey and P. Moores (ct 30/st 3); 32 – I.J. Gould and K.R. Brown; 31 – R.J. Maru; 28 – C.J. Tavare, G.A. Hick, G.A. Gooch, K.T. Medlycott, R.J. Blakey (ct 26/st 2) and M. Newell; 27 – A.R. Border; 26 – A.J. Stewart (ct 25/st 1); 25 – D.P. Hughes.

v. … 16–19 July	v. Surrey (Lord's) 23–6 July	v. Sri Lankans (Lord's) 30 July–2 Aug.	v. Lancashire (Old Trafford) 6–9 August	v. Gloucestershire (Lord's) 13–16 August	v. Somerset (Uxbridge) 17–19 August	v. Warwickshire (Uxbridge) 20–3 August	v. Yorkshire (Leeds) 25–9 August	v. Sussex (Hove) 30 Aug.–2 Sept.	v. Kent (Lord's) 9–12 September	M	Inns	Nos	Runs	HS	Av
3 53	22* 97*	21 39	19 35*	0 58*	0 20	4 0	48 18	31 —	92 60	24	43	6	1297	144	35.05
— —	— —	24 —	120 —	6 —	7* —			17 —	22* 59*	15	19	4	530	120	35.33
0	— 55		8 —	51 93*	27 51	4 45*	1 41	39 —	26 35	18	29	2	1431	210	53.00
* —		17 107*	38 —	3 —	73 1	16 2	2 18*		59 11	21	34	5	822	131*	28.34
— 8		41 10*	49 —	24 —	48 21	12 41*	67 27	134 —	0 10	19	29	3	796	134	30.61
		11 —			12 —			36 —	6 28	14	21	3	386	67	21.44
		43 —	0 —	82 —	13 0	102 —		73* —	7 14	16	21	4	627	102	36.88
		41 —	2 —	8* —	12 —	14 —		4* 2	6 4	23	27	9	223	41	12.38
		8 —		3 —	0 —	0 —		7 6*		18	21	5	321	53	20.06
		27* —		15* —	15* —	0 —	3* —			20	21	7	119	27*	8.50
										2	2	—	0	0	0.00
3* 105*	0* —		12 37*	56 0	1 0	44 4	75 83	40 —	5 80	19	32	5	1228	163*	45.48
					3* 1	25 —				8	11	2	186	63*	20.66
		88 —								9	13	1	292	88	24.33
										4	5	1	69	27*	17.25
										1	2	—	37	35	18.50
	5* 0		15 —		0* —	0* —			29 53	8	12	3	293	66*	32.55
										1	2	1	19	14	19.00
		1* —	2 —		0* —	0* —			1 20	11	12	4	44	20	5.50
										3	4	—	48	25	12.00
	— 24*	— 15*	0 20		45 43*	33 —	68* 49	66 —	54 4	9	13	4	421	68*	46.77
								10 —		1	1	—	10	10	10.00
2 3			5		3		4	7 1	9 1	2	1		4 8		
4 5	1 3	12 2	8		8 11	4 6	7 2	6 8	7		1 6				
		1		1			1 2	5 1	3		2 1				
2 1		1	16 7	2 1	5 3	2 6	3	9 5	3		5 11				
0 191	28 185	324 185	305 73	261 169	255 149	274 97	315 322	471 8	290 351						
3 1	0 3	10 2	10 0	8 1	8 6	10 3	6 9	9 1	10 10						
D	D	D	W	W	D	W	D	D	D						
5	2	—	22	22	6	23	4	5	5						

3 – J.F. Sykes and S.P. Hughes   † W.N. Slack retired ill
2 – M.R. Ramprakash and subs
1 – N.F. Wiliams and A.R.C. Fraser

REVIEW OF THE SEASON

A review of the 1988 season must start with mention of Worcestershire, Britannic Assurance County Champions, winners of the Refuge Assurance Sunday League, beaten finalists in the two knock-out competitions and semi-finalists in the Benson and Hedges Cup. It is a remarkable record, and one of which they can be justly proud even though they remain frustrated at having been now in six cup finals and having lost them all. Much praise has been lavished on Hick, and rightly so, but Worcestershire's success was based on team-work. Initially, there appeared to be a middle-order weakness, but Phil Neale enjoyed a splendid season, unobtrusively rectifying several uncertain situations and handling the side with dignity and intelligence at all times. Of the bowlers, Illingworth and Newport, in particular, deserve mention, and it was their advance above all else that turned Worcestershire into a championship winning side.

Kent ran them hard, and they were desperately unlucky to be denied at the last. In Cowdrey, they had an inspiring captain, and his treatment at the hands of the selectors was the most shameful event of the year. His appointment had promised a new age of joy, but all too quickly the selectors showed a lack of conviction, and English cricket was the poorer for their vacillations. Tavare, after an unhappy start, batted well for Kent, who were a team without stars. They were admirably served by Penn and by a corporate spirit which allowed everybody in the side to be making a contribution. They were a joy to watch.

The same could not be said of Derbyshire, who suffered from unenterprising leadership. Barnett is one of the most entertaining batsmen in the country and he well deserved his England cap, but one wishes he could adopt a less cautious approach in his captaincy. There were times when Derbyshire looked quite dreadful and dull, yet at others, especially with Barnett at the crease or Mortensen bowling, they could be delightful. Their problems were that Roberts never found form, and Malcolm, though very quick, was often wayward. On top of that, the paucity of their spin bowling is a serious weakness. On the credit side, the arrival of Bowler gave them a solid and dependable opening batsman, a perfect foil for Barnett, and next season, now that he is firmly established, it is likely that he will be able to bat with more freedom. It was certainly an

Middlesex CCC
First-Class Matches, 1988

BOWLING	N.G. Cowans	W.W. Daniel	S.P. Hughes	J.E. Emburey	A.R.C. Fraser	M.W. Gatting	N.F. Williams	J.F. Sykes	A.G.J. Fraser
v. Nottinghamshire (Lord's) 21–5 April	27–9–52–2 / 16–4–38–3	3–0–18–0	33–10–81–1 / 10.1–3–25–2	21–6–51–0 / 7–0–40–0	37.2–13–75–6 / 18–5–42–4	8–1–23–1 / 1–0–5–0			
v. Essex (Lord's) 28 April–2 May	21–7–54–1 / 19.4–5–45–4		25–6–63–2 / 17–4–45–3		13–7–14–1 / 24–6–44–1	1–0–1–0	22.2–5–42–6 / 16–3–28–2		
v. Surrey (The Oval) 5–9 May	15–5–22–3 / 14–5–20–4		3–0–7–0	21–8–31–3 / 30–6–78–2	9–5–7–0 / 13.4–2–36–2		8.2–1–28–3 / 11–0–38–2		
v. Leicestershire (Leicester) 18–20 May	16–6–22–2 / 21.3–2–75–3		10–3–28–0 / 18–4–51–2		12–2–16–3 / 26–10–55–0		13.5–2–46–5 / 20–5–60–4	1–0–1–0 / 1–0–13–0	
v. Cambridge University (Cambridge) 21–3 May			24–6–39–4 / 7–0–15–0					23–8–51–1 / 7–1–12–0	22–5–57–1 / 6–1–25–0
v. Sussex (Lord's) 28–31 May	6–2–8–1		3–0–5–0	2–1–4–0	6–3–7–0		8–4–25–1		
v. Worcestershire (Lord's) 4–7 June	21–3–66–1		29–5–92–2		31–11–56–3		24–3–65–1	5–0–26–0	
v. Kent (Tunbridge Wells) 11–14 June	10–3–29–2 / 21–6–48–3			6–0–16–1 / 37–15–70–1	11–3–30–4 / 14–4–54–0		10–3–32–2 / 9–2–23–0		
v. Hampshire (Basingstoke) 15–17 June	14–6–33–4 / 11–0–26–1		18–2–54–1 / 28.2–5–63–0		21.4–5–34–5 / 32–9–68–6	8–1–21–0		4–0–17–0	
v. Northamptonshire (Luton) 18–21 June			18–1–79–1 / 17–1–67–0		24–6–58–4 / 6–1–18–0	10–2–42–1	20–3–77–2 / 15–2–43–2		
v. Essex (Chelmsford) 25–8 June	15–4–43–1			47–16–86–3	28–7–59–5		1–0–4–0		
v. Yorkshire (Lord's) 29 June–1 July	15.1–3–39–3 / 8–3–21–1	12–2–16–2 / 1–0–3–0	16–2–68–3 / 11–4–19–1		18–2–56–2 / 17–6–32–2				
v. Derbyshire (Derby) 2–5 July									
v. Nottinghamshire (Trent Bridge) 13–15 July	21–5–60–3		11–0–49–2	5–0–13–0	21.1–4–43–5				
v. Glamorgan (Lord's) 16–19 July	14–1–36–0 / 7–3–11–2		11–4–27–0 / 2–0–4–0	36–8–91–1 / 29–8–78–1	20–5–42–2 / 13–2–32–0	13–2–41–0			
v. Surrey (Lord's) 23–6 July	12–4–43–1		9–0–33–0	43–12–94–6	13–2–29–0	9–3–26–0			
v. Sri Lankans (Lord's) 30 July–2 Aug.			19–5–61–1 / 6–3–7–0	33.4–19–50–3 / 13–5–26–2	23–5–66–3				
v. Lancashire (Old Trafford) 6–9 August	4–1–16–0 / 14.1–2–48–5			41.1–17–70–3 / 19–10–26–4	15–4–37–4 / 13–1–48–1				
v. Gloucestershire (Lord's) 13–16 August	13–3–50–3 / 5–0–19–0		18–2–46–1 / 6–0–45–0	21–7–46–3 / 21–9–24–6	23–7–51–0 / 7–2–13–1				
v. Somerset (Uxbridge) 17–19 August	16–6–36–1 / 9–2–20–1			34–7–97–3 / 14–4–30–1	20.2–7–52–1 / 13–1–37–0	1–0–8–0			
v. Warwickshire (Uxbridge) 20–3 August	17.2–2–49–6 / 22.1–6–48–4			25–9–54–2 / 17–6–35–3	26–1–61–2 / 19–7–25–3				
v. Yorkshire (Leeds) 25–9 August	20–5–52–0 / 6–1–26–0		31–5–86–0 / 14–5–20–0		30–11–50–0 / 7–1–22–0	20–7–36–1 / 9–2–51–0		19–0–85–0	
v. Sussex (Hove) 30 Aug.–2 Sept.			27–4–79–1	26–9–45–3	25–6–65–3	11–3–23–1			
v. Kent (Lord's) 9–12 September	35.5–9–105–5 / 4–0–30–1			31–5–80–0 / 10–5–42–3	38–10–89–2 / 9–2–27–5	5–1–10–0			
	491.5–123– 1290–71 av. 18.16	16–2– 37–2 av. 18.50	441.3–84– 1258–27 av. 46.59	589.5–191– 1277–54 av. 23.64	697.1–195– 1550–80 av. 19.37	96–22– 287–4 av. 71.75	178.3–33– 511–30 av. 17.03	60–9– 205–1 av. 205.00	28–6– 82–1 av. 82.00

a P. Whitticase absent hurt   b G.D. Rose retired hurt   c W.N. Slack 1–0–14–0   d W.N. Slack 1–1–0–0

P.C.R. Tufnell	J.D. Carr	K.R. Brown	N.R.C. MacLaurin	A. Needham	M.R. Ramprakash	M.A. Roseberry	Byes	Leg-byes	Wides	No-balls	Total	Wkts
							4	4		8	308	10
								5	2	1	155	10
								13		5	187	10
							2	11		6	175	10
								2		1	97	10
							3	3		3	178	10
							1			6	114	10
							1	10		11	265	9a
35–17–52–1	8–1–23–0	1–1–0–0					10	5	2	2	237	7
7–1–22–1			1–0–4–0				8	4			90	2
											49	2
							5	23		10	333	8
											0	0
							3				110	10
18–4–53–0	0.1–0–1–0							6		3	255	4
4–1–5–0							4	6		7	136	10
39–10–96–2							5	16		6	312	9
32.5–10–76–2							6		1	6	338	10
34–6–92–2	4–0–13–1							2		2	235	5
27–7–87–1							1	16		2	296	10
							8			13	187	10
							4	1	1	1	80	4
											0	0
								8		8	173	10
		1–1–0–0		20–3–51–1			4	6	1	4	298	4
				29–1–125–5				15		2	265	8
				29.4–8–93–1			4	12	1		334	9
											0	0
28–7–71–3	6–3–13–0						2	2		6	265	10
14–5–37–1	5–3–6–0				1–1–0–0		2	2			80	3
38–13–84–3				9–4–15–0			10	3		3	235	10
6–2–13–0							4	3			142	10
24–4–49–2	7–2–20–1							6		6	268	10
26.3–9–58–2							1	1		2	161	10
34–6–88–4								2		4	275	9b
8–2–17–0	2–0–4–1			5–0–46–0		7.1–1–41–1	4	11	1	2	232	4c
3–1–16–0	7–1–25–0						2	5		6	212	10
25–8–44–0								6	1	3	158	10
	27–8–52–1			20–3–78–1			4	20	1	7	463	3d
				7–0–37–0	1–0–1–0	4–0–19–0		9	5	4	185	0
	8–2–14–0				2–0–6–0	0.3–0–1–1	13	9	2	11	320	10e
24–3–86–1	10–2–25–1							17		1	412	10
6–3–12–0												
433.2–119– 1058–25 av. 42.32	84.1–22– 196–5 av. 39.20	2–2– 0–0 —	1–0– 4–0 —	114.4–19– 399–8 av. 49.87	9–1– 53–0 —	11.4–1– 61–2 av. 30.50						

e A.A. Barnett 27–9–65–0

Northamptonshire CCC
First-Class Matches, 1988

BATTING	v. Oxford University (Oxford) 20–2 April	v. Leicestershire (Leicester) 28 April–2 May	v. Gloucestershire (Northampton) 5–9 May	v. Warwickshire (Northampton) 17–20 May	v. Surrey (The Oval) 21–4 May	v. Leicestershire (Northampton) 28–31 May	v. Yorkshire (Northampton) 1–3 June	v. Somerset (Taunton) 4–7 June	v. West Indians (Northampton) 11–13 June	v. Middlesex (Luton) 18–21 June	v. Nottinghamshire (Trent Bridge) 25–8 June	v. Lancashire (Northampton) 2–5 July	v. Gloucestershire (Bristol) 13–15 July	v. Derbyshire (Derby) 16–18 July
G. Cook	14 —	8 7	3 12							3 124*	18 23	10 —	32 —	— 0
W. Larkins	9 —	32 9	9 0	19 33	2 22	42 0	14 12	7 81*	7 —	38 25	4 15	17 36	134 —	— 22
R.J. Bailey	101 —	27 1	66 21	76 60	48 0	55 18	19 72	59 0	45 —	19 48	14 4	8 10	21 —	— 5
A.J. Lamb	101* —	54 47	11 30			70 14			6 —		0 7		117 —	— 10
R.G. Williams	28 —	6 9	5 51	8 13	0 49*	33* 12	1 25	55 38*		14 1	28 2	39 33*	0 —	— 0
N.A. Stanley	66 —	22 4			18* —		4 1*	6 0*	0 —	55 —	62 5*	3 5	4 —	— 22
D. Ripley	41* —	1 0	15 35	14* 47		0 1	4 —	6 0*	0 —	8 —	49 —	8* 16	43* —	— 22
N.G.B. Cook	14* —	0 10	5 3	0 1			2 —	2 —	24 —	24 —	6 —			— 1
S.J. Brown		0 5	4 25*	0 0										
M.A. Robinson		1 0*						0 —		5 —				
A. Walker				11* 3	0 3*			21* —		1* —	0 4*	9 —		— 6*
W.W. Davis		14* 4		6 43			12* 16*	5 —		40 —	7 34		0 —	— 17
D.J. Capel			40 3	9 37	81 83*	75 8	6 46	33 —	2 —	92 21	9 6		28* —	— 47
D.K. Lillee		22 22					4* —							
A. Fordham				6 26	125* 1	25 0*	23 6	4 3	10 —			0 50*		
D.J. Wild		17 58			7 —	0 4	32 0	7 —		15 —	1 7	9 1	1 —	— 25
M.R. Gouldstone								5 2	16 —					
D.S. Hoffman									20* —					
Byes	2			2 5	5 8		2 3	2 3		6	6	2 5	1	
Leg-byes	5	9 4	5 7	5 10	11 7	11 3	3 4	6 3	17	2	5 2	10 2	5	3
Wides	1	2	1		5	1 1	1 1	1	1	4	1	1	1	
No-balls	7	9 4		8 22	1 4	5 1	5 6	20 6	8	6 2	1	3	8	6
Total	389	176 100	206 216	170 363	298 174	327 62	130 192	260 134	232	338 235	105 122	147 134	349 0	0 164
Wickets	5	10 10	10 10	10 10	5 3	8 6	10 7	10 3	10	10 5	10 10	10 2	5 0	0 10
Result	W	L	W	W	D	D	D	W	D	D	L	D	W	L
Points	—	4	22	19	5	8	4	23	—	8	4	3	20	2

Fielding Figures

81 – D. Ripley (ct 75/st 6)
23 – R.J. Bailey and W. Larkins
14 – G. Cook
13 – N.G.B. Cook and A. Fordham
8 – R.G. Williams
7 – A. Walker
6 – A.J. Lamb
5 – W.W. Davis
4 – D.J. Capel, M.R. Gouldstone and N.A. Stanley

---

inspired move on the part of the county's administration to acquire his services.

There were some surprising deficiencies at Essex, where, in spite of Gooch and Border, the batting looked rather fragile at times. Prichard did not appear to have recovered form and confidence after the injury that kept him out of most of the 1987 season, yet he played some excellent knocks on difficult wickets when they were most needed, for example at Worcester and Northampton. He is so sound technically, so rich in strokes, that one feels he must blossom into an outstanding player in the next two years. The Essex attack was inconsistent. Topley had some excellent moments and Childs bowled beautifully. Foster was always a threat, but the likeable Pringle has yet to fulfil the potential which has been apparent since his days at Felstead. With Fletcher spending most of his time directing operations from the pavilion balcony, Essex have to come to terms with the question of captaincy in the very near future. It remains to be seen if, since his experience at Test level, Gooch will take on the job again more happily than he did in the past.

Gloucestershire, too, have a captaincy problem, but of their own making. Few organizations can have done a worse public relations job than the Gloucestershire cricket committee, and Athey hardly looks the answer after the calm and dignified leadership of Graveney. There is much talent at the County, and Graveney has ironed out problems of unwilling bowlers and injury-list addicts to take the side to a challenging position in all competitions. For this, he was dismissed.

There will be a change of leadership in neighbouring Somerset, too, who are not the strongest of counties, particularly in bowling, and may well struggle if they have neither Waugh nor Crowe.

Andy Lloyd did a fine job at Warwickshire. He got the best out of Merrick, and Asif Din at last began to fulfil his promise. Munton made a good advance, but there is a weakness in spin. A fit Kallicharran would be a great boost to the side next season.

David Gower closed the season in glorious form, and one hopes that next year will see him consistently back to his best. There is no more lovely sight in English cricket than Gower at the crease and in form. The other Leicestershire batsmen tended to disappoint, sparkling intermittently, but pacemen Agnew and Ferris performed nobly. Agnew must be one of the unluckiest of bowlers. He

	v. Kent (Northampton) 20–2 July		v. Sussex (Northampton) 23–6 July		v. Worcestershire (Worcester) 30 July–2 Aug.		v. Essex (Northampton) 3–5 August		v. Warwickshire (Edgbaston) 6–9 August		v. Hampshire (Bournemouth) 13–16 August		v. Glamorgan (Wellingborough) 20–3 August		v. Derbyshire (Northampton) 25–9 August		v. Yorkshire (Scarborough) 9–12 September		v. Essex (Chelmsford) 14–17 September		M	Inns	Nos	Runs	HS	Av
	17	6	10	—	0	32	16	0	37	6	50	14	75	32	20	69	203	—	3	6	18	30	1	850	203	29.31
	2	112*	0	—	21	5	10	2	49	2	17	25	67	7	5	8					22	39	2	921	134	24.89
	63	4	127*	—	20	48					6	4	31	17	51	110	17	—	15	39	22	38	1	1349	127*	36.45
													20*	104*			76	—	155	16	11	17	3	838	155	59.85
	71*	—	28	—	10	15*	119	0									14	—	28	63*	19	32	7	798	119	31.92
									14	5											8	12	2	263	66	26.30
	0	—	5	—	0	—	8	0	11	15	12	31	—	—	14	1	12	—	9	11	24	32	6	439	49	16.88
	13	—	1	—	3	—	0	5	9	0	23	6	—	—	4	10	2*	—	3	—	22	26	2	171	24	7.12
																					4	6	1	34	25*	6.80
	0	—	0	—	4	—	0*	0	4	2	0*	—	—	—	0*	—	0*	—	19*	2*	15	17	7	37	19*	3.70
							8	2*	40*	10*	20	3*	—	—	21	33	13	—			17	19	10	208	40*	23.11
			26	—			18	18	9	8			—	—			29	—			15	18	3	306	43	20.40
	44	39*	7	—	70	51*					23	0			18	26	69	—	10	0	18	30	4	983	92	37.80
	0	—			1*	—					0	—			12	22			2	13	7	10	2	98	22	12.25
	30	52	0	—	44	29	1	31	10	20	2	19*	0*	13*			3	—	34	70	16	29	6	637	125*	27.69
	75	—	10	—	0	—	14	20	0	14					41	4			46	13	18	27	1	423	75	16.26
							71	10	50	2	36	0	—	—			0	47*			7	12	1	239	71	21.72
	20	20*																			1	1	1	20	20*	—

	Kent		Sussex		Worcs		Essex		Warw		Hants		Glam		Derby		Yorks		Essex	
B	2		5		1	1	2	1	4	4	8	5	1		6		4		2	
L-b	9	6	11		11	17	12		12	10	4	1	3	4	5	14	14		8	6
W	1		2								1		1		1	6	1			
N-b	5	4	1		6	7	4		12		4		4		1	6	7		8	2
Totals	29	226	233		191	205	283	89	261	98	205	108	201	178	193	362	464		340	243
Wkts	10	3	10		10	4	10	10	10	10	10	7	3	3	10	9	9†		10	8
Result	L		D		D		L		L		D		W		D		D		L	
Points	7		6		3		7		7		6		22		5		7		7	

3 – D.J. Wild, D.K. Lillee and M.A. Robinson   † N.G.B. Cook retired hurt
2 – S.J. Brown and sub (ct 1 /st 1)
1 – D.S. Hoffman

captures close to a hundred wickets every season, yet gets only fleeting recognition. He deserves more.

Middlesex added to their stock of trophies in recent years when they again won the NatWest Bank Trophy, but they promised more at the beginning of the season than they ultimately achieved. Gatting's problems and Emburey's loss of form could not have helped, but it was the loss of Williams, who has spent so much time injured that one must fear for his future, that caused their collapse. Hughes was expensive, and Tufnell found taking wickets harder than he seemed to do in 1987. Slack ended the year in fine style, and Carr, in spite of a bad patch, confirmed his class. Brown was very unlucky, but looks likely to make good the loss of Radley, while Downton remained, as ever, a fine wicket-keeper and an excellent team-man. The stars of the season, however, were Cowans, fully fit and consistent, and Angus Fraser, the most improved bowler in the country and a player of real quality.

Bailey prospered and was always good to watch with Northamptonshire, cynically referred to as the rest home for overseas pacemen. Capel disappointed with the ball, and the Northants tail looked alarmingly long at times.

Nick Cook bowled well and was desperately unlucky to miss his Test recall. Lamb remains an eminently joyous cricketer, but there are some doubts about the substance at Northamptonshire, which leads one to believe they may struggle for a couple of years. Curtley Ambrose could change that opinion.

If one had to point to a side to win trophies in 1989, one would choose Surrey. They are wonderfully led, and they have a mainly young and vigorous side. Greig himself is a constant source of inspiration. In 1988, Surrey fielded brilliantly on the ground and caught practically nothing. Neither Stewart nor Lynch, of whom so much was expected, found their form until late. If Clarke is fit and eager and if Martin Bicknell continues his advance, Surrey will take some stopping. They are strong in reserve, and the development of left-arm spinner Medlycott has given them an extra dimension.

Parker did well in difficult circumstances at Sussex, but the squad is generally immature, and there is a desperate need for a batsman to find consistent form to aid Parker. Sadly, Imran has been of little assistance to the Club on or off the field in his last season.

Lancashire, too, are in need of a batsman to help build

BOWLING	A. Walker	S.J. Brown	M.A. Robinson	N.G.B. Cook	W. Larkins	R.G. Williams	W.W. Davis	D.K. Lillee	D.J. Capel
v. Oxford University (Oxford) 20–2 April	22–9–40–2 12.4–5–20–3	21–13–25–2 16–8–20–3	21–5–43–3 7–2–13–0	15–8–18–1 24–7–32–4	9–9–0–1	4–3–6–1 5–2–7–0			
v. Leicestershire (Leicester) 28 April–2 May		33–5–107–2	27–5–82–2	16.2–9–9–2			36–5–115–4		
v. Gloucestershire (Northampton) 5–9 May	17.2–5–50–4 20–3–68–3	15–3–27–2 3–0–8–0		5–3–4–1 7–3–12–0	2–1–1–0			16–4–39–1 29–8–68–6	16–6–35–2 14–3–32–1
v. Warwickshire (Northampton) 17–20 May	25–9–67–2 14–1–40–3	14–5–34–0		34–11–57–0 1–0–3–0		3.2–0–10–2 6.4–3–9–3	36–5–141–6 19–3–44–4		22–5–75–0 1–0–6–0
v. Surrey (The Oval) 21–4 May	14–2–51–1 7–2–19–0			18–5–48–3 19–4–68–4		5–1–9–0 10–1–49–1	14–2–51–1 12.4–3–31–2		16–3–43–1 5–1–13–0
v. Leicestershire (Northampton) 28–31 May	15–5–40–3 26.1–5–59–4			31–18–33–2	3–0–17–0	6–3–4–0		12–1–39–0 2–1–9–0	14–3–40–4 31–9–72–3
v. Yorkshire (Northampton) 1–3 June			8–1–28–0 15–2–53–1	6–3–10–0 14–7–25–1		13–3–30–3	20.4–6–54–5 21–6–49–1		11–5–12–3 21–2–65–2
v. Somerset (Taunton) 4–7 June	2–1–5–0			4–1–7–0		2–0–3–0	24–5–92–5 15–0–54–4		17–3–52–2 10.5–0–63–3
v. West Indians (Northampton) 11–13 June			17–3–52–1 10–3–15–0	29.2–7–66–3 25–6–90–2	10–3–21–1				12–2–51–1 15–2–35–2
v. Middlesex (Luton) 18–21 June	5–0–12–0 4–1–20–2			29–4–61–4 29–4–73–0		18–4–64–1 19–3–76–2	21.1–3–54–5 11–4–22–0		12–2–52–0 12–2–40–1
v. Nottinghamshire (Trent Bridge) 25–8 June	13–4–36–2 15–4–50–1					7–2–17–0	15–3–42–2 20–5–43–3		13–3–35–1 23–2–68–3
v. Lancashire (Northampton) 2–5 July	18–3–63–1		22–6–63–3			19.2–5–28–2	21–0–66–0		
v. Gloucestershire (Bristol) 13–15 July	7–1–29–0			31.5–10–103–3			27–3–92–6		20–3–62–0
v. Derbyshire (Derby) 16–18 July	21–3–70–1			23.3–10–39–2		5–0–21–0	25–4–71–1		16–2–48–1
v. Kent (Northampton) 20–2 July			3–0–10–0	32–12–63–0 26–4–105–5		24–3–86–5 20.4–0–113–4		11–2–43–1 9–3–26–0	13–2–52–1 7–1–31–0
v. Sussex (Northampton) 23–6 July			17–1–64–2	8–4–13–1		21–8–43–0	16.5–0–52–7 24–5–84–3		16–2–59–3 15–2–67–1
v. Worcestershire (Worcester) 30 July–2 Aug.			29–7–102–4	15–5–38–0		3–0–6–0		30–6–106–1	20–3–92–1
v. Essex (Northampton) 3–5 August	24–6–68–3 13–1–32–1		18.3–3–34–3 7.1–1–18–0	17–6–29–0 21–9–30–3			28–6–102–3 23–6–41–2		
v. Warwickshire (Edgbaston) 6–9 August	23–2–86–2 14.3–6–28–2		23–4–68–2 6–1–13–0	15.1–2–26–1 2–1–7–0			27–4–76–5 11–1–32–2		
v. Hampshire (Bournemouth) 13–16 August	15–3–42–0 7–0–34–0		16–4–33–3 18–4–38–4	26–11–45–3 31–17–33–2				22–1–75–2 17–5–43–2	9.5–3–27–1
v. Glamorgan (Wellingborough) 20–3 August	21–4–64–5 7–0–26–0		27–10–48–3 12–2–19–4	12.4–6–30–2 23–12–34–2			28–7–66–0 14–2–42–1		
v. Derbyshire (Northampton) 25–9 August	26–6–68–3 10.5–1–43–2		23–4–61–2 16–4–24–3	15.3–8–25–2 21–9–40–3				28–1–96–3 20–5–58–0	
v. Yorkshire (Scarborough) 9–12 September	10–1–43–1 11.2–2–27–0		19–3–53–3 20–6–59–3	22–7–46–1 9–3–13–0		30–7–80–4 48–12–110–3	18–2–67–1 9–2–31–0		5–0–26–0 6–0–39–0
v. Essex (Chelmsford) 14–17 September			16–3–48–0 5–1–14–0	42.2–18–56–6 25–2–100–3		19–5–56–1 15–1–74–0		27–3–101–3 9–2–28–1	5–1–29–0
	440.5–95– 1300–51 av. 25.49	102–34– 221–9 av. 24.55	402.4–85– 1055–46 av. 22.93	725.4–256– 1491–66 av. 22.59	24–13– 39–2 av. 19.50	304–66– 901–32 av. 28.15	537.2–92– 1614–73 av. 22.10	232–42– 731–20 av. 36.55	398.2–72– 1321–37 av. 35.70

a J.P. Agnew absent ill

D.J. Wild	D.S. Hoffman	R.J. Bailey	A.J. Lamb	G. Cook	Byes	Leg-byes	Wides	No-balls	Total	Wkts
					3	2	1	11	137	10
						3		1	95	10
						14		27	327	10
					4	12		3	172	10
					7	6			201	10
9–0–22–0					1	8	9	14	415	10
					8	2		10	112	10
3–0–12–0						1		1	215	6
					1	7			188	7
11–3–18–2						6		3	143	9a
21–3–61–0					4	5	2	6	264	10
15–4–45–1					1	5		4	155	10
					2	4	1	12	228	9
14.4–3–38–3					4	14	1	1	215	10
17–6–50–3						11	11		178	10
18–2–62–2	13–3–43–1				4	10	1	3	288	10
5–2–15–0	19–3–54–1	17–2–77–2	4–0–19–0		6	13		2	345	8
6–0–28–0					6		1	5	277	10
					1	2	1		234	6
10.1–5–18–4					2	10	2	1	143	10
28–5–77–2					1	19	2	5	275	10
4–0–16–0					8	6	1	13	250	7
									0	0
12–3–44–0					9	9	1	11	348	10
11–0–47–1					3	9	2	3	308	6
									0	0
		2–0–3–0			5	6		4	268	7
						13			288	9
					1	6	9	8	118	10
		5–2–5–0				11		14	287	8
3–1–10–0						8	2	7	362	6
						5	1	18	238	10
					1	13		4	135	6
					7	15	2	13	278	10
						2			82	4
		2.1–0–11–1			1	5	2	6	239	10
		2–0–12–1				4		3	164	9
					4	8		11	220	10
		9–0–27–3				9		6	157	10
					2	8		11	260	10
				3–1–2–0		5	4	4	172	8
						5		15	320	10
		33–6–107–0	2–0–5–0		3	3		4	397	6
		6–0–36–0			8	14		4	312	10
					10	13			275	
187.5–37– 563–18 *av.* 31.27	32–6– 97–2 *av.* 48.50	76.1–10– 278–7 *av.* 39.71	4–0– 19–0 —	5–1– 7–0 —						

Nottinghamshire CCC
First-Class Matches, 1988

BATTING	v. MCC (Lord's) 16–18 April	v. Middlesex (Lord's) 21–5 April	v. Worcestershire (Worcester) 28 April–2 May	v. Lancashire (Trent Bridge) 5–9 May	v. Gloucestershire (Trent Bridge) 18–20 May	v. Sussex (Trent Bridge) 21–4 May	v. Derbyshire (Derby) 28–31 May	v. Kent (Dartford) 1–3 June	v. Warwickshire (Edgbaston) 4–7 June	v. Glamorgan (Trent Bridge) 11–14 June	v. Oxford University (Oxford) 15–17 June	v. Hampshire (Southampton) 18–21 June	v. Northamptonshire (Trent Bridge) 25–8 June	v. Middlesex (Trent Bridge) 13–15 July
B.C. Broad	49 32	68 10	53 27	4 32			41 —		23* —		2 15		3 47	24 —
R.T. Robinson	129 18	1 4	8 22	44 115	0 45	46 8	25 —	31 56	23* —					11 —
M. Newell	23 26*	80 3	1 2	0 0	2 25	14 26			18 10*	26 0	16 0	24 80	44 21	2 —
P. Johnson	61* 59*	13 60	1 2	17 4	14 24	20 24	3 —	0 30	18 19		104 58*	49 140	31 32	32 —
J.D. Birch	23* —	10 4	0 13	36 19	6 41	1 24	31 —	5 0	3 1	7 0	114* —	36 8	0 75	0 —
F.D. Stephenson	— —	63 24	8 0	79 15	35 13	63 1	0 —				6 65		10 0	1 —
B.N. French	— —	21 0	17 13											
E.E. Hemmings	— —	28* 23		11* 1			13		1* 1		15* 12		13 5	6 10
R.A. Pick	— —	0 19			1* 11									
K.E. Cooper	— —	0 0*	3* 33*	2 13	5 0	0* 12	12 —	3 5*	— 3	0 23*		21 0	30 0	0 0
K. Saxelby	— —	8 0	4 17			0 0	2 —	0 1	— 0		6* —			
D.W. Randall			10 69	9 10	2 58	64 15	24 —	7 44	69* 1	67 30		6 26	10 0	50
M.K. Bore			5 0											
J.A. Afford				3 0*	0 0*	0 1*		0 0						
C.W. Scott				0 11	20 3	5 7	16* —	1 21	22 0	2 34	20* —	5 0	0 3	5 5
K.P. Evans					4 3					1 29	29 —	6 34	4 13*	32
P. Pollard						44 19	0 —	2 142	28 6	39 1		16 11	8 34	
D.J.R. Martindale								6 15					29 52*	
C.L. Cairns								7* 15	7 0					
D.J. Millns											0 7	— —	7* 5*	0* 0
R.J. Evans													21 —	
C.D. Fraser-Darling													18 —	
D.J. Callaghan														
Byes	2	4	2	7 3		4		16	1	4	3		4	2 1
Leg-byes	9 2	4 5	8 9	9 8	5 5	9 4	8	3 8	9 1	4 9	6 2	7 13	10 19	8
Wides	1 2	2	1 1	1	2 2	3 5	7		3	2 3	11	1	2 2	
No-balls	1	8 1	5 4	2 4	1 4	1	2	4	4 2	3 2	12	4 10	1 5	8
Total	298 139	308 155	132 248	223 236	97 234	270 150	184	65 357	206 44	178 230	405 123	197 359	143 275	173
Wickets	3 2	10 10	10 10	10 10	10 10	10 10	10	10 10	6 9†	10 10	7 2	10 10	10 10	10
Result	D	L	L	L	L	W	D	L	L	W	D	D	W	W
Points	—	7	4	6	4	23	5	8	5	21	—	3	20	12

Fielding Figures

51 – C.W. Scott (ct 49/st 2)	17 – R.T. Robinson	12 – P. Johnson	7 – K.E. Cooper
28 – M. Newell	14 – J.D. Birch	10 – F.P. Stephenson	6 – P. Pollard
19 – K.P. Evans	13 – B.C. Broad and B.N. French	9 – D.W. Randall and E.E. Hemmings	4 – K. Saxelby and D.J. Millns

on the work of Mendis and Fowler. The call will be answered by Atherton, the most exciting young batting talent in the country after Hick. There is a blend of age and youth at Old Trafford, and their Refuge Cup win was welcome and deserved. Watkinson strove nobly to be an all-rounder, and Wasim Akram will give future entertainment. Simmons and Folley span the ball well, but chief honours should go to Paul Allott, who seems to have passed from the reckoning at Test level but who continues to be one of the best opening bowlers in the country, day in and day out.

Undoubtedly, the two most successful pacemen in the country were Stephenson and Cooper of Notts. Each took more than 100 wickets, and not all on the Trent Bridge pitch as some tried to suggest to try to diminish their remarkable achievements. Stephenson's 'double' marked him as the player of the year and underlined the fact that, as he had achieved all that Hadlee had achieved, the man Notts missed most was Clive Rice. His leadership and authority would have turned Notts into a championship winning side, and this only emphasizes the problems that faced Tim Robinson. He had a good season with the bat, but he was faced with impatience and discord over his captaincy, and he faces a hard time. He is a quietly effective and intelligent man, but whether he will be given time to establish his own brand of leadership and to learn about the job remains to be seen. Randall enjoyed an Indian summer, but Broad had a year he will want to forget in every way. He is such a dedicated and likeable man who has applied himself assiduously to the game that one hopes that all will come well for him again very quickly.

There were glimmers of hope at Glamorgan, who featured quite well in the one-day game, but there is still much unfulfilled promise. Greg Thomas was highly praised at the beginning of the season, yet his record at the end was moderate to say the least. Watkin gave hope of future success, but the batting was very fragile. Maynard won an England cap, but his technical deficiencies were patently obvious, which is a pity for he is a joy to watch when he is going well.

Hampshire at last won a final at Lord's, but there was little else to rejoice about. On paper the batting looked strong, but often it performed otherwise. Robin Smith alone showed consistent authority, but there were some pleasing all-round achievements from Ayling and some

v. Worcestershire (Trent Bridge) 16–19 July		v. Somerset (Taunton) 23–6 July		v. West Indians (Trent Bridge) 27–9 July		v. Leicestershire (Worksop) 30 July–2 Aug.		v. Yorkshire (Sheffield) 3–5 August		v. Sri Lankans (Trent Bridge) 6–8 August		v. Essex (Colchester) 13–16 August		v. Lancashire (Lytham) 17–19 August		v. Surrey (Trent Bridge) 20–3 August		v. Leicestershire (Leicester) 30 Aug.–2 Sept.		v. Derbyshire (Trent Bridge) 9–12 September		v. Yorkshire (Trent Bridge) 14–17 September		M	Inns	Nos	Runs	HS	Av
7	4					17	—	1	45	73	—	33	2	17	—	19	11	20	52	48	—	35	10	18	30	—	801	73	26.70
5	107*	50	13	6	—	35	—	6	.67			63	134*	19	—	13	2			11	—	10	14	20	33	3	1141	134*	38.03
8	24	21	2	0	—					25	31*					11	18	12	6	105	—	11	23	20	37	3	740	105	21.76
10	3	73	0	3	—			25	—	124	2	23	5	38	—	23	30	7	74	11	—	59	22	24	42	3	1389	140	35.61
0	34*					23	—	44	—	0	18*	20	—	9	75	48	—	0	10	11	16	11	—	24	39	4	776	114*	22.17
1	—	31	19	56	—	57	—	10	13			35	18	17	—	6	1	6	7	83	—	111	117	22	35	—	1018	117	29.08
11	0																	23	0*	11	—	11	28	7	11	1	135	28	13.50
		1	0*			13*	—	3	—			—	13	9	—	2	31*	18*	—	7*	—	6	3*	17	25	10	245	31*	16.33
																								3	4	1	31	19	10.33
39	—	0*	0	19	—	5	—	16	—					13*	—	14	7*	2	—	1	—	1	0	24	34	9	282	39	11.28
																		5*	4					10	13	2	47	17	4.27
0	33	0	4			134	—	12	29*			76*	1	28	—	0	2	3	90*	237	—	7	59	21	37	4	1286	237	38.96
																								1	2	—	5	5	2.50
																								4	8	3	4	3	0.80
47*	—	0	1	63*	—	18*	—	11	—					1*	40							30	0	19	27	6	356	63*	16.95
11	—	3	5									18*	—	31*	3	33*	4	24	0	54	—	30	0	15	24	4	406	54	20.30
										16	62*													9	17	1	428	142	26.75
				10	46	32	—	12	—	0	6	23	—	18	10	2	—							9	14	1	261	52*	20.07
				2	—					—	—													4	5	1	31	15	7.75
0	—	0	0	1	—					0*	—													11	12	5	20	7*	2.85
										50*	—													2	2	1	71	50*	71.00
																								1	1	—	18	18	18.00
				29	—																			1	1	—	29	29	29.00

v. Worcs		v. Somerset		v. W. Indians		v. Leics (Worksop)		v. Yorks (Sheffield)		v. Sri Lankans		v. Essex		v. Lancashire		v. Surrey		v. Leics (Leicester)		v. Derbyshire		v. Yorks (T.B.)	
	3	8		5				6		1		3				6	2	3		10			
3	12	3	6	3		1		7	12	6	2	6	6	6		4	10	6		13		2	10
1								1		2						2	2					2	
4	6	11	7	5		6		4		17	5	6	3			1		7	4	12		6	7
135	226	211	103	247		367		195	198	250	101	300	274	272	0	144	131	133	258	614		296	297
10	10	10	10	10		8		10	5	5	0	6	8	10	0	10	9‡	10	7	10		10	10
W		D		D		D		D		D		W		W		L		D		W		L	
20		6		—		8		5		—		24		19		4		3		22		5	

3 – D.J.R. Martindale
2 – R.J. Evans, C.D. Fraser-Darling and J.A. Afford
1 – R.A. Pick and sub

† R.T. Robinson absent hurt
‡ K.E. Cooper retired hurt

exciting bowling from Bakker at the season's end. Parks was as efficient as ever behind the stumps, and the return of Marshall and a fit Tremlett and Andrew should make a vast difference.

As the season drew to its close, Yorkshire began to show signs of stability and improvement, for earlier they had been a bitter disappointment after the promise of 1987. Moxon, Metcalfe and Blakey, of whom so much was expected, were late to find form, and the less publicized Robinson was the most dependable of their batsmen. If Jarvis could stay fit and partner Sidebottom, if he could remain fit, and thereby give support to the very much improved and very impressive Fletcher, and if Booth could blossom into the missing spinner, Yorkshire could be a power again. Perhaps that is really what is wrong with English cricket. It has never been strong when Yorkshire has been weak. We look to the White Rose with hope in our hearts. They won't walk alone.

WORLD RANKINGS
Brian Scovell of the *Daily Mail* talks to former England Captain Ted Dexter

A new symbol has started to appear on the TV screen when a batsman comes in to bat in a match these days – the fellow's world rating.

Australian captain Allan Border, for example, has been number two to India's Dilip Vengsarkar for much of last year. Having world ratings shown on TV represents a breakthrough for the man who thought of the idea, former England captain Ted Dexter.

When he first proposed a new type of averages two years ago he was greeted with scepticism. Ted always has been an ideas man. Some very good, others not so good. This one was put in the eccentric class.

He argues: 'Tennis and golf have world rankings, why not cricket? Feed the relevant information into a computer and you get answers.

'If you look at our rankings you will see we just about get it right. Malcolm Marshall, for example, took over from Richard Hadlee last year as the number one bowler

Nottinghamshire CCC
First-Class Matches, 1988

BOWLING	F.D. Stephenson	R.A. Pick	K.E. Cooper	K. Saxelby	E.E. Hemmings	J.D. Birch	M.K. Bore	J.A. Afford	K.P. Evans
v. MCC (Lord's) 16–18 April	15–1–58–1	11–5–37–3	10–3–40–0	7–2–21–3					
	10–1–21–1	12–2–61–1	11–1–44–1	6–0–41–0	13–2–47–1				
v. Middlesex (Lord's) 21–5 April	19–3–52–3	13–2–46–1	20.5–6–52–5	11–2–31–1	4–1–7–0				
	34–4–121–2	23–2–128–2	22–3–96–0	22–4–81–1	8–1–40–0	8–2–28–0			
v. Worcestershire (Worcester) 28 April–2 May	29–7–99–4		29–10–75–5	18–3–58–0		4–1–9–1	9–2–41–0		
	15–8–29–1		12–4–25–2	6–1–23–0		3.1–2–12–1			
v. Lancashire (Trent Bridge) 5–9 May	24–7–47–1		32–11–60–5		27.3–7–62–3	7–2–18–0		6–0–28–1	
	27.2–5–73–2		24–6–47–2		44–16–71–2			28–7–80–3	
v. Gloucestershire (Trent Bridge) 18–20 May	25–6–80–4	15–3–62–2	20.2–5–56–3						11–0–48–1
	13.1–4–36–3		13–5–42–1						
v. Sussex (Trent Bridge) 21–4 May	19.1–8–45–3		23–7–41–5	13–2–57–1		1–1–0–0		10–3–29–1	
	18.3–7–56–3		14–7–19–1	10–2–30–3				14–3–60–3	
v. Derbyshire (Derby) 28–31 May	21.2–9–44–6		19–5–54–2	8–1–16–1	3–1–2–0	7–2–15–1			
	22.3–5–59–6		13–5–19–0	22–4–71–1	2–0–7–0				
v. Kent (Dartford) 1–3 June			30–10–51–2	20–1–52–0		17–2–52–2		25–6–73–1	
			11.5–0–61–5	12–1–45–3					
v. Warwickshire (Edgbaston) 4–7 June			32–10–59–3	22–5–92–0	9.2–4–12–1	10–3–34–0			
			10–2–25–3		10–0–45–1				
v. Glamorgan (Trent Bridge) 11–14 June	22–7–42–5		17–10–15–3		5–2–10–1				6–2–12–0
	13–5–26–2		18–3–60–2		15–6–34–2				
v. Oxford University (Oxford) 15–17 June				18–5–42–0		19–4–63–0			17–4–52–2
				17–4–35–2		8–5–14–1			10–1–26–1
v. Hampshire (Southampton) 18–21 June	29–5–91–2		29–10–67–2		37–10–96–4				13.3–1–61–2
	7–4–25–2		6–3–15–2		5–4–1–1				
v. Northamptonshire (Trent Bridge) 25–8 June	16–5–39–3		15–5–25–4		5–2–7–0				6–3–8–1
	18–4–56–7		17–6–62–3						
v. Middlesex (Trent Bridge) 13–15 July	18–2–45–6		14–2–34–4						15–4–24–0
v. Worcestershire (Trent Bridge) 16–19 July	21–6–52–5		20–5–40–4						11–1–37–0
	20–6–42–3		19.5–2–71–2						10–4–37–2
v. Somerset (Taunton) 23–6 July	18–3–41–4		18.1–7–40–2		23–7–50–4				
	4.3–1–20–0		2–0–3–1		2–0–3–0				
v. West Indians (Trent Bridge) 27–9 July	18–3–49–2		19–3–60–1			1–0–7–0			
v. Leicestershire (Worksop) 30 July–2 Aug.	24.1–4–66–6		18–5–55–2		25–6–101–1				
	20–1–67–1		23–9–59–3		21–7–47–3				
v. Yorkshire (Sheffield) 3–5 August	31.5–7–91–3		33–7–83–2		25–4–73–4				
	3–0–13–0					7.3–1–46–0			
v. Sri Lankans (Trent Bridge) 6–8 August				4.2–2–8–0		17.4–6–44–1			22–8–66–1
						9–4–25–0			8–2–20–0
v. Essex (Colchester) 13–16 August	30–7–74–2		30–5–114–4		35–7–116–2				15–1–31–1
	9–0–43–1		14–3–54–1		22–2–88–2				8–1–31–2
v. Lancashire (Lytham) 17–19 August	17–8–25–5		19–4–42–4		13–7–31–1				7–2–17–0
v. Surrey (Trent Bridge) 20–3 August	22–5–66–2		22–5–90–3		16–3–49–3				10.5–0–59–2
						2–0–5–0			1.3–1–4–1
v. Leicestershire (Leicester) 30 Aug.–2 Sept.	30.4–7–107–4		28–8–80–2		28–8–66–2				24–4–73–1
v. Derbyshire (Trent Bridge) 9–12 September	33–11–91–5		37–6–88–2		33–7–87–3	2–0–7–0			17–2–64–0
	30–11–76–4		15–2–49–2		39–15–65–1				10.5–4–22–3
v. Yorkshire (Trent Bridge) 14–17 September	37–7–105–4		22–5–70–1	15–1–69–1	29–8–60–0				18.1–2–62–3
	34–2–117–7		13–5–37–0	14–2–65–0	10–2–35–0				17–2–75–0
	819.1–196– 2289–125 av. 18.31	74–14– 334–9 av. 37.11	816–220– 2179–101 av. 21.57	245.2–42– 837–17 av. 49.23	508.5–139– 1312–42 av. 31.23	123.2–35– 379–7 av. 54.14	9–2– 41–0 —	83–19– 270–9 av. 30.00	285.5–49– 829–22 av. 37.68

a T.E. Jesty retired ill   b C.W. Scott 1–0–10–0   c R.T. Robinson 4–0–38–0   d B.C. Broad 4–0–30–0; P Pollard 1.5–0–5–0

C.L. Cairns	M. Newell	D.J. Mills	C.D. Fraser-Darling	R.J. Evans	P. Johnson	D.J. Callaghan	Byes	Leg-byes	Wides	No-balls	Total	Wkts
								3		5	159	7
							1	7		6	222	5
							4	7			199	10
							11			3	505	5
								8		1	290	10
								3		1	92	4
							4	2	2	1	221	10
							7	11		2	289	9a
								8	1	1	254	10
								2		1	80	4
								10	4	6	182	10
							1	5		1	171	10
							4	8			143	10
							2	1		1	159	7
19–3–70–4							5	9		3	312	9
								5		1	111	8
25–2–89–4							3	11	3	5	300	8
5–1–20–0	1–0–11–0						5	5			111	4
		3–1–15–1						9		1	91	10
		10–1–37–3					1	5	1	4	175	10
		15–0–52–1	2–0–8–0				6	5	4		228	3
	3–2–1–0	5–0–15–0	10–4–22–0	20–8–40–3	2–1–1–0		4	4		1	162	7
		17–5–53–1					6	15	4	5	389	10
							3	1			45	5
		6–1–21–2						5			105	10
							2	2		1	122	10
		4–0–15–0						15	16		133	10
		9–3–26–1					1	3	1	5	159	10
		13–0–40–3					2	7		7	199	10
		5–0–26–0					2	8		8	167	10
								1			27	1
24–5–82–4		29–7–102–2				17–1–59–1		10	2	7	362	10
											17	0b
		5–0–24–0						11		5	257	10
		4–0–16–0					1	10		1	200	7
		19–1–83–1					1	6		1	337	10
		6–1–18–0					1	3			119	0c
19–2–70–3	2.4–0–13–1	15–0–95–1					2	9		9	307	7
17–3–53–0	11–2–38–2	14–2–45–3		5–1–23–0				5	4	12	244	7d
							2	10	5	10	347	9
							6	4		2	226	6
											0	0
								6		7	121	10
							1	4		4	269	10
								1			10	1
								6		1	332	9
							2	8		7	347	10
							5	9	4	5	226	10
								14		4	380	10
							4	7		2	340	7
109–16– 384–15 av. 25.60	17.4–4– 63–3 av.21.00	179–22– 683–19 av. 35.94	12–4– 30–0 —	25–9– 63–3 av. 21.00	2–1– 1–0 —	17–1– 59–1 av. 59.00						

Somerset CCC
First-Class Matches, 1988

BATTING	v. Sussex (Hove) 21–5 April		v. Glamorgan (Cardiff) 28 April–2 May		v. Worcestershire (Taunton) 5–9 May		v. West Indians (Taunton) 14–16 May		v. Worcestershire (Worcester) 18–20 May		v. Lancashire (Old Trafford) 28–31 May		v. Hampshire (Southampton) 1–3 June		v. Northamptonshire (Taunton) 4–7 June		v. Warwickshire (Bath) 11–14 June		v. Sussex (Bath) 15–17 June		v. Glamorgan (Taunton) 29 June–1 July		v. Essex (Taunton) 2–5 July		v. Gloucestershire (Bristol) 16–19 July		v. Nottinghamshire (Taunton) 23–6 July	
N.A. Felton	39	0	8	64*	24	36	10	4	16	13*	0	11	18	—	5	2												
P.M. Roebuck	12	19	40	24*	0	17			8	5											112*	—	—	24	22	26	0	5
N.J. Pringle	4	10															41*	2	40	20*					42	0	3	6*
M.D. Crowe	19	25			28	53	2	12	132	—	136*	80																
R.J. Harden	5	45	0	—	2	3																						
V.J. Marks	23	0	8	—	42	7	4	42	6	—	8	38	20	—	43	13	—	7	15*	40	—	—	—	—	21	—	9	—
N.D. Burns	16*	133*	66	—	32	11	0	0	3	—	16*	16	47	—	8	9	—	9	13	2	—	—	—	—	5	—	0	—
G.V. Palmer	0	23																										
N.A. Mallender	2	44	29*	—	3	1					—	3*							—	8*					0	—	1	—
A.N. Jones	0	6	6	—	8*	3*			0	—			3	—			10	—	—	8*					38	—	2*	—
D.J. Foster	9	1	9	—					6*	2*	0*	—	—	—	20	—	8*	2*	—	0*					9*	—		
J.J.E. Hardy			0	—	39	0	17	8	70	8*	30	18	0	—	12	0	81	29	1	40	12	—	—	6	6	52*	25	15*
S.R. Waugh			53	—			1	27			115*	—	13	—	37	40	103*	79	137	85	101*	—	—	33*	33	1*	0	—
G.D. Rose			27	—	12	30	12	14	20	—	—	12*	13	—	5	18	—	2	10*	0					0	—	22	—
C.H. Dredge					16	17	4	5									37	3										
J.G. Wyatt							42	19	45	—	47	1	20	—	30	69			16	4	6	—			2*			
M.W. Cleal							6	19	8	—	—	12	13	—					—	5								
R.J. Bartlett											31	4	19	—	0	0	28	0	38	35			—	15*	6	—	39	—
T.J.A. Scrivens																			—	—								
H.R.J. Trump																											48	
Byes		8	6	4		2		1				4	4		4		7	3	1	10	5				1	4	2	
Leg-byes	3	10	4	4	6	1	1	5	3	5	1	7	9		14	11	12	9	5	6	3			5	7	2	8	1
Wides				3					1	1			2				1	1	1	1								
No-balls	10	6	11	4	10	11	8	3	15	1	4		5		1		4	2			4				5	8	8	
Total	142	333	267	100	222	192	113	146	327	33	273	202	308		215	178	284	215	276	250	243		0	85	195	93	167	27
Wickets	10	10	10	0	10	10	10	10	10	1	5	8	10		10	10	3	9	6	7	2		0	2	10	2	10	1
Result	L		D		L		L		W		W		D		L		D		D		D		D		W		D	
Points	4		4		4		—		24		22		6		6		4		13		5		3		21		5	

Fielding Figures:
59 – N.D. Burns (ct 57/st 2)
23 – J.J.E. Hardy
20 – S.R. Waugh
12 – R.J. Bartlett
11 – G.D. Rose
9 – N.J. Pringle and J.G. Wyatt
8 – V.J. Marks, N.A. Mallender and A.N. Jones
7 – N.A. Felton and H.R.J. Trump
6 – P.M. Roebuck

and no one would argue with that.

'Vengsarkar stayed top of the batting because he had some very good innings in India against the West Indies. I thought Gordon Greenidge, Viv Richards or Richie Richardson might have dislodged him during the tour of England but none of them had a particularly good summer.

'It was left to Jeffrey Dujon and Gus Logie to improve their positions. Gus made the biggest advance of all, up 26 places to 13th.

'With normal averages you get people in them who shouldn't be there and we all know who they are, players who haven't done the hard work others have done. I am not saying our ratings should replace the traditional averages, but they are a useful addition.'

Dexter, together with the international accountants and management consultants Deloitte Haskins and Sells developed the scheme. With constant mentions on BBC for around 400 hours every summer, plus even more exposure on Channel 9 in Australia and on the TV network in New Zealand, Deloitte should be delighted with their investment.

It has increased their market awareness worldwide even if the British Press remains generally aloof. Records of more than 200 Tests played since 1981 are stored in the Deloitte computer. Every time a Test is played anywhere in the world, all the details are fed in.

The true value of players' performances are sought by 'weighting' them according to conditions. Dexter says that the average number of runs scored per wicket at Tests overall is 30.83. But at Headingley, that figure could drop to 20 or less. At Adelaide it could rise to 50 or more.

So a hundred at Headingly is looked upon as a far greater achievement and treated accordingly. That doesn't happen in normal averages.

Dexter doesn't claim the Deloitte system is the definitive answer. 'It adds to the debate really,' he says. 'Richie Benaud was for it from the start. He said it was something interesting, something fresh.

'It also enabled us to examine the performances of players we didn't know so much about. For example, someone like Ranatunga of Sri Lanka, who is a very good little player. Ranatunga doesn't play against Sri Lanka so he doesn't have any easy games. He is in at number seven through a series of good performances against good opposition and deserves it.'

v. Kent (Canterbury) 30 July–2 Aug.		v. Surrey (Weston-s-Mare) 3–5 August		v. Derbyshire (Weston-s-Mare) 6–9 August		v. Somerset (Scarborough) 13–16 August		v. Middlesex (Uxbridge) 17–19 August		v. Leicestershire (Hinckley) 20–3 August		v. Hampshire (Taunton) 25–9 August		v. Warwickshire (Edgbaston) 9–12 September		v. Gloucestershire (Taunton) 14–17 September		M	Inns	NOs	Runs	HS	Av
						21	61	88	7	11	24	36	57	17	0	21	127	14	27	2	720	127	28.80
68	—	10	47*	—	—					5	10							12	19	3	454	112*	28.37
54	—	9	0	4*	9													8	15	4	244	54	22.18
																		5	9	1	487	136*	60.87
												0	4*	63	43	78	52	6	11	1	295	78	29.50
—	—	0	—	46	11	25	33*	34	—	0	50	42	—	68	11	50	3	23	31	2	719	68	24.79
45*	—	35	25*	33	2	15	3	7	13*	11	17	9	—	1	48*	56	2	23	34	7	708	133*	26.22
																		1	2	—	23	23	11.50
—	—	5	0	2*	4	23*	3	11*	—	3	9			6	—			16	19	6	157	44	12.07
—	—	4	—	0	9*	—	0*	3	—	7	1*	17*	—	5	—			20	21	8	130	38	10.00
		4*	—													0*	2	13	14	9	72	20	14.40
14	—	23	26	60	25	97	10	26	28	0	2	19	50	40	23	5	10	22	39	3	927	97	25.75
61	—	31	4	44	1	2	31	83	112*									15	24	6	1314	161	73.00
—	—					69*	8	6*	—	0	6	34	—	37*	6*	14	8	20	25	6	385	69*	20.26
																		3	6	—	82	37	13.66
						1	44	0	19	57	14	8	5	29	26	23	0	15	26	1	578	69	23.12
										8*	13	1	—	0	—	9	3	9	12	1	97	19	8.81
02*	—	25	3	66	8	0	33	9	35	38	0	23	17*	67	4	3	0	18	29	3	648	102*	24.92
				7	4													2	2	—	11	7	5.50
—	—	4	—	8	0	0	0	2	—			0	—			0	0*	8	10	1	62	48	6.88
3		3							4				4	4	7	5							
4		6	5	10	2	9	5	2	11	12	9	10	9	18	13	5	3						
					2				1	1	3			2									
1				1	5	8	10	4	2	11	12	2	3	15	4	8	4						
52		159	110	281	82	270	241	275	232	164	170	201	149	372	185	277	214						
4		10	5	8	9†	8	9	9‡	4	10	10	10	3	10	6	10	10						
W		W		L		D		D		L		D		D		L							
23		21		5		3		6		5		5		6		6							

4 – M.D. Crowe
3 – R.J. Harden
2 – M.W. Cleal and subs

† P.M. Roebuck absent hurt
‡ G.D. Rose retired hurt

Slowly the critics came round to Dexter's way of thinking. Perhaps there was dissatisfaction about the averages we have accepted as inviolate over the years. A bowler who took a lot of wickets in a particular match on a pitch that suited him should be penalized but isn't.

A classic case is the Indian teenage leg-spin and googly bowler Nirwal Hirwani, who took 16 wickets in his first Test at Bangalore. In any accepted current list of Test bowlers, Hirwani would be top in terms of runs per wicket. But in Deloitte ratings he is discounted because he hasn't taken part in enough Tests.

Dexter claims that the bowlers who head his list are there on merit. 'Marshall overtook Hadlee because he had a great series in England,' he says. 'He saw that the pitches were easy paced and cut his pace down accordingly and moved the ball. That was intelligent, high class bowling.

'If you look at the top ten in our list you will see that they are all bowlers who do something with the ball. Hadlee is there in second place, Imran in third and the surprise packet, Winston Benjamin, in fourth.

'Benjamin started the year way down in 29th place but went shooting up because he got people out by moving the ball. He always seemed capable of taking wickets, unlike someone like Patrick Patterson, who was fast and nasty but didn't do anything with it.

'Graham Dilley did well. He battled away and got wickets and so did Neil Foster when he was fit. And a significant point about the bowling figures was that the Australians started to come through – Steve Waugh, Bruce Reid, Craig McDermott and Tony Dodemaide.

'Waugh varies his pace and tries to mix it up. On good pitches in Test matches you've go to do that as Ian Botham showed over the years. In county cricket you can just run up and put it on the spot and the pitch will help you do the rest. If you bowl like that in Tests, you're just playing the batsmen in.

'Botham never let the batsmen settle. He was always inviting batsmen to play shots against him and take risks.'

Top placed Englishman in the batting list was, inevitably, skipper Graham Gooch, who moved up to 10th from 21st, a reflection on his consistency against the world's best bowlers. His predecessor Mike Gatting dropped from 12th to 27th and there was a sudden fall for John Emburey, whose performances on the winter tour with the bat earned him unexpected promotion.

The Deloitte ratings are sent to around 150 outlets

Somerset CCC
First-Class Matches, 1988

BOWLING	D.J. Foster	A.N. Jones	N.A. Mallender	V.J. Marks	G.V. Palmer	N.J. Pringle	P.M. Roebuck	G.D. Rose	S.R. Waugh
v. Sussex (Hove) 21–5 April	16–1–67–4	12–2–49–2	27–7–59–2	18–4–55–1	8.2–0–26–1				
	8–1–35–0	15–2–35–0	17–3–46–1	17–6–49–2	10–2–28–0	1–0–6–0	0.4–0–4–0		
v. Glamorgan (Cardiff) 28 April–2 May	17–1–84–1	22–2–65–0	24–7–79–1	33–7–107–0			11–0–26–1	24–2–96–3	11–1–33–2
v. Worcestershire (Taunton) 5–9 May		32–4–97–0	32–9–86–1	50–6–141–1			10–0–48–0	31–8–101–3	
v. West Indians (Taunton) 14–16 May	17–2–77–3			6–2–13–0				21–4–71–3	
v. Worcestershire (Worcester) 18–20 May	18.3–2–46–4	19–1–43–1		22–6–40–1				19–5–51–3	
	15–6–31–2	14–3–28–3						7–1–37–1	
v. Lancashire (Old Trafford) 28–31 May	25–3–96–1		4–2–2–0	40.4–11–91–5				17.2–0–75–1	
	19–4–58–2			7–3–14–1				13.2–2–39–4	
v. Hampshire (Southampton) 1–3 June	16–2–41–1	18–9–30–7		46–11–111–3				16.3–5–53–2	
	15–3–40–0	13–2–42–0						15–3–44–1	
v. Northamptonshshire (Taunton) 4–7 June	13–5–25–1	20–1–81–3		8–5–14–0				28–8–81–3	9–3–17–1
	10–0–41–0	9–1–49–3		1–0–6–0				4–0–18–0	
v. Warwickshire (Bath) 11–14 June	17–5–43–0	11–0–53–0		46–13–108–3				22–6–47–6	
	12–0–40–2	12–2–35–1		28–8–75–4				12–4–29–0	
v. Sussex (Bath) 15–17 June		13–3–36–1	24–6–75–1	34–11–61–2				19–6–63–1	3–1–10–0
		8–0–29–0	7–1–21–1	23–4–81–1				6–0–30–0	
v. Glamorgan (Taunton) 29 June–1 July	23–5–72–4	14.2–1–48–0	21–8–33–0	20–5–43–2			2–1–1–0	19–7–40–1	
	12–1–52–1	10–2–49–0	15–3–53–1	17–7–37–0			1–1–0–0	10–3–16–1	
v. Essex (Taunton) 2–5 July	14–0–62–1	11.4–2–33–0	8–3–13–1	17–2–49–2			3–0–16–0	11.2–1–41–2	
v. Gloucestershire (Bristol) 16–19 July	12–2–36–1	11.3–4–47–3	16–0–47–4	2–0–11–0				8–0–20–2	
	2–0–12–0	6–1–26–1	9.3–2–20–2	10–3–25–4				12–2–31–3	
v. Nottinghamshire (Taunton) 23–6 July		7–0–28–0	21–6–49–2	32–10–73–5				10–1–31–0	
		14–3–42–3	8–3–8–2	12–1–43–5				3–1–4–0	
v. Kent (Canterbury) 30 July–2 Aug.		9–3–33–3	7–1–19–2	13–3–37–1				7–2–14–0	
		15–4–33–2	18–12–12–5	29–8–68–2		2–0–5–0		3–1–7–0	
v. Surrey (Weston-s-Mare) 3–5 August	5–0–24–0	11–2–36–2	19–6–22–4	16–4–32–1					
	4–0–18–0	13–3–29–1	16–5–18–3	20–7–41–5					
v. Derbyshire (Weston-s-Mare) 6–9 August		14–4–58–0	20.5–7–29–3	28–5–61–2		1–0–4–0			
		3–0–14–0	5–2–7–0	5–0–18–0		9–1–25–1	1–0–11–0		
v. Yorkshire (Scarborough) 13–16 August		20–5–71–0	17.1–3–46–1	31–6–98–0				16–3–71–1	
		8–0–26–0	11–4–19–2	14–3–63–2				4–2–8–0	
v. Middlesex (Uxbridge) 17–19 August		17–3–55–2	14–0–52–2	13–3–52–2				11–2–44–0	
		7–0–30–1	8–2–43–3	12.4–3–41–0				2–1–4–0	
v. Leicestershire (Hinckley) 20–3 August		15–1–55–2	17–3–49–1	13.4–3–34–3				17–6–40–2	
		9–2–40–1	7–0–20–0	2–2–0–0				10–2–41–1	
v. Hampshire (Taunton) 25–9 August		21.3–3–66–3		26–5–61–1				23–9–56–3	
		23–5–77–4						23.2–6–47–4	
v. Warwickshire (Edgbaston) 9–12 September		21–5–45–3	18–3–42–2	39.3–17–66–3				13–4–28–0	
		13–0–45–3		30–4–115–3				13–1–56–3	
v. Gloucestershire (Taunton) 14–17 September	6–1–34–0			50.2–14–118–7				15–3–43–0	
	3–2–10–0			30–10–62–2				19–5–50–3	
	299.3–46–	512–85–	411.3–108–	862.5–222–	18.2–2–	13–1–	28.4–2–	504.5–116–	23–5–
	1044–28	1658–55	969–47	2214–76	54–1	40–1	106–1	1527–57	60–3
	av. 37.28	av. 30.14	av. 20.61	av. 29.13	av. 54.00	av. 40.00	av. 106.00	av. 26.78	av. 20.00

a N.A. Felton 0.5–0–8–0   b I.T. Botham absent injured   c G. Fowler absent hurt   d J.J.E. Hardy 0.3–0–12–0

R.J. Harden	C.H. Dredge	M.W. Cleal	J.G. Wyatt	H.R.J. Trump	R.J. Bartlett	T.J.A. Scrivens	Byes	Leg-byes	Wides	No-balls	Total	Wkts
							6	4	2	8	266	10
							3	7		8	213	3
14–1–50–0								3		12	543	8
	34.5–8–133–2						6	16		4	628	7
	15–5–44–0	15–3–41–4						5		2	251	10
			1–0–4–0								12	0a
		13–2–49–1						11	2	11	240	10
		7.3–0–16–3						7	8	7	119	9b
		22–4–63–1			1–1–0–0			2	1	2	329	9
		9–2–27–2					4	3	2	4	145	9c
		9–3–27–0						5	1		156	10
		13–2–59–0			7–0–37–0		1	2		1	336	4
	15–7–34–1						2	6	1	20	260	10
	4–0–14–0						3	3		6	134	3
		15–3–47–0					7	10	1	7	315	9
		6.3–1–24–3						6		1	209	10
						32–6–71–0		4		14	320	6
						16–4–42–1		3		4	206	3
							1	14	1	16	252	8
			8–4–24–1		5–3–9–1			7	3	5	247	7
					5–0–20–1		1	11		10	258	7d
											0	0
								7		6	168	10
								5		3	119	10
				14–8–17–2	1–0–2–0		8	3	1	10	211	10
				1–1–0–0				6		7	103	10
				7.5–1–17–4				1			121	10
				21–4–53–1			5	2	1	5	185	10
				19.1–7–32–3				2		5	148	10
				7–3–9–1				4		4	119	10
				31–9–81–3		25–6–84–1	3	4			324	10
				17–2–58–1	7–0–48–1	23–9–40–1		1		1	222	4
				26–6–81–1				2	1	8	369	3
				10–3–56–1	1–0–9–1			1		4	182	7
				22–7–41–1			7	4	1	2	255	8
				5–1–24–1			1	6		6	149	6
		11–2–43–2	1–0–6–0				4	2		6	233	10
								2		2	103	3
		16–2–63–1		24–4–63–1			1	11		11	321	10
		1–1–0–1					5	6	1	3	135	9
2–0–11–0		14–0–51–2					12	2	1	5	257	10
		9–0–42–0			3–0–20–0			12	1	4	290	9
		7–0–30–0		39–10–96–2			5	9		4	335	10
				14–4–25–1			2	8			157	6
16–1– 61–0 —	68.5–20– 225–3 av. 75.00	168–25– 582–20 av. 29.10	10–4– 34–1 av. 34.00	258–70– 653–23 av. 28.39	30–4– 145–4 av. 36.25	96–25– 237–3 av. 79.00						

Surrey CCC
First-Class Matches, 1988

BATTING	v. Hampshire (Southampton) 21–5 April		v. Cambridge Univ. (Cambridge) 28–30 April		v. Middlesex (The Oval) 5–9 May		v. Northamptonshire (The Oval) 21–4 May		v. Essex (Chelmsford) 28–31 May		v. Sussex (The Oval) 1–3 June		v. Yorkshire (Harrogate) 4–7 June		v. Leicestershire (The Oval) 11–14 June		v. Cambridge Univ. (The Oval) 15–17 June		v. Derbyshire (The Oval) 25–8 June		v. Warwickshire (The Oval) 2–5 July		v. Hampshire (Guildford) 13–15 July		v. Kent (Guildford) 16–19 July		v. Lancashire (Southport) 20–2 July	
G.S. Clinton	11	3	74	—	2	3	50	8	12*	10	10	—	101	—	59	13			31	18*	23	—			43	71*	15	12
D.M. Smith	4	32*	45	—	28	8	0	10	10*	30	131		34		15	59					19	—	157*	23	15*	10*	73	45
A.J. Stewart	14	6*	13	—	3	6	—	5	—	0	39	—	31*	—							0	—	72	27	56	17	73	45
M.A. Lynch	39	—	103*	—	15	73			—	22	93		36		5	34			56	—	63	—	48*	44*	10	3	19	29
D.M. Ward	6	—	53*	31	14	10	51*	40	—	1	66		17		27	1	12	1	0	—	62*	—	—	6*	70*	0	23*	6
C.J. Richards	61	—			13*	6	85	26	—	5	102*	—	60*	—					77	—	49	—			30	2		
I.A. Greig	34	—	67	—	2	30	9	47	—	14					2	2			12	—	7	—			19	6	0	23
K.T. Medlycott	37	—	20*	—	0	5	12	19*	—	7			54*	—	24	71			0	—					10	0	0	24
M.A. Feltham	15	—			0	1	4*	8*	—	20					17	34*			7*	—					31	48	0	0*
N.H. Peters	0	—			2	5*			—		0				2*	25*	—	2*							0*	—	6	—
S.T. Clarke	14*	—			15	22			—		0										18*	—					4	—
C.K. Bullen			—	45													—	56	18*	—							4	—
M. Frost																												
D.J. Bicknell							2	17							0	7	62	29	16	28			6	15				
M.P. Bicknell							—	—			—	—															1	—
C.S. Mays										13*			—															
G.P. Thorpe															15	16	100*	8	19	0*								
G.E. Brown																	0	—										
P.D. Atkins																	114*	8									99	9
Zahid Sadiq																	5	64										
N.M. Kendrick																	—	8*										
A.H. Gray																												
J. Boiling																												
J.D. Robinson																												
Byes	1		8			3		1					2		4	4	6		1		4						1	2
Leg-byes	8	6	10	3	2	3	1	7		2	15		5		6	11	8	15	10	1	5		10	2	9	4	10	4
Wides			1												1		1				2		1		1	3	1	
No-balls	2		3		1	3	1			6	11		2		3	13	2		1		1		8	5	9	4	2	3
Total	246	47	310	166	97	178	215	188	22	130	467		342		179	291	309	192	250	47	233		301	122	303	168	253	158
Wickets	10	1	3	3	10	10	6	7	0	10	5		4		10	8	3	6	8	1	6		2	3	7	7	10	7
Result	W		W		L		D		L		W		D		D		W		D		W		L		D		D	
Points	22		—		4		4		4		24		8		4		—		5		22		5		8		7	

Fielding Figures
61 – C.J. Richards (ct 60/st 1)   22 – D.M. Ward   11 – S.T. Clarke   7 – G.E. Brown (ct 6/st 1)
28 – K.T. Medlycott   18 – M.A. Lynch   10 – M.A. Feltham   5 – N.H. Peters
26 – A.J. Stewart (ct 25/st 1)   16 – I.A. Greig   8 – G.S. Clinton and C.K. Bullen   4 – Subs

throughout the world on a regular basis and the England selectors are always on the mailing list. 'I think they read them,' says Dexter. 'I'm sure they find information there which is helpful to them.'

World rankings are accepted as gospel in tennis and golf but Dexter knows he has some way to go before that happens in cricket. But he is working hard on it and he is a persistent fellow.

IN DEFENCE OF ONE-DAY CRICKET
Christopher Cowdrey

Whenever things are not going too well with English cricket there is a tendency to put much of the blame onto the one-day game. As a passionate supporter of this form of cricket, it is an argument that I would refute.

In many ways, one-day cricket has helped to raise standards in this country, notably in fielding. There was a time in the past, as older players will admit, when fielding was a much neglected art. Veterans in the side would be placed in close to the wicket positions so that they did not have to run too often while the youngsters were dispersed to sprint around the boundary. That attitude was changing before the one-day game was introduced, but limited-over cricket accelerated the change and focused attention on how important fielding was in all forms of cricket. Crowds became more appreciative and more knowledgeable, and players responded so that every aspect of fielding was sharpened. Never was this more apparent than in the development of Derek Underwood as a fielder. In his early days with Kent, he was little more than a moderate fielder, but the amount of one-day cricket he played coupled with his application to the game made him a very good fielder indeed. He was missed as more than a great left-arm bowler when he retired at the end of the 1987 season.

Critics argue, too, that batting techniques suffer because of one-day cricket, and again I would refute this. Batsmen of the calibre of Gower, Gooch, Richards, Border and Javed have used the one-day game to enhance their approach to batting. It is possible to attain a sound technique with constant application and practice in county

Match column key:

- MID = v. Middlesex (Lord's) 23–6 July
- GLO = v. Gloucestershire (Cheltenham) 30 July–2 Aug.
- SOM = v. Somerset (Weston-s-Mare) 3–5 August
- GLA = v. Glamorgan (Swansea) 6–9 August
- SRI = v. Sri Lankans (The Oval) 13–15 August
- WOR = v. Worcestershire (The Oval) 17–19 August
- NOT = v. Nottinghamshire (Trent Bridge) 20–3 August
- LAN = v. Lancashire (The Oval) 25–9 August
- ESS = v. Essex (The Oval) 30 Aug.–2 Sept.
- SUS = v. Sussex (Hove) 9–12 September
- KEN = v. Kent (Canterbury) 14–17 September

MID		GLO		SOM		GLA		SRI		WOR		NOT		LAN		ESS		SUS		KEN		M	Inns	Nos	Runs	HS	Av
100	—	102	18*	16	10*							7	—					158	—	31	43	18	29	5	1054	158	43.91
																						11	18	5	630	157*	48.46
44	—	21	0	0	13	1	18	1	—	77	—	76	2*	70	—	133	—	119	—	11	13	22	32	3	1006	133	34.68
24	—	45	0			22	24*			4	—	11	—	103	—	14	—	13	—	8	36	21	29	4	996	103*	39.84
57	—	43	4	17	28	126	0	10	—	1	—	10	—	32	—	50	—	56	—	4	7	25	36	6	942	126	31.40
		43	18							87	—	80	—	38	—	31	—	11	—	2	35*	18	21	4	861	102*	50.64
20	—	0	35	20	22	25	45			26	—	10	—	2	—	7	—	42	—	1*	—	23	28	1	529	67	19.59
		1	17	0	21	43	4	51	—	77*	—	0	—	1	—	6	—	45*	—	0	5	23	28	4	554	77*	23.08
				18	2	0	0	15	—	1*	—	24*	—	15*	—	18*	—	74	—	0	15	22	25	9	367	74	22.93
24*	—	8	0	8*	0	3*	0															12	15	8	85	25*	12.14
5	—	16	11									2	—	28	—	28	—					12	10	1	141	28	15.66
2	—			10	7	24	3	59*	—	—	—	2	3	20	—	8	—					12	14	2	261	59*	21.75
								7	—									0	—	0	4	4	4	1	11	7	2.75
				8	21			5	—	11	5*					50	—	19	—	37	5	11	19	1	343	62	19.05
3*	—	8*	5	5	2			33	—	—	—	25	—			2	—	5	—	0*	3	17	13	3	93	33	9.30
																						2	1	1	13	13*	—
								10	—													3	6	2	158	100*	39.50
																						3	2	—	10	10	5.00
25	—	17	0	10	6	28	41															6	11	1	357	114*	35.70
13	—			37	0	16	—															4	6	—	135	64	22.50
																						1	1	1	8	8*	—
																						1					
				1	8*																	1	2	1	9	8*	9.00
						18	—	13	0*	20	4*											3	5	2	55	20	18.33
4						4	1					1				5		12		2	2						
12		7		2	4	8	3	8		2		4	1	7		7				7							
1		1		4		2						2									1						
1		4		5	4	4		6		3		4		1		3				13	10						
334 0	9 0	312	10	148	10	297	10	242	10	302	7	269	10	331	10	362	10	553	10	109	9†						
		115	10	119	10	171	9			5	0	10	1							179	9						

Results: MID D (3); GLO W (24); SOM L (4); GLA D (6); SRI —; WOR D (6); NOT W (23); LAN W (24); ESS D (6); SUS W (24); KEN L (4)

3 – D.M. Smith, G.P. Thorpe, D.J. Bicknell and M.P. Bicknell
2 – C.S. Mays and Zahid Sadiq
1 – N.M. Kendrick, M. Frost and J.D. Robinson

† I.A. Greig retired hurt, absent hurt

cricket, but to achieve greatness one needs the flair that comes with bravery and improvization. Batting in a one-day match demands a constant reassessment of the situation and of the needs of your side, and it teaches a batsman to be inventive and ever alert. The prime example at Kent was the great Alan Knott. He was the most thoughtful of cricketers, and every shot that he played was the result of calculating where best the ball should be hit and how to deal with a particular type of bowler. He reasoned all that he did, and for one who was chosen for England because he was the best wicket-keeper in the world it must have been very gratifying to himself and the selectors that he also scored five Test centuries and averaged more than 32 in Test cricket.

If batsmen learn to adapt and improvize so, too, do bowlers. They must be prepared for instant variation to counter an attack by the batsman. It may be necessary to adjust length or direction for every ball. The demands of one-day cricket provoke more thought in the bowler, ask of him that he make immediate response to the problems with which he is confronted, and such a constant need for reappraisal can only be for the good. My colleague Neil Foster has become an outstanding bowler at international level, yet in his early days he took some time to come to terms with the demands of one-day cricket. Application and much thought brought their reward, and Neil has become not only a highly successful bowler in the one-day game, but a bowler of more variety and more threat in the Championship and Test matches, for he now never allows the batsman to relax and is quick to exploit weaknesses and conditions.

On top of the developments it has encouraged in the techniques of batting, bowling and fielding, one-day cricket has brought crowds back to cricket. It is a very different experience playing in a county match at Derby or Swansea before a handful of spectators on a chilly day with a draw the only prospect to appearing before a capacity crowd in a Benson and Hedges or NatWest Cup game with all to play for. A misfield can cause an uproar, and the cricket can never become pedestrian when a maiden over is richly applauded and a good shot is thunderously received. To play before large crowds is an exhilarating experience and a test of character. A young player like Steve Marsh showed his true mettle and thrilled to playing at Lord's in the Benson and Hedges Cup final a couple of years ago. There are others who freeze in such circum-

Surrey CCC
First-Class Matches, 1988

BOWLING	S.T. Clarke	N.H. Peters	I.A. Greig	M.A. Feltham	M. Frost	K.T. Medlycott	C.K. Bullen	M.P. Bicknell	C.S. Mays
v. Hampshire (Southampton) 21–5 April	18–8–27–3 18–8–36–2	16–3–47–4 11–2–45–1	4–1–7–0 23.3–4–56–6	2.4–0–6–3 21–8–60–1					
v. Cambridge University (Cambridge) 28–30 April			19–8–34–6 12–1–27–2	23–9–51–2	17–7–49–1 23.5–5–56–4	16–4–35–1 36–9–76–4	11–4–37–0		
v. Middlesex (The Oval) 5–9 May	22.2–5–69–3 28.1–7–60–3	18–1–63–2 14–4–28–2	18–6–35–2 2–0–16–0	22–7–32–3 10–2–22–0		34–10–82–5			
v. Northamptonshire (The Oval) 21–4 May	24–5–48–3 8–4–11–3		20–3–48–0 7–0–36–0	30–9–90–2 9–4–33–0		13–3–52–0 9.3–4–19–0		23.4–10–44–0 14–2–60–0	
v. Essex (Chelmsford) 28–31 May	19–4–46–1		10–1–33–2	17.2–3–56–3		44–11–116–3			11–1–36–1
v. Sussex (The Oval) 1–3 June	13–5–36–3 17–6–31–0		17–4–44–4 21–2–74–3	8–0–36–0 26.4–8–70–3		20–7–36–2		20.5–1–66–3 17–5–47–1	
v. Yorkshire (Harrogate) 4–7 June			9–1–28–3 16–3–47–2	21–5–52–2 26–7–56–2		10.1–4–19–4 29–8–83–1		16–8–28–1 6–1–12–0	2–0–7–0 12–1–59–0
v. Leicestershire (The Oval) 11–14 June		19–4–59–0 5–1–18–2	21–3–50–2	26–9–57–1 5–1–17–0		17.4–9–45–2 1–0–3–0			
v. Cambridge University (The Oval) 15–17 June		13–2–32–0 2–0–15–0					18–4–56–4	16–5–42–0 13–3–45–9	
v. Derbyshire (The Oval) 25–8 June	32–6–92–3 1–0–10–0		19–5–52–2 7–2–21–0	22.3–4–66–1 8–1–19–0		25–9–51–1 8–0–34–0	13–2–34–1 5–0–18–0		
v. Warwickshire (The Oval) 2–5 July	16–2–40–4 19–5–40–4	15.2–5–31–6 16–4–36–4	4.5–1–15–2	2–0–16–0					
v. Hampshire (Guildford) 13–15 July		11–1–33–2 9–0–53–0	3–0–20–0 7–0–37–0	16–3–36–1 13–2–43–0		20–2–78–2		16–7–34–1 13–1–68–0	
v. Kent (Guildford) 16–19 July		14–2–51–0 19–3–96–2	16–6–45–0 3–1–8–0	13–1–52–2		28–8–80–4 27–2–112–6		24–3–84–2 14–5–44–0	
v. Lancashire (Southport) 20–2 July		20–7–35–2 21–6–70–2	21–10–26–4 19–4–89–2	8–1–39–1 13–2–64–0		1–0–4–0		20.1–7–35–3 16–2–36–3	
v. Middlesex (Lord's) 23–6 July	11.3–2–45–1	3–0–14–0 6–0–29–0	2–0–18–0				1–0–5–0 8–1–36–1	4–1–8–0 11–2–49–1	
v. Gloucestershire (Cheltenham) 30 July–2 Aug.	21.1–5–44–5 32.1–14–63–6	13–3–44–1 20–1–96–3	5–1–13–0 6–2–13–0			1–0–2–0		14–4–49–3 20–2–68–0	
v. Somerset (Weston-super-Mare) 3–5 August		4–0–16–0 2–0–16–0	20.1–4–40–4 12–2–21–0	6–1–19–1 3–0–11–0		24–10–55–5 15–5–33–5	6–1–14–0	7–2–20–0 2–0–10–0	
v. Glamorgan (Swansea) 6–9 August		5–1–9–0 2–0–18–1	15–3–36–2 2–1–4–0	24–6–58–3 5–0–27–1		40.5–8–122–5 7–1–25–0	4–1–14–0 2–0–3–0		
v. Sri Lankans (The Oval) 13–15 August				22.3–6–52–3 17–4–40–0	10–2–28–2 21–5–78–1	6–0–37–0 13–3–67–2	13–5–14–1 5–5–0–1	22–4–66–3 26–9–78–2	
v. Worcestershire (The Oval) 17–19 August			6–0–27–0 3–0–14–0	24–5–59–3 11–4–28–2		41–10–87–2 15–1–91–0	11–2–31–1 8–0–44–1	23–9–53–1 7–0–40–0	
v. Nottinghamshire (Trent Bridge) 20–3 August	23–5–47–2 21–5–52–6		5–1–10–0	17.1–6–43–4		2–2–0–0		24–9–34–4 18–4–67–3	
v. Lancashire (The Oval) 25–9 August	13.4–3–29–4 28.4–9–60–6		8–1–31–0	14–3–45–5 23–5–72–0		11–3–31–2		5–2–8–1 16–7–37–2	
v. Essex (The Oval) 30 Aug.–2 Sept.	10–0–27–1		4–0–11–0	16–3–58–0		14–2–62–1	2.1–0–10–1	21–4–80–3	
v. Sussex (Hove) 9–12 September			12–2–34–1	16–3–34–2 8–0–36–0	5–1–23–0 6–0–28–0	31–16–53–4 27–7–52–8		22–4–65–0 7.4–1–23–1	
v. Kent (Canterbury) 14–17 September			3–0–23–0	34.2–3–124–5	17–3–64–2	6–1–18–0		37–12–111–3	
	396.4–108– 913–63 *av.* 14.49	278.2–50– 954–34 *av.* 28.05	402.3–83– 1143–49 *av.* 23.32	584.1–135– 1679–56 *av.* 29.98	99.5–23– 326–10 *av.* 32.60	593.1–159– 1660–69 *av.* 24.05	107.1–25– 316–11 *av.* 28.72	516.2–136– 1511–50 *av.* 30.22	25–2– 102–1 *av.* 102.00

a C.J. Richards 4–1–26–0   b C.M. Wells retired hurt   c A.H. Gray 17–10–17–1; 9–3–21–1   d D.J. Bicknell 1–0–18–0

A.J. Stewart	N.M. Kendrick	M.A. Lynch	D.M. Ward	G.S. Clinton	G.P. Thorpe	J.D. Robinson	Byes	Leg-byes	Wides	No-balls	Total	Wkts
								4	3	4	91	10
								1	1	6	198	10
							4	3	4	5	176	10
							2	5		9	203	10
							4	4	4	2	207	10
								8			216	10
							5	11		1	298	5
							8	7		4	174	3
							6	9	1	1	302	10
4.1–0–16–0								3		2	45	0a
							5	1	4	9	188	10
2–1–2–0							1	7	3	6	268	9b
							4	4		4	142	10
		6–2–14–0	1–0–3–0	0.4–0–16–0			15	5	2	14	310	6
						14–2–33–2	1	10	4	3	255	7
											38	2
	26.5–6–92–1				6–1–17–1		1	9	1	7	266	7
	2–1–5–0									1	86	10c
					7–0–21–1		3	10	2	8	329	9
		2–0–9–1	4–0–28–0		3–0–6–0		8	8		1	171	1d
								3	6	3	74	10
							2	7	3	5	116	10
								2	6		125	4
		1.5–0–15–0						5	10		299	2
							1	11		6	324	9
3–0–9–0							16	3	1	10	288	8
								5		4	140	10
								8			271	9
								1			28	0
							5	3	1	1	185	3
							6	5		1	163	9
								3	1	2	243	9e
							3	6			159	10
								5			110	5
							4			9	262	10f
									1	2	98	3f
						3–0–16–0	4	2			219	10
1–1–0–0			1–1–0–0			6–3–22–0	4	10	3	2	300	6g
						9–1–41–2		5		14	303	10
						4–0–26–1		8		3	251	5
							6	4	2		144	10
							2	10	2	1	131	9h
							2		1	2	84	10
							7	8		1	246	10
							1	8	1	7	257	6
		5.3–1–10–3					6	4	1	3	229	10
4–1–18–1		14–5–40–0						8		6	205	10
							8	6	1	6	354	10
14.1–3– 45–1 av. 45.00	31.5–7– 97–1 av. 97.00	29.2–8– 88–4 av. 22.00	6–1– 31–0 —	0.4–0– 16–0 —	30–3– 77–4 av. 19.25	22–4– 105–3 av. 35.00						

e C.W.J. Athey absent hurt   f J. Boiling 7–1–19–0; 8–2–21–0   g D.J. Bicknell 1–0–1–0   h K.E. Cooper retired hurt

Sussex CCC
First-Class Matches, 1988

BATTING	v. Somerset (Hove) 21–5 April	v. Gloucestershire (Bristol) 28 April–2 May	v. West Indians (Hove) 7–10 May	v. Nottinghamshire (Trent Bridge) 21–4 May	v. Middlesex (Lord's) 28–31 May	v. Surrey (The Oval) 1–3 June	v. Derbyshire (Horsham) 4–7 June	v. Essex (Ilford) 11–14 June	v. Somerset (Bath) 15–17 June	v. Leicestershire (Leicester) 18–21 June	v. Yorkshire (Hove) 25–8 June	v. Kent (Hastings) 2–5 July	v. Gloucestershire (Hove) 20–2 July	v. Northamptonshire (Northampton) 23–6 July
R.I. Alikhan	18 6	46 7	29 —			9 8	56 1	11 18	98 20	9 0	71 1	0 21		
A.M. Green	29 44	18 9	32 —	54 28	28* —	5 9	0 1	23 23	7 10		9 18*			
P.W.G. Parker	101* 71*	18 55*	89 —	0 22			25 48	28 1	1 101*	4 3	29 2	10 117	12 6	13 4
A.P. Wells	4 25	69 24	17 —	74 0	17* —	34 11	36 2	4 9	64 38	8* —	20 37	10 11	69* 54	6 35
C.M. Wells	24 49*	33 0	1 —	21 0	— —	2 109*	16 7	27 0	0 30*	4 41	9 10	0 15	2 13	3 62
N.J. Lenham	6 —	32 8*	12 —	1 33	0 —	2 40	62 21	9 27	31 —	6 36*			8 38	15 52
I.J. Gould	13 —	20 —	33 —	6 20	— —	82* 11	32 10	13 26	69* —		11 56	35 5	2 8	8 33
A.C.S. Pigott	28 —			0 23	— —	20 1	12 45*	24 3		11 56	35 5	2 8	0* 8*	0 11*
A.R. Clarke	19 —	9 —	1 —	0 26			0* 3	0 3	— —	14 14*		7* 6*	12* 4	24* 4
M.W. Pringle	4 —	35 —	14 —			0 19					17 15			
A.M. Babington	0 —	1 —	2 —	6* 0*		9 0*	0 1				10 1	4 0*		— —
R.A. Bunting		11*	4*	0 3									5 1	3 —
D.K. Standing				0 9	4									
Imran Khan								11 16		55 0				4 30*
P.A.W. Heseltine						6 8					22 2	1 28	4 22	
P. Moores						0 35					2 15			
S.J.S. Kimber								8 5	0* 0*	32* —	8 1			
P.W. Threlfall										— —				
N.J. Falkner											55 14	5 45	20 18	8 27
M.P. Speight											8 3	14 50	35 0	10 4
Byes	6 3	4	5	1		5 1	1 1	4 1		4	4 2		4	1
Leg-byes	4 7	10 3	5	10 5		1 7	10 5	1 7	4 3	10 8	5	3 12	5 6	6 11
Wides	2		4	4		4 3	2 3					1	1	9
No-balls	8 8	18 10	4	6 1		9 6	12 2			14 4	15 18	7 7	5 10	8 14
Total	266 213	324 116	252	182 171	49	188 268	272 155	155 134	320 206	159 210	299 105	71 322	161 174	118 287
Wickets	10 3	10 4	10	10 10	2	10 9†	10 10	10 10	6 3	10 7‡	10 10	10 10	6 7	10 8
Result	W	D	D	L	D	L	L	L	D	L	L	L	D	D
Points	23	7	—	5	4	2	7	3	4	4	7	4	5	4

Fielding Figures
33 – P. Moores (ct 30/st 3) 17 – P.W.G. Parker 8 – C.M. Wells, R.I. Alikhan and A.M. Babington
32 – I.J. Gould 16 – A.C.S. Pigott 7 – A.R. Clarke and N.J. Lenham
18 – A.P. Wells 10 – A.M. Green 5 – M.P. Speight

stances and find the emotion of the occasion too much for them, yet if they aspire to play for their country, as all should, they must learn to play before large and critical crowds.

One-day cricket has brought dynamism into the game for both player and spectator. I cannot think that it has done cricket any harm, and, mostly, much good. Cricket is an entertainment, like all professional sport, and the one-day game has proved itself as top-class entertainment, attracting huge crowds and providing a sense of occasion. It is an exciting and joyful game to play, and at Kent, we are already looking forward to taking on Glamorgan, Essex, Hampshire and Sussex in next year's Benson and Hedges Cup and, we hope, to a visit to Lord's in July.

Book Reviews

THE BRADMAN ALBUMS. *Selection from Sir Donald Bradman's Collection;* Macdonald Queen Anne Press; 2 volumes; 800pp

This two-volume boxed set is a beautifully produced reproduction of the scrapbooks and diaries that Bradman kept throughout his career. There is some added comment and an abundance of photographs, and the whole constitutes one of the most important and impressive books concerned with cricket to have been published since the war. From the snips of diary and press cuttings emerges a picture of a man who was totally dedicated to the game, cool, calculating and always in charge of his own destiny. Lunch at The Savoy was followed by practice. The Cup Final between Arsenal and Huddersfield in 1930 was preceded by practice, and he left the game at half-time because he wanted to get to Leeds in time to acclimatize himself for the game against Yorkshire. There are reports by Robertson-Glasgow, Swanton, Arlott, Jack Hobbs, Arthur Mailey and many others, and controversy and criticism are not avoided. Rarely has the career of a cricketer been so fully and attractively documented. It is a fitting record of the greatest batsmen the world has known since the retirement of Jack Hobbs. It is also one of the finest books to have been offered us for very many years.

SOUTH LOUGHTON CRICKET CLUB 50 YEARS, 1938–1988. *Andrew Shield*; South Loughton CC, (01-580 8662); £2.50

One of the delights of recent years has been the number of club histories

v. Glamorgan (Eastbourne) 30 July–2 Aug.		v. Hampshire (Eastbourne) 3–5 August		v. Worcestershire (Kidderminster) 6–9 August		v. Lancashire (Hove) 13–16 August		v. Warwickshire (Hove) 17–19 August		v. Kent (Maidstone) 25–9 August		v. Middlesex (Hove) 30 Aug.–2 Sept.		v. Surrey (Hove) 9–12 September		v. Hampshire (Southampton) 14–17 September		M	Inns	Nos	Runs	HS	Av
						3	24	22	38	9	9	52	—	68	53	9	5	10	19	—	429	98	22.57
46	1	45	104*	4	12	6	36	79	61	0	124	32	—	1	24	1	23	16	29	2	639	68	23.66
50	44*	56	7	1	65	0	24	120	74*	39	30	16	—	21	9	40	12	21	40	5	1359	124	38.82
7	—	11	11	2	26	68	38	1	—	13	21	86*	—	9	13	92	31	23	42	5	1286	120	34.75
40	22	24	47	36	7	8	4	0	4	28	74							23	40	4	907	109*	25.19
1	32*	5	4	60	6	22	6	9	69*	23	50	30	—	47	40	44	51	18	32	2	733	74	24.43
52	—	16	35*	12	55	18	21	23*	—	47*	20	16	—	0	22*	24	15	19	31	4	875	82*	32.40
0	—	68	—	4	10	22	3	4	—	4	13	5	—	11	7	12	22*	20	34	8	668	56	25.69
																		21	32	8	337	68	14.04
																		5	7	—	104	35	14.85
2	—	0*	—	10	6*	7*	4	—	—	0	0*	5	—	0	4	12	3	19	26	8	87	12	4.83
11	—	5	—	1*	4	5	10	6	—	0	0	4	—	3*	0	17*	3	17	21	5	96	17*	6.00
																		2	3	—	13	9	4.33
																		4	6	1	116	55	23.20
																		2	2	—	14	8	7.00
38*	—	15	—	3	24	5	97*	8	—	8	2	12	—	22	19	2	9	14	24	2	395	97*	17.95
																		4	7	3	54	32*	13.50
																		1					—
6	7	10	4	1	12													7	14	—	232	55	16.57
												27	—	33	0	16	58	7	13	—	258	58	19.84
			5	4	1			8	2	1	1	13		6		3	3						
7	9	10	4	4	6	3	5	19	9	2	10	9		4	8	5	5						
1		1	1	2				2		4	1	2		1									
4		8	8	4	1	5	3	1		6	4	11		3	6	1							
265	115	279	225	146	237	172	275	300	259	184	359	320		229	205	278	240						
10	3	10	5	10	10	10	10	9	3	10	10	10		10	10	10	10						
D		D		L		L		W		W		D		L		L							
7		5		2		3		22		21		3		3		5							

4 – N.J. Falkner   † C.M. Wells retired hurt
2 – S.J.S. Kimber and R.A. Bunting   ‡ A.M. Green and N.J. Lenham retired hurt; A.P. Wells absent hurt
1 – M.W. Pringle and sub

that have been produced by the faithful and dedicated. South Loughton are not among the most renowned of Essex clubs, but they have issued a short history which is warm and readable. The numbering of pages would have helped, but this is a minor criticism of a delightful piece of work which is a credit to the author and the club.

LEADING FROM THE FRONT, THE AUTOBIOGRAPHY OF MIKE GATTING. *Mike Gatting (with Angela Patmore)*; Macdonald Queen Anne Press; 216pp; £12.95

One of the year's best-sellers, Gatting's 'autobiography' owed its sales to the TCCB's opposition and the unsavoury happenings in Pakistan. In truth, one learns nothing from this book that one did not know before, and there is very little of interest or vitality. The story is that Gatting plays cricket for a living and is not one of the world's great communicators.

MIDDLESEX COUNTY CRICKET CLUB REVIEW 1987/88. *Edited by Alvan Seth-Smith*; Middlesex CCC; 128pp; £4 (obtainable from the Club office)

This is the eighth edition of this delightfully produced annual which has maintained a consistently high standard. Like its predecessors, it is clear, balanced and literate. There is a fine sense of organization and dignity which never sap the vitality. An excellent publication.

KENT COUNTY CRICKET ANNUAL 1988. Kent CCC; 208pp; £2.50

A really beautiful club handbook, superbly produced by The Canterbury Printers Ltd with eight colour plates, the Kent annual contains an account of famous matches against Sussex by Derek Carlaw, who also contributes book reviews, an appreciation of Derek Underwood and a host of reports, score-cards and statistics. The book is alive and attractive, a fine advertisement for a well run county club.

ESSEX COUNTY CRICKET CLUB 1988 HANDBOOK. *Edited by Peter Edwards*; Essex CCC; 240pp; £3.50

Once again Peter Edwards presents a handbook which is crammed full of articles, statistics, pictures and information. It is good to note that a county for whom success has been a staple diet in the past decade remembers its administrative staff and supporters as well as its players and sponsors, and the article on Cathy Haw by Caroline Fardell is particularly welcome. When one looks at the Essex handbook of pre-Edwards days one realizes how great has been the secretary/manager's impact in every aspect of Essex cricket. The sadness of this issue is that the statistics are no longer by Leslie Newnham, who died last year. He was one of the great statisticians, precise and unflagging in his zeal and accuracy, and the world is the poorer for his passing.

SURREY COUNTY CRICKET CLUB HANDBOOK, 1988. *Edited by Anne Bickerstaff*; Surrey CCC; 148pp; £4

Few women have attained the higher levels of administration in county cricket, the major exception is Anne Bickerstaff at the progressive Surrey Club. The Surrey handbook is a testimony to her zestful approach to organization and to the vitality she brings to her work as assistant to the secretary. There is a clear presentation of all Surrey's matches, some lovely nostalgia by the late George Russ and a particularly interesting article on old Surrey captains by Tom Higgs. A very good handbook.

Sussex CCC
First-Class Matches, 1988

BOWLING	A.C.S. Pigott	M.W. Pringle	A.M. Babington	A.R. Clarke	N.J. Lenham	A.M. Green	A.P. Wells	R.A. Bunting	C.M. Wells
v. Somerset (Hove) 21–5 April	20.3–5–55–4 / 18.1–7–42–2	14–2–35–1 / 21–6–58–0	13–7–15–3 / 33.5–9–66–4	20–6–34–2 / 42–13–74–0	17.5–2–57–3	8–5–7–0	5–1–11–0		
v. Gloucestershire (Bristol) 28 April–2 May		17–4–51–2	15–1–59–0	22.2–3–47–3				25–4–86–5	
v. West Indians (Hove) 7–10 May		23–2–98–1 / 10–2–37–1	30–3–91–1 / 10–1–41–0	30–2–118–1 / 11–1–51–1	6–1–23–0 / 3–0–18–0	3–1–5–0	9–1–43–1	35–3–161–5 / 14–0–71–0	22–5–57–1 / 7–2–13–0
v. Nottinghamshire (Trent Bridge) 21–4 May	24–12–46–5 / 18.1–3–40–4		20–3–73–0 / 6–0–40–1	14–3–33–0				14–2–50–1 / 12–3–39–3	24.5–5–59–4 / 12–5–23–2
v. Middlesex (Lord's) 28–31 May	19–3–66–1		16–3–62–1					9–1–27–1	14–4–39–2
v. Surrey (The Oval) 1–3 June	20–2–107–1	19–0–82–1	25–2–84–2						19–5–77–0
v. Derbyshire (Horsham) 4–7 June	16–3–60–4 / 14–3–54–3		12–1–55–1 / 8.3–1–27–1	10–3–30–0 / 8.3–2–22–1	2–0–3–0				20–9–46–1 / 14–3–47–2
v. Essex (Ilford) 11–14 June	10–1–53–0			43.5–14–115–2		24–1–90–1			20–3–49–1
v. Somerset (Bath) 15–17 June				35.5–6–90–2 / 21–1–98–3		15–2–41–1		16–6–48–1 / 5–1–14–1	18–4–50–2 / 17–2–69–2
v. Leicestershire (Leicester) 18–21 June	35.4–5–100–6			14–5–30–1 / 3–1–11–0					24–7–66–2 / 5–2–15–0
v. Yorkshire (Hove) 25–8 June	9–2–14–0 / 17–1–67–2	17–4–62–1 / 10–3–35–1	20–1–66–4 / 10.5–1–45–1	18–6–32–2 / 5–0–12–1					19–2–40–3 / 12–4–23–2
v. Kent (Hastings) 2–5 July	29–5–78–3 / 4–0–8–0		15–3–47–2 / 12–3–23–2	7–0–23–0 / 5–0–18–2				13–1–39–0 / 4–1–18–1	33.3–7–94–4 / 9.1–0–37–1
v. Gloucestershire (Hove) 20–2 July	21–2–74–2 / 11–1–40–3		21–2–44–1 / 5–1–26–0	20–11–36–2 / 6–0–17–0				19.1–2–59–4 / 4–0–33–0	15–3–48–0 / 5–2–18–2
v. Northamptonshire (Northampton) 23–6 July	21–2–79–2			4.5–0–8–1				8–2–24–1	14–1–45–2
v. Glamorgan (Eastbourne) 30 July–2 Aug.	25.1–5–82–4 / 18–6–56–2		13–3–37–0 / 16–5–56–0	24–6–58–2 / 15–1–46–1				20–4–49–3 / 10–2–30–1	22–5–54–0 / 14–2–36–2
v. Hampshire (Eastbourne) 3–5 August	13–2–27–0 / 4–1–25–0		23.5–8–70–4 / 8–2–23–0	15–8–27–0 / 20.4–6–60–5				21–5–65–2 / 4–1–12–0	13–1–47–0 / 13–2–33–0
v. Worcestershire (Kidderminster) 6–9 August	21–3–85–3		26.3–5–83–4 / 2–0–7–1	34–9–92–3				14–1–47–0 / 1.5–1–7–0	12–2–44–0
v. Lancashire (Hove) 13–16 August	23–3–102–2 / 7–0–32–0		18–9–45–0 / 5–0–31–1	23–4–81–0 / 2–1–3–0				21–3–58–2 / 6–1–20–0	15–3–35–1 / 4–0–21–0
v. Warwickshire (Hove) 17–19 August	20–3–96–4 / 11.4–1–27–3		16–3–29–1 / 4–2–6–2	29–9–85–1 / 5–1–9–0		7–1–15–0 / 4–3–1–0		17–2–47–1 / 14–4–44–5	7–0–21–0
v. Kent (Maidstone) 25–9 August	24–3–77–3 / 29.4–5–86–4		25–6–63–3 / 27–8–58–3	3–2–3–0				20–7–40–0 / 14–4–39–2	19.1–5–43–4 / 25–7–55–1
v. Middlesex (Hove) 30 Aug.–2 Sept.	40–9–139–4		37–9–88–1	27–8–76–0				24–3–100–2	32–12–60–1
v. Surrey (Hove) 9–12 September	42–5–137–1		30–5–100–3	38–5–133–5		13–1–47–0		29–5–73–0	18–2–51–1
v. Hampshire (Southampton) 14–17 September	17–4–47–1 / 21–2–67–1		11–0–17–0 / 19.2–3–51–2	22–10–32–2 / 19–9–46–1		45.5–16–82–6 / 32–10–104–2		6–0–20–0	6–0–14–0
	624–109–2078–74 av. 28.08	131–23–458–8 av. 57.25	554.5–110–1628–49 av. 33.22	618–156–1650–44 av. 37.50	28.5–3–101–3 av. 33.66	151.5–40–392–10 av. 39.20	14–2–54–1 av. 54.00	400–69–1320–41 av. 32.19	524.4–116–1429–43 av. 33.23

a P. Moores 1–0–6–0; M.P. Speight 0.3–0–2–1   b P.J. Bakker absent hurt

R.I. Alikhan	Imran Khan	P.A.W. Heseltine	S.J.S. Kimber	P.W. Threlfall	I.J. Gould	P.W.G. Parker	Byes	Leg-byes	Wides	No-balls	Total	Wkts
								3		10	142	10
							8	10	3	6	333	10
							2	7		6	252	10
							9	4	7	9	561	9
7–0–19–2							1	6		6	305	5
								9	3	1	270	10
							4	4	5		150	10
	22.3–7–50–5	1–0–4–0					6	7	1	8	261	10
		27–5–102–1						15		11	467	5
			20–7–44–3				4	8	2	4	250	10
			8–0–26–2					2		3	178	9
	29–4–92–3		12–1–59–0					4			462	8
			13–4–28–0	8–2–13–0			1	5			276	6
			7–0–35–1	4–1–18–0			10	6			250	7
	20–10–45–1		14–3–63–0				2	3	1	5	309	10
0.3–0–7–0	7–2–7–1		9–4–17–1				4				61	2
								5		12	219	10
								4		2	186	7
							1	6	3	1	288	10
								2			106	6
								15	8		276	10
							3	4			141	5
	25–3–61–3						5	11	2	1	233	10
								3	3	4	283	10
								3	1	3	227	6
							1	6	2	2	253	10
					9–1–48–2			6		2	207	7
					7–1–16–0			3			370	10
											14	1
								16	4	2	337	6
						1–0–1–1	1	2	2	3	111	2
							1	9	2	2	303	8
							6	3	1	1	96	10
								10	4		233	10
								6	3	4	247	10
							1	7	3	3	471	9
											8	1a
							12			3	553	10
							6	4		3	222	9b
					5–0–20–0		5	5			298	6
73–0–26–2 av. 13.00	103.3–26–255–13 av. 19.61	28–5–106–1 av. 106.00	83–19–272–7 av. 38.85	12–3–31–0 —	21–2–84–2 av. 42.00	1–0–1–1 av. 1.00						

Warwickshire CCC
First-Class Matches, 1988

BATTING	v. Cambridge Univ. (Cambridge) 20–2 April		v. Lancashire (Old Trafford) 28 April–2 May		v. Yorkshire (Edgbaston) 5–9 May		v. Northamptonshire (Northampton) 17–20 May		v. Essex (Edgbaston) 21–4 May		v. Nottinghamshire (Edgbaston) 4–7 June		v. Somerset (Bath) 11–14 June		v. Yorkshire (Leeds) 15–17 June		v. Kent (Edgbaston) 18–21 June		v. Lancashire (Nuneaton) 29 June–1 July		v. Surrey (The Oval) 2–5 July		v. Worcestershire (Edgbaston) 13–15 July		v. Hampshire (Edgbaston) 16–19 July		v. Glamorgan (Cardiff) 20–22 July	
T.A. Lloyd	9	—	0	64	22	39	10	2	18	86	11	29	151	30	2	49	10	40	39	3	11	18	46	—	160*	—	17	13*
A.J. Moles	95	—	0	22	5	11	7	9	30	41	5	27	27	11	27	43	67*	21	115	17	25	2	42	—	60	—	33	15
M. Asif Din	158*	—	4	3	4	62*	131	48	2	33	6	14	45	44	5	77	10	52			2	8	14	—	13	—	65	1*
A.I. Kallicharran	117*	—	1	36	37	0	0	0	6	24									—	—								
G.W. Humpage	—	—	4	1	80	22*	3	3	22	14	58	22	9	23	10	—	0	1	21	8	1	3					19	—
P.A. Smith	—	—	68	22	31	—	47	5	0	32*	38	0*	17	31	0	—	1	8	0	3	0	0	20	—				
G.J. Parsons	—	—			10	—	18	8*	4	—							14*	—	12	17								
T.A. Merrick			23	19	8	—	34	1	24	—			19	—					0	11	23*	—						
G.C. Small			14	70	22	—							45*	—	6	14			0	6	5	32	1	—			29	—
A.R.K. Pierson			13*	8			18*	1					1*	0							0*	8*	5*	—			2*	—
N. Gifford			12	0*	0*	—	12	3	6*	—			1*	1	0	—			1	8	3	4*						
D.A. Reeve			11	36	0	—	103	12	36	2*			24	—	1	26*	13	—	—	—							26	—
T.A. Munton											0	—	4*	—	0	13*	1	1	9*	3	0	16	0	—				
A.C. Storie													68	9*	32	22	4	4*	6	35	0	4						
A.A. Donald															0	0	1	—	0	18*							1*	—
D.A. Thorne																			21	3	10	7	36	—	32*	—	20	—
S.J. Green																					0	28						
D.A. Banks																							47	—	1	—	19	—
P.C.L. Holloway																							2	—				
S.D. Myles																												
N.M.K. Smith																												
J.E. Benjamin																												
G.A. Tedstone																												
J.D. Radcliffe																												
Byes	5			9	9		1	8	6	1	3	5	7			10				2		2	1		5		3	
Leg-byes	12		3	5	3	1	8	2		9	11	5	10	6	4	8	1	1	13	3	3	7	7		23		11	2
Wides	4		1					9	1	4	1						1	7	3	2	6	3			6		10	1
No-balls	5		2	1	4		14	10	5	8	5		7	1	1	2	3		2	3	3	5	6		6		10	1
Total	405		155	297	235	135	415	112	160	254	300	111	315	209	81	206	107	174	234	129	74	116	250		300		255	32
Wickets	2		10	10	10	3	10	10	10	5	8	4	9	10	10	3	8†		10	10	10	10	9		3		8	1
Result	D		D		W		L		W		W		D		W		L		L		L		D		W		D	
Points	—		5		22		7		21		22		4		20		2		6		2		7		24		7	

Fielding Figures

57 – G.W. Humpage (ct 56/st 1)
18 – M. Asif Din
17 – D.A. Thorne
12 – D.A. Reeve and A.J. Moles
8 – G.A. Tedstone (ct 7/st 1)
7 – G.C. Small, T.A. Lloyd and P.C.L. Holloway (ct 6/st 1)
6 – A.C. Storie
5 – D.A. Banks and T.A. Merrick
4 – A.A. Donald and A.I. Kallicharran

THE CARPHONE GALLERY OF CRICKETERS. *Bill Frindall*; Macdonald Queen Anne Press; 222pp; £3.95

This is a pictorial autograph album, one of those ideas so simple and so good that it is hard to understand why nobody ever thought of it before.

HOWZZAT, A CENTURY OF CRICKET CARTOONS. *Alexyz*; The Marine Sports, Bombay

A hundred cartoons of varying quality from India.

THE TEST AND COUNTY CRICKET BOARD GUIDE TO BETTER CRICKET. *Vic Marks*; Octopus Books; 176pp; £12.95

The sponsorship of the National Westminster Bank has made this the most attractive cricket coaching book one has ever seen. It is, too, totally different in approach to other coaching manuals. Vic Marks draws his examples from professional cricket and talks to those who have played the game, like Brearley, Marsh and Kennedy, for their advice based on experience. One cannot think that there has ever been a better book of this type.

THE HISTORY OF HAMPSHIRE COUNTY CRICKET CLUB. *Peter Wynne-Thomas*; Christopher Helm; 275pp; £12.95

THE HISTORY OF KENT COUNTY CRICKET CLUB. *Dudley Moore*; Christopher Helm; 300pp; £13.95

THE OFFICIAL HISTORY OF MIDDLESEX COUNTY CRICKET CLUB. *David Lemmon*; *Christopher Helm*; 365pp; £14.95

Young publishers Christopher Helm launched their county history series with three titles in 1988, admirably chosen in that they were all counties who had success during the season. In each case, the books are beautifully produced with statistics provided by the Association of Cricket Statisticians and with an abundance of illustrations. John Arlott gives a personal view as an introduction to the Hampshire history, and Derek Underwood and Denis Compton make similar contributions to the Kent and Middlesex histories. While Peter Wynne-Thomas has tended to concentrate on facts and figures in the Hampshire book, Dudley Moore, close to the club, has given a warm, but always objective, view of Kent cricket. He knows the players and officials and has related their hopes and fears. He ends the book with comments from Chris Cowdrey which are honest and apt. The present writer was responsible for the Middlesex history, the first official history for 40 years, and was greatly assisted by all in the Club. The task was a pleasure. Glamorgan's story will be published late in 1988, and Surrey and Worcestershire are destined to follow in 1989 in what is an exciting and very important series.

THE BRITISH ACADEMY OF CRICKET MANUAL FOR GENTLEMEN AND PLAYERS. *Martin Ward*; Pavilion Books; 240pp, £12.95

The fun book of the year, the manual sets down codes of acceptable behaviour for cricket on and off the field. It makes gentle mockery of some ancient customs and attitudes. It is, perhaps, a little hard to sustain the humour for an entire volume, but it gives much light pleasure.

v. Sri Lankans (Edgbaston) 23–6 July		v. Derbyshire (Derby) 30 July–2 Aug.		v. Gloucestershire (Cheltenham) 3–5 August		v. Northamptonshire (Edgbaston) 6–9 August		v. Leicestershire (Edgbaston) 13–16 August		v. Sussex (Hove) 17–19 August		v. Middlesex (Uxbridge) 20–3 August		v. Worcestershire (Worcester) 25–9 August		v. Glamorgan (Edgbaston) 30 Aug.–2 Sept.		v. Somerset (Edgbaston) 9–12 September		M	Inns	Nos	Runs	HS	Av
0*	—	27	—	10	0	121	11	1	34	19	1	101	41	45	27	45	10	7	69	24	43	3	1448	160*	36.20
50*	—					35	—											20	64	18	31	2	968	115	33.37
59	—	52	—	84	26	26	31*	40	30	84	8	18	4	26	45	21	33	23	14	23	41	4	1425	158*	38.51
														1	60	63	18	47	8	9	15	1	418	117*	29.85
14	—	52	—	0	11	2	8													17	26	1	411	80	16.44
		50*	32											26	20	5	1	84*	1	16	27	4	542	84*	23.56
0*	—	23*	52			0	—	11	5											10	13	4	174	52	19.33
		0	—	—	6*	34	—	0	22	3*	16					4	0			16	21	3	256	34	14.22
		0	—			11	—	29*	0*	29	0	4	5	0	21*	31	69	22	56*	18	26	5	521	70	24.80
												1	0							9	12	7	57	18*	11.40
		0	—			1*	—	1	0	—	0*	7	0	15*	—	0*	23*	6	0*	18	25	11	104	23*	7.42
17	—			11	14	1	15*	3	0			14	41	3	22					16	23	3	431	103	21.55
		0	—	—	0*					15*	4	9*	24*	11	—	3	6	10	2	16	22	7	131	24*	8.73
22	—					2	7	7	11	7	15									9	17	2	255	68	17.00
—	—													29	9*	9	7			7	10	3	74	29	10.57
5	—	35	—	74	14	8	8	31	15	50	5	6	26	18	76	1	0	11	54	15	25	1	566	76	23.58
																				1	2	—	28	28	14.00
61	—	41	—			1	24*									0	1			7	9	1	195	61	24.37
																16	14	3	5	3	5	—	40	16	8.00
21	—							39	19	16	13	0	3							4	7	—	111	39	15.85
3	—																			1	1	—	3	3	3.00
—	—																			1					—
								4	32	50	17	34	0	10	4					4	8	—	151	50	18.87
								16	6	5	4									2	4	—	31	16	7.75
6					4	7				1	6	2			11	8	4	12							
14		4		4	4	15	2	7	1	9	3	5	6	5	14	8	2	2	12						
		3		2		2		2		2	1		1	1	4	3		1	1						
7		4		7	3	13		6	4	2	1	6	3	8	5	2	1	5	4						
212		285		307	191	278	82	181	173	303	96	212	158	198	318	215	189	257	290						
7		10		7	8	10	4	10	10	8	10	10	10	10	7	10	10	10	9						
D		D		D		W		L		L		L		D		L		D							
—		7		6		23		5		7		6		5		6		4							

3 – P.A. Smith and N. Gifford
2 – T.A. Munton and J.D. Ratcliffe
1 – G.J. Parsons and A.R.K. Pierson

† A.I. Kallicharran and D.A. Reeve absent hurt

CRICKET STATISTICS YEAR BY YEAR, 1946–1987. *Fred Trueman and Don Mosey*; Stanley Paul; 206pp; £14.95

This is the strangest publication of the year in that it offers a potted, very potted, outline history of cricket since the war. The aspect of the book of greatest value is Wendy Wimbush's statistical contribution although why this book ever saw the light of day remains a mystery, perhaps it was the names of the Yorkshiremen on the cover.

MARSHALL ARTS. *Malcolm Marshall (with Patrick Symes)*; Macdonald Queen Anne Press; 192pp, £5.95

Malcolm Marshall's autobiography is honest and straightforward in assessments. He may surprise some in rating Rowe above Viv Richards, but not those close to the game, and in being surprised as to how and why Essex have had so much success in recent years, but he is always offering a thoughtful comment, and the book is far better than many of its kind.

PLAYFAIR CRICKET ANNUAL 1988. *Edited by Bill Frindall*; Macdonald Queen Anne Press; 256pp; £1.75

This remains the indispensable pocket cricket annual. Full details and career records of all players in first-class cricket in England form the nucleus of this book, which is, unquestionably, the one book that no follower of the game should be without. It is accurate, ordered and excellent value.

HOMES OF CRICKET. *George Plumptre*; Macdonald Queen Anne Press; 224pp; £14.95

E.W. Swanton acted as consultant editor on this book of first-class cricket grounds in England and Wales. It is a delightfully produced book, very well illustrated, and is certainly a fine work of reference to have on one's shelves, but one wishes that there was a little more vitality in some of the writing. The book is heavily factual in description of the grounds, and although the information is of interest, there is little sense of the character of each ground and each county.

VIV RICHARDS' CRICKET MASTERCLASS. *Viv Richards (with Patrick Murphy)*; Macdonald Queen Anne Press; 160pp; £13.95

The latest offering from Viv Richards is a well-illustrated, well-designed book of instruction for those who already have some proficiency at the game. It is this fact which gives the book a particular interest and fascination, and it reveals some of the great man's secrets in dealing with certain types of bowlers and playing a wide variety of shots. One is doubtful that it is possible to learn cricket from a book, but this manual will aid those who have already mastered the rudiments of the game.

FROM BRISBANE TO KARACHI. *Edited by Peter Baxter*; Macdonald Queen Anne Press; 159pp; £10.95

The Test Match Special Team's diary of cricket in 1986 and 1987. There is not too much substance, but this amiable group of men have a worthy following to whom, no doubt, the book will give pleasure.

THE PAVILION LIBRARY – all published by Pavilion Books at £6.95:

END OF AN INNINGS. *Denis Compton*; 209pp

RANJI. *Alan Ross*; 256pp

Warwickshire CCC
First-Class Matches, 1988

BOWLING	G.C Small	T.A. Merrick	P.A. Smith	G.J. Parsons	N. Gifford	M. Asif Din	D.A. Reeve	A.R.K. Pierson	T.A. Munton
v. Cambridge University (Cambridge) 20–2 April	14–6–21–1	7.3–1–21–1	7–0–15–1	16–7–16–7	3–1–5–0				
v. Lancashire (Old Trafford) 28 April–2 May	25–4–60–5 9–3–15–0	22.5–4–67–5 8–1–11–0	6–0–21–0		22–10–24–0 10–3–20–1	3–1–22–0	7–2–11–0 6–0–17–0	10.4–4–19–0	
v. Yorkshire (Edgbaston) 5–9 May	23–10–29–5 22–7–55–5	15–2–40–0 23–5–77–4	3–0–13–0	22–8–52–1 12.3–4–23–1	2–1–1–0		16.5–5–50–4 10–5–9–0		
v. Northamptonshire (Northampton) 17–20 May		19.5–3–48–3 39–7–115–3	6–0–8–3 18–1–49–3	9–2–26–1 17–5–36–1	18–7–38–2 28–11–68–1	8–3–11–0	6–1–16–0 18.3–6–30–2	12–3–27–1 19–8–39–0	
v. Essex (Edgbaston) 21–4 May		20–6–39–4 26–7–72–3	5.3–1–7–3 7.1–0–45–1	12–3–48–1 11–4–25–2			4–2–12–0 12–2–31–0		16–2–47–1 19–3–62–3
v. Nottinghamshire (Edgbaston) 4–7 June	21–7–33–2 11.2–5–15–7	23–8–55–1 5–0–23–1	6–2–11–0 3–1–2–1		4–0–16–1		23–8–52–1 3–0–3–0		13–5–29–1
v. Somerset (Bath) 11–14 June	14–4–31–1 13–4–32–4		8–1–19–0		26–4–54–0 16–1–67–3	3–0–20–0	14–5–23–0 2–0–15–0	28–4–84–2 6–0–23–0	
v. Yorkshire (Leeds) 15–17 June			9–1–34–2 3.5–1–8–1	12–5–26–1 11–2–35–1			3–0–14–0		13–5–26–2 25–12–35–4
v. Kent (Edgbaston) 18–21 June			22–2–58–3	25–8–71–3	5.5–3–8–2		19–4–90–0		18–6–33–0
v. Lancashire (Nuneaton) 29 June–1 July	26–7–59–3 8–0–32–0	29–7–86–2 11.4–2–56–1	1–0–1–1 4–0–32–0						25–5–55–4 8–2–21–2
v. Surrey (The Oval) 2–5 July	19–4–76–0	14–2–61–0	2–0–18–0					3.3–0–19–1	17–4–50–5
v. Worcestershire (Edgbaston) 13–15 July	11–3–32–0 4–1–11–0	8–3–12–0 4–2–3–0	4–0–18–1					20–8–33–3	19–12–21–6
v. Hampshire (Edgbaston) 16–19 July	14–3–57–2 22–6–55–2	19.1–7–40–6 16–6–29–4					11–2–34–1	1–0–3–0	6–0–22–2 19–10–34–3
v. Glamorgan (Cardiff) 20–2 July	16–4–53–3 4–1–5–0					3–1–4–0	19–4–51–3	13.4–3–36–1 21–3–86–1	16–5–56–0 7–0–30–0
v. Sri Lankans (Edgbaston) 23–6 July				9–1–24–1		10–1–61–0			
v. Derbyshire (Derby) 30 July–2 Aug.	19–5–42–2 20–5–56–0	13–6–29–6 13–6–96–2			19–4–52–2 50–15–125–3	10–0–35–0	5–1–12–0 15–6–29–1		9–3–21–0 14–5–36–1
v. Gloucestershire (Cheltenham) 3–5 August		30–3–89–0 8–3–34–0	5–0–25–0 7–2–20–1	31–9–67–2 15–3–47–3		4–1–12–0 10–2–48–2	33–9–71–4 6–2–18–1		25–5–66–2 6–1–49–0
v. Northampton (Edgbaston) 6–9 August	19–4–51–1 14–5–27–1	26–7–85–4 14.2–2–26–5		12.3–5–22–1 8–3–17–3	14–6–32–1		18–2–55–3 7–1–14–1		
v. Leicestershire (Edgbaston) 13–16 August	14–4–38–1 10.2–2–30–1	19–4–64–6 6–0–34–2		5–0–18–0	15.1–7–32–2 15–4–42–2	6–0–27–1	15–2–47–1 3.4–0–8–1		
v. Sussex (Hove) 17–19 August	21–6–67–1 6–0–31–1	9.2–1–30–0			34–10–66–3 11–1–46–1	15–2–57–3 17–5–43–0			23.4–2–53–2 7–1–22–0
v. Middlesex (Uxbridge) 20–3 August	27.2–5–74–5 12–5–16–2				34–10–68–3 8–2–24–0	2–0–16–0	15–2–38–1	11–2–38–0 3–0–24–0	11–4–40–0 8–2–14–1
v. Worcestershire (Worcester) 25–9 August	27.3–5–95–5				19–7–33–1				12–3–46–1
v. Glamorgan (Edgbaston) 30 Aug.–2 Sept.	26.5–4–79–6 23.4–9–42–6		7–1–51–0 3–0–17–0		1–0–4–0 2–2–0–0				28–12–68–0 10–3–23–1
v. Somerset (Edgbaston) 9–12 September	29–10–56–3 18–4–26–1	18.5–0–95–2	27–7–68–2		34–8–68–1 34.1–4–83–2	8–0–25–0 2–1–6–0			21.3–7–38–2 29–7–50–3
	564.2–152– 1401–76 *av.* 18.43	468.3–105– 1437–65 *av.* 22.10	164.3–20– 540–23 *av.* 23.47	228–69– 553–29 *av.* 19.06	425.1–121– 976–31 *av.* 31.48	101–17– 387–6 *av.* 64.50	292–71– 750–24 *av.* 31.25	148.5–35– 431–9 *av.* 47.88	425.1–126– 1047–46 *av.* 22.76

a A.R. Border retired hurt   b R.T. Robinson absent hurt   c D.A. Banks 1–1–0–0; A.C. Storie 1–1–0–0

A.A. Donald	T.A. Lloyd	D.A. Thorne	J.E. Benjamin	S.D. Myles	N.M.K. Smith	G.W. Humpage	Byes	Leg-byes	Wides	No-balls	Total	Wkts
										3	78	10
							4	8	4	6	217	10
								1	1		83	1
							1	8		6	194	10
								11		3	175	10
							2	5		8	170	10
							5	10	5	22	363	10
							1	12		11	166	9a
								12	1	5	247	10
							1	9	3	4	206	6
								1		2	44	9b
11–4–34–0							7	12	1	4	284	3
11–0–66–1							3	9	1	2	215	9
19.4–2–57–5							2	4		8	163	10
22–9–36–4								9	1	1	123	10
20–3–45–2							6	16	9	9	327	10
								12	4	7	213	10
							5	6	4	3	152	4
							4	5		1	233	6
								14	4		130	10
										1	14	0
								3	2	5	122	10
								2	1	3	157	10
17–4–44–3								2	1	10	246	10
8–1–26–1	15–1–107–2	3–0–11–0					8	5	3	3	278	4
13–4–27–0			17–6–53–0	12–2–37–0	5–2–20–0			3		5	225	3c
								10		3	166	10
	4–0–29–0					3–0–10–0	4	8	6	4	428	7
							4	22	2	4	356	8
	1–0–14–0							4		2	234	7
							4	12		12	261	10
							4	10			98	10
							2	5			206	10
							4	4	1	1	149	9
							8	19		1	300	9
	11–0–58–0			6–0–28–0			2	9	2		259	3d
							9	7	1	3	274	10
							1	2	2		97	3
23–4–89–3							3	15	5	10	281	10
21–4–59–4								11		4	272	10
15–5–51–3							2	1	3	4	136	10
							4	18	2	15	372	10
							7	13		4	185	6
180.4–40– 534–26 *av.* 20.53	31–1– 208–2 *av.* 104.00	3–0– 11–0 —	17–6– 53–0 —	18–2– 65–0 —	5–2– 20–0 —	3–0– 10–0 —						

d A.C. Storie 6–0–20–0

Worcestershire CCC
First-Class Matches, 1988

BATTING

BATTING	v. Lancashire (Old Trafford) 21–5 April	v. Nottinghamshire (Worcester) 28 April–2 May	v. Somerset (Taunton) 5–9 May	v. Somerset (Worcester) 18–20 May	v. Leicestershire (Leicester) 21–4 May	v. West Indians (Worcester) 28–30 May	v. Lancashire (Worcester) 1–3 June	v. Middlesex (Lord's) 4–7 June	v. Hampshire (Worcester) 11–14 June	v. Derbyshire (Derby) 18–21 June	v. Gloucestershire (Worcester) 2–5 July	v. Warwickshire (Edgbaston) 13–15 July	v. Nottinghamshire (Trent Bridge) 16–19 July	v. Yorkshire (Worcester) 20–2 July
T.S. Curtis	49 11*	34 20	27 —	70 1	57 78	82 —	43 20	108 —	131 13*	0 76	— 41	26 5*	2 19	
G.J. Lord	30 —	1 41*	49 —	64 4	43 1	0 —	21 1	17 —	20 4*	28 53				11 85
G.A. Hick	212 —	86 14	405* —	8 11	6 7	172 —	0 8	78 —	177 —	47 31	— 20	23 —	8 76	198 17
D.B. d'Oliveira	11 —	4 6	0 —					37 —	0 —	0 20*				
P.A. Neale	40 —		0 —	8 10	72 2		6 17	12 —	38 —	125 8*	0 1	1 —	0 2	0 19*
S.J. Rhodes	28 10*	17 6*	56 —	35 11	20 31*		13 0*	22* —	0 —	108 —	— 26*		5 0	5 —
I.T. Botham	3 —	4 —	7 —	4 —										
P.J. Newport	13* —	33 —	27 —	11 16	6 6*		0 5*	1 —	6* —	8 —	— 40*	1 —	1 28	77* —
R.K. Illingworth	— —	9 —	31* —	8 12*	6 60		10 —	12 —		0 —		13 8*	58 10	— —
N.V. Radford	— —	28* —	— —				1 —	7* —		9* —	— —	13* —	65 0*	— —
G.R. Dilley	— —	21 —	— —									17 —	4* 0	
S.J. O'Shaughnessy		44 1		1 17	5 5	9* —					— 6	4 —	0 12	2 4
R.M. Ellcock				5* 13	0 —									
A.P. Pridgeon				2 2	1* —									
D.A. Leatherdale				27 11			3 20				— 26	12 —	0 28	
S.M. McEwan						— —		0* —		6 —				
M.J. Weston							18 45	1 —		5 —	— 20	1 —	6 8	10 24*
L.P. Vorster						16* —								
P. Bent														31 50
Byes			6		5 2	1	1	5	4	1 2	3		1 2	5 9
Leg-byes	21 8	8 3	16	11 7	13 14	13	2 2	23	13	13 9	1	14	3 7	6 5
Wides	1	1 1	4	2 8	8	2	1	10	2	2		4	1	2
No-balls	1	1 1	4	11 7	22 5	26	1	10	1	1	5		5 7	9 2
Total	409 29	290 92	628	240 119	291 222	321	119 118	333 0	397 17	367 200	0 233	130 14	159 199	356 215
Wickets	7 0	10 4	7	10 9†	10 7	3	10 6	8 0	10 3	10 3	0 6	10 0	10 10	7 4
Result	W	W	W	L	D	D	D	W	W	D	D	D	L	W
Points	23	23	23	6	5	—	4	19	24	7	1	4	5	22

Fielding Figures

78 – S.J. Rhodes (ct 70/st 8)	18 – R.K. Illingworth	8 – P.A. Neale and P.J. Newport
28 – G.A. Hick	15 – M.J. Weston	6 – D.B. d'Oliveira
19 – T.S. Curtis	14 – N.V. Radford	5 – S.J. O'Shaughnessy

JACK HOBBS. *Ronald Mason*; 212pp

FAREWELL TO CRICKET. *Don Bradman*; 319pp

One must confess to a great sense of disappointment with the year's offering from the Pavilion Library. This began as such an exciting venture, promising, as it did, to reprint some of the classics of cricket literature, yet this year we were offered two 'ghosted' books, and those not of the highest quality. The only reason for the inclusion of the Compton book was that 1988 saw the great man's 70th birthday, but surely there could have been better selections to commemorate this, books by Swanton or Peebles, for example. Bradman's 80th birthday gave cause for *Farewell to Cricket*, but what of Rosenwater or several other books on Bradman. Certainly the best of the four from Pavilion is Ronald Mason's biography of Jack Hobbs, which has never been bettered. Mason writes with clarity and understanding, and this book is a worthy addition to the series. Like a few other people, the present writer was a little disappointed with Alan Ross' *Ranji*.

THE GOLDEN AGE OF VILLAGE CRICKET. *Steven Garner*; Lennard Publishing; £4.95

More than a hundred cartoons by Steven Garner which capture the fun and character of village cricket very well indeed make up this delightful book. The artist is sure in his line, positive in the various characters he offers us. There have not been too many collections of cricket cartoons as good as this one.

THE PRIMARY CLUB'S MIDDLE AND LEG. *Edited by Jack Pollard*; Macmillan Australia; 205pp

An anthology of cricket writing related to the game in Australia. Some excellent pieces for a worthy cause.

THE OBSERVER ON CRICKET. *Edited by Scyld Berry*; Unwin Allen, 221pp, £11.95

One's only complaint about this collection of articles and reports from *The Observer* is that the paper has such a distinguished record of cricket writing that the offering Scyld Berry gives us seems insufficient. Perhaps it is just that the quality is so good that we ache for more. There are pieces by Altham, Peebles, Alan Ross and the incomparable Robertson-Glasgow, and many others. There should have been more Robertson-Glasgow and possibly less Hutton, but there is some lovely writing here.

FOX ON THE RUN. *Graeme Fowler (with Peter Ball)*; Viking; 206pp; £12.95

In 1984–5, Graeme Fowler was England's successful opening batsman in India, but a few months later, unable to find any sort of form, he was in the Lancashire second eleven. *Fox on the Run* is a diary of those days and goes some way towards giving us a sensitive picture of the triumphs, trials and tribulations of a professional cricketer. This particular diary also happens to be the work of a very likeable young man.

A CRICKET ODYSSEY. *Scyld Berry*; Pavilion Books; 214pp; £14.95

Scyld Berry's odyssey covers the World Cup and the tours of Pakistan and New Zealand. The strength of the book is that Berry sees so much more

v. Kent (Folkestone) 23-6 July		v. Northamptonshire (Worcester) 30 July-2 Aug.		v. Sussex (Kidderminster) 6-9 August		v. Glamorgan (Abergavenny) 13-16 August		v. Surrey (The Oval) 17-19 August		v. Essex (Worcester) 20-3 August		v. Warwickshire (Worcester) 25-9 August		v. Gloucestershire (Bristol) 9-12 September		v. Glamorgan (Worcester) 14-17 September		M	Inns	Nos	Runs	HS	Av
		45	—			24	86	86	17	10	33			2	13*	8	—	19	32	4	1237	131	44.17
0	13	47	—	10	5	56	2	13	43	15	1	0	—	41	101	42	—	20	33	2	862	101	27.80
21	—	132	—	18	2*	46	159	41	127	34	20	75	—	121	18	197	—	23	35	2	2615	405*	79.24
										8	29	17	—					8	11	1	132	37	13.20
108*	—	44	—	167	—	46*	51	36	35	0	31	23	—	102*	4	29	—	21	31	5	1036	167	39.84
7	31*	23	—	6	—	19*	1*	15	2*	17	11	0	—	1	24	46	—	23	33	10	597	108	25.95
																		4	4	—	18	7	4.50
16	—	6*	—	18	—			33	—	5	34*					30	—	21	24	8	421	77*	26.31
34	—			2*	—			3	—	31	20	15	—	38	8	16	—	23	22	4	404	60	22.44
6	—			1	—					18	11	15	—	15	1	10*	—	18	15	6	200	65	22.22
												3	—	36	3	5	—	9	8	1	89	36	12.71
						0	0	30	2	0	—							11	18	1	142	44	8.35
								9	—									5	4	1	27	13	9.00
4	—			11	—			4*	—	0*	0	5	—	1	1			10	11	3	31	11	3.87
22	34*	11	—	24	—									25	8	4	—	10	15	1	255	34*	18.21
																		6	2	1	6	6	6.00
0	—	37*	—	94	—	1	28*	14	14*	4	10	95*	—	0	12	2	—	18	24	1	514	95*	27.05
																		1	1	1	16	16*	—
5	2			16	7*													3	6	1	111	50	22.20

v. Kent		v. Northamptonshire		v. Sussex		v. Glamorgan		v. Surrey		v. Essex		v. Warwickshire		v. Gloucestershire		v. Glamorgan	
						1				1		3		3		5	
11	1	8		3		1	13	5	8	5	17	15		14	1	21	
2		2					2			5					3	2	
2		7				6	2	14	3	2		10		5	2	6	
238	81	362		370	14	200	344	303	251	150	217	281		404	199	423	
10	2	6		10	0	5	5	10	5	10	10	10		10	10	10	
D		D		W		W		D		L		D		W		W	
6		8		24		22		6		4		7		23		24	

4 – I.T. Botham and G.J. Lord
3 – D.A. Leatherdale and A.P. Pridgeon
2 – subs
1 – G.R. Dilley, R.M. Ellcock and S.M. McEwan
† I.T. Botham absent injured

---

than cricket, and one is led through the intricacies of a Moslem society with sensitivity and understanding. The Test matches become almost an irrelevance, or at least they are put in perspective. The book is written with Berry's usual fluidity of style and marked by his considerable wit.

THE SPINNERS' WEB. *Trevor Bailey and Fred Trueman*; Collins Willow; 224pp; £12.95

The main part of the analysis of spin bowlers from 'Tich' Freeman to John Emburey is done by Trevor Bailey, and there is comment from Fred Trueman. Bailey has become one of the great thinkers on the game and his analysis is clear, intelligent and quite fascinating. He draws on personal experience of those bowlers he faced during his career and the whole makes an eminently readable and most interesting addition to cricket literature.

THE JOURNAL OF THE CRICKET SOCIETY. *Edited by Clive Porter*; The Cricket Society; free to members, £3 to non-members, from Mrs V.A. Hoggarth, 26 Thirlmere Rise, London Road, Bromley, Kent BR1 4HY

A wonderfully high standard of writing and statistical and historical eccentricities is consistently maintained in this quarterly publication.

SWINGS AND ROUNDABOUTS. *Graham Dilley and Graham Otway*; Pelham Books; 160pp; £12.95

This is a very interesting book in that the author, while aiming to explain and justify his reasons for leaving Kent, does not always come out of it very well. It is this naïvety or frankness which gives the book its verve, and for this, co-author Graham Otway of *Today* must take much credit. Dilley talks about South Africa and Tests, and one is left with the feeling that he should, perhaps, have listened more readily to the advice of others on occasions.

ONE-DAY CRICKET. *David Lemmon*; Marks & Spencer; 190pp; £4.99

The present writer's study of the rise of one-day cricket with full coverage of all the major competitions is profusely illustrated and attractively produced by Marks & Spencer, whose second venture into the cricket book market this was.

TWO TOURS AND POLLOCK. *Chris Harte*; Sports Marketing; 320pp

Chris Harte has cornered the market of the Australian rebels' tours of South Africa. He writes with clarity and good sense. His facts are sure, and he has given a full and lucid account of the cricket and the politics as well as the wider implications. An important book.

SEVEN TESTS. *Chris Harte*; Sports Marketing; £5

An album of photographs and statistics of the matches between South Africa and the Australian rebels, 1985–7, this is a complementary offering to the same author's *Two Tours and Pollock*.

BOTHAM, A BIOGRAPHY. *Patrick Murphy*; J.M. Dent; 236pp; £12.95

If one feels that one has read enough biographies of Botham, one cannot doubt that Pat Murphy's book is the fullest and most detailed account we have had of the great all-rounder's career. The research has been assiduously carried out, and the book is the result of many hours of interviews over a long period of time. It is apparent that Pat Murphy responds to Botham's zestful approach to life and to cricket and that he is reluctant to

Worcestershire CCC
First-Class Matches, 1988

BOWLING	G.R. Dilley	N.V. Radford	R.K. Illingworth	G.A. Hick	P.J. Newport	I.T. Botham	R.M. Ellcock	A.P. Pridgeon	S.J. O'Shaughnessy
v. Lancashire (Old Trafford) 21–5 April	9–2–14–3	10–2–25–1	22.4–4–46–5	6–2–8–1					
	11.5–1–31–1	8–2–12–0	59–14–107–5	44–10–138–4	6–0–38–0				
v. Nottinghamshire (Worcester) 28 April–2 May	11–0–37–4	13.2–2–55–5			7–1–16–1	4–1–14–0			
	21–1–80–5	20–2–95–3			8.4–0–36–2	6–0–28–0			
v. Somerset (Taunton) 5–9 May	12–0–40–0	23.5–1–77–4	1–0–4–0	8–3–18–2	17–4–59–4	9–3–18–0			
	14–2–40–0	17–6–39–3	11–4–20–0	11–4–15–1	15.3–3–50–6	6–2–25–0			
v. Somerset (Worcester) 18–20 May			6–1–33–0		24–3–97–4	18–5–40–1	21–2–86–3	18.3–2–68–2	
							5.1–0–18–1	5–1–10–0	
v. Leicestershire (Leicester) 21–4 May			12–1–33–0		15–4–49–2		17–2–72–1	23–6–60–0	12–1–55–2
			9–3–22–1		10–2–39–2		6–1–19–0	7–0–19–1	
v. West Indians (Worcester) 28–30 May			19–5–45–2		9–1–40–1		13–2–51–2		2–0–9–0
v. Lancashire (Worcester) 1–3 June		14–1–52–2			21–8–51–6				
		12–1–39–3			15.5–1–61–3				
v. Middlesex (Lord's) 4–7 June		19–5–37–1	6–2–9–1		22–6–52–8				
v. Hampshire (Worcester) 11–14 June	17–4–37–1	16–3–62–2	2–0–7–0		20–3–61–5				
	23.1–5–65–5	28–3–82–3	5–4–1–0		14–3–45–0				
v. Derbyshire (Derby) 18–21 June		17–1–50–1	41–10–108–3	10–2–28–2	17–4–66–1				
		9–0–27–0	20–11–27–3	14–3–33–1	5–1–13–0				
v. Gloucestershire (Worcester) 2–5 July		23–4–85–1	23–5–55–0		24–5–59–1				6–0–35–1
v. Warwickshire (Edgbaston) 13–15 July	8–1–25–0	18–2–55–0	30.2–7–58–2	20–4–56–2	9–3–24–1				
v. Nottinghamshire (Trent Bridge) 16–19 July	17–2–46–5	21.3–0–67–5			5–0–19–0				
	15–7–25–1	15–5–46–2	21–9–41–1	6–0–18–0	13–2–37–0				1–0–7–0
v. Yorkshire (Worcester) 20–2 July		16–3–50–1	28–11–67–2	10–0–54–1	24.2–9–53–2				
		13.5–3–60–4	24–2–82–4		14–3–54–1				
v. Kent (Folkestone) 23–6 July		20–4–40–3	14–6–25–3		23.3–7–50–4			17–6–32–0	
v. Northamptonshire (Worcester) 30 July–2 Aug.		24.4–7–73–7	7–4–15–1		17–1–63–0			14–8–20–2	
		29.2–7–73–1	16–5–39–0		19.4–9–26–1			20–6–29–1	
v. Sussex (Kidderminster) 6–9 August		10–1–29–2	8.3–2–28–2		21–4–62–5			8–1–19–1	
		23–7–66–3	16–3–36–0	3–0–14–0	24.1–6–66–4			17–3–48–2	
v. Glamorgan (Abergavenny) 13–16 August			17–7–31–2		31.4–4–108–3		19–3–75–2	24–6–48–2	6–1–20–0
				4–0–13–0	3–0–9–0		3–0–13–0		9–1–35–1
v. Surrey (The Oval) 17–19 August			28–5–70–1	11–0–71–2	17.5–3–70–3		10–0–45–0	12–1–44–1	
					1–0–5–0				
v. Essex (Worcester) 20–3 August		30.1–8–80–2	14–5–29–0		31–9–70–5			26–7–61–2	
		14–3–39–2			21.5–3–56–4			19–2–68–3	
v. Warwickshire (Worcester) 25–9 August	24–7–53–4	18–4–72–1	13.4–10–4–2					16–1–39–2	
	28–3–75–1	32–3–126–3	28–9–51–3	5–3–8–0				15–1–33–0	
v. Gloucestershire (Bristol) 9–12 September	11–2–43–2	9.1–0–37–1	31–12–69–5	20–3–54–1				16–6–39–1	
		10–4–20–0	35.1–13–63–5	32–9–114–4				9–1–25–1	
v. Glamorgan (Worcester) 14–17 September	21–4–54–0	28–5–84–4	25–14–31–3		15–2–53–2				
	8–3–30–2	8–2–16–1	4.2–1–18–2		10–2–23–5				
	251–44– 695–34 av. 20.44	570.5–101– 1770–71 av. 24.92	597.4–189– 1274–58 av. 21.96	204–43– 642–21 av. 30.57	553–116– 1680–86 av. 19.53	43–11– 125–1 av. 125.00	94.1–10– 379–9 av. 42.11	266.3–58– 662–21 av. 31.52	39–3– 161–4 av. 40.25

a N.G. Cowley absent hurt

S.M. McEwan	M.J. Weston	T.S. Curtis	D.A. Leatherdale	P.A. Neale	Byes	Leg-byes	Wides	No-balls	Total	Wkts
					4	4		4	101	10
					6	4	3	10	336	10
					2	8	1	5	132	10
						9	1	4	248	10
						6		10	222	10
					2	1		11	192	10
						3	1	15	327	10
						5	1	1	33	1
					4	7		5	280	5
									99	5
7–0–21–0	4–0–4–0							2	170	5
14–2–61–1	6–2–13–1				4	8	4	9	189	10
11–0–43–4						4		1	147	10
									0	0
5–1–13–0	3–1–4–0				2	7	1	1	124	10
	12–4–26–2					10		3	203	10
	6–4–4–1				6	7	6	6	209	9a
13–0–61–2					4	5		5	322	9
		2–0–7–0			4	4			115	4
15–1–49–1	7–2–16–0	2–1–10–0	2–0–5–0			18		10	332	4
									0	0
	10–0–24–4				1	7		6	250	9
						3		4	135	10
	8–1–33–0	0.3–0–4–0			3	12		6	226	4
15–2–51–0	5–0–14–0					13	3	17	302	6
6–1–11–0	7–0–31–0				1	9	1	10	248	10
						5	1	1	152	10
	3–1–8–0				1	11		6	191	10
	4–2–8–0		4–3–12–1		1	17		7	205	4
					4	4		4	146	10
					1	6	2	1	237	10
	4–1–6–0					10	1	6	298	9
	9–0–51–1	10.2–0–53–1		14–1–62–0	4	2	3	5	242	3
						2		3	302	7
									5	0
					1	21		4	262	9
	7–3–16–1					3	1	2	182	10
	15–7–25–1					5	1	8	198	10
					11	14	4	5	318	7
	2–0–7–0		1–0–3–0		1	9		13	262	10
					3	2		4	227	10
	7–2–16–1				2	4		6	244	10
	5–1–14–0				1	1	2		103	10
86–7–	124–31–	14.5–1–	7–3–	14–1–						
310–8	320–12	74–1	20–1	62–0						
av. 38.75	av. 26.66	av. 74.00	av. 20.00	—						

Yorkshire CCC
First-Class Matches, 1988

BATTING	Derbyshire (Leeds) 28 Apr–2 May 1	2	Warwicks. (Edgbaston) 5–9 May 1	2	Kent (Canterbury) 21–4 May 1	2	Hampshire (Middlesbrough) 28–31 May 1	2	Northants (Northampton) 1–3 June 1	2	Surrey (Harrogate) 4–7 June 1	2	Cambridge Univ. (Cambridge) 11–13 June 1	2	Warwicks. (Leeds) 15–17 June 1	2	Essex (Sheffield) 18–21 June 1	2	Sussex (Hove) 25–8 June 1	2	Middlesex (Lord's) 29 June–1 July 1	2	Leicestershire (Leeds) 2–5 July 1	2	Worcestershire (Worcester) 20–2 July 1	2	Glamorgan (Cardiff) 23–6 July 1	2
M.D. Moxon	79	0	21	16	26	15	40	—	1	44	5	44							13	61					39	106	0	—
A.A. Metcalfe	11	8	3	29	67	0	28	—			3	87	52	—	4	25	6	5	9	22	0	12	—	21	28	0	2	—
R.J. Blakey	4	0	14	5					24	27	4	27	9	—	1	0			4	1			—	51				
J.D. Love	9	46	0	21	6	19	6	—	8	0	0	93*	7	—	1	0							—	68	36	19	52	—
P.E. Robinson	18	24	2	36	0	0	38	—	18	3	58	10	40	—	9	13	8	33	49	0	8	19*	—	0	51	33	63	—
D.L. Bairstow	14	5	68	1	1	0	0	—	15*	4*					27	10	7	14	5	0	41	—	—	—	9	23	33	—
A. Sidebottom	2	48	0	1	16	41	5	—	36	4	36	—			5	15	24	2	37*	27*	28	—	—	—	—	1		
P.W. Jarvis	11	0	1	13	13	0	11	—											0	6*								
P.J. Hartley	2	37	4	11																	16*	—			—	1	30*	—
P.A. Booth	0	2																										
C. Shaw	0*	6*	2*	0	3*	8*	4	—	0	0	2	—			4	2	6*	0	4	—	0	—			—	2*	26*	—
P. Carrick			64	28*	3	26	46*	—	29	47	3	6*	0	—	2	19	1	11	38	43	24	4*	—	22*	46*	20	14	—
I.G. Swallow					46	0	7	—	6	27	17	2			7*	8	37	27	30	21	5	12			48*	7	43	—
K. Sharp					57	14	36	—	8	48	2	5			33	0	22	5					—	10	12	15	24	—
S.D. Fletcher											0	5*	2	—					0	8*	1	—	18	—			13	—
D. Byas													69	—	57	6	4	0	16	0	4	14	—	28				
N.G. Nicholson													16	12*														
P.J. Berry													4	23*														
S.J. Dennis													36*	—			0	14*										
D.A. Towse													1	—														
S.N. Hartley																					22	12	—	26*				
C.S. Pickles																												
P. Anderson																												
Byes	3		1		1				1	2	4	15	3	4	2		2				8	4			1		1	
Leg-byes	2	9	8	11	3	8	6		5	4	4	5	7	2	4	9	5	1	5	4	1		15		13	9	9	
Wides	2	4			2				1		2		1				1				1		3		3	1	2	
No-balls	4	3	6	3		2	12		4	12	4	14	4		8	1	7	6	12	2	13	1	12		17	10	10	
Total	161	192	194	175	244	133	239		155	228	142	310	251	41	163	123	133	113	219	186	187	80	0	256	302	248	322	0
Wickets	10	10	10	10	10	10	10		10	9	10	6	10	0	10	10	10	10	10	7	10	4	6	10	6	10	9	0
Result	L		L		L		D		D		D		W		L		L		W		D		W		L		D	
Points	5		5		3		6		5		1		—		5		4		22		3		19		7		2	

Fielding Figures

33 – D.L. Bairstow (ct 38/st 1)	21 – P.E. Robinson	7 – P. Carrick, P.J. Hartley and S.D. Fletcher
28 – R.J. Blakey (ct 26/st 2)	12 – J.D. Love and D. Byas	5 – A.A. Metcalfe, A. Sidebottom and I.G. Swallow
22 – M.D. Moxon	9 – K. Sharp	3 – N.G. Nicholson

see faults in his subject, but he gives us the liveliest, fullest and closest account yet of a one of the great men of cricket history.

THE CRISIS OF CAPTAINCY. *David Lemmon*; Christopher Helm; 150pp, £12.95

A study of captaincy at Test and county level with the main emphasis on the days when cricketers were either gentlemen or players.

CRICKET MILESTONES. *Robert Brooke*; Marks & Spencer; 190pp; £4.99

Originally issued in monthly parts in *The Cricketer*, Robert Brooke's *Cricket Milestones* is an intriguing book of statistics and pictures pinpointing some of the important milestones reached by players and teams in the past decade and relating them to events in the past. Meticulously compiled, very well produced, and wonderful value.

DUMBLETON DAY. *Nico Craven*; Nico Craven (The Coach House, Ponsonby, Seascale, Cumbria, CA20 1BX); 12pp; £1.25

It will be a sad year when there is nothing new from Nico Craven upon which to comment. In comparison with Craven's earlier works, this 'August Occasion' is slight, but it is no less enjoyable. It tells the story of an August Sunday in Dumbleton when the home side met Eton Ramblers, and there was good tea and good lunch as well as good cricket. 'I saw home-made Cotswold cricket at its Sunday best – and its doesn't come much better – and I felt like a man refreshed,' writes Nico Craven. One feels a man refreshed for having read *Dumbleton Day*.

EMBUREY, AUTOBIOGRAPHY. *John Emburey (with Martin Rogers)*; Partridge Press; 167pp; £10.95

Emburey's cricketing life is told in a straightforward, uncomplicated manner. The passage dealing with the rebel tour of South Africa does nothing to explain nor justify the action, and, as one felt when reading Gooch's account, one feels it hard to forgive the duplicity and deceit which went on, particularly as it affected Keith Fletcher, who, Emburey says, would have been embarrassed if he had been in on the secret. In effect, the book reflects the man, cool and unruffled and never showing too much emotion – sorrow or joy.

THE CRICKETERS: WHO'S WHO 1988. *Compiled and edited by Iain Sproat*; Collins Willow; 512pp; £8.95

The most remarkable thing about the *Who's Who* is that it is still with us. After an initial period which saw almost as many errors as accuracies, the publication is now appreciably tighter with statistics and the facts are now more reliable.

WISDEN CRICKETERS' ALMANACK 1988. *Edited by Graeme Wright*; John Wisden; 1296pp; £16.50

Editor Graeme Wright has firmly and correctly stamped his own personality and authority on the famous annual in his second year as editor. His comments on events in international cricket over the past 12 months should be made compulsory reading by all who have authority in the game, indeed by all who have any concern whatsoever for the game. Thankfully, Graeme Wright sees cricket for what it is, a sport to be enjoyed, not a substitute for warfare or diplomatic wrangling sullied by national and commercial

v. Lancashire (Leeds) 30 July–2 Aug.		v. Nottinghamshire (Sheffield) 3–5 August		v. Gloucestershire (Cheltenham) 6–9 August		v. Sri Lankans (Leeds) 10–12 August		v. Somerset (Scarborough) 13–16 August		v. Derbyshire (Chesterfield) 17–19 August		v. Middlesex (Leeds) 25–9 August		v. Lancashire (Old Trafford) 30 Aug–2 Sept.		v. Northamptonshire (Scarborough) 9–12 September		v. Nottinghamshire (Trent Bridge) 14–17 September		M	Inns	Nos	Runs	HS	Av
2	9*	12	64*	31	21	132	1	81	10	0	—	57	89*	2	24	86	191	68	40	19	35	3	1430	191	44.68
13	9*	27	51*	15	33			98	31	115	9*	216*	78*	11	18	56	26	74	18	22	40	5	1320	216*	37.71
12	—	5	—	40	13*	5*	85*	—	30	38	—	—	—	3	0	0	45*			16	24	4	446	85*	22.30
77	—	69	—	2	—							70*	—	8	31	45	14	6	38	18	28	2	751	93*	28.88
27	—	129*	—	5	6	0	1	81*	53	10	—	88	—	9	4	32	17	98	80	24	40	3	1173	129*	31.70
15	—	4	—															26	94*	14	23	3	416	94*	20.80
55	—			37*	—			—	0*	51*	—	—	—					41	5	18	24	5	517	55	27.21
																				5	9	1	55	13	6.87
27	—	23	—	20	—			—	5*					127*	38	1	12*	7	3*	13	17	6	364	127*	33.09
						—	14							4	33*	28	0	15*	—	5	8	2	96	33*	16.00
6*	—	31	—	3*	—			—	—	24	—	—	—	2	16*	19*	—			21	25	12	170	31	13.07
37	—	26	—	81	17*	—	20	—	43	10	—	—	—	36	0	12	—	0	37	23	34	7	815	81	30.18
		2	—																	11	19	2	352	48*	20.70
						128	3	—	5	1	—									12	19	—	428	128	22.52
7	—	1	—	—	—			—	—	8	—	—	—	17	—	0	—	1	—	17	15	3	81	18	6.75
				112	9	4	4	98	0	17	16*	0	—	0	3	21	72	26	12	14	25	1	592	112	24.66
						15	4													2	4	1	47	16	15.66
																				1	2	1	27	23*	27.00
						—	0			0	—							1	—	4	5	2	50	36*	16.66
																				1	1	—	1	1	1.00
						3*	0													2	3	1	60	26*	30.00
						—	0													1	2	1	3	3*	3.00
																				1	1	—	0	0	0.00

v. Lancashire		v. Nottinghamshire		v. Gloucestershire		v. Sri Lankans		v. Somerset		v. Derbyshire		v. Middlesex		v. Lancashire		v. Northamptonshire		v. Nottinghamshire	
		1	1	8	1	1	2			4		4					3		4
15		6	3	11	2	5	8	2	1	4		20	9	4	4	5	3	14	7
				1					3	1		1		1	5				
		1				1	2	4	7	8	4	18		7	4	1		15	14	4	2
293	18	337	119	367	104	297	152	369	182	301	25	463	185	224	171	320	397	380	340
10	0	10	0	8	4	5	10	3	7	10	0	3	0	10	8	10	6	10	7
W		D		D		D		D		D		D		D		D		W	
23		8		8		—		7		5		4		6		5		24	

2 – C. Shaw
1 – S.J. Dennis, P.J. Berry, P.A. Booth, C.S. Pickles, D.A. Towse and P. Anderson

consideraitons. The annual presents its usual indispensable pages of scores and records. It remains the reference book supreme, and the 1988 edition will be remembered for the strength and substance of the editor's' comment, for which this writer, at least, is grateful and thankful.

THE TEST MATCH CAREER OF SIR JACK HOBBS. Clive Porter; Spellmount; 177pp; £12.95

So much has been written about Hobbs that one wondered what more Mr Porter could add, but in concentrating mainly, although not excusively, on Hobbs' Test career, he has managed to complement much of what has been said before and to draw our attention afresh to the greatness of the man. This is a scholarly work, though never dull, and gives a sharp perspective on the international career of one who has had no superior among English batsmen.

VISIONS OF SPORT. Pelham Books; 158pp; £14.95

This is a stunning collection of sports photography from Allsport, whose work has been a feature of *Benson and Hedges Cricket Year* for the past seven years, particularly the photographs of Adrian Murrell. *Visions of Sport* celebrates 25 years of the Allsport Picture Agency and is sold in aid of Sport Aid '88. It is a glorious achievement.

PAGEANT OF CRICKET. Compiled by David Frith; Macmillan; 640pp; £30

It is apparent that David Frith has approached this book, which is, in effect, an illustrated history of cricket, with much love and care. There are more than two thousand photographs and reproductions, many of which have never been seen before, and they present us with a fascinating panorama of the game from its earliest days. It would be idle to suggest that all the photographs are of the highest quality, but they blend into a complete picture of cricket and the social and technical changes it has undergone in the past two hundred and fifty years. The accompanying captions are precise and informative, and, like the *Bradman Albums*, the book should be at the centre of any collection. Mr Frith is to be thanked and congratulated for making this work available to us. It is a mighty achievement.

THE 1987 PROTEA CRICKET ANNUAL OF SOUTH AFRICA. Edited by Ted Partridge, Peter Sichel & Frank Heydenrych; 470pp

The 34th edition of this excellent annual which fully documents cricket in South Africa. There is a very fine records section.

GUILDFORD JUBILEE 1938–1988. Edited by David Frith; 44pp; £2

An absolutely splendid publication to celebrate fifty years of county cricket at Guildford, this brochure is full of fascinating facts, figures and articles and is lavishly illustrated. It has been carefully researched and the result is a publication of which the Guildford Club and, in particular, David Frith have every reason to be very proud.

Yorkshire CCC
First-Class Matches, 1988

BOWLING

	P.W. Jarvis	A. Sidebottom	C. Shaw	P.J. Hartley	P.A. Booth	P. Carrick	M.D. Moxon	A.A. Metcalfe	I.G. Swallow
v. Derbyshire (Leeds) 28 April–2 May	23–6–49–5	19–5–28–3	16–4–32–1	16–0–54–1	1–1–0–0				
	17–1–38–2	15–7–18–0	18.5–3–65–2	16–6–45–1					
v. Warwickshire (Edgbaston) 5–9 May	20–8–38–3	27–11–56–3	16–6–45–1	23–7–69–3		2–0–15–0			13–4–32–0
	13–3–40–1	3–1–13–0	9–2–31–0	10–1–40–2			2–0–8–0	0.5–0–2–0	
v. Kent (Canterbury) 21–4 May	25.2–3–75–4	19–7–38–1	21–6–56–4			24–7–56–0	4–2–7–0		
	16.3–7–40–6	13–8–21–1	7–1–34–0						
v. Hampshire (Middlesbrough) 28–31 May	16–5–36–2	18.2–6–30–5	10–3–27–1			18–4–35–2			
	19.2–6–45–2	14–2–32–0	6–1–17–1			21–9–33–1			4–0–19–0
v. Northamptonshire (Northampton) 1–3 June		19–4–48–3	23.5–8–50–4			3–1–3–0			
		16–1–51–3	13–1–53–0			14–7–34–1			1–0–2–1
v. Surrey (Harrogate) 4–7 June		6.3–2–19–0	21–2–84–1			24–6–89–0			25–6–91–1
v. Cambridge University (Cambridge) 11–13 June						18–7–42–4			
						12–6–17–3			
v. Warwickshire (Leeds) 15–17 June		15.2–7–25–3	12–5–17–4						
		18–7–43–1	23.4–10–46–2			8–5–10–0			
v. Essex (Leeds) 18–21 June		15.5–3–35–1	12–1–33–1			4–2–6–0			8–1–18–0
		8–0–29–1	5–0–13–0						
v. Sussex (Hove) 25–8 June	15–2–52–2	18–4–62–0	18–4–55–2			30–10–71–4			
	11–5–21–4	16.1–2–47–4							
v. Middlesex (Lord's) 29 June–1 July		18–6–51–1	22.3–3–54–4	19–2–75–1		20–4–55–0			8–1–26–0
v. Leicestershire (Leeds) 2–5 July		32–12–60–3	14–3–39–1			33.5–13–46–5			
v. Worcestershire (Worcester) 20–2 July		19–2–62–1	25.2–3–93–3	18–1–92–2		28–11–67–1			8–0–31–0
		5–1–15–0	17–3–52–1	6–0–33–0		14–1–52–3			8–0–38–0
v. Glamorgan (Cardiff) 23–6 July			14–4–18–2	10–0–27–1		19–9–27–1		2–0–5–0	13–3–54–0
v. Lancashire (Leeds) 30 July–2 Aug.		14–2–32–4	18–7–47–3	8.5–1–29–2					
		8–4–17–2	5–1–19–1	15–1–65–3					
v. Nottinghamshire (Sheffield) 3–5 August			15.4–1–44–3	21–3–85–5					
			12–1–41–0	8–0–40–0		17–1–51–0			
v. Gloucestershire (Cheltenham) 6–9 August		17–4–34–5	15–5–37–1	17–1–66–3		14–7–21–1			
		14–5–30–1	20–2–87–0	23–1–105–2		32–7–106–2			
v. Sri Lankans (Leeds) 10–12 August					26–8–80–2	17–3–45–1			
v. Somerset (Scarborough) 13–16 August		24–6–50–3	17–4–60–0	8–1–34–0		38–13–77–4			
		19–2–63–1	5–1–14–0	5–0–24–0		21–2–95–4			
v. Derbyshire (Chesterfield) 17–19 August		2.2–0–7–1	6–1–18–1			2–0–2–0			
		13.5–3–54–3	6–0–35–0			8–0–44–0			
v. Middlesex (Leeds) 25–9 August		22–5–74–1	15–6–49–0	17–2–61–0		28–9–67–4			
		5–0–27–0	18–2–77–1	18–1–66–2		21–2–89–1			
v. Lancashire (Old Trafford) 30 Aug.–2 Sept.			7–1–20–0	2–0–15–0	37.4–9–98–5	42–17–62–5			
v. Northamptonshire (Scarborough) 9–12 September			23–5–60–1	16–1–58–1	54–12–132–4	33.1–11–105–2			
v. Nottinghamshire (Trent Bridge) 14–17 September		26–4–89–7		14.4–3–51–2	13–3–42–0	14–3–53–1			
		12–2–43–1		16–0–85–3	4–2–9–0	15–2–76–0			
	176.1–46–	512.2–135–	507.5–110–	307.3–32–	135.4–35–	593–179–	6–2–	2.5–0–	88–15–
	434–31	1303–63	1522–46	1219–34	361–11	1551–50	15–0	7–0	311–2
	av. 14.00	av. 20.68	av. 33.08	av. 35.85	av. 32.81	av. 31.02	—	—	av. 155.50

a M.R. Benson absent hurt   b J.D. Love 2.3–0–11–1   c P.E. Robinson 1.2–0–12–0

S.D. Fletcher	S.J. Dennis	D.A. Towse	P.J. Berry	D. Byas	S.N. Hartley	K. Sharp	Byes	Leg-byes	Wides	No-balls	Total	Wkts
							4	3		4	170	10
							3	15			184	5
							9	3		4	235	10
								1			135	3
							4	6		2	274	9a
							4	5			104	7
								2		4	130	10
							1	2		4	149	4
16–5–24–3							2	3		5	130	10
15–3–45–2							3	4		6	192	7
24.3–5–52–2							2	5		2	342	4
15–5–31–2	9–4–20–1	9–2–24–1	15.2–5–35–2					4			156	10
12.2–2–25–4	11–5–26–2		23–8–56–1				3	8			135	10
	17–3–35–3							4		1	81	10
	19–4–73–0			4–0–16–0			10	8		2	206	3
24–6–58–8							5	3	1	2	158	10
6–0–35–0				2.2–0–8–0				4		4	89	1
20–4–50–2							4	5		7	299	10
6–0–35–2							2			7	105	10
22–0–108–4							9	10	1	13	388	10
22–3–78–1					5–1–25–0			5	1	8	253	10
											0	0
							5	6	2	9	356	7
						1–0–11–0	9	5		2	215	4
							4				20	1b
14–2–37–0							8	8		2	179	4
10–2–36–1								10	1	1	154	10
13–3–36–4							6	13	1	6	156	10
18–2–59–2								7	1	4	195	10
12–0–48–4							6	12			198	5
13–3–48–0								8	1	8	214	10
6–0–30–0				3–0–25–0			2	7	1	3	404	6c
	16–5–44–1						9	9		3	287	5d
	2–1–2–1										7	1e
15–2–40–1								9		8	270	8
15–1–40–4								5		10	241	9
3–0–29–0	11–1–27–1									2	83	3
7–2–15–2	16–1–61–1							7		7	216	6
17.2–5–56–1							2	6	5	9	315	6
19–1–55–3								8	1	5	322	9
5–1–14–0							2	7	1	4	218	10
25–3–91–1							4	14	1	7	464	9f
18–3–59–0								2	2	6	296	10
18.5–3–74–6								10		7	297	10
412–66– 1308–59 av. 22.16	90–19– 262–8 av. 32.75	20–7– 50–3 av. 16.66	38.2–13– 91–3 av. 30.33	9.2–0– 49–0 —	5–1– 25–0 —	1–0– 11–0 —						

d P. Anderson 17.3–4–47–1; C.S. Pickles 15–5–53–0   e C.S. Pickles 1.2–0–5–0   f N.G.B. Cook retired hurt